Ar De la Mare

A most generous gift of Andrew Watson

MEDIEVAL MANUSCRIPTS IN BRITISH LIBRARIES

MEDIEVAL MANUSCRIPTS IN BRITISH LIBRARIES

BY N. R. KER

III

LAMPETER–OXFORD

CLARENDON PRESS · OXFORD
1983

Oxford University Press, Walton Street, Oxford OX2 6DP
London Glasgow New York Toronto
Delhi Bombay Calcutta Madras Karachi
Kuala Lumpur Singapore Hong Kong Tokyo
Nairobi Dar es Salaam Cape Town
Melbourne Auckland
and associated companies in
Beirut Berlin Ibadan Mexico City Nicosia

Oxford is a trade mark of Oxford University Press

Published in the United States
by Oxford University Press, New York

British Library Cataloguing in Publication Data
Ker, N. R.
Medieval manuscripts in British Libraries.
3: Lampeter – Oxford
1. Manuscripts—Great Britain—Catalogs
I. Title
016.091 Z662.G7
ISBN 0-19-818195-7

Typeset by Joshua Associates, Oxford
Printed in Great Britain
at the University Press, Oxford
by Eric Buckley
Printer to the University

PREFACE[1]

The present volume begins with Lampeter and ends with Oxford. It is hoped that what still remains, including addenda, will fit into a fourth volume and that the general index will follow in a volume of its own. Nineteen of the 'larger collections' mentioned in the Preface to volume I are in the L–O section of the alphabet. They are the Bodleian Library, Oxford; Lincoln Cathedral; the John Rylands University Library of Manchester; and sixteen Oxford colleges. I am concerned with Lincoln Cathedral, the John Rylands University Library, and the sixteen Oxford colleges only in so far as they contain manuscripts not catalogued by Wooley (Lincoln), James (Manchester), or by Coxe (Oxford), and with the Bodleian Library only to provide a guide to catalogues and histories which supplement the main series of published catalogues. In Manchester the post-James material is extensive. My intention had been to provide somewhat abbreviated descriptions, on the lines of those provided for Canterbury Cathedral manuscripts in volume II, for all the Rylands manuscripts not catalogued by James but available in the handlists published in the *Bulletin of the John Rylands Library*. Descriptions of the manuscripts in question, in English, French, and other Western European languages, will be found in the present volume but not descriptions of manuscripts in Latin, save in a very brief form for those recent or fairly recent acquisitions which have not been described in *BJRL*. The decision to exclude the post-James Latin manuscripts was taken because it is the wish and intention of the John Rylands University Library to publish a complete catalogue of these medieval manuscripts and the cartularies and other business books outside the scope of *Medieval Manuscripts in British Libraries*. This catalogue is being prepared by Dr Frank Taylor and myself.[2]

The institutions with smaller medieval collections than the above, catalogued here, are of much the same kind as those in volume II

[1] When Neil Ker died in August 1982 proofs of this volume had begun to reach him and he had read pp. 1–120. Apart from minor corrections, and with two exceptions, the book is as he left it. The first exception is the description of Trinity College Oxford MS Danson 1, of the existence of which he learned only a few days before his death. The second exception is this Preface, of which he drafted only the first paragraph and part of the following sentence before tailing off into scribbled names. These names, and comparison with the Prefaces to volumes I and II do, however, make it clear that he had intended to follow their pattern, and the second paragraph here attempts to do that.

[2] Dr Ker's descriptions of these manuscripts have been handed over to the Library and will be used by Dr Taylor. The 'very brief form' of description used for the Latin manuscripts in the present volume follows the principles set out in the Preface to vol. I, p. vii.

(see there, p. vi),[1] although they may be grouped in nine categories rather than six: cathedrals; religious communities; universities; some libraries of Oxford University; theological colleges; public libraries and art galleries, museums, and record offices; churches; ecclesiastical archives; and miscellaneous. The cathedrals are Lichfield, Lincoln, Liverpool, Newcastle, and Norwich. The religious communities are the Community of the Resurrection, Mirfield, and the Cistercian Abbey of Mount St. Bernard. The universities are Leeds, Leicester, Liverpool, Newcastle, East Anglia (Norwich) and St. David's University College, Lampeter (a college of the University of Wales). The Oxford libraries are the college libraries of Hertford, Lady Margaret Hall, Mansfield, Pembroke, Regent's Park, St. Edmund Hall, St. Hilda's, Somerville, Wadham, and Worcester, and that of the Taylor Institution. The theological colleges are Oscott College and Blackfriars, Oxford. The public libraries, art galleries, museums, and record offices are at Leicester, Lichfield, Lincoln, Liverpool, Maidstone, Manchester, Newcastle, and Norwich. The churches are at Langley Marish, Maidstone, Malmesbury, Marlborough, Minehead, Norwich, and Oakham. The ecclesiastical archives are at Leeds, Leicester, Lichfield, Lincoln, and Norwich. The miscellaneous institutions are two societies (the Yorkshire Archaeological Society at Leeds and the Liverpool Athenaeum), a school (Queen Elizabeth's School for Boys, Mansfield) and two hospitals (the Wyggeston Hospital at Leicester, and Chetham's, Manchester). None of these smaller collections has been described in print until now, or not in a generally accessible publication, or only very briefly; they have been dealt with in the way referred to on pp. vii–xiii of the Preface to volume I.

From a few more words which Dr Ker scribbled on his draft it is possible to guess at two other matters on which he would have commented. First, in the Prefaces to volumes I and II (p. vii of each) he drew attention to his specimen Bible for each volume, i.e. an example of a common French type of Bible to which reference could be made throughout for comparison. In volume I the example was Lambeth Palace MS 1364, in volume II it was Bristol Public Libraries MS 15. In the present volume the specimen Bible is Liverpool Cathedral MS 13. Second, on p. vi of the Preface to volume II Dr Ker commented on his treatment of binding fragments: 'some space has been taken up in this volume by descriptions of binding fragments found in . . . capitular and diocesan records. . . . There seemed to me to be a case for including localizable material of this kind, some of which came certainly or probably from the medieval libraries in these places.'

[1] At this point Dr Ker's draft ends. The rest of this paragraph is modelled on the corresponding passages in volumes I and II.

In the present volume examples of such descriptions will be found under Leicester Archdeaconry, Lichfield Joint Record Office, Lincoln Dean and Chapter Muniments and Diocesan Records (both at the Lincolnshire Archives Office), Norwich Diocesan Record Office, and under All Souls, Corpus Christi, Magdalen, Merton, and Queen's Colleges in Oxford.

In the Preface to volume I Dr Ker set out his points of method, and users of the present volume are referred to it, with a reminder that in the Preface to volume II he drew attention to a change of mind over the use of 'med.' to indicate the middle years of a century. (In volume I 's. xiii' means the middle years of the thirteenth century; in volume II and in the present volume 's. xiii med.' is used to indicate these years.) On the matter of his conventions for indicating quiring he did not, however, say as much in the Preface to volume I as he might have done for, apart from a fairly general statement, he referred readers to his *Catalogue of Manuscripts containing Anglo-Saxon*, p. xxii. As this is now out of print and not everywhere readily available, these conventions are restated here:

The formulas used to show the construction of a quire are these:
(*a*) 1^8. (The eight leaves forming the quire are four conjugate pairs (i.e. four sheets), 1 and 8, 2 and 7, 3 and 6, and 4 and 5.)
(*b*) 1^8 3 and 6 are half-sheets. (Six of the leaves are conjugate pairs, 1 and 8, 2 and 7, and 4 and 5. Two of them, 3 and 6, are not conjugate.)
(*c*) 1^6 + 1 leaf after 5. (Six of the leaves are conjugate pairs, 1 and 6, 2 and 5, and 3 and 4. A seventh leaf lies between 1^5 and 1^6 and is an original part of the quire.)
(*d*) 1^6 + 1 leaf inserted after 5. (This differs from (*c*) in that the odd leaf is not an original part of the quire, but has been inserted at a later date.)
(*e*) 1^8 wants 2. (Formally this quire is identical with (*c*), but a gap in the text or some other evidence shows that the odd leaf, 1^7, was once paired with—but may not have been actually conjugate with—a leaf now missing after 1^1.)
(*f*) 1^8 wants 8, probably blank. (The scribe finished writing his text on or before the seventh leaf. The eighth leaf of the quire, now missing, was presumably blank. Formally the collation 1^6 + 1 before 1 is equally possible, but it seems unlikely that a scribe would deliberately begin his quire with a half-sheet. More probably he, or another scribe, or a binder, or a later owner or librarian in need of parchment removed the blank leaf at the end.)
(*g*) 1 five. (The quire consists of five leaves, but its construction is doubtful.)

The last paragraphs of Neil Ker's earlier prefaces were devoted to thanking people who had helped him, in particular the many librarians and curators whose manuscripts he described. In volume II, indeed, he remarked that in the Preface to volume I he did not express sufficiently how much he owed to librarians, especially of libraries where he had spent a long time. From the size of some of the collections in the present volume, and the complexity of some of the manuscripts in them, it may be possible to guess where his biggest debts lay, but a third person can do no more than express warm thanks on his behalf to all impartially.

As Dr Ker's literary executor I have incurred debts of my own to the following librarians and curators while seeing this volume through the press: Miss L. Gordon, University of Newcastle Library; Mr M. W. Grose, University of Leicester Library; Miss J. M. Kennedy, Archivist, Norfolk and Norwich Record Office; Dr S. M. Margeson, Norwich Castle Museum; Miss G. A. Matheson, Keeper of Manuscripts, John Rylands University Library of Manchester; Mr P. S. Morrish, Brotherton Library, University of Leeds; Mr M. R. Perkin, University of Liverpool Library; Miss A. C. Snape, Librarian, Chetham's Library, Manchester; Miss J. Williams, Librarian, Lincoln Cathedral Library. Dr Bruce Barker-Benfield, Mrs Ia McIlwaine, and Mr Andrew Wathey were frequently called on for help and deserve many thanks. I owe an enormous debt to Miss Grace Briggs and Dr Rodney Thomson, who both read all the proofs; to envisage the size of that task requires little imagination from anyone who glances at the book.

Users of volumes I–III of *MMBL* will wish to know whether the series can be completed as Dr Ker had intended, and I am glad to say that this should be possible. The typescript of a good deal of volume IV exists, in various stages of revision, and the Manuscripts Advisory Committee of SCONUL (the Standing Conference of National and University Libraries), whose predecessor, the Manuscripts Sub-Committee, asked Dr Ker to undertake the compilation of *MMBL*, has assumed the task of overseeing the completion. In 1982 Dr Ker estimated that he needed another five years to reach the end. Whether a co-operative effort can achieve a speedier completion than that remains to be seen, but it is unthinkable that this astonishing monument to Dr Ker's learning, vision, persistence over decades and, indeed, sheer courage, should be left uncompleted.

University College London ANDREW G. WATSON

Oxford University Press would like to acknowledge the generosity of the British Library Board in providing a subvention towards the costs of publication.

CONTENTS

LIST OF LIBRARIES AND MANUSCRIPTS

s before the short title shows that the name of the scribe or illuminator of all or part of the manuscript is known. *f* shows that the contents include fragments of manuscript used in binding: these are not taken into account in giving the short title and date. The country or place of origin is noted after the date, and also, in italics, the provenance, if the manuscript belonged to a particular institution in the Middle Ages or was then in a particular part of a country or was in a country different from that in which it originated. Bold type shows that a manuscript was both written in (or for) and belonged to a particular institution. An asterisk before a short title or pressmark shows that the manuscript in question is kept in a library other than that to which it belongs.

LAMPETER, Dyfed. ST DAVID'S UNIVERSITY COLLEGE

1. *s*Biblia. A.D. 1279. **S. Pierre-sur-Dives, O.S.B.** *England, Ord. Carth.*
2. Petrus de Capua. s. xiii^1. England.
3. *f*Letbertus, O.S.A.; T. à Kempis, O.S.A. s. xv^2. Low Countries (?).
4. Horae B.V.M. (Rome). s. xv^2. Italy.
5. *s*Ordinale sororum de Vadstena, Ord. Brig. s. xv ex. Vadstena.
6. Horae B.V.M. (Rome), etc. s. xv ex. Low Countries (?).
7. Horae B.V.M. (Rouen). s. xv/xvi. France.
8. Preces, etc. s. xvi^1. France.

LANGLEY MARISH, Buckinghamshire. PARISH CHURCH

227. P. Riga. s. xiii^1. N. France. *England.*
267. Evangelia. s. xi^1. England (Peterborough ?). *Windsor Collegiate Chapel.*

LEEDS, West Yorkshire

CATHOLIC DIOCESE OF LEEDS. Diocesan Archives.

Nicholas Love, Mirror (in English). s. xv^1. England.

UNIVERSITY LIBRARY

1. Manuel des Pecchez (in French). s. xiv^1. England.
2. Les Faits des Romains (in French). s. xv med. France.
4. *s*Juvenalis. s. xv^2. Italy.
122. *f*J. de Voragine, Legenda Sanctorum. s. xiii^2. Low Countries (?). *Liège, S. Jacques, O.S.B.*
123. Jacobus de Jüterbog. s. xv ex. Germany.
124. Evangelistarium. s. xv/xvi. Italy, for *S. Sixtus, Piacenza, O.S.B.*
498. Horae B.V.M. (Autun). s. xv^2. France.

Brotherton 1. Kalendarium, etc. s. xv med. France.
2. Psalterium, etc. s. xv med. France (Paris ?).
3. Horae B.V.M. (Sarum). s. xv med. Low Countries, for England. *England.*
4. Horae B.V.M. (Rome). s. xv^2. N.E. France.
5. Horae B.V.M. (Paris). s. xv med. France.
6. Horae B.V.M. (Rome). s. xv^2. Low Countries.

Brotherton 7. Horae B.V.M. (Utrecht: in Netherlandish). s. xv/xvi. Low Countries.
8. Horae B.V.M. (Bourges). s. xv/xvi.
9. Horae B.V.M. (Rome). s. xv ex. Low Countries (?).
10. Horae B.V.M. (Rome). s. xv^{2}. Italy.
11. Preces. s. xvi in. Germany.
12. Preces, etc. s. xvi in. Bavaria (Augsburg ?).
13. Ordo visitandi domos; G. de Pisis, De forma prima electionis. s. xv^{2}. Italy, for Ord. Carth.
14. Horae B.V.M. (partly in Netherlandish). s. xv^{2}. Low Countries.
15. Horae B.V.M. (Sarum). s. xv^{2}. England.
20. J. Duns Scotus, Quodlibeta. s. xv^{1}. England.
21. Cicero, De officiis. s. xii. Italy.
22. Beda, In Epistolas Canonicas. s. xii^{1}. S. Germany. *Reichenbach am Regen, O.S.B.*
23. J. de Voragine, Legenda Sanctorum. s. xiv in. Spain (?). *'Mosserhen'.*
24. Psalterium, etc. (in Netherlandish). s. xv^{2}. Low Countries. *Oudegein, O.S.A.*
100. 'Genealogie de la Bible', etc. (chronicle roll in French). s. xv^{2} (reign of Louis XI). France.
101. *sf*P. Burgensis, A.D. 1453–4. Bamberg. *Ebern.*
102. *s*Sermones, etc. A.D. 1412; s. xv^{1}. *Würzburg, O.F.M.*
103. *f*Distinctiones, Abstinencia–Zelus; etc. s. xv med. Germany (N.W. ?), for O.F.M.
500. Prick of Conscience (in English), etc. s. xiv/xv. England.
501. Prick of Conscience, etc. (in English). s. xv^{1}. England.
502. J. Mirk, Festial (in English); Sequentiae. s. xv med.–xv ex. England.

YORKSHIRE ARCHAEOLOGICAL SOCIETY, Claremont, Clarendon Rd.

MD 338 (part) + York, Borthwick Institute, BF 10. Aristoteles (fragm.). s. xv^{2}. France (?).

LEICESTER

ARCHDEACONRY

Fragments. See pp. 73–4.

OLD TOWN HALL LIBRARY

2. Biblia. s. xiii med. England (?). *England.*
3. J. Wyclif, Sermons (in English). s. xiv/xv. England.
4. Miscellanea (partly in English). s. xiii ex.–xiv ex. England.

BR II/3/1. Statuta Angliae. s. xiii/xiv–xv med. England.
BR II/3/3. Nova Statuta Angliae. s. xiv ex.–xv med. England.

UNIVERSITY LIBRARY

7. Biblia. s. xiii^{2}. England (?). *England.*
8. Biblia. s. xiii med. England.
9, 10. Biblia (2 vols.). s. xiii^{2}. Low Countries (?).
11A+B. G. Porretanus, In Psalterium. s. xii^{2}. England.
12. Horae B.V.M. (Rome). s. xiv ex. Flanders (?).
13. Horae B.V.M. (Rome). s. xv^{2}. Italy for Verona diocese.
14. Horae B.V.M. (Paris). s. xv/xvi. France.

15. Horae B.V.M. (Utrecht: in Netherlandish). s. xv in. Low Countries.
17. Graduale. s. xv². Germany, for Münster diocese.
18. Antiphonale. s. xvi in. Low Countries (?), for O.C.
20. Horae B.V.M. (Paris). s. xv². France.
21. *f*Prayers and devotions (in Netherlandish). s. xv/xvi. Low Countries, for nuns.
22. Horae B.V.M. (Utrecht: in Netherlandish). s. xv². Low Countries.
30. Historica quaedam. s. xv¹. England.
41. Ludolphus de Saxonia, Ord. Carth., Vita Christi. s. xv². **Trier, S. Maximinus, O.S.B.**
47. Brut Chronicle (in English). s. xv². England.
72. *s*P. Blesensis, Compendium de vita beati Job. A.D. 1443. Low Countries.
73. *f*Basilius, etc. s. xv². Italy.

WYGGESTON HOSPITAL

*10 D 34/6. J. Wyclif, Sermons (in English). s. xiv/xv. England.
*10 D 34/7. W. Peraldus, O.P., Sermones; etc. s. xv in. England.
*10 D 34/9. De vitiis et virtutibus. s. xiv². England.
*10 D 34/10. W de Pagula, Oculus sacerdotis. s. xiv med. England. *Leicester.*
*10 D 34/11. S. Boraston, O.P. s. xiv/xv. England. *Leicester, Collegiate Church of B. V.M.*
*10 D 34/12. *f*R. Rolle, etc. s. xv in. England.
*10 D 34/13. *f*J. Felton, Sermones; etc. s. xv med. England. *Leicester, Collegiate Church of B. V.M.* (?).
*10 D 34/14. Gesta Romanorum. s. xv¹. England.
*10 D 34/15. J. Rolle; J. Hanneton; etc. s. xiv med.–xiv/xv. England.
*10 D 34/16. Floretum. s. xv in. England. *Staffordshire.*
*1 D 50/xiii/3/1. *f*Narrationes, etc. s. xiv/xv. England.
*1 D 50/xiii/3/2, 3. Sermones, etc. s. xvi in. England.
*1 D 50/xiii/3/4. *f*T. Littleton (in French). s. xv ex. England.

LICHFIELD, Staffordshire

CATHEDRAL

1. *f*Evangelia ('The Lichfield Gospels'). s. viii med. (?). England or Wales. *Llandeilo-fawr; Lichfield Cathedral.*
9. Biblia (pars). s. xii ex. France (?). *England.*
10. New Testament (in English). s. xv in. England.
14. Bernardus, De consideratione. s. xiv med. France (?).
16. Prick of Conscience, etc. (partly in English and French). s. xv in. England.
20. Vigilius Thapsensis, etc. s. xiii in. England.
23. *s*Taxatio ecclesiastica Nicholai IV. s. xiv med. England.
28. *f*Annales. s. xiii²–xiv¹. England. *Lichfield Cathedral.*
29. Chaucer, Canterbury Tales (in English). s. xv¹. England.
30. Codex Justiniani. s. xiii ex. Italy. *France (?). England (Oxford).*
31. Decretales Gregorii IX et Innocentii IV. s. xiii/xiv. England. *Lichfield Cathedral.*
35. Dives and Pauper (in English). s. xv². England.
50. Prick of Conscience (in English). s. xiv². England.

JOINT RECORD OFFICE

Underwriting of 'Book of the Vicars'. s. xv.
Fragments: see p. 126.

LINCOLN

CATHEDRAL

300. Horae B.V.M. (Rome). s. xv^1. N.E. France.
301. Horae B.V.M. (Utrecht: in Netherlandish). s. xv^2. Low Countries.
302. *f*Psalmi paenitentiales, etc. s. xv med. France (for Troyes diocese ?).
303. Capitularium, etc. A.D. 1527. Italy, for O.P. (Bologna ?).
304. Psalterium. s. xv med. England. *Kent* (?).
305. Ordo baptizandi. s. xvi^1. Germany.
306. Psalterium, etc. s. xiv^2. Low Countries and England.
307. Horae B.V.M. (Rome). s. xv in. France.
308. Graduale. s. xvi^1. Italy, for O.S.A. (?).

DEAN AND CHAPTER MUNIMENTS, Lincolnshire Archives Office

A/1/11. Taxatio ecclesiastica Nicholai IV. s. xiv in. England.
A/2/3, ff. 1–48. J. de Schalby, Historia. s. xiv med.–xiv^2. Lincoln (?).
Fragments in A/2/18 and A/2/20: see pp. 140–2.
Di/20/2/B1, ff. 22–5. Officium J. de Dalderby, s. xiv^1. **Lincoln Cathedral.**
Di/20/3. J. de Hildesheim, Historia trium regum. s. xiv/xv. England.

DIOCESAN RECORDS, Lincolnshire Archives Office

Fragments: see pp. 143–6.

LINCOLNSHIRE ARCHIVES OFFICE, The Castle, Lincoln

2 Cragg/Bussy. Psalterium ('The Bussy psalter'). s. xv^1. England, for Bussy family.

LIVERPOOL, Lancashire

ATHENAEUM

Gladstone 13. Brevia placitata (fragm.). s. xiii^2. England.
27. Statuta Angliae; Registrum brevium. s. xiii/xiv. England.
49. Statuta Angliae, etc. s. xiv^1. England.
85. Statuta Angliae, etc. s. xiv^1 (*c.* 1330 ?)–xiv med. England.
Thompson 1. *s*Cicero, Orationes; etc. A.D. 1448–9 and s. xv med. Venice.

CATHEDRAL

*4. Breviarium. s. xv med. Germany, for Cologne diocese.
*5. Horae B.V.M. (Rome). s. xv med. N.E. France or W. Belgium.
*6. Horae angeli custodientis. s. xv^2. England.
*8. Horae B.V.M. (Utrecht: in Netherlandish). s. xv med. Low Countries.
*9. Horae B.V.M. (Paris). s. xv^2. France (Paris ?).
*10. Inhumatio defuncti. s. xv in. Italy.
*11. Breviarium romanum. s. xiv/xv. France, for Rodez diocese.
*12. T. Aquinas, etc. s. xv med. N. Italy.
*13. Biblia, s. xiii med. France.
*14. Manuale. s. xv in. Germany, for Cologne (?) diocese.
*15. *s*Horae B.V.M. (Bursfeld). A.D. 1496. Germany.
*17. Horae B.V.M. (Rouen). s. xv med. France.
*18. *s*Breviarium. A.D. 1503 (?). **Traunkirchen, O.S.B.**
*19. Antiphonale. s. xvi in. Germany, for O.S.A.
*20. *f*Manuale, cum notis. s. xiv ex. England.

*21. Ambrosius, In Ps. 118. s. xv med. N.W. Germany or Low Countries.
*22. Psalterium, etc. s. xiv med. England.
*23. Horae B.V.M. (Cologne), etc. s. xv². Germany, for Cologne diocese.
*27. *f*Psalterium, etc. s. xiii/xiv. England (?: for Seavington St Michael ?). *Somerset.*
*28. *f*Bernardus, Sermones; etc. s. xv in. Italy.
*29. Missale (Sarum), cum notis. s. xiv med.–xiv/xv. England. *Shepton Beauchamp Church.*
*30. W. de Pagula; Lyndwood. s. xiv/xv–xv in. England.
*34. *f*J. Damascenus, De fide orthodoxa, etc. s. xiii$^{1-2}$. Southern Low Countries. *Cambron O.C.*
*35. Processionale (Sarum). s. xiv²–xiv/xv. England.
*36. Horae B.V.M. (Sarum). s. xiv/xv. England, for Norwich diocese.
*37. Breviarium (Sarum). s. xiv². England.
*38. Graduale. s. xv². W. Germany.
*39. Pontificale. s. xiii/xiv. Italy. *Germany* (?).
*40. Missale (Sarum). s. xv med. England.
*41. Missale (Lyons). s. xv². France. *Nantua, chapel of Holy Cross.*
*42. Lectionarium. s. xv². Germany, for Münster diocese.
*50. Graduale (fragm.). s. xii med. Germany.
*51. Kalendarium (fragm.). s. xiii¹. England (London). *Writtle* (?).
*59. Agius, Compotus (fragm.). s. ix². Germany (Corvey ?).

MERSEYSIDE COUNTY MUSEUMS, Mayer collection

*12000. Sermones. s. xv². Germany.
*12001. Horae B.V.M. (Paris). s. xv med. France.
*12004 + 8951. *f*Psalterium, etc. s. xiii¹. S. Germany.
*12006. Horae B.V.M. (Rome). s. xv². Southern Low Countries (Bruges).
*12008. Biblia. s. xiii med. France (?).
*12009. Horae B.V.M. (Sarum). s. xv¹. Low Countries (Utrecht ?), for England.
*12010. Breviarium, pars hiemalis (Cologne). s. xv med. Germany.
*12012. Chronicon inrotulatum. s. xv med. England.
*12016. Psalterium, etc. s. xv med. England. *Cardington Church.*
*12017. P. Pictaviensis, Genealogia; etc. s. xiii med. England.
*12020. Horae B.V.M. (Carmelite: partly in Netherlandish). s. xv². Low Countries, for Ord. Carm.
*12022. Horae B.V.M. (Paris). s. xv in. France.
*12023. Horae (Utrecht: in Netherlandish). s. xv². Low Countries.
*12024. Horae B.V.M. (Rouen). s. xv med. France.
*12025. Horae B.V.M. (Paris). s. xv². France.
*12026. Breviarium ('Compendium diurni'). s. xv². S. Germany (?), for O.P.
*12027. Breviarium. s. xv in.–xv med. Italy (Florence ?). Added to for O.F.M.
*12028. Horae B.V.M. (Rome). s. xv med.–xv². N.E. France or Flanders.
*12032. *s*P. Lombardus, Sententiae. A.D. 1472. Italy.
*12033. Horae B.V.M. (Rouen). s. xv¹. France.
*12034. Processionale (Sarum). s. xiv², xiv/xv. England.
*12035. Schwabenspiegel (in German). s. xiv med. Germany.
*12036. Eugippius, etc. s. xiii/xiv. England. *Durham Cathedral Priory* (?); *Oxford.*
*12037. *s*T. Aquinas, Secunda secundae. s. xiii ex. France (?), for O.F.M. Koblenz (?). *Bredelar O.C.*
*12038. Biblia. s. xiii¹. France ('Alexander atelier').
*12039. Horae S. Spiritus, etc. (in Netherlandish). s. xv med. Low Countries.

*12046. *f*Sulpicius Severus; Coluccio Salutati; etc. s. xv/xvi. *S. Michael, Murano, Ord. Camald.*
*12047. Gaietanus de Thienis, In Physica Aristotelis. s. xv ex. Italy.
*12048. W. Peraldus, Summa de vitiis. s. xiii². England.
*12050. *s*Psalmi paenitentiales, etc. (in Netherlandish). A.D. 1432 (?). Delft (?).
*12055. Hugo Spechtshart von Reutlingen, Speculum grammaticae. s. xv med. Germany.
*12068. Eutropius; Festus. s. xv². Italy (Rome).
*12069. *s*Pseudo-Augustinus, Sermones. A.D. 1473, 1490. Germany.
*12070. *s*Juvenalis. A.D. 1471. Italy.
*12071. R. de Hengham, Summa magna (fragm.). s. xiii ex. England.
*12107. 'Distinctiones Magistri Mauricii'. s. xiii². France (?).
*12108. Horae B.V.M. (Rheims). s. xv². France.

PUBLIC LIBRARIES

091 CHO (8/80842). Officia liturgica. s. xv/xvi. Italy.
091 CHO (60/63395). Officia liturgica. s. xv². N. Italy, for diocese of Bressanone.
q091 HAL. Breviarium, pars hiemalis de tempore. s. xiii/xiv. Germany, for diocese of Halberstadt.
091 PSA 8/45329. Psalmi; Horae B.V.M. (Metz). s. xiii/xiv. E. France.
f091 PSA 65/32036. Psalterium cum comment. Petri Lombardi. s. xii/xiii. England (?).
f091 RAB. Rabanus Maurus, In Genesim; etc. s. xii med. England. *Peterborough, O.S.B.*
091 STA. Statuta Angliae, etc. s. xiv¹ (*c.*1330 ?). England.
096. 1 (64/22898). Horae B.V.M. (Rome). s. xv/xvi. N.E. (?) France.
q841. 1 JAC. J. de Longuyon, Voeux du Paon (in French). s. xiv in. France.
f909 HIG. R. Higden, Polychronicon (in English). s. xv med.
A. 13109. Pseudo-Jerome, Ad Celantiam (in Italian). s. xv med. Italy.
D. 435. Horae B.V.M. (Paris). s. xv¹. France, for Beauvais (?) diocese.

UNIVERSITY LIBRARY

F. 2. 1. Biblia. s. xiii med. Germany (?). Heinsberg, Ord. Praem.
F. 2. 2. Psalterium, etc. s. xv/xvi. Low Countries, for Ord. Brig. (Marienwater ?).
F. 2. 3. Psalterium, etc. s. xv². Italy (Naples ?), for O.F.M.
F. 2. 4. Psalterium, etc. s. xv in. Southern Low Countries (?).
F. 2. 5. Biblia. s. xiii med. England.
F. 2. 6. Horae B.V.M. (Rome). s. xvi in. France (for bishop of Albi ?).
F. 2. 7. Horae B.V.M. (Paris). s. xiv/xv. France.
F. 2. 8. Horae B.V.M. (Chartres). s. xv². France.
F. 2. 9. Lectiones breviarii. s. xv med. France (?), for Ord. Carth. *Villeneuve-lez-Avignon, Ord. Carth.*
F. 2. 11. Lectionary (in Netherlandish). s. xv². Low Countries.
F. 2. 12. *f*'Rapularius'. s. xv med.–xv². **Erfurt, Ord. Carth.**
F. 2. 13. *s*N. de Auximo, O.F.M., Supplementum Summae Pisanae. A.D. 1474. **Milan, O.F.M.** (?).
F. 2. 14. Horae B.V.M. (Châlons). s. xv². France.
F. 2. 17. Biblia. s. xiii med. France. *S. Denis, Rheims, O.S.A.*
F. 2. 18. Horae B.V.M. (Paris). s. xv med. France.
F. 2. 19. Horae B.V.M. (Rome). s. xv¹. Low Countries (Tournai diocese ?).
F. 2. 21. Horae B.V.M. (Paris). s. xiv med. France.
F. 2. 22. Horae B.V.M. (Rome). s. xv ex. France.

F. 2. 23. Horae B.V.M. (Rome). s. xv^2. Florence, for Taddei family.
F. 2. 24. Horae B.V.M. (Evreux). s. xv/xvi. France.
F. 3. 2. J. Curlus, In Terentium et Strabonem. s. xv^2. Naples, for Ferdinand of Aragon.
F. 3. 3. Ambrosius, De officiis ministrorum. s. xv med. Florence.
F. 3. 4. Quaestiones super Donatum minorem. A.D. 1490. Italy.
F. 3. 5. (*s*) Aulus Gellius. s. xv med. Florence.
F. 3. 6. Ovidius, Heroides. s. xiv^2. Italy.
F. 3. 8. L. Bruni, De studiis, etc. s. xv med. Italy (Veneto).
F. 3. 9. Graduale. s. xv^2. France, for O.P.
F. 3. 10. *f*P. Lombardus, Sententiae. s. xiii med. Italy.
F. 3. 13. *f*Gregorius, De cura pastorali. s. xiii in. Germany or Austria. *Ranshofen, O.S.A.*
F. 3. 14. Horae B.V.M. (Sarum). s. xiv^2–xv med. England.
F. 4. 1. *f*Parvum volumen, cum apparatu. s. xiii^1–xiii med. Italy.
F. 4. 2. Antiphonale, pars hiemalis. s. xiv^1. Italy.
F. 4. 4. Missale. s. xv^2. Austria, for Salzburg diocese.
F. 4. 5, ff. 1–12. Petrarch, Rime (fragm.: in Italian). s. xv med. Italy.
F. 4. 5, ff. 13–120. Lives and miracles of St Jerome (in Italian). s. xv/xvi. Italy.
F. 4. 6. *s*Marsilius de Inghen, Abbrev. Phisicorum Aristotelis. A.D. 1463. Italy. *Milan.*
F. 4. 7. Philippus Cancellarius, In Psalmos, etc. s. xiii^1. Low Countries (?). *S. Martin, Tournai, O.S.B.*
F. 4. 8. *f*Piers Plowman (in English). s. xv in. England.
F. 4. 9. William of Nassington, etc. (in English). s. xiv/xv. England.
F. 4. 10. Chastising of God's Children, etc. (in English). s. xv^2. England.
F. 4. 11. Registrum Brevium. s. xiv ex. England. *London* (?).
F. 4. 13. Officium Coronae Domini, etc. s. xiv^1, xv^1. Italy (Pisa). *Church of Santa Maria della Spina, Pisa* (?).
F. 4. 18. W. Peraldus, O.P.; R. Fishacre, O.P. s. xiii ex. England.
F. 4. 19. Missale romanum. s. xv^2. Italy (N. Umbria ?).
F. 4. 20. *s*Gregorius IX, Decretales. A.D. 1290. France.
F. 4. 22. *f*G. de Hoylandia, etc. s. xiv med. Germany.

MAIDSTONE, Kent

ALL SAINTS CHURCH

*A. 13. *f*Sermones, etc. s. xiii^1–xiv^1. England. *Northampton* (R. Helmdon, *Master of the Hospital of St John the Baptist and St John the Evangelist* ?).
*B. 91. Horae (Sarum); Psalterium. s. xiv ex. England.
*P. 5. Biblia, pars ii. s. xii med. England. *St Augustine's, Canterbury* (?).

CORPORATION MUSEUM

Mus. 4. Horae B.V.M. (Tournai: partly in Netherlandish). s. xv. Southern Low Countries.
Mus. 5. (A) Horae B.V.M. (Utrecht: in Netherlandish). s. xvi in. Low Countries.
(B) *s*Nine Virtues (in French). A.D. 1492. **Deynse** (near Kortrijk), **O.S.A.**
Mus. 6. Fervor amoris, etc. (in English). s. xv^1. England.

MALMESBURY, Wiltshire. PARISH CHURCH

1. *s*Biblia (4 vols.). A.D. 1457 (?). **Charterhouse of La Chapelle, Hérinnes-lez-Enghien.**

2 + YALE UNIVERSITY 86. Biblical history (in French), etc. s. xiv/xv. England.

MANCHESTER, Lancashire

CHETHAM'S LIBRARY

6680. Astrologica, etc. (partly in English). s. xv med. England (Enfield ?).
6681. *s*De situ universorum, etc. s. xiv ex. **Oxford, O.F.M.** (?).
6682. Augustinus, etc. s. xiii². England.
6687. F. Barbarus, De re uxoria. s. xv med. N.E. Italy.
6688. Biblia. s. xiii med. England (?).
6689. Biblia. s. xiii med. France (?).
6690. Mirror of life of Christ, etc. (in English). s. xv med. England.
6691. P. de Braco, Compendium juris canonici. A.D. 1466. France or Low Countries.
6696. (*s*)J. Gower, Confessio amantis (in English). s. xv/xvi. England (Nuthurst ?).
6709. *s*Lydgate, Life of Our Lady; etc. (in English). A.D. 1485, 1490, 1493. **Dunstable, O.S.A.**
6711. Mandeville's Travels (in English). s. xv¹. England.
6712. *s*M. Paris, Flores Historiarum; etc. s. xiii med.–xiv¹. St Albans, O.S.B.; Westminster, O.S.B.
6713. Missale (Sarum). s. xiv ex. England.
6714. Comment. in Ovidii Metamorphoseos. A.D. 1470 (?). France.
6717. Psalterium; Horae B.V.M. (Sarum); etc. s. xv med. England. *Godstow, O.S.B.*
6720. Terentius. A.D. 1427. Italy.
6721. Terentius. s. xv/xvi. Germany (?).
6722. P. Cantor, Verbum abbreviatum. s. xiii in. England.
6723. New Testament (in English). s. xv in. England.
8001. Aristoteles, Ethica. s. xv med. Italy (Florence).
8002. Aeschines, L. Bruni interprete. s. xv med. Italy.
8003. Jacobus de Cessolis, etc. s. xv². England.
8005. Justinus, Epitoma in Trogum Pompeium. s. xv². Italy.
8007. Horae B.V.M. (Besançon: partly in French). s. xv². France.
8008. Prick of Conscience (in English). s. xiv ex. Ireland (?).
8009. Ipomadon, etc. (in English). s. xv². England (London ?).
8023. Medica. s. xiii ex.–xiv med. France (?).
11362. Poems of Alain Chartier (in French). s. xv med. France.
11366. R. Bacon, Opera medica. s. xv ex. France (?).
11379. R. Higden, Polychronicon, etc. (in English). s. xiv/xv. England.
11380. Medica. s. xiii/xiv. France.
27857. Medica. s. xv². Italy (?). *England.*
27894. Evangelistarium (Sarum). s. xv med. England.
27900. (*s*)Aulus Gellius. s. xv². Italy (Florence, for F. Sassetti).
27902 (sold in 1980). G. de Chauliac (in English). s. xv². England.
27907. Hymnale (Sarum). s. xv². England, for Ord. Brig. (Syon).
27911. Life of Christ (in English). s. xv¹. England.
27929. Opera C. Salutati. s. xv in.–xv med. Italy; England. *England.*
27938. *s*Medical recipes (in English). s. xv/xvi. England.
27941 (sold in 1980). Medica. s. xv². England.
27971. Horae B.V.M. (Coutances). s. xv². France.
28024. *f*G. de Vino Salvo, Nova poetria; etc. s. xiv/xv, s. xv¹. England.
33667. Horae B.V.M. (Utrecht: in Netherlandish). s. xv ex. Low Countries.

PUBLIC LIBRARY

BR. 310 D. 5. J. Calderinus, Repertorium utriusque juris. s. xv med. Germany.
BRm. 343 Lt. 13. Officium in agenda mortuorum, etc. s. xv ex. Italy, for O.E.S.A.
BRm. 343 Lt. 15. Antiphonale, pars aestivalis. s. xv ex. Italy.
BRm. 360 Py. 35. Psalterium, etc. s. xv med. Germany, for Ord. Carth. (Erfurt).
G. 091 B. 1. Legenda, etc., Sanctae Bonae. s. xiii^1. **S. Martino, Pisa, O.S.A.**
G. 091 H. 2. Horae B.V.M. (Tournai). s. xv med. Low Countries.
q411. G. 2. G. Barzizius, De orthographia; etc. A.D. 1474. Germany (?).
f091. F. 9 ff. 20–1, 26–31, 36–41, 48–51, 77–8. Breviarium (fragm.). s. xv med. Denmark.
f091. F. 9 ff. 87–98. Exempla. s. xiii^2. England.
f091. J. 12. Codex Justiniani. s. xiii^2. France (?).

JOHN RYLANDS UNIVERSITY LIBRARY[1]

Dutch 8. Hours of B.V.M. (Utrecht). s. xv^2.
9. Imitation of Christ, etc. s. xv/xvi, xvi^1.
10. Usuard; Calendar. A.D. 1472. *St. Lucy, Amsterdam, O.F.M.*
12. Hours of B.V.M. (Utrecht). s. xv med.
13. Communion prayers, etc. s. xv med.
Eng. 1. Lydgate, Siege of Troy. s. xv med.
2. Lydgate, Fall of Princes. s. xv med.
3. Gospels, s. xv in.
7. 'Fourme of cury'. s. xv^2.
50. Prick of Conscience; Guy of Warwick. s. xiv ex.
51. Prick of Conscience, etc. s. xv in.
63. Chaucer, Canterbury Tales (fragm.). s. xv^2.
75. Pauline Epistles, etc. s. xiv/xv.
76. New Testament. s. xv in.
77. New Testament. s. xiv/xv.
78. New Testament. s. xv in.
79. New Testament. s. xv in.
80. New Testament. A.D. 1444 (?).
81. New Testament. s. xiv/xv. *Syon, Ord. Brig.*
82. Old Testament (part). s. xv^1.
83. Sapiential Books. s. xiv/xv.
84. Acts of Apostles. s. xiv/xv.
85. Commentaries on the Lord's Prayer, etc. s. xiv/xv.
86. John Wyclif, Tracts (mainly in Latin). s. xiv/xv.
87. Pore Caitif. s. xiv/xv.
88. Psalms and canticles. s. xiv^2.
89. Old Testament (part). s. xv in.
90. *f*Prick of Conscience, etc. s. xiv/xv.
91. Bible, vol. i. s. xv^1.
92. Apocalypse, with commentary. s. xiv ex.
94. Mirror of the Life of Christ, etc. s. xv med.
98. Mirror of the life of Christ. s. xiv/xv.
102. Brut Chronicle. s. xv med.
103. Brut Chronicle. s. xiv med.

[1] Language and country of origin are noted only if they differ from what is to be expected from the classification according to languages.

104. Brut Chronicle. s. xv ex.
105. Brut Chronicle. s. xv ex.
109 + Norwich Cathedral 5. 'Mirror' and other sermons (partly in Latin). A.D. 1432; s. xv^1. *Welbeck, Ord. Praem.*
113. *s*Chaucer, Canterbury Tales. s. xv^2.
206. Brut Chronicle. s. xv^2.
207. Brut Chronicle. s. xv^1, xv^2.
288. Littleton, Tenures (partly in French and Latin). s. xv/xvi.
404. Medical recipes, charms, etc. s. xv^2.
412. Pore Caitif, etc. s. xv in.
413. Mirror of the Life of Christ. s. xv in.
895. Passion and Resurrection of Christ, etc. s. xv med.
1310. On urines. s. xvi in.

Fr. 1 + Oxford, Bodleian, Douce 215. Arthurian romances. s. xiv in. N. France.
2. G. Deguileville, O.C., Pélérinages. s. xv^1.
3. Salutations to B.V.M., etc. s. xiv/xv.
4. J. de Courcy, La Bouquechardière. s. xv ex.
5. Illustrations of Genesis, with captions. s. xiii med.
6. Lives of saints, etc. s. xiii^1. England (?).
7. Régime de santé. s. xv^2.
54. Roll chronicle. s. xv^1–xv med. England.
55. *f*E. de Monstrelet, Croniques. s. xv ex.
56. History of the dukes of Normandy, etc. s. xiv^2.
57. *f*N. de Fribois, Cronique de France. s. xv/xvi.
58. *f*Customs of Brittany, etc. s. xv^2. Brittany.
62. Grandes Croniques de France. s. xv med.
63. Valerius Maximus, with commentaries (partly in Latin). s. xv in.
64. English chronicle. s. xiv in. England.
65. Guillaume de Tignonville, Dits moraux. s. xvi in.
66. Roman de la Rose, s. xiv med. N.E. France (?).
71. Accounts of Royal Artillery. s. xv^2.
72. Nova statuta Angliae. s. xiv ex. (1390?).
73. Customs of Normandy. s. xv^2.
74. Customs of Brittany. s. xv med.
75. Britton. s. xiii/xiv. England.
87. Theological tracts. s. xiv/xv–xv med.
88. Armorial roll. s. xv^1. England (Yorkshire ?).
98. Commentary on second statute of Westminster, etc. s. xv med. England.
99. Chronicle roll. s. xv^2 (after A.D. 1461).
142. La vie S. Edmund le rei. s. xiii/xiv. England.
143. Horae B.V.M. (partly in Latin). s. xv in.

Germ. 1. 'Vera sciencia alhimie in figuris'. s. xv/xvi.
11. *f*Büchlein von der Liebe Gottes, etc. s. xv^2. S. Germany, for nuns (?).
13, ff. 75–90, 93–102. Penitential psalms, etc. s. xv/xvi. S. Germany (Augsburg ?).
24. On diseases, etc. s. xv ex. S. Germany or Austria.

Ice. 1. Rimbegla, etc. s. xv.
5. Horae (?). s. xv in. (?).

Irish 35. Medical treatises. s. xv/xvi. W. Scotland or Ireland.

It. 1. *s*Petrarch, Rime; Dante, Canzoni. s. xiv^2. Florence, for Lorenzo di Carlo Strozzi.
2. Dante, Divina Commedia; etc. s. xv^2.

3. *s*Guido da Pisa, Ord. Carm., Istorie antiche. A.D. 1472 (?).
4. J. Climacus, Scala paradisi. s. xv in. Veneto (?).
43. *s*Description of Venice. A.D. 1464. Venice.
49. *s*Dante, Divina Commedia; etc. (partly in Latin). A.D. 1416, 1426, s. xv^1.
51. Fioretti of St Francis, etc. s. xv med. *Fabriano, O.F.M.*
53. Antoninus Florentinus, etc. (partly in Latin). s. xv med.

Lat. 448. Postilla studencium Pragensis super dominicalia ewangelia. s. xv med.
452. Horae B.V.M. s. xv med. France.
453. Horae B.V.M. (Angers). s. xv^2. France.
454. R. de Sancto Victore, In Ionam; Albertus Causidicus, De doctrina dicendi et tacendi. s. xiii med. France. *Paris, Sorbonne.*
458. *s*Speculum mortis maius, etc. 1458, 1459, 1464. Austria. **Melk, O.S.B.**
459. Nicholaus de Cusa, De visione Dei; etc. s. xv^2. Austria. *Melk, O.S.B.*
466. Horae B.V.M. (Rome). s. xv in. S. Low Countries.
467. Bernardus, etc. s. xv^1. Germany, *Gaesdonck, O.S.A.*
469. Horae B.V.M. (Tournai). s. xv in.
470. Missale 'secundum usum sancte romane ecclesie'. s. xiv/xv. Italy.
471. Cassiodorus, Variae, De amicitia. s. xiv^1. Italy. *Casali, O.P.*
472. Psalterium cum glossa Petri Lombardi. s. xiii^1. Italy. *Rimini, O.F.M.*
474. *f*Biblia. s. xiii med. England. *Christ Church, Canterbury.*
475. Correctiones Bibliae; Lucidarium Legendarum. s. xiii/xiv. Italy. *Siena (?), O.F.M.*
476. *s*Gregorius, Moralia in Job, lib. 17–24. s. xv^2. *Bethleem, near Louvain, O.S.A.*
477. Cassiodorus, In Psalmos 1–50. s. xv ex.
478. P. de Remis, Sermones. s. xiii med. Low Countries.
479. Pontificale. 1405. Venice.
480. Breviarium. s. xv in. France. *Le Château d'Oléron (?).*
481. Psalterium etc. s. xv in. Germany. **Steinfeld, Ord. Praem.**
482. Horae B.V.M. (Rome). s. xv^2. S. Low Countries.
483. Officium mortuorum (Sarum). s. xiv/xv. England.
484. Officium mortuorum, cum notis. s. xv med. Germany. *Hospital of the Holy Spirit, Horb am Neckar.*
485. Collectarium ad usum ordinis Carthusiensis. s. xiv^1. Spain (?) *Paular, Ord. Carth.*
486. Vita, Miracula et officium Sanctae Clarae de Cruce. s. xv^2. Italy.

Welsh 1. *s*Pedigrees by Gutun Owain. A.D. 1497 (?).

MANSFIELD, Nottinghamshire. QUEEN ELIZABETH'S SCHOOL FOR BOYS

Psalterium, etc. s. xiii in. France. *England* (?).

MARLBOROUGH, Wiltshire. VICAR'S LIBRARY

*E. 32. Sermones, etc. (mostly in English). s. xvi^1. England.

MINEHEAD, Somerset. PARISH CHURCH OF ST MICHAEL

Missale (Sarum). s. xiv/xv. England. *London.*

MIRFIELD, West Yorkshire. COMMUNITY OF THE RESURRECTION

*1. *f*Beda, Historia ecclesiastica. s. xiv med. England. *Lichfield diocese* (?).
*2. Miracula B.V.M.; Sermones; Exempla. s. xiii². Italy. *Ancona, O.P.* (?).
3. Graduale. s. xiii ex. Spain (?), for O.P.
4. Processionale. s. xiv/xv. England, for O.S.A. (Worcester diocese ?).
5. Officium mortuorum. s. xvi in. Spain (?).
6. Horae B.V.M. (Rome); Preces. s. xv/xvi. Italy (Naples ?).

MOUNT ST BERNARD ABBEY, Coalville, Leicestershire

1. Antiphonale, pars hiemalis. s. xiii¹. N. France (?), for O.C.
2. *f*Vita Sancti Bernardi, etc. s. xii/xiii. Low Countries (?).

NEWCASTLE-UPON-TYNE, Northumberland

CATHEDRAL

Biblia. s. xiii med. France (?). *Hexham, O.S.A.*

PUBLIC LIBRARY

*TH. 1678. Psalms and canticles in Latin, with Rolle's translation and commentary in English; etc. s. xiv². England.
*TH. 5045A. Peregrinus de Oppeln, O.P., Sermones. s. xv in. England.
*TH. 5403A. J. Calderinus, Repertorium utriusque juris. s. xv med. N.W. Germany or Low Countries. *England.*
*TH. 5405A. Sermones abbreviati. s. xv in. England.
091. 01173. H. de Novo Castro, O.F.M., De victoria Christi; etc. A.D. 1475; s. xv². Germany (Cologne ?).

UNIVERSITY LIBRARY

1. 'Passionarium'. s. xiii¹. N.E. (?) France. *St Mary, York, O.S.B.*
2. Missale (Sarum). s. xv in. England.
3. *f*P. Lombardus, Sententiae. s. xiii med. England (?).
4. F. Petrarch, Trionfi (in Italian). s. xv med. Italy (Florence ?).
5. Gualterus de Brugis, O.F.M., etc. s. xiii ex. England (?).
6. V. Ferrer, O.P., Sermones aestivales. s. xv². Germany.
7. Officia liturgica. s. xvi in. Italy.
8. Breviarium (Diurnale). s. xv². Low Countries, for **St Denis, Amsterdam, O.S.A.**
9. Horae B.V.M. (Paris). s. xiv². France.

Pybus Cv. 5. J. Arderne, etc. s. xiv¹–xiv ex. England.

NORWICH, Norfolk

CASTLE MUSEUM

99. 20. Glossaria. s. xiii ex. England. *Norwich Cathedral Priory, O.S.B.*
149. 938/1. Horae B.V.M. (Rome). s. xv in. France.
158. 926/4a. Psalterium, etc. s. xv/xvi. Low Countries (?), for England.
158. 926/4b. P. Riga, Aurora. s. xiii med. England.
158. 926/4c. Psalterium, etc. s. xv med. England (Norwich diocese).
158. 926/4d. Statuta Angliae. s. xiv¹–xiv med. England.
158. 926/4e. Processionale. s. xv in. England, for O.S.B. (Ord. Clun. ?), East Anglia (?).

158. 926/4f. Horae B.V.M. (Sarum: partly in French). s. xiv¹–xiv med. England (Norwich diocese).
158. 926/4g. 1. Nova Statuta Angliae. s. xv med., xv². England. *Norfolk* (?).
158. 926/4g. 2. Paupertas. s. xiv². England. *Canterbury, St Augustine's, O.S.B.*
158. 926/4g. 3. Theological treatises (in English). s. xv med. England.
158. 926/4g. 4. Processionale. s. xv med. England, for **Bury St Edmund's, O.S.B.**
158. 926/4g. 5. Theological treatises (in English). s. xv¹. England.
158. 926/4g. 7. Prophetae minores glosati. s. xii ex. England.
181. 27. Horae B.V.M. (Tournai). s. xv ex. Low Countries (Mechlen ?).
228.961. Horae B.V.M. (Sarum). s. xv med. England.

CATHEDRAL

*1. (*s*)Chronicon Angliae. A.D. 1270–2, s. xiii². **Norwich Cathedral Priory, O.S.B.**
*2. J. Boccaccio, De genealogiis deorum; etc. s. xv². England. *Norwich Cathedral Priory, O.S.B.*
*3. Psalterium. s. xv¹. England.
*4. Liber sextus cum tribus glosis. s. xiv¹. England.
*5. See above, Manchester, John Rylands University Library, Eng. 109.
Sequentiae, etc. s. xv/xvi. England, for O.E.S.A.
*Fragments in Dean and Chapter records. See p. 534.

DIOCESAN RECORD OFFICE

Fragments: see pp. 535–50.

NORFOLK RECORD OFFICE

Rye 38. (*s*)Book of arms, notes on French grammar (in English and French), etc. s. xv med. East Anglia.

PUBLIC LIBRARY

TC 27/1. *f*Berengaudus, In Apocalypsin; Qui bene presunt. s. xiii med.–xiii/xiv. England.
TC 27/2. Biblia. s. xiii². England.
TC 27/3. Medica. s. xiii med. France (?).
TC 27/4. *f*Manuale (Sarum), cum notis. s. xv in. England.
*TC 27/5. *f*Bible (in English). s. xv in.
TC 28/1. *f*Astronomica. s. xv², xv/xvi. England.
TC 28/2. Registrum brevium. s. xv med. England.
TC 28/4. P. Lombardus, Sententiae. s. xiv in. France (?). *England.*
S. A. 3. 7, ff. 150–67. De noviciis. s. xv med. England.

ST PETER MANCROFT CHURCH

Biblia. s. xiii². England.
Epistolae Pauli glosatae per Petrum Lombardum. s. xii/xiii. England. *Peterborough, O.S.B.*

UNIVERSITY OF EAST ANGLIA

PA 6280. Cicero, Philippica. s. xv². Italy.

OAKHAM, Leicestershire. PARISH CHURCH

Biblia. s. xiii¹. England.

OSCOTT COLLEGE, Chester Road, Sutton Coldfield, West Midlands

516 + 599. Missale (Sarum). s. xv med. England. (Norwich diocese).
518. A. de Villa Dei, Doctrinale. s. xv med. Italy.
519. Palladius, etc. s. xv med. Italy.
583. Horae B.V.M. (Paris). s. xv ex. France.
584. Horae B.V.M. (Langres). s. xv ex. France (Troyes ?).
585. *s*(?)Horae B.V.M. (Sarum). s. xv^1. England.
586. Prayers, etc. (mainly in Netherlandish). s. xvi in. Southern Low Countries.
714. Psalterium, etc. s. xv in. Low Countries, for England.
820. R. de Pennaforti, O.P., P. de Remis, O.P., etc. s. xiii^2. France, for O.P. (?).
1042. Horae B.V.M. (Rouen). s. xv med. France.
1043. J. Wallensis, O.F.M., Communiloquium, etc. s. xiv med. France (?). *England.*

OXFORD

ALL SOULS COLLEGE

302. Missale (Sarum). s. xv^1. England. *Oxford, All Souls College.*
315. Justinianus, Institutiones. s. xiii^2. S. France (?).
316. *f*Digestum novum. s. xiii med. Italy. Wiblingen, O.S.B.
322. *s*A. de Alexandria, In Aristotelem. A.D. 1477. Oxford.
331. Aphorismi Hippocratis cum expositione Magistri Cardinalis. s. xv med. England. *Oxford, All Souls College.*
332. Liber novem judicum, etc. (fragm.). s. xii ex. England. *Oxford, All Souls College.*
dd. 2. 9. Fallentiae regularum juris. s. xv ex. Italy.

ALLESTREE LIBRARY (at Christ Church)

F. 1. 1. Bernardus, Sermones; etc. s. xiii^1. England.
L. 4. 1. Clement of Lanthony (in English). s. xiv/xv. England.
M. 1. 10. Augustinus. s. xii med. England.

BLACKFRIARS

1. *f*Graduale. s. xiii^2. Spain (?), for O.P.
2. *f*P. Lombardus, Sententiae. s. xv med. Germany. *Ebern.*

BRASENOSE COLLEGE

*24. *f*Averroes, Colliget; etc. s. xiv^1. England.
*91. Genealogia regum Anglorum. s. xv^1. England, for J. Baten (?).

CAMPION HALL

1. Prayers, etc. (in German: fragm.). s. xvi^1. S. Germany (Nuremberg ?).
2. Horae B.V.M. (Rome). s. xv/xvi. France.
3. Horae B.V.M. (Sarum). s. xv med. Low Countries, for England.
4. Apollinaris Offredus; P. Mantuanus. A.D. 1442 (?), s. xv med. Italy. *Chiaravalle, O.C.*

CHRIST CHURCH (see also Oxford. Allestree Library)

507. Ovidius. s. xiv med. N. Italy (Milan ?).
508. Ovidius. s. xv med. Italy.

CORPUS CHRISTI COLLEGE

*261, ff. 70–115. *s*Clemens Cantuariensis, Collectanea. s. xv². **Canterbury, St Augustine's, O.S.B.** or **Oxford, Canterbury College, O.S.B.**
*394. Missale (Sarum). A.D. 1398. England. *Lapworth Church.*
*410. Pseudo-Bonaventura, Meditationes vitae Christi depictae. s. xiv med. Italy.
*431. South English Legendary, etc. (in English). s. xiv med. England.
*457 ff. 1–40, 42–7 + pastedowns of Exeter College 9K.1590.4. Pseudo-Augustinus, Sermones ad fratres in eremo; etc. (fragm.). s. xv in. England.
*479. Letters of Phalaris (in Italian). s. xv². Italy.
546. Virgilius. A.D. 1470. Louvain.

EXETER COLLEGE

186. (*s*)Suetonius. s. xiv med. Italy, for F. Petrarch.
187. F. Petrarch, Rime and Trionfi (in Italian). s. xv². Ferrara.
188. Terentius. s. xv². N.E. Italy (Ferrara ?).

HERTFORD COLLEGE

*1. Biblia. s. xiii med. France (?). *England.*
*2. Secreta secretorum. s. xiv ex. Hungary, for King Louis the Great.

JESUS COLLEGE

*146. J. de Rupella, O.F.M., Sermones; etc. s. xiii². Italy, for O.F.M.

LADY MARGARET HALL

*Borough 1. Horae B.V.M. (Rome); Preces. s. xv med. Umbria and N. Italy.
*Borough 3. Breviarium, pars aestivalis. s. xiv med. N. France. Haspres, O.S.B. (in s. xvii).
*Borough 4. Miscellanea theologica. s. xv². Italy.
*Borough 5. Commendatio animarum, etc. s. xv in.–xv². England.
*Borough 12. Antoninus Florentinus, O.P., Confessionale. s. xv med. Italy.
*Borough 19. Homiliarium (fragm.). s. xii med. N. Italy.

LINCOLN COLLEGE

*Lat. 129. *s*Miscellanea grammatica (partly in English). A.D. 1427–8, s. xv¹. England (Bristol).
*Lat. 131, ff. 9–32. Herbal (in English); etc. s. xv med. England.
*Lat. 131, ff. 45–69, 75. Jordanus Rufus, Cyrurgia equorum. s. xv in. England.
*Lat. 141, ff. 1–6, 9–20, 23–6. Verses (in English); Lat.–Eng. vocabulary. s. xv². England.
*Lat. 149. Horae B.V.M. (Rome). s. xv². Southern Low Countries.
*Lat. 150. Canon missae, etc. s. xiii². France.
*Lat. 151. Brut Chronicle (in English). s. xv². England.
*Lat. 152. Horae B.V.M. (Paris). s. xv¹. France.
*Lat. 153. Virgilius, Bucolica, Georgica. s. xv med. N.E. (?) Italy.

MAGDALEN COLLEGE

*Lat. 36. *f*Chronicon Angliae. s. xiii². England.
*Lat. 210. Cassiodorus, Historia ecclesiastica; Bernardus, Sermones; etc. s. xiv–xv. England; France (?).
*Lat. 213. John Gower, Confessio amantis (in English). s. xv². England.
Lat. 248. Chronicon inrotulatum regum Angliae. s. xv². England.

Lat. 251. Seneca, Epistolae. s. xv^2. Germany (?).
Lat. 252. Horae B.V.M. (Rome). s. xv med. Low Countries; Italy (?).
Lat. 253, ff. 1–33 + 257, ff. i, ii, 39, 40. Comment. in Decretales, etc. s. xiv ex. England.
Lat. 254. Biblia (fragm.). s. xiii^1. England.
Lat. 255. Huguitio (fragm.). s. xiv in. England.
Lat. 256. J. Lathbury, O.F.M., Distinctiones theologicae (fragm.). s. xv med. England.
Lat. 257, ff. 1–38. Quaestiones disputatae in philosophia. s. xiv ex.–xv in. England (Oxford ?).
Lat. 258. Justinianus, Institutiones (fragm.). s. xii/xiii. England.
Lat. 259, ff. 1–6. Replicationes scholasticae de Immaculata Conceptione B.V.M. s. xv med. England.
Lat. 259, ff. 7–18. Ludolphus de Saxonia, Ord. Carth., De vita Christi (extr.). s. xv^2 England.
Lat. 260. Evangelium Nicodemi. s. xv^2. England.
Lat. 261. Justinianus, Codex, cum apparatu. s. xiv med. England. *Cambridge.*
Lat. 262. Aristoteles; Avicenna (fragm.). s. xiii med. England.
Lat. 263. Henricus de Gandavo, Quodlibeta (fragm.). s. xiv in. France. *England.*
Lat. 264 + pastedowns of Arch. C.II.3.16. Comment. in Librum Pauperum Vacarii (fragm.). s. xii/xiii. England.
Lat. 405. Horae B.V.M. (Chartres). s. xv^2. France.

MANSFIELD COLLEGE

1. Missale. s. xv^1. Italy.

MERTON COLLEGE

256B. N. Trevet et T. Wallensis, In Augustinum de Civitate Dei. s. xiv^1. England. *Oxford, Merton College.*
297B. Vetera et nova Statuta Angliae. s. xv^1–xv med. *Canterbury, Christ Church, O.S.B.*
E. 3. 1, etc. R. Rolle (fragm.). s. xiv ex. England.
E. 3. 30, etc. Hugo de S. Victore, De sacramentis (fragm.). s. xii med. W. (?) England.
E. 3. 31. Psalterium (fragm.). s. xiii^2. England.

NEW COLLEGE

*358. Psalterium, etc. s. xiii med. England, for **St Albans, O.S.B.**
Mun. 9182. Statuta 2 Henrici V (extr.). s. xv in. England.

PEMBROKE COLLEGE

1. Missale (Sarum). s. xv^1. England.
2. J. Mirfeld, Breviarium Bartholomaei; etc. s. xiv/xv. England, at or for **Abingdon, O.S.B.** (?).
3. Beda, Historia ecclesiastica. s. xii/xiii. England.
4. P. Lombardus, Sententiae. s. xiii ex. England.
5. T. Wallensis, Lectura in Bibliam; Interpretationes nominum hebraicorum. s. xiii in.–xiv/xv. England. *Canterbury, Christ Church, O.S.B.*
6. Philippus Cancellarius, Sermones in Psalterium. s. xiii^1. England.
7. Biblia. s. xiii^1. England.
8. Alexander Trallianus, Therapeutica. s. xii/xiii. France (?).
9. R. de Pennaforti, Summa; etc. s. xiii ex. England.

10, ff. 1–107. Medica. s. xii med.–xiii in. France. England.
11, ff. 1–68. Recepta medica, etc. s. xiv/xv. England.
12. Medica. s. xii/xiii–xiii/xiv. England; France (?).
13. Medica. s. xiii in.–xiii med. England.
15, ff. 1–230. Medica. s. xii^2–xiii med. England.
18. Apocalypsis glosatus. s. xii ex. England.
20. Horae de S. Matthia, etc. s. xv in. Prague, for King Wenceslaus of Bohemia.
21. Medica. s. xiii ex.–xv med. England.

QUEEN'S COLLEGE

405. Horae B.V.M. (Bourges). s. xv med. France.
35. c. 1–15 + 35. d. 1–12. Johannes et Lucas glosati. s. xiii^1. England.

REGENT'S PARK COLLEGE

Angus d. 54. Horae (Rome). s. xv med. N.E. France.

ST EDMUND HALL

*1. Processionale (Sarum). s. xiv/xv. England.
*2. De sacramentis. s. xv^2. Italy.

ST HILDA'S COLLEGE

1. Horae (Utrecht: in Netherlandish). s. xv ex. Low Countries (Holland).

ST JOHN'S COLLEGE

256. Registrum brevium. s. xv med. England.
257. Nova Statuta Angliae (in French and English), etc. s. xv/xvi. England.
265. Breviarium Praemonstratense. s. xv ex. Southern Low Countries. Parc, Ord. Praem. (in s. xviii).
266. J. Lydgate, Siege of Thebes (in English). s. xv ex. England.
293. Psalterium, etc. s. xv med. England.

SOMERVILLE COLLEGE

1. Horae B.V.M. (Angers). s. xv ex. France.
2. Horae B.V.M. (Rome). s. xv med. Southern Low Countries.

TAYLOR INSTITUTION

8° E. 1. Statuta Angliae. s. xiv^1. England.
8° It. 1. Cecco d'Ascoli, Acerbo (in Italian). s. xiv med. N. Italy.
8° It. 2. Leonardus Bruni, Historiae Florentini populi. s. xv med. Italy.
8° It. 3. F. da Buti, Commentary on Dante's Paradiso (in Italian). s. xv in. Italy.
8° It. 4. F. Petrarch, Trionfi; etc. (in Italian). s. xv med. Italy.

TRINITY COLLEGE

*93. Summary of the Bible (in English). s. xiv/xv. England.
94. Missale (Sarum). s. xv med. England.
Danson 1. W. Peraldus, Summa de virtutibus. s. xiv^2. N.(?) Italy.

UNIVERSITY COLLEGE

*190 + 113, ff. 166–9. P. Comestor, etc. s. xiii in.–xiii med. England. *Beverley, O.P.*
*191. *f*Gregorius Magnus, Homeliae in Evangelia; etc. s. xii med. England, for O.C. (?).

WADHAM COLLEGE

A. 5. 28. Psalterium, etc. s. xiv med. England, for **Norwich Cathedral Priory, O.S.B.**

A. 7. 8. *s*Missale. A.D. 1521. Southern Low Countries, for **Parc, Ord. Praem.**

A. 10. 18. Cicero, etc. s. xv². Italy.

A. 10. 19. Horatius. s. xv². Italy.

A. 10. 20. Statius, Thebais. s. xv ex. Italy.

WORCESTER COLLEGE

213 + 213*. *f*Meditationes, etc. s. xiii². England, for **Reading, O.S.B.**

233. T. Netter, etc. s. xv med. England, for **John Whethamstede, abbot of St Albans.** *Oxford, Gloucester College.*

285. Eusebius, Historia ecclesiastica; etc. s. xiv¹. Salisbury, for R. Wivill.

SIGNS AND ABBREVIATIONS

In quotations from the manuscripts: round brackets are used to show editorial additions; square brackets are used where the text is illegible as a result of damage or where the space for an initial letter has not been filled and no guide-letter is to be seen; caret marks, ˋ ˊ, are used to show words or letters added to the text after it was written.

AFH	*Archivum Franciscanum Historicum.*
AFP	*Archivum Fratrum Praedicatorum.*
AGM	*Archiv für Geschichte der Medizin.*
AH	*Analecta Hymnica Medii Aevi*, ed. G. M. Dreves *et al.* Leipzig, 1886–1922. 55 vols.
Allen, *Writings*	H. E. Allen, *Writings ascribed to Richard Rolle.* 1927.
Anal. Boll.	*Analecta Bollandiana.*
Ancient Libraries	M. R. James, *Ancient Libraries of Canterbury and Dover.* 1903.
Andrieu, *Ord. Rom.*	*Les Ordines Romani*, ed. M. Andrieu. 5 vols. Spicilegium Sacrum Lovaniense, 11, 23, 24, 28, 29. 1931–61.
Andrieu, *Pont. Rom.*	M. Andrieu, *Le Pontifical romain au moyen âge.* 4 vols. (Studi e Testi, 86–8, 99.) 1938–42.
Aristoteles Latinus	G. Lacombe *et al.*, *Aristoteles Latinus*: Codices. Pars prior, Rome, 1939. Pars posterior, Cambridge, 1955.
ASOC	*Analecta Sacri Ordinis Cisterciensis.*
Axters, *BDNM*	S. G. Axters, O.P., *Bibliotheca dominicana Neerlandica manuscripta.* Bibliothèque de la Revue d'histoire ecclesiastique, fasc. 49. Louvain, 1970.
Bale, *Index*	J. Bale, *Index Britanniae Scriptorum*, ed. R. L. Poole and M. Bateson. Anecdota Oxoniensia, Mediaeval and Modern Series, 9. Oxford, 1902.
Bale, *Scriptores*	J. Bale, *Scriptorum illustrium maioris Britanniae . . . catalogus*, pt. i [Basel], 1557, pt. ii [Basel], 1559.
Beccaria	A. Beccaria, *I codici di medicina del periodo presalernitano.* Rome, 1956.
Berger	S. Berger, *Quam notitiam linguae hebraicae habuerint Christiani medii aevi temporibus in Gallia.* Paris, 1893.
BGPTM	*Beiträge zur Geschichte der Philosophie und Theologie des Mittelalters.*
BHL	*Bibliotheca Hagiographica Latina.* Ediderunt Socii Bollandiani. 1898–1901.
Biblia Sacra	*Biblia Sacra iuxta Latinam vulgatam versionem . . . iussu Pii PP XI . . . edita.* Rome, 1926– (in progress).
BJRL	*Bulletin of the John Rylands Library.*
B.L.	British Library, London.
Bloomfield	M. W. Bloomfield *et al.*, *Incipits of Latin Works on*

	the Virtues and Vices, 1100–1500. Mediaeval Academy of America Publications, lxxxviii. 1979.
BLR	*Bodleian Library Record.*
BQR	*Bodleian Quarterly Record.*
BMC	*Catalogue of books printed in the fifteenth century now in the British Museum.* 1908– (in progress).
B.N.	Bibliothèque Nationale, Paris.
Brev. ad usum Sarum	*Breviarium ad usum Sarum*, ed. F. Procter and C. Wordsworth. 3 vols. Cambridge, 1882–6.
Bruylants	P. Bruylants, *Les oraisons du missel romain.* 2 vols. Études liturgiques, i. Louvain, 1952.
CAO	R. J. Hesbert and R. Prévost, *Corpus antiphonalium officii.* 6 vols. Rerum ecclesiasticarum documenta, Series maior, Fontes vii–xii. 1963–79.
Carboni	F. Carboni, *Incipitario della lirica italiana dei secoli xiii e xiv* (Studi e Testi, clxxvii). 1977.
Carmody, 1956	F. J. Carmody, *Arabic Astronomical and Astrological Sciences in Latin Translation.* Berkeley, 1956.
Cat. of Romances	H. L. D. Ward and J. A. Herbert, *Catalogue of Romances in the Department of Manuscripts in the British Museum.* 3 vols. 1883–1910.
Catt. Vett.	*Catalogi Veteres Librorum Ecclesiae Cathedralis Dunelm.* Surtees Society, vii. 1838.
CC	*Corpus Christianorum.*
Clavis	E. Dekkers, *Clavis Patrum Latinorum.* Sacris Erudiri, iii, 1951. 2nd edn. 1961.
CMA	(E. Bernard), *Catalogi Manuscriptorum Angliae et Hiberniae.* Oxford, 1697.
CSEL	Corpus Scriptorum Ecclesiasticorum Latinorum.
Davis, *MC*	G. R. C. Davis, *Medieval Cartularies of Great Britain.* 1958.
de Bruyne, *Préfaces*	(D. de Bruyne), *Les Préfaces de la Bible.* Namur, 1920.
de Bruyne, *Sommaires*	(D. de Bruyne) *Sommaires, divisions, et rubriques de la Bible latine.* Namur, 1914.
de Haas and Hall	E. de Haas and G. D. G. Hall, *Early Registers of Writs.* Selden Society, lxxxvii. 1970.
de Morenas	H. Jougla de Morenas, *Grand armorial de France.* 6 vols. 1934–49. *Supplément*, 1952.
de Ricci, *Hand-list*	S. de Ricci, *A Hand-list of the Collection of Books and Manuscripts belonging to . . . Lord Amherst of Hackney at Didlington Hall, Norfolk.* 1906.
DNB	*Dictionary of National Biography.*
Dolezalek	G. Dolezalek, *Verzeichnis der Handscrhiften zum römischen Recht bis 1600.* 4 vols. Frankfurt-am-Main, 1972.
Dondaine and Shooner	H. F. Dondaine and H. V. Shooner, *Codices manuscripti operum Thomae de Aquino.* Rome, 1967– (in progress).
EBSB	J. B. Oldham, *English Blind-Stamped Bindings.* Cambridge, 1952.

EETS	Early English Text Society.
EHR	*English Historical Review.*
Emden, *BRUC*	A. B. Emden, *A Biographical Register of the University of Cambridge to 1500.* Cambridge, 1963.
Emden, *BRUO*	A. B. Emden, *A Biographical Register of the University of Oxford to A.D. 1500.* 3 vols. Oxford, 1957-9.
Emden, *BRUO 2*	A. B. Emden, *A Biographical Register of the University of Oxford, A.D. 1501-1540.* Oxford, 1974.
Emden, *Donors*	A. B. Emden, *Donors of Books to S. Augustine's Abbey, Canterbury.* Oxford Bibliographical Society, Occasional Publication no. 4. Oxford, 1968.
Essays presented to N. R. Ker	*Medieval Scribes, Manuscripts & Libraries: Essays presented to N. R. Ker*, ed. M. B. Parkes & A. G. Watson. 1978.
Foedera	T. Rymer, *Foedera.* Ed. 1704-35 (20 vols.).
Forshall and Madden	*The Holy Bible made from the Latin vulgate by John Wycliffe and his followers*, ed. J. Forshall and F. Madden. 4 vols. 1850.
Frere	W. H. Frere *et al.*, *Bibliotheca Musico-Liturgica.* Plainsong and Medieval Music Society. 2 vols. 1901-32.
Frere, *Use of Sarum*	W. H. Frere, *The Use of Sarum.* 2 vols. 1898, 1901.
GKW	*Gesamtkatalog der Wiegendrucke.* 1925- (in progress).
Glorieux	P. Glorieux, *Répertoire des maîtres en théologie de Paris au xiii*[e] *siècle.* 2 vols. Études de philosophie médiévale, xvii, xviii. 1933-4.
Goff	F. R. Goff, *Incunabula in American Libraries.* New York, 1964.
Haebler	C. Haebler, *Rollen- und Plattenstempel des xvi. Jahrhunderts.* 2 vols. Leipzig, 1928-9.
Haenel	G. H. Haenel, *Catalogi librorum manuscriptorum.* Leipzig, 1830.
Hain	L. Hain, *Repertorium Bibliographicum.* 2 vols. Stuttgart, etc., 1826-38.
Hauréau	*Initia operum scriptorum latinorum medii potissimum aevi ex codicibus manuscriptis et libris impressis alphabetice digessit B. Hauréau.* 6 vols. Turnhout, n.d.
Haymo	*Ordines of Haymo of Faversham.* Henry Bradshaw Society, lxxxv. [1961]. Corresponds to *SMRL* ii. 19-281.
HBS	Henry Bradshaw Society.
HMC	Historical Manuscripts Commission.
Holdsworth	W. S. Holdsworth, *A History of English Law.* All references are to vol. 2 (1903).
Horae Ebor.	*Horae Eboracenses*, ed. C. Wordsworth. Surtees Society, cxxxii. 1920.
Hoskins	E. Hoskins, *Horae Beatae Mariae Virginis.* 1901. Republished, 1969.

IMEV	C. Brown and R. H. Robbins, *Index of Middle English Verse*. New York, 1943. *Supplement* by R. H. Robbins and J. L. Cutler, Lexington, 1965.
JBAA	*Journal of the British Archaeological Association.*
Jolliffe	P. S. Jolliffe, *A Check-list of Middle English Prose Writings of Spiritual Guidance*. Pontifical Institute of Mediaeval Studies, Toronto, Subsidia Mediaevalia, ii. Toronto, 1974.
Kauffmann	C. M. Kauffmann, *Romanesque Manuscripts 1066–1190*. A Survey of Manuscripts Illuminated in the British Isles, ed. J. J. G. Alexander, iii. 1975.
Ker, *MLGB*	N. R. Ker, *Medieval Libraries of Great Britain*. Royal Historical Society, Guides and Handbooks, No. 3. 2nd edn. 1964.
Ker, *Pastedowns*	N. R. Ker, *Pastedowns in Oxford Bindings*. Oxford Bibliographical Society, new series, v. Oxford, 1954.
Ker, *Records*	N. R. Ker, *Records of All Souls College Library 1437–1600*. Oxford Bibliographical Society, new series xvi. Oxford, 1971.
Klebs	A. C. Klebs, 'Incunabula scientifica et medica', *Osiris*, iv, pt. 1 (1938).
Lacombe	see above, *Aristoteles Latinus.*
Långfors	A. Långfors, *Les incipit des poèmes français antérieurs au xvi*[e] *siècle*. Paris, 1917.
Lasko and Morgan	*Medieval Art in East Anglia 1350–1500*, ed. P. Lasko and N. J. Morgan. (Exhibition catalogue), Norwich, 1973.
Leroquais	V. Leroquais, *Les Livres d'heures manuscrits de la Bibliothèque Nationale*. 2 vols., plates, and supplement. 1927–43.
Lieftinck, *Maatschappij* (also Lieftinck)	*Codices 168–360 Societatis cui nomen Maatschappij der Nederlandsche Letterkunde descripsit G. I. Lieftinck*. Bibliotheca Universitatis Leidensis. Codices Manuscripti, V. i. Leiden, 1948.
Little, *Grey Friars*	A. G. Little, *The Grey Friars in Oxford*. Oxford Historical Society, xx. Oxford, 1891.
Lohr	C. Lohr, 'Medieval Latin Aristotle Commentaries', *Traditio*, xxiii. 317–413; xxvi. 135–216; xxvii. 251–351; xxviii. 281–396; xxix. 93–193; xxx. 119–44. 1967–74.
Lyell Cat.	A. de la Mare, *Catalogue of the Collection of Medieval Manuscripts bequeathed to the Bodleian Library, Oxford, by James P. R. Lyell*. Oxford, 1971.
MacKinney	L. MacKinney, *Medical Illustrations in Medieval Manuscripts*. Publications of the Wellcome Historical Medical Library, new series, v. 1965.
Manuale Sarum	*Manuale ad usum percelebris ecclesie Sarisburiensis*, ed. A. J. Collins. Henry Bradshaw Society, xci. 1960.

Manuscripts at Oxford	*Manuscripts at Oxford: an exhibition in memory of Richard William Hunt (1908–1979).* Oxford, 1980.
MBDS	*Mittelalterliche Bibliothekskataloge Deutschlands und der Schweiz*, ed. P. Lehmann *et al.* Munich, 1918– (in progress).
Mearns, *Canticles*	J. Mearns, *The Canticles of the Christian Church, eastern and western*. Cambridge, 1914.
Mearns, *Hymnaries*	J. Mearns, *Early Latin Hymnaries*. Cambridge, 1913.
Meertens	M. Meertens, *De Godsvrucht in de Nederlanden*, pts. i–iii, vi. 1930–4.
MERT	*Medieval and early Renaissance Treasures in the North West. [Catalogue of an Exhibition at the Whitworth Art Gallery, University of Manchester. 1976].* Manchester, 1976. (Manuscripts described by J. J. G. Alexander.)
MGH	Monumenta Germaniae Historica.
Missale Romanum	*Missale Romanum Mediolani 1474*, ed. R. Lippe. 2 vols. Henry Bradshaw Society, xvii, xxxiii (1899, 1907).
Missale Sarum, Burntisland edn.	*Missale ad usum insignis et praeclare ecclesiae Sarum. Labore ac studio F. H. Dickinson.* Burntisland, 1861–83.
Missale Westm.	*Missale ad usum ecclesie Westmonasteriensis*, ed. J. W. Legg. 3 vols. Henry Bradshaw Society, i, v, xii (1891–7).
MLR	*Modern Language Review.*
MMBL	N. R. Ker, *Medieval Manuscripts in British Libraries.*
MPE	*Manuale et processionale ad usum insignis ecclesiae Eboracensis*, ed. W. G. Henderson. Surtees Society, lxiii. 1875.
N.L.S.	National Library of Scotland, Edinburgh.
N.L.W.	National Library of Wales, Aberystwyth.
NLWJ	*National Library of Wales Journal.*
Notices et extraits	*Notices et extraits des manuscrits de la Bibliothèque du Roi* (or *Impériale*, or *Nationale*). 1787–1938. 42 vols.
NT	New Testament.
O.C.	Ordo Cisterciensis.
OED	*The Oxford English Dictionary.*
O.E.S.A.	Ordo Eremitarum Sancti Augustini.
O.F.M.	Ordo Fratrum Minorum.
Oldham	The context shows whether the reference is to J. B. Oldham, *English Blind-Stamped Bindings*, Cambridge, 1952, or to J. B. Oldham, *Blind Panels of English Binders*, Cambridge, 1958.
O.P.	Ordo Fratrum Praedicatorum.
Ord. Brig.	Ordo Brigittanorum.
Ord. Carm.	Ordo Carmelitarum.
Ord. Carth.	Ordo Carthusiensium.
Ord. Clun.	Ordo Cluniacensium.
Ord. Praem.	Ordo Praemonstratensium.

O.S.A.	Ordo Sancti Augustini.
O.S.B.	Ordo Sancti Benedicti.
OT	Old Testament.
Pächt and Alexander	O. Pächt and J. J. G. Alexander, *Illuminated Manuscripts in the Bodleian Library*. 3 vols. Oxford, 1966–73.
Parkes	M. B. Parkes, *The Medieval Manuscripts of Keble College Oxford*. 1979.
Parochial Libraries	*Parochial Libraries of the Church of England*, ed. N. R. Ker. 1959.
PCC	Prerogative Court of Canterbury.
Pfaff, *New Liturgical Feasts*	R. W. Pfaff, *New Liturgical Feasts in later Medieval England*. Oxford, 1970.
PG	J. P. Migne, *Patrologia Graeca*.
PL	J. P. Migne, *Patrologia Latina*.
PLS	*Patrologia Latina, Supplementum*.
PMLA	*Publications of the Modern Language Association of America*.
Pont. Rom.-Germ.	*Le Pontifical Romano-Germanique du dixième siècle*, ed. C. Vogel and R. Elze. Studi e Testi, ccxxvi-vii. 2 vols. 1963.
Potthast	A. Potthast, *Regesta Pontificum Romanorum*. 2 vols. 1874–5.
PRM	P. Glorieux, *Pour revaloriser Migne*. Supplement to *Mélanges de Sciences Religieuses*, ix. 1952.
P.R.O.	Public Record Office, London.
PS	*Processionale ad usum Sarum*, ed. W. G. Henderson. 1882.
RB	*Revue Bénédictine*.
Recueil	J. Leclercq, *Recueil d'études sur S. Bernard et ses écrits*. 3 vols. Rome, 1962–9.
Renzi	S. de Renzi, *Collectio Salernitana*. 5 vols. Naples, 1852–9.
RH	U. Chevalier, *Repertorium Hymnologicum*. 6 vols. 1892–1921.
Rietstap	J.-B. Rietstap, *Armorial général*. 2nd edn., 1884–7. Plates, 1903–26 and Supplements, 1926–51, by V. Rolland and H. Rolland.
Römer	F. Römer, *Die handschriftliche Überlieferung der Werke des heiligen Augustinus*, II, *Grossbritannien und Irland*. (2 vols.: (1) Werkverzeichnis; (2) Verzeichnis nach Bibliotheken.) Österreichische Akademie der Wissenschaften, Phil.-Hist. Klasse, Sitzungsberichte 276, 281. Vienna, 1972.
RS	Rolls Series.
RTAM	*Recherches de théologie ancienne et médiévale*.
SAO	*Sancti Anselmi Opera*, ed. F. S. Schmitt. 6 vols. 1946–61.
Sarum Missal	*The Sarum Missal, edited from three early manuscripts*, ed. J. W. Legg. Oxford, 1916.
Saxl and Meier	F. Saxl and H. Meier, *Verzeichnis astrologischer und*

	mythologischer illustrierter Handschriften des lateinischen Mittelalters. 3 vols. 1915–53.
SBO	*Sancti Bernardi Opera*, ed. J. Leclercq *et al.* 1957– (in progress).
Schenkl	H. Schenkl, *Bibliotheca Patrum Latinorum Britannica*. 3 vols. 1891–1908.
Schneyer	J. B. Schneyer, *Wegweiser zu lateinischen Predigtreihen des Mittelalters*. Munich, 1965.
Schneyer, *Rep.*	J. B. Schneyer, *Repertorium der lateinischen Sermones des Mittelalters für die Zeit von 1150–1350*. 5 vols. Beiträge zur Geschichte der Philosophie und Theologie des Mittelalters, xliii. 1969–79.
Schulte	J. F. von Schulte, *Die Geschichte der Quellen und Literatur des canonischen Rechts*. 3 vols. Stuttgart, 1875–80.
Shirley, *Cat.*	W. W. Shirley, *Catalogue of the Original Works of John Wyclif*. 1865.
Sinclair	K. V. Sinclair, *Prières en ancien français*. Hamden, Conn., 1978.
Singer and Anderson	D. W. Singer and A. Anderson, *Catalogue of Latin and Vernacular Alchemical Manuscripts in Great Britain and Ireland*. 3 vols. Brussels, 1928–31.
Singer and Anderson, 1950	D. W. Singer and A. Anderson, *Catalogue of Latin and Vernacular Plague Texts in Great Britain and Eire*. Collection de Travaux de l'Académie Internationale d'Histoire des Sciences, No. 5. 1950.
SMRL	S. J. P. van Dijk, *Sources of the Modern Roman Liturgy*. 2 vols. Studia et Documenta Franciscana, i, ii. 1963.
Sonet	J. Sonet, *Répertoire d'incipit de prières en ancien français*. Société de publications romanes et françaises, liv. Geneva, 1956.
Sonet–Sinclair	J. Sonet (above) taken in conjunction with K. V. Sinclair (above).
SOPMA	T. Kaeppeli, *Scriptores ordinis Praedicatorum Medii Aevi*. 1970– (in progress).
SR	*Statutes of the Realm*. References are to edn. 1810–28.
STC	A. W. Pollard and G. R. Redgrave, *A Short-title Catalogue of Books printed . . . 1475–1640*. 1926.
Stegmüller	F. Stegmüller, *Repertorium Biblicum Medii Aevi*. 11 vols. (vols. 9–11 adiuvante Nicolao Reinhardt). Madrid, 1950–80.
Stegmüller, *Sent.*	F. Stegmüller, *Repertorium Commentariorum in Sententias Petri Lombardi*. 2 vols. Würzburg, 1947.
STS	Scottish Text Society.
Sum. Cat.	*Summary Catalogue of Western Manuscripts in the Bodleian Library*. 7 vols. Oxford, 1895–1953.
Talbot and Hammond	C. H. Talbot and E. A. Hammond, *The Medical Practitioners in medieval England*. 1965.

Test. Ebor.	*Testamenta Eboracensia*. 5 vols. Surtees Society, (iv), xxx, xlv, liii, lxxix. 1836–84.
Thomson, *Grosseteste*	S. H. Thomson, *The Writings of Robert Grosseteste*. Cambridge, 1940.
Thorndike and Kibre	L. Thorndike and P. Kibre, *A Catalogue of Incipits of Mediaeval Scientific Writings in Latin*. 2nd edn. 1963.
VCH	*Victoria County History*.
Vising	P. S. Vising, *Anglo-Norman Language and Literature*. Oxford, 1923.
Walther	H. Walther, *Initia carminum ac versuum medii aevi posterioris Latinorum*. Carmina Medii Aevi Posterioris Latina, i. Göttingen, 1959.
Walther, *Sprichwörter*	H. Walther, *Lateinische Sprichwörter und Sentenzen des Mittelalters*. Carmina Medii Aevi Posterioris Latina, ii. 5 vols. Göttingen, 1963–7.
Watson, *B.L.*	A. G. Watson, *Catalogue of Dated and Datable Manuscripts c.700–1600 in the Department of Manuscripts The British Library*. 2 vols. 1979.
Watson, *Oxford*	A. G. Watson, *Catalogue of Dated and Datable Manuscripts c. 435–1600 in Oxford Libraries*. 2 vols. Oxford, forthcoming.
Weale	W. H. J. Weale, *Bookbindings and Rubbings of Bindings in the National Art Library, South Kensington Museum*. 1898.
Wells, *Manual*	J. E. Wells, *A Manual of the Writings in Middle English 1050–1400*. New Haven, 1916. With nine supplements, 1919–51.
Wickersheimer	E. Wickersheimer, *Dictionnaire biographique des médecins en France au moyen âge*. 1936.
Wordsworth and White	*Novum Testamentum ... Latine*, ed. J. Wordsworth, H. J. White, *et al.* Oxford, 1889–1954.
Zetzner	L. Zetzner, *Theatrum chemicum*. 6 vols. ed. Strasbourg, 1659–61.
ZRG	*Zeitschrift für Rechtsgeschichte*.
Zumkeller	A. Zumkeller, *Manuskripte von Werken der Autoren des Augustiner-Eremiten-Ordens in mitteleuropäischen Bibliotheken*. Cassiciacum, xx. 1966.

LAMPETER. ST DAVID'S UNIVERSITY COLLEGE

R. C. Rider, 'The Library of St David's College', *Trivium*, i (Lampeter 1966), 36–9.

1. *Biblia* 1279

A Bible which may have had the usual contents in the usual order (see below, Liverpool Cathedral 13), apart from the absence of Psalms and the presence of the prayer of Solomon after Ecclesiasticus, but probably forty leaves are missing: a quire after f. 268 with all between Isaiah 42: 2 'Uox eius' and Jeremiah 13: 17 'ritis in abscondito'; a quire after f. 328 with all between 'factam rem' in the prologue to Habakkuk and 1 Maccabees 3: 29 'de thesauris'; a quire after f. 410 with all between Philemon 1: 7 'requieuerunt' and Acts 18: 24 'eloquens'; two leaves after f. 183, where the text passes from Judith 11: 6 'indicatum est' to Esther 1: 10 'arbona'; one leaf after f. 119 with part of 3 Kings; one leaf after f. 150 with the end of the prologue and chapters 1–4: 4 of 2 Chronicles. The Prayer of Manasses is treated as 2 Chronicles 38. Proverbs and Isaiah begin on new quires. ff. 1^{rv}, 427^{v} left blank.

The prologues may have been the common set of sixty-four—eleven are now missing in gaps—together with nine further prologues after the common ones to each of the last nine Minor Prophets, but of these nine only Stegmüller, nos. 516, 522, 525, 527 survive. Stegm. nos. 519 and 517, usually run together as a single prologue to Obadiah, are here treated as two prologues. The common prologue to 1 Timothy, ending here 'a laodicia macedonia', is repeated as a second prologue to 2 Timothy (ending 'a macedonia'). Stichometric notes follow Genesis ('Habens versus' 3700), Leviticus (2300), Numbers (5000), Deuteronomy (27[..]), Joshua (1750).

Psalms 1–118: 136 were supplied between Job and Proverbs in a stiff anglicana formata, s. xv/xvi (ff. 198–222^{v}, quires 19–21): no doubt the rest was on now missing leaves. A reader at about this time expected to find more of Ezra and noted on f. 177 'Hic deest Esdre iiii cont' xvi^{a} ca.'. The same person, perhaps, put 'totum legi' or 'legi totum' at the end of Genesis, Exodus, Leviticus and Judges and made some notes in current anglicana in the margins, chiefly in the Genesis–4 Kings and Ecclesiasticus–Maccabees sections. Some words of these notes are in English, for example at Exodus 10: 12 (f. 25) 'gressehoppers and thyk dirkneth'.

Carthusian lection marks, 'P(rima)', 'S(ecunda)', 'T(ercia)', have been added often in the margins, s. xv; also 'in Retect' ' and here and there letters, A–H.[1] The A–H marking covers all 1, 2 Maccabees, but occurs elsewhere mainly at the beginning of books, as at Exodus and Leviticus, or against Sunday lections where these are marked, as at Numbers 15: 1 (1st Sunday in Lent) and Deuteronomy 1: 1 (2nd Sunday in Lent). Occasions of reading are seldom given: first week of Lent (Numbers from 15: 1); second week of Lent (Deuteronomy); 4th week of Lent (Judges); 'Feria 2^{a}'–'Feria 6^{a}' against Jeremiah 19–29; 'Dominica secunda'–'Feria 6^{a}' against Acts 19: 23–27: 1; 'Dominica 3' at the prologue to James; 'In natali Iohannis Euangeliste leccio prima littera A' in pencil at Apoc. 1: 1 (f. 421^{v}); 'In festo innocencium leccio prima littera A' at Apoc. 6: 1 (f. 423).

[1] See below, Malmesbury, Bible.

ff. iv + 427 + iv. 335 × 250 mm. Written space 245 × 170 mm. 2 cols. 47 lines. Collation: 1^4 2–8^{12} (7^9, f. 73, torn) 9^{10} 10^{12} 11^{12} wants 10 after f. 119 12^{12} 13^{10} 14^{12} wants 8 after f. 150 15–16^{12} 17^{12} wants 6, 7 after f. 183 18^{10} 19–20^{8} 21^{8} (ff. 215–22) 22–23^{12} 24^{10} 25–34^{12} 35^{10} 36–38^{12} 39 five (ff. 423–7). Leaves in the first halves of some quires have been given *ad hoc* quire marks and leaf marks a–f or i–vi, for example, ff. 53–8, 65–70, 77–82, 99–104 (quires 6–8, 10). Initials: (i) of books and f. 2, blue or pink patterned in white on grounds of colour and gold, historiated: the *O* beginning Song of Songs, f. 233ᵛ, depicts B.V.M. and Child and a figure in black kneeling before them holding a pastoral staff: facsimile in *St David's School and College Magazine*, ix (1906); f. 2, *F* of *Frater*, Crucifixion and in the prolongation a child riding a chained bear; f. 5, *I* of *In*, the days of creation in seven compartments; (ii) of prologues, as (i), but smaller and not historiated: the decoration is often zoomorphic, especially centaurs and grotesques; (iii) of chapters, 2-line, red or blue with saw-pattern ornament in both colours the height of the written space. Capital letters in the ink of the text filled with pale yellow: in the first line on a page they are often elaborate cadel-like letters. Rebound at the National Library of Wales in 1947: formerly in red morocco, s. xviii. Secundo folio *ret. ignorabat.*

Written during more than three years and finished in 1279 by G. of Fécamp, presumably with money provided by James, abbot of Saint-Pierre-sur-Dives (near Lisieux, Calvados, O.S.B.: †1273), as appears from twelve couplets on f. 427, printed in *St David's School and College Magazine*, ix (1906), 146 (transcription and translation by Falconer Madan) and in *Bibliothèque de l'École des Chartes*, lxxiv (1913), 743–4: 'Scriba manum siste. consummatur liber iste G. fiscampnensi. flores per rura legensi Perpetuum lumen. habeat G. claude uolumen. Hoc qui scripsisti. dentur tibi gaudia xpisti Huius scripture. fuit auctor dispare crure. G. de fiscampno. quarto perfecit in anno. Ad sanctum petrum sub diua credere metrum. Hoc potes in camera cantoris. profero uera. Abbas modestus. bibliotam fecit honestus. Hanc scribi iacobus. uir pius atque probus. Anno milleno. bis. centum. septuageno. Scribitur hec nono. bibliota dei bona dono'. Presumably Abbot James is depicted on f. 233ᵛ (see above) and it may be his mitred head which adorns the *T* of *Trahe me post te* (Song of Songs 1: 4) in the top line on f. 234—as is suggested in a note pencilled on a slip of paper inserted at this point.

In England by s. xv/xvi and perhaps rather earlier, when the ownership was apparently Carthusian. Scribbles in English hands, s. xvi, include: f. 1, 'W. Crofton (*or* Croston)'; f. 164, 'John Laye'; f. 290, 'Richard Whitney'; f. 315, 'Richard Whitney the poitarie'; f. 427ᵛ, 'John Ley'; f. 427ᵛ, alphabets and 'by me John Weard ded writ this same'. Bequeathed by the founder: 'Collegio Sancti Davidis . . . T. L. Thomas Burgess, S.T.P. Episcopus Sarisburiensis et Collegii Fundator. MDCCCXXXVII'.

2 +Oxford, Bodleian Library, Lat. th. c. 10, f. 102. *Petrus de Capua, Distinctiones theologicae* s. xiii[1]

(*begins imperfectly*) dicitur durus id est firmus. Pau. Nec mors nec uita . . . ne anbules (*ends imperfectly*). A very defective copy of the distinctions Alpha-Christus (Xristus), a numbered series of words under each letter of the alphabet, compiled by Peter of Capua, cardinal-deacon of St George, †1242.

Headings and numbers, both in red, and biblical references are ranged in the margins. Each letter of the alphabet is preceded by a numbered table of the words discussed. The first words now are in D xxix (*Defectus*) and the last in S xiii (*Surditas*) and there are thirteen gaps between these points, including a large gap after quire 6: from E xli to F i (ff. 20, 21); from F xiiii to F xix (ff. 26, 27); from F lxxi to G vi (ff. 43, 44); from G xiiii to G xvi (ff. 47, 48); from G xxi to L ii (ff. 51, 52); from M xxxii to M xl (ff. 79, 80); from item 33 in the table of chapters of letter O to O iiii (ff. 90, 91); from O xxxi to P iiii (ff. 100, 101); from P xvi to P xxi (ff. 104, 105); from P lix to Q iiii (ff. 118, 119); from Q ix to R iii (ff. 119, 120); from R xxvii to R xxxii (ff. 126, 127), and from R xxxiii to S ix (ff. 128, 129). All leaves on which a new letter of the alphabet began are now missing, except ff. 7, 82 (E, N), which have been mutilated for the sake of their initials. f. 46 is out of place: it should follow f. 31. Many leaves have been mended at the edges.

The gap after f. 80 is closed by the Bodleian leaf which contains M xlvi, xlvii and parts of M xlv, xlviii.

The only complete copy in an English library seems to be Hereford Cathedral P. vi. 6. A 'pars secunda' from the Charterhouse of Witham belongs to Mr H. Sanders (Ker, *MLGB*, p. 205). A. Wilmart lists eleven copies in continental libraries in *Memorial Lagrange*, 1940, pp. 339–41: cf. Glorieux, i. 265.

ff. i + 129 + i in Lampeter 2; f. 1 in Bodleian Library. *c.*300 × 285 mm, the height much cut down. Written space *c.*255 × 160 mm. 2 cols. 48 lines. The first line of writing above the top ruled line. Pricks in both margins to guide ruling. Collation of ff. 1–71: 1^8 2^{12} 3^8 wants 1 and 8 4^8 (ff. 27–31, 46, 32, 33) 5^{12} wants 11, 12 after f. 43 6^8 wants 4 (ff. 44–5, 47–51) $7\text{–}8^{10}$: uncertain after this. Initials: (i) missing; (ii) 2-line, red or green with ornament of the other colour; (iii) in tables of chapters (ff. 82, 90^v), 1-line, red or blue. Binding of s. xix.

Written in England. According to a printed cutting pasted inside the cover 'found near Bangor, supposed to have belonged to the Monks of that Monastery, who were murdered by the command of Ethelred the 2nd, and thought to be stained with their blood [*there are indeed dark stains on ff. 127–9*], having been discovered with a quantity of human bones'. Printed book-plate, 'Collegio Sancti Davidis . . . D.D.D. Thomas Phillips, de *Brunswick Square* apud Londinenses, Armiger, 1841'. Shown to George Borrow when he visited Lampeter in 1854: cf. his *Wild Wales* (Norwich edn., 1924), ii. 324. The Bodleian leaf was given by N. R. Ker in 1949.

3. *Letbertus, O.S.A., In Psalmos; T. à Kempis, O.S.A., Opuscula; etc.* s. xv^2

1. ff. 1–312 Galterus magalonensis episcopus . . . in domino. Salutem. Cum vobiscum. dudum . . . semper habetote. Sunt superscriptionum . . . (f. 2) esse dissimilem. Beatus uir qui non abiit. De domino nostro ihesu xpisto . . . a deo mors est. omnis spiritus laudet dominum. Explicit.

Stegmüller, no. 5395. *PL* xxi. 641–960. Part 2 (Pss. 51–100), f. 88; 3 (Pss. 101–50), f. 175. f. 312^v blank.

2. (*a*) ff. 313–20 Uenite ad me omnes . . . Hec sunt verba tua criste veritas eterna . . . ineffabilia dicenda. Explicit liber 4us tractans de sacramento altaris. (*b*) ff. 320–9 Incipit liber quintus de disciplina claustralium in quibus consistit disciplina claustralis. Capitulum primum. Apprehendite disciplinam . . . vbi cristus est in gloria dei patris per eterna secula. amen. Explicit libellus de disciplina claustralium. (*c*) ff. 329–30 Sequitur Recommendatio humilitatis que est fundamentum totius sanctitatis et perfectionis. Discite a me quia mittis sum . . . nisi sint humiles. Explicit de humilitate quam quidem doctrinam composuit quidam canonicus regularis de ordine sancti augustini ad laudem dei beateque virginis marie. (*d*) ff. 330–4 Incipit libellus spiritualis exercicii. de feruida exhortacione

ad virtutes. Renouamini autem spiritu mentis vestre ait beatus paulus. Solent deuoti religiosi . . . deo et hominibus subiectus. Explicit libellus spiritualis exercicii. (*e*) ff. 334–336v Sequitur libellus de recognitione proprie fragilitatis. Cognoui domine quia equitas iudicia tua et in veritate tua . . . ad te vespertinum et placeat in eternum Amen. Explicit libellus de recognitione proprie fragilitatis. (*f*) ff. 336v–337v Incipit epistola quedam satis vtilis ad quendam regularem seu religiosum. Ista sunt precipue vtilia et necessaria pro conseruacione deuotionis . . . vsque in finem amen. (*g*) ff. 337v–340v Sequitur de eleuatione mentis ad summum bonum. Vacate et videte quoniam ego sum deus. Ecce inquiro te deus meus . . . precibus et lamentis Amen. Explicit. (*h*) ff. 340v–342 Sequitur de mortificata vita pro cristo. Gloriosus apostolus paulus docet me mortificatam gerere vitam . . . est voluntas dei. (*i*) ff. 342–343v Incipit quedam breuis ammonitio spiritualis exercicii. Ab exterioribus peruenitur ad interiora . . . et celestis sapiencia. Deo gracias. Opuscula predicta composuit frater thomas kemper canonicus regularis de ordine sancti augustini.

(*a*). The fourth book of De imitatione Christi. Eighteen chapters. (*b*). Thomas à Kempis, *Opera*, ed. Sommalius 1759, ii. 131–50. Apparently reckoned here as bk. 5 of De imitatione Christi. Sixteen chapters. (*c*). ibid. ii. 273–5. One paragraph. (*d*). ibid. ii. 198–207. Twelve chapters. (*e*). ibid. ii. 243–8. Eight chapters and a final prayer. (*f*). ibid. iii. 178–80 (Epistola 6). One paragraph. (*g*). ibid. ii. 258– (*ends differently*). Eight paragraphs. (*h*). ibid. ii. 270–3. Six paragraphs. (*i*). ibid. ii. 208– (*ends differently*). Twelve paragraphs.

3. ff. 343v–345v Incipit Reuelatio facta sancto bernardo abbati a beata maria virgine de dolore ipsius quem habuit in passione dilectissimi filii sui domini nostri ihesu cristi. Quis dabit capiti meo aquam . . . O vos filie iherusalem . . . in eternum et vltra cum ihesu filio tuo. qui . . . amen. Et sic est finis huius operis. Deo gracias. Scriptor qui scripsit cum cristo viuere possit. Amen.

One paragraph. Only partly the same as the piece printed in early editions of St Bernard (edn. Paris 1517, sign. EE viv–viii).

4. ff. 346 and 348 were flyleaves and ff. 347 and 349, each a double thickness, pastedowns used presumably in the old binding. They contain fragments of a noted breviary, s. xii med., with offices for Advent (347v, 346 in that order), Laurence (10 Aug.: 348rv, 349v), and Assumption of B.V.M. (15 Aug.: 349r).

ff. 6. Written space 253 × 160 mm. 2 cols. 30+ lines. 2-line red initials.

ff. ii + 345 + vi. Paper. For ff. 346–9, parchment binding leaves, see art. 4. The foliation is medieval as far as '124'. 285 × 210 mm. Written space 200 × 145 mm. 2 cols. 39–57 lines. Frame ruling, at first (ff. 1–38v) in red ink. Collation: 1 nine 2 nine (ff. 10–18) $3–5^{10}$ 6^{12} 7^{10} 8^{12} $9–31^{10}$ $32–33^{12}$ 34 nine (ff. 337–45). Traces of signatures of the usual late medieval kind, for example 'd. ii' on f. 30: probably a new series began at quire 10, since the letters on quires 29–31 are t, v, and x. Art. 1 in cursiva, set at first, changing to current hybrida by another hand on f. 104ra/27. A third hand wrote arts. 2, 3 in admirable cursiva: ascenders are only sometimes looped. Initials: (i) ff. 1, 2, in red and the ink of the text; (ii, iii) 2-line (or 3-line) and 1-line, red: not filled in on ff. 205–14 (quire 21). Capital letters in the ink of the text lined with red. Binding of s. xix. Secundo folio *vt in primo*.

Written in the Low Countries (?). English owners, Anthonye Gatonbye (s. xvi ex.) and H. Dodwell (s. xvii): the names are at the head of f. 1. A late pressmark 'Y. 11. 10', f. 1, top right.

4. *Horae* s. xv^{2}

1 (quire 1). ff. 1–12^{v} Full calendar in gold, blue, green, and red, the three colours usually alternating.

Feasts in gold include the Visitation of B.V.M. and Reparata (2 July, 8 Oct.); in colour 'Altonis confessoris', 'Gomberti abbatis', 'Dedicatio sancte marie ad martires (?)', 'Oldorici episcopi et confessoris', 'Ysaiae prophete', 'Guilibaldi episcopi' (9 Feb., 20 Mar., 13 May, 4, 6, 7 July).

2 (quires 2–9). ff. 13–87^{v} Hours of B.V.M. of the use of (Rome).

Two leaves missing. Psalms on particular week days, ff. 67^{v}–76^{v}. Special offices at Advent, etc., ff. 76^{v}–87^{v}. f. 88^{rv} blank.

3 (quires 10–12). ff. 89–111^{v} Incipit offitium sacratissime passionis domini nostri ihesu cristi . . . Hymnus. In passione domini . . .

Hours of the Passion. One leaf missing.

4 (quires 13–17). ff. 112–159^{v} Incipit offitium mortuorum.

5 (quires 18–20). ff. 160–182^{v} Penitential psalms and (f. 172^{v}) litany.

The first leaf missing. Monks and hermits: Bernard, Dominic, Thomas, Francis, Anthony. Nine virgins, not Anne or Mary of Egypt: . . . (8, 9) helysabeth clara. The prayers after Deus cui are: Exaudi; Ineffabilem; Deus qui culpa; Omnipotens sempiterne deus miserere famulo tuo; Ure igne; Deus a quo; Fidelium; Actiones; Omnipotens sempiterne deus qui uiuorum.

6. ff. 183–193^{v} Incipiunt psalmi graduales. Ad dominum cum tribularer (Ps. 119) . . .

7. ff. 193^{v}–198 Incipit offitium sacratissime crucis. quod fecit papa iohannes. dans indulgentiam omnibus dicentibus. centum dierum . . . Ymnus. Patris sapientia . . . Explicit offitium sacratissime crucis. Deo gratias. f. 198^{v} blank.

ff. ii + 198 + ii. 163 × 127 mm. Written space 93 × 70 mm. 14 long lines. Collation: 1^{12} 2^{10} wants 1 before f. 13 3^{10} 4^{10} wants 3 after f. 38 $5–8^{10}$ 9^{8} (ff. 81–8) 10^{10} 11^{10} wants 8 after f. 105 12^{4} (ff. 108–11) $13–16^{10}$ 17^{8} (ff. 152–9) 18^{10} wants 1 before f. 160 19^{10} 20^{4} (ff. 179–82) 21^{10} 22^{6} (ff. 193–8). Initials: (i) 6–8 line, blue or pink, patterned in white and decorated in colours, on historiated gold grounds: in art. 2 the subjects are (matins) *missing*, (lauds) Visitation, (prime) Presentation, (terce) *missing*, (sext) flight into Egypt, (none) Christ in the Temple, (vespers) B.V.M. in glory, (compline) Coronation of B.V.M.; art. 3 begins with Pietà, followed by (f. 98) Last Supper and a passion series (none missing); arts. 4, 6, 7 begin with Francis (?), a saint at prayer, and Gethsemane respectively and the *K* of *Kyrie*, f. 172^{v} contains two figures; (ii, iii) 3-line and 2-line, as (i), but smaller and not historiated; (iv) 1-line, gold on grounds of blue or pink patterned in white. Line fillers of many patterns, blue, pink, yellow or green, decorated with gold. Borders of gold and colours on pages with initials of type (i): continuous on ff. 89, 112, 183. English black morocco, gilt, s. xix[1], lettered on the spine 'Liturgie de l'eglise romaine. On vellum with painting', and with gilt doublures. Secundo folio (f. 13) *faciem*.

Written in Italy, but the presence of Alto, Gumbert, Ulric, and Willebald in art. 1 suggests an interest in southern Germany. Given by Phillips (cf. MS. 2): the printed ex-dono label is dated 1846. A Church Congress Exhibition label marked '316' is inside the back cover.

5. *Ordinale sororum ordinis sancti Salvatoris de Vadstena, etc.*

s. xv ex.

For this manuscript and especially art. 2 see M. Hedlund in *Eranos*, lxxix (1981), 121-36.[1]

1. ff. 1-8 Incipit ordo cantus et lecture sororum Ordinis sancti saluatoris in horis diurnis pariter et nocturnis inpermutabiliter obseruandus. Primo igitur est sciendum . . . variatur. In aduentu domini obseruetur ordo feriarum . . . Regina celi letare Cum versu.

Printed by R. Geete, *Jungfru Marie Örtagård*, 1895, pp. 273-81, from a presumably rather later manuscript, Florence, Magliabecchi xxxvi. 62. The chief differences from the printed text are in the ordo after Christmas and at the end, where the paragraphs beginning *Item sciendum est, Item dum processiones*, and *Hec sunt festa* (edn., pp. 280-1) do not occur. The Visitation of B.V.M. is not included among feasts when Salve regina is sung: cf. edn., p. 281/11, and art. 3. Other copies are in B.L., Add. 38604, f. 7; Bodleian, Canonici Liturg. 49 (*Sum. Cat.* 19249), f. 1.

2. ff. 8-51 Ihesu cristi nomine inuocato sequitur prologus cum rubricis in ordinem et ordinarium super horis et officiis diuinis atque missis sororum ordinis sancti saluatoris. Infrascriptus ordo cantus et lecture est sororum ordinis sancti saluatoris in horis diurnis pariter et nocturnis . . . (f. 8^{v}) uariatur. Sed quia ordo . . . (f. 12^{v}) dissensiones. Ordinarius sororum hic incipit. Incipit ipse ordinarius seu ordo cantus et lecture . . . (f. 49^{v}) vniformiter habeantur. Igitur propter premissa . . . hic ordinarius . . . secundum veras instituciones magistri petri confessoris beate birgitte etc. Que quidem instituciones habentur in libro maiori chori sororum monasterii vatzstenensis . . . (f. 51) Acta sunt hec anno domini quadragentesimo quinquagesimo in crastino sancti petri ad uincula. Hic explicit ordinarium sororum vatzstinensis sancti saluatoris ordinis Orate deum pro scriptrice sorore cristina filia iohannis.

The ordinal of the nuns of Vadstena otherwise known only in a translation into Scandinavian in Stockholm, Royal Library, Holm. A. 51. The contents of the twenty-five chapters are set out on ff. 10-12^{v}. The first verses of hymns are provided with musical notation. On f. 50 are the names of the six nuns who checked the translation of the ordinal 'in swecam seu goticam linguam' (in or about 1450).

[1] I am indebted to Mr R. C. Rider for details about art. 1 and to Mrs Hedlund for telling me of the printed edition of art. 1, the vernacular version of art. 2, and the identity of the scribe.

3. ff. 51v–54v In aduentu domini usque ad natiuitatem ad uesperas et ad matutinas et terciam Capitulum Ecce virgo concipiet . . .

Capitula and collects for B.V.M. at special seasons and at her seven feasts, Conception, Purification, Annunciation, Visitation, Assumption, Nativity, and Compassion.

4. ff. 54v–56 Infrascripta capitula habeantur omni die per totum annum nisi in precipuis sollempnitatibus beate marie et earum octauis. Ad matutinas In omnibus requiem . . .

Daily capitula at the hours and collects at matins, prime, vespers and compline.

5. f. 56v Nos soror margareta clawsadotter abbatissa Frater Martinus Confessor generalis necnon conuentus . . . protestamur . . . librum siue ordinarium suprascriptum fore et esse excopiatum transcriptum et demum collacionatum sine fraude ex et cum nostro vero ordinario quo nos sorores in monasterio nostro vtimur in diuinis officiis qui collectus sollicite et conscriptus est secundum instituciones magistri petri confessoris sancte matris nostre beate birgitte vt habetur in prologo huius libri sigillatusque est sigillis vtriusque conuentus vna cum sigillo venerabilis patris et domini domini nicholai dudum episcopi lyncopen' . . . In horum igitur omnium mayoris euidentie et fidei robur et munimen sigilla vtriusque conuentus sororum et fratrum dicti monasterii vatzstinen' huic libro ordinem et ordinarium continenti ex nostro vnanimi consensu et certa sciencia dorsotenus sunt appensa Anno domini mcdlxxxprimo In vigilia assump (*ends imperfectly*).

ff. vi + 56 + xxii. 177 × 120 mm. Written space 120 × 80 mm. 22 long lines. Ruling in red ink. Collation: $1\text{–}5^{10}$ 6^{8} wants 7, 8 (ff. 51–6). Hybrida, not current: the scribe wrote some way above the ruled line. Initials: (i) f. 56v, 3-line *N*, blue patterned in white with red ornament; (ii) 2-line, blue, sometimes patterned in white; (iii) 1-line, blue or red. English binding, s. xix^{1}. Secundo folio *psalmi.*

Written at Vadstena, Ord. Brig., probably in or soon after 1481 (cf. art. 5). The scribe is the Vadstena nun Kristina Hansdotter Brask. For other manuscripts written by her see M. Hedlund, *Katalog der datierten Handschriften in lateinischer Schrift vor 1600 in Schweden*, i (1977), 47, 53 and pls. 139, 157; ii (1980), 38 and pl. 106: Margareta Clausdotter was abbess of Vadstena, 1473–86. Given by Phillips as MS. 2: the printed label is dated 1847.

6. *Horae, etc.* s. xv ex.

1. ff. 1–12v Calendar in red and black, with some gradings (maius duplex, duplex, semi duplex (a few only) or soll').

Franciscan calendar. Feasts in red include 'Berardi accursii petri adiutoris et ottonis martirum festum ordinis minorum Maius duplex', Bernardine, and Bonaventura (16 Jan., 20 May, 3 July), the Visitation, Presentation, and Conception of B.V.M. (2 July, 21 Nov, 8 Dec.), the Transfiguration (6 Aug.), Servatius, Lambert, and Hubert (13 May, 17 Sept., 3 Nov.).

2. ff. 13–41 Item Commendatio pro defunctis. Non intres in iudicium . . . (f. 20^{v}) Finita oratione . . . dicant clerici has antiphonas In paradisum deducant te . . .

The office of burial begins on f. 20^{v}.

3. ff. 41–51 Ordo commendationis anime. In primis pulsetur campana . . . Et sollempniter cantent totam uigiliam cum ix lectionibus.

4. ff. 51–59^{v} Feria sexta in parasceue Passio domini nostri ihesu cristi secundum Iohannem. In illo tempore Egressus est ihesus . . . Ibi ergo propter paras' (*ends imperfectly*: John 18: 1–19: 42).

Direction at 19: 38 Hic legitur in tono ewangelii.

5. ff. 60–86^{v} Hic incipiunt hore beate marie uirginis. Use of (Rome).

6. ff. 88–104^{v} Hic incipiunt uigilie defunctorum.

Office of the dead.

7. ff. 105–16 Hic incipiunt septem psalmi. Litany, f. 111.

Nine pontiffs and confessors: . . . (8, 9) bonauentura ludouice. Five monks and hermits: benedicte francisce antoni dominice bernardine. Nine virgins: . . . (8, 9) clara elizabeth. The prayers after Deus cui are Exaudi, Deus qui culpa, Omnipotens sempiterne deus miserere famulo tuo ministro nostro, Deus a quo, Ure igne, Actiones, Omnipotens sempiterne deus qui uiuorum.

8. ff. 116^{v}–120 Special forms of art. 5 for use in Advent, etc.

9. ff. 120–2 Hic incipiunt xv gradus beate marie uirginis et dicitur absolute . . .

Fifteen gradual psalms: cues only of first ten. In the collect 'Absolue quesumus domine animas famulorum famularumque tuarum ab omni uinculo . . .' the scribe went wrong after *tuarum* and wrote 'remissionem cunctorum tribue peccatorum ut indulgenciam quam semper optauerunt piis supplicationibus consequantur' before 'ab omni uinculo': these twelve words are crossed through in red.

10. ff. 122^{v}–127^{v} Incipit preparamentum dicendum ante celebrationem misse. Deus in adiutorium . . . Ueni creator spiritus . . .

Psalms 83, 85, 115, 129 (cue), prayers, Aures, Deus cui omne, Ure igne, Mentes nostras, Assit nobis, Deus qui corda, Conscientias, and form of confession, 'Confiteor deo omnia peccata mea . . .'.

11. ff. 127^{v}–130 Super gracias post missam. A'. Trium puerorum. Ps' Te Deum . . .

Te deum, Benedicite, Laudate, Nunc dimittis, Trium puerorum, Deus qui tribus, and prayers, Gratias tibi ago, Ineffabilem, Sit michi ihesu dulcissime and Agne dei qui tollis.

12. ff. 130^{v}–132 Hic incipiunt septem hore de sancta katherina. Castitatis lilium alma katherina . . .

The hymn—four lines at each hour—is *RH*, no. 2672; *AH* xxx. 167.

13. ff. 132^{v}–133^{v} Incipit oratio Venerabilis Bede presbiteri de septem ultimis uerbis . . . morietur. Domine ihesu criste fili dei uiui . . .

14. ff. 133^{v}–136 Quicumque subscripta septem gaudia in honore beate marie uirginis semel in die dixerit c dies indulgencie obtinebit a domino honorio papa quinto (*sic*) qui hec septem gaudia proprio stilo composuit. Uirgo templum trinitatis. deus summe bonitatis . . . *RH*, no. 21899.

15. ff. 136–7 Deuota oratio ad beatam uirginem mariam. O intemerata . . . orbis terrarum. Inclina . . . Masculine forms.

16. ff. 137^{v}–140 Deuota meditatio de nomine Ihesu. Ihesu dulcis memoria. dans uera cordis gaudia . . .

Ed. A. Wilmart, *Le 'Jubilus' dit de saint Bernard*, 1944. Forty-three stanzas, one more than in the 'texte pur'. 'Tu vere lumen . . .' follows stanza 38 (cf. edn., p. 216). Stanza 17 begins 'Qui ihesu' (cf. edn., p. 205) and stanza 40 'Ihesus potenter'. Stanzas 35 and 36 are in reverse order.

17. ff. 140–141^{v} Aue mundi spes maria. Aue mitis . . . *RH*, no. 1974.

18. ff. 141^{v}–142 Bonefacius papa VI concessit omnibus orationem sequentem dicentem (*sic*) ob reuerentiam uenerabilis sacramenti inter eleuationem corporis cristi et agnus dei duo milia annorum indulgentiarum ad supplicationem domini philippi regis franscie qui deuote ea(m) dixerit. Domine ihesu criste fili dei uiui qui hanc sacratissimam carnem . . .

19. ff. 142–145^{v} Incipit dulcissima meditatio et amantissima oratio scilicet corona marie uirginis gloriose. Cum iocunditate memoriam . . . Ymnus. Gaude uirgo mater cristi que per aurem concepisti . . .

The hymn at the hours is *RH*, no. 7017.

20. f. 145^{v} Antiphona. Celorum candor splenduit . . .

Memoria of Francis. *RH*, no. 3589.

21. f. 146 Ad `te' fontem et mare magnum . . .

22. f. 146^{rv} Oratio. Suscipe sancte pater clementissime deus precibus et meritis beate marie semper uirginis et beati patris nostri francisci et omnium sanctorum atque sanctarum officium seruitutis nostre . . .

23. ff. 146^{v}–147 Psalmus dauid. Retribue seruo tuo . . . Ps. 118: 17–24.

24. ff. 147–9 Incipiunt septem hore de beato francisco. Ad matutinas. Crucis arma fulgentia uidit franciscus dormiens . . .

25. f. 149^{rv} Oratio ad sanctam barbaram. Gaude barbara regina. summe pollens in doctrina . . .

Memoria of Barbara. *RH*, no. 6714.

26. ff. 149^{v}–151 Psalmi sequentes cum suis orationibus dicuntur in conuentu pro benefactoribus uiuis atque defunctis. Ps. Ad te leuaui . . .

Pss. 122 and 129 followed by versicles, responses, collect, Ecclesie tue quesumus domine, and prayers, Omnipotens sempiterne deus qui facis mirabilia, Pretende, Adesto domine, Fidelium.

27 (added, s. xvi in.). f. 151^{v} Gaude pia magdalena spes salutis . . .

Memoria of Mary Magdalene. *RH*, no. 6895.

ff. 151 + iii. Parchment (ff. 1–12, 87) and paper. f. 152 is a parchment flyleaf. 132 × 98 mm. Written space 78 × 58 mm. 12–18 long lines or 4 long lines and music. Collation: $1\text{–}2^{6}$ $3\text{–}7^{8}$ 8^{8} wants 8 after f. 59 9^{8} 10^{4} (ff. 68–71) 11^{8} 12^{8} + 1 leaf inserted before 8 (f. 87) $13\text{–}20^{8}$. Quires 3–8 are signed n–s in the usual late medieval manner: the signatures suggest that arts. 2–4 were meant to come after art. 26. A crude full page picture on f. 87^{v} (the recto blank): Christ in judgement on the rainbow: continuous framed floral border. Initials: (i) ff. 60, 88, blue patterned in white with red ornament; (ii–iv) 3-line, 2-line, and 1-line, blue or red. Capital letters in the ink of the text lined with red. Contemporary binding of wooden boards covered with brown leather: fifteen repetitions (three rows of five) of a stamp of a pelican in its piety form a rectangular panel within triple fillets: a small fleur-de-lys stamp at each corner of the panel and three repetitions of a lozenge dragon stamp outside it: three bands: three clasps, now missing, fastened from back to front.

Written in the southern Low Countries (?) for male Franciscan use by a scribe named John who wrote in the space below *Fidelium* on f. 151,

Si io pona > tur < et han sibi associa > tur.
Et nes adda > tur < qui scripsit ita uoca > tur.

Given by Phillips as MS. 2: the ex-dono label is dated 1848.

7. *Horae* s. xv/xvi

1. ff. 1–4 Sequentiae of the Gospels. The prayer 'Protector in te sperancium . . .' follows John.

2. ff. 4–5^{v} Deuota oracio ad beatam virginem mariam. Obsecro te . . . Masculine forms.

3. ff. 5^{v}–7^{v} De beata virgine maria. O intemerata . . . orbis terrarum. De te enim . . . Masculine forms.

4. ff. 8–36^v Hours of B.V.M. of the use of (Rouen).

Hours of Cross and Holy Spirit worked in.

5. ff. 36^v, 38–47^v Septem psalmi penitenciales. Litany, f. 44.

Martial last of apostles and evangelists. Ursinus as disciple. Thirty-three confessors: . . . (8–13) mellone gildarde et medarde romane audoene ausberte euode. Fourteen virgins: . . . (7–10) austreberta barbara anna genouefa: Mary of Egypt omitted. Only two prayers, Ure igne and Animabus, after Deus cui proprium. f. 37^{rv} blank.

6. ff. 48–63^v Office of the dead.

7. ff. 63^v–67^v Sequuntur suffragia plurimorum sanctorum: Trinity; Michael; John Baptist; Peter and Paul; Sebastian; Nicholas; Romanus; Anne; Mary Magdalene; Katherine; Barbara; Margaret; All Saints; of peace.

8. ff. 67^v–71^v Deuotissima oratio dicenda diebus sabbati in honorem intemerate virginis marie. Missus est gabriel angelus . . . et seculum per ignem Amen. Te deprecor ergo mitissimam . . .

The refrain Dominus tecum is said eighty-two times. Arts. 9–12 were added in s. xvi^1.

9. ff. 72–76^v Memoriae: (*a*) B.V.M., Stabat mater dolorosa . . . ; (*b*) B.V.M., Gaude flore virginali que honore speciali . . . ; (*c*) Barbara, Gaude barbara beata summe pollens . . . ; (*d*) Julian; (*e*) Martin; (*f*) 'De archiepiscopis et episcopis nostris'; (*g*) Trinity; (*h*) B.V.M., Inuiolata integra et casta . . . ; (*i*) B.V.M. 'In tempore paschali', Regina celi letare . . . ; (*j*) Scholastica.

(*a–c*). *RH*, nos. 19416, 6810, 17170.

10. ff. 76^v–77^v Prayers to Father, Son, and Holy Spirit severally.

11. ff. 77^v–78^v Oraison tresdeuote a dieu le pere. Mon benoist dieu. ie croy de cueur et confesse de bouche . . . Sonet–Sinclair, no. 1150.

12. f. 79 Oraison de la +. Saincte vraye croix aoree . . .

Sonet–Sinclair, no. 1876. f. 79^v blank.

ff. x + 79 + vi. ff. v–x, 80–1 are parchment leaves ruled for 24 lines of writing: x^v has offset of a blue initial on it. ff. iv^v, 82 have engravings pasted on them, St Michael and Holy Face, s. xvii. 177 × 127 mm. Written space 115 × 77 mm. 25 long lines. Ruling in red ink. Collation: 1^8 wants 8, perhaps blank $2\text{–}4^8$ 5^6 (ff. 32–7) $6\text{–}9^8$ 10 two (ff. 70–1) 11^8: probably a quire (or two quires) with a calendar are missing before quire 1. Catchwords written vertically. *Lettre bâtarde* (almost). Nine pictures within architectural frames: the four in art. 4 and those beginning arts. 1, 5 (David and Bathsheba) are full page; the three others, 23-line, precede lauds and compline in art. 4 and art. 8 (B.V.M. and Child, who holds a parrot: the owner, a woman, kneels before them: three trumpeting angels on the roof-top). Initials: (i) 2-line, black and white on grounds of gold paint; (ii) 1-line, gold paint on grounds of red or blue. Each page is framed on three sides with branches cut straight across and coloured brown in the inner margin and either green or blue in the upper and lower margins: the outer margin is filled with a framed floral border on gold-paint ground the height of the written space. Line fillers blue or red or, if long, in both colours, patterned in gold paint. Capital letters in the ink of the text filled with pale yellow. Gilt binding, s. xvi (?), rebacked in England, s. xix[1], and labelled 'MISSAL'.

Written in France for use in the diocese of Rouen, apparently for a woman (see above). Arms in the lower margin, f. 8 are parti per pale argent two crescents sable gules two fleur-de-lis or. 'Charles Boddam Jun[r] Trin: Coll: Camb: June 1st 1782', f. vii. Printed ex-dono label of Thomas Phillips, as in MS. 4. Label of Church Congress Exhibition numbered 315 inside the back cover.

8. *Preces, etc.* s. xvi[1]

An owner broke art. 5 to make a two-picture double opening, ff. 26v–27. Probably ff. 27–32 originally followed the memoriae which now end on f. 74. I describe them in that order.

1. ff. 1–5 Thirteen paragraphs: Pater noster . . . ; Aue maria . . . ; Credo in deum patrem . . . ; Benedicite dominus nos et ea que sumus sumpturi . . . ; Agimus tibi gratias . . . ; Misereatur nostri . . . ; Confiteor deo omnipotenti . . . (masculine forms); Sanctus . . . ; Agnus dei . . . ; Aue salus mundi verbum patris . . . ; Aue sanguis domini nostri ihesu xpristi . . . ; In manus tuas . . . ; Dominus pars hereditatis mee . . .

2. ff. 5–14 Quando surgis de mane. Domine sancte pater omnipotens eterne deus qui nos . . . Oratio. In manus tuas . . . hodie commendo . . . Oracio.[1] Domine deus omnipotens patrum nostrorum . . . Oracio. Domine ihesu xpriste redemptor mundi defende me de manu inimicorum meorum . . . Oratio. Domine deus omnipotens pater et filius et spiritus sanctus da michi famulo tuo N. da michi victoriem (*sic*) . . . Oracio. Deus in nomine tuo saluum me fac . . . Oracio. Libera me domine ihesu xpriste . . .

3. ff. 14–16v Inuocatio dei omnipotentis ad morum et vite reparacionem ab augustino edita. Domine deus meus da cordi meo . . . celestia sitire Amen.

4. ff. 16v–26 Salutations and prayers at mass in nineteen paragraphs: (*a*) In eleuacione corporis cristi. Aue verum corpus natum . . . ; (*b*) Oratio. Aue caro xpristi cara . . . ; (*c*) Oratio. Aue corpus incarnatum in altari consacratum vita panis . . . ; (*d*) Oratio. Aue uerbum incarnatum in altari . . . ; (*e*) Oratio. Aue solacium nostre expectacionis aue salus . . . ; (*f*) In eleuatione sanguinis. Calicem salutaris accipiam . . . ; (*g*) Oratio. Sanguinis domini nostri ihesu xpristi custodiat animam meam in vitam eternam. Amen; (*h*) Oratio. O vere sanguis me protege morcibus anguis inferni sorte me dira protege morte; (*i*) Oratio. Aue domine ihesu xpriste verbum patris filius virginis. Aue . . . laus angelorum . . .

[1] The scribe settled for *Oratio* after art. 2.

(five aves); (*j*) Oratio. Aue santissimum et preciocissimum corpus xpristi in ara crucis . . . ; (*k*) Oratio. O sanctissimum corpus adoro te . . . ; (*l*) Oratio. Aue ihesu xpriste inmaculatus aue falso iudicatus aue sic ludificatus . . . ; (*m*) Oratio. Anima xpristi sanctifica me . . . ; (*n*) Alia oratio. Salue sancta caro dei per quem salui fiunt rei . . . ; (*o*) Oratio. Domine ihesu xpriste fili dei viuit (*sic*) qui hanc sacratissimam carnem . . . ; (*p*) Oratio. Domine ihesu xpriste gracias ago tibi qui nos per sacratissimam carnam (*sic*) . . . ; (*q*) Oratio. In presencia corporis et sanguinis tui domine ihesu xpriste commando (*sic*) tibi . . . ; (*r*) Quando datur pax. Da pacem . . . ; (*s*) Oratio. Deus a quo sancta desideria . . .

(*a–d*). *RH*, nos. 2175, 1710, 1741, 2169.

5. ff. 26rv, 57–8 Sainct gregoire a donne xiiii mille ans de vray pardon a tous ceulx qui diront deuotement sept fois. Pater noster Aue maria. auec les oraisons qui sensuiuent. O domine ihesu xpriste adoro te in cruce pendentem . . .

Seven Oes of St Gregory.

6. ff. 58–62 Oratio deuotissima ad beatissimam virginem mariam. Obsecro te . . . Masculine forms.

7. ff. 62–6 Alia oratio ad beatam virginem mariam. O intemerata . . . orbis terrarum. De te enim . . . Masculine forms. f. 66v blank.

8. ff. 33–56v, 67–74 Thirty-six memoriae: Holy Trinity, with prayers to the three Persons severally; Holy Face, Salue sancta facies . . . ; Michael; John Baptist; John Evangelist; Peter; Paul; James; Stephen; Laurence; Christopher; Sebastian; George, Fideles hic attendite . . . ; Denis 'cum sociis'; Adrian, Aue martir adriane qui martyrium immane . . . ; Nicholas, Salue presul gloriose sancte . . . ; Three Kings; Claud; Anthony hermit, Anthoni pastor inclite . . . ; Julian; Martin; Roche, Aue roche sanctissime . . . ; Francis; Anthony of Padua; Severinus; Ivo; Anne; Mary Magdalene; Katherine; Margaret; Barbara, Gaude barbara beata summe pollens . . . ; Apollonia; Avia; Susanna; Oportuna, Oportuna piissima roga deum dulcissima . . . ; Radegund.

The metrical pieces for Holy Face, George, Adrian, Nicholas, Anthony hermit, and Barbara are *RH*, nos. 18189, 6923, 2106, 33178, 1203, 6711.

9. f. 27rv Monsieur sainct iehan et son aigneau. Saint cristofle et son fardeau. Nostre dame et sa brassee. Me doint ennuyt bonne iournee. In nomine patris et filii et spiritus sancti. Amen.

10. ff. 28–31v Dignes armes de iesu crist. En qui nostre vray sauueur fist . . . de ton doz partit Amen. Sixty-eight lines. Sonet, no. 451.

11. f. 32 Saincte vray croix aouree . . . Sonet–Sinclair, no. 1876. f. 32v blank.

ff. ii + 74 + ii. 250 × 175 mm. Written space 147 × 82 mm. 16 long lines. Ruling in red ink. Collation of ff. 1–26, 57–66, 33–56, 67–74, 27–32 in that order: 1–4[8] (ff. 1–26, 57–62) 5[4] (ff. 63–6) 6–9[8] (ff. 33–56, 67–74) 10[8] wants 7, 8, perhaps blank (ff. 27–32). Very few abbreviations. Catchwords in *lettre bâtarde*. An 8-line picture not the full width of the written space before art. 1 (God the Father blessing), art. 4 (sacrifice of Isaac), and art. 5 (vision of Gregory). A twelve-line picture before art. 9 (B.V.M., Child, John Baptist, Christopher) and art. 10 (Arma Christi). Each has an elaborate border which has been damaged by a binder at the edges (ff. 1, 16v, 26v, 27, 28): in the border on f. 28, three roundels and two rectangles contain scenes from the Passion in an all-over blue colour: a similar technique in bronze on f. 1, where an angel is on the base of one pillar and B.V.M. on the base of the other. Initials: (i) blue and white on red ground patterned in gold paint; (ii) 2-line, gold paint on grounds of red or blue patterned in gold paint. Line fillers in red patterned in gold paint. Capital letters in the ink of the text stroked with pale yellow. French binding, s. xix[1], gilt with small stars on the spine and lettered 'HEURES MANUSCRI'. Secundo folio *ferna*.

Written in France. Arms in the border of each picture page, barry nebuly argent and gules (Rochechouart ?). Armorial book-plate of John Symmons inside the cover: he wrote his name and 'March 15th 87 No 29' on f. iv: his gift to Bishop Burgess. No doubt given as MS. 1.

LANGLEY MARISH. CHURCH, KEDERMINSTER LIBRARY

Parochial Libraries, pp. 85, 109.

227. *P. Riga, Aurora* s. xiii[1]

Prologus in aurora editus a magistro petro. Omnis scriptura diuinitus inspirata . . . debeat sustinere. De preparatione. Porro hii obmutescant qui circa figmenta poetarum . . . (f. 1v) diaboli a cristo. His ita dictis ad sequentia transeamus. Incipit prologus super pentateucum. Frequens sodalium meorum peticio . . . patenter illuxit. Explicit prologus. Incipit pentatheuc' moysi. Incipit aurora et primo agit de vii diebus. Prima facta die duo. celum. terra leguntur . . . (f. 211v) Ense necat paulum par lux dux urbs cruce petrum. Explicit aurora magistri petri rige. super uetus et nouum testamentum. Vermiculos post uersiculos tu petre sequeris. Versiculosus eras uermiculosus eris.

A copy with some of the features of Aegidius's first revision of the Aurora, as described in the introduction to P. E. Beichner's edition, p. xx, but Job and Song of Songs precede the Gospels. 'Omnis scriptura' and 'Frequens' are Beichner's prefaces II, III. Traces of the division of Genesis into four books (cf. edn., p. xvii) remain in the headings 'Explicit primus liber. Incipit secundus' and 'Incipit quartus liber' before 'Dicturus moyses . . .' and 'Sem cum centenos . . .' (lines 523, 706). The scribe was copying a defective exemplar and left some lines blank, for example line 34 of Numbers, and smaller spaces to take a word or two, noting usually 'deerat' or 'deest' against them. 'Vermiculos' is Walther, no. 33162. f. 212rv is blank, except for some computistical notes in an English hand, s. xv.

ff. iii + 212 + iii. 244 × 165 mm. Written space 180 mm high. 42 long lines. The first line of writing above the top ruled line. Collation: 1–26[8] 27 four (ff. 209–12). Quires, except the last, numbered at the end. Initials: (i) of books and prologues, 4-line or more, either gold on patterned grounds of red and blue framed in gold, or, f. 136 onwards, red or blue with ornament of the other colour; (ii) after each red heading, 2-line, red or blue with ornament of the other colour. Binding of s. xix. Secundo folio *ut pentateuchum*.

Written probably in northern France. In England in s. xv and probably at Langley Marish by 1631: see the next item.

267. *Evangelia*[1] s. xi[1]

A gospel book, written, like other English gospel books of this period, in many numbered paragraphs, following the Ammonian section numbers: the top numbers are (Matthew) 'ccclv', (Mark) 'ccxxxiiii', (Luke) 'cccxlii', (John) 'ccxxxi'. One of the books discussed by T. A. M. Bishop, 'The Copenhagen Gospel Book', *Nordisk Tidskrift för Bok- och Biblioteksväsen*, liv (1967), 33–41. Briefly described in *British Museum Quarterly*, vi (1932), 93, with reduced facsimiles of ff. 80v, 99. Trinity College, Cambridge, 215 (B. 10. 4) and B.L., Royal 1 D. ix are closely related manuscripts.

The point at which the passion story begins is marked in Matthew by a line of rustic capitals (f. 31v), in Mark by a heading in gold 'Secundum Marcum' and a line of gold capitals (f. 56), in Luke by a heading in gold 'Secundum Lucam' and a line of uncials (f. 92), and in John by a heading in gold 'Passio domini nostri iesu cristi secundum Iohannem' (f. 120). In the Matthew passion story interlined letters, *c, s,* and *t*, indicate respectively Christ's words, words spoken by others, and the connecting narrative. The scribe put cross references to other Gospels in the margins and also, in red, Eusebian canon numbers and, in Luke and John only, a broken series of capitula numbers, which run (Luke) III, III (*sic for* IIII), V–X, XIII–XVIII and (John) III, V, X (*sic for* VII), VIIII–XI, XIIII.[2]

f. 38 and unnumbered leaves after ff. 4 and 63 are modern parchment blanks.

1. ff. 1–4v The prologues Novum opus, Plures fuisse, Ammonius quidem, and Sciendum etiam: Wordsworth and White, i. 1, 11, 6, 5.

2. ff. 4v–36v The prologue to Matthew, 'Matthaeus ex Iudaea . . . apprehendere expetunt' (*ends imperfectly*: Wordsworth and White, i. 17/1), and, after a gap, the Gospel, beginning on f. 5 at 1: 18, 'cristi autem'.

The gap contained no doubt capitula and at least one display page (see below, decoration) and perhaps Eusebian canons: cf. Trinity 215, ff. 5–18.

3. ff. 36v–37, 39–60v The prologue to Mark, 'Marcus euangelista . . .' (Wordsworth and White, i. 171), unnumbered capitula, 'De iohanne baptista . . . diuitem intrare' (*ends imperfectly in the eighth paragraph*, f. 37v: as C of Wordsworth and White, i. 174–182/10), and the Gospel.

[1] On permanent deposit in the British Library, Loans 11.

[2] Almost the same broken series is in Royal 1 D. ix, which has the same two errors and the same exceptional placing of the bracket—which distinguishes a capitula number from a canon number—after instead of before the number at each of the two numbers X in John.

4. ff. 60^{v}–97 The prologue to Luke, 'Lucas syrus . . .' (Wordsworth and White, i. 267), unnumbered capitula, 'Zacharias uisio . . . petrus ubi (*sic*). ter' (*ends imperfectly in the seventeenth paragraph*, f. 63^{v}: as C of Wordsworth and White, i. 274–304/19), and the Gospel, beginning imperfectly on f. 64 at 1: 21, 'Et erat plebs'.

5. ff. 97^{v}–125 The prologue to John, 'Hic est Iohannes . . .' (Wordsworth and White, i. 485), unnumbered capitula, 'Phariseorum . . . resurrectio eius', in fourteen paragraphs (as C of Wordsworth and White, i. 492–504), and (f. 99) the Gospel.

A leaf missing after f. 107 contained 7: 37 *autem die* . . . 8: 23 *deorsum estis*. The text was supplied in s. xvi on ff. 108–9. f. 98^{v} blank: the lower half of the leaf has been cut off, but the text on the recto is complete.

6. ff. 125^{v}–131 A table of gospel lections for the year, beginning at Christmas, 'In primis in uigilia natalis domini de nona . . . de turba ait ad iesum' (*ends imperfectly at Saturday in the eighth week after Pentecost*).

Also in Trinity 215 and Royal 1 D. ix.

ff. ii + 126 + ii, together with two supply leaves and three inserted blanks. The foliation, (i, ii), 1–131, (132–3), takes account of the supply leaves (ff. 108–9) and one of the three blanks (f. 38). 310 × 210 mm. Written space 223 × 138 mm. 20 long lines. Collation impracticable: leaves are missing after ff. 4, 37, 63, 107, 131.

Arts. 2 (from f. 5)–5 are in the same admirable hand as the Trinity and Royal gospel books, the 'Missal of Robert of Jumièges' and three fragments, and as leaves added to the Copenhagen gospel book: see Bishop, loc. cit., for all but the fragment at Oslo, RA 227.[1] Art. 1 and the prologue to Matthew on f. 4^{v} are in a hand which Bishop identifies as that of the scribe who wrote Pembroke College, Cambridge, 301 (gospel book) and Bodleian Library, Bodley 163 (Bede, Historia ecclesiastica) and completed the general prologues in Royal 1 D. ix (see his fig. 2, p. 10).

The principal decoration consisted originally of at least four display openings with pictures of the evangelists on the left hand pages and elaborate initials on the right hand pages, but of all this only two right hand pages, ff. 39, 99, remain, each with an initial *I* as its main feature, within 'Winchester style' frames.[2] On f. 39 (Mark) the *I* has beside it ten golden lines of rustic capitals (1), square capitals (2–7), and uncials (8–10): SE*C*U*N*D*U*M MARCUM / NI / TIVM / EVANGE / LII IH̄U / XP̄I FILII / D*E*I SICVT / SCRIPTUM / EST IN ISAIA / PROPHETA. On f. 99 (John) the *I* has above and beside it eleven golden lines of rustic capitals (1–3, 9), square capitals (4–7), uncials (8), and minuscules (10, 11): INITIVM SANCTI / EVANGELII SECVNDVM / IOHANNEM / N / PRIN / CIPIO / ERAT / VERBVM / ET UERBUM / erat apud deum / et deus erat uerbum. Except on these two pages and on f. 35^{v} initials are in gold in four sizes: 10-line for the *B* of *Beatissimo*, f. 1; 3-line and 4-line for the *L* and *M* on ff. 4^{v}, 60^{v}; 1-line (but usually outside the written

[1] The Bailey fragment is at Salisbury, not Winchester. A facsimile of it is Bodleian, MS. Facs. c. 27, f. 8. Dr. L. Gjerløw kindly told me of the Oslo fragment.

[2] The leaves missing after ff. 37 and 63 contained, no doubt, the pictures of Mark and Luke. Trinity College 215 has five display openings and B.L., Add. 34890 and Pembroke College, 301, have four display openings. The collation suggests that there were once pictures facing the initials in Royal 1 D. ix.

space) where a new paragraph begins; 1-line for the *Q* of *Qui* in the genealogy, Luke 3: 23–8. Binding of s. xix/xx by F. Bedford. Secundo folio *apud nos*; tertio folio *niaeque partibus.*

Written in England. Bishop, loc. cit., draws attention to the evidence for Peterborough as the place of origin. At the royal collegiate chapel of Windsor in s. xv, as appears from an entry added to the book-list in Bodleian, Ashmole Roll 36: 'Vnum vetus textus Euangeliorum iii° folio maque partibus'. 'Liber collegii de Wyndesore' at the head of f. 1, s. xv/xvi. A gift to Langley Church, presumably from Sir John Kederminster, †1631: see E. C. Rouse, 'The Kederminster Library', *Records of Bucks*, xix (1941–6), 50–66.

LEEDS. CATHOLIC DIOCESE OF LEEDS, DIOCESAN ARCHIVES

Mirror of the Life of Christ (in English) s. xv[1]

1. ff. 2–114 (*begins imperfectly*) þ[t] is to say as deuoute ymaginacions and lyknesses . . . (f. 3[v]) firste Chapitre. [The] first parte hath v chapitres . . . saluacion. [After the] tyme þ[t] man was exiled . . . (f. 114) of al the blessed lyf byfore writen. Amen. Here folweth a short deuoute praier to hym and his blessed body in the sacrament of the auter. the which (f. 114[v]) [. . . .] at messe with inwarde deuocion. [. . . .] Ihesu crist [. . . . c]onteined here in this moost . . . with fire of thy loue and myn (*ends imperfectly*).

The ruins of a fine copy of Nicholas Love's translation of Pseudo-Bonaventura, Meditationes Vitae Christi, in sixty-three numbered chapters. The first words now are in the 'Proheme' (ed. L. F. Powell, 1908, p. 9/11) and the last in chapter 63 (edn. p. 324/16, six lines from the end of the text).

f. 1 (only a small fragment remains) and a leaf missing after f. 1 contained a table of chapters: ch. 33 is the last listed on 1[v].

A small piece of f. 115 remains. The text ended on its recto and the verso was left blank: the ends of five added lines can be read, three ending 'wat*er*', 'full' and 'and of' and two, in another hand, ending 'xxvii' and '[. . .]lfford'.

2 (flyleaf). (*a*) f. 116 Christofer Mustchamp was christened the 24th of Jan' 1566 diones Mustchampe wieff to Barron Mustchamp and mother to the foresaid Christopher departid her lyeffe the xv[th] of Jan' Anno 1567. (*b*) f. 116[v] A recipe 'for the pestylens', s. xvi: 'Take a quantyte of wormwod Rew Tansey . . .'.

ff. 115 + i. For f. 116 see above. 287 × 200 mm. Written space 182 × 110 mm. Thirty-four long lines. Seventeen quires, all originally eights. The missing leaves are $1^{2,3}$, 2^2, $3^{3,4}$, 4^3, 5^6, 6^3, $7^{1,8}$, 8^2, 9^1, $11^{2,8}$, 12^2, 13^6, $14^{3,4}$, $15^{1,7}$, 16^8. 1^1, and 17^8 (ff. 1, 115) are very small fragments. Quire and leaf signatures in the usual late medieval form: the last is 'R iiii' on f. 111. Written in anglicana formata, with short and sometimes backward-sloping *r*. Initials: (i) of main divisions, missing, together with the leaves on which they came; (ii) of chapters 29, 31, 38, 2-line, gold on red and blue grounds patterned in white, with short sprays into the margin: the rest of this type either on missing leaves or cut out of existing leaves.

Paragraph marks, blue with red ornament or gold with violet ornament are used: (*a*) in the text; (*b*) in front of each of the three constituents of the running title (for example in front of 'Pars iii^{ta}', 'Die iouis', and 'Capitulum xxxvii^{m}' on f. 68); (*c*) in the margins in front of the word 'Nota' or other annotations in the main hand, of which there are three or four to a page. Line fillers of gold and blue. Parchment binding, s. xvii (?).

Written in England. Art. 2 suggests ownership by Christopher Muschamp, †1579, baron of the exchequer, 1577-9 (E. Foss, *Judges of England*, v. 529). Book-plates, inside the cover, of the Northern District, s. xix^{1}, and of the Leeds Seminary, s. xix^{2}: (1) Ex libris vic. ap. sep. distric.; (2) E libris Bibliothecæ Seminarii Diœcesani S. Josephi Loidis Donum (*blank*)'.

LEEDS. UNIVERSITY LIBRARY

The six medieval manuscripts which do not form part of the Brotherton Collection were acquired in 1921 (MS. 4), 1925 (MSS. 1, 2), 1948 (MSS. 122-4), and 1952 (MS. 498). The Brotherton Collection was formed by Edward Allen Brotherton (created Baron Brotherton of Wakefield in 1929, †1930), during the last years of his life. It was handed over to the University of Leeds in 1935 in accordance with his wishes. Each volume contains his book-plate. Most of the medieval manuscripts were bought from Charles Sawyer, Grafton St., London. They are listed on pp. 3-7, 14-31 of J. A. Symington, *Catalogue of the Ancient Manuscripts and Early Printed Books in the Brotherton Collection*, 1931. MSS. 500, 501, 502 were added to the Brotherton Collection by purchase in 1950 and 1958.

1. *Manuel des Pecchez (in French)* s. xiv^{1}

'Le manuel des pecchez'. Li vertu del seint espirit . . . (p. 200) En piere. fiz et seint espirit amen. Explicit.

Described by E. J. Arnould, *Le manuel des péchés*, Paris, 1940, p. 384 and collated as Z in his specimens from the text, pp. 399-436. Bk. 6 does not occur, bk. 9 is abbreviated and there are smaller gaps in the text, bringing the total number of lines here to 9,508. The line in the epilogue in which the name of the putative author occurs is 'Que pur William prie de Widitton': cf. Arnould, pp. 245-56, 436. pp. 201-2 are blank, except for a recipe on the recto, 'Pernetz gromoyl saxifrage . . .'.

ff. ii + 101 + ii, paginated (i-iv), 1-202, (203-6). 272 × 170 mm. Written space *c.* 180 mm. in height. 2 cols. 24 lines. Collation: 1-12^{8} 13^{6} wants 6, blank. Textura. Initials: (i) f. 1, 8-line, red and blue with ornament of both colours; (ii) 2-line, blue with red ornament. Each line of verse begins with a capital letter in the ink of the text: the letter is filled with pale yellow in the first line of each couplet and stroked with red in the second line. Binding of s. xix^{1} covered with red velvet. Secundo folio *Echiet.*

Written in England. Armorial bookplate of William Constable-Maxwell (1804-76) of Everingham Park, Yorkshire,[1] and (Everingham ?) shelfmark

$$A\frac{2\ \text{Sh}}{4\ \text{Place}}$$

inside the cover. Given by Colonel Sir E. A. Brotherton in 1925.

[1] The copy of Manuel des Pecchez now at San Marino, Huntington HM 903, is listed among the Everingham manuscripts in HMC, 1st Report, App. p. 45, but not this copy.

2. *Les Faits des Romains (in French)* s. xv med.

'Cest le liure des fays des Romains conpille en[sem]ble de la[. .]uste et de suetoyne et du lucain et cest premier liu[r]e est de Iuilles cesar et de ces ouures' iusques a sa mort.[1] Chascuns homs a qui dieu a donne cens et entendement . . . (f. 247) mise la cendres (*ends abruptly*).

Printed in 1490 and 1500 and by L.-F. Flutre and K. Sneyders de Vogel, *Li fet des romains*, Paris, vol. 1 (text), undated, vol. 2 (introduction, etc.), 1938. Listed as X_1 by Flutre, *Les manuscrits des 'Faits des Romains'*, Paris 1932, who knew it only from the 1901 sale catalogue. Noticed by B. Woledge in *Romania*, lix (1933), 564-6. The last words are within a printed page of the end, edn. p. 743/6. ff. 247^v, 248 blank (248^v is pasted down). The outer columns of text on ff. 6-10 are missing.

ff. 248, the columns numbered in a modern hand. Thick parchment. 405 × 305 mm. Written space *c.*275 × 210 mm. 2 cols. 39-42 lines. Frame ruling in pencil. Collation: 1-20^{12} 21^{12} wants 8-10, 12: 11, f. 248, is pasted down. Written in fairly large current cursiva. Initials: f. 1, 6-line, red and blue-green with ornament prolonged to make an odd and ugly continuous border; (ii) 3-line, blue with red ornament or red with blue ornament. Capital letters in the ink of the text are covered with a yellow wash. Binding of s. xviii: 'Faits et geste de I. Cesar MS' on a label on the spine. Secundo folio *therantres*.

Written in France. 'Ex bibliotheca minimorum Guichiensium', f. 14, s. xvii: the Poor Clares of La Guiche, near Blois, owned also the copy of the *Faits* now in the Archives départmentales of Saône-et-Loire, as Woledge noted in *Neophilologus*, xxiv (1939), 41. 'CRS/Vol (?) lil (?)' inside the cover, bottom left, s. xix in. From the Paul Barrois collection obtained by Lord Ashburnham: sale at Sotheby's, 10 June 1901, lot 278, to Leighton for £2. 2*s*. 0*d*. 'Presented with the aid of funds subscribed by Mrs Nellie Emsley of Bradford, Dr W. Gough of Park Square, Leeds, and Colonel T. Walter Harding of Madingley Hall, Cambridge' in 1925.

4. *Juvenalis* s. xv^2

Iunii Iuuenalis aquinatis satyra prima. Semper ego auditor . . . orbita culpæ (*ends imperfectly, at Sat. xiv. 37*).

No scholia. Facsimiles: of f. 1, reduced, and f. 52^v, slightly reduced, accompanying a notice by R. H. Martin in *Leeds Phil. and Lit. Soc. Proceedings*, VI, pt. v (1948), 361-3; of f. 52^v, actual size, in the University of Leeds publication *Greek and Latin* [1968]; of ff. 46^v-47, slightly reduced, by J. Wardrop, *The Script of Humanism*, 1963, pl. 38. The plates show the two distinct Greek 'nota bene' signs added in red in the margins by a reader to draw attention to certain passages: cf. Wardrop, p. 34.

ff. iii + 64 + iii. 208 × 125 mm. Written space 137 × 65 mm. 26 long lines. Ruling with a hard point. Collation: 1-6^{10} 7 four. Quires 1-6 signed A-F at the end between the inner pair of bounding lines: cf. Wardrop, pl. 22. Written in a sloping humanistic hand. The ink looks browner on hair sides than on flesh sides. On f. 1 the text has been made to look as though it were written on a monument, with entablature and base, the latter bearing an empty wreath. Initials: (i) f. 1, 6-line, gold paint on a decorated green ground; (ii) 2-line, blue. The first word of each satire after the initial letter is in red rustic capitals. Binding of English russia, s. xix in. Secundo folio *Aut Lugdunensem*.

[1] The heading, except the last four words, is over erasure by a scribe who seems to have been unable to see or understand all he was copying. The eleventh word should be *salluste*.

Written in Italy. Wardrop recognized that the scribe was Bartolomeo Sanvito, op. cit., p. 34. Book-plate with the name 'Henrici Alani', s. xix. No. 512 in catalogue 31 (new series) of Davis and Orioli, 1921, at £5. 5*s.*: the relevant cutting is attached to f. ii^{v}. Acquired 25 October 1921.

122. *J. de Voragine, Legenda Sanctorum* s. xiii^{2}

1. ff. 3–195 Incipit prologus super legendis sanctorum quas compilauit frater Iacobus Ianuensis. de ordine fratrum predicatorum. Uniuersum tempus . . . ad aduentum. Explicit prologus super librum de legendis sanctorum in quatuor tempora distinctum. Incipiunt capitula . . . (*numbered table of 178 items*) . . . (f. 4) 1. De aduentu domini. Aduentus domini per quatuor . . .

As compared with Graesse's edition of Legenda Sanctorum there are the same five omissions as in Brotherton Collection 23 (q.v.) and the order is the same, except at Graesse nos. 132–9, here in the order 134–8, 132, 139, 133, Cornelius following Chrysostom and Lambert Eugenia. The life of Elizabeth of Hungary ends abruptly on f. 174^{v} at the words 'sic afflixit: ut' (edn., p. 769/3): the rest of f. 174^{v} and f. 175^{rv} are blank. A break at the end of quire 2, where f. 22^{v} is partly blank: no text is missing and f. 23 seems to be in the same hand. A reader noted 'Hec Legenda beati Lamberti non est propria set alia maior' at the foot of f. 142^{v}, s. xiv.

2 (added in s. xv). f. 195^{v} De sancto Godehardo episcopo hildensemensi et confessore. [S]anctus godehardus in altahensi monasterio . . . dominus operatus est etc. ff. 196–198^{v} blank.

3. ff. 1, 199 were pastedowns in a former binding: (*a*) f. 1, a leaf of Josephus in a neat hand of s. x in. (?); (*b*) f. 199, a leaf of an antiphonal, s. xii.

(*a*) is back to front. The text begins on the verso with the last six of a table of chapters of Antiquitates, bk. 15, '. . .]diata partem eorum ab antonio . . . duplum condidit', followed by the beginning of bk. 15, '(*blank*) qualiter hierosolimam ceperunt. Nec non et antigonum'. It ends abruptly in the second column on the recto 'ubi nauem in qua nauigarent ad egyptum' (edn. 1514, f. 139^{v}/42). Written space 250+ × 210 mm. 3 vols. 55 out of 56 (?) lines remain. (*b*). Part of the office for Good Friday and Easter Eve. 19+ long lines.

ff. iii + 196 + ii, foliated (i), 1–199, (200). For ff. 1, 199 see above, art. 3. f. 2 is a medieval parchment flyleaf. 295 × 205 mm. Written space 200 × 130 mm. 2 cols. 46 lines. Collation of ff. 3–198: 1^{12} 2^{8} (ff. 15–22) $3\text{–}16^{12}$ 17^{8}. *Ad hoc* signatures in pencil. Initials: (i) blue and red with ornament of both colours; (ii) 2-line, blue or red, with ornament of the other colour; (iii) in the table of chapters, 1-line, blue or red. Capital letters in the ink of the text touched with red. 'Bound by J. Clyde', s. xix. Secundo folio (f. 5) *nostram.*

Written in the Low Countries (?). A gift to the Benedictine abbey of St Jacques, Liège, in or before 1312: 'Notandum quod anni domini renouantur in kalendis ianuarii. siue in natiuitate domini. Anno igitur domini M^{o} ccc^{o} xii^{o} in kalendis ianuarii. obiit D*ominus* iacobus dictus godar sacerdos. capellanus ecclesie sancti bartholomei in leodis. Qui dedit nobis hunc librum quem dicunt uitam auream. siue nouam legendam de sanctis. ad refectionem [. . . .]um. Quam ob rem oretur pro eo ab omnibus in hoc eodem libro legentibus. quatinus anima eius per misericordiam dei requiescat in pace. Amen. Liber iste est ecclesie sancti Iacobi in leodio', f. 195. 'Aurea liber iste est monasterii sancti Iacobi in Insula Leod' ', f. 2^{v}, s. xiv. 'Ex libris Diui Iacobi Leodii in Insula', f. 2, s. xvii. 'I 28' and 'B 35', f. 3, are post-medieval pressmarks. Belonged to Paul Barrois: 'Barrois No. (*blank*)' inside the cover.[1] Ashburnham-Barrois sale, Sotheby's, 10 June 1901, lot 614, to Quaritch (£11). Book label of Silvanus P. Thompson, F.R.S., inside the cover. Given by Dr T. E. Harvey in 1948.

123. *Jacobus de Jüterbog* s. xv ex.

1. ff. 1-53 Tractatus de Statu et officio prelatorum. Iosias factus rex iuda diuine legis feruentissimus . . . mecum glorificet cui laus et gloria semper sit in secula Amen. Explicit tractatus de Statu et officio ecclesiasticarum personarum et de canonico ingressu ad beneficia ecclesiastica editus a sacratheologie doctore Iacobo ordinis Cartusien' erfordie cuius anima in domino requiescat feliciter. Laus deo pax viuis Requies eterna defunctis.

See L. Meier, *Die Werke des Erfurter Kartaüsers Jakob von Jüterbog, BGPTM* xxxvii. 5 (1955), pp. 37-9 (no. 39). ff. 53^v-54^v blank.

2. ff. 55-69 Rogamus vos ne terreamini per spiritum. Verba sunt apostolica ad plebem tessalonicam missa in epistola 2^a . . . ad hoc instigante. Pro quo deus sit benedictus in secula Amen. Tractatus de animabus exutis a corporibus editus a fratre Iacobo doctore sacratheologie ordinis Cartusien' Erforden' domus finitur feliciter.

Meier, pp. 58-9 (no. 70). Printed often: Goff, J., 19-27.

3. ff. 69^v-72^v De anno iubileo seu plenarie remissionis de quo oportune . . . Currente anno domini M^o $cccc^o$ lxxiii autorisante in ecclesia militante domino Sixto papa quarto de ordine minorum. Explicit tractatus de anno iubileo magistri Iacobi ord' Cartusien' domus Erforden' cuius memoria apud superos sit in benediccione.

Meier, pp. 69-70 (no. 87).

ff. iii + 72 + ii. Paper. For ff. ii, 73 see below. 280 × 202 mm. Written space *c.* 205 × 135 mm. 2 cols. 38-41 lines. Frame ruling in pencil. Collation: 1-6^{12}. Written in cursiva. Initials 4-line or 3-line, metallic red or blue. Capital letters in the ink of the text marked with red. Binding of s. xx: formerly in marbled covers, s. xix, retained as ff. ii, 73. Secundo folio *quatuor*.

Written in Germany. Perhaps part of a larger book. From the Kloss library, with book-plate, s. xix, inscribed 'Georgius Kloss M.D. Francofurti ad Moenum'. 'Phillipps MS. 9539', f. 1. Phillipps sale 5 June 1899, lot 776. Item 684 in a Dobell catalogue, the cutting from which is attached to f. ii^v. 'Ex libris T. Edmund Harvey, London 19.vi.1903', f. iii. Given by Dr T. E. Harvey in 1948.

[1] A note here by Lord Ashburnham (?) dated September 1856: 'The number was lost in re-binding, before Mr Holmes made his Catalogue, but it is entered in that Cat. and by error in index as B 334 it should be s.n. 'Now entered as no. 30'.'

124. *Evangelistarium* s. xv/xvi

1. ff. 1–42 Dominica prima aduentus. Sequentia sancti euangelii secundum mattheum. xxi ca. In illo tempore quum[1] appropinquasset iesus hierosolimis . . . Temporal for the year from Advent.

2. ff. 42v–51 Sanctoral.

Twenty-six proper lessons: Andrew, Conception of B.V.M., Thomas apostle, Maur, Fabian and Sebastian, Purification of B.V.M., Annunciation of B.V.M., Philip and James, John before the Latin Gate, Nativity of John Baptist, Peter and Paul, Visitation of B.V.M., octave of Peter and Paul, Mary Magdalene, Apollinaris, B.V.M. 'ad niues', Sixtus, Transfiguration, Laurence, Assumption of B.V.M., Decollation of John Baptist, Exaltation of Cross, Matthew, Michael, Placidus, All Saints. Among feasts with cues only are 'In sancti patris nostri benedicti' (cues to Maur), 'In festo sancti antonini mar' patroni placentini' (cues to Maur), 'In translatione sancti xysti' (cues to common of martyr), 'In sancte iustine de padua' (cues to common of virgin).

3. ff. 51–58v Common of saints.

4. f. 58v In ipsa die dedicationis ecclesie. et in anniuersario.

5. ff. 58v–59v In agendis missis pro defunctis.

6. f. 60rv A selective table of contents, with leaf numbers.

The reference to art. 4 is in the words 'In dedicatione ecclesie s. xisti. 58'.

ff. i + 60 + i. ff. 1–59 have a medieval foliation in red. 340 × 245 mm. Written space 215 × 165 mm. 2 cols. 31 lines. Collation: $1–7^8$ 8 four (ff. 57–60: 58 and 60 are a bifolium). Initials: 3-line and on f. 1 7-line, blue or red patterned in white, the blue initials ornamented in red, blue, and green and the red initials in violet and green. Binding of s. xix. Secundo folio *ei. Quid.*

Written in Italy, no doubt for the use of the Benedictine abbey of St Sixtus, Piacenza, a member of the congregation of Monte Cassino: a shield in the lower margin of f. 1, flanked by dolphins, bears a cross and upon it an *S*. An erasure at the foot of f. 1. Listed in an English book-seller's catalogue, s. xix ex. (?), at 12 guineas: the relevant strip is pasted inside the cover. Given by Dr T. Edmund Harvey in 1948.

498. *Horae* s. xv^2

1. (*a*) f. 1rv Pape boniface a donne a tous ceulz et celles qui diront deuotement ceste oraison qui sensuit entre le leuation du corp*us* domini et le dernier agnus dei deux mille ans de uray pardon. Domine ihesu criste qui hanc sacratissimam carnem . . . (*b*) ff. 2–4v Le rosaire de nostre dame. Pour bien uouloir complaire A la vierge de bonnaire . . . se son lescriptures. (*c*) ff. 5–6 Auete omnes anime

[1] So regularly for *cum*. For an earlier example of this revived spelling—by Niccolò Perotti in 1446 at the age of 18—see *Duke Humfrey and English Humanism* (Bodleian Library Exhibition Catalogue), 1970, p. 28. See also C. R. Cheney in *Bulletin of the Institute of Historical Research*, xxiv (1951), 44.

fideles quarum corpora . . . Oremus. Domine ihesu criste salus et liberatio . . . (*d*) f. 6^{v} Quant on lieue le calice. Aue uere sanguis domini nostri . . . (*e*) f. 6^{v} Salue sancta caro dei per quam salui fiunt rei . . . Vnda que de te manauit a peccato nos (*ends imperfectly*).

(*b*). Cf. Sonet-Sinclair, no. 1690 (six huitains). Here 46 + 27 lines, consisting of (1) twenty couplets and two triplets and (2) nine triplets, beginning 'Le chapelet deuotement', perhaps added rather later. Only six lines are written on the recto of f. 4: see below. (*e*). *RH*, no. 18175.

2. ff. 7–12^{v} Sequentiae of the Gospels.

3. ff. 13–69 Hours of B.V.M. of the use of (Autun).

As in other Autun hours, capitula (prime and none, Uirgo verbo concepit and Felix namque es) are not preceded by antiphons. Memoriae of the Annunciation and Conception follow lauds.

4. ff. 69–72^{v} Sequuntur hore de sancta cruce . . . Hymnus. Patris sapiencia . . .

5. ff. 73–6 Hours of the Holy Spirit. . . . Hymnus. Nobis sancti spiritus . . .

6. ff. 76–94^{v} Sequuntur septem psalmi penitentiales: followed on f. 88^{v} by litany (of Autun), ending imperfectly.

Three disciples: lazare marcialis saturnine. Thirty-seven martyrs: (2–4) nazari nazari et celse leodegari . . . (14, 15) andochi tyrse. Twenty-six confessors: (9–13) amator racho siagri brici aniane. Twenty-three virgins: (1) anna.

7. ff. 95–9 Obsecro te . . . Masculine forms.

8. ff. 99–101 De beata maria oratio deuota. Stabat mater dolorosa . . . Oratio. Interueniat pro nobis quesumus . . . *RH*, no. 19416.

9 (added, s. xvi). f. 99 (at foot) Dulcis amica dei. Rosa vernans stellaque decora. Tu memor esto mei Dum mortis venerit hora. *RH*, no. 25737.

ff. 101. 140 × 110 mm. Written space *c*.90 × 65 mm. 14 long lines. Collation: 1^{6} $2–12^{8}$ 13^{8} wants 1 before f. 95. The quire signatures, b–o, show that there was a now missing quire (calendar ?) before art. 1. On f. 4 a full-page picture of B.V.M. and Child within a rosary extends into the upper and lower margins and is partly 'concealed' by six lines of art. 1*b* which occupy the eighth to thirteenth lines on the page. Blank spaces on ff. 4^{v} and 99 were used in s. xvi (?) for small pictures: skull and crossbones; B.V.M. beside the cross with a sword in her breast: only a short section of the cross, and of the body on it only the feet are shown. Initials: (i) f. 1, 4-line, blue patterned in white, historiated (Christ crowned with thorns) on a gold ground; (ii) 4-line (f. 13), 3-line or 2-line, gold on red and blue grounds; (iii, iv) 2-line and 1-line, red or blue. A poor and damaged framed floral border on f. 13. French binding of gilt leather over pasteboard, s. xvi^{1}.

Written in France for use in the diocese of Autun. Two inscriptions of s. xvii: (1) inside the cover, 'Ce present liure este a moy Denis grison de Villangrette (*Jura*) Je prie a ceux qui les treuueront que moi les rande et Je poyeres le Vin a la Sainct mor (?) et le pain blan a la Sainct Jean et la Viande a la Sainct Anne Faict ce dixsiesme de Januier mil six cen trante neux Denis Grison'; (2) f. 101^{v}, 'Ces presante heures sont a moy emilland gey et me sont este donnes par eschange par himbert Jolicwe (?) Contre des aultre que Je luy ay donnes. Je prie a Ceux ou Celle (?) quy les trouueront quy moy (?) les rande et Je les peiriray (?) en r(e)conpanse. Faict a bouches (?) anges ce trantiesme octobre mil six sent [. . . .] deux (?). Emilland gey'.[1] Given by R. A. Hellewell in 1952.

Brotherton Collection 1. *Kalendarium, etc.* s. xv med.

A fragment of a book of hours.

1. ff. 1–12^{v} Full calendar in gold, blue, and red, the two colours alternating.

Translation of Nicholas, Yvo, Louis king, Giles, Denis, Nicholas, Thomas archbishop (9, 19 May, 25 August, 1 September, 9 October, 6, 29 December) are among feasts in gold. Visitation of B.V.M. not entered, 2 July.

2. ff. 13–18 Sequentiae of the Gospels.

3. ff. 18–20^{v} Oracio de beata maria. Obsecro te . . . (*ends imperfectly*).

Masculine forms. Altered in s. xvii (?) and made to begin 'Obsecro te domine orphanorum'.

4. ff. 21–36^{v} Penitential psalms and (f. 34) litany.

Ends imperfectly in the list of martyrs: . . . (6, 7) iustine lucane . . . (14) georgi (15 catchword), 'Sancte cosma. ora pro nobis'. Facsimiles of f. 21 and of ff. 31^{v}–32 (reduced) are in *Catalogue*, pp. 14, 15.

ff. vii + 36 + xviii. 202 × 150 mm. Written space 100 × 60 mm. 15 long lines. Ruling in red ink. Collation: 1^{12} $2\text{–}4^{8}$. Profusely illuminated. An 11-line picture on f. 21 (David). Initials: (i) f. 18^{v}, 3-line, pink, patterned in white, on gold ground, historiated (B.V.M.); (ii, iii) as (i), but 2-line and 1-line and decorated. Borders of art. 1: (i) in each lower margin, the occupation of the month and sign of the zodiac in a double compartment measuring 62 × 40 mm.; (ii) in other borders, 85 figures of saints, usually 4 on each verso and 3 on each recto, some of them worked up into small scenes. Borders of arts. 2–4: (i) f. 21, continuous, including 8 scenes from the life of David; (ii) on three sides of all other pages, of gold ivy leaves, with grotesques and other figures among them and in art. 2 the evangelists and their symbols. French binding, s. xvi: narrow border, centrepiece, and corner-pieces, these last gilt.

Written in France. The illumination is of the Bedford Master group.[2]

Brotherton Collection 2. *Psalterium, etc.* s. xv med.

1. ff. 2–7^{v} Calendar in red and black, graded.

In red: Genouefe uirginis duplum; Dyonisii rustici et eleutherii martirum Duplum; Marcelli episcopi Duplum (3 Jan.; 9 Oct., with octave in black, Duplum; 3 Nov., with octave in black,

[1] In the first inscription I owe the surname and place-name to Mr Peter Morrish: I had misread them. The second inscription has been read in a photograph taken in ultra-violet light.

[2] Information from Dr J. J. G. Alexander.

of nine lessons). In black: Rigoberti archiepiscopi semiduplum; Guillelmi archiepiscopi bitur' semiduplum; Inuentio corporum dionisii sociique eius semiduplum; Erblandi abbatis memoria; Guenal' abbatis memoria; Clari episcopi et martiris semiduplum; Maximini abbatis memoria (8, 10 Jan., 22 Apr., 18 Oct., 3, 5 Nov., 15 Dec.). No Visitation of B.V.M., 2 July.

2. (*a*) ff. 8–9 Hymns 'In pasione domini', Vexilla regis, Pange lingua gloriosi prelium, Lustra sex, with lesson and collect. (*b*) f. 9v Hymns at matins and lauds, Nocte surgentes and Ecce iam noctis. (*c*) f. 9v Eleven benedictions, (1) Benedictionem perpetuam tribuat nobis pater eternus . . . (11) Splendor lucis eterne illuminet nos sine fine.

3. ff. 10–102 Liturgical psalter.

4. ff. 102–4 Benedicite, Benedictus, Magnificat, Nunc dimittis, Te deum (called 'Canticum angelorum').

5. ff. 104–107v Litany.

Eighty-five martyrs: . . . (20) dyonisi. Forty-seven confessors: . . . (8, 9) marcelle gendulphe . . . (47) rigoberte. Thirty-two virgins: . . . (16) genouefa . . .

6. ff. 108–15 Abbreviated hours of B.V.M. of the use of (Paris). Nine lessons in matins.

7. ff. 115–117v Septem psalmi penitenciales.

Cues only of psalms. Litany: 21 martyrs; 20 confessors: . . . (20 clodoalde); 19 virgins.

8. ff. 117v–118v Hore de cruce. Abbreviated.

9. ff. 118v–119v De sancto spiritu. Abbreviated hours.

10. ff. 119v–124v Office of the dead, abbreviated.

11. ff. 124v–126v Commendaciones. Subuenite . . .

12. ff. 127–265v Breviary offices of Christmas, Circumcision, Epiphany, Purification of B.V.M., Annunciation of B.V.M., Thursday, Friday, and Saturday in Holy Week, Easter, Ascension, Pentecost, Trinity, Corpus Christi, John Baptist, Peter and Paul, Mary Magdalene, Laurence, Assumption of B.V.M., Nativity of B.V.M., Exaltation of Cross, All Saints, Martin, Katherine, Nicholas, Conception of B.V.M.

Catalogue, pp. 16–18, shows ff. 162v (Good Friday), 245v (Martin), 251 (Katherine), slightly enlarged.

13. ff. 265v–266v Hymns in Advent, Conditor, Verbum supernum, and Vox clara, and in Lent, Iam ter and Criste qui.

14. ff. 266v–276 Secuntur memorie sanctorum.

Memoriae in the order of the church year: Andrew, Thomas apostle, Stephen, John evangelist, Innocents, Genovefa, Vincent, Conversion of Paul, Agatha, Chair of Peter, Mathias, Gregory, Benedict, Mary of Egypt, Anthony confessor, Mark, Philip and James, Invention of Cross, Germanus, Barnabas, Margaret, Christopher, Apollonia, Transfiguration, Anne, Chains of Peter, Bartholomew, Louis king and confessor, Augustine, Decollation of John, Francis, Matthew, Michael, Denis et socii, Luke, Marcellus, Maturinus, Clement, Cosmas and Damian.

15. ff. 274v–276 Suffragia communia sanctorum.

16. f. 276. Memoriae of Yvo and De pace.

17. ff. 276v–278 Sequentiae of Gospels.

18. Devotions to B.V.M.: (*a*) ff. 278v–279 Obsecro te . . . ; (*b*) ff. 279v–280 Ant'. Inuiolata integra et casta es maria . . . ; (*c*) f. 280 Oracio ad deuocionem . . . Salue regina . . . ; (*d*) ff. 281v–282 Stabat mater . . . ; (*e*) ff. 282–283 Alia oratio. O sancta uirgo uirginum que peperisti dominum . . . ; (*f*) f. 283 Oratio ad nostram dominam. Aue maria gracia plena. dominus tecum ita tu mecum sis nunc et semper et in hora exitus . . .

(*a*). Masculine forms. (*b*). *RH*, no. 9094. (*c*). A memoria for each day of the week, Saturday–Friday: (1) Salue regina (*RH*, no. 18147); (2) Alma redemptoris mater and, at Easter, Regina celi letare (*RH*, nos. 861, 17170); (3) Aue regina celorum aue domina angelorum (*RH*, no. 2070); (4) Aue regina celorum mater regis angelorum (*RH*, no. 2072); (5) Vidi speciosam; (6) Tota pulcra es; (7) Beata dei genitrix. (*d, e*). *RH*, nos. 19416, 13694.

19. (*a*) f. 283rv Pater noster . . . (*b*) f. 283v Aue maria . . . (*c*) f. 283v Credo in deum patrem . . . (*d*) f. 283v Benedicite domine nos . . . (*e*) ff. 283v–284 Agimus tibi gracias . . . (*f*) f. 284 Misereatur nostri . . . (*g*) f. 284 Confiteor deo omnipotenti . . . (*h*) f. 284 Aue salus mundi uerbum patris . . .

20. Prayers before and at mass: (*a*) f. 284rv Quando uolueris recipere corpus domini. Oratio. Domine ihesu criste fili dei uiui non sum dignus . . . Quando reciperis dic. Uera susceptio corporis et sanguinis . . . (*b*) f. 285 Oratio ualde deuota que dicenda est post eleuacionem corporis cristi. Domine ihesu criste qui hanc sacratissimam carnem . . .

21. (*a*) f. 285rv Memoria quinque sanctorum martirum . . . Dionisi radius grecie . . . (*b*) f. 285v Similiter memoria de quinque uirginibus martiribus. Katherina tyrannum superans . . .

(*a, b*). *RH*, nos. 4707, 2691. The ten martyrs are Denis, George, Christopher, Blaise, Giles; Katherine, Margaret, Martha, Christina, Barbara.

22. ff. 285v–286 Quinque gaudia beate marie uirginis. Aue cuius conceptio . . . *RH*, no. 1744.

23. f. 286^{rv} Salutacio ad deum. Aue ihesu criste uerbum patris . . . (five aves).

24. f. 286^{v} Anima cristi sanctifica me . . . *RH*, no. 1090.

25. f. 286^{v} Versus sancti bernardi. Illumina oculos meos . . . Oremus. Omnipotens sempiterne deus qui ezechie . . .

Eight verses.

ff. iii + 286 + ii, foliated (i, ii) 1–193, 193B, 194–286 (287–8). f. 1 is a medieval flyleaf ruled like the rest of the leaves from f. 10. A medieval foliation of ff. 11–107 in red, ii–iii^{xx} xviii. 182 × 130 mm. Written space 100 × 77 mm. 2 cols. 27 lines. Ruling with red ink. Collation of ff. 2–286: $1–12^{8}$ 13^{10} (ff. 98–107) $14–35^{8}$ 36^{4} (ff. 283–6). A 24-line picture in front of art. 3. 17-line pictures in front of arts. 6, 10 (burial: an angel rescues a soul from the devil) and in front of all the offices of art. 12, except Annunciation and Ascension: the three Holy Week pictures are of Gethsemane, Christ before Pilate, and the Descent from the Cross. Initials: (i) 9-line, blue patterned in white on gold grounds, historiated, begin Pss. 26, 38, 52, 68, 80, 97, 109 in art. 3; (ii) 3-line or 4-line, as (i), but decorated; (iii) 3-line, blue and red, with red and blue-grey ornament; (iv, v) 2-line and 1-line, red with blue ornament or gold with blue-grey ornament. Line fillers of blue and gold or blue and red. Continuous framed floral borders on picture pages and shorter borders on pages with initials of type (i) and with the type (ii) initials on ff. 151^{v} (Annunciation) and 278^{v}. The nineteenth-century binding of red morocco, covered with purple velvet and with a heavy metal frame round each board, is now kept separately: the present binding of wooden boards, quarter covered with pigskin over the spine, is by D. Cockerell and Son in 1954.

Written in France (Paris ?). The illumination is related to the work of the Mansel master.[1]

Brotherton Collection 3. *Horae* s. xv med.

A book of hours like Dulwich College 25 (*MMBL*, i. 46) and Edinburgh Univ. Libr. 303 (*MMBL*, ii. 593) in contents and order, but lacking the commendatory psalms, which should follow art. 16, and St John Evangelist in art. 4. The singleton leaves with pictures on the versos sometimes have writing on the rectos which is an integral part of the text of arts. 4, 5, for example ff. 46, 98, 102, but this writing is not in the main hand: at one point the scribe wrote on the wrong leaf (see below, art. 5).

1. ff. 3–14^{v} Calendar in red and black.

Feasts in red include 'Translatio hugonis' and 'Hugonis episcopi' (6 Oct., 17 Nov.) and the July and December feasts of St Thomas of Canterbury, neither erased. 'Translatio zwichini' in black, 15 July. Visitation of B.V.M. not entered, 2 July. ff. 1–2^{v} were left blank: see art. 20.

2. ff. 16–27 Oratio deuota ad xpristum. O ihesu criste eterna dulcedo . . .

The 15 Oes of St Bridget. f. 27^{v} blank.

[1] Information from Dr J. J. G. Alexander.

3. ff. 29–31^{v} Memoria de sancta trinitate. Domine deus omnipotens pater et filius et spiritus sanctus da michi famulo tuo N . . . Oracio. Libera me domine . . . f. 32^{rv} left blank: cf. art. 20.

4. ff. 33–52 Memoriae of nine saints, John Baptist, Thomas of Canterbury, George, Christopher, Anne, Mary Magdalene, Katherine, Barbara, Margaret.

The antiphons are the usual ones, Gaude iohannes baptista, Gaude lux londaniarum (*sic*), Georgi martir inclite, Sancte cristofore martir, Gaude felix anna, Gaude pia magdalena, Gaude uirgo katherina, Gaude barbara regina, Gaude uirgo margareta (*RH*, nos. 26988, 26999, 7242, 18445, 6773, 6895, 6991, 6714, 7011). *Catalogue*, p. 19, shows ff. 35^{v}–36 much enlarged. f. 52^{v} left blank: cf. art. 20.

5. ff. 53–115 Incipiunt hore beate marie uirginis secundum consuetudinem anglie.

Memoriae at the end of lauds of *Holy Spirit*, Holy Trinity, Holy Cross, SS. *Michael*, John Baptist, *Peter and Paul, Andrew, Stephen, Laurence,* Thomas of Canterbury, *Nicholas*, Mary Magdalene, Katherine, Margaret, *All Saints*, and peace.[1] Hours of the Cross are worked in. None of the Cross ends 'Terra tunc' on f. 105^{v} and the rest of it is on f. 98^{r}, before the picture for sext. On ff. 114^{v}–115 is the metrical 'Recommendatio. Has horas canonicas cum deuotione . . .' (*RH*, no. 7679).

6. Devotions to B.V.M.: (*a*) ff. 115^{v}–116 Salue regina, followed by the versicles Virgo mater ecclesie; (*b*) ff. 116^{v}–117^{v} Oratio de domina nostra. Gaude virgo mater cristi: que per aurem . . . ; (*c*) ff. 117^{v}–119^{v} Ad honorem beate marie uirginis. Gaude flore virginali: que honore speciali . . . ; (*d*) ff. 120–126^{v} Has uideas laudes . . . , followed by the farsing of Salve regina with Salve virgo virginum.

(*a*). *RH*, nos. 18147, 21818. (*b, c*). *RH*, nos. 7014, 6809. (*d*). *RH*, nos. 7687, 18318.

7. ff. 126^{v}–129 Ad uirginem mariam. O intemerata . . . orbis terrarum inclina . . . Masculine forms.

8. ff. 129–133^{v} Item alia oratio ad mariam. Obsecro te . . . Masculine forms.

9. ff. 133^{v}–136 Oratio de domina nostra. Aue mundi spes maria: aue mitis . . . *RH*, no. 1974.

10. ff. 136^{v}–141 Quicumque hec septem gaudia in honore beate marie uirginis semel in die dixerit centum dies indulgenciarum optinebit a domino papa clemente qui ea proprio stilo composuit. Uirgo templum trinitatis . . . *RH*, no. 21899.

11. ff. 141–7 Ad ymaginem xpristi crucifixi. Omnibus consideratis . . .

AH, xxxi, 87–9. *RH*, no. 14081 (etc.).

[1] Italics show that there is a picture.

12. (*a*) ff. 147–50 Oratio uenerabilis bede presbiteri de septem uerbis . . . (*b*) ff. 150–1 Oratio. Precor te piissime . . .

13. ff. 151–2 Oratio. Deus qui uoluisti pro redemptione mundi . . .

14. (*a*) ff. 152–3 Salutationes ad sacrosanctum sacramentum altaris. Aue domine ihesu criste uerbum patris . . . (*b*) f. 153^{rv} Aue principium nostre creationis . . . (*c*) ff. 153^{v}–154 Aue uerum corpus cristi natum . . . (*d*) f. 154 Aue caro cristi cara . . . (*e*) f. 154^{rv} Anima cristi sanctifica me . . . (*f*) ff. 154^{v}–155^{v} Omnibus confessis . . . Domine ihesu criste qui hanc sacratissimam carnem . . . , with heading conveying indulgence of 2,000 years granted by Pope Boniface 'ad supplicationem Philippi regis francie'.

(*b–e*). *RH*, nos. 2059, 2175, 1710, 1090.

15. ff. 157–83 Incipiunt septem psalmi penitenciales . . . (f. 169^{v}) Incipiunt quindecim psalmi . . . (cues only of the first twelve) . . . (f. 172^{v}) Letania.

Twenty-nine martyrs: . . . (21–24) eduuarde osuualde alane geruasi . . . Fifteen confessors: . . . (14, 15) suuichine birine.

16. ff. 184–235^{v} Office of the dead.

17. ff. 237–244^{v} Incipit psalterium de passione domini. Pss. 21–30.

18. ff. 244^{v}–265^{v} Beatus uero iheronimus in hoc modo psalterium . . . regnum eternum. Oratio. Suscipere digneris . . . (f. 248) Incipit psalterium beati iheronimi. Uerba mea auribus percipe . . .

19 (added). f. 266^{rv} Domine ihesu criste te adoro in cruce pendentem . . .

In the 2nd to 5th paragraphs the words after *adoro* are 'uulneratum', 'in sepulcro positum', 'pastor bone' and 'per illam amaritudinem'. For the use of a woman. At the end 'xlvi M^{1} X xx^{ti} ȝeris. and liii dayis of pardon'.

20 (added in blank spaces, s. xvi in.). (*a*) ff. 1^{v}–2 This orison sent Pope Sixtus to the kyng to sey deuoutly for the pestelence. Sancte deus sancte fortis . . . Pater noster Aue maria iii tymes. (*b*) ff. 31^{v}–32 A memoria of St Roche, who is invoked against pestilence. (*c*) f. 52 A memoria of St Elizabeth.

(*a, c*) in one hand. (*b*) in hand of art. 19.

ff. ii + 266 + ii. 95 × 65 mm. Written space 52 × 30 mm. 16 long lines. Collation uncertain: mainly eights, but 1^{12} + 2 leaves after 12, 4^{4} (ff. 34, 36, 37, 39), 5^{4} (ff. 41, 43, 45, 47): 22 singleton picture pages put into quires or placed in front of them, ff. 15, 28, 32, 35, 38, 40, 42, 44, 46, 48, 50, 52, 64, 86, 93, 98, 102, 109, 156, 183, 236, 247. The pictures, usually on versos, are: before art. 2, Christ standing on the orb, blessing, an angel on each side; before art. 3, the Father with the wounded Son on his lap, no dove; nine in art. 4; seven in art. 5, a passion series—the vespers picture missing—as in Edinburgh, Univ. Libr. 303; before arts. 15–18 (15, Christ on the rainbow, and bodies rising; 16, raising of Lazarus; 17, Christ sitting in the tomb and instruments of the Passion; 18, Jerome). Initials: (i) pink or blue patterned in white, historiated: eight in art. 5, and beginning arts. 6*d* (B.V.M. and Child in glory), 7 (Christ on the lap of B.V.M.), 10 (B.V.M. kneels before a priest), 11 (Christ and the thieves on crosses); (ii) on pages which face pictures, as (i), but on decorated gold grounds; (iii) 3-line, gold on blue and red grounds patterned in white; (iv) 1-line, blue with red ornament or gold with blue ornament. Line fillers of gold or blue in the litany. Binding of red velvet over wooden boards, s. xix. Secundo folio (f. 17) *gustie.*

Written in the Low Countries for the English market. Arts. 19, 20 were presumably added in England, art. 19 for a woman owner.

Brotherton Collection 4. *Horae* s. xv^2

A book of hours consisting originally of arts. 1, 2, 3*c*, 3*f*, 5–13. A second hand rewrote art. 7 from the words 'me condempnare. Quia peccaui' near the end of the first nocturn to 'impietatibus nostris tu propiciab-' in Te decet hymnus, added to art. 3, and added arts. 4 and 32. A third hand added arts. 14–31.

1. (*a*) ff. 1^v–2 O Gregori sanctissimum sancti spiritus organum . . . (*b*) f. 3^{rv} Memoria of St John Evangelist.

(*a*). Memoria of St Gregory, *RH*, no. 13074. ff. 1^r, 2^v blank.

2. ff. 3^v–9^v Sequentiae of the Gospels.

3. ff. 10–35^v Hours of Holy Spirit (ff. 16–21) and Holy Cross (ff. 28–31) amplified to make a series of hours for each day of the week: (*a*) of Holy Trinity on Sunday; (*b*) of the dead on Monday; (*c*) of Holy Spirit on Tuesday; (*d*) of All Saints on Wednesday; (*e*) of Corpus Christi on Thursday; (*f*) of Holy Cross on (Friday); (*g*) of B.V.M. on Saturday.

(*a*, *c*–*g*). The hymns are *RH*, nos. 16566, 12022, 18373, 3936, 14725–6, 25443; *AH* xxx. 10, 15, 143, 29, 32, 123. (*b*). Begins 'Deus qui hominem de limo'. f. 36^{rv} blank.

4. ff. 37–44^v Rosarium beate marie virginis.

The five tens begin: (i) Aue maria gratia plena; (ii) Cum quo; (iii) Qui in ortum; (iv) Quem vestibus; (v) Cuius sacrati.

5. ff. 45–97^v Hours of B.V.M. of the use of (Rome). The Advent office begins on f. 92. A leaf missing after f. 72.

6. ff. 98–112^v Penitential psalms and litany.

Sixteen confessors: . . . (11–16) Claude Gaugerice Vedaste Amande Amate Maxime. Sixteen virgins: . . . (16) Genovefa.

7. ff. 113–42 Office of the dead. f. 142v blank.

8. ff. 143–146v Oracio deuota. Obsecro te . . . et michi famulo tuo Anthonio . . .

9. ff. 147–162v Memoriae of (*a*) apostles, (*b*) Christopher, (*c*) Sebastian, (*d*) Adrian: Aue martir adriane Qui martirium immane . . . , (*e*) George, (*f*) Hippolitus, (*g*) martyrs, (*h*) Anthony hermit, (*i*) Claude, (*j*) Nicholas: Copiose caritatis . . . , (*k*) Bernardine: Gaudeat ordo minorum . . . , (*l*) Martin, (*m*) confessors, (*n*) Katherine, (*o*) Barbara: Aue trini (?) lucifera . . . , (*p*) 11,000 virgins.

(*d*). *RH*, no. 2106. (*h*). The memoria and its picture are on f. 154. Facing them, f. 153v, are the words 'O Anthoni dei sancte: Exorat te suppliciter: [. . . . .] Stirpe natus. Vt clementer. Ores deum et benigne. Vt saluetur perhenniter' and above them a picture of a suppliant looking towards St Anthony on f. 154. Over the erasure is 'Hugo de Mazijnghem'. (*j, k*). *RH*, nos. 3864, 7095. *Catalogue*, pp. 20–1, shows f. 148 (Christopher) and, reduced, ff. 153v–154 (Anthony).

10. ff. 162v–165 Cum intraueris in cubiculo antequam vadis cubitum dic deuote hunc psalmum. Qui habitat . . .

An office consisting of Ps. 90, antiphon, hymn 'Criste qui lux es . . . , capitellum, Nunc dimittis, and prayers 'Illumina . . .' and 'Angele qui meus es . . .'.

11. ff. 165–171v Prayers before and at mass, the first, on going 'ad missam', 'Vias tuas domine . . .' and the last 'Deus qui nobis sub sacramento mirabili . . .'.

Includes the 'Psalmus Anastasii. Quicumque uult . . .'.

12. Prayers: (*a*) ff. 171v–176 Oracio valde deuota. Domine ihesu criste qui de sinu patris . . . ; (*b*) ff. 176–177v Sequitur alia oracio composita a beato Augustino. Valde humilis et deuota. et vtilis ad Remissionem suorum peccatorum dum tamen fuerit lecta cum emendacionis proposito. Concede michi misericors deus que tibi placita sunt . . . ; (*c*) ff. 177v–178 Alia pro peccatis. Omnipotens misericors et mitissime deus. respice in me . . .

13. ff. 178–180v Contra Inimicos fidei cristiane. que debet dici a militantibus cristianis R'. Congregati sunt inimici . . .

Prayers and Pss. 69 and 78.

14. ff. 181–3 Oroison de venerable Bede . . . Domine ihesu xpriste qui septem uerba . . .

15. f. 183rv Oroison. Anima xpristi . . . *RH*, no. 1090.

16. ff. 183v–185 Oroison. Stabat mater dolorosa . . . *RH*, no. 19416.

17. ff. 185–6 Oroison a son bon angele. Angele qui meus es custos pietate . . . *RH*, no. 22954.

18. Devotions to B.V.M.: (*a*) ff. 186–8 Oroison de nostre dame. Aue mundi spes maria . . . (4) Aue uirgo mater cristi . . . ; (*b*) ff. 188–9 Florat stilla de mamilla. gloriose uirginis . . . ; (*c*) ff. 189–90 Sensuiuent les quinze gaudes de la glorieuse uierge marie mere de dieu. Gaude uirgo mater cristi Que per aurem concepisti . . . ; (*d*) ff. 190–1 Les v aue de nostre dame. Aue cuius concepcio. solempni plena gaudio . . . ; (*e*) ff. 191–193v Deuote oroison a la uierge marie. O intemerata . . . orbis terrarum. Inclina . . . ; (*f*) ff. 193v–199 Oroison de la uierge marie. He tres doulce marie mere de ihesucrist le vray dieu . . . ; (*g*) ff. 199–200 O trescertaine esperance defenderesse et dame . . .

(*a*). *RH*, no. 1974. (*c, d*). *RH*, nos. 7015, 1744. (*e*). Masculine forms. (*f, g*). Sonet, nos. 755 (?), 1538.

19. ff. 200–1 Omnibus confessis et contrictis sequentem orationem dicentibus inter eleuacionem corporis cristi et tercium agnus dei Dominus papa bonifacius concessit dua millie annorum indulgenciarum ad supplicacionem philipi regis francorum. Domine ihesu xpriste qui hanc sacratissimam carnem . . .

20. ff. 201–202v. Oracio. Deus propicius esto michi peccatori . . .

21. f. 202v Oroison deuote a ihesucrist. Doulx (MS. Oulx) ihesus vraye sapience Tresor de grace et de science . . . (10 lines).

22. ff. 202v–205 Oroison a son propre angele. Sains angeles de dieu a qui ie suis baillie . . .

23. ff. 205–12 Memoriae: (*a*) Memoire de la sainte croix; (*b*) Three Kings; (*c*) B.V.M., Aue regina celorum Aue domina angelorum . . . ; (*d*) Margaret; (*e*) Francis, Celorum quandor splenduit . . . ; (*f*) Jerome; (*g*) Holy Trinity; (*h*) All Souls, Auete omnes anime fideles . . . ; (*i*) Quintin; (*j*) Elizabeth; (*k*) Susanna.

(*c, e*). *RH*, nos. 2070, 3589.

24. ff. 212–13 Les vii vers saint bernard. Illumina . . .

25. (*a*) ff. 213–214v Aue maria gracia plena dominus tecum . . . Magnificat anima mea . . . Oremus. Concede nos famulos tuos . . . (*b*) ff. 214v–219 Aue maria au long. Ad dominum cum tribularer . . .

(*b*). Four aves, each consisting of psalm, antiphon, and collect. The psalms are 119, 118 Gimel, 125, 122.

26. ff. 219–20 Aue domine ihesu criste uerbum patris . . . (five aves).

27. ff. 220–223v Quicuncques requiert que sa priere soit oye . . . en disant Adoramus te criste . . .

Psalms (122, 53, 66, 150), etc., to be said before a crucifix.

28. f. 224^{rv} Ceste oroison qui sensuyt est escripte en leglise saint iehan de latran a romme . . . et pour le temps perdu. Domine ihesu xpriste Rogo te amore illius gaudii . . .

The heading conveys an indulgence of 80,000 years.

29. f. 224^{v} Ceste oroison fist pape iehan le xii^{e}. Et donna a tous ceulx qui le diront deuotement xl iours de vray pardon. Aue ihesu xpriste puer amabilis totus desiderabilis . . .

30. ff. 224^{v}–226 Sensuiuent les lxxii noms de la glorieuse uierge marie. Aue digna. virgo. flos . . .

31 (added in the hand of arts. 14–30). (*a*) ff. 226^{v}–228 [O] bone ihesu. O piissime ihesu. O dulcissime ihesu . . . (*b*) f. 228^{rv} [O] domine ihesu xpriste adoro te in cruce pendentem . . .

(*a*). Prayer of the Holy Name. (*b*). Five oes, as Brotherton 3, art. 19.

32. ff. 229–244^{v} Psalterium beati iheronimi. Verba mea . . . Oremus. Omnipotens sempiterne deus clementiam tuam suppliciter deprecor ut me famulam tuam N. . . .

ff. ii + 244 + ii. 198 × 140 mm. Written space 100 × *c.*65 mm. 17 long lines. Ruling in red ink. Collation: 1^2 2^8 wants 8, probably blank (ff. 3–9) 3^{18} (originally 3^6, ff. 16–21: see above) 4^4 + 1 leaf before 4 (f. 28) 5^4 (ff. 33–6) 6^8 (ff. 37–44) 7^4 + 1 leaf after 4 (ff. 45–9) 8^8 + 1 leaf before 1 (f. 50) 9^8 10^8 wants 7 after f. 72 $11–16^8$ 17 two (ff. 122–3) 18^8 19^6 + 1 leaf before 1 (f. 132) 20^4 (ff. 139–42) 21^4 + 1 leaf before 1 (f. 143) 22^8 23^6 24^8 25^6 26^4 + 1 leaf before 1 (f. 176) $27–32^8$ 33^8 + 1 leaf before 1 (f. 229) 34^6 + 1 leaf after 6 (f. 244): when first written the manuscript consisted of quires 1, 2, 3^{7-12}, 7–17, 22–26. Three cursiva hands (see above), the earliest a rather scrawly *lettre bâtarde*. Thirty-eight 12-line pictures: before art. 1*a* (Vision of Gregory); four in art. 2; seven in art. 3 (Trinity, raising of Lazarus, Pentecost, saints, mass—a man kneels and a woman stands in the background, Crucifixion, B.V.M. and Child); before art. 4; seven in art. 5—the terce picture, shepherds no doubt, is missing and after this the pictures are Circumcision (sext), kings, all white (none), Presentation (vespers), flight into Egypt (compline); before art 6; before art. 7; fifteen in art. 9; before art. 32. In art. 9, only Hippolitus has no picture: Nicholas and Bernardine share a picture, f. 156^{v}, Nicholas on the left and Bernardine on the right with scroll inscribed 'Pater manifestaui nomen tuum hominibus I xvii^{o}' (John 17: 26) and with three mitres at his feet to represent the refused bishoprics of Siena, Ferrara, and Urbino; Katherine and Barbara share a picture, f. 160. The memoria of Bernardine (art. 9*k*) is also illustrated by a head and shoulders side view of the saint placed in the space remaining blank on f. 157^{v}. Initials in parts by hand 1: (i) 4-line or 3-line, red or blue, patterned in white, on decorated gold grounds; (ii) as (i) but 2-line; (iii) 1-line, blue with red ornament or gold with blue-grey ornament. Initials in parts by hand 2: (i) and (iii) as (i) and (iii) above; (ii) 2-line, gold on blue and red grounds patterned in white. Initials in parts by hand 3: (i) 3-line, gold and blue, with red and blue-grey ornament; (ii) as (iii) above, but 2-line. Line fillers in gold and blue. Continuous framed borders on picture pages. Binding of brown calf, s. xvi: a narrow border roll, angle-pieces and large centrepiece, all gilt: the remaining space *semé* with gilt stars. Secundo folio *vt hoc*.

Written for use in a French-speaking area, presumably for someone called Anthony, but his name has been erased on f. 153^{v} (art. 9*h*) and 'Hugo de Mazijnghem' substituted not much later. The suppliant figure in the picture on this page bears arms, azure a bend argent and gules, with a crescent for difference. Perhaps used by a woman when the parts in hand 2 were added: cf. art. 32. L. M. J. Delaissé attributes the picture on f. 1v to Guillaume Vrelant, most of the pictures to the 'maître du Mansel avec la collaboration probable de Simon Marmion, jeune' working probably at Valenciennes, and the pictures on leaves written by hand 2 (art. 3*a*, *b*, *d*, *e*, *g*; art. 4; art. 32) to the 'maître d'Edouard IV' (*La miniature flamande*, 1959, p. 64, no. 57). 'De Hornes', f. 149, s. xvi. 'sr f pot' in the margins of ff. 78, 116, 124, 181, s. xvii (?). Exhibited at Brussels in 1959.

Brotherton Collection 5. *Horae* s. xv med.

1. ff. 1–12v Full calendar in French in gold, blue, and red, the two colours alternating.

Feasts in gold include Geneviève, 'S' Leu S' Gille', Denis (3 Jan., 1 Sept., 9 Oct.). No Visitation of B.V.M., 2 July.

2. ff. 13–18v Sequentiae of the Gospels.

3. ff. 18v–29v In illo tempore. Egressus ihesus cum discipulis . . . posuerunt ihesum.

Chapters 18, 19 of St John.

4. ff. 29v–30v Illumina oculos meos . . . Oremus. Omnipotens sempiterne deus qui ezechie regi . . .

The Seven Verses of St Bernard and the prayer which commonly follows them.

5. ff. 31–34v Obsecro te . . . Masculine forms.

6. ff. 35–37v O intemerata . . . orbis terrarum. Inclina . . . Masculine forms. f. 38rv blank.

7. ff. 39–111 Hours of B.V.M. of the use of (Paris). f. 111v blank.

8. ff. 112–129v Penitential psalms and (f. 125) litany.

Fifteen virgins: (12) Genovefa . . . (15) Radegundis.

9. ff. 129v–133v Hore de sancta cruce. Patris sapiencia . . .

10. ff. 133v–137 Hore de sancto spiritu. Nobis sancti spiritus . . .

11. ff. 137–186v Office of the dead.

12. ff. 187–192v Doulce dame de misericorde mere de pitie . . .

Sonet–Sinclair, no. 458. *Catalogue*, p. 22, shows f. 187 slightly enlarged.

13. ff. 192v–196 Doulx dieu doulx pere . . . Sonet, no. 504. f. 196v blank.

14. ff. 197–211v Saint gregoire pape de rome composa les xv deuotes oroisons qui cy apres sensuiuent . . . O ihesu crist doulceur eternelle iubilation et leese de tes amans . . .

The Fifteen Oes of St Bridget in French. Sonet–Sinclair, no. 1393. The heading conveys an indulgence of 7007 years and as many quadragenes granted by Pope Gregory and later popes and says that 'les choses qui sont icy escriptes sont a rome en la chapelle de sancta sanctorum de saint iehan de latheran en vng tableau de boys couuert par dessus dung clervoirre' and also in letters of gold before the high altar of St Paul without the Walls.

15. ff. 212–13 Pape benedic donna a tous vrays catholicques . . . laquelle est icy translatee en francoys. Ie te deprye tres debonnaire seigneur ihesu crist par icelle charite par laquelle toy roy celeste pendoye en croix . . .

Sinclair, nos. 3027, 3029. The heading conveys as many days of pardon as Christ had wounds.

16. ff. 213–215v Cest vng seruice qui entre tous les seruices que on fait a la benoitte vierge marie cest cil qui mieulx lui plaist et de quoy on peut plus grace acquerir ce nous tesmoingne s' lyon. Benedicta et dulcissima domina . . .

Adorations, ten in all, to the feet, womb, heart, breasts, hands, eyes, ears, mouth, nose, and, in general, body and soul of B.V.M.

17. ff. 216–217v Prayers: (*a*) Deus cui omne cor patet . . . , for grace of the Holy Spirit; (*b*) Omnipotens in(u)ictissime deus respice propicius . . . , against ill thoughts; (*c*) Omnipotens sempiterne deus qui iusticia legis . . . , for faith, hope, and charity; (*d*) Nostre dame aprist ceste oroison a vng preudomme pour la seruir. Benedictus es domine ihesu criste splendor . . . ; (*e*) Domine adiutor et protector noster adiuua nos . . . , against temptations of the flesh.

18. ff. 217v–218v Hic est titulus triumphalis. Ihesus (MS. Ohesus) nazarenus rex iudeorum crucifixus miserere mei. Hely hely . . .

19. ff. 218v–220v Prayers: (*a*) Deus qui beatos tres magos orientales . . . , on going a journey; (*b*) Saluator mundi salua me qui per crucem . . . ; (*c*) Domine ihesu xpriste qui me creasti et redemisti . . . ; (*d*) Deus qui liberasti susannam de falso crimine . . . , against tribulation.

ff. vi + 221 + xxii, foliated (i–vi), 1–126, 126B, 127–220, (221–42). ff. iii, iv are blank leaves ruled like the rest. 180 × 125 mm. Written space 100 × 60 mm. 15 long lines. Ruling in red ink. Collation impracticable. Twelve 12-line pictures, the usual set in art. 7 and one before each of arts. 8–10, 11 (Death on horseback points his spear at a crowd of people). Initials: (i) 4–6 line, blue, patterned in white, on gold grounds, historiated, beginning arts. 2, 3, 5, 6, 12 (a woman in red kneels before B.V.M. and Child), 13 (Trinity); (ii, iii) 3-line and 2-line, as (i), but decorated instead of historiated; (iv) 1-line, gold on grounds of red and blue patterned in white. Line fillers of blue and red with roundels or short bars of gold. Continuous framed floral borders on picture pages, compartmented, the grounds partly of gold paint: a bar of decorated gold lies between picture and border on the outer and lower sides. Borders on three sides of pages with initials of type (iii). Binding of gilt red morocco, s. xviii: 'Rogabis eum et exaudiet te' on the spine.

Written in France.

Brotherton Collection 6. *Horae* s. xv^2

1. ff. 1–12^v Full calendar in gold, blue, and red, the two colours alternating for effect.

'Ponciani', 'Seruacii', 'Bonifacii', 'Lebuini', 'Lamberti', 'Wilibrordi' in gold (Jan. 14, May 13, June 5, 25, Sept. 17, Nov. 7).

2. ff. 13–88^v Hours of B.V.M. of the use of (Rome).

Begins with lauds. f. 77^v blank before the beginning of the Advent office. ff. 89–92^v blank.

3. ff. 93–120^v Penitential psalms and (f. 109^v) litany.

4. ff. 120^v–125 Hore de sancta cruce.

5. ff. 125–129^v Incipiunt hore de sancto spiritu.

6. ff. 129^v–189 Incipiunt vigilie mortuorum. f. 189^v blank.

7. f. 190^{rv} Qui dicit istam orationem in honore domini nostri ihesu cristi cotidie nunquam subitanea morte morietur. Ihesus nazarenus rex iudeorum et omnium populorum . . .

8. ff. 190^v–215^v Memoriae: (*a*) of St James (of Compostella); (*b*) of Sts Peter and Paul; (*c*) for twenty-six saints' days in the order of the church year: Stephen, John Evangelist, Innocents, Sebastian, Paul, Matthias, Chair of Peter, George, Mark, Philip, Barnabas, John Baptist, Laurence, Bartholomew, Holy Cross, Arnold (confessor and bishop), Matthew, Michael, Denis, Luke, Simon and Jude, Quintin, All Saints, Martin, Andrew, Thomas apostle; (*d*) of Sts Anthony hermit, Adrian, Nicholas, Holy Spirit, 'In exultatione sancte crucis', Holy Trinity, Three Kings, Christopher.

The antiphon for Arnold (f. 202) is 'Confessor domini arnoldi astantem plebem corobora . . . . . (cf. *CAO*, no. 1862)' and the collect 'Exaudi quesumus omnipotens deus preces nostras quas in beati arnoldi confessoris tui atque pontificis solennitate deferimus . . .'. The day should be in the third week of September.

9. ff. 215^v–220^v Orationes de quinque vulneribus domini nostri ihesu cristi. Ad uulnus dextere manus. Laus honor et gloria . . .

10. ff. 220v–221v Oratio breuis et deuota de passione domini. Obsecro te domine ihesu criste ut tua sancta passio sit michi . . .

11. ff. 221v–223 Oratio deuota ualde. O bone et dulcissime iesu per tuam misericordiam esto michi iesu . . .

12. ff. 223–6 Oratio sancti thome de aquino. Concede michi queso omnipotens et misericors deus que tibi placita sunt . . .

13. ff. 226v–228 Oratio de angelis. Superne curie ciuis angele sancte qui ad custodiam . . .

14. f. 228rv Oratio ad omnes angelos valde deuota. Obsecro vos omnes sancti angeli et archangeli throni . . .

15. ff. 228v–229v Oratio bona. Inenarrabile nomen magnitudinis tue . . .

16. ff. 230–4 Memoriae of B.V.M., (*a*) for general use and (*b–e*) for Purification, Annunciation, Nativity, and Assumption.

17. ff. 234–239v Memoriae of Anne (Anna pie mater aue anne nomen est suaue: *RH*, no. 1109), Apollonia, Katherine, Barbara, Margaret, Mary Magdalene, Agatha, and Agnes.

18. ff. 239v–246v Incipit missa nostre domine. Introibo . . .

19. Hours of (*a*) ff. 247–251v St Katherine and (*b*) ff. 252–6 St Barbara.

The antiphons are (*a*) Nobis florem protulit, *RH*, no. 12010, and (*b*) Matutino tempore barbara beata, *RH*, no. 11392, *AH* xxx. 146.

20. f. 256rv Memoria of 11,000 virgins.

21. Memoriae of B.V.M.: (*a*) ff. 256v–257v Antyphona de nostra domina. A'. Salue regina . . . ; (*b*) ff. 257v–259 Ant'. Alma redemptoris mater . . .

(*a, b*). *RH*, nos. 18147, 861.

22. ff. 259–61 Antiphons of B.V.M., Anima mea liquefacta es(t) . . . , Aue regina celorum aue domina angelorum salue radix . . . , Regina celi letare . . . , Nigra sum sed formosa . . . , Tota pulchra es amica mea . . . f. 261v blank.

23. ff. 262–4 Auete uos omnes anime fideles . . .

24. ff. 264–6 Oratio ualde deuota. Miserere pie iesu per gloriosam resurrectionem tuam miseris animabus . . . Oratio. Reminiscere clementissime deus miserationum . . . Respice quesumus domine iesu christe animas omnium fidelium . . .

25. ff. 266–267v Prayers for the dead, 'pro patre', 'pro fratribus', 'pro omnibus amicis'.

26. ff. 268–9 Aue domine ihesu criste uerbum patris . . . (5 aves).

27. f. 269 Aue uerum corpus natum . . . *RH*, no. 2175.

28. f. 269v Domine ihesu criste pastor bone conserua . . .

29. ff. 270–274v Prayers for special occasions, thirteen in all, the first 'Pro transeuntibus aquam oratio deuota. Deus qui transtulisti patres nostros . . .'.

30. ff. 274v–277v Dominus ihesu(s) cristus apud me sit ut me defendat . . . , and four prayers for help, each beginning 'Benedicat me deus'.

ff. iii + 277 + iii. 108 × 77 mm. Written space 52 × 32 mm. 15 long lines. Ruling in red ink. Collation: 1^{12} 2^{8} + 1 leaf before 1 (f. 13) $3–10^{8}$ 11^{10} wants 8–10 blank after f. 92 $12–13^{8}$ 14^{6} + 1 leaf before 1 (f. 109) $15–23^{8}$ 24^{2} (ff. 188–9) $25–31^{8}$. Fourteen 11-line or 12-line pictures, seven in art. 2 and one before each of arts. 3–5, 6 (Job: his comforters play musical instruments), 18 (f. 240, a man kneels before B.V.M. and Child: facsimile in *Catalogue*, p. 23), 19*a*, *b*. Initials: (i) 3-line, blue patterned in white on decorated gold grounds; (ii) 3-line, gold and blue; (iii, iv) 2-line and 1-line, gold or blue. Line fillers in gold and blue. Continuous framed floral borders on picture pages: gold paint is only used to compartment the ground on f. 240. Binding of s. xix. Secundo folio *flumina* (f. 14).

Written in the Low Countries. The borders on ff. 13 and 61 contain a merchant's mark, [mark], A J above and V H below the horizontals.

Brotherton Collection 7. *Hours of B. V.M. (in Netherlandish)*

s. xv/xvi

1. ff. 8–16v Full calendar in red and black.

The usual Utrecht saints in red. 22 lines to the page: no breaks between months. ff. 4–5v, blank, originally followed f. 16: see collation.

2. ff. 18–36v Hier beghint der ewigher wijshet getide.

3. ff. 38–59v Hier beghint des heilighen geests getide.

4. ff. 61–85v Hier beghint des heilighen cruys getide.

5. ff. 87–119v Hier beghint onser vrouwen getide: use of (Utrecht).

6. ff. 121–141v Hier beghint alre heilighen ghetide.

7 (in another hand). ff. 143–7 Een seer deuote meditacie ende oefeninge van den vii weden ofte droefheiden onser lieuer vrouwen . . . Dat eerste wee ende grote droeuicheit die die lieue moeder gods . . .

The Seven Sorrows of B.V.M. f. 147v blank.

8. ff. 149–65 Hier beghinnen die seuen psalmen. Litany, f. 156v.

9. f. 165v Memoria of peace.

10. ff. 165v–168v Dese na ghescreuen ghebeden plach sinte franciscus dagelix te lesen. Des sonnendaechs. O heer ihesu crist dope mi in dijn reuerencelike ende edele bloet . . .

A prayer for each day of the week.

11. f. 168v Merct wel. Dat nu dorret sel noch bloeyen . . . (5 lines).

12. ff. 170–198v Hier beghint die vigelie van ix lessen.

Office of the dead.

13. ff. 198v–199v A memoria of Francis and prayers to Elizabeth 'weduwe' and Mary Magdalene.

14 (added, s. xvi). f. 200rv O heere ihesu criste ic aenbede di hanghende in den cruce . . .

The Seven Oes of St Gregory. Meertens, vi. 16. f. 201rv blank.

ff. iv + 2 + ii + 194 + xviii, foliated i, 1–219. ff. i, 1–3, 216–9 are medieval parchment flyleaves and ff. 6, 7, 202–15 modern parchment flyleaves. 182 × 130 mm. Written space 105 × 70 mm. 22 long lines. Collation of ff. 4, 5, 8–201: 1^{12} wants 10 blank after f. 16 (ff. 8–16, 4, 5: now made into two quires, 11, 12 being folded back before 1, 2) $2–9^{8}$ 10^{2} (ff. 84–5) 11 three (ff. 87–9) 12^{8} 13^{6} + 1 leaf after 2 (f. 100) $14–17^{8}$ 18^{8} (ff. 138–41, 149–52) 19^{8} 20 three (ff. 161–3) 21^{8} wants 6–8 blank after f. 168 22 four (ff. 170–3) $23–24^{8}$ 25^{6} 26^{8} wants 7, 8 blank after f. 201; together with eight inserted picture pages, ff. 17, 37, 60, 86, 120, 142, 148, 169 and five leaves for art. 7. All in a handsome black hand, except arts. 7, 14. Eight full page pictures on versos, the rectos blank: before art. 2, Coronation of B.V.M., and a kneeling man and woman; before arts. 3–6; before art. 7, Pietà surrounded by the other six sorrows, each in its roundel; before art. 8, Christ in judgement; before art. 9, the risen Christ stands in the tomb. Smaller pictures, *c.* 50 × 50 mm., on ff. 18 (baptism of Christ), 38 (a priest kneels at an out-of-doors altar), 61 (Gethsemane), 87 (Adam and Eve and a human-headed serpent), 121 (creation of Eve), 170 (Resurrection). The initial letters of arts. 2–6, 12 are in the top right corners of the smaller pictures. Other initials: (i) at each hour of arts. 2–6, 4-line, shaded blue or pink, historiated: a passion series in art. 4, Innocents at vespers, and flight into Egypt at compline of art. 5, B.V.M. at prime, Michael at terce, John Baptist at sext, Peter at none, Paul at vespers, and Katherine and Barbara at compline of art. 6; (ii) 2-line, gold on blue and red grounds patterned in white; (iii) 1-line, gold or blue. Capital letters in the ink of the text marked with red. In the litany (art. 8), line fillers are blue and red patterned in white and gold. Continuous framed floral borders on the eight main picture pages and the rectos facing them. Shorter floral borders on pages with initials of type (i) contain some historiations, for example the descent from the Cross on f. 79v. Binding of s. xix, wooden boards covered with red velvet, repaired and rebacked by Douglas Cockerell and Son in 1954: engraved silver clasps. Secundo folio (f. 19) *die glorie.*

Written in the Low Countries. A shield between the kneeling figures on f. 17v bears vert two bands or between 8 martlets sable, 3, 2, 3. 'Ex musæo Huthii' stamp on f. 1v: Huth sale, Sotheby's, 2 June 1913, lot 3799.

Brotherton Collection 8. *Horae* s. xv/xvi

1. ff. 1–12v Calendar in French in gold, blue, and red, the two colours alternating. Many days have no feast.

Guill*erme*, Francoys, Denis, Ursin in gold (10 Jan., 4, 9 Oct., 29 Dec.).

2. ff. 13–18v Sequentiae of the Gospels.

The prayer, 'Protector in te sperantium . . .' follows John.

3. ff. 18v–27 Passio domini nostri ihesu cristi secundum iohannem. Egressus est dominus ihesus . . . posuerunt ihesum. Deo gracias. Per euangelica dicta deleantur nostra delicta. amen. . . . Deus qui manus tuas . . .

4. (*a*) ff. 27–8 Oratio ante receptionem corporis cristi. et fecit eam sanctus thomas de aquino. Omnipotens et misericors deus ecce accedo ad sacramentum . . . (*b*) f. 28rv Oratio post receptionem corporis cristi. Vera perceptio corporis et sanguinis . . .

5. ff. 29–66 Hours of B.V.M. of the use of (Bourges).

6. ff. 66–68v Officium de cruce . . . Patris sapiencia . . .

7. ff. 68v–71 De sancto spiritu . . . Nobis sancti spiritus . . . ff. 71v–72v blank.

8. ff. 73–84 Penitential psalms and (f. 81) litany.

Eleven martyrs: . . . (5) Denis . . . Fourteen confessors: . . . (11–14) Guillerme Ursine Benedicte Ludouice. f. 84v blank.

9. ff. 85–106 Office of the dead.

10. ff. 106–7 Pro defunctis antiphona. Auete omnes anime fideles . . . Domine ihesu criste salus et liberatio . . . ff. 107v–108v blank.

11. ff. 109–11 Te inuocamus te adoramus te laudamus . . .

Memoria of Holy Trinity and prayers to the three persons of the Trinity individually.

12. ff. 111–12 De sancta facie. Salue sancta facies . . . *RH*, no. 18189.

13. Devotions to B.V.M.: (*a*) ff. 112–115v Oratio ad mariam uirginem. Obsecro te . . . ; (*b*) ff. 115v–118v Alia oratio. O intemerata . . . orbis terrarum. De te

enim . . . ; (*c*) ff. 118v–120 Contemplacio. Stabat mater dolorosa . . . Interueniat pro nobis quesumus domine . . . ; (*d*) f. 120rv Salutacio marie uirginis. Salue regina . . . ; (*e*) f. 120v Aue regina celorum aue domina angelorum. Salue radix . . . ; (*f*) ff. 120v–125 Ceste oroison qui sensuit se doit dire chescun sabmedy a lhonneur et louenge de nostre dame. Missus est gabriel angelus . . .

(*a*). Masculine forms. (*c–e*). *RH*, nos. 19416, 18147, 2070.

14. ff. 125–128v Sensuiuent pluseurs deuotes louenges peticions oroisons et requestes qui a toute personne ayant entendement sont necessaires a dire a nostreseigneur ihesucrist. Premierement au matin quant tu te leueras de ton lit tu diras. In matutinis . . .

Single prayers on getting up, on going out, on taking holy water, before the crucifix, and five mass prayers, Salue saluator mundi deus atque creator . . . , O (MS. A) sanguis cristi qui fusus amore fuisti . . . (*RH*, no. 31018), Anima cristi sanctifica me . . . (*RH*, no. 1090), Aue vere sanguis domini . . . , In presencia veri corporis et sanguinis tui . . . : the headings, except the last, are in French.

15. ff. 128v–138v Memoriae of Sts Michael, John Baptist, John apostle, Peter and Paul, James, all apostles, Stephen, Christopher, Sebastian, all martyrs, Nicholas, Claud, Anthony hermit, Anne, Mary Magdalene, Katherine, Margaret, Barbara (Gaude barbara beata summe pollens . . . : *RH*, no. 6711), Apollonia.

16. ff. 139–140v O domine ihesu criste adoro te in cruce pendentem . . .

The Seven Oes of St Gregory. f. 141rv blank.

ff. ii + 141 + ii. 188 × 125 mm. Written space 100 × 60 mm. 20 long lines. Ruling in red ink. Collation: $1\text{–}2^6$ $3\text{–}9^8$ 10^4 (ff. 69–72) $11\text{–}14^8$ 15^4 (ff. 105–8) $16\text{–}18^8$ 19^8 + 1 leaf after 6 (f. 139). Written in *lettre bâtarde*. Twenty full page pictures, four in art. 2, one, the best of a poor lot, before art. 3, eight in art. 5, one before each of arts. 6 (Christ bears His Cross), 7, 8 (David and Goliath: facsimile in *Catalogue*, p. 24), 9 (three dead and three living), 11 (Baptism of Christ), 13 (B.V.M. and Child attended by angels), 16 (vision of Pope Gregory): ff. 13, 14v, 16, 17v, 19, 29, 41, 48v, 52v, 55v, 58, 60v, 63, 66, 68v, 73, 85, 109, 112v, 139. Smaller pictures, 35 × 30 mm, on ff. 109v (Trinity), 111 (Holy Face), 115v (B.V.M. and Child), 118v (Pietà), 121 (Annunciation) and illustrating the memoriae in art. 15, except All Apostles and All Martyrs. In art. 1 the signs of the zodiac are in the margins on the right and the occupations of the months in framed pictures in the lower margins. Initials: (i, ii) 2-line and 1-line, gold paint on blue or dark red grounds. Binding of s. xix (?), covered with light blue velvet.

Written in France. On f. 5 Gemini is half seen behind a shield bearing vert a cross argent between 4 oxheads or: cf. the arms of Bouer given by Rietstap. 'Seur Marie de cumieres (?) bonne fille', f. 1, s. xvi. 'des liures de mr guyon de sardiere' (†1759), ff. 1, 140v.[1]

Brotherton Collection 9. *Horae* s. xv ex.

1. ff. 1v–13 A rather empty calendar in red and black, each month on a double opening.

[1] For Guyon, see below, Manchester, John Rylands University Library, Fr. 62.

Names in red include Bonifacii, Eligii, Egidii, Remigii et Bauonis, Dyonisii, Donaciani, Eligii (5, 26 June, 1 Sept., 1, 9, 14 Oct., 1 Dec.). ff. 1r, 13v blank.

2. ff. 14–15 Deuota oracio ad sanctam ueronicam. Salue sancta facies . . .

Memoria of the Holy Face (*RH*, no. 18189). f. 15v blank.

3. ff. 16–20v Incipiunt hore sancte crucis.

4. ff. 21–5 Incipiunt hore sancti spiritus. f. 25v blank.

5. ff. 26–30 Incipit missa beate marie virginis. Et introibo . . .

6. ff. 30–4 Sequentiae of the Gospels. f. 34v blank.

7. ff. 35–87 Incipit officium beate marie virginis secundum consuetudinem romane ecclesie.

A leaf with beginning of vespers missing after f. 71. The Advent office begins on f. 81. ff. 87v–88v blank. *Catalogue*, p. 25, shows f. 62.

8. ff. 89–105 Incipiunt septem psalmi penitenciales.

Litany, f. 97v. Eight confessors: . . . (8) ludouice. Seven monks and hermits: francisce benedicte anthoni bernardine dominice elziari ludouice. f. 105v blank.

9. ff. 106–137v Incipiunt uigilie mortuorum.

'Partem beate resurrectionis . . .' at the end.

10. ff. 138–140v Deuota oracio ad uirginem mariam. Obsecro te . . .

The words 'Et in nouissimis diebus meis ostende michi faciem tuam Et annuncies michi diem et horam obitus mei' have been struck out near the end. Masculine forms.

11. ff. 141–142v O intemerata . . . orbis terrarum. Inclina mater . . .

Masculine forms.

12. ff. 143–4 Oracio ad dominum nostrum ihesum cristum. O bone ihesu. O dulcissime ihesu. O ihesu . . . f. 144v blank.

13. ff. 145–147v Canticum beati athanasii episcopi. Quicunque uult . . .

14. ff. 148–56 Passio domini nostri ihesu cristi. Secundum Iohannem. In illo tempore Egressus est ihesus . . . posuerunt ihesum. ff. 156v–160v blank.

ff. ii + 160 + ii. 142 × 100 mm. Written space 75 × 55 mm. 17 long lines. Collation: 1^2 2^{14} wants 14, blank after f. 15 3^6 $4-9^8$ 10^8 wants 3 after f. 71 11^8 12^4 (ff. 85-8) $13-21^8$. Catchwords written vertically. Humanistic *g*—which takes up more vertical space—is used only in the bottom line on a page. Initials: (i) 5-line or 6-line, pale pink shaded or patterned in white on grounds of gold paint slightly decorated or, five times, historiated: ff. 89, 138 (Pietà), 143 (a naked figure holding orb and sceptre and attended by angels stands beside the Cross), 145 (Athanasius), 148 (Gethsemane); (ii, iii) 2-line and 1-line, gold paint on dark red grounds patterned in gold paint. Capital letters in the ink of the text touched with pale yellow. Line fillers in the litany in gold paint and dark red. Continuous framed floral borders on grounds of gold paint on pages with initials of type (i): they include grotesques, birds, insects, and a few figures, a man and woman gardening on f. 21, a hunt on f. 62. In art. 1 the signs of the zodiac are at the foot of rectos and the occupations of the months at the foot of versos. A skull in the margin, f. 106 (art. 9): labelled 'mors impia nulli parcit'. Binding of s. xix. Secundo folio (f. 15) *terris*.

Written in the Low Countries (?). 'Erissouan (?) de Saa de Albuquerque', f. 156, s. xvi.

Brotherton Collection 10. *Horae* s. xv^2

1. ff. 1-12v Calendar in gold and black.

Gold names include 'Antonii de ordine minorum' (but 'Francisci' is black), 'Marie de niuibus', 'Clare virginis', 'Remigii episcopi et confessoris' (13 June, 4, 12 Aug., 1 Oct.).

2. ff. 13-101v Hours of B.V.M. of the use of (Rome). The Advent office begins on f. 88. f. 102rv blank.

3. ff. 103-109v Hours of Holy Cross.

Catalogue, p. 26, shows f. 103. f. 110rv blank.

4. ff. 111-139v Penitential psalms and (f. 126v) litany.

Eleven virgins: (8) restituta. f. 140rv blank.

5. ff. 141-192v Office of the dead.

6. ff. 193-198v Oratio deuotissima ad beatam uirginem mariam. Ad sanctitatis tue pedes dulcissima uirgo maria . . .

7. ff. 198v-202v Oratio ad beatam uirginem. O intemerata . . . orbis terrarum. inclina . . . Masculine forms.

8. ff. 203-6 Domine iesu criste redemptor mundi defende me . . . (f. 203v) dona michi famulo tuo Nicolao ueram penitentiam . . . (f. 204) Domine iesu illumina famulum tuum nicolaum . . . f. 206v blank.

The scribe wrote Finis at the end of arts. 2-5.

ff. v + 206 + v. 148 × 105 mm. Written space 73 × 48 mm. 12 long lines. The ink has faded slightly on hair sides. Collation: 1^{12} $2\text{–}6^{8}$ 7^{8} wants 5 after f. 56: f. 57 is an ill-written supply leaf $8\text{–}11^{8}$ 12^{10} (ff. 93–102) $13\text{–}16^{8}$ 17^{6} (ff. 135–40) $18\text{–}23^{8}$ 24^{4} (ff. 189–92) 25^{8} 26^{8} wants 7, 8 blank. Pictures, 10-line or less, before arts. 2 (B.V.M. and Child), 3–5. Initials: (i) 4-line or 3-line, shaded red or blue, patterned in white, on decorated grounds of gold, gold paint, and colour; (ii) 2-line, gold on grounds of red and blue patterned in white and of green patterned in yellow; (iii) 1-line, blue with red ornament or gold with violet ornament. Continuous framed floral borders on picture pages (on f. 13, picture and border are one composition). Shorter borders of gold and colours with floral terminals on pages with initials of type (i). Binding of blue velvet with silver clasp and cornerpieces, s. xix.

Written in northern Italy for a person named Nicholas. The arms in the border on f. 13 are gules on a chevron azure between three mullets argent three bezants: in chief or a demi-eagle displayed sable. 'Henricus Joannes Milbank Trin. Coll. Cambridge Anno 1845', f. iv.

Brotherton Collection 11. *Preces* s. xvi in.

1. (*a*) ff. 1–9 Heu mihi infelix anima in tantis peccatis . . . Solue priusquam moriar meorum vincula peccatorum Amenn. (*b*) ff. 9–11v Item oracio s. augustini ad impetrandum veniam peccatorum. Deus iusticie deus misericordie deus inuisibilis . . . claritatis ostende. (*c*) ff. 11v–13 Item confessio peccatorum eiusdem beati augustini. Miserator et misericors magne et terribilis deus Tibi confiteor . . . et scis miserere mei. Amenn. (*d*) ff. 13–16v Sequitur oracio beati Gregorii pape pro fine bono impetrando et gracia lacrimarum pro peccatis. Domine exaudi oracionem meam quia iam cognosco . . .

(*b*). Cf. *PL* ci. 1384–5. (*c*). *PL* ci. 1386–7. f. ivrv blank.

2. ff. 16v–81 Sequuntur oraciones seu contemplaciones multum deuote cum graciarum accionibus de omnibus beneficiis a deo humano generi impensis et specialiter in opere nostro redempcionis et passionis cristi Et primo ponitur oracio excitatiua humane mentis ad laudandum deum. Domine deus meus laudare te desidero quia . . .

Forty-two prayers, all beginning 'Laudo et glorifico' or 'Gracias tibi ago', except the first two and the twenty-fourth. Blank pages: f. 17rv before the first prayer; ff. 35rv, 55v after the seventeenth and the twenty-sixth prayers. The eighteenth prayer is headed, f. 36, 'De resuscitatione Lazari et humili ingressu in ciuitatem iherusalem in die Palmarum et eiectione vendencium et emencium de Templo' and the twenty-seventh is headed, f. 56, 'De baiulacione crucis ad locum caluarie et crucifixione Ihesu'. The last pieces are (f. 78v) 'Canticum Sanctorum Ambrosii et Augustini. Te deum laudamus . . .' and (f. 80) 'Collecta. Deus qui contritorum non despicis . . . Amenn. Explicit totus processus de vita passione Resurreccione et Ascensione domini nostri Ihesu christi nec non spiritus sancti missione omnibusque aliis beneficiis hominu(m) a deo collatis'. f. 81v blank.

3. (*a*) ff. 82–6 Oracio sancti Ambrosii de passione domini quam Anastasius papa primus confirmauit dans singulis eam dicentibus quingentos dies indulgenciarum. Domine iesu criste fili dei viui creator et resuscitator . . . peruenire. Qui . . . (*b*) ff. 86–87v Oracio sancti Augustini a spiritu sancto sibi reuelata . . . infernus eam non possidebit. Deus propicius esto michi peccatori et custodi me sis . . .

(*b*). For manuscripts in British libraries cf. Römer, i. 374.

4. (*a*) ff. 87v–88 Commendacio ad beatissimam virginem mariam. O domina mea sancta maria me in tuam benedictam fidem . . . (*b*) ff. 88–89v Item alia oracio de eadem pulcrior. Spes anime mee post deum virgo maria . . .

5. (*a*) ff. 89v–90 Postquam mane surrexeris primo dic (*sic*) flexis genibus. Gracias tibi ago domine . . . (*b*) f. 90rv Cum mane surgeris quoquaque pergere velis dic. Bene+dicat me imperialis maiestas . . .

6. Devotions at mass: (*a*) ff. 90v–92 Item Oracio in eleuacione uel post vel aliunde coram ymagine crucifixi dicenda . . . Precor te amantissime domine Ihesu criste propter illam eximiam caritatem . . . (*b*) f. 92rv Item post eleuacionem dic oracionem sequentem . . . Domine ihesu criste qui hanc sacratissimam carnem . . . (*c*) ff. 92v–93 Alia oracio in eleuacione corporis cristi. Aue caro cristi caro (*sic*) . . . (*d*) ff. 93v–94 Item salutaciones domini nostri ihesu cristi reuelate cuidam deuoto viro . . . salutare ammonuit. Aue ihesu criste uerbum patris. filius virginis . . . (five aves). (*e*) Secuntur nunc tres oraciones de passione domini multum deuote . . . Et dicitur quod dominus Innocencius papa tercius concessit cuilibet illos deuote dicenti remissionem omnium peccatorum suorum. (1) Domine ihesu criste filii (*sic*) dei viui. qui pro redemptione nostra nasci . . . (2) Auxilientur nobis pie domine ihesu criste omnes passiones . . . (3) Domine deus de deo lumen de lumine qui humanum genus . . .

(*a*). The heading conveys an indulgence of as many days as Christ had wounds, that is, 6,666. (*b*). The heading conveys an indulgence of 20,000 days from Pope Innocent VI 'ad supplicacionem domini Philippi regis francie'. (*c*). *RH*, no. 1710. (*e*). These prayers may be said by the priest at mass as collects before the epistle, secret, and complenda, according to the heading.

7. Devotions to B.V.M.: (*a*) f. 97rv Aue maria ancilla sancte trinitatis . . . ; (*b*) ff. 97v–98 Subscriptam oracionem edidit Sixtus papa Quartus et concessit eam deuote dicentibus coram ymagine Beate virginis in sole vndecim milia annorum vere indulgencie. Aue sanctissima maria mater domini . . . ; (*c*) ff. 98–103v Quicumque subscriptam oracionem triginta diebus deuote dixerit . . . sepius probatum est. Sancta maria perpetua virgo . . . ; (*d*) ff. 103v–108v Quicumque subscriptam oracionem quottidie dixerit . . . sepius repertum. O Clementissima domina et dulcissima virgo . . . ; (*e*) ff. 108v–110v Item alia Oracio de eadem similis efficacie cum predicta. Ad sanctitatis tue pedes dulcissima virgo Maria . . . (*ends imperfectly*).

(*d*). The heading carries an indulgence of 300 days from Pope Innocent: B.V.M. will appear to the suppliant three days before his death, 'Sicut in quodam monasterio ordinis Sancti Benedicti reuelatu(m) est cuidam abbatisse in extremis laboranti'.

8. ff. 111–114v Five oes, the first beginning imperfectly near the end 'fleuerunt quando mortuus es' and the others 'O mitissime agne dei ihesu criste immaculate moneo te', 'O vnice amator meus ihesu moneo te', 'O refugium delectabile omnium desolatorum ihesu criste moneo te', and 'O dulcissime ihesu moneo te'. A collect follows the fifth prayer.

9. ff. 114v–116v Sequitur oracio Venerabilis Bede presbiteri de Septem Verbis . . . Domine ihesu criste qui septem verba . . .

For ascriptions to Bede in Brussels manuscripts see H. Silvestre, *Les manuscrits de Bède* . . ., 1959, pp. 21–3.

10. (*a*) ff. 116v–128 Oracio deuotissima beati Bernardi abbatis Clareuall' quam cum semel diceret ante ymaginem Crucifixi ipsa ymago de cruce se inclinans eum amplexata est. Salutacio ad Pedes. Salue mundi salutare Salue salue Ihesu care . . . Collecta. Domine ihesu criste rogo te per misterium . . . (*b*) ff. 128–9 Legitur in vita sancti Bernardi abbatis Clareuall' quod demon . . . sunt autem hii que sequuntur. Illumina . . .

(*a*). *RH*, no. 18073. (*b*). The eight verses of St Bernard.

11. ff. 129–130v Subscripte tres oraciones habentur Rome in quadam capella que dicitur Sancte crucis septem romanorum . . . (1) Domine ihesu criste ego miser peccator Rogo . . . (2) Domine ihesu criste saluator et redemptor tocius mundi Rogo . . . (3) Domine ihesu criste rogo et ammoneo . . . Three Joys.

12. ff. 130v–141 Secuntur nunc quindecim oraciones de passione domini reuelate sancte Brigitte regine Suecie deuotissime mulieri cum esset rome reclusa apud sanctum Paulum . . . data est. Prima oracio. O domine ihesu criste eterna dulcedo . . .

The Fifteen Oes of St Bridget, but the last part of no. 15, from the words 'O dulcis ihesu uulnera cor meum', is here called 'Oracio Sedecima'.

13. f. 141rv Item salutacio uulnerum. O salutifera vulnera dulcissimi amatoris mei . . .

14. Devotions to B.V.M.: (*a*) ff. 141v–143 Secuntur oraciones de septem gaudiis spiritualibus que beata virgo maria nunc habet in celis . . . Gaude virgo mater cristi que tu sola meruisti o virgo dulcissima . . . ; (*b*) ff. 143–5 Oracio ad virginem gloriosam valde deuota dicentibus. Aue mundi spes Maria. Aue mitis . . . ; (*c*) ff. 145–50 Item oraciones de quinque doloribus beate marie quas sanctus An`s´helmus Capellanus eius composuit . . . Prima oracio. Mediatrix dei . . .

(*a, b*). *RH*, nos. 7021, 1974. (*c*). Five prayers each beginning with a letter to make up the word MARIA: cf. Leroquais, *Livres d'heures*, Index.

15. ff. 150–2 Oracio ad proprium angelum Dicenda. Obsecro te angelice spiritus cui ego ad prouidendum . . .

16. ff. 152–159v Prayers and memoriae: Peter (2); Paul; John Evangelist (2); George, 'Georgi martir inclite . . .': *RH*, no. 7242; Katherine, 'Aue virgo Katherina Aue martir et regina . . .': *RH*, no. 2180; Barbara, 'Aue martir gloriosa Barbaraque generosa . . .': *RH*, no. 1915.

George and Katherine are drawn attention to by continuous borders, ff. 156, 157.

17. ff. 159v–178v Item de magnis festiuitatibus. Et primo de Natiuitate domini ad sanctam Mariam virginem oracio. Sancta maria mater domini nostri ihesu christi . . .

Prayers, (*a*) at Christmas, (*b*) at Easter, (*c*) at Pentecost, and (*d, e*) two for Holy Trinity: (*d*) ff. 171–4 Oracio beati augustini doctoris. Adesto mihi verum lumen pater omnipotens . . . semper inspicere; (*e*) ff. 174–178v Item alia oracio eiusdem de Sancta Trinitate. Deus ineffabilis et incircumscripte nature . . . pacis sequi. Per . . . Amen. (*d*). Cf. Römer, i. 371 and *PL* xl. 967–9.

18. ff. 178–183v Secuntur nunc oraciones multum deuote ante sanctam communionem dicende. Ad mensam dulcissimi conuiuii tui . . . (f. 180) Alia oracio ante sanctam communionem. Ne irascaris queso . . . (f. 182) Item alia oracio . . . Domine deus meus non sum dign(u)s . . .

19. ff. 183v–195v Item oraciones post sanctam communionem dicende. O sacratissimum corpus et sanguis . . . (f. 186v) Benedictus es potentissime domine ihesu christe . . . (f. 192) Ineffabilem misericordiam tuam domine . . . (f. 193) Serenissima et inclita mater domini . . . (f. 193v) Gracias ago immense maiestati . . . (f. 195) Anima cristi sanctifica me . . . : *RH*, no. 1090.

20. ff. 195v–197v Item oracio ad sanctam crucem. Signum sancte crucis defendat me a malis preteritis . . .

21. ff. 198–201v Secuntur oraciones de septem gaudiis corporalibus beate marie virginis . . . Uirgo templum trinitatis . . . : *RH*, no. 21899.

22. ff. 201v–208 Incipit Rosarium beate marie virginis cum articulis vite christi . . . Suscipe rosarium virgo deauratum ihesu per conpendium . . . Collecta. Interueniat pro nobis quesumus domine . . .

RH, no. 19951. ff. 208v–213v ruled, but blank.

ff. iii + 214 + vii, foliated i–iv, 1–218, (219, 220). ff. iii, 214–18 are contemporary flyleaves, ruled like the text. 142 × 100 mm. Written space 80 × 52 mm. 18 long lines. Ruling in violet or red ink. Collation of ff. iv, 1–213: $1\text{–}9^{10}$ 10^{8} wants 8, blank, after f. 96 11^{10} 12 seven (ff. 107–13) 13^{10} 14^{10} wants 9 after f. 131: f. 132 is a supply leaf $15\text{–}22^{10}$. Written in good hybrida, with few abbreviations: 'ihesus' and 'mihi' are normal spellings and both 'christus' and 'cristus' occur. Black ink. Initials: (i) ff. 1, 18, 36, 56, 82, 97, 104, 198, 11-line or less, in colour shaded and patterned on grounds of gold paint decorated and (ff. 97, 104) with naturalistic landscapes (enlarged facsimile of f. 97 in *Catalogue*, p. 27: tree, village, mountains);[1] (ii), as (i), but smaller; (iii) on ff. 74v–80 and in art. 22, 2-line or 1-line, gold or blue. Floral borders: (i) on pages with initials of type (i) and on ff. 156, 157, continuous, framed, on grounds of gold paint: a pelican in its piety, f. 91; (ii) on pages with initials of type (ii), partial and not framed. Binding of red morocco by Douglas Cockerell and Son, 1954: the brass clasps, s. xix, of the former pink velvet binding have been retained.

Written in Germany.

[1] Dr J. J. G. Alexander suggested to me that the artist might be Jacob Elsner and referred me to Edmund Schilling, 'Dürer und der Illuminast Jacob Elsner', *Phoebus* i (1946), 135–44.

Brotherton Collection 12. *Preces, etc.* s. xvi in.

1. ff. 1–11v Full calendar in red and black, not graded.

Feasts in red include 'Affre martyris', 'Magni abbatis', 'Dedicacio ecclesie august' ', 'Othmari abbatis', 7 Aug., 6, 28 Sept., 16 Nov. May is missing.

2. Prayers, etc.: (*a*) f. 12 Cum vadis dormitum sequentem premitte confessionem ac oraciones subsequentes. Confiteor tibi domine deus omnipotens creator celi et terre: omnia peccata . . . ; (*b*) ff. 12v–13 Oratio dicenda dormituro. O Iesu dulcissime: iesu pater dilectissime: tu mecum queso maneas . . . ; ff. 13v–14, 14rv Two other prayers 'dormituro': (*c*) Omnipotens sempiterne deus tibi gracias . . . ; (*d*) Gracias tibi ago domine sancte pater. lux es et dies: noctis . . . ; (*e*) ff. 14v–15v ymnus. Criste qui lux es . . . ; (*f*) ff. 15v–16 Sequuntur Tres veritates Gersonis noctu et mane ab omnibus dicende. Prima veritas est. Domine sic vel sic contra tuam . . . ; (*g*) ff. 17–19 Oraciones cum mane surgit . . . ; (*h*) ff. 20–21 Oracio ad deum pro bono fine; (*i*) f. 22rv Oracio ad beatam virginem pro bono fine impetrando. O domina dulcissima . . . (*ends imperfectly*); (*j*) ff. 23–24v Obsecro te angelice spiritus: cui ego indignus peccator . . .

3. ff. 25v–69v, 72–87v Thirty-eight prayers: (1–6) to John Baptist, patriarchs and prophets, Peter, Paul, James the greater, Bartholomew; (7–14) to Sebastian, George, Erasmus, 10,000 martyrs, Kylian, Christopher, Stephen, fourteen helpers; (15–22) to Erhard, Anthony hermit, Gregory, Ambrose, Bernard, Augustine, Jerome, Francis; (23–37) to Katherine, Barbara, Agnes, Bridget (O beata brigita late collaudata . . . : *RH*, no. 12671), Agatha, Dorothy, Apollonia, Anne, Gertrude, Sophia and her daughters, Margaret, Mary Magdalene, Martha, 11,000 virgins, Elizabeth; (38) to the Three Kings.

A leaf cut out after f. 69. For ff. 70, 71 see below, art. 8.

4. ff. 88v–93 Prayers at and after mass: (*a*) Aue verum corpus cristi . . . ; (*b*) Aue caro cristi chara . . . ; (*c*) Salue lux mundi: verbum patris . . . ; (*d*) Sanguis tuus domine Ihesu criste pro nobis effusus . . . ; (*e*) Oratio beati thome de aquino in eleuacione corporis cristi dicenda. Adoro te deuote latens deitas . . . ; (*f*) Domine ihesu criste fili dei viui qui hanc sacratissimam carnem . . . ; (*g*) Anima cristi sanctifica me . . .

(*a*, *b*). *RH*, nos. 2175, 1710. (*e*). Walther, no. 542; *RH*, no. 519. (*f*). The heading conveys an indulgence of Pope Innocent VI. (*g*). *RH*, no. 1090. The heading conveys an indulgence of 300 days of Pope John XXII.

5. ff. 93–104 Sequitur nunc de missa . . . Missam in primis Dominus noster ihesus cristus . . .

6. ff. 105–109v Nunc sequuntur oraciones pro mortuorum (*sic*). Ad primam pro parentibus. Deus qui nos patrem . . .

Fifteen prayers.

7. ff. 110^{v}–112 Pius papa secundus largitus est . . . Miserere mi domine animabus que singulares . . .

The heading conveys indulgences of Pius II and John IV (*sic*).

8 (added. s. xvi ex.). ff. 70, 71, 113–135^{v} and blank spaces contain prayers, etc., written in 1596 (see below) in a good italic hand.

ff. 70, 71 are two leaves which take the place of one leaf cut out of art. 3 after f. 69. They contain the end of the prayer to Apollonia (the rest is on f. 69) and prayers to Christina, Ottilia, and All Virgins.

ff. iii + 135 + iii. ff. 12–134 were foliated in 1596 (?) 1–123. 105 × 80 mm. Written space *c.* 80 × 58 mm. 15 long lines. Collation impracticable. Written in hybrida. A full page picture before art. *2g* (a man lying in bed, hands clasped), *2h* (Christ scourged and tied to a pillar: a kneeling priest with scroll 'Aufer a nobis cunctas iniq.), *2i* (B.V.M. and Child in glory), each prayer of art. 3, and arts. 4 and 6, forty-three in all: for two of them see *Catalogue*, p. 28. 3-line and 2-line initials, blue or red. Binding of red velvet, with elaborate brass clasps, s. xix. Secundo folio (f. 13) *dilectissime*.

Written in Bavaria (Augsburg ?: cf. art. 1). At Überlingen (on Lake Constance) in 1596, when art. 8 was added, apparently for J. Reutlinger, since the two inscriptions are in the hand of art. 8: (1) f. 120^{v} Iste liber de Nouo est renouatus et scriptus Per Fratrem Iohannem Singerium, Vberlingensem, Franciscanum, Anno Domini 1596. Die 17 Februarii; (2) f. 135^{v} Iacobus Reutlinger Vberlingen: est possessor huius libri anno 1596.

Brotherton Collection 13. *Ordo visitandi domos ordinis Carthusiensis; Guido de Pisis, De forma prima electionis; etc.* s. xv^2

1. ff. 1–18^{v} Incipit ordo uisitandi domos ordinis Cartusiensis. Eliguntur a domibus ordinis aut ordinantur et mittuntur per capitulum generale duo priores . . . (f. 2) et discordia inter domos ordinis terminanda. In nomine sancte et indiuidue trinitatis. Ob statum Cartusiensis ordinis . . . (f. 4^{v}) Sequitur Quedam ordinatio facta in capitulo generali anno 1389 de uisitationibus fiendis. Cum propter priorum nostri ordinis euagationes . . . poterunt iudicio terminare reseruent. Hic est finis.

Basically Statuta antiqua, part 2, chapter 30, sect. 1–33 in *Statuta et privilegia ordinis Cartusiensis*, Basel 1510. The text was added to in s. xvi^2 and on ff. 4–7 it was altered by erasure. In additions in the margins of ff. 16^{v}, 17 the words spoken by the visitor 'in capitulo conuersorum' are in Spanish.

2. ff. 18^{v}–22 De uisitatione priuata. Est et alia species uisitacionis . . . non obstantibus.

Also in Keble College, Oxford, 34, ff. 94–104^{v}.

3. ff. 22–24^{v} Forma reconciliandi fugitiuos. Reconciliandis coram priore . . . Et pro penitentia dicetis etc.

4. (*a*) ff. 24^{v}–31 'Sermo in visitatione' Apprehendite disciplinam . . . Psalmus secundus. Cum propter fragilitatem humane corruptionis . . . (*b*) ff. 31–39^{v} Omnis anima potestatibus sublimioribus subdita sit. Ad Romanos xiii . . . Non enim sine ingenti misterio dei sapientia . . .

5. ff. 40–103 De forma prima electionis. Incipit tractatus. Sciendum est itaque primo quod tres sunt forme electionis . . . (f. 102) quicquid loquitur doctrina sit aliorum. Finis. Prologus. In nomine patris et filii et spiritus sancti amen. Anno domini M^{o} ccclxxvii^{o}. de mense ianuarii. Cum essemus in ciuitate Bononie reclusi propter guerras ut uacaret mihi tempus Ego frater Guido de pisis monachus domus Bononie Cartu. ordinis . . . de materia postulationis. 'Deo gratias et Beatæ virgini'.

Four parts: 2, f. 74; 3, f. 79^{v}; 4, f. 82^{v}. f. 103^{v} blank.

ff. ii + 103 + iii. 160 × 102 mm. Written space 105 × 60 mm. 20 long lines. Ink ruling. Collation: 1–12^{8} 13^{8} wants 8, blank. Upright humanistic hand. Flex punctuation is not used. Initials: (i) f. 1, 3-line, gold on blue and green ground, with violet penwork in the margin; (ii) 2-line, blue or red. Binding of s. xx. Secundo folio *legere*.

Written in Italy (north east ?).[1] Probably in Spain in s. xvi. A stamped *A* within a double border at the foot of f. 1.

Brotherton Collection 14. *Horae (partly in Netherlandish)* s. xv^{2}

A book of hours in which arts. 1, 10, 11 and rubrics throughout are in Netherlandish.

1. ff. 1–4 Calendar in Netherlandish, in red and black, beginning imperfectly at 10 Sept.

Written continuously, 17 lines to the page. f. 4^{v} left blank.

2. ff. 5–8 Die vii getiden van den heiligen cruce . . . Prosa. Patris sapiencia . . . f. 8^{v} left blank.

3. ff. 9–55^{v} Hours of B.V.M.

Antiphon and capitulum at prime O admirabile and Ego sapiencia; at none Germinauit and Et radicaui.[2] A leaf missing at the end.

4. ff. 56–69^{v} Die vii psallem. Litany follows, f. 65^{v}, and ends imperfectly.

Seventeen confessors: . . . (13–17) seruaci anthoni egidi alexi machari. Twenty-four virgins: (15–22) gertrudis walburgis waldetrudis aldegundis iuliana dympna ursula cum sodalibus suis cordula.

[1] Information from Dr A. de la Mare.
[2] Madan records this only from a manuscript of Adelberg, Ord. Praem.

5. ff. 70–74^{v} Office of the Five Joys of B.V.M., beginning imperfectly in the first Joy, 'cere Aue maria gracia plena'.

The hymn is 'Gaude virgo mater cristi', *AH* xxiv. 571 (Die Martis, prosa 1). Erased text on f. 74^{v}.

6. ff. 75–6 Gaude flore uirginali que honore speciali . . .

Seven Joys of B.V.M., *RH*, no. 6810. f. 76^{v} blank.

7. ff. 77–101^{v} Hier beghinnen die vigilien.

The ninth lesson is 'Ecce misterium . . .', 1 Cor. 15: 51–7.

8. ff. 102–111^{v} Die x psalmen. Deus deus meus . . .

The psalms of the Passion, Pss. 21–30.

9. ff. 112–116^{v} Memoriae of Sts Katherine, Barbara, Cecilia, Margaret, Dympna, and Waldetrudis, with headings in Netherlandish: (*a*) ff. 112–13 Aue felix katherina. virgo martir et regina . . . ; (*b*) f. 113^{rv} Gaude virgo gloriosa barbaraque generosa . . . ; (*c*) ff. 114–15 Aue uirgo gloriosa toti mundo gaudiosa beata tu cecilia . . . ; (*d*) f. 115^{rv} Aue margarita prefulgida . . . ; (*e*) f. 116 O virgo decus regium tuis instantes laudibus . . .; (*f*) f. 116^{v} Uualdetrudis o mater alma per te detur nobis palma . . .

(*a*). *RH*, no. 35516. (*b*). Cf. *RH*, no. 2204. (*c*). *RH*, no. 2208. f. 117^{v} left blank.

10. ff. 118–30 Hier beghint dat anbacht ende officie der kanonix ghetiden sijnte Katherine der maghet gheset bi onsen gheesteliken vader den paues van romen vrbaen den vierden . . . Here luket opp mijn lippen . . . O maghet katherine bidt voer mi . . .

Hours of St Katherine. f. 130^{v} left blank.

11. ff. 131–3 Die sijnte agneten der wtuercoren bruyt cristi gheerne eren sonde . . . Te mettentijt. Ic minne cristum in welc slaepcamer . . .

Short hours of St Agnes, ending imperfectly in none.

ff. iii + 133 + ii. 140 × 100 mm. Written space 80 × 53 mm. 17 long lines. Collation: 1–6^{8} 7^{8} wants 8 after f. 55 8^{8} 9^{8} wants 7, 8 after f. 69 10^{10} wants 6 after f. 74 and 9, 10, probably blank, after f. 76 11–12^{8} 13^{8} + 1 leaf after 8 (f. 101) 14–17^{8}. Changes of hand at ff. 56, 77, and 118. Initials: (i) blue or pink patterned in white on decorated gold grounds; (ii) blue patterned in white, with pale violet ornament; (iii, iv) 3-line or 2-line and 1-line, red or blue. Capital letters in the ink of the text stroked with red. Continuous framed floral borders on pages with initials of type (i). Brown morocco binding by Baynton, Bath, s. xx. Secundo folio (f. 6) *Exaudi*.

ff. iii^{v}, 8^{rv}, 101^{v}, 117^{rv}, 130^{rv} have pasted-on initials cut from a handsome book, s. xiii^{1}: the only historiation is a standing saint, f. iii^{v}.

Written in the Low Countries.

Brotherton Collection 15. *Horae* s. xv^{2}

A book of hours in which pains have been taken to erase parts of the text, especially invocations of B.V.M. and other saints and headings referring to them. Art. 7 is perhaps worst affected.

1. ff. 1–6^{v} Calendar in red and black.

Feasts in red include: Transfiguracio domini, 6 Aug.; Festum dulcissimi nominis Ihesu, 7 Aug.; Translatio sancti Erkenwaldi, 14 Nov.; Deposicio Sancti Osmundi, 4 Dec. St Thomas of Canterbury erased at 7 July and 29 Dec.

Many added births, marriages, and deaths, mostly of the families of Braddyll and Talbot, the earliest probably at 27 Oct., 'hodie natus fuit edwardus Braddyll receptor Cumbriæ Anno domini 1533'; also the birth of his daughter Dorothy, 3 Oct. 1572, and her marriage, 2 July 1595, to John Talbot; also the birth of John, son of John Talbot, 13 Dec. 1607 'in the greate froste'; also, 'In die martis videlicet secundo die decembris 1628 et Caroli 4° in unvera natus fuit thome whyt filius Ro: Whyt de magna eccleston (*Great Eccleston, Lancashire*) inter horam sextam et septimam eiusdem diei'. The latest date is 19 Dec. 1645, the marriage of Leonard Tomlinson and Ann Smyth.

Four lines of verse were added in s. xvi at the foot of each page: The fyrst vi yeres of manys birth and aege / May well be compared to Ianyuer . . .

2. (*a*) f. 8^{rv} Passio domini nostri ihesu cristi Secundum Iohannem. In illo tempore Apprehendit pilatus . . . testimonium eius. Oremus. Oratio. Deus qui manus tuas . . . (*b*) f. 8^{v} Ad matutinas beate marie pro pace memoria. Da pacem domine . . .

(*a*). Cf. *Lyell Cat.*, p. 65.

3. ff. 9–12^{v} Thes prayers folowynge ought for to be said or ye departe out of youre chambre at your vprysyng. Auxiliatrix sis michi . . .

Prayers on particular occasions: getting up; going out; going into church; taking holy water —the text and English rubrics erased, but the text replaced; Whan thou begynnest to pray thus begynne knelynge. Discedite a me maligni . . . O bone ihesu tu nouisti . . . ; Pro carnali dileccione; Pro temptacione carnis; Pro vera penitencia; at the hours; (f. 12) Oracio sancti augustini in nocte. Deus pater noster qui ut oremus . . . ; (f. 12^{rv}) Oracio sancti Anselmi. Domine deus meus si feci ut essem reus . . .

4. ff. 12^{v}–14^{v} Iste oraciones sequentes debent dici in agonis mortis per sacerdotem pro infirmo . . . Kyrieleyson . . . Oratio. Domine ihesu criste per agoniam et oracionem tuam . . .

Ends with a form of confession, 'Confiteor tibi domine ihesu criste omnia peccata mea quecumque feci ab infancia . . .': asks for intercession of B.V.M., Michael, John Baptist,

John Evangelist, Peter, Paul, George, Christopher, Martin, Nicholas, Katherine, Margaret, and Barbara.

5. ff. 14v–23 Matutine de passione domini nostri Ihesu cristi sequuntur . . . Ymnus. In passione domini qua datur salus homini . . .

Hours of the Passion, *RH*, no. 8722.

6. ff. 24–47 Hours of B.V.M. of the use of (Sarum). Lauds is followed by memoriae of Holy Spirit, Holy Trinity, Holy Cross, Sts Michael, John Baptist, Peter and Paul, John Evangelist, Andrew, Stephen, Laurence, (Thomas of Canterbury), all martyrs, Nicholas, all confessors, Mary Magdalene, Katherine, Margaret, all virgins, All Saints, and for peace. Hours of the Cross worked in.

Many headings and some of the text, especially memoriae of saints erased, but replaced, except for St Thomas of Canterbury.

7. Devotions to B.V.M.; (*a*) f. 47rv Salue regina . . . , followed by Virgo mater ecclesie . . . ; (*b*) ff. 47v–48 Gaude uirgo mater cristi que per aurem . . . ; (*c*) ff. 48–9 Gaude flore uirginali . . . ; (*d*) ff. 49–50v O intemerata . . . orbis terrarum. Inclina . . . ; (*e*) ff. 50v–52 Obsecro te . . . ; (*f*) f. 52rv Stel[. . . . . .] dignetur sidera compescere . . . ; (*g*) ff. 52v–54 Oracio deuotissima beate marie virginis. Sancta maria regina celi et terre mater domini nostri . . . ; (*h*) ff. 54–63v Hee sunt hore [compassionis beate] marie virginis . . . Ymnus. Uenite mares et femine ploramus cum maria . . . ; (*i*) ff. 63v–65 Has uideas laudes . . . , followed by the farsing of Salue regina with Salue virgo virginum. (*j*) ff. 65–68v Oracionem subsequentem confirmauit dominus Innocentius [papa] quartus. O domina mea sancta maria perpetua virgo . . . ; (*k*) ff. 68v–71v Quicumque [. . . . .] proprio stillo composuit. Uirgo templum trinitatis . . . ; (*l*) ff. 71v–74 Letania de uirgine maria . . . ; (*m*) f. 74rv Oratio sancti petri apostolorum principis. Salue mater saluatoris que deorum deum paris . . . ; (*n*) ff. 74v–75v Oracio ad virginem mariam. Stabat mater dolorosa . . . ; (*o*) ff. 75v–76 Alia oracio. Mater fili nouis more fecundata sacro rore . . . ; (*p*) f. 76 Peticio cuiuslibet deuoti cordis cum paciencia. Pia mater fac nos flere mala tecum ut gaudere . . . ; (*q*) ff. 76–7 Alia oracio. Aue nostra domina plena caritate. Aue felix . . . ; (*r*) f. 77rv Oracio. O domina sancta maria filia dei patris . . . ; (*s*) Alia oracio. Nesciens mater uirgo uirum peperit . . .

(*a*). *RH*, nos. 18147, 21818. (*b*). Five Joys, *RH*, no. 7017. (*c*). Seven Joys, *RH*, no. 6810. (*e*). Masculine forms. (*h*). *RH*, no. 34405; *AH* xxxi. 155. (*i*). *RH*, nos. 7687, 18318. A leaf missing after f. 63. (*j*). The heading conveys 500 days of indulgence and a quadragene. (*k*). Seven Joys, *RH*, no. 21899. (*m*). Thirteen stanzas, one attributed to each apostle and the thirteenth to 'omnes pariter'. *RH*, no. 33139; *AH* xxxi. 207. (*n*). *RH*, no. 19416. (*o*). 8 × 6. (*p*). 1 × 9. (*q*). 16 × 6.

8. ff. 78–85v Hours of Holy Trinity.

The hymns are Pater fili paraclite (*RH*, no. 14660), Adesto sancta trinitas (*RH*, no. 487), Pater deus qui omnia uerbo creasti, Qui trinus ante secula, Te trinum dei colimus, Tu trinitatis unitas (*RH*, no. 20714), O lux beata trinitas (*RH*, no. 13150), Rex celorum. lux angelorum: twenty-nine stanzas (5, 5, 4, 3, 3, 3, 3, 3).

9. ff. 85^{v}–86^{v} De sancta trinitate Oracio. Domine deus omnipotens pater et filius et spiritus sanctus da michi N famulo tuo . . .

10. ff. 86^{v}–90^{v} Sequuntur quindecim oraciones. O domine ihesu criste eterna dulcedo . . .

The Fifteen Oes of St Bridget.

11. ff. 90^{v}–92 Salue sancta facies nostri redemptoris . . . *RH*, no. 21204.

12. f. 92^{rv} Oraciones beati gregorii. O domine ihesu criste adoro te in cruce pendentem . . .

Five Oes, as MS. Brotherton 3, art. 19.

13. ff. 92^{v}–93 Ueni creator spiritus mentes tuorum uisita . . . *RH*, no. 21204.

14. Devotions to God the Son: (*a*) f. 93^{rv} Ora[cio . . . .] in auxilium sibi preparatam. Oracio. Deus propicius esto michi peccatori et custos mei . . . ; (*b*) ff. 93^{v}–94^{v} Alia oracio. O bone ihesu. O dulcissime o piissime ihesu . . . ; (*c*) ff. 94^{v}–95 Benedicatur hora in qua deus natus est . . . ; (*d*) f. 95 O Ihesu pie ihesu bone . . . ; (*e*) f. 95^{rv} Benedic domine hodie et custodi me . . . ; (*f*) f. 95^{v} Benedicat te imperialis maiestas . . . ; (*g*) ff. 95^{v}–96 Ihesu fili dei omnium cognitor . . .

(*a–d*). Cf. *Lyell Cat.*, pp. 373, 386, 371, 388.

15. ff. 96–99^{v} Pss. 30, 3, 53, 56, 58, 69, 101.

16. Further devotions to God the Son: (*a*) ff. 99^{v}–100 O bone ihesu duo in me agnosco . . . ; (*b*) ff. 100–101^{v} Dominus [. . . .] composuit [. . . .] indulgencie. O pie crucifixe redemptor omnium populorum . . . ; (*c*) ff. 101^{v}–102 O rex gloriose inter sanctos tuos . . . ; (*d*) f. 102 Sanctifica me domine ihesu criste signaculo tue sancte crucis . . .

(*b*). A prayer of the Five Wounds. (*c*). A memoria of the Holy Name. (*d*). Cf. *Lyell Cat.*, p. 62.

17. (*a*) f. 102^{rv} Ad proprium angelum. Angele qui meus es custos pietate . . . (*b*) ff. 102^{v}–103 Oracio ad omnes angelos. Deus qui sanctorum angelorum tuorum . . .

(*a*). *RH*, no. 22954.

18. ff. 103–15 Memoriae of twenty-four saints: (*a*) Sebastian; (*b*) Christopher (Martir cristofore . . .); (*c*) George (Georgi martir inclite . . .); (*d*) Giles; (*e*) Augustine (Magne presul augustine. Ierarchie comes trine . . .); (*f, g*) Leonard (Salue pater pietatis leonarde desolatis . . . ; Aue pater deo digne. aue dulcis et benigne . . .); (*h*) 11,000 virgins; (*i*) Apollonia (Virgo cristi egregia pro nobis appollonia . . .); (*j*) All Saints; (*k*) John Baptist (Gaude iohannes baptista qui in uentris clausus cista . . .); (*l*) John Evangelist (Gaude iohannes electus virgo a deo dilectus . . .); (*m*) Thomas of Canterbury (Gaude lux londoniarum . . .); (*n*) Anthony hermit (O anthoni sancte pater . . .); (*o*) Roche; (*p*) Erasmus; (*q*) Martin; (*r*) Nicholas (Salue gemma confessorum et conciuis angelorum . . .); (*s*) Anne (Gaude felix anna que concepisti prolem . . .); (*t*) Mary Magdalene (Gaude pia magdalena spes salutis . . .); (*u*) Katherine (Gaude uirgo katherina qua doctores . . .); (*v*) Barbara (Gaude uirgo barbara generosa paradisus . . .); (*w*) Margaret (Gaude uirgo gloriosa margareta preciosa . . .); (*x*) Winefred (Ad laudes regis glorie hoc extat memorabile . . .).

(*b, c, f, g, i, k*). *RH*, nos. 29471, 7242, 33166, 35650, 21744, 26988. (*m, n, s, t, u w*). *RH*, nos. 26999, 30215, 6773, 6895, 6991, 7002. The *incipits* of (*e, l, r, v, x*) are not in *RH*. ff. 115ᵛ–116ᵛ left blank.

19. ff. 117–29 Penitential psalms, (f. 122) Quindecim psalmi (cues only of the first twelve), and (f. 123ᵛ) litany.

The names in the litany partly erased. f. 129ᵛ left blank.

20. ff. 130–148ᵛ Sequuntur vigilie mortuorum.

21. ff. 149–156ᵛ Commendaciones animarum. Pss. 118, 138.

22. ff. 157–63 Psalmi de passione domini.

Pss. 21–30 and prayers 'Respice quesumus domine super hanc familiam . . .' and 'Aue benigne ihesu gracia . . .'. f. 163ᵛ blank.

23. ff. 164–71 Psalterium beati Ieronimi.

Followed by prayers, 'Omnipotens sempiterne deus clementiam tuam . . .' and 'Dona michi queso omnipotens deus vt per hanc sacrosanctam psalterii . . .'.

24. ff. 171ᵛ–172 Oracio ad sanctum Ieronimum. Aue amator quam famose. Ieronime gloriose . . .

A memoria of St Jerome, not in *RH*.

25. f. 172ʳᵛ O blessid trinite. fader sone and holy ghost. thre persones . . . all the seyntes of heuen. Amen.

Horae Ebor., p. 86.

26 (added in s. xvi^2). (*a*) f. iii^v Prognostications from thunder. (*b*) f. iii^v, in English, The vii ages of mans lyuyng in thys worlde . . . (*c*) ff. 115^v–116 Litany of B.V.M. (*d*) f. 116^v Psalm 6, signed 'Nicholas White'.

ff. iii + 172 + ii. f. iii is a medieval flyleaf. 265 × 185 mm. Written space 160 × 105 mm. 23 long lines. Collation: 1^6 2^8 + 1 leaf inserted before 1 (f. 7) 3–5^8 6^8 wants 1 before f. 40 and 7 after f. 44 7–8^8 9^8 wants 3 after f. 63 10–22^8. A full page picture on the singleton leaf before art. 2 (f. 7^v: the recto blank) shows the burial service and probably ought to be before art. 18. A smaller picture, 55 × 55 mm, defaced (probably B.V.M., seated, and Child), before art. 7*g* (f. 53). Initials: (i) in colours, patterned in white, on decorated gold grounds; (ii) 2-line, gold on blue and red grounds patterned in white, with short sprays of gold and green into the margins; (iii) 1-line, blue with red ornament or gold with blue-grey ornament. Capital letters in the ink of the text filled with pale yellow. Continuous floral borders on ff. 7^v (framed), 24 (framed) 117, 130, 149, and on three sides of other pages with initials of type (i). Gold and blue line fillers in the litany. Binding of s. xix^1 lettered 'Missale'. Secundo folio (f. 9) *Thes prayers.*

Written in England. Belonged probably to Edward Braddyll, born in 1533, and later to Talbots and perhaps Whites (cf. arts. 1, 26*d*). 'William Sproate Booke', f. 105^v, s. xvii. J. I. Jefferson wrote on a sheet of paper kept loose with the manuscript: 'This book belonged formerly to Miss Ann Ingleby, then Robert Ingleby 1860 then John Ingleby 1863 then John Ingleby Jefferson 1897. Entries relate to Talbot family of Bashall.'

Brotherton Collection 20. *J. Duns Scotus, Quodlibeta* s. xv^1

1. ff. 1–174^v Cuncte res difficiles ait salomon ecc' primo et cur intelligit eas esse difficiles subdit . . . ut dictum est etc' patet ad rationes. Explicit quodlibetum Duns.

For the manuscripts, see *Opera*, edn. 1950, i. 150*, and Glorieux, no. 344*s*. A table of the twenty-one quodlibets is on f. 176. Corrections and many notes throughout, s. xv med.: Ware is referred to in them, ff. 84^v (hec Ware super 4^m sentenciarum q. 18), 85, 108; also Woodford, f. 164^v. ff. 29, 48, 157, 165 are inserted slips with additions: 29 contains a reference to 'inceptor Cowton libro primo q. 49'; 157 quotes 'Scharp'; 165, called a 'scedula' in the direction at the foot of the recto, 'Verte hanc scedulam', contains a story of Pope Benedict derived from 'Cestrensis in suo policronicon libro 6 ca. 16'. *Catalogue*, p. 31, shows f. 1.

2. Notes in the blank space at the end of the last quire include verses, s. xv: (*a*) f. 174^v Omnibus assuetam iubeo seruare dietam . . . (3 lines); (*b*) f. 175 Dum ruit interius ordo sacer irreuerenter . . . (2); (*c*) f. 175 Vos qui gustatis mel mundi. fel caueatis; (*d*) f. 177^v Iustus abel pares habraham . . . (4); (*e*) f. 177^v Anna solet dici tres concepisse marias . . . (6); (*f*) f. 177^v Tu peruerteris peruerso si socieris . . . (2); (*g*) f. 177^v Hoc verbum do das iungit amicias; (*h*) f. 177^v Hic iacet Alanus qui totum scibile sciuit.

(*a*). Walther, *Sprichwörter*, no. 20108 (1 line). (*e*). Walther, no. 1060. (*f, g*). Walther, *S.*, nos. 31698, 11077.

ff. i + 177 + i. 210 × 160 mm. Written space 145 × 98 mm. *c.*30 long lines. Frame ruling. Collation, excluding inserted leaves and slips: 1–13^{12} 14^{14}. Quires 3–14 signed a–m in red. The script is secretary, except for the 8-shaped *g*. Initials: (i) f. 1, 8-line, blue and red with red ornament; (ii) 2-line, blue with red ornament. Red morocco binding, s. xix[1]: gilt crest and motto '**NOBILIS IRA**' on the front cover. Secundo folio *essencia*.

Written in England. The explicit, f. 174v, is followed by a name (of the scribe or an early owner ?) 'Wyllelmus' and what might be 'Sampton'. Tempsford Hall book-plate and cuttings from a sale catalogue and a bookseller's catalogue, s. xix, inside the front cover; not apparently in the William Stuart (of Tempsford Hall and Aldenham Abbey) sales at Sotheby's, 17 June 1875 and 6 Mar. 1895.

Brotherton Collection 21. *Cicero, De officiis* s. xii

Marci tulii ciceronis de officiis liber primus. Quamquam te marce . . . que letabere. Marci tullii ciceronis de officiis liber explicit. D(eo) G(ratias) A(men). Tullius Arpinas . . . supposuit tumulo (6 verses).

Cf. R. H. Martin, *Classical Quarterly*, new series i (1951), 35–8, where the verses at the end are printed from this copy (p. 37) and the gaps are noted, single leaves after ff. 13, 30 and probably eight leaves after f. 23. All after iii. 105 'non mediocrem' was missing by s. xv, when the rest of the text was supplied on ff. 39–41 and many notes added in the margins and between the lines throughout. f. 41v blank.

ff. ii + 41 + ii. 277 × 190 mm. Written space 220 × 150 mm. *c.*31 long lines. Ruling with a hard point. Collation: 1^8 2^8 wants 6 after f. 13 3^8 4^8 wants 8 after f. 30 5^8 6 three (ff. 39–41, s. xv). Quires 1–5 numbered i–iii, v, vi in s. xv. Initials: f. 26, beginning bk. 3, 5-line *S*, interlacing outline on ground of pale yellow, brown, and red; f. 21, beginning bk. 2, 3-line *Q* in the ink of the text, decorated with interlace; f. 1, 2-line red *Q*. Bound by D. Cockerell and Son in 1954: fragments of the spine of the former binding, 'diced brown calf', s. xviii, are laid down on f. 43v and a specimen of the marbled endpapers is pasted to the endleaf on which Cockerell has described his rebinding. Secundo folio *partes*.

Written in Italy, and there in s. xv. Probably belonged to Anthony Askew, †1774, and lot 442 in his sale, 7 Mar. 1785: cf. Martin, loc. cit.

Brotherton Collection 22. *Beda, In Epistolas Canonicas* s. xii[1]

1. ff. 1–84 Incipit expositio uenerabilis bede presbyteri in epistolas beati Iacobi apostoli. Iacobus dei et domini nostri . . . alicuius sed ante omne sęculum et nunc et in omnia sęcula sęculorum. amen. Explicit expositio uenerabilis bede super canonicas septem epistolas.

PL xciii. 9–130. This copy not listed by M. L. W. Laistner and H. H. King, *A handlist of Bede manuscripts*, 1943, pp. 31–7. *Catalogue*, p. 6, shows part of f. 22v and of f. 78v.

2. (added, s. xii). f. 84 Noscat omnes hec scripta legentes . . . qualiter quedam femina irmgarth uocata. predium quod `uocatur´ tomnignin . . . sancte marie ad richinb' dedit dono per manum nobilis uiri Cunradi de biburch . . . in presentia marchionis P*er*tholdi et comitis Gebehardi de sulcipach est actum atque confirmatum: the names of fifteen witnesses follow.

3 (added, s. xii). f. 84v In sapientia disponens omnia superna deitas . . . sortem parentis.

Verses (Walther, no. 9092; *RH*, no. 8754), with musical notes.

4. The pastedowns are sliced-up bits of service-books (?), s. xii and s. xiv.

ff. 84. 302 × 220 mm. Written space c.215 × 140 mm. 26 long lines. Ruling with hard point. Collation: $1-10^{8}$ 11^{4}. Quires numbered at the end. An ugly sloping hand, the same throughout. Initials, ff. 1, 22v, 42, 54, 77v, 78v, 80, outlined on decorated blue, or blue and green grounds and touched with red. Binding of wooden boards, covered with red leather, repaired in 1968: five bosses on each cover and two clasps now missing: two labels on the front cover, one of them, formerly under a piece of horn secured by six nails, inscribed 'Exposicio Bede presbiteri super septem canonicas epistolas' and the other, smaller, below it, bearing a pressmark 'A v. p'. Secundo folio *omnibus*.

Written in southern Germany. Belonged to the Benedictine abbey of Reichenbach am Regen, Bavaria, in s. xii: cf. art. 2. 'Lambach', f. 84, s. xix or s. xx.

Brotherton Collection 23. *J. de Voragine, Legenda Sanctorum* s. xiv in.

Incipit prologus super legendas sanctorum quas [compilauit frater] Iacobus [Ianuensis] de ordine fratrum predicatorum. Uniuersum tempus presentis . . . ad aduentum domini. Explicit prologus super legendas sanctorum. Incipiunt capitula . . . (table, with leaf numbers from i to cclxxxix) . . . Expliciunt capitula totius libri. Incipit de aduentu domini. Aduentus domini per quatuor . . .

The lives of Sophia, Timothy, Fabian, Apollinaris, and Boniface, nos. 48, 52, 64, 66, 71 in the edition by T. Graesse, 1846, do not occur here. The order differs from Graesse's in three places: Giles (G. 130) follows Felix (G. 126); Cornelius (G. 132) follows Chrysostom (G. 138); Lambert (G. 133) follows Eufemia (G. 139). Noticed in *Catalogue*, pp. 29–30, with a reduced facsimile of ff. 118v–119.

ff. ii + 292 + ii. The medieval foliation (roman) is one too high after f. 45. Parchment with holes. 220 × 155 mm. Written space c.157 × 105 mm. 2 cols. 39 lines. Collation: $1-24^{12}$ 25^{4}. Quires numbered at the end and catchwords. Initials: (i) f. 1, 10-line, blue patterned in white, on gold ground, historiated; (ii) ff. 15v, 52, 83v, 117v, in colour on gold grounds decorated in colour; (iii) 5-line, red and blue (or blue-green) with saw pattern of both colours running the height of the page; (iv) beginning etymologies, 3-line, as (iii), or blue with red ornament; in quire 1 only, the 5-line and 3-line initials are of gold on pink and blue patterned grounds. Capital letters in the ink of the text filled with pale yellow. Bound by Riviere and Son. Secundo folio (f. 3) *tus utilitas*.

Written in Spain (?). 'Anno domini M° CCCC° XXIX et die xxviii mensis Iulii. Frater Pontius lau*te*rii ordinis predicatorum conuentus montispess*ulani* Indignus Sp*iritus* Troiam existens in Valencia Regni Aragonie dedi (*sic*) amore dei conuentui Mossernen' istum librum intitulatum Flores sanctorum ut orent deum pro eo', f. 292. Armorial book-plate of 'Thomas Evelyn Scott-Ellis VIII Baron Howard de Walden'.

Brotherton Collection 24. *Psalter, etc. (in Netherlandish)* s. xv^{2}

1. ff. 2–10v Full calendar in red and black.

Written without break between the months. Some gradings, among them 'Ponciane martir dubbe feest', 'Odhulf confes' ix lessen', 'Lambert half dub' ', 'Willibroort b' dubb' ' (13 Jan., 12 June, 17 Sept., 6 Nov.).

2. ff. 10v–11 Des donderdages metten . . .

Psalms on Thursdays, Fridays, and Saturdays.

3. Preliminaries to the psalter: (*a*) ff. 11–12v Die sanc der ps'. Die sanc der ps' heylicht dat lichame. Het verciert die ziele . . . becoringe liden; (*b*) f. 13rv Dat prologius op dien souter metten virtuten. Alsoe als iheronimus seit . . . of sonderlinge; (*c*) f. 13v Beatus vir. Dese psalm seggen die meysters dat esdras bescreuen heeft . . .

(*a*). Lieftinck, pp. 48, 49.

4. ff. 14–180 Hier beghint dien souter in duutsche. Die eerste int'. Laet ons aenbeden den here . . . Salich is die man . . .

Liturgical psalter. Ps. 118 is numbered cxviii–cxxxix and the total number is, therefore, 171 instead of 150.

5. ff. 180–194v Six ferial canticles, Benedicite, Benedictus, Te deum, Magnificat, Nunc dimittis, 'Quequmque ult'.

Numbered clxxii–clxxxiii, in continuation of art. 4.

6. ff. 194v–207 Litany.

f. 200v Hier beghinnen die lettanien van der preces. O gesondmaker der werelt . . . (f. 202) Die corte preces. Ic heb geseit den heer . . . Collects 'voer onsen pastoer', etc., begin on f. 203.

7. ff. 207–72 Hier beghint dat comunum sanctorum.

8. ff. 272v–287 Die cleer eer . . .

Twenty-one hymns of the temporal, followed by 'O licht van den lichte . . .' for the Transfiguration and single hymns for St Remigius and for St Martin 'onsen pateroen'.

9. f. 287 Antiphons at particular seasons. f. 287v blank.

ff. i + 287 + i. 170 × 118 mm. Written space 105 × 80 mm. 2 cols. 24–6 lines. Frame ruling. Collation: 1^{12} + 1 leaf after 11 $2–34^{8}$ 35^{8} + 1 leaf after 5 and 1 leaf after 8 (ff. 283, 287). Signatures, mostly cut off, began with 'a' on f. 14 and with 'A' on f. 222 (quire 28). Rough textura, an unusual script for a manuscript with frame ruling. Initials: (i) gold, either on blue and red grounds patterned in white, or with blue ornament; gold and coloured prolongations into the margins; (ii) 3-line, red and blue with blue ornament or blue with red ornament; (iii, iv) 2-line and 1-line, red or blue. Capital letters in the ink of the text stroked with red. Small coloured buttons set on strips of parchment project from the fore-edge and mark the main divisions of the text. Contemporary binding of wooden boards covered with calf bearing a pattern of fillets: rebacked: two clasps.

Written in the Low Countries. 'totten nonnen te nazareth int geyn', f. 1^v^, s. xv/xvi, shows ownership by the Augustinian canonesses at Oudegein, near Jutfaas, in the province of Utrecht: cf. M. Schoengen, *Monasticon Batavum*, ii (1941), 104.[1] 'N° 8', f. 1, s. xviii (?).

Brotherton Collection 100. *'Genealogie de la bible', etc. (in French)* s. xv^2 (1461–83)

Cy sensuit la genealogie de la bible qui monstre et dit Combien chascune aage a dure . . . Et si trouueres ou nouuel testament des papes qui ont este a romme depuis sainct pierre iusques en lan mil iii^c iiii^{xx} et des empereurs de romme iusques en lan mil iii^c xxviii et des rois de france iusques en lan mil iii^c li et des roys dangleterre iusques en lan (mil) iii^c iiii^{xx}. Et si trouueres des roys crestiens qui ont este en iherusalem puis godefroy de billon etc. In principio creauit deus celum et terram etc. Cest a dire que au commancement du monde . . . A present regne le roy louys son filz ainsne dieu luy doint si bien regner que ce soit au prouffit de luy et du royaulme et a son salut et victoyre contre ses ennemis Amen. Deo gratias.

A long and wide roll set out in two columns to begin with, but from 'Roboam / Ieroboam / siluius / Briut' in four columns to show the lines of popes, emperors, kings of France, and kings of England. Col. 1 ends with the consecration of Urban VI in 1378, 'Cy ne parle plus des papes pour la diuision qui a este depuis en saincte eglise que dieu veulle amender'. Col. 2 ends 'En lan mil iii^c xxxvii (*sic*) fut couronne empereur de romme louys de bauiere et lors les romains firent a romme vng antipape etc. Explicit. Cy finent les empereurs de romme etc'. Col. 4 ends 'et fut hanry de lanclastre couronne roy dangleterre le quel a fait mourir des plus nobles du royaulme dangleterre sicomme les croniques le disent plus a plain etc' '. Towards the end, the French history (col. 3) takes over other now blank columns and for the reigns of Charles VI and Charles VII it occupies the whole width of the written space. For these reigns the text is very much fuller than in Manchester, John Rylands University Library, Fr. 99, q.v., and is in annalistic form for 1422 to 1461.

Illustrated by 64 captioned pictures within roundels, numbered in modern pencil 1–16, 17a–d, 18–61. The subjects are usually the same as in the Manchester manuscript, but the style tends to be more formal and elaborate. The following list gives in italics the picture-number in Fitzwilliam Museum, Cambridge, MS. 176, as given by M. R. James in his *Catalogue*, and after it the Leeds number in brackets: the main differences between Fitzwilliam and Leeds seem to be at nos. 11, 12, 38, 42, 43. The column in which the roundel occurs is shown by a number at the end of each entry.

(1–6) are in one horizontal row.

1 (1) Creation of 'le ciel la terre (*sic*) et les estoilles'. Fitzwilliam has here the expected caption, 'Comment dieu crea le ciel et la lune et les estoilles'.

2 (2) Creation of earth, herbs, and trees.

3 (3) Creation of waters and fishes.

4 (4) Creation of beasts and birds.

5 (5) Creation of angels.

6 (6) Fall of wicked angels.

7 (7) 'Comment dieu de paradis fist adam et eue quant les mausuais anges furent trebuches etc'. (2)

[1] I owe the identification and reference to Professor G. I. Lieftinck.

8 (9) God instructs Adam and Eve beside the tree. (1)
9 (8) Adam and Eve and, in the tree, the serpent. (1)
10 (10) God upbraids Adam and Eve, who kneel wearing short green skirts. (2)
11 *Expulsion*. (No picture)
12 *Angel clothes Adam, Eve already dressed*. (No picture)
13 (11) A blue-trousered Adam with raised mattock. (Centred)[1]
14 (12) The Ark: Noah walks up the gangplank. (Centred)
15 (13) Tower of Babel. (2)
16 *Abraham and Isaac* (14) Abraham, seated alone. (1)
17 (15) Joshua. (2)
18 (18) David. (1)
19 (16) Destruction of Troy. (2)
20–23 (17a–d) Aeneas, Priamus, Turtus, Helenus: four roundels of ships full of soldiers in one horizontal row.
24 (19) 'Comment bruit occist les geans (*sic*) etc' '. (4)
25 (20) Samarie. (2)
26 (22) 'Sedechias roy de iudee'. (1)
27 (23) The corpse of Nebuchadnezzar in pieces. (2)
28 (21) Sincambre. (4)
29 (24) Founding of Rome. (3)
30 (26) Killing of Baltasar. (2)
31 (27) Rape of Sabines. (3)
32 (25) Building of Paris. (4)
33 (28) Vashti: reproduced in Symington's *Catalogue*, pl. 7. (2)
34 (29) Alexander: stock 'warrior' picture, as Joshua. (2)
35 (30) Judas Machabeus: nearly as Joshua and Alexander. (1)
36 (31) Birth of Christ. (1)
37 (32) 'Ihesus nazarenus rex iudeorum'. A small naked figure in a field among trees, a city behind. It is in a mandorla and has the Cross under its arm. (1)
38 *Resurrection* (34) Annunciation, under the heading 'Comment ihesucrist sist en humanite en ce monde comme premier pape etc' '. (1)
39 (35) Killing of Julius Caesar. (2)
40 (33) London. (4)
41 (36) Sicambrians and Romans fight: reproduced in Symington's *Catalogue*, pl. 7. (3)
42 *Constantine and Bishops* (38) 'Cy parle du premier roy cristien le quel ordonna les arceuesques et les euesques etc' ': the text calls him 'bucie'. (4)
43 *Le duc Priant* (37) 'Comment les francois desconfirent les romains etc' '. (3)
44 (39) Conain. (4)
45 (40) Crowning of Pharamond. (3)
46 (41) Baptism of Clovis. (Centred)
47 (42) 'Comment le roy anglist occist xxx^{m} bretons en trahison etc' '. (3)
48 (43) Founding of St Denis. (Centred)
49 (44) Arthur kills Mordred in a battle on horseback. (4)

[1] In Fitzwilliam 176 11–13 are in a row horizontally.

50 (45) A city with soldiers outside it, apparently to illustrate the destruction of Britain. (4)
51 (46) Crowning of Pepin. (3)
52 (47) Gregory the Great. (1)
53 (48) William I, enthroned, no doubt, but all cut out except a piece of the canopy of the throne. (4)
54 (49) Crowning of Hugh Capet. (3)
55 (50) Godfrey de Bouillon on board ship. (4)
56 (51) Charlemagne. (2)
57 *Conquest of Jerusalem* (52) Godfrey de Bouillon enthroned. (4)
58 *Louis* (53) 'Comment monsieur s' Louys desconfit le roy dangleterre'. (Centred)
59 (54) Beranger I. (2)
60 (56) Edward I. (4)
61 (55) Philip de Valois. (2)
62 (57) Capture of John 'deuant poitiers'. (Centred)
63 (58) Charles V. (Centred)
64 (59) Charles VI. (2)
(60) Charles VII. (Centred)
(61) Louis XI. (Centred)

A roll about 18 metres long and *c.*630 mm wide. Membranes are as a rule about 450 mm long. Columns, if four in number, are each about 82 mm wide. When cols. 1, 2, 4 come to an end the one remaining column is 400 mm wide. Written in handsome set cursiva. Pictures in roundels with toothed edges (see above), usually about 75 mm across. Initials: (i) *C* of *Cy*, blue on decorated gold ground; (ii) 4-line, gold on grounds of pink and blue patterned in white. A floral border 480 mm across the top of the roll and the first 600 mm down each side. Kept on rollers in a glass-topped box made by Sangorski and Sutcliffe, s. xx[1].

Written in France.

Brotherton Collection 101. *Paulus Burgensis* 1453–4

1. ff. 1–344v Incipiunt addiciones super postille (*changed to* postilla) biblie magistri Nicolai de lira edite a R.P. magistro paulo. Episcopo Burgen' in sacra pagina professore quas venerabili viro Alfonso legum doctore de cauo (*or* cano). Compostellan' filio suo ex legittimo matrimonio suscepto. direxit premittens ei prologum sub hac forma. Prologus. Quid tibi vis ut viuens donem dilectissime fili . . . nunc per gratiam et in futuro per gloriam Amen. Deo gracias. Scriptor Nicolaus notulista In Ba. infra montem sancti Steffani Anno etc' liii° (*these twelve words in red*).

Stegmüller, nos. 6329–30. A projecting piece of parchment marks where a new book of the Bible begins.

2. ff. 345–449 Incipiunt addiciones super postillam magistri Nicolay de Lyra in psalterio. In prologo ubi dicitur in postilla . . . Addicio. Oppositum videtur . . .

et uox laudis. Ad quod nos perducat dei filius Amen. Et sic est finis pro quo deus gloriosus sit benedictus Amen. N. scriptor Anno etc. liiii^{o} (*these sixteen words in red*).

Stegmüller, no. 6329.

3. The pastedowns are two leaves of a paper manuscript of theological questions written in German cursiva, s. xiv: 2 cols., *c.*53 lines, frame ruling.

One question is whether 'omnia sacramenta antique legis in noua lege sint totaliter euacuata et uidetur quod non'.

4. A strip of parchment from a manuscript of s. xi (?) lies down the central opening of each quire.

ff. 449. Paper. A medieval foliation at the foot of each recto, 1–472, repeats '277' and '334' and jumps from '342' to '347' and from '435' to '456'. 310 × 210 mm. Written space *c.*235 × 150 mm. 2 cols. 44 lines. Ruling with a hard point. Collation: $1\text{–}28^{12}$ 29^{12} wants 9–12, probably blank, after f. 344 $30\text{–}37^{12}$ 38^{12} wants 10–12, blank. Written in cursiva. 4-line and 3-line metallic red initials. Capital letters in the ink of the text touched with red. Binding perhaps contemporary, pigskin over wooden boards: five large metal bosses on each cover: two strap-and-pin fastenings: a label formerly on the front cover: a chain of three links at the head of the back cover (facsimile in *Catalogue*, p. 4). Secundo folio *ceteros.*

Written at Bamberg by a named scribe in 1453 and 1454 (see above). 'per[. . .]' inside the cover, s. xv. Later marks are 'Poss. Ebern. X' (s. xviii ?) and 'N° 270' inside the front cover and 'N^{o} X' in the top compartment of the spine. No. 10 in the chained Pfarrbibliothek at Ebern, near Bamberg, which is said to have consisted of 42 manuscripts and 14 printed books and was sold in 1878 to Friedrich Böhm, a Munich bookseller: cf. E. G. Krenig, 'Nachrichten zur ehemaligen Pfarrbibliothek in Ebern', *Mainfränkisches Jahrbuch*, xii (1960), 293–9, which includes (pp. 296–9) descriptions of this manuscript and of MSS. 7–9, 11–14, derived from the notes of J. W. Rost in Staatsarchiv Würzburg f. 1218 Hist. Verein. taken in 1833/4. For this and other Ebern manuscripts see also Sigrid Krämer, 'Neue Nachrichten über die ehemalige Pfarrbibliothek von Ebern', ibid. xxviii (1976), 36–47. The inscription inside the cover, now cut out except for the first three letters, was no doubt that found in other Ebern manuscripts, 'pertinet ad Iohannem de Helb plebanum in opido Ebern'. Helb founded the library in 1463. Cf. below, Oxford, Blackfriars 2.

Brotherton Collection 102. *Sermones, etc.* 1412; s. xv^{1}

Sermons and other pieces in the hand of John Sintram, OFM, of Würzburg. For manuscripts, including this one, written by him see D. Coveney in *Speculum*, xvi (1941) 336–9; also T. C. Petersen in *Speculum*, xx (1945), 77–83, and Emden, *BRUO*.

1. ff. 1–6 O munde inmunde quare dileximus te . . . oculis considerare et tandem omnibus dimissis sola visione dei eternaliter in celesti patria gaudere quod nobis conce. etc. Explicit Hugo venerabilis de vanitate mundi script' anno m^{o} cccc xii^{o} in anglia.

PL clxxvi. 703-720/14: bk. 1 and most of bk. 2. For this and other manuscripts see Rudolf Goy, *Die Überlieferung der Werke Hugos von St Viktor*, 1976, pp. 245-8.[1] The explicit is repeated in the margin, f. 6, plus 'feria 6 ante natalem domini' after the year.

2. ff. 6v-76 Dominica 16. Cum vocatus fueris . . . luc. 14. Karissimi habetur Ione 1o quomodo ionas fuit in mari . . .

Sermons, mainly of the temporale. The 'processus' and other heads of each sermon are set out in the margins, where, too, there are cross references. Some notes are in German, e.g. on ff. 10v, 33v.

3. ff. 76v-82 Tractatus bonauenture Cardinalis albanensis de ordine minorum qui intytulatur Itinerarium mentis in deum. Beatus vir cuius est auxilium . . . posuit. Cum beatitudo nichil aliud sit . . . et dicet omnis populus fiat fiat. Amen Explicit. Explicit speculacio pauperis in deserto habet tamen iste tractatus aliud nomen recte notificans eum videlicet Itinerarium mentis in deum edidit dominus cardinalis albanensis sacre theologie doctor approbatus frater bonauentura de ordine fratrum minorum.

Opera (Quaracchi edn.), v. 296-313.

4. f. 82v A hand, with texts beginning 'Meditare' on the thumb, each finger and two places of the palm. Above is 'Mane Techel Phares' and below ''Hic nota metra in pollice'. Nunc locus est flendi . . . flebit' (Walther, *Sprichwörter*, no. 19352).

The recto has further notes on 'Mane Thecel Phar(es)' with reference to the hand 'in alia latere'.

5. ff. 83-140, 150-82. Sermons, mainly for saints' days, including (ff. 126-7) 'Sermo ad clerum in concepcione virginis quem predicaui Oxoniis Mo cccco xiio Iohannes Sintram. Orietur stella Numeri 24 et prothemate hodierno. Reuerendi p.d. atque magistri Cum sine omnipotentis gracia . . .', and (f. 135v) 'De sancto Iacobo et est sermo elucidarii'.

Marginalia as in art. 2: German occurs on ff. 98, 102v, 111v, 164, 171, and elsewhere. A reference on f. 150v is to 'alia pars huius libri folio 220'[2] and one on f. 111 is to a book 'qui incipit zachee festinans descende folio 176 in libro rubio huic simile'. On f. 150 a piece about evil thoughts ends with the words 'Item materiam applica in fasciculo morum folio 2o ibi contra malas cogitaciones[3] vel hic in libro 'folio 22 et folio 23' vbi introduccio thematis vel alibi de custodia cordis et malis cogitacionibus'. A note on f. 162v is dated 1427. f. 182v blank.

[1] Information from Mme. M.-C. Garand.

[2] Dr Nigel Palmer tells me that this reference is to Princeton, Univ. Libr. MS. Garrett 90, also written by Sintram, and that there are references there to ff. '110' and '136', now 111 and 137, of Brotherton 102: Garrett 90 was originally intended to follow on from Brotherton 102, f. 137.

[3] Now New York, Pierpont Morgan Library, MS. 298 (information from Dr Palmer).

6. ff. 140–50 `Tractatus de homine spirituali'. Ex quo creator tocius vniuersi inter cetera creaturas quandam `creaturam' aliis nobiliorem . . . equanimiter et pacienter ferre non possum.

7. ff. 183–8 Tabula sermonum de tempore et de sanctis istius libri.

With leaf references. Sintram wrote at the end 'Plures sermones in libro gerhardi et in libro rubeo paruo. CV^{m}'. f. 188^{v} blank.

8. The pastedowns are from the sanctoral of a missal, s. xii: written space 173 × 100 mm, 20 long lines, ruling with a hard point. The exposed sides have all or part of the collect, secret, and post-communion of (1) the vigil and day of St Laurence and (2) St Arnulf and the octave of St Laurence.

ff. ii + 187 and an inserted slip (f. 14). Paper—and for the outside and central bifolia in each quire—parchment. Foliated (i, ii), 1–188. A medieval foliation omits the slip and passes from '137' on f. 138 to '150' on f. 139. 220 × 145 mm. Written space *c.*170 × 100 mm. 29–51 long lines. Frame ruling. Collation: 1^{24} + a slip after 13 2^{20} 3^{18} 4^{18} + 1 leaf after 9 (f. 73) 5^{20} 6^{16} 7^{18} + 1 leaf after 9 (f. 128) 8^{14} wants 2–13 (ff. 138, 139: see above) $9–11^{16}$. Written in cursiva. Initials mainly 2-line in red or the ink of the text, sometimes decorated in red. Contemporary binding of wooden boards covered with red leather, re-backed: four bands: central clasp: a chain of five links attached to the top of the back cover (cf. facsimile in *Catalogue*, p. 4): a paper label was pasted to the front cover, but has gone, except for a scrap. Secundo folio *in pastum.*

'Librum istum scripsit Iohannes Sinttram de herbipoli', f. 1: see above.

Brotherton Collection 103. *Distinctiones, Abstinencia-Zelus, etc.* s. xv med.

Collections for Franciscan use (cf. arts. 4–6). A table of contents, s. xv, inside the front cover, headed 'Infrascripta continentur in isto libro', lists arts. 1–3, 6, 8 and in last place a now missing piece 'Item de partibus seu statibus atque condicionibus vltramarinis nec non de terra sancta'. Tabs show where arts. 3, 4, 5, 8 begin.

1. ff. 1–111 Abstinencia est Meriti augmentatiua . . . ducens eos in damascum act' 13.

Biblical distinctions, Abstinencia-Zelus, printed often: see *BMC* under Guerri (Bindus) and Goff, R. 12–20 (Antonius de Rampigollis). Stegmüller, nos. 1419, 1765.

2. ff. 111–13 Quomodo Iosias rex iudicauit sacerdotes . . .

Old Testament types of New Testament events. ff. 113^{v}–119^{v} blank.

3. ff. 120–43 Corpus iuris diuiditur in ius canonicum et in ius ciuile . . .

Includes: f. 121^{v} Divisions of the Bible; rubrics of the Decretals (f. 123), Digest (f. 126), and Codex of Justinian (f. 130^{v}) in alphabetical order; f. 138 Versus decreti et prima distinccio. Vt iudicet quisque diuinum ius hominisque . . . ; f. 143 Versus decretalium. Pars prior officium curat ecclesieque ministros . . . (5 lines: Walther, no. 13719). Directions to a copyist at the beginning, 'Hic incipite', and on f. 123, 'Usque huc et non plus'.

4. ff. 143–148v Decet in altissima paupertate cristo famulantes benigno fauore sic prosequi ut . . . et pro nunc hec dicta sufficiant etc' laus deo. Explicit opusculum excellentissimi legum doctoris domini bonifacii (*de Amatinis* ?) cardinalis sacrosancte romane ecclesie pie determinantis pro fratribus minoribus in altissima paupertate fundatis.

A legal opinion as to whether friars minor are able to inherit property. Refers often to the Minorita of 'Bertoldus de Saxoferrato' (Bartolus de Saxoferrato, †1354, *De minoritis: GKW*, no. 3647).

5. ff. 149–150v Incipit tabula priuilegiorum ordinis fratrum minorum. Absoluere possunt fratres curatis irrequisitis Clemens 4us *ad audienciam* . . . Item quod predicatores non possunt recipere fratres minores nec nos eorum. Innocencius 4us *qui nos in cristo*. Omnia hec priuilegia tabulata hic sunt in Colonia in sacristia in quadam cista et multa alia.

An alphabetical list.

6. ff. 150v–151v Item bonifacius priuilegium dedit . . . ad tumulandum etc. Explicit etc. Nota. Actum consilium domini Io. andree. coram vniuersitate bononiensi. Ordinamus quod fratres minores et predicatores de obuencionibus omnibus etc. Glosa. Non simpliciter set si defunctus qui eligit sepeliri apud ecclesiam dictorum fratrum ordinauit illa in vltima voluntate debetur quarta . . . debet de relictis ecclesie. Explicit etc.

The privilege of taking burials 'processionaliter' and, in the words of the table of contents, 'Consilium domini Ioh' Andree de porcione canonica danda': cf. Wadding, *Annales Minorum*, ed. 1931, v. 382 (1295).

7 (added). f. 151v Nota hic versus infrascripti monstrant questio causarum que numero 36 sunt Despice / preclaro / specialiter / optimo / florum . . . supplicium/ve. ff. 152–155v blank.

8. ff. 156–68 De libro apum. et tantum pro hiis etc. Triplex viuendi modus distingwiter in clericis . . . ad superna transiit. Item elemosyna multum valet pro defunctis.

With the last words compare T. Cantimpratensis, O.P., *Bonum universale de apibus*, edn. 1627, p. 506. ff. 168v–177v blank.

ff. i + 176. Paper. 217 × 100 mm. Written space *c.*150 × 95 mm. Arts. 3–7 in 2 cols. 30–3 lines. Frame ruling in pencil. Collation: 1^{12} wants 1, perhaps blank, $2–14^{12}$ 15^{10}. Written in cursiva. Spaces for coloured initials, 3-line and 2-line, have not been filled. Contemporary binding of wooden boards covered with white skin, rebacked: 3 bands: 2 clasps, fastening from the front to the back cover: a chain of four links attached by a ring to the front cover (cf. the facsimile in *Catalogue*, p. 4). Secundo folio *oracio cum.*

Written probably in north-west Germany (cf. art. 5). Armorial book-plate of Samuel Bowne Duryea, s. xix.

Brotherton Collection 500. *Prick of Conscience (in English), etc.*

s. xiv/xv

1. Hic incipit quidam tractatus [Roberti Grost]hed episcopi lincolliensis qui nomina[tur sti]mulus consciencie.[1] Prima pars qualiter homo factus est et omnia propter eum. þe myȝt of þe fader almyȝty . . . vs alle brynge Ihesus kyng ouer vch kynge. Amen.

Cf. K. W. Humphreys and J. Lightbown in *Leeds Studies in English*, nos. vii–viii (1952), 29–30, with a reduced facsimile of f. 121; also Allen, *Writings*, p. 377. The scribe took care to begin the section on purgatory (line 2690) on a new quire, quire 7. *IMEV*, no. 3428. 75.

2 (additions in Latin). (*a*) f. 44, Querunt multi cur deus hominem fecerit qui peccare potuit . . . semper mori: nine reasons why God created man. (*b–d*) f. 44v Notes on the five sheddings of the blood of Christ, on feigned (Samuel), imperfect (Lazarus), and perfect (Christ) resurrection, and on the Seven Words from the Cross. (*e*) f. 147v Examples from OT of pride, envy, and sloth.

(*a*) is in the main hand in a blank space at the end of quire 6.

ff. xii (foliated after two unnumbered leaves i–x) + 147 + ii. 205 × 125 mm. Written space 185 mm high. 27–35 long lines. Frame ruling in pencil. Collation: 1^8 2^6 + 1 leaf after 3 (f. 12) and 1 leaf after 6 (f. 16) $3\text{–}4^8$ 5^8 + 1 leaf after 3 (f. 36) 6^4 want 4, perhaps blank, after f. 44 $7\text{–}9^8$ 10^6 + 1 leaf after 4 (f. 72) $11\text{–}16^8$ 17^{10} 18^6 + 2 leaves after 3 (ff. 137–8) 19^6. Written in large current anglicana (single compartment *a*), probably all by one hand: sudden changes of ink, ff. 116, 124. Red initials, 3-line (f. 1) and 2-line: some spaces remain blank. Binding of 1954 by Douglas Cockerell and Son: the previous binding was made in 1896. Secundo folio *loueþ.*

Belonged to T. C. Neale, whose notes are on ff. iv–viv and to his grandson, Frederick A. Harrison, whose notes are on f. vii (dated 1898) and on f. viii. Harrison sale at Sotheby's, 30 Jan. 1920, lot 116. Sir L. Harmsworth sale at Sotheby's, 15 Oct. 1945, lot. 2086 (£125). Bought from Maggs Bros. in 1950.

Brotherton Collection 501. *Prick of Conscience, etc. (in English)*

s. xv[1]

The Prick of Conscience and other pieces[2] described by K. W. Humphreys and J. Lightbown in *Leeds Studies in English*, nos. vii–viii (1952), 30–4, with a reduced facsimile of f. 38.

[1] In the heading the letters shown here within square brackets have faded and were restored by a later hand.

[2] I owe the references at arts. 5, 10, 13, 14, 15 to Dr A. I. Doyle.

1. ff. 1–58v (*begins imperfectly*) Omne quod est in mundo . . . þt for oure hele on rode ded hyng. Amen. Explicit tractatus qui vocatur Stimulus consciencie.

Prick of Conscience, ed. R. Morris, 1863, beginning at line 1130. *IMEV*, no. 3428. 89.

2. ff. 59–67v Here beginnyth a notabill matyr extracte in the maner of a sermoun . . . publyshid and prechid at Poulis cros in london the ȝeris of oure lord crist ihesus þt tyme beyng mccc. iiiiti (*sic*) and viii. Modo attende diligenter. Redde racionem villificacionis tue . . . My dere frendys ȝe shuln vndyrstand . . . into worldis of worldis Amen. Explicit sermo notabilis secundum M.R.

Thomas Wimbledon's sermon (1388 ?). Printed often. Seventeen manuscripts recorded, thirteen in the edition by I. K. Knight, 1967, and four others, including this one, by E. Wilson in *Neuphilologische Mitteilungen*, lxxiv (1973), 90.

3. ff. 68–74 VII dedly synnys. Here begynneth a notabyll tretys of the Sevyn dedly synnys and of her braunchis . . . Cryst that deyde on þe tre . . . (3 lines of verse). These thingis that y haue purposid . . . eternall place. Amen. Explicit tract' prefat' etc.

The 'Litil tretys' of Richard Lavenham, Ord. Carm., ed. J. P. W. van Zutphen, Rome 1956. Jolliffe, p. 79 (F. 2a). Cf. *IMEV*, no. 621.5. A leaf is missing after p. 70.

4. ff. 74v–81 Here beginnyth a tretys of the ten commaundmentis as folwith here. O ye crystyn men ye shal vnderstande. that all manyr of pepill . . . he hath promysid vs of his mercy and charyte. Amen. Explicit 10 precept'.

5. f. 81rv A declaracion of þe vii dedis of mercy þat arn bodily here folwith. Of the seuyn dedys of mercy god shal speke . . . bodyly ne gostly. Explicit.

Cambridge, U.L., Nn. 4. 12, f. 37v and Trinity College, Dublin, 245, f. 219, begin thus.

6. ff. 82–86v/10 O þu my brothyr þt art yong of age. qwiche kanst not confesse thiself . . . the maner of informacion. Confiteor deo. beate marie . . . I am aknowe to god . . . in werefull thowtys.

Jolliffe, p. 73 (C. 39).

7. ff. 86v–88v The apostill seynt poule seyth In a mans wyll . . . ioye and solace wt hym to regne wt outen ende. Amen. Explicit.

Jolliffe, p. 121 (K. 8b).

8. ff. 89–90 Here begynnyth a lytyl matyr of the glorious virgyne oure lady . . . Wurshypfull frendys we rede among myraculys of oure lady . . . wt god and oure lady. To whiche ioyes god vs alle brynge. Amen.

9. f. 90^{v} Here þu shal weten how þu shalt plese most god of all thingis:' attende. Synt Poule the fyrst hermyte . . . for she wyll gete the þ^{e} blysse of heuyn. Amen.

Nine things pleasing to God. Jolliffe, p. 107 (I. 12f).

10. f. 91^{rv} (*begins imperfectly*) ʒyf þu offre thin herte to him . . . to ihesu endeles spouse þ^{t} he vs graunte the lyf þat euyr shal last. Amen.

Tribulations. Jolliffe, p. 117 (J. 4). Chapter 15 of Walter Hilton's translation of pseudo-Bonaventura, Stimulus Amoris, ed. C. Kirchberger, 1952, pp. 122/11–124/11.

11. ff. 92–99^{v} Here begynnyth a notabyll matere and a gret myracule don be oure lord ihesus cryst . . . as I fynde þus wretyn. Augustinus in libro de fide ad petrum dicit. Miraculum est . . . ostendere etc. Incipit Spiritus guydonis ut sequitur. Lorde and god alway . . . When we make oure endyng.

Gast of Gy. *IMEV*, Supplement, no. 2785. This copy described by J. Lightbown, 'A shorter metrical version of the "Gast of Gy" ', *Modern Language Review*, xlvii (1952), 322–9.

12. ff. 107^{r}–101^{v} (*going back leaf by leaf*) Here begynneth a proces and a declaracion of the holy cros . . . The holy Rode the swete tre . . . that neuyr shal haf ende. Amen. Explicit virtus sancte crucis vt supra.

IMEV, Supplement, no. 3389/20. Invention and Exaltation of the Cross from the South English Legendary: this copy listed by M. Görlach, *The textual tradition of the South English Legendary*, Leeds Texts and Monographs, New Series 6 (1974), 121–2.

13. ff. 101^{v}, 100^{rv}, 114^{r}–109^{v} (*going back leaf by leaf*) Iam incipit passio domini nostri. Here begynnyth the passyon of oure lord cryst ihesus . . . Owre swete lady seynt marie . . . and reygnyth w^{t} out ende. Amen. Here endith the passion of crist and the compassion of his modir of the tellyng of the same modyr of cryst.

The version here is that in Magdalene College, Cambridge, Pepys 2498, p. 449 and San Marino, Huntington, HM 144, f. 21. Cf. J. F. Drennan in *Manuscripta*, xxiv (1980), 165.

14. ff. 109^{v}, 108^{rv}, 115^{r} And now here begynnyth the Epystyll of Nichodemus . . . The gode and the Nobyll prynce Nichodemus . . . he of hys mercy vs alle bryng. Amen. Explicit epistola Nichodemi.

As Pepys, p. 459 and Huntington, f. 47. f. 109^{v} ends 'ytt befyll in thys mornyng a gret erthe' and f. 108 begins 'wykkydnes. that we ded onwetyng to the': a leaf is missing in between.

15. ff. 115^{v}–116^{v} O þ^{u} my frend y wyll teche þ^{e} a lityll lesson:' how þ^{u} shal loue god and forstere thy self to kyndele thin herte in to his loue:' qwich lesson ys callyd Stimulus amoris. drawyn of Bonauenture cardynal and doctor. ʒyf þ^{u}

wylt ben steryd for to loue god . . . Qwerfor lete vs hertly loue oure blyssid lorde þ^{t} we may duell w^{t} hym w^{t} out ende. Amen. Explicit stimulus amoris.

As edn., Kirchberger (see art. 10), chapter 11.

16. ff. 117–122^{v} Here biginnith Miraculis of our ladi seint Marie . . . Seint Teophile was a grete man . . . where thi blyssid sone and the arn inne. Amen. Expliciunt Miracula sancte Marie.

IMEV, Supplement, no. 3266/13. Theophilus from the South English Legendary: this copy listed by Görlach, op. cit.

ff. iii + 122 + iii. Paper. 222 × 200 mm. Written space *c.* 193 × 140 mm. 36–46 long lines. Collation: 1–8^{8} 9 six (ff. 65–70) 10^{8} wants 1 before f. 71 11^{8} 12 six (ff. 86–91) 13^{8} 14^{8} (ff. 100–7 in reverse order) 15^{8} wants 7 (ff. 108–14 in reverse order) 16^{8}. Written in a good set current anglicana by one hand throughout:[1] headings and Latin lemmata are in anglicana formata or textura. 3-line or 2-line red initials with muddy green-brown ornament in arts. 2–16. Binding of s. xx.

Written in England. Humphreys and Lightbown, p. 34, list the scribbles of s. xvi, which include the names George Sheldrake twice, Marke Sheldrake twice (f. 6^{v} 'Marke Sheldrake ow this booke . . .') and Thomas Pell three times. Maggs Bros., cat. 542, no. 132; cat. 555, no. 204; cat. 580 (1933), no. 450. Sale at Sotheby's, 14 March 1949, lot 309. Bought from Francis Edwards in 1950.

Brotherton Collection 502. *J. Mirk, Festial (in English); Sequentiae* s. xv med.–xv ex.

1. ff. 1–116^{v} (*begins imperfectly*) Olyffe and palme and ther' dyed . . . to ye chyrch (*ends imperfectly*).

The Festial of John Mirk, ed. T. Erbe, EETS, Extra Series, xcvi, 1905. A copy of the 'B' type: cf. M. F. Wakelin in *Leeds Studies in English*, New Series, i (1967), 110–11. Temporal to Corpus Christi and (f. 34) sanctoral beginning with Andrew. The former begins near the end of the homily for Quinquagesima Sunday (edn. 78/1) and the latter ends in the homily for All Saints (edn. 266/5). A gap after f. 19 which ends 'And then wyll criste' (edn. 124/21): f. 20 begins 'hym from yees processions' (edn. 149/20). Most of f. 33 was left blank. Later scribbles in this space include 'Explicit liber quod Iohn Slareffe (?)'. Many leaves are damaged, especially the first leaf and the last two leaves.

2. ff. 117–138^{v} (*begins imperfectly*) ethera. Rex in eternum . . . in exelsis voce dulcisono (*ends imperfectly*).

Sequences widely spaced for Latin and English interlinear glosses. In Laus devota (f. 138) 'scismata' is glossed 'lollere'.

(*a*) Temporal: (Easter) Fulgens preclara; (within the octave of Easter) Zima vetus, Prome casta, Concinat orbis, Dic nobis, Victime pascali; (Sunday after Easter) Laudes saluatori; (Ascension) Rex omnipotens; (Pentecost and within the octave) Sancti spiritus, Resonet

[1] According to Humphreys and Lightbown, p. 34, there are changes of hand at ff. 59, 100, 108, 117, but these seem to me minor changes by a skilful scribe: his *d*, pointed at the foot, is distinctive.

sacrata, Eya musa, Lux iocunda, Alma chorus, Laudes deo; (Trinity) Benedicta sit; (Corpus Christi) Lauda syon.

(*b*) Sanctoral and common: De sancto andrea. Sacrosancta; De sancto nicol[ao]. Congaudentes; (Vincent) Stola iocunditatis; (Paul) Solemnitas; (Purification) Hac clara die; (Annunciation) Aue mundi; (Alban) Eya gaudens; (Invention of Cross) Salue crux; (Nativity of John Baptist) Sancti batiste; (Peter and Paul) Laude iocunda; (Martin) Sacerdotem; (Mary Magdalene) Mane prima; (Chains of Peter) Nunc luce; (Laurence) Stola iocunditatis; (Assumption of B.V.M. and within the octave) A rea virga, Post partum, Aue maria, Letabundus . . . alleluia rerem (*sic*) regum, . . . ,[1] Hodierne lux, Missus gabriel; (Nativity of B.V.M.) Alle celeste; (Dedication of church) Ierusalem et syon, Quam delicta (*sic*); (Exaltation of Cross) Laudes crucis; (Michael) Ad celebres; (Dedication) Letabundus . . . celi curie; (Apostles) Clare sanctorum, Alleluya nunc decantet; (Anne) Testamento veteri; (All Saints) Cristo inclito; (Evangelists) Laus deuota; (Martyr) Organicis canamus; (Martyrs) Mirabilis deus.

After Ad celebres (Michael) the ink varies in colour, as though pieces had been added from time to time.

ff. ii + 138 + iii. 'The nvmbar of ye leves in this booke xiiii and vi score', f. 83^{v}, s. xvi, probably refers to art. 1 when it was already incomplete, but less so than now. Paper. 208 × 140 mm. Written space *c.*150 × 95 mm. 28-36 long lines (art. 1). 17-23 long lines (art. 2). Frame ruling with a hard point. Collation: 1 one 2^{12} 3 ten (ff. 14-23: a large gap after f. 19) 4^{10} (ff. 24-33) $5\text{-}10^{12}$ 11^{12} wants 12 after f. 116 12^{22} (ff. 117-38: perhaps once 12^{24} wants 1 and 24). Art. 1 is basically secretary, but with anglicana *e, g,* and *r*. Art. 2, s. xv ex., is a current mixture of anglicana and secretary. Initials: in art. 1, 2-line, red; in art. 2, not filled in. Bound by Katharine Adams, s. xx, for £6. 3*s.*

Written in England. 'Henry Chicetor (?) ous thes boke', f. 90. Bought by Wilfred Merton from Bertram Dobell (Tunbridge Wells), 17 May 1913, for 16*s.* Bought from M. Breslauer, 4 June 1958.

LEEDS. YORKSHIRE ARCHAEOLOGICAL SOCIETY

MD 338 (part) + York, Borthwick Institute, BF 10. *Aristoteles, Corpus Naturalium (fragm.)* s. xv^2

De memoria, De motu animalium, and fragments of De generatione in the translation of William of Moerbeke and fragments of De anima and Physics in a later translation.

1. Two leaves of De anima, the first (York, f. 1) and another (Leeds, f. 1). Bk. 1, chapters 1, 2, 3 (part), 11 (part), 12 (part). The first words of an older translation and a summary precede each chapter.

(York, f. 1) Bonorum honorabilium noticiam oppinantes et cetera. Capitulum primum declarat nobilitatem sciencie de anima propter quam racionabile sit tractare de ipsa et cognoscere tam subiectum quam proprias passiones ipsius licet hoc sit multum difficile. Quoniam

[1] The scribe left a space for the initial (elsewhere in art. 2 the spaces for initials contain guide letters) and then wrote what might be 'torum' above which 'c̄' is interlined. The sequence continues 'decus angelorum Aue maria Visita tuorum mentes famulorum dulcis maria O fons bonitatis nostre paupertatis delue maria. Nobis eue natis sinum (?) pietatis aperi maria. Ne nos pro peccatis simus cum dampnatis succurre maria'.

sciencia est bonum honorabile ita quod vnam nobiliorem alia reddit certitudo modi aut nobilitas subiecti . . .

(Leeds, f. 1v/14) Capitulum 12m quod sic incipit. Alia autem opinio et cetera. introducit quamdam opinionem dicentem animam esse quamdam armoniam et ipsam improbat. Quedam opinio alia a predictis (Bekker, 407b. 27). The last words (1v/36), 'fieri mixtio. Neutro autem' and catchword 'modorum' are 408a. 10.

Some marginal and interlinear glosses.

2. Twelve consecutive leaves from bks. 2 and 3 of the Physics (Leeds, ff. 2–4; York, f. 2; Leeds, f. 5; York, ff. 3–5; Leeds, ff. 6–8; York, f. 6), beginning in bk. 2, ch. 8 and ending in bk. 3, ch. 13.

Examples of beginnings of chapters: 2. 14 Peccatum autem accidit in hiis que fiunt ab arte sicut gramaticus; 3. 11 (205b. 1) Anaxagoras autem inconuenienter loquitur ex quiete infinita dicens se ipsum sustentare.

A summary of each chapter is in the margin opposite the beginning of the chapter, except at 3. 1 (Leeds, f. 5), where the summary is in the text space and is preceded by the first twelve words of bk. 3 in an older translation: Quoniam autem natura est principium motus et mutacionis eius in quo est et cetera. Huius libri capitulum primum ostendit necessitatem determinandi de motu . . . ipsius motus. Some marginal and interlinear glosses.

3. Leeds, ff. 9–11; York, f. 7 'Incipit liber de memoria et reminiscentia . . .' De memoria autem et memorari dicendum quid est et propter quam causam . . . et propter quam causam dictum est.

Lacombe, p. 139. As edn. Venice 1496, ff. 323–324v. Some marginalia and many interlinear glosses.

4. ff. 12–17 'Incipit liber de motu animalium . . .'. De motu autem eo qui animalium quecumque circa vnumquodque genus ipsorum . . . non tantam aut tallem. De partibus quidem igitur vniuscuiusque animalium et de anima adhuc et de sensu et sompno et memoria et comuni motu diximus causas. reliquum autem de generatione dicere.

Lacombe, pp. 177–8. ff. 12–17 are consecutive leaves. As edn. Venice 1496, ff. 330–333v. The upper and lower margin of each page contains a full commentary and the space on either side of the text is reserved for short glosses and headings. The commentary has usually lost a line or two in the upper margin and the beginning of the first paragraph is therefore lacking on the first page (12v): this paragraph deals with five main topics, of which the second is how De motu differs from (i) Physics, De celo, De generatione and Metheora, (ii) De anima, (iii) the Liber animalium, and (iv) De progressu animalium and the third, fourth, and fifth paragraphs are 'De intitulatione libri', 'De ordine eius', and 'De libri processu' respectively. The second paragraph begins 'Intentio philosophi in isto libelo est tractare de causa motus animalium. scilicet ex quibus principiis fiat'. Interlinear glosses.

5. ff. 18–21 From De generatione et corruptione.

Lacombe, p. 130. The only paragraph is on f. 19v: Quia vero sunt quedam generabilia et corruptibilia generacio contingit eis que sunt circa medium . . . (335a. 24). Some marginalia.

ff. 21 + 7. Paper. 298 × 210 mm. Written space 190 × 110 mm and (Leeds, ff. 9–17; York, f. 7) 150 × 105 mm. 36 long lines on Leeds, ff. 1–8 and York, ff. 1–6; 30 on Leeds, ff. 9–17 and York, f. 7; *c.* 26 on Leeds, ff. 18–21. Current hybrida by three hands, the first good (Leeds, ff. 1–8; York, ff. 1–6) and the last scribbly and widely spaced for interlinear glosses (Leeds, ff. 18–21). Spaces for initials, 4-line (Leeds, f. 5), 3-line, and 2-line not filled. No binding.

Written probably in France. Used as a pad in a binding: patterns of wormholes suggest that Leeds, ff. 1–8 and York, ff. 1–6 were at one end and Leeds, ff. 9–21, and York, f. 7, at the other end and marks made by the leather turned in from the covers on York, ff. 1 and 7, show that these were the top (inmost) leaves of the pad at either end. Given to Canon J. S. Purvis in 1949 by F. A. Hyde, headmaster of Lady Lumley's Grammar School, Pickering. MD 338 given by Miss H. M. Purvis in 1970.

LEICESTER. ARCHDEACONRY

The records were transferred on deposit from the Registry of the diocese of Leicester to the Archives Department of Leicester City Museum in 1941 (cf. *Handlist of Records of Leicester Archdeaconry*, 1954, p. 4) and (probate records) in 1949: the City Archives Department was amalgamated with the County Record Office at 57 New Walk in 1974. Used parchment for purposes of binding seems to have been in short supply or not in favour and most of the sixteenth-century Archdeaconry books are in plain parchment covers.

1 D 41/11/19. *A bifolium of sermons* s. xiv²

A paragraph begins on f. 1ᵛ 'Eadem dominica sermo secundus. Quecumque scripta sunt etc. homo con[. . .] letificat patrem. vt le. prouerb. Written space 195 × 132 mm. 2 cols. 42 lines. Textura. 2-line blue *Q* with red ornament.

Written in England. Formerly the wrapper of an act book containing instance court business for 1586–8; now, after repairs in 1951, inside the new cover (*Handlist*, p. 14).

1 D 41/13/2. *A bifolium of a treatise on civil law* s. xiii¹

The leaf in front contains a section headed 'De satisdando' and beginning 'Quia in arbitriis de quibus dicendum est' and a section headed 'De iureiurando propter calumpniam dando' and beginning 'In principio causarum. immo a causis primordium'. Almost the whole of the leaf at the back has been torn off: a section is headed 'De [. . .]is diuersorum [. . .]' and begins 'Audiuimus de postulantibus'. Written space 215 × 113 mm. 2 cols. 70 lines. Initials blue or red, outside the written space.

Written in England (?). The wrapper of a 'Liber correctionis' for 1537–51 (*Handlist*, p. 21).

1 D 41/13/3. *A leaf of a priest's guide* s. xiii/xiv

A section, 'De transitu clericorum' begins 'Quinque sunt cause transitus clericorum de una ecclesia ad aliam' and a second (main ?) section '[. . .] regu[. . .]' begins 'Prima regula est. Qui peccauerit mortaliter post baptismum non potest promoueri': running number III in upper margin. Pieces in smaller script are inset, for example, 'Nunquid diacono licet corpus domini deferre ad infirmum et eum communicare R d' xciii. d. presente presbitero diaconus . . .'. Written space 195 mm high. 2 cols. 23 lines. 2-line red *P* of *Prima* with saw pattern ornament in red and blue the height of the written space.

Written in England. Used in the binding of a Correction Book for 1561-2 (*Handlist*, p. 21); half the leaf cut vertically is tied in as a partial cover in front and half at the back.

1 D 41/13/5. *A leaf of psalms* s. xiv/xv

Pss. 56: 11-62: 10, with noted antiphons: cf. *Brev. ad usum Sarum*, ii. 116-20. 430 × 297 mm. Written space 305 × 210 mm. 2 cols. 42 lines.

Written in England. Used as the wrapper of a Correction Book for 1569-70 (*Handlist*, p. 21).

1 D 41/13/7. *A leaf of an antiphonal* s. xiv/xv

Common of Apostles: cf. *Brev. ad usum Sarum*, ii. 366-8. 410 × 282 mm. Written space 310 × 185 mm. 14 long lines and music.

Written in England. Used as the wrapper of a Correction Book for 1571 (*Handlist*, p. 21).

Will Registers 6-9, 12 (1564-7, 1570) had leaves of service books as wrappers: offset traces remain.

Will Register 15, 1573. Original decree of Pope Paul II. 7 June 1465.

Dispensation to William Westbury, canon of Salisbury,[1] 'Paulus episcopus . . . Litterarum scientia . . .' (*Calendar of Papal Registers*, xii. 424). Signed at the foot on the left by the hands of 'B. de Maffeis / Adrianus / A. de Viluno / f. Agn[. . .]'. Written space *c.* 155 × 360 mm. 23 lines.

Index of wills and administrations, 1660-79. Contemporary copy of episcopal letter. Sleaford Castle, 26 July 1416

Philippus permissione diuina lincoln' Episcopus dilecto filio Offic' Archidiaconi nostri Leycestr' Salutem graciam et benediccionem. Presentarunt nobis . . . Permission to the prioress and convent of Harrold, O.S.A., to appropriate the parish church of Shackerston, Leicestershire, as in J. Nichols, *History and Antiquities of the County of Leicester*, ix (1811), 909-10, where the date is given as 26 May. Written space 255 × 160 mm. 2 cols. 42 lines.

A bifolium as wrapper.

[1] Westbury was provost of Eton 1447-77, canon of Salisbury 1449-77, canon of Lincoln from September 1465 until at latest June 1469, and canon of St Stephen's Westminster from November 1465 until October 1468, when he exchanged this canonry for one at St Paul's, held till death in 1477 (Emden, *BRUO*).

LEICESTER. OLD TOWN HALL LIBRARY[1]

MSS. 2–4 are noticed briefly by C. Deedes, J. E. Stocks, and J. L. Stocks, *The Old Town Hall Library of Leicester*, 1919, p. 167; MSS. 2–4, BR II/3/1 and BR/II/3/3 by J. C. Jeaffreson in HMC, *Eighth Report* (1881), Appendix pp. 419–20, 425.

2. *Biblia* s. xiii med.

1. ff. 1–295 An imperfect Bible, with the usual contents in the usual order.[2] The first leaf and probably nearly a hundred other leaves are missing and the lower margins of many leaves have been cut off. The chief gaps are from Ecclesiasticus 3 to Isaiah 32 and from 2 Corinthians 1 to Hebrews 2. Most of Psalms is missing. Proverbs begins a new quire, f. 145. Annotations in an English hand, *c.*1300.

The remaining prologues are thirty-one of the common set and eleven others shown here by *: Stegmüller, nos. 284, 285, 323, 328, 330, 332, prologue to Tobit, 'Liber tobie in superficie littere est salubris . . . signantur in subiectis*', 335, 344 + 349* (linked by 'finit hic additum est'), 457, 468, 487, 494, 495*, 500, 507, 515, 512 (. . . uerbum dei), 519 + 517, 516*, 524, 522*, 526, 525*, 528, 527*, 531, 529*, 538 (Moriente dario rege medorum . . .), 535*, 539, 540*, 551, 590, 624, 685, 699, 640, 631*, 809.

2. ff. 295–315 Aaz apprehendens . . . consiliatores eorum.

The usual dictionary of Hebrew names.

ff. v + 329 + iii, foliated (i–v), fourteen unnumbered leaves, 1–315, (316–8). ff. iv, v are medieval flyleaves. Parchment thicker than is usual in Bibles. 254 × 175 mm. Written space 153 × 100 mm. 2 cols. (art. 2, 3 cols.). 55 lines. Collation of ff. (vi–xix), 1–315 impracticable: the quires are mainly sixteens: f. 199ᵛ is marked 'x pec' ' at the foot. A small rather poor hand. Initials: (i) of books, red and blue with ornament of both colours; (ii) of prologues, 5-line or less, and (iii) of chapters, 2-line, red or blue, with ornament of the other colour—the type (ii) initials are more often blue than red; (iv) of psalm verses and in art. 2, 1-line, blue or red. Binding of s. xx: the sides of an earlier binding, s. xvii, pasted on, bear a cancelled gilt centrepiece of the royal arms of England. Secundo folio (f. vi) *De ueteribus.*

Written probably in England. 'Caucio (?) Iohannis Wis[. . .] die [. .] ante festum sancti Matthie in quadragesima anno gracie M° CCCVI°', f. v, erased. 'W. Stanlay. alio nomine Walne. Scripsit', f. 315, s. xv. 'Ihon Coke', f. 315ᵛ, s. xvi; also in pencil 'John Stoone / Lestere', s. xvii (?).

3. *J. Wyclif, Sermons (in English)* s. xiv/xv

For the manuscripts of these sermons see Anne Hudson in *Notes and Queries*, 218, 1973, p. 451, and *Medium Aevum*, xl (1971), 142. Her α.

[1] The Leicestershire Record Office acts as supervisor of the Old Town Hall Library.
[2] See below, Liverpool Cathedral 13.

1. ff. 1–58v Epistole dominicales per annum. Dominica prima aduentus domini. epistola. Scientes quia hora est Ro. 13o. We take as bileue . . . 7 begyle hem fro tru lore. Expliciunt Epistole Dominicales per annum.

Set 5. Sermons on the Sunday Epistles throughout the year, beginning at Advent, as printed in *Select English Works of John Wyclif*, ed. T. Arnold, 1869–71, ii. 221–376.

2. ff. 59–99v In vigilia sancti Andree apostoli. Euangelium. Stabat iohannes. þis gospel telles . . . goddes law 7 his wille.

Set 3. Sermons on the Gospels for saints' days from St Andrew to All Saints. As Arnold, i. 295–412, except that the sermon for Ascension Day (edn., pp. 360–2) is absent and the sermon for St Mary Magdalene printed in edn., ii. 205–7, here comes between the sermons for Seven Brothers and St James (f. 86).

3. ff. 99v–143 In vigilia vnius apostoli siue plurimorum apostolorum euangelium. Ego sum vitis vera . . . Io. 15. As comyne þinge is bettir . . . þei shul dye. Here ende þe godspelles of comyn sanctorum.

Set 2. As Arnold, i. 165–294.

4. ff. 143–7 Exposicio textus Mt 23 de 8 ve scribis et phariseis. Crist byddes vs be ware . . . nede to trete.

As Arnold, ii. 379–89 (*Vae octuplex*).

5. ff. 147–158v Egressus ihesus de templo Mt 24o. þis godspel telles mycle wisdom . . . hope to criste.

As Arnold, ii. 393–423 (*Of mynystris in the chirche*).

6. ff. 159–216v Cum appropinquasset ihesus . . . Math' 1o. þis gospel tellis of þe secund aduent . . . and holde hym here kynge. Expliciunt euangelia Dominicalia per annum. Amen.

Set 1. As Arnold, i. 65–162, and 1–64. Sermons on the Sunday Gospels throughout the year, beginning at Advent. Below the explicit are the words 'Ista euangelia dominicalia corriguntur [per] primum originale' in a contemporary hand.

ff. ii + 216 + ii. 243 × 170 mm. Written space 175 × 125 mm. 2 cols. 40 and 41 lines. Collation: $1–6^8$ 7^{10} (ff. 49–58) $8–16^8$ 17 eight (ff. 131–8) $18–22^{10}$ $23–24^8$ $25–26^6$. The only remaining signatures are g [iiii] on f. 52, h iii[i] on f. 162 and + o iiii on f. 62: cf. below. Written in anglicana formata, probably all by one hand, but if so, the quires were written in the order 1–7, 20–6, 8–19, that is to say art. 6 was written before arts. 2–5: the writing becomes gradually more expert and less personal. 2-line blue initials with red ornament. Binding of s. xix, but the leather of a mid-sixteenth-century binding bearing Oldham's rolls HE. k. 1 and MW. a. 4 has been pasted to the new covers: rust from a former chain-staple has damaged ff. 210–16 at the foot. Secundo folio *to experte men*.

Written in England. A scribble on f. 36, s. xvi, 'To you and to noe other Till deathe vs towe departe I geue uou Thys ryng w[t] Wyllyng hert By me Robert Ormes'.

4. *Miscellanea (partly in English)* s. xiii ex.–xiv ex.

A miscellany written at different times. Four main parts: arts. 1–10, s. xiv med.; arts. 11, 12, s. xiii ex.; art. 13, s. xiv ex.; art. 14, s. xiv med. A table of contents on pp. 143–5 is signed by William Kelly, Borough Accountant, February 1851.

1. pp. 1–6 (*begins imperfectly*) moab et agarem . . . Passus id est tollorauit. Explicit exposicio psalterii.

Brief notes on Psalms and Canticles, beginning at Ps. 82. Some glosses are in English, for example (Ps. 82) 'stipula anglice stubbyl'.

2. Includes: (*a*) pp. 6–7 Forty-two lines of verse, 'Ignota vocabula mult' exponentur Metris in sequenciis annoque legentur'; (*b*) pp. 7–9 'Magister dicit hic quod omne nomen compositum . . .' and other grammatical notes.

Some English glosses in (*b*), for example, 'hoc fimarium anglice myddyng. hec sagina anglice horspanel'. Blank space on p. 9 was filled early, partly with notes on liturgical customs.

3. pp. 10–28, 35, 36, 39 Short pieces, including: (*a*) p. 10 'Discipuli rogauerunt dominum quod doceret eos . . .' on the Lord's Prayer; (*b*) p. 12 Quare cantantur tres misse in die natalis domini . . . ; (*c*) p. 12 Notandum quod canon misse consistit in duobus . . . ; (*d*) pp. 13–15 Notes on liturgical customs, in which many paragraphs begin 'Queritur quare', for example (p. 15) 'Queritur quare pax non datur in missa pro fidelibus . . .': verses include a couplet on holy water, 'Aufert purgat . . .', and fifty-nine lines beginning 'De superpellicio. Illud superpellicium quod presbiter induit ante', and ending with four couplets 'De sursum corda. Verba sacerdotis digitisque purificatur . . .'; (*e–h*) Notes on the seven 'gradus ecclesie' (p. 16), the nine 'pene infernales' (p. 18), the seven sacraments (p. 19), and the seven petitions of the Lord's Prayer (p. 24); (*i*) p. 27 Salue plus decies quam sunt momenta dierum . . . (7 lines).

(*d*). For the verses 'Illud . . .' see Walther, no. 8376 (Hildebert, De missa). They are in Oxford, Bodleian, Digby 53, ff. 20–2. (*i*). Walther, no. 17138.

4. pp. 29–32 Qui me iudicat dominus est karissimi: beatus basilius in quodam sermone . . . Explicit sermo de deo et de peccatoribus.

5. pp. 33–4 Hic incipit sompnarius danielis prophete quem composuit in babilonia . . . Aues uidere in sompnis contra se demicantes iracundiam significat . . . Zonam singere lutrum significat.

Cf. Thorndike and Kibre. Printed from six manuscripts by Max Förster, 'Beiträge zur mittelalterlichen Volkskunde, V', *Archiv für das Studium der neueren Sprachen*, cxxvii (1911), 53–83.

6. p. 37 Omnia ista verba pertinent presbitero scire. hic calix a chalix . . . hoc ferum a nobley.

Sixty-three words, Latin and English.

7. pp. 37–8 (*a*) Woys hatawyf *and* loȝt fort to suync . . . (*b*) Lord ihesu crist ȝat sitit abow hous . . . (*c*) Al clercyn lou clercyn low ys y wyrc at oxinfort on ȝe scolowys dor . . . (*d*) Latin verses and notes on grammar, etc.

(*a–c*). Four, four, and six lines of verse, each set followed by its equivalent in Latin, 'Qui prauam habet coniugem . . .', 'Ihesu criste domine qui supra nos sedes . . .', 'Omnis amor clerici . . .'. *IMEV*, Suppl., nos. 4128.5, 1963.5, 173.5. Printed from this manuscript by (T.) W(right) in *Retrospective Review*, i (1852), 419. (*d*). Includes: Sunt tria que nullus (?) poterit . . . proferre latinum (3 lines); Ira res mira Idio non iris in ira . . . (9 lines); Fercula sunt epule . . . (3 lines); Ierusalem ierusalem vnde gaudet ierusalem . . . (10 lines).

8. (*a*) pp. 39, 40 A note on the declension of numerals and (p. 40) a series of numbers expressed in roman figures and in words, ending 'Explicit numerus secundum vsus tocius mundi'. (*b*) p. 40 Verses: (1) Si tibi sit vita semper saligia vita; (2) Si digne capiatur dumentum seruat ab igne . . . (2 lines).

(*b*1). Walther, *Sprichwörter*, no. 29292. Followed by an explanation of *saligia*, a word made up of the initial letter of each deadly sin. (*b*2). On the body of Christ.

9. (*a*) pp. 41–2 Four stories: (1) the bowman in the wood; (2) the hermit in the desert; (3) the rich man's penitence; (4) the householder who loved a boy 'carnaliter', ending with nine couplets in English spoken by the dying boy, 'Fadir y may no lagir (?) duhel . . . y am yput from god is fas et tunc obiit et demones rapuerunt eum a manibus patris sui'. (*b*) p. 42 Verses: (1) Mater quid fili poto te dul[. . .] ba ba O pater o fili michi placet oscula da da (2 lines); (2) Diues diuicias non congregat absque labore . . . (10 lines); (3) Quatuor ex puris vitam . . . (3 lines).

In several more or less contemporary hands. (*a*). The English is *IMEV*, Suppl. no. 782. 8, printed in *Retrospective Review*, i. 419, after art. 7*a–c*. (*b*2). Walther, *Sprichwörter*, no. 6059 (2 lines). (*b*3). Walther, *Initia*, no. 15306; Renzi, v. 50 (4 lines).

10. pp. 44–73 Cum plures ecclesiastici uocabula exotica grammatice non intelligentes . . .

On difficult words in the temporal, sanctoral, troper (p. 50), and lectionary (p. 70: Hic incipiunt omnia deficilia verba epistolarum et euangeliorum . . .). Some English glosses. p. 74 blank, except for scribbles.

Arts. 11, 12 are probably on a quire of twelve leaves.

11. pp. 75–87 Templum dei sanctum quod estis uos . . . esse in temperancia.

R. Grosseteste, Templum domini. For the manuscripts see Thomson, *Grosseteste*, pp. 138–40.

12. pp. 37–98 Sepius rogatus a condiscipulis quasdam questiunculas enodare . . . ex inferno infernorum amen.

Honorius, Elucidarium. *PL* clxxii. 1109–1159C. The last words here come near the beginning of bk. 3.

13. pp. 99–128 Carta est quoddam scriptum sigillatum de re immobili cum condicione uel sine condicione . . . vel decem solid' sterling' (*ends imperfectly*).

A formulary. The last chapter now remaining is headed 'Scriptum de tenementis concessis ad terminum vite. pro necessariis sibi inueniendis'. Initials only for names of persons and places.

14. pp. 129–42 Verba singularum coniugationum conpendiose tractarum (*sic*) secundum ordinem alphabeti. Verba primi coniugacionis habencia b ante o. Labo. as aui atum. for to slyd tutibare to stumly . . . (*ends imperfectly*).

The first conjugation runs from 'b ante o' to 'z ante o'. Only five lines of the second conjugation remain. Many interpretations in English. Two leaves appear to be missing after p. 136 where the list passes from -lo words to -to words (from Pabulo to Lito); also one leaf after p. 138.

ff. iii + 71 + iv, paginated (i–vi), 1–(150). 270 × 198 mm, except in art. 13, where the height is 255 mm. Written space *c.*220 × 140–70 mm. 2 cols. and (arts. 11, 13, 14) long lines. 40-50 lines. Frame ruling in art. 13. Collation: 1^{10} (pp. 1–20) 2^{12} wants 11, 12, perhaps blank, after p. 40 3 one (pp. 41, 42) 4^{16} (pp. 43–74) $5\text{-}6^{6}$ (pp. 75–98) 7^{10} 8^{4} 9^{10} wants 5, 6, 8 (pp. 129–42). Arts. 11, 12 are in textura and the rest in more or less current anglicana. Initials: (art. 1) 2-line, blue with red ornament or red with violet ornament; (arts. 2–14) 2-line, red. In arts. 1–3 capital letters in the ink of the text are filled with red. Smears of red or pale yellow pick out leading words in art. 10 and the headings in art. 14. Rebound by W. Cross (Leicester) Ltd. in March 1939.

Written in England. 'Iste liber attinet ad me Iohannem Wilkock', p. 129, s. xvi in.

BR II/3/1. *Statuta Angliae* s. xiii/xiv–xv med.

1 (quires 1–5). ff. 1–58 Magna Carta and statutes (etc.) of various dates to 29 Edward I (1300/1) or without dates.

(*a*) f. 1 Magna Carta: the inspeximus of 28 Mar. 1300. *SR* i, Charters, p. 38.
(*b*) f. 4 Carta Foreste: the inspeximus of 28 Mar. 1300. *SR* i, Charters, p. 42.
(*c*) f. 5 Provisions of Merton. *SR* i. 1.
(*d*) f. 7 Statute of Marlborough. *SR* i. 19.
(*e*) f. 12 Statute of Westminster I. In French. *SR* i. 26.
(*f*) f. 20 Statute of Gloucester. In French. *SR* i. 45.
(*g*) f. 23 Explanaciones Glouc'. *SR* i. 50.
(*h*) f. 23^{v} Statute of Westminster II. *SR* i. 71.
(*i*) f. 40 Quia emptores . . . *SR* i. 106.
(*j*) f. 40 Contra religiosos. *SR* i. 51.
(*k*) f. 40^{v} Statutum de mercatoribus. In French. *SR* i. 98.
(*l*) f. 42^{v} Statutum de Finibus Leuandis. Quia fines . . . *SR* i. 128.
(*m*) f. 43^{v} Statutum de Bigamis. *SR* i. 42.

(*n*) f. 44 Statuta de presentibus vocatis ad War'. *SR* i. 108.
(*o*) f. 44v De vasto. *SR* i. 109.
(*p*) f. 45 Statutum Lincolnie de Escaetoribus. *SR* i. 142.
(*q*) f. 45v Statutum ubi Regis Prohibicio tenet locum. Sub qua forma . . . *SR* i. 101/24.
(*r*) f. 46 Circumspecte agatis . . . *SR* i. 101. 1–23.
(*s*) f. 46 Noui articuli super magnas cartas. In French. *SR* i. 136.
(*t*) f. 49 Statutum de Scaccario. In French. *SR* i. 197.
(*u*) f. 51v Districciones eorundem. Pur ceo que la communalte . . . *SR* i. 197b.
(*v*) f. 52 Statutum de Recognitoribus. *SR* i. 113.
(*w*) f. 52v Statutum quod dicitur Quo waranto. Cf. *SR* i. 45 and footnote.
(*x*) f. 53v Statutum de Quo waranto. In French and Latin. *SR* i. 107.
(*y*) f. 54 Statutum de terris et parcis perquirendis. In French. *SR* i. 131.
(*z*) f. 54v Modus calumpniandi Essonia. *SR* i. 217.
(*aa*) f. 55 Composicio De ponderibus et mensuris. Nunc dicendum est de ponderibus . . . *SR* i. 205.
(*bb*) f. 55v Le Roi voet qe de trespas faitz deci en auaunt en ses forestes . . . la puralee faite.
(*cc*) f. 56 Statutum de Chaumpartours. Come il soit apartement defendu . . . Cf. *SR* i. 216.
(*dd*) f. 56v Conspiratours. Dominus rex mandauit nunciante G. de Roubury . . . *SR* i. 216.
(*ee*) f. 56v Communes Dies in Banco. *SR* i. 208.
(*ff*) f. 56v Communes Dies de dote. *SR* i. 208.
(*gg*) f. 57 Assisa panis et Deinde Assisa Ceruisie. In French. Cf. *SR* i. 199.
(*hh*) f. 57v Visus Franci Plegii. In French. *SR* i. 246.
(*ii*) f. 58 Modus faciendi Homagium. In French. *SR* i. 227. f. 58v is blank, except for seven lines on weights and measures added in s. xiv.

Arts. 2, 3 were added later to make a complete set of statutes of Edward I and II.

2 (quires 6–9, added in s. xv med.). Twenty-eight pieces.

(*a*) f. 59 Prerogatiua Regis. *SR* i. 226.
(*b*) f. 60v De coniunctim feoffatis. *SR* i. 145.
(*c*) f. 61v Addicio foreste. *SR* i. 147.
(*d*) f. 62v De aportis religiosorum. *SR* i. 150.
(*e*) f. 64 Articuli pro clero. *SR* i. 171.
(*f*) f. 65v Articuli super cartas. In French. Repeats art. 1*s*.
(*g*) f. 69 De consultatione et prohibicione. *SR* i. 108.
(*h*) f. 69v De fine pur terres purchaces. In French. Repeats art. 1*y*.
(*i*) f. 70 De malefactoribus in parcis. *SR* i. 111.
(*j*) f. 70v De clericis vic' retournantis breuia. *SR* i. 213.
(*k*) f. 71 Statutum de Appellatis et Appelatores. *SR* i. 141.
(*l*) f. 71 Statutum Exon'. Articuli Itineris. In French. *SR* i. 210.
(*m*) f. 74 Ordinacio Inquisicionum. *SR* i. 143.
(*n*) f. 74v De proteccionibus Allocandis etc. In French. *SR* i. 217.
(*o*) f. 74v De religiosis etc. Repeats art. 2*d*.
(*p*) f. 76 Ordinacio de foresta. In French. *SR* i. 144.
(*q*) f. 76v De waranto in hustengis. In French. *SR* i. 52.
(*r*) f. 77 Acton' Burnell'. In French. *SR* i. 53.
(*s*) f. 78 Westmonasterium quartum siue districciones Scaccarii. In French. *SR* i. 180.
(*t*) f. 78v De prisonis prisonam frangentibus etc. Five lines. *SR* i. 113.
(*u*) f. 78v De gaueletto. *SR* i. 222.
(*v*) f. 79 Reuocacio ordinacionum nouorum. In French. *SR* i. 189.
(*w*) f. 80 Enroulement en la Chancell'. In French. *SR* i. 190.
(*x*) f. 81v De terris templariorum. *SR* i. 194.
(*y*) f. 82v De Moneta. In French. *SR* i. 219.
(*z*) f. 83v Iudicium Pillorie. *SR* i. 201.

(*aa*) f. 84v Exposicio uocabulorum etc. Sok hoc est secta . . . pro aueragio domini regis.
(*bb*) f. 85v Officium coronatorum. *SR* i. 40. Ends abruptly after thirteen lines. f. 86rv blank.

3 (quires 10, 11). ff. 87–94v Statutes of 5 and 12 Edward II. s. xiv in.

(*a*) f. 87 Noue ordinaciones. In French. *SR* i. 157.
(*b*) f. 93v Statuta Ebor'. *SR* i. 177–8.

ff. iv + 94 + iv. f. 95 is a medieval flyleaf. 225 × 160 mm. Written space 185–165 × 108 mm. 32 long lines. Frame ruling on ff. 67–85. Collation: $1\text{–}4^{12}$ 5^{12} wants 11, 12, probably blank, after f. 58 $6\text{–}8^{8}$ 9 four (ff. 83–6) $10\text{–}11^{4}$. Written—art. 1 excellently—in current anglicana, s. xiii/xiv (art. 1), s. xiv in. (art. 3), and s. xv med. (art. 2). Art. 2 is in a hand like that of the latest scribe in BR II/3/3, q.v. The spaces for initials left blank in arts. 1, 3, were filled by the same hand, s. xv, as put in the initials of art. 2, but only as far as f. 74: blue initials with red ornament in the same style as in BR II/3/3. 'Rebound by Wm. Cross (Leic.) Ltd March 1939'. According to Jeaffreson in *Eighth Report*, App. p. 419, the binding in 1881 was of medieval boards, newly recovered and stamped with the arms of the borough. Secundo folio *ad debitum*.

Written in England. 'Iste liber constat Iohanni (*above erasure*) Welford', s. xiv, is on f. 58v, the last page of art. 1. This page, the last until arts. 2, 3 were added, shows signs of exposure. Cf. BR II/3/3.

BR II/3/3. *Nova Statuta Angliae (mainly in French)*

s. xiv ex.–xv med.

1. (*a*) ff. 2–11v Tables of chapters of statutes of 1 Edward III–9 Richard II. (*b*) ff. 12–19v An alphabetical subject index of statutes of Henry III–Richard II, beginning imperfectly in the letter *p*.

(*a*). The first hand ends at 6 Richard II. f. 1rv is blank, except for two couplets in English, s. xv: (1) In euery place wher I can goo for lack of a forewytt ys cause of woo; (2) Wt a Betyll be he beton' that all hys godez to hys chylder leyton (?) And gyffez awey all hys thyng and goys hym selff a beggynge: cf. *MMBL* ii. 362. (*b*). s. xv in.

2 (quires 3–14). ff. 20–117v Forty-seven statutes of 1–50 Edward III and (no. 15), a statute of 17 Edward II (*SR* i. 193) here said to be of 17 Edward III.

As compared with *SR* the two statutes of anno 9 are in reverse order; the second statute of anno 10 ends at edn. 277/27 after which is 'vide de capitulo vio quia hic deest'; the statutes of anno 14 are in the order 1, 3, 4, 2; the statute of anno 15 and the first statute of anno 18 are said to be of anno 17; the statutes of anno 25 are in the order 2, 7, 6, 3, 5, 1, 4; the first three statutes of anno 31 are in the order 1, 3, 2 and the fourth statute is placed under anno 36 and dated at the end 20 May anno 36. The statutes in *SR* and not here are on pp. 278, 295, 297, 299, 327, 394 (10 E. III, no. 3; 15 E. III, nos. 1, 2; 17 E. III; 25 E. III, no. 7; 46 E. III).

3 (quires 15–20). ff. 118–164v Nineteen statutes of 1–15 Richard II.

The nine statutes of 1–6 Richard II on ff. 118–37, as *SR* ii. 1–31, are in the same hand as art. 2 and the collection probably ended originally at this point (cf. art. 1*a*). The ten other statutes were added early, the two of 7, 8 Richard II, as *SR* ii. 32–9, by perhaps four hands on ff. 137–42, and the eight of 9–15 Richard II by one hand on ff. 143–164v. As compared with *SR*, the first part of the statute of anno 11 is here said to be of anno 10 and the second part beginning at Come nostre seignur (ii. 46) is a separate statute of anno 11. The statute of anno 10 and the third statute of anno 13 do not occur here.

4. (*a*) ff. 164v–180v. Statutes of 16–21 Richard II. (*b*) ff. 180v–217v. Statutes of Henry IV. (*c*) ff. 217v–243. Statutes of Henry V. (*d*) ff. 243–268v Statutes of 1–8 Henry VI, ending imperfectly.

(*a–d*). As *SR* ii. 82–254/11.

ff. iii + 268 + iv. 225 × 160 mm. Written space 168 × 100 mm. 25–37 long lines. Frame ruling. Collation: 1^{12} wants 1, probably blank, $2\text{–}13^{8}$ 14^{10} (ff. 108–17) $15\text{–}19^{8}$ 20^{6} + 1 leaf before 1 (f. 158) $21\text{–}26^{6}$ 27^{8} wants 8 after f. 219: f. 220 is a contemporary supply leaf $28\text{–}33^{8}$. Quires 3–20 signed a–s and quires 21–33 +, a–m. Current anglicana by several hands of s. xiv ex. (see above art. 3) and (art. 4) one hand of s. xiv med. Initials all of s. xv in the same style as in BR II/3/1, q.v.: the illuminator put in many wrong letters. Bound by W. Cross in 1939 in the same style as BR II/3/1: both volumes were uniformly bound when Jeaffreson described them for HMC in 1881. Secundo folio *ont par cause.*

Written in England. Art. 1*b* suggests that arts. 1, 3 of BR II/3/1 and arts. 1–3 here may have been bound together until the collection was greatly enlarged, provided with coloured initials, and split into two volumes in s. xv.

LEICESTER. UNIVERSITY LIBRARY

7. *Biblia* s. xiii^{2}

A Bible in the order Genesis–2 Chronicles, 1 Ezra, 'Esdras II' (Nehemiah), 'Esdras III' (3 and 5 Ezra, Stegmüller, nos. 94, 1 and 96), Judith, Esther, Tobit, Job–Lamentations, Baruch 1–5, Ezekiel–Pauline Epistles, Catholic Epistles, Acts, Apocalypse. Ecclesiasticus ends with the Prayer of Solomon. The Prayer of Manasses is an addition after 2 Chronicles and Baruch 6 was added in s. xiv on f. 278 in the blank space after 2 Maccabees.

The prologues are 38 of the common set of 64[1] and 11 others shown here by *: Stegmüller, nos. 285, 311 + 307*, 315*, 323, 328, 330, 335, 341 + 343, 551 (after Esther: repeated in its place), 332, 344, 357, 457, 455* (as prologue to Wisdom), 482, 487, 491, 492, 494, 500, 527*, 529*, 532*, 535*, 540*, 544*, 551 (see above), 590, 607, 624, 677, and thirteen more as usual to 793 (765, . . . de laodicea), 809, 812*, 818*.

Two leaves are missing at the beginning, with Jerome's general prologue (no. 284) and the beginning of his prologue to Desiderius (no. 285), and two leaves after f. 227 with part of Jeremiah. f. 279rv is blank: NT begins at f. 280 on a new quire (24^{1}). Within books the text is written continuously: sometimes a coloured initial and sometimes a blue paragraph mark shows the beginning of a new chapter. The chapters of Job have a double numeration, 1–35, and, later, in red, 1–42; so also the chapters of Jeremiah, 1–52, and, later, in red arabic figures, 1–177.

[1] See below, Liverpool Cathedral 13.

ff. i + 355 + i. 240 × 162 mm. Written space c. 155 × 92 mm. 2 cols. 59 lines. Collation of OT: 1 eleven (ff. 1-11) $2\text{-}5^{12}$ 6^{10} (ff. 60-9) $7\text{-}19^{12}$ 20^{12} wants 3, 4 after f. 227 $21\text{-}22^{14}$ 23^{16} (ff. 264-79). Collation of NT doubtful. Small clear script, changing at f. 70 (6^{1}). Initials: (i) blue and red with ornament of both colours; (ii) of prologues and psalms, 3-line, blue or red with ornament of the other colour; (iii) of chapters and verses of psalms, 1-line, blue or red. Capital letters in the ink of the text filled with red. Rebound in August 1907 by J. S. Bates.

Written probably in England. Baruch 6 and marginalia are in current anglicana, s. xiv. Sale at Sotheby's, 27 July 1907, lot 431, to H. H. Peach, Belvoir Street, Leicester: cf. the note on the pastedown. Label in front, 'This book was given by The Robjohns Bequest': the first five words are printed. The bequest was in 1922.

8. *Biblia* s. xiii med.

A Bible in the order Genesis–4 Kings, 1 Ezra, 2 Ezra (Nehemiah), 1, 2 Chronicles, Prayer of Manasses, Tobit, Judith, Esther, Proverbs–Lamentations, Baruch 1-5, Ezekiel, Daniel, Minor Prophets, Job, 1 Maccabees–Pauline Epistles, Catholic Epistles, Acts, Apocalypse, and as additions by a main hand on f. 299rv, chapter 6 of Baruch and the Epistle to the Laodiceans.

The prologues are 57 of the common set of 64 (cf. below, Liverpool Cathedral 13) and 18 others shown here by *: Stegmüller, nos. 284, 285, 311, 323, 330, 332, 335, 336*, 341 + 343, 457, 468, 482, 487, 491, 492, 494, 495*, 344 + 357 (but in the space left blank between Daniel and Minor Prophets, instead of before Job), 500, 503* + 506*, 510 (. . . continentur), 512 (. . . uerbum dei), 516*, 522*, 525*, 527*, 529*, 532*, 535*, 540*, 544*, 551, 590, 607, 620, 624, 677, and thirteen more as usual to 793 (765 . . . laodicea), 809, 806*, 807*, 818*, 640, 631*, 839; also, as additions by a main hand on ff. 296-9, nos. 462, 456* (as prologue to Song of Songs: ends '. . . nescit se regem') and the common prologues to Minor Prophets, 507, 511, 515, 519 + 517, 524, 526, 528, 531, 534, 538, 539, 543.

Nehemiah ends abruptly at 10: 27, where f. 112v ends; space was left for the rest of the text on f. 113, the first page of a quire written by scribe 3 (see below), but it was never filled. The Psalter is absent. The five sapiential books, Isaiah and Jeremiah have a double numeration of chapters: the modern divisions are in the text and other divisions are shown by red numbers in the margins (Proverbs, 58; Ecclesiastes, 30 (?); Song of Songs, 12; Wisdom, 45; Ecclesiasticus, 127; Isaiah, 203; Jeremiah, 180. Marginalia of s. xiii/xiv are fairly numerous, especially in Pauline Epistles. A note against Laodiceans is in red: 'Hec epistola non est communiter in bibliis. de ipsa tamen mentionem facit in precedenti epistola'. f. 3v blank.

Three recipes in English against swelling and sores were added in s. xiv on f. 299v: *the* is written 'yo'.

ff. iv + 299 + iv. 212 × 150 mm. Written space c. 136 × 90 mm. 2 cols. 28 lines. Collation: $1\text{-}8^{12}$ 9^{16} 10^{14} + three leaves after 14 (ff. 127-9) $11\text{-}12^{16}$ 13^{12} 14^{14} 15^{14} + 1 leaf after 14 (f. 202) 16^{12} 17^{16} $18\text{-}19^{12}$ $20\text{-}21^{14}$ 22^{12} 23 five (ff. 295-9). Written in probably four small and rather poor hands: (1) ff. 1-93v; (2) ff. 94-112v (quire 9 and the last leaves of quire 8) and ff. 130-202v (quires 11-15); (3) ff. 113-129v (quire 10) and ff. 231-99 (quires 18-23); (4) ff. 203-30 (quires 16, 17). Probably scribes 2-4 were working at the same time and leaves were added to quires 10 and 15 to fit in what scribes 2 and 3 had to copy. Initials: (i) red and blue, with ornament of both colours, and in the *F* and *I* on ff. 1, 4, also green; (ii) 3-line, blue with red ornament; (iii) within chapters occasionally, 1-line, blue or red. Capital letters in the ink of the text filled with red. Binding of s. xix. Secundo folio *celis sileam*.

Written in England. Notes in the margins are in English hands. 'Fras. Lucas', s. xvi, and a short erasure, f. 299v. Book-plates of Edward Hailstone (probably lot 305 in his sale at Sotheby's, 23 April 1891) and E. Crawshaw. Bequeathed as MS. 7.

9, 10. *Biblia* s. xiii²

1. vol. 1, ff. 1–343v; vol. 2, ff. 1–348v A 2-volume Bible with the usual contents, except that Baruch was originally absent, and in the usual order: see below Liverpool Cathedral 13. Baruch was added by another hand after art. 2 (ff. 413–16) and 'Require librum baruc in fine istius biblie post interpretaciones' was written after Lamentations.

The prologues are all but five of the common set of 64 (all but 341 + 343 to Esther, 491 (Baruch), 513 to Amos and 589 to Matthew), together with five others, Stegmüller, nos. 326 (to 1 Chronicles, added in s. xv), 349 to Job after 517, 414 and 430 to Psalms and 669+ 'Romani namque tam infirmi . . . suscepistis' to Romans before 677. The second and third words of 430 are 'remedii dum' instead of 'rome dudum' and 640 begins 'Lucas antiocensis natione titus cuius laus . . .'! The letter to Desiderius, 285, is run together with the general prologue 284.

1 Chronicles, Psalms, and Proverbs begin on new quires (19^1, 27^1, and 30^1) with blank spaces before them or (f. 344rv of vol. 1) a blank leaf. Proverbs begins vol. 2. The Pauline and Catholic Epistles were marked for lections in s. xiv.

2. vol. 2, ff. 349–411v Hee sunt interpretaciones nominum hebraicorum. Aaz apprehendens . . . consiliatores eorum.

The usual dictionary of Hebrew names. f. 412rv blank.

3. vol. 1, f. iv Notes added in s. xiv begin 'Considerandum est quod materia confessionum est peccatum . . .'.

4. vol. 1 f. vrv A list of books of the Bible and the number of chapters in each book, s. xiv in., and (added rather later) leaf numbers.

ff. vii + 344 + i in vol. 1, foliated (i–vii) 1–345. ff. iii + 416 + i in vol. 2. Vol. 1, ff. iv, v are medieval flyleaves: see above, arts. 3, 4. A faulty medieval foliation begins with 1 on f. 1 of vol. 1 and runs through to the end of art. 1: the last legible number is '682' on f. 337 of vol. 2. 174 × 120 mm. Written space 111 × 76 mm. 2 cols. 36–8 lines. Collation: 1^{14} 2^{10} $3\text{–}25^{12}$ 26^8 $27\text{–}29^{12}$ (vol. 1, ff. 309–44) $30\text{–}52^{12}$ 53^{10} $54\text{–}61^{12}$ $62\text{–}63^{10}$ 64^8 65^4. *Ad hoc* pencil signatures. Written in a clear hand, larger than is usual in this size of bible. Initials: (i) in colours on gold grounds, historiated (vol. 1, f. 1 only: Jerome at his desk) or decorated (vol. 1, f. 5 only); (ii, iii) of books, 8-line and of prologues, 5-line, blue and red with ornament of both colours; (iv) of chapters and psalm-verses, 2-line, red or blue with ornament of the other colour. Capital letters in the ink of the text filled with red. Germanic bindings of wooden boards covered with brown leather, s. xvi, rebacked: a border roll dated 1557, NP 34 in Haebler, i. 339, encloses a panel containing a centrepiece and anglepieces: the roll was used by a binder at Groningen, Holland (see Kluyver in *Het Boek*, xi. 4). Secundo folio *per quam sunt* (vol. 1); *inferos* (vol. 2).

Written in the Low Countries (?). Sale of the Duke of Sassano Serra, London, 5 February 1828, lot 5, to Frederic Madden, Deputy Keeper of Manuscripts in the British Museum, as

Madden noted at the beginning of vol. 1: in his diary entry for this day (Oxford, Bodleian, Eng. hist. c. 147) he mentions having bought 'a very capital Latin vulgate of beginning of xiv cent. in two vols. for 1.15.0'. Bequeathed as MS. 7.

11A + B. *Gilbertus Porretanus, In Psalterium* s. xii^2

(11A, f. 1) Cristus integer caput cum membris . . . singulariter in libro psalmorum. (f. 1^v) Beatus uir. Huic psalmo non est ausus hesdras apponere titulum . . . ita conclusit omnis spiritus laudet dominum.

Stegmüller, no. 2511. The author died in 1154. f. 1^r of 11A is hardly legible. Sixteen leaves went astray before the rest were put into binding. Fourteen of them, now 11B, were found among the effects of the late P. L. Muschamp and were acquired by the University Library in November 1965: for their places in 11A, see below. The two still missing leaves are from the commentary on Ps. 118. f. 139^v is blank.

ff. iii + 139 + iii in 11A. ff. i + 14 + i in 11B. 320 × 235 mm (11B). 295 × 220 mm (11A).[1] Written space 235 × 170 mm and on leaves in long lines 235 × 100 mm. 2 cols. and (11A, ff. 1–29, 128–39, 11B, ff. 1, 10^v–14) long lines: the 2-column part begins on the first leaf of quire 5 (f. 30) and continues as far as the recto of the third leaf of quire 18 (11B, f. 10). 42 lines. In the part in long lines one of the side margins is 70 mm wide and has a pair of vertical lines ruled down it: from 11B, f. 10^v, every horizontal line, from 11B, f. 12, every second horizontal line, and from 11A, f. 134^v, every fifth horizontal line is prolonged across this margin. Collation: 1^8 (ff. 1–7, 11B, f. 1) 2^8 3^6 $4\text{–}5^8$ 6^{10} $7\text{–}15^8$ 16^8 wants 4, 5 (11B, ff. 2–7) 17^8 (ff. 120–7) 18^4 (11B, ff. 8–11) 19^8 (11B, f. 12, ff. 128–33, 11B, f. 13) 20^8 wants 8, blank (11B, f. 14, ff. 134–9).

Written, f. 30 apart, in three hands, probably: (1) ff. 1–29^v, 128–133^v, and 11B, ff. 1^{rv}, 12–13^v; (2) ff. 31–55^v, 88–127^v, 134–9 and 11B, ff. 2–11^v, 14^{rv}; (3) ff. 56–87^v (quires 8–11). f. 30, the first leaf of quire 5, is in three hands which do not occur elsewhere. Initials: (i) ff. 1^{rv}, 14, red and blue, with ornament of both colours; (ii) 2–4 line, red, blue or green, with ornament in one or two of the other colours. 11A was bound in s. xix/xx and 11B in 1966. Secundo folio *ab uno*.

Written in England. 11A was bequeathed by James Johnson in 1929. For 11B see above.

12. *Horae* s. xiv ex.

1. ff. 1–12^v Calendar in red and black.

Entries in red include 'Amandi episcopi', 'Baselii episcopi', 'Remigi et bauo', 'Donaciani episcopi' (6 Feb., 14 June, 1, 14 Oct.). 'Visitacio marie' in black, 2 July (other feasts of B.V.M. are in red).

2. ff. 13–18 Hours of the Cross . . . Patris sapiencia . . . f. 18^v blank.

3. ff. 19–38 Incipit missa beate Marie uirginis. Introibo . . . f. 38^v blank.

4. ff. 39–110^v Incipiunt hore beate marie uirginis secundum usum romane ecclesie.

[1] This is a good example of the large amount of margin a binder may cut off.

5. ff. 112–137^v Penitential psalms and (f. 131^v) litany.

Martial last of apostles. Eight martyrs. Eight confessors. Twenty-four virgins: . . . (13–16) gertrudis phitildis walburgis genouefa.

6. ff. 139–66 Office of the dead. f. 166^v blank.

7. Blank spaces after arts. 4, 5 (ff. 111^{rv}, 137^v–138^v) contain prayers to follow the litany written in brown ink in a small clear hand.

ff. iii + 166 + iii. 72 × 50 mm. Written space 42 × 30 mm. 10 long lines. Collation: 1–2^6 3–10^8 11^6 + 1 leaf after 1 (f. 78) 12–21^8 22^4 wants 4, probably blank. Initials: (i) beginning arts. 2–6, blue or pink patterned in white, on grounds of decorated gold: damaged borders; (ii, iii) 3-line and 2-line, gold on grounds of blue and pink patterned in white; (iv) 1-line, blue with red ornament or gold with blue-grey ornament. Green morocco binding, s. xviii. Secundo folio *cem tuam* (f. 14).

Written probably in Flanders: cf. art. 1. The leather book-plate of E(dward) H(ailstone) is inside the cover: not identified in his sale, 23 April 1891. Bequeathed as MS. 7.

13. *Horae* s. xv^2

1. ff. 1–12^v Calendar in red and black.

Feasts in red include 'Sancti zenis (*sic*) episcopi et confessoris', 'Sancti zenonis episcopi et confessoris', 'Visitacio uirginis marie', 'Conceptio virginis marie et sancti zenonis episcopi et confessoris' (12 April, 21 May, 2 July, 8 Dec.).

2. ff. 13–107 Incipit officium beate marie uirginis secundum consuetudinem romane curie.

3. ff. 107–12 Incipit officium sanctissime crucis compositum a summo pontifice domino iohanne papa uigesimo secundo. et concessit omnibus fideliter dicentibus centum dies indulgencie . . . Hymnus. Patris sapiencia . . .

4. ff. 113–41 Penitential psalms, beginning imperfectly, and (f. 127^v) litany.

Eighteen confessors and doctors: (7–9) nicholae zeno theodore. ff. 141^v–142^v blank.

5. ff. 143–202 Incipit officium defunctorum. f. 202^v blank.

ff. ii + 202 + i. 98 × 70 mm. Written space 55 × 40 mm. 13 long lines. Collation: 1^{12} + a blank leaf inserted after 12 2–10^{10} 11^{10} wants 10, probably blank, 12^{10} wants 1 before f. 113 13^{10} 14^{10} + a blank leaf, f. 142, inserted after 10 15–20^{10}. Initials: (i) ff. 14, 143, in colours on gold grounds, historiated (B.V.M. and Child; skull); (ii) as (i), but decorated instead of historiated; (iii) 2-line, red or blue with ornament in pale red (?); (iv) 1-line, red or blue. Continuous borders framed in gold on ff. 14, 143. Binding of s. xix.

Written in Italy, for use in the diocese of Verona, where Zeno, †371, was bishop. An armorial shield within a wreath in the lower border of f. 14. Bequeathed as MS. 7.

14. *Horae* s. xv/xvi

1. ff. 2–7v Full calendar in French in gold, blue, and dark red, the two colours alternating. Geneviève and Denis in gold.

2. ff. 9–10v Sequentiae of the Gospels.

3. ff. 10v–12 Oroison de nostre dame. Obsecro te . . . Masculine forms.

4. ff. 12v–13v O intemerata . . . orbis terrarum. De te enim . . .

5. ff. 14–32v Hours of B.V.M. of the use of (Paris).

6. ff. 34–40v Penitential psalms and (f. 38) litany.

Twenty confessors: . . . (5) marcialis . . . (14–20) guinale yuo patrici alexis germane marcelle bernardine.

7. ff. 40v–41 Hours 'de la croix'.

8. ff. 41v, 43–4 Hours 'du saint esperit'.

9. ff. 44–60v Office of the dead.

10. ff. 60v–64v Memoriae of Michael and all angels, John Baptist, John Evangelist, Peter, Paul, James, James and Philip, Bartholomew, Thomas, Andrew, Matthew, Mark, Simon and Jude, Matthias, Barnabas, Christopher, Sebastian, Germanus (Aue presul gloriose aue sydus iam celeste . . . : cf. *RH*, no. 2054), Laurence, Genovefa. Cf. art. 28.

11. f. 65 Hymns, Christe qui lux es and Vexilla regis.

12. ff. 65v–66 Les viii vers saint bernard.

13. f. 66rv Prayers: (*a*) Anima cristi . . . ; (*b*) Domine ihesu criste qui hanc sacratissimam carnem . . . ; (*c*) Domine ihesu criste redemptor mundi defende me . . . ; (*d*) Domine ihesu criste fili dei viui. redemptor mundi pius et misericors . . . Te laudo . . .

14. ff. 67–68v Passio . . . secundum iohannem. In illo tempore. Apprehendit pilatus . . . testimonium eius.

John 19: 1–35, abbreviated, followed by the prayers 'Deus qui manus tuas . . .' and 'Deus qui voluisti pro redemptione mundi . . .'.

15. ff. 68v–69v Versus que sequuntur (*sic*) Domine non secundum peccata mea . . .

16. ff. 69v–71 Devotions to B.V.M.: (*a*) De beata maria prosa. Gaude virgo mater cristi. Que per aurem concepisti . . . ; (*b*) De beata maria oratio. Per te

accessum habemus . . . ; (*c*) De beata maria oratio. O domina glorie. regina leticie . . . ; (*d*) Alia oratio. Gaude dei genitrix uirgo immaculata . . .

17. ff. 71–2 Septem peticiones ad dominum. Domine ihesu criste qui septem uerba . . .

18. ff. 72–3 Oratio ad dominum. Deus propicius esto michi peccatori . . .

19. f. 73^{rv} Quinque adorationes ad dominum. Domine ihesu criste adoro te in cruce pendentem . . .

20. ff. 73^{v}–74^{v} Orationes ad sumendum corpus domini. O salutaris hostia que celi pandis hostium . . . (*RH*, no. 13680: other prayers follow).

21. f. 74^{v} Oratio s. augustini. Gracias ago tibi domine qui me dignatus es . . .

22. f. 74^{v} Quando fueris excitatus a sompno. Excita domine potenciam tuam . . .

23. f. 75 Oratio deuota sancti augustini. Domine ihesu criste uerbum patris qui uenisti . . .

24. ff. 75^{v}–76 Pro defunctis antiphona. Auete omnes anime fideles . . .

25. f. 76^{rv} Quinque salutaciones ad dominum. Aue domine ihesu criste uerbum patris . . .

26. Prayers: (*a*) f. 76^{v} In eleuatione corporis et sanguinis. Aue uerum corpus natum . . . ; (*b*) f. 76^{v} Alia oratio ad dominum. Aue principium mee creationis . . . ; (*c*) f. 76^{v} Salue lux mundi uerbum patris . . . ; (*d*) ff. 76^{v}–77 In eleuatione sanguinis domini. Aue sanguis sanctissime . . . ; (*e*) f. 77 Aue sanguis. aue uita . . . ; (*f*) f. 77 Alia oratio. Domine ihesu criste rogo te amore illius gaudii . . . ; (*g*) f. 77^{rv} O passio magna. o profunda uulnera . . .

27. ff. 77^{v}–80^{v} Oratio sancti petri de lucembourc. Deus pater qui creasti . . . *RH*, no. 4477. Thirty-five 4-line stanzas.

28. ff. 80^{v}–88 Memoriae of B.V.M., Innocents, Stephen, Lazarus, Vincent, Denis, Eustace 'cum sociis suis', Blaise (Aue presul honestatis . . . : *RH*, no. 2056), Gregory, Jerome, Nicholas, Claude, Bernard, Louis (Lilium uirginitatis. regale signaculum . . . : not in *RH*), Anthony of Padua, Maur, Mary Magdalene, Katherine (Aue uirgo speciosa clarior syderibus . . . : *RH*, no. 2253), Barbara (Aue trini lucifera . . . : *RH*, no. 23902), Margaret, De sanctis priuilegiatis, All Saints, 'Des cinq sains martirs priuilegiez' (Denis, George, Christopher, Blaise, Giles, beginning 'O dionisi radius . . .': *RH*, no. 4707), 'Des cinq saintes priuilegiees' (Katherine, Margaret, Martha, Christina, Barbara, beginning 'Katherine tirannum . . . : *RH*, no. 2691), Cosmas and Damian, Martin, Ama 'virgo et martir'.

A leaf is missing after f. 86 (All Saints).

ff. ii + 88 + iii. f. 89 is a parchment flyleaf. 146 × 105 mm. Written space 97 × 67 mm. 26–7 long lines. Collation: 1^6 $2\text{–}10^8$ 11^8 wants 5 after f. 86 and 8 after f. 88, together with four inserted singletons (see below). Written in *lettre bâtarde*. The four full-page pictures are probably of s. xvii, ff. 1^v, 8^v, 33^v, 42^v: rectos blank. Two nearly full-page pictures in rectangular frames before arts. 5 and 13 (Christ carrying the Cross). Initials: (i) blue and gold with ornament in red and blue-grey; (ii, iii) 2-line and 1-line, blue or dark red. English red morocco binding, s. xviii.

Written in France. Armorial book-plate of John Lewis Petit: not identified in his sale, 6 February 1786. Given as MS. 7.

15. *Horae (in Netherlandish)* s. xv in.

1. ff. 1–12^v Full calendar in red and black.

2. ff. 13^v–60^v Hier begint onser lieuer vrouwen marien getide in duutsche.

Use of (Utrecht). The first and one other leaf missing. The translation of Salve regina at the end (f. 60^{rv}). f. 13^{rv} blank, except for the title of art. 2 in red at the foot of the verso: the titles of arts. 3–6 are similarly placed on otherwise blank pages.

3. ff. 61^v–88 Hier beghint dat getide van det ewigher wijsheit.

The first leaf missing. f. 61^r blank.

4. ff. 88^v–119 Hier beghint dat lange cruce getide. f. 119^v blank.

5. ff. 120^v–141^v Hier beghint dat getide van den heilighen gheest.

The first leaf missing. f. 120^r blank.

6. ff. 142^v–164^v Hier beghint die souen psalmen van penitencien.

The first leaf and the last missing. Litany, f. 153^v. Forty-one confessors: (18, 19) Bauo Willibrort. f. 142^r blank.

7. ff. 165–205^v Office of the dead, ending imperfectly.

ff. v + 205 + iii. f. v is a medieval parchment flyleaf. 118 × 85 mm. Written space 75 × 50 mm. 17 long lines. Collation: 1^8 wants 1–3 2^8 (ff. 6–13) 3^{10} wants 1 and 10 (ff. 14–21) $4\text{–}6^{10}$ 7^8 8^{10} wants 3 after f. 61 $9\text{–}12^{10}$ 13^{12} 14^{10} wants 1 before f. 121 15^{10} 16^{12} wants 4 after f. 142 17^{10} 18^{10} wants 5 after f. 164 19^8 $20\text{–}21^{10}$ 22^8. Initials: (i) ff. 89, 165, blue or blue and red patterned in white, with red, gold, and green ornament; (ii) 3-line, blue with red ornament or red with violet ornament; (iii, iv) 2-line and 1-line, blue or red. Capital letters in the ink of the text marked with red. Borders on ff. 89, 165. Rebound in 1972 (?). Secundo folio (f. 14) *sijn want.*

Written in the Low Countries. Bequeathed as MS. 7.

17. *Graduale* s. xv²

1 (quires 1–11). ff. 1–82ᵛ Ad te leuaui . . . a morte suscitari. Alleluia.

Temporal from Advent to Easter Eve.

2. ff. 83–100ᵛ Resurrexi et adhuc tecum . . .

Temporal from Easter to octave of Pentecost.

3. ff. 101–114ᵛ Offices for Trinity, Corpus Christi, Holy Cross, 'De lancea domini', B.V.M., Eternal Wisdom, 'Pro pestilencia', 'In anniuersario seu commemoracione defunctorum', 'In die deposicionis et in exequiis defunctorum', 'In dedicacione ecclesie', 'In dedicacione altaris' and (perhaps as an addition) 'In festo sanctissimi Nominis iesus'.

4 (quires 16, 17). ff. 115–131ᵛ Kyries, Gloria, Credo in unum deum, Sanctus, Asperges me.

5 (quires 18, 19). ff. 132–147ᵛ Domine in tua misericordia . . .

Temporal from the first Sunday after the octave of Pentecost.

6. ff. 148–169ᵛ Sanctoral, beginning with Andrew.

The proper offices are of Andrew, Thomas apostle, Paul first hermit, Joseph, Paul, Purification of B.V.M., Chair of Peter, Annunciation of B.V.M., Philip and James, Achilleus and Pancras, Gervase and Protase, John Baptist, Peter and Paul, Anne, Laurence, Assumption and Nativity of B.V.M., Michael, Martin. Cues for the feast of Relics between Septem Fratres and Benedict (so 10 or 11 July), Magdelberta (7 Sept.), Ludger and his translation (26 Mar., 27 Apr., 3 Oct.). Additions were made in s. xvii, for example, f. 154ᵛ (Joseph), f. 163 (Joachim).

7. ff. 169ᵛ–201ᵛ Incipit commune sanctorum.

Additions in the space at the end of the quire include: f. 202ᵛ, a mass of St Anne; f. 203, Aue verum corpus natum . . . (*RH*, no. 2175); f. 203ᵛ, a table of arts. 8, 9.

8 (quires 27–34). ff. 204–61 Noted sequences for the year from Christmas (Grates nunc omnes reddamus domino . . .), for the common of saints, and the dedication of a church.

Includes Alme confessor et professor for Anthony hermit, Hodierne festum lucis for Holy Lance, Inclite psallamus omnes for Ludger, Aue verbi dei parens for Visitation of B.V.M., Cleri decantet concio for translation of Ludger, and Celi enarrant gloria for 'In divisione apostolorum' (*RH*, nos. 833, 7944, 8837, 2165, 3398, 3488).

9. A supplement to art. 8 in the same hand in the space remaining blank at the end of quire 34: (*a*) f. 261 De sancto paulo si est patronus in commemmoracione.

Sancte paule merita tua colentes . . . ; (*b*) f. 261v Laudes deo dicat per omnia . . . , for the Transfiguration, ending imperfectly.

RH, nos. 18493, 10372.

10. ff. 262–5 Four paper leaves added in s. xvii contain offices of (*a*) Joachim, (*b*) Joseph, (*c*) the Transfiguration, (*d*) 'In festo sancti Iosephi Calasanctii confessoris' (†1648), (*e*) on the sixth Sunday after Pentecost 'Missa in festo S. Iosephi Sponsi B.M.V. Confessoris', and (*f*) 'Die 20ti Iulii in festo s. Hieronymi Aemiliani confessoris (†1537) duplex minus'.

ff. ii + 265 + ii. Medieval foliation in red i–clxxv on ff. 1–114, 132–202. 285 × 202 mm. Written space 240 × 155 mm. 10 long lines and music. Black ink. Collation: $1–2^8$ 3 eight $4–10^8$ 11 two (ff. 81, 82) $12–16^8$ 17^8 + 1 leaf after 8 (f. 131) $18–32^8$ 33^6 34^6 wants 5, 6 after f. 261 35^4 + 1 leaf after 4 (f. 265). A new hand begins at art. 8. Initials: (i) ff. 1, 83 on gold (?) grounds decorated with green and pink; (ii) f. 204, 4-line, red and blue, with violet ornament; (iii, iv) 2-line and 1-line, blue or red. Cadels and capital letters in the ink of the text lined with red. Binding of s. xix. The metal clasps and corner-pieces of an older binding have been preserved: the latter are inscribed 'aue maria gracia plena'. Secundo folio *Populus.*

Written in Germany for use in the diocese of Münster, Westphalia. 'Pet Br M *par* a', f. 203, s. xvii. Given as MS. 7.

18. *Antiphonale* s. xvi in.

The spring volume of an antiphonal. The title on the spine, s. xviii (?), is 'LXXa vsque ad pascha'.

1. ff. 6–185 Temporal, Septuagesima–Easter. ff. 5rv, 185v blank.

2. ff. 186–279v Sanctoral: f. 186 Agnes (21 Jan.); f. 209 Purification of B.V.M. (2 Feb.); f. 239 Agatha (5 Feb.); f. 261 Annunciation of B.V.M. (25 Mar.)

3. ff. 280–288v Three sets of monastic canticles: f. 280, for Sundays, Domine miserere nostri, Audite qui longe, Miserere domine plebi; f. 282v, 'In purificatione', Populus qui ambulabat, Letare iherusalem, Urbs fortitudinis; f. 286, for the common of virgins, Audite me diuini, Gaudens gaudebo, Non vocaberis.

See Mearns, *Canticles*, pp. 87, 92.

4 (added). (*a*) f. 1 Feria quinta ad magnificat antiphona. Domine non sum dignus . . . (*b*) f. 2 In principio et ante secula . . . (*c*) ff. 2v, 4rv Magi uiderunt stellam . . . (*ends imperfectly*). (*d*) f. 3rv Commemoratio scolastice. virginis (10 Feb.) ad vesperas antiphona. Quinque prudentes virgines . . .

(*a*). s. xviii, on a paper leaf. (*b*–*d*). s. xvi in.

5. The pastedown and flyleaf at each end are a bifolium of a well-written French (?) gradual, s. xii/xiii: f. i^{rv} Septuagesima and Sexagesima Sundays; pastedown in front, verso, Friday in the first week of Lent and the first Sunday in Lent; f. 290^{rv} and pastedown at the end, recto, Friday in Easter week to the first Sunday after Easter.

Written space 255 × *c.*170 mm. 10 long lines and music. As *Missale Romanum*, i. 43–4, 53–6, 221–3, except that the versicle before the offertory on Friday after Easter is In die resurrectionis, not Dicite in nationibus.

ff. i + 288 + ii. For ff. i, 290 see above, art. 5. f. 289 is a blank flyleaf. 280 × 195 mm. Written space 230 × 135 mm. 2 cols. 7 long lines and music (arts. 1, 2) and 17 long lines (art. 3). Collation of ff. 5–288: 1^8 2^8 + 1 leaf after 8 (f. 21) 3^6 + 1 leaf after 6 (f. 28) 4–22^8 23^{10} 24–32^8 33^{10} 34^8. A large hand and black ink: letters about 7 mm high: flex punctuation in art. 3. Clumsy metallic red initials. Capital letters in the ink of the text lined with yellow. Binding of wooden boards covered with leather bearing a floral roll and a crested roll, s. xvi: five bosses on each cover: metal corner-pieces: metal strips, two on each cover, project below the tail: two straps fasten to pins on the front cover.

Written in the Low Countries (?), for monastic (Cistercian) use.[1] Given as MS. 7.

20. *Horae* s. xv^2

Mutilated for the sake of its pictures. Arts. 2, 4–9, 11 are imperfect at the beginning.

1. ff. 1–12^v Full calendar in French, in red and black.

'S' Fremy' and 'S' Fulcien' (*sic*) in red (25 Sept., 10 Dec.).

2. ff. 13–17^v Sequentiae of the Gospels.

'Protector in te sperancium . . .' after St John.

3. ff. 17^v–20^v Deuota oracio beate marie. Obsecro te . . . Ends imperfectly. Masculine forms.

4. ff. 21–23^v (O intemerata . . .).

5. ff. 24–68^v Hours of B.V.M. of the use of (Paris). Nine leaves missing.

6. ff. 69–85^v Penitential psalms and (f. 81) litany.

Ten confessors: . . . (8–10) anthoni ludouice dominice.

[1] In a letter of 28 March 1958, Father J. Morson O.C.R. pointed out to me Cistercian features of this antiphonal: (Purification) the antiphon Salue regina for Magnificat at 1st vespers and the hymn at terce O quam glorifica; (Agnes) hymn at vespers Agnes beate virginis (*RH*, no. 735); (Agatha) hymn at vespers Agathe sacre virginis (*RH*, no. 716).

7. ff. 86–88^{v} De sancta cruce.

8. ff. 89–91^{v} De sancto spiritu.

9. ff. 92–138^{v} Office of the dead.

10. ff. 138–143^{v} Doulce dame de misericorde . . .

The Fifteen Joys of B.V.M., ending imperfectly. Sonet, no. 458.

11. ff. 144–146^{v} The Seven Requests, in French, beginning imperfectly. Sonet, no. 504.

12. f. 146^{v} Sainte uraye croix aouree . . . Sonet, no. 1876.

13. ff. 146^{v}–148^{v} Memoriae: Trinity; Michael; John Baptist, ending imperfectly; Anne.

14 (added). f. 149^{rv} Salve Regina and Regina celi letare, the former beginning imperfectly. f. 150^{rv} blank.

ff. i + 150 + i. 158 × 110 mm. Written space 85 × 58 mm. 15 long lines. Collation: twenty-two quires, 1^{12}, 3 four (ff. 20–3), 10^{6} wants 1, 5, 6 (ff. 66–8), 13^{6} wants 3 after f. 85, 22 two (ff. 149, 150), the rest regular eights, but now lacking twelve leaves, 2^{1} before f. 13, 4^{1} before f. 24, 6^{8} after f. 45, 7^{4} after f. 48, 8^{2} after f. 53, 8^{6} after f. 56, 9^{2} after f. 59, 11^{1} before f. 69, 14^{1} before f. 89, 14^{5} after f. 91, 21^{2} after f. 143, and 21^{8} after f. 148. Thirteen or fourteen pictures once probably, but only one now remains, 11-line, before lauds in art. 5 (f. 34). Initials: (i) blue or pink patterned in white on gold grounds, all removed, except ff. 17^{v}, 34, 138^{v}; (ii, iii) 2-line and 1-line, gold on blue and pink grounds, patterned in white. Line fillers in red, blue, and gold. Floral borders: continuous on f. 34; on three sides of ff. 17^{v}, 138^{v}; the height of the written space in the outer margin of all other pages: versos are usually 'mirror images' of rectos. Purple velvet binding, s. xviii. Secundo folio (f. 13) *ex sanguinibus*.

Written in France. Art. 1 suggests Amiens. Erasures on f. 1. Given as MS. 7.

21. *Devotions and prayers (in Netherlandish)* s. xv/xvi

Many pieces here occur also in Leyden, University Library, Ltk. 321, from the nunnery of IJsselstreek, described by Lieftinck, *Maatschappij*, pp. 150–3.

1. ff. 3–10 O allmechtige ewige god gloriose weerde . . .

Hours of the Holy Trinity, as Ltk. 321, f. 44.

2. ff. 10–16^{v} Ic bid u lieue mynliche ihesus . . .

A 'Dornencroen' to Christ Crucified.

3. ff. 17–18 Prayer of St Gregory, as Ltk. 321, f. 15^{v}.

4. f. 18^{rv} Op die penetencie en gebet. O lieue heer hemelsche vader . . . As Ltk. 321, f. 43.

5. ff. 20–6 Salutations to the Five Wounds, beginning 'O gi costelicke wonden'. Illustrated by a coloured woodcut of the Wounds and Instruments of the Passion on an inserted leaf (f. 19^{v}: 19^{r} blank).

6. ff. 26–29^{v}, 32–33^{v} Hier begint dat auentmael. Voer den hoechtijt van paesschen wiste ihesus . . . St John 13, 14.

7. ff. 33^{v}–42^{v} The Passion according to St John (18, 19), preceded by six lines of Latin, 'O crux aue spes unica . . .'.

8. ff. 45–48^{v} Ic aenbede O alre saechtmoedichste heer . . .

The seven 'bloetstoringe'.

9. Prayers at mass: (*a*) ff. 49–52^{v} O ouerste priester . . . ; (*b*) f. 52^{v} O suete milde bermhertige vader ic aenbede dijn edel . . . ; (*c*) f. 54 O alre suetste heer dien ic begeer . . . ; (*d*) f. 55 O du suete gast mijnre sielen ende alre liefste lief . . . ; (*e*) f. 55^{v} O lieue heer suete mijnlicke vader . . . ; (*f*) f. 56 Ic bid di O edel coningynne maria . . . ; (*g*) f. 56^{v} Weest wilcom mijn heer . . . ; (*h*) f. 57 O lieue heer ihesus cristus lof dy . . . ; (*i*) f. 58^{v} O lieue heer ihesus cristus ic danc di . . . ; (*j*) f. 59 Weest gegruet alre sueste spise . . . ; (*k*) f. 60^{v} O almechtige ewige god want ic di nu ontfangen heb . . . ; (*l*) f. 61^{v} O alre suetste ihesu O alre mijnlicste mijnner O alre genaedichste vader . . . ; (*m*) f. 62 O eeweerdige moeder gods . . .

(*b–f*) are headed 'voer die ontfenckenisse' and (*g–m*) 'naeder ontfenckenisse'.

10. f. 63^{rv} The seven 'Gloria Patri'. Cf. Ltk. 321, f. 219.

11. ff. 64–74 Mijn siele gebenedijt den heer . . . O lieue heer ihesu cristi. ic doe di danckberen lof . . . Pater noster. O lieue heer ihesu cristi ewige sueticheit . . . The Fifteen Oes of St Bridget.

12. (*a*) f. 74^{rv} Dese gebeden salmen voer die cribbe lesen . . . Mijn heer ende mijn god . . . (*b*) f. 74^{v} Berna(r)dus voer die cribben. Weest gegruet throen . . . (*c*) ff. 74^{v}–75^{v} Weest gegruet du cleyn kyndeken . . . (*d*) ff. 75^{v}–76 Tot onser vrouwen . . . Verblijt di keyserlicke moeder . . . (*e*) f. 76 Van onser vrouwen. O du hoge steern der see . . .

(*a–d*). Ltk. 321, ff. 40^{v}–42.

13. ff. 76–79^{v} Heer du salste opdoen . . . Hours of the Cross.

14. (*a*) ff. 80–87ᵛ Den du reyne ioncfrouwe van herten . . . (*b*) ff. 87ᵛ–90 Dese aue maria leerden onse lieue vrouwe enen clerck . . . O maria hemelsche conigynne die ierste twee . . .

(*a*). Five tens, four of them ending with a prayer 'Ghegruet sijstu maria . . .'.

15. ff. 90–112ᵛ Dit is onsen vrouwen salter van den leuen ons heren. O eerweerdige ende hoge onscheidelicre drieuoldicheit . . .

Three 'rosencransen'. Cf. Ltk. 321, f. 84ᵛ.

16. ff. 133–147ᵛ, 30–31ᵛ, 148–171ᵛ Hier begint onser vrouwen psalter. Heer doet op mijnen mont . . .

Divided into nocturns. Pss. 1, 2 were on a leaf missing after f. 114.

17. ff. 171ᵛ–178 Die letanien.

Litanies of B.V.M.

18. Devotions to B.V.M.: (*a*) ff. 178–82 Soe wie dit ghebet alle dage leest . . . O maria een ioncfrouwe alre ioncfrouwen . . . ; (*b*) ff. 182–4 Totten mijnlicken herten onser lieuer vrou (*sic*). O hertelicke ioncfrouwe maria moeder . . . ; (*c*) ff. 184–5 Die selige ioncfrouwe maria heuet . . . Verblijt di bloem der ioncferscap die mit eeren der sunderlingheit . . . ; (*d*) f. 185 Soe wie dit gebet leest . . . Ic gruet v maria een opgewassen lelye . . . ; (*e*) f. 186 Soe wie dit gebet alle dage leest op sijn knyen . . . Coemt ader der genaden . . .

(*a*). The heading conveys an indulgence from Pope Gregory of 100 days of venial and two days of deadly sin. (*c*). According to the heading, the Seven Joys revealed to St Thomas of Canterbury: cf. Ltk. 321, f. 82ᵛ.

19. ff. 186–187ᵛ Dit gebet salmen ducksprecken mit ihesus ende maria gebet. O lieue heer ihesu cristi ic bekenne dat ic des onweerdichi bijn . . .

20. ff. 187ᵛ–190ᵛ Selich sijn alle die . . . God gruet u enyge rose gesproten wtter wortel van yesse . . .

The Five Sorrows of B.V.M., as Ltk. 321, f. 113ᵛ.

21. ff. 190ᵛ–191ᵛ Tot desen drien Aue maria . . . O heilige moeder gods ic biddi want god . . .

22. ff. 191ᵛ–194ᵛ Hier begint dat gebet van acht dagen. Ic bid u O heilige ioncfrouwe sancta maria doer alle die groete gnade . . .

23. ff. 194v–197 Prayers to Sts Giles, Katherine, Barbara, and Agnes: Egidius heilige confessoer cristi . . . ; O alre heilichste katharina . . . O heilige maget sancta barbara . . . ; O onbeulecte lelye des hemelschen paradijs . . .

24. f. 197rv Cruus gods si mit mi + Cruus gods in mijn toeuerlaet . . .

25. ff. 198–202v Hier begint een schoen gebet va(n) den liden ons lieuen heeren . . . O alre bermhertichste . . . As Ltk. 321, f. 28.

26. ff. 202v–204v Four paternosters 'als een mensche op sijn verscheiden leget', for use by nuns, beginning 'In den handen dijnre onuerscheidelicker bermherticheit'. As Ltk. 321, f. 172v.

27. ff. 204v–217 Devotions for the dying and the dead, beginning 'Kerieleyson . . . Gesontmaker der werlt . . .': cf. Ltk. 321, f. 169v.

Includes seven and three paternosters 'om den kerckhof voer die zielen' (f. 207v, as Ltk. 321, f. 175), 'die vier ewangelien voer die zielen' (f. 210), and 'die xv graden voer die zielen' (f. 214v). f. 217v blank.

28. ff. 218–28 Soe wie sancta anna wille eeren . . . Gegruet sijstu heilige vrouwe Anna een eer alre vrouwen een stam der bomen . . .

A 'croen' for Anne, seven sets of salutations, one for each day of the week. Cf. Ltk. 321, f. 126v.

29. ff. 228–233v Hier begint Sancte Anna roesencransken. O heilige moeder Sancte Anna weest ons een ewich triest . . .

The heading conveys an indulgence of 10,000 years. Cf. Ltk. 321, f. 118, ff. 234–235v blank.

30. ff. 1–2 (added early). [E]xurge domine adiuua nos et libera nos . . . collecta. [P]retende domine famulis et famulabus tuis dexteram celestis (*ends abruptly at the foot of f. 2, unless the text continues underneath the woodcut pasted to f. 2v*).

Prayers and cues to psalms. A sentence begins '[S]urgite sancte dei de mansionibus vestris'.

31. f. 236, a binding leaf, is from a manuscript of s. xv, containing prayers of a litany in Latin. Current hand.

ff. iii + 235 + ii. Paper, except the three leaves with initials of type (i) and the binding leaves (ff. ii, 236). For f. 236 see art. 31. 136 × 100 mm. Written space 92 × 67 mm. 19 long lines. Frame ruling in ink. Collation uncertain: mainly eights. The only pictures are inserted coloured cuts: f. iii, adoration of the Child, so probably meant to precede art. 12; pasted to the verso of f. 2, the coronation of St Katherine of Sweden, with printed legend 'S' Katherina de swecia filia S' birgitæ';[1] f. 19^{v}, see above, art. 5. Initials: (i) ff. 34, 64, 80, gold on coloured grounds patterned in white: gold frames and continuous borders; (ii) beginning arts. 1, 5, 9, 15, 18, 19, 28, in gold and colours: part borders; (iii, iv) 2-line and 1-line, blue or red. Capital letters in the ink of the text touched with red. English binding of s. xix, labelled 'Missal'. Secundo folio (f. 4) *suete*.

Written in the Low Countries for use in a nunnery. 'Mary Anne Fraser November 1st 1831 '—to Edward Hornor 1840'', f. i. Given as MS. 7.

22. *Horae (in Netherlandish)* s. xv^{2}

1. ff. 1–12^{v} Full calendar in red and black.

Utrecht saints in red include 'Ieroen martir', 17 Aug. 'Onse vrou' in red, 2 July.

2. ff. 13–40^{v} Hier begint die vrouwe ghetide.

Use of (Utrecht).

3. ff. 42–53^{v} Hier beghint die seuen salm Dauid.

Penitential psalms and (f. 49^{v}) litany. Fifteen confessors: . . . (3) Williboert.

4. ff. 54–58^{v} Hours of the Cross. One leaf missing.

5. ff. 60–72^{v} Hier beginnen die vigilien iii lessen. Mi hebben ombefangen . . .

Office of the dead, ending imperfectly.

6. f. 73^{rv} Memoriae of B.V.M., 'Ghegroet sijstu coninginne der ontfermherticheit des leuens . . .', and apostles.

ff. i + 73 + i. 188 × 125 mm. Written space 95 × 71 mm. 19 long lines. Collation (excluding ff. 41, 59): 1–6^{6} 7^{4} (ff. 37–40) 8–9^{6} 10^{6} wants 5 after f. 57 11–12^{6} 13 two (ff. 72, 73, a bifolium). Two full page pictures on versos of inserted leaves, the rectos blank: f. 41^{v} Christ carrying the Cross; f. 59^{v} Christ rising from the Tomb. Initials: (i, ii) gold on coloured grounds: the larger, beginning arts. 2–5, have floral borders, each containing a peacock, on three sides; (iii, iv) 2-line and 1-line, red or blue (blue with red ornament on ff. 72–73^{v}). Contemporary binding of brown stamped leather over wooden boards: on each cover a pineapple stamp within a central lozenge is surrounded by small stamps of four patterns.

Written in the Low Countries (Holland). Given as MS. 7.

30. *Historica quaedam (partly in French)* s. xv^{1}

A single quire, probably taken from a larger manuscript. The notice of it in the *Leicester Daily Post*, 15 March 1915, is pasted to f. ii. Arts. 1–3 are in B.L., Royal 20 D. x, arts. 3, 6, 7.

[1] Apparently as W. L. Schreiber, *Handbuch der Holz- und Metallschnitte des XV Jahrhunderts*, ii, 1927, no. 1347.

1. ff. 1–5 Six documents of the years 1362–5 concerning the Black Prince's principality of Aquitaine: (*a*) A Regali solio velut a sole . . . , 19 July 1362; (*b*) Combien que au iour present nous auions donnez . . . , 19 July 1362; (*c*) Inspeximus quasdam litteras patentes carissimi primogeniti . . . , 20 July 1362; (*d*) Vt licium et causarum continuata . . . , 23 May 1365; (*e*) Come pur certains que a ce nous ont meuz . . . , 19 July 1362; (*f*) Come nous auons a receuoir les homages . . . , 10 July 1362.

(*a–f*). *Foedera*, ed. 1816–30, iii (2), 667, 669, 668, 766, 668, 665.

2. ff. 5v–11 Seven documents concerning English rights in Gascony: (*a*) Nouerunt vniuersi presentes . . . , 22 April 1292; (*b*) Cum Regalis celsitudo viros clare propaginis . . . , 1 Nov. 1292; (*c*) Pridem volentes pro nobis . . . , 1 Feb. 1362/3; (*d*) De vestris legalitate circumspeccione . . . , 8 Feb. 1362/3; (*e*) Alia Commissio, 8 Feb. 1362/3; (*f*) Sciant . . . quod pridem internis . . . , 1 Mar. 1362/3; (*g*) Qualiter predictus Rex Castelle fecit alligancias predictas . . . (6 lines).

(*a–f*). Op. cit. i. 300, 310; iii (2), 686, 688, 688, 690.

3. ff. 11v–15v The treaty of Berwick on Tweed, 3 Oct. 1357 in French (*Foedera*, iii (1), 372), followed by a memorandum about Scotch hostages 'in quorum custodia sunt'.

4. ff. 15v–16v Post obitum Alexandri regis Scocie . . . qualiter concordat psalterium cum cithara.

An outline of events connected with the English claim to Scotland from the treaty of Norham in 1291 to 1357.

ff. vi + 16 + vi. 290 × 210 mm. Written space 190 × 128 mm. *c.*40 long lines. One quire. Written in a good rather upright secretary. Elaborate and skilful penwork initials tinted in brown and sometimes on a brown ground. Binding by Baynton, s. xx.

Written in England. In Leicester in 1915: see above. The relevant cutting from a bookseller's catalogue (Bernard Halliday's ?) is pasted to f. ii. Given as MS. 7.

41. *Ludolphus de Saxonia, Vita Christi* s. xv²

Nunc secundum iheronimum aspergamus . . . et anima singulorum. amen. amen. amen.

Chapters 51–89 of the Vita Christi (Stegmüller, no. 5437). Called 'Ludolphus De vita christi, liber 4us' in a title of s. xviii (?) on f. 1. Three leaves are missing.

ff. i + 234 + i. The foliation in red, i–ccxxxvii, is contemporary: the now missing leaves are xliiii, xlv, liii. 325 × 220 mm. Written space 248 × 162 mm. 2 cols. 39–44 lines. Collation: 1–5^8 6^8 wants 4, 5 7^8 wants 5 8–29^8 30^6 wants 6, blank. Several formal hybrida hands: black ink. Flex punctuation by the first hand, quires 1–6. Initials: (i) f. 1, 15-line red and blue *N*, historiated (the Flagellation); (ii) of chapters, red or blue (or both red and blue), in various sizes and with varying ornament. A border in three margins of f. 1. Capital letters in the ink of the text touched with red. Binding of wooden boards covered with pigskin bearing a roll and stamped on the front cover 'Anno 1749': the roll is of sixteenth-century type (not in Haebler), with four scenes: (1) Adam and Eve at the Tree, (2) Sacrifice of Isaac, (3) Crucifixion dated 1559, (4) Resurrection, each above a 2-line inscription; the words below (2) are TENTAT AB / RAM DOMI and the words below (4) MORS ERO / MORS TVA. Secundo folio *perbiam.*

Written in Germany. The ex-libris of the Benedictine abbey of St Maximinus, Trier, is on ff. 108, 236 in the hand of the scribe: 'Codex monasterii sancti maximini archiepiscopi ordinis sancti benedicti extra muros treuerorum'. On f. 108 it is followed by 'si quis abstulerit anathema sit. Amen'. Pressmark 'N. 159', f. 1, s. xviii (?). '135' on a label on the spine. Phillipps MS. 520, from the collection of Leander van Ess (no. 142): Phillipps sale, 26 Apr. 1911, lot 657, to Leighton: his catalogues, n.d. (1912), 205, and 1918, 422. Given as MS. 7.

47. *Brut Chronicle (in English)* s. xv^2

Here may a man here how England was first called Albyon and thorow whome it had his name. In the noble londe of Surrye ther was a worthi kynge . . . (f. 106^v) went to the (*ends imperfectly*).

The last words here are in chapter 230 in Brie's edition (EETS, cxxxvi, 1908), p. 310/11, except for a few words corresponding to edn., pp. 339–40 which can still be read on recto and verso of the small fragment of the leaf conjugate with f. 104: see below, collation.[1] The leaves missing from quires 2 and 5 contained the text between 'towarde ye Erle' and 'was made kynge', between 'glad enough' and 'at the table' and between 'and this was' and 'and saide' (edn., pp. 41/3–49/13, 70/12–78/19, 173/8–178/18).

ff. i + 106 + i. 310 × 230 mm. Written space 232 × 165 mm. 37–46 long lines. Collation: 1^{12} 2^{14} wants 2, 3 after f. 13 and 11–13 after f. 20 $3\text{–}4^{14}$ 5^{14} wants 7, 8 after f. 55 $6\text{–}8^{14}$ 9^{14} wants 3–13: 14, f. 105, is a small fragment. A fairly large clear hand, mainly of secretary type. 2-line blue initials with red ornament. Binding perhaps contemporary: wooden boards covered with brown leather: on the back cover only a shield is incised, 160 × 115 mm, bearing a saltire chequy (?) between four columbines. Secundo folio *with gode.*

Written in England. The arms on the cover are perhaps of Collingbourn, who bore azure a saltire chequy or and azure between 4 columbines proper (J. W. Papworth, *Dictionary of Coats of Arms*, 1874, p. 1073). 'Codex edmundi chadertun', f. 77, and 'Wilielmus Chaderton', f. 102: both inscriptions are in legal hands, s. xvi. Notes by Harry Place, rector of Marnhull, Dorset, dated 30 May 1823, are on two pieces of paper pasted to f. i: '. . . Many leaves . . . are Lost and Missing from Time, and the Book being thrown by and neglected; a poor Return for the Pains and Labour the Author must have Taken in Compiling and Writing it'. Belonged to Lord Ashburnham: his 'Appendix' sale at Sotheby's, 1 May 1899, lot 57. Given as MS. 7.

72. *Petrus Blesensis, Compendium de vita beati Job* 1443

Incipit compendium de vita beati Iob compilatum a Magistro Petro Blesensi. Prologus. Henrico dei gracia . . . uel legisse. Incipit narrare. Uir erat in terra hus . . . (f. 35) altissimus altissimi filius. Ihesus cristus qui . . . Amen. Explicit compendium de vita beati Iob compilatum a magistro Petro Blesensi excellentissimo

[1] For edn. 339/6 *Minstralcye* this manuscript has 'nakeurs': cf. *OED Naker.*

magistro. Scriptum per manus fratris Hugonis de Tsgrauensande ordinis Beate marie theutonicorum anno 1443º In die sancti Anthonii.

The text is divided into forty-nine sections with headings in red (De simplicitate . . . De morte, Exhortacio). These are listed in a table on ff. 35v–36: leaf numbers are given. f. 36v blank.

ff. iii + 36 + iii. Paper. Medieval foliation in red. 193 × 128 mm. Written space 140 × 88 mm. 23 long lines. Collation doubtful: a catchword at f. 28v. Current hybrida, the ascenders often split at the top. Initials: 4-line red *H*, f. 1, and 2-line black *U*, f. 2v. Capital letters in the ink of the text stroked with red. English binding, s. xix. Secundo folio *quia cum*.

Written in 1443 by a named scribe. T. Thorpe's catalogue for 1836, item 89 (£2. 2*s*.) Phillipps MS. 9279: this number on f. iv and on a paper label near the foot of the spine. Sale of Phillipps manuscripts, 10 June 1896, lot 127 (Webster, £13), and 15 June 1908, lot 99. 'This book was given by Mr. H. H. Peach' inside the cover.

73. *Basilius, De legendis gentilibus libris; etc.* s. xv²

1 (quire 1). ff. 1–10 Ego tibi hunc librum Coluci ex media (ut aiunt) grecia delegi . . . hinc sumens initium. 'Explicit prologus. Incipit liber.' Nos quidem o filii hanc humanam vitam . . . nunc recta consilia spernantes. Magni Basilii libri Teaos (*sic*). finis.

Basil, De legendis gentilibus libris, in the translation of Leonardo Bruni. Printed first *c.* 1470/1 and often later (*GKW*, 3700–18). 'ihs' at the head of f. 1. f. 10v blank.

2 (quire 2). (*a*) ff. 11–26 [M]aiores nostros Angele mi suauissime non admirari . . . plutarcum audiamus. [Q]uidnam est quod de ingenuorum educatione . . . constat ingenio. finis. (*b*) f. 26 Pii Virgilii metra quedam perpulcra de virtute et vitio sua in adolescentia edita. Littera pythagore discrimine secta bicorni . . . transsiget euum (12 lines). (*c*) f. 26 Nota simul facili vicia ipsa assumere captu . . . durissima quondam (7 lines).

(*a*). Pseudo-Plutarch, De liberis educandis, in the translation of Guarino Veronensis. Printed in 1472 and later (Goff, P. 821–5). (*b*). Walther, no. 10361. Printed in *Anthologia latina*, no. 632 and by Baehrens, *Poetae minores*, iv. 149, as 'Carmen Maximini de Y littera', one of the series of Carmina duodecim sapientum. f. 26v blank.

3 (quires 3, 4). (*a*) ff. 27–34v Etsi non dubitabam. quin hanc epistolam multi nuntii . . . diligentissime seruias. finis. (*b*) ff. 35–42v [E]tsi tibi omnia suppetunt que consequi ingenio . . . omni ratione perfectum. finis. (*c*) ff. 43–4 Vellem equidem Colendissimi patres Virique prestantissimi [. . .]dius mearum orationum publice agendarum . . . O spes mortalium cassas (*ends abruptly*).

(*a, b*). Cicero, Ep. I. 1, ad Quintum fratrem and Commentariolum petitionis consulatus ad M. fratrem. (*c*). A funeral oration containing the passage 'domini mei precipui domini petri Columne prouintie huius equissimi fortissimique rectoris. iussu magistri fratris eius ludouici'. ff. 44v–46v blank.

4 (quire 5). ff. 47–55 Inter multos saepe dubitatum est a quo potissimum monachorum heremus habitari coepta est. quidam enim . . . qui domos marmoribus vestiunt (*ends abruptly*).

Jerome, Vita Pauli heremitae. *PL* xxiii. 17–28/21. ff. 55^v–56^v blank.

5 (quire 6). ff. 57–67^v Vita P. Virgilii Maronis Poetae Maximi feliciter Incipit. Publius Virgilius Maro parentibus modicis fuit . . . omnibus aliis prætulit. Explicit Vita Virgilii.

Begins with the same words as the life formerly ascribed to Aelius Donatus, but now to Suetonius, printed in Heyne's edition of Virgil, 1830, and by H. Nettleship, 1879. f. 68^{rv} blank.

6. f. ii, formerly the pastedown, contains: (*a*) part of a brief grammatical text in a good round hand, s. xiv: 'Quid est nomen. Nomen est diccio per quam fit nominatio . . . Quid est coniunctio . . . ceteras partes orationis in oratione'; (*b*) in part of the space remaining blank on f. ii^v, a table of contents, 'In hoc libro Continentur Infrascripta videlicet (*two lines blank*) Magnus Basilius . . . P. Virgilii Maronis vita. Ouidius de remedio amoris. (*Two lines blank*) [. . . . .] anno domini 1477 mense Madio'.

(*b*) refers to arts. 1, 2*a*, 3*a*, 4, 5 and a now missing text in last place.

ff. ii + 68 + i. Paper, except the binding leaf, f. ii. 208 × 150 mm. Written space 142–165 × 85–105 mm. 29–33 long lines. Ruling with pencil in arts. 1–3 and with hard point in arts. 4, 5. The first line of writing above the top ruled line. Collation: 1^{10} 2^{16} $3\text{–}5^{10}$ 6^{12}. Three humanistic hands: arts. 1–3; art. 4; art. 5. The first two hands are current. Binding of s. xix^1 —by C. Lewis, according to the Phillipps sale catalogue. Secundo folio *minus ego*.

Written in Italy. Belonged to H. Drury, who noted the absence of Ovid, De remedio amoris (f. i): not identified in the catalogue of his sale, 19 February 1827. Phillipps 3366 (this number on a paper label at the foot of the spine): Phillipps sale, 6 June 1898, lot 97, to Dodson for 6*s*. Given as MS. 72.

LEICESTER. WYGGESTON HOSPITAL

The hospital was founded by William Wigston (1467–1536) in 1513. Ten medieval manuscripts and six early printed books (10D34/1–5, 8) were deposited in the City Archives Office[1] in 1934 and three manuscripts (1D50/xiii/3/1, 2–3, 3–4) in 1950. The collection, partly manuscript and partly printed, is comparable to that at All Saints Church, Bristol (*MMBL* ii. 183–6).

[1] See above, Leicester, Archdeaconry.

10D34/6. *J. Wyclif, Sermons (in English)* s. xiv/xv

Four sets of sermons on the Gospels and a set on the Epistles, all defective, and other sermons printed, except art. 3, by Arnold, *Select English Works of John Wyclif*. More than sixty leaves are missing. Dr Hudson's β (see above, Leicester, Old Town Hall Library, 3).

1. ff. 1–58 (*begins imperfectly*) almes for we schal sue criste . . . sawmple after þe tirnite (*sic*).

Set 1. As Arnold, i. 6/2–162, sermons on the Sunday Gospels through the year, beginning at Trinity. Numbered 3–54. Two leaves missing at the beginning and four elsewhere.

2. ff. 58–62v Expositio textus mathei xxiiio capitulo de ve octuplici . . . Crist biddiþ us be war . . . nede to trete.

As Arnold, ii. 379–89 (*Vae octuplex*).

3. ff. 62v–63 De sacramento. 1a (*sic for* contra) fratres. Of al þe feiþ of þe gospel gederen trew men . . . weryn open heritikes etc.

As F. D. Matthew, *The English Works of Wyclif hitherto unprinted* (EETS lxxiv (1880), 357–8).

4. ff. 63–109v Commune sanctorum. Incipit 2a pars. Ego sum vitis vera . . . As commune þing is better . . . þei shal be dede.

Set 2. As Arnold, i. 165–294, sermons on the Gospels for the common of saints. Numbered 1–31. Probably five leaves are missing.

5. ff. 109v–126v Stabat iohannes. In vigilia andree . . . þis gospel telliþ in storie . . . is pouderid wiþ (*ends imperfectly*).

Set 3. As Arnold, i. 295–350/19, sermons on the Gospels for saints' days through the year from Andrew, ending imperfectly in Cathedra Petri (22 Feb.). Numbered 32–46 in continuation of art. 4. Lacks two quires after f. 126, a leaf after f. 114, and two leaves after f. 118.

6. ff. 127–133v (*begins imperfectly*) feme prelatis . . . þer hope in crist.

As Arnold, ii. 407/1–423 (*Of mynystris in the chirche*).

7. ff. 133v–212v 3a pars euangel(i)orum ferialium. feria iiiia dominice prime aduentus . . . Sermo primus. As men shulden trowe in crist . . . as poul spekiþ. Heere endene þe gospelis.

Set 4. As Arnold, ii. 1–217, sermons on the ferial Gospels through the year from Wednesday in the first week of Advent. Numbered 1–120. Five leaves are missing.

8. ff. 212^{v}–223^{v} de ecclesia et membris eius. cristis chirche is his spouse . . . vertu stablid.

As Arnold, iii. 339–65 (*The Church and her Members*). Follows art. 7 without break.

9. ff. 224–277^{v} Epistole dominicales per annum. Scientes quia hora est . . . Sermo primus. We taken as bileue . . . dayes come (*ends imperfectly*).

Set 5. As Arnold, ii. 221–354/13 up and (f. 277) 373/11–375/24, sermons on the Sunday Epistles through the year, beginning at Advent. Numbered, except on f. 277, 1–55. For missing leaves see below.

ff. ii + 279 + ii, foliated (i, ii), 1–33, 33*, 33**, 34–277, (278–9). 315 × 220 mm. Written space 238 × 150 mm. 2 cols. 40 lines. Ruling in red ink. Collation: 1^{12} wants 1, 2 2^{12} wants 5 after f. 14 3^{12} 4^{12} wants 9 after f. 39 5^{12} wants 8 after f. 49 6^{12} wants 5 after f. 57 7^{12} wants 5–7 after f. 68 and 10 after f. 70 8^{12} 9^{12} wants 1 before f. 85 10^{12} 11^{12} wants 8 after f. 114 12^{12} wants 1, 2 before f. 119 and 11, 12 after f. 126 13^{12} 14^{12} wants 12 after f. 149 15^{12} wants 12 after f. 160 16^{12} wants 1 before f. 161 17^{12} wants 4, 5 after f. 174 18–20^{12} 21^{6} (ff. 218–23) 22–24^{12} 25^{12} wants 11 after f. 269 26^{12} wants 2 after f. 271 26^{12} wants 8–12 after f. 276 27 one (f. 277). The signatures, in three series, show that two quires are missing after quire 12: a–k on quires 1–10 (ff. 1–107); +, a, d–m on quires 11–21 (ff. 108–223); a–e on quires 22–6 (ff. 224–76). In quire 22 the two middle sheets are now bound in the wrong order. Written in a fairly large textura by one hand, except the fifth sheet of quire 20 (ff. 210, 213) which has been supplied in another contemporary hand. Blue initials with red ornament, (i) 6-line or less, (ii) 2-line or 3-line: the style is not different on ff. 210 and 213. Binding of s. xix.

10D34/7. *W. Peraldus, O.P., Sermones; etc.*[1] s. xv in.

1. (*a*) ff. 4–79^{v} Hora est iam nos de so(m)pno surgere Ro 13. Hoc tempus tempus dicitur aduentus quia cantus ecclesie . . . crinibus alienis. Explicit tractatus super epistolas dominicales. (*b*) ff. 1–3 Additions to (*a*).

(*a*). The sermons on the Sunday Epistles by Guillaume Peyraut, O.P., †1275. Printed in 1494, 1519, and 1576. Schneyer, *Rep.*, ii. 543–51 (nos. 129–233). *SOPMA*, no. 1623. The text has been much altered and added to, and additions for which there was not room were assembled under a series of letters, A–R, on a preliminary quire. (*b*). E, G, O, and R in this series are complete sermons which were taken into account when an annotator numbered the sermons of art. 1 from 1 to 119.

2. ff. 80–98^{v} De apostolis. Qui sunt isti qui ut nubes volant etc. Profectus apostolorum volatui nubium et columbarum comparatur . . .

Sermons on the common of saints by Petrus de Remis, O.P. Only thirty of the forty-five sermons listed by Schneyer, *Rep.*, iv. 752–5, nos. 462–505, occur here: the last is no. 505, 'Ecce sponsus venit. Est triplex aduentus. in carnem in mentem . . . In via cordis recipe etc.'.

[1] A letter, s. xvi, lies loose inside the cover. It begins 'Mother haue my commened vnto you' and is subscribed 'from lecester be your louinge sun henry suttun'.

3. ff. 99–101 A table of the sermons of art. 1. References are by sermon number and letter, the letters corresponding to letters written in the margins of art. 1.

ff. i + 101 + ii. The endleaves are medieval, ff. i, 103 former pastedowns and f. 102 a flyleaf. 318 × 215 mm. Written space *c.* 255 × 160 mm. 2 cols. *c.* 53–62 lines, the number varying from column to column. Frame ruling. Collation: 1^4 wants 4, probably blank, $2–9^{12}$ 10^2. Written in a current mixture of anglicana and secretary and (art. 3) in textura. Art. 1*b* and the alterations to art. 1*a* are in current anglicana. 2-line initials, red or (ff. 4–27 only) blue with red ornament. Binding of s. xix ex. Secundo folio *suspenditur* (f. 5) or *Pax locus* (f. 2).

Written in England. 'Willelmo Wyrght sibi datus fuit anno 1.4.8.7' and 'Iste liber constat d*omi*no Willelmo Wyrght', f. 102^v.

10D34/9. *De vitiis et virtutibus* s. xiv^2

1. ff. 2–83 De uiciis et uirtutibus auctoritates sacre scripture et sanctorum ac philosophorum et notabilia de diuersis tractatibus in hoc libello continentur. Sed quia per sapienciam discernitur inter uirtutes et uicia primo loco de sapiencia scriptum est. De sapiencia et sciencia uera et falsa. Capitulum primum. Vani sunt omnes homines in quibus non est sciencia dei . . . in regnum celorum. Quod nobis . . . Explicit.

Seventy-two chapters are listed on f. 2. According to the copy in Merton College, Oxford, 67, this 'De vitiis et virtutibus' (Bloomfield, no. 6323) is an abbreviation of Peraldus called 'Speculum Beatorum'. An alphabetical list of subjects is on the flyleaf, f. 1^v. f. 83^v, left blank, was filled later with the alphabet written many times over in the main hand (?), and *inter alia* a list of nine vices and those most addicted to them, 'Simoniam prelatus ecclesie . . . luxuria discurrit inter omnes quasi publi(c)a meretrix' and four lines of verse, 'Post hominem vermis post vermem fetor et horror . . .' (Walther, *Sprichwörter*, no. 22007: 2 lines).

2 (added, s. xv in.). f. 84 A bidding prayer in English.

Prayers are asked 'for ye brethore and ye sisteris of seynt wylliam hous of yoork and of seynte mari hous of Soutwell'. A copy, made in 1903, is in Oxford, Bodleian, Eng. Liturg. c. 2. f. 84^v is blank, except for two couplets, 'Perd[. . .] . . . perdita sola dies' and 'Quid melius auro Iaspis . . .' (Walther, *Sprichwörter*, nos. 21317, 25072).

ff. i + 83 + i, foliated 1–85. For f. 1 see above. 268 × 180 mm. Written space 210 × 130 mm. 2 cols. 39 lines. Collation of ff. 2–83: $1–8^8$ 9^6 10^8 11^8 wants 6–8, probably blank. Fairly large textura, changing at f. 58 (8^1). Blue initials, usually 2-line, with red ornament. Binding of limp vellum, s. xix. Secundo folio *dencia dulcius* (f. 3).

Written in England. Belonged probably to a priest in the diocese of York.

10D34/10. *W. de Pagula, Oculus sacerdotis* s. xiv med.

(*begins imperfectly*) et ad pacem habenda . . . de dote accessoria (*ends imperfectly*).

Manuscript listed by Bloomfield, no. 1088 and L. E. Boyle, 'The *Oculus Sacerdotis* and some other works of William of Pagula', *Trans. Royal Hist. Soc.*, fifth series, v (1955), 81–110.

This very imperfect copy contains the end of the Pars Oculi on ff. 1–33v, the beginning of the Dextera Pars on ff. 34–59v and part of the Sinistra Pars on ff. 60–75v. The remains correspond to Bodleian, MS. Hatton 11, ff. 114vb–140v, 173v–181v.

A fragment of a medieval endleaf pasted to the modern flyleaf, f. 76, bears scribbles like 'Si mea penna valet melior' and a receipt dated in 12 Richard II: Pateat vniuersis per presentes me Iohannem Howdby de suburbiis leycestr' vnum collect' de Gertr' hundr' . . . recepisse de Thomas Maundeayle de belgraue v s' pro redditibus . . . in villa et campis de houghton . . .'.

ff. i + 75 + i. For f. 76 see above. ff. 3–33 are foliated in a medieval hand xxix–lix. 252 × 175 mm. Written space *c.*205 × 132 mm. 32–48 long lines. Frame ruling. Collation: 1^{10} $2\text{–}6^{8}$ 7^{6} + 1 leaf after 2 (f. 53) 8^{2} (ff. 58, 59) $9\text{–}10^{8}$. 'cor' ' at the end of quire 2. Written in current anglicana by more than one hand. Red initials, 3-line (f. 34) and 1-line. Binding of s. xx in.

Written in England. In Leicester by s. xiv ex.

10D34/11. *Simon Boraston, O.P., Distinctiones et Sermones* s. xiv/xv

1. ff. 1–150 Abicere. secundum auctorem de natura rerum Columba propter calorem quem habet . . . pietas vult videri. Expliciunt distinctiones maiores parisiensis.

S. L. Forte, 'Simon of Boraston, his Life and Writings', *AFP* xxii (1952), 331–4, records eight manuscripts, but not this one. See also Emden, *BRUO*, p. 221. Stegmüller, no. 7641.

2. ff. 150–90 Hora est iam nos de somno surgere. Ro. 13. Volentibus transire mare precipue est . . . in tribulacione sua consurgent ad me.

168 short sermons on the Sunday Epistles and Gospels. Forte, loc. cit., records only one manuscript, Merton College, Oxford, 216: its sermons are set out by Schneyer, *Rep.*, v. 449–59. f. 190v, left blank, contains a costing note of the number of flourished letters (correct), paragraph marks, and quires: 'de litteris floretis. v C. xxxvi litteris. Item de paraffis xv C. di*m*. xxxvi. de quaternis xxix' (*sic*, but the first 'x' may be an addition).

ff. iv + 190 + ii. ff. i–iv, 191–2 are medieval flyleaves. 275 × 180 mm. Written space *c.*218 × 140 mm. 2 cols. *c.*52 lines. Frame ruling. Collation: $1\text{–}19^{10}$. Slightly sloping anglicana formata. Initials: f. i, 5-line red and blue *A* with ornament of both colours; (ii) 3-line, blue with red ornament (see above). Binding of s. xix ex. Secundo folio *mortem.*

Written in England. Belonged in s. xv ex.–xvi in. successively to a canon of Newark (Leicester) and two vicars of Bradford, West Yorkshire, and was a gift to Newark College by the later of the two vicars. The inscriptions are on f. ivv: (1) Ex dono Magistri Iohannis Blakewyn (Emden, *BRUO*, p. 196 (Blackweyn): canon of Newark, presented 1472, † by September 1485) successori suo Ric' Stratberell' per W. Blakewyn fratrem eiusdem ac executorem suum; (2) Iste liber quondam erat magistri Ricardi Stratbarell' vicarii perpetui de Bradford (Emden, *BRUC*, p. 563: admitted vicar, 21 Dec. 1488) quem postmodum prefatus M' Gilbertus becansaw successor suus in eodem beneficio habuit de executoribus suis pro dilapidacione beneficii sui antedicti: Becansaw was admitted to Bradford on Stratberell's death in 1503; (3) Ex dono Magistri Gilberti Becansaw (†1537) Ecclesie noue collegiate beate marie Leycestrie imperpetuum. (2) was written after (3), perhaps at Newark and presumably to explain how Becansaw came to own this book. 'Precium xxvi s' viii d' ', f. ii^{v}.

10D34/12. *R. Rolle, etc.* s. xv in.

1. ff. 1–63 Parce michi domine . . . tu criste corona ricardum. Expliciunt lecciônes de seruicio mortuorum secundum exposicionem Ricardi heremite de Hampol. Respice illas bene.

This and forty-one other manuscripts of this exposition of the nine lessons in the office of the dead are listed by Allen, *Writings*, pp. 130–5. Printed at Oxford in 1483, at Paris in 1510, and at Cologne in 1536. ff. 63^{v}–64^{v} blank.

2. ff. 65–104^{v} Speculum consciencie sancti Bernardi . . . Quomodo edificanda sit consciencia. Domus hec in qua habitamus . . . quam terrestrium occupacione etc'. Explicit speculum consciencie Beati Bernardi et cetera non plus.

Pseudo-Bernard. Four books, each preceded by a table of chapters. *PL* clxxxiv. 505–52. Bloomfield, no. 1787.

3. The flyleaf and the now raised pastedown at the end, ff. 105–6, are two leaves of a year book in French, s. xiv in., written in current anglicana.

Cases concern John Holkham, John Falstolf, among others. Lawyers named include Cambridge, Denham, Herle, and Toudeby.

ff. i + 104 + ii. For ff. 105–6 see above. 245 × 170 mm. Written space 180 × 115 mm in art. 1 and 200 × 115 mm in art. 2. Art. 1 in 2 cols. of 30 lines ruled in ink. Art. 2 in 32 long lines: frame ruling. Collation: 1–13^{8}. Textura and (art. 2) anglicana formata. Initials of art. 1, 2-line, blue or red. In art. 2 spaces for initials remain blank, except on the first seven pages where they have been filled in the ink of the text. Medieval binding of wooden boards covered with white leather, repaired: two strap-and-pin fastenings, the straps modern. Secundo folio *amicis calumpniatus*.

Written in England. 'Willelmo constat derby liber vt nota monstrat', f. 104^{v}, s. xv/xvi. Erasures on f. 104^{v} are not legible by ultra-violet light.

10D34/13. *J. Felton, Sermones dominicales; etc.* s. xv med.

1. ff. 1–157 Incipit prologus in opus sermonum dominicalium secundum Iohannem Felton 'vicarium beate marie Magd''. Penuria studencium . . . (f. 146^{v}) concordia dulcis. Ad illa gaudia eterna perducat nos ihesus cristus amen. Expliciunt dominicales per annum compilati per vicarium sancte marie magdal' oxon'. ff. 147–57 contain an index, Abraham–Zodioco.

Fifty-eight numbered sermons on the Sunday Gospels by John Felton, † by June 1434: for the manuscripts cf. Emden, *BRUO*, p. 676 and *MMBL* i. 283. References in the index are to sermon numbers and the divisions of sermon by letters corresponding to letters in the margins of the text.

2. ff. 157v–161v Pater noster qui es in celis. Docuit nos superius dominus et saluator noster peruenire posse ad beatitudinem . . . in hoc quod peccant homines sunt. amen.

A sermon on Beati pauperes spiritu. f. 162rv blank.

3. ff. 163–6 are two leaves of a noted missal, s. xii med., laid sideways and folded to make four leaves in binding. 163 + 166 is from the common of saints: 163v + 166r is the recto side. 164 + 165 is from the office of the dead: 164v + 165r is the recto side.

f. 163v begins 'dominus dilexit illam' in the lesson from Wisdom (8: 3), which is followed by three noted pieces, the gradual Dilexisti iusticiam and versicles Propterea and Specie tua and lessons from Matthew, Simile est regnum celorum decem uirginibus . . . neque horam, and Luke, Simile est regnum celorum fermento . . . in regno dei.

The true verso (163r + 166v) contains: (*a*) the noted offertories Filie regum and Offerentur regi; secret Offerimus tibi domine preces; noted communion Simile est regnum celorum homini . . . omnia sua; postcommunion Indulgentiam nobis domine beata N. uirgo. (*b*) under the heading 'Alia missa', the collect, secret and postcommunion in *Missal of the New Minster* (HBS xciii, 1962), p. 205; (*c*) under the heading 'In natale unius uirginis et martiris', the offertory Loquebar and cues for psalms, Beati immaculati and Me expectauerunt peccatores and prayers, Deus qui inter cetera (*New Minster*, p. 204) and Domine deus meus exaltasti . . . assidue (*ends imperfectly*).

The leaf from the office of the dead begins (f. 164v) with the Epistle, Stimulus autem mortis . . . uictoriam (1 Cor. 15: 56–7), and ends with the prayer, Deus qui inter apostolicos sacerdotes famulum tuum N (*Sarum Missal*, p. 434). As compared with *Sarum Missal* the lessons from St John are in the order 1 (Dixit martha), 3, 2, 4.

Written space *c.*252 × 175 mm. 2 cols. 34 lines. Good English hand. 3-line or 2-line initials in red, blue or green.

ff. ii + 162 + v. Medieval endleaves: for ff. 163–6 see art. 3. 252 × 175 mm. Written space *c.*180 × 120 mm. 33 long lines. Frame ruling. Collation: $1–3^{8}$ $4–15^{10}$ 16^{12} 17^{6}. The hand changes at f. 17/5 from secretary to an ugly stilted anglicana formata (secretary *g*). Initials: (i) 7-line *P*, shaded blue and pink on a pale yellow decorated ground; (ii) 2-line, red or blue, plain or with rough ornament. Binding of wooden boards, re-covered. Secundo folio *filia iuda.*

Written in England. 'Iste liber constat collegio', f. 162v, s. xv ex., may indicate provenance from the collegiate church of Leicester: cf. MS. 11.

10D34/14. *Gesta Romanorum* s. xv¹

1. (*begins imperfectly*, f. 2) me ab ista infirmitate curarem. Ait imperator dic michi . . . (f. 68v) et iusti ibunt in vitam eternam. Ad quam nos perd'.

Apparently the standard collection of 101 tales found in English manuscripts of Gesta Romanorum: cf. the copy (Harley 5259) described in *Cat. of Romances*, iii. 199–212. It begins in the middle of no. 26 and lacks nos. 88–98 and parts of nos. 87 and 99 in the gap after f. 62. Numbers in the main hand against six tales, '29', '30', '32', '33', '34', '39' are five behind the expected numbers and suggest that there were only twenty, not twenty-five tales on the 21 (?) leaves missing at the beginning.

2. Added notes: (*a*) f. 68^{v}, s. xv, that the abbot of Abingdon 'nunc existens' had not for the past two years been fulfilling the obligation imposed on him by an agreement of 1208 to provide a priest at the chantry chapel of Watchfield, Berks; (*b*) f. 1^{v}, s. xvi, of legal charges.

(*b*) is 'For an alias plurias x^{d} for an origenall ix^{d} for an capias primo x^{d} for an capias alias x^{d} for ye ynputtyng yn to ye cowrt xvi^{s}. For myn Eturney for ye terme xx^{d}'.

ff. i + 67 + i, foliated 1–69. Paper and, for the outside and middle sheets of each quire, parchment. f. 1 is a medieval parchment flyleaf. *c.*215 × 145 mm. Written space *c.*163 × 102 mm. 35–41 long lines. Frame ruling. Collation of ff. 2–68: 1 three (ff. 2–4) 2^{12} 3^{10} wants 10 after f. 24 4–6^{12} 7^{12} wants 2–5 after f. 62 and 12, probably blank. Quires signed as usual in s. xv, beginning with c. 1 on f. 5. The script is current anglicana. From f. 53^{v} 2-line initials are in the ink of the text: before this point spaces for initials remain blank. Binding of s. xx in.

Written in England. Belonged to someone with an interest in the chantry chapel at Watchfield, Berks.

10D34/15. *R. Rolle; J. Hanneton; etc.* s. xiv med.–xiv/xv

1. ff. 2–16^{v} 'Hic libellus per Ricardum hampole compositus est de emendacione uite . . .'. Ne tardes conuerti . . . eternaliter laudare cui . . . amen. Explicit hic amen.

R. Rolle, De emendatione vitae. The manuscripts, including this one, listed by Allen, *Writings*, p. 237.

2. ff. 16^{v}–62 'Incipit exposicio eiusdem super illo Iob parce michi domine'. Parce michi domine . . . Exprimitur autem in hiis verbis . . . in sensu ignis inhabitans in eternum.

Allen, op. cit., p. 134. The explicit is followed here and in seventeen other manuscripts by four lines of verse, '[Tal]entum traditum . . . corona ricardum Amen': Allen, p. 130.

3. ff. 62^{v}–67 'Speculum peccatorum'. Quoniam karissime in huius vite via . . . prudenter prouideas. etc.

Speculum peccatoris. *PL* xl. 983–92. A common text variously ascribed. Bloomfield, no. 4918. Cf. Allen, op. cit., p. 353, and Römer, i. 173–5.

4 (filling quire 5). (*a*) f. 67^{rv} Augustinus de laude psalmorum. Canticum psalmorum animas decorat . . . offerre sacrificium eukaristie. (*b*) ff. 67^{v}–68^{v} Bernardus de dignitate sacerdotum. Quantam dignitatem contulit nobis deus O sacerdotes . . . vobis dico omnibus dico. (*c*) ff. 68^{v}–69^{v} De vita beate marie virginis. Circa virginem vero ex qua incarnacio . . . vnquam fuerit. Huc usque de sanctis reuelacionibus. (*d*) f. 69^{v} Beatus vero Ieronimus de vita ipsius ita scribit hanc regulam. Beata virgo statuerat vt a mane . . . obtemperabant ei. Huc vsque Ieronimus. (*e*) ff. 70–71 'De regimine sacerdotum'. Bernardus. Si vis esse a fornicacione

tutus . . . sanguinem illum dedit. etc. (*f*) f. 71rv 'regula perfecte viuendi'. Omnibus in cristo ihesu pie viuere volentibus . . . possunt reperire.

(*a*). Cf. Stegmüller, no. 369. (*e*). 'Notate sacerdotes istud capitulum' in the margin of f. 70. (*f*). At the end the writer refers those who may wish 'amplius in hac regula proficere' to arts. 5, 6.

Arts. 5-7 are on quires 6-8.

5. ff. 72-78v 'Compendium amoris'. Diligamus deum. Io. 4 Cum iam in tant' libri multiplicentur. vt pene nemo sit: qui omnes scire vel legere queat . . . de dileccione dei . . . compendiose scribere curaui . . . continuum incrementum. Explicit compendium amoris editum per fratrem I. hanneton' cordelat' die et anno superius memorat'.

6. ff. 79-93 'de meditacionibus'. 'N'uper (S *changed to* N) adueniente tempore sacris meditacionibus pro solacio spiritus . . . effectu conetur et studeat adimplere. Explicit. Meditacio fratris. Iohannis de Hanneton' humilis cordilati.

This and arts. 4*f*, 5 noticed by Allen, op. cit., p. 134, footnote.

7. ff. 93v-107v 'Liber de amore dei secundum Ric' Hampull' contra amatores mundi et de contemptu mundi'. Quoniam mundanorum . . . commendo sine fine amen. Explicit liber de amore dei contra amatores mundi secundum Ricardum uenerabilem heremitam.

Allen, op. cit., p. 205.

8 (quire 9). ff. 109-16 Multi multa sciunt . . . vnum eundemque dominum glorie qui viuit et regnat in secula seculorum.

The popular meditations often attributed to St Bernard and printed among his works, *PL* clxxxiv. 485-500.

9 (added). (*a*) in the space remaining blank on f. 116rv, notes, s. xiv ex., on the texts 'Epulemur non in fermento' (1 Cor. 5: 8) and 'Oritur sol et occidit' (Eccl. 1: 5) and a miracle of B.V.M. (*b*) on f. 108, a blank leaf, three notes, s. xiv/xv, one of them referring to the good example of St Chad and the bad example of 'Lollardi'. (*c*) on the flyleaf, f. 1, a note in English, s. xiv/xv, 'þese aren þe ix poyntes þt owre lord ihesu crist onswered an holi mon þat coueyted gretly to wyte what þyng most pleseþ god. þe first is to do almesdede . . . þe ix is þu loue god . . . for godes sake etc.'.

(*c*). Cf. Allen, op. cit., pp. 134, 317-20. Jolliffe, pp. 106-8 (I. 12), but not including this copy, which seems to resemble I. 12*h*.

ff. i + 115 + i, foliated 1-117. f. 1 is a medieval flyleaf conjugate with the pastedown. 198 × 150 mm. Written space *c*.152 × 108 mm. 29-40 long lines. Collation of ff. 2-116: 1^{16}

2-3^{12} 4^{14} 5^{16} 6-8^{12} 9^{8} + 1 leaf inserted before 1 (f. 108). Anglicana—formata, except in quires 6, 7—by four hands: (i) arts. 1-4*e*, s. xiv²; (2) arts. 5, 6 and art. 4*f*, s. xiv ex.; (3) art. 7, s. xiv/xv; (4) art. 8, s. xiv med. The second hand, a good one, becomes current after a few pages. Binding of s. xx in. over old boards. Secundo folio (f. 3) *Set nondum se.*

Written in England. An erasure on the front pastedown.

10D34/16. *Floretum* s. xv in.

Absolutio. Dominus noster ihesus cristus dicit beato petro . . . Vtrumque crescere vsque ad messem. dicit dominus noster ihesus cristus cui sit honor et gloria per secula sempiterna amen.

The collection of theological 'distinctiones', Absolutio-Zizannia, called Floretum, in which there are many references to the works of Wyclif: see Anne Hudson in *Journal of Theological Studies*, n.s. xxiii (1972), 65-81 and xxv (1974), 129-40. The preface and table of contents, here absent, but found in Bodleian MS. Bodley 55 (*Sum. Cat.* 1976), and two other manuscripts, give the title and show that it was divided into 509 tituli. At the end of the text here, f. 544ᵛ, the scribe began to copy an alphabetical index in which the first words are 'Aa dixi', and in which the tituli and their subdivisions by letters are referred to, for example, 'Aaron interpretatur mons fortis 18.114.117a. 335 b et 428 a.g'. He desisted after a column, presumably because this index would be of no use in a manuscript which has no numbering of tituli or letter-divisions. ff. 545-51 remain blank.

ff. iv + 552 + vi, foliated 1-177, 177*, 178-557. Parchment roughish. Flyleaves of medieval parchment, blank or lined for music. 162 × 110 mm. Written space 135-120 × 80 mm. 2 cols. 31-44 lines. Frame ruling from f. 65ᵛ. Collation: 1-69^{8}. Textura as far as f. 65; after this a mixed more or less current script in which the letter-forms are mainly anglicana and the duct mainly secretary. Initials: (i) f. 1, 3-line *A*, blue with red ornament; (ii) 2-line, red or blue. After f. 325 spaces for initials remain blank. Old (?) wooden boards, re-covered and the old leather pasted on: each cover has a panel of 'triple' type, the two main divisions of which bear the words IHESVS MARIA between rows of five roundels, four of them containing a bird and one a monkey. This panel is not recorded by Oldham. Secundo folio *ut eadem uirtus.*

Written in England. 'Liber M' Io. Bayll precium xx s', f. iiiᵛ, s. xv ex. 'Liber M' Iohannis Geffrey Decani Staffordie', f. ivᵛ, s. xv ex. For John Bayly, legatee of his uncle John Geffray, prebendary of Ryton in Lichfield and canon of Tamworth, †1493, see Emden, *BRUO*, p. 135, and for Geffray, ibid., p. 753. Among other books, named and unnamed, Geffray left him a Breviloquium vocabulorum, which could be the present manuscript (P.C.C., 3 Vox).

1D50/xiii/3/1. *Narrationes, etc.* s. xiv/xv

1. ff. 1-16ᵛ Tales—'exempla' and 'narraciones'—mainly against the vice of avarice, taken from various sources, some English.

Named sources include Odo de 'sericon' (Cheriton), f. 13ᵛ, and 'allexander (Nequam) de naturis rerum', f. 14ᵛ. A story 'De virtute sancte crucis', f. 3ᵛ, is about Warin Sowth, O.F.M. of the Shrewsbury convent, a man 'simplicissime litterature', who was teased by devils on his death-bed with hard questions about the Trinity and the catholic faith: cf. *Cat. of Romances*, iii. 688.

2. ff. 17–18 Two stories from Gesta Romanorum, no. 101 (Fridolin) and no. 75 (Fair and Ugly) in the Anglo-Latin series: cf. above, 10D34/14. No. 101 begins imperfectly. ff. 18^{v}, 19 are blank.

3. ff. 19^{v}–20 A 'narracio bona', beginning 'Fuit quidam papa qui dum ad extrema peruenisset', on the importance of a good friend at hand at the time of death.

A signe de renvoi, 'lege super cedulam', at the end of the text on f. 20, refers to its continuation on a slip of parchment inserted between f. 19 and f. 20. A reader wrote on f. 19^{v} 'Nota bene ista duo latera'.

4. (*a*) ff. 20^{v}–21^{v} Sermo de sepultura domini. Notandum quod quatuor leguntur . . . (*b*) f. 21^{v} Verses, 'Cum sapiens loquitur expectat . . .' (6 lines) and 'Si sapiens fore uis . . .' (2 lines). (*c*) ff. 21^{v}–23^{v} Notes 'De corpore cristi', 'De dei misericordia et gracia', 'De elemosina', etc.

(*b*). Walther, *Sprichwörter*, nos. 4217 (2 lines), 29127.

5. The wrapper is part of a bifolium, the whole of one leaf and half the other, taken from a large liturgical psalter, s. xv: Pss. 54–67.

Written space 276 × 202 mm. 36 long lines.

ff. 23. *c.*235 × 170 mm, and some smaller leaves. Written space *c.*195 × 125 mm. *c.*33 long lines. Half frame ruling on ff. 1–16^{v}, the inner vertical line and the upper horizontal line only. Collation: 1^{16} 2 seven. Current anglicana, perhaps all by one hand. No ornament. The wrapper (above, art. 5) had two strips of leather attached to its spine, but only the upper strip now remains, with the strings from the quires attached to it at two points. Secundo folio *ex quo.*

Written in England.

1D50/xiii/3/2, 3. *Sermones, etc.* s. xvi in.

Sermons and other short pieces, 1–6 on the first of two quires and 7–10 on the second.

1. ff. 1–8 Two sermons under the heading 'De confessione. 2–5. Pieces under the headings 'De decem preceptis' (f. 8^{v}), 'Cur deus permittit electos cadere in peccatum' (f. 11), 'Ad sanctitatem sive puritatem vel mundiciam' (f. 11^{v}), 'De scala virtutum' (f. 12). 6. f. 12^{rv} Exemplum. Contra murmurantes de austeritate ordinis. Legitur in quodam libro quod quidam cruce signatus intrauit cisterciencium in anglia ordinem . . . 7. ff. 13–15 On the seven petitions of the Lord's Prayer, the first page illegible. 8. ff. 15–16^{v} A sermon 'De salutacione angelica'. 9. ff. 16^{v}–22^{v} De cimbalo apostolico. Sine fide impossibile est . . . terminare non timuerunt. Explicit. 10. f. 23^{rv} A sermon (?) 'De septem horis' ending imperfectly.

8. Each phrase is attributed to an apostle and rendered in an English couplet, 'I leue in god father of myght y^t^ heuen and erthe made and dyght . . . And in ye lyfe y^t^ lastey ay þys ys ye yought of godes lay' (cf. *IMEV*, no. 1326). **10.** On the application of each hour to Christ's Passion.

ff. 23. Paper. 210 × 158 mm. Written space *c.*175 × 135 mm. *c.*31 long lines. No ruling. Collation: 1^{12} 2^{12} wants 12. Very current anglicana. No coloured initials. No binding: kept loose in two brown paper covers.

Written in England.

1D50/xiii/3/4. *T. Littleton, New Tenures (in French)* s. xv ex.

1. (f. 3) Tenaunt en ffe simple est celuy qui . . . (f. 102) Reuersion etc.

The Tenores novelli of Sir Thomas Littleton, †1481, in three books, ending in bk. 3 with chapter 'De attornamentis' (edn. 1841, p. 573). ff. 1-2^v^, 102^v^ remain blank, except for notes about impounding cattle, s. xvi, on 102^v^.

2. Fragments of a common-law text in French, s. xii ex., on the strips of parchment used as strengthening in the middle of the quires and between them.

Strips cut probably from a roll, the writing on one side only. Two chapter-headings remain, 'De tenement demande quant li emplede vouche warant' and 'De pasture a mesuree'. The written space is *c.*155 mm wide.

ff. i + 102. Paper. f. i is a medieval parchment leaf. 190 × 130 mm. Written space *c.*130 × 105 mm. 24 long lines. No ruling. Collation: 1^{20} wants 1, 2, probably blank. $2\text{-}3^{16}$ 4^{20} $5\text{-}6^{16}$. Written in current legal anglicana. No coloured initials. Parchment wrapper, with thick leather pieces on the spine pierced with holes through which the strings are taken at four points. Secundo folio *par discent.*

Written in England. Scribbles of s. xvi suggest ownership by the family of Grene of Humberston, near Leicester, in s. xvi: 'That I Robert Grene', f. i; 'That I francys grene of Humberston gatherar (?)', f. 102^v^.

LICHFIELD. CATHEDRAL

Catalogues of or including manuscripts: (1) by Patrick Young in 1621 (MS. 39) printed by N. R. Ker in *Mediaeval and Renaissance Studies*, ii (1950), 154–9, describes a collection which was mostly destroyed or dispersed in the seventeenth century: only MS. 31 has any claims to be identified with an item in this catalogue; (2) of the manuscripts of the Duchess of Somerset in 1671 (MS. 60): these manuscripts were part of the gift by the Duchess in 1673, and the catalogue lists MSS. 16, 29, 30; (3) by John Wills, D.Th., in *CMA* ii. 32, nos. 1381–1445: it lists MSS. 1, 16, 23, 29, 50 (nos. 1387, 1393, 1413, 1382, 1412) and also (no. 1399) Postillæ vet. Lat. cum Regulis S. Augustini, et Urbani Papæ,

Clero et Populo Carnotensi. 4to; (nos. 1414–19) Six old imperfect Glossaries upon some parts of Scripture; (nos. 1420–6) Seven imperfect Postillators; (nos. 1427–44) Eighteen old and imperfect Canon and Civil Law Books; (4) by Samuel Smalbroke, canon of Lichfield 1744, †1803 (MS. 43), a good catalogue made probably in 1771 (see MS. 43, f. 22), which includes descriptions of MSS. 1, 7, 16, 20, 23, 30, 35, 50, and, as an addition, MS. 31; (5) *Catalogue of the printed books and manuscripts of Lichfield Cathedral*, 1888, pp. 119–20 (MSS. 1, 16, 20, 23, 29, 30, 31, 35, 50); (6) by B. S. Benedikz (typescript), 1974. (7) J. C. Cox, *Catalogue of the muniments and manuscript books pertaining to the Dean and Chapter of Lichfield* (Staffordshire Record Society, vi, pt. 2, 1886) includes notices of the Vicars Choral Evidence Book and the Dean and Chapter muniments now numbered D30.

The numbers assigned by Smalbroke remained in use until 1974 and manuscripts acquired after 1771 were given numbers (19–40) in continuation of his numbers. I have noted these 'Smalbroke' numbers in brackets after the current numbers. MS. 28 was not numbered until 1974.

Only MSS. 28 and 31 have escaped rebinding. Handsome eighteenth-century bindings cover six medieval manuscripts: see below, MS. 16.

1. (1). *Evangelia: 'The Lichfield Gospels'* s. viii med. (?)

1. 118 leaves, paginated 1–236, of a Gospel Book ending imperfectly at Luke 3: 9 'exciditur'. Described by E. A. Lowe, *Codices Latini Antiquiores*, 2nd edn., ii (1972), no. 159: bibliography there and in *Supplement* (1971), p. 46. See also for the decoration, J. J. G. Alexander, *Insular Manuscripts*, 1978, no. 21, with bibliography and facsimiles of seven of the eight illuminated pages (pp. 5, 142–3, 218–21, but not p. 1, which is badly damaged); also for the parchment and quiring and the new binding of 1962, R. Powell, 'The Lichfield St Chad's Gospels: Repair and Rebinding, 1961–2', *The Library*, 5th series, xx (1965), 266–76, with 9 plates.

Matthew, pp. 1–141 (ff. 1–71^{r}). Portrait and symbol of Mark, p. 142 (f. 71^{v}). Mark, pp. 143–217 (ff. 72–109^{r}). Portrait and symbol of Luke, p. 218 (f. 109^{v}). Four-symbols page, p. 219 (f. 110^{r}). Cross-carpet page, p. 220 (f. 110^{v}). Luke, pp. 221–36 (ff. 111–118^{v}). The portrait of Matthew and presumably canon tables are missing. f. 110, a singleton (?) between the portrait of Luke and his Gospel, is likely to be out of place and to have been originally at the beginning as a 'frontispiece' before Matthew: the beginning is the usual place for a four-symbols page (Alexander, p. 72). The designs of pp. 5 and 143, the 'Xt̄i' page of Matthew, and the 'Initium' page of Mark (Alexander, pls. 76, 50) suggest a special relationship with the Lindisfarne Gospels (ibid., pls. 44, 46).

2. pp. 241–4 Two complete leaves and part of a third leaf of a manuscript written in France (?) in s. x^{2} and used presumably in the medieval binding of art. 1.

pp. 241–2 contain Boethius on the Categories of Aristotle from 'perpenserit' to 'in qualitatibus posse', *PL* lxiv. 249/7 up–251/12 up. pp. 243–4 are the two conjoint leaves of a bifolium laid sideways, one leaf complete and the other a half leaf cut down the middle. The complete leaf contains an abbreviation of the text of Boethius from 'conuertuntur' (287/14) to 'quod sub se aliquas partes spetiesque contineat quando' (294/end: the text here seems to be unfinished). The half leaf contains most of chapters 10 and 11 of the Boethian translation of Aristotle, De interpretatione (*Aristoteles Latinus* II. 1, pp. 23/3-29/5 = Bekker 20b/19-22a/10).[1] Written space of pp. 241-2 212 × 140 mm. 34 long lines. pp. 241-2 are in one good hand and pp. 243-4 in two other less good hands.

ff. iii + 118 + xi. Of the fourteen flyleaves: two are medieval leaves, above, art. 2; one, pp. 247-8, contains notes about the manuscript by Archdeacon Smalbroke drawn up in 1750 and 1758 and copied here in 1783; two, pp. 251-4, are leaves on which Powell recorded his account of the rebinding; nine, pp. i-vi, 237-40, 245-6, 249-50, 255-8, are blank leaves inserted by Powell. 308 × 223 mm. Written space *c.*250 × 190 mm. 20 long lines.

Cut into single leaves by a binder (Powell, p. 259), now reassembled as nineteen six-leaf quires and one four-leaf quire (Powell, p. 264). Originally, fifty-four bifolia in 12 quires and ten singletons (ff. 35, 50, 59, 70, 71, 80, 96, 108, 110, 118: pp. 69-70, 99-100, 117-18, 139-40, 141-2, 159-60, 191-2, 215-16, 219-20, 235-6) are posited in Powell's reconstruction (pp. 266-76).

Two older bindings are kept separately, one of *c.*1707 and one of 1862 by F. Bedford, on whom, in this connection, see Henry Bradshaw, *Collected Papers*, p. 459.

For the provenance, not Llandaff, but Llandeilo-fawr in Ystrad Tywi, Dyfed, until s. x^1 and then Lichfield, see M. Richards, 'The "Lichfield" Gospels (Book of "Saint Chad")', *Journal of the National Library of Wales*, xviii (1973), 135-46. An entry in Old English made at Lichfield in s. xi^1 is on p. 4: see N. R. Ker, *Catalogue of Manuscripts containing Anglo-Saxon*, 1957, no. 123.

9. (40). *Biblia (pars)* s. xii ex.

The five sapiential books in the usual order, followed by the Prayer of Solomon, Pauline and Catholic Epistles, and Job.

The Prayer of Solomon, Et inclinauit . . . coram te (Ecclesiasticus 51), has an *explicit* of Ecclesiasticus both before and after it. Romans follows on the same page (f. 50^v). Hebrews is followed by Catholic Epistles on a new leaf, but in the same quire (f. 92). Jude ends on f. 100: 100^v blank. Job fills the last two quires.

Missing leaves contained the end of Ecclesiastes, the beginning of Song of Songs, the end of Philemon, and the beginning of Hebrews, and a leaf of Hebrews is missing after f. 91. Part of f. 1 has gone and f. 2 is badly stained.

Books are written in unnumbered paragraphs, each introduced by a coloured initial: for example, Wisdom is in 61 and 1 Corinthians in 22 paragraphs. Chapter numbers and running titles were added later. The only prologues are the common ones to Pauline Epistles, Stegmüller, nos. 677-783: that to Hebrews is missing in the gap after f. 86. The heading is in each case 'Argumentum'. The introduction to Ecclesiasticus, 'Multorum nobis . . .', is absent.

ff. iv + 116 + iv. 218 × 140 mm. Written space 170 × 95 mm. 38 long lines. Collation: 1^8 2^8 wants 7, 8 after f. 14 $3\text{-}11^8$ 12^8 wants 2 after f. 86 and 7 after f. 91 13^{10} wants 9, 10, probably blank, $14\text{-}15^8$. Initials on ff. 1-100: (i) 5-line, blue with red ornament, or blue and green with red ornament, or red and green with green ornament; (ii) 2-line or 3-line, blue,

[1] I owe this identification of De interpretatione to Dr L. Minio-Paluello.

green, or red, with ornament in one of the other colours. Initials on ff. 101–16 are red, without ornament. Binding of s. xx by Birdsall, Northampton. Secundo folio *enim erit*.

The writing looks more French than English, but marginalia of s. xiv are in English hands, ff. 51, 73. Armorial book-plate of E. R. O. Bridgeman, rector of Blymhill, Staffs. (prebendary of Lichfield, †1940). Bequeathed by him.

10. (41). *New Testament (in English)* s. xv in.

1. ff. 1–124v Matheu þat was of iudee as he is set firste in ordre of þe gospeleris ... The book of þe generacioun of ihesu crist: þe sone of dauiþ ...

Four Gospels, Pauline Epistles, Acts, Catholic Epistles, and Apocalypse in the later Wycliffite version, with the usual prologues. Not known to Forshall and Madden.

2. f. 124v I þonke þe lorde god full of myht ... saue me oute of synne amen.

IMEV, no. 1369. 8 stanzas, 64 lines, of the text printed from the Vernon manuscript in EETS cxvii. 744–6. Stanzas 4–6 there do not occur here. Printed by B. S. Benedikz in *Studies in English Language and Early Literature in honour of Paul Christopherson*, Coleraine, 1981, pp. 33–9.

ff. iii + 126 + iii, foliated (i–iii), 1–41, 41A, 42–50, 50A, 51–124, (125–7). 268 × 203 mm. Written space 205 × 152 mm. 2 cols. 44 lines. Collation: $1\text{–}15^8$ 16^8 wants 7, 8, probably blank. Quire signatures p, q are to be seen; the rest cut off. One good textura throughout art. 1. 4-line and 2-line blue initials with red ornament. Binding of s. xx in. by Birdsall, Northampton. Secundo folio *in þe desert*.

Written in England. Armorial bookplate of E. R. O. Bridgeman. Given as MS. 9.

14. (39). *Bernardus, De consideratione* s. xiv med.

Incipit primus liber bernardi. abbatis clareuallensis. ad dominum papam (*cancelled and replaced later above the line*) eugenium. de consideratione. Subit animum dictare ... sit finis libri set non querendi. Explicit.

SBO iii (1963), 393–473. Five books. 'Assit principio sancta maria meo. ne scribam [uanum] duc pia uirgo manum' at the head of f. 1 in the scribe's hand.

ff. iii + 27 + iii. 225 × 165 mm. Written space 165 × 120 mm. 35–6 long lines. Collation: $1\text{–}6^4$ 7^4 wants 4, blank. Initials: (i) 4-line on f. 1, red and blue with ornament of both colours; (ii) 2-line beginning bks. 2–5, red or blue. Capital letters in the ink of the text filled with pale yellow. Gilt calf binding, s. xix in., for Sir William Betham, as Canterbury Cathedral, Add. 66 (*MMBL* ii. 308) and Cambridge, Fitzwilliam Museum, McClean 134. Secundo folio *non est alternam*.

Probably French and part of a larger volume. In England by s. xvi, to judge from scribbles on ff. 26v–27v and the cancelling of 'papam'. Sir W. Betham[1] sale by Sotheby and Wilkinson, 1 June 1854, lot 14. Bought by Lord Ashburnham from Upham and Beet. Acquired

[1] Sir William Betham was a collector who increased the number of his manuscripts by disbinding them and rebinding parts separately.

with other 'Ashburnham Appendix' manuscripts by H. Yates Thompson in May 1897: his label 'Ashburnham Appendix N° LXXX May 1897' inside the cover: Appendix sale, 1 May 1899, lot 33. 'Presented to the Lichfield Cathedral Library by the Rev. Thomas Barns, Vicar of Hilderstone. Sept. 18 1899', f. ii.

16. (6). *Prick of Conscience, etc. (in English, Latin, and French)*

s. xv in.

1 (quires 1, 2). ff. 1-15 Cum omnes homines natura scire desiderent. O summa et eterna sapiencia . . . ac felicitatis eterne. Explicit tractatus. qui scire mori merito nuncupatur necessarius perlectori.

Henricus Suso, Horologium Sapientiae (*SOPMA*, no. 1872), bk. 2, ch. 2. ff. 15v-16v blank.

2 (quires 3, 4). ff. 17-34v Incipit tractatus qui scire mori appellatur. Syþþe al manere men desireth by kynde . . . and ioye þat is in heuyn. Amen.

A translation of art. 1 into English. Jolliffe, L. 8(a).

3 (quires 5-23). ff. 35-189v The m'yh'te (*perhaps from* miȝtte) of þe fader almyȝtty . . . þt for oure loue made al þynge Amen. Here endeþ þe bok þt ys cleped þe pryk of concyens.

IMEV, no. 3429. 13. A text of the 'Southern Recension' of Prick of Conscience, lacking two quires (16 leaves): f. 123v ends at line 4536 of R. Morris's edition (1863) and f. 124 begins at line 4914; f. 163v ends at line 7122 and f. 164 begins at line 7857. Probably 352 lines are missing in each gap. Readings of this copy are noticed by K. D. Bülbring in *Transactions of the Philological Society*, 1888-90, pp. 279-83. A letter from him to Furnivall written in September 1889 is loose inside the cover.

4 (quires 24, 25). ff. 190-205v Incipit libellus Beati Anselmi episcopi de quatuordecim partibus beatitudinis hoc modo. Nunc inuestigare iuuat quantum boni sibimet ipse faciat . . . et imperium nunc et imperpetuum Amen. Explicit libellus beati Anselmi Archiepiscopi Cant' (de) xiiii partibus beatitudinum.

Chapter 5 of the Dicta Anselmi of Alexander of Canterbury in the earlier recension: ed. R. W. Southern and F. S. Schmitt, *Memorials of St Anselm*, 1969, pp. 127-41.

5 (quires 26-9). ff. 206-32 Incipit libellus beati anselmi episcopi de xiiiicim partibus beatitudinis. Nunc inuestigare iuuat etc. The sentence of thys chapitur is þus in enghische (*sic*). Hit is spedful . . . Whare fro god defende vs. A.M.E.N.

A translation of art. 4 into English. f. 232v blank.

6. ff. 233-247v Incipit libellus beati Anselmi episcopi de quatuordecim partibus beatitudinis. etc. Ore il eide a sercher quant de bien celui fait . . . il suffrera. Purce en y (*ends imperfectly a few lines from the end of the text*).

A translation of art. 4 into French.

ff. ii + 246 + ii, foliated (i, ii), 1-225, 227-47, (248-9). f. ii, a medieval flyleaf ruled for 25 lines, is perhaps an unfilled leaf of quire 31. 258 × 185 mm. Written space 165 × 110 mm. 21 long lines in arts. 1, 2, 22 in art. 3, and 25 in arts. 4-6. Collation: $1\text{-}3^{8}$ 4^{10} $5\text{-}10^{8}$ 11^{8} + 1 leaf after 8 (f. 91) $12\text{-}22^{8}$ 23^{10} $24\text{-}28^{8}$ 29 two (ff. 231-2) 30^{8} 31^{10} wants 8-10. Quires 5-23 signed a-l, n-r, t-x. Large textura, changing at ff. 17, 35, 83, 190, 206 (3^{1}, 5^{1}, 11^{1}, 24^{1}, 26^{1}): art. 1 is in a skilled hand. Initials: (i) beginning arts. 3-6, in colour, patterned in white, on gold grounds decorated in blue and red patterned in white: prolongations into the margins form continuous borders or (arts. 4, 5) short sprays; (ii) beginning arts. 1, 2, gold on blue and red grounds patterned in white: prolongations into the margins. Capital letters in the ink of the text filled with red (arts. 3 (to f. 82^{v}), 5, 6) or pale yellow: the change from red on f. 82^{v} to yellow on f. 83 goes with a change of scribe. Binding of red morocco, s. xviii, gold tooled and with handsome black and green title labels on the spines and handsome marbled endpapers.[1] Secundo folio *ut uix eam.*

Written in England. Given by Frances, widow of William Seymour, Duke of Somerset, in 1673.

20. (7). *Vigilius Thapsensis, Ambrosius, etc.* s. xiii in.

1. ff. 1-20^{v} Incipit proemium in libro sancti ath*anasii* episcopi contra Arrium. Sabellium. atque fotinum de fide catholica. Cum apud niceam urbem . . . (f. 1^{v}) sacra legatur. Epistola constantini. Constantinus constantius. pius. perpetuus . . . gestis indatur. Probus. Perspiciens in idolorum . . . sorte capessant. Explicit liber Athanasii.

Vigilius Thapsensis, De fide catholica (cf. A. Wilmart in *RB* xxx (1913), 272) in an unusual arrangement. *PL* lxii. 155-157/12, 179/39-238/11. f. 3^{v} ends 'denique idem ad Patrem' (edn. 186/30) and f. 4 begins 'Nec potest' (edn., 192/6: two leaves are missing). Bk. 2 begins on f. 6 'Quoniam uos' (edn., 197) and bk. 3 on f. 13^{v} 'Probus. Quia in hoc hodie descendimus . . . coangustet. Arrius. Ego spiritum sanctum' (cf. edn., 220/15).

This version divided into three books has three short passages which belong presumably to the original form of the work: at the end of bk. 1, 'Probus. Iam quia tandem postmeridianum sol . . . auditores'; at the end of bk. 2 after 'proferre' (edn., 220/14), 'nisi forte huic disputationi hodierni diei . . . lucta rimetis'; beginning bk. 3 (see above). They spread the talks over three days.[2] Two of twelve manuscripts in London and Oxford, B.L., Arundel 370 and Add. 15608, have them.

2. f. 21 Epistola Gratiani imperatoris ad sanctum Ambrosium. Ambrosio Religioso . . . quem colimus ihesu cristi.

PL xvi. 875-6.

3. ff. 21-34^{v} Incipit liber sancti Ambrosii orthodoxi episcopi de trinitate ad Gratianum augustum. Regina austri uenit audire . . . trophea mereatur.

De fide, bks. 1, 2. *PL* xvi. 527-90. *CSEL* lxxviii. 1-107: cf. there the heading of MS. *U*. Bk. 1: introductory section and 8 chapters. Bk. 2: introductory section and 4 chapters.

[1] Dr B. S. Benedikz tells me that this binding and the similar bindings on MSS. 23, 29, 30, 35, and 50 are likely to have been made when Canon Smalbroke was caring for the library: the flyleaves usually bear numbers and notes of contents in his hand.

[2] A trace of this arrangement remains in the *textus receptus* in the words *Et alia die* (edn., 197).

4. ff. 34v–66 Incipiunt capitula libri primi de spiritu sancto . . . Incipit liber primus. De spiritu sancto. Iherobáál sub arbore . . . qui alta scrutatur dei? Explicit liber iiius de spiritu sancto.

PL xvi. 703–816. Three books. A table of chapters (19, 12, 22) precedes each book.

5. ff. 66–73 Incipit liber sancti ambrosii de incarnatione domini. Debitum cupio . . . intelligibilium. Explicit liber sancti Ambrosii mediolanensis episcopi De incarnatione domini contra Arrianos.

PL xvi. 818–46. The running title is De incarnatione verbi. f. 66 was annotated in s. xiv.

6. ff. 73v–112v Incipit liber sancti ambrosii mediolanensis episcopi de officiis. primus. Non arrogans . . . instructionis conferat. Explicit liber tercius beati Ambrosii mediolanensis episcopi de [o]fficiis.

PL xvi. 23–184. Bk. 2, f. 93. Bk. 3, f. 102v. Written continuously within books, but chapter numbers covering the three books in one series are pencilled in the upper margins as far as 'xxxiv' midway in bk. 3. ff. 93–113 are damaged by damp and some text has been lost on ff. 110–12. ff. 73v–76 were annotated in s. xiv. f. 113rv blank.

ff. i + 116 + i, foliated (i) 1–12, 12*, 13–27, 27*, 28–32, 32*, 33–113, (114). 285 × 190 mm. Written space 212 × 130 mm. 35 long lines. Writing above top ruled line: 1, 2, 5, 6, 30–1, 34–5 of the ruled lines are prolonged into the margins throughout. Collation: 1^8 wants 4, 5 after f. 3 $2\text{–}12^8$ 13^{10} 14^8 15^4. All in one hand. Initials: (i) ff. 21, 73v, blue and red with ornament of both colours, and edged with green on f. 21; (ii) 4-line (f. 1) and 2-line, blue with red ornament; (iii) 1-line, blue or red. Binding of s. xvii/xviii. Secundo folio *lium et inuisibilium.*

Written in England. An ex-libris of s. xiv (?) cut from the foot of f. 1, except for the tops of two tall letters.

23. (4). *Taxatio ecclesiastica Nicholai IV* s. xiv med.

A list of all benefices in England and Wales with their value, compiled in 1291–2. This handsome copy is not in the same order as that printed for the Record Commission in 1802 and is sometimes verbally different. The order of dioceses is: f. 3 Canterbury; f. 4v Rochester; f. 5v London; f. 22v Winchester; f. 32v Chichester; f. 38 Salisbury; f. 51 Worcester; f. 67 Exeter; f. 75 Bath and Wells; f. 80 Hereford; f. 91 Lincoln; f. 135 York; f. 143v Durham; f. 145v Carlisle; f. 146v York (Richmond, Catterick, Boroughbridge, Amounderness, Lonsdale and Kendal, Copeland, Ripon: edn., pp. 306–8); f. 148 Coventry and Lichfield; f. 165v St Asaph; f. 167v Bangor; f. 169v Llandaff spiritualia; f. 171 St David's spiritualia; f. 174 Llandaff temporalia; f. 177v St David's temporalia; f. 181 Norwich; f. 214v Ely.

The Worcester, Exeter, Bath, Lincoln, York, and Norwich lists begin on new quires (quires 8, 10, 11, 13, 20, 27). The first two leaves are missing and the text begins now (f. 3) 'Archidiaconatus. De incertis prouentibus archidiaconatus Cant' xx li' (edn., p. 4, col. 1/17). The other missing leaves were all at quire ends and were probably all blank, with one exception, the leaf after f. 153: the Coventry list now ends imperfectly, f. 153v 'Item habet apud' and the leaf which followed it probably contained only the few lines of text in the edition, p. 255, col. 2, near the foot, *Horewelle . . . Crulefeld in eodem dec.*'. Quire 14 (ff. 99, 100) is at present bound out of order after quire 15 (ff. 101-8). ff. 216-18 are badly damaged. 'exur' is written at the end of most quires and once, in full, 'examinatur'.

f. iii has pasted to it part of a page of medical notes on circulation, s. xviii.

ff. iii + 209 (foliated in a medieval hand 3-215, [216-18]) + ii. The medieval foliation, which has not been replaced, takes account of the nine leaves now missing from quires 1, 9, 10, 19, 22, 26.[1] 312 × 230 mm. Written space 240 × 190 mm. 2 cols. 40 lines. Collation: 1^8 wants 1, 2 (ff. [1, 2]) $2\text{-}6^8$ 7^2 8^8 9^8 wants 7, 8 (ff. [65-6]) 10^8 wants 8 (f. [74]) $11\text{-}13^8$ 14^2 (ff. 99, 100, now bound after quire 15) 15^8 16^{10} 17^4 18^8 19^4 wants 4 (f. [134]) 20^{10} 21^8 22^2 wants 2 (f. [154]) 23^8 24^4 25^8 26^6 wants 5, 6 (ff. [179, 180]) 27^8 28^4 wants 4 after f. 191 $29\text{-}30^8$ 31 eleven (ff. 208-18). Quires 1-12, 15, 16, 18-21, 25-30 numbered at the end I-VI, VIII-XXV. Quires 8-10 numbered at the beginning 'prima'-'Tercia'. Written by more than one hand in anglicana, usually current, and, for headings only, textura. Two scribes, Lond(on) and Welburn, seem to be named at the ends of quires: 'Lond' ius quaternus' on 11^8 (f. 82v); 'Lond' iius quaternus' on 12^8 (f. 90v); 'Welb' ' on 16^8 (f. 118v); 'Lond' ' on 18^8 (f. 130v); 'Welburn' x. examinatur' on 27^8 (f. 188v). No coloured initials. Binding as on MS. 16: a piece of the old red skin is pasted to f. ii.

Written in England.

28. *Annales* s. xiii^2-xiv^1

The Registrum Album, a register of Lichfield Cathedral (Davis, *MC*, no. 563) written mostly by one hand in the early fourteenth century, is described by R. L. Poole, HMC, *14th Report*, Appendix viii (1895), pp. 206-26, and edited by H. E. Savage, *Magnum Registrum Album*, William Salt Archaeological Society xlviii (1926): see especially pp. xiii-xv, xix, xxii-xxv. The first eight quires are not part of the Register and they and the endleaves—the binding is contemporary wooden boards covered with white leather—are noticed here, together with the flyleaves of Dean and Chapter Muniments, D. 30 (XXIVb) which is part of the same manuscript as art. 4.

1. ff. 1-5 (modern foliation) M.CC.XXVI. Obiit Dompnus Hug' abbas . . . pro dicta licencia.

Annals of the Benedictine abbey of St Werburg, Chester, from 1226 to 1259, written in current anglicana of legal type, s. xiii^2, small on ff. 1-4, but larger on ff. 4v-5 when the scribe saw that he had more than enough space at his disposal. The leaves were evidently the first five of the last quire of a larger manuscript used as flyleaves of the Registrum: the space remaining blank on ff. 5v-8v was used for the beginning of an index to the Registrum, s. xiv^1, which is continued on ff. 9-12 (modern foliation). The annals are printed by R. C. Christie, *Annales Cestrienses* (Lancashire and Cheshire Record Society, xiv), 1887, from a later copy which begins with the birth of Christ. MS. 28 is collated with it by Poole, pp. 207-9. In two places the word 'Lich' ' is over erasure of a word likely to be 'Cestr' ' (Poole, p. 207). A reader noted at 1257 that there was a famine also in 1317.

Written space 200 × 125 mm. 40 long lines. Collation: 1^8.

[1] The leaves in question are shown by square brackets in the collation.

2. ff. 1–77 (medieval foliation) Anno ab incarnacione domini m^{o} iiii^{o} indiccione ii^{a}. Tempore Athelredi . . . Obiit Iohannes filius Galfridi.

Annals of the Benedictine abbey of Burton-on-Trent from 1004 to 1258, written in an incipient formal anglicana, s. xiii^{2}, not for Burton itself, according to Poole, p. 211.

Printed from another copy by Luard, *Annales Monastici* (RS, 1864–9), i. 183–461: cf. Poole, pp. 211–12. ff. 77^{v}–82^{v} were left blank.

Written space 215 × 140 mm. 2 cols. 40 lines. Pricks in both margins to guide ruling, ff. 1–12. Collation: 1–6^{12} 7^{10}. The ink becomes darker at f. 39^{v}/1. No coloured initials on ff. 1–39. 2-line blue initials with red ornament from f. 40.

3 (added in the blank space after art. 2). (*a*) f. 77^{rv} A table of years 1259–1312. (*b*) ff. 78–81 Anno dominice incarnacionis sexcentesimo xx^{mo} sexto post mortem Hengistii Anno c^{o} xxx^{mo} nono. Penda quidam . . . Kenelmus decapitatus. (*c*) ff. 81–82^{v} A writ of 1 Edward III and documents concerned with the church of Lichfield.

(*a*). Continues art. 2, but the only entries of events are in 1264, 1265, 1272, 1274, 1280, 1291, 1295, and 1305. They are printed by Poole, p. 212. (*b*). Items of Mercian and Lichfield interest collected from William of Malmesbury, *Gesta Regum* (RS edn., i. 74–95). Additions in the margins printed by Poole, pp. 212–13. (*c*). Poole, pp. 213–16.

4. The pastedowns now raised from the boards (ff. i, 310) and six flyleaves, ff. ii–iv at the beginning and ff. 307–9 at the end, form a complete quire of the temporal of a missal written in England, s. xiii^{1}. The order is i, ii, 307–10, iii, iv: f. i begins '. . . Lux et origo . . .' followed in the same line by the heading of the office of St Thomas of Canterbury; f. iv^{v} ends 'edebant et bibebant' (Luke 17: 27) in the Gospel lesson for Friday after Sexagesima. In the office of Thomas of Canterbury only collect, cue for Epistle (Ego sum pastor, as *Missale Romanum*), secret (Hostias tibi domine beati thome martyris tui atque pontificis dicatas . . . : common of martyrs in *Missale Romanum*, adapted) and postcommunion are provided.

Four more leaves of this missal are inside the parchment cover of Lichfield Dean and Chapter Muniments, D. 30 (XXIVb), which contains documents relating to the church of Lichfield in a hand of s. xv^{2} (1454 or later) written on 'cotton paper', now ten leaves only, but once part of a larger book, no doubt: cf. Cox, p. 99. The leaves are flyleaves between the cover and f. 1, but the two first (ff. i, ii) are sewn to the central parchment tie, so that only corners of i^{rv} and ii^{r} can be seen. f. ii^{v} contains lessons for the common of a martyr, Matthew 10: (23)–32, beginning imperfectly at verse 26, Matthew 10: 34–42 and Luke 14: 26–9, ending imperfectly 'illudere'. ff. iii–iv^{v} are two leaves of continuous text containing lessons for the common of martyrs, Matthew 5: (1)–12, beginning imperfectly at verse 7 'ipsi misericordiam', Matthew 10: 23–32, Matthew 24: 3–13, Luke 21: 9–19, Luke 21: 14–19, Luke 6: 17–23 celo, Luke 12: 1–8, Luke 11: 47–54, Mark 13: 1–13, Mark 13: 5 (only), followed (f. iv^{v}) by smaller script for officia and psalm cues as in *Sarum Missal*, p. 372 (common of confessor and bishop) and the officium Sacerdotes eius induant salutari (*sic*: *Sarum Missal*, p. 377, common of confessors). The text in MS. 28 agrees as a rule with the printed Rouen missal of 1531, ff. xii–xxi^{va}/2. Thus it has Multifarie as the Epistle and Letabundus as the sequence at the Circumcision and Confiteor tibi as the Gospel for the 5th Sunday after the octave of Epiphany. For Rouen influence at Lichfield see Savage, op. cit., pp. xxv–xxvii.

Written space 232 × 150 mm. 31 and (in D. 30) 30 long lines. Initials: (i) 2-line, red or green with ornament of the other colour or blue without ornament; (ii) 1-line, red or green.

29. (2). *Chaucer, Canterbury Tales* s. xv^1

. . . (f. 292^v) Here endeth the boke of the tales of Canterbery compiled by Geffray Chaucers of whoos soule Ihesu crist haue mercy. Amen.

This copy fully described by J. M. Manly and E. Rickert, *The Text of the Canterbury Tales*, 1940, i. 322–8, with a much reduced facsimile of f. 41^v (pl. IIIb) to show the similarity of the decoration of the first thirteen quires here and the Petworth Chaucer. They note that the text is close to New York, Pierpont Morgan 249. Five leaves are missing, but four of them were supplied in s. xvi^2 (ff. 1, 93, 125, 206).

A pencil note on f. 104^v (13^8) sums up the decoration of quires 1–13: 'i hole venett and vii d' (*seven half vinets*) parafys vi^c xl champes xliii'. The 'hole venett' is missing. Six of the seven half vinets are the type ii initials beginning the tales of Knight, Miller, Reeve, Cook, Man of Law, and Squire (ff. 12, 41^v, 51, 59, 70^v, 84^v): the seventh vinet, for the Merchant's tale, was on the leaf now missing after f. 92. Thirty-nine of the forty-three champs (type iii initials) remain on pages of quires 1–13. The decoration of quires 14–37 is by a competent, but less skilled illuminator. The running title of the Miller's tale is 'The Meller'.

ff. ii + 288 + ii, together with four supply leaves, foliated (i, ii), 1–208, 210–92, 294, (295–6). 345 × 245 mm. Written space 213–205 × (Parson's tale) 125 mm. 39 or (ff. 201–94) 40 long lines. Light ruling within frame. Collation: 1^8 wants 1 (supplied, f. 1) $2\text{–}11^8$ 12^8 wants 5 (supplied, f. 93) $13\text{–}15^8$ 16^8 wants 5 (supplied, f. 125) $17\text{–}25^8$ 26^8 wants 6 (supplied, f. 206) 27^8 wants 1 before f. 210 $28\text{–}36^8$ 37^6 wants 5, blank, after f. 292. Quires 1–25 signed a–z, +, ɔ. Quires 26–36 signed (a)–l. Anglicana formata by two hands, changing at f. 196^v (25^4). Initials: (i) missing: see above; (ii) beginning each tale (four missing), 4-line, blue or pink (both colours on ff. 12, 41^v), patterned in white, on decorated gold grounds, with prolongations into three margins; (iii) beginning prologues and parts of tales and at twenty-three points in the Prologue, 2-line, gold on blue and pink grounds patterned in white, with short sprays into the margin; (iv) ff. 13^v, 73 and beginning each stanza of the Man of Law's tale, 1-line, gold with violet ornament or blue with red ornament: elsewhere minor divisions are shown by paragraph marks in the same style. Binding like MS. 16. Secundo folio *with hym*.

Bequeathed by the Duchess of Somerset in 1673.

30. (3). *Codex Justiniani* s. xiii ex.

In nomine domini nostri ihesu cristi codicis domni iustiniani repetite perleccionis liber primus incipit de nouo codice faciendo . . .

Bk. 6 begins a new quire, f. 148: f. 147^{rv} was left blank. Bk. 9 ends on f. 264: ff. 264^v–266^v, left blank, contain (264^v–265) a table of chapters of each book added in s. xiii/xiv and (ff. 265^v–266^v) legal notes and scribbles, mostly of s. xiv.

The commentary in the margins is not continuous and not in the hand of the text, although probably nearly of the same date. It was written later than references to points of law in the Authentica, which are in the margins by the main hand, preceded by the letters CN: see, for example, f. 9. Further marginalia are in English hands, s. xiv. They include verses: f. 1, Prima sacrat . . . (6 lines: Walther, no. 14596); f. 95, Discant illustres stipulari . . . (4 lines); f. 110, Coniugii iura sunt hec specialia plura . . . (17 lines). Four lines of verse on f. 217, 'Exsul abit sine spe . . .', are probably earlier than others and not in an English hand. An erased couplet in English, s. xiv, is on f. 264: the first line begins with 'W' and ends 'no more at þ^e^ iewry (?) scole' and the second begins 'For þ^t^ þ^u^ hast her' '. 'Ihon nycoll our' boteler' on this page is later.

ff. iv + 266 + iv, foliated (i–iv), 1–37, 37*, 38–267, (268–9). ff. iii, iv, 266–7 are medieval pastedowns and the flyleaves conjugate with them. 410 × 245 mm. Written space of text 225 × 115 mm. 2 cols. 49 lines. Wide lower margin. Collation: $1\text{–}14^{10}$ 15^{8} (ff. 140–7) $16\text{–}26^{10}$ 27^{8} (ff. 258–65). The decoration consisted originally of the word 'Imperator' at the beginning of each book in elongated blue capitals with red ornament and, outside the written space, blue initials for the words *Idem* and *Imperator* beginning each paragraph of the text. Later: (1) a picture, *c.*60 × 55 mm, was painted over the word *Imperator* at the beginning of each book, except bk. 3, where it is fitted into a blank space at the end of bk. 2; (2) if the word *Imperator* begins a new titulus, the blue initial *I* is converted nearly always into a human or animal figure, often with a grotesque above and below it running most of the height of the written space; (3) drawings, sometimes illustrating the text, shields, and grotesques were added in the margins, for example on ff. 1^{rv}, 7^{v}, 18^{rv}, 63^{v}, 64^{v}, 76^{v}, 77^{v}, 98, 110. All this added work is English and probably all of one date in s. xiv. Binding like MS. 16. Secundo folio *interagentes.*

Written, text and commentary, in Italy. Later perhaps in France: 'de dono magistri Dyonisii de crienchiis', f. 264, s. xiii/xiv. In England in s. xiv, when the decoration was added, probably for a member of the Gorges family of Litton, Somerset, whose arms, argent and azure a whirlpool, are in the *I* of *Imperator* on ff. 22, 76^{v}, are incorporated into the picture beginning bk. 7 (f. 188^{v}), and clothe a female figure standing in the narrow space on the left of the picture on f. 37^{v}, col. 2: in this figure the left foot turns through a right angle to make the letter *L*, after which 'uton' is written very small. 'Kelseye' at the head of f. 1, s. xiv, is in a hand rather like that which supplied a good deal of annotation: for one of this name at the right date see Emden, *BRUO*, p. 1030. Pledged three times by Richard Harden (Emden, *BRUO*, p. 870: fellow of New College 1395, vac. 1403) in the common college chest (f. 266^{v}): C harden' exposita in cista communi collegii pro xiii s iiii d (*altered to* xxvi s viii d) in vigilia Gregorii pape Anno domini M^o^ CCCC^mo^ primo et habet supplementum 3° folio in textu Seruus non preferatur; C harden' exposita in cista communi coll' pro xvi s' viii d' in festo sancti Aldelmi anno m^o^ cccc iii^o^ et habet supplementum 3° folio in textu Seruus non preferatur; (iii) Caucio Ric' harden' exposita in cista communi collegii pro xx^ti^ s' in crastino sancti Iohannis Baptiste Anno domini m^o^ cccc^o^ iiii^o^ et habet supplementum 3° folio in textu Seruus non preferatur et vnam sonam de viridi serico cum xii stipis argenteis et cum mordente et pendente de argento. Scribbled names are 'harden' ', f. 266^{rv}, 'harden harden Malachias Mullachuy' in one hand, f. 265^{v}, and 'Grenehurst' (f. 266: cf. Emden, *BRUO*, p. 816, for Ralph Grenehurst, fellow of New College 1391, vac. 1401).

Bequeathed by the Duchess of Somerset in 1673, if, as is likely, this is 'A large Civill Law Manuscript in vellum' entered under the mark I.1.5 in the 1671 catalogue of her books.

31. (29). *Decretales Gregorii IX et Innocentii IV, etc.* s. xiii/xiv

1. ff. 1–255^{v} (*text*) Gregorius episcopus . . . dilectis filiis doctoribus et scolaribus uniuersis parisius commorantibus . . . Rex pacificus . . . homagium compellatur.

(*apparatus*) In huius libri principio . . . scilicet de pactis pactiones. Bernardus. Explicit iste liber scriptor sit crimine liber. Amen.

Decretals of Gregory IX surrounded by the apparatus of Bernardus de Botone (Schulte, ii. 124). Bk. 2, f. 68; 3, f. 124; 4, f. 177; 5, f. 199. Bks. 2-4 begin on new quires (7^1, 12^1, 17^1).

2. ff. 256–265^v (*text*) Innocencius iiii^{tus} in concilio lugdune . . . Innocencius episcopus . . . dil' fi. vniuersitati magistrorum et scol' bonon' salutem . . . Cum nuper in concilio . . . consulere supradicti. Expliciunt constituciones Innocencii quarti. (*apparatus*) Cum in multis et infra. infinitas. Nota quod \`infinitas′ in multis articulis . . . procuretis. vsque huc est suspensiua ab inicio. Explicit expliceat ludere scriptor eat.

Constitutions of Innocent IV, surrounded by the apparatus of Bernardus Compostellanus junior (Schulte, ii. 119). The running title is 'Liber V', as on ff. 199–255. After the bull Cum nuper the order is 1–5, 'Cum inter uenerabiles . . . constituta sunt hec', 6, 8–41, 7: cf. Kessler in *Zeitschrift der Savigny-Stiftung für Rechtsgeschichte*, lxii, Kan. Abt. xxxi (1942), 200–2, and Kuttner in *ZRG* lvii, Kan. Abt. xxvi (1937), 442–3. 'Cum inter . . .' is marked 'vacat': on it, cf. Kessler, loc. cit. 300–4, and Kuttner, loc. cit. 450–1. 37 has the passage 'Ecclesiastica censura . . . presenti de cetero' before 'Statuimus . . .'.

An early addition marked 'Innoc' ' is in the lower margin of f. 265^v: Iste sunt dec' que corrupte erant et secundum veram registi (*sic*) litteram emendate. prima est scilicet de electione bone memorie magistri fufi vbi dicebatur . . . de prebenda et canonia etc'.

3 (in the blank space at the end of bk. 3 of art. 1, in the hand of the apparatus to arts. 1, 2). (*a*) f. 176 Ad honorem summe trinitatis et indiuidue vnitatis . . . incipit commentum arboris con(sanguinitatis) per compendium versificat' et per iura probat' a magistro Iohanne de deo yspano per xviii rubricas declaratam . . . a scolaribus vniuersis. Principio nostro etc. Cum super computacionem arboris diuersi diuersa sensissent. . . . Idcirco ego Iohannes de deo yspanus elegi de omnibus sentenciis . . . veniam postulo a scolaribus et magistris. Iohannes de deo yspanus. (*b*) f. 176^v Ad honorem summe trinitatis et indiuidue unitatis incipit comentum arboris affinitatis . . . a scolaribus. Cum enim celeritas locucionum molestias fugiat . . . Idcirco Ego magister Iohannes de deo yspanus sacerdos elegi regulas . . . translato Io. de deo. Explicit arbor consanguinitatis et affi. secundum Io de deo.

Commentaries of Johannes de Deo (cf. Schulte, ii. 94–107), (*a*) surrounding a tree of consanguinity and (*b*) a table of affinity.

4. The endleaves (ff. ii–v^v, 266–269^v) and blank spaces on ff. 255^v, 265^v are thickly covered with formulary documents in hands of s. xiv med. Headings are, for example, 'Procuratorium generalissimum' (f. ii), 'Littera institucionis' (f. ii^v), 'Procuratorium generale valde' (f. v^v), 'Resignacio simplex' (f. v^v), 'Resignacio in curia romana' (f. v^v), 'Littera missa parentibus' (f. 268), 'Supplicacio de appropriacione beneficii' (f. 269), 'Supplicacio pro pluralitate' (f. 269^v: begins 'Supplicat s. vestre deuota filia vestra Isabella dudum regina Anglie').

The abbot and convent of Sulby (Northants) are named on ff. ii, 269. A form of supplication on f. 269v is in the name of William La Zouch. The 'Processus permutacionis M' R' de Hesillebech', Ripon, 28 Sept. 1346 (f. iv: cf. Emden, *BRUO*, p. 883, Adam de Haselbeche), is the chief piece to give names and dates. It is followed (f. ivv) by the bull 'de Reseruacione ecclesie de Stretton', Avignon, 3 Feb., 6 Clement (VI). The lower part of f. 267 has been cut off. It may have contained some part of the text now beginning at the head of the verso '[. . . .] per magistrum Iohannem de merton in scolis M' Ioh' Stepdve[1] (?) Oxon' hora immediata Set quia non est bacularius non audit opponentes': several sentences begin 'Quero'. Notes of the taxation of 'Schutlindon' (Shillington), Barnack, Byfield, and Towcester (Bedfordshire and Northamptonshire) and in whose collation they were are on f. 265v, one with the date 1349. Two writs on f. 255v are addressed to the sheriff of Northampton and name Alan la Zouch, clericus, one with the date 1347, 'Anno Regni regis Anglie xxi regni vero Francie octauo'.

ff. v + 265 + v. f. 270 is a modern parchment flyleaf. For ff. ii–v, 266–9 see art. 4. 340 × 200 mm. Written space of text *c.* 160 × 100 mm. 2 cols. *c.* 45 lines. Collation: 1^{12} 2^{10} $3–5^{12}$ 6^{8} + 1 leaf after 4 (f. 63) $7–9^{12}$ $10–11^{10}$ 12^{8} 13^{10} 14^{12} 15^{12} wants 12 after f. 164 $16–22^{12}$ 23^{8} 24^{10} wants 10, probably blank. Quires 3–24 signed at the beginning a–y in pencil. Written in more than one hand. Initials 2-line, red or blue, with ornament of the other colour. Elongated blue letters with red ornament are used for the first line of each book and for the first two lines on f. 1 (GREGORI/VS EP̄C). Medieval binding of white leather over wooden boards, repaired: six bands: central clasp now, but two straps earlier: the mark of a chain attachment is at the foot of the front cover. Secundo folio in the text *astruebat*; in the apparatus *in deum.*

Written in England. An erased inscription at the top of f. iv. An owner in s. xiv med. was perhaps beneficed in Northamptonshire: see art. 4. 'Iste liber post mortem domini Roberti Snapp presbiteri tradatur ecclesie Cath' lichefeld' de dono M' Thome Chestrefeld' quondam eiusdem ecclesie Canonici Residen' ', f. iiv, s. xv: for the donor, † by Sept. 1452, see Emden, *BRUO*, p. 2088. Perhaps included in Patrick Young's list of the manuscripts of Lichfield Cathedral: no. 35 is 'Decretales libris quinque cum glossa. fol.' and no. 52 'Decretales cum gloss. fol.' (see N. R. Ker in *Mediaeval and Renaissance Studies*, ii (1950), 163). Alienated at some time. Given by John Haworth, chapter clerk, in 1839, as is noted in the library account for that year (MS. 43, f. 22).

35. (5). *Dives and Pauper (in English)* s. xv²

ff. 11–214v Diues et pauper obuiauerunt sibi . . . prouerb' xxi. These been þe wordes of Salomon' þus moch to sayn in englisch . . . ffor þe wys man seyth Qui cito (*ends imperfectly: the catchword is* credit).

Collated as L in P. H. Barnum's edition, EETS cclxxv, cclxxx (1976–80). A member of the 'B' group: cf. edn., I. xiii. Ends in ch. 5 of pt. 9, on the eighth commandment (edn., ii. 220/8). For the unknown author and the date see edn., I. ix. Printed in 1493 and later. The table on ff. 1–10v, 'Riche and pore . . . Powle and Moyses. Explicit', is printed from this copy by Barnum, i. 25–50. The running title of the preliminary section (ff. 11–17: edn., i. 70–80, 65–9) is 'Of holy pouerte'.

ff. ii + 216 + ii, foliated (i, ii), 1–93, 93*, 94–138, 138*, 139–214, (215–16). 290 × 195 mm. Written space 200 × 112 mm. 34–41 long lines. Collation: $1–27^{8}$. Traces of quire signatures remain from 'e' on 6^{1} to 'v' on 21^{1}: the series probably began with '+'. Written in noncurrent secretary, probably all by one hand, which becomes better towards the end. Facsimile

[1] One Stephen rented a school in Cat Street in 1352 (Emden, *BRUO*, p. 1772).

of f. 182 in edn., ii, opposite p. 129. Spaces for the initial beginning each part, usually 2-line, remain blank. f. 11 has a neat 4-line *D* in the ink of the text. Binding as MS. 16. Secundo folio *ungeth his sentence* (f. 2) or *ȝe alleged* (f. 12).

Written in England. Not listed in *CMA*. No. 5 in Smalbroke's catalogue (1771).

50. (18). *Prick of Conscience (in English)* s. xiv^2

ff. 1–109^v The myth of the fader of heuene . . . And to drede out to do aȝeins godis wille (*ends imperfectly*).

Prick of Conscience in the 'Southern Recension', as in MS. 16, art. 3. *IMEV*, no. 3429/14. Ed. R. Morris, 1863. This copy noticed by K. D. Bülbring in *Transactions of the Philological Society*, 1888–90, pp. 279–83. The last words are at a point where six lines of the 'Southern Recension' represents lines 9573–4 of the edition. f. 110 is a waste leaf retained as a flyleaf: it has the same text as f. 105^{rv}, the first leaf of quire 14, but stops abruptly at line 13 on the verso.

ff. ii + 109 + iii. For f. 110 see above. 180 × 130 mm. Written space *c.* 135 mm high. 28–39 long lines: the number increases towards the end. Collation: $1–13^8$ 14 five (ff. 105–9). Written in modified textura: as Bülbring noted, p. 280, there is probably a change of hand at f. 59, where the writing becomes larger. Initials usually 3-line, red, plain or with rough ornament. The capital letter beginning each line is touched with red. Binding of s. xviii. Secundo folio *þanne creatures.*

Written in England, probably in west Norfolk: cf. A. McIntosh in *Medium Aevum*, xlv (1976), 44–5. 'Galfridus Glasier / Reg(ist)rarius' upside down on f. 1, s. xvii: he was chapter-clerk, †1668, and perhaps the donor. Probably *CMA* ii, no. 1412 ('An old Book of English Verses 4to').

Dean and Chapter Muniments[1]

D30 (Vicars Choral, 'Evidence Book', *c.* 1535)

A fifteenth-century parchment book in contemporary binding (Davis, *MC*, no. 570; Cox, pp. 163–7). All the original text has been erased to make way for documents relating to the Vicars Choral, except an initial *D* on f. 1, which was preserved to make the first letter of the word 'De'. By ordinary light a little can be made out here and there and probably all the text not actually written over in s. xvi could be read by ultra-violet light, for example some lines on ff. 2, 6^v ('sue vere et efficacis virtutis prestantissimum donum'), 29^v, 48, 75 ('Ego sum Nemaal spiritus auertens'), 103. General appearances would suit a book of hours, but a book of charms or magic is a possibility. In the last quire each page began with a new text which did not reach all the way down it. A sixteenth-century coloured drawing of David and Bathsheba is on f. 108^v.

ff. iii + 111 + ii. 170 × 132 mm. Written space 112 × 77 mm (f. 48). 22 long lines. Collation: $1–7^8$ 8^8 wants 2 after f. 57 $9–13^8$. Quires signed a–k, a–(c). Written in textura. Gold

[1] Transferred to the Lichfield Joint Record Office, Bird St., in 1973.

2-line *D* on blue and red ground, f. 1. Contemporary binding of wooden boards covered with white leather: four bands: two strap-and-pin fastenings missing.

Written in England.

Fragments in bindings of muniments

D30 (XXI). A bifolium of Augustine on the Psalms. s. xiv med.

Parts of the commentary on Pss. 76–8, corresponding to *PL* xxxvi. 981/27–984/last line and 1005/8 up–1009/26. Written space 255 × 170 mm. 2 cols. 48 lines. Probably the outside sheet of a quire. 2-line and 1-line initials, blue with red ornament.

Written in England. Used as the wrapper of an index of wills made *c.*1611 and headed 'Alporte' after the first name in the index (Cox, p. 97); bound in after rebinding.[1]

D30 (XXIV). Four damaged leaves of a commentary on the Institutes of Justinian. s. xiii ex.

Headings are 'De adopcionibus' and 'De fideiussoribus' (bk. 1, tit. 11; 3, tit. 21). Written space 277 × 180 mm. 2 cols. 82 lines. Spaces for initials remain blank.

Two leaves at each end of a cartulary of s. xv (Davis, *MC*, no. 567; Cox. p. 99). Rebound in s. xix[2]. Presumably taken over from an older binding, perhaps a medieval binding.

D30 (XXIVb). See above, Lichfield Cathedral MS. 28, art. 4.

LICHFIELD. DIOCESAN ARCHIVES[2]

B/A/27ii. *Eight leaves (four bifolia) of a noted missal* s. xiii/xiv

Three bifolia are from the first quire of the temporal and one bifolium is from the second quire. The eight visible pages contain: (1, 2) the beginning and end of the Holy Water service; (3–7) parts of the offices for Saturday in the 3rd week of Advent and for the 4th Sunday in Advent; (8) parts of the offices for Holy Innocents and Thomas of Canterbury. Cf. *Sarum Missal*, pp. 10–12, 21–4, 32–4. Written space 210 × 135 mm. 2 cols. 30 lines.

In use as covers of a volume containing lists of personal names drawn up in 1532–3 and arranged by families (edited by A. Kettle, *A list of families in the Archdeaconry of Stafford 1532–3* (Staffordshire Historical Collections, 4th series viii), 1976), found in the Cathedral Library in 1960 together with the register of Bishop Geoffrey Blythe's visitations (ed. P. Heath, Staffordshire Historical Collections, 4th series vii, 1973). The covers consist of a double thickness of parchment, two bifolia laid sideways and pasted together, at each end. The visible pages are 5 and 2 outside in front, 6 and 1 inside in front, 7 and 8 inside at the back, and 4 and 3 outside at the back.[3]

[1] On rebinding in 1886 twenty-two more leaves were added and the index now runs to 1626.

[2] Transferred to the Lichfield Joint Record Office, Bird St., in 1968.

[3] The pages I have called 4, 5, 6, 7 are the left-hand pages of each sideways pair. 6 and its other side and 7 and its other side may have been adjacent leaves, the last in quire 1 and the first in quire 2 respectively.

LINCOLN. CATHEDRAL[1]

R. M. Woolley, *Catalogue of the manuscripts of Lincoln Cathedral Chapter Library*, 1927, lists MSS. 1-298. The series of 'modern manuscripts' begins at 247. 298 is a collection of binding fragments. Ninety-two of the medieval manuscripts are listed by Ker, *MLGB*, under Lincoln Cathedral. Some thirty others were the gift of Michael Honeywood, dean of Lincoln 1660–81.

300. *Horae* s. xv^1

1. ff. 1–24 Hours of B.V.M. of the use of (Rome), beginning imperfectly near the end of prime.

The leaves on which sext, none, vespers, and compline began are missing.

2. (*a*) ff. 24–5 Ad laudes et ad vesperas ante psalmos dicuntur antiphone. O admirabile commercium creator generis humani . . . (*b*) Item nota quod a pascha usque ad ascensionem. ad benedictus. Magnificat et Nunc dimittis dicitur hec antiphona. Regina celi . . .

3. ff. 26–43 Penitential psalms, the first leaf missing, and (f. 36) litany.

Eighteen martyrs: (12–18) lamberte quintine adriane cosme damiane iohannes paule. Fourteen confessors: (11–14) huberte guillerme iuliane francisce. Seventeen virgins: (7–17) anna agnes auia katherina barbara marguarita geneuefa oportuna fides spes caritas elyzabeth. The prayers after Deus cui proprium are Exaudi, Deus a quo, Inclina domine . . . ut animam famuli tui N . . . , Deus qui nos patrem, Fidelium.

ff. i + 43. 160 × 115 mm. Written space 90 × 62 mm. 17 long lines. Collation: 1 one (f. 1) 2^8 wants 4 after f. 4 and 7 after f. 6 3^8 wants 3 after f. 9 4^8 wants 1 before f. 15 5^4 (ff. 22–5) 6^8 wants 1 before f. 26 7^8 8^4 wants 4 (ff. 41–3). Offsets of pictures with curved tops show on ff. 25^v and 43^v: probably the office of the dead followed art. 3. Initials: (i) f. 1, 4-line blue *D* patterned in white on a decorated gold ground; (ii, iii) 2-line and 1-line, gold on blue and red grounds patterned in white. Framed floral borders in gold and colours, probably continuous on picture pages (a fragment of the border on the leaf missing before f. 26 still remains, misbound after f. 31), on three sides of f. 1. Line fillers in red and blue patterned in white and a central blob of gold. Capital letters in the ink of the text filled with pale yellow. English (?) binding, s. xviii/xix.

Written in north-east France or the southern Low Countries. Given by Archdeacon Hubert Larken between 1933 and 1937.

301. *Horae (in Netherlandish)* s. xv^2

1. ff. 1–8^v Full calendar in red and black, written with 1-line intervals between the months.

[1] Lincoln Cathedral is not included in *CMA*. The earliest printed list seems to be that by Haenel, pp. 799–801. According to him the manuscripts were damp and neglected in 1827 and had been so for sixty years.

Thomas Aquinas, Anthony of Padua, 'Maria int snee' are additions, 7 Mar., 13 June, 5 Aug.; also 'lodewicus mynre broeder', 19 Aug. Certain feasts are marked with letters of the alphabet, A–G, for example, Circumcision with A, Conversion of Paul with B, Ignatius with C: the key is at the end (f. 8^{v}), 'A Sinte pieters kerc . . . G Sinte ians kerc te latranen'.

2. f. 9^{rv} Dit is des conincs manasses ghebet dat hi self ghemaect heuet. Almachtige god onser vaderen . . .

The Latin is Stegmüller, no. 93, 2.

3 (added, s. xvi in., in space left blank at the end of quire 1). ff. 9^{v}–10^{v} A list of the twelve 'gulden vrijdagen'.

4. ff. 11–36^{v} Hier beghinnen die getiden van onser lieuer vrouwen. Use of (Utrecht).

5. ff. 37–51^{v} Hier beghint dat getide van der ewiger wijsheit.

6. ff. 52–71 Hier begint dat lange cruus ghetide.

7. ff. 71–88^{v} Hier beghinnen die ghetiden van den heilighen gheest.

8. ff. 89–102^{v} Hier beghinnen die seuen psalmen van penitencien.

Litany, f. 95: fifty-three martyrs, thirty-nine confessors, and thirty-four virgins. Arts. 9–12 are Meertens, i, nos. 16–19.

9. ff. 103–120^{v} Dit sijn die hondert articulen of gedencknisse van den liden ons heren seer deuoot. Soe wie begheert te gedencken dat minlike liden . . . (f. 104) te houden. Hier endat dat prologus. Hier beghinnen die hondert articulen. Die eerste artikel Des sonnendaghes. Ay ewige wijsheit . . . ende die heilighe geest. Amen. Hier einden die hondert articulen . . . ende hem onse lieue heer verleent (*eleven lines in red*).

H. Suso, Centum meditationes. Ed. H. U. Meyboom in *Archief voor Nederlandsche Kerkgeschiedenis*, i (1885), 177–89.

10. ff. 120^{v}–131^{v} Hier beghinnen die lxv gebeden die iordanis bescriuet. Te metten tijt. O heere ihesu criste des leuendigen gods soen Die te metten tijt voer mi arme sondaer . . .

Jordan of Quedlinburg, O.E.S.A. Zumkeller, no. 646C.

11. ff. 131^{v}–137^{v} Hier begint een goet gebet van den xv pater noster. O mijn alre soetste here ihesu criste een ewighe honichuloeyende soeticheit alle den ghenen die di minnen een bliscap bouengaende alle bliscap . . . O ihesu een waerachtige . . .

The Fifteen Oes of St Bridget.

12. ff. 137v–143 Dese nagescreuen bedinge sel men lesen ter eeren den wonden ons liefs heren . . . O vader der ontfermherticheit ic arme ongeraecte sondige mensche danc di dijnre vaderliker ontfermherticheit ende trouwe die du . . .

Prayers to the Five Wounds.

13. ff. 143–5 Een goet innich ghebet van onsen lieuen heer Ende men macht lesen als men ten heiligen sakerment wil gaen. O du hoghe heerscap godliker volcomenheit . . .

Cf. Meertens, vi, no. 26 art. 1. Lieftinck, p. 139 (Ltk. 317, f. 36v).

14. ff. 145–148v Een ghebet van alle die ghewonde ende ghepijnde leden ons liefs heren ihesu xpristi. Almachtige ewige god ende scepper alre dingen goedertieren verlosser der menscheliker naturen . . .

Lieftinck, p. 155 (Ltk. 322, f. 123v).

15. ff. 149–150v Een ynnich ghebet van der passien ons lieues heren ihesu xpristi. O god hemelsche vader ic arme sondige deerne offer di huden dinen eengeboren soens.

Cf. Meertens, vi, no. 5, art. 5.

16. ff. 150v–154 Dit is een ynninghe beclaghinge der voerledenre sonden ende daer op een suuerlic ghebet om ghenade. O mine siele keer di *omm*e ende ganc in di seluen . . .

17. ff. 154–7 Alle die ghene die aendencken die wapenen ons heren ihesu xpristi . . . O waerdige mes welke besneetste det heilige vleysche . . .

The heading is long and conveys indulgences of three years from St Peter, first pope, of 100 days from each of thirty other popes and of 200 days from Pope Innocent IV.

18. ff. 157–60 Dit gebet maecte sinte augustijn ende soe wie dattet leest . . . Oratio. O alre suetste heer ihesu criste die wt den scoot des almachtigen vaders ghesent biste in deser werelt . . .

Cf. Meertens, vi, no. 6, art. 12.

19. ff. 160v–162 Van der heiliger drieuondicheit een deuoot ghebet wie dattet dagelix ynnichlic leest god en laten sonder gracie ende ghenaden leuen noch steruen. Heer god almachtich du biste drieuoudich in den personen mer een so bistu in den wesen . . .

Cf. Meertens, vi, no. 6, art. 13.

20. ff. 162–3 Sinte augustijns gebet. O god wes genadich mi sondaer ende wes een behoeder . . .

Meertens, vi, no. 23, art. 10.

21. ff. 163–5 Een goet gebet dat sinte augustijn plach te lesen ende wie dattet leest op dien tach en mach hem die viant niet quetsen noch gheen quaet of boos mensche. O suete heer ihesu criste du quaemste in die werelt van dinen vader om ons . . .

22. f. 165^{rv} Dit is sinte Augustijns gebet tegen die doot. Mijn god mijn god mijn ontfermherticheit . . .

Lieftinck, p. 140 (Ltk. 317, f. 112^{v}).

23. ff. 165^{v}–170^{v} Hier beghinnen vijf suuerlike gebeden die ghemaect heuet sinte thomas van aquinen. Dat eerste ghebet. O heer mijn god ic arme sondaersche come . . . Dat ander ghebet. Almachtige god alle dingen wetende . . . Dat derde ghebet van sinte thomas. Verleent mi ontfermhertige god die dingen . . . Dat vierde ghebet. Ic loue ende glorificeer ende benedie . . . Dat vijfte ghebet. Ic aenroep di god alles troostes . . .

24. f. 171^{rv} Totten vijf wonden. Wes gegruet o fonteyn der ghenadicheit . . .

25. ff. 171^{v}–174^{v} Tot onsen heer een deuoet ghebet. Ic roep tot di mijn god ic roep tot di want du biste . . .

Cf. Meertens, vi, no. 14, art. 23.

26. ff. 174^{v}–175^{v} Soe wie dese drie pater noster deuotelic leest in node onsen lieuen (*sic*) heer wil hem troosten ende te hulpe comen. O lieue heer ic vermaen di dijnre vaderliken trouwen die du mi arme sondaer . . .

Three sections. Pater noster between each.

27. ff. 175^{v}–177 Dit ghebet selmen lesen in der missen voer den heiligen sakerment. Ic bidde v heer hemelsche vader duer dijn almachticheit ende doer dinen claren eengeboren soen . . .

28. ff. 177–178^{v} Dese bedinge maechte die eersaem priester beda ende is van den seuen woorden . . . Heer ihesu criste die in den lesten daghe . . .

29. ff. 178^{v}–179^{v} Dit is sinte Ancelmus ghebet. O heer mijn god al heb ic arme sondaer ghemaect dat ic dijn sculdenā bin doch en mocht ict niet maken dat ic dijn creatuer . . .

Meertens, i. 57; vi, no. 22 ter, art. 7.

30. Prayers at mass: (*a*) ff. 179^{v}–182 Een deuote bedinge voer die ontfangenisse des heligen sacraments. Oratio. O mijn heyl ghif mi dat mijn siel . . . ; (*b*) ff. 182–3 Noch voer die ontfangenisse des heiligen sakerments. O heer ihesu criste ic geloue in di volcomeliken ende sette alle mijn troest . . . ; (*c*) f. 183^{rv} Oratio. O heer ic coem totti als een kint tot sinen vader . . . ; (*d*) ff. 183^{v}–184^{v} Dit selmen lesen nader ontfangenisse des heilighen sakerments. Dit sijn die werscappen die di behagen welke werscappen du hebste . . . ; (*e*) ff. 184^{v}–185^{v} Nader ontfangenisse oratio. O alre ghemintste ende alre soetste here ihesu criste Sich ic ongeuallige ende onwaerdige sondaer N bin hier . . . ; (*f*) f. 185^{v} Nader ontfanghenis des heiligen sacraments. O gloriose moeder ons heren ihesu cristi maria die den seluen scepper . . .

(*d*). Meertens, vi, no. 7, art. 5.

31. ff. 185^{v}–218^{v} Hier beghinnen sominige deuote gebede die men lesen sel totter eren der reynre maget marien der moeder gods.

(*a*) ff. 185^{v}–188 Ende eerst die viertien benedictien die hoer seer behaechlic sijn. Aue maria gratia plena dominus tecum. Ghebenedijt so moetstu sijn o alre suetste maecht maria in der ewiger ewicheit . . .

(*b*) ff. 188–191^{v} Dese vijf bliscappen maechte sinte bernaert ter eren onser lieuer vrouwen voer die rouwe der vijf wonden cristi. Ic spreec goedertieren maget tot dinen loue . . .

(*c*) ff. 191^{v}–194 Tot onser lieuer vrouwen. O maecht der maechden ende vrouwe o coninginne der engelen . . . want ic hebbe tegen v . . .

(*d*) ff. 194–195^{v} Om troost ende genade te vercrigen in bangicheit so les dese bedinge die sinte baernaert maecte. O maria coninginne des hemels ende sterre der see en versmade niet dat ghebet . . .

(*e*) ff. 195^{v}–197 Tot onser vrouwen een goet gebet. Ic gruet v. ghebenedide spiegel der ewiger glorien . . .

(*f*) ff. 197–9 Tot onser vrouwen. O heilige ende sonder smitte maget ende moeder des ouersten gods soon . . .

(*g*) f. 199^{rv} Een goet gebet van onser lieuer vrouwen ende heuet gemaect sinte bernaert. O ghebenedide vinster der genaden winster des leuens moeder der salicheit . . .

(*h*) ff. 199^{v}–201 Tot onser lieuer vrouwen een ghebet. God gruet v maria seer blenckende bloem der duerbaerre cruden. O rose . . .

(*i*) ff. 201–3 Die paeus innocencius gaf elken mensche die dese nagescreuen bedinge leest . . . O waerde vrouwe marie moeder ende dochter des alren ouersten conincs . . . Ic bid v bi der heiliger onsprekeliker blijscappen . . .

(*j*) ff. 203–205^{v} Hier beghint een suuerlic gebet van onser lieuer sueter vrouwen. Wes gegruet heilige maget maria dochter des conincs van israel . . .

(*k*) ff. 205^{v}–207 Hier beghint dat alre suetste gebet des heiligen sinte bernaerts tot dat herte der heiligher maget marien daer hi grote genade mede bi haer vant. Ic spreec tot dijnre herten ende aenbede dat als een heilich tempel gods. Ende ic aenbede . . .

(*l*) ff. 207^{v}–208^{v} Tot onser vrouwen. O maria reyne maecht ende moeder des hemelschen conincs een sonderlinge treulucht ende toeuerlaet alre creaturen . . .

(*m*) ff. 208v–209v Soe wie dit gebet alle daghe deuotelic leest voor onser vrouwen beelde die en sel sijn notruft niet oncbreken opter aerden ende hi sel niet steruen sonder biecht ende hi sel dat waerde heilige sacrament ontfangen voer sijn doot. O hoghe edel vrouwe moeder gods maria ic bidde v dat ghi mi nu doet penitencie . . .

(*n*) ff. 209v–211v Tot onser lieuer vrouwen gebet. O grondelose barmhertige moeder . . .

(*o*) ff. 211v–214 Onser lieuer vrouwen lxxii namen. O maria onbeulecte maget . . .

(*p*) ff. 214–15 Soe wie in ghenaden staet ende dit gebet innichlic leest die verdient seuen iear oflaets ende viertich karynen van den paues bonifacius. Die moeder gods vol van rouwen stont bi den cruce . . .

(*q*) ff. 215–18 Die sijn die xxii Aue maria van onser lieuer vrouwen Aue maria. Weest gegruet gebenedide moeder gods maria . . .

(*r*) f. 218rv Die heilige maget machtelt bat onser vrouwen dat si bi haer wesen woude in die vre hare doot . . . O gloriose ewige maget maria ende moeder ons heren uwe onsprekelike ontfermherticheit bidde ic . . .

(*a, d, e, k*). Lieftinck, p. 110. (*c, k, p, r*). Meertens, vi: no. 26, art. 25; no. 12, art. 14; no. 22 *ter*, art. 8; no. 31, art. 23 (three aves of Mechtild van Hackeborn). The 24-line heading of (*i*) conveys an indulgence of 100 days from Pope Innocent and 300 days from Pope John XXII and relates the vision of an abbess 'die lach op hore versceiden' and was surrounded by devils. (*q*) is ten, not twenty-two aves.

32. ff. 218–28 Hier beghint die palmwijnghe in duytsche die men doet opten palmen sonnendach . . . Wi bidden di dauids soen . . .

Blessings, etc., on Palm Sunday.

33. ff. 228–234v Hier beghint die wijnghe der kaers opten den paeschauont . . . Heer heilige vader almachtich ewich god in dinen naem ende dijns soens . . .

34. ff. 234v–239 Hier beghint die wijnge van onser lieuen vrouwen lichtmisse . . . Erudi quesumus domine plebem tuam. Oratio. O heer wi bidden leer dijn volc . . .

35. f. 239rv Van onsen goeden enghel. O mijn alre heilichste engel trouwe behoeder des hemeschen houes edel creatuer . . .

36. ff. 239v–240v Van s' michiel gebriel ende raphahel. O sinte michiel prince ende trouwe behoeder der heiliger kerken ende ouerstarcke verwinre der helscher vianden O sinte gabriel . . .

Meertens, vi, no. 84, art. 41c.

37. ff. 241–264v Hier beginnet die lange vigelie van ix lessen. Mi hebben ombeuangen die suchten des doots . . .

ff. ii + 264 + ii. 167 × 120 mm. Written space 107 × 70 mm. 25 long lines. Collation: 1^{10} $2\text{-}29^{8}$ 30^{6} (ff. 235–40) $31\text{-}33^{8}$. Quires 2–27 signed a–z, ꝛ. Initials with good penwork ornament: (i) blue and red patterned in white with ornament of blue, red, and green (on f. 11 picked out with gold and prolonged into a continuous border); (ii) 4-line, blue, patterned in white, with red ornament; (ff. iii, iv) 2-line and 1-line, blue or red. Capital letters in the ink of the text lined with red. 'Bound by J. Clarke', s. xix^{2}.

Written in the Low Countries. Belonged to A. G. H. G. Gibbs, 2nd Baron Aldenham: Aldenham House book-plate inside the cover and on it in pencil 'Horae N° 9 4 C.9': sale 23 March 1937, lot 186. No. 373 at £15 in a bookseller's catalogue: the relevant strip, marked 'catalogue 236 1943' is pasted inside the cover. Armorial book-plate of William Maurice Wright, Wold Newton: bequeathed by him in 1954.

302. *Psalmi penitentiales, etc.* s. xv med.

1. ff. 1–20 Penitential psalms and (f. 15) litany.

Fifteen martyrs: . . . (7) sauiniane . . . (12, 13) urbane blasi. Fifteen confessors: . . . (4) lupe. Eighteen virgins: . . . (10–15) helena mastidia oyldis syria sauina susanna. f. 20ᵛ blank.

2. ff. 21–70ᵛ Office of the dead.

The ninth lesson is 'In diebus illis. Audiui uocem . . . secuntur illos' (Apoc. 14: 13).

3. ff. 70ᵛ–71ᵛ Si commencent les uers saint bernart. Illumina . . . Oracio. Omnipotens sempiterne deus qui ezechie regis . . .

Eight verses.

4. The pastedown at the end is part of a document, s. xv, apparently a letter to the bishop of Angoulême in favour of Jacques Dautry of Tours, O.F.M., and master of theology.

ff. i + 71 + i. ff. i, 72 are parchment flyleaves. 190 × 138 mm. Written space *c.*93 × 67 mm. 13 long lines. Collation: $1\text{-}2^{8}$ 3^{4} 5 three (ff. 29–31) $4\text{-}8^{8}$. The hand changes at f. 32 (4^{1}). 10-line pictures on ff. 1, 21. Initials: (i) 3-line, blue patterned in white on decorated gold grounds; (ii) 2-line, blue or pink patterned in white on decorated gold grounds; (iii) 1-line gold on blue and red grounds patterned in white. Continuous borders of flowers, gold ivy leaf, etc., on ff. 1, 21: they are separated from the text by bands of colour and gold projecting from the *D* of *Domine* and the *D* of *Dilexi*. Borders on all pages with initials of type (ii) enclose three sides of the text: the right margin is empty both on rectos and versos. Line fillers in red and blue patterned in white and picked out with gold. French binding of gilt black morocco, s. xvi.

Written in France. Probably once part of a book of hours of the use of Troyes: cf. art. 1. The relevant strip from a sale catalogue, s. xix/xx, is inside the front cover and the label of Kerr and Richardson, 89 Queen St., Glasgow, inside the back cover. Obtained by W. M. Wright, 19 Nov. 1927, from Edgar Backus, bookseller, 44–6 Cank Street, Leicester, for £35: item 174 in an undated Backus catalogue kept with the manuscript. Given as MS. 301.

303. *Capitularium, etc.* 1527

1. ff. vi–xii^v Calendar in red and black, graded 'totum duplex', 'duplex', 'simplex', 'iii lec(tiones)', 'memo(ria)'.

Written with a gap of one line between the months. Feasts in red include Joseph, Presentation of B.V.M., and 'Sanctificatio beate marie virginis' (19 March, 21 Nov., 8 Dec.), all 'totum duplex'. A column is provided for the day of the month as well as one for nones, ides, and kalends. 'Aureum autem numerum sic inuenies, nam anno domini mcccccxxvii . . .' occurs in a computistical note at the end of March. ff. i–v^v were left blank: cf. art. 10.

2. Capitula and prayers and noted cues of antiphons: (*a*) ff. 1–68, of the temporal through the year from Advent; (*b*) ff. 68–69^v, 'In dedicatione ecclesie'; (*c*) ff. 70–142, of the sanctoral from Andrew to Saturninus; (*d*) ff. 143–8, of the common of saints; (*e*) ff. 148^v–150, in commemorations of B.V.M.

(*a*) begins 'Ecce dies ueniunt . . . terra. Ad magnificat. a'. Ecce nomen. Oratio. Excita quesumus domine potentiam tuam . . . (*c*). Thirteen feasts are distinguished by an historiated initial: Andrew; Agnes (larger than others); Purification and Annunciation of B.V.M.; Vincent O.P.; Peter Martyr O.P.; Antoninus O.P.; Dominic O.P.; Assumption and Nativity of B.V.M.; Michael; 11,000 virgins; All Saints. Six feasts have an initial of type (iii): Holy Innocents, Conversion of Paul; Joseph; translation of Dominic; Peter and Paul; Petronius (of Bologna, 4 Oct.). Adalbert precedes George at 23 April.

3. ff. 150^v–152 Orationes in offitio defunctorum.

4. f. 152^rv De disciplinis post complet'.

5. ff. 152^v–153 De officio in receptione nouic'.

6. ff. 153–157^v De oratione pro capitulo et pro iter agentibus.

ff. 157^v–163^v were left blank: cf. art. 10.

7. ff. 164–71 Litany.

Fifteen martyrs: (15) Achatii cum sociis tuis. Twenty confessors: (8) Petroni; (9–13), over erasure, Antonini Dominice Thoma Vincenti. A prayer invokes Dominic, another Agnes, and a third—over erasure, but perhaps in the main hand—Peter, Thomas, Vincent, Antoninus, and Katherine. At the end are prayers, 'Omnipotens sempiterne deus in cuius manu sunt omnium potestates et omnium iura regnorum: respice in auxilium christianorum ⁊ ut gentes paganorum . . .', and 'Sancti martialis episcopi et confessoris Oratio. Omnipotens sempiterne deus: qui beatum martialem confessorem tuum atque pontificem ecclesie tue sancte preesse uoluisti . . .'.

8. f. 171^v Cues of an antiphon of St Martha.

9. ff. 174–6 Benedictions. ff. 176^v–177^v blank.

10 (added in blank spaces). (*a*) ff. i–v^v, s. xvii, Collects of SS. Hyacinth, Bonaventura, Joachim, Raymond, Louis, Joseph, and of the rosary of B.V.M.;

(*b*) 157v–158, s. xvi, Prayers of SS. Francis de Paola (†1507) and Monica; (*c*) f. 159, s. xvii, Collects of SS. Agatha and Dorothea; (*d*) f. 176, Collect of St. Louis Beltrand (O.P., †1581).

ff. 189, foliated (an unnumbered leaf pasted down), i–xii, 1–115, 115*, 116–71, 174–7. The foliation 1–177 is sixteenth century. 250 × 180 mm. Written space 158 × 120 mm. 16 long lines. Collation: 1^{12} + 1 leaf after 11 (pastedown and ff. i–xii) 2–6^{10} 7–8^{8} 9^{10} 10–11^{8} 12 four (ff. 93–6) 13–18^{10} 19^{8} (ff. 156–63) 20^{10} wants 9, 10, probably blank, after f. 171 21^{4} (ff. 174–7: 177 is pasted down). Punctuation includes the flex. Initials: (i) 5-line or 6-line (8-line, f. 13) in shaded colours on gold grounds, historiated (f. 13 B.V.M. and Child in glory, f. 41v Resurrection, f. 51v Pentecost, f. 55v Corpus Christi, and in art. 2*c*, see above); (ii) 3-line or 4-line, as (i), but decorated, not historiated; (iii, iv) 3-line and 2-line, blue or red with ornament of the other colour; (v) 1-line, blue or red. Contemporary binding of wooden boards, bevelled on the inside, covered with brown calf: a framed border filled with intersecting circles encloses a panel in which are corner-pieces and a centrepiece within a large diamond the frame of which contains circles smaller than those in the border and not intersecting: a central strap and pin from front to back cover is missing. Secundo folio (f. 2) *inus.*

Written in Italy for Dominican use, perhaps at Bologna (cf. arts. 2, 7). 'II. Cms. 22' inside the cover, s. xviii (?); also '13224' and a fairly recent pencil note in Italian. Item 902 at £10 10*s.* in a catalogue of T. Thorp, Strathfieldsaye, Guildown Road, Guildford: the relevant leaf was loose inside the cover in 1976, but is now missing. Book-plate of W. M. Wright. Given as MS. 301.

304. *Psalterium* s. xv med.

1. ff. 1–6v Calendar in red and black.

'Visitacio beate marie' in red, 2 July. Feasts of St Thomas of Canterbury and the word 'pape' erased. Aelphege, John of Beverley, Botulph, Edward King and Martyr, Arnulph, the Transfiguration and 'De nomine ihesu' added (18 Apr., 7 May, 17, 20 June, 8 July, 6, 7 Aug.); also at 17 Jan. 'S. Sulplicii conf. et pon. S. Antonii' and at 3 Oct. 'dedicacio per totam Canciam', also 'Anno domini 1488 intraui' at 30 Nov., the battle of Blackheath, 1497, at 16 June, and 12 obits (of parishioners ?): Henry Cowe, 1497, at 26 March; John Symson, 1504, at 8 April; John Denne at 20 Apr.; John Wex, 1503, at 24 Apr.; William Denne, 1502, at 3 May; Laurence Burdon and Agnes his wife at 9 Aug.; 'semper hac die in perpetuum 20 d'; John Mayre at 22 Aug.; Margaret Broun at 31 Aug.; R. Byrd and Joan his wife at 30 Sept.; Robert Ballard 1498 at 4 Oct.; Geo(r)ge Crosby 1507 at 9 Nov.; John Tomlynson at 26 Nov.; Alice Yonger, 1507, at 6 Dec.

2. ff. 7–124v Psalms 1–150. Seven leaves missing.

3. ff. 124v–137v Six ferial canticles, Te Deum, Benedicite, Benedictus, Magnificat, Nunc dimittis, Quicumque vult.

4. ff. 137v–141v Sarum litany, ending imperfectly in Fidelium deus.

The saints are almost exactly those in *Brev. ad usum Sarum*, ii. 250–1.

ff. ii + 141 + ii. 237 × 155 mm. Written space 145 × 97 mm. 19 long lines. Collation: 1^{6} 2^{8} wants 5 after f. 10 3^{8} wants 6–8 (ff. 14–18) 4–7^{8} 8^{8} wants 5 after f. 54 9–10^{8} 11^{8} wants 1, 2 before f. 74 12^{6} + 1 leaf after 4 (ff. 80–6) 11–16^{8} 17^{8} wants 8 after f. 141. Quires

5–17 signed c–r in the usual late medieval manner. Initials: (i) 4-line (5-line, f. 7), gold on blue and red grounds patterned in white, with sprays of green and silver into the margins; (ii) 2-line, blue with red ornament; (iii) 1-line, blue or red. English binding, s. xviii: a gilt elephant at the foot of the spine.

Written in England. Art. 1 was annotated, *c.*1500, by a parish priest, probably in Kent. 'N° 17' and 'N° 50', f. 1. 'E libris A. J. V. Radford', f. i. The number 233 and the armorial book-plate of W. M. Wright f. i^{v}. Given as MS. 301.

305. *Ordo baptizandi* s. xvi^{1}

Primum interroget sacerdos quod nomen habere debeat infans quem patrina supra dexterum brachium tenebit. sic quod caput infantis aspicit occidentem. Sufflet in facie eius ter frigido spiritu dicens. Exi ab eo + sathana + da honorem deo viuo et vero . . .

The last forms are on f. 15^{v}, 'Accipe lampadem ardentem . . .' and on f. 16^{v} a form for use when it is doubtful whether the rite of baptism has already been performed. A final rubric is for the baptism of the children of lepers, 'Pueri leprosorum non baptizantur supra communem fontem sed supra piscinam seu peluim aquam baptismalem continentem. que re acta funditur in piscinam'.

ff. i + 16 + i. A medieval foliation i–xvi in red. 208 × 157 mm. Written space *c.*132 × 90 mm. 13 long lines. Collation: 1–2^{8}. Written in debased textura. Initials: (i) f. 1, blue with red ornament; (ii, iii) 2-line and 1-line, blue or metallic red. Red velvet binding, s. xix. Secundo folio *ut suscipias.*

Written in Germany. Arms of Copinger inside the cover, s. xix. The crest and motto 'Virtute et fidelitate' are those used by W. A. Copinger, †1910: cf. Fairbairn, *Book of Crests*, 1905, i. 132. Item 687 in a catalogue of T. Thorp, Guildown Rd., Guildford, Surrey, at £3 3*s.* Given as MS. 301.

306. *Psalterium, etc.* s. xiv^{2}

1. ff. 1–230^{v} (*begins imperfectly*) Qui non abiit in consilio . . .

A liturgical psalter. All Ps. 51 and the beginnings of Pss. 68, 80, 97, and 109 are missing on single leaves after ff. 74, 93, 116, 138, 163. Vespers (f. 164) is interrupted after feria 2 by prime, terce, sext, and none (ff. 174–198^{v}). f. 1 is a fragment.

2. ff. 230^{v}–248 Six ferial canticles followed by Te deum, Benedicite, Benedictus, Magnificat, Nunc dimittis.

3. ff. 248–254^{v} Litany.

Nineteen confessors: . . . (14–19) Nicholae Seuerine Seruati Egidi Eligi Wido. Twenty-seven virgins: . . . (19–24) Benedicta Genofeua (*sic*) Gertrudis Gudila Ramildis Brigida.

4. ff. 255–262^{v} Prayers, (*a–h*) before and (*i–m*) after mass: (*a*) f. 255 Ante perceptionem corporis et sanguinis domini oracio. Domine ihesu criste qui celum et terram fecisti et me ad ymaginem . . . ; (*b*) f. 256 Item de eodem Oratio. Domine

ihesu criste qui patre disponente . . . ; (*c*) f. 258 Item de eodem ad beatam mariam. Misericordissima mater misericordie misericordissimi saluatoris . . . ; (*d*) f. 259 Item ante perceptionem oratio. Fiat michi domine ihesu xpriste . . . ; (*e*) f. 259 Item de eodem oratio. Domine ihesu xpriste fili dei uiui te supple queso . . . ; (*f*) f. 259^{v} Item de eodem oratio. Domine sancte pater omnipotens eterne deus, da michi corpus et sanguinem . . . ; (*g*) f. 260 Item de eodem Oratio. Domine ihesu criste fili dei uiui qui ex uoluntate patris spiritu sancto cooperante . . . ; (*h*) f. 260^{v} Item Oratio. Aue in eternum sanctissima xpristi caro . . . ; (*i*) f. 260^{v} Post perceptionem oratio. Corpus domini nostri ihesu xpristi quod accepi . . . ; (*j*) f. 261 Item post percepcionem. Domine ihesu criste qui ex hoc mundo . . . ; (*k*) f. 261^{v} Item post percepcionem Oratio. Gratias ago tibi domine deus meus qui me peccatorem satiare dignatus es . . . ; (*l*) f. 261^{v} Item post percepcionem oratio. Corpus et sanguis (*etc., nearly as i*). (*m*) f. 262 Item post percepcionem oratio. Domine sancte pater eterne deus exaudi digneris oracionem meam pro me famulo tuo N quia benigna est misericordia tua . . .

5. ff. 263–268^{v} (*begins imperfectly in a prayer to God the Father*) cam et noctibus horis . . . propicius esto michi peccatori N famulo tuo. et omnibus cristianis cultoribus catholice fidei Amen.

6. ff. 268^{v}–269^{v} Oratio bona ad filium. Domine ihesu xpriste fili dei uiui. gloriosissime conditor benignissime redemptor mundi . . .

7. ff. 269^{v}–271 Ad spiritum sanctum. Domine sancte spiritus domine omnipotens coeterne et consubstancialis. patri et filio . . .

8. ff. 271–7 Ad trinitatem Oratio. Adoro te domine. pater. fili. spiritus sancte. trine et et une deus . . . Benedictus sis . . .

9. Prayers to B.V.M.: (*a*) ff. 277–279^{v} Ad sanctam mariam Oratio. Ecce ad te confugio uirgo nostra saluatatio (*sic*) spes salutis . . . ; (*b*) ff. 279^{v}–280^{v} De sancta maria oratio. Beata mater et innupta uirgo gloriosa . . . ; (*c*) ff. 280^{v}–281^{v} De sancta maria. Te supplico uirgo maria mater cristi inmaculata. Puerpera grata . . .

ff. i + 281 + i. 105 × 80 mm. Written space 58 × 43 mm. 15 long lines. Collation of ff. 1–254: $1–5^{12}$ 6^{10} 7^{12} wants 5 after f. 74 8^{10} 9^{14} wants 3 after f. 93 10^{12} 11^{12} wants 1 before f. 117: from here doubtful, but ff. 183–254 appear to be regular twelves: a leaf is missing after f. 138 and a leaf after f. 163. Collation of ff. 255–81: 1^{8} 2^{8} wants 1 before f. 263 3^{8} 4^{4}. Initials of arts. 1–3: (i–iii) 7-line (ff. 34, 56^{v}, 141^{v}, 230^{v}) 4-line, and 3-line, pink patterned in white on decorated blue grounds edged with gold; (iv) 1-line, red or blue. Initials of arts. 4–9: (i) f. 255, 4-line, gold on coloured ground; (ii) 2-line, blue with red and blue ornament; (iii) 1-line, blue. In arts 1–3 capital letters in the ink of the text are touched with red. Binding of s. xx. Secundo folio *Qui non* (f. 1).

Written in the southern Low Countries and (ff. 255–81) in England. 'James Grunnel 1749', f. 222^{v}. Bought by W. M. Wright for £8 8*s*. from William C. Elly, 17a Sweeting Street, Liverpool, whose bill dated 28 June 1926 is kept with MS. 306. Given as MS. 301.

307. *Horae* s. xv in.

Incipit officium beate marie secundum usum romane curi(e).

Hours of B.V.M. in a confused order: (*a*) ff. 1–18, matins; (*b*) ff. 42–52^{v}, 53–56^{v}, lauds and prime; (*c*) ff. 33–35^{v}, 36–38^{v}, 39–41^{v}, terce, sext, and none; (*d*) ff. 28–32^{v}, 19–21^{v}, 21^{v}–22, 23–27^{v}, vespers, compline, Salve regina, special office in Advent (ending imperfectly). Each hour begins on a new leaf and ff. 18^{v}, 22^{v} are blank.

ff. ii + 56 + ii. 112 × 75 mm. Written space 65 × 43 mm. 16 long lines. Collation: 1–2^{8} 3^{2} (ff. 17, 18) 4^{8} (ff. 42–9) 5^{8} wants 8, blank (ff. 50–6) 6^{10} wants 10, blank (ff. 33–41) 7^{6} (ff. 28–32, 19) 8^{8} (ff. 20–7). Initials: (i) beginning each hour and the Advent office, 4-line, pink or blue, patterned in white, on decorated gold grounds; (ii) 2-line, gold on pink and blue grounds patterned in white; (iii) 1-line, blue with red ornament or gold with blue-grey ornament. Capital letters in the ink of the text filled with pale yellow. Continuous floral borders on pages with initials of type (i). Binding of s. xviii. Secundo folio *dominus deus*.

Written in France. Given by Miss Rennell, The Old Posting House, Partney by Spilsby, in November 1957.

308. *Graduale* s. xvi^{1}

1. ff. 1–259^{v} Ad te leuaui . . .

Temporal from Advent to the 24th Sunday after Pentecost. In the Easter Eve litany, ff. 177–84, the apostles are Peter, Paul, John, and James, the martyrs Stephen, Laurence, and Vincent, the confessors Gregory, Martin, Augustine (Sancte pater augustine ora pro nobis), and Nicholas de Tolentino, and the virgins Mary Magdalene, Agnes, and Monica (Sancte mater monicha ora pro nobis). Rubrics apart, the text seems to agree with *Missale romanum*. One leaf missing (Wednesday–Thursday in the week after Easter).

2. ff. 260–265^{v} Kyrieleyson, Gloria, Sanctus, Asperges me, Vidi aquam egredientem. f. 266^{rv} blank.

ff. i + 266. Contemporary foliations at foot of versos in pencil and in side margin of versos in red ink. 535 × 370 mm. Written space 380 × 270 mm. 6 long lines and music. Collation: 1–19^{10} 20^{10} wants 2 after f. 191 21–26^{10} 27^{10} wants 8–10, blank. Minims 11 mm high. Initials on nine pages: (i) green and red or blue and gold on grounds of silver and colour, historiated: continuous border on f. 1; (ii) as (i) but decorated, not historiated; (iii) blue with red ornament or red with blue or violet ornament; (iv) blue with red ornament or red with violet ornament. Capital letters in the ink of the text filled or lined with yellow. Thick wooden boards, re-covered, but retaining the stamped metal (yh̄s and lamb and flag stamps) corner- and side-pieces and on the front cover only a metal centrepiece. Two projecting studs at the head and on the side of each cover.

Written in Italy, probably for Augustinian use. A blank shield in the lower border on f. 1. Armorial book-plate of W. M. Wright. Given as MS. 301.

Muniments of the Dean and Chapter

J. A. Bennett's report on the contents of the muniment room of Lincoln Cathedral, HMC, *12th Report*, Appendix ix (1891), 553–72, describes or notes the existence of A/1/11 (p. 560), A/2/3 (p. 561), A/2/18 (p. 563), A/2/20 (p. 563), Di/20/2/Bl (p. 568), Di/20/3 (p. 566). The muniments were transferred to the care of the Lincolnshire Archives Office in 1949. The portfolio of fragments mentioned in the last lines of the HMC report (p. 571) has not been found.

A/1/11. *Taxatio ecclesiastica Nicholai IV* s. xiv in.

A list of all benefices in England and Wales, with their values, compiled in 1291-2. Unlike the edition printed for the Record Commission in 1802, this copy is in two parts, 'spiritualia' (ff. 1-207) and 'temporalia' (ff. 212-391). In the first part Lincoln is in first place, ff. 1-39^{v}: Hic incipiunt taxaciones dignitatum ecclesie Lincoln' et prebendarum eiusdem . . . Anno regni regis Edwardi primi vicesimo. Lincoln is followed by: f. 40 Ely; f. 43^{v} Carlisle; f. 47 York; f. 64 Durham; f. 70 Worcester; f. 82 London; f. 93 Norwich; f. 120^{v} Canterbury; f. 125^{v} Rochester; f. 128 Salisbury; f. 142 Winchester; f. 150 Chichester; f. 158 Bath and Wells; f. 165^{v} Exeter; f. 176 Hereford; f. 183^{v} Coventry and Lichfield; f. 194 St David's; f. 199 Llandaff; f. 201^{v} Bangor; ff. 203^{v}-207 St Asaph. The temporalia are in the order: f. 212 Canterbury; f. 214 Rochester; f. 215^{v} London; f. 241^{v} Chichester; f. 245^{v} Winchester; f. 252^{v} Salisbury; f. 262^{v} Bath and Wells; f. 266^{v} Exeter; f. 273 Worcester; f. 294 Hereford; f. 306^{v} Coventry and Lichfield; f. 328 Lincoln; f. 369 Ely; f. 374^{v} York; f. 376^{v} Durham; f. 377^{v} Carlisle; f. 377^{v} St David's; f. 380 Llandaff; f. 386^{v} Bangor; ff. 388^{v}-391 St Asaph. No Norwich temporalia.

The York, Worcester and London lists of spiritualia begin on new quires (5^1, 7^1, 8^1). f. 391 is blank, except for the first two lines on the recto, 'remittebatur eidem (*sic*) Abbatisse propter paupertatem suam. Inde Decima', which are in the anglicana formata used for summaries and so are, no doubt, the last words of the summary for the diocese of St Asaph. The abbey referred to is probably Llanllugan, but the entry about it is now lost: f. 390 is much damaged and fragmentary. Notes about Carlisle and Lincoln were added early in the margins of ff. 68 and 369: 'pro spiritualibus dioc' Karliolens' et eciam ipsius Episcopi si que fuerunt deficiunt vt videtur set require in proximo quaterno precedente'; 'pro temporalibus Episcopi linc' hic deficiunt et in particulis et in summa'. Running titles added on ff. 1-63. ff. 46^{rv}, 68^{v}, 69^{rv}, 207^{v}-211^{v} blank.

ff. 380-90 have been damaged by damp: 381-90, five bifolia, are at present loose.

ff. xi + 391 + xli. ff. x, xi are a conjugate pair of medieval parchment leaves, once pastedown and flyleaf. 350 × 245 mm. Written space 270 × 172 mm. 40 long lines. Collation: 1-3^{12} 4^{14} wants 11, 12, blank, after f. 46 5^{12} 6^{12} wants 11, blank after f. 69 7-17^{12} 18^{12} wants 11, 12 blank (ff. 202-11) 19-32^{12} 33 twelve (see above). Quires 7-17 are numbered on last versos i-xi and quires 19-32 in the same place i-xiiii. Current anglicana and, for headings and summaries, anglicana formata, probably by three hands, 1-45^{v}; 47-68^{v}; 70-390^{v}. Ascenders are sometimes split and sometimes looped: the splitting is usual on ff. 1-68^{v}[1] and these leaves look rather earlier than the rest, because of this feature and the heavier diagonal of *d*. No coloured initials. Rough calf binding, s. xvii. Secundo folio *Vicaria eiusdem*.

'This Book belongs to ye Church of Lincoln', f. ii, s. xvii.

[1] But the looped *b* is used in the word *alibi*: the disadvantages of splitting the tops were easily seen in this word.

A/2/3 ff. 1–48. *J. de Schalby, Historia episcoporum ecclesiae Lincolniensis, etc.* s. xiv med.–xiv^2

1. ff. 1–45v Cathedralis ecclesie Lincoln' fidelibus vniuersis Iohannes de Schalby Canonicus eiusdem ecclesie vitam bonam exitumque felicem. Quoniam ob defectum scripture rerum bene gestarum memoria sepe perit: ego Iohannes quedam contingencia statum ecclesie Lincoln' predicte quorum aliqua scripta reperi in archiuis ecclesie memorate. aliqua a senioribus meis didici veritate fulciri et aliqua fieri vidi censui redigere in scripturam ad certitudinem presencium et memoriam futurorum. De prima fundacione ecclesie Lincoln'. Tempore Willelmi Regis anglorum primi . . .

Printed as far as f. 30 'plenius continetur' in *Giraldi Cambrensis opera*, vii (ed. J. F. Dimock, RS, 1877), 193–216. English translation by J. H. Srawley, Lincoln Minster Pamphlets, no. 2 (1949). The latest date seems to be 1330 (f. 34) and the latest bishop is Henry de Burghersh (1320–40). John de Schalby signs a document of 1324 as one of the chapter (f. 30). A space was left on f. 34v—filled later with a document of 1467—after which is the heading (f. 35) 'Rubricelle J. de Schalby facte super probacionibus suis propriis': this section (ff. 35–36v) begins 'Inspecta submissione facta' and ends 'Tradit' per Iohannes de Schalby etc' '. ff. 37–43v contain a continuously written piece on the customs of the church, 'Cum consuetudinis vsusque longeui non sit vel auctoritas . . . propter solempnitatem exposicionum' and ff. 44–45v a list of obits and payments, and between them, f. 43v, is an added piece on the ceremonies at the installation of John de Bokyngham as bishop, 23 Oct. 1363. On f. 28 the word 'papa' has been erased in a reference to Pope John XXII. f. 19 is half torn away.

2 (added by another hand to fill quire 6). ff. 46–48v Ut quilibet qui filius ecclesie censeri desiderat . . . villa.

Customs of the church of Lichfield: f. 46 is headed 'Lich' '. f. 48v is worn from exposure.

ff. 48. ff. 1–46 have a medieval foliation. *c.*290 × 195 mm. Written space 202 × 145 mm. 35 long lines. Collation: 1–6^8. Art. 1 is in anglicana, current at first, but as a rule anglicana formata after the turn from the recto to the verso of f. 3. Art. 2 is in current anglicana, s. xiv^2. Red initials, mostly 2-line: at first they tend to be too small for the spaces left for them. Bound in s. xvii in the same style as A/1/11, together with ten leaves of a sixteenth-century book numbered 28–37 and containing (28–33) a visitation of the church of All Saints, Derby and (34–7) a rental of 'Eyton', etc. Secundo folio *Robertus.*

Written probably at Lincoln. 'Liber Willelmi Snawdun notarii publici', f. 48v: Bennett, p. 561, notes that he was an officer of the Chapter, s. xvi med.

A/2/18/7. *A bifolium of the astronomical tables of John Holbroke* s. xv^1

ff. 1v, 2r contain the introductions to Holbroke's tables, 'Gloriosus et sublimis deus a rerum exordio . . . secundum eundem' and 'Quoniam celestium motuum . . . propositum sit': cf. Thorndike and Kibre. For the author, master of Peterhouse, Cambridge, by July 1437, see Emden, *BRUC*, p. 309, and *DNB*. The words 'Radix cantabrig' ' and 'Argumentum lune 1433' occur in headings to tables. Written space 200 × 130 mm.

Written in England. Probably used as a wrapper.

A/2/18/8. *A leaf of Isidore, Etymologiae* s. xiii[1]

End of bk. 4, table of 39 chapters of bk. 5, beginning of bk. 5. *PL* lxxxii. 197/8–207/3. A handsome copy. Written space 260 × 150 mm. 2 cols. 72 lines. Initials: (i) of bk. 5, 4-line blue *M*; (ii) 2-line, blue or red with ornament of the other colour.

Written in England. Formerly a wrapper. Marked 'Willelmi Smith episcopi' (bishop of Lincoln, 1495–1514).

A/2/18/30. *A leaf of Jerome, Epistolae* s. xii med.

Part of letter 77: *PL* xxii. 695. Written space 237 × 145 mm. 2 cols. 36 lines.

Written in England.

A/2/20/1. *A bifolium of a lectionary* s. ix

Dominical and ferial lessons after Easter. Written space 222 × 140 mm. 26 long lines.

Written in France.

A/2/20/2. *A leaf of a lectionary* s. xi med.

Lessons for Wednesday, Thursday, and Friday after Easter. Written space 205 × 130 mm. 24 long lines.

Written in England.

A/2/20/3. *Horae (fragm.)* s. xv in.

Parts of two adjacent quires of a Sarum book of hours of the kind described in *MMBL* i. 46–8. In the similar book of hours in Edinburgh Univ. Libr. MS. 40, the pieces here occur: (1) on ff. 67v–68v, 71–3; (2) on ff. 74v–75v, 78–80v; (3) on f. 81rv; (4) on ff. 82v–84v.

1. ff. 1rv and 2–3v A leaf of vespers and two leaves of compline of B.V.M.

2. ff. 4–9 (*a*) Oratio de sancta maria. Salue regina . . . : followed by (*b*) the versicles 'Uirgo mater ecclesie . . . uentris tui', (*c*) the first word of a heading 'Oratio', (*d*), after a missing leaf, the farsing of Salve regina with Salve virgo virginum, beginning in *Exules* at the words 'priuati paradisi gaudio' (f. 6), and (*e*) a collect, 'Deus qui de beata maria . . .' (f. 9).

(*b*). *RH*, no. 21818. (*d*). *RH*, no. 18318. Almost the whole of f. 5 has been torn away.

3. f. 9rv Ad salutandum mariam. O intemerata . . . orbis terrarum inclina mater . . . dileccionis sue con- (*ends imperfectly*).

4. ff. 10–11v Oratio de sancta maria uirgine. Obsecro te . . . futura moderetur. Vitam (*ends imperfectly*).

ff. 11. 205 × 135 mm. Written space 115 × 65 mm. 19 long lines. Collation: 1^8 wants 2, 3, 6, 7 (ff. 1–4) 2^8 want 6 after f. 9, and nearly all 1 (ff. 5–11). Initials: (i, ii) 3-line and 2-line, gold on blue and red grounds patterned in white; (iii) 1-line, gold with blue-grey ornament or blue with red ornament.

Written probably in the Low Countries for use in England. Among fragments assembled in s. xix: not, apparently, leaves used in binding.

Di/20/2/B1, ff. 22–5. *Officium Iohannis de Dalderby* s. xiv[1]

A contemporary copy of letters to the pope, mostly dated in 1327–9, in favour of the canonization of John de Dalderby, bishop of Lincoln 1300–12 Jan. 1320 (Emden, *BRUO*; *DNB*) is followed by an office for John de Dalderby written by the same hand, but on leaves of smaller size. (f. 22) Istoria de sancto Iohanne de Dalderby quondam Episcopi (*sic*) Lincoln' ad vesperas A'. Forma morum doctor veri fac nos pater promereri vt possimus intueri wltum regis glorie . . . R' Iohannes Lincolnie presul cristo care . . . Or' Deus qui beatum Iohannem confessorem tuum atque pontificem . . . Ad mutat' Inuitat' Confessorem dominum venite adoremus confesoris Iohannis festa celebremus. P' Venite . . .

Consists of vespers, matins (three nocturns), (f. 23) lauds, vespers, and compline (cue only, 'complet' vt supra'). All antiphons and responses are rhymed; also at matins the prose 'Iohannes est cristo datus annis puericie Studio fit occupatus non vacans stulticie . . .'. The first of the nine responses at matins is 'Dum legit Lincolnie nondum infulatus . . .'. No musical notation. ff. 2^v–4^v ruled, but not written on.

ff. 4. 208 × 150 mm. Written space 150 × 115 mm. 31 long lines. Anglicana formata. 2-line and 1-line red initials.

Written at Lincoln, no doubt.

Di/20/3. *J. de Hildesheim, Historia trium regum* s. xiv/xv

1. ff. 1–39^v Cum venerandorum trium magorum ymmo verius trium regum . . . (f. 37) tres reges virgines fuerunt deo gracias. (f. 37^v) In primo capitulo huius libri qui est collectus de gestis . . . In 45 capitulo describuntur laudem regum reperte et conscripte in diuersis temporibus et locis transmarinis. Explicit tractatus de tribus regibus Colonie.

John of Hildesheim, Ord. Carm., †1375. Printed often. C. Horstmann in footnotes to his edition of the English translation (EETS lxxxv, 1886: cf. *MMBL* i. 119) gives the last words of the text here from two English manuscripts (p. 312). They are followed by a table of forty-five chapters: edn. cit., pp. 206–11. The verses of f. 36^v, 'Ab helena . . .', are Walther, no. 115, and *RH*, no. 22299.

2. f. 40^{rv} Misericordia et veritas obuiauerunt sibi . . . Quidam paterfamilias quidam rex potens quatuor habuit filias . . . celestis reconciliacionis perducat nos qui amen. Secundum Lincolniensem doctorem.

3. ff. 41–42^v (binding leaves). secuturis. Iuxta finem . . . simplicitate sua. Est ad hoc quartus modus per [. . .]

A fragment of the Documentum de arte versificandi of Geoffrey of Vinsauf, ed. E. Faral, *Les arts poétiques du xiie et du xiiie siècle*, 1924, pp. 282 (last word of II. 2. 55)–297 (beginning of II. 3. 70).[1]

s. xiii[1]. French (?). Written space 195 × 135 mm. Closely written in two columns of 43–8 lines. The first line of writing is probably above the top ruled line. The central bifolium of a quire.

ff. 40 + ii. 220 × *c.* 140 mm. Written space 167 × 105 mm. Mainly in 39 long lines. Frame ruling. Collation: $1\text{–}2^{10}$ 3^{8} $4\text{–}5^{6}$. Secretary hand (*r* long-tailed or 2-shaped). Initials: (i) 3-line, blue with red ornament or red with violet ornament. Loose in perhaps contemporary English binding of wooden boards covered with pink skin: four bands: central clasp. Secundo folio *vaus de India.*

Written in England. 'liber willelmi Gaske Anno cristi 1493°', f. 42. 'Robertus Colyn de Connesbe (Conisby, Lincs)', f. 41^v, s. xvi in.

LINCOLN. DIOCESAN RECORDS

Fragments from the bindings of diocesan records

The fragments in Box 73 in the Lincolnshire Archives Office (formerly the Diocesan Record Office) have been taken from the bindings of diocesan records. Fragments in two other collections in the Archives Office come, certainly or probably, from the same source. They appear to have been collected by Canon A. R. Maddison, †1912: one collection forms part of the Maddison Deposit received in 1950 from Canon Maddison's nephew, Major George Maddison; the other was given by Canon Maddison to the Lincoln County Museum in 1907 and was transferred in 1976.

Box 73, no. 20. Two leaves of a medical text. s. xiv[1]

Paragraphs begin 'Splen est membrum rarum spogiosum oblongum a sinistra parte' and 'Intelligendum quod duo renes quorum vnus'. Written space 232 (+ ?) × 165 mm. 2 cols. 53 (+ ?) lines. Anglicana formata. 3-line red or blue initials.

Written in England. Used in binding, probably as pastedowns of a business book of s. xvi[1]: memoranda of that date on one leaf include 'Robert Skynner de yerburgh vexatur per Willelmum Thorne de Cockryngton' . . . et non prosequitur' and 'Thomas Sewger de donyngton decessit'. Cf. Box 73, no. 24.

Box. 73, no. 21 + Maddison Deposit, 2/13. Two bifolia and two single leaves of the commentary of Johannes Andreae on Liber sextus decretalium. s. xiv[1].

The bifolia are Box 73, no. 21, the single leaves 2/13. Written space 277 × 165 mm. 2 cols. 57 lines. 2-line blue initials with red ornament.

Written in England. The bifolia were used as wrappers: 'S 9' is on one of them. 'Vis . . . domini Episcopi 1694' is recorded as having been seen on 2/13 under ultra-violet light.

[1] I owe the identification to the late Dr R. W. Hunt.

Box 73, no. 22 + Lincoln County Museum Deposit, 10/7, 8. A bifolium and two single leaves of Gratian, Decretum. s. xiii med.

The bifolium (Box 73, no. 22) is from Distinctions 93 and 95. The single leaves are from Causa I. Surrounding apparatus in another hand. 425 × 290 mm. Written space of text 285 × 175 mm. 2 cols. 48 lines. Apparatus in 91 lines.

Written in England. Box 73, no. 22, was a wrapper, marked '1573–4', the edges folded in to make a cover measuring 320 × 225 mm.

Box 73, no. 23. A leaf of an antiphonal. s. xv in.

Sanctoral, Annunciation of B.V.M.—Philip and James. Cf. *Brev. ad usum Sarum*, iii. 245–6, 258, 265. Written space 385 × 230 mm. 2 cols. 19 lines and music.

Written in England. A wrapper on which is a note that 'This Book was . . . produced to Francis Berners Esq. upon his Examination . . .' in a lawsuit, 8th September 1741.

Box 73, no. 24. Two leaves of a medical text.

Not the same hand as no. 20, but perhaps the same book. Written space 260 × 165 mm. 2 cols. 61 lines. Anglicana formata.

Written in England. Used in binding, probably as pastedowns of a will register (?), s. xvi[1]: a torn memorandum of this date records that 'a greate pare of coral beads gawdyd with gairdys of Sylver and gylte' were to be given 'vnto our lordys warke of lincoln' accordyng aftyr the last will of the sayd fader William willesforthe'.

Maddison Deposit, 2/1. A bifolium of a Lincoln cathedral register. s. xiv in.

Lists of ordinations at Pinchbeck in Hoyland, 24 May 1309, and at 'Kynebau[. . .]' (Kimbolton, Huntingdonshire, ?): see D. M. Smith, *Guide to Bishops' Registers of England and Wales*, 1981, p. 110. Formerly the wrapper of 'Correctiones 1602'.

Maddison Deposit, 2/2/1–4. A bifolium and three half-leaves of an antiphonal. s. xiv/xv.

Common of virgins and vigil and day of Andrew (4); Circumcision (1, 2); octave of Stephen (3). Cf. *Brev. ad usum Sarum*, ii. 458; iii. 1–12; I. cclxxxiv–ccxcix. Written space 340 × 225 mm. 2 cols. 14 long lines and music. The recto of (4) was a principal page with an upper and inner and, no doubt, lower border: the initial beginning the sanctoral came, no doubt, on the missing lower half of this page.

Written in England. Used in binding. (2) is marked '1560' and (4) '1553'.

Maddison Deposit, 2/3. A bifolium of a manual. s. xiv ex.

Canon of mass: *Manuale Sarum*, pp. 84–5, 89. Written space 180 × 110 mm. 24 long lines.

Written in England. Formerly the wrapper of a small book, 215 × 150 mm. Marked 'Subscriptions'.

Lincoln County Museum Deposit, 10/3, 4. Two leaves of a gradual. s. xv in.

(3) contains part of the office for Friday in the 2nd week of Lent: cf. *Sarum Missal*, pp. 70–2. Written space 323 × 207 mm. 10 long lines and music. (4) contains part of the office for Good Friday: cf. *Sarum Missal*, pp. 109–13. Written space 300 × 207 mm. 10 long lines and music. The hand looks a little older than the hand of (3).

Written in England. (3) is marked '1560' and '1562'.

Lincoln County Museum Deposit, 10/5, 6. Two leaves of a missal. s. xv^1.

Prefaces (noted) for apostles and feasts of B.V.M. (5); canon of mass (6). Cf. *Sarum Missal*, pp. 214–15, 223–4. Written space 260 × 165 mm. 2 cols. 24 lines.

Written in England. (5) is marked 'Repertorium Inventariorum [. . .]', s. xvi.

Other Maddison fragments have no claims to any special connection with Lincoln. I include those which seem to be of some interest.

Maddison Deposit, 2/4. Two bifolia of a treatise on music. s. xiii med.

A paragraph begins 'Sciendum est quod octo sunt toni quibus tocius cantus natura distinguitur seu dinoscitur' and the first words of one page are 'Primus igitur tonus in quatuor literis regulariter incipit idest . . . in antiphonis inuenimus. Set in missarum officiis duobus locis vt est . . .'. Includes passages of music. 25 long lines. Pricks in the inner margin at every second line.

Written in England (?). Pastedowns formerly: on one of them a reader entered memoranda, for example 'Mors an sit natura vel pena cap. 4 lect. 48b'.

Maddison Deposit, 2/6. Parts of two leaves of the poem Aliscans (in French).[1] s. xiii/xiv.

A wide strip across the foot of a bifolium. 52 complete lines are on f. 2, the last thirteen in each of four columns. 24 complete and 22 very incomplete lines are on f. 1, the last 11 or 12 in each of four columns. The first and last lines in each column are: 1ra, lines 640d, 'Oueke les angles honorer et seruir' and 645 in the edition by E. Wienback, W. Hartnacke and Paul Rausch, 1903; 1rb, lines 671 and 680; 1va, doubtful: lines end '-ant'; 1vb, lines 738 and 748; 2ra, lines 1083b and 1089; 2rb, lines 1112 and 1123; 2va, lines 1146 and 1154; 2vb lines 1171/15 and 1171/24. There are many variations from the printed text. A 2-line space was left for the *O* beginning line 643.

Maddison Deposit, 2/11. Two bifolia of Richard Rolle's commentary on the Psalms (in English). s. xiv^2.

The two outer bifolia of a quire, containing Pss. 26: 20–8: 8 and 30: 22–31: 6. For other copies see H. E. Allen, *Writings of Richard Rolle*, 1927, pp. 171–6. Written space 220 × 150 mm. 2 cols. 47 lines. A good anglicana formata in two sizes.

Formerly pastedowns.

[1] I owe the identification to Professor Larry Crist.

Maddison Deposit, 2/12. Two bifolia of a year book (in French). s. xiv[1].

The names of law-men include Par, Pole, Stouf, Herle, Trow'. Written space 293 × 195 mm. 74 long lines. Current anglicana.

LINCOLN. LINCOLNSHIRE ARCHIVES OFFICE

2 Cragg/Bussy. *Psalterium ('The Bussy psalter')* s. xv[1]

1. ff. 1–6v Sarum calendar in blue, red, and black.

Entries include Albinus, 1 March, and Chad in red, 2 March. Gradings occasional, mainly in January, July, and August. Additions, s. xv, include David, William of York (red), Anthony O.F.M. (blue), Visitation of B.V.M. (blue), Martha (red), Ordination of Gregory, Francis (blue), 1 March, 8, 13 June, 2 July, 1 Aug., 3 Sept., 4 Oct. 'pape' crossed through; also the entry of Thomas of Canterbury at 7 July, but not at 29 Dec. 'Hic natus est iohannes filius et heres domini iohannis buschi anno domini m° cccc° 22°' is in red in the main hand at 21 October, and the obit of John Bussy, 30 July 1399, may have been added at about the same time. Later entries include obits of John Bussy, 4 March 1458, master George Comberworth, vicar of Coton, 7 July 1462, John Cumberworth 14 Nov., and many members of the family of Bussy of Hougham and Haydor, Lincs, up to 1609. They are printed by James Creasey, *Sketches of New and Old Sleaford*, 1825, pp. 227–30 (thence, E. Trollope, *Sleaford*, 1872, pp. 378–80), with errors and omissions made good by A. Gibbons in *Lincolnshire Notes and Queries* ii (1891), 1–3, with facsimile of the March page. A Bussy, s. xv, was proud of John Bussy, †1399, adding 'apud Brystow' to the obit at 30 July and 'Iste Iohannes fuit filius et heres Iohannis Bussy qui obiit apud Brystow pro Ricardo secundo in Anno regni regis sui (x)xii°' at 4 Mar.

2. ff. 7–147 Psalms, lacking probably forty-two leaves, including the first leaf: f. 7 begins 'Dirumpamus' (Ps. 2: 3).

The two largest gaps are a quire after f. 21 with Pss. 17–20 and parts of Pss. 16 and 21 and three quires after f. 28 with Pss. 28–42 and parts of Pss. 27 and 43.

3. ff. 147–63 Six ferial canticles, followed by Benedicite, Benedictus, Te deum, Magnificat, Nunc dimittis and Quicumque vult. One leaf missing.

4. f. 163rv Litany. Only the first leaf remains.

5. ff. 164–5 (*begins imperfectly*) ne qua ita tunc ore dominico uelut mater et filius inuicem coniuncti estis. Uobis duobus ego peccator hodie et in omnibus omni tempore commendo corpus meum et animam meam in omnibus horis . . . cum eis regnat deus per omnia secula seculorum amen. ff. 165v–167v blank.

ff. iii + 167 + i. ff. ii, iii are medieval parchment endleaves. 220 × 150 mm. Written space 135 × 85 mm. 16 long lines. Collation: 1^6 2^8 wants 1 before f. 7 3^8 4^8 wants 7 after f. 27 5^8 6^8 wants 2 after f. 37 7^8 8^8 wants 3 after f. 53 9^8 10^8 wants 5–7 after f. 70 $11–14^8$ 15^8 wants 7 after f. 109 16^8 wants 7 after f. 117 17^8 18^8 wants 5 after f. 129 $19–20^8$ 21^8

wants 2 after f. 149 22^8 23 four: two inner bifolia (ff. 164–7). Remains of two series of signatures: the first begins with b. ii on f. 7 (2^2) and ends with q. iii[i] on f. 83 (12^4) and the second begins with a. ii on f. 90 (13^2) and ends with h. iiii on f. 159 (22^4). In the first series the quires marked d, f–h are missing. In the second series b–h have a stroke over them as a distinction. Initials: (i) of principal psalms, removed; (ii) of other psalms, 2-line, gold on blue and red grounds patterned in white, with short sprays into the margins; (iii) 1-line, blue with red ornament or red with violet ornament. Line fillers in red and blue. Old boards (?) covered with red morocco, s. xix, stamped back and front 'The Bussy Psalter MS. of the xvth century'. Secundo folio (f. 7) *Dirumpamus*.

Written in England, perhaps in or soon after 21 Oct. 1422 for John Bussy of Hougham and Haydor, Lincs, †4 Mar. 1458. Belonged to the Bussy family until s. xvii in. (cf. art. 1) and to Edward James Willson of Lincoln in 1825 (cf. Creasey, op. cit.). Willson sale at Sotheby's, 30 May 1888, lot 355, to E. L. Grange, F.S.A., of Grimsby (cf. Gibbons, loc. cit.). Grange sale at Sotheby's, 14 March 1892, lot 426. Belonged later to 'Mr Wake of Fritchley' (cf. below, Manchester, Rylands Eng. 412, 413) and bought from his executors by E. S. Pickard, bookseller, 16 Stonegate, York, according to W. A. Cragg in *Lincolnshire Notes and Queries*, xiv (1917), 116–17. In Pickard's catalogue 9 (1914) at £21: the relevant cutting is pasted to f. 168^v. 'Wm. A. Cragg, Threekingham 1914' and Cragg's armorial book-plate inside the cover: his sale at Sotheby's, 10 Dec. 1962, lot 147. Bought then by the Lincolnshire Archives Committee for £328, with the aid of a contribution of £100 from the Friends of the National Libraries: cf. their *Report* for 1963, p. 13.

LIVERPOOL. ATHENAEUM

Gladstone 13. *Brevia placitata (fragm.: in French)* s. xiii^2

Explanations of eight forms of writ: (*a*) f. 1, of right (see below); (*b*) f. 2^v, of right, 'Le Rey salue etc'. Nus ws comaundums . . . ; (*c*) f. 5^v, Pone; (*d*) f. 7^v, Precipe in capite; (*e*) f. 8^v, right of advowson; (*f*) f. 10, darrein presentment; (*g*) f. 10^v, Quare impedit; (*h*) f. 12, claim as right and heritage (?) on the recto, illegible on the verso. Probably the first quire of the manuscript.

Cf. G. J. Turner, *Brevia placitata* (Selden Soc., lxvi, 1951), pp. 2, 1, 1, 11, 6, 34, 33, 7 (?). (*a*). An almost wholly illegible underlined text, f. 1^r–1^v/17, is followed on 1^v/18–2/11 by the *Ceo vous mustre* paragraph in edn., p. 2. The arrangement of (*b–g*) seems to vary: (*e*) and (*g*) consist of four paragraphs each, (1) the writ, (2) an underlined passage beginning 'Ore deuez sauer ke cest bref' (not in edn.), (3) 'Ceo vous mustre . . .', (4) 'Tort e force . . .'. In (*c*) the writ is followed by a long underlined passage, ff. 5^v/19–7^v/6, 'Pur ceo ke nus sum' ore aiurne en baunk par le Pone vus deuez sauer ke ces sunt les delays des brefs ke sunt plaidez deuant Iustices en bank'. Primes esson' . . .'. The *Ceo vous mustre* of (*h*) contains the words 'en tens le Rey H pere le Rey ke ore est'; so too (*a*), f. 2/2, 3.

ff. 12. 150× 95 mm. Written space 115 × 70 mm. 22 long lines. Collation: 1^{12}. Ugly current anglicana. 2-line red initials. No binding: kept in an envelope.

Written in England. Robert Gladstone noted on the envelope 'Bt from Dr Philip Nelson of Liverpool in 1914 for 30/. it was part of Dunn. no. 1101, 3 Feb. 1914': in the catalogue of the George Dunn sale, lot 1101 is described as a collection of legal fragments in a medieval binding. Part of the Robert Gladstone bequest in 1940.

Gladstone 27. *Statuta Angliae; Registrum Brevium* s. xiii/xiv

1. (*a*) f. 1 Table of arts. 2–43. (*b*) ff. 1v–4 Tables of chapters of arts. 2, 6–9, 24. f. 4v blank.

2. ff. 5–8v Magna Carta de libertat*ibus*. Edwardus dei gracia . . . Sciatis quod inspeximus . . . Dat' per manus venerabilis patris domini R. Dunelm' Episcopi Cancellar' nostri apud Sanctum Paulum London' vi° die Nouembris anno regni nostri secundo.

Inspeximus of the charter of 6 November 1217, for which see H. J. Lawlor in *EHR* xxii. 514–18. Thirty-four chapter numbers in the margins.

3. ff. 8v–10v Incipit carta de Foresta. Edwardus . . .

Dated as art. 2.

4. ff. 10v–11 Sentencia lata super cartas. Anno domini m° cc quinquagesimo quarto . . .

Cf. *SR* i. 6 and for this year-date, *MMBL* i. 407.

5. ff. 11–12 Confirmacio cartis predictis. Edward par la grace dieu . . . Anno xxv. *SR* i. 124.

6. ff. 12–13v Incipiunt prouisiones de Mertona. *SR* i. 8.

7. ff. 13v–18v Incipiunt statuta de Mar(l)eberg'. *SR* i. 19.

8. ff. 18v–28v Incipiunt prima statuta Westm'. *SR* i. 126.

9. ff. 28v–31v Incipiunt prouisiones Gloucestr'. Pur les granz Meschefs . . . Com auant ces houres . . .

SR i. 47, with short introduction in place of i. 45–6. Cf. art. 17.

10. f. 31v Explanaciones de eisdem. *SR* i. 50.

11. ff. 32–4 Incipit Dictum de Kenilworthe. *SR* i. 12.

12. ff. 34v–35 Incipiunt districciones de scacario. In French. *SR* i. 197*b*.

13. ff. 35–7 Incipiunt statuta de scaccario. In French. *SR* i. 197.

14. ff. 37–8 Incipit statutum de iusticiariis assignatis. In French. *SR* i. 44.

15. ff. 38–9 Statuta de Mercatoribus edita apud Actone Burnel. In French. *SR* i. 53.

16. ff. 39–40v Incipiunt Statuta de Moneta. In French. *SR* i. 219.

17. ff. 40v–41v Statutum de libertate clamanda quo Warranto. Anno domini M° cc° lxxviii° Regni autem . . .

The preamble of the statute of Gloucester in Latin. Cf. *SR* i. 45–6. Includes four writs.

18. f. 42rv Incipit statuta de bigamis. *SR* i. 42.

No personal names in the first sentence.

19. ff. 42v–43 Incipit statutum de Religiosis. *SR* i. 51.

20. f. 43rv Statutum de presentibus vocatis ad Warrantum. *SR* i. 108.

21. ff. 43v–44 Statuta Milicie. *SR* i. 229.

22. f. 44v Statutum contra regiam prohibicionem allocandam. Circumspecte agatis . . . si porrigatur et non ad penam pecuniariam agatur. *SR* i. 101/1–23.

23. ff. 44v–45 Statutum contra regiam prohibicionem. quod laici impetrant. Sub qua forma . . . non obstante. *SR* i. 101/24.

24. ff. 45–63v Incipiunt secunda statuta Westm'. *SR* i. 71.

25. ff. 63v–65 Incipiunt statuta Wyntonie. In French. *SR* i. 96.

26. ff. 65v–68 Incipiunt statuta Exestrie. In French. *SR* i. 210.

27. f. 68rv Incipit nouum quo warranto. In French. *SR* i. 107.

28. ff. 68v–69 Incipit tercium statutum Westm'. Quia emptores . . . *SR* i. 106.

29. f. 69rv Statutum de recogn' et iuratis. *SR* i. 113.

30. f. 69v Incipit statutum de conspiratoribus. In French. *SR* i. 216.

The second writ is addressed to the sheriff of Northampton.

31. f. 70 Incipit statutum de Gaulette. *SR* i. 222.

32. ff. 70v–71 Incipit statutum de vasto facto tempore alieno. *SR* i. 109.

33. ff. 71–3 Addicio super statutum de Actone Burnel. Pur ceo qe marchaunz auant ces houres . . .

The fourth paragraph begins 'Le Rey a son parlement a Westmouster apres la pasch' lan de son regne xiii fist rehercer la auauntdit estatut fet a actone burnel'.

34. f. 73 Qualiter procedendum ad homagium faciendum. In French. *SR* i. 227.

35. (*a*) ff. 73v–74 Incipit assisa panis que obseruand' est in Anglia. (*b*) f. 74 Lucrum pistoris. (*c*) f. 74 Assisa ceruisie. (*d*) f. 74rv Iudicium pillorie.

(*a–d*). *SR* i. 199, 200, 200, 201.

36. ff. 74v–75 Exposicio quorundam vocabulorum. Sok. Hoc est secta de homagio . . .

The thirty-four Old English words, Sok–Brigg'bote, are ranged in the margin. Cf. *MMBL* i. 253.

37. f. 75rv Incipit extenta manerii. *SR* i. 242.

38. ff. 75v–92 Incipit summa Magnum Hengham. Licet ordo placitandi in Curia domini Regis . . . rei petite tempore Ricardi Regis auunculi Regis Henrici patris Regis Edwardi sic peremptorie dedic*io* (*sic for* dicitur) actio actoris.

W. H. Dunham, *Radulphi de Hengham Summae*, 1932, pp. 1–50.

39. ff. 92–98v Incipit paruum Hyngham. Notandum quod quinque sunt esson'. Primum est de ultra mare . . . compertus fuisset tenens.

Ibid. pp. 52–71.

40. ff. 98v–105 Incipit summa que vocatur cadit assisa. Rex vic' salutem. Si A fecerit te securum . . . Cadit assisa si petatur . . . remanebit posse loco suo ut predictum est.

41. ff. 105–116v Incipit summa que vocatur fet asauer. Fet asauer ke en le comencement de chescune play . . . le Rey si com auuaunt est dist.

Ed. G. E. Woodbine, *Four thirteenth century law tracts*, 1910, pp. 53–115.

42. ff. 116v–122 Incipiunt Iudicium essoniorum. Primum capitulum de difficultate esson' circa viros et mulieres siue circa plures tenentes . . . ad alia placita iuxta eorum discrecionem.

Ibid. pp. 116–42.

43. ff. 122v–125 Excepciones contra breuia. Excepcioun pur bref abatre . . . les disseisistes de lour frank' ten' puys le terme etc'.

Ibid. pp. 160–82/15.

44. f. 125v Per discrecionem tocius populi Anglie fuit mensura domini Regis Edwardi filii Henrici Regis composita . . . octaua pars quarterii. Cf. *SR* i. 204.

45. f. 125rv Chescun play ou il est de {Tere / Trespas} . . .

Writs suited to particular kinds of pleas.

46 (added, s. xiv^2). f. 126rv Dominus rex habebit custodiam omnium terrarum eorum qui de eo tenent in capite . . . saluo custodiantur sine vasto (*ends imperfectly*). f. 127rv blank.

47. ff. 128–94 Edwardus dei gracia Rex anglie . . .

A register of writs beginning with an undated writ of right. The collection falls between the registers called CC and R by de Haas and Hall. The order is nearly that of CC, but there are many more writs, for example on ff. 144v–146, seven ecclesiastical writs between CC 83 and CC 85 (CC 84 does not occur) and on ff. 153–5 fifteen writs between CC 110 and 111. Writs of debt are more numerous than in CC and are placed before the writ CC 123 (ff. 162v–165). Twenty-seven writs come between CC 174 and 175 (ff. 174v–177v): they include writs of association and 'Quod Iustic' procedant ad capcionem assise'. After a writ of entry on f. 187 (CC 209) there is no further agreement with CC, apart from CC 229 and 231 (ff. 187v, 192v). This final miscellaneous section has fifty-six writs (ff. 187–94), including one of trespass, 'De transgressione ouium et aliorum animalium' (f. 190), one for paving the town of Boston (f. 191),[1] one 'De tornamento proibendo' (f. 192), and seven exemptions from assizes (f. 193rv), including R 629 and R 625 and a writ which refers to the new statute of Westminster (Westminster 2, ch. 38). The last three headings are 'Quod nemo distringatur nisi principalis debitor', 'De aueriis iniuste captis', and 'De forisfactura Maritagii formatum pro executore' (of the will of Ralph Basset).

Notes and rules are rather more frequent than in CC. A long rule not in CC follows CC 61 (f. 142), 'Modo dicendum est in quibus casibus regia prohibicio . . . prohibicione non obstante'. The limit at CC 100 is 'post coronacionem domini H. Regis patris nostri' (cf. de Haas and Hall, p. xlviii). f. 194v blank.

ff. ii + 195 (foliated 1–59, 59*, 60–194). 202 × 140 mm. Written space *c.*155 × *c.*98 mm. 32–3 long lines. Collation: 1 four (ff. 1–4) 2–16^8 17^4 (ff. 124–7) 18–24^8 25 three (ff. 192–4). Current anglicana: ascenders split at the top. Initials red and blue with ornament of both colours. Binding of s. xix, perhaps by 'Thompson', whose name is stamped on f. iv, top left. Secundo folio (f. 6) *quadraginta*.

Written in England. 'Ihon bond', f. 45 (cf. ff. 5, 128), s. xvi. 'Thomas lukas', f. 2.

[1] This appears to be the writ of 6 Nov. 1281 (*Calendar of Patent Rolls 1272–81*, p. 462), with a change of year, 'secundo' for *nono*. I owe the reference to Mr C. P. C. Johnson.

Gladstone 49. *Statuta Angliae, etc.* s. xiv[1]

1. ff. 10v–17 Tables of chapters of arts. 3–7, 9, 11, 13.

The scribe began on f. 10 and after writing fifteen lines decided to start again on f. 10v.

2 (filling part of the blank space in quire 1). ff. 17v–20 Primes deyt homme enquer' de chateus . . . cheant par an. Explicit Extenta Manerii.

Cf. *SR* i. 242 (Latin). ff. 20v–21v blank.

3. ff. 22–30 Carta de libertatibus Anglie. Edwardus dei gracia . . . salutem. Sciatis quod intuitu dei . . .

Henrician, except for the king's name. Fifty-three chapters.

4. ff. 30–33v Henricus dei gracia . . .

Charter of the Forest in twenty chapters.

5. ff. 34–38v Prouisiones de Merton. *SR* i. 1.

6. ff. 38v–50v Stat' de Marleb'. *SR* i. 19.

7. ff. 51–82 Westminster 1. In French. *SR* i. 26.

8. ff. 82rv–85v Stat' primum de quo waranto. Rex vicecomiti . . . Cum in vltimo parliamento . . .

Consists of three writs, the second (f. 83rv) 'Rex vic' salutem precipimus tibi quod pupplice proclamare facias etc'. et ponatur in breui . . .' and the third (ff. 83v–85v) 'Rex vic' salutem precipimus tibi quod per totam balliuiam tuam videlicet tam . . . debeant in itineribus.' Cf. *MMBL* i. 187, 252.

9. ff. 85v–94v Incipiunt statuta Glouc'. Pur les grauns damages . . . Cum auaunt ces houres . . . venue des iustices. *SR* i. 47/1.

10. f. 95rv Explanaciones. *SR* i. 50.

11. ff. 96–101v Wynton'. *SR* i. 96.

12. ff. 101v–102v Incipit officium Coronatoris. Primes deit le coroner demaunder si les quatre villes seyent venuz . . . de ces chateus.

13. ff. 103–148v Westminster 2. *SR* i. 71.

14. ff. 149–50 Soc est de sauer sywte de vos hommes . . .

Explanations of thirty-one old law terms, Soc–Frefare.

15. f. 150^{v} Notandum est quod quatuor modis dicitur excepcio . . . responsionem.

16. ff. 151–152^{v} Statut' de Religiosis. Cum iadys esteyt . . . Cf. *SR* i. 51 (Latin).

17. ff. 152^{v}–158^{v} Incipiunt Statuta de Mercatoribus. In French. *SR* i. 53.

18. ff. 159–66 Statuta de Scaccario. In French. *SR* i. 197.

19. ff. 166–167^{v} De Ministris distringentibus pro debito Regis. *SR* i. 197*b*.

20. ff. 167^{v}–169 Statut' de Emptoribus Terre. Quia emptores . . . *SR* i. 106. The running title is 'Westm' Ter' '.

21. f. 169^{rv} Statut' de quo waranto. De breui quod dicitur . . . Cf. *SR* i. 107 (in French).

22. f. 170^{rv} Statut' de Chaunpartour'. *SR* i. 216/1–14. No writs.

23. ff. 170^{v}–171 Circumspecte agatis . . . licet porrigatur. *SR* i. 101/1–23.

24. ff. 171–3 Incipit statutum de Iure. Quia dominus rex per pupplicam et frequentem . . .

SR i. 113. Writ follows, 'Quia ad communem vtilitatem populi Regni nostri . . .'.

25. ff. 173–5 Incipiunt de iusticiariis assignatis. In French. *SR* i. 44.

26. f. 175^{rv} Statutum de anno bisextili. *SR* i. 7.

27. ff. 175^{v}–178^{v} Statuta Monete. In French. *SR* i. 219.

28. f. 179 Statut' Composicionis Monete. Per discrecionem . . . quarterii London'. Cf. *SR* i. 204 and *MMBL* i. 38.

29. ff. 179–87 Incipiunt Statuta eccestrie. Purueu est . . . *SR* i. 210.

30. ff. 187^{v}–198^{v} Tractatus de Bastardia. Sciendum quod si Bastardus se clamando . . . id est extrahitur.

31. ff. 199–219^{v} Hengham Minor. Notandum quod quinque sunt essonia . . . si compertus fuisset tenens. Explicit Hengham minor.

W. H. Dunham, *Radulphi de Hengham Summae*, 1932, pp. 52–71.

32. ff. 219v–220v Hic incipit modus faciendi homagium et fidelitatem. In French. *SR* i. 227.

33. f. 220v Vous deues sauer que la ou relef serra done . . . lour seygnur. *SR* i. 228/1–9.

34. f. 221 Socage put estre destincte en treys maners . . . fere ne deyuent. et cetera.

35. ff. 221v–222v Quando quarterium frumenti venditur pro xii den' . . . per tote la tere. Explicit assisa panis et ceruisie.

SR i. 199. The last paragraph here is in French.

Arts. 36–8 are additions on flyleaves, ff. 1–9, 223–39.

36 (s. xv). (*a*) f. 1 A list of kings of England, William I–Henry VI. (*b*) ff. 1v–2 Tables of 'Dies communes in banco (et) in placito dotis'. *SR* i. 208.

37 (s. xv). ff. 224v–228 Incipit statutum de finibus. *SR* i. 215.

38 (s. xvi). (*a*) ff. 229–32 Bound' de Mariscis de Elye vbi et quomodo Conabuntur. Ad quem pertinet quidam Mariscus qui vocatur Cauldewell' fen . . . et vltra magnam ripam in Cherchfen' sed non falcare. Finis. (*b*) f. 232v A pitmansdike ex vna parte . . . (7 lines).

ff. xi + 213 + xix, foliated (i, ii), 1–240, (241). For the parchment flyleaves see above, arts. 36–8. f. 240, a parchment leaf, was pasted down to a former binding. 138 × 87 mm. Written space *c.*102 × 55 mm. 21–6 long lines. Collation of ff. 10–222: $1\text{–}2^{12}$ 3^{10} + 1 leaf after 10 (f. 44) $4\text{–}5^{12}$ 6^{10} $7\text{–}18^{12}$. Current anglicana. 3-line red initials. Binding of s. xix in. Secundo folio (f. 23) *tamen quod.*

Written in England. An owner, s. xvi, was interested in the Ely marches (art. 38). 'Thomas Bryan Richards 22 April 1803', 'David Constable MDCCCXVII' and a number '224 A' on f. ii: probably item 2896 in the David Constable sale, Edinburgh 19 Nov. 1828 (13*s.*). Item 42 in Thomas Thorpe's catalogue for 1836: bought by Sir Thomas Phillipps. 'Phillipps MS. 8824', f. ii. Phillipps sale, 15 June 1908, lot 14. 'R. Gladstone Junr bought from Ellis of London for £5. 10. 0. Nov. 1908', f. iv.

Gladstone 85. *Statuta Angliae, etc.* s. xiv¹ (*c.*1330 ?)–xiv med.

1. ff. 1–8 Tables of chapters of arts. 2, 3, 5–8, 10–47, the last two added in a later hand; also of two statutes now missing after art. 43, 'Westminster vi' and Northampton (*SR* i. 255 and 257: 1 Edward 3, Stat. 2, 2 Edward 3). f. 8v blank.

2. ff. 9–12 Edwardus dei gracia . . . Inspeximus magnam cartam . . . *SR* i. 114. Dated 12th Oct., anno 25. Thirty-five chapters.

3. ff. 12–13v Incipit carta de foresta. Edwardus . . . Inspeximus . . . *SR* i. 120.

4. ff. 13v–14 Sentencia lata super Cartas. *SR* i. 6.

5. ff. 14–16 Incipiunt prouisiones de Merton'. *SR* i. 4.

6. ff. 16–20v Incipit statutum de Marleberg'. *SR* i. 19.

7. ff. 20v–29v Incipit Westm' primum. In French. *SR* i. 26.

8. ff. 30–2 Gloucestr'. Pur les grantz meschiefs . . . Come auant ces houres . . . des iustices errantz.

See above, Gladstone 27, art. 9.

9. f. 32rv Incipiunt explanaciones Glou[. . .]. *SR* i. 50.

10. ff. 32v–50 Incipit Westm' secundum. *SR* i. 71.

11. f. 50rv Incipit Tercium. Quia emptores . . . *SR* i. 106.

12. ff. 50v–51 Incipit statutum Religiosorum. *SR* i. 51.

13. ff. 51–3 Incipit statutum Mercatorum. In French. *SR* i. 53.

14. f. 53rv Incipit statutum de Bigamis.

SR i. 42. No personal names in the first sentence.

15. ff. 53v–54v Incipit statutum de Iusticiariis assignatis. In French. *SR* i. 44.

16. ff. 54v–55v Incipit statutum de quo waranto. Anno domini mcclxxviii . . . in forma breuis subscripti. Rex vic' etc' salutem. Cum nuper in parliamento . . . ex parte nostra. Cf. *MMBL* i. 252.

17. ff. 55v–56 Incipit quo waranto nouum. In French. *SR* i. 107.

18. f. 56 Incipit statutum de anno et die bisextili. *SR* i. 7.

19. ff. 56–57v Incipit statutum Wynton'. In French. *SR* i. 96.

20. ff. 57v–59v Incipit statutum de scaccario. In French. *SR* i. 197.

21. f. 60 Districciones scaccarii. *SR* i. 197*b*.

22. ff. 60v–61v Statutum de coniunctim feoffatis.

SR i. 145. Dated 27 May 'anno regni nostri xiii'.

23. ff. 61v–62 Incipit Statutum de Militibus. *SR* i. 229.

24. ff. 62–3 Incipit Statutum de Moneta. In French. *SR* i. 219.

25. f. 63rv Incipit statutum de vasto facto. *SR* i. 109.

26. ff. 63v–64 Incipit statutum de Defensione Iuris. *SR* i. 110.

27. f. 64 Incipit statutum de Champart. Come il soit apartement defendu . . . a la volunte le Rey.

Differs much from *SR* i. 216/1–12.

28. f. 64rv Incipit statutum de [Conspiratoribus]. Dominus rex [. . .] . . . grauiter redimatur.

Cf. *SR* i. 216/15 and footnotes.

29. ff. 64v–65 Incipit statutum de presentibus vocatis ad Warantum. *SR* i. 108.

30. f. 65rv Incipit statutum de hiis qui ponendi sunt in assisis et Iur'. *SR* i. 113.

31. ff. 65v–66v Incipit statutum de finibus. *SR* i. 215.

32. ff. 66v–70v Incipiunt noui articuli super Cartas. In French. *SR* i. 136.

33. f. 70v Incipit statutum de prisonibus. De prisonibus . . . (7 lines). *SR* i. 113.

34. ff. 70v–71v Incipit statutum Lincoln' primum. *SR* i. 142.

35. f. 71v Incipit statutum de proteccionibus non allocandis. In French. Dated 33 Edward I. *SR* i. 217.

36. ff. 71v–73 Incipit statutum Carlioli Primi. *SR* i. 150.

37. f. 73rv Incipit statutum Karlioli secundum. *SR* i. 215.

38. ff. 73v–74 Incipit statutum Circumspecte agatis. Edwardus etc. Iusticiariis suis Itinerantibus in com' Lincoln' salutem. Scire facias nobis . . . licet porrigatur. Sub qua forma . . . In defamacionibus libere corrigant prelati non obstante Regis prohibicione.

SR i. 101. As one statute of nine chapters. Cf. Graves in *EHR* xliii (1928), 14 and *MMBL* i. 408 for the variant of Circumspecte agatis beginning *Scire*.

39. ff. 74–6 Incipiunt articuli cleri. Edwardus etc' . . . salutem. Sciatis . . . *SR* i. 171–4/2.

40. f. 76^{rv} Incipit statutum Lincoln' secundum. In French. *SR* i. 174. No writ.

41. ff. 76^{v}–78 Incipit statutum de Ebor'. In French. *SR* i. 177.

42. ff. 78–9 Incipit Westm' quartum. In French. *SR* i. 180.

43. ff. 79–80^{v} Incipit Westm' quintum. Come hugh le Despenser le piere . . . (*ends imperfectly*). *SR* i. 251.

44. f. 81 (*begins imperfectly*) deuant les Iustices . . .

SR i. 264/41 (4 Edward III). Called 'Westm' septimum' in the table of contents: cf. above, art. 1.

45. ff. 81–4 Incipit statutum Westm' viii.

In the main hand, but perhaps an addition. In French. *SR* i. 269 (9 Edward III).

Arts. 46–50 were added in s. xiv med.

46. ff. 84–86^{v} Incipit statutum Ebor' secundum. In French. *SR* i. 269 (9 Edward III).

47. ff. 86^{v}–87^{v} Incipit statutum Westm' nonum de cartis adnull'. *SR* i. 275 (10 Edward III).

48. ff. 88–89^{v} Edward par la grace de dieu . . .

SR i. 192 (14 Edward III). A leaf missing after f. 88 contained i. 293/23 up–294/33.

49. ff. 89^{v}–98 Incipit statutum Westm' vndecimum. In French. *SR* i. 281 (14 Edward III).

50. ff. 98–100 Incipit [. . .] . . .

In French. *SR* i. 295 (15 Edward III). f. 100^{v} blank.

Arts. 51–63 are on quire 15.

51. ff. 101–102^{v} Incipit prerogatiua Regis. *SR* i. 226.

52. ff. 102^{v}–103 De antiquo dominico corone. Licet in antiquo . . . et quod alii faciunt. Cf. *MMBL* i. 142.

53. f. 103^{rv} Incipiunt dies communes in banco. *SR* i. 208.

54. ff. 103^{v}–104 Incipiunt dies communes in placito dotis. *SR* i. 208.

55. f. 104^{rv} Incipit visus francipleg'. In French. *SR* i. 246.

56. f. 104^{v} Hec sunt inquirenda in proxima Curia Domini post visum. De molendinar' capientibus tolnetum . . . vicinorum. De hiis (*ends imperfectly*).

Some twenty heads remain, the last seven damaged. Nos. 2, 5, 10, 13 begin 'De Natiuis' (2, 'De natiuis domini qui terram liberam emunt') and no. 7 is 'De filiis Natiuorum ordinatis sine licencia domini'.

57. (*a*) f. 105 Assise of bread, beginning imperfectly. (*b*) f. 105^{v} Assisa Ceruisie. (*c*) ff. 105^{v}–106 Incipit iudicium Pilorie.

(*a–c*). *SR* i. 199, 200, 201.

58. f. 106^{v} Incipit assisa ponderum et waiarum. Notandum quod carrata plumbi constat ex xxx fodmall' . . . Cf. *SR* i. 205/1.

59. f. 107 Incipit composicio monete. Sciendum quod denarius . . . bussellum London'. Cf. *SR* i. 204.

60. f. 107 Incipit assisa pollicis vlne et pertice. Sciendum quod tria grana . . . vnam acram.

61. f. 107^{rv} Incipit extenta manerii. *SR* i. 242.

62. f. 108^{rv} Incipit modus faciendi Homagium et fidelitatem. In French. *SR* i. 227.

63. f. 108^{v} De ward' et relef. Vous deuez sauoir qe la ou relef . . . (*ends imperfectly*). *SR* i. 228.

ff. 108. (?) × 118 mm: the foot of each page has been eaten away. Written space 125 × 80 mm. 33–8 long lines, the last ten or so not wholly legible. Collation: 1^{6} 2^{2} $3–12^{8}$ 13^{2} (ff. 89–90) 14^{10} (ff. 91–100) 15^{10} wants 5, 6 after f. 104. Sewing all gone, except that quires 10, 11 are still connected by the top string. Quire 15 may not be in its original position. Arts. 1–45, 51–63 in good anglicana by one hand: the scribe tends to write currently, especially towards the end. Arts. 46–50 in one hand: current anglicana. 5-line initials, blue with red ornament: the internal ornament is sometimes in the form of hatching and suitably includes a stag on f. 12: a dog hunts a hare in the border on the same page. The back wooden board of the medieval binding remains: five bands: two holes for the pins which held the straps: a paper label, s. xix, on the outside of the board, 'A curious Epitome of old English Law (much damaged at corners) with coloured capitals. sec. xiv'. Secundo folio (f. 10) *terras*.

Written in England. 'Given to me by E. Gordon Duff. In November 1903' is on a label kept in the same cardboard box as the manuscript.

Thompson 1. *Cicero, Orationes; etc.* 1448-9, s. xv med.

Arts. 1-20, 22-34 are speeches of Cicero. The titles of arts. 2-14 were not filled in. Many brown-ink scholia in a humanistic hand in the margins of arts. 12, 13, 15, 16, 24.

1. ff. 1-13v M. T. Ciceronis oratio pro sexto roscio ad iudices feliciter incipit. Crede ergo vos . . .

The scribe left a space of 27½ lines on ff. 11v-12 after 'erucius' (xlv. 132) and noted 'Hic deficit. tantumdem enim in codice uetustissimo deficiebat'.

2. ff. 13-23 Iam ne sentis bellua . . .

In Pisonem. The scribe noted at the beginning 'Hic deesse creditur principium huius orationis. Sic enim erat in exemplari'. On f. 19v, after 'appara argentum', the words 'quod doctum' were altered to 'decoctum' by a sixteenth-century reader who added a reference in the margin to G. Budé 'in Annotationes in pandectas Iuris': cf. edn. Lyons 1551, p. 512, where this passage (xxv. 61) is quoted in the discussion of *decoquere.*

3. ff. 23-29v Hesterno die p.c. cum me . . .

De haruspicum responsis. The first eight lines are in capitals.

4. ff. 29v-34 Si quis vestrum p.c. expectat . . . *De prouinciis consularibus.*

5. ff. 34-37v Si p.c. pro vestris immortalibus . . . *Post reditum suum.*

6. ff. 37v-39v Quod præcatus á ioue . . . *De reditu suo.*

7. ff. 40-47v Cum in maximis periculis . . . *Pro L. Flacco.*

8. ff. 47v-63 Animaduerti iudices omnem . . . *Pro A. Cluentio.*

9. ff. 63-71v Si quantum in agro . . . *Pro A. Caecinna.*

10. ff. 71v-80v Quę deprecatus a diis . . .

Pro L. Murena. Small blank spaces, 1½ lines each, were left on ff. 78v, 80 for the gaps at xxxiv. 72 and xxxix. 85.

11. ff. 80v-83 Si quid est in me ingenii . . . *Pro A. Licinio.*

12. ff. 83-6 Nouum crimen . . . *Pro Q. Ligario.*

13. ff. 86-89v Cum in omnibus causis . . . *Pro Regi Deiotaro.*

14. ff. 89v-92 Diuturni silentii . . . *Pro M. Marcello.*

15. ff. 92–8 Eiusdem oratio de laudibus magni pompeii feliciter incipit. Quanquam mihi semper frequens . . . *De lege Manilia.*

16. ff. 98–107 Eiusdem oratio pro milone feliciter incipit. Etsi vereor iudices . . .

17. ff. 107–12 Eiusdem oratio pro cornelio balbo incipit feliciter. Si auctoritates patronorum . . .

18. ff. 112–24, 210rv Eiusdem pro publio sextio incipit feliciter. Si quis ante iudices . . .

A note on f. 120v refers to the part of this speech left out at 120v/31 and added in the main hand after art. 36: 'Nota quod hic deficit una pars huius orationis quę scripta est in fine libri huius in cartis 213 ubi est simille signum huic'. 'Cum omnes certanti . . . gens ista clodiana quod' (xxxiv. 74–xxxviii. 81) is on f. 210rv.

19. ff. 124–38 Eiusdem oratio pro domo sua ad pontifices vel in P. Clodium incipit. Cum multa diuinitus . . .

20. ff. 138–46 Eiusdem pro P. Quintio incipit feliciter. Quę res in ciuitate . . .

21. ff. 146–148v Eiusdem oratio ad equites R. priusquam iret in exilium incipit. Si quando inimicorum . . . conseruetis.

Pseudo-Cicero. Teubner edn., iii, pt. 4, pp. 425–34.

22. ff. 148v–156 M.T.C. oratio pro M. Celio incipit feliciter. Si quis iudices forte . . .

The middle sheet of a quire of the exemplar was probably bound the wrong way round, since the scribe copied 'Quod quidem in hac etate . . . conuitium renuerit' (vii. 18–xi. 27) on ff. 151/14–152/9 instead of after f. 150/22: a contemporary note at 151/14 points out the mistake.

23. ff. 156v–159 Eiusdem oratio in vatinium testem incipit feliciter. Si tua tantummodo vatini . . .

24. ff. 159v–167v Eiusdem oratio pro P. Silla incipit feliciter. Maxime vellem iudices . . .

25. ff. 167v–177v Eiusdem oratio pro gneo plantio incipit feliciter. Cum propter egregiam . . .

26. ff. 177v–180v Eiusdem oratio pro Rabirio Perduellionis reo incipit feliciter. Etsi quirites . . .

At the end, beside the last words, 'improborum ciuium', is '[I]n exemplari deficiebant duo folia quę abscisa fuerunt'.

27. ff. 180v–184 M.T.C. Oratio pro roscio commedo. fragmenta principium est. Malitiam naturę crederetur . . . Roscio debebat.

In the margin, beside the last words, is 'Deest reliquum'.

28. ff. 184–6 M.T.C. Oratio contra P. Seruilium rullum de lege agraria oratio I. Fragmenta. Quę res aperte patebatur . . .

29. ff. 186–194v M.T.C. Oratio contra P. Seruilium rullum de lege agraria oratio II incipit feliciter. Est hoc in more positum . . .

Small blank spaces on ff. 193v, 194, the first between 'M. bruti' and 'atque auspitia' (xxxiii. 92) and the second between 'compleretis nouo' (edn. *exploraretis nova*) and 'Vrbi ad' where two words *urbem nouam* are missing (xxxvi. 98).

30. ff. 194v–196 M.T.C. Oratio contra P. Seruilium Rulum de lege agraria oratio III incipit. Commodius fecissem . . . conuocauerunt disserant.

The scribe wrote 'sic erat in exemplari' opposite the last words.

31. ff. 196–9 M.T.C. Oratio contra lutium catilinam incipit I. Quousque abutere . . .

32. ff. 199–202 M.T.C. contra lutium catilinam II incipit. Tandem aliquando quirites . . .

33. ff. 202–204v M.T.C. Oratio contra lutium catilinam III incipit. Rem p. quirites vitamque . . .

34. ff. 204v–207 M.T.C. Oratio contra lutium catilinam IIII incipit. Video p.c. in me omnium ora . . .

35. ff. 207v–208 Crispi salustii oratio in M.T.C. Incipit. Grauiter et iniquo animo . . .

Ciceronis Opera, ed. G. Baier and C. L. Kayser, xi (1869), 147.

36. ff. 208–10 M.T.C. Responsio in Crispum salustium incipit. Ea demum magna uoluptas . . .

Ibid. xi. 149. The scribe wrote 'Laus deo. Pax viuis. requies defontis' at the end. For the text on f. 210rv see above, art. 18.

37. ff. 210v–216 [S]i quid precibus apud deos immortales sanctissimi iudices . . . genere calamitatis. Laus deo. Scripsit de Lusdiis leonardus qui uocitatur.

For this 'supposta quinta Catilinaria, esercizio rettorico dell'età imperiale' see R. Sabbadini, *Storia e critica de testi latini*, 2nd edn., 1971, pp. 136–41. Ed. K. Zimmerer, Munich 1888. First printed in a 1490 edition of Sallust (Goff, S. 75). f. 216v left blank.

ff. ii + 219 + iii. The modern foliation 1-216 repeats the number 107, misses the number 119, and does not mark single leaves after 157, 182, and 191. Traces of a contemporary correct foliation, for example '191' on f. 189 and '210' on f. 207: cf. art. 18. 293 × 220 mm. Written space 215 × 135 mm. 44 long lines. Collation: 1-21^{10} 22^{10} wants 10, blank. Written in more or less current fere-humanistica: single-compartment *a*: non-humanist *g* common at first: a distinctive abbreviation for *quod*. Art. 37 by another scribe, in humanistica. Initials: 6-line, pink on punched gold grounds, with blue or green and blue ornament. Bound by C. Lewis, s. xix^1. Secundo folio *questioni*.

Arts. 1-36 written in Venice by a named scribe in just under seven months: 'Scriptum per me Andream del Zeno notarium placentinum in ciuitate Venetiarum a die xii° octobris M° cccc° xlviii vsque ad diem vi^{to} Maii M° cccc° xlviiii° quod die gratia altissimi compleui', f. 210^v. For the scribe of art. 37 see above. An armorial shield at the foot of f. 1, azure a bend argent between two stars gules, is flanked by the letters A and S and has above it the letters CO with mark of abbreviation. Belonged to Henry Drury in s. xix^1: 'H. Drury Harrow Scr. 1449 comp: C. Lewis', f. i. His sale, 19 February 1827, lot 1200. Belonged to Joseph Brooks Yates (†1855) of West Dingle, Liverpool (f. i). Given by his grandson Henry Yates Thompson, in 1898: the *ex-dono* is stamped on the outside of the front cover.

LIVERPOOL. CATHEDRAL

A collection made by Sir Frederick Radcliffe (†1953), expressly for Liverpool Cathedral, mainly in the 1930s and with the advice of Dr F. C. Eeles.[1] The more or less immediate pre-Radcliffe history of about half the medieval manuscripts is known: see below, MSS. 6, 14, 19, 20, 23, 27, 29, 30, 35, 36, 37, 39, 40, 41, 50.[2]

4. *Breviarium* — s. xv med.

1. ff. 1-12^v Calendar in red and black, graded.

Of Cologne feasts, 'Obitus tercii regis', Three Kings, Gereon et soc., 11,000 Virgins, Severinus, Anno, are marked 'Duplex festum' (11 Jan., 23 July, 10, 21, 23 Oct., 3 Dec. Et anticipabitur hic propter festum barbare) and, except at 11 Jan., are in red; Cunibert is 'Semiduplex' and in red, 12 Nov.; Agillofus is 'ix lc' and in red, 9 July 'Et anticipabitur hic festum propter oct' visitacionis marie'. Visitation and Presentation of B.V.M. in red, duplex, 2 July, 21 Nov. 'Anne matris marie duplex' added over erasure, 26 July. Transfiguration added, 5 Aug., and a note that the 'festum sixti anticipabitur'. f. 12*^{rv} blank.

2. ff. 13-130^v Liturgical psalter, matins-vespers: cf. art. 5.

3. ff. 130^v-132^v Canticles of the Psalter.

Cues of Confitebor-Benedicite; then Benedictus, Magnificat, Nunc dimittis, Te deum in full.

[1] See E. G. W. Bill, *A catalogue of manuscripts in Lambeth Palace Library*, 1972, pp. 142-3, description of MS. 1518. The manuscripts were deposited in Liverpool University Library in 1980.

[2] The medieval manuscripts not described here are: 1, a bull of Pope Innocent III in favour of the abbey of St Bertin, O.S.B., 8 March 1202 (Phillipps 3587); 48, 49, 52-8, binding fragments or cuttings. Many of these fragments were acquired probably at the same time as MS. 50, q.v.

4. ff. 132v–136v Letania.

Apostles end with Timothy and Barnabas. Twenty-two confessors: (12–22) kuniberte bricti seruati seuerine udalrice galle anthoni bernarde materne dominice heriberte. Mary of Egypt last of twenty-two virgins: Anne absent.

5. ff. 136v–138 Item sic obseruandum est ad completorium per annum. Conuerte nos . . .

6. ff. 138–140v Item iste preces dicuntur ad matutinas et ad vesperas quando nocturnus seruatur . . . Preces. Ego dixi domine miserere mei . . .

Twenty-one short prayers follow Ego dixi.

7. ff. 140v–142v Suffragia dicuntur secundum tempus . . .

Memoriae for bishop, for the dead and for sins.

8. ff. 142v–145 Memoriae of Holy Cross, B.V.M., Peter, Three Kings (including a collect for Felix, Nabor, and Gregory), All Saints, and for peace, in various forms according to the status of the feast on which they are said.

9. ff. 145–148v Incipit cursus beate marie uirginis.

Hours of B.V.M. of the use of (Utrecht).

10. (*a*) ff. 148v–150 Oratio sacerdotis preparantis se ad missam. Adiutorium etc. Sancti spiritus assit nobis gracia . . . (*b*) ff. 150v–151 Oratio sacerdotis post missam. An'. Trium puerorum . . .

(*a*). Psalms (cues only) and six prayers, the last 'Conscientias nostras . . .'. (*b*) ends with 'Famulorum tuorum quesumus domine delictis . . .'. f. 151v blank.

11. ff. 152–157v Incipiunt vigilie defunctorum.

12. ff. 158–251v Temporal from Advent.

13. ff. 252–335v Incipit de sanctis.

Saturninus–Linus. The Visitation and Presentation of B.V.M. are included, as well as the Transfiguration, but not Anne; also Walburga, Cassius and Florentius, Servatius, Udalricus, Agillolfus, Three Kings, Madelberta, Gereon et soc., Eliphius, Severinus, Kunibertus, Brice.

14. (*a*) ff. 335v–337v Item sic obseruandum est de regibus terciis feriis . . . ; (*b*) ff. 337v–339 Item sic obseruandum feriis quintis de sancto petro apostolo; (*c*) ff. 339–46 item sic obseruandum est sabbatis diebus de domina nostra.

(*c*). ff. 343–6 contain four sets of three lessons 'quando seruatur de domina per annum', Creatoris . . . , Ad te domina . . . , Quando enim . . . , Magne deuocionis . . . f. 346v blank.

15. ff. 347–366^{v} Common of saints, ending imperfectly in the common of a virgin.

16. ff. 375–391^{v} Hymns.

(1–4) O lux beata, Lucis creator, Te lucis, Criste qui lux; (5–20, Advent–Easter) Conditor, Veni redemptor, Vox clara, A solis ortus, Hostis herodes, Ibant magi, Ex more docti, Audi benigne, Ihesu quadragenarie, Summi largitor, Clarum decus, Vexilla regis, Rex cristi factor, Ad cenam agni, Ihesu nostra redemptio, Vita sanctorum decus, headed 'De sanctis'; (21–3, Saints' days, 23 Apr.–3 May) Martir egregie (George), Pange lingua gloriose lancee preconium (Holy Lance), Salue crux sancta; (24–6, Ascension, Pentecost, Corpus Christi) Festum nunc, Veni creator spiritus, Pange lingua gloriosi corporis; (27–45, saints' days on and after 24 June) Ut queant laxis, Aurea luce, In mariam, Sidus solare, Imnis laudum (Three Kings: *RH*, no. 8210), Petre pontifex, Ymnizemus regi cristo (Mary of Egypt: *RH*, no. 8220), En martyris, Gaude visceribus, Bernardus doctor, Aue maris stella, Tibi rex splendor, Rex sempiterne lucis (Gereon: *RH*, no. 17520), Ihesu saluator seculi, Nouum sydus (Elizabeth), O dei sapiencia (Presentation), Aue katherina martir, Andrea pie, Gratuletur ecclesia laudum promat (Barbara); (46–50, Common of saints) Exultet celum, Deus tuorum, Rex gloriose, Iste confessor, Ihesu corona; (51) De commendacione beate marie. Lauda mater ecclesia (*RH*, no. 10211); (52) De Transfiguratione domini. Gaude mater pietatis in valle; (53, Dedication of church) Criste cunctorum; (54, added, s. xvi) In fest' gaudiorum gloriose virginis marie ymnus. Laudes perpetue (*RH*, no. 29043). ff. 392–394^{v} blank. In s. xvi art. 16 followed art. 11 (see below).

ff. i + 368 + viii + i, foliated (i, ii), 1–12, 12*, 13–394, (395). ff. 367–74 are blank paper, s. xvi (?). 82 × 70 mm. Written space 63 × 45 mm. 22 long lines. Collation of ff. ii, 1–366, 375–94: 1^{6} wants 1 (ff. ii, 1–4) 2^{10} wants 10, blank (ff. 5–12, 12*) $3–12^{10}$ 13 nine (ff. 113–21) $14–16^{10}$ 17^{6} (ff. 152–7) $18–25^{10}$ 26^{8} 27^{6} (ff. 246–51) 28^{8} $29–36^{10}$ 37^{6} (ff. 341–6) $38–41^{10}$ (ff. 347–66, 375–94). Quires signed in s. xvi in the usual late medieval way A–P (ff. 13–147), a–y (ff. 158–366), Q, R (ff. 375–94). Small script: *u* has often a small *o* over it as a distinguishing mark. Initials: (i) red and blue, with ornament of red, green, and violet; (ii, iii) 3-line and 1-line, blue or red. Rubrics are usually in the ink of the text, underlined in red. Binding of thin wooden boards bevelled on the inside and also in the middle of the edge at head and foot outside: a broad floral framing roll encloses a small panel containing two ornaments: three bands: two clasps missing. Secundo folio (f. 14) *quod plantatum est.*

Written for use in the diocese of Cologne.

5. *Horae* s. xv med.

1. ff. 5–16^{v} Calendar in red and black.

Feasts in red include Amandus, Basil, 'Translatio thome', Remigius and Bavo, Donatian, Nichasius (6 Feb., 15 June, 3 July, 1, 14 Oct., 13 Dec.). 'Visitacio Marie' in black, 2 July: other feasts of B.V.M. are in red.

2. ff. 18–22 Hore sancte crucis . . . Patris sapientia . . . f. 22^{v} blank.

3. ff. 24–8 Hore sancte (*sic*) spiritus . . . Nobis sancti spiritus . . .

4. ff. 28–33^{v} Obsecro te . . . Masculine forms.

5. ff. 34–37^{v} O intemerata . . . orbis terrarum inclina mater . . .

6. ff. 39–97^v Hore beate marie.

Of the use of (Rome). Salve regina as a memoria of B.V.M. after compline. No special forms for Advent, etc.

7. ff. 98–119^v Septem psalmi peni(tenciales) and (f. 114^v) litany.

Timothy last of apostles. Thirteen martyrs: . . . (7) nicasii cum sociis tuis. Six confessors: . . . (4) amande.

8. ff. 121–42 Office of the dead. 'Partem beate resurrectionis . . .' at the end. f. 142^v blank.

9 (added in s. xvi in.). ff. 143–149^v Incipiunt preparat' sacer(dotis) . . . Quam dilecta . . .

Pss. 83–5, 115 and prayers.

ff. vii + 145 + iii, foliated (i–iii), 1–149, (150–2). 92 × 65 mm. Written space 68 × 40 mm. 15 long lines. Collation of ff. 5–149: 1–2^6 3–6^8 7^4 (ff. 51–4) 8–13^8 14^6 (ff. 103–8) 15 eight (ff. 109–16) 16–19^8, together with three singleton picture pages, the rectos blank, ff. 17, 23, 120. Set cursiva, not good, near to *lettre bâtarde*. A full-page picture before each of arts. 2, 3, 6, 8. Initials: (i) blue or red patterned in white on grounds of the other colour and gold: continuous borders on picture pages and on pages facing them, badly damaged by the binder; (ii) 3-line gold on grounds of red and blue patterned in white: sprays into the margins; (iii) 2-line, as (ii), but without sprays; (iv) 1-line, blue with red or gold with violet ornament. Binding of s. xx in. Secundo folio (f. 19) *pone passionem*.

Written in N.E. France or W. Belgium. 'Alex Boswel [. . . .] Paris 1729', f. 1.

6. *Horae angeli custodientis* s. xv^2

1. ff. 2–4 Euerlastinge welthe withe oute disconfeture . . .

Sixteen lines of verse printed in the Quaritch catalogues: see below. The initial letters of the first nine lines spell **ELISABETH**: the other seven letters are **ATIMWAW**. The verses are addressed to 'a Lady souereyne princes' by the donor, who says that 'it shulde haue bene moche more illumynid withe pleasure Ande if I had tyme'. ff. 1^{rv}, 4^v, 5 blank.

2. ff. 6–77 Domine labia mea aperies . . .

Hours of the guardian angel: a full description in the Quaritch catalogues. A hymn, 'Salus tibi sit cum gaudio', is distributed through the hours: 25 stanzas in all and the refrain 'Gloria tibi domine qui tali me munimine custodis a discrimine in hac mundi caligine'. f. 77^v blank.

ff. 78 + ii. 90 × 65 mm. Written space 50 × 30 mm. 10 long lines. Collation: 1^6 (1^1, unnumbered, is the pastedown) 2–10^8. A full-page picture, f. 5^v: a kneeling woman gives a book to a queen seated on her right: above the woman a scroll 'w^t euerlastyng ioy'. Initials: (i) beginning each hour, a 4-line (f. 6) or 3-line *D*, shaded pink and blue on gold grounds, decorated with a flower (a red and white rose, f. 6); (ii) 2-line, gold on blue and red grounds patterned in white: green and gold sprays into the margins; (iii) 1-line, blue with red ornament or gold with blue-grey ornament. Capital letters in the ink of the text marked with red. Borders are continuous on ff. 5^{v}, 6 and in three margins of other pages with initials of type (i). Binding of thin wooden boards covered with worn woven fabric the threads of which are crimson and gold: central silver clasp: kept in a red levant morocco case made by Riviere. Secundo folio (f. 7) *lenti*.

Written in England, presumably by the donor, a woman, as a gift to an English queen: 'It has been supposed that the queen is Elizabeth, queen of Henry VII, married in 1486, since on f. 6 the initial contains a white rose superimposed on a red one. On stylistic grounds, however, her mother, Elizabeth Woodville, who married Edward IV in 1464 and died in 1492, is more likely' (*MERT*, p. 29). 'Num^{b} 425' inside the cover. 'This MS was given to my Father in December 1828 by our old neighbour in Suffolk and pleasant acquaintance for many years Mrs Plumpin widow of the late elegant scholar and right worthy man the rector of Whatfield near Hadleigh E. W. H. Drummond Hay' inside the cover. A pencil note on f. 1 by G(eorge) D(unn) is dated 'July 1898' and his printed label with number '219' on it is at the end: his sale 2 February 1913, lot 593. Listed in two Quaritch catalogues, both with facsimiles of ff. 5^{v}–6: *Catalogue of illuminated and other manuscripts*, 1931, item 73; catalogue 532 (1937), item 403 (£250). *MERT*, no. 49.

8. *Horae (in Netherlandish)* s. xv med.

1. ff. 3–14^{v} Calendar in red and black.

ponciaen pancraes seruaes bonifacius odulf lebuijn lambert remigius willibrort lebuijn among feasts in red.

2. ff. 15–46^{v} Hier beghint onser vrouwen ghetijde. Use of (Utrecht).

3. ff. 47–67 Hier beghint die lange cruys getyde. f. 67^{v} blank.

4. ff. 68–82^{v} Hier beghint des heiligen ghiestes Tyde. f. 83^{rv} blank.

5. ff. 84–102^{v} Hier beghint die wijsheits getijde.

6. ff. 103–119^{v} Hier beghint die souen psalmen.

'Letenie' f. 110^{v}. Forty-eight martyrs. Forty-three confessors, beginning with Martin. Thirty virgins, beginning with Agnes.

7. ff. 120–51 Hier beghint die lange vigilie. Circumde. Mi hebben ommebeuangen die suchten des doets . . .

ff. ii + 149 + ii, foliated 1–153. 147 × 102 mm. Written space 88 × 63 mm. 20 long lines. Collation of ff. 3–151: 1–2^{6} 3–8^{8} 9^{4} + 1 leaf after 4 (ff. 63–7) 10–13^{8} 14^{2} + 1 leaf after 2 (ff. 100–2) 15^{8} 16^{8} + 1 leaf after 8 (ff. 111–19) 17–20^{8}. Initials: (i) 10-line or 11-line, blue shaded to white or patterned in white on decorated grounds (f. 1 historiated: B.V.M. crowned, with the Child); (ii) 5-line, gold on grounds of red and blue patterned in white; (iii) 2-line, blue with red ornament; (iv) 1-line, red or blue and, in the litany, gold or blue. Capital letters in the ink of the text marked with red. Continuous borders of flowers, etc., on pages with initials of type (i): the grounds are usually of pink dots. On pages with initials of type (ii) the border decoration consists of sprays of red and blue springing from head and foot of a bar of blue and gold lining the written space on the left: free standing gold stars. Binding of s. xviii: on spine 'Almenac oste Getij Boeck'.

Written in the Low Countries. Armorial book-plate inside the cover, s. xix, with motto 'Vertu force avec'. *MERT*, no. 37.

9. *Horae* s. xv^2

1. ff. 1–12ᵛ Full calendar in French in gold, blue, and red, the two colours alternating.

Entries in gold include Geneviève at 26 Nov. and 4 Jan., Louis, 'Sain leu s' gille', Denis, Marcel (25 Aug., 1 Sept., 9 Oct., 3 Nov.). No entry of Visitation of B.V.M., 2 July.

2. ff. 13–22ᵛ Sequentiae of the Gospels. The prayer 'Protectio in te sperantium ...' after John.

3. ff. 22ᵛ–27ᵛ Oratio. Obsecro te ... Masculine forms.

4. ff. 27ᵛ–31 Alia oratio de beata maria. O intemerata ... orbis terrarum. Inclina ... Masculine forms.

5. ff. 31ᵛ–47ᵛ Passio domini nostri iesu cristi secundum Iohannem. Egressus est dominus ... posuerunt iesum. Per euangelica dicta deleantur nostra delicta Amen.

John 18: 1–19: 42, divided into nine sections at 18: 10, 29, 19: 1, 5, 14, 16, 25, 38, each preceded by a picture.

6. ff. 48–110ᵛ Hours of B.V.M. of the use of (Paris).

Hours of Holy Cross and Holy Spirit are worked in. Ends imperfectly in terce.

ff. iii + 110 + ii. 135 × 93 mm. Written space 73 × 45 mm. 14 long lines. Ruling in red ink. Collation: $1\text{–}2^6$ $3\text{–}6^8$ 7^2 (ff. 46–7) $8\text{–}15^8$. Eight 10-line or 11-line pictures, six in art. 6 (matins, lauds, prime, terce and (ff. 92, 94) matins of Cross and Holy Spirit), one before art. 2, and one before art. 5 (Christ in the garden). Eleven smaller pictures, *c.*37 × 30 mm, three in art. 2 and eight, a Passion series, in art. 5. Initials: (i, ii) 3-line and 2-line, blue patterned in white on decorated gold grounds; (iii) 1-line, gold on blue and red grounds patterned in white. Capital letters in the ink of the text filled with pale yellow. Line fillers blue and red patterned in white with a piece of gold between the colours. Borders: (*a*) continuous on pages with larger pictures; (*b*) on three sides, not the inner margin, of pages with smaller pictures; (*c*) the height of the written space in the outer margin of pages with initials of type (ii): a bar of blue and gold separates them from the text. Binding of red velvet, s. xix. Secundo folio (f. 15) *perhiberet*.

Written in France (Paris ?). '128/924' at the end.

10. *Inhumatio defuncti* s. xv in.

1. Incipit ordo ad benedicendum tumulum. Cum autem peruenerit ad tumulum sacerdos cum feretro stet iuxta tumulum: et cantatis antiphonis. dicat orationem absolute. Deus qui fundasti terram . . .

Prayers, psalms and antiphons as in *Sacerdotale ad consuetudinem s. Romanę ecclesię*, Venice 1564, ff. 145–9.

2. Two 8-line stanzas were added in s. xvi^2 on f. ii^v, 'Corre di sponda in sponda / Senza timor del onda . . . '

ff. ii + 23 + i. Strong parchment. f. ii is a medieval flyleaf. 252 × 170 mm. Written space 147 × 108 mm. 12 long lines, each bounded above and below by a ruled line. Collation: 1–2^8 3^8 wants 8. Initials: f. 1, two initials, pink on blue grounds, one historiated (a priest reading), the other decorated in colours and gold; (ii, iii) 2-line and 1-line, blue with red ornament or red with violet ornament. Capital letters in the ink of the text lined with yellow. Binding of s. xx in. Secundo folio *nostrum ihesum.*

Written in Italy.

11. *Breviarium* s. xiv/xv

Use of Rome, according to the headings of arts. 5, 8.

1. ff. 1–6^v Graded calendar. No entries in red, except at 18 Sept.

Gradings are 'duplex maius', 'duplex minus' 'ix lc' and 'commemoratio'. 'Duplex maius' includes Mark, Martial, Floregius, Raphael, Anne, B.V.M. de niuibus, Transfiguration, Amancius, Thomas of Canterbury (25 Apr., 30 June, 1, 8, 26 July, 5, 6 Aug., 4 Nov., 29 Dec.); 'Duplex minus', 'Prelium sancti michaelis', translation of Andrew (8, 9 May); 'ix lc', Tarcicia, Robert abbot, Quiteria, Troecia, Namacius, Dalmacius, Anianus (15 Jan., 24 Apr., 22 May, 8 June, 2, 3, 17 Nov.). The one red entry, 'Ferreoli (? *sic*) martiris duplex' (18 Sept.) is probably an addition. Marciana and Amarandus were added in s. xvi, 5, 7 Nov.

2. (*a*) ff. 7–9 Aduentus domini celebratur . . . O sapientia. (*b*) f. 9 Item notandum quod quandocumque fit officium beate marie . . . Laus tibi domine. (*c*) f. 9^{rv} Rubrice infrascripte collecte multas dubitaciones prout patebit. Est sciendum quod capitula et benedicciones . . . (*d*) f. 9^v Notandum quod anno domini m^o ccc^o lx^o et in festo kathedre sancti petri contigit feriam iiii^{am} cinerum occurreret. tunc fuit ordinatum in auinione in consilio domini pape clementis sexti et dominorum cardinalium quod ratione incoationis tam solemniorum ieiuniorum in v^a feria amodo uoluerint transfieri quam ordinacionem per totum orbem miserunt obseruari.

(*a*). *SMRL* ii. 114–21. f. 10^{rv} blank.

3. ff. 11–101v Temporal, beginning imperfectly with the capitulum Qui timet for John Evangelist and ending imperfectly in the response for the first Sunday after Pentecost, Preparate corda vestra.

The office for Wednesday after Corpus Christi is followed on f. 101 by a decree of Pope John (XXII) about duplex and other feasts falling on Corpus Christi Day and within the octave, 'Bene gestis et congrue ordinatis . . . Sane nonnullorum clericorum querela ad nos peruenit quod in festo eucaristie . . . et in missa dicitur credo'.

4. ff. 102–120v Common of saints, beginning imperfectly.

5. ff. 120v–125 Incipit officium beate marie uirginis secundum consuetudinem romane ecclesie.

A leaf missing after f. 120.

6. ff. 125–7 In dedicatione ecclesie. *SMRL* ii. 158.

7. ff. 127–129v Incipit agenda defunctorum. *SMRL* ii. 164.

8. ff. 130–189v Incipit proprium sanctorum secundum consuetudinem romanam.

Saturninus–Assumption of B.V.M., ending imperfectly. A pattern of wormholes on ff. 184–9 is not continued on f. 190.

9. ff. 190–259 Liturgical psalter.

The right order of the first three quires (19–21) is 190–2, 194, 193, 196, 195, 197–9, 212, 200–11, 214–17, 213, 218–22. Three leaves are missing.

10. ff. 259–261v Letania.

Ten confessores: . . . (5–10) amancii floregii dalmacii iheronime marcialis nicholai. Thirteen virgins, Anne not among them: . . . (8) radegundis.

11. ff. 261v–268v Forty-one hymns.

(1–21, Advent–Pentecost) As *Haymo*, pp. 21–89 and *SMRL* ii. 17–101. (22–39, Sanctoral, 24 June–1 Nov.) Ut queant, Antra, O nimis felix; Aue maris stella, Quem terra, O gloriosa; Iam bone, Quodcumque uinclis, Doctor egregie, Aurea luce; Nardi; Petrus beatus; O nata lux and Festiua sat (for Transfiguration: *RH*, nos. 13298, 6193); Tibi criste, Criste sanctorum decus; Criste redemptor, Ihesu saluator. (40, 41, Dedication) Urbs beata, Angularis.

12. ff. 269–86 Temporal, beginning imperfectly at the third Sunday after Pentecost.

Haymo, pp. 93–100; *SMRL* ii. 105–14. A leaf missing after f. 278. f. 286v blank.

ff. 286. 150 × 105 mm. Written space 87 × 67 mm. 2 cols. 28 lines. Collation: 1^{6} 2^{4} (ff. 7–10) 3^{10} wants 1, 2 before f. 11 $4\text{-}9^{12}$ 10^{12} wants 12 after f. 101 11^{12} wants 1 before f. 102 12^{12} wants 9 after f. 120 $13\text{-}17^{12}$ 18 six (ff. 184-9) 19^{12} wants 1 (ff. 190–9, 212, the two central sheets reversed and the last leaf misplaced: see above, art. 9) 20^{12} 21^{12} wants 2 after f. 214 and 7 (6 is misplaced: see above, art. 9) $22\text{-}24^{12}$ 25^{10} (ff. 259–68) 26^{10} wants 1-3 27^{12} wants 4 after f. 278. The catchwords, written vertically and centred, are prettily decorated. Initials: (i) gold and blue with ornament in several colours; (ii) 3-line, blue and red with red and violet ornament; (iii) 2-line, blue with red ornament or red with violet ornament; (iv) 1-line, blue or red. Binding of limp parchment, s. xvii (?). Secundo folio (f. 8) *si festum*.

Written for use in the diocese of Rodez (Aveyron), as appears from calendar and litany; perhaps for use at Estaing, 35 km north-north-east of Rodez, where Floregius, here Duplex maius in the calendar and after Amantius in the litany, was the local saint: cf. *Acta Sanctorum*, July I. 38–41.[1]

12. *Thomas Aquinas, etc.* s. xv med.

1. (f. 5) Incipit compendium theologie secundum beatum thomam de Aquino ordinis predicatorum. Et primo que sit auctoris intencio. Eterni patris verbum . . . (f. 143) ad vltimam suam perfectionem. Que secuntur non sunt beati thome. (f. 143^{v}) Dupliciter autem restat . . . in quantum appetitum quietat. Explicit compendium S. B. T. de Aquino.

Glorieux, no. 14*cs*. *Opuscula*, ed. Mandonnet (1927), ii. 1–210/34: the fourteen lines said not to be by St Thomas are edn., p. 210/22–34. Pt. 1, bk. 1, is in three sections corresponding to edn., chapters 1–36, 37–67, 68–184: a numbered table on ff. 1–4^{v}. Pt. 1, bk. 2, begins on f. 88^{v} and corresponds to edn., pt. 1, chapters 185–246: a table of chapters on ff. 84^{v}–88^{v}. Pt. 2 begins on f. 135^{v}. Only a few chapters are numbered in the text, for example, no. '41' of bk. 2 (edn., ch. 223). Contemporary marginalia were written first in a very small current hand and then copied in textura, for example on f. 55. A reader noted on f. 143 'Sanctus thomas morte preuentus non compleuit residuum de spe et totum de caritate'.

2. ff. 143^{v}–172^{v} Incipit tractatus de obseruancia mandatorum secundum eundem. De mandatis seu decem preceptis. secundum beatum thomam. Si vis ad vitam ingredi serua mandata. Naturale desiderium inest cuilibet homini ad beatitudinem . . . Fili concupiscis sapienciam serua iusticiam.

A shortened reworking of Aquinas, Collationes 29 in Decem Praeceptis: cf. J. P. Torrell, 'Deux remaniements anonymes des 'Collationes in Decem Praeceptis' de s. Thomas d'Aquin', *Mediaeval Studies*, xl (1978), 1–29.[2] Bloomfield, no. 5647.

3. ff. 172^{v}–186^{v} Incipit exposicio dominice oracionis secundum eundem beatum thomam de Aquino. Pater noster etc. Inter alias oraciones oracio dominica

[1] For Roman breviaries in the diocese of Rodez see V. Leroquais, *Bréviaires manuscrits des bibliothèques publiques de France*, v, Index, s. v. Rodez, and add Toulouse 71, 75 (ibid. iv. 178, 185). Leroquais does not refer to St Floregius.

[2] I owe this identification and reference to Mme M.-C. Garand.

. . . remouendum petimus. Sed libera nos a malo. Explicit exposicio oracionis dominice.

Glorieux, no. 14*db*. Ed. Mandonnet (1927), ii. 389–411 (Opusc. 34).

4. ff. 187–256 Incipit prologus in opusculo quatuor nouissimorum. Memorare nouissima tua. et in eternum . . . Sicut dicit Augustinus . . . Si placet imponatur. Incipit opusculum quatuor nouissimorum. Memorare . . . Sola autem peccati feditas . . . ac nouissima prouiderent. Explicit tractatus qui cordiale dicitur.

Often printed: *GKW* 7469–7514. Bloomfield, no. 3057. The fifty-six verses 'Vado mori mors certa . . . sic bene vado Mori' are on ff. 195–6: cf. Walther, no. 19965.

5. f. 256^v Incipiunt peticiones que debent fieri infirmo exeunte in agonia mortis edite a beato Anselmo in libro de oracionibus . . . Prima peticio est. Si firmiter credit . . . loco prenominato.

Cf. R. W. Southern and F. S. Schmitt, *Memorials of St Anselm*, 1969, pp. 352–3.

6. ff. 257–275^v Incipit tractatus de arte bene moriendi. Cum de presentis exilii miseria . . . gaudiis potiaris in secula seculorum amen. Proficiscere anima cristiana de hoc mundo in nomine patris . . . in ierusalem celeste per eundem dominum nostrum Amen.

Printed often: *GKW* 2597–2614. Cf. M. C. O'Connor, *Art of Dying well*, 1942, pp. 48–60.

ff. i + 275 + i. 147 × 110 mm. Written space 97 × 63 mm. 31 long lines. Collation: 1^4 2^{10} $3\text{–}23^{12}$ 24^{12} wants 8, cancelled, after f. 273 and 11, 12 blank. From f. 5 the quires are signed in the usual late medieval way. ff. 208^v–275^v (except 218^{rv}) are in a distinctive and good fere-humanistica, which occurs earlier in the margins. Initials: (i) ff. 5, 88^v, 187, 257, blue or red on gold grounds: sprays into the margins; (ii, iii) 3-line and 2-line, blue with red ornament or red with violet ornament. Capital letters in the ink of the text stroked with red. Binding of thin wooden boards recovered in s. xviii: four bands. Secundo folio (f. 6) *quidem essencie*.

Written in northern Italy. A title label on the spine bears the number 83, s. xix.

13. *Biblia* s. xiii med.

ff. 1–518 A Bible in the usual order,[1] Genesis–2 Chronicles + Prayer of Manasses, Ezra, Nehemiah, 2 Ezra (= 3 Ezra: Stegmüller, no. 94, 1), Tobit, Judith, Esther, Job, Psalms, Proverbs, Ecclesiastes, Song of Songs, Wisdom, Ecclesiasticus (without the Prayer of Solomon at the end), Isaiah, Jeremiah, Lamentations, Baruch, Ezekiel, Daniel, Minor Prophets, 1, 2 Maccabees, Gospels, Pauline Epistles, Acts,

[1] By usual order I mean the order of books commonly found in manuscripts written in France in s. xiii: see *MMBL* I. vii, II. vii.

Catholic Epistles, Apocalypse. The prologues are the common set of 64, except that by some casual error the scribe failed to copy nos. 707, 765 (Galatians, 1 Timothy).[1]

No notes in the margins. f. 518^{v} blank. A parchment tab marks the beginning of each book. Chapter numbers were entered at the foot of pages as a guide to the rubricator.

	Stegmüller no.		
1	284	General prologue	Frater Ambrosius
2	285	Pentateuch	Desiderii mei
3	311	Joshua	Tandem finito
4	323	1 Kings	Viginti et duas
5	328	1 Chronicles	Si Septuaginta
6	327	2 Chronicles	Quomodo Graecorum
7	330	1 Ezra	Utrum difficilius
8	332	Tobit	Mirari non desino
9	335	Judith	Apud Hebraeos
10 + 11	341 + 343	Esther	Librum Esther + Rursum
12	344	Job	Cogor per singulos
13	357	Job	Si aut fiscellam
14	457	Proverbs	Iungat epistola
15	462	Ecclesiastes	Memini me
16	468	Wisdom	Liber Sapientiae
17	482	Isaiah	Nemo cum prophetas
18	487	Jeremiah	Ieremias propheta
19	491	Baruch	Liber iste
20	492	Ezekiel	Ezechiel propheta
21	494	Daniel	Danielem prophetam
22	500	Minor Prophets	Non idem ordo est
23	507	Hosea	Temporibus
24	511	Joel	Sanctus Ioel
25	510	Joel	Ioel filius Phatuel
26	515	Amos	Ozias rex
27	512	Amos	Amos propheta
28	513	Amos	Hic Amos
29 + 30	519 + 517	Obadiah	Iacob Patriarcha + Hebraei
31	524	Jonah	Sanctum Ionam
32	521	Jonah	Ionas columba
33	526	Micah	Temporibus Ioathae
34	528	Nahum	Nahum prophetam
35	531	Habakkuk	Quattuor prophetae
36	534	Zephaniah	Tradunt Hebraei
37	538	Haggai	Ieremias propheta
38	539	Zechariah	In anno secundo
39	543	Malachi	Deus per Moysen
40	547	1 Maccabees	Cum sim promptus
41	553	1 Maccabees	Memini me
42	551	1 Maccabees	Maccabaeorum libri
43	590	Matthew	Matthaeus ex Iudaeis
44	589	Matthew	Matthaeus cum primo

[1] The number of prologues is sixty-four, both in the Bibles and by Stegmüller's reckoning. In the Bibles, Stegmüller's nos. 343 and 517 are not separated from nos. 341 and 519 and, on the other hand, two biblical texts, the introduction to Ecclesiasticus, *Multorum nobis* . . . and Luke 1: 1–4, are considered as prologues. The latter usually precedes prologue no. 620, as here.

45	607	Mark	Marcus evangelista
46	620	Luke	Lucas Syrus
47	624	John	Hic est Iohannes
48	677	Romans	Romani sunt
49	685	1 Corinthians	Corinthii sunt
50	699	2 Corinthians	Post actam
51	(707	Galatians	Galatae sunt)
52	715	Ephesians	Ephesii sunt
53	728	Philippians	Philippenses sunt
54	736	Colossians	Colossenses et hi
55	747	1 Thessalonians	Thessalonicenses sunt
56	752	2 Thessalonians	Ad Thessalonicenses
57	(765	1 Timothy	Timotheum instruit)
58	772	2 Timothy	Item Timotheo
59	780	Titus	Titum commonefacit
60	783	Philemon	Philemoni familiares
61	793	Hebrews	In primis dicendum
62	640	Acts	Lucas natione Syrus
63	809	Catholic Epistles	Non idem ordo est
64	839	Apocalypse	Omnes qui pie[1]

2. ff. 519–567v Hic incipiunt interpretationes hebraicorum nominum. Aaz apprehendens . . . consiliatores eorum.

The common dictionary of Hebrew names, Stegmüller, no. 7709, usually anonymous, sometimes attributed to Remigius.

ff. i + 566 + ii. The present foliation of art. 1 is a late medieval one: it takes account of the leaf now missing from quire 1 and goes wrong several times, righting itself later without correcting the errors. 170 × 110 mm. Written space 115 × 73 mm. 2 cols. 49 lines and—quire 23—46 lines. Collation: 1^{24} wants 3 $2\text{–}21^{24}$ 22^{18} wants 15–18, blank, after f. 518 23^{24} 24^{26} wants 26, blank. Leaves numbered a–m in the first halves of some quires, for example quires 12–14 (ff. 265–336), with *ad hoc* quire marks above or beside the letters. Initials: (i) of books, 6-line, blue or pink patterned in white on pink or blue grounds, historiated: a little gold: some minor prophets hold scrolls with their names; (ii) of prologues, 4-line, as (i), but decorated instead of historiated; (iii) of chapters, 2-line, blue or red with ornament of the other colour: the exterior ornament is saw-pattern down the margins; (iv) of verses of psalms and in art. 2, 1-line, blue or red. Gilt-tooled binding, s. xviii, rebacked: 'BIBLIA SACRA MS SUR VELIN AVEC MIGNATURES' on the spine. Secundo folio *debant*.

Written in France. An erased shield with 'I H' above it, f. 567v, is perhaps fifteenth-century.

14. *Manuale* s. xv in.

1. ff. 1–7 Incipit ordo ad baptizandos masculos.

2. ff. 7–10v, 12–13v Incipit ordo ad baptizandos feminas.

f. 11 is an inserted paper leaf, s. xvi, with Credo in deum patrem and Pater noster on it.

[1] I follow Stegmüller's spelling and wording. The manuscripts have usually *Iona*, not *Ionas* (this one has *Ionas*, but the *s* is expunged), at no. 521, *Iudea* not *Iudeis* at no. 590, and *ita*, not *idem*, at no. 509. No. 528 ends usually as here, *sicut in consequentibus libri huius demonstratur*, not *futurus est dominus*, that is to say it lacks the final section, *Sciendum autem quoniam niniue . . .*

3. ff. 13v–15 Incipit ordo ad baptizandum infirmum puerum.

4. ff. 15–32v Incipit ordo ad visitandum et ungendum infirmum.

Litany, f. 18v. Eleven martyrs: . . . (7–11) gereon c(um) s(ociis) t(uis) dionisi c.s.t. kyliane c.s.t. georgi blasi. Eight confessors: nicolae seuerine martine kuniberte seruacii brichi anno anthoni. Thirteen virgins: . . . (10–13) antonina geirtrudis irmetrudis. Omnes vndecim milium virginum.

5. f. 32v Incipit comendacio omnium fidelium defunctorum.

Only two lines remain.

6. ff. 33–49v Ordo in vigilia pasche ad benedicendum ignem . . . Incipient duo scholares cantare Imnum etc. Inuentor rutuli . . . An' super Magnificat. Vespere autem sabbati. Deinde sicut notatum est in libro missali etc.

Exultet noted, f. 34. Litany noted, f. 39v: the seven confessors are Silvester, Leo, Gregory, Martin, Severinus, Nicholas, and Kylian (cf. art. 4).

7. The pastedowns (the one at the back now raised, f. 50) are two bifolia, probably the four middle leaves of a quire of a small breviary (?) of s. xiv^2 with a written space of *c.* 100 × 68 mm and 28 long lines to the page. Of the eight pages, two are still pasted to the front board. The rest contain mainly an office of Corpus Christi.

The hymn at lauds of Corpus Christi is O quam magnum quam preclarum (*RH*, no. 13527: *AH* xii. 33, terce); at prime, Summe ihesu clemencie qui ob salutem (*RH*, no. 19638: *AH* lii. 28); at terce, Sacro tecta uelaminis (*RH*, no. 17727: *AH* lii. 28). Cf. the early Liège office discussed in *AH* lii. 27–30 and partly printed in *Acta Sanctorum*, Apr. I, p. 903.

f. 10 + i + 38 + i, foliated 1–49, (50). For f. 11 see above. 195 × 145 mm. Written space 150 × 112 mm. 18 long lines. Collation: 1^8 2^6 (ff. 9, 10, 12–15) 3^8 (2 and 6 are half-sheets) 4^8 5 one (f. 32) 6^8 7^8 + 1 leaf after 8 (f. 49). Red initials, 2-line and 1-line. Contemporary stamped binding of wooden boards covered with brown leather: the stamps are fleur de lis, flower head and lamb and flag within a frame of fillets and a small round eagle stamp outside the frame: three bands: central clasp missing. Secundo folio *pietatis*.

Written in Germany, probably for use in the diocese of Cologne. 'Johannes C. Jackson clericus ex dono Willelmi Burges MDCCCLXX' in a gothic hand at the foot of f. 1: for Jackson cf. *Sum. Cat.* vii. 555. After his death, his books and manuscripts—but not this one?—were sold at Sotheby's, 13 Dec. 1895. J. M. Falkner sale at Sotheby's, 12 Dec. 1932, lot 262.

15. *Horae* 1496

1. (*a*) ff. 2–12 Incipit accessus altaris . . . (*b*) ff. 12v–14v Placeat tibi sancta trinitas . . . An'. Trium puerorum . . . (*c*) ff. 15–18 Oracio dicenda ante missam. Summe sacerdos . . . sitiam in eternum Saluator mundi qui viuis.

Forms of service, (*a, c*) before and (*b*) after mass. (*a*) consists of hymn Veni creator, psalms (83, etc.) and prayers, the last 'Domine ihesu criste fili dei viui qui per manus sacerdotum sacramentum corporis et sanguinis tui in hora misse confici voluisti . . .'. (*c*). A. Wilmart, *Auteurs spirituels*, pp. 114–24. f. 1rv blank, except for 'Assit in principio beata virgo maria' on the recto and a shield (see below) on the verso. f. 18v blank.

2. ff. 19–63 Incipit Cursus beate ac gloriose virginis marie secundum modum bursfeldenum.

3. f. 63 A memoria of the Crucifixion.

4. ff. 63v–65v Hore de passione domini . . . Patris sapiencia . . .

5. ff. 65v–67 Oratio Bernhardi. Illumina oculos meos . . . Prayers follow: 'Omnipotens sempiterne deus qui ezechie . . .'; 'Protector in te sperancium . . .'.

6 (added, s. xvi). f. 67 Aue sanctissima maria regina celi . . .

7. ff. 67v–88v Incipiunt septem psalmi penitenciales. Litany, f. 77.

Twenty-one martyrs: . . . (7, 8) Emmeramme Lamperte . . . (11, 12) Ianuarii Kiliane. Twenty-eight confessors: . . . (12–14) Burcharde Vdalrice Gotharde . . . (27, 28) Allexi Karole. Twenty virgins: . . . (13–20) Affra Gerdrudis Margaretha Scolastica Walburga Elizabeth Kinegund Ursula cum sociis tuis. Of the fifteen prayers after 'Deus cui proprium . . .', the last but one is 'Tu domine qui hanc congregacionem . . .' and the last, 'Domine ne respicias . . .', asks for the intercession of St Martin and all saints 'quorum reliquie recondite sunt in isto loco'.

8. ff. 89–122v Office of the dead.

One leaf missing. f. 122v contains an addition in the hand of art. 6. f. 123rv blank.

9. ff. 124–5 De sancta trinitate ante communionem. O uera summa sempiterna trinitas. O inmensa deitas . . . f. 125v blank.

10. ff. 126–7 Oratio de beata virgine pro bono fine. Queso te clementissima virgo maria ostende michi . . .

11. ff. 127–32 Quicumque subscriptam orationem quotidie dixerit in honorem beatissime virginis marie ccc dies indulgenciarum habebit ab innocencio papa qui eam instituit . . . sicut in quodam Monasterio ordinis sancti benedicti reuelatum est cuidam abbatisse in extremis laboranti et post sepius expertum. O clementissima domina et dulcissima virgo . . . Obsecro te per illam sanctam et ineffabilem leticiam . . .

12. (*a*) f. 132rv Oratio dormituro dicenda. O Ihesu dulcissima Ihesu pater dilectissime Te queso mecum maneas . . . (*b*) ff. 132v–133 Oratio mane dicenda ad cor Ihesu. Laudo benedico . . . (*c*) f. 133rv Cum mane surgeris vel quoquaque pergere velis dic Benedicat me + Imperialis maiestas . . .

13. ff. 133v–135 Oratio sancti augustini a spiritu sancto sibi reuelato. Deus propicius esto michi peccatori . . . ; rubric follows, 'Notandum quod qui suprascriptam oracionem sancti augustini deuote legerit . . . in illa die non peribit . . . possidebit'.

Römer, i. 374.

14. ff. 135v–136v Oratio ad proprium angelum. Obsecro te angelice spiritus cui ego . . .

15. ff. 136v–138v Prayers to Simon, to Jude, and 'Ad omnes apostolos' (two forms).

16. ff. 138v–141v Memoriae of Sebastian and Christopher: at the end 'Scriptum per me marcum rothaubt herbipolen' dioc' Finitum per eundem die xxii mensis augusti Anno domini M° cccc° lxxxxvi'.

17 (added in hand of art. 6). f. 142 Media vita in morte sumus . . .

18. ff. 142v–154 Psalms 21, 34, 54, 68, 108 and at the end 'Deo gratias (in red). Finis'.

19 (added). (*a*) f. 154rv Deus deus (*sic*) qui uoluisti pro redemptione mundi . . . (*b*) f. 155 Deus a quo et iudas . . . (*c*, *d*) f. 156rv Two memoriae of Apollonia. (*e*) f. 157 Memoria of Matthew. (*f*) f. 158 Memoria of Anne, 'Anna pia mater aue . . .' (*RH*, no. 1109). ff. 155v, 157v, 158v blank.

ff. 158. 132 × 95 mm. Written space 87 × 55 mm. 18–19 long lines. Collation: $1–11^8$ 12^8 wants 7 after f. 94 $13–18^8$ 19^8 wants 6 after f. 148, except for a blank strip about 20 mm wide of a leaf which was either passed over in error or on purpose, because of some defect, 20^8. Written in cursiva. Initials: (i) gold or blue on grounds of colour or gold: border ornament, ff. 2, 19; (ii–iv) 3-line, 2-line and 1-line, blue or red. Binding of pasteboard covered with brown leather, s. xvi: a roll frames a blank panel: three bands: two clasps missing. Secundo folio (f. 3) *et turtur*.

Written, except arts. 6, 17, 19, by a named scribe, a clerk of the diocese of Würzburg (art. 16). Art. 2 is according to the use of the Benedictine congregation of Bursfeld. On f. 1v a shield is outlined: within it, a horizontal branch, with a smaller side branch of leaves and buds rising from it.

17. *Horae* s. xv med.

The leaves are disordered and arts. 2, 6–8, 11 have lost their first leaves.

1. ff. 1–12v Calendar in French in gold paint, blue, and red, the two colours alternating.

'geruais', 'eloy', 'sauueur', 'romain' in gold, 19, 25 June, 6 Aug., 23 Oct. 'romain' in red, 17 June.

2. ff. 19^{rv}, 22–24^{v} Sequentiae of the Gospels, beginning imperfectly. 'Protector in te sperantium . . .' after John.

3. ff. 24^{v}–25^{v}, 20–1 Oratio beate marie, Obsecro te . . . Masculine forms.

4. ff. 21^{rv}, 26–28^{v} O intemerata . . . orbis terrarum. De te enim . . .

5. f. 28^{v} Salutacio beate marie. Salue regina . . . (*ends imperfectly*).

6. ff. 29–48^{v}, 13–18^{v}, 49–56^{v} Hours of B.V.M. of the use of (Rouen).

Memoriae of Holy Spirit, Nicholas, and Katherine after lauds. The beginning of prime and the end of compline are missing.

7. ff. 58–71^{v} Seven penitential psalms and (f. 67) litany.

Martial is last of apostles. Fourteen confessors: (6–10) mellone romane audoene seuere laude.

8. ff. 78^{rv}, 71^{rv} Hours of the Cross.

9. ff. 71^{v}–75 Hours of the Holy Spirit.

10. ff. 75–77^{v}, 85–94^{v}, 79–84^{v}, 95–97^{v}, 57^{rv} Office of the dead.

11. ff. 100–103^{v}, 99^{rv} Fifteen Joys of B.V.M. in French. Sonet–Sinclair, no. 458.

12. ff. 99^{rv}, 98^{rv}, 104^{rv} Les vii requestes nostre seigneur: in French. Sonet–Sinclair, no. 504.

13. ff. 104^{v}–105 Saincte vraye croix aouree . . .

Sonet–Sinclair, no. 1876. Most of the leaf has been cut off and the verso, presumably blank, covered with thick paper.

ff. ii + 105 + i. 152 × 110 mm. Written space 97 × 65 mm. 17 long lines. Collation impracticable: art. 1 is a twelve. The only remaining picture—14-line—is before art. 10 (f. 74^{v}). Initials: (i) 3-line, blue patterned in white on decorated gold grounds; (ii, iii) 2-line and 1-line, gold on blue and red grounds patterned in white. Capital letters in the ink of the text filled with pale yellow. Line fillers red and blue patterned in white, the colours separated by one or two blobs of gold. A compartmented border of flowers and strawberries, f. 74^{v}. Framed borders on three sides (not the inner margin) of pages with initials of type (i). Binding of s. xix, titled on the spine, 'Heures anciennes Provenant du père Antoine' in capitals.

Written in France for use in the diocese of Rouen. 'Ex libris Fred. Raisin adv' genevens. 1882', f. 2. His book-plate inside the cover.

18. *Breviarium* 1503 (?)

1. ff. 1–314 Temporal from Advent to the Saturday after Trinity and sanctoral from 21 Jan. to 30 Nov.

Twelve lessons. Saints Days are in three blocks: ff. 60^{v}–90, Sebastian (21 Jan.)–Annunciation of B.V.M. (25 Mar.) before Septuagesima Sunday; ff. 175^{v}–186, Mark (25 Apr.), Invention of Cross, Florianus, John before Latin Gate (6 May), before Ascension Day and immediately after the common of saints 'paschali tempore'; ff. 202^{v}–314, Vitus (15 June)–Andrew (30 Nov.), after Saturday after Trinity: includes Achatius, Udalricus, 'De S. Henrico Imperatore', Chunegundis, Pantaleon, Affra, 'Translacio Sancti Ruperti', Gallus (27 June, 4, 13, 13 (?), 27 July, 5 Aug., 24 Sept., 16 Oct.). Probably fourteen leaves are missing between f. 1 and f. 2, which begins in the office of the Conception of B.V.M. (8 Dec.). One leaf missing before f. 195.

2. ff. 314–317^{v} In dedicatione ecclesie.

3. ff. 317^{v}–343 Incipit Commune.

4. ff. 343–357^{v} Sequitur historia de Corpore Cristi.

Corpus Christi and within the octave.

5. ff. 357^{v}–405^{v} Sequitur dominica prima post octauas penthecostes.

Temporal, first to twenty-fourth Sundays after the octave of Pentecost.

ff. i + 405 + i. A foliation in pencil 1–401 (s. xix (?), before rebinding) is incorrect after f. 152. Paper. 273 × 210 mm. Written space 210 × 140 mm. 2 cols. 25 lines. Collation: 1 two (ff. 1, 2, outermost bifolium) $2\text{–}13^{16}$ 14^{16} wants 1 before f. 195 $15\text{–}18^{16}$ 19^{16} + 1 leaf after 16 (f. 291) $20\text{–}26^{16}$ 27 three. Written by one hand in expert hybrida. Initials: (i) blue or red patterned in white; (ii, iii) 2-line and 1-line, red. Binding of s. xix. Secundo folio *namque*.

Written by a named scribe to the order of Margaret Stainnacherin, cellaress (and later, 1522–34, abbess) of the nunnery of Traunkirchen, O.S.B., diocese of Passau: the colophon is on f. 405^{v} in two paragraphs, the Latin in red ink and the German in blue ink, 'finis huius codicis Anno et cetera xv^{co} Et Anno Tertio. Iohannes Richthofen. Das puech hatt schreiben lassen dy Erwurdig vnd Geistlich Klosterfraw Margareta Stainnacherin dye zeit kelnerin des wurdigen Gotzhawss Trawnkirchen vnd welche fraw das nach Irem abgang Brauchen oder Nutzen ist dy soll Ir durch Gotswillen gedencken mit ainen Pater noster vnd Aue maria. Vnd dem Schreiber. ain Aue Maria'.

19. *Antiphonale* s. xvi in.

1. ff. 1–93^{v} Temporal beginning imperfectly at Easter and ending at the twenty-fifth Sunday after Pentecost.

2. ff. 93^{v}–101 In dedicacione ecclesie. f. 101^{v} blank.

3. ff. 102–5 Venite exultemus domino . . .

Laid out for four settings, but the music has not been filled in. ff. 105v–106v left blank: additions on 106 are of s. xvii (?).

4. ff. 107–262 Sanctoral, beginning with Compassion of B.V.M., Philip and James (1 May) and Invention of Cross (3 May).

Feasts include Monica, Visitation of B.V.M., Divisio apostolorum, Anne, Transfiguration, Helen, Augustine, translation of Augustine (ff. 123v, 152, 157v, 166, 173v, 193, 199v, 226v). ff. 262v–263v blank.

5. ff. 264–300 Common of saints.

6. ff. 300–7 Office of B.V.M. ff. 307v–310v blank.

7. ff. 311–330v Hymns, beginning with the first Sunday after Easter: the first verse of each hymn is noted.

Proper of time, common of time (f. 315), dedication of church (f. 316v), B.V.M. (f. 317), Holy Cross (f. 318), sanctoral (f. 318v), common of saints (f. 325v) and settings of Iam lucis orto and other hymns (f. 328v). Proper hymns of the sanctoral include: Imperatrix clemencie (*RH*, no. 8483) for Compassion of B.V.M.; Eterne regi glorie and Lauda fidelis concio (*RH*, nos. 629, 10204) for Crown of Thorns; Alma mater augustini and Celi ciues applaudite . . . matris nostre . . . (*RH*, nos. 848, 3470) for Monica; Lauda mater ecclesia and Eterni patris unice for Mary Magdalene; Factor orbis et omnium and its division Hec circa ministerium (*RH*, no. 5943) for Helen; Magne pater augustine and Celi ciues applaudite . . . patris nostri . . . for Augustine; Iste confessor domini sacratus (*RH*, no. 9140) for Remigius; Gaude sancta colonia and Nocte surgentes virginum laudes (*RH*, nos. 6934, 12037) for Eleven thousand virgins; Katherine collaudamus, Pange lingua gloriose virginis martirium and Presens dies expendatur (*AH* lii. 220–4) for Katherine. ff. 331–332v left blank: 332v is pasted down.

8 (added, s. xvi). f. 331 Office of Augustine, with hymn Alma parente genitus, *RH*, no. 855.

ff. 332. Paper: many leaves damaged and repaired in s. xvii (?). 363 × 250 mm. Written space 265 × 170 mm. 9 long lines and music and (art. 6) 27 long lines. Horizontal ruling with hard point—the writing in arts. 1–6 between a pair of ruled lines—and vertical ruling in ink. Collation: 1 three 2–9^{8} 10^{8} 8 cancelled after f. 74 11–33^{8} 34^{8} wants 6–8, blank, after f. 263 35–39^{8} 40^{8} wants 6, blank, after f. 308 41–42^{8} 43^{8} wants 7, 8, blank: 6, f. 332, is pasted down. Red initials in three sizes, 6-line, 3-line, and 1-line. Cadels lined with red. Binding of wooden boards covered with brown leather: the front board and the leather over it, bearing a pattern of pineapple stamps in lozenges, framed by a border of stamps, may be original: the back board is bevelled and has a cover with a centre-piece of *c.*1600: four bosses on the front cover.

Written in Germany, probably for Augustinian canons with a special devotion to St Helen in the region of Cologne. A letter to Sir Frederick Radcliffe from W. H. Randoll Blacking, F.R.I.B.A., 21 The Close, Salisbury, 9 December 1946, is inside the cover: apparently Blacking owned this and another music book in the Radcliffe collection.

20. *Manuale, cum notis* s. xiv ex.

1. ff. 1–5 Omnibus dominicis per annum . . .

Manuale Sarum, pp. 1–4.

2. ff. 5v–10 Ordo ad cathecuminum faciendum. In primis inquirat . . .

Ibid., pp. 25–31.

3. ff. 10–20v Quando fons fuerit mundandus . . .

Blessing of font and order of baptism. Ibid. pp. 31–8/1, 40/1–7, 38/6–8. On f. 18v 'Si dubitet sacerdos . . . ut supradictum est', nine lines on whether the child has been baptized already, follows edn., p. 36/29.

4. ff. 20v–31 Ordo ad facienda sponsalia.

Ibid. pp. 44–59. English on f. 22v: in both forms the nine words 'to haue . . . forwarde' (edn., pp. 47, 48) are omitted. Second marriages on ff. 28–29v: the 79-line rubric differs from edn., referring to Hostiensis and 'quedam constitucio que creditur fuisse Ioh. xxii sic incipiens Concertationi antique vbi dicitur . . .'.

5. ff. 31–50v Ordo ad uisitandum infirmum. Ends imperfectly 'penarum. et de'.

Ibid. pp. 97–100/19, 106/29–118/5 (omitting 112/16–27 on f. 46v). The rubric on f. 37v agrees with H. Extreme unction begins on f. 38v.

6. ff. 51–84v Commendation of souls, beginning imperfectly, and (f. 56) office of the dead, ending imperfectly in Ps. 141.

Ibid. pp. 124/26–142. The office of the dead is preceded by 215 lines of rubric on ff. 51–55v: Incipiantur solemniter uigilie mortuorum . . . sedere licet.

7. ff. 85–8 Commendation of souls, beginning imperfectly.

Ibid. pp. 142–4.

8. ff. 88v–101v Post missam accedat . . .

Office of burial. Ibid. pp. 152–62. A leaf missing after f. 95.

9. ff. 101v–109 Ad missam pro defunctis.

Ibid. pp. 144–52, but secrets and postcommunions are arranged differently.

10 (added). (*a*) f. 109 In anniuersariis et trigentalibus. (*b*) ff. 109v–113v Masses of Holy Trinity, Holy Cross, Holy Spirit, and B.V.M., ending imperfectly. (*c*) f. 114 A form of absolution 'virtute huius bulle et papalis indulgencie'.

(*a, b*). s. xv in. (*a*) supplements art. 10 with lessons from Maccabees and tract, De profundis. ff. 114–115^{v} were left blank: (*c*) was added on the first page in a current hand, s. xv.

11. f. i, a now raised pastedown, is the lower half of a leaf of a fourteenth-century missal: cf. *Sarum Missal*, p. 159.

ff. i + 115 + ii. 212 × 143 mm. Written space 135 × 90 mm. 24 long lines. Collation: 1–6^{8} 7 four (ff. 49–52: the two outer bifolia) 8–11^{8} 12^{8} wants 1–5 before f. 85 13^{8} 14^{8} wants 1 before f. 96 15^{8} 16^{8} wants 4 after f. 113 and 7, 8 blank. Quires signed in the usual late medieval way. Initials: (i) gold on grounds of pink and blue patterned in white and decorated with gold: nearly continuous borders; (ii) 2-line, blue with red ornament; (iii) 1-line, blue or red. Cadels lined with pale green. Medieval binding of white skin over wooden boards: two strap-and-pin fastenings missing. Secundo folio *cristum*.

Written in England. 'Richard Savage March the 25 Anno domini [. . .]' f. 115^{v}, s. xvi/xvii. Label of 'N. C. S. Poyntz (*1846–1920*) Dorchester Vicarage Wallingford' inside the cover: his (?) printed label on the spine, '[1]872 / Catalogued / B', above an older printed label, 'M/252': his sale at Sotheby's, 28 June 1921, lot 602. J. M. Falkner sale at Sotheby's, 12 December 1932, lot 264.

21. *Ambrosius, In Ps. 118* s. xv med.

Licet mistice quoque veluti tube . . . postquam in ortis passus est cristus.

PL xiv. 1197–1526. A tab or button shows the beginning of each of the twenty-two chapters. The scribe left spaces for the Greek. Some spaces were filled later, for example on f. 110, but most of them remain blank. ff. 151–153^{v} blank.

ff. 153. Paper. 283 × 215 mm. Written space 195 × 135 mm. 2 cols. 40 lines. Frame ruling. Collation: 1–12^{12} 13^{10} wants 10, blank. A strip of parchment down the centre of each quire as strengthening. Quires signed in the usual late medieval way; also by numbers at the head of each first recto on the right. Written in good current hybrida: punctuation within the sentence by flex and colon. Initials: (i) f. 1, 10-line, blue and red with red, violet, and green ornament prolonged into the margins: blue and red roundels in the outer margin in three groups of three; (ii) 4-line, blue with red ornament or red with violet ornament. Contemporary binding of wooden boards covered with stamped calf: on each cover double fillets form a broad rectangular frame in which are sixteen stamps of nine patterns, (1–4) roundels, one at each corner, each containing an evangelist's symbol, (5, 6) in the middle of each long side a 'ihesus' and in the middle of each short side a 'maria' rectangular stamp, (7–9) square stamps set lozenge-wise above and below (5) and flanking (6), one of them a displayed eagle: the panel within the frame is divided by diagonal double fillets into twenty-four lozenges and sixteen triangles, each containing a stamp: outside the frame a pair of double fillets runs from each band to a point at which there is a small fleur-de-lis stamp: five bands: two clasps: curving metal pieces at the outer corners: five bosses missing from each cover and a title label from the front cover. Secundo folio *quo moralem*.

Written in north-western Germany or the Low Countries. An erasure at the head of f. 1, another at the foot and a third on the pastedown at the end. Above this last is 'registratum (?) non indiget'.

22. *Psalterium, etc.* s. xiv med.

1. ff. 1–6v Graded calendar in blue, red, and black.

Calendar as in *Sarum Missal*, pp. xxi–xxxii, together with the ten English saints commonly found in later Sarum books, Oswald, Richard, Wulfstan, Edmund, Richard, Botulph, Cuthburga, Hugh, Frideswide, Hugh (28 Feb., 3 Apr., 7, 9, 16, 17 June, 31 Aug., 6, 19 Oct., 17 Nov., the first five, eighth and tenth in red); also Anthony of Padua, 13 June, and feast of relics, 15 September. Emerentiana and Milburga added, 23 Jan., 23 Feb. Feasts of St Thomas and the word 'papa' not cancelled. Three added obits: 'Obitus Iohanne hunte', 18 Feb.; 'Obiit Rex Edwardus Tercius', 21 June (1377); 'Obiit philippa Regina', 15 Aug. (Philippa of Hainault, †15 August 1369).

2. ff. 7–128 Psalter, beginning imperfectly at 12: 6, 'domino qui bona': the first quire is missing and the leaf on which Ps. 68 began.

3. ff. 128v–141v Six ferial canticles, followed by Te deum, Benedicite, Benedictus, Magnificat, Nunc dimittis, Quicumque vult. The couplet 'Ter quinquagenos . . .' (Walther, *Sprichwörter*, no. 19209) at the foot of f. 141v.

4. ff. 142–147v Litany.

Thirty martyrs: . . . (23–30) albane eadmunde oswalde edwarde iuste thoma elphege kenelme. Seven prayers as in *Brev. ad usum Sarum*, ii. 254–5.

5. ff. 148–59 Placebo domine . . .

Office of the dead, noted. f. 159v left blank.

ff. i + 159 + ii. 163 × 115 mm. Written space 118 × 72 mm. 20 long lines. Collation: 1^6 $2\text{–}7^8$ 8^8 wants 1 before f. 55 $9\text{–}19^8$ 20^{10}. Initials: (i) of principal psalms, including 51 and 101 on a smaller scale, 6-line and 4-line, blue or pink patterned in white on grounds of the other colour and gold, historiated: the grounds are sometimes in squares or diamonds of colour and gold; (ii) 2-line, gold on red and blue grounds patterned in white, with decoration extending into the margin; (iii) 1-line, blue or red. Cadels in art. 5. Contemporary binding of white skin over wooden boards: four bands: central strap and pin.

Written in England. 'Iste liber constat Iohanni Maylarde', f. 159v, s. xv/xvi. 'Hawtrey', f. 160, s. xvi in.

23. *Horae, etc.* s. xv^2

Arts. 2–5, 11, 12 and parts of arts. 8, 10 are in editions of *Hortulus Animae*, usually in the same order as here and with the same headings.

1. ff. 1–24v Incipiunt hore de domina nostra secundum ordinarium maioris ecclesie Colon'.

2. ff. 24v–41v Prayers and graces, beginning with a form of confession on going to bed and ending with a prayer of the Eternal Wisdom.

All occur in the same order and with the same headings in *Hortulus Animae* (edn. Basel 1522, ff. 61–7), except 'Sumendo aquam benedictam. Presta michi domine deus per hanc creaturam aque . . .' and 'Adhuc alia pulcherima oracio ad sanctissimam Trinitatem. O summa vera et sempiterna trinitas atque unitas . . .' (ff. 37rv, 39–41v). Everything in this section of *HA* is here, except the three verities of Gerson on f. 62. The last prayer (*HA* f. 67v) ended imperfectly 'arden', since a leaf or more is missing after f. 41: a later hand completed it 'ti desiderio adherere Per dominum'.

3. ff. 42–56v Incipit cursus Sancti Bonauenture de passione ihesu cristi. *HA*: edn. 1522, f. 21v.

4. ff. 56v–58v Sequitur officium passionis cristi compositum per dominum Iohannem papam xxii qui singula horas deuote dicentibus dedit unum (annum) Indulgenciarum. Ibid. f. 18, but without the heading.

5. ff. 58v–77 Nine pieces which occur in the same order in *HA* (edn. 1522, ff. 27v–35) and with the same headings. (*a, c*) are ascribed to Ambrose and Bede respectively and (*d, e*) to Gregory. (*a, c, i*) are indulgenced.

The incipits are: (*a*) f. 58v Domine ihesu criste fili dei viui creator et resuscitator; (*b*) f. 62 Aue ihesu splendor; (*c*) f. 64 Domine ihesu criste qui septem verba; (*d*) f. 65v Aue manus dextera; (*e*) f. 66v O domine ihesu criste adoro te in cruce pendentem; (*f*) f. 68 In mei sint memoria (*RH*, no. 8682); (*g*) f. 71 Culter qui circumscidisti (*RH*, no. 4052); (*h*) f. 74v Precor te amantissime; (*i*) f. 76 Salue tremendum cunctis potestatibus. The heading of (*a*) begins 'Sequitur nunc oracio . . .': *HA* omits *nunc*. f. 77v blank.

6. ff. 78–89v Penitential psalms and litany.

Cologne litany.

7. ff. 90–100v Preparamentum sacerdotis celebrantis. Adiutorium nostrum in nomine domini. Qui fecit celum . . . Veni creator spiritus . . . Veni sancte spiritus reple tuorum . . . (f. 96v) Ego dixi domine miserere mei . . . Oremus. Aures tue pietatis . . . Assit nobis quesumus domine virtus spiritus sancti . . . Ure igne sancti spiritus . . . Deus qui corda fidelium . . . Conscientias nostras . . . Omnipotens et misericors deus Ecce accedo . . . ad mensam tui dulcissimi conuiuii . . .

The psalms after Veni creator spiritus are 83–5, 115–16, 118 Tau, 129, 25, 42.

8. Prayers before mass: (*a*) ff. 100–1 Oracio beati Augustini. Accende illumina et sanctifica me vas tuum . . . ; (*b*) f. 101rv Ante Communionem. Domine ihesu criste pater misericordissime. rogo corde toto . . . ; (*c*) ff. 101v–102 Cum immediate vis accedere. Domine non sum dignus . . . ; (*d*) ff. 102–3 Ante Communionem. O dulcissime atque amantissime domine . . . quem nunc deuote desidero . . . ; (*e*) ff. 103–4 Ante Communionem. O fons totius misericordie . . . ; (*f*) f. 104rv Alia oracio ante communionem. Aue sanctissima caro cristi et sanguis . . .

(*c, d*). *Hortulus Animae*, edn. 1522, ff. 123, 121v.

9. ff. 104^{v}–106 Ad exuendum Capam vel Superpel. Exue me domine veterem . . . Ad Albam . . . Ad Cingulum . . . Ad Stolam . . . Ad Casulam . . . Alia. Fac me queso omnipotens deus ita iusticia indui . . .

10. Prayers after mass: (*a*) f. 106^{v} Post communionem. O benignissime domine . . . inspice super me indignum . . . ; (*b*) ff. 106^{v}–107 Sit michi dulcissime ihesu criste hoc sacrosanctum misterium . . . ; (*c*) f. 107^{rv} Ineffabilem misericordiam tuam . . . ; (*d*) ff. 107^{v}–109 Post Missam. Benedicite omnia opera . . . Laudate dominum in sanctis . . . Nunc dimittis . . . Trium puerorum cantemus . . . Protector in te sperancium deus sine quo . . . ; (*e*) f. 109^{rv} Post Communionem. Vera perceptio corporis . . . ; (*f*) f. 109^{rv} Gracias tibi ago domine sancte pater omnipotens eterne deus qui me indignum peccatorem . . . ; (*g*) f. 110 O serenissima et inclita virgo maria mater . . .

(*c, e, f, g, a*) are in *Hortulus Animae*, edn. 1522, ff. 123^{v}–124, in that order.

11. ff. 110^{v}–112^{v} Sequuntur oraciones ante et post eleuacionem dicende.

Five prayers Aue uerum corpus natum . . . , Aue caro cristi cara . . . , Salue lux mundi . . . , Sanguis tuus domine iesu criste . . . and (attributed to Aquinas) Adoro te deuote latens deitas . . . (*RH*, no. 519), as in *Hortulus Animae*, edn. 1522, ff. 124^{v}–125.

12. ff. 112^{v}–113^{v} Three prayers, (*a*) Miserere mi domine animabus . . . , (*b*) Saluete uos omnes fideles anime . . . and (*c*) Respice quesumus omnipotens deus super animas . . .

As in *Hortulus Animae*, edn. 1522, ff. 157–8. There as here (*a*) is indulgenced by Pope Pius II (1464–71) and Pope John IV (*sic*). After (*c*) are the first four words of another prayer 'Hanc oracionem compilauit papa'.

13 (added, s. xvii ?). ff. 114–17 Oratio Manasses regis Iude cum captus teneretur in Babilone. Domine omnipotens deus patrum . . . Amen. Secundo Paralipo. ultimo cap.

Stegmüller, no. 93, 2. f. 117^{v} blank.

ff. 117 + i. 128 × 90 mm. Written space 90 × 52 mm. 20 long lines. Collation: $1\text{–}5^{8}$ 6 one (f. 41) 7^{6} (ff. 42–7) $8\text{–}9^{8}$ 10^{6} (ff. 64–9) 11^{8} wants 2 after f. 70 + 1 leaf after 8 (f. 77) 12^{4} + 2 leaves after 4 (ff. 82–3) 13^{6} (ff. 84–9) $14\text{–}15^{8}$ 16^{6} + 2 leaves after 6 (ff. 112–13) 17^{4}. Well written in a small hybrida. A small good picture of Christ on the Cross, alone and with a background of hills, 50 × 35 mm, f. 67. Initials: (i) f. 1, blue with red and green ornament; (ii, iii) 2-line and 1-line, blue or red. German binding, s. xvi. Secundo folio *meam*.

Written for the use of a priest in the diocese of Cologne. Quaritch, *Catalogue of Illuminated Manuscripts*, 1931, item 34 (£20), with facsimile of f. 42.

27. *Psalterium, etc.* s. xiii/xiv

1. ff. 3–132^{v} Liturgical psalter.

2. ff. 132^{v}–136^{v} Te deum, Benedicite, Benedictus, Magnificat, Nunc dimittis and Quicumque vult.

3. ff. 136^{v}–141 Litany.

Angels: michael gabriel michael. Monks and hermits: francisce (*erased*) benedicte antoni dominice (*erased*).

4. ff. 141–159^{v} Hymns: (*a*) temporal, Advent–Pentecost; (*b*) sanctoral, Conversion of Paul–All Saints; (*c*) common of saints; (*d*) dedication of church.

As set out in Haimo's breviary, *Haymo*, pp. 21–159 and *SMRL* ii. 17–185, together with the three hymns for Anthony of Padua, *AH* iv. 90–1.

5. ff. 159^{v}–164^{v} Mass of B.V.M. at the Annunciation and at six seasons, the five set out in *Haymo*, pp. 271–2 and *SMRL* ii. 319–20 and in fourth place 'A septuagesima ad feriam quartam maioris ebdomade'.

6. ff. 164^{v}–170^{v} Masses of Holy Spirit, Holy Trinity, 'In dedicatione sancti michaelis' and 'Pro defunctis'.

Haymo, pp. 270, 270, 254, 281 (o) and *SMRL* ii. 319, 318, 300, 330.

Arts. 7–10 are in another hand.

7. ff. 171–7 Prefaces (not noted) and canon of mass.

A leaf missing after f. 176.

8. ff. 177–182^{v} Collect, secret and postcommunion of fifteen votive masses: (*a*) of All Saints; (*b*) Pro prelatis; (*c*) Pro rege et regina; (*d*) Pro pace; (*e*) Pro amicis; (*f*) Pro familiaribus; (*g*) Pro penitentibus; (*h*) Pro peccatis; (*i*) Pro itinerantibus; (*j*) Pro tribulacione amici; (*k*) Pro quacumque tribulacione; (*l*) Ad pluuiam postulandam; (*m*) Pro [serenitate aeris]; (*n*) (*Pro mortalitate hominum*); (*o*) Pro infirmis.

Except (*n*), as *Sarum Missal*, pp. 394, 396, 398, 395, 399, 392, 400, 402, 405 (but the postcommunion is Deus infinite misericordie), 408, 403, 403, 404, 409. The forms in (*n*) are Deus qui non uis mortem, Protegat nos, Sumptis domine salutis.

9. ff. 182^{v}–186^{v} Masses for the dead.

Twelve forms, collect, secret, and postcommunion only: (*a*) Pro episcopo; (*b*) Pro sacerdote; (*c*) Pro defuncto; (*d*) (*Pro familiaribus viris*); (*e*) Pro defuncta; (*f*) In anniuersario; (*g*) Pro requiescentibus; (*h*) [Pro patre et matre]; (*i*) Pro benefactoribus; (*j*) Pro defunctis; (*k*) Pro congregatione; (*l*) Pro fidelibus. (*e–h, j–l*) agree with *Sarum Missal*, pp. 441, 437, 441, 436, 439, 438, 442. (*a–d, i*) differ in one or two of the three pieces from *Sarum Missal*, pp. 434, 435, 442 note 5, 440, 437. f. 185 is damaged.

10. ff. 186v–187v Pro uiuis et defunctis.

The first set and the collect and secret of the fourth set in *SM*, pp. 442–3, 445.

11. ff. 188–193v Calendar in red and black, rather empty and originally without gradings.

A papal calendar. Entries of Peter, O.P., Dominic, Francis (in red), erased (29 Apr., 5 Aug., 4 Oct.). Feasts were added at 4, 7, 11, 15, 17, 20 July, three with gradings, s. xiv: translation and ordination of Martin, Thomas martyr (ix lc), Benedict, Swithun, Kenelm (ix lc), Margaret (ix lc); also by the same hand obits at 6, 27 Apr., 11 Aug., 21 Nov., 3 Dec.: O' Isabell' de lastone quondam vxoris gregorii de lastone; Obitus Alicie fuit (?) vxor Iohannis de spina anno domini mccc; Obitus Magistri Ricardi de spina persona Ecclesie de seuenhamton anno domini m° ccc xi (*he was instituted at Seavington St Michael, Somerset, in 1297*); Obitus Iohannis atte stone anno domini m° ccc xix; Obiit petronilla atte Stone et Elizabet fil' eius anno M (ccc) xlviii.

12. Flyleaf additions in English hands: (*a–c*) f. 2rv Devotions to Holy Cross, Holy Trinity, and B.V.M., including 'Hodierna festiuitas matris ihesu cristi . . .', eight (?) couplets for the Assumption of B.V.M.; (*d*) f. 2v Per sancte (*sic*) luce dicta nos iuuet crux benedicta; (*e*) f. 194 [. . .] pronum fac nobis criste patronum . . . ; (*f*) f. 194 Mundet nostrorum: mentes Petrus miserorum . . . ; (*g*) f. 194 Qui natus est de virgine. sit nobis clemens hodie Puer qui (*ends abruptly*); (*h–l*) ff. 194v–195v Rhyming couplets 'De natiuitate', 'De cruce', 'De apostolis', 'De sancta agatha', 'De ascensione'.

(*a–d*) in current anglicana, s. xv. (*e–g*) in fere-textura, s. xiv/xv. (*h–l*) in a mainly secretary hand, s. xv.

(*e*), 16 lines (4 + 4 + 8) and (*f*), 8 lines (4 + 4) ask for the intercession of John Baptist and Peter respectively. The rhyming couplets are: (*h*) Puer qui nobis est natus . . . (30 couplets); (*i*) [N]os cruce signatos. faciat crux uere beatos . . . (24); (*j*) Cetus apostolorum. aperi nobis ianua celorum . . . (8); (*k*) Interuentrix assidua. sit pro nobis uirgo cristi agatha . . . (10); (*l*) Qui sedes super astra benedicas agmina nostra . . . (10).

13. f. 1, a binding leaf from a service book, s. xiv, contains parts of the blessing of ashes on Ash Wednesday.

28 long lines. Large hand. Initials not filled in. As *Manuale Sarum*, pp. 11/24–12/18. f. 1r, really the verso, was pasted down.

ff. iv + 191 + iv, foliated (i, ii), 1–195, (196–7). For ff. 1, 2, 194–5 see above arts. 12, 13. 245 × 165 mm. Written space 150 × 100 mm. 21 long lines. Collation of ff. 3–193: 1–14¹² 15¹² wants 7 after f. 176 16 six (ff. 182–7) 17⁶. A Crucifixion picture at f. 174v, 78 × 62 mm on a ground of patterned gold. Initials: (i) blue on pink and gold grounds, decorated or

(f. 4) historiated (*B* of *Beatus*), and with prolongations: on f. 4 one prolongation turns into the lower margin where David and Goliath fight on a sloping bar; (ii) ff. 173^v, 174^v, gold *P* of *Per, U* of *Uere*, and *T* of *Te igitur*, on red and blue grounds patterned in white; (iii) 2-line, gold with blue ornament or blue with red ornament or (f. 7^v) red with blue ornament: the ornament is prolonged into saw-pattern and tendril runners the height of the written space; (iv) 1-line, red or blue with ornament of the other colour. Capital letters in the ink of the text lined with red. Binding of marbled pasteboards, s. xviii. Secundo folio (f. 4) *Beatus*; (f. 5) *tribulant*.

Written probably in England and perhaps for use at Seavington St Michael: cf. arts. 3, 6. In or near Seavington in s. xiv: cf. art. 11, where the obits suggest ownership by a family named Stone. '5' on the spine and 'N° 5 Bruce 1728' on f. 1: 'Bruce' here and in MS. 29 (q.v.) is probably Charles Bruce, 1682–1747, who succeeded his father as 3rd Earl of Ailesbury in 1741. Armorial book-plate of R. S. Sievier (1860–1939) who married the granddaughter of the 3rd Marquis of Ailesbury in 1892. Quaritch, *Catalogue of Illuminated Manuscripts*, 1931, item 85 (£42). *MERT*, no. 18.

28. *Bernardus, Sermones; etc.* s. xv in.

1. pp. 1–38 Domus hec in qua habitamus: ex omni parte . . . quam terrestrium occupatione. Deo gratias amen.

PL clxxxiv. 507–52. p. 38* blank.

2. pp. 39–72 Scribere me aliquid et deuotio iubet . . . deuotissime destinaui. Laus tibi sit pia genitrix dei uirgo Maria.

Four sermons: *SBO* iv. 13–58. The scribe wrote 'Adsis uirgo tuis scribendis rogito sacris' at the head of p. 39. p. 73 blank.

3. The pastedown at the front is part of a leaf of the commentary of Aquinas on the De causis: ed. Saffrey, 1954, pp. 51/22–56/25 on the exposed side.[1] s. xiii ex. 2 cols. 60 out of probably 62 lines.

ff. 37, paginated 1–38, 38*, 39–73. 255 × 185 mm. Written space 165 × 105 mm. 34 long lines. Collation: $1\text{–}4^8$ 5^6 wants 6, probably blank. Handsomely written and decorated. Initials: (i) pp. 1, 39, 6-line *D* and 7-line *S*, pink patterned in white on gold and blue grounds, decorated: a border at head and foot of p. 1; (ii, iii) 4-line and 3-line, red or blue. Contemporary binding of wooden boards covered with brown leather bearing a pattern of triple fillets: nine small bosses once on each cover in three rows of three: three bands: two clasps missing. Secundo folio *Munda igitur*.

Written in Italy. A shield flanked by *N* and *O* at the foot of p. 1: barry of six gules and argent. Erased inscriptions at the foot, pp. 1, 72. '36 feuillets', p. 1, top right, s. xix. Phillipps MS. 4773, so from James Taylor. Phillipps sales at Sotheby's, 5 June 1899, lot 185 to Ware (£2, presumably bought in) and 27 Apr. 1903, lot 138. 'δηλ G.D. Ap. 1903' on the pastedown. George Dunn sale at Sotheby's, 11 Feb. 1913, lot 405. Forshaw sale at Sotheby's, 13 December 1920, lot 376.

[1] I owe the identification to Professor Charles Lohr.

29. *Missale, cum notis* s. xiv med.–xiv/xv

A Sarum missal described briefly by J. A. Robinson, *Muchelney Memoranda*, Somerset Record Society, xlii (1929), pp. 179–81. A later hand altered arts. 3, 4 and wrote art. 14*a–d* and another hand of about the same date added art. 15. Projecting pieces of parchment slotted through slits show the main divisions.

1. ff. 1–3ᵛ Graded calendar in red and black, lacking Mar.–June and Nov., Dec.

As *Sarum Missal*, pp. xxi–xxxii, except for: the absence of Lucian, feast of relics and Francis (8 Jan., 15 Sept., 4 Oct.); the presence of one feast in red, 'Translacio s' Hugonis episcopi iii lc'' (6 Oct.) and of four feasts in black, Anne, Cuthburga, translation of King Edward confessor, Frideswide (26 July, 31 Aug., 13, 19 Oct.): these four were marked 'non Sarum', but the 'non' has been erased, except at 19 Oct. 'In dedicacione ecclesie de schepton: beuchamp duplex [. . . .]' was added early in red, 7 Feb. The word 'pape' and feasts of St Thomas of Canterbury have not been cancelled.

2. ff. 4–109 Temporal, Advent–Easter.

The secret for the 2nd Sunday after the octave of Epiphany is Ut tibi grata.

3. (*a*) f. 109 Hanc oracionem dicat sacerdos ante altare recumbatus priusquam missam incipiat. Deus qui de indignis dignos facis . . . (*b*) ff. 109–10 Ordinary of mass. (*c*) ff. 110–111ᵛ Prefaces of mass, ending imperfectly 'Habemus ad dominum. Gra' (*Sarum Missal*, p. 219/29). (*d*) ff. 112ᵛ–114ʳᵇ/7 Canon of mass. (*e*) f. 114ʳᵇ/10–114ᵛᵇ Pro pace psalmus cum oracione Deus uenerunt gentes . . . (*f*) f. 114ᵛᵇ [G]racias tibi ago . . . Placeat tibi . . .

(*a*). *Missale Sarum*, Burntisland edn., col. 573. (*b*) differs much from *Sarum Missal* and all but one of the prayers Ad manus (etc.), edn. p. 216 footnote, are different. (*c*). A small corner remains of the leaf cut out after f. 111: a little border decoration can be seen on its verso. (*d*). All in the later hand on supply leaves (ff. 112–13) and over erasure (f. 114). The erased text was the canon, as appears from 114ʳᵇ/8, 9, which alone can be read, 'miserante propiciabile Qui uiuis et regnas per omnia secula' (*SM*, p. 229/2, 3). The rewritten text ends in line 7 'faciat esse consortes amen' (*SM*, p. 228, n. 2): the scribe then left art. 3*e* undisturbed and finished the canon (art. 3*f*) in the space remaining blank on f. 114ᵛ. On f. 112ᵛ prayers were entered *c.*1500 'pro bono statu magistri Henrici Wogan' and for the soul of Amete Wogan 'deffuncta' and for their six children, living and dead. f. 112ʳ is blank. (*e*). Prayers in prostration. After Deus qui admirabili (*Sarum Missal*, p. 210), the later hand added two more prayers, Rege quesumus domine and Da quesumus omnipotens deus (Burntisland edn., col. 634). (*f*). See above, (*d*). The first seven lines are over erasure.

4. ff. 115–162ᵛ Temporal from Easter to Sabbato quatuor temporum mensis septembris.

On ff. 115–25 much of the text, but not the music, has been written over in blacker ink by the hand of art. 3*d*. Trinity Sunday, f. 137ᵛ. Corpus Christi absent: see art. 13.

5. ff. 162ᵛ–164 In dedicatione ecclesie.

6. ff. 164–201v Sanctoral, Andrew–Saturninus.

'In festo reliquiarum saluberiensis ecclesie' is a July feast, f. 193. Anne not in her place, but added by the main hand after Saturninus: the office here differs from that in art. 14*b* and has secret Deus qui beate anne and postcommunion Deus bonorum creator.

7. ff. 201v–221 Common of saints.

8. ff. 221–223v Masses of Holy Trinity, Holy Spirit, Holy Cross, B.V.M., and angels.

Sarum Missal, pp. 384–91 (nos. 1–6) and p. 459.

9. ff. 223v–227 Twenty-eight votive masses, (*x*) a full office, the rest collect, secret, and postcommunion only.

(*a*) In memoria saluatoris (Burntisland edn., col. 825*). (*b*) De reliquiis (p. 401, footnote).[1] (*c*) De omnibus sanctis (8). (*d*) Pro uniuersali ecclesia (10). (*e*) Pro pontifice (12). (*f*) Pro prelatis (13). (*g*) Pro rege (15). (*h*) Pro rege et regina (16). (*i*) Pro sacerdote (18). (*j*) Pro familiaribus (7). (*k*) Pro penitentibus (20). (*l*) Contra temptaciones (21). (*m*) Contra cogitaciones (22). (*n*) Pro peticione lacrimarum (24). (*o*) Pro peccatis (25). (*p*) Pro pace (11). (*q*) Contra aduersitates (Pretende quesumus omnipotens deus fidelibus . . . ; Placidus aspice domine . . . ; Protege quesumus domine famulos tuos . . .). (*r*) Pro peccatis (26, collect; secret, Purificet nos . . . ; postcommunion, Presta domine quesumus ut terrenis affectibus . . .). (*s*) Ad pluuiam postulandam (27: postcommunion as MS. B). (*t*) Pro aeris serenitate (28: secret and postcommunion as MS. B). (*u*) Pro iter agentibus (30). (*v*) Contra aereas potestates (32). (*w*) Pro infirmo (39). (*x*) Pro sapientia postulanda in quadragesima (33). (*y*) In tempore belli (43: secret and postcommunion as MS. B, p. 393, footnote). (*z*) Pro peste mutorum animalium (42: secret Sacrificiis domine placatus . . .). (*aa*) Pro mortalitate hominum (Deus qui non mortem . . . ; Protege nos . . . ; Sumptis domine salutis . . .). (*ab*) Pro febricitantibus (p. 406, footnote 2). (*ac*) Pro infirmo qui uidetur appropinquare finem (p. 410, footnote). (*ad*) Pro amico (20). (*ae*) Pro amico (19).

10. ff. 227–30 Missa pro defunctis.

Fifteen of the nineteen sets of collects, secrets, and postcommunions in *Sarum Missal*, pp. 434–42. They are here in the same order as in *SM*, nos. 1, 2, 4–6, 8–14, 15 (the postcommunion left out), 18, 19.

11. ff. 230–1 Missa generalis.

Four sets, nos. 1, 2, 4 (postcommunion as in MSS. A, B) of the four in *Sarum Missal*, pp. 442–5, and in fourth place Accinctus . . . , Exaudi . . . , Munda . . .

12. f. 231 Collect, secret, and postcommunion 'De omnibus sanctis', Conscientias . . . , Munera . . . , Purificent . . .

[1] For the bracketed references by page or number, see below, Oxford, All Souls College 302, art. 9.

13. ff. 231–232^v Cibauit eos . . .

Mass of Corpus Christi: *Missale Sarum*, edn. Burntisland, col. 455.

14. Additions filling quire 21, (*a–d*) in the hand which rewrote art. 3*d*: (*a*) f. 233 Salus populi ego sum . . . ; (*b*) f. 233^{rv} Gaudeamus omnes in domino . . . ; (*c*) ff. 233^v–234 Deus qui es summa spes nostre redemptionis . . . ; (*d*) f. 234 Istud euangelium sequens compositum fuit per do*mp*nu*m* Iohannem xx (*sic*) apud auinionem iii die ante decessum suum . . . Passio domini nostri ihesu cristi secundum Iohannem. In illo tempore. Apprehendit . . . testimonium eius . . . Oremus. Deus qui manus tuas . . . ; (*e*) f. 234^v Gloria in excelsis . . .

(*a*). Missa Salus Populi, as *Missale Sarum*, Burntisland edn., col. 741*. (*b*). Office of St Anne, as ibid., col. 825: cf. art. 6. (*c*). Trental of St Gregory, followed by 'Ordo trigintalis quod quidam apostolicus . . .' (*Sarum Missal*, p. 460). (*d*). The catena from John and Matthew attributed to Pope John XXII in 1334: *Missale Sarum*, Burntisland edn., col. 890*; cf. *Lyell Cat.*, p. 65. As there it carries an indulgence of 300 days. (*e*). Added in current anglicana, s. xv/xvi.

15. ff. 235–251^v Sequences, not noted.

Temporal (including Corpus Christi), sanctoral (including Anne), common of saints, B.V.M., dedication, cross (Salue crux sancta . . .).

ff. ii + 251 + ii. 340 × 215 mm. Written space 245 × 145 mm. 2 cols. 39–42 lines. Collation: 1^{12} wants 2, 3, 6 (ff. 1–9) 2^{10} $3\text{–}9^{12}$ 10^{12} wants 9–11 after f. 111: ff. 112–13 are supply leaves in place of $10^{10,11}$ $11\text{–}13^{12}$ 14^{10} $15\text{–}17^{12}$ $18\text{–}19^{10}$ 20^{8} (ff. 217–24) 21^{10} (ff. 225–34) 22^{8} 23^{8} + 1 leaf after 8. Initials: (i) ff. 111, 112^v *P* of *Per omnia* and *T* of *Te igitur*, gold and blue, with red and blue ornament; (ii) red and blue with ornament of both colours; (iii) 2-line, blue or red with ornament of the other colour; (iv) in art. 15, 1-line, blue or red. Binding as on MS. 27. Secundo folio (f. 5) *Excita.*

Written in England. The dedication of the church of Shepton Beauchamp, Somerset, was added early to art. 1. The missal may have continued in use there until *c.*1500, or later: as Robinson noted, a John Wogan with Shepton Beauchamp connections in s. xvi may be the John listed fifth among the Wogan children in art. 3*d*. '9' on the spine and 'N° 9 Bruce 1728' on f. 1: cf. MS. 27. Book-plate of Robert Standish Sievier, as in MS. 27. J. M. Falkner sale, 12 December 1932, lot 294 (£110).

30. *W. de Pagula, Dextera pars oculi; Lyndwood; etc.*

s. xiv/xv–xv in.

1. (*a*) ff. 1–56^v Liber secundus videlicet dextera pars oculi sacerdotis. Multi sunt sacerdotes . . . separatim nominatur. (*b*) ff. 57–92 Incipit cilium 'oculi' sacerdotis . . . Omnis vtriusque sexus . . . cause humilium populi mei etc. Explicit cilium Sacerdotis.

(*a*). The second part of Oculus sacerdotis: see L. Boyle, 'The Oculus Sacerdotis and some other works of William of Pagula', *Trans. Royal Historical Soc.*, 5th series, v (1955), 84–110, where this manuscript is not listed. (*b*). Cf. Boyle, p. 84 ('added about 1330–40').

2. ff. 92v–97v (filling quire 12) Incipit quidam tractatus paruus abstractus a sanctis doctoribus et ab aliis viris sapientibus contra fetentem et fumigantem impudicam et excecatam letargicam et freneticam intollerabilem et luciferinam superbiam prelatorum et aliorum temporalium dominorum . . . regere et prodesse. Superbia istorum olim ascendebat . . . sine fine permansura. Item protestor . . . (*ends abruptly*).

Taken mainly from the Opus imperfectum on Matthew of Pseudo-Chrysostom: 'Os aureum' in the margins.

3. ff. 98–161v De summa Trinitate et fide Catholica. Peccham. Ignorancia sacerdotum et infra. Ne quis per ignoranciam . . . canonice compellandos.

No apparatus. C. R. Cheney lists fifty-seven copies of Lyndwood's Provinciale—not this one—in his *Medieval texts and studies*, 1973, pp. 182–4.

ff. viii + 161 + ii. 203 × 150 mm. Written space 150 × 100 mm. 41–4 long lines and (art. 3) 31 long lines. Frame ruling, arts. 1, 2, with the first line of writing above the frame line. Collation: $1–12^8$ 13^8 wants 2–8 after f. 97 (perhaps blank leaves intended for the continuation of art. 2) $14–21^8$. Quires 14–21 signed a–h in the usual late medieval way. Well written, arts. 1, 2 in a current mixture of anglicana and secretary and art. 3 in secretary. Initials: (i) 4-line (f. 98) or 3-line (ff. 1, 57), blue with red ornament; (ii) as (i), but 2-line; (iii) in art. 3, 1-line, blue or red. Binding of s. xviii (?): 'Binding repaired and new back by R. Audrey, Salisbury, 2 Mar. 1894' inside the cover in the hand of Rev. Christopher Wordsworth: label, 'Audrey Binder Salisbury' at the end. Secundo folio *corripiendi*.

Written in England. 'Heb Dhun heb dhim E.B.', f. 1, s. xvii. Belonged to Christopher Wordsworth, bishop of Lincoln, †1885, and to his son, Christopher Wordsworth, canon of Salisbury, †1938. The former placed his name stamp—motto 'Veritas'—at the foot of f. 1 and inside the back cover. The latter wrote his name on f. i and notes on ff. i–viii, 162v–163v and a note inside the back cover to the effect that other writing here, consisting of reproductions of letter-forms and expansions of abbreviations, 'is in the handwriting of Dr Chr. Wordsworth (the Bishop of Lincoln)'.

34. *Johannes Damascenus, De fide orthodoxa; etc.*

s. xiii^1 (arts. 4–6)–xiii^2

1. ff. 1–64v ˋIncipit Dam'ˊ. Deum nemo uidit unquam . . . (f. 63v) ab ipso est gaudium fructificantes. Explicit liber Iohannis presbiteri damasceni . . . (f. 64v). Explicit iste liber scriptor sit crimine liber.

The translation by Burgundio of Pisa in four books of 18, 34, 37, and 19 chapters, without numbers or titles: a table of them is on ff. 63v–64v.

2. ff. 65–142v ˋphilippus cancellarius super spalteriumˊ Domine dominus noster quam am. est nomen tuum in uni. terra. Nomen domini est emmanuel . . . eius. Secunda (*ends abruptly*).

Sermons numbered 1–85, the last, for Christmas, beginning 'Quasi diluculum . . . Hodierna die fratres karissimi filius dei de uirginali utero'. f. 142vb blank.

3. ff. 143–169^{v} Aleph. Quomodo sedet sola ciuitas p.p. Aleph: interpretatur doctrina quomodo sola et plena populo . . . sicut aqua ne crescas quia etc.

Sermons on Lamentations 1, 2, the same text as in Liverpool, Univ. Libr. F.4.7, art. 2 (q.v.), but divided rather differently: forty-one paragraphs. f. 170^{rv} blank.

4. ff. 171–175^{v} Hic notantur principia epistolarum et euangeliorum tocius anni. cum libris et capitulis in quibus continentur. In aduentu. Dominica prima. Epistola. Ro xiii f. Scientes . . .

Tables of lessons of the temporal, dedication of church, sanctoral (Stephen–Thomas apostle), common of saints, 'In commemoracione de sancta cruce', 'Pro familiaribus', 'Pro tribulacione ecclesie', 'Pro quacumque necessitate', 'Pro infirmo', and for the dead, followed on f. 175 by a list of sixty-one saints, with a red letter and a black letter against each name. The saints are in the order of the church year, Thomas the Martyr–Lucy, and include William (of Bourges), Robert abbot, Peter (of Tarentaise) and Malchi, but not Bernard. The red and black letters refer back to the table of the common of saints in which each of the twenty-two Epistle lessons is marked with a red letter and each of the twenty-two Gospel lessons with a black letter, a–y.

5. (*a*) ff. 175^{v}–177^{v} Incipiunt capitula seu distincciones sequentis operis. Titulus i^{us} habet iii partes. De uitando consortio colloquio et exemplo prauorum pars i^{a} . . . (*b*) ff. 177–262^{v} Ps. i. Beatus uir qui non abiit . . . Leui. xii. in m. Expletis diebus.

(*a*), the table for (*b*), lists nineteen tituli, each divided into parts, the last (19, pt. 9) 'Quod integra sit confessio. peccatique detestacio'. (*b*) is a subject index of biblical texts. The part of a chapter referred to is shown by 'in principio', 'ante medium', 'post medium', 'in fine', and the like.

6. ff. 263^{v}–269^{v} Breuis concordia euangeliorum. A generat. B magos vocat. egyptum petit. exit . . . Agnos committit in se librum ioha finit. explicit.

309 lines. Walther, no. 37. Each Gospel is taken chapter by chapter. ff. 263^{r}, 270^{v} left blank: on the latter a contemporary hand wrote a note 'De duobus serpentibus Corcodrillo et ydro' and a rather later hand wrote 'Bernardus. Ve tibi amator peccatorum meorum propter que filii dei traditio fuit necessaria'.

7 (on end flyleaf). f. 271^{v} Verses in a hand of s. xv ex.: O mors quam dura . . . (2 lines); O homo si scires quid esset (*sic*) . . . (2); Sunt tria que vere faciunt me sepe dolere . . .

Walther, *Sprichwörter*, nos. 19509, 19477, 30847.

8. f. ii, a binding leaf, is from a manuscript of sermons, s. xiii, with many exempla.

2 cols. 32 lines. A sermon (for the beginning of Lent ?) begins 'Ecce nunc tempus acceptabile . . . Wlgariter dicitur ki ne fait quant il puet il ne fait quant il wet. qui non facit quando . . .'. The leaf or the sermon is numbered xli.

ff. ii + 270 + i. 188 × 135 mm. Written space: (arts. 1, 3) *c.*130 × 95 mm; (art. 2) 120 × 95 mm; (arts. 4–6) *c.*150 × 90 mm. 2 cols. of 32 lines (art. 2). 2 cols. of 44 lines (art. 3). 24 long lines (art. 6). 29 long lines (art. 1). 38 long lines (arts. 4, 5). In arts. 4–6 the first line of writing is above the top ruled line. Collation: $1–5^{12}$ 6 four (ff. 61–4) $7–12^{12}$ 13 six (ff. 137–42) $14–15^{14}$ $16–26^{8}$ 27^{4} (ff. 259–62) 28^{8}. Initials in arts. 1, 2: (i) blue and red with ornament of both colours; (ii) 2-line, red or blue, with ornament of the other colour. Initials in art. 3, 2-line, blue or red. No coloured initials in arts. 4–6. Medieval binding of wooden boards covered with brown leather, rebacked and with new leather on the back board: the front cover bears a large X of double fillets with a star at each corner and small stamps of four patterns in the triangles made by the fillets. Secundo folio *enim esse*.

Written in the southern Low Countries (?). Art. 4 is for Cistercian use. The fifteenth-century ex-libris of the Cistercian abbey of Cambron, near Mons, Belgium, 'de Camberone', is written at the foot of f. 1 and throughout at the foot of every third or fourth leaf.[1] 'John Kennedy C.S. 1833', f. i^{v}; also the number '47'. A cutting from an English auction or bookseller's catalogue is pasted inside the cover. 'E libris Ronaldi Coates 1917' inside the cover.

35. *Processionale Sarisburiense, etc.* s. xiv^{2}–xiv/xv

1. ff. 1–108^{v} Omnibus dominicis diebus per annum . . .

Temporal through the year from Advent. *PS*, pp. 1–134. The office of Thomas of Canterbury (ff. 13^{v}–14^{v}: *PS*, p. 21) has been crossed out lightly. The litany in Lent (f. 30) agrees with that at Easter Eve (f. 67: edn., pp. 85–6). Corpus Christi, ff. 103^{v}–105^{v}.

2. ff. 108^{v}–110 In dedicacione ecclesie. Ibid., pp. 134–5.

3. ff. 110^{v}–139^{v} Sanctoral.

Includes Anne. As compared with edn. the only feast, apart from 'nova festa', there and not here is Margaret (p. 151) and the only feast here and not there is the Invention of Stephen, f. 127. On f. 125^{v} the office of the Translation of Thomas of Canterbury is crossed out and his name is erased. On f. 134^{v} at 'Sancte edwarde' (*PS*, p. 158) the name is erased and replaced by 'N'.

4. ff. 139^{v}–142^{v} Common of saints.

5. ff. 142^{v}–143^{v} Fiunt autem quedam processiones ueneracionis causa . . . *PS*, pp. 169–70.

Arts. 6–8 (quires 19–28) were written in s. xiv/xv.

6. Breviary offices: (*a*) ff. 145–155^{v} 'In festo corporis' and within the octave; (*b*) ff. 155^{v}–163 'In festo reliquiarum'; (*c*) ff. 163–80 'In dedicacione ecclesie' and within the octave; (*d*) ff. 180–186^{v} of St Anne, ending imperfectly.

[1] As commonly in Cambron manuscripts. The Cambron manuscripts were dispersed in the late 1820s. Sir Thomas Phillipps obtained thirty-four, most of them now in Brussels. The present manuscript is probably the one noticed by A. Sanderus in his Cambron list, *Bibliotheca Belgica*, 1641, p. 362.

(*a*). Cf. *Brev. ad usum Sarum*, I. mlxi–mxcviii. (*b*). Cf. ibis., iii. 451–66. The office is preceded by a notice of the change of date from September to July. The homily of the third nocturn is ascribed to Gregory: cf. edn., col. 460, footnote. (*c*). Cf. ibid., I. mccccxlix–mccccxcii. (*d*). Ibid., iii. 539–553/17.

7. ff. 187–215 In uigilia mortuorum . . .

Noted office of the dead: *Manuale Sarum*, pp. 133–42.

8. ff. 215–26 Sciendum est quod quandocumque corpus adest presens . . . Beati inmaculati . . .

Commendatory psalms (ibid., pp. 142–4), preceded by a 28-line heading. f. 226v blank.

ff. i + 220 + i, foliated i, 1–143, 145–82, 184, 185, 187–94, 196–219, 222–7. 192 × 133 mm. Written space 130 × 85 mm. 8 long lines and music (or 24 long lines) on ff. 1–143. 21 long lines on ff. 144–226. Collation: $1\text{–}17^8$ 18^8 wants 8, blank, after f. 143 $19\text{–}27^8$ (3 and 6 half-sheets in quire 23) 28^6 wants 6, blank. A series of signatures begins with *a* on quire 19. Initials: (i) ff. 1, 187, 215v, in colour on patterned gold grounds, decorated: part borders; (ii) f. 1, gold with violet ornament; (iii) 2-line, blue with red ornament; (iv) 1-line, blue or red. The illuminator put in a wrong letter rather often, especially *N* in place of *U*. Contemporary binding of pink skin over wooden boards: four bands: two strap-and-pin fastenings: kept in a box. Secundo folio *Deus qui*, but the illuminator put *Q* instead of *D*.

Written in England. 'Edgecott', f. 2, s. xvi. 'Edgecott Cloueshale' (?), f. 1, s. xvi. '443' at the foot of f. 1, on the left. '1125/£TL' on a round label inside the cover. J. M. Falkner sale at Sotheby's, 12 December 1932, lot 397 (£17 10*s*).

36. *Horae* s. xiv/xv

1. ff. 4–8v Sarum calendar in red and black, lacking January and February. Some gradings.

Entries in red include the translation of Edmund martyr and 'Dedicacio ecclesie Norwyc' ' (29 Apr., 24 Sept.); in black, Felix, Botulph (8 Mar., 17 June). John of Beverley, Richard of Chichester, Erkenwald absent. The word 'pape' and entries of Thomas of Canterbury not damaged.

2. ff. 9–41v Hours of B.V.M. of the use of (Sarum), beginning and ending imperfectly.

The memoriae after lauds are the usual sixteen (cf. *MMBL* i. 47) and four more, James and Edmund (Aue rex gentis anglorum . . . : *RH*, no. 23810) after Stephen, Cecilia after Katherine and relics after Margaret. Hours of the Cross worked in. Two (?) leaves missing after f. 11.

3. ff. 42–58v Penitential psalms, beginning imperfectly, (f. 50) 'quindecim psalmi' (cues only of the first twelve), and (f. 52) litany.

Nineteen martyrs: . . . (8) thoma . . . (18, 19) edmunde edwarde. Twenty-one confessors: . . . (9) dunstane . . . (16–21) wilfride maure edmunde taurine edwarde antoni. Twenty-one virgins: (1) anna . . . (16–20) elena etheldreda radegundis praxedis brigida.

4. ff. 58v–90v Office of the dead.

Manuale Sarum, pp. 132–42.

5. ff. 90v–102 Sequuntur commendaciones . . . Beati immaculati . . .

Ibid., pp. 143–4.

6. ff. 102–17 Hic incipit psalterium beati Ieronimi . . . cum hac oracione ante psalterium dicenda nam post psalterium sequatur alia oracio. Suscipe domine . . . Verba mea auribus . . . Omnipotens sempiterne deus maiestatem tuam . . .

7. ff. 117v–126v, 146rv A woman solitare and recluse coueytyng to knowe the numbre of the woundis . . . his soule to heuene. Summa indulgencie cuilibet dicenti has oraciones xl dies. tociens quociens si uere confessus fuerit et contritus (*74 lines in red ink*). (f. 119) Aue benignissime domine ihesu criste. O ihesu criste eterna dulcedo . . .

The Fifteen Oes of St Bridget and prayer 'Gracias tibi ago . . .'. The English heading (cf. *Lyell Cat.*, p. 62) was perhaps an afterthought. It fills the space remaining blank after art. 6 (ff. 117v–118v) and is continued in the next blank space (f. 146).

8. ff. 126v–127v Illumina oculos meos . . .

The Eight Verses of St Bernard and prayer 'Omnipotens sempiterne deus qui ezechie . . .'.

9. ff. 127v–129 Domine ihesu criste qui septem uerba . . .

10. f. 129 Benedicat me imperialis maiestas . . .

11. Prayers for a soul: (*a*) ff. 129v–133 Deus summe pacis et dileccionis domine celi . . . precor te ut suscipias animam famuli tui N . . . ; (*b*) f. 133 Domine sancte pater omnipotens eterne deus qui sedes . . . ; (*c*) ff. 133–134v Commendo animam famuli tui in manus tuas . . . Commendo animam eius in manibus sanctorum innocencium et sanctorum martirum. stephani. clementis. leodegarii. alphegi. Laurencii. mellori. uincencii. cristoferi. georgii. willelmi. et omnium martirum . . . ; (*d*) ff. 134v–135v Qui in cruce positus latronem suscepisti penitentem eius deprecor pie peccata dilue. libera domine animam famuli tui . . .

(*a*). Feminine forms interlined. (*c*). Five confessors and twelve virgins are named: Nicholas, Benedict, Giles, Martin, Leonard; Mary Magdalene, Mary of Egypt, Sexburga, Margaret, Katherine, Edith, Faith, Cecilia, Agnes, Lucy, Constantia, Barbara.

13. ff. 135v–137 A repetition of art. 9.

14. ff. 137–8 O bone ihesu. o piissime ihesu. o dulcissime ihesu. o ihesu fili . . . See *Lyell Cat.*, p. 386.

15. f. 138^{rv} Saluator mundi saluum me fac . . . See ibid., p. 394.

16. ff. 138^{v}–140 O beata et intemerata . . . orbis terrarum. Inclina . . . et esto michi peccatrici N pia . . .

17. ff. 140–1 Sancte leonarde sancte dulcis sancte pie sancte deo multum care ad me precor . . . Ego peccatrix te requiro . . . Ora ergo pro indigna . . . et in cunctis iuua bonis.

The word *leonarde* is followed by a blank space of about twelve letters.

18. ff. 141–2 In bona recordacione quinque plagarum ihesu cristi. Confiteor tibi domine ihesu criste saluator mundi omnia peccata mea . . .

19. Forms of commendation: (*a*) f. 142^{rv} In manus tuas et in misericordia tua domine deus meus creator meus . . . commendo animam meam . . . ; (*b*) ff. 142^{v}–146 Domine deus omnipotens qui es trinus et unus . . . Commendo animam meam in manus potencie tue . . .

(*a*). Cf. *Lyell Cat.*, p. 383. (*b*). On f. 145 *peccatorem* is changed to *peccatricem*. f. 146^{v} contains the end of the heading of art. 7.

20. ff. 147–150 Quicumque hec letania semel in die in honore beate marie dixerit in triduo ante mortem suam eam uidebit. Kyrieleyson . . . (f. 149^{v}) Oracio. Omnipotens sempiterne deus te deprecor domine ut \`non' sinas me terroribus demonum . . .

Litany of B.V.M. and prayer.

21. f. 150^{rv} Domine ihesu criste qui hanc sacratissimam carnem . . . A rubric follows conveying an indulgence of 2,000 years 'a domino Bonifacio papa x^{o} (*sic*) ad instanciam domini philippi Regis Francie'. Cf. *Lyell Cat.*, p. 379.

22. The flyleaves (?), ff. 1–3, a bifolium and a singleton, contain: (*a*) f. 1, the end of a prayer to B.V.M. which begins now 'pauperum miseratrix'; (*b*) ff. 1^{v}–2, Oracio. Aue sanctissima caro ihesu cristi. Si cum ieo crai uerament que uous preistes char . . . ; (*c*) ff. 2–3, Beaus sire duz ihesu crist que le uostre benoit seinte cors e uostre precious sanc donastes . . . ; (*d*) f. 3^{rv} Veni creator spiritus mentes tuorum uisita . . .

(*a*). s. xv, in a current hand. (*b–d*). In the main hand. (*c*). Sinclair, no. 2565.

ff. ii + 150 + iii. 178 × 117 mm. Written space 108 × 77 mm. 17 long lines. Collation of ff. 4–150: 1^{6} wants 1, 2 three (ff. 9–11, probably leaves 4–6 of a quire of 8) $3–5^{8}$ 6^{8} wants 7, 8 after f. 41 $7–15^{8}$ 16^{4} + 1 leaf after 4 (f. 118) $17–19^{8}$ 20^{4} (ff. 143–6) 21^{4} (ff. 147–50). Skilful writing: a new hand at f. 83^{v}. Initials: (i) 4-line or 3-line, in colours on decorated gold grounds: borders continuous or on three sides: a brown curled-up dog-like creature is here and there in the decoration, for example on f. 30; (ii) 2-line, gold on grounds of blue and pink patterned in white; (iii) 1-line, blue with red ornament or gold with violet ornament. Red and violet line fillers of many different patterns. English brown calf, gilt, s. xviii: 'MISSALE' on the spine.

Written in England, apparently for the use of a woman in the diocese of Norwich (arts. 1, 15, 16, 18). Armorial book-plate of John Skottowe Esqr inside the cover, s. xviii: on it are the words 'to Charlton Lancs'. Armorial book-plate of 'Boies Penrose II', f. i. Quaritch, *Catalogue of Illuminated Manuscripts*, 1931, item 53 (£60).

37. *Breviarium* s. xiv^{2}

1. ff. 1–8^{v} Dominica prima aduentus domini . . . sed psalmorum seruetur.

Directions for services, especially (ff. 7–8^{v}) on the feast of the dedication.

2. ff. 9–178 Temporal, beginning imperfectly at Wednesday in the first week of Advent: *Brev. ad usum Sarum*, I. lxii.

On f. 143^{v} the main hand ends with the 'lecciones feriales' after Trinity (cf. edn., I. mlviii). The office of Corpus Christi is provided at this point by another hand, over erasure on f. 143^{v} and on five inserted leaves, 144–6, 146*, 147: 146* is a half-leaf of rubric, 'In octauis de corpore . . . in crastino Sancti Iohannis baptiste' (cf. edn., I. mciv–v); 146^{v} ends at 'impleta gracia et' (edn., I. mlxxv/3), after which a leaf or more is missing; f. 147^{r} has three 'Alie lecciones per ebdomadam. Nam et in eodem . . . Unde omnibus . . . Huius igitur sacramenti figure . . . mortui sunt'. The same scribe continues (f. 147rb/32) with the office for the first Sunday after Trinity and wrote the first eight lines on f. 148 over erasure; the main hand begins again at 148ra/9, 'Cognouerunt omnes' (edn., I. mclxxi).

On ff. 38–40^{v} the office of St Thomas of Canterbury, 'Tunc est processio ad altare sancti thome . . . Deus pro cuius ecclesia . . .', has not been disturbed.

3. ff. 178–82 In dedicatione ecclesie.

Offices for the dedication of a church, the anniversary, and within the octave.

4. ff. 182–3 Seruicium de omnibus sanctis in ferialibus diebus . . . Sancti et iusti . . .

5. f. 183^{rv} (*a*) Diuisio festorum duplicium in ecclesia sarum. Hec sunt festa . . . (*b*) Hec sunt festa cum regimine chori secundum usum sarum. Debet autem chorus regi . . . petri et pauli.

Cf. the 'Tabula de festorum divisione', *Brev. ad usum Sarum*, ii. 462–75.

6. ff. 184–188^{v} Calendar lacking Nov., Dec., in blue, red, and black, graded.

Sarum calendar. Additions: (i) s. xiv/xv (?), (1) octave of Thomas of Canterbury, (2–6) David, Chad, Felix, John of Beverley, Thomas of Hereford (1, 2, 8 Mar., 7 May, 2 Oct.: (2, 4) marked 'synod' ' and (3, 5) 'prouinc' ' and (2–4, 6) graded for nine lessons), (7) in red, Anne, 26 July; (ii) s. xv, 'Obitus Agnetis Towrney', 27 Mar.; (iii) s. xv ex., Etheldreda, Frideswide (17, 19 Oct., not graded).

Feasts of Thomas of Canterbury have not been touched either here or in art. 11, but 'pape' was erased at 12 Mar. and erased, but later restored, at 28 June. A red entry at 18 Sept. erased. At 8 July a red note that the feast of relics is on the Sunday after St Thomas.

7. ff. 189–232. Liturgical psalter. Four leaves missing.

8. ff. 232–7 Six ferial canticles, followed by Te deum, Benedicite, Benedictus, Magnificat, Nunc dimittis and Quicumque vult.

9. ff. 237–240^{v} Litany: a set for each day of the week.

10 (added, s. xv). f. 240^{v} A rule for the office of Exaltation of the Cross, to which there is a cross reference on f. 338.

11. ff. 241–379 Sanctoral, Andrew–Saturninus.

12. ff. 379–94 Common of saints.

The part of art. 12 on f. 394 is in the hand of art. 13*a*.

13 (added on quires 53, 54). (*a*) ff. 394–401^{v}, 407^{rv}, 403 Hec festa sequencia non sunt sarum sed synod' et prouincial': there follow offices for David, Chad, Felix, translation of Edmund king and martyr, Anne, Dominic, Thomas of Hereford, Francis, translation of John of Beverley, Winefred and Hugh of Lincoln (1, 2, 8 Mar., 29 Apr., 26 July, 5 Aug., 2, 4, 25 Oct., 3, 17 Nov.). (*b*) ff. 403–4 'Regula de historia In principio incipienda' and other rules in red, ending imperfectly. (*c*) ff. 405–406^{v} Benedictions, beginning imperfectly. (*d*) f. 406^{v} Office 'In festo reliquiarum', ending imperfectly. (*e*) f. 402^{r} Further lessons for St Hugh (cf. (*a*) above). (*f*) Nine lessons for the common of martyrs filling the space after (*e*).

(*a*) is a supplement to art. 11 where there are no offices for these eleven feasts. Nine lessons, except for Edmund, John of Beverley, and Hugh. (*d, e*). *Brev. ad usum Sarum*, iii. 451, 398. (*e*) and (*f*) are on an inserted leaf.

ff. iii + 407 + iii. 152 × 97 mm. Written space 120 × 75 mm. 2 cols. 35 lines. Collation: 1^{8} 2^{8} wants 1 3–18^{8} 19 five (ff. 144–6, 146*, 147: see above art. 2) 20–23^{8} 24^{4} (ff. 180–3) 25^{6} wants 6 after f. 188 26^{8} wants 1 before f. 189 and 8 after f. 194 27^{8} 28^{8} wants 1 before f. 203 29^{8} wants 3 after f. 211 30–51^{8} 52 one (f. 393) 53 six (ff. 394–9) 54^{8} wants 6 after f. 404 (ff. 400–1, 407, 403–6) + 1 leaf, f. 402, inserted after 3. Initials: (i) f. 241, punched gold on patterned blue and red grounds, with prolongations into the margins; (ii) f. 143^{v}, gold on red and blue grounds, with ivy leaf sprays into the margin; (iii) 2-line, blue with red ornament; (iii) 1-line, red or blue. Binding of s. xix: gilt edges. Secundo folio *omnibus sanctis*.

Written in England. Book-plate, s. xix, with motto 'Sic vos non vobis mellificatis apes': the centrepiece is a bee. Belonged to the Revd W. J. Blew, according to a note on f. i. Quaritch, *Catalogue of Illuminated Manuscripts*, 1931, item 23 (£45).

38. *Graduale* s. xv²

1. f. i Ad aspersi: aque bened: fer. die. Exaudi nos domine quoniam . . . f. iv blank.

2. ff. ii–iiiv (*a*) Eight settings of Gloria patri. (*b*) Antiphons of the holy-water service, Asperges me and Vidi aquam, and their versicles all noted and prayer Exaudi nos domine . . . et mittere dignare angelum tuum . . .

3. ff. 1–57v Uniuersi qui te expectant . . .

Temporal, Advent–23rd Sunday after octave of Pentecost. Noted litany, ff. 25–9: thirteen confessors: . . . (3) martine . . . (7) seruati . . . (9, 10) dominice francisce . . . (13) anthoni; thirteen virgins: (1, 2) maria magdalena felicitas . . . (10–13) odilia vrsula cum sodalibus helena elysabeth; eight names interlined, huberte above martine, bernarde leonarde above anthoni, anna above maria magdalena; martha above felicitas, margareta above barbara, gertrudis above odilia, appollonia above ursula, and monica added after elysabeth. Two leaves missing.

4. ff. 57v–59 In dedicacione ecclesie et in anniuersario eiusdem.

5 (added) f. 59v In presentatione beate virginis. Ends imperfectly, a leaf missing.

6. ff. 61–83 Sanctoral.

Visitation of B.V.M., f. 74v. Cues for Thomas Aquinas, Peter Martyr and Hubert. Additions in the margins: Gertrude and Joseph, f. 68v; Quiriac, f. 72; 11,000 virgins, f. 72v. One leaf missing.

7. ff. 83–106 Common of saints.

8. ff. 106–11 Settings of Kyrieleyson, Gloria, Credo in unum deum, Sanctus and Agnus dei 'In festis totis duplicibus', 'In semiduplicibus', 'In dominicis et semiduplicibus' and 'In simplicibus'.

9. Sequences: (*a*) ff. 111–18 seven of the temporal: Letabundus exultet for Christmas and the next two days; Victime paschali for Easter and the next two days; Omnes gentes plaudite for Ascension Day; Sancti spiritus assit nobis gratia and Veni sancte spiritus et emitte celitus for Pentecost; Profitentes vnitatem for Trinity Sunday; Lauda syon saluatorem 'In festo venerabilis sacramenti'; (*b*) ff. 118–119v Rex salomon fecit templum 'In die consecracionis et in anniuersario ecclesie'; (*c*) ff. 119v–135 thirteen of the sanctoral: Aue maria gracia plena for Annunciation of B.V.M.; Precursorem summi regis for John Baptist; Iubar mundo geminatur (*RH*, no. 9786) for Peter and Paul; Aue preclara maris stella for Visitation of B.V.M.; Salue mater saluatoris for Assumption of B.V.M.; Ad honorem summi regis (*RH*, no. 162) for Helen; De profundis tenebrarum for Augustine; Natiuitas marie virginis que nos for Nativity of B.V.M.; Honor crucis dilatetur et deuote celebretur eius exaltatio (*RH*, no. 7990) for Exaltation of

Cross; Laus erumpat ex affectu for Michael; Virginalis turma sexus for 11,000 Virgins; Superne matris gaudia for All Saints. ff. 135^{v}–136^{v} left blank.

10 (added, s. xv ex.). ff. 135^{v}–136^{v} Virginis odilie solemnitas hodie . . . et ab hamis erue nos scelesti.

Ten stanzas. Not in *RH*.

ff. 135, foliated (i–iii) 1–6, 8–54, 56–9, 61–74, 76–136 in a medieval hand in red. Paper. 382 × 277 mm. Written space 297 × 190 mm. 10 long lines and music or 30 long lines. Collation of ff. i–iii, 1–136: 1^{10} wants 1, blank (ff. i–iii, 1–6) 2^{10} wants 1 before f. 8 3–5^{10} 6^{10} wants 9 after f. 55 7 three (ff. 57–9) 8^{10} 9^{10} wants 5 after f. 74 10–14^{10} 15^{8} wants 7, 8, blank (ff. 131–6). Good set hybrida. Punctuation includes the flex. Initials: (i) ff. 6, 61, blue patterned in white; (ii) red, plain or patterned in white. Cadels lined with red. Binding of contemporary wooden boards covered with brown leather bearing a pattern of fillets, rebacked: metal pieces removed.

Written in western Germany (?). Arts. 3, 10 suggest a special interest in St Otilia (of Hohenbourg, diocese of Strasbourg).

39. *'Ordo romanus tocius pontificalis offitii'* s. xiii/xiv

A pontifical which derives texts from various sources. Arts. 3, 4, 18 belong to the 'Pontifical de la curie romaine au xiiie siècle' (Andrieu, *Pont. Rom.*, ii) and arts. 6, 7 to the tenth-century 'Pontifical romano-germanique' (*Pont. Rom. Germ.*). Cf. also art. 1. Many texts differ more or less from those printed by Andrieu, especially in the rubrics. Art. 8 is not recorded by Andrieu or by V. Leroquais, *Les pontificaux manuscrits des bibliothèques publiques de France*.

1. ff. 1–22 Incipit ordo romanus tocius pontificalis offitii. In primis sciendum est quod hostiarii . . . et subdiaconi ante epistolam debent ordinari. post epistolam uero diaconi et sacerdotes consecrari debent. Ordo ad clericum faciendum. In primis aspergat episcopus . . . Oremus dilectissimi fratres . . . pro hoc famulo . . . custodias. per. Salmista id est cantor . . . comprobes. De officio hostiarii . . .

f. 2^{v} Hostiarius: Hostiarium oportet percutere . . . ; f. 3^{v} Lector; f. 4^{v} Exorcista; f. 5^{v} Acolitus; f. 7^{v} Subdiaconus: the blessing (Andrieu, *Pont. Rom.*, i. VIII. 5) is followed on f. 9 by 'Tunc episcopus tradat ei fanonem in sinistra manu dicens. Accipe hunc fanonem ad expugnandas spiritalis inimici insidias. In nomine . . . amen (cf. Andrieu, ii. 335, footnote). Tunc det ei tunicam dicens. Constringat cor et corpus tuum timor domini castus et sanctus permanens in seculum seculi amen'; ff. 14–22 Presbiter: Presbitero licet offerre. benedicere. sed super populum benedictionem ei dare non licet . . . (f. 15) Sequitur allocutio episcopi ad populum. Quoniam dilectissimi fratres rectori nauis et naufragium (*sic*) deferentibus (*sic*) . . . Tunc interroget episcopus eum qui consecrandus est dicens. Vis presbiteri gradum . . . (f. 19^{v}) Item consecratio presbiteri. Deus sanctificationum . . . (f. 22) Super populum. Da quesumus domine populis . . . frequentant per.

For the bishop's address and questions, f. 15 sqq., see Leroquais, op. cit. i. LXX, LXXX, 220. Sections corresponding to Andrieu, ii, nos. II, IV do not occur.

2. ff. 22–39 Incipit ordo ad ad (*sic*) uocandum et examinandum seu consecrandum electum episcopum. Set sciendum est quod si electus fuerit de ecclesia romana non examinabitur prerogatiua romane ecclesie. Sabbati uero die . . . ualeamus. per.

Title as Andrieu, ii, no. XI. At XI. 13 (f. 27) the third interrogation is 'Vis sancte romane ecclesie et michi ac sucessoribus meis fidem et subiectionem exibere ?'. As in *Pont. Rom.-Germ.* the 'Benedictio baculi. Deus sine quo . . .' and 'Benedictio anuli. Creator et conseruator . . .' precede the order of mass. The formula 'Accipe mitram qua utaris ad laudem et gloriam . . .' is an addition in the margin, f. 39: the same form was in the margin, f. 38v, but has been erased there. Andrieu, ii, no. XII does not occur.

3. ff. 39–41v Incipit ordo qualiter romanus pontifex aput basilicam beati petri apostoli debeat ordinari. Primicerius cum scola . . . uicem recipiat. Qui uiuis.

Andrieu, ii, nos. XIIIA, XIV.

4. ff. 41v–52 Incipit ordo ad benedicendum imperatorem quando coronam accipit facit hanc promissionem. In nomine cristi . . . ianuam auxiliante . . .

Andrieu, ii, no. XVA.

5. ff. 52–64v Incipit ordo ad benedicendum regem quando nouus a clero et populo sublimatur . . . Oratio. Omnipotens sempiterne deus qui famulum tuum . . . dispe(n)satione redemptus. per.

Cf. Andrieu, *Ord. Rom.* i. 194.

6. ff. 64v–69v Incipit ordinatio abbatis. Capitulum ex canone theodori. In ordinatione abbatis . . . dicens. Ecclesie nostre fratres karissimi pater electus . . . pietate conseruet. per.

Nearly as *Pont. Rom.-Germ.*, nos. XXVI, §§1–4, 6, 7, 9, 12, 15–17; no. XXVII, §§2–5.

7. ff. 69v–73v Incipit ordinatio abbatisse monasticam regulam profitentis. Capitulum ex canone theodori anglorum archiepiscopi. In ordinatione abbatisse . . . placere contendat. per.

Nearly as *Pont. Rom.-Germ.*, no. XXXII, §§1–5, 7, 9, 10, 12–14.

8. ff. 73v–77 Ordo ad recludendum quemlibet. uitam contemplatiuam eligentem. Quando episcopus uel abbas aut sacerdos . . . Verba mea . . . Oratio. Pie domine qui attriti cordis gemitum . . .

Consists mainly of Pss. 5, 22, 26, 41, 60, 73, 137, 141, each followed by a prayer. At the end is a direction, 'Post hec accipiat eum . . . (*takes to house*)' and a blessing 'Benedic deum omnipotens locum istum ut sit in eo famulo tuo . . .' and prayer 'Consolatio tuorum omnium domine . . . in unitate eiusdem'.

9. ff. 77–81 Ordo ad monachum faciendum. In primis faciat subdiaconus letanias. deinde episcopus dicat hanc orationem. Adesto domine . . . consortium per do. n. i. x.

Andrieu, i, no. XVI; ii, no. XVII, but the rubrics of XVII. 6, 7 are here 'Benedictio uestimenti. Hic exuat se uestimentis mundanis dicente episcopo' and 'Hic tribuat ei episcopus uestimentum et induat se dicente episcopo'.

10. (*a*) ff. 81–94 Consecratio sacre uirginis que in epyphania uel in secunda feria pasce. aut in apostolorum natalitiis celebratur. Omnes qui ad sacros ordines debent promoueri . . . Oremus. Deus eternorum bonorum . . . confidit per dominum. (*b*) ff. 94–95^{v} Incipit ordo ad ancillas cristi uelandas que omnibus dominicis et festiuis diebus . . . Oremus fratres karissimi misericordiam dei ut illud donum . . . consolatione percipiat. per.

(*a*). Heading and incipit as *Pont. Rom.-Germ.*, no. XX. Collect, secret, and postcommunion as there, no. XXI. (*b*). Cf. *Pont. Rom.-Germ.*, no. XXIII. Collect, secret, and postcommunion as there.

11. ff. 95^{v}–98^{v} Incipit ordo ad uelandam uiduam que fuerit castitatem professa. Vidue . . . solis episcopis uirgines. Benedictio uestimentorum uidue or'. Uisibilium et inuisibilium . . . florietur. per.

Cf. *Pont. Rom.-Germ.*, no. XXV and Andrieu, i, no. XIII. In the mass the collect is Deus castitatis, as Andrieu's L.

12. ff. 98^{v}–101 Ad diaconissam consecrandam . . . inuenias. per.

Cf. Andrieu, i, no. XIV. 1–5, 14, 15, 9, 11, 13; *Pont. Rom.-Germ.*, no. XXIV.

13. ff. 101–5 Incipit ordo ad eiciendos penitentes de ecclesia. Feria iiii in capite ieiunii penitentes cum ad ecclesiam uenerunt laneis tantummodo . . . his uerbis. Scitis filii karissimi quia primus parens . . . cordis poposcerit.

14. ff. 105–125^{v} Incipit ordo qualiter agendum sit feria v in cena domini. Hora tercia sonet signum ut omnes conueniant in ecclesia. in qua crisma . . . factus est pro nobis. Sequitur oratio. Descendat in hanc pinguidinem . . . diurnale insimul cantentur.

Rubric nearly as Andrieu, *Pont. Rom.*, ii. 68. The bishop's sermon, 'Sacrosanctam nostri saluatoris sententiam cum summa cordis deuotione fratres karissimi . . .', is on ff. 108^{v}–111. The order ends with Benedictio incensi (Andrieu, *Pont. Rom.*, i, nos. XXV; ii, no. XXXII) and long rubric, 'Tunc pontifex lauet . . .'.

15. ff. 125^{v}–130 Feria vi^{a} parasceue hora diei v^{ta} conueniant omnes clerici ac laici. et preparent se presbiteri . . . Sed hiis omnibus expletis. unusquisque cum pace et absque confabulatione recedat.

Begins as Andrieu, *Pont. Rom.*, ii. 56, 194, 222. A rubric in the reading of the Gospel is (f. 127) 'Et cum peruenerit diac'. ad locum. ubi legitur Partiti sunt uestimenta mea sibi. duo acoliti auferant eas (*sic*) hinc inde ad modum furantis . . .': cf. Andrieu, *Pont. Rom.*, i. 235/14-17.

16. f. 130rv Benedictio primi lapidis . . . Oratio. Exaudi nos domine sancte pater omnipotens eterne deus et lapidem istum serenis oculis . . . defensare digneris per.

17. ff. 130v-158 Incipit ordo ad benedicendam seu dedicandam ecclesiam. In primis erunt preparata in ecclesia queque sunt necessaria id est ysopus . . . augmentis. per.

Noted. Cf. Andrieu, ii, no. XXIII. Ends with XXIII. 88-90, after which comes a second post-communion, Deus qui de uiuis et electis lapidibus (*Pont. Rom.-Germ.* i. 182). A large X fills f. 138, the Latin alphabet strung along the first diagonal and the Greek along the second. Additions with musical notes in the lower margins, ff. 130v-131 and f. 136v: Exaudi nos domine quoniam benigna est . . . ; Exurge domine adiuua nos . . .

18. f. 158rv Benedictio poliandri uel cimiterii. Domine sancte pater omnipotens eterne deus locorum omnium . . . occurrant. per eundem.

Andrieu, ii, no. XXIV.

19. ff. 159-62 Incipit ordo ad reconciliandam ecclesiam uiolatam. Primus ueniat episcopus et ante ipsam . . . uota sanctifica. Qui cum.

Ibid., ii, no. XXVI.

20. (*a*) ff. 162-4 Benedictio lapidis `quando primitus ponitur in fundamento noue structure' (*these seven words partly over erasure and partly in the margin*). Deum omnipotentem fratres dilectissimi . . . (f. 162v) Consecratio lapidis. Exaudi nos deus . . . in tabulis scripsisti lapideis. Per. (*b*) ff. 164-166v Incipit consecratio altaris. In primis benedicatur aqua . . . dicens. Sanctifice+tur hoc altare . . . Item alia. Omnipotens sempiterne deus altare hoc (*no more*). (*c*) ff. 167-8 Incipit consecratio altaris itinerarii. Supplices tibi . . . Omnipotens sempiterne deus altare hoc ut supra.

(*a*). Cf. ibid., i, no. XIX, the BO text, §§2, 5, 6, 13, 14; ii, no. XXVII. 1-4, 11, 12. (*b*). Cf. ibid., ii, no. XXIII. 39, 40, 55-64, 66-70, 72, 73, 75-9. (*c*). Cf. ibid., ii, no. XXVII. 12-14, no. XXIII. 79. A long addition in the margin, f. 167, s. xiv: Rubrice noue et antique. In primis dicitur oratio. Supplices. Deinde aspergatur lapis consecrandus . . .

21. ff. 168-74 Incipit ordo romanus qualiter concilium agatur. Conueniente uniuerso cetu . . . Omnipotens sempiterne deus qui misericordia tua . . . in domos suas.

Ibid., i, no. XXXVI; ii, no. XLV.

22. ff. 174–7 Benedictio crucis noue. Bene+dic domine ihesu criste hanc figuram crucis tue . . . sanitatem. Per. In unitate eiusdem.

Ibid., i, no. XXVI, ii, no. XXXI, but without the prayer Sancti+fica.

23. f. 177rv Prefacio patene consecrande. Consecra+mus . . . domino nostro. Qui.

Ibid., ii, no. XXVIII.

24. ff. 177v–178v Prefacio calicis. Oremus dilectissimi . . . In unitate eiusdem.

Ibid., ii, no. XXIX.

25. ff. 178v–179 Benedictio corporalis. Clementissime domine . . .

Ibid., i, no. XXI, ii, no. XXX, but with a third prayer, 'Domine deus qui iam sanctificare . . . (*Pont. Rom.-Germ.*, no. XL, §83).

26. ff. 179–81 Benedictio planete. dalmatice. et aliarum uestium sacerdotalium ac leuitarum. Omnipotens sempiterne deus qui per moysen . . . peruenire per.

Ibid., i, no. XX, ii, no. XXXIII, but with a third prayer, 'Omnipotens sempiterne deus qui moysi famulo tuo sacerdotalia seu leuitica indumenta . . .'.

27. ff. 181–2 Ordo ad consignandum pueros. Omnipotens sempiterne deus qui regenerare . . . et maneat semper. Amen.

Cf. ibid., ii, no. XXXIV: ends with 'Benedictio dei . . .', not *Benedicat te* . . . ff. 182v–185v and part of f. 182r were left blank: f. 185 was at one time the last leaf.

28 (added early in the space remaining blank in quire 23). (*a*) ff. 182–184v Ordo ad benedicendum signum. In primis dicatur letania . . . protectio sempiterna. per. Explicit de campana. (*b*) f. 185 A repetition of the alphabets on f. 138.

(*a*). For the incipit here cf. ibid., ii. 122.

29. ff. 187–190v Litany.

Martyrs: Stephane Clemens Laurenti Uincenti Blasi [. . .] (*two names erased*). Confessors: Siluester Martine Nicholae Gregori Ieronime Ambrosi Augustine. Monks and hermits: Benedicte Leonarde Antoni. Virgins: Maria Magdalena Helena Perpetua Agatha Agnes Lucia Cecilia. Many erasures in the *A(b), Per, Ut* sections. The *Ut ecclesiam* formula is 'Ut ecclesiam tuam sanctam catholicam atque apostolicam regere et conseruare digneris' and the *Ut domum* formula (f. 190) 'Ut domum istam regalem aulam tibi domino deo nostro benedicere et consecrare digneris'. Perhaps imperfect at the end: the three prayers after *Et ne nos* are 'Deus qui de diuersis ordinibus . . .', 'Sicque uos altaris . . .' and 'Quatenus corpore et mente . . .'.

An addition in the margin of f. 190 has been erased: 'Ut hos penitentes . . . confirmare digneris'.

30 (added, s. xiv). (*a*) ff. 191–198^{v}, 186^{rv} Incipiunt Benedicciones Episcopales per anni circulum. Et primo in vigilia Natiuitatis domini. Populum tuum quesumus domine celesti fauore . . . (*b*) f. 186^{v} De corpore cristi. Deus qui sui sacratissimi corporis . . .

(*a*). Seventy-two blessings: for Christmas Eve, Christmas Day (in gallicantu, in aurora, ad publicam missam), Stephen, John Evangelist, Innocents, Circumcision, Epiphany, 1st and 4th Sundays after Epiphany, Conversion of Paul, Purification of B.V.M., Chair of Peter, Annunciation of B.V.M., seven Sundays from Septuagesima to the 4th in Lent, Passio Domini, Palm Sunday, Passio Domini, Thursday and Saturday in Holy Week, Easter, Wednesday after Easter (two forms); 1st and 4th Sundays after the octave of Easter, Invention of Cross, Pentecost, John Baptist, Peter and Paul, Laurence, Assumption of B.V.M., Decollation of John Baptist, Nativity of B.V.M., Michael, All Saints, Martin, Andrew; apostle and apostles, martyr, confessor and confessors, virgin; dedication of church and anniversary of dedication; 1st, 3rd, 5th, 7th, 9th, 11th, 13th, 15th, 17th, 19th, 21st, 23rd Sundays after Pentecost, 1st, 2nd, and 3rd Sundays in Advent, Sabbato quatuor temporum; Holy Cross, Holy Trinity; 'Benedicciones cottidiane' (two forms).

31 (added on flyleaf, s. xiv). f. 199 Ordo ad reconciliandum Cimiterium uiolatum. In primis benedicatur aqua . . .

Cues, except for the first prayer, 'Domine pie qui agrum figuli . . .' (Andrieu, *Pont. Rom.*, iii. 512).

ff. ii + 198 + ii. Thick parchment of good quality. 247 × 170 mm. Written space 152 × 98 mm. 17 long lines. Collation: 1–16^{8} 17^{6} + 1 leaf after 2 (f. 131) 18–19^{8} 20^{10} 21–23^{8} 24^{4} (ff. 187–90) 25^{8} + 1 leaf after 8 (ff. 191–8, 186). Well written. Initials (arts. 1–26, 28): (i) f. 1, 6-line *O*, dark green on patterned pink ground, historiated (Priest at altar): a border of green and vermilion contains climbing cherubs and a suppliant tonsured figure: the initial and border are probably later additions; (ii) outside the written space, blue or red with ornament of the other colour; (iii) 1-line, as (ii), but with simpler ornament. Initials of art. 29: (i) 4-line, blue and red with ornament in colours; (ii) 2-line, red with violet ornament or blue with red ornament; (iii) 1-line, blue or red. Germanic binding of brown calf over wooden boards, partly bevelled at head and foot and on the sides: a double border made of two rolls, the inner one with four scenes marked 'APPARVIT / BENIGNI', 'ECCE AN/GNVS. DEI', 'DATA. EST / MIHI. OM' and 'DE. FRVCT/V. VENTRI' (cf. Weale, nos. 736, 811) encloses a panel which contains two strips of a four-evangelists roll cut to leave room for a blank space above and below: on the front cover only, the upper space contains the letters VEG and the lower space the date 1572. Secundo folio *atur eternam*.

The main hand (arts. 1–27, 29) is Italian and so is the hand of art. 28: the book may have been written for a royal chapel (cf. art. 29). It seems to have been in a Germanic area in s. xiv, to judge from the hands of arts. 30, 31, and in s. xvi, to judge from the binding. Quaritch, *Catalogue of Illuminated Manuscripts*, 1931, item 80 (£60).

40. *Missale Sarisburiense* s. xv med.

1. ff. 1–2^{v} Calendar, May–August, in red and black, with some gradings.

The entry at 2 July is 'Visitacio beate marie uirginis ix lc' (*so far in red*). Sanctorum swithini et processi et mar' iii lc' '. The entry at 8 Aug. is 'Festum transfiguracionis domini (*in red*). Sancti ciriaci martiris (*in black*) ix lc' (*in red*)'. Translation of Wulfstan, 6 June. Augustine (28 Aug.) absent. The word 'pape' and entries of St Thomas of Canterbury have been erased.

2. ff. 3–4^{v} (*begins imperfectly*) incipiens ab acholito qui crucem deffert . . . Holy water service.

3. ff. 4^{v}–116^{v} Temporal from Advent to Easter Eve.

The secret for the second Sunday after the octave of Epiphany is Ut tibi grata. The office of Thomas of Canterbury has not been cancelled on f. 23, only the word Thomas erased each time it occurs. 'Oremus . . . n' erased, f. 102: cf. *Sarum Missal*, p. 110/25. The central bifolium of quire 8 seems to be a replacement, since the script and initials are different from the rest. Single leaves missing after ff. 105, 111.

4. (*a*) ff. 116^{v}–118^{v} Oracio sancti Augustini dicenda est a sacerdote in missa dum cantatur officium et Kyrie et Gloria in excelsis et Credo vel tota dicatur ante missam quod melius est et cetera. Summe sacerdos et uere pontifex . . . siciam in eternum. Qui . . . (*b*) ff. 118–26 Ordinary of mass. (*c*) ff. 126–127^{v} Noted prefaces of mass, ending imperfectly. (*d*) ff. 128–131^{v} Canon of mass, beginning imperfectly. (*e*) ff. 131^{v}–132 Cum uero sacerdos exu(e)rit casulam . . . (*f*) f. 132^{rv} Predictus modus et ordo . . . (*g*) ff. 132^{v}–134 Preterea in omni missa que de feria agitur . . . (*h*) f. 134^{rv} Settings of Benedicamus domino and Ite missa est. (*i*) ff. 134^{v}–136^{v} De diuersis casibus et periculosis (*sic*) in missa contingentibus. Presbiter potest supplere . . .

(*a*). Ed. A. Wilmart, *Auteurs spirituels*, pp. 114–24. (*e*). Gratiarum actio post missam. (*g*). Psalms and prayers in prostration.

5. f. 136^{v} Aspersing of water and directions for Easter procession, ending imperfectly.

6. ff. 137–87 Temporal from Easter, the first leaf missing and a leaf after f. 150, with the beginning of Ascension Day.

A tab marks Trinity (f. 161). Corpus Christi, f. 162. A reader noted at the foot of f. 152 'lakkis þ^{e} pistill and þ^{e} gospel [. . . .] feria': cf. *Sarum Missal*, p. 158, where Epistle and Gospel are provided for the Friday after Ascension Day.

7. ff. 187^{v}–189 Dedication of church and within the octave, consecration and reconciliation. A leaf missing after f. 187.

8. ff. 190–244^{v} Sanctoral, Andrew–Katherine (ending imperfectly).

Two leaves missing after f. 221 with feasts of 24–9 July and single leaves after ff. 199, 226, 240, with the beginnings of the offices for the Purification of B.V.M., the Assumption of B.V.M. and All Saints respectively. The Visitation of B.V.M. occurs (f. 217), but not the Transfiguration (cf. art. 1).

9. ff. 245–259^{v} Common of saints.

10. (*a*) ff. 259^{v}–260^{v} In commemoracione Petri et Pauli. (*b*) ff. 260^{v}–261 In commemoracione sancti thome.

(*a*). Fuller than on f. 219v. The sequence is Plaudat ergo tellus. plaudat celorum curia. (*b*). Collect, sequence (Gaude thomas de cuius uictoria: *RH*, no. 37580; *AH* xl. 296), secret, and postcommunion for Thomas of Canterbury, all lined through.

11. ff. 261–71 Nine masses, three for Friday and one for the other days of the week: (*a*) Holy Trinity; (*b*) Angels; (*c*) 'Pro fratribus et sororibus'; (*d*) Holy Spirit; (*e*) Corpus Christi; (*f*) Holy Cross, with long heading, 'Feria via Sanctus bonifacius papa egrotauit . . . : sequence, Cenam cum discipulis; (*g*) as second Friday mass, Holy Name, 'Feria vi. Decimo nono die mensis iulii anno domini millesimo ccccmo ix xi (*sic*) Robertus episcopus Sacro in castro suo de scirebor' consessit omnibus uere confessis et contritis . . .': sequences, Dulcis ihesus nazarenus and Dulce nomen ihesu cristi; (*h*) as third Friday mass, Crown of Thorns: sequence, Si uis uere gloriari; (*i*) B.V.M., with long heading, 'Sabbato celebratur . . .'.

(*a–d, i*). *Sarum Missal*, pp. 384, 459, 392, 385, 388. (*a–f, h, i*). *Missale Sarum*, Burntisland edn., cols. 735*–782*. The headings of (*f, g*) have been cancelled. (*g*). On this indulgenced mass issued by Robert Hallum, see R. W. Pfaff, *New liturgical feasts in later medieval England*, 1970, pp. 62–5. The heading here conveys an indulgence of forty days. (*h*). Ibid., pp. 92–3.

12. ff. 271–273v Collect, secret, and postcommunion of eleven votive masses: (*a*) Pro penitentibus (25);[1] (*b*) De resurrectione; (*c*) De omnibus sanctis (8); (*d*) Pro uniuersali ecclesia (10); (*e*) Pro pace (11); (*f–i*) 'De Generalis' (*sic*: four sets); (*j*) Pro febricitantibus (p. 406, footnote 2); (*k*) Pro muliere pregnante.

(*b, k*). *Missale Sarum*, Burntisland edn., cols. 826*, 822*. (*f–i*). *Sarum Missal*, pp. 442, 443, 445, no. 1, 445, no. 2.

13. ff. 273v–274v Missa de recordare. Recordare domine . . .

Missale Sarum, Burntisland edn., col. 886* (Missa pro mortalitate evitanda).

14. ff. 274v–284v Thirty-eight votive masses: (i) Pro pace (11, but full office: cues to art. 12*e*); (ii) Pro rege nostro (15, but full office); (iii) Item alia oratio pro rege et regina (16); (iv) Ad inuocandam graciam spiritus sancti (23, but full office); (v) Pro semetipso (17, but full office) . . . (xxxviii) Ad memoriam de sanctis Katerina margareta et maria magdalena.

For nos. v–xxxviii see below, All Souls College, Oxford, 302, art. 9, nos. x–xliv, which, with one exception, are the same forms as here, in the same order and with the same variation between a full office and the priest's prayers only. The exception is no. xxix, Pro universali ecclesia, in MS. 302, but omitted here, because it occurs above in art. 12.

[1] The bracketed numbers and page reference here and in art. 14 refer to the series of forty-three votive masses printed, but not actually numbered, in *Sarum Missal*, pp. 384–412. See below, Oxford, All Souls College 302, art. 9 and footnote.

15. ff. 284v–288 Ordo ad faciendum sponsalia. Queritis quando potest . . .

English forms on f. 285v. Nothing on second marriages since a leaf is missing after f. 287 which ends at *Manuale Sarum*, p. 54/11: f. 288 begins at p. 58/23.

16. ff. 288–90 Ordo ad seruicium peregrinorum faciendum. Ibid., pp. 60–3.

17. ff. 290–2 The eleven blessings in *Manuale Sarum*, pp. 63–70/7.

The heading of the blessing of eyes is 'Benedictio oculorum Willelmus magister de montibus matricis ecclesie lincoln' cancellarius benedictiones oculorum infirmorum quando necessitas inducit et potest fieri in hunc modum': cf. below, Oxford, Corpus Christi College 394, art. 17, and Pembroke College 1, art. 12.

18. ff. 292–295v Ordo ad uisitandum infirmum. In primis induat se . . . (*ends imperfectly*).

Manuale Sarum, pp. 97–100, 106–12/15, 114–17/23. Extreme unction begins on f. 293. The litany is that in edn., but includes Barbara in last place among virgins.

19. f. 296rv Commendation of souls, beginning imperfectly.

Ibid., pp. 120–4/25. The words Diri vulneris (120/24) appear here as 'Dixi mulieris'.

20. ff. 297–8 Mass of the dead, beginning imperfectly in 1 Thess. 4: 14. Ibid., pp. 147–52/4.

21. ff. 299–300v Collect, secret, and postcommunion of masses for the dead, beginning imperfectly.

The remaining forms are thirteen of the nineteen in *Sarum Missal*, pp. 434–42, in the order 19, 3, 4, 6, 7, 5, 15, 13, 14, 16, 17, 12, 18.

22. ff. 300v–301 Ordo trigintalis quod quidam apostolicus . . .

Collect, secret, and postcommunion. *Missale Sarum*, Burntisland edn., col. 883*.

23. f. 301 Pro quibus orare tenemur. Ibid., col. 878*.

24. f. 301rv Post missam accedat sacerdos . . . (*ends imperfectly*).

Office of burial. *Manuale Sarum*, pp. 152–4/16.

ff. i + 301 + i. 387 × 270 mm. Written space 265 × 180 mm. 2 cols. 35 lines. Collation: 1^6 wants 1, 2, 5, 6 2^8 wants 1 $3\text{–}14^8$ 15^8 wants 1 before f. 106 and 8 after f. 111 $16\text{–}17^8$ 18 three (ff. 128–30) 19^8 wants 7 after f. 136 20^8 21^8 wants 6 after f. 150 $22\text{–}25^8$ 26^8 wants 4 after f. 187 27^8 28^8 wants 1 before f. 200 29^8 30^8 wants 8 after f. 221 31^8 wants 1 before f. 222 and 7, 8 after f. 226 32^8 33^8 wants 7 after f. 240 34^8 wants 4 after f. 244

35–38[8] 39[8] wants 8 after f. 287 40[8] 41[8] wants 1 before f. 296, 3 after f. 296 and 6 after f. 298 42 one (f. 301). Signatures of the usual late medieval kind begin with b 1 on f. 10. A new series, red instead of black, begins on f. 200 (quire 28). Initials: (i) 7-line or less, in colours, including green and vermilion, on decorated gold grounds, with prolongations into the margins in colours and a little gold: on f. 20, Christmas, and on f. 190 the borders are continuous; (ii) f. 27, 6-line, pale green and white *E* of *Ecce* (Epiphany) on a decorated red ground: this style of initial is only here; (iii) 2–4-line, gold on blue and pink grounds, patterned in white: short sprays into the margin; (iv) 2-line, blue with red ornament; (v) 1-line, blue with red ornament or red with blue-grey ornament. Capital letters in the ink of the text filled with pale yellow. 'Bound by Riviere and Son', s. xix. Secundo folio (f. 3) *incipiens*.

Written in England. J. M. Falkner sale, 12 December 1932, lot 299.

41. *Missale* s. xv^2

1. ff. 1–6^v Calendar in red and black, not graded.

'Claudii confessoris' in red, 6 June. Fifteen entries in black have the word 'Lugd' in front of them: 'Desiderii', 11 Feb.; 'Nicecii', 'Ipypodii', 'Alexandri et sociorum', 'Rustici', 2, 22, 24, 26 Apr.; 'Hyrenei', 28 June; 'Viuencioli', 'Panthaleonis', 12, 28 July; 'Aduentus sancti iusti in heremo', 4 Aug.; 'Iusti', 'Pacientis', 'Lupi', 'Annemundi', 2, 12, 25, 28 Sept.; 'Antyochi', 15 Oct.; 'Eucherii', 16 Nov. 'Consecracio altaris Lugd' ', 9 July, in black. 'Dedicacio sancti stephani', 15 Sept., in black. No entries for Visitation of B.V.M. (cf. art. 5) or Transfiguration.

2. ff. 7–133 Temporal from Advent to Saturday after Easter.

The office for Good Friday includes prayers for heretics, Jews, and pagans, as in the printed Lyons missal of 1510, f. 66^v, and there are three litanies on Easter Eve, 'Letania prima ad incensum cerei' (f. 119), 'Letania secunda ad descensum fontis' (f. 121), and a third 'expleto baptismo' (f. 123^v), as there, ff. 69–72: in the second litany the apostles after Jude are 'sylea timothee tite'. A prayer at the end of the office for Easter Sunday is headed 'Ad sanctum andream'; so, too, prayers within the octave of Easter. The initial at Easter has been cut out of f. 125.

3. ff. 133–52 Incipit ordo de uestimento altaris. Indue me domine . . .

Ordinary, noted prefaces, and (f. 147^v) canon of mass. ff. 145–146^v, 152^v blank.

4. ff. 153–225^v Temporal from the first Sunday after Easter to the second Sunday before Advent, ending imperfectly.

5. ff. 226–80 Sanctoral from Andrew (beginning imperfectly) to Saturninus, followed by the rubric 'Eodem die vigilia sancti andree que est in principio sanctuarii'.

Visitation of B.V.M., f. 253. A prayer at the Purification of B.V.M., 'Exaudi quesumus domine plebem tuam . . .' (f. 233), is headed 'Ad sanctum adrianum'.

6. ff. 280–281^v In dedicacione ecclesie.

7. ff. 281v–300 Incipit commune sanctorum.

8. ff. 300–1 Ad sponsam benedicendam.

9. ff. 301v–302v Masses of Holy Cross and B.V.M.

10. ff. 302v–309 Collect, secret, and postcommunion of thirty masses: de communione domini nostri ihesu cristi (Corda, In mentibus, Presta); All Saints; Missa spiritualis sacerdotis (2 forms); pro amico (2 forms); pro familiari; pro salute viuorum; pro familiaribus; pro abbate vel congregacione; pro iter agentibus; pro peccatis; in tempore belli; pro pace; pro quacumque tribulacione; contra iudices malos; pro infirmis; pro reddita sanitate; in contencione; pro peste animalium; ad pluuiam postulandam (2 forms); pro serenitate habenda; contra tempestatem; contra paganos; ad graciam sancti spiritus postulandam; pro lacrimis; contra temptacionem carnis; contra malas cogitaciones; pro semetipso. Two postcommunions are often provided.

11. ff. 309–313v Pro defunctis. Ends imperfectly. ff. 314–315v left blank.

12 (added). (*a*) f. 314v Dies ire dies illa . . . (*b*) f. 315v Officium beate anne.

(*a*). *RH*, no. 4626. (*b*). Not the same office as on f. 257.

13. Additions on the flyleaf, f. 316, some referring by leaf number to offices in the sanctoral.

ff. i + 315 + i. The medieval foliation in red i–cccxiiii on ff. 7–315 takes account of five missing leaves. 340 × 240 mm. Written space 230 × 150 mm. 2 cols. 30 lines (21 lines, ff. 147–52). Ruling in violet ink. Collation: 1^6 $2\text{–}10^8$ $11\text{–}12^6$ (ff. 79–90) $13\text{–}19^8$ 20^6 (ff. 147–52) $21\text{–}29^8$ 30^8 wants 2 after f. 225 $31\text{–}40^8$ 41^8 wants 3–6 after f. 313. Catchwords vertical in *lettre bâtarde*. Quires signed in the usual late medieval way. Initials: (i) blue or red patterned in white or shaded to white on grounds of gold or on grounds of gold paint decorated with naturalistic flowers (cf. for the two styles ff. 246, 280); (ii) f. 147v, gold *T* of *Te igitur* on blue and red ground decorated in gold paint; (iii) 2-line, blue or red with ornament of the other colour. Capital letters in the ink of the text filled with pale yellow. Binding of thick wooden boards, with pigskin over the spine and 70 mm of each board, s. xvi (?): 'Missale Lugdunense' on the spine. Secundo folio (f. 8) *in iordane*.

Written in France and given in or before 1489 for use in the chapel of Holy Cross at Nantua (Ain, 70 kms north-west of Lyons), as appears from the entry in the calendar at 30 Sept.: Hac die fiat anniuersarium R.p.d. domini anthonii bertrandi qui dedit hunc librum sue cappelle sancte crucis qui erat decretorum doctor canonicus sancti pauli off*icialis* lugd' et curatus nantuaci et dedit pro suo anniuersario dec' octo gross' soluend' per rectores dicte sue cappelle sancte crucis. de quibus xviii g' percipiat curatus tres g'. tam pro luminari quam pro sua missa dicenda in dicta sua cappella et dicatur missa de sancto iheronimo et dicti rectores quilibet duos gross' et vndecim gross' diuidantur inter presbiteros ville nantuaci presentes et adiuuantes et obiit die octaua marcii anno domini millesimo iiiic octuagesimo octauo `et fuerunt primi rectores dicte cappelle dominus glaudius goyffonis (?) et dominus anthonius motillieti nepos dicti domini anthonii bertrandi'. The arms of the Lyonnais family of Bertrand, gules six hawk's bells or (de Morenas, no. 4543), are in the initial on f. 7.

'Joseph Cuet', f. 316, s. xviii (?). A scribble, 'Monsieur Rossord' (?), on f. 291, s. xviii. Sotheby sale, 3 April 1939, lot 108.

42. *Lectionarium* s. xv[2]

One hundred and twenty single leaves, probably the unwanted remains of a book from which other leaves were taken for the sake of their decoration. Most principal feasts are headless.

1. ff. 1–72v Temporal from Easter.

2. ff. 73–75v Dedication of church, followed on f. 75v by a note on vespers 'De sanctis' from the octave of Easter to the octave of Pentecost.

3. ff. 76–120v Sanctoral, May–October.

Nineteen separable portions: f. 76, 3–6 May; ff. 77–8, 24–6 June; f. 79, 2 July; ff. 80–1, 9–14 July; f. 82, 18–22 July; ff. 83–6, 25 July–1 Aug.; ff. 87–9, 10–13 Aug.; ff. 90–1, 15–19 Aug.; ff. 92–3, 20–2 Aug.; ff. 94–5, 28 Aug.; ff. 96–7, 29–30 Aug.; f. 98, 1, 5 Sept.; ff. 99–100, 8 Sept.; ff. 101–2, 14, 15 Sept.; ff. 103–13, 17 Sept.–2 Oct.; ff. 114–15, 4 Oct.; ff. 116–17, 4–9 Oct.; f. 118, 11 Oct.; ff. 119–20, 14–28 Oct. Nine and three lessons. Feasts include Florianus, Visitation of B.V.M. (headless), translation of Augustine, Victorinus, translation of Ludger, and 'Duorum Ewaldorum' (4 May, 2 July, 11 Aug., 5 Sept., 3 Oct.).

ff. 120. 363 × 270 mm. Written space 270 × 185 mm. 2 cols. 32 lines. Catchwords ff. 61v, 91v. A signature, G, f. 20. Handsome black script. Initials: (i) f. 63, 4-line blue with red ornament, and ff. 43, 55, red with violet ornament; (ii, iii) 2-line and 1-line, red or blue. Capital letters in the ink of the text marked with red. Kept loose between pieces of cardboard.

Written in Germany for use in the diocese of Münster, where Ludger was bishop and the bodies of Victorinus and Florianus were principal relics.

50. *Graduale (fragm.)* s. xii med.

The musical parts of the office of mass. In s. xv ex. new texts were added in the margins, interlinear leaf references were written in above cues and some parts of the original text were written afresh, the ink having faded, for example most of f. 47r. The remaining pieces are from the temporal for the week after Pentecost and the sanctoral from 2 June which here follows Trinity Sunday immediately.

ff. 42–3 (Wednesday after Pentecost), beginning 'tur inimici' in Ps. 67: 1, followed by Friday and Saturday and 'De sancta Trinitate'.

ff. 43/5–47v Sanctoral, 2 June–9 Aug.: Marcellinus and Peter, Primus and Felician, 'Basilidis. Cyrini. N.', Marcus and Marcellinus, Gervase and Prothase, vigil and day of John Baptist, John and Paul, vigil and day of Peter, 'Festiuitas S. Pauli', Processus and Martinianus, 'Septem fratrum filiorum S. Fe.', Apollinaris, Felix Simplicius and Faustinus, Stephen, Sixtus Felicissimus and Agapitus, Cyriacus et soc., vigil of Laurence, ending in the offertory 'Oratio mea munda est et ideo peto ut detur lo'.

f. 49^{rv} Sanctoral, 15 Aug.–8 Sept.: Assumption of B.V.M. (only the last words of the communion 'us deus tuus' remain), 'Octaua sancti laurentii', Agapitus, Timothy and Simphorian, Hermes, decollation of John Baptist, Sabina, Felix and Adauct, Nativity of B.V.M., ending at 'clara ex stirpe' in the alleluia verse 'Natiuitas gloriose virginis marie'.

f. 56^{rv} 11th–14th Sundays after the octave of Pentecost, ending with the introit for the 14th Sunday. The forms are the same as the small print in *Bec Missal* (HBS xciv), pp. 107–10.

ff. 8. Medieval foliation xlii–xlvii, xlviiii, lvi. Written space 147 × 95 mm. 22 long lines: notes of music interlined. Collation: probably 1^8 wants 1 and 8 2^8 wants 2–8, these being originally the fifth and sixth quires. 2-line and 1-line red initials.

Written in Germany and there in s. xv ex. Used later in bifolia as pastedowns and flyleaves at either end of two volumes of a theological book, as appears from a reference note on f. 46^{v} 'Maria sine originali peccato concepta 81 L 83 L. 3'. Part of lot 531 in a Sotheby sale, 21 Dec. 1937: facsimile of f. 42 in the sale catalogue.[1]

51. *Kalendarium (fragm.)* s. xiii[1]

Two leaves containing a calendar for May–August in blue, red, and black.

Printed by F. C. Eeles, 'Part of the kalendar of a xiiith-century service book once in the Church of Writtle', *Transactions of the Essex Archaeological Society*, xxv (1955), 68–79. Original entries include: in blue, 'Sancti Ælberti regis et martiris' (20 May); in red, 'Translatio sancti Andree et sancti Nicholai' (9 May); in black, 'Silee apostoli' (13 July), 'Sixti episcopi. Felicissimi. et Agapiti. et transfiguratio domini' (6 Aug.). Much added to, mainly by two hands, one probably of s. xiii med. who added Potentiana, Petroc, Germanus, Martial, Mildred, Edith, Paulinus and Aidan (19, 27, 28 May, 7, 13, 15 July, 31 Aug.), the other, rather later, who wrote at a time when the 'beaver-tailed' *S* was in fashion[2] and added the translation of Richard (of Chichester), Anne, and Helena (16 June, 26 July, 18 Aug.), and gradings throughout, which agree closely with those given in Bishop Baldock's statutes for St Paul's Cathedral, 1294–5 (*Registrum Statutorum*, ed. W. S. Simpson, 1873, pp. 52–4), as Eeles noted: 'i^{e} dig.', ii^{e} dig.', iii^{e} dig.', 'ix lc' ', 'iii lc' ', 'pron' ' (*standing for* cum pronuntiatione euangelii), 'com.', 'festum' (for Dunstan and Augustine of England, 19, 26 May, only). Three other additions appear to pre-date the grading, Edmund confessor, Botulf, and translation of Thomas the Martyr (9, 17 June, 7 July). The grading hand is probably responsible for the interlined 'a' and 'b' at 9, 16 June and 18 Aug., which show that the added feast is to take precedence over the feast originally written; also for 'va cat' above Osith and Neot (3 June, 31 July). 'Non sarum' against John of Beverley, translation of Andrew and Nicholas, Petroc, Quirinus, Botulf, Leufridus (7, 9, 27 May, 4, 17, 20 June) looks later and is perhaps by the same hand as 'Nichomedis Martiris' (3 June, s. xiv/xv ?).

A conspicuous addition is handsomely written at 20 May: 'Obitus Magistri (*erased*) Iacobi de ciuitate sancti angeli custodis ecclesie omnium sanctorum de Writtele (*erased*) Anno domini Millesimo ccc^{o} xl^{o} viii^{o}. cuius anime propicietur deus'.

ff. 2. Written space 245 × 180 mm. Large gold KL partly cut off at the top on each page.

[1] Lot 531 was a collection of 58 examples of calligraphy each mounted on a card, 100 leaves or parts of leaves in all.

[2] This *M*-like *S* was common for forty years or so. The earliest specimen of it in C. Johnson and H. Jenkinson, *English Court Hand*, 1915, is of 1265 and the latest of 1303.

Written in England for use in, or in a church belonging to, St Paul's Cathedral London, where Ethelbert had an altar and was considered the founder: cf. *Documents illustrating the history of St Paul's Cathedral*, ed. W. S. Simpson (Camden Soc., new series xxvi, 1880), p. 56. The added grading is of St Paul's: Ethelbert is 'i^{e} di[g']'. The obit of 1346 points to a connection with Writtle, Essex, or at least with one of the wardens of the church there, which belonged to the hospital of Holy Spirit in Rome from 5 John until 14 Richard II, when it was bought by New College, Oxford. Used as pastedowns: May and August were the pasted sides. Probably part of the same collection of fragments as MS. 50, q.v., since the leaves show signs of having been mounted on cards.

59. *Agius, Compotus (fragm.)* s. ix^{2}

1. f. 1 A table of lunar epacts, etc.

The signs of the zodiac are set out one below the other on the left of the first of eleven columns: Arios Tauros Didim (?) Cancros Leon Parthinos Zichos Scorpeios Tenentis (?) Eleaceros Ydrochos Ichtis. Seven headings are one below the other in the first column: (1) Epacte lun*e*; (2) Ciclus lun*e*; (3) Linea angl'; (4) Regula; (5) Dies sol*is* ii lun' init'; (6) Ætas *lune* in k' Ian'; (7) Prime lun*e* primi mens*is* dies sol*is*. Figures and month dates for each year of a decennovenal cycle are set out against each of these headings in the remaining columns, ten in one horizontal line and nine in the next. The cycle starts with (1) xxv, (2) xvii, (3) n' ap*relis*, (4) v, (5) viii k' mar', (6) viiii, (7) x k' ap*relis*: 25 Mar. and 22 Apr. were Sundays in the year 882.

2. ff. 1^{v}–2^{v} COMPOTUS AGII INCIPIT PRAEFATIO. ILLUSTRI DOMINĘ REGINĘ MORIBUS ALMĘ LEODGARDAE FIDUM. AGIUS OBSEQUIUM. Cum cunctę penitus dentur diuinitus artes . . .

The first page and the last two pages of the computistical verses of Agius of Corvey, O.S.B., known hitherto only from a Basel manuscript printed in MGH, *Poetae Latinae Aevi Carolini*, iv (1923), 937–43.[1] Dedicated here to Queen Liutgard (wife of King Louis III of the East Franks, 876–82). The 20 lines on f. 1^{v} are I. 1–4, 7–22 in edn., but only 'omine claro' and 'agius obsequium' can be read there in lines 1, 2. f. 2/1, 2 = edn., VIII. 9, 10, and f. 2/12 Quocirca si nosse cupis . . .-21 = edn., VIII. 17–26: 2/12 is preceded by a heading (2/11) 'QUALITER XL ET PASCHA INUENIATUR'. The rest is not in edn.: (f. 2/3–10) Qua concurrentum numerus congestus habetur . . . Post septem plenas atque octoginta decadas'; (f. 2/22–2^{v}/22) Quot sint ebdomadae. quot soles forte supersint . . . AEUI PLASMATOR UOSMET CONSERUET IN AEUUM.

ff. 2. Cut down to 205 × 165 mm (f. 2) and 190 × 140 mm (f. 1). Written space 158 mm high. Pricks to guide ruling ranged along the outer of the two vertical bounders. 22 long lines. Bifolium. Headings, etc., in uncials. Red initials, 6-line *I* of *Illustri*, 2-line *Q* of *Quocirca* and 1-line *H* of *Hic* and *Haec* (f. 2/4, 2^{v}/9).

Written in Germany (Corvey ?). In use formerly in a binding, no doubt. Marked at the foot of f. 1 'Nro 8 Saec. IX', s. xix.

[1] I owe the reference and the date and localization to Professor Bernhard Bischoff. See also P. E. Schramm and F. Mütherich, *Denkmäle der deutschen Könige und Kaiser*, 2nd edn., 1981, pp. 474–5.

LIVERPOOL. MERSEYSIDE COUNTY MUSEUMS

Mayer Collection

The collection of antiquities formed by Joseph Mayer (†1886: *DNB*) was given by him to the City of Liverpool in 1867. It includes thirty-nine medieval manuscripts, twenty-five of which are described more or less briefly by C. T. Gatty, Liverpool Free Public Museum: *Catalogue of mediaeval and later Antiquities contained in the Mayer Museum*, 1883, pp. 6–11: MSS. 12001, 12006, 12010, 12017, and 12038 are illustrated by good facsimiles. The manuscripts are on deposit in Liverpool University Library.

12000. *Sermones* — s. xv^2

1. pp. 1–217 Incipit commune sanctorum. Sermo primus. De apostolis. Species celi gloria stellarum ecclesiastici 43(: 9) per celum enim proprie ecclesia designatur . . . non potest aput filium esse cassa. Amen.

Thirty-six sermons on the common of saints. Reference numbers in the upper margin, '1' to '16'. Each of these numbers is subdivided by letters in the side margins, 'a' to 'z' at irregular intervals. Also in Sélestat 21 (43), ff. 86–158, copied in Alsace in s. xv med.[1]

2. Two tables: (*a*) pp. 217–33 Actiua vita . . . 13 f . . . Vxor non est ducenda 6 b Amen. (*b*) pp. 233–9 Item alia Tabula. Dominica prima aduentus. Erunt signa in sole . . . Queras in sermone stelle manentes in Custodiis suis l. i . . . Item de dedicatione. domus mea . . . sermone ora(te pro inuicem) 11 d.

In (*a, b*) reference is to the numbers and letters in art. 1. (*b*) seems to be designed as a means of finding suitable texts in art. 1 for sermons on the Epistles of the temporal and dedication.

3. Pastedowns: (*a*) at the front on the exposed side, questions and answers on distinctions 93–6 and causa 1 of the Decretum of Gratian, for example, 'D xxiii (*sic for* xciii) c. Si inimicus . . . aduersum. contra c. vi q. ii c. Episcopus. si alieni . . . Respondeo. Istud generaliter de aliis episcopis istum specialiter pro priuilegio de summo pontifice intelligitur'. (*b*) at the back, questions on canon law: a section begins 'Episcopus quidam tam forensem. quam ecclesiasticum gerens amministrationem . . . primo queritur an episcopus secularem iurisdiccionem': references are to the Decretum.

(*a*) and (*b*) are each parts of a bifolium in long lines, s. xii ex. The hands differ. Strips from the same manuscript (?) lie as strengthening between and in the middle of quires.

ff. 120, paginated 1–(240). Paper, except art. 3. 215 × 145 mm. Written space 153 × 100 mm. 28 long lines. Collation: $1\text{–}10^{12}$. Written in cursiva: two-compartment *a* often. Red initials: (i) f. 1, 4-line; (ii) 3-line. Medieval binding of wooden boards covered with white (now brownish) leather: a label pasted to the front cover bears a 3-line title 'Commune

[1] Information from Mme M.-C. Garand.

sanctorum bene tabulatum / et portabilis per totum / annum de tempore et de sanctis': a chain of eight links is attached to the head of the back cover. Secundo folio *ab uxoribus*.

Written in Germany. 'N° 7' top left inside cover.

12001. *Horae* s. xv med.

1. ff. 1–12v Full calendar in French in gold, blue, and red, the two colours alternating.

'Saint denis' in gold. Visitation of B.V.M. and Transfiguration not entered.

2. ff. 13–20. Sequentiae of the Gospels. 'Protector in te sperancium . . .' after John.

3. ff. 20–5 Oratio de beata maria. Obsecro te . . . Masculine forms.

4. ff. 25–30v Oratio. O intemerata . . . orbis terrarum. De te enim . . .

5. ff. 31–36v Salue sancta parens . . .

Mass of B.V.M. Salve regina and Omnipotens sempiterne deus qui gloriose . . . follow the postcommunion.

6. ff. 37–116v Hours of B.V.M. of the use of (Paris). Nine lessons at matins.

7. ff. 117–140v Penitential psalms and (f. 131) 'Letania'.

Denis sixth of martyrs. Among confessors Dominic precedes Francis. Twenty-three virgins: . . . (12) Genouefa. The prayers after Deus cui are Pretende, Ineffabilem, Actiones, Deus a quo, Absolve, Deus qui es sanctorum.

8. ff. 141–154v Hours of Holy Cross, . . . Patris sapiencia . . .

Two leaves for each hour.

9. ff. 154v–163v Du saint esperit, . . . Prosa. Nobis sancti spiritus . . .

10. ff. 163v–219v De mors.

11. ff. 220–238v Memoriae of Holy Trinity, Michael, John Baptist, Peter and Paul, Thomas apostle, Stephen, Christopher, Sebastian, Eustace, Benignus, Adrian (Aue sancte adriane . . . (12 lines): *RH*, no. 2106), Peter martyr (O petre martyr inclite . . . : *RH*, no. 30815), Hippolytus, Vincent, Claude, Nicholas, Fiacre (O qui cuncta fabricasti . . . : *RH*, no. 13579), Katherine (Aue gemma claritatis . . . : *RH*, no. 1809), Avia, Geneviève, Mary Magdalene, All Saints.

12. ff. 239–46 Doulce dame de misericorde, mere de pitie . . . Sonet–Sinclair, no. 458.

13. ff. 246–249^{v} Les viii requestes. Doulx dieu doulx pere saincte trinite . . . Sonet–Sinclair, no. 504.

14. f. 250 Saincte uraye crois aouree . . . Sonet–Sinclair, no. 1876.

15. ff. 250–2 Les uers saint bernart. Illumina oculos . . . Oratio. Omnipotens sempiterne deus qui ezechie . . . f. 252^{v} blank.

16 (added). f. 253 Pour endurer mainte chose ilicite pour peu challoir et quanmode profite . . .

14 lines of verse, s. xvi. Below them 'Souffrir pour parvenir'.

ff. v + 212 + viii. ff. (iv, v), 253–(257) are flyleaves ruled like the rest of the manuscript. 216 × 155 mm. Written space 95 × 58 mm. 15 long lines. Ruling in red ink. Collation: 1^{12} $2\text{–}31^{8}$. Twenty-eight 11-line pictures, eight in art. 6, seven in art. 8, four in art. 2, one before each of arts. 3 (B.V.M. and (large) Child, who holds a harp on which an angel is playing), 4 (B.V.M. and (small) Child and two angels playing musical instruments), 5 (B.V.M. and Child in manger: Joseph kneels, cooking), 7, 9, 10, 12 (B.V.M. with book and Child: angels play musical instruments), 13 (Christ in glory on the day of judgement), and one at All Saints in art. 11 (the owners, man and wife, and a child kneel before the heavenly host: *MERT*, pl. 8; Gatty, pl. 4, reduced). Initials: (i) blue, patterned in white, on decorated gold grounds; (ii) 2-line, as (i), but the colours are blue or red; (iii) 1-line, gold on grounds of blue and red patterned in white. Continuous floral borders on picture pages: they include four or more roundels with appropriate scenes on the pages beginning arts. 6, 7, 8, 10. Borders on three sides of all other pages, usually mirror image, except for the sign of the zodiac half way down the outer border on each page of art. 1 and sometimes for the bird or other ornament which occupies this position on other pages. Line fillers red and blue patterned in white, the colours separated by blobs of gold. Capital letters in the ink of the text filled with pale yellow. Binding of indigo velvet, s. xix, with silver clasp-work, s. xviii, bearing the mark of the town of Amsterdam:[1] the designs on the clasps themselves are (upper) Moses and (lower) Aaron: the attachments on the front and back covers have each an evangelist's symbol: the title on the spine is 'Missale Romanum'. Secundo folio (f. 14) *ut testinomium.*

Written in France: 'related in style and iconography to later products of the workshop of the Bedford Master' (*MERT*, p. 25). The label of the 'National Exhibition of Works of Art, Leeds, 1868' is inside the cover. *MERT*, no. 32. Gatty, no. 12.

12004 + 8951. *Psalterium, etc.* s. xiii^{1}

H. Swarzenski, *Die lateinischen illuminierten Handschriften des xiii Jahrhunderts in den Ländern an Rhein, Main und Donau*, 1936, no. 53. H. Bober, *The St Blasien Psalter*, New York 1963, pp. 14–15, 27–9. W. Irtenkauf in *Bibliothek und Wissenschaft*, i (1964), 23–49 and ii (1965), 59–84. Paris, B.N., nouv. acq. lat. 187 (described by V. Leroquais, *Les psautiers manuscrits des bibliothèques publiques de France*, ii. 133–4), is a closely related psalter in a similar hand: cf. especially Bober, p. 14.

[1] I am grateful to Mrs Anthea James for the reference to Jan Divis, *Silver Marks of the World*, 1976, no. 1953.

1. pp. 1–12 Calendar all in black and without gradings. See Irtenkauf, i. 27–8, ii. 60–1.

As in the 'St Blasien Psalter' (Dyson Perrins 127) the illuminator has not bothered to keep within the spaces left by the scribe for pictures and initials here and in art. 2.

2. pp. 23–257 Psalms 1–150. Preceded by pictures (pp. 13–22).

3. pp. 257–8 Memoriae of Holy Spirit, B.V.M., John Evangelist, and Katherine.

4. pp. 259–81 Six ferial canticles, followed by Benedicite, Benedictus, Magnificat, Nunc dimittis, Pater noster, Credo, Te deum, Quicumque vult.

5. pp. 281–9 Litany.

The lists of martyrs, confessors, and virgins printed by Irtenkauf, ii. 61–3. The prayers after Deus cui proprium are Omnipotens sempiterne deus qui facis, Pretende domine famulis, Deus a quo, Ure igne, Actiones nostras, Animabus quesumus, Fidelium. p. 290 left blank.

6. p. 290 Prognostications by day of the week and from dreams in German (Swabian dialect), s. xiv.

Printed by R. Priebsch in *Bulletin of the Liverpool Museums*, i (1898), 121–2. Backward sloping fere-textura.

7. MS 8951, ff. 1–2^{v}, formerly pastedowns of 12004. 271 lines of the Parcival of Wolfram von Eschenbach, s. xiii med.

Printed ibid., pp. 119–21, with facsimiles of all four sides. The text corresponds to the edition by Lachmann, pp. 770/3–774/18, 783/19–788/3. Written space 153 × 120 mm. 2 cols. 34 lines. The first line of writing below the top ruled line. Ruling in ink. 2-line initials, blue or red with ornament of the other colour.

ff. 145. Paginated 1–290. Thick parchment. 257 × 185 mm. Written space 165 × 105 mm. 22 long lines. The first line of writing above the top ruled line. Collation: 1^{6} 2^{8} wants 1–3 (pp. 13–22) 3–16^{8} 17^{6} (pp. 247–58) 18–19^{8}. Clumsy hand. Black ink. The (once sixteen) full-page pictures in front of art. 2 (pp. 13–22) contain scenes from the life of Christ: see *MERT*, p. 18 and pl. 3 for a facsimile of p. 13. A protecting piece of fabric is still attached to p. 15. Signs of the zodiac and occupations of the months in art. 1. Initials: (i) of Pss. 1, 51, 101 and at p. 259, full-page or nearly, in colour on gold grounds historiated and framed in green: at Ps. 1 'EAT / VS / VIR' is in gold within the framed space: Ps. 101 is protected by a piece of fabric; (ii) of other principal psalms, as (i), but smaller, 7-line or 8-line, historiated at Pss. 26, 119, and elsewhere decorated; (iii) 3-line and (art. 4) 2-line, gold on grounds of green and blue or green and red patterned in white; (iv) 1-line, red filled in silver or blue filled in gold. Green and red line fillers in all sorts of shapes, often zoomorphic, were added in s. xiv. Contemporary (?) binding of wooden boards covered with green leather: three bands: two brass clasps in the form of a dove (Swarzenski refers to Manchester, John Rylands University Library, Lat. 95 and London, B.L., Add. 22280) fasten from front to back.

Written in southern Germany, much more probably for lay use than, as has been suggested from the evidence of arts. 1, 5, for the use of the Benedictine priory of St Blaise at Ochsenhausen, a cell of St Blasien. The Benedictine divisions of psalms do not occur, nor is Audite celi divided in art. 4. *MERT*, no. 10. Frere, no. 622. Gatty, no. 1.

12006. *Horae* s. xv²

1. pp. 1–24 Calendar in red and black.

Entries in red include 'Amandi episcopi', 'Bauonis et remigii', 'Donaciani episcopi', 'Thome canthuar' ' (6 Feb., 1, 14 Oct., 29 Dec.). 'Theobaldi episcopi' in black, 1 July. 'Visitacio marie' in black, 2 July. No entry of Transfiguration.

2. pp. 27–30 Oracio beate veronice cristi. Salue sancta facies . . .

Memoria of Holy Face.

3. pp. 30–9 Canticum beati athanasii. Quicumque vult . . .

4. pp. 41–55 Incipiunt hore de sancta cruce . . . Ymnus. Patris sapiencia . . . p. 56 left blank.

5. pp. 59–70 Incipiunt hore de sancto spiritu . . . Ymnus. Nobis sancti spiritus . . .

6. pp. 73–86 Missa beate marie virginis. Et introibo . . .

7. pp. 86–98 Sequentiae of the Gospels.

8. pp. 101–270 Incipiunt hore beate marie virginis secundum vsum Romanum.

p. 208 blank. Advent office, p. 253.

9. pp. 271–80 Deuota oracio ad mariam. Obsecro te . . . Masculine forms.

10. pp. 280–6 Alia oracio ad mariam. O intemerata . . . orbis terrarum. Inclina . . .

11. pp. 289–334 Septem psalmi penitenciales. Litany follows, p. 315.

Ten confessors: (9, 10) anthoni francisce. Eleven virgins: (6) clara . . . (11) elyzabeth. Deus cui proprium is preceded by Ps. 69 and by Saluos fac seruos . . . and followed by Exaudi, Ineffabilem, Deus qui culpa, Deus a quo, Ure igne, Fidelium, Actiones, Omnipotens sempiterne deus qui viuorum.

12. pp. 335–433 Office of the dead. pp. 434–6 blank.

13. pp. 437–59 Memoriae of John Baptist, Peter, Paul, James, Nicholas, Christopher (O martir cristofore . . . : *RH*, no. 29471), Sebastian, Francis (Salue sancte

pater patrie . . . : *RH*, no. 40727), Anthony of Padua (O proles hyspanie . . . : *RH*, no. 13447), Katherine, Barbara (O pulcra precipuum . . . : *RH*, no. 30857; *AH* xviii. 31), Mary Magdalene, Margaret. pp. 460–2 left blank.

14 (added). Memoria of Piatus added, s. xvi: 'O gloriose testis cristi piate salus et decus sicliniensis ecclesie . . .'.

ff. i + 231 + i, paginated 1–462, (463–4). 140 × 105 mm. Written space *c.* 77 × 53 mm. 15 long lines. Ruling in red ink. Collation: $1\text{–}2^6$ $3\text{–}8^8$ 9^8 + 2 leaves before 1 (pp. 131–4) $10\text{–}15^8$ 16^6 (pp. 275–86) $17\text{–}24^8$ 25^{10} (pp. 417–36) 26^8 27^4 + 1 leaf after 3 (pp. 459–60), together with twelve singleton leaves, with blank rectos and pictures on versos, pp. 26, 40, 58, 72, 100, 146, 174, 186, 198, 220, 240, 288. Written in *lettre bâtarde*. Seven full-page pictures in art. 8 (no picture now at none before p. 209; slaughter of Innocents at vespers; flight into Egypt at compline), and one before each of arts. 2, 4 (Gatty, pl. 5a), 5, 6 (angels crown B.V.M.), 11. Initials: (i) pp. 30, 253 and thirteen in art. 13, 7-line, dark blue patterned in white on grounds of pink patterned in gold paint, historiated: Gatty, pl. 5b shows p. 452, Katherine; (ii) 5-line, as (i), but with decoration on gold grounds instead of historiation; (iii) 3-line, blue patterned in white on decorated gold grounds: sprays into the margin; (iv) 2-line, gold on grounds of blue and pink patterned in white; (v) 1-line, blue with red ornament or gold with grey-blue ornament. Line fillers only in the litany: gold and blue. Continuous framed floral borders on pages with pictures and initials of types (i) and (ii), except in art. 13, where the borders are only above and below the written space: they include grotesques, birds, etc., at the mid point in the outer border. Binding of s. xviii. Secundo folio (p. 29) *tui domine*.

Written in the southern Low Countries (Bruges). The pictures and initials 'painted in tones of grey with some blue, silver and gold . . . are from the atelier of William Vrelant' (*MERT*, p. 26). Arms on p. 56, s. xvi (?), quarterly 1 and 4 argent an eagle displayed sable 2 and 3 quarterly or and sable: a swan as crest. 'Liuinus Brakelman habuit hunc librum 1666, 29 Iulii', p. 1. *MERT*, no. 38. Gatty, no. 16.

12008. *Biblia* s. xiii med.

1. pp. 1–930 The usual books of the Bible in the common order: cf. above, Liverpool Cathedral 13. The prologues are the common set of 64, Haggai missing, together with two others, Stegmüller no. 540 before 539 (Zechariah) and a prologue to 2 Maccabees not recorded by Stegmüller, 'Secundus liber machabeorum licet breuior . . . Vnde idem ita incipit . . .'. Two more prologues, no. 516 (Obadiah) and no. 532 (Zephaniah) are in the main hand in the margins.

The Prayer of Manasses is set off from 2 Chronicles by a type (ii) initial and is headed 'Oracio salomonis (*sic*)'. The last chapters of Job are squeezed in and partly in the margins of pp. 405–6: the psalter begins on a new quire (p. 407) and in a new hand: psalms are abbreviated sometimes. The heading of Proverbs, 'Parabole salomonis secundum hebraicam . . .', is written as though it were part of the prologue. p. 696 breaks off in the prologue to Zephaniah and p. 697 begins in the prologue to Zechariah: two leaves are missing.

2. pp. 933–1024 Aad (*sic*) apprehendens . . . consiliatores eorum.

The usual dictionary of Hebrew names. On pp. 1024–5, left blank, a hand of s. xiv added a list of the books of the Bible and the six ferial canticles.

ff. i + 513, paginated (i, ii), 1-1026. Thin parchment. The pastedowns and f. i are medieval leaves. 153 × 105 mm. Written space 102 × 70 mm. 2 cols. (3 cols., pp. 933-1024). 48 lines. Collation: $1-8^{20}$ 9^{22} 10^{20} + 1 leaf after 20 (pp. 405-6) 11^{20} 12^{18} + 1 leaf in the first half of the quire 13^{20} 14^{22} $15-17^{20}$ 18^{20} wants 5, 6 after p. 696 $19-22^{20}$ $23-24^{24}$ 25^{20} 26 three. *Ad hoc* signatures in red and blue inks, the latter in quires 18-22. Very small writing. Initials: (i) of books and the eight main divisions of the Psalms, usually 6-line, in colour on coloured grounds, historiated; (ii) of prologues and Ps. 51 (but not Ps. 101) as (i), but decorated, instead of historiated, and usually smaller; (iii) of chapters, 2-line, blue or red, with ornament of both colours running the height of the written space; (iv) of verses of Psalms, 1-line, blue or red. Capital letters in the ink of the text marked with red. Binding of s. xix. Secundo folio *librum teneret*.

Probably written in France. '3.13.6' top left, f. i^{v}. Gatty, no. 2.

12009. *Horae* s. xv^{1}

For this type of hours see *MMBL* i. 46, ii. 593. The leaves are in disorder. The original positions of arts. 2, 3 before art. 4 and of the pictures illustrating arts. 2, 10, 17 are inferred from other books.

1. pp. 1-24 Calendar in red and black.

Many English saints (cf. Gatty, *Cat.*, p. 9), but, Thomas apart, the only ones in red are Hugh (17 Nov.: octave in black) and his translation (6 Oct.: octave in black) and Edmund, king and martyr (20 Nov.). Added births and deaths of the Ewer family of Pinner (Middlesex), 1565-89, are printed by T. C. Gatty, *Transactions of the Historical Society of Lancashire and Cheshire*, xxxiii (1880), 158-63. Earlier is 'Obitus willelmi Boleyn' Militis qui obiit anno domini m. ccccc^{o}. quinto' at 10 Oct. (of Blickling, Norfolk: will PCC Holgrave 40, 8 Oct. 1505, proved 27 Nov. 1505). The word 'pape' and entries of Thomas of Canterbury cancelled.

2. pp. 65-70, 75-9 Oracio deuota ad cristum. O ihesu criste eterna dulcedo . . .

The Fifteen Oes of St Bridget. p. 80 blank.

3. pp. 41-2, 45-6, 49-50, 53-4, 57-60, 63-4, 81-2 Memoriae of eight saints, Christopher, Katherine, John Baptist, Thomas of Canterbury (crossed through), Margaret, Barbara, George, Mary Magdalene.

The antiphons are the same eight as in Dulwich College 25 (*MMBL* i. 47), *RH*, nos. 18445, 6991, 26988, 26999, 7011, 6714, 7242, 6895. The arrangement is by pairs of saints, one on the first leaf and one on the second leaf of each of four bifolia: the pairs which go together are Christopher and Katherine, John Baptist and Barbara, Thomas and Margaret, George and Mary Magdalene. The present order is unlikely to be original.

4. pp. 27-30, 87, 88, 31-4, 93-4, 35-8, 71, 72, 83-6, 89-92, 95-8, 73-4, 99-121 Incipiunt hore beate marie uirginis secundum consuetudinem anglie.

Memoriae after lauds of Holy Spirit, Holy Trinity, Holy Cross, Michael, John Baptist, Peter and Paul, Andrew, Stephen, Laurence, Thomas of Canterbury (Tu per thome . . . , crossed out), Nicholas, Mary Magdalene, Katherine, Margaret, All Saints and for peace. Hours of the Cross worked in. p. 100 is blank after prime.

5. pp. 121, 112*–113* Salue regina . . . V'. Virgo mater ecclesie . . .

RH, nos. 18147, 21818. p. 114* blank.

6. pp. 117*–121*, 122–4 Has uideas laudes . . . Salue. Salue uirgo uirginum . . .

7. pp. 124–7 Oracio deuota ad mariam. O intemerata . . . orbis terrarum inclina . . . ego miserrimus peccator . . .

8. pp. 127–31 Item alia oracio ad mariam. Obsecro te . . . michi famulo tuo . . .

9. pp. 131–3 Aue mundi spes maria aue mitis aue pia . . . *RH*, no. 1974. p. 134 blank.

10. pp. 137–41 Quicumque hec septem gaudio (*sic*) . . . Uirgo templum trinitatis . . .

The heading conveys indulgence of 100 days from Pope Clement 'qui hec septem gaudia proprio stilo composuit'. p. 142 blank.

11. pp. 143–7 Ad ymaginem cristi crucifixi. Omnibus consideratis . . .

AH xxxi. 87–9. *RH*, no. 14081 (etc.). p. 148 blank.

12. (*a*) pp. 149–51 Oracio uenerabilis bede . . . sibi preparatam. Oracio. Domine ihesu criste qui septem uerba . . . (*b*) p. 151 Precor te piissime . . .

13. pp. 152–3 Deus qui uoluisti pro redempcione mundi . . .

14. (*a*) pp. 153–4 Aue domine ihesu criste uerbum patris . . . (*b*) p. 154 Aue principium . . . (*c*) pp. 154–5 Aue uerum corpus domini nostri ihesu cristi natum . . . (*d*) p. 155 Aue caro cristi cara . . . (*e*) p. 155 Anima cristi sanctifica me . . . (*f*) pp. 155–6 Omnibus confessis . . . Domine ihesu criste qui hanc sacratissimam carnem . . . , with heading conveying indulgence of 2,000 years from Pope Boniface 'ad supplicacionem philippi regis francie'.

(*c*–*e*). *RH*, nos. 2175, 1710, 1090.

15. pp. 157–83 Incipiunt septem psalmi penitenciales . . . (p. 171) Litany.

Sixteen confessors: . . . (15, 16) swithine vrine. Twenty-five virgins: . . . (15) editha. The prayers after Deus cui proprium are Pretende, Animabus, Omnipotens sempiterne deus qui facis, Deus qui caritatis, Ineffabilem, Exaudi, Absolue, Concede, Fidelium, Pietate tua. p. 184 blank.

16. pp. 187–90, 193–4, 191–2, 195–202, 205–6, 203–4 Office of the dead. p. 220 blank.

17. pp. 221–39 Incipiunt commendaciones animarum . . .

Pss. 118, 138 and prayers Tibi domine and Misericordiam. p. 240 blank.

18. pp. 243–9 Incipit psalterium de passione domini. Deus deus meus . . . p. 250 blank.

19. pp. 250–71 Beatus uero iheronimus in hoc modo . . . regnum eternum amen. Oracio. Suscipere digneris . . . amen. Incipit psalterium sancti iheronimi. Verba mea auribus . . . Oracio. Omnipotens sempiterne deus clemenciam tuam . . . pp. 272–4 blank.

ff. ii + 242 + ii, paginated (i–iv), 1–112, 112*–121*, 122–274, (275–8). 180 × 132 mm. Written space 105 × 72 mm. 21 long lines. Collation: 1 six (pp. 1–12) 2^{6} (pp. 13–24) 3^{6} (pp. 65–70, 75–80) $4–7^{2}$ (see above, art 3) 8^{8} (pp. 27–30, 87–8, 31–4, 93–4, 35–8) 9^{8} (pp. 71–2, 83–6, 89–92, 95–8, 73–4) 10^{8} (pp. 99–114) 11^{8} (pp. 115–21, 112*–14*, 117*–21*, 122) 12^{8} (pp. 123–34, 137–40) $13–14^{8}$ (pp. 141–72) 15^{8} (pp. 173–84, 187–90), $16–18^{8}$ (pp. 191–238) 19^{8} (pp. 239–52, 255–8) 20^{8} (pp. 259–74), together with twelve inserted leaves with blank rectos and full-page pictures on the versos. The twelve pictures—probably there were once a dozen more—are: five in art. 4 (Barbara, Christopher, Katherine, Thomas, Mary Magdalene: pp. 26, displaced, 40, 44, 52, 56, displaced); one before art. 2, displaced at p. 48 (Christ with orb: angels attend Him); one before art. 6 (B.V.M. and Child in glory); one before art. 10, displaced at p. 136 (B.V.M. on the steps of the Temple); one before art. 16 (p. 186); one before art. 17, displaced at p. 62 (two haloed figures are carried to heaven by angels); one before art. 18 (p. 242, Christ rises from the tomb); one before art. 19 (p. 254, Jerome). Initials: (i) 5-line, red or blue patterned in white, on decorated gold grounds; (ii) 2-line, gold on grounds of red and blue patterned in white; (iii) 1-line, blue with red ornament or gold with blue-grey ornament. Line fillers in litany only: gold and blue or red and blue. Capital letters in the ink of the text stroked with red. Nearly continuous borders on pages with initials of type (i). On pp. 124, 127 a bar of gold and colours beside the written space marks the beginnings of arts. 7, 8. Binding of red velvet over wooden boards, s. xix: silver corner-pieces. Secundo folio (p. 29) *adorant*.

Written in the Low Countries for use in England. 'The illumination is by the Master of Nicholas Brouwer working in Utrecht' (*MERT*, p. 25). 'Iohn Serne owe thys boke `sometyme'', f. 1, s. xv/xvi. Belonged to the Ewer family, s. xvi^{2}: cf. art. 1. 'B. Chandler', p. 272, s. xix. A letter from J. (?) Brownbill, 32 Windsor Road, Tuesbrook, 9 Dec. 1893, is loose inside the cover. *MERT*, no. 34. Gatty, no. 15.

12010. *Breviarium, Pars hiemalis* s. xv med.

1. ff. 1–6v Calendar in red and black, graded—usually in a specially ruled column—Summum festum, Duplex, Semiduplex, Collecta, Off', ix l', iii l', omelia.

Entries in red include 'Albini martiris ix lc' x^{m} martirum', 'Gereonis et uictoris et sociorum martirum duplex', 'Vndecim milium virginum duplex', 'Kuniberti episcopi semiduplex' (22 June, 10, 21 Oct., 12 Nov.); also the Visitation and Presentation of B.V.M. (2 July, 21 Nov., both duplex), 'Festum uenerabilis sacramenti' (26 May, no grading) and the Transfiguration (5 Aug., duplex). The Three Kings, 23 July, and 'Obitus tercii regis', 12 Jan., are duplex, but not in red. A line of Cisiojanus (Cisioianus ephy sibi vendicat oc feli mar an . . .) at the foot of each month.

2. f. 7^{rv} Table of a great cycle of 532 years and circular diagrams of solar and lunar cycles, accompanied by explanations, (f. 7) Ista tabula docet inuenire in quo signo luna sit . . . , (f. 7^{v}) Volens scire ex hac figura ciclum solarem . . . , (f. 7^{v}) Volens scire ex hac figura ciclum lunarem . . .

3. ff. 8–100 Liturgical psalter.

Some fifteen leaves are missing. On f. 77, after lauds, is the heading 'Hee preces obseruande sunt ad matutinas et ad vesperas quando legitur nocturnus': the series beginning 'Ego dixi domine miserere mei' is complete in Liverpool Cathedral 4, art. 6 (q.v.), but breaks off here at no. 15, owing to the loss of a leaf after f. 77. ff. 8^{r}, 66^{r} were damaged in s. xviii (?), in order to conceal imperfections: cf. below, decoration.

4. ff. 100–3 Sancta letania.

'Sancti tres reges' after Innocents. Thirty-one confessors: . . . (5–8) seuerine cuniberte heriberte anno. Twenty-six virgins: . . . (10, 11) walburgis geirthrudis . . . (25, 26) pinnosa cordula.

5. (*a*) ff. 103–106^{v} In summis festis in primis vesperis Suffragia. (*b*) ff. 106^{v}–108^{v} Item hic sequuntur preces quadragesimales. (*c*) f. 108^{v} Ab octauis pasche usque ad vigiliam penth' inclusiue sabbato suffragium ad vesperas. Cristus resurgens . . . (*d*) ff. 108^{v}–111^{v} De sanctis suffragiis.

(*a*). Memoriae of Holy Cross, B.V.M., Peter, Three Kings, and All Saints. (*d*) includes proper offices for Peter and feasts of B.V.M. at vespers.

6. ff. 111^{v}–118^{v} Per aduentum domini. Ad uesperas ympnus. Conditor . . .

Twenty-three hymns of the temporal and sanctoral in one series, Advent–Ascension, and six hymns of the common. The former are nos. 5–7, 44, 45, 8, 10, 32, 11–24 of the series in Liverpool Cathedral 4, art. 16, together with Fit porta for the Annunciation of B.V.M., between Passion Sunday (17) and Easter (18).

7. ff. 119–322^{v} Temporal from Advent to the vigil of Pentecost, beginning and ending imperfectly. f. 119 is damaged: see below.

8. ff. 323–404 Sanctoral from Andrew (begins imperfectly) to Servatius (30 Nov.–13 May), followed by Quirinus (ff. 400–4, 4 June: nine lessons) and (f. 404) the words 'et hec sufficiunt de sanctis usque ad festum pentecostes pro parte hyemali etc'.

9. ff. 404^{v}–422 Incipit commune sanctorum secundum verum ordinem maioris ecclesie Coloniensis.

Four leaves missing, one at the beginning, one after f. 407, and one after f. 414.

10. ff. 422^{v}–424^{v} Directions for services, headed 'In duplicibus festis', 'In festo nouem leccionum', 'Item in semiduplici festo', 'Item de festo officiato nota',

'Item de festo trium leccionum', 'De tempore aduentus', 'Item de septuagesimo', 'De festo pasche. nota bene'.

ff. 424. 183 × 140 mm. Written space 105 × 82 mm. 25 long lines. Mainly in eights: many leaves missing. Well written in good black ink. Initials: (i) in colour on gold grounds, historiated or decorated, the latter sometimes supported by pictures in the borders, for example at Ps. 131 (f. 90), Christ washing feet: cf. *MERT*, p. 27): on ff. 19, 37, 189, 367v, 387 the layout of the page permits the initial in the first column to extend to the right so that it covers some 15 mm of the second column and on f. 367v the text is out of its proper order in order to accommodate the initial in a suitable position on the page; (ii–iv) 4-line (or more), 3-line and 2-line, gold on grounds of red and blue with floral patterning in white; (v) 1-line, blue or red. The quality of the gold and colours is outstanding. Gatty, pl. III, shows f. 194v, with initials of types (ii, iii), and f. 367v, with an initial of type (i), both slightly reduced; *MERT*, pl. 9b shows f. 19 much reduced. Borders on main pages contain distinctive gold sprays and knotwork: on ff. 19, 37 they are crowded with further ornament, including coats of arms (cf. *MERT*, p. 27). In s. xviii (?) damage due to missing leaves was made less obvious by painting over part of the text on ff. 8, 66. Binding of wooden boards, bevelled on the inside and covered with dark brown leather (s. xvi ?).

Written for use in the diocese of Cologne. '**BOUDOT 1666**' and '**MARIA**' in the margin, f. 230v. Gatty, no. 11. *MERT*, no. 43: 'Two leaves from an Antiphonal illuminated by the same hand are in the Fitzwilliam Museum, Cambridge, MSS. 205, 275. The style of decoration is comparable to that in a group of Books of Hours which have been attributed to Stefan Lochner'. Frere, no. 618.

12012. *Chronicon inrotulatum* s. xv med.

Joseph Mayer exhibited this chronicle at the Chester Congress of the British Archaeological Association in 1849 (*Journal*, vi (1851), 149–50) and William Bell read a paper on it to the Association on 3 April 1850 and printed a translation of it, *Thomas Sprott's Chronicle of Profane and Sacred History*, Liverpool 1851, which is accompanied by an 'Anastatic Fac Simile of the Entire Original Codex'. The membranes contain art. 1 on one side and art. 2 on the other.

1. [C]onsiderans sacre historie prolixitatem . . . ad nostrum ordine perduxi. Adam in agro damasceno . . .

The genealogy, Adam to Christ attributed to Peter of Poitiers, lies on each side of the line of descent. Stegmüller, no. 6778. Cf. P. S. Moore, *The Works of Peter of Poitiers*, 1936, pp. 97–117, 188–96. The last words here are on the sixth membrane (F), 'antonius cum eo regnauit'; the next and last paragraph of the text, *Iste Tiberius* . . . (see below, Mayer 12017) does not occur here.

2. [T]emporum summam lineamque descendentem ab exordio mundi . . . nos admonent. Formatus itaque adam . . .

The descent of the kings of England from Adam. The prologue *Temporum* . . . *admonent* is an abbreviation of the prologue of Flores historiarum, ed. Luard (RS), i. 1/1–2/4. Ends imperfectly at the foot of the twelfth membrane (M) at 'de sanguine propinquiori Regum defu(n)ctorum'. These words come shortly after a notice of the death of Edward I and below roundels containing his name and the names of his eleven children.

The line of descent, strung with small and a few larger roundels, is flanked on each side by text. The lines of the kings of Kent, the East Saxons, South Saxons, and West Saxons are in four columns as far as the coronation of Egbert.

Now twelve membranes, separated and laid flat and numbered A–M. B–L are each about 840 mm long, A and M shorter (780 and 580 mm). Width *c.* 285 mm. Ruling is with a hard point on the side containing art. 2. Untidy anglicana formata: single compartment *a.*[1] Larger roundels, up to 80 mm across, contain coloured penwork pictures, (1–8) in art. 1 and (9–17) in art. 2: (1) on A, Adam and Eve at the tree; (2) on A, gathering grapes; (3) on A, Abraham's sacrifice; (4) on C, David harping; (5) on D, Zedekiah; (6) on F, Manger; (7) on F, Crucifixion; (8) on F, Christ rising from the tomb, the names of the twelve apostles in roundels about it and of Paul, Barnabas, and Matthias in roundels below it on membrane G: (9) on A, as (1); (10) on A, as (2); (11) on A, rainbow; (12) on B, Brutus; (13–16) on G, the four kings Hengistus, Kynwynus, Elle, Cerdicus in a row; (17) on L, William I holding a drawn sword.

Written in England. Belonged to Joseph Mayer in 1849. Gatty, no. 20.

12016. *Psalterium; Hymni cum notis; etc.* s. xv med.

1. (*a*) pp. 1–7 Settings of Venite exultemus domino, beginning imperfectly. (*b*) p. 7 Settings of Gloria patri. (*c*) pp. 8–10 Examples of the eight tones, 'Primus Tonus. Primum querite regnum dei . . . Octauus tonus ut sic. Octo sunt beatitudines . . .'. (*d*) pp. 10–12 Setting of Benedicamus domino and Ite missa est.

2. pp. 13–118 Omnibus dominicis diebus a Domine ne in ira usque ad sexagesimam quando die dominica agitur Inuitatorium Preocupemus . . .

Liturgical psalter. A quire now missing after p. 110 contained Pss. 109–31: the text recommences at 134: 2, 'tum in capite: quod descendit'. Two-leaf gaps after pp. 34, 94.

3. pp. 119–24 Litanies.

Brev. ad usum Sarum, ii. 250–60. The phrase 'Ut dompnum apostolicum . . .' is untouched.

4. pp. 124–6 Noted office of the dead, ending imperfectly 'oculi mei'.

Ibid. ii. 271–4/2 up.

5. Noted hymns, often in more than one setting: (*a*) pp. 127–46 Temporal to Corpus Christi, beginning imperfectly at line 7 of Aeterna celi; (*b*) pp. 146–7 In dedicatione ecclesie; (*c*) pp. 147–9 O lux beata trinitas, Nocte surgentes, Ecce iam noctis; (*d*) pp. 149–64 Sanctoral, Vincent–All Saints, Andrew, Thomas, Matthew, John Evangelist; (*e*) pp. 164–86 Common of saints; (*f*) pp. 186–94 Iam lucis orto, Nunc sancte nobis, Rector potens, Rerum deus.

Ibid. III. ciii–v: (*a*) nos. 32–63; (*b*) nos. 67–8; (*c*) nos. 64–6; (*d*) nos. 82, 83, 86, 87, 85, 88–91, 108, 96, 97, 99–101, 109, 110, 113, 111, 112, 114, 115, 79, 84, 98; (*e*) nos. 69–78;

[1] The anastatic facsimile gives a good idea of the script, but does not reproduce it exactly.

(*f*) nos. 5–8. In (*d*), p. 161, 'require in fine libri' in the margin against 'Impleta sunt' refers to art. 8*d*.

6. Noted offices: (*a*) pp. 194–200 In nocte Natiuitatis domini dum canitur . . . Liber generationis . . . (p. 196) Te deum . . . (p. 198) Laudes deo dicam . . . ; (*b*) pp. 200–4 Benedictio cerei paschalis . . . Exultet iam angelica . . . ; (*c*) pp. 204–6 Sequencia sancti euangelii secundum Lucam . . . Factum est autem cum baptizaretur . . . ; (*d*) pp. 206–9 Omnipotens sempiterne deus adesto . . . Per omnia . . . Vere dignum et iustum . . . infanciam renascatur. Per dominum . . . amen.

Manuale Sarum: (*a*) p. 5; (*b*) p. 23, In vigilia pasche; (*c*) p. 7, Evangelium in nocte epyphanie; (*d*) pp. 33–5/16 Benedictio fontis.

8. pp. 210–16 Ten noted hymns, supplementing art. 5: (*a*) Visitation of B.V.M. (3); (*b*) Transfiguration (3); (*c*) Epiphany (2); (*d*) Invention of Cross (2).

(*a–d*) in the main hand. (*a–c*). *Brev. ad usum Sarum*, III. ciii–v, nos. 92–4, 102–4, 13, 14. (*d*). Ibid. iii. 274 (stanzas 4–8 of Vexilla regis) and 279 (stanzas 3, 5 of Lustra sex).

9 (added, s. xv^2). (*a*) pp. 217–19 Ympni de festo nominis ihesu. (*b*) pp. 219–25 Subuenite sancti dei . . . vel saltem De profundis etc. (*c*) pp. 225–6 Two forms of Tristes erant apostoli and Claro paschali gaudio.

(*a*), (*b*) and (*c*) are in different hands. (*a*). Ibid. III. cv, nos. 105–7. Noted. (*b*). Psalms and noted antiphons of the burial office: *Manuale Sarum*, pp. 123–4, 153–62/2. (*c*). *Brev. ad usum Sarum*, ii. 356, 358.

ff. i + 113, paginated (i, ii), 1–226. 275 × 200 mm. Written space 205 × 152 mm. 32–6 long lines and (pp. 127–219) 13 long lines and music. Collation: 1^2 2^4 3^8 4^8 wants 4, 5 after p. 34 $5–7^8$ 8^8 wants 4, 5 after p. 94 9^4 + 1 leaf after 4 (pp. 109–10) $10–11^8$ 12^2 (pp. 143–6) 13^8 14^4 + 1 leaf after 6 (pp. 175–6) $15–16^8$ 17^4 (pp. 209–16) 18^2 19^2 + 1 leaf after 2 (pp. 225–6). Initials: (i) 6-line, blue patterned in red, with red ornament; (ii) 2-line, blue with red ornament; (iii) 1-line, blue or red. Cadels have greenish ornament. Contemporary binding of wooden boards covered with pink leather, now dirty white, except on the turn-ins: four bands: two strap-and-pin fastenings, the pins missing: three nails at the foot of the front cover and two nails at the foot of the back cover have left rust marks on pp. 1, 225.

Written in England. 'Iste liber constat ecclesie de Cardyngton (*Bedfordshire*) ex dono Thome Swetbon', p. 216, s. xv/xvi. Other names in scribbles, s. xvi, are: 'Thomas Dignam', p. 216; 'Wellam Welfard', p. 12; 'Francys buttman. Frances Allen otherwise buttman', p. 81; 'lenarde butman ys a knaue', p. 146; 'simon canon', p. 223. Gatty, no. 13. Frere, no. 621.

12017. *P. Pictaviensis, Genealogia; etc.* s. xiii med.

A roll, now of fourteen membranes.

1. Membrane 1. Quod dicitur pater noster qui es in celis. breuis est captio beneuolentie . . . et paupertas spiritus. Amen.

On the Lord's Prayer. Bloomfield, no. 8378.

2. Membrane 1. A diagram headed 'Hec figura ualet ad intelligendum quod dicitur in numeris de disposicione tribuum . . .

The same heading and diagram, but much smaller, are in art. 4.

3. Membrane 2. A drawing of a seven-branched candlestick and text to go with it, 'De candelabro. Tres calami id est tria brachia ex vno latere . . .'. Cf. *Lyell Cat.*, p. 214.

4. Membranes 2–10. A red and yellow stem down the middle, with small and some larger roundels strung on it, is flanked by texts in columns about 85 mm wide. The first paragraph on the left is 'Considerans hystorie sacre prolixitatem . . . secundum nostrum ordinem perduxi' and the first on the right 'Incipit historia de Adam et Eua. Adam in agro damasceno . . .

The genealogy from Adam to Christ: cf. above, Mayer 12012. The last few paragraphs on each side are reproduced by Gatty, pl. 2. The last on the right is the usual ending, 'De Tyberio cesare. Iste Thyberius . . . passus est Qui cum patre . . . amen'. The last on the left is 'De cibis a domino sumptis. Sciendum est cibos a domino sumptos post resurrexionem . . . solis candens', which follows the paragraph 'De Paulo et Barnaba'. Roundels to left and right of the two columns of text contain names of kings (Antioch, Babylon) and other persons.

5. Membrane 11. A short membrane, 175 X 200 mm, containing a two-compartment picture, 80 X 170 mm: on the left, Christ and his disciples; on the right, a king, named in a much later hand 'Octauianus Augustus tocius orbis monarchus'.

6. Membranes 12–14. 'Cathalogus siue Cronica omnium pontificum et imperatorum' in two columns: (*a*) popes on the left, 'Dominus noster ihesus cristus primus et summus pontifex . . . Iohannes Natione Rom' sedit Annis x Mensibus ii (*ends imperfectly*); (*b*) emperors on the right, 'Octauianus Augustus imperauit . . . Eo quod franci non adiuuabant Romanos contra longobard . . . (*ends imperfectly*).

(*a*) ends now at John (VIII, 872–82) and (*b*) at Berengar (915–24). Under Mauricius the 'Pantheon Magistri Godefridi' of Viterbo is noticed.

7. Dorse, membrane 1. Notes on the ark and the golden candlestick.

8. Dorse, membranes 2, 3. Notes: (*a*) 'Ieronimus in annalibus libris hebreorum inuenit signa xv dierum ante diem iudicii . . .'; (*b*) Three paragraphs on the tabernacle, the priestly vestments, and the sanctuary within the tabernacle; (*c*) One paragraph, beginning 'Dixit dominus ad Moysen faciant michi filii israel sanctuarium' and ending with Alexander's translation of the sepulchre of Jeremiah to Alexandria; (*d*) On the ten commandments, 'Non habebis deos alienos . . . nec omnia que illius sunt. Hic autem prohibet concupiscentiam rei mobilis et secundum Origenem vnum est preceptum'.

(*c*). Epiphanius is referred to as a source.

Membranes measure *c.*520 mm in length (but 1, 2, 10, 11 are shorter) and *c.*210 mm (later *c.*200 mm) in width. A small back-sloping informal textura. The small roundels on the main stem are alternately red and green. In art. 4 larger roundels, up to 65 mm across, contain pictures on blue or blue and pink grounds: (1) Christ blessing; (2) Adam and Eve at the tree; (3) entry into the ark; (4) Abraham's sacrifice; (5) David; (6) Zedekiah; (7) Babylon; (8) Manger; (9) Crucifixion; (10) Resurrection; (11) Ascension: (9–11) are shown in the slightly reduced facsimile of the lower part of membrane 10 by Gatty, pl. 2. Six pictures in art. 6, three popes, Silvester, Gregory the Great, and Leo, and three emperors, Constantine, Eraclius, and 'Carolus' (Charlemagne), in roundels within square frames. See also art. 5. The style is 'reminiscent of Matthew Paris . . . and particularly in the grotesque faces in profile, of the Apocalypse at Trinity College, Cambridge (R. 16. 2)' (*MERT*, p. 20). Initials: (i) beginning art. 6, blue and red *D* and *O*, with ornament of both colours; (ii, iii) 2-line and 1-line, red or blue with ornament of the other colour; (iii) in art. 6, 1-line, red or blue.

Written in England. *MERT*, no. 14. Gatty, no. 6.

12020. *Horae* s. xv²

1. pp. 3–14 Calendar in Netherlandish in red and black, the black feasts graded, the red usually not.

The only entries marked 'duplex' are two in black: 'Sanctarum sororum marie' and 'Commemoratio solemnis marie' (25 May, 17 July). Feasts in red include Apollonia (9 lessons), Adrian, George, Basil, Donatian (9 Feb., 4 Mar., 23 Apr., 14 June, 14 Oct.); also the Visitation and Presentation of B.V.M. Dominican feasts in black include 'S' vincent predicaere ix lc' ', 6 Apr. 'S' thomas van aqwyn', 'Sint Iob propheta' and 'S' niclaes van tollentum' are later additions (7 Mar., 10 May, 19 Sept.).

2. pp. 19–23 (*begins imperfectly, Deus cui proprium est mi*)sereri semper et parcere . . . : followed by Pss. 124–6, 128 (cues only), the prayer Pretende domine famulis, Pss. 129–33 (cues only of 129, 130) and the prayer Absolue quesumus domine animas famulorum famularumque . . .

Ps. 124 marked 'souet te sexte', Pss. 125–6 'souet dese ii te noenen' and Pss. 128–9 'souet dese te complie'.

3. (*a*) pp. 24–92, 15–18 Hier beghinnen de daghelijexe ghetiden van onser vrouwe na der vsage van den Carmers. (*b*) pp. 93–110 (*begins imperfectly*) uirgo dei genitrix. Lauda anima mea dominum . . . (*c*) pp. 110–74 In deser dauolghende maniere sult ghi gheminde alle zondaghe van paesschen toten aduente uwe mattene segghen van marien met ix lessen ende ix psalmen. (*d*) pp. 174–88 Hier na volghet tofficie van onser vrouwen in den aduent. (*e*) pp. 188–206 Hier na volghet tofficie van onser vrouwen van kermesse toot lichtmesse van den aduent.

(*a*). Weekday office, matins–compline of Carmelite use, ending with three anthems, Aue regina celorum Aue domina angelorum Salue radix, Aue regina celorum mater regis angelorum O maria, and Salue regina (*RH*, nos. 2070, 2072, 18147). (*b*). Weekday office: special forms of vespers and compline, the first leaf missing. (*c–e*). Sunday offices.

4. pp. 207–8 Ter eeren den name der maghet marien . . . Ymnus. Maria mater gratie mater misericordie tu nos ab hosti . . .

Office of the name of Mary, ending imperfectly. The hymn is *RH*, no. 11114.

5. pp. 209–10 (Obsecro te begins imperfectly) lacritate eciam habundanciam . . .

6. pp. 210–14 Een ander oratie van onse vrouwe van sint Ian ewangeliste. O intemerata . . . orbis terrarum. Inclina . . . Feminine forms.

7. p. 214 Onse vrouwe seyde toot eenen monic. So wie dat dese x versekins eens daechs segt ende des saterdaghes v. weruen sal ic sijns ghedijncken ende bi hem wesen in de doot. Stella poli regina soli tu proxima proli . . . (10 lines).

8. pp. 215–39 Hier beghinnen de vii psalmen van penitencien. Litany, p. 230.

Fifteen virgins: (1) anna . . . (13–15) tecla scolastica appolonia. Prayers at the end are Fidelium, Ecclesie tue, Exaudi, Omnipotens sempiterne deus qui facis, Deus qui caritatis, Absolue quesumus, Deus qui es sanctorum.

9. pp. 240–81 Hier beghinnen de vigilien van den dooden.

Office of the dead.

10. pp. 282–92 Memoriae of Francis (Franciscus vir catholicus . . .), Margaret, Holy Spirit (Veni creator spiritus mentes tuorum . . . : *RH*, no. 21204), Corpus Christi, Jerome, Cornelius, Christopher, Nicholas, Barbara (Aue martir o barbara aue uirgo deo cara . . .), Ontcommer.

11. Pieces in Netherlandish, added in s. xv ex.: p. 1 och wat vruechden daer wesen moch daer dusent iaer . . . ; p. 1 vier quatuor temperen zii int iaer . . . ; p. 2 Maria die moedre . . . ; p. 2 viif `beden' Eerst. O heere verleent mii cracht voort te gane in huwe minne . . . (*ends imperfectly*).

ff. i + 145, paginated 1-292. 160 × 110 mm. Written space 115 × 73 mm. 21 long lines. Collation of pp. 3-292: 1^6 2^8 wants 1 before p. 19 $3\text{–}5^8$ 6^8 wants 1 + 1 leaf after 8 (pp. 81-92, 15–18) 7^8 wants 1 before p. 93 $8\text{–}13^8$ 14^8 wants 4, 5 after p. 208 15^6 + 1 leaf after 6 (pp. 215–28) $16\text{–}19^8$. Eleven 12-line pictures, seven in art. 3*a*, a Passion series, lacking the vespers picture on a leaf missing after p. 80 (pp. 24, 47, 61, 68, 73, 77, 87), two in art. 10 (Francis—a nun in black kneels before him—and Margaret), and one before each of arts. 7, 8: 'school of Vrelant' (*MERT*, p. 26). Initials: (i) blue or pink patterned in white on decorated gold grounds; (ii) 2-line, gold on grounds of blue or pink patterned in white; (iii) 1-line, blue with red ornament or gold with blue-grey ornament. Borders are continuous on picture pages and on three sides of other pages with initials of type (i). Capital letters in the ink of the text filled with pale yellow. Panel binding, s. xvi in., rebacked: on each cover two repetitions of a 'Flemish animals' panel, two rows of four with floral border, separated by a strip bearing stag, lion, 2-headed eagle, and wyvern, each in a compartment: two clasps.

Written in the southern Low Countries for female (art. 6) and Carmelite (art. 3) use. Gatty, no. 24. Frere, no. 624.

12022. *Horae* s. xv in.

1. pp. 1–24 Full calendar in French in red and black.

Entries in red include 'Geneuieue', 'Yues', 'Loys roy', 'Saint leu. s. gille', 'Denis', 'Marcel'. (3 Jan., 19 May, 25 Aug., 1 Sept., 9 Oct., 3 Nov.). Anne in black, 28 (*sic*) July.

2. pp. 25–34 Sequentiae of the Gospels, ending imperfectly.

3. pp. 35–175 Hours of B.V.M. of the use of (Paris), beginning imperfectly.

Nine lessons at matins. No special offices at the end.

4. pp. 176–182 Obsecro te . . . et michi famulo tuo N. . . .

5. pp. 183–8 O intemerata . . . orbis terrarum. de te enim . . . et esto michi peccatori . . .

6. pp. 189–227 Penitential psalms and (p. 216) 'Letania'.

Nineteen martyrs: . . . (12) dyonisii cum sociis. Thirteen confessors: . . . (5) seuerine . . . (8) yuo. Thirteen virgins, but not Genovefa, nor Anne. At the end only Fidelium follows Deus cui proprium.

7. pp. 228–236 Hours of the Cross, . . . Patris sapiencia . . .

8. pp. 236–44 Hore sancti spiritus . . . Nobis sancti spiritus . . .

9. pp. 244–344 Incipiunt vigilie mortuorum. Plabo (*sic*). Dilexi . . .

Office of the dead.

ff. iii + 172 + iii, paginated (i–iv), 1–344, (345–50). 180 × 127 mm. Written space 93 × 62 mm. 14 long lines. Collation: 1^{12} 2^{6} wants 6 (pp. 25–34) 3 eight (pp. 35–50) 4^{8} $5\text{–}6^{6}$ 7^{10} wants 10, blank, after p. 108 $8\text{–}17^{8}$ 18^{8} 7, 8 cancelled (pp. 269–78) 19^{8} 20^{10} 21 three (pp. 315–20) 22^{8} 23 four. Catchwords in cursiva, middle of lower margin. Eleven 10-line flat-topped pictures, seven in art. 3 (Flight into Egypt at none, Presentation at vespers: at prime (Manger) a haloed figure (midwife) holds the Child; and one before each of arts. 6 (Christ seated, orb in left hand and right stretched out to take a chalice: tables of law on His left), 7–9. Initials: (i) 3-line, blue or pink, patterned in white on decorated gold grounds; (ii) 2-line, as (i), with sprays into the margins; (iii) gold on grounds of red and blue patterned in white. Line fillers in red and blue patterned in white with pieces of gold between them: usually there is a regular alternation, blue and red followed by red and blue, but in the litany the colours go in blocks, so that, for example, on p. 221, lines 1–8 are all red and blue and lines 9–14 all blue and red. Continuous borders on picture pages, with a strip of gold decorated with flower heads between border and picture. Borders of ivy leaves springing from a narrow vertical bar of gold and colours extend over three margins of all other pages. Capital letters in the ink of the text filled with pale yellow. Red velvet binding, s. xviii: a silver clasp is engraved on the inside '1757 *die* 30 Julii Eva Margaretha Rehfussin'.

Written in France. For an owner, s. xviii, see above. *MERT*, no. 24. Gatty, no. 10.

12023. *Horae (in Netherlandish)* s. xv^2

Arts. 2, 4, 5, 7, 8 are the translations of Geert Grote. Arts. 3, 6, 9 are quire fillers.

1. pp. 1–24 Full calendar in red and black.

Entries in red include the usual Utrecht saints and (17 Aug.) Jeroen.

2. pp. 27–80 Hier begint die vrouwe getide. Here du selte opdoen . . . Use of (Utrecht).

3. (*a*) pp. 80–1 Een gebet als men totten heiligen sacramente wilste gaen. O almachtighe ewige god Ick arme sondighe mensche . . . (*b*) p. 81 Dit gebet seltu lesen alstu dat heilige sacrament onfanghen hebste. Ic dancke dij lieue hemelsche vader . . . (*c*) pp. 81–2 Een gebet tot maria. Ic bidde dij gloriose moeder ende maget Maria dochter . . .

4. pp. 85–105 Hier begint die seue salm dauid. Litany, p. 98.

Eighteen virgins, not Anne: . . . (12) Walburth. p. 106 blank.

5. pp. 109–14 Hier begint die cruus getide.

6. pp. 117–22 Hier begint een gebet van sinte anna. Verblijt v heilige anna salige vrouwe die alsoe groten dochter . . .

7. pp. 125–56 Hier beghint die wijsheit getide.

8. pp. 159–84 Hier begint die heilige geest getide.

9. pp. 185–6 Memoria of Cornelius pope and martyr and Anthony hermit, jointly: O scone sterren des hemels . . .

10. pp. 189–212 Hier begint die vigilie van iii lesse. Mi hebben ombeuangen . . . Office of the dead.

ff. i + 106 + i, paginated (i, ii), 1–212, (213–14). Thick parchment. 195 × 135 mm. Written space 93 × 75 mm. 20 long lines. Ruling in red ink. Collation: $1\text{–}2^6$ $3\text{–}5^8$ 6^4 (pp. 75–82) 7^8 8^2 + 1 leaf after 2 (pp. 105–6) 9^6 (pp. 109–14, 117–22) $10\text{–}12^8$ 13^6 (pp. 175–86) 14^8 15^4, together with seven singletons with blank rectos and pictures on the versos, pp. 25–6, 83–4, 107–8, 115–16, 123–4, 157–8, 187–8. Seven full-page pictures in an impressionistic style, pp. 26, 84 (Christ on the rainbow), 108, 116 (B.V.M. and Child, Anne, and two angels), 124, 158, 188: the two on pp. 26 and 116 'are taken from engravings by Schongauer and the Master I.A.M. of Zwolle respectively' (*MERT*, p. 27). Initials: (i) blue shaded to white on gold grounds, historiated, pp. 27 (B.V.M. in glory), 85 (David), 109 (vision of Gregory); (ii) as (i), but decorated, not historiated; (iii, iv) 3-line and 2-line, red or blue with ornament of the other colour; (v) 1-line, blue or red. Line fillers in litany blue and gold. Capital letters in the ink of the text stroked with red. Borders on picture pages are continuous and framed; on pages facing picture pages in three margins and without frames. Contemporary stamped binding, rebacked: triple fillets and stamps of four kinds, rosette, fleur de lis, fleuron and star, forming a symmetrical pattern, the same on each cover: two clasps.

Written for use in the diocese of Utrecht: Jeroen suggests Holland. A note in Dutch, s. xix, inside the cover. 'N° 6' inside the cover. 'N° 7', p.i. *MERT*, no. 40. Gatty, no. 23.

12024. *Horae* s. xv med.

1. pp. 1–24 Calendar in French in gold, blue and red, the two colours alternating.

Entries in gold include Gervais, Eloy, Marcial, Anne, Saint sauueur, Denis, Romain, Thomas (19, 25 June, 3, 26 July, 6 Aug., 9, 23 Oct., 29 Dec.).

2. pp. 25–36 Sequentiae of the Gospels. Prayers, Protector in te sperantium and Ecclesiam tuam, after John.

3. pp. 36–42 Oracio beate marie. Obsecro te . . . Masculine forms.

4. pp. 42–9 Alia oracio. O intemerata . . . orbis terrarum. De te enim . . . Masculine forms. p. 50 blank.

5. pp. 51–139 Hours of B.V.M. of the use of (Rouen). Memoriae of Holy Spirit, Holy Trinity, Michael, John Baptist, Peter and Paul, Laurence, Nicholas, Katherine, Margaret, All Saints, and for peace after lauds. pp. 140–2 blank.

6. pp. 143–76 Penitential psalms and (p. 166) litany.

Ursinus as disciple. Seventeen confessors: . . . (8–11) audoene benedicte mellone romane. Seventeen virgins: . . . (6) honorina. The only prayer after Deus cui is Fidelium.

7. pp. 176–82 Hours of Holy Cross. Patris sapiencia . . .

8. pp. 182–8 Hours of Holy Spirit. Nobis sancti spiritus . . .

9. pp. 188–244 Office of the dead.

10. pp. 244–56 Les xv ioys nostre dame. Doulce dame de misericorde . . . Sonet-Sinclair, no. 458.

11. pp. 256–62 Doulz dieu doulz pere saincte trinite . . . Sonet–Sinclair, no. 504.

12. pp. 262–3 Saincte vraye croix aouree . . . Sonet–Sinclair, no. 1876. p. 264 blank.

ff. ii + 132 (paginated 1–264) + ii. 200 × 142 mm. Written space 92 × 62 mm. 15 long lines. Ruling in red ink. Collation: 1^{12} 2^{8} 3^{4} + 1 leaf after 4 (pp. 49, 50) 4–8^{8} 9^{6} (pp. 131–42) 10–16^{8} 17 five (pp. 255–64). Catchwords in cursiva. Thirteen 12-line pictures, seven in art. 5 (for lauds see below) and one before each of arts. 2 (a four-compartment picture), 6–9, 10 (pietà). Aquarius in a roundel at the foot of p. 1. Initials: (i) 3-line, blue patterned in white on gold grounds, historiated on p. 70 (Visitation) and elsewhere decorated in colours; (ii) as (i), but 2-line; (iii) 1-line, gold on grounds of red and blue, patterned in white. Continuous borders of fruits, flowers and leaves on pages with initials of type (i) and mirror-image borders the height of the written space in the outer margin of all other pages, apart from blank pages: the border on p. 51 is specially treated with a gold paint ground and has various creatures, including a siren with comb and mirror, among the flowers. Line fillers in red and blue patterned in white, the colours separated by blobs of gold. Capital letters in the ink of the text marked with pale yellow. Handsome olive green morocco binding, s. xix, by 'Thouvenin': the name is at the foot of the spine and a title 'Preces Piæ' is higher up.

Written in France for use in the diocese of Rouen. Gatty, no. 24.

12025. *Horae* s. xv²

1. pp. 1–24 Full calendar in French in red and black.

Entries in red include Loys, Remy, Eulalie, Thomas (26 Aug., 1 Oct., 14, 29 Dec.).

2. pp. 25–32 Memoriae of Sebastian (O sancte sebastiane. Semper uespere et mane . . . : *RH*, no. 13708) and B.V.M. (Salue sancta parens enixa . . . : *RH*, no. 18197).

3. pp. 32–9 Office of Holy Spirit.

4. pp. 39–44 Domine ihesu criste qui septem verba . . .

5. pp. 44–7 De s' cristofle. Saint cristofle martir tres doulx. pries le roy des roys pour nous . . . Sonet–Sinclair, no. 1816.

6. pp. 47–54 Oracio. O intemerata . . . orbis terrarum inclina . . . Masculine forms.

7. p. 54 Oracio. Domine ihesu criste qui hanc sacratissimam carnem . . . (*ends imperfectly*).

8. pp. 55–68 Sequentiae of the Gospels. pp. 69–70 blank.

9. pp. 71–197 Hours of B.V.M. of the use of (Paris). p. 198 blank.

10. pp. 199–206 Hours of Holy Cross. Patris sapientia . . .

11. pp. 207–14 Hours of Holy Spirit. Nobis sancte (*sic*) spiritus . . .

12. pp. 215–59 Penitential psalms and (p. 246) litany.

Twenty-one virgins: . . . (16) Sufrasia (*sic*) . . . (21) Castitas.

13. pp. 260–70 Obsecro te . . . Masculine forms.

14. pp. 271–389 Office of the dead.

15 (added early). pp. 380–395 Tres piteux et benigne redempteur ihesus Ie te requier en grant humilite . . . (*ends imperfectly*). Cf. Sonet–Sinclair, nos. 2235, 2239.

ff. 198 (paginated 1-396) + i. 97 × 73 mm. Written space 52 × 37 mm. 14 long lines. Collation: 1^{12} 2^{8} 3^{8} wants 8 after p. 54 $4-16^{8}$ 17^{4} (pp. 263-70) $18-24^{8}$ 25^{4} (pp. 383-90) 26^{4} wants 4 after p. 396. Inexpert *lettre bâtarde*. Eight pictures, 10-line or 11-line, two in art. 9 (matins and prime, the latter not the usual scene, but two saints with palm and book, one on each side of a palm tree) and one before each of arts. 10-12, 13 (vision of Gregory: better than the rest), 14, 15 (Crucifixion). Initials: (i) blue or red patterned in white on decorated gold grounds; (ii, iii) 2-line and 1-line, gold on red and blue grounds patterned in white. Borders: continuous on picture pages; on three sides of other pages with initials of type (i); the height of the written space in the outer margin of all other pages, including pages with no writing on them. Line fillers of blue and red patterned in white, the colours separated by a piece of gold. Binding of wooden boards covered with green morocco, s. xvi (?). Secundo folio (p. 27) *Tu semper*.

Written in France. The four divisions made by a St Andrew's cross within a shield on p. 260 contain the initials I U C B. 'N° 300', p. 398. A monogram (?) stamped on pp. 1 and 396. An armorial book-plate, s. xviii (?), inside the cover, gules a garb proper on a chief azure three stars: a coronet above the shield.

12026. *Breviarium ('Compendium diurni')* s. xv^{2}

1. pp. 1-24 Calendar in red and black, graded.

Entries in red include: eight Dominican feasts, all graded 'Totum duplex', among them Vincent confessor and Katherine of Siena (5 Apr., 2 May); Visitation and Presentation of B.V.M. (2 July, 21 Nov.); Transfiguration (6 Aug.). pp. i, ii, 25-6 are blank and unruled.

2. pp. 29-179 Incipit compendium diurni secundum ordinem fratrum predicatorum. Dominica prima in aduentu domini Sabbato precedenti Ad vesperas. Capitulum. Ecce dies veniunt . . .

Temporal to the 25th Sunday after Trinity.

3. pp. 179-84 In dedicacione ecclesie et in anniuersario eiusdem.

4. pp. 185-338 Incipit compendium diurni de sanctis.

Andrew-Saturninus.

5. pp. 339-58 Common of saints.

6. pp. 359-65 Sequitur officium beate virginis.

7. pp. 366-457 Common of time, (*a*) at prime, terce, sext, and none, (*b*) p. 396, at vespers, (*c*) p. 428, at compline, (*d*) p. 433, at lauds.

8. pp. 458-66 Litany.

Twelve martyrs: . . . (10-12) thoma petre adalberte. Twenty-one confessors: . . . (8) Dominice, doubled . . . (18-21) vdalrice conrade galle othmare. Sixteen virgins, not Mary of Egypt: . . . (15, 16) anna elysabeth. The prayers at the end are Protege, Concede, Ineffabilem, Pretende, Ecclesie, Deus a quo. pp. 467-70 blank, the first two ruled.

ff. i + 236 + xvii, paginated (i–iv), 1–466, (467–504). 128 × 90 mm. Written space 85 × 60 mm. 24 long lines. Collation of pp. iii, iv, 1–470: 1^8 2^6 $3\text{–}29^8$ 30^6. Good set fere-textura: single compartment *a*; *s* and *f* descenders; ascenders looped: punctuation within the sentence by colon: no punctuation at the end of a sentence. Initials: (i) p. 29, blue *E* shaded to white on gold ground, historiated (Annunciation): frame parti-coloured pink and green: part border; (ii) 5-line, blue and red; (iii, iv) 2-line and 1-line, blue or red. Contemporary binding of wooden boards covered with stamped brown leather: on the front the pattern is formed mainly by rectangular crested and floral border stamps: on the back are eagle and fleur de lis stamps and a large six-pointed star: two clasps.

Written for Dominican use, probably in southern Germany. An erasure, p. i. Gatty, no. 18. Frere, no. 620.

12027. *Breviarium* s. xv in.–xv med.

1. pp. 1–143 In nomine domini. Amen. Dominica prima post pentecosten. Inuit'. Adoremus dominum . . .

Liturgical psalter.

2. pp. 143–4 Antiphons of B.V.M., Alma redemptoris, Salue regina, Regina celi, Aue regina celorum, Aue stella matutina (*RH*, nos. 861, 18150, 17170, 2070, 2135), Quam pulcra es, and prayers.

3. pp. 144–5 Ymnus sanctorum ambrosii et augustini. Te deum . . .

4. pp. 145–6 Pater noster and Credo in deum patrem.

5. pp. 147–51 Litany.

Twelve martyrs: . . . (5–7) siste blasii ansane. Fourteen virgins: . . . (9–14) iustina ursula cum sociis tuis anna monica helysabeth brigida. p. 152 blank.

6. pp. 153–4 A single leaf of the temporal for Easter.

7. pp. 155–364 Sanctoral, Andrew–Katherine.

The first leaf is missing. Offset on p. 152 may be from the historiated initial it contained. Single leaves are also missing after pp. 284 and 342.

8. pp. 365–408 Incipit comune sanctorum.

9. pp. 408–14 In dedicatione uel in anniuersario dedicationis ecclesie.

10. pp. 414–26 Notandum quod officium beate uirginis non dicitur . . .

Office of B.V.M., with introductory rubric as *SMRL* ii. 185–6/30.

11. pp. 426–8 Ordo ad comunicandum infirmum.

12. pp. 428–33 Ordo ad ingendum infirmum.

Litany, pp. 432–3. The three martyrs are Stephen, Laurence, and Ansanus.

13. pp. 433–44 Deinde pro uicino morti cum in agone . . .

Office of burial.

14. pp. 445–60 Incipit officium in agenda defunctorum . . . An'. Placebo . . .

Office of the dead. Rubric as *SMRL* ii. 191.

Arts. 15, 16 (quires 25–7) are in another rather later hand.

15. pp. 461–7 In festo sanctissime trinitatis.

16. pp. 467–520 Franciscan offices supplementing art. 7: (*a*) 467, translation of Francis; (*b*) 478, Clare; (*c*) 486, Louis, bishop; (*d*) 494, Louis, king; (*e*) 496, stigmata of Francis; (*f*) 498, 'In festo beatissimi patris nostri francisci'; (*g*) 509, 'De festiuitatibus que infra octauam sancti francisci ueniunt'.

(*a–g*). 25 May, 12, 19, 25 Aug., 17 Sept., 4 Oct., 5–10 Oct. (*a*). Rubric as *SMRL* ii. 140–1. (*g*). Rubrics as *SMRL* ii. 166–7, followed by six sets of nine short lessons, 'Ecclesiarum itaque trium . . . ac nomine benedixit. Explicit minor uita beati francisci. Deo gratias. Amen'. Bonaventura, *Opera* (1888–1902), viii. 566–78 (end of lectio 4).

17 (added). (*a*) pp. 521–4 Office of the Transfiguration (5 Aug.: hymn, Gaude mater pietatis). (*b*) p. 526 An incomplete 12-column table, each column headed with the name of the month in Italian.

ff. i + 263 + i, paginated (i, ii), 1–525 (527–8). A medieval foliation is partly cut off. 138 × 95 mm. Written space 80 × 63 mm. 2 cols. 28 lines. Collation (omitting pp. 153–4): $1–7^{10}$ 8^{6} (pp. 141–52) 9^{10} wants 1 (pp. 155–72) $10–14^{10}$ 15^{10} wants 7 after p. 284 $16–17^{10}$ 18^{10} wants 7 after p. 342 19^{10} wants 9, 10, blank, after p. 364 $20–23^{10}$ 24^{8} (pp. 445–60) $25–27^{10}$ 28 three (pp. 521–6). Punctuation includes the flex. Initials: (i) in colours, blue, red, green, on grounds of gold and colour, with yellow as a frame within the initial, historiated; (ii), as (i), but smaller and filled with patterned colours, not historiated; (iii) 2-line, red or blue with ornament of the other colour; (iv) 1-line, red or blue. Part borders on main pages and short projections on other pages with initials of type (i): the decoration includes tall narrow birds and stalked gold balls. Binding of s. xviii/xix. Secundo folio *die ac nocte.*

Written in Italy: probably Florentine,[1] but the litanies suggest a special devotion to the Sienese saint Ansanus. Later supplemented for Franciscan use. 'N° 5', f. i^{v}. Gatty, no. 8. *MERT*, no. 68. Frere, no. 619.

[1] Information from Dr A. de la Mare.

12028. *Horae* s. xv med.–xv^2

Arts. 8 (except three leaves), 9–12 are rather later than the rest.

1. pp. 1–12 Calendar in red and black, rather empty.

Entries in red include the Visitation of B.V.M., Divisio apostolorum, and Nichasius (2, 15 July, 14 Dec.).

2. pp. 13–17 Incipiunt hore de sancta cruce . . . Hymnus. Patris sapiencia . . . p. 18 blank.

3. pp. 19–23 Incipiunt hore de sancto spiritu . . . Hymnus. Nobis sancte (*sic*) spiritus . . .

The five lines on p. 23 are in a later hand. p. 24 blank.

4. pp. 25–32 Incipit missa beate marie virginis.

5. pp. 32–8 Sequentiae of Gospels.

John, Luke, Matthew, Mark as usual, but the portion of Luke is ascribed to Matthew, and vice versa.

6. pp. 41–106 Incipiunt hore beate marie virginis secundum usum Romane ecclesie.

A memoria of All Saints is added by the hand of arts. 8–12 at the end of each hour from prime onwards. pp. 54, 68 blank.

7. pp. 107–26 Incipiunt Septem psalmy. Litany, p. 124.

The scribe missed part of his text and went straight on from the seventh martyr 'Laurenti' with fourteen names, 'Gregori . . .', all confessors except the second, 'Georgi': . . . (10–14) Francisce Huberte Benedicte Arnoude Bernarde. Fourteen virgins: . . . (3, 4) Gudula Clara. The prayers at the end are Deus cui proprium and Fidelium only.

8. pp. 127–94 Incipiunt vigilie mortuorum.

Office of the dead. Only pp. 127–8, 145–8 are in the hand of arts. 2–7. A rubric in French before Venite exultemus, p. 137: 'Ceste psalme qui sensieut ne se doibt dire si non au iour des ames . . .'.

9. pp. 194–7 Ceste anthienne et orison doibt on dire en vne cymentiere por les tresp'. Auete omnes anime . . .

10. pp. 197–200 Deuote orison de saincte anne. Aue sancta anna mater matris domini . . .

A notice at the end that those who say the prayer 'par deuotion' will have 'pour chascun iour viii mil ans et mil quarantaines de vray pardon'.

11. pp. 201–6 Oratio de domina nostra. Obsecro te . . .

12. pp. 206–9 Oratio de domina nostra. O intemerata . . . orbis terrarum. Inclina . . . Masculine forms. p. 210 left blank.

13. pp. i–iv contain washed out writing, s. xv (?).

ff. ii + 105 + i, paginated (i–iv), 1–210, (211–12). 170 × 125 mm. Written space 93 × 65 mm. 18 long lines. Ruling in violet ink. Collation: 1^6 2^6 (1, 3, 4, 6 half sheets) 3–7^8 8^8 wants 8 after p. 128 9–12^8 13^4 (pp. 193–200) 14^6 wants 6, blank (pp. 201–10), together with four singleton leaves with blank rectos and full-page pictures on the versos, pp. 74, 80, 86, 92. The pictures illustrate terce, sext, none, and vespers in art. 6 and are probably the remains of a larger set. Initials: (i) blue patterned in white on decorated gold grounds; (ii) 2-line, gold on blue and pink grounds patterned in white; (iii) 1-line, blue with red ornament or gold with slate-grey ornament (or green ornament on later leaves). Line fillers in litany only, gold and blue. Continuous framed borders in colours and gold on picture pages and pages with initials of type (i). Capital letters in the ink of the text stroked with pale yellow. Binding of wooden boards covered with dark brown calf, s. xvi: a floral roll of Oldham's type FL.(b) encloses a panel in which are two rows of the same roll: four bands: two clasps missing.

Written in north-east France or Flanders. Two crossed out inscriptions on p. iii on top of art. 13: the first, s. xvi^1, ends 'Iaspar le Roy'. '[. . . .] le Roy de Tournoy (?) 1568', p. iv. 'Sum Simonis Cazier et Amicorum 1568', p. ii. 'Jan Canette (?)', p. 210, s. xvi. Gatty, no. 22.

12032. *P. Lombardus, Sententiae* 1472

1. Magistri Petri Lombardi sentenciarum liber foeliciter Incipit. Prefatio. Ueteris ac noue . . . (f. 170) ducė peruenit. Laus deo Petrus `h'ędus scripsit (*this word in red*) 1472 die 15 Februarii iiii uero (?) xl^e.[1]

2. The outer part of the last leaf (f. 170) has been cut off, with the beginning of a piece on paradise added on the verso of the last leaf of art. 1 by the main hand. The text ends in col. 2 'delectatio completa. Hec dicit magister Albertus in secundo super sentencias'.

Not, that I can see, in the commentary by Albertus Magnus on the Sentences of Peter Lombard, bk. 2, distinctio 17.

ff. i + 170 + i. Paper. 337 × 240 mm. Written space 205 × 140 mm. 2 cols. 45 lines. Pencil ruling. Collation: 1–17^{10}. Strips of parchment as strengthening between and in the middle of quires. Written in humanistica. Initials: (i) red or blue with ornament of the other colour; (ii) 2-line, blue with red ornament. Pasteboard binding, s. xviii (?). Secundo folio *iam non.*

Written in Italy. '816 / Pietro Lombardo / Sententiarum / Libri iv' and 'Ms / N^o / 299' on the spine. A cancelled number '8328' at the end.

[1] Ash Wednesday was on 12 Feb. in 1472.

12033. *Horae* s. xv^1

1. ff. 1–12v Calendar in French in red and black.

Entries in red include 'marcial apostre', 'ouen' (octave in black), 'romain' (octave in black), 'senestre pape' (3 July, 24 Aug., 23 Oct., 31 Dec.). Translation of Evodius and 'Les reliques de nostre dame' in black, 8 July, 3 Dec.

2. ff. 13–18v Sequentiae of Gospels, in the unusual order Luke, Matthew, Mark, John, followed by 'Protector in te . . .' and 'Ecclesiam tuam . . .'. ff. 19–20v blank.

3. ff. 21–72v Hours of B.V.M. of the use of (Rouen).

Memoriae of Holy Spirit, Nicholas, Katherine, Holy Trinity, John Baptist after lauds.

4. ff. 73–90 Penitential psalms and (f. 85) litany.

Martial absent. Ten confessors: . . . (4) lupe . . . (9, 10) audoene romane. Sixteen virgins: . . . (15, 16) radegondis genouepha.

5. ff. 90–4 Hours of the Cross: . . . Ymnus. Patris sapiencia . . .

6. ff. 94v–98 Hours of Holy Spirit: . . . Nobis sancti spiritus . . .

7. ff. 98–102 Cy en apres ensieut vne deuoste oroison de nostre dame. Obsecro te . . . et michi famulo tuo . . .

8. ff. 102–5 Vne oroison de nostre dame. O intemerata . . . orbis terrarum. De te enim . . . michi miserrimo peccatori . . . ff. 105v–107v blank.

9. ff. 108–52 Office of the dead. One leaf missing.

10. ff. 152v–157v Douce dame de misericorde mere de pitie . . . Sonet–Sinclair, no. 458.

11. ff. 157v–161v Les v plaies nostre seigneur ihesucrist. Quiconques veult estre biens conseilliez . . . Dous dieux dous pere sainte trinite . . . The nine requests, Sonet–Sinclair, no. 504.

12. f. 161v Sainte uraie crois aouree . . . Sonet–Sinclair, no. 1876.

13 (added on the last leaf of quire 21 and on flyleaves in several hands). (*a*) f. 162rv Douce vierge plaisante et coye Qui au monde aportas ioye. Si vrayement . . . vraye contriction Amen (20 lines). (*b*) f. 162v Douce dame saincte marie qui portat' le Roy Qui deuint mortel homme . . . (7 lines); (*c*) f. 163rv [O] beata virgo maria quis digne tibi valeat . . . ; (*d*) ff. 163v–164 Saluator mundi salua nos omnes sancta dei genitrix . . . Omnipotens sempiterne deus qui nos omnium sanctorum merita . . .

(*a*). Sinclair, no. 2792.

ff. i + 163 + v, foliated (i), 1–104, 104*, 105–64, (165–7). For ff. 163–4 see above, art. 13. 190 × 135 mm. Written space 95 × 65 mm. 15 long lines. Collation: 1^{12} $2–8^{8}$ 9^{4} (ff. 69–72) $10–13^{8}$ 14^{4} (ff. 104*, 105–7) $15–17^{8}$ 18^{8} wants 5 after f. 135 $19–21^{8}$. Thirteen 11-line or 12-line flat-topped pictures, eight in art. 3 and one before each of arts. 4–6, 9, 11 (Christ on the rainbow showing His wounds, feet on globe: angels, one trumpeting: grass field with flowers, but no resurrection): ivy-leaf borders set off from the pictures by a band of colour and a little gold, 4 mm wide. Initials: (i) 3-line, red or blue patterned in white on decorated gold grounds; (ii) 2-line, gold on blue and red grounds patterned in white: gold ivy-leaf sprays into the margin; (iii) 1-line, blue with red ornament or gold with blue-grey ornament. Gold and blue line-fillers. Capital letter in the ink of the text filled with pale yellow. Binding of s. xviii: an elaborate silver clasp. Secundo folio (f. 14) *tissimi*.

Written in France. A piece containing probably one line of writing has been cut out of f. 164. Below it is 'Guerapin mil quatre cent dix Guerapin' and a paraph and at the foot of the page 'MCCCC X', both of s. xvi. Armorial book-plate of Henry Francis Lyte (†1847). A printed label, 'National Exhibition of Works of Art, Leeds, 1868. Museum of Art Liverpool (this word by hand) Proprietor' is inside the cover, bottom left. Gatty, no. 9. *MERT*, no. 25.

12034. *Processionale ad usum Sarum* s. xiv², xiv/xv

Quires 8–18, on thinner parchment (ff. 55–141: art. 1 from Easter and beginning of art. 2), look rather later than the rest.

1. ff. 1–140 (*begins imperfectly*) a deo in ciuitatem . . .

Temporal. The first words are in *PS*, p. 6/14. The forms for rain and fine weather in edn., p. 165, are here at Monday in Rogationtide, ff. 78–83ᵛ. Seven penitential psalms in full, ff. 83ᵛ–90. The rubric with the name of St Thomas (of Canterbury) on f. 12 and the words 'dompnum apostolicum' in the litany on f. 94 (edn., pp. 21, 110) have been erased. Offset from a now missing initial *A* (*Asperges* ?) shows on f. ivᵛ.

2. ff. 140–142ᵛ Dedication of church.

3. ff. 142ᵛ–180 Sanctoral.

Differs from edn.: by including Invention of Stephen, 'Sanctus iohannes episcopus . . .', f. 162ᵛ; by omitting (besides 'nova festa') Thomas of Canterbury and feast of relics in July, Denis in October, and Edmund of Canterbury and Edmund king and martyr in November. 'rubrysch' in margins against headings, ff. 147–8.

4. ff. 180–7 Common of saints. f. 187ᵛ blank.

5. The flyleaf, f. 188, has a four-part setting of Nunc dimittis on the verso, s. xv.

ff. iv + 187 + i. Thick parchment, ff. 1–52, 142–87. 127 × 93 mm. Written space *c.*80 × 55 mm. 18 long lines or 6 long lines and music. In the older part the writing is between double ruled lines. Collation: 1^{6} $2–6^{8}$ 7^{6} + 1 leaf after 6 (f. 53) $8–23^{8}$ 24^{6} (ff. 182–7). Signatures of the usual late medieval kind, beginning with *a* on quire 2 and recommencing with *a* on f. 54. Initials: (i) on quires 8–18 only, mainly for proses, 3-line, gold on grounds of blue and red patterned in white: sprays into the margins: (ii) 2-line, blue with red ornament or (in the older part) without ornament; (iii) 1-line, red or blue. Cadels of various patterns, some elaborate. Medieval binding: bare wooden boards: three bands: a central strap and pin missing.

Written in England. Names 'John Robinson' and 'D. Walker' on f. ii, s. xvii. Gatty, no. 14. Frere, no. 623.

12035. *Schwabenspiegel (in German)* s. xiv med.

The 'Normalform' of the Schwabenspiegel. Art. 1 corresponds to pp. 330–94 (Lehnrecht) of the edition in Bibliotheca rerum historicarum, ed. K. A. Eckhardt, *Studia Juris Suecici, V, Schwabenspiegel Normalform*, 1972, art. 2 to pp. 150–260 (Erster Landrechtsteil), and art. 3 to pp. 261–328 (Zweiter Landrechtsteil).

1. ff. 1–49 Hie vat man an zellenne wa von daz rehtlehen bůch an. Die dez herschiltes darbent . . . (*table of 139 heads*) . . . (f. 2ᵛ) Hie hebet sich daz edele vnde daz rehte lehen bvch an. Swer lehen reht kvnnen welle. der volge diz bůchez lere. Aller erst . . . daz verliehe vns der vater vnd der svn vnd heilige geist Amen Amen Amen.

References to leaf numbers, 'Vier'—'Nun vnde vierzig', have been added to the table. f. 49ᵛ, left blank, was filled with now washed out writing in s. xv.

2. ff. 50–126 Hie vat man an zellenne wa von daz recht bůch saget. Von die vrien . . . (*table of 218 heads*) . . . (f. 52ᵛ) Hie hebet sich daz lant recht bůch an. Herre got himelscher vater dvr dine milte gůte . . . vf swelhen tac der man bescheidet. Hie ist daz lant reht bůch vz.

3. ff. 126–77 Hie vahet man an zellenne wa von daz reht lehen bůch seit. Nv seit ez da von wie wit dez kvniges strazzan svln sin . . . (*table of 148 heads*) . . . (f. 128) Hie vahet daz edel bůch an daz da heizzet von lehen rehte. Ob ein kint sin lar zal beheltet vntz an den tac . . . vor allem weltlichem gerihte mit rehte.

4. The pastedown at the front was once the flyleaf of another manuscript. It has on it a well-drawn pen-and-ink initial *Q* and grotesques, s. xiii.

ff. i + 177. 246 × 170 mm. Written space 173 × 122 mm. 31 long lines. Collation: $1\text{–}5^8$ 6^{10} wants 10, blank, after f. 49 $7\text{–}8^{10}$ $9\text{–}19^8$ $20\text{–}21^{10}$. Medieval foliation in German words, beginning afresh at arts. 2, 3; also 1–74 in art. 2 on rectos, at the foot. Well written in textura. Initials: (i) blue and red, with ornament of both colours; (ii, iii) 2-line and 1-line, blue or red. Medieval binding of wooden boards covered with brown leather bearing a pattern of fillets and stamps, one of them 'maria' on a scroll: three bands: five bosses on each cover: two strap-and-pin fastenings missing.

Written in Germany. Inscriptions of s. xv: (i, ii) on f. iᵛ and inside the back cover, 'Das buch ist iacob nordlingers'; (iii) inside the front cover, 'Daz buch ist `[. . . .] im 69 Iar an sant Gals (?) abent [. . . .] wardsz Im′'. 'R' and (s. xix) 'Nᴼ 26353' and initials R.N. inside the front cover.

12036. *Eugippius, etc.* s. xiii/xiv

Tables of contents on f. ivv, s. xiv and s. xv, refer to arts. 1–7.

1. ff. 1–109v Liber egyppii viri eruditissimi quem `de´ nonnullis operibus sancti augustini excerpsit. Liber ad ieronimum presbiterum de sentencia iacobi apostoli . . . Ex sermone de laude caritatis (*list of 37 titles*). Incipit prologus. Domino merito uenerabili et fructu sacre uirginitatis . . . ultimus enutrite laudem. Liber ad ieronimum presbiterum . . . (f. 4v) Item de caritate sermo sancti fulgentii episcopi. cccliii. Expliciunt capitula. Quod ad te scripsi honorande michi in cristo . . . set etiam breuis. ccclii. De caritate in sermone. supra fulgentii episcopi. Quantum cupio sanctitati uestre debitum reddere . . . discrimine possidetur.

PL lxii. 599–1088, followed by *PL* lxv. 737–40, but the text here continues a dozen lines further than in edn. *Clavis*, nos. 676, 832. The table on ff. 1–4v has 353 heads, but the numbering in the text is 1–352. For this and other copies see M. Gorman in *Revue Bénédictine*, xcii (1982), 7–32. 'Nota manbe' is in the margin of f. 109 beside a drawing of a kneeling man whose long index finger points to 'caritatem omnibus hominibus esse reddendam' (*PL* lxv. 738D). Similar drawings are on ff. 5, 105, 108v, 109: cf. art. 7. f. 110rv is blank and not ruled.

2. ff. 111–177v Incipiunt quedam excepta ex opusculis beati Gregori(i) pape . . . Incipit liber primus de deo. In scriptura sacra aliquando deus nuncupatiue. . . Re. in capitulo de dextera. Expliciunt capitula.

317 chapters, each on a particular subject and its significance, the first De deo and the last De lagena. The chapters are in sixteen books, each preceded by a table of chapters and the tables are also set out all together on f. 178, '. . . Expliciunt capitula beati Gregorii pape'. Normally each chapter begins in a set form, for example, the last, 'Lagenarum nomine corda nostra designantur . . .'. f. 178v blank.

3. ff. 179–82 Incipit liber sancti augustini episcopi de conflictu uitiorum atque uirtutum. Apostolica uox clamat per orbem . . . et aliis tradere debes. Explicit liber de conflictu uitiorum atque uirtutum.

PL xl. 1091–1106. Cf. Römer, i. 49–51 for other manuscripts in British libraries.

4. ff. 182–8 De fide ad petrum. Epistolam fili petre tue caritatis . . . quoque illi dum reuelauit. liber explicit.

Fulgentius Ruspensis: *PL* lxv. 671–706B; *PL* xl. 753–78. *Clavis*, no. 826. Cf. Römer, i. 89–90, for other manuscripts in British libraries.

5. ff. 188–191v Aurelii augustini de beata uita ad ma`u´lum theodorum uirum magnificum liber incipit. Si ad philosophie portum . . . disputacionis fine discessimus.

PL xxxii. 959–76. *Clavis*, no. 254. Cf. Römer, i. 199, for other manuscripts in British libraries.

6. ff. 191v–202v Incipit prefatio libri anselmi cantuariensis archiepiscopi: Cur deus homo. Opus subditum . . . non despitiat. Hic incipiunt capitula huius libelli

. . . (*table of 25 chapters*) . . . Incipit cur deus homo liber anselmi archiepiscopi cantuariensis. Sepe et studiosissime . . . attribuere debemus. Qui est . . . amen.

SAO ii. 42–133. Bk. 2, f. 200, is preceded by a table of 22 chapters.

7. ff. 203–270^{v} Prologus in librum sequentem \`qui' remediarium conuersorum dicitur. Reuerendo patri ricardo ecclesie londoniensis episcopo tertio (*Richard FitzNeal, 1189–98*): suus petrus archidiaconus eiusdem ecclesie sic currere per temporalia . . . (f. 203^{v}) feliciter apprehendere. amen. Explicit prologus. Incipiunt capitula primi libri . . . (*table of 26 chapters*) . . . De condicione hominis dignissima . . . animam petri commendet deo . . . cui . . . amen. Anima eius et anime omnium fidelium defunctorum: per misericordiam dei requiescant in pace amen.

Bloomfield, no. 2819. Extracts from Gregory's Moralia on Job by Peter of Waltham, archdeacon of London.[1] Two parts, each of six books: pt. 2, f. 240. John Manbe took a particular interest in this piece, which his (?) table of contents on f. iv^{v} calls 'opus solempne Petri Ruff' qui vocatur remediarium conuersorum'.[2] 'Nota manbe' is on f. 223 beside an arm and hand with index finger pointing to 'Melior est ira risu: quia per tristiciam uultus corigitur animus delinquentis', on f. 225^{v} against 'Malum igitur luxurie: aut cogitacione perpetratur: aut opere', on f. 230, and on f. 242, 'Nota bene manbe totum capitulum'.

ff. iv + 270 + iii. ff. iii, iv, 271–2 are medieval endleaves: iii was pasted down. 283 × 200 mm. Written space 220 × 143 mm. 2 cols. 61–5 lines. Pricks in both margins to guide ruling in quire 22 only. Collation: 1^{12} $2\text{–}10^{10}$ 11^{8} (ff. 103–10) $12\text{–}16^{12}$ 17^{8} (ff. 171–8) $18\text{–}28^{8}$ 29^{6} wants 5, 6, probably blank. Arts. 1, 3–7 probably all in one hand, which becomes larger towards the end; art. 2 in another hand. Initials: (i) in art. 7 only, beginning each book but the first, red and blue with ornament of both colours; (ii) 2-line, blue with red ornament or red with blue or blue-green ornament; (iii) in art. 2 only, 1-line, blue or red. Binding of s. xix med. Secundo folio *fatali*.

Written in England. A fifteenth-century pressmark (?), 'A' in the middle of the upper margin and '3' in the top right corner of f. 1. Connections with Durham or Durham College, Oxford, are not apparent, but a Durham monk, John Manbe (at Durham College, Oxford, in the 1470s; sub-prior of Durham Cathedral Priory, 1490: *BRUO*, p. 1212), used the book as though it were his own[3] and pledged it in an Oxford loan-chest: 'Caucio d*ompn*i Iohannis manbe exposita in cista de Da(n)ver[s] 3° die Nouembr' Anno domini M CCCC^{mo} lxxv^{to} et est liber Egippii cum multis aliis 2° fo. fatali. et iacet pro xxvi s' viii d' ', followed by the monogram of the Oxford stationer Thomas Hunt and 'xxvi s' viii d' ', f. 271. Another pricemark, 'precium xxxiii s' iiii d' ' on the same page. Gatty, no. 7.

[1] Not Peter of Blois: cf. J. le Neve, *Fasti Ecclesiae Anglicanae 1066–1300, I. St. Paul's, London*, compiled by D. E. Greenway, 1968, pp. 9, 10.

[2] A treatise on vices and virtues now Bodleian, Lyell 16, belonged to Manbe, and is attributed by him to Petrus Ruffensis: cf. *Lyell Cat.*, p. 39 and pl. xxxivc.

[3] Manbe's distinctive annotations (see above, arts. 1, 7) occur also in Lyell 16. He wrote 'Nota manbe' in Durham Cathedral B. II. 18, f. 52 and in Cambridge, Univ. Libr., Gg. 4. 33, f. 6^{v} (see R. A. B. Mynors, *Durham Cathedral Manuscripts*, 1939, nos. 56, 119): both these manuscripts belonged to Durham Cathedral Priory long before Manbe's time.

12037. *Thomas Aquinas, Secunda secundae* s. xiii ex.

Continuacio libri precedentis ad sequentem. Post communem considerationem de uirtutibus et uiciis aliis ad materiam moralem pertinentibus . . . (f. 223) super omnia deus benedictus in secula amen. Explicit summa secondi libri fratris thome de aquino edita ab illo deo gracias. A table of the 189 questions follows in the same hand, ending on f. 228, 'Explicit ordo et signatio questionum secundi libri secunde partis fratris thome de aquino benedictus deus Amen. Leduc. c. s'.

A leaf missing after f. 113 contained parts of questions 95 and 96. Pecia marks in the margins run from 'ii^{a} pecia' to 'xx pecia': they occur on ff. 13, 24, 33, 44, 54, 65 (top margin), 76, 87, 99 (top margin), 110, 121^{v}, 134^{v}, 147, 157^{v}, 167, 177^{v}, 187^{v}, 198^{v}, 209^{v}, against points in Q. 10, 19, 25, 33, 43, 53, 62, 72, 83, 92, 102, 115, 128, 141, 152, 158, 168, 177, 185 respectively. The marks show that this copy is derived from the exemplar in twenty-one pieces completed in Lent, 1291 (cf. *Scriptorium*, xii (1958), 86–8), as noted by G. Fink-Errera in *Revue philosophique de Louvain*, lx (1962), 211: pecia 21 begins in question 189 in the Mazarine copy.[1] A good many notes in the margins, s. xv. Additions of s. xv on the blank pages at the end: f. 228^{v}, a table 'Abstinencia q. 146 . . . Zelus q. 36'; f. 229, a diagram of vices. f. 229^{v} is pasted down.

ff. 229. 365 × 260 mm. Written space 250 × 180 mm. 2 cols. 54 lines. Collation: $1–4^{12}$ 5^{10} 6^{6} (ff. 59–64) $7–8^{12}$ 9^{10} 10^{12} 11^{12} wants 4 after f. 113 $12–20^{12}$ (12 pasted down). Initials: (i) 9-line (f. 1) and 3-line, blue and red; (ii) 2-line, blue or red. Binding of s. xv ex., wooden boards covered with stamped brown leather, an X pattern using six stamps, the four largest a rectangular foliaged staff used within fillets as a border and three handsome round stamps filling the triangles formed by the X, lamb and flag, Moses at the burning bush (?), and a standing female figure: eight bands: two clasps missing: five bosses formerly on each cover: a small fragment of a title label (?) on the front cover. Secundo folio *uel propter euidenciam*.

Written by a named (French?) scribe, probably for the use of the Franciscan convent at Koblenz, whose ex-libris, s. xiii ex., is in large red letters on f. 228: 'Liber beati Francisci apud fratres Minores in Confluentia quem frater Theodericus de Bopardia ad usum et utilitatem eiusdem Conuentus cum maximo labore pariter et sollicitudine procurauit Cuius anima requiescat in sancta pace Amen. `De licencia conuentus predicti pro conuentu Zegenen´ (*these seven words, s. xv/xvi*)'. Later at the Cistercian abbey of Bredelar, diocese of Paderborn, Westphalia: 'Liber bibliothecæ Breidelariensis', f. 1, s. xvii. '236 Blätter' inside the front cover may be a bookseller's note. Gatty, no. 19.

12038. *Biblia* s. xiii[1]

1. ff. 1–349^{v} Apparently a regular Bible, as to contents, order and prologues (see above, Liverpool Cathedral 13), but of the variant type which does not have the prologue to Wisdom, Stegmüller, no. 328.

Nine missing leaves contained, no doubt, prologues to 1 Ezra, Esther, Hosea, Haggai, Zechariah, Titus, and the beginnings of Genesis, Ruth, 4 Kings, 1 Ezra, Esther, Hosea, Haggai and Zechariah (on one leaf), Titus and 1 Peter. The prologue to 1 Timothy ends 'a laodicia', as is usual in regular Bibles.

[1] Information from Dr H. V. Shooner.

2. ff. 350–384^{v} Aaz apprehendens . . . consiliatores eorum.

The common dictionary of Hebrew names. f. 385^{rv} was left blank: the recto has the beginning of a table of lections, s. xiii. In s. xv a list of the books of the Bible was added in the space remaining blank on f. 384^{v}.

ff. ii + 385 + iii. ff. ii, 386 are parchment flyleaves, perhaps post-medieval. 185 × 120 mm. Written space 130 × 82 mm. 2 cols. 55 lines. Collation: originally 1–2^{20} 3^{22} 4–11^{20} 12^{16} 13^{20} 14–18^{16} 19^{20} 20^{16} 21^{20}, but single leaves are missing after ff. 2, 69, 97, 125, 142, 252, 261, 329, 342 (1^{3}, 4^{9}, 5^{18}, 7^{7}, 8^{5}, 13^{20}, 14^{10}, 18^{15}, 19^{13}). Initials: (i) of books and the eight main divisions of the Psalms, usually 6-line, blue or pink, patterned in white, on gold and coloured grounds, historiated: according to F. Avril 'attributable to an artist who signed a Bible now in Paris (B.N. lat. 11930–1): Alexander me fecit' (*MERT*, p. 18);[1] (ii) of prologues and Ps. 51 (but not Ps. 101), as (i), but smaller and decorated, not historiated; (iii) of chapters, 2-line, blue or red, with ornament of the other colour; (iv) of verses of psalms and in art. 2, 1-line, blue or red. Gatty, pl. I, shows initials of types (i–iii) on f. 328. Pencil sketches in the margins of ff. 107, 132^{v}, 137, 179^{v}, 181 are beside initials of type (i), but are not particularly like them. Binding of pasteboard covered with light green velvet, s. xviii. Secundo folio *ea habet*.

Written in France. Gatty, no. 3. *MERT*, no. 8.

12039. *Hours of Holy Spirit, etc. (in Netherlandish)* s. xv med.

Three quires of a larger book.

1. ff. 1–22 Here du salte opdoen mine lippen . . .

Hours of Holy Spirit.

2. ff. 22–23^{v} Hier navolghen seuen corte ghetiden van den heilighen gheest. Com heilighe gheest . . .

Seven paragraphs begin thus: 'Pater noster Aue maria' after each of them.

3. ff. 23^{v}–24^{v} Tot aensichte cristi. veronica. Ues ghegruet o heilighe aensicht ons verlossers . . .

4. f. 24^{v} Die langhe cruus ghetiden.

Missing, apart from the heading.

ff. i + 24 + i. 127 × 95 mm. Written space 85 × 60 mm. 20 long lines. Collation: 1–3^{8}. Written in non-current hybrida. Initials: (i) 12-line blue *H*, patterned in white on a decorated gold ground; (ii) 4-line, red with violet ornament or blue with red ornament; (iii, iv) 2-line and 1-line, blue or red. Parchment cover of s. xix (?), but the quires are loose inside it.

Written in the Low Countries.

[1] For the 'Alexander atelier' see R. Branner, *Manuscript Painting in Paris during the Reign of St Louis*, 1977, p. 203.

12046. *Sulpicius Severus; Coluccio Salutati; etc.* s. xv/xvi

1. ff. 1–35v Cum in unum locum ego et galus conuenissemus. vir michi et propter martini memoriam . . . dolore dissessus est. Scriptum muriani In abbatia sancti michaelis.

PL xx. 183–222. *Clavis*, no. 477. Dialogus 2, f. 16; 3, f. 25v. Spelling is wild here and in arts. 2, 3, for example on f. 1r *ominem* for *hominem, conscedimus* for *consedimus, traere* for *trahere, consenderem* for *conscenderem, ade* for *adeo, tam tum* for *tantum*. f. 36r blank.

2. ff. 36v–40v Quarta restat causa que maxime angere atque solicitam habere nostram etatem . . . probare possitis. Explicit feliciter Amen.

Cicero, Cato maior de senectute, ch. 19–23 (§ §66–85).

3. ff. 41–99v Incipit liber primus de Seculo et Religione a Colucio P'i'eri de stig[nano] Cancelario Florentino. ad fratrem Ieronimum de Vzano ordinis Camaldul[en]sium in monasterio sancte Marie de florentia. Et primo prohemio. Memor semper fui uenerabilis . . . (f. 42) et exoro. explicit prohemium. Incip(i)t tratatus in (q)uo premisso ordine dicendorum quid sit mundus multis difin(i)tionibus explicatur. Capitulum primum. Hec igitur tantisper exordiendo . . . quem monstrauero tibi (*ends abruptly*).

Colucii Salutati De seculo et religione, ed. B. L. Ullman, 1957. Book 2, f. 79: the end here is in ch. 10 (edn., 132/10). On f. 90v, 'volta carta a.b.' is in the margin, because the scribe had written the leaf in the wrong order, verso before recto. f. 100rv blank.

4. The parchment strengthening strips in the central openings of quires are from a canon law manuscript, s. xiii.

The subject is 'electio', for example at f. 56, 'Quid si electus propria beneficia . . .'. 'nec obstat c. Winton' occurs at f. 26.

ff. 100. Paper. ff. 8–90 are damaged at the foot, but the written space is not affected. 212 × 140 mm. Written space 155 × 107 mm. 27–33 long lines. Collation: $1–10^{10}$. Parchment strips in the middle of quires: see art. 4. Perhaps all by one hand, except f. 96rv (fere humanistica), f. 97/24–8, and ff. 97v–99, a current cursiva with long-tailed *i* commonly in medial and final positions. 2-line initials, blue or red, with ornament of the other colour, or no ornament, or, if the initial is red, red ornament. Capital letters in the ink of the text filled with pale yellow. Binding of contemporary wooden boards, one third covered with leather: two scraps of manuscript, s. xiii, pasted to the leather: three bands: central clasp missing. Secundo folio *possum*.

Written in Italy, art. 1 in the Camaldolese abbey of St Michael between Murano and Venice, if the inscription on f. 35v refers to this actual copy: art. 2 is in the same hand. Lot 130 in a sale catalogue, s. xix: the relevant cutting is inside the cover and has 'From Sir W. Betham's collection' written on it. Not, it seems, in the Betham sale catalogue, 6 July 1830: cf. below, Mayer 12048. 'Cod. lix, lx' inside the cover; also '7/6'. 'XII' on f. 100v.

12047. *Gaietanus de Thienis, In Physica Aristotelis* s. xv ex.

Quedam utilia super libros physicorum aristotelis: edita a subtilissimo ac formosissimo: artium et medicinę doctore: gaietano de tienis: philosophorum principe. Sepe animaduerti insignes ac literatissimi viri ex ueteri consuetudine . . . (f. 87^{v}) sunt in occidente cum moueant opposito motu.

Thorndike and Kibre. Lohr, p. 390. Printed *c.* 1476 and later (Goff, G. 33–6). A lively caricature head, f. 77^{v}, and pointing hand, f. 83^{v}, as 'nota bene' signs. ff. 88–89^{v} blank.

ff. ii + 89. Paper. 435 × 290 mm. Written space 275 × 175 mm. 2 cols. 56–8 lines. Collation: $1\text{–}4^{10}$ 5^{8} 6 nine (ff. 49–57) 7^{10} 8 nine (ff. 68–76) 9^{8} 10^{8} wants 4–6 (blank (?): ff. 85–9, 89 once pasted down). Quires numbered in the usual late medieval way. A strip of parchment down the middle opening of each quire as strengthening. Written in current hybrida. Initials: (i) f. 1, pink on ground of gold, green, red, and blue, the colours patterned in white: border ornament in gold and colours; (ii, iii) 9-line and 4-line, blue or red with pale red (?) ornament. Binding of wooden boards covered with sheepskin, stained blue inside: decorated metal centrepieces and corner pieces, the latter stamped with 'yh̄s' in a roundel and 'maria' in an oval, with 'Aue dn̄e yh̄u xp̄e' on each side of the oval: four bands: four clasps missing, but two of the metal pieces which held them remain on the back cover and are stamped 'yh̄s' and 'S'. Secundo folio *aptitudine*.

Written in Italy, probably the north-east.[1]

12048. *W. Peraldus, Summa de vitiis* s. xiii^{2}

Incipit tractatus moralis de vii viciis capitalibus et peccato lingue. Tractatus iste continet ix partes . . . (*table of the parts and their chapters*) . . . (f. 5^{v}) Dicturi de singulis uiciis incipiemus a uicio gule . . . angelus malus ad eum ueniet. ut cum (*ends imperfectly*).

SOPMA ii. 133–42, no. 1622. A Dondaine in *AFP* xviii (1948), 193–7. Bloomfield, no. 1628. Many manuscripts and printed editions (Goff, P. 84–90). Here, as often, anonymous. A leaf is missing after f. 144 with the end of the first part and beginning of the second part of De peccato linguae and another leaf with the end of the text from a point in ch. 10 of part 2 (edn., Antwerp 1588, ii. 190).

ff. v + 154 + x. 195 × 110 mm. Written space 130 × 85 mm. 2 cols. 48 lines. The columns on ff. 6–154 are numbered 1–600 and lines are numbered between the columns at intervals of 5 lines, 5, 1, 5, 2, 5, 3, 5, 4, 5. Collation: $1\text{–}12^{12}$ 13^{12} wants 1, 12 (ff. 145–54). Initials: (i) blue and red with ornament of both colours; (ii) 2-line, blue or red with ornament of the other colour. Binding of marbled pasteboards: gilt brown leather over the spine stamped 'Tractatus morum'. Secundo folio *quos uidentur*.

Written probably in England. Armorial bookplate of Sir William Betham dated 1783 inside the cover. Not identifiable in the catalogue of the Betham sale by Evans, 6 July 1830. '21/', f. v^{v}. Gatty, no. 5.

[1] Information from Dr A. de la Mare.

12050. *Penitential psalms, etc. (in Netherlandish)* 1432 (?)

1. f. 1 Golden number and Sunday letter roundels, dated 'mcccc' in red at the top. The series in the first roundel begins with xv and in the second roundel with bagfdc.

Cf. *Brev. ad usum Sarum*, i. 15. Explanatory texts in the middle of the roundels: 'Wiltu weten dat guldene ghetal soe soeke yn dessen cirkel mcccc ende telle . . .'; 'Wilstu weten die litter van den sondaghe soe soeke yn desen cirkel mcccc ende telle . . .'. A later user changed the first 'mcccc' to 'mccccxcvi' and the second 'mcccc' to 'mccclxxx[v]'. f. 1v blank.

2. ff. 2–13v Calendar in red and black.

The usual Utrecht saints in red: Jeroen absent, 17 Aug. Additions at 16 Jan., 'Op desen dach starf he[. . . . .] Werninck [. . .]ken to s' merten in den Iaren [. . . .] mccc[. . . . .]', and 24 Nov., 'Op desen dach starf gherbrich Wernynck onse moder'. f. 14rv left blank.

3. ff. 15–39v Hier beghinnen die seuen psalmen van penitencialis. Litany, f. 27.

Fifty-one martyrs, Forty-five confessors: (1) Mertijn . . . (16) Remigius . . . (19, 20) Vedast Bavo. Thirty-four virgins: . . . (18, 19) Walbruch Ghertruet.

4. ff. 39v–44v Hier beghint dat guldene ghebet dat men lesen sal voer die sielen. O here Ihesus cristus Ic arme sundighe creatuer bidde dy om dine hillighe viif wonden . . .

5. ff. 45–51v Hier beghint dat meere gehebet voer die sielen. O vader hemelsche god Ic bidde dy doer dinen eengheboernen soene . . .

6. ff. 51v–53v Tot onser lieuer vrouwen ende alden hemelschen gheselscap vor die sielen. O alre hefste myldeste moeder godes onse enighe hoepe naest gode . . .

7. ff. 54–65v Hiir beghynnet die Comendacie. O alre barmhertichste god die voer onse armoede heuest gheleden den doet . . . Ic beuele dy die sielen . . .

Sixteen saints are called upon, ff. 59v–60, the last four Hubertus, Lutgerus, Remygius, Iorgius.

8. ff. 65v–68v Dit sal men dertich daghe lesen. Ic bidde dy hillighe vader Adonay in den namen der hilligher maystaet . . .

9. ff. 68v–117v Hiir beghinnet die vigilie. My hebben ommebeuanghen . . .

The ninth lesson is 'Broeders sin wy allene . . .'.

10. ff. 117v–121v Hiir beghinnet souen bedroefnisse onser lieuen vrouwen. Aue. Ic vermane dij vrouwe der verueernisse . . .

11. ff. 121v–124v Dit ghebet sal men des sondag van sunte herasmus een ghebet lesen. O hillighe presciose martelaer godes . . .

12. ff. 125–141v Prayers and (*a–c, e, s–u, w*) memoriae: (*a*) Anthony and Paul, hermits; (*b*) Bernardine; (*c*) Jerome; (*d*) George; (*e*) Christopher; (*f*) Cornelius; (*g*) Peter; (*h*) Andrew; (*i*) John Evangelist; (*j*) James the Greater; (*k*) James the Less; (*l*) Thomas; (*m*) Philip; (*n*) Bartholomew; (*o*) Matthew; (*p*) Simon; (*q*) Jude; (*r*) Matthias; (*s*) Mary Magdalene; (*t*) Clare; (*u*) Margaret; (*v*) Apollonia; (*w*) Barbara; (*x*) guardian angel.

(*a*). The collect names, after Christopher, Eustace, Blaise, Vitus, Pantaleon, Silvester, Denis, Magnus, Ciriac, Erasmus, George, Katherine, Margaret, Barbara, and 10,000 Martyrs.

13. ff. 142–157v Thirty-eight short prayers, the first 'Voer die hillighe kerke. Wy bidden dy here weset versoent . . .', the sixteenth 'Voer vasticheit der stede', the twentieth 'Voer onsen prior. God die een here bist ende een regierre alre creatueren sich an ghenadelike dinen knecht N. onsen prioer . . .'. The three last are not for particular occasions or persons: 'Ene ghemene collecta'; 'Ene ghemene collecte voer die sielen'; 'Voer alle gheloenighe sielen coll*ecta*'.

ff. ii + 157 + ii. 115 × 73 mm. Written apace 72 × 50 mm. 18 long lines. Collation: 1^{14} $2\text{–}5^{8}$ 6^{8} wants 8, blank, after f. 53 $7\text{–}8^{8}$ 9^{8} + 1 leaf after 4 (f. 74: 4, 5, ff. 73, 75, are very thick parchment) 10^{8} + 1 leaf after 4 (ff. 79–87) 11^{8} + 1 leaf after 4 (ff. 88–96) 12^{8} + 1 leaf after 4 (ff. 97–105) 13^{8} + 1 leaf after 2 and 1 leaf after 4 (ff. 106–15) 14^{8} + 1 leaf after 4 (ff. 116–24) 15^{10} 16 seven (ff. 135–41) $17\text{–}18^{8}$. Written in non-current hybrida: the hand changes at f. 54. 2-line and 1-line blue or red initials. Binding of s. xviii: 'Manuscrip' on spine: fore-edge pattern. Secundo folio (f. 16) *ommeghelriert*.

An inscription on f. 157v, s. xviii (?), is presumably a copy of the inscription on a now missing flyleaf: Dit boeckijn is ghescreven to Delf in Hollant int iaer mccccxxxii by mi P. van Os den tienden dach der monmaent'. 'Limtu (?) albritstun (?) hort dit bock . . .', f. 14, s. xvi. '5/' inside the cover.

12055. *(Hugo Spechtshart von Reutlingen), Speculum grammaticae*[1] s. xv med.

(*begins imperfectly*) Secundo modo accipitur . . . ethymologye sequitur. Vt speculum uarias rerum formas manifestat . . . (4 lines). Iste liber in quo author determinat de deriuacione composicione et significacione vocabulorum . . . terminauit Pro quo . . . in secula seculorum amen etc. Te deum laudamus et sic est finis huius libri etc. Et sic est finis illius operis.

For the text, partly verse (Walther, no. 19880, listing six copies, s. xv) and partly prose, see A. Diehl, 'Speculum Grammaticae und Forma discendi des Hugo Spechtshart', *Mitteilungen der Gesellschaft für deutsche Erziehungs- und Schulgeschichte*, xx (1910), 1–26. The author died *c.* 1360. One leaf with the beginning of the prologue missing at the beginning. Bk. 2, f. 117 ('Explicit primus liber speculi gramatici. PP', f. 116v); 3, f. 152; 4, f. 229 ('Et sic est finis tercii libri speculi', f. 288v). Some German glosses in the upper margins, ff. 69–80.

ff. iii + 259 + iii. Paper. 303 × 215 mm. Written space 225 × 160 mm. 2 cols. *c.* 54 lines of commentary in prose: the verse text is in 19 lines on f. 190 and in 25 lines on f. 257.

[1] The identification is Dr R. W. Hunt's.

Collation: 1^{12} wants 1 $2\text{-}8^{12}$ 9 eleven (ff. 96–106) $10\text{-}12^{12}$ 13^{10} (ff. 143–52) $14\text{-}21^{12}$ 22^{12} wants 12, blank (ff. 249–59). Quires numbered at the head of the first recto up to 21; the number 13 is repeated in error: words, not numbers, are used at first, 'secundus sexternus' to 'octauus sexternus'. Written in cursiva, the hand changing at ff. 113, 142, 156. Spaces for coloured initials left blank. Binding of s. xix.

Written in Germany. '12/6', f. i^{v}.

12068. *Eutropius; Festus* s. xv^{2}

1. ff. 1–126^{v} M. EVTROPII CLARISSIMI HISTORICI DE GESTIS ROMANORVM L. PRIMVS I.F. Primus in italia . . . Anastasius presbiter ordinatus est. Explicit liber Eutropii.

Eutropius and the additions of Paulus Diaconus. Ed. H. Droysen, MGH, Auct. Antiq. ii (1879), 6–182 (Eutropius), 185–224 (Paulus), 396–405 (ex Pauli Historia Langobardorum). Seventeen books. Learned notes on Eutropius, s. xvii, are on ff. i, 139^{v} and the back pastedown: on 139^{v} a manuscript belonging to Theodore Pulman is mentioned.[1]

2. ff. 127–138^{v} Rufi Festi Pio Valentino (*sic*) imperatori compendiosa abbreuiatio historie romane. Pio perpetuo domino Valentiniano . . . Breuem fieri clementia tua precepit . . . tibi palma pacis accedat. Explicit Breuiarium Festi Rufi etc.

This copy not listed by J. W. Eadie, *The* Breviarium *of Festus*, 1967, pp. 26–31.

ff. i + 138 + i. 200 × 127 mm. Written space 128 × 68 mm. 29 long lines. Faint ruling with hard point. Collation: $1\text{-}13^{10}$ 14^{8}. Catchwords written vertically. Fairly large upright humanistica. Initials: (i) beginning each book of art. 1 and on f. 127, 6-line, gold on blue, purple, and green grounds decorated with dots in groups of three and white vine interlace; (ii) 2-line, blue. The white-vine border on f. 1 includes a flower with a butterfly perched on it. Contemporary Italian binding of wooden boards covered with brown leather tooled in interlace and stud patterns: two clasps missing. Secundo folio *posthumum fratrem*.

Written in Italy, in Rome according to *MERT*, p. 35. Arms, azure a lion mask or, are in the lower border on f. 1. 'Histor. O. 2', f. 1, is perhaps the shelfmark of this manuscript in the library of the scholar whose notes are referred to above, art. 1. *MERT*, no. 70. Gatty, no. 25.

12069. *Pseudo-Augustinus, Sermones ad fratres in eremo* 1473, 1490

1. ff. 1–30^{v} Incipiunt sermones sancti Augustini ad heremitas etc. et nonnulli ad sacerdotes suos et ad aliquos alios. Et primo de institucione regularis vite. Fratres mei et leticia cordis mei . . . virtus et salus Amen dicant omnia. Expliciunt sermones sancti augustini ad heremitas finiti anno domini 1473 6^{a} feria ante dominica palmarum.

Twenty-five sermons, nos. 1–4, 6–22, 43, 5, 26, 44 of the series beginning at *PL* xl. 1235. Cf. art. 2.

[1] Theodore Pulman (Poelman: 1511–81) owned many manuscripts now in the Plantin Moretus Museum, Antwerp, among them MS. Lat. 38, which contains Eutropius.

2. (*a*) f. 31 A table of the sermons of art. 1, followed by an incomplete table of the sermons of art. 2. (*b*) ff. 31^v–58^v De ieiunio Sermo. Frequenter audistis . . . feliciter inueniamus Amen. Expliciunt sermones sancti Augustini ad heremitas scripti per N Schelhammer Anno domini 1490 circa festum vrbani episcopi.

Twenty-eight sermons, nos. 23–5, 27–44, 46–51 of the series beginning at *PL* xl. 1235, together with a sermon in place of no. 45 in *PL*, 'De penitencia sermo. Venite penitentes et non sitis deridentes. Penitentes mutate vitam . . . in regno celesti iudicari Amen' (ff. 51–2). This sermon occurs as no. 45 in early editions of Ad fratres in eremo. The last eleven sermons are numbered xli–li.

For a note on the probable nationality and date of the author see J. B. Bonnes in *Revue Bénédictine*, lvi (1957), 174–9.

ff. i + 58 + i. Paper. 297 × 210 mm. Written space 207 × 127 mm. 43–55 long lines. No ruling, apart from vertical bounders in quires 1–4: frame ruling in quire 5. Collation: 1^{10} $2–5^{12}$. Two cursiva hands, changing at f. 31. The black ink of art. 1 showed through the paper and the scribe had to leave many versos partly blank and two (14, 15) entirely blank: he sometimes wrote 'Nullus defectus' in the space. Initials: (i) f. 1, 6-line, red with red and black ornament; (ii) 2-line, red. Capital letters in the ink of the text stroked with red. Binding of s. xix. Secundo folio *te nullo modo*.

Written in (southern ?) Germany, art. 1 in 1473 and art. 2 by a named scribe in 1490. Perhaps once part of a larger manuscript. '5/' inside the cover.

12070. *Juvenalis* 1471

Iunii Iuuenalis [. . . . .] / Sat[. . . . . . .] / Materiam et causas satyrarum. Semper ego auditor . . . (f. 68) et torquibus omnes. τελωσ. Huic Iuuenalis operi per me Antonium Lulmanum impossita finis fuit hora 3ª Martii die octauo 1471.[1]

Satires 1–16 in five books (1–3; 6; 7–9; 10–12; 13–16). At 9. 37 the Greek was put in by another hand, together with a translation in the margin: the same hand probably wrote 'vacat' and 'supersunt hi quattuor versus' against the first four lines on f. 2 where 6. 548–51 were copied in error. Immediately before this 1. 58–62 were left out: they have been added by another hand at the foot of f. 1^v. f. 27^r was left blank after 6. 522, but nothing is missing. A line or couplet precedes each satire, except the first and last, as in Blickling 6898 (*MMBL* ii. 139). The line 'Immanes . . .' is written both in its place in front of Sat. 15 and in error as the last line of Sat. 14. The 3-line heading on f. 1 is in faded red capitals, hard to read.

Interlinear glosses and a few scholia. f. 68^v blank.

ff. 68 + ii. 210 × 152 mm. Height of written space *c.*143 mm. 27–30 long lines. Collation: 1 nine $2–6^{10}$ 7 nine. Catchwords on and after f. 19 written vertically. Humanistica by more than one hand, current except Sat. 16. 1–3 and the last two lines and the colophon on f. 68 which may be all that A. Lulmanus wrote: his script is handsome, with long *s* and *f*. 3-line or 4-line red initials, plain except at bks. 2, 4, 5, where there is ornament in a pale colour: some spaces were not filled. Binding of s. xix. Secundo folio *Spondet*.

[1] I misread the date as 1476 and owe the correction to Dr A. de la Mare.

Written in Italy. Inscription label, etc., inside the cover: 'Purchased at the sale of Dr Kloss's Library 23rd Octr 1828';[1] 'No 6'; bookseller's label 'H. Coxhead 4 Newman's Row Lincoln's Inn Fields (*London*); book-plate of Samuel Brent, and motto 'Nunquam Non Paratus'; '8/'.

12071. *R. de Hengham, Summa magna (fragm.)* s. xiii ex.

(*begins imperfectly*) Capitulum primum. que placita pertinent ad Maiorem Curiam et que . . . uel quasi in fine alicuius termini (*ends imperfectly*).

W. H. Dunham, *Radulphi de Hengham Summae*, 1932, pp. 5–29/13. The text here includes the two references to the first statute of Westminster (1275) printed by Dunham in footnotes (p. 25, notes 1, 5): in the second the reading is 'In primis statut' Westm' Cap. xlio', not *in sexagesimo articulo constitucionum illarum*. The name at edn. 23/15 is here 'H. de Bathon' '. The running title is 'Hengham'.

ff. 6, foliated lxxxiv–lxxxix in a medieval hand: the same number is on recto and verso. 246 × 172 mm. Written space 195 × 135 mm. 38 long lines. The three innermost bifolia of a quire. Business hand. 2-line red initials with yellow fillings and sometimes a little ornament in red. Stitched into a paper folder, s. xix.

Written in England.

12107. *'Distinctiones Magistri Mauricii'* s. xiii²

1. (*a*) ff. 1–334v Incipiunt distinctiones magistri Mauricii. Circa abiectionem nota . . . circa pectora zona aurea etc. (*b*) ff. 335–9 A numbered list of the words treated in (*a*) under each letter of the alphabet (A. i–lxxxix . . . Z. i, ii), ending 'Expliciunt Capitula'.

Distinctions, Abiectio–Zona. Stegmüller, no. 5566. Bloomfield, no. 0088. Closely written in the style of a small Bible, but numerous red and blue paragraph marks and underlining in red help the reader. The foliator added leaf numbers to (*b*) and as a result any word in (*a*) can be found very rapidly from (*b*). Very few marginalia.

2. f. 339rv Ego C questionem hic non facio sed q*uasi* raciones pono quia si questiones facerem: necesse esset ut magnam disputacionem inirem . . . equiuocacionem cauere. et hec dicta sufficiant.

An early addition. The subject is distinction of words.

3. (*a*) ff. 340v–341v Ego quasi fluuius dorix exiui de paradiso ecclesiastici xxiiii. Sacra misteria et altissima sacramenta natiuitatis uirginis matris dei . . . remanet accensa (*ends abruptly*). (*b*) f. 345 Notes for a sermon 'pro mortuis'. (*c*) f. 345v Memoranda of the use of art. 1, for example, 'In capitulo de spe bona materia de gaudiis paradisi'.

(*a*). A sermon for the Nativity of B.V.M., s. xiii ex. (*b*). s. xiv/xv. (*c*). s. xiii ex. f. 340r blank.

[1] The New York Public Library has a copy of the catalogue of the Kloss sale at Hodgson's (London), 20 Oct. 1828.

ff. ii + 343 + ii, foliated in a medieval hand, s. xiii/xiv ?, (i, ii), 1–194, 194–341, 345, (346–7). 188 × 132 mm. Written space 135 × 98 mm. 2 cols. 44 lines. Collation: $1-8^{16}$ 9^{14} 10^{10} (ff. 143–52) $11-21^{16}$ 22^{12} 23 three. Initials: (i) at each new letter of the alphabet, red and blue with ornament of both colours, the exterior ornament saw-pattern; (ii) 2-line, blue with red ornament or red with pale violet ornament. Binding of s. xix in. Secundo folio *nicam*.

Written in France (?). 'Ex libris d*omin*ici Riui', f. 341^v, s. xvi. 'Ex libris Sebastiani Riparii', f. 345, s. xvi/xvii. Book-plate of the Duke of Sussex, shelfmark VI. H. g. 12: no. 113 in Pettigrew's catalogue of the manuscripts, *Bibliotheca Sussexiana*, i (1827). Duke of Sussex sale, 31 July 1844, lot 301: the relevant slip is inside the cover. '2/2' (for £2. 2*s*. ?) in pencil inside the cover. Gatty, no. 4.

12108. *Horae* s. xv^2

1. ff. 1–12^v Calendar in French in red and black.

Entries in red include 'S' Remy s' hilaire', 'Inuention s' estienne', 'Saint remy' (13 Jan., 3 May, 1 Oct.). No Visitation of B.V.M.

2. ff. 13–19 Sequentiae of the Gospels.

3. ff. 19–23^v Oratio de beata maria. Obsecro te . . . Masculine forms.

4. ff. 23^v–27 Oratio. O intemerata . . . orbis terrarum. Incline . . . Masculine forms.

5. ff. 27–28^v Memoriae of Marculf, abbot and confessor, and of Peter and Paul.

6. ff. 29–83^v Hours of B.V.M. of the use of (Rheims). f. 84^{rv} blank.

7. ff. 85–103^v Penitential psalms and (f. 98) litany.

Thirteen confessors: . . . (4) remigi . . . (13) huberte. Seventeen virgins: . . . (8) genouefa . . . (13, 14) gertrudis boua.

8. ff. 104–107^v Hours of Holy Cross. Patris sapientia . . .

9. ff. 108–11 Hours of Holy Spirit. Nobis sancti spiritus . . .

10. ff. 111^v–159 Office of the dead.

11. ff. 159^v–167 Memoriae of (*a*) Christopher, (*b*) Barbara, (*c*) Sebastian, (*d*) Godo, (*e*) Veronica.

Antiphons are: (*a*) Sancte martir cristofore. pro salutis honore . . . ; (*b*) Regali progenie ciuis nichomedie . . . ; (*c*) O sancte sebastiane. Semper vespere et mane . . . (40 lines: *RH*, no. 13708; *AH* xxxiii. 167); (*d*) Godo, abbot (of Oye) and confessor, invoked against plague; (*e*) Salue sancta species (*sic*) . . . (*RH*, no. 18189); f. 167^v blank.

ff. ii + 168 (foliated 1–137, 137*, 138–67) + iii. 107 × 70 mm. Written space 60 × 40 mm. 15 long lines. Collation: 1^{12} $2-20^{8}$ 21 four (ff. 164–7). Written in *lettre bâtarde*. A 14-line picture before art. 11*a*. Eleven 11-line pictures, seven in art. 6 (no picture at lauds, Visitation at sext) and one before each of arts. 7–10. Initials: (i) 5-line and 4-line, blue or red, patterned in white, on decorated gold grounds: continuous borders in colours and gold ivy leaf; (ii) 2-line, gold on grounds of blue and red, patterned in white; (iii) 1-line, blue with red ornament or gold with grey-blue ornament. Capital letters in the ink of the text filled with pale yellow.

Written for use in the diocese of Rheims. Crossed-out inscriptions inside the cover: also 'B.H.' and a pencilled note of the number of leaves in German, s. xix. Monogram of AB (?) at the foot of f. 1. 'D. J. Bles 1843', f. i. Gatty, no. 17.

LIVERPOOL. PUBLIC LIBRARIES

091 CHO (8/80842). *Officia liturgica* s. xv/xvi

A repertory of hymns, antiphons, etc., preceded by a short treatise on music. Noted throughout, except for art. 1*c*, 10, 11, 14. Arts. 9–14 are for the dead.

1. (*a*) f. 1, blank, except for 'La sol la quartus ut mi sol sit tibi quintus Septimus fa mi fa sol. sic recorderis'. (*b*) f. 1v A hand showing the gamut. (*c*) ff. 2–3 Nota quod in musica plana sunt vii principalia quorum duo cantantur per naturam . . . Octaui toni est. ff. 3v–4v blank.

2. ff. 5–29 First stanzas of hymns of the proper of time, beginning with Conditor alme (Advent) and ending with Verbum supernum (Corpus Christi), followed by the proper of saints from Paul to All Saints, the common of saints, dedication of church, and lastly Nunc sancte, Rerum deus, O lux beata, and Lucis creator.

Includes hymns for Antony of Padua (2), Clare (3), Stigmata of Francis, Francis (3); also all nine stanzas of Aures ad nostras for Lent.

3. ff. 29–39 Toni festiui primus tonus . . .

Settings of Dixit dominus domino meo sede a dextris meis, Magnificat, Benedictus dominus, Gloria in excelsis, Ite missa est, and Benedicamus domino.

4. ff. 39–76v Responses and versicles for various feasts, the first Christmas (Criste fili dei uiui Miserere nobis) and the last Palm Sunday.

5. ff. 76v–85 Antiphons (or parts of antiphons) and versicles for B.V.M.: (*a*) Salue regina . . . ; (*b*) Virgo mater ecclesie eterna porta . . . ; (*c*) Quam pulcra es et quam (*no more*); (*d*) Alma redemptoris mater . . . ; (*e*) V'. Marie virginis fecundat uisera (*sic*) . . . ; (*f*) O sumens illud aue peccatorum miserere (*no more*); (*g*) Aue regina celorum Aue domina angelorum; (*h*) V'. Septa choris angelorum . . . Tu stas pulchra velut luna . . . Consolamen miserorum . . . ; (*i*) Regina celi letare. alleluya . . . ; (*j*) V'. Uirgo mater resurgentis . . . Tu fermenti corrumpentis . . . Ueri lumen orientis. fac nos.

(*e, h, j*) are each three stanzas to accompany the antiphons (*d, g, i*): (*e*) *RH*, no. 11167; (*h*) not in *RH*; (*j*) *RH*, no. 21829, referring only to F. J. Mone, *Hymni latini*, ii. 202.

6. ff. 86–87^{v} Incipit lamentatio yeremie . . . Quomodo sedet . . . inimici deum tuum (Lamentations 1: 1–12). Hierusalem h. conuertere ad dominum deum tuum.

7. ff. 88–91^{v} Incipit oratio yeremie prophete. Recordare . . . de choro psallentium (Lamentations 5: 1–14). Ierusalem ierusalem conuertere ad dominum tuum.

8. ff. 91^{v}–98 Passio domini nostri yhesu cristi secundum matheum. In illo tempore dixit ihesus discipulis suis Scitis quia post biduum . . . Satis est. Satis est. Non sum. Sitio Sitio.

Phrases from the Passion according to St Matthew and other evangelists.

9. ff. 98–114^{v} Antiphons, responses, and versicles of the office of the dead.

10. ff. 114^{v}–116 Oratio. Omnipotens et mitissime deus qui omnibus paruulis renatis . . . Postea antiphona. Iuuenes et uirgines senes cum iunioribus . . . Oremus. Omnipotens sempiterne deus sancte puritatis amator . . . Oremus. Deus qui corda fidelium . . . Dum portatur ad tumulum dicitur psalmus Benedicite. Postea antiphona Iuuenes et uirgines . . . Dominus uobis. Et con spiri.

Office for a dead child.

11. f. 116^{v} Prayers: Concede nos famulos tuos . . . Oremus. Deus qui miro ordine . . . Oratio pro mortuis. Non intres in iudicium . . .

12. ff. 117–130^{v} Sung parts of the mass for the dead, including all of Dies ire dies illa (ff. 120^{v}–127).

13. ff. 130^{v}–133^{v} Chirieleyson . . . , Sanctus . . . , Agnus dei . . . , Requiescant in pace, In manus tuas domine: Comendo . . . , Nunc dimittis . . . , Cum inuocarem exaudiuit me deus.

14. f. 134 [D]eus cui omnia viuunt . . . [F]ac quesumus domine hanc cum seruo tuo defuncto misericordiam. ut.

15 (added, s. xvi). ff. 134^{v}–151 De apostolis. Tradent enim uos in conciliis . . .

Antiphons of the common of apostles, All Saints (f. 139), In die pasche et per octauam (f. 143), In die penthecostes et per octauam (f. 146^{v}), In sancto Michaele Archangelo (f. 149), De corpore cristi (f. 150^{v}).

ff. i + 151 + i. Paper and (ff. 1–4) parchment. 117 × 83 mm. Written space 85 × 60 mm. 4 long lines and music. Collation: 1^{4} 2–12^{10} (ff. 5–134), then doubtful. The hand changes to a handsome rotonda for arts. 12, 13. Initials blue (red ornament, f. 117) or red. Capital letters in the ink of the text filled with pale yellow. Parchment binding, s. xviii (?).

Written in Italy. At Ferrara in s. xvi, probably, when the scribe of art. 15 wrote on f. 151 'MDLVI fu fatto et creato ret[ore] de santo Bartholomeo delle M[. . .]gan' il R^do^ Do' geminian' Roio capellano di santo siluestro di ferrara Adi 27 de 7mb' da donnę patrone'. A number 'LXXIX' and 'Iugli 1812 (?)', f. i. Bought 28 Oct. 1958 from M. Morton-Smith.

091 CHO (60/63395). *Officia liturgica* s. xv^2

1. Noted masses at eleven principal feasts: (*a*) ff. 1–8 In dedicacione ecclesie; (*b*) ff. 8–13 Anthonii abbatis (17 Jan.); (*c*) ff. 13–17 Christmas; (*d*) ff. 17–23 Purification of B.V.M.; (*e*) ff. 23–5 Annunciation of B.V.M.; (*f*) ff. 25–28^v Easter; (*g*) ff. 28^v–31^v De sancto spiritu; (*h*) ff. 31^v–34 De corpore cristi; (*i*) ff. 34–37^v Assumption of B.V.M.; (*j*) ff. 37^v–39^v Valentine; (*k*) ff. 39^v–41^v Barbara.

(*b*) begins 'Super ps' ad uesperas an'. Domine rex eterne . . . Set secundum chorum brixin' habentur psalmi feriales. R'. Seruus meus es tu . . .'.

2. ff. 41^v–48^v De veneracione b.v' Sabbatis. Salue sancta parens . . . (f. 46) Item Sequencia. Uerbum bonum et suaue . . . Noted.

3. ff. 49–56^v Settings of Kyrie eleyson and Gloria in excelsis for apostles, dedication and 'De beata virgine'.

4. ff. 56^v–63 Sequitur Sanctus de beata uirgine . . .

Eight settings of Sanctus. ff. 63^v–64^v were left blank.

5. ff. 65–67^v Incipiunt quatuor ewangeliorum inicia contra tempestates.

John 1: 1–14, Mark 1: 2–7, and Matthew 1: 3 (beginning imperfectly)–16, each piece followed by 'Per istos sermones sancti euangelii bene+dicat deus hanc creaturam frumenti et sic benedicta ab omni fulgure et tempestate' (or, after Matthew, '. . . benedicat dominus noster ihesus cristus fructus nostros a grandine et tempestate'), versicle and prayer 'A domo tua quesumus . . .': cf. A. Franz, *Die kirchlichen Benediktionen im Mittelalter*, 1909, ii. 88.

6. Blessings: (*a*) ff. 67^v–68^v Benedictio vini in die sancti Iohannis ewangeliste. Exorcizo te creatura vini . . . Oratio. Domine sancte pater . . . te suppliciter deprecamur . . . Oratio. Deus qui malignorum spirituum destruis . . . Qui uenturus. Omnipotens sempiterne deus tu primos parentes nostros ita creaueras . . . (*naming St John*). Domine deus omnipotens criste qui ex quinque . . . Sequitur. In principio erat uerbum. Per istos sermones sancti ewangelii domini nostri ihesus cristi benedicere dignetur . . . (*b*) ff. 68^v–69^v Benedictio super euntibus ad limina sanctorum. Domine noster ihesu criste mundi redemptor qui beatis apostolis . . . coronandi. Hic dantur eis fustes et capsella. Accipe has capsellas et hos fustes . . . Omnipotens sempiterne deus humani generis reformator . . . preualeant. (*c*) ff. 69^v–70 Benedictio elemosine siue panis in dedicatione ecclesie. Oracio. Sanctum et uenerabilem retributorem bonorum operum . . . Oracio. Da quesumus domine famulis tuis sperata . . . Deus qui post baptismum . . .

(*a*). Cf. ibid., i. 310–23, especially p. 323, footnote, with reference to the Brixen *Agenda* printed in 1567. (*b*). Ibid., ii. 275–7.

7. f. 70^{rv} Incipit exorcismus salis et aque minori(bu)s dominicis.

Ends imperfectly. The leaf missing after f. 70 contained two blessings, 'Benediccio mulieris post partum' and 'In die s. pasce benediccio lardi', according to art. 9: cf. ibid., ii. 208–13 and i. 589.

8. f. 72 Blessings at Easter: (*a*) of sheep, beginning imperfectly 'prenotatum dignare domine omnipotens benedicere'; (*b*) of cheese, 'Bene+dic domine hanc creaturam casei quam ex adipe . . .'; (*c*) of eggs, 'Subueniat domine quesumus tue benediccionis gracia . . .'; (*d*) of milk and honey, 'Bene+dic domine has creaturas lactis et mellis . . . ; (*e*) Ad omnia que uolueris. Bene+dic domine istam creaturam ut sit remedium . . .

(*a, d, e*). Andrieu, *Pont. Rom.* i, nos. XLI, XXXVIII, XL. (*c*). Franz, i. 592.

9 (perhaps in main hand). f. ii^{v} A table of arts. 1–8, with leaf references i–lxxii: the unit is the recto of one leaf and the verso of the leaf facing it.

10 (added on a flyleaf and in blank spaces, s. xvii ?). (*a*) f. ii^{r} Salue regina . . . (*b*) ff. 63–4 Uiri galilei . . . (*c*) f. 64^{v} Credo in unum deum. Patrem . . . (*d*) f. 72^{v} Credo in vnum deum, PATREM . . .

(*b*) for Ascension Day, is noted. (*c, d*). Two copies, the first spaced for music and incomplete.

11. The binding leaves are: (*a*) a flyleaf, f. 73, a well-written leaf of a 2-column missal, s. xv; (*b*) the two pastedowns, leaves with noted prefaces from a missal, s. xiv/xv.

(*b*). A preface on the pastedown at the end is 'De Ascensione domini binaliter et per octauam'.

ff. ii + 70 + i. Arts. 1–8 are foliated in red in a contemporary hand i–lxv, lxvii–lxx, lxxii. For ff. ii, 73 see above. 243 × 192 mm. Written space *c.* 192 × 117 mm. 7 long lines and music and (arts. 5–8) 24–7 long lines. Collation: $1\text{–}8^{8}$ 9^{8} wants 2 and 7. Initials: (i) f. 1, blue *S* with red ornament; (ii–iv) 3-line, 2-line, and 1-line, blue or red. Capital letters in the ink of the text marked with red. Binding of carved oak, s. xvii (?): brass corner-pieces on the outer corners and eleven six-petalled brass studs round the edges of each cover.

Written for use in the diocese of Bressanone (Brixen), Trentino, and probably for a church of St Anthony, abbot: cf. arts. 1*b*, 6*a*, and a faded inscription on f. i^{v}, 'Cantate [. . .] iss[. . .] Sancti Anthonii / 1554 `Iar 12 Mayus'': script and decoration are Germanic in style. Cancelled inscriptions of ownership in German and Italian on f. i^{v}: 'Peter de Varda aus Puechenstein den 25 Sebt' [. . .] 1672'; 'Pietro da Varda de Liuinollongo Adi 25 7^{bris} 1672'. The shields carved on the covers bear (front) a wing pierced by an arrow and (back) three trefoils: each is surmounted by a visor and above it a displayed eagle. Bought from Sawyer (London), 18 Nov. 1960.

q091 HAL. *Breviarium, Pars hiemalis de tempore* s. xiii/xiv

1. ff. 1–6v Calendar in red and black.

Entries in red include the octave of Stephen (2 Jan.) and Sixtus, Felicissimus and Agapitus (6 Aug.). No original gradings, but some were added, mainly for nine lessons. Nineteen added entries are mostly in one hand, s. xiv: 14 Jan., *Obiit* Konegundis. dabo xvi sol'; 15 Jan. O' Barbantinus . . . ; 17 Mar., O' Wernerus de schermbeke. dabo xxvi sol'; 23 April, O' Vrbanus Dabo xi sol'; at head of May (referring to 2 May ?), In translatione sancte elyzabeth dabo x sol'; 2 May, Item dabo ix sol' scolaribus de dormitorio; 10 May, a later entry than the others, O' Borchardus de Asseborch et fuit feria 2a in anno domini Mo ccc lxxviii. cuius anima requiescat in pace; 18 May, O' Volradus. dabo xxiiii sol'; 6 July, O' Konegund' de asseburch; 17 July, O' lucia dabo viii sol'; 22 July, Dabo x sol'; 6 Sept., O' hermannus de hertb' (?) dabo x sol'; 30 Sept., Canonicis s' bonifacii dabo iiii sol' et duos sol' aliis prebendariis; 1 Oct., O' ghenehardus dabo xiiii sol'; 20 Oct., O' domina de werberghe; 30 Oct., O' anno dabo xxv sol'; 8 Nov., O' borchardus de asseborch. O' Bertha dabo x sol'; 20 Nov., Dabo tria tal' et xiiii denarios; 20 Dec., O' Wernerus dabo x solidos.

For the family of Asseburg at Falkenstein, Lower Saxony, see Brockhaus, *Enzyklopädie*.

2. ff. 7–54v Liturgical psalter.

3. ff. 54v–59 Six ferial canticles, Benedicite, Benedictus, Magnificat, Te deum, Quicumque vult, Nunc dimittis.

4. ff. 59v–64 Hymns: (*a*) the proper of time (17); (*b*) the common of saints (10); (*c*) the common of time (14); (*d*) additions.

(*a*). Conditor alme, Veni redemptor, Vox clara for Advent. A solis ortus and Corde natus for Christmas. Hostis herodes, Ortum sydus (*RH*, no. 14309) and Ihesus refulsit for Epiphany. Quod chorus for Purification and Aue maris stella for Annunciation of B.V.M. Ihesu quadragenarie, Criste qui lux, and Clarum decus for Lent. Summe largitor and Ex more docti for 3rd Sunday in Lent. Vexilla regis and Rex criste factor for Passion Sunday. (*d*) Presepe iam fulget for Christmas Eve in the margin of f. 59v, s. xiii/xiv, Sancte dei for Stephen on f. 64, s. xiv, and Iam bone pastor (stanzas 3, 4, 6 of Aurea luce) on f. 64v, s. xiv.

5 (added, s. xiv). f. 64v Office for the vigil of Epiphany.

6. ff. 65–154v Temporal of breviary, Advent to Easter Eve.

Leaves are missing after f. 65 where the text passes from the first to the fourth Sunday in Advent. On Friday in the fourth week a sermon follows the antiphon O virgo virginum: Uos inquam conuenio (?) o iudei qui usque in hodiernum diem negastis filium . . . (ff. 69v–71). Proper offices for Stephen and the octave of Stephen are on ff. 76v–78v, 87rv. Three lines erased at the foot of f. 153.

7 (added, s. xiv). f. 154v Memoria of Barbara.

8 (added, s. xiv/xv) Mnemonic verses in blank spaces of art. 1, (*a–g*) on f. 1 and (*h, i*) on f. 2: (*a*) Sunt quinque sensus . . . (2 lines); (*b*) Dic michi saligia . . . (2); (*c*) Vnum crede deum nec . . . (4); (*d*) Ordo coniugium . . . (2); (*e*) Iussio consilium . . . (2); (*f*) Vescio poto cibo . . . (1); (*g*) Fortitudo timor . . . (1); (*h*) Qui facit incestum . . . (9); (*i*) Ad papam ferens clerum falsarius . . . (3).

(*a–g*). On the five senses, seven mortal sins, ten commandments, seven sacraments, nine sins, seven works of corporal mercy, seven gifts of the Holy Spirit: (*a–f*). Walther, nos. 18869, 4370, 19669, 13452, 9990, 20271. (*h–i*). Walther, nos. 15482, 411. (*d–f*) come at the end of printed editions of *Peniteas cito* (Deventer edn., 1491, signs. d. 3, 4).

ff. i + 154 + i. 245 × 160 mm. Written space *c.* 185 × 110 mm. 2 cols. 35 lines and (art. 6) 30 lines. Ruling with ink. Collation: 1^6 $2\text{–}7^8$ 8^{10} (ff. 55–64) 9 two (ff. 65–6) $10\text{–}20^8$. Quires 2–7 numbered at the end i–vi. Initials: (i) of principal psalms, including 51 and 101, 9-line (f. 7) and 4-line, red and blue with ornament of both colours; (ii, iii) 2-line and 1-line, red. Binding of s. xx.

Written in Germany, for use, no doubt, in the diocese of Halberstadt where the cathedral is dedicated to St Stephen: Ortum sidus (art. 4) is recorded in *RH* only from a Halberstadt breviary. An owner in s. xiv was presumably a member of the family of Asseburg (art. 1). Bought from Alan G. Thomas (his catalogue 5, 1959, no. 5), 2 June 1959, for £75.

091 PSA 8/45329. *Psalmi, etc.* s. xiii/xiv

1. ff. 1–164 Psalms 1–150.

A late medieval numbering runs from 1 to 172: the divisions of Ps. 118 have each a number.

2. ff. 164–79 Six ferial canticles, Te deum, Benedicite, Benedictus, Magnificat, Nunc dimittis, Quicumque vult, numbered 173–84 in continuation of art. 1.

3. ff. 180–211 Hours of B.V.M. of the use of (Metz: antiphon and capitulum at prime, Sub tuum presidium and Hec est virgo; at none, Beata mater and Per te dei),[1] preceded by a short prayer 'Sancta maria piissima domina deprecare pro nobis . . . hostiam laudis'.

4. ff. 211v–222v VIItem psalmi . . . (f. 219) Incipit letania.

Twelve confessors: . . . (8) remigi. Deus cui proprium est is the only prayer.

5. ff. 222v–250v and pastedown (f. 251) Office of the dead.

The ninth lesson is Ecce mysterium. A leaf missing after f. 250.

ff. 251. Traces of a medieval foliation throughout: f. 250 was '260'. 132 × 90 mm. Written space 88 × 60 mm. 17 long lines. Collation: $1\text{–}11^{10}$ 12^8 13^6 + 2 leaves after 4 (ff. 123–4) $14\text{–}21^{10}$ 22^8 23^{10} 24^8 25^{10} 26^8 27 one (pasted down). Initials: (i) of principal psalms and beginning arts. 3–5, 11-line (f. 1) or less, pink and blue patterned in white on gold and coloured grounds, historiated: B.V.M. and Child at art. 3; God the Father holding orb at art. 4: the *B* of *Beatus*, f. 1, has a picture in each compartment, (1) David harping, (2) David and Goliath; (ii) beginning lauds and later hours in art. 3, as (i), but decorated, not historiated; (iii) 2-line, gold on grounds of red and blue patterned in white; (iv) 1-line, blue or gold with ornament in red or blue. Panel binding, s. xvi: a blurred haloed figure with sword on the front cover and Christopher with the Christ Child on the back cover.

[1] For other Metz hours see *MMBL* ii. 78 and Sotheby catalogue, 13 July 1977, lot 40. Three are listed by Leroquais.

Written in eastern France (?). 'Hic Liber dono oblatus ab Illustri. Magnif. Domino Petro Przyiemski Fundatore Conventus Raviz pro Bibliotheca Ravien' Gierlachoviæ' inside the cover, s. xviii (?); also 'Antonina Przyiemská h Pomorska Curká Piotra Prziemskiego' and two lines in Polish asking prayers for their souls.[1] Bought from Francis Edwards, 4 July 1958.

f091 PSA 65/32036. *Psalterium cum comment. Petri Lombardi* s. xii/xiii

Described by Sir George Warner, *Catalogue of illuminated manuscripts in the library of C. W. Dyson Perrins*, i (1920), 33–4 and pl. ix (see below). See also *MERT*, no. 6 and G. Haseloff, *Die Psalterillustration im 13 Jahrhundert*, 1938, pp. 13–18, 100. Haseloff notes how like this psalter is to a psalter in the Biblioteca comunale at Imola, MS. 111, which can be dated *c.* 1204–16.

1. ff. 1–250v Beatus uir . . . Beatus cui omnia optata . . . eterne uox est: omnis spiritus lau. do.

The commentary, *PL* cxci. 61–1296, follows the text verse by verse, in smaller script. No preface. Lemmata underlined in red.

The broad margins contain almost no annotation, apart from 'nota bene' signs, a few of them in the form 'd.m.'.

2. ff. 251–257v Six ferial canticles and Quicumque vult, with glosses in the margins and between the lines.

The heading of Ego dixi is 'Scriptura ezechie regis iuda'. The first gloss in the margin begins 'Prophetauerat isaias quod deus'.

ff. i + 258 + i. Fine parchment. 393 × 260 mm. Written space 215 × 117 mm. 2 cols. 58 lines (commentary) and 29 lines (text) and in art. 2 23 long lines widely spaced for an interlinear gloss on specially ruled lines. Writing above the top ruled line in art. 2 and for the commentary, but not the text in art. 1. Pricks in both margins to guide ruling. Collation: 1^{10} $2–31^{8}$ 32^{10} wants 9, 10, blank. Initials: (i) of the eight principal psalms and Pss. 51, 101, gold on pink and blue grounds, the blue patterned in white, historiated: facsimiles of Pss. 1, 109 by Warner, pl. ix (a, b) and of Ps. 109 in *MERT*, pl. 1(c); (ii) C of *Confitebor*, f. 251, pink on blue ground, the space within the initial filled with interlacing circles: facsimile by Warner, pl. ix(c); (iii) of other psalms and for the first letters after initials of types (i, ii), 2-line, gold on pink and blue grounds patterned in white; (iv) of verses, 1-line, blue with red ornament; (v) beginning the commentary on a new psalm or verse, 1-line, red. Elaborate gilt binding, s. xix. Secundo folio *qui uite.*

Written probably in England. A blue panel edged with gold in the upper margin of f. 1 bears a blank shield or, flanked by initials L. G., s. xv (?). Beside it on the left a panel of green edged with blue bears six fancy letters, the first two OR and the last A. Armorial book-plate of 'Thomas Brooke, F.S.A.' (Sir Thomas Brooke, Bt., †1908) and the signature of W. Ingham Brooke, Barford Rectory, Warwick, dated 1908, inside the cover. Brooke sale at

[1] I am indebted to Mr John Simmons for help in reading and for the interpretation of these inscriptions. Antonina names herself as Peter's daughter. Rawicz is between Poznań and Wrocław.

Sotheby's, 7 March 1913, lot 11, to C. W. Dyson Perrins. Perrins MS. 9: sale at Sotheby's, 29 Nov. 1960, lot 103. Bought in 1966: cf. *Friends of the National Libraries, Annual Report for 1966*, p. 9.

f091 RAB. *Rabanus Maurus, In Genesim; etc.* s. xii med.

1. ff. 1–104v Incipit epistola Rabani ad Freculfum episcopum. Reuerentissimo patri Freculfo Rabanus peccator in xpisto salutem. Magnorum uirorum conamen . . . uetustate firmetur.

On Genesis. *PL* cvii. 441–667B (end of bk. 4, ch. 16: Gen. 50: 3). Stegmüller, no. 7021. Bk. 2, f. 26; 3, f. 56v. No indication of the fourth book, f. 89. Two leaves are missing after f. 5 and presumably two leaves at the end; also single leaves after ff. 4 and 57 and all but a corner of f. 17: the gaps are between 'qualitate. sed et' and 'deinde lux', between 'fulgorem' and 'ginem et similitudinem', between 'eius nomine posuimus' and 'uolatilia cęli' (a few words survive on f. 17) and between 'stirpibus latuisse' and 'postea puteus' (edn., 448C–450D, 453A–457C, 482B–484B, and 563D–565C). 1½ lines were left blank after 'firmetur' at the foot of f. 104v, col. 2.

QS and Sol' (for Questio and Solutio) and the names of patristic authorities, including Albinus, are in the main hand in the margins. Contemporary corrections, some in the main hand: as a signe de renvoi θ is sometimes used, both in text and margin, for example on f. 19.

2. (*a*) f. 105 (*begins imperfectly*) concupiscentia. quo pudore sacrificare usurpabit . . . nichil proprium possidebant. (*b*) f. 105rv De heresibus cristianorum a sancto ysidoro ex aliis patrum dictis collectis. Ait itaque inter cetera ita. cap' i. Quidam etiam heretici . . . in hoc mundo utuntur. (*c*) f. 105v Quod proprie posse uel nosse . . . etiam si uenerari uideantur. (*d*) f. 105v Ex decretis innocentii papę. Quid enim prodest illi suo errore non pollui . . . prestat erranti. (*e*) f. 105v Ex dictis gregorii papę. Consentire uidetur erranti . . . non concurrit. (*f*) f. 105v Fabianus papa. Qui uero omnipotentem deum metuit . . . agere aliquid (*ends imperfectly*).

(*b*). From Isidore, Etymologiae, bk. 8 (*PL* lxxxii. 298B–299C). (*c*) is one paragraph said to be mainly from Gregory, Moralia, 'pro defensione iusticie'. (*d–f*) are Decretum Gratiani, Dist. 83, c. 4, 5 and Causa xi, q. 3, c. 95: they are taken from (*d, f*) the decretals of Pseudo-Isidore (ed. Hinschius, pp. 117, 166) and (*e*) Gregory, Registrum, bk. ix (*PL* lxxvii. 1044 A). The scribe wrote 'Sancti spiritus assit nobis gracia' at the head of ff. 105 and 106.

3. ff. 106–15 Incipit prologus subsequentis libri. Dilectissimo filio uuidoni comiti. humilis leuita alchuinus salutem. Memor petitionis tuę . . . dignetur dilectissime fili. Explicit prologus. Incipiunt capitula omeliarum numero triginta quinque in libro salutari Alcquini . . . euitandis . . . (*table of 35 homilies*) . . . (f. 106v) De sapientia. Omelia prima. Primo omnium querendum . . . dignus ęfficietur. auxiliante domino nostro . . . amen. Explicit liber salutaris. Iterum epistola Alcquini diaconi ad Vuidonem comitem. Hęc tibi dulcissime fili . . . coronabitur gloria.

PL ci. 613–38. f. 111v ends 'de meritricum immu(n)di—' and f. 112 begins 'hoc est de presentis uite': one leaf is missing with the text in edn., 626D–629A.

4. ff. 115v–123v Incipiunt glosulę super quasdam epistolas pauli apostoli. et super alia quedam plurimis necessaria. Saulus inquietus siue temptatus interpretatur. Sed ei mutatis operibus . . . quę apostolus dixit?

At first five paragraphs of brief glosses on Romans 1: 1–16: 1, 1 Corinthians 1: 1–9, 1 Corinthians 1: 11–16: 18, 2 Corinthians 1: 11–5: 18 and Hebrews 1: 1–5: 9, divided by headings in large red capitals, 'Iterum (*or* Item) unde supra'. The 'alia . . . necessaria' begin on f. 121: the headings are 'De leuitis' and (f. 121v) 'De ministeriis sacri baptismatis sicut a sanctis patribus traditum est incipiunt pauca'. f. 122 is a corner only. f. 123rv treats of angels, the significance of sanctus, osanna, etc.

5. ff. 124–125v Quomodo dominus docuit discipulos suos orare. O uos mei clientes nouis regulis . . . opera eorum recepturos.

On Pater Noster and Creed.

6. ff. 126–146v Incipit liber scintillarum. Dominus dicit in euangelio. Maiorem caritatem . . . donentur uictoribus premia sempiterna. Explicit liber scintillarum.

Defensor, Liber scintillarum, ed. H.-M. Rochais, *CC* cxvii. 102 numbered chapters (instead of the normal 81), as in Corpus Christi College, Cambridge, 439, no. 29 of the 285 manuscripts listed by Rochais in *Scriptorium*, iv. 296–305, where also the ending is *premia sempiterna*. The titles of the first fifty-two chapters agree with those of edn., chapters 1–10, 50–5, 13–24, 56–62, 65–81 in that order; the rest, liii De eucharistia–cii De quindecim gradibus, differ. The last fifteen chapters do not begin *Dicit* and the last five are not attributed to any author.

The scribe of arts. 1–4 began his copy in col. 2 of f. 125v and may have continued it on leaves now missing after f. 125. A new scribe made a fresh start on f. 126. Two leaves missing after 143 contained chapters 80–2, part of ch. 79, and nearly all ch. 83.

7. ff. 146v–149 Incipiunt quedam miracula de Imagine domini. (*a*) Eleuate oculos sensus uestri in filio suo. Est ciuitas que uocatur biritho . . . diem quintum iduum nouembris solemnem agi. in quo hec facta sunt ad laudem domini nostri . . . amen. (*b*) Item unde supra. Adhuc fratres audite quod factum est uerbum in diebus nostris et obstupescite . . . id est quinto idus nouembris celebremus. ad laudem . . . amen. (*c*) Vnde supra. Puer itaque etate minusculus . . . uoluit etiam non ignorari. (*d*) Item unde supra. Aliud nichillominus in eadem regione . . . morientium letatur. Qui cum . . . amen.

(*a*). *BHL*, no. 4230. *PG* xxviii. 819–24. (*b*). *BHL*, no. 4231a. *Romania*, xxix. 521–2. (*c*). Boy offers bread to image, which tells him he will die in three days and be in heaven. (*d*). Soldier of evil life. The blank (?) part of the first column on f. 149 has been cut off. The verso was left blank.

8. Five pieces: (*a*) ff. 150–2 `Tractatus cuiusdam de dedicatione ecclesie'.[1] Quoniam ad dedicationem . . . implere studeatis. prestante domino . . . amen; (*b*) ff. 152–5 Quoniam populus ad fidem uocatus . . . rationem reddant; (*c*) ff. 155–8 `De clericis ordinandis'. Quia cristianam militam . . . in diem proficiat;

[1] The titles of (*a*), (*c*), and (*e*) are in a hand of s. xiv on f. 149v. They agree exactly with the titles given in the late fourteenth-century Peterborough catalogue.

(*d*) ff. 158^{v}–159^{v} Quia sanctitas ministerii . . . in nobis est fide (*ends imperfectly*); (*e*) ff. 160–163^{v} 'De conueniencia noui et veteris testamenti' (*begins imperfectly*) sacramentorum concordiam intelligere possimus . . . (162^{v}) ea que fiebant in altari (*ends imperfectly*): f. 163 is a small fragment only, see below.

Five pieces by Ivo of Chartres, printed in *PL* clxii. 505–62, here in the order 4, 1, 2, 3, 5. In (*a*) a leaf missing after f. 151 contained the text between 'deo illa opera' and 'Interea mittit pontifex' (edn., 532A–534C). For (*c*) see R. E. Reynolds, 'Ivonian opuscula on the ecclesiastical officers', *Studia Gratiana* xx (1976), 311–22, and in *Law, Church, and Society, Essays in Honor of Stephan Kuttner*, ed. K. Pennington and R. Somerville, 1977, p. 126: he lists fifty-two manuscripts of s. xii and earlier. (*d*) ends at edn. 523B. (*e*) begins at edn. 536A and ends at 543A, apart from slight remains of 549D–551D on f. 163^{rv}.

All that remains of the text on f. 164 is in the bottom line. 'sicut accep[. . .]' on the recto and 'humerus' on the verso.

ff. i + 164. f. i was formerly and is still partly pasted down. 300 × 215 mm. Written space 215 × 138 mm and (art. 8) 235 × 150 mm. 2 cols. 35–8 lines and (art. 8) 40 lines. Pencil ruling. Collation: 1^{10} wants 4, 6, 7 2–6^{10} 7^{10} wants 1 before f. 58 8–10^{10} 11^{10} wants 11, 12 after f. 104 12^{10} wants 2, 3 after f. 105 and 10 after f. 111 13^{10} 14 four (ff. 122–5) 15^{10} 16^{8} 17^{8} wants 1, 2 before f. 144 18^{10} wants 3 after f. 151 19^{8} wants 2 after f. 159 and 6, 7 after f. 162: for the small remains of 8 (f. 163) see above, art. 8, 20 one (a small fragment: see above, art. 8). Probably four hands, changing at f. 124 (art. 5), 126 (art. 6) and—for the better—150 (art. 8): see also above, art. 6. Occasional punctuation by means of the flex in arts. 1, 4, is perhaps by the corrector, who uses it for example on f. 18^{v}: the shape of the mark above the point is more like an open *a* than a figure 7. Initials: (i) f. 1, a handsome 14-line blue and green *R* patterned in white with red and green ornament, the final limb a dragon: reduced facsimile in Thomas's catalogue, pl. 2; (ii) ff. 26, 56^{v}, red and green with ornament of both colours: reduced facsimile of f. 26 in Sotheby catalogue; (iii) blue, red, or green, with ornament of two of the other colours; (iv) 2-line, red or green, or (arts. 5, 6) blue. Capital letters in the ink of the text filled with red only on ff. 121^{v}–123^{v}. Contemporary binding of white skin over thick wooden boards, rebacked: two bands: the tunnels for the bands are more than 70 mm long:[1] double headband and tailband, the cords mixed white and blue. Secundo folio *sic intellegerent*.

Written in England. Identifiable with P. ii in the catalogue of the Benedictine abbey of Peterborough, s. xiv ex., where arts. 3, 4, 6–8, 10, 11 are listed, as M. R. James saw (*Lists of manuscripts formerly in Peterborough Abbey Library*, Supplement to the Bibliographical Society's Transactions, no. 5, 1926, p. 36).[2] Long in the Tollemache library at Helmingham Hall, Suffolk, where the modern shelfmark was L.J.I (*altered to* V).6. Tollemache sale at Sotheby's, 14 June 1965, lot 3, to A. G. Thomas. Thomas's catalogue 17 (1966), item 1. Bought in April 1966. Schenkl, no. 4701. *MERT*, no. 2.

091 STA. *Statuta Angliae, etc.* s. xiv[1] (*c.* 1330?)

A collection made probably immediately after the legislation of the parliament of 1330: cf. arts. 56, 57. Arts. 8, 9, 10, 13, 14, 52 are marked 'ex*aminat*ur' in the margin. Some damage from damp.

[1] This is much longer than 'between one and two inches' which Graham Pollard notes as normal in his 'The Construction of English twelfth-century bindings', *The Library*, fifth series xvii (1962), 10.

[2] The Peterborough catalogue we have omits the first item in each volume and all volumes containing only a single text, presumably because a short-title catalogue giving first items already existed: cf. the two parts of the Dover catalogue of 1389 printed in *Ancient Libraries*. Probably N ii and O ii, the two volumes listed before P ii, also began with a work of Rabanus.

1. ff. 7–12^{v} Edwardus . . . Dat' apud Westm' per manum nostram. decimo octauo die Marcii. Anno regni nostri decimo viii^{o}. Explicit magna carta de libertatibus anglie.

Inspeximus of Magna Carta. A note of s. xvii ex. at the foot of f. 9^{v} draws attention to the presence here of clause 27 of the charter of 1215, 'Si autem aliquis liber homo intestatus decesserit catalla sua per manus propinquorum parentum et amicorum per visum ecclesie distribuantur saluo tantum cuilibet debito quod defunctus ei debuit', which is marked 'vacat' by the main hand and omitted from the numbering: cf. *SR*, Charters 11/4, 5. The clause was left out of the re-issue of 1216 and subsequently: cf. J. C. Holt, *Magna Carta*, 1969 edn., p. 271. f. 7 is badly damaged.

2. (*a*) ff. 12^{v}–15 Incipit carta de Foresta. Henricus dei gracia . . . salutem. In primis concedimus quod omnes foreste . . . mobilium suorum. Nos autem predictas consuetudines donaciones et libertates ratas habentes et gratas eas presenti sigillo nostro signatas innouamus et pro nobis heredibus et successoribus nostris Regibus Angl' concessimus et imperpetuum confirmamus. Explicit assisa Foresste (*sic*). (*b*) ff. 15–16^{v} Incipit assisa foreste. Si quis forestarius iuratus . . . de exercitu (*sic*) porcorum. Explicit carta (*sic*) Foreste.

(*a*). *SR*, Charters, p. 27. The sentence 'Nos autem . . .' is not printed in the examples of the charter in *SR*. (*b*). Often verbally different from *SR* i. 243–4/36.

3. ff. 17–20 Prouisum est . . . Expliciunt statuta de Merton'. *SR* i. 1.

4. ff. 20–9 Incipiunt statuta de Marlebergh'. *SR* i. 19.

5. (*a*) ff. 29–33^{v} Incipiunt statuta Gloucestr'. Pur les grauntz meschiefs . . . tenuz en son Roialme. Come auant ces houres . . . (*b*) ff. 33^{v}–34^{v} Incipiunt explanaciones Glouc'.

(*a*). *SR* i. 47, with short preamble in place of the longer text in *SR* i. 45–6: cf. *MMBL* i. 407. (*b*). *SR* i. 50.

6. ff. 34^{v}–54^{v} Incipiunt statuta Westm' primi. In French. *SR* i. 26.

7. ff. 54^{v}–88 Incipiunt statuta Westm' secundi. In French. *SR* i. 71.

8. ff. 88–9 Incipit statutum Westm' tercii. Quia emptores . . . *SR* i. 106.

9. ff. 89–90 Incipit statutum de bigamis. *SR* i. 42.

10. ff. 90–1 Incipit statutum de religiosis. *SR* i. 51.

11. f. 91^{rv} Incipit statutum de quo waranto. In French. *SR* i. 107.

12. f. 91^{v} Incipit statutum de Chaumpart. In French. *SR* i. 216.

13. ff. 91^{v}–94^{v} Incipit statutum Wyntonie. In French. *SR* i. 96.

14. ff. 94^{v}–97 Incipit statutum de Finibus. *SR* i. 128.

15. f. 97^{rv} Incipit Circumspecte agatis. Rex talibus . . . Circumspecte agatis . . . cognoscere contra prohibicionem. *SR* i. 101/1–23.

16. ff. 97^{v}–98 Incipiunt articuli contra prohibicionem. Sub qua forma . . . Parisius anno xiiii. *SR* i. 101/24–102.

17. ff. 98–100 Incipit statutum de coniunctim feoffatis. *SR* i. 145. Dated here 17 May anno 30.

18. ff. 100–101^{v} Incipit Visus franci pleg'. In French. *SR* i. 246.

19. ff. 101^{v}–102^{v} Incipit Officium Coronatoris. Officium coronatoris est quod statim . . . regnum exierit.

20. ff. 102^{v}–103 Incipiunt dies communes ˋinˊ Banc'. *SR* i. 208.

21. f. 103^{rv} Incipiunt dies communes in placito dotis. *SR* i. 208.

22. ff. 103^{v}–104 Incipit modus faciendi homagium et fidelitatem. In French. *SR* i. 227.

23. ff. 104–5 Incipit assisa panis. *SR* i. 199.

24. f. 105 Sequitur assisa seruicie. *SR* i. 200.

25. f. 105^{rv} Pena delinquencium. Shorter than *SR* i. 201 and rather different.

26. ff. 105^{v}–106^{v} Incipit statutum Lyncolnie. In French. *SR* i. 174.

27. ff. 106^{v}–110 Incipit statutum de Ebor'. In French. *SR* i. 177.

28. ff. 110–111^{v} Incipit statutum Westm' quarti. In French. *SR* i. 180.

29. ff. 111^{v}–112 Incipit statutum de anno bisextili factum apud Wyndessore. *SR* i. 7. Dated 44 Henry III.

30. ff. 112–13 Incipit tractatus de antiquo dominico Corone.

Printed by A. J. Horwood in *Year Books 20–21 Edward I* (RS, 1866) from a manuscript in which it is said to be the opinion of Anger de Rypon.

31. ff. 113–14 De wardis et releuiis. In French. *SR* i. 228.

32. ff. 114–15 Incipit statutum de vasto. *SR* i. 109.

33. ff. 115–120^{v} Incipit statutum Norht'. In French. *SR* i. 257.

34. ff. 121–8 Articuli super cartas. In French. *SR* i. 136.

35. f. 128rv Incipit statutum de socagio. Socage poet estre destreinte (*sic*) . . .

Cf. B.L., Royal 10 A. vi, art. 30, and *MMBL* i. 33, 140.

36. ff. 128v–129 De ponderibus et mensuris. Per discrecionem . . . faciunt acram. Cf. *SR* i. 204/1–9 and 206, footnote.

37. ff. 129–132v Incipit statutum de Mercatoribus. In French.

SR i. 98–100 and (writ) 100, footnote.

38. ff. 133v–134v De recognicionibus.

SR i. 113 and writ 'Quia ad communem vtilitatem . . . nullo modo omittas', 13 Dec., anno 22. Between art. 37 and art. 38 the scribe made a second copy of art. 12 and the first six lines of art. 11 (f. 133): these are marked 'vacat' and crossed out.

39. ff. 134v–136v Purueu est et ordeine . . . enqueste de eaux.

SR i. 210–11/40 (Statute of Exeter). The running title is 'Oxonoford'.

40. ff. 136v–137v Incipit compotus Ponderum. *SR* i. 205.

41. f. 137v Incipit lucrum Pistoris. Memorandum quod Pistor . . . allocando ob' (6 lines).

42. ff. 138–140v Prerogatiua Regis. *SR* i. 226.

43. ff. 141–143v Al honour de dieu . . .

SR i. 255 (1 Edward III). The running title is 'Al honour de dieux (*or* dieu). Dated at the end 7 Feb., anno 1.

44. ff. 144–5 Lincolnie de Escaetis (running title). *SR* i. 142.

45. f. 145 Incipit statutum de frangentibus prisonam. *SR* i. 113.

46. f. 145 Incipit assisa de mensuris. *SR* i. 204/1–9. Nearly as art. 36.

47. f. 145v Assisa pollicis vlne et pertice. *SR* i. 206, footnote. Repeats the last paragraph of art. 36.

48. ff. 145v–146 Incipit statutum de hibernia etc. *SR* i. 5.

49. f. 146rv Excepcio dicitur quatuor modis . . . responsionem (13 lines). Cf. *MMBL* i. 53.

50. ff. 146v–147 Cum quis itaque terram cum vxore in maritagio ceperit si ex eadem vxore . . . primo siue non (16 lines).

The running title is 'Statutum Legis Anglie'.

51. f. 147 Statut' de forstallis. Precipue . . .

SR i. 203–4, but after 'fauorem' there is a further sentence 'Omnes vero culpabiles in primis articulis . . . scilicet pillorie et Trebuchetun etc.'.

52. ff. 147v–152 Incipiunt articuli cleri. *SR* i. 171.

53. ff. 152–3 Quant le bref original . . . Explicit statutum de finibus.

SR i. 214. The running title is 'Modus leuandi fines'.

54. f. 153rv Et quia malefactores in forestis . . . *SR* i. 111.

55. f. 154rv Iuramentum vicecomitis. *SR* i. 247.

56. ff. 154v–161 . . . Explicit statutum Westm' vltimi. In French. *SR* i. 261 (4 Edward III).

57 (a nearly contemporary addition). ff. 161v–168v Au parlement semon a Westm' lendemeyn du seint michel . . . *SR* i. 265–8 (5 Edward III).

58 (added, s. xiv). (*a*) ff. 168v–169 De anno xlv regis E tercio. (*b*) f. 169rv De esson' calumpniand'. Demonstratur quot modis . . . (*c*) ff. 169v–170v Brief notes in French headed Dilaciones in placito terre, En ple de dette, En breue du trespas. (*d*) f. 170v De proteccionibus non allocandis. In French. Ends imperfectly.

(*a*). *SR* i. 393, para. 4. (*b*). *SR* i. 217: cf. *MMBL* i. 409.

59. (*a*) f. 1 Table of contents of arts. 1–57, numbered i–lvii. (*b*) ff. 2–6v . . . Expliciunt Capitula Magne Carte et carte Foreste Gloucester' Mertone et aliorum Statutorum immediate sequencium.

(*a*). I have followed this numbering. The table omits arts. 2*b*, 5*b*, and the texts written by mistake on f. 133. (*b*). Tables of chapters of arts. 5*a*, 1, 2*a*, 4, 6, 7. f. 1v blank.

ff. i + 170 + i. 120 × 80 mm. Written space *c.*87 × 55 mm. 22–6 long lines. Collation of ff. 7-170: 1^{8} 2 eight (ff. 15–22) 3 eleven (ff. 23–33) 4^{8} 5 three (ff. 42–4) $6\text{–}9^{8}$ $10\text{–}11^{10}$ $12\text{–}19^{8}$ 20 ten (ff. 161–70). Written in anglicana of a business kind and usually current: the hand changes at f. 45 (6^{1}). Initials: (i) f. 7, gold *E* and *H*, both much damaged; (ii) 4-line or less, blue with red ornament. Binding of s. xix. Secundo folio (f. 8) *hominibus*.

Written in England. Item 6 in catalogue 5 of Alan G. Thomas (1959) at £70: bought 2 June 1959.

096.1 (64/22898). *Horae* s. xv/xvi

1. ff. 1–12v Calendar in French in red and black.

Entries in red include 'Le iour des roys', 'Les v Ioyes nostre dame', 'Saint eloy', 'Saint iehan de colasce' (*sic*), 'Saint denis' (6 Jan., 8, 25 May, 29 Aug., 9 Oct.).

2. ff. 13–18 Sequentiae of the Gospels.

3. ff. 18v–22 Deuota oracio beate marie virginis Obsecro te . . .

Masculine forms.

4. ff. 22–26v Sensieut aultre oroison mout deuote a la vierge marie. O intemerata . . . orbis terrarum de te enim . . .

5. ff. 27–69v, 75v–81v Hours of B.V.M. of the use of (Rome).

The special offices in Advent, etc., follow arts. 6, 7. f. 82rv blank.

6. ff. 70–72v Hours of the Cross . . . Patris sapiencia . . .

7. ff. 73–75v Hours of the Holy Spirit . . . Nobis sancti spiritus . . .

8. ff. 83–96v Penitential psalms and (f. 92v) litany.

The only prayer after Deus cui proprium is Fidelium deus.

9. ff. 97–124v Office of the dead.

10. ff. 125–130v Memoriae of the Trinity, Michael, John Baptist, John Evangelist, Peter and Paul, Sebastian, Nicholas, Anne, Mary Magdalene, Katherine, Margaret.

The last memoria is followed by the words 'De sancta trinitate. Sancta trinitas vnus deus miserere nobis'.

ff. i + 130 + i. 127 × 98 mm. Written space 68 × 48 mm. 17 long lines. Collation: $1\text{–}2^6$ 3^8 4^6 (ff. 21–6) $5\text{–}17^8$. Written in *lettre bâtarde*, but its typical form of *d* occurs only in arts. 2–4. 12-line pictures within arches, ff. 27, 70, 73, 83, 97 (Job): the ground below the written space is bronze coloured and decorated with a winged cherub's head. Initials: (i) 3-line, in shaded colour on grounds of red patterned in white and gold paint decorated with strawberries or flowers: a compartmented border in the outer margin the height of the written space; (ii) 2-line, gold paint on red ground patterned in gold paint; (iii) 1-line, gold paint on grounds of blue or red patterned in gold paint. Binding of brown leather over boards, s. xvii (?), rebacked. Secundo folio (f. 14) *nomine eius*.

Written in France (north-east ?). Bought from Seligman for £185, 25 Feb. 1964.

q841.1 JAC. *Jacques de Longuyon, Voeux du paon (in French)* s. xiv in.

Apres ce qualixandre ot de desur conquis . . . Tel prince ne nasqui ne iamais ne naistra. Explicit.

This copy noticed by E. B. Ham, 'Three neglected MSS. of the *Voeux du Paon*', *Modern Language Notes*, xlvi (1931), 78–84; also by D. J. A. Ross, *Alexander Historiatus*, 1963, p. 16. Partly erased scribbles below the end of the text, f. 131v, include the name 'Ieh'm bourgoys'.

ff. i + 131 + i. 252 × 183 mm. Written space 200 mm high. 32 long lines. Collation: 1–6[8] 7[6] 8–16[8] 17[6] wants 6, probably blank. Twenty pictures, 14-line (85 × 75 mm) on f. 1 and 12-line (*c.* 75 × 65 mm) elsewhere. Initials: 2-line, blue with red ornament or gold with blue-green ornament. The ruled space for the initial or capital letter at the beginning of each line is 6 mm wide. The capital letter of the line following one beginning with an initial is written with the rest of the verse to the right of the vertical rule. Binding of mottled calf, s. xix[1], lettered on the spine '**ALEXAND / LE GRAN / ROMAN. M.**'.

Written in France. No. 16487 in Thomas Thorpe's catalogue for 1824, bought by Sir Thomas Phillipps. Phillipps MS. 2582. Still in the Phillipps collection in 1929. Bought from Sawyer, London, 28 June 1957. *MERT*, no. 21.

f909 HIG. *R. Higden, Polychronicon (in English)* s. xv med.

1. Tables to art. 2: (*a*) ff. 1–7 in Latin, 'Abraham 2. 10 . . . De Zerobabel et cetera 3. 10'; (*b*) ff. 7–13 in English, 'Appolyn delphicus his temple 1. 22 . . . Wynchilsee ybrend 7. 44'. Reference by numbers to book and chapter.

2. ff. 13–220v After solempne and wise writers . . . fyue and þritty.

Polychronicon, ed. C. Babington, *RS* 1865–86. Nine copies, but not this one, are listed by J. Taylor, *The Universal Chronicle of Ranulf Higden*, 1966, p. 138. Bk. 2, f. 48; 3, f. 71; 4, f. 108v; 5, f. 135v; 6, f. 167v; 7, f. 189v. ff. 47v, 220v blank. Probably five leaves are missing, three after f. 208 where the text passed from 'prince. Also the' (edn., viii. 87/17) to 'curssynge' (viii. 139/10) and single leaves after ff. 38 (ends 'water wolde', edn., ii. 25/16: f. 39 begins 'knette', edn., ii. 43/3), 214 (ends 'bycause of', edn., viii. 251/7: f. 215 begins 'of kinges', edn., viii. 267/15). The last four leaves should be in the order 217, 219, 218, 220. Some notes to the text and on f. 15 the six verses printed in the Sotheby and Traylen catalogues are of s. xvi.

ff. ii + 220 + ii. 365 × 255 mm. Written space 252 × 170 mm. 2 cols. 53 lines. Collation of quires 1–25 (ff. 1–197): 1–4[8] 5[8] wants 7 after f. 38 6–11[8] 12[6] (ff. 88–93) 13–25[8]; of ff. 198–200, doubtful. Traces remain of quire signatures of the usual late medieval kind. Textura modified by secretary, which influences especially the forms of *d, e, r,* and *s*. Initials: (i) blue or pink and blue shaded to white on decorated gold grounds; (ii) f. 13, 6-line, gold on decorated coloured ground; (iii) 3-line, blue with red ornament. Ornament springs from the initials of types (i) and (ii) to form borders, continuous on f. 1, on three sides of f. 48 and on one side of other pages: cf. the reduced facsimile of f. 108v in the Sotheby and Traylen catalogues. Binding of s. xix: the two clasps of a former binding show on ff. 218–20. Secundo folio *Canutus* or (f. 14) *trays*.

Written in England. Arms in the initials on f. 1 are party per pale sable and gules, but no more can be made out. Belonged to Canford School, Wimborne, and traditionally to Sir A. H. Layard, †1894: sale at Sotheby's, 12 December 1966, lot 202, to Traylen. Traylen catalogue 77 (1972), item 18: acquired from him.

A. 13109. *Pseudo-Jerome (Pelagius), Ad Celantiam (in Italian)* s. xv med.

Incomincia il tractato di sancto hieronymo ad celantia del modo di ben uiuere. El si lege nella scriptura sancta una sententia anticha . . . opera de iustitia esser peruenuto al fine. FINIS FOELICITER (*in gold*).

A translation of *PL* xxii. 1204–20 (Ep. 148). *Clavis*, no. 745. Written without break.

ff. iii + 53 + iii. 172 × 120 mm. Written space 105 × 70 mm. 15 long lines. Vertical lines ruled with a hard point, horizontal lines with ink. Collation: $1\text{-}5^{10}$ 6 three. Written in a good upright humanistica. Damaged green *E* on gold and blue ground, historiated (Jerome writing ?) on f. 1, which has also a continuous gold-framed border in which are red, green, and blue flower heads, birds in two roundels, and small rayed gold roundels. There is no other decoration apart from the 3-line heading on f. 1 and the last two words on f. 53^v which are in gold capitals. Pasteboard binding, s. xix in., with red leather corners and gilt red leather on the spine: a title label on the front cover and 'MS' in the second compartment on the spine. Secundo folio *tue preghe*.

Written in Italy. A damaged shield in the lower border, f. 1: the third quarter is silver and the others are blue: angels as supporters. 'From T. Campbell (*Thomas Campbell, 1777–1844: DNB*) to his revered friend W. Roscoe', f. iii. Bequeathed by a descendant of William Roscoe (1753–1831) in January 1950.

D. 435. *Horae* s. xv^1

Fifteen quires of a book of hours: the signatures show that nine quires are missing after f. 72 and a calendar preceded art. 1, no doubt.

1. ff. $1\text{-}3^v$ Sequentiae of the Gospels, John and Luke only. f. 4^{rv} blank.

2. ff. $5\text{-}71^v$ Hours of B.V.M. of the use of (Paris). Nine lessons at matins.

3. Prayers at mass: (*a*) ff. 71^v–72 Quant on lieue le corps nostres'. Aue uerum corpus natum . . . ; (*b*) f. 72^{rv} Quant on lieve le calisce. Anima xpristi sanctifica me . . . ; (*c*) f. 72^v Quant on lieue le calisce. Sanguis preciosissime domini nostri . . .

(*a, b*). *RH*, nos. 2175, 1090. 'Domine ne' is the catchword on f. 72^v, so the penitential psalms came first of the missing items.

4. Prayers in French: (*a*) ff. 73–74^v Orison de la messe. He sire tres bien puissies uous estre uenus . . . (f. 74) Et puis si dittes a lui. He sire dieus doulces graces uous rens . . . ; (*b*) ff. 74^v–78 Tres deuote orison. Tres doulx sauueur ihesus plain de misericorde Ensaigne moi comment a toi ie me racorde . . . ; (*c*) ff. 78–81

Deuotte orison. Tres doulz et souuerain euesque pere et pasteur de nos ames . . . Ie tres poure pecheresse . . . ; (*d*) ff. 81–83^{v} Deuote orison. Tres doulz ihesu crist qui estes la doulce refection des ames . . . ; (*e*) ff. 83^{v}–86 Ainsi que on trouue es fais de saint iehan leuuangeliste ihesus apres lascencion acorda a marie le sainte mere que ceulx qui lui demanderont ce qui sensieut en lorison quinte parte en ramenbrance des v doulours qui nommees y sont les aront. Doulce uierge marie fontaine de pitie Ihesus mere et amie qui pour moy fus pene . . . dont ie ny faille ia. Ihesus. Amen. Maria.

(*b*). Fifty-four lines of verse. (*c, d*). Sonet-Sinclair, nos. 2180, 2103. In (*e*), Five Sorrows of B.V.M. in forty-four lines of verse, line 11, Et pour celle tristour . . . , begins with a type (ii) initial.

5. f. 86^{rv} Le pape iehan donna a tous ceulx et a toutes celles qui diront deuotement ceste orison vi cens iours de urai pardon. qui seront en estat. Benedicatur hora qua deus homo . . .

6. ff. 86^{v}–89 Saint gregoire pape composa cest orison et donna a tous le disant deuotement en le ramenbrance de la passion nostre seigneur ihesucrist et des doleurs de la benoite mere. sept ans de urai pardon. Et est escripte de lettre dor en lesglise de S. pierre de romme. In nomine patris et filii et spiritus sancti. Amen. Salue mater dolorosa. Iuxta crucem lacrimosa . . . *RH*, no. 18018.

7. ff. 89–90 Oracio. Domine ihesu xpriste adoro te ascendentem in cruce . . . uulneratum . . . mortuum . . . descendentem . . . resurgentem . . . uenturum . . .

For this prayer see L. Gjerløw, *Adoratio Crucis*, 1961, pp. 16–21, 26.

8. ff. 90–93^{v} Memoriae of (*a*) John Evangelist, (*b*) Stephen and Laurence, (*c*) Francis, (*d*) James, (*e*) Eustace, (*f*) 'De Saint lucien et de ses compagnons', (*g*) Peter Martyr.

(*b*). O sanctissimi stephane et laurenti qui uno tumulo iacetis . . . Propiciare nobis famulis tuis quesumus domine per horum sanctorum martyrum tuorum stephani et laurencii atque aliorum qui in presenti requiescunt ecclesia . . . (*c*). Salue sancte pater patrie lux forma minorum . . . : *RH*, no. 40727). (*f*). Lucianus, Maximianus and Julianus.

9. Masses: (*a*) ff. 93^{v}–99^{v} Cest la messe du Saint esprit; (*b*) ff. 99^{v}–101^{v} Missa de beata maria uirgine; (*c*) ff. 101^{v}–104^{v} Missa pro defunctis.

10. ff. 104^{v}–105^{v} Memoriae of the Trinity and Nicholas. f. 106^{rv} blank.

ff. i + 106 + i. 195 × 135 mm. Written space 100 × 75 mm. 15 long lines. Collation: 1^{4} $2\text{-}9^{8}$ 10^{4} (ff. 69–72) $11\text{-}14^{8}$ 15^{2}. e, h, i, k, v, x of a series of signatures remain (quires 5, 8–12). Eight 11-line pictures in art. 2. Initials: (i) blue patterned in white on gold grounds decorated with ivy leaves in red and blue; (ii, iii) 2-line and 1-line, gold on blue and red grounds patterned in white. Line-fillers in red and blue patterned in white and decorated with gold. Capital letters in the ink of the text touched with pale yellow. Continuous floral borders on picture pages. A border the height of the written space in the outer margin of all pages with initials of type (ii). Early sixteenth-century panel binding, rebacked:

on the front cover acorns above a shield on which are initials GP (?); on the back cover, God the Father within a broad border containing figures: the panels are framed by a border made of repetitions of a lattice stamp. For a similar acorn panel cf. E. P. Goldschmidt, *Gothic and renaissance bookbindings*, no. 135.

Written in France for the use of a woman (art. 4*c*) and perhaps in the diocese of Beauvais (art. 8).

LIVERPOOL. UNIVERSITY LIBRARY

Brief descriptions of all manuscripts but F. 3. 13, F. 3. 14, F. 4. 20, F. 4. 22 in *A Guide to the Manuscript Collections of Liverpool University Library*, Library Publications, no. 1, Liverpool 1962.

F. 2. 1–4, 6–9, 11, 12, F. 3. 2–4, F. 4. 1, 2, 4–7 are more fully described in John Sampson, *A Catalogue of the Books, printed and in manuscript, bequeathed by the late Thomas Glazebrook Rylands of Highfields Thelwall Cheshire, Esquire, to the Library of University College, Liverpool*, Liverpool University Press 1900: referred to as Sampson, *Cat.*

F. 2. 1. *Biblia* s. xiii med.

1. ff. 1v–367 A Bible which differs from the common thirteenth-century Bible[1] by not having the prayer of Manasses after 2 Chronicles, 3 Ezra after Nehemiah, and Psalms after Job, and by including the Epistle to the Laodiceans among Pauline Epistles (after Philemon). Song of Songs was omitted in its place and put in at the end: a contemporary note on f. 189v reads 'Cantica Require post apocal' '.

The prologues are 42 of the common set of 64[1] and 7 others shown here by *: Stegmüller, nos. 284, 285, 311, 323, 328, 330, 332, 335, 341 + 343, 465* (Salomon . . . producunt), 482, 487, 492, 494, 500, 507, 511, 515, 519 + 517, 524, 526, 528, 530*, 534, 538, 590, 607, 614*, 620, 624, 628* (. . . commendauit. Iohannes interpretatur dei gracia . . . humanis mentibus), a third prologue to John, 'Contra eos qui temporalem natiuitatem dicebant . . . posset nosci a paruulis'*, 677, a second prologue to Romans, 'Paulus vocatus apostolus fidem romanorum predicare . . . et de oleastro et de oliua'*, 685, 699, 707, 715, 728, 736, 747, 752, 765 (. . . a laodicia), 772, 780, 783, a prologue to Hebrews, 'Paulus in hac epistola tacuit suum nomen . . . non posuit'*.

Five leaves are missing with Genesis 19: 17–22: 29, 27: 22–30: 14, 4 Kings 9: 11–14: 4 and Lamentations 2: 17 to Baruch 1: 10. Three of the four gaps are marked by leaves of modern paper, ff. 9, 12, 237. The last gap may have contained the prologue to Baruch, Stegmüller, no. 491. Quire 28 is misplaced after quire 24: the right order of leaves is 288–321, 276–87. The recto of f. 1, a now damaged leaf, was left blank. Books are numbered in a single series from 1 to 72 in the top right corner of each recto, s. xv (?).

2. ff. 367v–375v Aaz apprehendens . . . Thagetra liber leuitarum. uel liber leuiticus (*ends imperfectly*).

The usual dictionary of Hebrew names.

[1] See Liverpool Cathedral 13.

ff. iii + 8 + i + 2 + i + 224 + i + 138 + v, foliated i–iii, 1–380. 237 × 170 mm. Written space 175 × 115 mm. 2 cols. 55 lines. Pricks in both margins to guide ruling. Collation of ff. 1–8, 10, 11, 13–236, 238–375: 1^{12} wants 1, presumably blank and 9 2^{12} wants 1 before f. 13 $3–10^{12}$ 11^{12} wants 6, 7 after f. 124 $12–15^{12}$ $16–17^{10}$ $18–20^{12}$ 21^{12} wants 4 after f. 236 $22–24^{10}$ 25^{10} (ff. 288–97) $26–27^{12}$ (ff. 298–321) 28^{12} (ff. 276–87) $29–32^{12}$ 33^{10} wants 7–10. Quires 1–16 are numbered at the beginning and sometimes at the end. Some *ad hoc* pencil signatures. The quires were numbered a–x, i–xii, probably in s. xvi, after quire 28 was misplaced. The hand and the style of the decoration change in quire 15, where Job begins (f. 174, col. 2). Initials on ff. 1–174: (i) of the first two prologues and of Genesis, in colours on coloured grounds, decorated in colours and gold; (ii) of books and some prologues, blue and red with ornament of both colours, sometimes in saw pattern the whole height of the leaf; (iii, iv) of most prologues, 5-line, and of chapters, 3-line, blue or red with ornament of the other colour. Initials from f. 174: (i) 5-line, red or, rarely, blue, with ornament of the other colour; (ii) 2-line, red with blue ornament; (iii) in art. 2 only, 1-line red. Binding of s. xix by 'Ramage, London'. Secundo folio *nocte*.

Written probably in Germany. A gift to the Premonstratensian canonesses of Heinsberg, near Jülich, Rhineland: 'dominus prepositus h*ericus* de wesel concessit nobis librum istum et pertinet conuentui et monasterio heynsbergen' ', f. 1, at top, s. xv.[1] Book-plate of W. H. Rylands. Bequeathed by T. G. Rylands in 1900.

F. 2. 2. *Psalterium* s. xv/xvi

1. (*a*) ff. 1–9 Calendar in red and black. (*b*) f. 9v Circular diagrams to find the golden number and Sunday letter in any year, with accompanying text in Netherlandish.

(*a*) is written straight through without any gaps between the months. Usual Utrecht saints in red; also 'Canonizatio sancte Birgitte' on 7 Oct. The feasts of St Bridget on 28 May and 23 July are in black, underlined with red. (*b*) is perhaps an early addition. It is dated 1500, 'MvC' to the left of the cross. For the diagrams see *Brev. ad usum Sarum*, i, the page following the calendar.

2. ff. 10–113v Psalms 1–150.

3. ff. 113v–122 Six ferial canticles, followed by Te deum ('Canticum ambrosii et augustini'), Benedicite, Benedictus, Magnificat, Nunc dimittis. Audite celi is divided at Ignis succensus.

4. ff. 122–6 Litany.

Thirty-eight martyrs: . . . (14–18) olaue erice hinrice eskille botwide. Twenty-six confessors: . . . (8) sigfride. Thirty-six virgins: Birgitta (a capital letter is not used for other names) is in fourth place after Mary Magdalene, Mary of Egypt, and Anne.

5. ff. 126–32 Sequuntur vigilie mortuorum. An abbreviated office.

6. f. 132rv Forms headed 'De ingredientibus coquinam', 'Horista soror' and 'De egredientibus coquinam'.

[1] Mr D. A. Clarke noted, 25 November 1963, that Henricus de Wesel occurs in Heinsberg records of 1479 and 1491.

7. ff. 133–5 Hore de sancto spiritu.

8. ff. 136–208 Trinum deum et unum . . .

Hours of B.V.M. as said by the Bridgettines every week, Sunday to Saturday. Printed in 1512 and later. Salue regina, Uirgo mater ecclesie and Regina celi letare at the end of compline. A leaf missing after f. 165.

9. ff. 208–12 Antiphons, capitula, and collect at Advent, Christmas, and feasts of the Conception, Purification, Annunciation, Visitation, Assumption, Nativity, and Compassion of B.V.M.

10. f. 212 Collecte ad Aue maris stella ante vesperas. Two collects. f. 212^v left blank.

11 (added). ff. 212–13 Collects and capitula at the hours and (f. 213) Domine sancte pater qui corpus . . . f. 213^v blank.

ff. iv + 212 + iii. ff. iii, iv, 213 are medieval parchment flyleaves. 225 × 150 mm. Written space 135 × 90 mm. 23 long lines. Collation: 1^8 + 1 leaf after 8 (f. 9) $2–9^8$ 10^8 7 cancelled after f. 79 $11–19^8$ 20^8 7 cancelled after f. 165 $21–25^8$ 26^6 + 1 leaf after 6 (f. 212). Signatures in the usual late medieval manner, many cut off. Written in good hybrida and (ff. 10–17/8, 136–41) textura. A flex-like mark of punctuation is used in place of :' on ff. 20^v–39/8. Initials: (i) blue *B* of *Beatus*, f. 10, and *T* of *Trinum*, f. 136, 15-line and 16-line, the full width of the page, decorated on decorated green grounds: continuous borders; (ii) 9-line, blue or red and blue, patterned in white, with ornament in red and green; (iii) 3-line, blue or red patterned in white: ornament in red; (iv, v) 2-line and 1-line, blue or red. Capital letters in the ink of the text lined with red. Binding of s. xix in which is inlaid a triple 'flemish animals' panel in duplicate on each cover, like but not Weale no. 350: the inscriptions are, on the left 'Notam fac / michi uiam in qua ambulam / quia ad te / leuaui animam meam' and on the right 'Miserere / mei deus secundum / mangnam / misericordiam tuam'. Secundo folio (f. 11) *intelligite*.

Written for the use of a Bridgettine convent in the diocese of Utrecht: Miss U. E. Sander Olsen suggests Marienwater near 's-Hertogenbosch. Armorial book-plate of T. G. Rylands. Acquired as F. 2. 1. *MERT*, no. 41.

F. 2. 3. *Psalterium, etc.* s. xv^2

1. ff. 1–124 Psalms beginning at 19: 15.

Thirteen leaves are missing from extant quires.

2. ff. 124^v–139^v Benedicite, six ferial canticles, Benedictus, Te deum, Magnificat, Nunc dimittis, Quicumque vult, Credo in deum patrem, Pater noster, Gloria in excelsis deo.

3. ff. 139^v–143^v Litany.

The order of monks and hermits is Benedict, Francis, Anthony, Dominic, Bernard, Leonard. Twelve virgins: . . . (8–9) clara elyzabeth. The fourth of nine prayers after 'Deus cui proprium est' is 'Omnipotens sempiterne deus miserere famulo tuo ministro nostro . . .'.

ff. i + 143 + i. Good parchment. 212 × 160 mm. Written space 127 × 85 mm. 20 long lines (23, f. 143v). The collation was $1\text{-}19^8$ 20^4: the missing leaves are $1^{7,8}$, 3^5 after f. 18, 5^2 after f. 30, 7^1 before f. 45, 9^2 after f. 60, 11^1 before f. 75, 11^3 after f. 75, 13^4 after f. 91, 13^8 after f. 94, 14^1 before f. 95, 16^2 after f. 110 16^8 after f. 113. Initials: (i) on now missing leaves; (ii) in Ps. 118, beginning terce, sext, and none, and beginning Pss. 121, 126, and 143 (but this last initial has been cut out), 4-line or 5-line, crimson or blue, patterned in white, on decorated grounds of the other colour and gold: sprays into the margins; (iii) 2-line, gold on crimson and blue grounds patterned in white; (iv) of verses of psalms, 1-line, blue with red ornament, or gold with violet ornament. At Pss. 121, 126, 143, the first six or seven letters after the type (ii) initial are made like type (iii) initials. Binding of olive-green morocco over wooden boards, s. xvi, the front cover stamped in gold '**LIBER**' at the head and '**PSALMORVM**' at the foot.

Written in Italy (Naples ?)[1] for Franciscan use. Book-plate of W. H. Rylands and note of contents by him, f. i, dated 24 March 1874. Given as F. 2. 1.

F. 2. 4. *Psalterium, etc.* s. xv in.

1. ff. 1–237v Psalms 1–150.

2. ff. 237v–260v Six ferial canticles, followed by Te deum, Benedicite, Benedictus, Magnificat, Nunc dimittis, Quicumque vult.

3. ff. 260v–269v Litany.

Twenty-eight martyrs: (13–25) dyonisi thoma alane geruasi prothasi quintine cristofore lamberte ualentine agapite cosme damiane iuliane. Sixteen confessors: (10–16) remigi uedasti bauo leonarde anthoni germane amande. Twenty-four virgins: (1) anna . . . (6) aghata . . . (11) genouepha . . . (21–4) susanna elizabeth anastasia iuliana. Ten prayers follow Deus cui proprium, the last Pietate tua.

4. f. 270rv Deus qui uoluisti pro nostra redemptione . . . perduc me miserum peccatorem. Qui uiuis . . . Amen. ff. 271–272v blank.

ff. ii + 272 + ii. 115 × 85 mm. Written space 68 × 50 mm. 15 long lines. Ruling in red ink. Collation: $1\text{-}34^8$. The quires are numbered in fairly modern pencil 2–35, as though a first quire (calendar ?) was once here. Initials: (i) of principal psalms, including 51, 101, 118, 131, but not 26, in colour patterned in white on decorated gold grounds: a frame of gold and colours between the text and a continuous border; (ii) 2-line, gold on grounds of blue and red patterned in white; (iii) 1-line, blue with red ornament, or gold with grey-blue ornament. Line fillers in gold and blue. Binding of s. xix. Secundo folio *et proiciamus*.

Written in the southern Low Countries (?). Probably in England by s. xvi. 'This b[. . .]' is scribbled on f. 27v, s. xvi (?). The psalms were numbered by an English hand, probably in s. xviii. 'I.M.', f. 1. Armorial book-plate of T. G. Rylands. Given as F. 2. 1.

F. 2. 5. *Biblia* s. xiii med.

1. ff. 1–312v A Bible in the order Genesis–2 Chronicles (no prayer of Manasses), Ezra, Nehemiah (the running title is 'Esdre II'), Tobit, and thence as usual[2] to

[1] Information from Dr A. de la Mare. [2] See Liverpool Cathedral 13.

Apocalypse. The prologues are 23 of the common set[1] and 14 others shown here by *: Stegmüller, nos. 284, 285, 311, 323, 328, 330, 332, 335, 341, 344, 457, 455* (. . . dubiis commodare, before Wisdom, not Proverbs), 482, 487, 492, 494, 500, 507, 512 (. . . uerbum dei), 527*, 529*, 532*, 535*, 540*, 544*, 551, 590, 607, 620, 624, 677, 703*, 708*, 717*, 729*, 740*, 750*, 640, 835*.

Two leaves are missing, one in Proverbs and one with the end of Romans and the beginning of 1 Corinthians and probably a prologue to 1 Cor., Stegm., no. 686. Psalms are numbered and have a running title—this is unusual—'Psalterium'. The running title calls Philemon 'Prologus in Hebreos'. The general prologue, no. 284, is not divided into chapters. The prologues to 2 Cor., Gal., Eph., Philipp., Col., 1 Thess. are unusual: they are printed by de Bruyne, *Préfaces*, p. 242, from Munich 21215 and two other manuscripts.

After Ecclesiasticus an annotator wrote 'Quidam habent Et inclinauit (*the prayer of Salomon*) sed non est de libro' and in the margin where Leviticus begins, in red, 'Radulphus exposuit librum istum. vnde vbicumque inueneris Ra :' in [. . . .] significant Radulfum non Rabanum', s. xiii. Many corrections. Alternative readings in the margins in contemporary hands, with references to authorities, show use of a correctorium, for example at Leviticus 3: 12 *obtulerit eam domino* 'He. coram. An. Ra non habent'.

2. ff. 313–331v Aar (*sic*). apprehendens . . . Zuzim . . . vel consiliatores eorum.

The usual dictionary of Hebrew names.

ff. v + 332 + v, foliated in a modern hand (i–v), 1–101, 103–41, 141*, 142–252, 252*, 253–336. ff. iv, v, 332–3 are post medieval (?) parchment flyleaves. 188 × 125 mm. Written space 137 × 83 mm. 2 cols. 59 lines. Line numbering by fives between the columns on ff. 156–7, 189, and partly on f. 53. The vertical ruling is with a pair of ruled lines in the outer margin and a single line in the inner margin of each page. Collation: $1–8^{12}$ 9^{12} wants 6 after f. 101 $10–23^{12}$ 24^{12} wants 5 after f. 283 $25–27^{12}$ 28^{10}. On 27^{3}, f. 312v, is '26 sextar' et 3 fol.', as a memorandum that art. 1 takes up twenty-six twelves and three leaves. Initials: (i) of many books, the usual eight psalms and Ps. 101 (but not Ps. 51), 6-line, blue patterned in white with interior curled-leaf decoration edged with green on a purple ground and exterior ornament in red: (ii) of some books, 8-line, red and blue with ornament of both colours; (iii) of prologues, 6-line, blue or red with ornament of the other colour; (iv) of chapters, 2-line, blue or red with ornament of the other colour; (v) of psalm verses, 1-line, red or blue. English gilt red morocco binding, s. xviii. Secundo folio *et regnum*.

Written in England. 'Fulco Wallwyn prætium', f. 1, s. xvi, suggests a Herefordshire provenance: to the right of 'prætium' is a word beginning 'Sat'. Armorial book-plate of 'Matthew Gregson Armiger', s. xix. Transferred from the Gregson Institute, Wavertree, Liverpool, in 1938.

F. 2. 6. *Horae, etc.* s. xvi in.

1. ff. 1–11v Calendar in gold, blue, red, and black.

January badly faded. August missing. 'Dedicacio ecclesie Sal' ' in red, 18 Nov. 'Magnabodi episcopi' (of Angers) and 'Anthonilę uirginis' in black, 16 Oct., 19 Dec. The scribe failed to enter two gold feasts, the Visitation and Conception of B.V.M., for which octaves are provided.

[1] See Liverpool Cathedral 13.

2. ff. 12–42^{v} Hours of B.V.M. of the use of (Rome).

Originally seven quires, but one quire is missing after f. 32 with all sext and none and only the first quire (ff. 12–19) is still complete. Advent office, f. 39. A memorial of B.V.M., 'Aue stella matutina peccatorum medicina . . .' (*RH*, no. 2135) at the end of lauds. f. 28^{v} blank before prime.

3. ff. 43–45^{v} Hours of Holy Cross beginning imperfectly at prime.

4. ff. 46–9 Hours of Holy Spirit. f. 49^{v} blank.

5. ff. 50–62^{v} Penitential psalms, beginning imperfectly, and (f. 56) litany.

Twenty-eight martyrs: (12) clare. Monks and hermits: maure placide geralde guillerme anthoni radulphe francisce. Fifteen virgins: (2) cecilia, doubled, . . . (11) martiana . . . (15) carissima.

6. ff. 63–80^{v} Office of the dead, beginning imperfectly.

7. ff. 80^{v}–82^{v} Five memoriae: Cecilia (only the heading remains); Mary Magdalene; Martha; against enemies; for peace.

8. ff. 82^{v}–83^{v} Sequuntur antiphone que singulis diebus debent dici post complectorium. (1) Aue regina celorum . . . (2) Mater patris et filia . . . (*RH*, no. 11349). (3) Alma redemptoris mater . . . (4) Inuiolata integra . . . (5) Aue . . . (as 1). (6) Alma . . . (as 3). (7) Salue regina . . .

9. ff. 83^{v}–89 Pontifex uolens missam celebrare dicat ea que sequuntur . . . Psalmus. Quam dilecta . . .

Before and after mass. Pss. 83–5, 115 and seven prayers, followed by 'Orationibus huiusmodi completis dicat Pontifex . . . Calcia me domine . . . Calcia domine . . . Deinde exuitur a scutiferis cappa dicens Exue me . . . Dicat lauando manus. Da domine. Antiphona. Trium puerorum . . . Deus qui tribus . . . Actiones nostras . . . Amen.

10. (*a*) ff. 89^{v}–90 De sancto hieronymo. Antiph. Tue decus monachorum . . . (*b*) f. 90 Oratio. Benignissime iesu qui pro credentibus . . . (*c*) f. 90^{v} Memoria of Mary Magdalene. (*d*) ff. 90^{v}–97 Ab ista feria quarta Cinerum usque in cena domini et nullo alio tempore . . .

(*a*). Memoria of Jerome. (*d*). The fifteen gradual psalms (119–33) in three groups of five, each group followed by a prayer. ff. 97^{v}–98^{v} blank.

ff. ii + 98 + ii. 207 × 140 mm. Written space 130 × 70 mm. 20 long lines. Collation: 1^{6} 2^{6} wants 2 3^{8} 4^{8} wants 1 before f. 33 and 8 after f. 25 5^{8} wants 6 after f. 30 6^{8} wants 1, 2 before f. 33 and 7, 8 after f. 36 7^{8} wants 4, 5 after f. 39 8^{8} wants 1 before f. 43 9^{8} wants 1 before f. 50 10^{8} wants 7 after f. 62 11^{8} 12^{8} wants 1 before f. 72 13 two (ff. 79, 80) 14^{10} (ff. 81–90) 15^{8} (ff. 91–8). Written in good humanistica. Initials: (i) f. 12, blue and purple on ground of gold paint, historiated: continuous framed renaissance-style border on a bronze ground: other initials of type (i) were either not filled in or are now missing: the offset of a missing side border shows on f. 32v; (ii) 2-line, gold paint on blue or red grounds decorated in gold paint; (iii) 1-line, gold paint on blue, red, or green grounds. Line-fillers in blue, red, or green patterned in gold. Binding of s. xvii, rebacked. Secundo folio (f. 13) *Gloria patri*.

Written in France, probably for the use of a bishop (art. 9). The litany points to Albi (Clarus, Martiana, Carissima) and suggests a special devotion to Cecilia. 'Libro de [. . .]', f. 98. Book-plate of W. H. Rylands. Given as F. 2. 1.

F. 2. 7. *Horae* s. xiv/xv

A handsome book of hours from which many leaves have been removed. Other leaves are damaged by cutting letters out, for example the *D* on f. 60 and nine of the principal initials of art. 14. Arts. 6–12 begin imperfectly.

1. ff. 1–12v Full calendar in French in gold, red, and blue: the two colours are used so that whenever possible two entries in blue follow two in red.

2 (added in s. xvi). ff. 13–18v Passio domini nostri iesu christi secundum Iohannem. Egressus est . . . posuerunt iesum . . . Deus qui manus tuas . . .

John 18, 19 and concluding prayer.

3. ff. 19–20v Sequentiae of the Gospels, ending imperfectly.

4. ff. 21–22v Obsecro te, beginning imperfectly. Masculine forms.

5. ff. 22v–26 Oratio beate marie virginis. O intemerata . . . orbis terrarum. de te enim . . .

Masculine forms. f. 26v blank.

6. ff. 27–62v Hours of B.V.M. of the use of (Paris).

7. ff. 63–74v Penitential psalms and (f. 74) litany, ending imperfectly.

8. ff. 75–78v Hours of the Cross.

9. ff. 79–81v Hours of Holy Spirit.

10. ff. 82–85v The Fifteen Joys of B.V.M. in French. Sonet–Sinclair, no. 458.

11. ff. 85v–87v Sequitur septem requeste . . .

In French. Incomplete at both ends. Sonet–Sinclair, no. 504.

12. ff. 88–123 Office of the dead.

13. Devotions to B.V.M.: (*a*) ff. 123–124v Les aues nostre dame. Aue uirgo semper pia dei genitrix maria aue diu predicata . . . ; (*b*) ff. 124v–125v Les gaudes

nostred'. Gaude uirgo mater cristi que per aurem concepisti . . . ; (*c*) ff. 125^{v}–126 Les aues de v festes nostred'. Aue cuius concepcio . . . ; (*d*) f. 126^{rv} Oroison de nostre dame. Sancta maria mater dei domini nostri ihesu cristi ora pro me famula tua . . .

(*a*). *RH*, no. 35840, from a Rheims manuscript. (*b*). Five Joys of B.V.M. *RH*, no. 7017. (*c*). *RH*, no. 1744.

14. ff. 127–134^{v} Memoriae of Holy Trinity, John Baptist, Peter, Michael, James, Stephen, Laurence, Nicholas, Louis confessor and bishop (Aue proles clari francorum cicilis . . .), Denis, Anne, Mary Magdalene, Katherine, Margaret.

15. Masses: (*a*) ff. 135–138^{v} Missa de sancto spiritu; (*b*) ff. 138^{v}–140^{v} Missa beate marie uirginis. Salue sancta parens . . . ; (*c*) ff. 140^{v}–143 Missa de sancta cruce; (*d*) ff. 143^{v}–144^{v} Missa pro defunctis, ending imperfectly.

ff. 140–1 have been badly damaged.

16. ff. 145–150^{v} (*begins imperfectly*) Dame du ciel dame des anges . . . (22 lines, the last) Merci uierge merci uous pri. Pater noster Aue maria. E tres certaine esperance dame et deffenderesse . . . auoir pitie et mercy mes malfaiteurs (*ends imperfectly*).

For *E tres certaine* see Sonet–Sinclair, nos. 1538, 2816. Feminine forms, for example 'poure pecheresse'.

ff. 150. 185 × 130 mm. Written space 95 × 63 mm. 14 long lines. Collation: 1^{12} 2^{6} (ff. 13–18) 3 four (ff. 19–22, two outer bifolia) 4^{4} 5^{8} wants 7 after f. 32 6^{8} 7^{8} wants 2 after f. 42 and 7 after f. 46 8^{8} wants 3 after f. 49 and 7 after f. 52 9^{8} wants 1 before f. 54 and 3 after f. 54 10 three (ff. 60–2) 11^{8} wants 1 before f. 63 12 five (ff. 70–4) 13^{8} wants 1, 2 before f. 75 and 7 after f. 78 14^{8} wants 3 after f. 81 and 8 after f. 85 15 five (ff. 86–90: 87 and 89 are conjoint) 16–17^{8} 18^{8} wants 7 after f. 112 19^{6} 20^{8} wants 4 after f. 122 21^{8} 22^{6} (ff. 135–40) 23^{8} wants 5 after f. 144 24 three (ff. 148–50). Initials: (i) removed; (ii) 2-line, pink or blue, patterned in white on gold grounds with ivy-leaf decoration and sprays of ivy into the margin: many cut out; (iii) 1-line, gold on coloured grounds. Line fillers in red and blue patterned in white and decorated with pieces of gold. A gold and blue bar runs down every outer margin and is usually linked to an initial of type (ii) if there is one: it gives off leafy branches at head and foot and in the middle: sometimes on rectos a dragon, not leaves, decorates a head branch. Capital letters in the ink of the text are filled with pale yellow. Binding of s. xix by the same binder as F. 4. 7.

Written in France for the use of a woman, as appears from arts. 13, 16, but arts. 4, 5 were not adapted. 'Carmeli Sedanen' ', s. xvi, and '[...]tionis Jalienensis (?)', s. xvii (?), at the foot of f. 1. Book-plate of W. H. Rylands. Given as F. 2. 1.

F. 2. 8. *Horae* s. xv^{2}

1. ff. 1–12^{v} Full calendar in French in red and black, the colours alternating: principal feasts are distinguished by being given a blue initial.

2. ff. 13–18 Sequentiae of the Gospels. 'Protector in te sperantium . . .' follows the extract from St John.

3. ff. 18–21^{v} Oratio deuotissima ad beatam mariam. Obsecro te . . . Masculine forms.

4. ff. 21^{v}–23^{v} O intemerata . . . orbis terrarum. Inclina . . . Masculine forms.

5. ff. 24–82^{v} Hours of B.V.M. of the use of (Chartres). Hours of Cross and Holy Spirit worked in. Salve regina, f. 50^{v}, between matins of Holy Spirit and prime of B.V.M.

6. ff. 83–96 Penitential psalms and (f. 93) litany.

Eleven confessors: (9–11) brice benedicte germane. The prayers at the end are only Deus cui proprium and Fidelium.

7. ff. 97–134^{v} Office of the dead.

8. ff. 135–141^{v} Memoriae of Holy Trinity, Michael, John Baptist, Peter and Paul, Laurence, Sebastian, Nicholas, Anne, Mary Magdalene, Katherine, Barbara (Gaude barbara beata summe pollens . . . : *RH*, no. 6711). f. 142^{rv} blank.

ff. ii + 142 + iii. 168 × 120 mm. Written space 100 × 63 mm. 17 long lines. Ruling in red ink. Collation: $1\text{–}2^{6}$ $3\text{–}10^{8}$ 11^{6} (ff. 77–82) $12\text{–}18^{8}$ 19^{4}. Fourteen 12-line pictures, ten in art. 5 and one before each of arts. 2, 3 (pietà), 6 (David and Bathsheba), 7. Fifteen smaller pictures, three in art. 2, eleven in art. 8 and one before art. 4 (B.V.M. in glory). In art. 5 the pictures precede matins and lauds of B.V.M., matins of the Cross, matins of Holy Spirit and all hours of the Cross from prime to compline. For the subjects of these twenty-nine pictures see Sampson, *Cat.* Initials: (i) blue shaded to white on decorated grounds of gold paint and red; (ii–iv) 4-line, 2-line, and 1-line, gold on grounds of red and blue patterned in white. Capital letters in the ink of the text filled with pale yellow. Line fillers red and blue, patterned in white and picked out with a few blobs of gold. Framed flowers-and-fruit borders, continuous on pages with larger pictures, on three sides of pages with smaller pictures, and the height of the written space in the outer margin of pages with initials of type (ii). On principal pages the borders are sometimes compartmented, strips of white alternating with strips of gold paint. Red morocco binding, s. xviii. Secundo folio (f. 14) *In propria.*

Written in France. 'André francois de paule le fevre Dormesson', f. i^{v}, s. xviii. Armorial book-plate of T. G. Rylands inside the cover below an Aldenham Abbey book-plate: sale of William Stuart of Aldenham Abbey, 17 June 1875, lot 89. Given as F. 2. 1.

F. 2. 9. *Lectiones breviarii* s. xv med.

1. ff. 1–44 Lessons of the temporal, beginning imperfectly at Sexagesima Sunday and running to the twenty-fifth Sunday after Pentecost.

The foliation suggests that 121 leaves are missing at the beginning.

2. ff. 44–81 Incipit legenda sanctorum per anni circulum. In natali sancti antonii abbatis et confessoris . . .

For feasts of twelve lessons, 17 Jan.–21 Dec. (Thomas apostle), forty-seven in all, and within the octaves of Assumption and Nativity of B.V.M. The feast of Relics lies between 1 and 11

Nov. Cues for Hugh (of Grenoble), 1 Apr., 'per omnia sicut sancti Martini', and Hugh (of Lincoln), 17 Nov.

3. ff. 81–2 Lessons for the common of martyrs, martyr, confessor and bishop, confessor not bishop, and virgins: for the last three the reader is referred by cues to Gregory, Ambrose, and Agatha in art. 1.

4. ff. 82–3 In dedicacione ecclesie.

5. f. 83^{rv} Post oct' penthecostes die quacumque festum trium leccionum occurrerit . . . sine festo occurrerit.

Rubric on readings. ff. 84–86^{v} blank.

6. ff. 87–127 . . . Explicit dominicale xii leccionum secundum ordinem cart'. deo gracias et sue genetrici marie gloriose.

The first leaf is missing.

7. ff. 127–144^{v} Incipit sanctorale.

26 Dec. (Stephen)–21 Nov. ('Sanctificatio beate marie'), largely by cues. The dedication of church is in August between the Assumption of B.V.M. and the Decollation of John. A note in the lower margin of f. 136^{v}, 'De visitacione beate marie quere in principio libri' refers to a now missing text.

8. ff. 144^{v}–152 Incipit commune sanctorum.

9. ff. 152^{v}–154 Tabula infrascripta docet responsa que dicenda sunt in festis trium leccionum . . .

The fifty-seven feasts are divided under apostles, martyrs (20), martyr (14), confessor and bishop (5), confessor not bishop (6), and virgins and each is marked with its Sunday letter. The order is for a church year beginning in May.

10 (added, s. xv). ff. 154^{v}–157^{v} Noted preface and canon of mass, ending imperfectly in the Lord's Prayer.

11. f. 158 (flyleaf, s. xvi, backed by modern paper). Benedictione perpetua benedicat nos pater eternus . . .

ff. v + 157 + ii. A sixteenth-century foliation runs 122–200 on ff. 1–79, 210, 220, 23(0), 240, 250, 260, 270 on ff. 80–86, 263–9 (erased) and 216 (erased) on ff. 87–94, 217–79 on ff. 95–157. 133 × 100 mm. Written space 93 × 70 mm and from f. 87 93 × 70 mm. 2 cols. 25 lines and from f. 87 29 lines. Ruling with violet ink. Collation: 1^{8} wants 1, 2 2–11^{8} 12^{8} wants 1 before f. 87 13–20^{8}. Initials 2-line or 1-line, red or blue. Capital letters in the ink of the text filled with pale yellow. Blue morocco binding, s. xix.

Written in France (?) for Carthusian use. From the Charterhouse of Villeneuve-lez-Avignon: [Istud] Breuiarium est domus vallisbenedictionis secus auinionem Mutuatum domno Iohanni de mannis professo eiusdem domus per d' Iohannem vientis (?) priorem dicte domus xviii[a] Septembris anno domini 1500 quod promisit restituere fideliter dicte domui, f. 152v. A slip from an English bookseller's catalogue, s. xix, in which this was item 557 is inside the cover. Armorial book-plate of W. H. Rylands. Given as F. 2. 1.

F. 2. 11. *Lectionary (in Netherlandish)* s. xv^2

Epistle and Gospel lessons of the temporal beginning imperfectly (f. 2) in the heading of the Epistle for St Stephen, 'telaers dach die Epistel int werck der apostelen int seste capittel. In dien daeghen Stephanus . . .' (Acts 6: 8) and ending imperfectly (f. 197v) in the Epistle for the 15th Sunday after the octave of Pentecost, 'en is die bedrieghet' (Galatians 6: 3).

Probably four leaves are missing after f. 123, where the text of the Gospel for Good Friday passes from John 18: 23 to John 19: 14.

ff. i + 196 + i, foliated 1–198. 115 × 85 mm. Written space 87 × 63 mm. 17 long lines. Ruling in red ink. Collation: 1–15^8 16^8 wants 3–6 after f. 123 17–25^8. Written in a set sloping hybrida: no marks of punctuation. Initials: (i) f. 155v (Pentecost), 4-line, blue patterned in white, with violet (?) ornament; (ii) 2-line, red or blue. Capital letters in the ink of the text stroked with red. Binding of gilt red morocco, s. xviii: floral centrepiece.

Written in the Low Countries. Arms on f. 1, s. xvii (?), azure a chevron between three cocks or armed gules: over all an inescutcheon barry of eight gules and or. Belonged to W. H. Black, †1872: 'Nigri codex Lond 4/11/56', f. 1v; 'Bought of Lumley 4/11/[56] W. H. Black' inside the cover; not in his sale, 28 July 1873, apparently. Book-plate of T. G. Rylands. Given as F. 2. 1.

F. 2. 12. *'Rapularius'* s. xv med.–xv^2

A book in which various people, all probably monks of the Charterhouse of Erfurt, have entered extracts from the Fathers, especially St Bernard, and many other short pieces. Arts. 13, 14 bear dates of compilation or writing. The pieces thought to be of special interest were marked by parchment tabs projecting from the head: all these—arts. 3–8, 12–16—and a few others, are noticed here. The title is on the front cover. The late medieval Erfurt cataloguer used it several times as a term for a collection of odds and ends: cf. *Asinarius und Rapularius*, ed. K. Langosch (Sammlung mittellateinischer Texte x, 1929), pp. iii, iv, and Paul Lehmann's article on the Rapularius of Heinrich Token, *Erforschung des Mittelalters* iv (1961), 187–205.[1]

1 (quire 1, ff. 1–8). ff. 1–8v [. . .] Wyllelmi (?) de contractu doctore sacre theologie. Quinto videndum est an licitum sit emere et vendere pro pecunia . . . Ad quod respondendum suppono primo . . .

Henricus de Hoyta, De contractibus. The extract here is printed in *Opera Gersonis*, Cologne 1484, iv. 237v–240v. f. 1 is damaged at the foot.

[1] I owe both references to Dr S. Krämer.

2 (quire 2, ff. 9–12). ff. 9–11v Ex tractatu Magistri heinrici de hassia qui incipit In sudore vultus tui etc. Ex 2a eius parte de origine censuum. Capitulum x. Contra contractum reuendicionis Obligacio emptoris extorta ad reuendendum rem emptam . . . potest inueniri.

Printed op. cit., iv. 209v–210v (chapters 10–12).

3 (quire 3, ff. 13–24). f. 15rv Corona beate virginis. Cum iocunditate memoriam nominis marie celebremus ut ipsa presens intercedat ad dominum ihesum cristum. Gaude virgo mater cristi que per aurem . . . (*RH*, no. 7017). A psalm, antiphon and prayer after each Joy.

f. 13 is headed 'Ihesus xc'. ff. 16v, 20v blank.

4 (quire 4, ff. 25–34). ff. 31–3 Incipit epistola Thome de aquino de norma viuendi religiosorum. Quoniam vt ait apostolus 1a ad Chorint' 4o Omnia honeste . . . ob reuerenciam beate uirginis matris dei Marie Amen. Explicit Epistola beati thome . . . utilis valde pro direccione incipiencium. etc.

Attributed to Rogerius, O.F.M., in Paris Mazarine 995, f. 139 and to Rogerius in Paris, Ste Geneviève 1363.

5 (quire 5, ff. 35–49). (*a*) ff. 35–6 Tractatus bonus de diffinicione et diuisione peccatorum. Quid sit peccatum beatus augustinus describit dicens . . . (*b*) ff. 37–46v On the seven deadly sins, beginning with the first 'quod est inanis gloria'. (*c*) ff. 47–49v Modus confitendi. Sensus precepta mortalia suscipe sacra . . .

(*c*) partly in verse. Numbers are interlined above the key words, thus 5, 10, and 7 above the first three.

6 (quire 6, ff. 50–69). (*a*) ff. 51–3 Sequitur de Institut' Cartusien'. Cum singulis personis nostre carthus' ordinis institutis cupientibus eadem verbotenus enarrare nobis satis sit tediosum nostreque paci et silencio valde contrarium visum est nobis . . . quod ei opus erat. (*b*) ff. 53v–56v Regula minorum fratrum. Honorius episcopus seruus . . . Solet annuere sedes apostolica . . . Data laterani in kalendis decembris pontificatus nostri anno octauo. (*c*) ff. 57–63v Notes on the rule of St Francis, extracts from it and, finally, a list of thirty-eight 'casus in quibus frater minor potest dici proprietarius'.

(*b*). The papal confirmation in which the rule of the Franciscans is set out, 29 Nov. 1223. (*c*). The text on the inserted bifolium, ff. 57, 62, includes (62v) a reference to the opinion of 'doctor Gotschalcus decanus' (cf. art. 8). f. 65v blank.

7 (quire 7, ff. 70–9). (*a*) f. 70rv, the end of a piece about spiritual exercises, which includes some sentences in German, for example (f. 70/9) 'Och leue sote fader wanner sol wy kommen togader'. (*b*) f. 72rv Extracts from 'Clymachus', the first 'De obediencia de quodam sane octogenario . . .'. (*c*) ff. 78v–79v 'De sancto Anthonio': on his temptations.

(*b*). Cf. J. Climacus, Scala paradisi, in *Cassiani opera*, Cologne 1540: Gradus 4 is De obediencia (f. 149), but I do not see art. 7*b* there.

8 (quire 8, ff. 80–3). (*a*) ff. 80–2 O ihesu criste eterna dulcedo . . . (*b*) f. 83^{rv} Probleuma doctoris etc ut infra. Quare cristus vt est in sacramento corporaliter non potest uideri . . . Istud probleuma cum questione alia determinatum est in quotlibeto studii Errforden' Anno domini 1448 per doctorem Godschalcum sacre theologie (professorem) decanumque ecclesie ad grad' ibidem. Item idem godschalcus remouebat in questione dubium . . .

(*a*). The Fifteen Oes of St Bridget.

9 (quire 9, ff. 84–100). ff. 85^{rv}, 99^{rv} A prayer headed 'Pro fine bono obtinendo oracio'.

Apparently thirteen leaves of excerpts, ff. 86–98, were inserted into a quire of four leaves. ff. 86^{v}, 97^{v}, 98^{r}, 100^{rv} blank.

10 (quire 10, ff. 101–17). (*a*) f. 101 Incipit deuotus trac(ta)tulus de spiritualibus ascensionibus . . . Beatus vir cuius est auxilium . . . (*ends abruptly*).

The scribe headed f. 101 'Ihesu maria A(ndreas)', but he wrote only the one page of Gerhart Zutphen's De spiritualibus ascensionibus (cf. *MMBL* ii. 185). ff. 101^{v}–102^{v}, 116^{rv} blank.

11 (quire 11, ff. 118–29). f. 128^{rv} De sancto francisco.

f. 120 is headed 'Ihesus maria andreas'.

12 (quire 12, ff. 130–7). (*a*) ff. 130–133^{v} Si diligenter et attente considerentur vita mores atque doctrina suprascripte virginis alme. videlicet beate katherine de senis . . . omnia venerandus. cui est honor et gloria in secula seculorum. Amen. Exemplar prescripti huius apportauit venerabilis pater dompnus Stephanus prior domus papie nostri ordinis quibusdam monachis domus Cartusie. requirentibus eum super nonnullis de prefata sacratissima virgine mirabilibus intimandis sua propria manu scriptum Anno domini mcccc^{o} xviii^{o} tempore nostri capituli generalis. frater Gerardus schultet monachus Carth'. `istud non scribatur ad legend''. Venerabilis pater et dilecte domne Alberte noueritis quod . . . predictum dompnum Gerhard' et me cordialissime commendando. Dompno Alberto de suntram monacho domus Errford' presentetur. Echardus filius vester quem noscitis. (*b*) ff. 134–135^{v} Sermo capituli in epiphania anno 1423. Et intrantes domum . . . In serie sancti euangelii presentis pro instruccione nostra spirituali. Tria notari possunt que isti sancti magi fecisse leguntur . . . (*c*) f. 137^{v} Explicit legenda de vita et moribus virginis Katherine de senis . . . Sequitur attestatio vite et legende predicte uirginis domni Steffani prioris et rectoris tocius ordinis carthus' tempore scismatis . . . quem attestationem ego frater petrus de A[. . . .] (*these five words crossed out*) domnus Albertus de Suntram huius uirginis deuotus recepit a Cartusia.

(*a, c*). Apparently matter accompanying the copy of the life of St Katherine of Siena sent to the Charterhouse of Erfurt. ff. 136–7 blank. f. 130 is headed 'Ihesu bone adesto prone'.

13 (quires 13, 14, ff. 138–57). ff. 138–55 Registrum sermonum Scientes quia etc' `et sunt sermones melliflui' . . . Accelerare . . . Xpistus. Et sic finis . . . 1446 circa festum natiuitatis Marie.

References are by numbers, the highest a little over 300, and subdivisions, a–d. ff. 155^{v}–157^{v} blank.

14 (quire 15, ff. 158–63). ff. 158–62 Registrum in materiam subsequentem. De auersione 1 . . . De zelo domini 21. Explicit registrum 1449.

On vices and virtues. Numbers range from 1 to 49. ff. 162^{v}–163^{v} blank.

15 (quire 16, ff. 164–71). (*a*) ff. 164–70 Table of chapters of the fifteen books of Augustine, De trinitate. (*b*) ff. 170^{v}–171 Table of the fifty-six letters of St Bernard 'ad Carthusienses'.

(*b*). The first letter is 'De contemptu mundi contra sapientes. Sinite', and the last 'De dileccione dei et proximi. Hec est species'. The first word or two of each letter is given. f. 171^{v} blank.

16 (quire 17, ff. 172–7). ff. 172–176^{v} A sermon, 'Eum constitues tibi regem . . . deutronomio xvii°. Teste sacra scriptura in multis locis . . .'. f. 177^{rv} blank.

17. Pastedowns now raised: (*a*) f. i^{rv}, the lower part of a leaf, with 23–30 Apr. and 25–31 May of a calendar, s. xi: 'Obiit Manegoldus' added at 28 May, s. xii. (*b*) f. 178^{rv} Missa de visitacione beate marie virginis, s. xv.

(*b*). The sequence is 'Aue uerbi dei parens virginum humilitas . . .', *RH*, no. 2165.

ff. i + 177 + i. Paper, except art. 17. 142 × 105 mm. Written space *c.* 110 × 80 mm. 28–45 long lines (2 cols., ff. 80–2). Frame ruling. Collation: 1^{8} 2^{4} 3^{12} 4^{10} 5^{16} wants 16 after f. 49 6^{18} + a bifolium, ff. 57, 62, inserted between sheets 7 and 8 7^{10} 8^{8} wants 5–8, blank, (?), after f. 83 9^{16} + a slip, f. 89, after 5 10^{18} wants 18, blank after f. 117 11^{10} + a leaf inserted after 4 (f. 122) and a slip, f. 125, after 6 12^{8} 13^{12} 14^{8} 15^{6} 16^{8} 17^{6}. Parchment strips, some taken from a manuscript, lie in some quire centres. Hands mainly cursiva or hybrida or (f. 80^{rv} only) more or less humanistic. Red initials, ff. 1, 138. Contemporary binding of wooden boards: a piece of brown leather over the spine and some 37 mm of each board bears triple fillets, a cinqfoil and a small round stamp on each cover and a quatrefoil on the spine: three bands: clasp missing: kept in a perhaps contemporary leather case.

Written at least in part by monks of the Charterhouse of Erfurt: cf. arts. 8, 12. A label on the front cover bears the title 'Rapularius [. . .]us' which suggests that this is the Rapularius primus or secundus, H 81^{2} or H 81^{3}, in the late medieval catalogue of the Erfurt Charterhouse, *MBDS* ii. 412. Bülow sale, 10 October 1836, lot 568. 'G. Sumner, Woodmansey, 1855', f. i: his sale at Beverley, 31 Oct. 1877, part of lot 562: the lot number is on f. i.[1]

[1] The Sumner sale catalogue describes lot 562 as '2 old vols. MSS.': it went for 5*s*.

F. 2. 13. *Nicholaus de Auximo, O.F.M., Supplementum Summae Pisanae* 1474

1. ff. 1–329v Quoniam Summa que magistrucia seu pisanella nuncupatur propter eius compendiositatem . . . Abbas in suo monasterio . . . apud locum nostrum prope mediolanum sancte marie de angelis vulgariter sancti angeli nuncupatum Mo cccco xliiii Nouembris xxviii die sabbati proximi ante aduentum hora quasi sexta. Et circa que in eo ac ceteris opusculis per me compilatis compilandisue incaute seu minus bene posita continentur peritiorum et presertim sacrosancte ecclesie submitto correctioni. Iste liber est ad usum fratris mathei de campo sibi concessum per R' p.f. 'Laurentium de pina' (?) tempore vicariatus sui anno domini Mo cccco lxxiiii quem egomet manu propria scripsi et pertinet ad eundem locum. laus deo amen.

An alphabetical series, Abbas–Zelus, a reworking of the Summa casuum of Bartholomaeus Pisanus, †1347: Schulte, ii. 435–6. Printed in 1478 (Hain 2149 and 1482) (Goff, N. 56) and often later. Followed on ff. 330–41 by a short list of the words treated, 'Incipiunt capitula litterarum predicti libri. In primis A. . . .'.

2. (*a*) ff. 341–2 Ista est rubricarum tabula quinque librorum decretalium . . . 5. 1 Accusacionibus Inquisicionibus Denunciacionibus . . . 3. 12 Vt ecclesiastica beneficia . . . (*b*) f. 342 Diuisio decretalis per versus. Prima creat clericos . . . (5 lines).

(*a*). An alphabetical table. The heading explains what the figures mean. (*b*). Walther, no. 14547. ff. 342v–343v blank.

ff. iii + 343 + iii. 190 × 135 mm. Written space 135 × 95 mm. 2 cols. 40 lines. Only the vertical ruled lines project into the margins. The first line of writing is above the top ruled line. Collation: $1\text{–}34^{10}$ 35^{4} wants 3, blank. Initials: f. 1, 7-line, shaded red *Q* on gold and blue ground: border; (ii) 2-line, red with violet ornament or blue with red ornament. Capital letters in the ink of the text filled or lined with pale yellow. Binding of s. xix in.: fore-edge pattern. Secundo folio *innuitur.*

Written in 1474, presumably by fr. Matheus de Campo, O.F.M. (see above), at Milan, if 'et pertinet ad eundem locum' refers back to 'apud locum nostrum' of the author's colophon. '9^{i} 35. C 334', f. 1, at foot, s. xvii (?). Bought from Marks in November 1937.

F. 2. 14. *Horae* s. xv^{2}

1. ff. 3–14v Calendar in French in red and black.

Feasts in red include 'Saint remy. s. hylaire', 'Saint alpin', 'Linuencion saint estienne', 'Saint menge', 'La dedicace S. estienne' (13 Jan., 2 May, 3, 5 Aug., 26 Oct.). No entry of the Visitation of B.V.M.

2. ff. 15–16 Inicium euangelii secundum iohannem. Gloria tibi domine. In principio . . . et ueritatis.

John 1: 1–14. f. 16v blank.

3. ff. 17–64 Hours of B.V.M. of the use of (Châlons). f. 64^v blank.

4. ff. 65–81 Penitential psalms and (f. 76) litany.

Twenty-seven confessors: . . . (12, 13) memmi alpine . . . (20–7) elaphi egidi florentine leonarde gerarde theobalde bernarde leo. Twenty-four virgins: . . . (6–8) genouefa helena syria . . . (15) poma. f. 81^v blank.

5. ff. 82–112^v Office of the dead.

The ninth lesson is Clama ad te (Job 30: 20–4).

ff. iii + 110 + ii, foliated (i), 1–114. Thick parchment. Of the flyleaves, 2, 113 are old parchment, and i, 114 modern paper. 180 × 125 mm. Written space 98 × 63 mm. 17 long lines. Ruling in red ink. Collation of ff. 3–112: 1^8 2^6 $3\text{–}9^8$ 10^8 + 1 leaf after 8 (f. 81) $11\text{–}14^8$. Catchwords are written vertically in *lettre bâtarde*. Ten 12-line pictures, eight in art. 3, one before art. 4 and 1 before art. 5 (Death leads pope, king, and nobleman). A smaller picture before art. 2. Continuous compartmented borders on picture pages, including animals and grotesques, make a rich show. Initials: (i) red or blue shaded to gold paint on blue or red grounds patterned in gold paint; (ii, iii) 2-line and 1-line, gold paint on grounds of red or blue patterned in gold paint. Capital letters in the ink of the text filled with yellow-brown. Line fillers are mainly broken branches of red (or sometimes blue) and gold paint. Side borders on ff. 19^{rv}, 42^v, 46^v only. Contemporary brown leather over wooden boards, rebacked: seven vertical rows of stamps of four patterns, 1, 2, 3, 4, 3, 2, 1. Secundo folio (f. 16) *luntate*.

Written in France for use in the diocese of Châlons. Inscriptions on f. ii: 'Ces presentes heures appartiennent a Margueritte Iacobe femme de Anthoine du Boys marchant dem' a chaalons a la Rue de Naulx (?)'; 'Ian (?) fais present a ma fille margueritte Caills (?) de ces presentes heures ce iourdhui 20 fevriers (?) 1625 . . . Caills'. Given by Miss C. G. Coltart in 1945.

F. 2. 17. *Biblia* s. xiii med.

A Bible in the usual order and with the common set of prologues: cf. Liverpool Cathedral 13. Acts ends imperfectly at 7: 21, 'exposito autem illo su–', and Catholic Epistles and Apocalypse are missing. The introduction to Ecclesiasticus, *Multorum nobis . . . vitam agere* has been left out. There are two tables of chapters, one of 24 chapters before 1 Chronicles, 'De adam usque ad ioab . . . et obitu dauid' and the other of 20 chapters before 2 Chronicles, 'De hostiis oblatis a salomone . . . regis persarum': see *Biblia sacra*, vii, Series unica, forma b. They follow the prologues.

Subject headings and references to other Gospels were added in the margins of Matthew, Mark, Luke, and John in s. xiii, for example at Mt 21: 19, 'De malediccione ficus et sessione super asellam M^r xi L' 19 Io 12' (f. 476): they have been much damaged by the binder. The initials of Romans and of the prologue to Romans have been cut from f. 514.

ff. iii + 547 + ii. 245 × 177 mm. Written space 165 × 110 mm. 2 cols. 40 lines. Collation: $1\text{–}2^{12}$ $3\text{–}23^{24}$ 24^{24} wants 20–4. Initials: (i) of books and to mark the eight divisions of the psalter and on f. 1, pink or blue patterned in white on gold (or gold and blue or gold and pink) grounds, historiated: a gold frame often; (ii) of prologues, as (i), but decorated instead of historiated: the *H* of the prologue to St John contains his eagle; (iii) of chapters, 2-line, blue or red, with ornament of the other colour; (iv) in the two tables of chapters, 1-line, blue or red. Capital letters in the ink of the text filled with red. English binding, s. xix[1]. Secundo folio *perdam inquit*.

Written in France. An erasure at the head of f. 1. The ex-libris of the Augustinian abbey of St Denis, Rheims, 'De conuentu sancti dionisii remen' a[. . . .]', f. 5, s. xiv (?). 'Nathaniel George Philips' (1795–1831), f. i^v. 'Theodore W. Rathbone', f. ii: a note by him, dated 1832, follows, and his book-plate, 'Theodore W. Rathbone Allerton Priory' is inside the cover. Given by Miss May Rathbone in 1917.

F. 2. 18. *Horae* s. xv med.

1. ff. 2–13^v Full calendar in French, in gold, blue, and red, the two colours alternating.

Entries in gold include 'S^e geneuiefue', 'S leu s' gile', and 's' denis' (3 Jan., 1 Sept., 9 Oct.). No visitation of B.V.M.

2. ff. 14–20 Sequentiae of Gospels.

3. ff. 20–4 Obsecro te . . . Masculine forms.

4. ff. 24–26^v O intemerata . . . orbis terrarum. Inclina . . . Masculine forms. f. 27^{rv} left blank: see art. 12.

5. ff. 28–112 Hours of B.V.M. of the use of (Paris). Hours of the Cross and of the Holy Spirit worked in. f. 112^v blank.

6. ff. 113–32 Penitential psalms and (f. 127) litany.

Thirteen confessors: . . . (9–13) francisce yuo guillerme ludouice anthoni. Twelve virgins: . . . (9) genouefa.

7. ff. 132^v–183 Office of the dead.

8. f. 183^v Gratissime domine ihesu criste respicere digneris super me miseram peccatricem . . .

9. (*a*) f. 184 Salue regina . . . (*b*) f. 184^{rv} Alia oracio. Regina celi letare . . .

10. ff. 184^v–185^v Les sept uers s' bernard. Illumina . . .

Eight paragraphs: (2–8) Locutus, Et, In manus, Disrupisti, Periit, Clamaui, Fac mecum.

11. ff. 185^v–191^v, 193–196^v, 192^{rv}, 197^{rv} Memoriae: John Baptist, John Evangelist, James, Adrian, Blaise, Christopher, Sebastian, Anthony hermit, Laurence, Nicholas, 'De bono angele' (Angele qui meus es . . .), Avia, Mary Magdalene (Gaude pia magdalena spes salutis uite uena . . . : *RH*, no. 6895), Margaret, Katherine, Anne, Barbara, Genovefa, 'xi mille uierges', Apollonia, All Saints.

12 (added, s. xviii ?). 'Les Litanies De La Vierge Marie' were added on a leaf left blank, 27^{rv}, and in the lower margins, ff. 28^{v}–29.

ff. i + 196 + i, foliated 1–198. ff. i, 198 are unused blank leaves ruled in red: 15 lines. 150 × 105 mm. Written space 73 × 50 mm. 15 long lines ruled in red ink. Collation of ff. 2–197: 1^{12} 2^{8} 3^{6} (ff. 22–7) 4–10^{8} 11^{8} wants 7 blank after f. 88 12^{8} wants 7 after f. 95 13–23^{8} 24^{6} (ff. 185–90) 25 seven (ff. 191, 193–6, 192, 197). Eleven 11-line pictures, nine in art. 5 (the vespers picture is missing) one before art. 6 and one before art. 7. Four smaller pictures, *c.*40 × 35 mm, in art. 2. Initials: (i) blue, patterned in white, on gold grounds decorated in colours; (ii) 2-line, blue or pink patterned in white on gold grounds decorated in colours; (iii) 1-line, gold on blue or pink grounds patterned in white. A different style is used occasionally, with flowers and fruits on gold-paint grounds (ff. 20, 24, 43^{v}). Capital letters in the ink of the text filled with pale yellow. Line fillers red and blue patterned in white and picked out with gold. Continuous framed floral borders on picture pages and similar borders the height of the written space in the outer margins of pages with initials of type (ii): in these latter the verso is the reversed image of the recto. Binding of red morocco, s. xviii, lettered 'Missale romanum': the bird centrepiece and shell angle-pieces are devices of Thomas Rawlinson, †1725. Secundo folio (f. 15) *eum non.*

Written in France for the use of a woman (art. 8: cf. arts. 3, 4). Arms at the foot of f. 66 and in the initial on f. 132 are party per pale (1) gules cross keys or between four fleur de lys of the same (2) barry of six azure and argent in chief or a demi eagle displayed. (1) occurs also in the initial on f. 28 and (2) in the initial on f. 113. Belonged to Thomas Rawlinson, to judge from the binding. '104' inside the cover; also at the end '197' and, later, 'Hon Lady Simeon'. Advertised at £28 in a bookseller's catalogue, s. xix: the relevant slip is pasted inside the back cover.

F. 2. 19. *Horae* s. xv^{1}

1. ff. 1–12^{v} Calendar in French in red and black.

Entries in red include 'S' eloy', 25 June and 1 Dec., 'S' remi S' piat', 1 Oct., and 'S' denis S' Guillam' (Ghislain: 9 Oct.). Spellings: franchois, mahieu, bietremieu.

2. ff. 13–15^{v} Hours of the Cross.

3. ff. 16–18^{v} Hours of the Holy Spirit.

4. ff. 19–87^{v} Hours of B.V.M. of the use of (Rome).

Headings in French. Salve regina, f. 78. Advent office, f. 79.

5. ff. 88–106^{v} Penitential psalms and (f. 99^{v}) litany.

Thirteen martyrs: (13) lamberte. The scribe failed to copy a list of confessors, although he wrote 'Omnes sancti confessores orate' after Lambert. Fourteen virgins: (14) anna.

6. ff. 107–145^{v} Office of the dead.

At the end is the prayer 'Deus qui nos patrem . . .' for the souls 'patris mei et matris mee'.

7. ff. 146–147^{v} Sens' les commendasses. Subuenite sancti dei . . .

8 (added). f. 148v Orison a son bon ange. Angele qui meus es custos pietate . . .

ff. ii + 147 + ii. 178 × 140 mm. Written space 100 × 72 mm. 16 long lines ruled in red ink. Collation: 1–2[6], then difficult: each art. and each section of art. 4 begins on a new quire and all picture pages are singletons. Twelve 12-line pictures 'by the "Master of the Gold Scrolls" ', eight in art. 4 and one before each of arts. 2, 3, 5 (Christ in judgment on the rainbow), 6. Initials: (i) 4-line, blue or pink patterned in white on decorated gold grounds; (ii, iii) 2-line and 1-line, gold on pink and blue grounds patterned in white. Continuous borders on picture pages of mixed flowers and grotesques, partly gold, separated from the text by a broad band of gold decorated in colours: the border on f. 19 contains a scroll with 'ue[.]ar me weil' on it. Capital letters in the ink of the text touched with red. Line fillers in blue and red patterned in white and decorated with a little gold. Binding of s. xix. Secundo folio (f. 14) *li dei*.

Written for use in the French-speaking Low Countries, probably in the diocese of Tournai. 'Votre bonne sur Florence de lesan', f. 100, s. xvi. Belonged to 'Francis Jack, second Earl of Kilmorey', †1880: his book-plate inside the cover. Henry White sale at Sotheby's, 26 April 1902, lot 1125. Given by J. W. Hughes in 1903. *MERT*, no. 36.

F. 2. 21. *Horae* s. xiv med.

1. ff. 1–46 Hours of B.V.M. of the use of (Paris).

Headings in French. Four leaves missing.

2. ff. 46v–53 Ci apres ensuiuant commencent les heures de la croiz . . . Ymne. Patris sapiencia . . . f. 53v blank.

3. ff. 54–68v Penitential psalms and (f. 63v) litany.

Nineteen confessors: (7) ludouice . . . (19) yuo. Ten virgins: (4) genouefa . . . (10) clara.

4. ff. 69–102v Office of the dead. Two leaves missing. ff. 103–105v left blank.

5 (added, s. xv). (*a*) ff. 104v–105 A memoria headed 'Vessi le seruice Sainte Katherine' and followed by directions for saying it in French. (*b*) f. 105 Aspice in me infelicem . . . (*c*) f. 105, at the foot, 'Sancta yma Sancta Clema (?) Sancta Custancia'.

ff. i + 105 + i. 145 × 110 mm. Written space 95 × 67 mm. 17 long lines. Collation: 1[8], 1 and 8 singletons 2–3[8] 4[8] wants 1, 3, 6, 8 (ff. 25–8) 5–9[8] 10[8] 1 and 8 singletons 11[8] wants 3 after f. 78 and 6 after f. 80 12–13[8] 14[8] wants 8, blank. A 7-line picture of the Annunciation, 38 × 38 mm, on f. 1. Initials: (i) 7-line, blue or pink patterned in white on grounds of the other colour and gold, decorated with ivy leaves and with sprays of ivy into the margins; (ii) as (i), but 2-line and the grounds all gold; (iii) 1-line, blue with red ornament or gold with slate-grey ornament. Line fillers blue and gold or red and blue. Capital letters in the ink of the text filled with pale yellow. Binding by D(ouglas) C(ockerell) dated 1902.

Written in France. Writing on ff. 8v, 48v, s. xvii (?) is in Netherlandish. Item 270 in a bookseller's catalogue at £40: the relevant strip is pasted in at the end and on it is 'Purchased by CSJ 1 Feb. 1913'. Book-plate of the C. Sydney Jones gift to the University of Liverpool. *MERT*, no. 20.

F. 2. 22. *Horae* s. xv ex.

1. ff. 2–13^v Calendar in gold, blue, and red, the two colours alternating.

Entries in gold include 'Gregorii pape', 'Urbani pape' and Denis (12 March, 25 May, 9 Oct.).

2. ff. 14–21^v Sequentiae of the Gospels.

3. ff. 22–7 Obsecro te . . . Et michi famulo tuo . . . ff. 27^v–29^v blank.

4. ff. 30–126 Hours of B.V.M. of the use of (Rome). Hours of the Cross and of the Holy Spirit are worked in.

No break before the Advent office, f. 117^v. f. 126^v blank.

5. ff. 127–153^v Penitential psalms and (f. 144^v) litany.

Nine martyrs: . . . (9) dionisii cum sociis tuis. Twelve virgins: . . . (8) genouefa.

6. ff. 153^v–200^v Office of the dead. ff. 201–206^v were left blank.

7 (added, s. xvi in., in the blank space at the end of quire 26). (*a*) ff. 201^v–202 Credo in deum patrem . . . (*b*) ff. 202^v–203 [Auete] omnes anime fideles quarum corpora . . . Domine ihesu criste salus et liberacio . . . (*c*) ff. 204^v–205^v The Seven Oes of St Gregory.

(*a*), (*b*), and (*c*) each in a different hand.

ff. iii + 203 + ii, foliated (i, ii), 1–208: the foliator left out the numbers 70 and 79. f. 1 is a parchment flyleaf. 127 × 88 mm. Written space 60 × 40 mm. 13 long lines. Ruling in red ink. Collation of ff. 2–206: 26 quires, all once regular eights, except 1–2^6, but one blank leaf is missing after f. 126 (16^8) and four leaves of text are missing (10^7, 12^5, 17^1, 20^4) and have been supplied later (see below). *Lettre bâtarde*, except ff. 77, 92^v, 127^v, 154^v, which are in poor cursiva, s. xix (?). A full-page Annunciation picture, f. 30, incorporates three lines of text. Nine 10-line pictures, eight in art. 4 and one before art. 2. The pictures before matins of Holy Spirit and sext of B.V.M. in art. 4 and before arts. 5 and 6 are missing and were supplied in s. xix (?) on ff. 77^v, 92, 127, 154: Descent of Dove, Three Kings, David and Bathsheba, Raising of Lazarus.[1] In art. 1 the occupations of the months are on rectos and the signs of the zodiac on versos in rectangles measuring 35 × 20 mm. Initials: (i, ii) 3-line and 2-line, blue or partly red and partly gold paint on grounds of the other colour decorated in gold paint; (iii) 1-line, gold paint on blue or red grounds decorated in gold paint. Line fillers in blue and red, patterned in gold paint. Continuous framed floral borders on picture pages. 'Mirror image' borders the height of the written space in the outer margin of all other pages with writing on them: the style differs on ff. 204^v–205^v. Binding of s. xix in., lettered 'Officium'. Secundo folio (f. 15) *vt testimonium*.

Written in France. A shield in the blank space on f. 21^v, gules on a chevron sable 3 escallops argent in base a fox statant, is set in a rectangular floral design on gold ground, 52 × 40 mm, s. xvi: á scroll inscribed 'IAIME QVI MAIME' above, below, and on each side of it. Armorial book-plate of William Harcourt Cooper, s. xix, inside the cover. Book-plate on f. i as in F. 2. 21.

[1] Information from Dr J. J. G. Alexander.

F. 2. 23. *Horae* s. xv^{2}

MERT, no. 73 and pl. 16 (ff. 13^{v}–14): 'The style is close to that of Attavante and the manuscript should be compared with the Bible of Federigo da Montefeltro, 1476–8 (Vatican, Urb. Lat. 1–2)'.

1. ff. 1–12^{v} Calendar in red and black.

Entries in red include 'Georgii (*sic*) pape et confessoris' (12 March), 'Translacio (*sic*) domini nostri Ihesu cristi' (6 Aug.), 'Raphaelis archangeli' (30 Dec.) and nine Franciscan feasts, Bernardinus (20 May), Francis (25 May and 6 Oct.), Antony (13 June), Clare (12 Aug., 4 Oct.), Louis, bishop (19 Aug., 8 Nov.), 'Helysabeth uidue', 19 Nov.

2. ff. 14–103 Incipit offitium beate marie uirginis secundum modum romane curie.

Special office in Advent, etc., f. 92. Salve regina precedes the special psalms for Tuesdays and Fridays (f. 80). f. 103^{v} blank.

3. ff. 104–59 Incipit officium mortuorum. ff. 159^{v}–161^{v} blank.

4. ff. 162–88 Incipiunt septem psalmi penitentiales.

'Incipiunt letanie', f. 176. 'niccholae lodouice' last two of eight 'Doctores'. 'Monaci et heremite': benedicte francisce bernardine dominice. Eight virgins: . . . (7, 8) clara elisabeth. Nine prayers follow Deus cui proprium. ff. 188^{v}–191^{v} blank.

5. ff. 192–227 Incipit offitium sanctissime passionis domini nostri yhesu cristi.

Hours of the Passion. The hymn is 'In passione domini . . .' (*AH* l. 568). A heading in Italian, f. 202^{v}. f. 227^{v} blank.

6. ff. 228–231^{v} Incipit offitium sanctissime crucis editum per dominum papam iohannem . . . Ymnus. Patris sapientia . . .

7. ff. 232–245^{v} Incipiunt psalmi graduales.

Pss. 119–33. ff. 246–247^{v} blank.

ff. i + 247 + ii. 132 × 92 mm. Written space 68 × 50 mm. 13 long lines. Collation: 1^{12} 2^{10} + 1 leaf before 1 3–15^{10} 16^{10} wants 9, 10, blank, after f. 161 17–22^{10} 23^{6} (ff. 222–7) 24^{4} (ff. 228–31) 25^{10} 26^{8} wants 7, 8, blank. A full-page picture, f. 13^{v}. Initials: (i) 8-line or less, historiated, ff. 14 (Nativity), 104 (Death mounted on a black bull), 162, 192 (Christ bears the Cross), 228 (a saint), 232 (B.V.M. (?), reading); (ii) 3-line, in colours on gold and coloured grounds, decorated; (iii) 2-line, blue with red ornament or gold with blue ornament; (iv) 1-line, blue or red. Capital letters in the ink of text are decked out like small cadels and touched with pale yellow. Continuous borders on f. 13^{v} and on pages with initials of type (i): they include roundels in the lower margins in which are shields (ff. 13^{v}, 14), a crowned skull and crossbones (f. 104), the head of Goliath (f. 162), Christ standing in the Tomb (f. 192), Crucifixion (f. 228): cherubs flank the roundels, or (f. 104) lie dead below. Binding of s. xviii: gay endpapers.

Written in Florence. Arms on f. 13^{v}, azure 3 chevrons compony gules and or, of the Taddei of Florence: on f. 14, sable an eagle displayed argent. A slip from a sale catalogue, s. xx in., attached to f. i^{v}. Item 54 at £50 in a catalogue of Henry Young and Son Ltd: the relevant slip is attached to f. 249 and 'Bought by C. S. J. July (19)22' is written on it. Book-plate of Liverpool University as in F. 2. 21.

F. 2. 24. *Horae* s. xv/xvi

The leaves are in disorder after f. 52.

1. ff. 1–12^{v} A rather empty calendar in French, in gold, blue, and red, the two colours alternating.

Entries in red include 'Saint mausse', 'Abdon et Sennes', 'Taurin', 'Les maries' (25 May, 30 July, 11 Aug., 22 Oct.). 'Invencio s' taurini' in blue, 5 Sept.

2. ff. 13–18 Sequentiae of Gospels. 'Protector in te sperancium . . .' after John.

3. ff. 18–21 Oratio valde deuota de beata virgine maria. Obsecro te . . . Masculine forms. f. 21^{v} blank.

4. ff. 22–52^{v}, 108–115^{v}, 101^{rv} Hours of B.V.M. of the use of (Evreux).

5. ff. 102–103^{v} Hours of the Holy Cross, beginning imperfectly.

6. ff. 104–106^{v} Hours of the Holy Spirit. f. 107^{rv} blank.

7. ff. 93–100^{v}, 85–92^{v} Penitential psalms and (f. 87^{v}) litany.

Sixteen martyrs: . . . (12) maxime et uenerande. Twenty confessors: . . . (7–13) taurine aquiline gaude landulphe nicolae romane audoene.

8. ff. 77–84^{v}, 69–76^{v}, 61–68^{v}, 54^{rv}, 53^{rv}, 55–58^{v} Office of the dead.

9. (*a*) f. 59^{rv} Oratio ad deum patrem. Pater de celis deus miserere nobis. Domine sancte pater omnipotens eterne deus qui coequalem . . . (*b*) ff. 59^{v}–60 Oratio ad filium. Fili redemptor mundi deus miserere nobis. Domine ihesu criste fili dei viui . . . (*c*) f. 60^{rv} Oratio ad spiritum sanctum. Spiritus sancte deus miserere nobis. Domine spiritus sancte deus qui coequalis . . .

10. f. 60^{v} De sancto michaele antiphona (*heading only*).

ff. iii + 115 + ii. 172 × 108 mm. Written space 100 × 58 mm. 17 long lines. Ruling in red ink. Collation: 1–2^{6} 3–7^{8} (ff. 13–52) 8^{8} (ff. 108–15) 9^{8} wants 2 after f. 101 (ff. 101–7) 10–14^{8} (ff. 93–100, 85–92, 77–84, 69–76, 61–8) 15 eight (ff. 54, 53, 55–60: 55, 59 are a bifolium and 56–7 a central bifolium). Twelve 14-line pictures, eight in art. 4 and one before each of arts. 2, 6, 7 (David and Bathsheba), 8 (Christ on the rainbow in judgement): a picture is missing no doubt at art. 5. Three smaller pictures in art. 9. Initials: (i) f. 18 5-line purple and white *O* on gold ground, historiated (B.V.M. and Child); (ii, iii) 3-line and 2-line, white and a colour on gold paint grounds, decorated with flowers; (iv) 1-line, gold paint on dark red grounds. Line fillers of two kinds, either dark red patterned in gold paint or broken branches in dark red and gold paint: the two kinds alternate in the litany and the branch kind is sometimes used vertically over two lines when the whole of the written space was not filled, for example on f. 24. On picture pages borders are of beasts, birds, and grotesques among flowers on gold paint grounds. On all other pages there is a floral border in the outer margin, compartmented on grounds of gold paint or white. Binding of s. xvii (?), light brown morocco, gilt on the spine and round the edges.

Written in France, for use in the diocese of Evreux. University of Liverpool book-plate, as in F. 2. 21.

F. 3. 2. *Jacobus Curlus, In Terentium et Strabonem* s. xv²

1. ff. 1–92 I[ACO]B[I CURLI EPI]TOMA DONA[TI IN T]ER[E]NTIV[M.] PROLOGVS INCIPIT. Superioribus mensibus Rex inclyte atque prędarissime Diuus Alfonsus pater tuus . . . (f. 8ᵛ) gloriam inmortalem. Vale. (f. 9) Abducere est per fraudem auferre Cicero . . . bona femina lauit et unxit. FINIS.

An alphabetical list, Abducere–Vxor, preceded by a preface printed by De Marinis, 1969 (see below), p. 34, from this copy. P. O. Kristeller notes this and five other copies in *Manuscripta*, v (1961), 37–8. The first leaves and especially the first of all have been damaged by damp. f. 92ᵛ blank.

2. ff. 93ᵛ–155ᵛ In quarto comentario Strabonis hec insunt de hispania et mauri-thania. Artoterbas uocabant aliqui . . . latinis finitimi sunt.

Extracts from the fourth, fifth (f. 106), and sixth (f. 129) commentaries arranged alphabetically in three alphabets. ff. 93ʳ, 156ʳᵛ blank: 156 is not ruled.

ff. ii + 156 + ii. 280 × 203 mm. Written space 178 × 100 mm. 26 long lines. Ruling with a hard point. Collation: $1–11^8$ 12^8 wants 1 before f. 89 $13–19^8$ 20^6 wants 5, blank. Quires, except the last, signed A–T on last versos a little below and to the right of the bottom line of text. Humanistica in one large hand remarkable for the form of *s* used commonly before *p*: the *p* is wrapped in the curving head of the *s*. Initials: (i) ff. 1, 9, 93ᵛ, 8-line, gold on blue, green, and purple grounds powdered with white dots and decorated with a thick interlace of white vine-stem; (ii), as (i), but 3-line or 4-line. A continuous border on f. 1 includes a roundel of Terence (?), arms (see below), and a bird like a parrot: 'attributable to Gioachino dei Gigantibus' (*MERT*, p. 36). 'Bound by Woolstencroft, Warrington', s. xix.

Written in Italy (Naples). Arms of Ferdinand of Aragon (King of Naples 1458–94) supported by cherubs in the lower border, f. 1: cf. T. De Marinis, *La biblioteca napoletana dei re d'Aragona*, ii (1947), 57–60, and *Supplemento* (1969), pp. 7, 34. Belonged to C. Minieri-Riccio (1818–82). Given as F. 2. 1. *MERT*, no. 74.

F. 3. 3. *Ambrosius, De officiis ministrorum* s. xv med.

Incipit liber primus sancti Ambrosii de Offitiis feliciter. Non arrogans . . . instructionis conferat.

PL xvi. 23–184. Bk. 2, f. 56; 3, f. 88.

ff. iii + 116 + ii. 198 × 128 mm. Written space 128 × 75 mm. 23 long lines. Ruling with ink: double vertical bounders: horizontal lines are not prolonged into the margins. Collation: $1\text{-}11^{10}$ 12^{6}. Written in small upright humanistica: if the first letter of a sentence comes at the beginning of a line it is placed outside the written space, between the double bounders. Initials: (i) f. 1, 5-line gold *N* on blue, red, and green ground, decorated with white vine-stem ornament: the blue ground is powdered with white dots: prolongations into the margins; (ii) ff. 56, 88, 4-line, gold on coloured grounds, blue, green, red on f. 56 and blue and red on f. 88: the blue and green are patterned in white and the red in black. 'Bound by Ramage, London', s. xix. Secundo folio *complures*.

Written in Florence.[1] A smudged shield at the foot of f. 1. The relevant cutting from an English bookseller's catalogue, s. xix, is pasted to f. iii: the price was £1. 8*s*. T. G. Rylands book-plate. Given as F. 2. 1.

F. 3. 4. *Quaestiones super Donatum minorem* 1490

(f. 1) Circa initium Donati minoris queritur primo utrum tantum septem sint artes liberales pro cuius questionis declaratione . . . accidentia principaliora. Finis huius operis. 1490 die 30 Ianuarii hora 17.

The forty-nine questions are listed in a contemporary hand on ff. iii–iv. Each question is usually in two paragraphs beginning respectively 'Queritur' and 'Contra'. The last is 'Vtrum tantum vnum est accidens interiectionis'. ff. iv^{v}–vi^{v} blank.

ff. ii + 64 + ii, foliated (i–vi), 1–60, (61, 62). The foliation is contemporary. Paper. 203 × 150 mm. Written space 143 × 93 mm. 2 cols. 32 lines. Ruling with hard point. Collation: 1^{4} (ff. iii–vi) $2\text{-}7^{10}$. Catchwords written vertically. Written in current humanistica. A new hand begins at f. 11 and continues to the end. Spaces for initials (4-line and (f. 43) 6-line) not filled. Binding of s. xix. Secundo folio *Sed ars*.

Written in Italy. 'N^{O} 55', f. iv^{v}. W. H. Rylands bookplate. Given as F. 2. 1.

F. 3. 5. *Aulus Gellius, Noctes atticae* s. xv med.

(f. 2^{v}) A. Gellii noctium atticarum liber i incipit. (f. 3 *begins imperfectly*) idiotas uocas non quimus . . . (f. 240^{v}) transeundisque multis admodum (*ends imperfectly*).

Begins in i. 2. 6. Ends in 'xx. 12' in the Praefatio of Gellius (Teubner edn., p. 3/8), here counted as part of bk. 20. Three leaves are missing between these points with the beginnings of bks. 3, 10, 17. A table of contents before each book. When he came to Greek words the scribe at first wrote 'G' and later 'g'' in the text and left no space. Later he left small spaces and from f. 114 large enough spaces for at least some of the Greek to be fitted in. He does not use the 'g'' after f. 128. On the last leaf, f. 240^{v}, when copying the Praefatio, he reverted to his first practice, writing 'G' and leaving no space. The Greek words were written in by one expert hand. Some marginalia are preceded by 'al'', for example on f. 3 'al' festinanter' opposite 'firmiter' (i. 2. 7) where the accepted reading is 'festiuiter'. f. 245^{rv} blank.

ff. iv + 240 + iv + 1. Fine parchment. f. ii was pasted to a former binding: it may have been the missing blank leaf of quire 26. 268 × 170 mm. Written space 168 × 90 mm. 28 long lines. Inconspicuous hard-point ruling. Collation: 1 two (ff. 1, 2) 2^{10} wants 1–3 before f. 3 $3\text{-}5^{10}$ 6^{10} wants 1 before f. 40 $7\text{-}12^{10}$ 13^{10} wants 2 after f. 109 $14\text{-}21^{10}$ 22^{10} wants 1

[1] Information from Dr A. de la Mare.

before f. 198 23–25^{10} 26^{8} wants 5–7: 7 probably blank (ff. 237–40, 245: 245 was pasted to a former binding). Quires signed in the usual late medieval way. Written in sloping humanistic cursive: *a, f, g, s* are cursiva forms. Initials: (i) of books, gold on blue, green, and red grounds, decorated with stems of white vine: the blue ground is sprinkled with white dots in groups of three; (ii) 2-line, blue. Binding of s. xviii (?).

Written in Italy (Florence) by a scribe who worked for Vespasiano da Bisticci, the Greek added by Giorgio Antonio Vespucci, †1514:[1] cf. A. de la Mare, *The handwriting of Italian humanists*, i (1973), pp. 106–38 and pls. XXIII–XXV and, for Greek added by Vespucci in other manuscripts, pp. 137–8 and pl. XXIV*g, h*. 'Vinc. Vagnucii', f. 2^{v}, and 'Vagnucii' f. 1, s. xvi (?). Phillipps MS. 6750 (from Payne): sale 21 March 1895, lot 44, to Nichols (£15). H. B. Weaver sale, 29 March 1898, lot 140. Bequeathed by J. P. Postgate, Professor of Latin in the University of Liverpool, in 1926.

F. 3. 6. *Ovidius, Heroides* s. xiv^{2}

\`Ouidii Epistolarum \`liber' feliciter Incipit'. Hanc tua penelope lento tibi mittit ulyxe . . . ne uelis esse michi. Explicit liber ouidii epistolarum. Finito libro referatur gloria cristo.

Ends as usual at Ep. xxi. 14. f. 1^{r} contains lines 1–30 in a later hand than the rest of the manuscript. On f. 42^{v} poor parchment caused the scribe to cancel seven lines and begin again on f. 43. On f. 9^{v} a reader noted in a humanistic hand, s. xv, against Ep. iv. 133 'Hoc carmen id est Iuppiter esse pium est omnium ouidii versuum turpissimum'.

ff. i + 55 + i. Thick parchment. 232 × 165 mm. Written space 167 mm high. 28 long lines. Collation: 1^{10} wants 1 2^{4} (ff. 10–13) 3–5^{8} 6–7^{6} 8^{4} 9^{2}. Written in rotonda: a new scribe at f. 10 (2^{1}). 2-line initials, red or blue with ornament of the other colour, but there is very little ornament after f. 30. Binding of s. xvii (?). Secundo folio *misimus*.

Written in Italy. 'Iste liber est virmilei (*or* virnulei) condam damati de gadio', f. 55^{v}, s. xv ex.: also scribbles, including 'Questo libro [. . .] mazo [. . .]'. Phillipps MS. 4199, so from Payne and Foss. 'N° 101' inside the cover. The relevant entry from a bookseller's catalogue in which this was item 315 at £4. 4*s*. is pasted inside the cover. Bequeathed as F. 3. 5.

F. 3. 8. *L. Bruni, De studiis, etc.* s. xv med.

1. ff. 1–16 Leonardi Aretini de literis et studiis ad (*these seven words in a later hand over faded red*) illustrem dominam baptistam de malatestis. Compulsus crebro rumore . . . ad gloriam cohortari. VALE.

Printed *c.*1470 and later: *GKW*, nos. 5614–20. f. 16^{v} blank.

2. ff. 17–38^{v} [. . . .] Leonardus Aretini Isagogicum moralis disciplini ad Galeottu(m) Richasulanum. [S]icut uiuendi Galeotte sicut etiam bene uiuendi . . . uirtutesque exerceamus. LAVS DEO.

Printed *c.*1470 and later: *GKW*, nos. 5621–4.

[1] Information from Dr A. de la Mare, who tells me in a letter of 20 June 1980 that she has identified the scribe as the Florentine notary Ser Agnolo di Jacopo de' Dinuzi of San Gimignano.

ff. iii + 38 + iii. 185 × 130 mm. Written space 110 × 80 mm. 21–3 long lines. Ruling in ink. Collation: $1–3^{10}$ 4^{8}. Quires 1–3 lettered at the end, A–C, sideways. Written in humanistica. Initial *C*, f. 1, 3-line, pink on blue ground, decorated in red and green. Space for *S*, f. 17, not filled. Binding of red morocco, s. xix. Secundo folio *lio augustino*.

Written in Italy (Veneto).[1] The bookplate reads 'Liverpool University College . . . Presented by Liverpool County Council'. *Guide* says 'Purchased c.1900'.

F. 3. 9. *Graduale* s. xv^2

1. ff. 1–2v Eight settings of Gloria patri.

2. ff. 2v–3v Ad aspersionem aque benedicte. Asperges me . . . Tempore paschali. Vidi aquam egredientem . . . In die pasc'. Hec est dies . . . In residuo tempore resurre. vsque ad penth' Confitemini domino . . . In die pentheco. Emitte spiritum tuum . . .

3. ff. 3v–210 Dominica prima aduentus. off'. Ad te leuaui . . .

Temporal. Sundays are reckoned from Trinity. No Corpus Christi: cf. art. 10. Cibauit is the officium for Monday after Pentecost.

4. ff. 210–212v In festo dedicationis ecclesie.

5. ff. 213–61 Sanctoral.

Corona domini, f. 234. Dominic, f. 245 (. . . V'. Pie pater dominice tuorum memor operum . . .). Translation of Dominic, f. 235, by cues.

6. ff. 261–308v Common of saint.

7. f. 308v Cues for Holy Spirit and Holy Cross.

8. ff. 308v–314v B.V.M.

9. ff. 314v–326v Settings of Kyrie eleyson, Gloria in excelsis, Credo in unum deum, Sanctus, Agnus dei, (f. 314) 'In toto duplici et duplici' and at feasts of lesser importance (ff. 319, 321, 323v, 325) and (f. 326) 'In missis defunctorum'.

10. ff. 327–339v Sequitur rubrica officiorum de sanctis cum aliquibus officiis festiuitatum que non habentur superius.

A supplement to art. 5 in the main hand, consisting of eight proper offices, six sets of cues and at the end (f. 339v) Kyrie eleyson 'In precipuis festiuitatibus'. The proper offices are for: Aquinas, f. 327v; 'In festo nostre domine de pietate', f. 328; Vincent confessor (. . . Tractus. O uincenti pater gloriose . . .), f. 331v; Katherine of Siena, f. 333v; Corona domini, f. 333v; 'In festo sancti sacramenti', f. 334v; Visitation of B.V.M., f. 336; 'De beato dominico in feria iiia infra sept' (. . . Tractus. Pie pater sancte dominice celi ciuis . . .), f. 337v.

[1] Information from Dr A. de la Mare.

The cues include translation of Aquinas, Adalbert bishop and martyr, translation of Peter Martyr, Anthony, Anne, 'Wanzeslai'.

ff. ii + 339 + ii. Medieval foliation in red on ff. 1–326 'I–XVI^{XX} [VII]: a number missed after IX^{XX} V[III]'. ff. 152 × 110 mm. Written space 105 × 70 mm. 8 long lines and music. Collation: 1–11^8 12^8 + 1 leaf after 1 (f. 197) 26–40^8 41^2 (ff. 325–6) 42^8 43^4 + 1 leaf after 4 (f. 339). The scribe spells *Christus* and *Iesus* correctly. Initials: (i) at Advent, Christmas, Easter, Ascension, Pentecost, ff. 4, 26, 139, 163, 169, blue patterned in white on decorated gold grounds; (ii) 1-line, blue or red. Capital letters in the ink of the text filled with pale yellow. Cadels decorated with pale green or yellow within a frame. Binding of s. xix by Sotheran and Co.

Written in France for Dominican use. The relevant slip from an English sale catalogue, s. xix/xx, is inside the cover. '£20' and '1/5/1901' f. i. Bought for the Department of Education from the C. Sydney Jones Fund. Transferred to the main library in 1959.

F. 3. 10. *P. Lombardus, Sententiae* s. xiii med.

1. Cupientes aliquid . . . (f. 1^v) premissimus. di. i. Omnis doctrina est de rebus (f. 3^v) ccxi Vtrum passiones sanctorum debeamus uelle. Incipit primus liber sentenciarum. R'. Omnis doctrina est de rebus . . . (f. 4) Veteris[1] ac noue legis . . . (f. 245^v) duce peruenit.

Bk. 2, f. 75^v; 3, f. 144; 4, f. 182^v. A table in front of each book: bks. 1, 2, 211 and 258 chapters; bk. 3, no numbers; bk. 4, six numbered paragraphs, 2–6 at points corresponding to dist. l. x (De parvulis defunctis), 8, 14, 24, 26. Red and blue distinction numbers in the margins, but distinctions are not referred to in the tables. Paragraphs numbered in the text only as far as 'xxix' (= 'xxx' in the table) on f. 16. Broad margins, but few marginalia. The link 'Que ad misterium . . . transeamus' (edn. Ad claras aquas, 1971, i, pt. 2, 329) follows bk. 1 (f. 72^v). Part of dist. 32 of bk. 2 on f. 124^{rv} was copied again by the main hand on f. 246 and is followed there by a couplet, 'Tempore sit sanus longo bene cremosianus Cartas qui pingit post ueraque carmina fingit'. f. 246^v blank.

2. The nineteenth-century binder used fragments of a copy, s. xv, of Richard of St Victor on the Apocalypse as covers for his pasteboards. The text on the exposed side of the front cover is from bk. 7 (*PL* cxcvi. 865A–C). Written space 145 × 110 mm. 2 cols. 29 lines.

ff. i + 246 + i. 192 × 140 mm. Written space 105 × 73 mm. 2 cols. 42 lines. Collation: 1–13^{12} 14^{10} (ff. 133–42) 15^{12} 16^{10} (ff. 155–64) 17–22^{12} 23^{10}. Small expert hands, changing at f. 143. Initials: (i) beginning books, red and blue with ornament of both colours: in frames, ff. 143, 144, 182^v; (ii) blue or red with ornament of the other colour: in bks. 1, 2, 3-line in first columns and outside the written space of second columns; in bks. 3, 4, outside the written space; (iii) in tables, 1-line, blue or red. The style changes at bk. 3 and type (ii) initials become smaller. Capital letters in the ink of the text stroked with red. Binding of s. xix. Secundo folio (f. 4) *Cum enim*.

Written in Italy. Phillipps MS. 2194, so obtained from James Taylor, 162 Great Surrey Street, London. Phillipps sale, 21 March 1895, lot 589, to Nichols for £9. 9*s*. H. B. Weaver sale, 29 March 1898, lot 289. The relevant extract from a catalogue of Henry Young and

[1] But the rubricator put in a *C* instead of a *V*.

Sons is pasted inside the cover: this was item 262 at £13. 13*s*. Bought from the C. Sydney Jones fund, 1 Feb. 1913: book-plate as in F. 2. 21.

F. 3. 13. *Gregorius, De cura pastorali* s. xiii in.

1. (f. 1v) Ne uenire imperiti . . . (f. 2) predicacio extollat. Pastoralis cure me pondera . . . (f. 90v) meriti manus levet. Pande michi limen celi deus ablue crimen. Est textum stamen. benedicito (?) nos deus amen.

PL lxxvii. 1–128. Not divided into books: f. 32v where bk. 3 begins was headed later 'Secundus liber pastoralium' and the admonitions of bk. 3 are marked with later chapter numbers 1–36. The text is preceded by a table of chapters covering all four books. 'Gregorius de Cura Pastorali' in a frame on the pastedown, s. xiv.

2. f. 1r, left blank, was filled in s. xiii: (*a*) Mella patent. dum fella latent . . . (2 lines); (*b*) A note on the ten commandments; (*c*) Medical recipes in 41 lines, beginning 'Epar asini'.

3. The pastedown at the end is from a manuscript written in cursiva, s. xv: [Q]uid est littera. respondetur littera est minima pars vocis composite que scribi potest indiuidua . . .'.

ff. 90 + i. Thick parchment. 165 × 122 mm. Written space 120 × 85 mm. 25 long lines. The first line of writing above the top ruled line. Collation: $1–4^8$ 5^4 $6–10^8$ 11^6 12^8. Quires numbered at end or beginning. The hand changes at ff. 12v, 29v, and 61 (9^1). Scribe 3 begins to use 7 instead of the ampersand on f. 31v and to cross it on f. 36. Initials: (i) f. 2, 5-line space not filled; (ii) 3-line, red. Capital letters in the ink of the text touched with red. Medieval binding of bevelled wooden boards covered with white leather: three bands: the clasp fastens from the front to the back cover. Secundo folio (f. 3) *gisterium*.

Written probably in Germany or Austria. From Ranshofen, O.S.A., Austria: 'Iste libellus est Canonicorum regularium Monasterii S. pangracii in Ranshofen', f. 1v, s. xv. 'lviii Pastorale greg' ', f. 2, at the head, s. xv ex. Belonged to James P. R. Lyell: cf. Lyell Cat., p. xxviii. Quaritch catalogue 699 (1952), item 67, at £100. Given by Robert George Morton, Beacon Tor, West Kirby, Cheshire, in 1969.

F. 3. 14. *Horae* s. xiv² (arts. 1, 5)–xv med.

1. (*a*) pp. 2–25 Calendar in blue, red, and black. (*b*) p. 26 Qui se seignera au diz et septime iour de mars . . .

(*a*). Arranged so that a month is on a double opening, not, as usual, a recto and verso. Anne in red, 26 July. David and Chad added. The word 'pape' and feasts of St Thomas of Canterbury erased. (*b*). Good and bad days for bloodletting. p. 1 left blank.

2. pp. 27–124 Hours of B.V.M. of the use of (Sarum).

Memoriae of Holy Spirit, Holy Cross, Angels, John Baptist, Peter and Paul, Andrew, John Evangelist, Laurence, Stephen, Thomas of Canterbury (erased), Nicholas, Mary Magdalene, Katherine, Margaret, relics, All Saints and for peace follow lauds. Hours of the Cross (but not hours of the Holy Spirit) are worked in. pp. 82, 92, 104, 116 blank.

3. Devotions in honour of B.V.M.: (*a*) pp. 124–7 Salue regina . . . , followed by the verses Virgo mater ecclesie . . . ; (*b*) pp. 127–8 Gaude virgo mater cristi que per aurem concepisti . . . ; (*c*) pp. 129–33 Gaude flore virginali honoreque speciali . . . ; (*d*) pp. 133–5 Stella celi extirpauit . . .

(*a*). *RH*, nos. 18150, 21818. (*b, c*). Five and Seven Joys, *RH*, nos. 7107, 6809. (*d*). *RH*, no. 19438. p. 136 blank.

4. pp. 137–77 Penitential psalms and (p. 162) litany.

Twelve confessors: . . . (11, 12) swithune birine. Twelve virgins: . . . (6) genouefa . . . (12) editha. p. 178 blank.

5. pp. 179–272 Ici commence li offices des mors. Cest assauoir quon ne dist mie le office des mortz selonc le coustume de leglise de rome. Car on ne dist mie le office des mors quant on fait ix lesons ou dou sanctorum ou del temporalite. on ne le dist mie dou mekerdi en le peneuse semaine deuant pasques iusques a le trinite ne le uigile de noel son ne le dist pur corps present ou pour ses biens-faiteurs. mes en tout lautre tans del an le dist on quant on fait trois lecons soit dou sanctorum soit de le fere. Ad uespres. A'. Placebo. Psalmus. Dilexi quoniam . . .

The original text has been altered in three places by removing and supplying leaves and by erasing:
1. Ps. 145 and the versicles and responses following it (pp. 191–4: *Manuale Sarum*, p. 134/8–13) and the prayers Deus qui inter, Deus venie largitor and Fidelium deus (pp. 194–5: *M.S.*, p. 137/21–37) were followed immediately by 'Inuitatorium. Regem cui omnia uiuunt . . .' and 'Ps. Venite exultemus . . .' (pp. 195–6). The invitatory and as much of Ps. 94 as was on p. 196—to verse 5, 'ipsius est mare et'—have been erased, except for the coloured initials and line fillers, and the next leaf was removed. The first three prayers in *M.S.*, p. 135, were added in s. xv on a new leaf, pp. 197–8, in the order 1, 3, 2. The original text begins again on p. 199 in a rubric 'Cest a sauoir qon ne dist on*que*s Inuitatoire ne Uenite fors qe lendemain de tous saintz. Et quant on les dist pur corps present'. Then comes the first nocturn (*M.S.*, p. 136);
2. On p. 244 the versicle 'Nunc criste te . . . redemptos' (*M.S.*, p. 139) is followed by 'Cest respons qui ci apres uient dist on ades quant on dist uigiles a trois lecons. R'. Libera me domine . . . erant in' (*ends imperfectly*). After this a leaf has been removed and p. 245/1–4, containing the end of Fidelium deus from 'torum ut', have been erased. Lauds follows (*M.S.*, pp. 140–1);
3. Benedic domine (*M.S.*, p. 141/6) was followed by 'Ps. De profundis . . .'. As much of Ps. 129 as was on pp. 267–8—to a point in verse 8—has been erased and the next leaf removed. The texts in *M.S.*, pp. 141/14–142/9, except the prayer Deus qui nos patrem, were added in s. xv on two new leaves (pp. 269–72). pp. 273–6 blank.

6. pp. 277–314 Beati immaculati . . . Tibi domine commendamus . . .

Commendation of souls: *Manuale Sarum*, pp. 142–4.

7. pp. 313–30 Deus deus meus respice in me . . .

Psalms of the Passion and prayer 'Respice quesumus domine super hanc familiam tuam . . .'. Rubrics in English.

8. pp. 331–50 O domine ihesu criste eterna dulcedo . . .

The Fifteen Oes of St Bridget.

9. pp. 351–80 Incipiunt (*sic*) psalterium sancti Ieronimi.

ff. ii + 192 + iv, paginated (i–iv), 1–384, (385–8). pp. 381–4 are a bifolium of blank parchment ruled like the later part of the manuscript. 172 × 125 mm. Written space 108 × 65 mm. 15 long lines. Ruled in red ink. Collation: 1^8 2^6 wants 6 after p. 26 *3–11^8 12^4* (pp. 171–8) 13^{12} wants 10 after p. 196 + *1 leaf added after 9* (pp. 197–8) 14–15^8 16^8 wants 8 after p. 244 17^8 18^8 wants 5–8 after p. 268 + *4 leaves added after 4* (pp. 269–76) *19–20^8 21 seven* (pp. 309–22) *22^4* (pp. 323–30) *23–25^8*.[1] One picture, p. 180, before art. 5, 85 × 68 mm, including the frame, shows a woman as chief mourner at a burial service: 'In style this belongs with the group of the Fitzwarin psalter (Paris, BN, latin 765) and the early Bohun manuscripts' (*MERT*, p. 22). Initials in art. 5: (i) 2-line, blue or pink patterned in white on decorated gold grounds; (ii) 1-line, gold on grounds of pink and blue patterned in white. Initials in arts. 2–4, 7–9: (i) 3-line, blue and red shaded to white on gold grounds decorated in colours, including green; (ii) 2-line, gold on blue and red grounds patterned in white, with sprays of green and gold into the margins; (iii) 1-line, blue with red ornament or gold with slate-grey ornament. Line-fillers: in art. 5, blue, red, and (predominantly) gold; in arts. 2–4, 7–9, blue or gold. Gilt morocco binding by Waters, Newcastle, s. xix ex. Secundo folio (p. 29) *fecit nos*.

Written in England. Item 564 in a bookseller's catalogue, s. xx^1: the slip from it is preserved separately in a loose-leaf folder. Book-plate of R. G. Morton: given as F. 3. 13. *MERT*, no. 23.

F. 4. 1. *Parvum volumen, cum apparatu* s. xiii^1–xiii med.

(1) Institutes of Justinian, (2) Authenticum, and (3) Tres libri Codicis, each surrounded by the apparatus of Accursius entered by other hands. For many manuscripts in which these texts occur together, this one among them, see Dolezalek, iii, s.v. Accursius, and for the texts and apparatus, *Accursii glossa in Volumen*, Corpus Glossatorum Juris Civilis, xi (1959), a reprint of the Venice editions of 1489 (*GKW*, nos. 7621, 7762). Art. 3 looks rather later than arts. 1, 2.

In arts. 1, 2 the *signes de renvoi* to the apparatus are tied to the column, the series beginning with '–.' in each first column and 'a' in each second column of art. 1 and with '–a' in each first column and either 'a' or 'a–' in each second column of art. 2. In art. 3 the series beginning with 'a' is tied to pages, not columns, that is it extends over the two columns of a page. On the last eighteen leaves of art. 2 the signs have been entered as usual in the apparatus, but there is nothing corresponding to them in the text space.

1. ff. 1–54^v Imperator cesar flauius. iustinianus. alamanicus. gothicus. franticus (*sic*). germanicus. anticus. guandalicus. affricanus. pius. felix. inclitus. uictor. semper augustus. cupide legum iuuentuti. Rubrica. *Imperatori mai.*[2] non

[1] Italics show the quires and leaves added in s. xv.

[2] The italicized letters here and in arts. 2, 3 are tall red or blue letters. They are used also after the initial to begin books on ff. 10, 28, 42^v, 183.

solum[1] armis decoratam . . . aduentura est Amen. Explicit liber dumpni iustiniani.

Bk. 2, f. 10; 3, f. 28; 4, f. 42^{v}. The apparatus begins 'In nomine ex hoc no. quod cristianus fuit'.

2. ff. 55^{v}–139^{v} De heredibus et falcidia. [*I*]*nperator iustinianus*. [O]ccupatis nobis . . . per omnia custodiri prouideat.

Collationes i–ix of Authenticum. The apparatus begins 'In nomine domini. Iustinianus opus suum laudabile' and ends 'de re iudex. ad que. accursius'.

f. 55 contains a table of relationship with names in twenty-nine circles from 'tritauus vi' and 'tritauia vi' at the top to 'trinepos vi' and 'trineptis vi' at the bottom: in the middle is 'Pater fillius/Mater fillia'. Underwriting on this page is in sixteen lines beginning 'Circa rectoriam primo querendum est vtrum sit proprium'.

3. ff. 140–211^{v} Incipit liber x de iure fisci. *Ulpianus*. Si priusquam fisci . . . quatiatur.

Codex Justiniani, bks. 10–12. Bk. 11, f. 161^{v}; 12, f. 183. The apparatus begins 'De iure fisci. occasione criminum' and ends in a gloss on *officium* 'id est iudices cum suis officialibus. ac', after which is 'cur(sius) subdit florentinus', perhaps in the main hand.

4. f. 212 is a binding leaf taken from a legal (?) manuscript, s. xiii, in 27 long lines: the text has been washed out, but the verso may probably be read by ultra-violet light. Verses were scribbled over the recto in s. xv, 'Mitto tibi primas animosi martis olimpi Et cum fine caput Interiora dei' repeated six times, and 'Cum sol est occiduas celeri . . .' (3 lines); also, at the top 'flo 2° de mense decembris die' and 'flo de mense ianuarii die circa finem mensis'; also, recto and verso, scribbled names (see below).

ff. ii + 211 + iii. For f. 212 see above, art. 4. 363 × 225 mm. Written space 220 (205 in art. 3) × 100 mm. 2 cols. 46 lines in art. 1, 48 in art. 2, and 43 in art. 3. Collation: 1–6^{8} 7^{8} wants 8, blank, after f. 54 8^{6} + 1 leaf before 1 (f. 55) 9–17^{8} 18^{6} (ff. 134–9) 19–26^{8} 27^{6} (ff. 204–9) 28^{2}. *Ad hoc* signatures in red. Initials in art. 1: f. 1, gold *I*, historiated (a dragon with human head); (ii) of books 2–4, gold on blue grounds patterned in white; (iii) of tituli, outside the written space, blue or red with ornament of the other colour. Initials in art. 2: (i) f. 56, space not filled; (ii) *I*s of *Imperator*, outside the written space, red and blue; (iii) of paragraphs, outside the written space, red or blue with ornament of the other colour. Initials in art. 3: (i) of bks. 10, 12, spaces not filled; (ii) of bk. 11 and the *I*s of *Imperator* or *Idem*, outside the written space, red or blue; (iii) of tituli, 1-line, red or blue. Binding of s. xix. Secundo folio *est lex*.

Written in Italy. Two ex-libris inscriptions: 'Iste institutiones sunt Iohannis de A[. . . .]bus filii d. pauli vtriusque Iuris doctoris anicii. Qui est legum Scolaris etc' ', f. 212^{v}, s. xiv; 'Librum quem cernitis poscidet audire dicti Iacobi de stupo (?) dignaui vere creati', f. 212, s. xv. Other names occur in scribbles, s. xv: on f. 212^{v} 'Andreas Arzonus Dominus Iacobus Arzonus', 'd. Iohannis de Arzonibus', 'presbiter paulus de riboldis de lexonia' and 'Petrus martir molgula iuris utriusque scolaris doctissimus', this last in capital letters; on f. 1, at

[1] In this copy the six words 'In nomine Domini Nostri Iesu Christi', which should precede 'non solum', have been left out.

foot, 'dominus [. . . . .] de Mlo Iohanne [. . . .]'. According to a note on f. iv this came (to W. H. Rylands ?) from J. Arthur, like an Epistolary from Bobbio and a 'Speculum Gulielmi Duranti from same library'. W. H. Rylands book-plate. Given as F. 2. 1.

F. 4. 2. *Antiphonale, Pars hiemalis* s. xiv^1

Temporal from Advent to the Saturday before Easter, beginning imperfectly (f. 2) 'nus ueniet' in the antiphon Ecce in nubibus for the second Sunday in Advent.

The text seems to agree with Haymo's (*SMRL* ii. 23–88). f. 1 should follow f. 210. The office for Easter Eve ends on f. 215 and is followed by the office for Easter Day, which was later cancelled by pasting f. 215v to the end cover. The pasted side, now raised, ends with the first two words of the response Angelus domini (*SMRL* ii. 88). Eight quires are now incomplete and probably eighteen leaves missing in all: see below.

ff. ii + 216 + ii, foliated (i, ii), 1–5, 5bis, 6–215, (216–7). 420 × 300 mm. Written space 295 × 200 mm. 7 long lines and music. Minims 6 mm high. ff. 2–210 are twenty-three quires, all once regular tens, except 1^8, 16^8 (ff. 139–46), 19^8 (ff. 167–74): the missing leaves are 1^1, 5^1 before f. 38, 8^3 after f. 68, 8^7 after f. 71, $10^{1,2}$ before f. 85, $12^{1,2}$ before f. 103, 12^6 after f. 105, 12^{10} after f. 108, 20^1 before f. 175, 21^{10} after f. 192, $22^{1,2}$ before f. 193; ff. 1, 211–15 are the remains of a twenty-fourth quire, probably a ten lacking 1, 2, 8 and either 9 or 10. Initials: (i) of principal responses, in colour, on red and blue grounds, the red historiated: only three survive, f. 45 Stephen, f. 51 John Evangelist, f. 183 *I* of *In die* (Palm Sunday); (ii) of nineteen responses, all listed by Sampson, *Cat.*, except the damaged *A* of *Angelus*, f. 215v, pink, grey, or brown, patterned in white, on blue grounds decorated in colours and gold; (iii) blue or red with ornament of the other colour: 'There are stylistic similarities with Umbrian illumination' (*MERT*, p. 33). Binding of s. xix ex.: for an older binding, see Sampson, *Cat.*, p. 5.

Written in Italy. W. H. Rylands book-plate. Given as F. 2. 1. *MERT*, no. 64.

F. 4. 4. *Missale* s. xv^2

1. ff. 1–6v Calendar in red and black, partly graded.

Among entries in red are 'Depositio sancti Ruperti', 'Translatio sancti Valentini episcopi', translations of Rupert and Virgil, and 'Depositio sancti Virgilii episcopi' (27 Mar., 4 Aug., 24, 26 Sept., 27 Nov.), all graded for nine lessons, except at 4 Aug. Octaves in black of the September feasts of Rupert and Virgil.

2. ff. 7–115v Temporal, Advent–Corpus Christi.

3. ff. 115v–116v In dedicatione ecclesie.

4. f. 116v Sequitur Iubilacio. Antiphona. Gloria in excelsis deo . . . De Beata Virgine. Gloria in excelsis deo . . .

5. ff. 117–130v Prefaces with and (ff. 125–6) without musical notes, (f. 125) Credo in unum deum, noted, and (f. 127) canon of mass.

Tabs to show main divisions are fixed to the foot of leaves in art. 5 (127, 128, 129). Elsewhere they project from the side. f. 124rv blank.

6 (added in blank spaces). (*a*) ff. 124^{v}–125 Magnificat, noted. (*b*) f. 130^{v} Canon minor. Sacerdos faciat crucem super patenam. In nomine . . . Suscipe sancta trinitas . . . Orate pro me . . . deo. Sequitur secretum sine salutacione.

7. ff. 131–64 Temporal from Sunday after octave of Pentecost to Friday before 1st Sunday in Advent.

8. ff. 164–215^{v} Incipit de Sanctis. per totum annum.

Andrew-Virgil, mainly cues, and at the end (215^{rv}) collects, secrets, and postcommunions for Mary of Egypt and Joseph.

9. ff. 215^{v}–234 Incipit commune sanctorum.

10. ff. 234–9 In agendis mortuorum.

11. Incipiuns (*sic*) votiue misse: (*a* 1–7) ff. 239–42 Trinity, Wisdom, Holy Spirit, Angels, De caritate, Holy Cross, B.V.M., one for each day of the week; (*b* 1, 2) ff. 242–3 Transfiguration and Crown of Thorns; (*c*) ff. 243–7 Incipiunt misse pro diuersis necessitatibus: (1) Missa iudicii; (2) Pro peccatis; (3) Pro quacumque tribulacione; (4) Pro pace; (5) Pro pluuia; (6) Pro iter agentibus; (7) Pro concordia; (8) Pro elemosinariis; (9) De omnibus sanctis; (10) Pro se ipso; (11) Pro temptacione cordis; (*d*) ff. 247–52 Collect, secret, and postcommunion of thirty-three masses: (1) In veneracione domini nostri ihesu cristi; (2–7) Generalis; (8) Pro viuis et defunctis; (9) Pro omni gradu ecclesie; (10) Pro vniuersis ordinibus; (11) Pro aduersitatibus tocius ecclesie; (12) Pro papa; (13) Pro Episcopo; (14) Pro e(xe)rcitu uel pro rege et populo catholico; (15) Pro inimicis; (16) Pro discordantibus; (17) Pro hiis qui persecucionem paciuntur; (18) Pro amico viuente; (19) Pro vna virgine; (20) Pro vidua; (21) Pro liberacione mulieris inpregnate; (22) Pro Confitente; (23) Pro infirmo; (24) Pro mortalitate hominum; (25) Pro temptacione cogitacionum; (26) Pro peticione lacrimarum; (27) Pro peccatis; (28) Pro tempestate; (29) Pro agonizante; (30) Pro demoniaco; (31–2) Sacerdos pro se ipso; (33) Pro hereticis.

In a new and more stylish hand. (*a* 1, 5) are as *SMRL*, ii. 325–6 (nos. 48–9). (*d* 7). A cunctis, Exaudi, Mundet: names B.V.M., Peter and Paul, and Augustine. (*d* 14). In the collect Deus qui conteres a later hand has written 'Imperatori' opposite 'regi'.

12 (added in another hand). f. 252^{rv} De transfiguratione domini. Speciosus forma pre natis hominum iesus . . .

Sequence: *RH*, no. 19257.

ff. i + 252 + i. 400 × 300 mm. Written space 285 × 188 mm. 2 cols. 36 lines and (ff. 127–130^{v}) 26 lines. Collation: 1^{8} wants 7, 8 2–12^{10} 13^{10} wants 8, 9, perhaps blank, after f. 123 14–24^{10} 25^{10} 6 cancelled after f. 239 26^{10} wants 10, blank, after f. 252. Arts. 1–10 in a modified textura: cursiva forms of *a*, *g*, and sometimes *s*: *v* initially. Pictures: f. 126^{v}, Crucifixion, full page; f. 129^{v}, at foot, a roundel, Christ rising from the tomb. Initials: (i) in shaded colour, usually green, on grounds of colour, usually dark red, patterned in gold paint, and punched gold: prolongations of delicate foliage in pink, blue, and green; (ii–iv) 3-line, 2-line, and 1-line, blue or red. Capital letters in the ink of the text stroked with red. Binding of wooden boards covered with brown leather, s. xvi, rebacked: four rolls on each cover, one with figures labelled **CARI, SPES, FIDE, FORT**: metal centrepieces and cornerpieces.

Written for use in the diocese of Salzburg: 'It is attributable to the so-called "Master of the Lehrbuch of Maximilian" ' (*MERT*, p. 28). '38' top left inside cover, s. xviii (?). 'N° 5' and, later, 'M. J. Johnson', f. i. Book-plate of T. G. Rylands. Given as F. 2. 1. *MERT*, no. 44.

F. 4. 5, ff. 1–12. *Petrarch, Rime (fragm.: in Italian)* s. xv med.

Described by N. Mann in *Italia medioevale e umanistica*, xviii (1975), 203.

1. ff. 1–8 A pie de colli oue la bella uesta. S fo 2 . . . Zeffiro torna el buon tempo rimena. S fo 109.

An alphabetical table of first lines of art. 2, with leaf numbers, which show that its three remaining leaves are the first three of about 130. There are 372 entries. The right order of leaves is 1–4, 6, 5, 7, 8. ff. 8^v–9^v blank.

2. ff. 10–12^v Rime 1, 3, 2, 4–12, four to a leaf.

ff. 12. Paper, repaired at the edges. The old leaf number '3' remains on f. 12. 290 × 200 mm. Written space *c.*177 mm high. *c.*30 long lines in art. 1. Collation: 1 eleven 2 one (f. 12): catchword, f. 11^v. Written in hybrida influenced by humanistica. Initials: (i) f. 10, 4-line, blue and red, with red ornament; (ii) 2-line, red or (f. 12^v) blue.

Written in Italy. Bound with F. 4. 5, ff. 13–20, q.v.

F. 4. 5, ff. 13–120. *Lives and miracles of St Jerome (in Italian)* s. xv/xvi

1. ff. 14–15 Table of chapters of art. 2. ff. 13^{rv}, 15^{rv} left blank.

2. ff. 16–120 Inchomincia lapistola del beato Eusebio . . . Al padre reuerendissimo damasio . . . santo Ierolimo intorno agli anni del nostro Signore yhesu cristo ccclxxxviii A dio sia honore laude e gloria imperio e forteza in sechula sechulorum Amen. Finito el libro de beato e glorioso messer S. Ierolimo confessore e dottore excelentissimo Amen.

Sixty chapters, numbered 1–59, 61, translating *BHL*, nos. 3866–8, 3875: (i) ff. 16–60^v, chapters 1–31, Pseudo-Eusebius: *PL* xxii. 239–82; (ii) ff. 60^v–67, chapters 32–5, Pseudo-Augustine to Cyril: *PL* xxxiii. 1120–6; (iii) ff. 67–115, chapters 36–59, Pseudo-Cyril to Augustine: *PL* xxxiii. 1126–53; (iv) ff. 115^v–120, chapter 61, 'Hierolimo figluolo di Eusebio nobile huomo fu nato di chastello stridone . . .: the Latin partly printed in *PL* xxii. 235–8: references in the text, ff. 116, 118^v to 'Giovanni Beleth' (fl. s. xii^2).

3. f. 120^v O falso mondo pieno di molti inghenni . . . facendo bene paradiso aspetto.

Six 3-line stanzas and a final two lines.

ff. 108. Paper. ff. 16–120 paginated in s. xvi 1–210. 290 × 200 mm. Written space 190 × 125 mm. 26–32 long lines. Frame ruling in pencil. The first line of writing above the frame line. Collation: $1\text{–}9^{12}$. The leaves in the first halves of quires are numbered in a single series 1–54, bottom right. Current hybrida and (art. 1) cursiva. 2-line initials, red with violet ornament or blue with red ornament. Binding of s. xviii lettered '**VITA DI S GIRO**'.

Written in Italy. 'N° 544 C' f. 13. In s. xviii, or later, ff. 1–12 (q.v.) were inserted at the beginning. A cutting from an English bookseller's catalogue, s. xix, inside the cover. Bookplate of W. H. Rylands. Given as F. 2. 1.

F. 4. 6. *Marsilius de Inghen, Abbreviata phisicorum Aristotelis* 1463

(f. 5) Incipit liber primus phisicorum marsilii. Circa librum phisicorum sunt ali^{ca} nunc videnda. diuina fauente clementia. prima abreuiacionum parte . . . (f. 84) de toto isto octauo libro phisicorum de quo deus benedicat in secula seculorum amen. Expliciunt abreuiata libri phisicorum composita et tradita parisii. ab excelentissimo doctore Magistro Marsilio medicine monarcha et artium doctore famossisimo. que sunt scripta per me *Euange*listam de car[. .][1] xxii decembris 146iii hora secunda noctis sequentis diey ad laudem dei o(mn)ipotentis ac beate marie virginis. amen. amen. amen. Deus qui nos patrem ac matrem honorare precepisti miserere clementer animabus patris ac matris mee eorumque peccata dimitte meque eos in eterne claritatis gaudio fac videre. (f. 85) Tabula questionum super octo libris phisicorum marsilii . . . (f. 86) Et sic finita est tabula questionum libri phisicorum aristotelis. 1463 die xxviiii° decembris hora 4^{a} decima. Deo gracias amen.

Thorndike and Kibre, s.v. Divina and Prima. Printed *c.* 1480; Goff, M. 281. The scribe wrote 'Deo dante. ac per cuius graciam possumus bene studere. Amen' at the end of bk. 2. He dated bks. 3 and 4 at the end 22 June and 17 June 1463, respectively, ff. 30^{v}, 43^{v}, but bk. 4 can hardly have been written before bk. 3: presumably the scribe wrote 'xvii' for 'xxvii' or June for July. The table is of 21, 18, 19, 21, 13, 12, 10, and 17 questions. On f. 84 all from *Expliciunt* to *viuere* is in capital letters. ff. 69^{v}, 84^{v}, 86^{v}–89 left blank, except for an ex-libris on f. 89^{v} (see below).

ff. iv + 85, foliated 1–89. Paper. 280 × 210 mm. Written space 185 × 130 mm. 2 cols. 38–42 lines. No horizontal ruling after quire 2. Collation of ff. 5–89: 1^{10} 2^{10} 7 cancelled after f. 20 $3\text{–}8^{10}$ 9^{6}. Narrow strips of parchment between quires and down the middle openings of quires. Written in very current but clear fere-humanistica. Initials: (i) red or blue patterned in white; (ii) red or blue. Contemporary binding of square-cut wooden boards: three bands: a clasp at head and foot and two clasps on the side. Secundo folio *eo quod.*

Written in Italy by a named scribe. His name occurred again on f. 89^{v}, since the ex-libris there is in his hand: 'Iste liber est mei [. . . .] de [. . . .] artium scolaris et completus est ab ipso die xxviii decembris hora 4^{a} decima. ad laudem dei omnipotentis gloriossime (*sic*) virginis marie tociusque curie triumphantis amen amen amen'. Belonged a little later to J. M. Ferrarius de Gradibus, †1472: 'Est mei Iohannis matthi ex ferrariis de gradi Mediolanum medici etc' emptus a Iohanne francisco de guateris bidello in papia (?) anno 147 (*sic*) die 14° februarii est quoque et amicorum ad usum', f. 89^{v}. 'Pretium est adnunc (?) duc' l auri',

[1] Letters in italics can be read by ultra-violet light.

f. 84. 'N° 167' on the front board, outside. The relevant slip from an English bookseller's catalogue, s. xix, inside the front cover. Book-plate of T. G. Rylands. Given as F. 2. 1.

F. 4. 7. *Philippus Cancellarius, In Psalmos; etc.* s. xiii^{1}

1. ff. 2–154^{v} Exurge psalterium et cythara. etc'. Prouerbiis xi. dicitur bene consurgit . . . Qui habitas in ortis. et Cetera.

Stegmüller, no. 6952 (Philippus Cancellarius Parisiensis, Sermones in Psalmos). Printed in 1523 and later. The sermons are numbered in pencil up to 'cclxlvii' (i.e. 297). Blank spaces here and there, either following the exemplar or because the scribe could not read it. A larger blank on f. 110^{v} where scribe 1 gave up.

2. ff. 155–171^{v} Quomodo sedet sola ciuitas plena populo. Aleph. Interpretatur doctrina. Quomodo sola . . . effusus es sicut aqua. et cetera.

Sermons on Lamentations 1, 2. Stegmüller, no. 6953, refers only to A. Sanderus, *Bibliotheca Belgica*, 1641. Other copies are Paris, B.N., lat. 3862, f. 127 and Sorbonne 77, and Liverpool Cathedral 34, art. 3, q.v. Attributed in the ex-libris (see below) to Philip the Chancellor. Some blank spaces like those in art. 1.

3. ff. 172–198^{v} Domine ne in furore tuo arguas . . .

A commentary on the psalms in the form of distinctions beginning at Ps. 6 and ending abruptly (?) in the last section but one of Ps. 118, 'G. quicumque. mat' xviii'. *Lectus* (Ps. 6: 7) is the first word: it is distinguished as 'sacre scripture', 'contemplacionis', 'ecclesie', 'consciencie', 'voluptatis', 'pene eterne', and 'vite eterne'. ff. 199–201^{v} left blank.

4 (added, s. xiii, on blank pages after art. 3, in the lower margin of ff. 142^{v}–143 and on flyleaves). (*a*) f. 200 [I]n seruo peruerso preter alia hec sunt precipue uicia . . . (*b*) ff. 142^{v}–143, 200^{rv}, 201^{v} Theological notes, usually set out as distinctions. (*c*) f. 201^{v} Disce quid es quid eras . . . (4 lines). (*d*) f. 1^{v} Ordo librorum veteris testamenti . . . Ordo librorum noui testamenti . . . (*e*) f. 202 The first words of sermons 1–42 of art. 1 and, for nos. 1–17, brief subject notes.

(*a*). Seven vices of a bad servant. (*c*). Walther, *Sprichwörter*, no. 5881. (*d*). OT: Genesis–4 Kings, Isaiah–Minor Prophets, Job, Psalms–Ecclesiasticus, 1, 2 Chronicles, 1, 2 Ezra, Esther, Tobit, Judith, Maccabees. NT in the common order.

ff. iv + 200 + iii, foliated (i–iii), 1–202, (203–4). ff. iii, 202 are medieval end-leaves: iii^{r} was pasted down. 278 × 200 mm. Written space of art. 1 changes from 202 × 130 mm to 182 × 125 mm at f. 111; of art. 2, *c.*195 × 130 mm. 2 cols. 51–4 lines: a change from 53 to 51 at f. 111. The first line of writing above the top ruled line in arts. 2, 3. Pricks in both margins to guide ruling in arts. 1, 2. Collation of ff. 2–201: 1–13^{8} 14^{4} + 1 leaf after 4 (f. 110) 15–17^{8} 18^{4} (ff. 135–8) 19–21^{8} 22^{8} + 1 leaf after 8 (f. 171) 23–25^{8} 26^{6}. Quires 1–13 have numbers at the end as well as catchwords, quires 15–19 catchwords only, quires 23–6 numbers at the beginning. Four hands, two in art. 1, changing at f. 111, and one for each of arts. 2, 3. Initials of art. 1: (i) f. 1, 8-line *E*, a blue and pink dragon and, for the horizontal central bar, a lion (or dog), on a decorated gold ground; (ii) 2-line, blue or red with ornament of the other colour: the style changes where the scribes change. Initials of art. 2, 2-line, red. Small blank spaces were left for initials of art. 3 and of art. 4*a*. Binding of s. xix. Secundo folio *in luca.*

From St Martin, Tournai, O.S.B.: 'Liber ecclesie sancti Martini torn' in quo continentur. phalterium cancellarii par'. Item expositio eiusdem super trenos Iheremie. Item distinctiones quedam super phalterium', f. 2, s. xiii; 'Liber sancti martini torn' ', f. 201^{v}, s. xiii. A number 'clxxxxv' cancelled and replaced by 'clv', f. 201^{v}, s. xv (?); also a later number '28' on ff. 1, 201^{v}. A. 39 in the list of Tournai manuscripts, given by Sanderus, op. cit., p. 92. Assigned the number 2023 by Sir Thomas Phillipps, but this manuscript and a good many other Tournai manuscripts never reached Phillipps, 'the scoundrel Eeman at whose house I left them having sold them during my absence' (A. N. L. Munby, *Phillipps Studies*, iii. 22). Book-plate of W. H. Rylands. Given as F. 2. 1. *MERT*, no. 7.

F. 4. 8. *Piers Plowman (in English)* s. xv in.

1. In a somer seisonne when softe was the sonne . . . (p. 202) til I gan awake. Explicit liber Willelmi de petro le plowȝman.

Described by J. H. G. Grattan in *MLR* xlii (1947), 1–8; also by G. Kane, *Piers Plowman, the A version*, 1960, pp. 2–3. An 'A' text, ending as usual at xi. 313, with a 'C' continuation. Collated as Ch by Kane.

A reader, s. xvi, wrote paraphrases of the original in the margins occasionally throughout, for example at vii. 288 (p. 50) 'when honger was gone and harvest come wast(er)s began to wax wilfull agean'. The same person (?) added running numbers from 'i' to 'iiii': the numbers change at Passus ix, xix, xxii.

2. pp. 207–10 are two adjacent leaves of Ezekiel, with the gloss, in an ugly English hand, s. xiii med.

Contains 20: 42–21: 7 on pp. 209–10 and 21: 10–23 on pp. 207–8. 26 lines of text and 52 of gloss. Formerly pastedowns in this or possibly some other book: 'Mr John Denman oweth this boucke god graunt hyme longe lyf wth muche encrease of wyrshype' is on p. 208, s. xvi, and a pressmark, probably of s. xviii, 'T. 2. 10' on p. 210.

ff. iii + 103 + iv, paginated (i–vi), 1–202, (203–14). 262 × 200 mm. Written space 182 mm high. 31 or 32 long lines. Frame ruling. Collation: 1–12^{8} 13^{8} wants 7, blank. Hair outside all sheets. Quires 1–10 lettered in red at the end, [A]–K. Written in anglicana formata (short *r*). Initials: (i) f. 1, 3-line, gold with violet ornament; (ii) 3-line, blue with red ornament. Binding of s. xviii. Secundo folio *And he buncheth*.

Written in England. A scribble, 'Isabell poniell', p. 11, s. xvi. 'Walt: Stonehouse p^{re} 10^{s}', f.. 1, s. xvii: he was fellow of Magdalen College, Oxford, 1617–29 (W. D. Macray, *Register of St Mary Magdalen College*, iii. 147) and owned Bodleian, MS. Bodley 435, and other manuscripts: a note by him on p. 202. Armorial book-plate of 'Sr William Horton Bar^{t} / Chaderton' (created 1764) inside the cover, s. xviii. For another possible owner, see above, art. 2. Given by Mrs Clara Hornby in 1944.

F. 4. 9. *William of Nassington, etc. (in English)* s. xiv/xv

1. ff. 2–203 All myghty god in trinite . . . þat on þe crosse for vs all' walde hyng.

The Mirror of Life attributed to William of Nassington in B.L., Royal 17 C. viii. *IMEV*, no. 245/35.

2. ff. 203v–207v þe worthyest thing maste of godenes . . . In goddes name ga þi way.

Not used for the edition by T. F. Simmons, *Lay folks mass book*, EETS lxxi (1879), 2–58. *IMEV*, no. 3507/8. 353 lines, the last corresponding to line 356 of MS. C. The text resembles MS. D, a much later manuscript. Directions are in red ink.

ff. iv + 206 + iv, foliated (i–iii), 1–208, (209–11). ff. 1, 208 are parchment flyleaves. 200 × 137 mm. Written space *c.*165 mm high. 40 long lines. Collation of ff. 2–207: 1–16[12] 17[8] 18[8] wants 7, 8. Quires 1–17 signed in pencil a–g, a–c, a–g. Written in anglicana formata (short *r*). Initials: (i, ii) 6-line (f. 2) and 3-line, blue with red ornament. The capital letter at the beginning of each line is filled with pale yellow. Binding of s. xviii for the family of Gower, whose coronet and (dog-like) wolf are on the spine below the title 'Gower's Poems'.[1] Secundo folio *þare fore.*

Written in England. Armorial book-plate of 'Gower Earl Gower', s. xviii, inside the cover: the earldom dates from 1746. '27. 4', f. ii and 'N. 5. 4' on the book-plate. Belonged to Messrs Quaritch, *c.*1925 (catalogue 328, item 577). Sir L. Harmsworth's sale, Sotheby's 15 Oct. 1945, lot 2123. T. Thorp, catalogue 246, item 444. Bought in 1946.

F. 4. 10. *Chastising of God's Children, etc. (in English)* s. xv²

1. ff. 1–42v Here begynneth and folowin the chapeturs of this boke which is clepede the chastisynge of goddis childyrn. The first is howghe that . . . (*table of 26 chapters*) . . . (f. 2) In drede of almyghty god religious sistir a shorte pistel . . . haue m*er*cie on us synful. Amen.

Collated as L for the edition by J. Bazire and E. Colledge, 1957: see p. 6. A poor text. Two leaves are missing with parts of chapters 1, 2, 4, 5.

2. ff. 42v–51 Prayinge is a gracious gifte of oure lorde god . . . melodie of heuene to the whiche. god us brynge. Amen. In nomine patris et filii et spiritus sancti. Amen.

Another complete copy is Bodleian, e Mus. 35, pp. 452–67: cf. H. E. Allen, *Writings of Richard Rolle*, p. 81, footnote. Printed from the imperfect Thornton manuscript by C. Horstmann, *Yorkshire Writers*, i. 295–300.

3. ff. 51v–53v In the begynnynge thou shalte make it knowin to thyne `harte´ . . . And therefore I rede. that thei be thyne not (*ends imperfectly*).

An 'inferior recension' of the Pistle of Preier, more or less as edn. by P. Hodgson, EETS ccxxxi (1955), pp. 48/5–58/9: see pp. xv, xvi.

4. ff. 54–100v (*begins imperfectly in a table of 90 chapters*) certayne but trouble the steringis of theim that be in deuocion' c. xxix . . . (f. 55) Gostely brothir or systir in ihesu criste. I praye the þt . . . it shall teche the alle that the (*ends imperfectly*).

[1] The words 'The mirrour of lyfe' are on f. 1, s. xvi, and, lower down, by the same hand, 'Vox clamantis / Speculum meditantis / Confessio amantis' and against these three lines 'Iohn Gower'. This explains the false title.

Walter Hilton, Scale of Perfection, bk. 1, ending in ch. 91 (numbered 'lxxxix' in the table: ed. E. Underhill, p. 218/19). A manuscript of type C: see Helen Gardner in *Medium Aevum*, v (1937), 17.

ff. i + 100 + i. f. is a modern parchment leaf. Thick parchment. 273 × 190 mm. Written space *c.* 190 × 130 mm. 37 long lines. Collation: 1^8 wants 3 and 7 2–6^8 7^8 wants 8 after f. 53 8–12^8 13^8 wants 8 after f. 100. Quires signed in the usual late medieval way, *a–n*. Catchwords in distinctive frames. Textura: *þ* and *y* are indistinguishable. Initials: (i) blue patterned in white and shaded to white on decorated gold grounds: a continuous framed border on f. 1 and a border on three sides—not the outer margin—of f. 2; (ii) 2-line, gold on grounds of pink and blue, with sprays into the margins; (iii) 1-line, blue or red. Line fillers in blue and red. Medieval binding of bevelled wooden boards covered with stamped brown leather: rebacked, but the old leather has been pasted on the spine: on the front cover a pattern of fillets encloses three vertical rows of stamps; on the back cover fillets and a border stamp enclose two horizontal and three vertical rows of stamps separated by fillets: the stamps are of six patterns, a cinquefoil for the border: five bands.[1] Secundo folio *In drede of*.

Written in England. Scribbles, s. xvi, include 'Thomas Barker is my name', f. 23, 'Deuonshire debebat' (f. 89v) and '6000 to stowes wharff 11000 Mr Secreatory' (f. 101). '27/3/13' inside the back cover. Quaritch, Catalogue no. 344 (1916), item 10 at £80. Belonged to Sir Leicester Harmsworth: his sale 15 Oct. 1945, lot 1957. Liverpool University book-plate marked 'The Gift of Mrs Harold Cohen': given in 1949.

F. 4. 11. *Registrum brevium* s. xiv ex.

1. ff. iv–xiiv Kalendare. Litera resignacionis causa permutacionis . . .

A table of the contents of art. 2, leaf by leaf or by batches of leaves: thus, the last sixteen entries, 'Breue de vasto versus mulierem in dote . . . Breue de ventre inspiciendo. etc' ', are followed by references to ff. 273–80. The numbering from 'xiiii' is one behind that of art. 2. f. xiiirv is blank.

2. ff. 1–280v In dei nomine amen Ego H. de W. Rector ecclesie de N. Lingcolnie dioc' . . .

A register of writs in which the name of the king issuing the writ occurs in two places, on f. 21 at the first entry under 'Assisa noue disseisine', 'Ricardus dei gracia . . .' a writ of 2 August anno 4, and on f. 72 at the first entry under the heading 'Breue de recto patens', 'Ricardus dei gracia . . .', a writ of 6 July anno 4. f. 1 begins with a letter of resignation 'causa permutacionis'. Letters of presentation come next. The last writ, 'De ventre inspiciendo', is as edn. 1595, f. 227. Notes in explanation of the writs are written in the margins throughout by the main hand. One of them is 'Nota de breuibus de recto que iam non sunt in vsu' (f. 75). 'Hic est quaternus qui debet scribi' is on the verso of the last leaf of quire 9. ff. 281–283v left blank.

3. ff. 284–310v Registrum Iudiciale. Primum. Ricardus dei gracia . . . vic' Notyngham salutem. Quia Iohannes de Westhorp' . . .

213 numbered writs, the first 'Quando vicecomes mandauit quod pleg' non inuenit' and the last 'Episcopo ad inquirendum de Bastardia'. Probably the same collection as in Bodleian,

[1] Dr Ian Doyle tells me that three of the stamps, cinquefoil, rosette, and lion, are also on the binding of a Lydgate, Fall of Princes, belonging to Mr R. H. Taylor: the facsimile of one cover in Quaritch catalogue for 1931, item 100, shows the cinquefoil and the rosette.

Rawlinson C. 941, s. xv. As there the first writ gives a king's name and a date, 8 June anno 14. de Haas and Hall, p. xxvii, list seventeen registers of judicial writs, but not this one. f. 311^{rv} left blank.

4 (added, s. xv). A dozen writs in blank spaces, ff. 280^{v}–283, 310^{v}–311^{v}, and in the lower margins of ff. 166, 197^{v}, 203^{v}, 253 include a licence to Humfrey, Duke of Gloucester, and Eleanor his wife to empark 200 acres at Greenwich, Westminster 6 March, no year (f. 280^{v}), and two copies of a writ to the sheriffs of London on the burning of Lollards, 14 June 18 (Henry VI) (ff. 166, 197^{v}): the first copy is signed 'haslen' and is entitled in the margin 'Breue quod vocatur Dormant pro lollardes'.[1] On f. iii is a note of a case at Guildhall, Henry Fereby and other citizens of London in debt to Robert de Heworth, gentleman, 12 Dec. 33 Henry VI.

ff. iii + 321 + ii, foliated i–xiii, 1–311, (312–13). The medieval foliation of art. 1 runs i–ccxlix, ccxlx–ccxlxxxx. f. iii is a medieval parchment flyleaf. 262 × 190 mm. Written space 195 × 120 mm. 40 long lines. Frame ruling in art. 3. Collation of ff. iv–xiii, 1–311: 1^{6} 2 four $3\text{–}37^{8}$ 38^{4} + 2 leaves before 1 (ff. 281–2) $39\text{–}40^{8}$ 41^{8} + 1 leaf after 8 (f. 311). Quire 3 is marked on all leaves 'quaternus i^{us}'. Quires 16–37 are signed at the beginning *a–y*. Written in current anglicana of a legal kind by three hands, the second, looser and more spreading than the first, beginning at f. 105 (16^{1}) and the third at f. 284. Initials: (i) f. 1, 5-line, blue with red ornament; (ii) 3-line and 2-line not filled: spaces occur only on ff. 37^{v}–94. Binding of s. xix. Secundo folio (f. 2) *nostrum C.*

Written in England. Perhaps in London in s. xv. 'Mr J. B. Hostage' and 'John Hostage Chester 1863' inside the cover. The University of Liverpool book-plate is marked 'The Gift of Mrs Stella Permewan in memory of William Muspratt Permewan MCMXLVIII'.

F. 4. 13. *Officium coronae domini, etc.* s. xiv^{1} (arts. 1, 2) s. xv^{1} (art. 3)

1. (*a*) ff. 1–2^{v} [D]ies ire dies illa . . . (*b*) ff. 2^{v}–3 [S]alue regina . . . (*c*) ff. 3–4 [U]irgo mater ecclesie . . . (*d*) f. 4^{rv} [R]egina celi letare . . . (*e*) f. 4^{v} Aue regina celorum aue domina angelorum Salue radix . . .

RH, nos. 4626, 18147, 21818, 17170, 2070. All noted. (*e*) is an addition, s. xiv.

2. ff. 5–46^{v} In uigilia sanctissime spinee corone domini. ad vesperas super psalmos Ant'. Gaude felix mater ecclesia . . .

The musical parts of offices of the Crown of Thorns. The metrical antiphons are printed in *AH* xlv. 16–18. The hymns at vespers, matins and lauds are Cor(o)nam syon, Eterne regi glorie, Lauda fidelis contio (ff. 7, 9, 29^{v}: *RH*, nos. 3933, 629, 10204). Office of mass, ff. 32–44; prose, f. 37^{v}, Dyadema salutare, *RH*, no. 4558. Credo in unum deum, ff. 44^{v}–46^{v}.

3. (*a*) ff. 47–53 In uigilia beatissimi Mathei apostoli et eu'. In primis uesperis. Ant.' Hoc est preceptum . . . (f. 49^{v}) Ad missam. Os iusti meditabitur . . . (f. 52)

[1] As Miss Barbara Harvey tells me, the writ is probably to be connected with the burning of Richard Wyche (Emden, *BRUO*, p. 2101) in London, 17 June 1440.

In secundis uesperis. a'. Intrauit dominus et non penitebit . . . (*b*) ff. 53^{v}–60 In missa de beata uirgine ab aduentu usque ad nat. Introytus. Rorate celi . . . (*c*) ff. 60^{v}–63 Kyrieleyson, Gloria, Sanctus, Agnus. (*d*) ff. 63^{v}–65 [G]audeamus omnes in domino diem festum celebrantes sub honore sanctarum uirginum . . . (*e*) ff. 65^{v}–66^{v} [A]sperges me domino . . . Vidi aquam etc.

All noted. (*a–c*) in one hand. (*d, e*) in two other hands.

ff. i + 66 + i. 325 × 235 mm. Written space 210 × 145 mm. 7 long lines and music. Collation: 1^{4} 2^{10} $3\text{-}5^{12}$ $6\text{-}7^{8}$. Initials of art. 2: (i) ff. 5, 11^{v}, 32^{v}, 41^{v}, blue or pink on gold and coloured grounds, historiated or decorated, with prolongations: the historiations are (f. 5) the Crowning with Thorns (facsimile in *MERT*, colour plate 2) and (f. 32^{v}) Christ in Glory: a saint on each side of Him, one holding lance, nails, and scourge, the other a crown: the prolongation on f. 5 forms a continuous border and at each corner an evangelist's symbol in a roundel; (ii) pink on decorated grounds of deep blue: prolongations into the margins; (iii, iv) 2-line and 1-line, blue with red or red with violet ornament. Initials of art. 3: (i) ff. 47, 49^{v}, 52, elaborate penwork, lightly tinged with green, with penwork borders: an historiation, Matthew, f. 49; (ii, iii) 2-line and 1-line, red with blue or blue with red ornament. 1-line spaces in art. 1 have not been filled. Binding of s. xix in. Secundo folio *lapsus*.

Written in Italy. Dr Alexander identifies the decoration of art. 2 as Pisan and suggests provenance from the Pisan church of Santa Maria della Spina, so called from 1333 when it received a relic of the Crown of Thorns. '[. . . . .] Pisa Sept. 1837 [. . .]', inside the cover. C. W. Reynell sale at Sotheby's (property of his daughter, Miss Reynell), 15 May 1895, lot 10: acquired thence by Henry Young, 12 Castle St., Liverpool, as appears from the slip from a Young catalogue pasted inside the cover. Belonged to Cedric H. Boult. Given by his son, Sir Adrian Boult, in 1950. *MERT*, no. 66.

F. 4. 18. *W. Peraldus, Summa de vitiis; etc.* s. xiii ex.

1. ff. 1–72 Titulus incipit tractatus moralis de vii uiciis capitalibus. Tractatus iste continet ix partes. prima pars . . . (*summary of contents*) . . . (f. 3) Incipit summa de uiciis et post (*sic for* primo) de uicio gule R*ubrica*. Dicturi de uiciis incipiemus a uicio gule propter hoc . . . loqutam esse aliquando penituit tacere uero nunquam. Explicit de lingua cristo gloria qui est benedictus deus in secula. Explicit summa de uiciis.

For manuscripts and printed editions see A. Dondaine, 'Guillaume Peyraut', *AFP* xviii (1948), 189, 193–7, *SOPMA* ii. 133–42 no. 1622, Bloomfield, no. 1628. For printed editions see also Goff, P. 84–90. Notes and corrections in English hands. f. 72^{v} blank.

2. ff. 73–96^{v} [S]ap. 6 Quid est sapientia et quemadmodum facta sit referam . . . et ideo minori quam habuit surrexisse (*ends abruptly*).

Richard Fishacre, O.P., on bk. 4 of the Sentences of Peter Lombard. Stegmüller, *Sent.*, no. 718, iv. No breaks in the text. No signs of use. The last words are in the discussion of *nec minus tribuit* towards the end of Dist. 14 (*PL* cxci. 871/4 up). In the copy in Oriel College, Oxford, 43 they occur at f. 381vb/10.

ff. ii + 96 + ii. 333 × 228 mm. Written space 245 × 142 mm and (art. 2) 160 mm. 2 cols. 71–7 lines. Collation: $1\text{-}6^{10}$ 7^{12} $8\text{-}9^{10}$ 10 three (ff. 94–6). Initials of art. 1: (i) f. 1, 7-line, blue on decorated pink and gold ground; (ii) 2-line, blue with red ornament. A 4-line space for *S* on f. 73 not filled and initials outside the written space on ff. 75v, 83 not supplied. 'Bound by W. Pratt', s. xix ex.: perhaps long without a cover, since ff. 1, 96v show signs of exposure. Secundo folio *sit nequam*.

Written in England. '29/3/95' and '£20', f. 1. University of Liverpool book-plate, the space for donor's name blank.

F. 4. 19. *Missale romanum* s. xv²

1. ff. 1–6v Calendar in red and black.

No gradings, apart from Duplex for a few principal feasts. Marianus and Jacobus at 30 April and Ubaldus (bishop of Gubbio) at 16 May, both in black, seem to be the only saints not usually in the Roman calendar of this date. 'sancti bernardini confessoris' added at 20 May and 'et sancti facundini episcopi et confessoris' (bishop of Gualdo Tadino, Umbria: Gams, *Series Episcoporum*, p. 710) added at 28 Aug.

2. ff. 7–121 Incipit ordo missalis secundum consuetudinem romane curie.

Temporal, Advent–Easter Eve. The Exultet noted, ff. 106v–111.

3. ff. 121v–122 Aduentus domini celebratur . . . ecclesiarum et altarium.

Except the first two items, not the text in *SMRL* ii. 114.

4. ff. 122–36 Paratus sacerdos cum intrat ad altare . . .

Ordinary, (ff. 123v–130) noted prefaces, (ff. 130–1) Communicantes, and (ff. 131v–136) canon of mass.

5. ff. 136–80 Temporal, Easter–24th Sunday after Pentecost.

6. ff. 180–225v Incipit proprium sanctorum de missali.

Andrew–Katherine.

7. ff. 225v–250 Incipit commune sanctorum de missali.

8. ff. 250–255v (*a*) Missa de trinitate. (*b, c*) In anniuersario dedicationis ecclesie; In ipsa die dedicationis altaris. (*d*) Missa in honore sanctorum quorum corpora . . . (*e*) Missa de spiritu sancto. (*f*) Missa in honore sancte crucis. (*g*) in commemoratione beate marie. (*h*) Missa pro peccatis.

SMRL: (*a*) p. 318, no. 2, but a full office; (*b, c*) pp. 317–18; (*d*) p. 318, no. 1; (*e, f*) p. 319; (*g*) pp. 319–20; (*h*) p. 323, no. 25.

9. ff. 255v–265v Collect, secret, and postcommunion of votive masses, the first 'In postulandam gratiam sancti spiritus' and the last 'Pro infirmo qui proximus est morti'.

SMRL ii. 318–27, nos. 3, 7–9, 6, 10–17, 19, 20, 24, 23, 25, 27–9, 31–8, 41–4, 46–54, 56, 57, 59–61, 55, 45, 62.

10. ff. 265v–270v Missa in agenda defunctorum.

SMRL ii. 327–30, nos. 63a–m, o–q, s.

11. ff. 270v–271 Collect, secret, and postcommunion Pro desiderantibus penitenciam and Pro cuius anima dubitatur.

SMRL ii. 330–1, nos. 64–5.

12. ff. 271–272v Missa pro sponso et sponsa. Intr. Deus israel sit uobiscum . . .

Missale Romanum, ii. 321, but the first prayer is 'Exaudi nos omnipotens et misericors deus ut quod nostro . . .'.

13. f. 272v In festo sancte marthe.

Collect, secret, and postcommunion. Cf. *SMRL* ii. 291.

14. ff. 272v–274 Incipit benedictio salis et aque.

15. f. 274rv In festo uisitationis gloriose virginis marie. Introitus. Gaudeamus . . .

Missale Romanum, ii. 208.

16. ff. 274v–275v Missa fraternitatis. Salus populi ego sum . . .

Ibid. ii. 361.

17 (added, s. xv ex. ?). (*a*) ff. 275v–276 In conceptione uirginis ordinata a Systo pont'. Q. (*b*) f. 276rv In uisitatione beate uirginis. Introitus. Transite . . . (*c*) f. 277 Seven settings of the words 'Kyrie. Gloria in excelsis deo. Ite missa est'.

(*a*). Ibid. ii. 165. (*b*) Ibid. ii. 275 (mass attributed to Sixtus IV).

ff. i + 277. 350 × 250 mm. Written space 210 × 160 mm. 2 cols. 25 lines, or, on pages with music, 7 lines. Collation: 1^{6} $2\text{–}27^{10}$ 28^{10} + 1 leaf after 10. Catchwords written vertically. A Crucifixion picture, 158 × 165 mm, including the frame, on f. 131v. Initials: (i) ff. 190v, 204v, 6-line, in colour on gold grounds, historiated (Annunciation of B.V.M., James the Greater); (ii) f. 131v, 4-line *T* of *Te igitur*: elaborate penwork ornament in the margins; (iii) 2-line, blue with red ornament or red with violet ornament; (iv) 1-line, blue or red. Capital letters in the ink of the text filled with pale yellow. Contemporary binding of wooden boards covered with brown leather bearing a pattern of 4-line fillets and small ornaments of two patterns: five bands: clasps (missing) fastened from front to back.

Written in Italy (northern Umbria ?: see art. 1). '4575' and 'Milan 1/9/95', f. i. Liverpool University book-plate marked 'Presented by C. Sydney Jones to the Department of Education'. Transferred to the main library in 1959.

F. 4. 20. *Gregorius IX, Decretales* 1290

Gregorius episcopus seruus seruorum dei dilectis filiis doctoribus et scolaribus parisius et ubicumque commorantibus . . . Rex pacificus . . . (f. 354) homagium compellatur. Expliciunt decretales gregorii noni. Tradite magistris et scolaribus parisien'. Anno ab incarnatione domini M CC XXXIIII. Tercio nonas nouembris pontificatus nostri anno octauo. Deo gracias.

The text is surrounded by the apparatus of Bernardus (Parmensis): In huius libri principio quinque sunt precipue prenotanda . . . scilicet de pactis. pactiones. b'. Explicit apparatus decretalium editus a bernardo cum omnibus additionibus nouis et ueteribus. deo gratias. amen. Thoma normanno milleno scribitur anno / et ducenteno domini nouies quoque deno.

Bk. 2, f. 97; 3, f. 185^{v}; 4, f. 257; 5, f. 281^{v}. Some contemporary annotations in neat textura, for example on ff. 3, 96^{v}, and in anglicana, for example on ff. 96^{v}, 118^{rv}; others of s. xiv^{2} (?) in cursiva.

ff. 354 + i. 415 × 247 mm. Written space, including apparatus, 395 × 230 mm. 2 cols. 38–41 lines (text) and up to 92 lines (apparatus). Collation: 1–28^{12} 29^{16} 30 two. Textura based on an Italian model: the two sizes of script for text and apparatus are probably by the same hand. Anglicana is used (by the scribe of the text ?) in headings written at the foot of the page as a guide for the rubricator. A picture before each book, that for bk. 1 erased and repainted in s. xiv^{2}. Initials: (i) of books, blue or pink patterned in white on grounds of the same colours, patterned in white, and of decorated gold; (ii, iii) 3-line (in text) and 3-line (in apparatus), as (i) but smaller and on grounds of one colour only; (iv, v) outside written space of text and 2-line in apparatus, red or blue with ornament of the other colour. All or most part of the first column of each book is in red or blue cadel-like letters with elaborate penwork ornament in green alternating with lines of ordinary script in blue ink. Facsimiles of part of f. 97 in the Quaritch catalogues (see below) and of part of f. 257, reduced, in *MERT*, pl. 5b, show pictures, type-(i) initials, and fancy writing. Late medieval binding of wooden boards covered with white skin: six bands: two clasps: the flyleaf and pastedown at the end have been taken over from an earlier binding. Secundo folio *a tota trinitate* or (apparatus) *passum*.

Written in France by a named and perhaps English scribe (see above). A French owner wrote notes on the pastedown at the end in the 1370s: (1) Anno domini m^{o} ccc^{o} lxx^{o} die mercurii post festum natiuitatis beati Io. bap. (26 June) Recessit magister cristianus magister magnarum scolarum tienen (Tirlemont) ad curiam romanam causam quare bene scitur quare etcetera; (2) die xii^{a} februarii anno 1371 fuit tonitruum magnum horribile cum magna coruscacione circa horam none nostre domine et hoc parisius quia tunc (?) morabar in claustro brunelli et ista dies fuit prima kadragesime (? *sic*);[1] (3) die xxv^{a} mensis septembris venit G. curel ad domum nostram que dies fuit dies Iouis post festum mathei apostoli et nobiscum illa die cenauit et prima nocte ad domum iacuit.[2] Other notes are: (4), below (3), die viii^{a} mensis septembris recessit; (5) decima octaua die septembris fui ad domum ma. thome [. . .]; (6) Penultima die mensis aprilis fui ad domum ma. alani; (7) die Iouis ante festum sancti Io. Bap. fui ad balistam [. . . .] et cetera. Printed book-label of William Morris (†1896): his sale, Sotheby's, 7 December 1898, lot 561. Lent by Bruce S. Ingram to the

[1] Ash Wednesday was the 11th of February in 1372 and the 20th in 1371. The Clos Bruneau in the Rue St Jacques de Beauvais was the seat of the faculty of law of the University of Paris.

[2] The 25th of September was a Thursday in 1376.

Burlington Fine Arts Exhibition of Illuminated Manuscripts, 1908: *Catalogue*, p. 46, no. 94. Quaritch cat. 532 (1937), item 241; cat. 629 (1945), item 5. Book-plate of R. G. Morton: given as F. 3. 13.

F. 4. 22. *G. de Hoylandia, etc.* s. xiv med.

1. ff. 1–56 Osculetur me osculo oris sui etc. Antequam ad [. . .] littere accedatur sunt aliqua premittenda. ad introductionem sequencium . . . (f. 2) per dileccionem coniungere. Osculetur me osculo oris sui. Liber iste qui cantica canticorum intitulatur prima sui diuisione habet . . . carnis lacrime fluant.

Divided into six parts, each called a 'dragma' or 'corda': see f. 46. f. i^{rv} left blank.

2. ff. 56–108^{v} Incipit Gilbertus super Cantica Sermo primus. In lectulo meo etc'. Varii sunt amancium affectus . . . approximat igni.

PL clxxxiv. 11–252. Stegmüller, no. 2493. Forty-seven numbered sermons, not forty-eight as in *PL*, since no. 11 here corresponds to nos. 11, 12 there. ff. 61–70 are out of order: see collation, below.

3. ff. 108^{v}–113 Dilectus meus. Hic describitur et laudatur sponsus a sponsa . . . et scripturarum et sic de aliis.

On Song of Songs 5: 10–8: 14. ff. 113^{v}–114^{v} were left blank: some notes have been added on 113^{v}–114.

4. ff. 116^{v}–134 Erat lux vera que illuminat . . . Legimus in genesi sic. Vniuerse creature corporee . . .

On John 1–4 and 5: 1, ending abruptly. Begins as Stegmüller, no. 10328. A leaf missing after f. 130. ff. 134^{v}–136^{v} contain added 'Notabilia de aduentu', notes on Song of Songs, etc. ff. 115–16 were left blank: a list of the sermons of art. 2 and six others has been added on f. 115^{v}.

5. The pastedowns are parts of two bifolia of a closely written commentary, s. xii/xiii, on an early compilation of decretals. Strips of the same manuscript were used also as strengthening between quires and in the middle of quires. Headings are 'Qui clerici uel uouentes matrimonium contrahere possunt', 'Qui matrimonium accusare non possunt uel testificari' and at the back 'De purgatione vulgari' and 'De sententia excommunicationis et absolutionis', as Compilatio I, iv. 6, 18 and v. 35, 39: this last begins '*Cum sit* hoc c. expositum est supra de appellationibus c. ii. *Super eo canonem* xvii. q. iiii (Decretum Gratiani, Causa 17, q. 4. 29). Si quis suadente *excommunicatus*, et hoc v^{m} est de doli'.

References are mainly to the Decretum.

ff. 137, foliated i, 1–136. Paper. 280 × 215 mm. Written space *c.*240 × 170 mm. 2 cols. 54–63 lines. Frame ruling. Collation: 1–9^{12} (ff. i, 1–60, 67–70, 65, 66, 61–4, 71–107) 10 seven (ff. 108–14: 112–13 is the central bifolium) 11 eight (ff. 115–22: 115–18 are the two central bifolia) 12^{12} wants 9 after f. 130 13 three (ff. 134–6). Written mainly in a modified textura which tends to be current at first; from f. 109 in the German equivalent of anglicana formata. 2-line blue or red initials: 'ix^c parua littera', a memorandum in the lower margin of f. 59^v, cannot refer to them. Contemporary binding of bevelled wooden boards, the spine and 35 mm of each board covered with leather: a chain of five links is attached by a ring to the point of a piece of metal 33 mm wide at the base and 83 mm long, which is fastened by three nails half way along the top of the front cover: three bands: title on the back cover, 'Lectura super Cantica canticorum et alia bona super Iohannem'. Secundo folio *anagogico*.

Written in Germany. Book-plate of R. G. Morton. Given as F. 3. 13.

MAIDSTONE. ALL SAINTS CHURCH

Parochial libraries of Great Britain, ed. N. R. Ker, 1959, pp. 88–9, 109–10. S. W. Kershaw, 'On manuscripts and rare books in the Maidstone Museum', *Archaeologia Cantiana*, xi (1877), 187–98. The library, of which a nucleus, including P. 5, existed already by 1716, was kept in the vestry until 1867: in May that year the Vestry decided that it should be deposited in the Town Museum (*Maidstone and Kentish Journal*, 13 May 1867).[1] A. 13 and P. 5, but not B. 91, are listed in the catalogue made by Robert Finch in 1815 (manuscript at Maidstone Museum).

A. 13. *Sermones, etc.* s. xiii¹, xiii/xiv, xiv¹

A closely written mass of sermons and pieces useful to a preacher, all in small hands, except art. 14. For arts. 3, 11, 12, see C. Brown in *Modern Language Review*, xxi (1926), 1–12, 249–60.

1 (quire 1). (*a*) ff. 1–5^v De incarnacione. Luc' 1. Colloquium gabrielis et mulieris. Dicit deus serpenti . . . (*b*) ff. 6^v–9^v Amor est coniunccio diligentis ad dilectum . . . (*c*) ff. 10–11^v A table of Epistle and Gospel lessons through the year for temporal, sanctoral, and common of saints.

(*a*). OT types of NT events under 136 headings, the first 'De incarnacione' and the last 'Sedens ihesu in iudicio'. The references to OT under each heading are sometimes followed by verses, mainly couplets, the first 'Serpentis fragile territur capud a muliere . . .' (Walther, *Initia*, no. 17577, which refers only to Vat. Reg. lat. 29, s. xvi) and the last 'Ut crucis ascensor latronum fit quasi censor . . .'. 'Incipit ii^a pars. Iohannes in deserto . . .' is on f. 1^v and 'Incipit iii^a pars. Andreas et alii . . .' on f. 2. (*b*) Definitions in alphabetical order, ending imperfectly in P. A few are ascribed to particular authors, for example 'Arbitrium est liberum de uoluntate animi iudicium' has 'Magistri Willelmi de montibus li. nu.' against it. Most of each page was left blank.

2 (quires 2–7). (*a*) ff. 12–91^v De unitate et concordia prelatorum. Gen. xlvi Ioseph proficiscentibus . . . (*b*) f. 12, at foot, Videbo te bone ihesu. Videbo te occulis fidei quos aperuisti michi . . . (*c*) f. 92^rv, mainly blank until s. xix (cf. art. 14) has on it a few earlier notes, including four lines of verse, 'Crede michi mitos . . .' on the verso.

[1] I owe the reference to Mr Graham Hunter.

(*a*). Some 315 subject headings, each followed by references to the Bible and patristic and other authorities, perhaps all the work of one scribe at various times. Some verses are included, for example on f. 71^{v} under 'De Resurrectione domini', seventeen lines beginning 'Quinquies in prima dominus se luce reuelat'. Spaces were left for additional entries which include a couplet in French on f. 46 and maxims, etc., in English on f. 46^{v} (see below, art. 3*b*), f. 49^{v} (couplets, 'Lo man u ich luuede þe . . .' and 'Also god is he þat holdt . . .') f. 54 (an early version of *IMEV*, Suppl. no. 4020.6)[1] and ff. 55^{v}, 86, 87. The authorities include Seneca, 'Philosophus', Aristotle 'in libro de animalibus', Anastasius (f. 43^{v}) and 'Magister Blesensis' (f. 51). 'Versus de fratre Ricardo. Siste. locum signa. Iacet hic caro viuere digna . . .' (4 lines) is in the margin of f. 61^{v}. (*b*) A brief meditation, added early.

3–5 (quire 8). Pieces in English, French and Latin, partly at least in a hand which occurs in art. 2.

3. *English*. (*a*) f. 93 Dicta alfredi. þe erl and the þe aþeling . . . (*b*) f. 93 Swines brede is Swiþe Swete . . . (*c*) f. 93^{v} Man mei longe him liues wene . . .

(*a*). 266 lines of the 'Proverbs of Alfred', printed from this copy by Brown, loc. cit., pp. 252–5; see also H. P. South, *The Proverbs of Alfred*, 1926, where part of f. 93 is reproduced double size. (*b*). Lines 149, 150 of 'Poema Morale', printed by Brown, loc. cit., p. 250. The same couplet is also on f. 46^{v} and on f. 253. (*c*). Five 10-line stanzas, the first with musical notes, printed from this copy by Carleton Brown, *English Lyrics of the Thirteenth Century*, 1933, pp. 15–16 (*Death's Wither-Clench*). *IMEV*, no. 2070.

4. *French*. (*a*) f. 93^{v} Preum an chantant la mere ihesu . . . (*b*) f. 102^{rv} Mort ki prenz ceus sudenement . . .

(*a, b*) printed from this copy by Brown in *MLR* xxi. 2. 4. (*a*), Sinclair, no. 3473, is five 14-line stanzas to B.V.M. (*b*) is stanzas 19, 34, 41, 35–8, 30, 49, 50, 48 of a 50-stanza poem printed by F. Wulff and E. Walberg, *Les vers de la mort par Hélinant, moine de Froidmont*, Société des anciens textes français, 1905.

5. *Latin*. (*a*) ff. 94^{rv}, 103^{rv} Seventeen tales, mainly miracles of B.V.M. (*b*) ff. 95–101^{v}, 104. Miscellaneous theological notes. (*c*) f. 99^{v} Letters: (1) from a bishop to the abbots, priors, archdeacons, deans, parsons, vicars and chaplains of his diocese, 11 July 1229, asking that 'cum Canonici Sancti N illius loci ad vniuersitatem vestram accedent pro sua necessitate vestras elemosinas petituri' they should be treated generously; (2) from a dean to the incumbents of his deanery on the same matter.

(*a*) occupies the second sheet of the quire and runs straight on from f. 94^{v} to f. 103^{r}. (1) Erat quidam monachus `h´oroscopus valde luxuriosus . . . (2) Clerk of Chartres who loved chess, dicing, etc. (3) Clerk who said 'Gaude dei genitrix'. (4) Poor man who honoured B.V.M. (5) Ebbo, a robber. (6) Monk of St Peter's, Cologne. (7) Layman who lay with his mistress the night before he proposed to go on pilgrimage to St James. (8) Chaplain who said Salve sancta parens instead of mass. (9) Rich clerk who left his benefice to get married. (11) Girl has vision of her mother who led a bad life. (12) Arrogant abbess. (13) Thais. (14) Man who never smiled. (15) Holy man sees a dying pilgrim surrounded by angels. (16) Vision of a Cistercian monk. (17) Man with three friends. (*c*) is over writing in pencil among the notes forming (*b*).

[1] Information from Mr J. E. Maddrell.

6 (quire 9). ff. 105–108^{v} Cogitis me o paula et eustochium . . .

Extracts from Jerome, De assumptione Beatae Virginis (*PL* xxx) and other treatises and letters of Jerome. The numbers in the margins of f. 107^{v} VII, VIII, IX, XII, XIII, XXI, CXIII are the numbers assigned to the letters in the common collection of 121 letters, for example in New College, Oxford, MS. 129.

7 (quires 10–13). Four sets of sermons and (*e, f*) quire fillers: (*a*) ff. 109–146^{v} In die pasche. Non inmerito hodie propheta precepit . . . ; (*b*) ff. 146^{v}–151^{v} Saulus adhuc spirans etc. Ex persecutione cristianorum . . . ; (*c*) ff. 151^{v}–157 De apostolis. Respondit ihesus dix' Confiteor tibi domine . . . In fronte huius leccionis ewangelice. questio oritur Cum nec superius . . . ; (*d*) ff. 157–189^{v} Scientes quia hora est . . . Mos sacre scripture est horam sepissime . . . (*e*) f. 190^{rv} Cum appropinquasset dominus ihesus . . . Presens euangelium bis in anno legitur . . . qui timet pruinam irruet (*ends imperfectly*); (*f*) ff. 192–194^{v} Notes on Gospel texts.

(*a*). Temporal from Easter to the 25th Sunday after Pentecost, mainly abbreviations of patristic homilies. The first sermon is *PL* lvii. 363 and most of the next dozen are from the series of Haymo's sermons printed in *PL* cxviii. 455 sqq. (*b*). Sanctoral from Conversion of Paul to Andrew. (*c*). Common of saints. Four leaves (153–6) are missing after f. 152. (*d*). Temporal from Advent to Easter Eve. Cf. Schneyer, p. 310. (*e*). Schneyer, p. 100 (Odo of Cheriton).

8 (quires 14, 15). ff. 195–219^{v} Ex`i´it qui seminat . . . Gregorius. Lectio sancti Ewangelii quam modo . . .

Abbreviations of sermons of Gregory, Bede, Jerome, Augustine, Leo, Maximus and others, Easter to Advent.

9 (quire 16). ff. 223–9 Dixit ihesus D. S. Ego sum vitis uera . . . Augustinus. Iste locus euuangelicus fratres ubi se dicit dominus vitem . . .

A sanctoral series (cf. art. 8) beginning with the sermon printed in *PL* lxv. 913. The next sermon is for Philip and James. The scribe wrote 'Auxilium nobis saluator mitte salutis' at the head of f. 223.

10 (quires 17, 18). ff. 230–256^{v} Sermons and notes for sermons, beginning imperfectly.

The first complete piece begins on f. 230^{v} 'Sermo ad prelatos. Ego sum pastor bonus. Verba dei valent ad omnia . . .'. Several hands. Bernard and Seneca are quoted. Six English verses, 'þru tidigge us cumet . . .', are written as prose near the end of a note on Memorare novissima tua, f. 243^{v}: printed by C. Brown, *English Lyrics of the Thirteenth Century*, p. 18 (*Three Sorrowful Tidings*). A little higher up the same page is 'fo is ute biloce he his inne sone forþide' (cf. Proverbs of Alfred, B 554).

11 (added, s. xiii/xiv, in the blank space at the end of quire 15). Fourteen prayers and devotions, all to B.V.M., except (*g–i, k*): (*a*) f. 219^{v} Aue stella mater maris clemencie pare carens paris regem iusticie . . . ; (*b*) f. 219^{v} Rosa sine spina flos pudicitie . . . ; (*c*) f. 220^{v} Ecce ad te confugio uirgo nostra saluacio . . . ; (*d*) f. 220^{v} Gaude sancta maria cristi genitrix gloriosa . . . ; (*e*) f. 220^{v} O gloriosa et

misericordissima o uirgo uirginum . . . ; (*f*) f. 221 Aue maria gloriosa regina celorum que peperisti . . . ; (*g*) f. 221 Gracias agimus tibi domine ihesu criste rex glorie . . . ; (*h*) f. 221 Sanctorum mitissime andrea qui sequenda saluatorem . . . ; (*i*) f. 221v Aue redemptor et saluator mundi aue rex regum . . . ; (*j*) f. 221v Sancta dei genitrix uirgo semper maria maris stella . . . ; (*k*) f. 222 Confiteor tibi domine deus quia peccaui nimis . . . ; (*l*) f. 222 Aue uirgo singularis porta uite stella maris summi regis propria. aue mundi dei cella florens Rubens ac nouella . . . in celesti gaudio; (*m*) f. 222 O intemerata et in \`e´ternum benedicta . . . orbis terrarum. Inclina . . . ; (*n*, in another hand) f. 222 Intemerata uirgo deprecor te . . .

(*c*). *RH*, no. 5087. (*l*). Cf. *RH*, no. 2250. (*m*). Ed. A. Wilmart, *Auteurs spirituels*, 1932, p. 488.

12 (added in the same hand as art. 11, between 11*l* and 11*m*). f. 222 Richard, master of the hospital of St John the Baptist, Northampton, grants fifteen acres of land in Gayton (Northants) to A. de G.

Richard Helmdon was master 1291-1323 ?: cf. J. Bridges, *History of Northamptonshire*, i. 456.

13 (added in the same hand as arts. 11, 12 in blank spaces of art. 1*b*). ff. 6v-7 Accounts of the hospital of St John the Baptist and St John the Evangelist, Northampton.

Printed by C. Brown in *Modern Language Review*, xxi. 7-8.[1]

14 (added in s. xiv med.). Sermons added in blank spaces on ff. 9rv, 20-21v, 28, 45v, 48rv, 53rv, 54, 57rv, 58v, 68v-69, 71v-73v, 76rv, 77v-79v, 81-5, 86v-92v, 95-97v, 101v, 102v, 103v-104, 107, 191rv, 219v-220, 248rv, 253.

All in one hand. Includes a little English, for example on f. 104, '3yf they munde is most of god . . .', on f. 248v, Of oure sunnes furȝyuing . . .' and on f. 253 (see above, art. 3*b*). A sermon 'De sancto hugone' begins on f. 77v and one 'De sancto Clemente' on f. 78. The sermon on f. 191 begins 'Ego sum pastor bonus . . . In his verbis notantur tria circa summum pastorem' and the sermon on f. 219v 'Probauit me quasi aurum . . . Hec verba dicuntur de iob'.

15 (binding leaves). ff. 257-60 are four leaves of a Sarum ordinal in rough textura, s. xiv med. A fifth leaf was in the binding until Dec. 1979: see below.

ff. 257-60 are the four inner leaves of a quire and contain continuous text, 'Item tu autem miserere nostri. Per totum aduentum legantur lect' de propheta ysaya . . . P' Dixit iniustus. Gloria': cf. *Brev. ad usum Sarum*, I. xx-li (first Sunday in Advent and the following day). The missing leaf contained cues for offices, 'V' Israel . . . Responsorium. Non': cf. ibid. I. lxxxiii/4-cxxiii/11. Verbally different from the 'old ordinal' in B.L., Harley 1001. No music.

ff. iv + 242 + viii. The foliation of arts. 1-10, 1-29, 40-152 (the numbers 30-9 were missed in error), 157-256, is medieval and probably a little earlier than art. 14: cf. f. 248. For four

[1] Brown was misled by art. 11*h* into supposing that the accounts were of the Cluniac priory of St Andrew, Northampton. K. B. McFarlane, without knowledge of art. 12, identified them for me as accounts of the hospital.

(once five) flyleaves see art. 15. 270 × 195 mm. Written space of arts. 6–10 *c.*220 × 145 mm. 2 cols. (3 cols. on ff. 1–5, 93). *c.*60 lines. The first line of writing below the top ruled line. Collation: 1^{12} wants 10 after f. 9 2 eleven (ff. 12–22) 3 twelve (ff. 23–9, 40–4) 4^{12} 5 thirteen (ff. 57–69) 6^{12} 7^{10} + 1 leaf after 10 (f. 92) 8^{12} 9 four (ff. 105–8) 10^{20} 11^{22} 12^{24} wants 3–6 after f. 152 (ff. 141, 152, 157–74) 13^{24} wants 17 after f. 190 and 22–4, probably blank, after f. 194 14^{16} 15^{18} wants 13–18, probably blank, after f. 222 16^{10} wants 8–10 after f. 229 17^{12} 18^{16} wants 12 after f. 252: the manuscript had only four more leaves than at present (12^{3-6}) at the time the leaves were numbered. Arts. 6–10 are in small clear textura, at its best on ff. 190^{rv}, 251–254^{v}. Arts. 1–5 are in more current writing, perhaps mainly by one scribe at different times: he wrote art. 5*c* in or soon after 1229. Arts. 11–13 are in small anglicana by one hand, current, except in art. 11*l*, *n*. Art. 14 is in larger anglicana, sometimes current and sometimes not. Spaces for initials have not been filled. 'Medieval binding of wooden boards covered with leather, once pink: seven bands: two clasps now missing.'[1] Secundo folio *Ieiunat rex.*

Written in England. Belonged in s. xiii/xiv to a member of the hospital of St John the Baptist and St John the Evangelist in Northampton, and perhaps to the master of the hospital, Richard Helmdon: see above, arts. 12, 13. 'An old Latin MS imperfect A 13' is an addition to the 1815 catalogue.

B. 91. *Horae; Psalterium* s. xiv ex.

1. pp. 1–12 Sarum calendar in red and black, graded.

The word 'pape' and feasts of St Thomas of Canterbury erased.

2. pp. 12*–32 Hours of B.V.M. of the use of (Sarum), with hours of the Cross worked in.

The beginning of each hour, except terce, has been removed. The memoriae at the end of lauds are for Holy Spirit, Holy Trinity, Holy Cross, angels, John Baptist, Peter, Andrew, Stephen, Laurence, Thomas of Canterbury (Tu per thome sanguinem: crossed out), Nicholas, Mary Magdalene, Katherine, Margaret, All Saints, peace.

3. pp. 32–3 Salve regina farsed with Virgo mater ecclesie (*RH*, no. 21818) and followed by the prayer 'Omnipotens sempiterne deus qui gloriose virginis et matris marie corpus . . .'

4. p. 34 Gaude virgo mater cristi que per aurem . . . (*RH*, no. 7017). Omnipotens sempiterne deus qui diuina gabrielis salutacione . . .

5. pp. 34–6 O intemerata . . . orbis terrarum. Inclina . . .

6. p. 36 Quilibet dicenti . . . ad supplicacionem philippi regis francie. Domine ihesu criste qui hanc sacratissimam carnem . . . (*ends imperfectly*).

The heading carries an indulgence of 2,000 years from Pope Boniface (name erased).

[1] So my description, made before December 1979 when this manuscript was rebound and the old boards (but not the old leather covers) were stuck on outside the new binding. Six medieval parchment flyleaves were discarded at this time, five in front and one at the back: these were blank leaves except the second of the five in front which was a leaf of art. 15. The text of the missing leaf can be read in a positive microfilm kept in the County Record Office (TR 1758/25/2) and in a negative microfilm and photographic print kept at Maidstone Museum.

7. pp. 37–42 Penitential psalms, beginning and ending imperfectly.

8. pp. 43–74 Office of the dead, beginning imperfectly.

9. pp. 75–210 Psalter, ending imperfectly at 118: 129.

10. pp. 211–17 Ferial canticles, beginning in Audite celi, followed by Te deum, Benedicite, Benedictus, Magnificat, Nunc dimittis (these five abbreviated) and Quicumque vult. Part of pp. 213–14 cut away.

11. pp. 218–26 Litany. 'Thoma' among martyrs erased and put in again. Rachelfledis 40th of forty-five virgins.

12. pp. 227–8 are blank, except for the words 'deus propicius esto michi peccatori' on the recto, which seem to have stood below a now missing full-page pasted-on picture.

13. pp. 229–32 Hymns 1, 3–8, 2, 9, 10 of the list in *Brev. ad usum Sarum* III. ciii: Conditor, Verbum supernum, Vox clara, Iam lucis, Nunc sancte Rector, Rerum deus, Te lucis, Veni redemptor, Saluator mundi (*ends imperfectly*).

ff. 117, paginated 1–12, 12*, 12**, 13–232. 203 × 148 mm. Written space 125 × 86 mm. 2 cols. 23 lines. Ruling in red ink. Fourteen quires, normally twelves (1^6), but 2–14 are all imperfect and probably at least fifty leaves are missing. For the only surviving picture page (no picture now) see above, art. 12. Initials: (i) only four remain, pp. 29 (terce), 75, 133 (Ps. 51), 134 (Ps. 52), 6-line, in colours on decorated gold and coloured grounds, with continuous borders in gold and colours; (ii) 2-line, gold on coloured grounds, patterned in white; (iii) 1-line, blue with red ornament or gold with violet ornament. Medieval binding of wooden boards covered with white leather: the upper of two clasps remains. Secundo folio (p. 12*) *nomen tuum*.

Written in England. The inscription 'Maidstone Parochial Library' is on the pastedown at the end, and the number 'B 91' inside the front cover.

P. 5. *Biblia, pars ii* s. xii med.

The second volume of a 2-volume Bible. The first volume is now Lambeth Palace, London, 3. The second contains Psalms (from 4: 1, latasti michi), including Ps. 151, Proverbs–Ecclesiasticus + Prayer of Solomon (called ch. 128 of Ecclesiasticus), 1, 2 Chronicles, Ezra + Nehemiah (running title 'Liber Ezre'), Esther, Tobit, Judith, 1, 2 Maccabees, Gospels, Acts, Catholic Epistles, Pauline Epistles, including (f. 290^v) the Epistle to the Laodiceans before 1 Thessalonians, Apocalypse. Lambeth Palace 4 has the same contents and order. The notice 'Hic psalmus in hebreis codicibus non habetur sed nec (*sic*) a lxx interpretibus additus est et iccirco repudiandus' follows Ps. 151, f. 39^v: the same notice is in Lamb. 4, but reading *hic*, not *nec*.

Described by E. G. Millar in *Bulletin de la Société française de réproductions de manuscrits à peintures*, viii (1924), 29–30; by C. R. Dodwell, *The Canterbury School of Illumination*,

1954, p. 49; by C. R. Dodwell, *The Great Lambeth Bible*, 1959; by Kauffmann, no. 70. See also M. Kershaw in *Archaeologia Cantiana*, xi (1877), 189.

As far as Mark a new book begins usually on a new page, if not on a new recto. f. 84^{v} is blank before 1 Chronicles and f. 146^{r} blank before 1 Maccabees. A blank verso (49^{v}) and a now missing blank (?) leaf (8^{8}) preceded Ecclesiastes, which begins a new quire (9^{1}). A now missing blank (?) leaf (25^{3}) and a blank recto, f. 176^{r}, preceded Matthew.

At least twenty-five leaves on which there were probably major initials have either been removed or exist only as small fragments. ff. 10–14 were damaged at the head in or before s. xv ex. and some lines on each page were rewritten then on new parchment by a scribe who repaired similar damage in Lamb. 3. The preliminaries to the Psalter were recopied and probably added to at about the same time (ff. 1–9).

For corrections entered first in the margins and then fitted neatly into the text, see ff. 28^{v}, 41, 306.

Prologues. Except on ff. 1–9 (see below), the prologues are 29 of the common set (see Liverpool Cathedral 13) and 26 others, shown here by *: Stegmüller, nos. 457, 462, 328, 327 (both to 1 Chronicles), 326* (after capitula of 1 Chronicles), 330, Ezras et Nehemias adiutor . . .'*, 341 + 343, 332, 335, 551 (cut out of f. 146^{v}), 595*, 601*, 581*, 596*, Mattheus Marcus Lucas et Iohannes quadriga . . . flatus sancti spiritus duxerit* (headed 'Beatus Ieronimus de Quatuor ewangelistis'), 590, 607, 620, 624, 640, 631*, 809, 807*, 806*, 815*, Discipulo[s] saluat[oris . . .]*, 818*, 819*, 822*, 823*, 824*, 825*, 662* + 663*, 651*, 654*, Concordia epistolarum. De unitate . . . (ends imperfectly: Wordsworth and White, pp. 12–16)*, 677, 685, 699, 707, 715, 728, 726*, 736, 747, 765 (. . . ab urbe roma), 772, 780, 783, 793, 834*, 829*. Probably nos. 456* and 455*, 670* and 674*, 689*, 752, all in Lamb. 4, were once here in the gaps after ff. 39, 263, 270, 292, and probably no. 551 has been cut out of f. 147.[1] Luke 1: 1–4 is not treated as a prologue.

Tables of chapters as in Lamb. 4, except at 1, 2 Chronicles and Mark, and the same curious arrangements, apparently, at 1 Corinthians, where Lamb. 4 has (1) Stegmüller's prologue 689, (2) a table giving incipits of 22 chapters, (3) prologue 685, (4) a table of 72 chapters: owing to the loss of a leaf after f. 270 the first and most of the second of these four pieces are missing. The table of Proverbs, which comes in Lamb. 4 after the three prologues 457, 456, 455, is likely to have been on the leaves now missing after f. 39.

Ecclesiastes. Quod uanitas . . . obseruanda. 31 chapters. Series A, forma b.
Wisdom. De diligenda . . . (ends imperfectly in ch. 10, 'coturnices. de'. Series B).
Ecclesiasticus. Quod omnis sapientia . . . Oratio Salomonis. 126 chapters. Series A, forma a.
1 Chronicles. Generationes ab adam . . . et de obitu regis [dauid]. 23 chapters. Cf. forma a. (Lamb. 4 has 108 chapters, 'Descriptio . . . filius eius', as de Bruyne, *Sommaires*, p. 124 (A etc.).)
2 Chronicles. De hostiis quas salomon . . . (ends imperfectly in ch. 16, 'ab ezechia rege cęle-'). Cf. forma a. (Lamb. 4 has 74 chapters, 'Confortatus . . . templum domini', as ibid. p. 132 (A etc.).)
1 Maccabees. Ubi euersa . . . perdere eum. 60 chapters. de Bruyne's series A.
2 Maccabees. Vbi occisus est . . . [. . . .]. de Bruyne's series A.
NT. The tables, except to Apocalypse, are printed by Wordsworth and White: to Matthew, as B, etc.; to Mark, as C, etc.; to Luke and John, as K, etc.; to Acts, James 1, Peter, as A, etc.; to 2 Peter–Jude, as B, etc.; to Pauline Epistles, as A, etc. The table to Apocalypse is

[1] ff. 1–9 apart, the only differences between the prologues in Lamb. 4 and Maidstone were probably these: (1) in L. and not in M., Stegm., no. 336 (to Judith) before no. 335; (2) in M. and not in L., no. 327 (to 1 Chronicles) after no. 328, and 'Mattheus Marcus . . .' to Gospels after no. 596; (3) in L., no. 596 precedes no. 581 and no. 651 precedes nos. 662 + 663.

in 24 chapters, 'De septem ęcclesiis quę sunt in asia . . . De comminatione et conclusione prophetię libri huius'. (Lamb. 4 has a table to Mark of 50 chapters, De baptismo . . . discipulis apparuit, as K, etc., in Wordsworth and White).

Stichometric notes. Probably the same selection and, with one exception, the same figures as in Lambeth 4, but Romans and 1 Thessalonians end imperfectly, so that the stichometry is missing: Psalms 5,000, Proverbs 1,740, Ecclesiastes 800, Song of Songs 270, Wisdom 1,800 (Lamb., 1,700), Ecclesiasticus 2,800, 1 Chronicles 2,040, 2 Chronicles 2 . . . , Esther 700, Tobit 900, Judith 1,100, 1 Maccabees 2,300, 2 Maccabees 1,800, Mark 1,700, Acts 3,600, 1 Corinthians 880, 2 Corinthians 892, Galatians 213, Ephesians 317, 1 Timothy 230. Cf. *MMBL* ii. 655.

Preliminaries to the Psalms were added in s. xv ex. on eleven leaves of which two are missing, two (ff. 3, 5) are no more than stubs, and four (ff. 1, 2, 6, 8) are more or less badly damaged: f. 1, Stegmüller, no. 430, nearly complete: the last words are 'contempnere uideri' (*PL* xxix. 124/10); f. 1^{v} part of Stegm., no. 389, ending at 'Sine nomine qui tantum' (*PL* xxvi. 1380/35); f. 2, end of Stegm., no. 405; ff. 2–7 part of Stegm., no. 451: a leaf is missing after f. 2 and a leaf after f. 4 and ff. 3 and 5 are stubs; ff. 7–8^{v} a table of Pss. 1–150, 'Primus psalmus ostendit. quod dominus ihesus cristus . . . collaudandus'; f. 9^{rv} Stegm., no. 431.

ff. 306. The modern foliation 1–310 includes four numbers on stubs of missing leaves, 3, 5, 52, 163 ($1^{3,6}$, 9^{3}, 23^{6}) and six numbers on small fragments, 27, 28, 162, 178, 264, 292. 500 × 357 mm. Written space 375 × 230 mm. 2 cols. 46 lines. Ruling with pencil. Pricks to guide ruling in both margins. Collation: 1^{8} wants 3, 4 after f. 2 and 6, 7 after f. 4 2^{4} wants 4, blank, after f. 9 3^{8} wants 1–5 before f. 10 4–6^{8} 7^{8} wants 4, 5 after f. 39 8^{8} wants 8, blank, after f. 49 9^{8} wants 3 after f. 51 10–12^{8} 13^{8} wants 5 after f. 84 14–16^{8} 17^{8} wants 6 after f. 116 18–20^{8} 21^{8} wants 2 after f. 143 22^{8} 23^{8} wants 6 after f. 162 24^{8} 25^{8} wants 3, blank, after f. 175 26–35^{8} 36^{8} wants 5 after f. 264 37^{8} wants 4 after f. 270 38–40^{8} 41^{8} wants 7, 8 after f. 304 42^{6}. Leaves in the first halves of quires 9 (where Ecclesiastes begins)–22 are marked in pencil, s. xiv, with numbers running from (i) to xiiii, each followed by 'qua' and a leaf number from i to iiii. Quires 23–42 are marked on first rectos only in pencil with numbers 16–35. Later, perhaps when the present binding was made, quires and leaves in the first halves of quires 5–42 were marked in ink in a continuous series from b. 1 on f. 21 to oo. 3 on f. 307: the letters run b–z, +, ɔ, aa–oo, and as far as v. 4 (f. 161) are placed half way down the outer margin of recto sides. At the same time all the leaves in quires 3, 4 (ff. 10–20), except the last leaf, were marked with the letter 'a' and a number, the numbers running 2–4 on ff. 10–12, 1–3 on ff. 13–15, 4 and 8 on f. 16, 9–11 on ff. 17–19. Yet another marking, B vi, B vii, B viii on ff. 10–12, presumably dates from a time when there were thirteen (?) now missing leaves before the present f. 10: the present ff. 1–9 are not marked in any way.

ff. 10–196 are by the same scribe as Lambeth Palace 3. The hand is less good than that of Lambeth Palace 4. The decoration probably included several full-page or three-quarter-page pictures like those in Lambeth Palace 3, but all are now missing and only one is referred to by Joseph Ames in July 1752, when the Bible was already 'sadly mutilated' and 'many of the Illuminated Innitials cut out': 'One large design of Wisdom is before the Song of Songes, with a great nº of figures, most of them holding Rolls of writing. over the heads of several of them its wrote Sapientia edificavit sibi domum exidit columna septem. under, Fluminis impetus letificat civitatem Dei. etc.':[1] this was, no doubt, on f. 52^{v}. Initials: (i) of principal psalms, in colours and sometimes a little gold on coloured grounds, historiated: six out of nine remain, Pss. 26, 38, 51, 52, 68, 109, but not Pss. 1, 96, 101; (ii) beginning Pss. 80, 119,

[1] Oxford, Bodleian, Top gen. e. 58, f. 23. I owe the reference to Mr Timothy Rogers. Ames travelled by coach from London on 17 July 1752 and had a thorough look at the Bible on the 18th, presumably.

Ecclesiasticus, Luke, Acts (ff. 26, 35, 63, 205^{v}, 237^{v}), and the prologue to Ecclesiasticus (f. 61^{v}), in colour on decorated coloured grounds; (iii) of some Catholic and Pauline Epistles, Apocalypse (f. 304) and some prologues (but not before f. 83), in colours with ornament of two or three colours; (iv) of the prologue to Judith (f. 139^{v}) in gold and colours; (v) of most prologues, 4-line or more; (vi) of chapters, psalms (except as above), and a few prologues and to mark the beginnings of Gospel sections from Luke 4: 14 to the end of John, 3-line or 2-line; (vii) beginning verses of psalms and Gospel sections from Matthew to Luke 4: 2, and in tables of chapters, 1-line. Initials of types (v–vii) are monochrome, red, blue, green, or, rarely, brown, (v–vi) usually and (vii) always without ornament. Initials of type (vii) are usually in the order red, blue, red, green.

Millar, pl. xi*a–f*, reproduces the initials on ff. 14, 19^{v} (2), 22^{v}, 26, 32^{v} (Pss. 26, 51, 52, 68, 80, 109). Dodwell, 1954, pls. 24c, 40b, 29e, reproduces the initials on ff. 17, 22^{v}, 32^{v} (Pss. 38, 68, 109). Kershaw provides approximate facsimiles of the type (ii) initials on ff. 63, 237^{v}, 304 and of one type (iii) initial, that of the prologue to Matthew on f. 173^{v}. From Proverbs to Mark all main initials have been removed, except on f. 63 (Ecclesiasticus), but from Luke onwards more use was made of initials of types (ii) and (iii) at the beginning of books, and more have survived. More type (i) initials existed in 1752 than now, as appears from Ames's account. He noted: (1) 'Incipiunt cantica canticorum quod hebraice dicuntur sirasitim. Begins with a large O filled up with the crucifixion of Christ on a Cross, a Lady crownd kissing him, and holding out a Roll with these words [SC̄A ecclesia] this on the right side. Another Lady on the left with an^{r} Roll written [SINAGOGA] and an old man with another with [LEX Ī Umbra] another man on the right side with a red glory seems to be looking on'; (2) 'Liber Tobie . . . Tobie blind and 3 other figures in the Letter T'; (3) 'Liber Judith with la. Cut of her etc.'.[1] These initials were cut out of ff. 53, 135, and 140 in or after 1752.

Binding of s. xv/xvi, uniform with that of Lambeth Palace 3: thick wooden boards covered with goat skin bearing a pattern of fillets, faint stamps, one of them an *M*, and roughly incised trefoils, quatrefoils, etc.: nine bands: two clasps missing. Secundo folio missing (3^{2}) or (*superscriptiones*): the latter was the now missing first word on f. 2.

Written in England as a continuation of Lambeth Palace MS. 3. Perhaps written at St Augustine's, Canterbury, and very probably once there, but not, apparently, any of the three two-volume Bibles listed in the late medieval catalogue: see especially Dodwell 1954, pp. 49–52 and Dodwell 1959, pp. 8, 14. The sixteenth-century memoranda on f. 310 are set out by Millar, p. 17. They suggest that very soon after the Dissolution the Maidstone volume was in the hands of John Colyar of Lenham, Kent, where St Augustine's was patron until 1539, and that it belonged rather later to John Pery (not Perys), who notes that his daughter Mary, born on 9 Feb. 1559[/60], had Mary Colyar as godmother (probably John's daughter Mary whose birth in 1542 is also recorded on f. 310). Pery was principal of Staple Inn, London, and died 30 Oct. 1577: the memorial to him in Lenham Church is mentioned by E. Hasted, *History of Kent*, ii (1782), 452, footnote (x). Presumably the 'Manuscript Latin Bible' in the list of 32 books in the 'vestry library' at All Saints on 24 June 1716 entered at the end of the Burial Register for 1678 to 1716 recorded by C. E. Woodruff, *Inventory of the parish registers and other records in the Diocese of Canterbury*, 1922, p. 119.[2] Seen by Ames at Maidstone in 1752 (see above).

[1] Bodleian, Top. gen. e. 58, f. 23^{v} (1) and f. 23 (2, 3).
[2] I owe the reference to Mr Graham Hunter.

MAIDSTONE. CORPORATION MUSEUM

The Museum was founded under the will of Thomas Charles, †1855: see W. B. Gilbert, *Antiquities of Maidstone*, 1865, p. 164. It was opened in 1858.

Mus. 4. *Horae (partly in Netherlandish)* s. xv

1. ff. 1–12^{v} Calendar in Netherlandish, red and black.

Entries in red include Amant, Amelberghe, Baue, Lieuin (6 Feb., 10 July, 1 Oct., 12 Nov.).

2. f. 14^{rv} Deus qui manus tuas et pedes tuas . . . f. 15^{rv} blank.

3. ff. 17–82^{v} Hours of B.V.M. of the use of (Tournai).

4. ff. 84–105^{v} Penitential psalms and litany.

Twenty martyrs: (20) Bauo. Eighteen virgins: (17, 18) Gudila Allegunda.

5. ff. 107–12 Dit es obsecro te domina. Obsecro te . . .

Masculine forms. f. 112^{v} blank.

6. ff. 113–16 Oratio deuota de domina nostra. O intemerata . . . orbis terrarum. Inclina . . .

7 (added). ff. 116^{v}–118^{v} O heere ihesu criste ic aanbede dij hanghende . . .

The Seven Oes of St Gregory. Lieftinck, p. 227; Meertens, vi. 16.

8. ff. 120–57 Officium mortuorum.

9 (in another hand). (*a*) ff. 157^{v}–161 Hier volghet eene deuote oratie to segghene tot onsen here. O hemele vader ic offere dijns eenichs gheborens soons . . . (*b*) ff. 161–162^{v} Hier navolghen de vii veersen sente bernaerde. Illumina oculos . . . Omnipotens sempiterne deus qui ezechie regi . . .

(*a*). Cf. Meertens, vi. 140.

10 (in another hand). ff. 163–165^{v} Die dit nauolghende ghebet . . . O du alder mulicste. o alder histe heste . . .

To B.V.M. The heading conveys an indulgence of 83 years and 'also vele alst dropelen reghenen moghen in eenen daghe'. ff. 166–169^{v} blank.

ff. iv + 169 + i. ff. iii, iv are unused leaves, perhaps the blanks from quires 22, 23. Collation: $1–2^{6}$ 3 two (ff. 14, 15) $4–15^{8}$ (ff. 115–18) $17–18^{8}$ 19^{6} $20–21^{8}$ 22^{6} wants 6, perhaps blank, after f. 162 23^{8} wants 8, blank; together with five singleton leaves with pictures on versos and blank rectos (ff. 13, 16, 83, 106, 119). A full-page picture on a chequered ground in front of arts. 2–5, 7: 2, Crucifixion; 4, Christ in judgement; 5, B.V.M. and Child and kneeling angel. Initials: (i) on twelve pages, 5-line, blue or pink patterned in white on grounds of decorated gold and the other colour; (ii) 2-line, gold on coloured grounds patterned in white; (iii) 1-line, blue with red ornament or gold with iron-grey ornament. Continuous borders on picture pages and pages with initials of type (i): some contain figures on diapered grounds. Contemporary panel binding, rebacked: the Annunciation with a 'Flemish animals' border is on both covers.

Written in the southern Low Countries for someone whose motto 'Sans anoy' comes repeatedly in borders: a damaged shield in the lower border, f. 17. 'Desen boeck hoert toe [. . .] . . .', f. 169v: 'Gofvrouwe' (?) is written over part of the erasure. Book-plate of 'Thomas Charles, Maidstone'.

Mus. 5. *A. Horae (partly in Netherlandish)* s. xvi in.
B. Nine virtues (in French) 1492

A. 1. ff. 1–8 A rather empty calendar in Netherlandish, red and black, 1 Mar.–29 Apr., 29 July–31 Dec., graded for duplex and nine lessons. No spaces between the months.

2. f. 8v Die paus Iulius die tweeste heeft dese nauolghende oratien ghemaect vleenende allen den ghenen diese deuotelijc leest smorghens ende sauonts als men Aue maria clipt telker reysen lxxvm Iaren aflaets.

Heading only. The prayer is missing.

3. ff. 9–49v Hours of B.V.M. of the use of (Utrecht).

4. ff. 50–67v Hic incipiunt septem psalmi. Litany, f. 61.

Nineteen virgins: (16–19) Gudila Anna Monica Elyzabeth. On f. 66v the heading 'Incipiunt preces minores is followed by 'Ego dixi domine miserere mei . . . Exaudi quesumus domine supplicum preces . . . Deus cui proprium est . . . Ineffabilem misericordiam . . . (*ends imperfectly*)'.

Arts. 5–16 are in Netherlandish.

5. ff. 68–81 Hours of the Passion, beginning imperfectly.

6. ff. 81–121v Twenty-one prayers, mainly to God the Son, (*f–m*) prayers at mass: (*a*) 81–5 Heere iesu christe ghii swetet water ende bloot on mynen wille . . . ; (*b*) 85–87v Ic bidde v mynnelijcke heere ihesu christe Om der hoogher mynnen . . . : the heading conveys an indulgence of Pope John II of as many days as Christ had wounds, that is 6,666 'ende sijn heylige v wonden'; (*c*) 87v–90 Men leest van sinte siluester den paus doen hij op sijn dootbedde . . . O heere iesu christe ontfaet dit ghebet . . . : the heading conveys as much indulgence 'als op eenen dach druppelen waters moghen reghenen'; (*d*) 90–91v I liue heere iesu christe ghii wondet om die verlossenisse . . . : attributed in the heading to Pope Innocent; (*e*) 91v–92v Ach alder hoocste godeste alder ontfermhertichste ewich god . . . ; (*f*) 92v–93 Ghegruet sijstu o salicheyt der werelt . . . : indulgenced by Popes Innocent, Gregory, and John III; (*g*) 93rv Sijt ghegruet in der

ewicheyt . . . (*h*) 93^{v}–94^{v} Sijt ghegruet onsprekelijc weerdich sacrament . . . ; (*i*) 94^{v} God gruete minnelijke heere iesu christe ende uwen werdighen heylighen lichaem . . . ; (*j*) 94^{v}–95 Willecome heere willecome coninck willecome scoene maria . . . ; (*k*) 95–97^{v} Soe wie dit nauolghende gebet leest verdunt C^{m} iaer aflaets ende xc k*ar*enen. In die teghenwoerdicheyt uvs lichaems ende vus helighen dierbaren bloete . . . ; (*l*) 97^{v}–98 So wie dit ghebet leest in der missen als ons heere ghehauen es . . . O heere iesu christe almechtich god want ghij dat alder heylichste vleesh ontfaen hebt . . . ; (*m*) 98–9 Siele christi heylicht mij . . . ; (*n*) 99–100 Een minnelijke ghebet tot onsen here. God sijt ghenadich mijns sondaren . . . ; (*o*) 100–2 Een oracie tot onsen heere. Mijn heere mijn god ontfanct mij in den schoot . . . ; (*p*) 102–105^{v} O hemelche vader ic offer v heden uwen eneghen gheborenen soene . . . ; (*q*) 105^{v}–109 O goedertieren iesu O alder sueste iesu . . . ; (*r*) 109–113^{v} O alder goedertierenste heere iesu christe . . . ; (*s*) 113^{v}–116^{v} Hier beghinnen die v oracie van sinte franciscus die men lesen sal . . . O heere iesu christe ic kniele hier voer v ghebenedide oghen . . . ; (*t*) 116^{v}–118 S' bernaerts ghebet. Sijt ghegruet o heere iesu christe woert des vaders . . . ; (*u*) 118–122^{v} O alder sueste lam christi goedertieren suete vader ende ewige sueticheyt Ic vermane . . .

(*c*). Three divisions: each begins with these seven words. (*e*). To the Trinity. (*g*). Two parts, one of the Body and one of the Blood of Christ. (*q*) is of the Holy Name and (*r*) of the Five Wounds. (*s*). The first, third, and fifth are said kneeling, and the second and fourth standing.

(*k, m, n, u*). Cf. Lieftinck, pp. 230, 229, 227, 228. (*k, l, o, p, q, t, u*). Cf. Meertens, vi. 76, 76, 108, 25, 75, 25, 25.

7. Prayers to B.V.M.: (*a*) ff. 122^{v}–125 O gloriose vrouwe alderheylichste maghet maria Ic beuele heden . . . ; (*b*) ff. 125–126^{v} Weest ghegruet alder oetmoedichste dienstmaert . . . ; (*c*) f. 127^{rv} (*begins imperfectly*) ende dat ic die xii poenten van den heylighen gheloue . . . ; (*d*) ff. 127^{v}–128 Weest ghegruet alder heylichste maria moeder gods coninghinne des hemels. poorte des paradijs . . . ; (*e*) f. 128^{rv} O gloriose maghet maria moeder christi alle die goede wercken dat ic . . . ; (*f*) ff. 128^{v}–129^{v} O alder goedertierenste vrouwe maria verhoert dat ghebet des gheens die bidt voer alle leuende ende doode . . .

(*b*). The verses given to St Bernard by an angel. 9-line heading. Meertens, vi. 74. A gap of probably six leaves between (*b*) and (*c*). The first three words of the heading of a missing piece are in the last line on f. 126^{v}. (*d*). Meertens, vi. 172. The heading conveys an indulgence of 11,000 years from Pope Sixtus IV.

8. (*a, b*) ff. 129^{v}–135^{v} A prayer to St Anne in eight paragraphs beginning 'Weest ghegruet edele roese angelier bloeme' and (f. 134) another 'dat men leesen sal des dyschdaechs', 'O heylighe vrouwe ende werde moeder sinte Anna ghi sijt . . .'.

(*b*). Cf. Lieftinck, p. 152.

9. f. 135^{v} Een deuoet (ghebet) van onsen goden ynghel. O heylighe ynghel gods die nu . . .

Cf. Meertens, vi. 22. Ends imperfectly: three leaves missing.

10. ff. 136–43, 145–152^{v} Prayers to saints: (*a*) 136–7 John Baptist, beginning imperfectly; (*b*) 137^{rv} John Evangelist; (*c*) 137^{v}–138 Augustine; (*d*) 138–40 Peter; (*e*) 140–1 apostles; (*f*) 141–142^{v} martyrs, naming Stephen, Laurence, Vincent, Ignatius; (*g*) 142^{v}–143^{v}, 145 confessors, naming Gregory, Augustine, Martin, Jerome, Nicholas, Benedict, Bernard, Francis, Dominic: a leaf missing after 143; (*h*) 145^{rv} Mary Magdalene (in Latin: Aue maria magdalena. gratia redemptoris plena . . .); (*i*) 145^{v}–147 Katherine; (*j*) 147–148^{v} Barbara, 'God gruete v hooghe martelesse ende heylighe maghet barbara . . .'; (*k*) 148^{v}–149^{v} Apollonia, 'O wtuercoren bruyt iesu christi appollonia . . . ; (*l*) 149^{v}–151 virgins, naming Katherine, Barbara, Agnes, Margaret, Cecilia, Agatha, Christina, Gudila, Lucy, Ursula; (*m*) 151–152^{v} All Saints.

11. Prayers: (*a*) ff. 152^{v}, 155^{rv} Een antiffene van den heyligen gheest. Coemt heylighe gheest veruullen . . . ; (*b*) ff. 155^{v}–160^{v} Een ghebet van den heylighen sacrament eert men ontfanghen heest. O almachtich god scepper hemelrijcs ende eerterijcs . . . ; (*c*) ff. 160^{v}–164 Als men dat sacrament ontfanghen heest noch een deuoet ghebet. O suete heere iesu christe minnelijcke scepper . . . ; (*d*) ff. 164–5 Een ghebet totter heyligher driuuldicheyt. O heylighe driuuldicheyt ontfermt dij onser . . . ; (*e*) ff. 165–6 Ghebet totter ewichs wijsheyt. O wijsheyt die vten mont des alderoppersten . . . ; (*f*) ff. 166–7 Noch een oracio van der heyligher driuuldicheyt. Ach alder hoochste alder godste . . .

12. Devotions to B.V.M.: (*a*) ff. 167–9 God gruete v gloriose ioncfrouwe moeder alder ontfermherticheyt . . . ; (*b*) f. 169^{rv} Soe wat mensche die dit ouer hem draecht die er mach met steruen onghebrecht . . . O weerde moeder gods een ghenade ende licht des hemels . . . ; (*c*) ff. 169^{v}–173 Hier na volghen die seuen wee van onser liuer vrouwen. O lieue heere iesu christe in der eeren des bitteren wees . . . ; (*d*) ff. 173–6 Een salighe broder scap van die x duechden van Maria . . . Prudentia. Weest ghegruet o alder wijste moeder ende maghet maria . . .

(*d*). The paragraphs are headed 'Prudentia', 'Humilitas', 'Castitas', 'Charitas', 'Gratiarum actio', 'Obedientia', 'Pacientia', 'Paupertas', 'Fides et pietas', 'Martirium'.

13. ff. 176–178^{v} Een oracie van sinte Erasme om sondaechs te leesen. O heylighe martelare christi erasme die opten sondach . . .

Lieftinck, p. 113. Meertens, vi. 12.

14. (*a*) f. 178^{v} Hier beghint sinte ians ewangelie. In den beghinne . . . (*ends imperfectly at John 1: 5*). (*b*) ff. 179–80^{v} In dien tyde dije ynghel gabriel . . . moet mi ghescien. Amen (*Luke 1: 26–38*).

15 (added). (*a*) ff. 180^{v}–182 O alder suetste here Iesu christe ouermits die weerdicheyt vus heyleghen lichaems . . . (*b*) The Seven Oes of St Gregory.

(*a*). Seven requests. f. 183^{v} blank.

16. ff. 144 and 153–4 are inserted paper leaves with (144) a prayer to St Mary Magdalene, (153–154^{v}) hymn, 'Comt scepper gheest . . .', etc.

B. ff. 184–186v (*begins imperfectly*) a une creature. Qui desirans estoit. et voloit faire cose qui plaisist a lui. Premiers ihesu crist li dist donne a moy e as poures tant que tu vis . . . qui trencassent ta char. Explicit. Escript et finet de par moy seur ysabeel de halewijn Religieuse en nostre cloestre de sainte margrite en bethleem. en la ville de doinse en lan mile cccc iiiixx et douze le premier iour de Septembre Priies pour moy. et prenes en gret. Deo gracias.

Begins in the heading of the Nine Virtues, a few words only missing: cf. Jolliffe, p. 107, I. 12*g*, for a similar heading and incipit in English.

ff. 186. 102 × 75 mm. Written space of (A) 68 × 48 mm: 16 long lines. Written space of (B) 67 × 45 mm: 14 long lines. Collation: 1 four 2^4 3^8 wants 1, 2 before f. 9 4–17^8 18 two (ff. 126–7, outside bifolium) 19^{12} wants 11, 12 after f. 135 20^8 wants 1 before f. 136 21^8 wants 2 after f. 143 22–24^8 25^8 wants 3 after f. 178 26 three (ff. 184–6): together with three inserted leaves (art. 16). Hybrida. Initials of (A): (i) f. 50, blue patterned in white on patterned red ground: continuous border; (ii) 3-line, blue with red ornament or red with violet ornament; (iii, iv) 2-line and 1-line, blue or red. Capital letters in the ink of the text are stroked with red. Initial of (B): 2-line gold-paint *P* on a blue ground. Binding of s. xvi.

(A) and (B) were written in the Low Countries, (B) for or perhaps by Isabel de Halwijn, nun of the Augustinian priory of St Margaret of Bethlehem 'en la ville de doinse' (Deynse, near Kortrijk).

Mus. 6. *Fervor amoris, etc. (in English)* s. xv[1]

1. ff. 1–40v Ardeat in nobis diuini feruor amoris. This schorte pistel þat folowith ys diuided in sundri maneres . . . (*table of 24 chapters*) . . . (f. 2) In þe beginning and ending of alle goode werkes . . . y can schewe. Goode broþer or suster praie þan. for me. which bi þe teching of almiȝti god haue write to þe þese fewe wordis. in help of þi soule. `Ardeat in nobis diuini feruor amoris. Amen.' `Benedictus dominus ihesus cristus marie filius.'

Jolliffe, H. 15. Printed by C. Horstmann, *Yorkshire Writers*, ii. 72–105, from de Worde's 1506 edition. In the table the chapters are marked with large letters, A–Z, AB, but in the margins of the text the alphabet only reaches E (f. 10). Three lines erased after 'marie filius', f. 40v.

2. ff. 41–57v This boke spekis of a place . . . deyde on þe rode tre. Amen. Thus endis the abbey of þe holy ghost.

Jolliffe, H. 9(b). Printed by Horstmann, i. 337–62. A leaf is missing after f. 49 with the text in edn., 350/13–351/22. A line erased after 'holy ghost', f. 57v.

3 (added in s. xv in blank space at the end of quire 8). (*a*) f. 57v O rex glorie domine uirtutum qui triumphator mortis . . . bona tua qui uiuis et regnas deus in secula. (*b*) f. 58rv Exortacio Iohannis Crisostomi ad quemdam episcopum amicum suum. Nouam tibi dominus contulit dignitatem nouam ergo debes . . . ut desideremus coronas de hiis vi cogitacionibus anima iusti proficit. (*c*) f. 58v Si vis saluari . . .

(*c*). Walther, *Sprichwörter*, no. 29412.

4 (added in s. xv). f. ii^{rv} Ihesu thy swetnesse hose miht yt se . . . he roos aȝen þrou his godhede.

IMEV, no. 1781/18. Ten (out of fifteen) 8-line stanzas.

ff. vii + 59 + iv. For ff. v, vi (parchment flyleaves) and f. vii see below. 195 × 136 mm. Written space 125 × 80 mm. 26 long lines (art. 1) and 25–7 long lines (art. 2). Collation: $1\text{–}6^8$ 7^8 wants 2 after f. 49 8^4 (4 was pasted down). Quires 1–5 signed +, a–d. Art. 1 in very formal short-*r* anglicana formata, different from that of art. 2 in which long-tailed *r* occurs towards the end. Initials: (i) 4-line or 5-line and (ii) 3-line, blue with red ornament. 'Binding of wooden boards covered with once pink, but now dirty brown leather: four bands: two clasps missing.'[1] Secundo folio *ward vppon*.

Written in England. The erasures on ff. 40^v, 57^v (see above) may conceal the scribes' names. Belonged to Sir Henry Bosvile, †1638, and handed down in the Bosvile, Boteler, Hinton, and Baverstock families: 'This Booke the Ladie Bosvile my Mother in Law gave me out of your grandfather Sr Henerie Bosviles Closet who prized it as a great Antiquitie. Tho. Boteler. 'N.B. This Tho. Boteler was living in the reign of Charles 1st and was my Grandmother Hintons Great Grandfather. J. Hinton Baverstock January 1806', f. vi^v; 'J. Hinton Chawton', f. v (he was rector of Chawton, Hants, †1802). Armorial book-plate of 'James Hinton Baverstoke F.S.A.', †1837, who added a paper leaf, f. vii, on which he set out his descent through six generations from 'Sir Henry Bosville of Eynsford in Kent, who died 27 Apr. 1638 æt. 51'. 'This leaf was gone when I first discovered the M. S. in the Charles Museum Library Feby 1866. W. J. Lightfoot' is on the stub of the leaf missing after f. 49. 'This book was returned from Mr Murrial Nov. 24 1876 it was taken away by mistake when Mr Lightfoot died', f. v.

MALMESBURY. PARISH CHURCH

1. *Biblia* 1457 (?)

A Bible in four volumes: (1) 1–4 Kings, Proverbs, Ecclesiastes, Wisdom, Ecclesiasticus, Job, Tobit, Judith, Esther; (2) Maccabees, Daniel, Ezekiel, Minor Prophets, Isaiah, Pauline Epistles; (3) Genesis–Ruth; (4) Jeremiah, Lamentations, Ezra, Nehemiah, Acts, Catholic Epistles, Apocalypse.

Vol. 1 runs from the first Sunday after Pentecost: the rubric at the beginning is 'Si tribus diebus ante festum sacramenti occurrit festum trium lectionum celebrandum. tunc libri regum incipiuntur in ecclesia. Sin autem. inchoantur sequenti dominica. in refectorio'. Vol. 2 runs from the first Sunday in October. Vol. 3 should run from the Sunday before Septuagesima, but there is no indication of this. Vol. 4 runs from Passion Sunday. The volumes agree in contents and order with those of the Bible from the charterhouse of Utrecht, now Brussels, Bibliothèque Royale, 107, 205, 106, 204.[2] As there, Psalms, Song of Songs, Baruch, and the four Gospels are omitted. In vol. 2, Pauline Epistles, and in vol. 4, Acts begin on new quires. The usual Carthusian marks to show where lections begin are in the margins, i–viii by the main hand and P(rima), S(ecunda), T(ertia) and 'In Refectorio' by another hand.

[1] So my description made before December 1979 when this manuscript was rebound and the old boards (but not the old leather covers) were stuck on outside the new binding.

[2] For this Brussels Bible and the order in which the volumes should be taken see P. Gumbert, *Die Utrechter Kartäuser und ihre Bücher*, 1974, pp. 134–6, 342. MSS. 49, 201–3 in Brussels are another 4-volume Carthusian Bible: see Van den Gheyn's catalogue, i. 23.

The text was carefully corrected. Marginalia of s. xv include: (vol. 2, f. 144^{v}: cf. ff. 147, 149^{v}) 'Quando b vel c est littera dominicalis sequere P.S.T. reliquo vero tempore A.B.C.' against Isaiah 45: 14; (vol. 3, f. 194) 'exemplar habet confortate' against 'comportate iam fruges' at Judges 15: 5; (vol. 4, f. 102^{v}) 'Secundum correctionem Carthusie. Illa clausula. Durum est tibi contra stimulum calcitrare staret post illa verba. Saule saule quid me per' in an excellent hybrida: in the text 'Durum . . . calcitrare' follows 'Ihesus nazarenus quem tu persequeris' (Acts 22: 9). A later correction, s. xvii (?), at vol. 1, f. 87, 'Ochozias pro ahazias semper legendum'.

The prologues are only eighteen: Stegmüller, nos. 323, 457, 344, 332, 335, 341 in vol. 1; nos. 494, 492, 500, 482, 670 in vol. 2; nos. 285, 311 in vol. 3; nos. 487, 330, 640, 809, 328 in vol. 4. All but one of them (670) belong to the common set: see above, Liverpool Cathedral 13.

In s. xix a title-page in Latin and a description in English were added on two paper leaves, ff. iii, iv, at the beginning of vol. 2.

ff. ii + 223 + i in vol. 1: f. ii, a medieval leaf, was formerly the pastedown at the end. ff. iv + 211 + i in vol. 2: f. ii, a medieval leaf, was formerly the pastedown at the end. ff. i + 201 + i in vol. 3, foliated (i), 1–135, 137–54, 156–203, (204). ff. ii + 215 + i in vol. 4, foliated (i, ii), 1–147, 147*, 148–214, (215): f. ii is a medieval flyleaf. 575 × 405 mm. Written space 370 × 245 mm. 2 cols. 32 lines. Collation: (vol. 1) $1\text{–}27^{8}$ 28^{8} wants 8, probably blank; (vol. 2) $1\text{–}19^{8}$ 20 three (ff. 153–5) $21\text{–}27^{8}$; (vol. 3) $1\text{–}23^{8}$ 24^{8} + 1 leaf after 8 (f. 203); (vol. 4) $1\text{–}9^{8}$ 10^{4} + 1 leaf after 4 (f. 77) $11\text{–}26^{8}$ 27^{8} + 2 leaves after 8 (ff. 213–14). Some quires numbered at the beginning, for example (vol. 3, quire 9) 'nona quat' '. Punctuation within the sentence by flex and colon. Good illumination. Initials: (i) of books, usually 7-line or 6-line (the larger *c.* 80 × 80 mm), in colours, historiated by more than one artist, and framed in gold; (ii) of prologues, as (i), but rather smaller: Jerome and his lion is the usual subject; (iii) of chapters, 1-line, red or blue. Capital letters in the ink of the text are touched with red. Penwork ornament, a paragraph mark, or sometimes a coloured letter at the point where a new lection begins. Borders, sometimes continuous, accompany initials of type i: they are in gold and colours, including green: the lower border has been cut from f. 1 of vol. 1, and pieces of the border from f. 64 and f. 138 of vol. 4. The bindings are medieval, repaired and rebacked: wooden boards covered with brown leather, each cover bearing a pattern of intersecting diagonal triple fillets, and, except the back covers of vols. 2 and 4, four repetitions of a small circular stamp containing B.V.M. and Child and the word 'CAPELLE': metal corner-pieces and centrepiece now missing. Secundo folios: (1) *que prophetarum*, (2) *ad insidias*, (3) *tiora sunt*, (4) *Et factum est.*

Written by Gerard Brilis for the charterhouse of La Chapelle at Hérinnes-lez-Enghien, 25 km south-west of Brussels. His receipt is in a current hand on a piece of paper now pasted to f. ii of vol. 1: 'Ic gheraerdus brilis kenne ende lide my ten volle vernoucht ghepayt ende wel betaelt vanden prioer vander capellen als vander heeler biblen die ic voer tgods huys ghescreuen hebbe in vier volum*in*a bede van scriuene punsene linen ende al dat ic daer toe ghedaen hebbe In kennisse der waerheyt heb ic dese sedule ghescreuen met miner proper hant Int Iaer m^{cccc} `ende´ [.]vii quinta die maii': in the date the word *ende* is over erasure and may be followed by a half erased *l* or possibly *xl*. In the initial beginning Judith in vol. 1 'anton [. . .]hes. maria ihesus ma[. . .] oro' is on the canopy of the bed of Holofernes. Probably still in use in s. xvii. 'Cole Park', vol. 1, f. ii, s. xix: sold by Mrs Audley Lovell of Cole Park, Malmesbury, at Sotheby's, 19 June 1914, lot 138, to Henry M. P. Howard, 19th Earl of Suffolk and Berkshire (†1917): his gift to the Church in 1914.

2 (i, ii) + Yale University, 86. *Biblical history, etc. (partly in French)* s. xiv/xv

One hundred and seven leaves of a manuscript of more than 200 leaves originally. Made into three volumes by J. P. R. Lyell: see below and *Lyell Cat.*, p. xxix. 2(i), ff. i^{v}–ii^{v} and 2(ii), ff. i^{v}–iii^{v} contain calligraphically written descriptions of each volume signed by Lyell. The signatures have been erased, but that in 2(i) was replaced, presumably when Lyell repurchased it.

1. 2(i), f. 1^{rv} (*begins imperfectly* ?) Absque viri natus semine cristus adest . . . Absque labore quies et sine nocte die[s]. In omnibus operibus tuis memorare [nouissima].

Verses on the Gospels (87 lines).

2. 2(i), ff. 2–46 Genesis–4 Kings in Anglo-Norman rhyming couplets. To judge from Corpus Christi College, Oxford, 36, ff. 48–158^{v}, s. xiii, less than half the text remains. For other manuscripts see Paul Meyer in *Bulletin de la société des anciens textes français* for 1889, pp. 77–82.

The blocks of consecutive text are:

ff. 2–8 (Gen.).	As Corp., ff. 49ra/16–56vb/3.
ff. 9–13 (Jud.–Ruth).	As Corp., ff. 75vb/11–80vb.
ff. 14–28 (1, 2 Kings).	As Corp., ff. 98vb/27–115va/22.
ff. 29–32 (3 Kings).	As Corp., ff. 127va/25–132ra/37.
ff. 33–5 (3 Kings).	As Corp., ff. 138vb/5–142ra/9.
ff. 36–42 (4 Kings).	As Corp., ff. 143ra/25–150vb/18.
ff. 43–5 (4 Kings).	As Corp., ff. 151vb/39–155rb/9.
f. 46 (4 Kings).	As Corp., f. 158va/22–37.

Many leaves are damaged and the text is complete only on ff. 14–16, 18–36, 38–46. The stubs of three leaves missing before f. 2 now appear after f. 8, and are followed there by ten more stubs: they contain a few complete words and many first letters. Another stub after f. 42.

The last words on f. 46, 'Ed de ceux disrael auaunt parler', are also the last words in Corp. 'ολβιον πολυ' and 'Caue mihi ne inuidias. Nutritus Amore: Perditus Dolore' are in the margin of f. 35^{v}, s. xvii. f. 46^{v} blank.

3. 2(ii), ff. 1–9^{v} Fragments of Guido de Columnis, Historia troiana: f. 1^{rv} A table of chapters of bks. '1' to '21', giving the first word of each chapter; ff. 2–8^{v} Seven consecutive leaves of bks. 1–4; f. 9^{rv} One leaf of bk. 30.

The text corresponds to N. E. Griffin's edition, 1936, pp. 7/33–37/16, 232/13–236/17. According to the divisions of this manuscript f. 1 begins in ch. 2 of bk. 1, f. 8 ends in ch. 2 of bk. 3 and f. 9 contains chs. 4–6 of bk. 28.

4. 2(ii), ff. 10–33^{v}, 35–40^{v}, 34^{rv}, 41^{rv} Fragments of Martinus Polonus, Chronica pontificum et imperatorum: (*a*) ff. 10–25 Sixteen out of twenty-five leaves of the chronicle of the popes, ending at 1287; (*b*) ff. 25–41^{v} The chronicle of the emperors, lacking only the end of the last annal. The two chronicles are not written on facing pages, as often, but one after the other.

(*a*). MGH, Scriptores, xxii. 401/9–443 (with gaps), 476–82, ending 'sepelitur iuxta sepulcrum Nicholai tercii. Explicit cronica Pontificorum Romanorum'. (*b*). Incipit de Imperatoribus. Post natiuitatem domini nostri . . . que est prope thunicam potenti manu (*ends imperfectly*). Edn. 443–474/9 (a.d. 1270).

Arts. 5–9 are at Yale University.

5. Yale, f. 13rv (*a*) recto, Henry IV's consecration in 1399 and his descent from Adam. (*b*) verso, 'Nomina Regum Anglie quorum Cronicke consecuntur', followed by the names of eighty-six kings, Brutus–Edward III.

The heading of (*b*) and the offset of a large initial show that art. 5 was originally in front of art. 6.

6. Yale, ff. 1–12v Fragments, twelve bifolia derived from three quires of a Brut chronicle in French, beginning in a chapter numbered 36 'Rome et oscist touz lez mescreauntz' (cf. the English in Brie's edition, EETS cxxxi, p. 40/20) and ending 'ou il fuist ioyeusement resceu'.

At first the text ended at f. 12/6, in a chapter numbered 86, 'en la feste seint Lucie' (4 Edward III, execution of Simon de Bereford, 13 Dec. 1330). A short continuation, 1331–57, was crowded in by the main hand on the rest of f. 12rv: it begins 'En lan E le Roys v le Comite Dasseles'. f. 7 should precede f. 6.

7. Yale, ff. 14–19v. Two pieces in French, (*a*) f. 14, a list of those taken and killed at Poitiers in 1356 and (*b*) ff. 14–19v, the terms of the treaty of Bretigny.

8. Yale, ff. 19v–20v. De modo parliamenti. Hic describitur modus quomodo parliamentum . . . inteligerint et sencierint (*ends imperfectly*).

Ed. N. Pronay and J. Taylor, *Parliamentary Texts of the later Middle Ages*, 1980, pp. 67–72/11. Recension A.

9. Yale, cover. A lease on parchment by John Merewether of Chippenham, Bachelor of Physic, to Thomas Hamblett in 1766 of part of the manor of Whitechurch and Milbourne (in Malmesbury) and inside it as additional strengthening a Wiltshire legal document on paper, s. xviii.

No doubt the cover of the whole manuscript when Lyell first had it. In 2(ii), f. ii he refers to it as a grant of lands in the parish of Malmesbury, s. xviii.

10 (missing). A fragment, one or two leaves, of a French version of Mandeville's travels.

Two papers loose inside Yale 86 refer to this fragment: (1) s. xix, 'These old Parchments were found in Malmesbury abbey during excavations . . . The 2 loose pages belong apparently to a book of travels probably Sir John Mandeville's (2) a letter to 'My dear Sparke' dated at Ashburton, Devon, 3 Feb. 1882 and signed John S. Amery. Amery records that the text began 'estre appelle Collos et vncore les Turkes lappellent ensynt. Et seint Poul en ses pistres escriuoit a eux dicele Isle ad Colocenses ceste Isle est bien' and went on to describe Cyprus and in last place Mount Carmel. The words quoted belong to the insular version and are near the end of ch. 4 in the Roxburghe Club edition by G. F. Warner, 1889, p. 13/39.[1]

[1] Information from Mr Michael Seymour.

ff. iii + 46 + i in 2(i). ff. iii + 41 + i in 2(ii). ff. 20 in Yale 86. 366 × 245 mm (Yale). 359 × 240 mm (Malmesbury). Written space 275 × 165 mm (Yale). *c.*260 × 175 mm (Malmesbury). Long lines and (arts. 1, 2) 2 cols. 44 lines and (arts. 5–8) 41 lines. Collation of art. 2 1^{10} wants 1–3 (ff. 2–8) 2^{8} wants 1–3 (ff. 9–13) 3^{8} (ff. 14–21) 4^{8} wants 8 (ff. 22–8) 5 four (ff. 29–32: two innermost bifolia) 6 three (ff. 33–5: three consecutive leaves) 7^{8} wants 8 (ff. 36–42) 8^{6} wants 4, 5 (ff. 43–6). Collation of art. 3: 1^{8} wants 1 2 one (f. 9). Collation of art. 4: 1^{8} wants 1, 2, 4–7 (ff. 10, 11) 2^{8} wants 2, 4, 5, 7 (ff. 12–15) 3–5^{8} (ff. 16–33, 35–40) 6 two (ff. 34, 41: the first two leaves). Collation of art. 6: 1 four (ff. 2–5: two innermost bifolia) 2 four (ff. 6, 8, 7, 9) 3^{8} wants 3–6 (ff. 10–13). Collation of arts. 7, 8: 1^{8} wants 1. Two series of quire letters, one, b, d, g, h, k–o, referring to the nine quires of arts. 2, 3, and the other, a–f, to the six quires of art. 4. Written by one hand throughout in pointed current anglicana of a rather legal type: single compartment *a*. Initials: (i) of art. 4*b*, in colours on gold and coloured ground, decorated and with prolongations into the margin; (ii) of art. 2, ff. 13^{v} (Ruth) and 45^{v} (in 4 Kings at a point corresponding to Corp. f. 154rb/1), gold on coloured grounds, with prolongations into the margin; (iii) 2-line, blue with red ornament. Capital letters in the ink of the text touched with red. 2(i) and 2(ii) are in bindings of s. xx^{1}. For the cover of Yale 86 see above, art. 9.

Written in England. At Malmesbury in s. xvi med., probably, when 'James Stumpe knight / Androwe Baynton esquier / Androw / Baynton' was written on f. 1^{v} of 2(i), the last two words in a more or less humanist script: James Stumpe was son of William Stumpe, †1552, who bought the abbey of Malmesbury at the Dissolution, and Andrew Baynton was his brother-in-law, son of Sir Edward Baynton of Bromham, Wilts. 'Some leaves of early English history in Norman French supposed to have come from Malmesbury Abbey' was written on art. 9 in s. xix: cf. also art. 10. Belonged apparently to – Sparke in 1882: see above, art. 10. Bought and later sold by James P. R. Lyell: see above. He repurchased MS. 2(i) on 8 April 1942, according to his note on f. i^{v}, and gave it to Malmesbury Church before his death in 1949. MS. 2(ii) was acquired by the Church in 1961. MS. 86 was a gift to Yale University from Henry Fletcher in 1950.

MANCHESTER. CHETHAM'S LIBRARY

The library was founded by Humphrey Chetham, †1653. The manuscripts are listed briefly in *Bibliotheca Chethamensis* (6 vols.): 6680–6723 in ii (1791), 618–22; 7995–8029 in iii (1826), 165–74; 11362–11398 in iv (1862), 424–49; 27842–28047 in vi. 367–82.[1] J. O. Halliwell, *An account of the European Manuscripts in the Chetham Library, Manchester*, Manchester 1842, covers 6680–6723, 7995–8029, and lists also as '8031', '8037' and '8038' three medieval manuscripts which were not listed in 1826 and were given the numbers 11362, 11379, and 11380 in 1862.[2]

So far as is known 6712 is the first medieval manuscript acquired by Chetham's Library. Early library records refer to 6681, 6689–90, q.v. 6682, 6690, 6712, 6688, 6689, 6696 are listed in *CMA* ii. 222, in that order. 8003, 8005, 8009, 11362, and 11366 were bought at auction. 27857 and ten other manuscripts

[1] The 1791 volume and its supplements are all alphabetical lists by authors in which the manuscripts are taken in blocks. vi. 367–82 provides a general index.

[2] Two manuscripts given by Byrom, 27902 and 27941, were sold at Christie's 19 November 1980, lots 286–7. I have included descriptions in order to preserve a complete list of the Byrom manuscripts. Facsimiles in the sale catalogue of 27902, f. 1 and 27941, f. 19.

belong to the Byrom collection given in 1870: see under 27857. All of them except 27911 bear the signature of J. Byrom, †1763, and all are listed in the catalogue of the Byrom library printed in 1848.

Concordance of Mun. and *Bibliotheca Chethamensis* numbers.[1]

Mun.	*B.C.*	Mun.	*B.C.*	Mun.	*B.C.*
A. 2. 160	6723	A. 4. 91	11380	A. 6. 18	6682
A. 2. 161	8007	A. 4. 92	6722	A. 6. 31	8009
A. 2. 162	6687	A. 4. 94	8001	A. 6. 59	6720
A. 2. 163	33667	A. 4. 96	6688	A. 6. 74	6717
A. 2. 164–5	6689	A. 4. 99	6680	A. 6. 88	8005
A. 2. 166	27911	A. 4. 100	6681	A. 6. 89	6712
A. 2. 171	27941	A. 4. 101	11366	A. 6. 90	11379
A. 3. 127	27938	A. 4. 102	8003	A. 6. 91	11362
A. 3. 128	27894	A. 4. 103	8008	A. 6. 96	8023
A. 3. 129	27907	A. 4. 104	6709	A. 7. 1	6691
A. 3. 130	28024	A. 4. 106	6714	A. 7. 48	6696
A. 3. 131	27929	A. 4. 107	6711	E. 8. 21	6713
A. 3. 132	27971	A. 4. 109	6721	E. 8. 23	27900
A. 4. 90	8002	A. 5. 14	27902		

6680 (Mun. A. 4. 99). *Astrologica, etc. (partly in English)* s. xv med.

Described in some detail by Halliwell, pp. 1–3. The diagram 'inserted loosely', formerly kept in a pocket of the binding, belongs to MS. 6681, q.v.

1. f. 1^{v} A volvelle of three revolving circles mounted on a base on which the points of the compass are marked. Each circle consists of three thicknesses of parchment. The outermost and largest of the three is marked with the months and the signs of the zodiac and the next largest bears numbers from 1 to 29. The metal pointer remains. f. 1^{r}, blank, was pasted down.

2. f. 2 A volvelle, the mount of which is divided into compartments to show the dominant planet in each part of the world, for example 'Dominacio Saturni in ynde and Ethiope and þ^{er} aboute'. It is of two thicknesses of parchment and has seven projections, each bearing the name of a planet.

3. f. 2^{v} He þat wole wite whanne it is good tyme to be leten blood byholde þe doctrine of galien and of ypocras. In februar' it is good . . . for al maner of diseses. Explicit.

The text is written circularwise from the outside inwards. The name of an evangelist is on a scroll at each corner of the page.

4. f. 3 A table of years 1348–1475.

Some events are noted as far as 1422, for example the first, second and third plagues at 1348, 1361, and 1368, 'romo^{r} com' ' at 1381, 'romo^{r} lord*is*' at 1387, 'romo^{r} cobham' at 1414.

[1] The manuscripts are kept in Mun. order.

5. f. 3v A table of a great cycle of 532 years, beginning at 1140. Some of the events noted in art. 4 are marked here also.

6. f. 4 A table headed 'Contratabula quinti festorum mobilium'.

7. ff. 4v–16 (*a*) Sarum calendar in red and black, graded, on rectos, ff. 5–16. (*b*) Tables of eight decennovenal cycles beginning at 1482, 1501, 1520, 1387, 1406, 1425, 1444, and 1463 respectively, on versos, ff. 4v–15v.

(*a*). The occupation of each month is shown in a roundel and by a line of verse, printed by Halliwell, 'Ouer this feer I warme myn hondes . . . Welcome Cristemasse wyth ale and wyn' (6 couplets). 'Dominica prima post festum petri et pauli dedicacio ecclesie apud Enefeld' below June and 'In vndecimo die mensis Nouembris obiit Gilbertus benete anno domini 1419' below November, both in the main hand (ff. 10, 15). The word 'papa' and feasts of St Thomas of Canterbury erased. (*b*). 'Commemoraciones Solis et lune secundum Magistrum Walterum Elueden et Iohannem Somur . . .' at the foot of f. 15v in the main hand.

8. f. 16v Tabula ad sciendum quis planeta regnat in qualibet hora diei et noctis.

9. f. 17 This spere telleþ at what tyme of þe day or nyȝt þat þe planet*is* entre.

A volvelle divided into 360 degrees. The page on which it is mounted has a scroll at each corner bearing the name of an evangelist.

10. f. 17v Spera planetarum. f. 18rv blank.

11. ff. 19–20 A table over three pages, four months to a page, headed on f. 19v 'This 3 tabules tellen what quantite a planete regneþ bi dai and bi niȝt euery day in þe ȝer for to departe þe day and þe nyȝt on 12 be it schort or long'.

12. ff. 20v–21 Tabula salamonis ad sciendum in quo signo sit luna et in quo gradu illius Signi omni die in anno secundum almagest'.

13. f. 21v (*a*) Diagram of a human body marked with the twelve signs of the zodiac: silver on a red ground framed in gold. (*b*) Duodecim sunt signa celi. scilicet Aries . . . Et quia Aries in prima mundi origine . . . illud signum. (*c*) Table of the signs according to the element to which each belongs. (*d*) Tabula domus planetarum.

(*b*). Cf. Thorndike and Kibre.

14. f. 22 Hic incipit tabula de gradibus altitudinis Solis.

15. ff. 22v–27v Tables of eclipses of sun and moon for 1330–1462 and diagrams to show the amount of totality of eclipses of the sun (f. 24rv) and of the moon (ff. 26v–27v).

A total eclipse of the sun is shown as occurring on 18 June 1443. 'mccccIxxv' at the head of f. 24v in a hand of that date, probably.

16. f. 27^{rv} Tabula continuacionis motus Solis.

For 1385–1465.

17. f. 28 Tabula medie coniunctionis et opposicionis Solis et lune in annis cristi expansis.

18. f. 28^{v} Tabula equacionum solis.

19. ff. 29–31^{v} Hic incipiunt Tonitrua Mensium et Signorum Solis et Lune.

Prognostications of weather, etc., in Latin prose and English verse from (*a*) thunder and (*b*) the zodiacal signs of each month. The Latin begins 'Mense Ianuar'. Si tonitruum fit mense Ian' ventus validus: cf. Thorndike and Kibre. The English begins: (*a*) Whan þonder comeþ in Ianiuer þou schalt haue þ^{t} ilke ȝer; (*b*) The sonne is her in þis signe: *IMEV*, nos. 4053, 3479. The signs of the zodiac are in 10-line roundels on gold and coloured grounds.

20. ff. 29–31, below art. 19 Hic incipiunt Septem ann[orum] . . . Littera dominica A a warm wynter and esy. þe somer stormy . . . grete plente of gras and hey schal be. and þese ȝeres ben ytake out of þe brute for substaunce. Expliciunt septem annorum.

Prognostications of weather from the Sunday letters, A–G.

21. f. 31, after art. 20 Lists of 'Dies periculi'.

22. f. 31^{v}, below art. 19 A list of the twelve fasting Fridays.

23. f. 32 The mount for a volvelle, with the names of the signs of the zodiac marked on it. The volvelle itself is missing. f. 32^{v}, blank, was pasted down.

ff. v + 32 + i. 186 × 186 mm. Written space *c.*165 × 155 mm. Collation of ff. 4–31: 1^{8} 2^{8} + a bifolium (ff. 17, 18) inserted after 5 3^{10}. Written in anglicana formata. For pictures see arts. 7 and 19. 2-line initials, gold with blue ornament or blue with red ornament. Binding of s. xix, stamped 'Kalendrier des Bergers'.

Written in England, perhaps at Enfield, Middlesex: cf. art. 7. Given by 'Dr Mainwaring' according to Halliwell.

6681 (Mun. A. 4. 100 + 100*). *De situ universorum, etc.* s. xiv ex.

1. ff. 1^{v}–2^{v} De tribus habitaculis. C.p^{m}. Cum enim dicitur in sacra scriptura. Celum sursum et terra deorsum. prouerb. 25. Et eciam dicitur Iosue 2 . . . quorum omnium pars (*ends imperfectly in ch. 6*). f. 1^{r} blank.

2. ff. 3–100^{v} (*preface*) De situ vniuersorum reminiscemini:ʼ et cuncta creata in vno concludi . . . creauit omnia . . . (*text*, f. 7) Uniuersorum creator in quo sunt omnes thesauri sapiencie . . . in ista figura magna sequenti aliqualiter demonstratur. Explicit compilacio de situ uniuersorum creatorum:ʼ omnipotenti deo gracias.

The author relates on ff. 49v–50 that George, a young pilgrim from Apulia, visited St Patrick's Purgatory (in Lough Derg, Donegal, Ireland) in 1353 and entered paradise and that he carried letters of credence to this effect on his way home 'quas in conuentu fratrum minorum oxon' iii Nonas aprilis anno supradicto presentibus magistro sacre theologie et bacularijs et gardiano et multis aliis fratribus:' sub sigillis auctenticis oculis meis `ego scriptor istius' vidi': he spoke with George on this occasion. Roger Bacon is referred to occasionally, for example on f. 48. The 117 chapters are listed in a table between the preface and the text (ff. 3–5v). f. 6rv was left blank.

3. ff. 101–4 De descensu a summo habitaculo ad ymum habitaculum. Ca. pm. Cum enim dicitur Celum sursum et terra deorsum et sub terra esse infernus quem distat ortus ab occidente. Qui hoc dubitant siue negant . . . a gaudiis celorum remotissimi. Explicit compilacio de descensu a summo habitaculo ad ymum habitaculum. 1392.

Seven chapters.

4. Mun. A. 4. 100*. The 'figura' mentioned in the last words of art. 2 is a folded sheet of parchment measuring 423 × 405 mm, now kept separately. It shows twenty-three circles round the earth, each marked with its name.

The outermost circle is marked at the top 'Celum siue locus cristi ascendentis super omnes celos in celo empyreo' and at the foot 'Inferni profunditas'. 'Limbus puerorum' is below the twelfth sphere. 'Celum cristallinum siue aqueum' is four spheres deep on each side of the entrance to 'Puteus inferni'.

ff. iii + 104 + ii and a diagram now kept separately. f. iii is a medieval flyleaf. 225 × 150 mm. Written space *c.*175 × 115 mm. 40 long lines. The first line of writing is above the top ruled line, as in MS. Digby 90. Collation: 1 six (ff. 1–6) 2^8 6 cancelled after f. 11 (ff. 7–13) $3\text{–}10^8$ 11^{12} 12^{10} + a slip (f. 92) tied in after 2 13 four (ff. 101–4). Quires 2–12 signed a–l in the usual late medieval way. Well written in current anglicana, arts. 1 and 3 perhaps rather later than the rest: the same scribe wrote MS. Digby 90 (cf. below). 3-line (ff. 3, 7) and 2-line red initials. Capital letters in the ink of the text touched with red. Binding of s. xix. Secundo folio *volubilitate* (f. 2) or *vigent* (f. 8).

Written in England, art. 2 after 1353 and before 1392 if that is the date of art. 3. An author's autograph, to judge from *ego scriptor istius* in art. 2. 'Iste liber est fratris Iohannis de Tewkesbury', ff. 1v, 3, erased, s. xiv/xv. The owner is no doubt the John of Tewkesbury who gave Bodleian MS. Digby 90 to the Oxford Franciscans in 1388 and it seems likely that both manuscripts were of Tewkesbury's own making: if so, he was at the Oxford convent in 1353 and is the author of De situ universorum. 'Liber M Io Bayll' prec' v s' ' and 'liber cli', f. 1, s. xv. 'Liber Bibliothecæ Chethamensis Ex dono Dmni Ricdi Johnson', f. 1: the Donors' Book records at 1699 the gift of 'An old MS. in 8vo, a treatise of Natural Philosophy or Astronomy by Mr Richard Johnson, apothecary'.

6682 (Mun. A. 6. 18). *Augustinus, etc.* s. xiii²

1. ff. 1–6v Liber boetii de trinitate incipit prologus. Inuestigatam diutissime questionem . . . perpetua creatoris.

The five 'opuscula sacra' in the order of the Teubner edition, but here treated as three: (*a*) ff. 1–2v, the two first in three chapters; (*b*) ff. 2–3, the third under the title 'Liber boetii de bono', in two chapters; (*c*) ff. 3–6v, the fourth and fifth under the title 'De duobus naturis et una persona cristi', in six chapters.

2. ff. 6v–10v Uestra nouit intentio de scolarium disciplina . . . inquinamenta permanebunt. Amici (*sic*) boecii seuerini ex consultis patritii: liber de disciplina scolarium explicit. Explicit.

Pseudo-Boèce. De disciplina scolarium, ed. O. Weijers, 1976.

Arts. 3–13 are listed by Römer, ii. 218.

3. ff. 11–14v Incipit liber de bono coniugali. Quoniam unusquisque homo . . . patres fuerunt. Explicit liber beati aug' de bono coniugali. *CSEL* xli. 187–230.

4. ff. 14v–21 Incipit liber beati aug' de adulterinis coniugiis. Prima questio est frater dilectissime . . . occasio castitatis. *CSEL* xli. 347–410.

5. ff. 21–24v Aurelii augustini doctoris egregii de presentia dei ad dardanum presbiterum liber incipit. Fateor me frater dilectissime . . . qua concedis et ueniam. Explicit liber ad dardanum presbiterum.

CSEL lvii. 81–119 (Ep. 187). The relevant extract from Retractationes is in front of the text.

6. ff. 24v–30 Aurelii aug' doctoris liber primus incipit de predestinatione sanctorum ad prosperum et hylarium. Dixisse quidem apostolum . . . nimia longitudo. Explicit liber primus de predestinatione. *PL* xliv. 959–92.

7. ff. 30–7 Incipit liber secundus de bono perseuerantie. Iam de perseuerantia . . . nosce quod scribo. *PL* xliv. 993–1034.

8. ff. 37–42v Aurelii aug' [doc]toris egregii contra mendatium incipit ad consen[tium]. Multa michi legenda misisti . . . quem loco isto fiximus ueniremus. Aurelii augustini doctoris egregii contra mendatium explicit. *CSEL* xli. 469–528.

9. ff. 42v–48 Aurelii augustini doctoris egregii liber de mendatio incipit. Magna questio est . . . ut possitis sustinere. Explicit liber de mendatio. *CSEL* xli. 413–66.

10. f. 48rv Augustinus ut non solum lingua . . . tale quod procedit in opere. Resurrectio et clarificatio (*sic*) domini nostri ihesu cristi . . . uite mentis comparemus. *PL* xxxix. 2211 (Appendix, Sermo 252).

11. ff. 48v–52v Incipiunt questiones orosii ad sanctum augustinum. Licet multi ac probatissimi . . . non prodesse. Expliciunt questiones orosii ad sanctum augustinum.

Numbered I–LXIII, since the twelfth and fourteenth of the sixty-five questions have been left out: 'hic deficit multum' is in the margin where the gap occurs, f. 49.

12. ff. 53–90 Incipit prologus libri confessionum sancti augustini episcopi. Et in hoc corpore continentur libri numero xiii. Magnus es domine et laudabilis . . . sic aperietur. Amen.

CSEL xxxiii. 1-388. The relevant extract (from Retractationes is in front of the text. 'In hoc corpore continentur' is in the title of Paris B.N., lat. 1913A (edn., p. xxx) and—of English copies of Confessiones—Bodley 815 and Lambeth Palace 365.

13. ff. 90^{v}-204 . . . (f. 91) Domino illustri et merito prestantissimo filio volusiano . . . uel faciendum esse reperias.

The same collection of 144 letters[1] as in B.L. Royal 5 B. v. (Römer, ii. 189). As compared with Eton 105 (*MMBL* ii. 717-18) there are five more letters here and one difference in order: nos. 81, 82 after no. 143 (Eton vii); nos. 130 (in last place in Eton 105), 147 after no. 164 (Eton xlv); no. 165 after no. 101 (Eton liv); App. no. 16 after App. no. 15 (Eton cvii). The numbering in the text is I-CXLIIII, but in the table on ff. 90^{v}-91, where there were no numbers originally, it is 1-141, since the scribe failed to enter the three letters numbered in the text LXIII, LXXVI and LXXXVIII. f. 204^{v} blank.

ff. ii + 204 + ii. 375 × 260 mm. Written space 258 × 135 mm. 2 cols. 68 lines. Collation: 1^{10} 2^{14} $3\text{-}17^{12}$. Small hands, changing at ff. 109 (first leaf of quire 10, where the ruling changes from double to single vertical bounders), 183. Initials on ff. 1-108: (i) red and blue with ornament of both colours; (ii) in art. 11, 1-line, red or blue with ornament of the other colour. Initials on ff. 109-204, red or blue at first, but from f. 109 the spaces for the blue initials and from f. 191 all the spaces remain blank. Capital letters in the ink of the text touched with red on ff. 118^{v}-154^{v}. Binding of s. xix. Secundo folio *Maxime enim*.

Written in England. In the library in 1697: *CMA* ii, no. 7146.

6687 (Mun. A. 2. 162). *F. Barbarus, De re uxoria* s. xv med.

(f. 4) Francisci barbari veneti ad insignem virum laurentium de medicis ciuem florentinum de re vxoria liber incipit feliciter. Maiores nostri laurenti carissime . . . (f. 94^{v}) certe tibi deditissimo proficiscitur. Preceded on ff. 1-3^{v} by letters from Poggio and Vergerio in praise of De re uxoria.

Printed together with the two letters in 1513 and later. One leaf missing. Damaged by damp throughout and by the excision of initials on ff. 8, 27, 38, 49, 67, 78. 'Found mutilated Ap. 3 1913 H(orace) C(rossley)', f. 99. ff. 95-97^{v} blank.

ff. iv + 97 + ii. ff. iii, iv are medieval endleaves: iii was pasted to a former binding. 164 × 118 mm. Written space 105 × 60 mm. 21 long lines. Collation: 1^{10} 2^{10} wants 9 after f. 18 $3\text{-}9^{10}$ 10^{8}. Written in humanistica. Initials: (i) 6-line, gold on grounds of blue, green, and purple, decorated with white vine stems and dots and edged with red: (ii) '1-line', red or blue, outside the written space. Binding of s. xix. Secundo folio *git probatque*.

Written in Italy, almost certainly in the north-east (Padua ?).[2] '[. . . .] liber est [. . . . .]ganore apud [. .]ibium: 1533', f. iv^{v}, partly cut off. In England by s. xvii med. when the date '20 [. . .] 1649' and name '[. .]oodall' were written on f. iv.

[1] 142 letters according to Römer's numbering: his Ep. 26 is here and in Eton 105 counted as three numbers (xxiii-xxv = Eton xxi-xxiii).

[2] Information from Dr A. de la Mare.

6688 (Mun. A. 4. 96). *Biblia* s. xiii med.

A Bible in the order Genesis–2 Chronicles, Ezra, Nehemiah, 'Item liber Esdre' (5 Ezra, chapters 1, 2: Stegmüller, no. 96), Judith, Esther, Tobit, Job, five sapiential books, Psalms, Isaiah, Jeremiah, Lamentations, Baruch, Ezekiel, Daniel, Minor Prophets, 1, 2 Maccabees, Gospels, Pauline Epistles, Catholic Epistles, Acts, Apocalypse. Psalms are on two independent quires, 16, 17.

The prologues are 39 of the common set of 64 (see Liverpool Cathedral 13), and twelve others shown here by *: Stegmüller, nos. 284 (not divided into chapters), 285, 311, 315*, 323, 319* (before 3 Kings), 328, 330, 335, 341 + 343, 332, 344 + 357, 457, 462, 455* (as prologue to Wisdom), 443*, 482, 487, 491, 492, 494, 500, 527*, 529*, 532*, 535*, 540*, 544*, 551, 590, 607, 620, 624, 677 and thirteen more as usual to 793 (the prologue to 1 Timothy (765) ends 'antopoli uel de laodicea'), 809, 812*, 818*.

Many books have both the usual chapter-numbers in red and blue roman figures and also numbers in red arabic figures, according to which Hosea, Jeremiah, and Apocalypse, for example, are divided into 46, 179, and 38 chapters respectively. Within books the beginning of a new chapter is shown only by a blank space a few letters wide and in it a coloured initial. Many pencilled marginalia in current hands.

ff. iii + 329 + ii. 232 × 170 mm. Written space *c.* 170 × 105 mm. 2 cols. 54–6 lines. Collation: 29 quires, all twelves, except 2^{10}, 6^{6} (ff. 59–64), 15^{8}, 17^{6}, 18^{14}, 22^{10}: 29 wants 12, probably blank. Initials: (i) of books, Pss. 1, 26, 38, 51, 52, 68, 80, 97, 101, 109, and some prologues, red and blue with ornament of both colours; (ii) of psalms (except as above) and some prologues, 2-line, red or blue with ornament of the other colour; (iii) of chapters and psalm-verses, 1-line, red or blue. Rebound in s. xix by Thomas Carter, 7 Bridgewater Place, Manchester: the covers of the older binding, s. xvii, bearing a large gilt centrepiece and with the mark of a chain on the side are pasted to the new covers. Secundo folio *naue qui*.

Written in England, probably. 'Memoria vicarii de scartheburg' nomine', f. 1, at top, s. xiii. Presumably the 4to Bible listed in the Chetham shelf-list of 1680. *CMA* ii, no. 7149.

6689 (Mun. A. 2. 164–5). *Biblia* s. xiii med.

1. vol. 1, vol. 2 ff. 1–301v A Bible with the usual contents in the usual order (see above, Liverpool Cathedral 13), bound in two volumes: the break is after Psalms.

The first leaf is missing. The prologues are the usual set of sixty-four, except that the prologue to Jonah is Stegmüller, no. 522, not no. 521, and that there are two prologues to Daniel, Obadiah, and Acts, no. 495 after no. 494, no. 516 before nos. 519 + 517 and no. 631 after no. 640.

2. vol. 2, ff. 302–347v Aaz apprehendens . . .

The usual dictionary of Hebrew names, ending imperfectly in the interpretation of Zabuth.

ff. ii + 292 + ii (vol. 1). ff. ii + 347 + ii (vol. 2). Thin parchment. 142 × 105 mm. Written space 103 × 75 mm. 2 cols. 45 lines. Collation: (vol. 1) 1^{24} wants 1 2^{22} 3–10^{24} 11^{28} 12^{26}; (vol. 2) 13–24^{24} 25^{16} wants 14–16, probably blank, after f. 301 26^{24} 27^{22} wants 22 after f. 347. Small hand. Initials: (i) of books, Pss. 1, 26, 38, 52, 68, 80, 97, 109, and prologues, and at each new letter of art. 2, red and blue with ornament of both colours; (ii) of psalms (except as above) and of chapters, 2-line, red or blue with ornament of both colours; (iii) of verses of psalms and in art. 2, 1-line, red or blue. The ornament runs nearly the length of the page. Capital letters in the ink of the text touched with red. Bindings of s. xix: gilt edges. Secundo folio (f. 1) *duodecim prophete*.

Written in France, probably. 'Olim peculium Thomæ Hodden' according to Halliwell. Probably the 8° Bible given by Roger Kenyon, according to the Gift-book, and recorded in the first register of accessions in or soon after 1674 and in a shelf-list of 1680. *CMA* ii, no. 7150.

6690 (Mun. A. 7. 1). *Mirror of the life of Christ, etc. (in English)* s. xv med.

1. ff. 1–116 Attende lector huius libri sic prout scribitur consequenter in anglico quod ubi in margine ponitur littera N uerba sunt translatoris siue compilatoris alia quam scribuntur de meditacionibus uite cristi in latino. a uenerabili doctore Bonauentura secundum communem opinionem. Et quando peruenitur ad processum et uerba eiusdem doctoris inseritur in margine littera B. prout poterit lucide apparere librum ipsum de uita cristi diligencius intuenti. Here biginneth þe proheme of þe boke þat is clepid þe merour of the blisside lyfe of ihesu criste. Quecumque scripta sunt . . . spem habeamus. This bene þe wordes of þe grete doctour . . . moder marye now and euere wiþ outen ende. Amen. Explicit Speculum Vite cristi. Amen.

The translation by Nicholas Love of the Speculum vitae christi, in sixty-three chapters, edited by L. F. Powell, 1908, pp. 7–301, preceded by the Latin notice printed by Powell, p. 6. Running titles, Die lune, Die martis, etc.

2. ff. 116v–130 Here begynneth a techynge þat Rychard hermyte made and sente it to ankres. In ilke a synful man . . . þe grace of ihesu be wiþ þee. Amen. þis teching made Rychard Hermyte and sent it to an Ankres that was cleped Margarete.

Ed. H. E. Allen, *English writings of Richard Rolle*, 1931, pp. 85–119 (Form of living): cf. Allen, *Writings*, p. 261.

3. f. 130rv A sely soule asked of god . . . I telle þee forsoþe Kateryne dougter dere. Explicit.

Three things to do 'if þou wolt haue clennes'. Jolliffe, I. 7 (c).

4. ff. 130v–132 þise arn þe fyftene orysons wt þe fiftene Pater nosters and Aue maries of þe passion of oure lord ihesu cryste. A þou lord Ihesu cryste endeles swetnes . . . wt all þi seyntes wiþowten ende Amen. Pater noster. Aue maria.

A translation of the Fifteen Oes of St Bridget.

5. ff. 132v–133 Incipit oracio uenerabilis Bede presbiteri. Oracio. A þou lord ihesu cryste⸝ þat seydest seuene worde . . . and duelle þurgh endeles werlde. Amen. Explicit.

A translation of the prayer of the Seven Words commonly attributed to Bede. Cf. F. Wormald in *Laudate* for 1936, p. 168.

6. ff. 133–134v Incipit oracio deuota ad dominum Ihesum. Oracio. Ihesu Ihesu mercy I cry . . . Ihesu mercy for my mysdede. Ihesus Amen. Maria Amen.

Twenty-two 8-line stanzas. Carleton Brown, *Religious lyrics of the fifteenth century*, 1939, pp. 222–7, no. 144. *IMEV*, no. 1732.

7. f. 134v Alia Oracio Deuota. Ihesu þi name honoured mot be . . . And graunte me blysse wt outen ende. Amen.

Five 8-line stanzas. Brown, op. cit., pp. 227–9, no. 145. *IMEV*, no. 1780.

8. ff. 135–45 Here beginneth þe tretys þat is clepid media vita. þt is best for comon simple leuyng. þe grace and þe goodnes of oure lord ihesu crist . . . to dwelle with him in his swete place. Amen. Here endith a tretys þat is clepid Media vita.

Ed. D. Jones, *Minor works of Walter Hilton*, 1929, pp. 8–75/17. Ends as B.L. Harley 2254 (edn., p. 75, footnote).

9. ff. 145–154v De corpore cristi. Memoriam fecit mirabilium . . . timentibus se. þise wordes of dauid in þe sawtier seyde . . . as for a ful ende of al his blyssid lif bifore wryten. Heir folweþ a schort deuout prayer . . . atte messe wyth inwarde deuocioun. Heyle holiest bodi of our lord ihesu Crist . . . of þi lif blissed wt outen endynge. Amen. Lord ihesu þi blissed lif ∴ helpe and conforte oure wrecchid lif. Amen.

The last part of Love's translation of pseudo-Bonaventura: see below, Manchester, John Rylands Univ. Libr., Eng. 94. Ed. Powell, pp. 303–23. ff. 115–157v and the pastedown are blank, but ruled.

ff. ii + 157. 262 × 190 mm. Written space 168 × 115 mm. 34 long lines. Collation: $1\text{–}16^8$ 17^6 (ff. 129–34) $18\text{–}20^8$ (20^8 is pasted down). Written in modified textura, probably by one hand throughout. Initials: (i) f. 1, 6-line *A*, blue and red with red ornament; (ii) 2-line, blue with red ornament. Contemporary binding of wooden boards covered with white leather: six bands: two strap-and-pin fastenings: a chain of 16 links attached to the side of the front cover just above the lower of the two straps. Secundo folio *as for a princypale*.

Written in England. Given before 1697: *CMA* ii, no. 7147.

6691 (Mun. A. 7. 1). *P. de Braco, Compendium iuris canonici* 1466

Compendium domini petri de braco super iure canonico. (*preface*) Quoniam inter cetera dampna que suis posteris intulit prothoplaustoris transgressio non minimum fuit obliuio . . . Idcirco ego petrus de braco inter decretorum doctores minimus . . . Breue compendium ex diuersis textibus et glosis iuris canonici . . . compilare concepi . . . (*text*) A quod a est prima littera grecorum . . . extra de elec. licit. Explicit compendium domini petri de braco super iure canonico. 14 Ianuar' 1465 Pro [. . . . . .].

For P. de Braco, s. xiv², see Schulte, ii. 262. ff. 333v–335v blank.

ff. v + 335 + v. Paper and—the outside and central leaves of each quire—parchment. ff. iv, v, 336–7 are medieval (?) parchment endleaves. 368 × 270 mm. Written space 277 × 185 mm. 2 cols. 60 lines. Collation: $1\text{–}27^{12}$ 28^{12} wants 12, probably blank. Written in a set hybrida. Initials: (i) blue, patterned in white on gold grounds decorated with ivy leaves; (ii) 2-line, red or blue. Capital letters in the ink of the text filled with yellow. Binding of s. xix/xx. Secundo folio *Item abbas*.

Written in France or the Low Countries. 'E libris Chr. Byron 1721', f. iv. Given by Byron.

6696 (Mun. A. 7. 48). *J. Gower, Confessio amantis (in English)* s. xv/xvi

(*begins imperfectly*) To thinke apon the daies olde . . . Oure Ioie may ben endles Amen Amen Amen. Explicit Iste liber . . . grata britannis (4 lines) Quam cinxere freta . . . stat sine meta (4 lines) Amen.

This copy described by G. C. Macaulay, *Works of John Gower*, II. cxli. The four missing leaves contained lines 1–192 of the prologue, lines 1092–491 of bk. 1 and lines 2111–343 of bk. 8. The scribe omitted many passages.

ff. iii + 126 + ii. Paper. 385 × 262 mm. Written space *c.*315 × 155 mm. 2 cols. 47–61 lines. Frame ruling, the horizontals with a hard point and the verticals with pencil. Collation: 1^{12} wants 1 and 12 2^{12} wants 1 before f. 11 3^{12} 4^{14} $5\text{–}7^{12}$ 8^{14} 9^{12} 10^{18} wants 14 after f. 123. Quires numbered at the beginning (A)–K. Written in a current and basically secretary hand by the same scribe as the copy of the Troy Book, now Glasgow, Hunterian 388. Penwork initials in the ink of the text, as in the Glasgow manuscript. Binding of s. xix. Secundo folio *To thinke*.

Written in England. The word 'Notehurste' is in the scribe's hand on a scroll a little below the last words of the text. It occurs also in the scribe's hand at the end of the Glasgow manuscript, which belonged in s. xvi med. to John, son and heir of Thomas Chetham 'late of Notehurst (*Nuthurst, Lancashire*) Decessyd . . . to be an heyrelome at Notehurst according to ye tenour and effect of my fathers will'.[1] 'William yate oeth this book god', f. 21. Entered in the 1680 shelf-list. *CMA* ii, no. 7151.

6709 (Mun. A. 4. 104). *Lydgate, Life of Our Lady; etc. (in English)* 1485, 1490, 1493, s. xv ex.

Religious poems in English in the hand of William Cotson, canon of the Augustinian priory of Dunstable. Affected by damp throughout. f. 1 has a table of contents in Cotson's hand listing arts. 1–7 and before art. 3 a 1-leaf life of St. Thomas, now missing: references to quires and leaves of quires are given.

1. ff. 6–159 O Thowghtfull Harte plungyd in dystresse . . . That we regne in hevyn w^t the ordres Nyne. Explicit libellus de vita beate virginis marie compilatus per Dompnum Iohannem lydgate . . . et scriptus propriis manibus dompni

[1] For the Chetham family of Nuthurst see *Life of Humphrey Chetham* (Chetham Soc., new series 50), 1903, Appendix, pp. 9–31. Thomas Chetham died in 1503, his son John in 1516, his grandson Thomas in 1546, and his great-grandson John in 1573. C. A. Luttrell showed in *Neophilologus*, xxiv (1958), 38–50, that the scribe is probably Thomas Chetham, †1546.

willelmi Cotson Canonici . . . vltimo (?) die Aprilis hoc anno domini Millesimo cccc nonagesimo tercio calamum relaxaui . . .

Lydgate, Life of Our Lady, 848 7-line stanzas copied from the printed edition of Caxton (1484): cf. R. A. Klinefelter, 'Lydgate's "Life of Our Lady" and the Chetham ms. 6709', *Papers of the Bibliographical Society of America*, xlvi (1952), 396–7, for evidence of copying from Caxton's edition. *IMEV*, no. 2574. Ed. J. A. Lauritis, 1961. ff. 1^{v}–5^{v} contain a table of contents. f. 159^{v} blank.

2. (*a*) ff. 160–73 Vita Sancte Cecilie sic incipit. The mynystre and Noryssh to all vicis . . . Men do to Cryste and to his sayntis service. Explicit vita Sancte Virginis et Martiris Cecilie. scripta per manus Dompni Willelmi Cotson Canonici In mense Marcii Anno domini Millesimo cccclxxxx^{mo}. (*b*) ff. 173–178^{v} Hic incipit Miraculum Beate Marie Virginis. Dominus dominus noster. quam admirabile est nomen tuum in vniuersa terra. Lorde oure lord thy Name euer meruelous . . . moder Marye.

(*a, b*). The Second Nun's and Prioress's Tales copied from Caxton's second edition of the Canterbury Tales: cf. Manly and Rickert, *The text of the Canterbury Tales*, i (1940), 82–4. *IMEV*, no. 4019 (85) and (74). f. 179^{rv} left blank: the verso contains two extracts from Augustine, De civitate Dei, bks. 16 and 22, in Latin.

3. ff. 180–192^{v} Hic incipit vita Sancte Margarete C[. . . . .] Compilata per Dompnum Iohannem Lydgate Monachum de Bury Anno viii^{o} Henrici Sexti. At the Reuerence of Seynt Margarete . . . thy seruauntis sette at ease.

IMEV, no. 439. Seventy-seven 7-line stanzas. Ed. MacCracken, *Minor Poems of John Lydgate* (EETS, Extra series cvii, 1911), pp. 173–92.

4. ff. 193–198^{v} Incipit vita Sancti Georgii. O ye folkys that here present be . . . As he repayred home to his Mansyon. Explicit secundum lydgate scripta per manus dompni Willelmi Cotson Canonici in mense Iulii (?) Anno domini Millesimo cccclxxxv[. .].

IMEV, no. 2592. Thirty-five 7-line stanzas. Ed. MacCracken, op. cit., pp. 145–54.

5. ff. 199–284 Vita Sancti Edmundi Regis et Martiris. The Noble story to put in Remembraunce . . . Where thow faylest to do Correcyon. Explicit quod Willelmus Cotson Godde grawnte vs grace. Anno domini Millesimo cccc^{mo} lxxxv^{to} . . . finem feci In Die Sancte Barnabe Apostoli. Amen.

IMEV, no. 3440. Lydgate. Printed by K. Horstmann, *Altenglische Legenden, Neue Folge*, 1881, pp. 378–440/7. 7-line and for the final prayer 8-line stanzas. In bk. 1 the scribe did not copy lines 158–206 (7 stanzas) and lines 697–703 (1 stanza). Here also he copied lines 214–55 (f. 200^{rv}: 6 stanzas) before lines 123–57, 207–13, and lines 382–423 (f. 204^{rv}: 6 stanzas) before lines 339–81: probably in the exemplar the second bifolium of a quire was misplaced after the third bifolium. Lines 1037–43 of bk. 3 are illustrated by a pen and ink drawing of Edmund and Sweyn in a castle room (f. 272^{v}). In the last stanza of the prayer line 5 reads 'And to Sixte herry Ioye and felycyte' (edn., p. 439, bk. 3, line 1517).

6. ff. 284^{v}–285^{v} Stella celi extirpauit Que lactauit Dominum. Thow hevenly quene of grace owre loode sterre . . . for her merytes save us fro Pestylence. Amen et Explicit secundum Lydgate.

IMEV, no. 3673. Seven 8-line stanzas. Printed from this copy by C. Brown, *Religious lyrics of the fifteenth century*, 1939, pp. 208–10.

7. ff. 286–287^v De sancta Maria contra pestilenciam. O hevynly sterre. most Comfortable of lyght . . . Off grace and mercy be w^t vs present Amen. Explicit secundum Lydgate God grawnte vs grace quod Willelmus Cotson Canonicus.

IMEV, no. 2459. Eleven 7-line stanzas. Printed from this copy by Brown, op. cit., pp. 206–8. Both leaves are damaged.

ff. iii + 287 + iv. Paper and—for the outside and middle sheets of each quire—parchment. ff. 288–9 are medieval parchment flyleaves. 185 × 125 mm (parchment) and 197 × 130 mm (paper). Written space *c.* 150 mm high. Three stanzas (21 lines) to a page, as a rule. Collation: 1 five (ff. 1–5) 2–8^{20} 9^{14} (ff. 146–59) 10^{20} (ff. 160–79) 11^{20} wants 1 before f. 180 12^{20} 13^{18} + 1 leaf after 17 (f. 236) 14 ten (ff. 238–47) 15–16^{20}. In quires 2–16 every leaf of every quire is signed at the head of the recto with its quire and leaf number, for example (f. 18) 'Quaterno 1° folio 13°'. An expert current mixture of anglicana and secretary by William Cotson, canon of Dunstable, O.S.A. 2-line initials, either red or of flourished pen-work in the ink of the text. The latter are touched with red, as is the capital letter which begins each line of verse. Gilt red morocco binding, s. xviii: one of the ornaments, two linked Cs, back to back below a crown, is used on the spine as well as on the sides. Secundo folio (f. 7) *Of aurora*.

'Iste liber pertinet dompno Willelmo Cotson Canonico et propriis ipsius manibus scriptus extitit', f. 86; also 'Willelmus Cotson de Dunstaple Canonicus', ff. 261^v–262, and 'Libellus W^i Cotson de Dunstaple Canonici', f. 274^v, and other similar inscriptions in the hand of the text. Cotson also gives his name in five colophons and dates four of them: see above.

6711 (Mun. A. 4. 107). *Mandeville's Travels (in English)* s. xv^1

Here begynneth the book of Iohn Mawndevyle knyght the whilk techeth the right way to ierusalem fro diuerse c[ont]re[s] and of the maruay[les] off ynde. and of diu*er*site off the contr'. off the grete chame and off the sawdon of babyloyne . . . For als mekel as the land ouer the se that ys to say the holyland . . . (f. 79^v) god w^{t}outen ende. Amen. here endeth the book of Iohn Maundevyle knyght of wayes to Ierusalem and of þe meruayles of ynde and of other contres translatus in anglicum de lingua Gallicana.

The English translation of Mandeville's Travels, edited last by M. C. Seymour, 1967: this copy listed by him and assigned to Sub-group D (p. 275). ff. 80–82^v left blank: 80 and 82^v were filled with notes, s. xv/xvi, the first of them 'in thys bok ben vii quayrres . . . her ben in thys bok iii skore leffys and xviii leffys And more than halfe a leffe'.

ff. ii + 82 + ii. 193 × 136 mm. Written space *c.* 145 × 92 mm. 2 cols. 30 lines. Collation: 1–4^{12} 5^{10} 6–7^{12}. Written in anglicana formata by one hand. 4-line or 3-line red initials. Binding of s. xix. Secundo folio *the whilk*.

Written in England. 'Iste liber constat `Ed*mundo* Wyghton Militi'', f. 80, s. xv ex.[1] 'Gerard legh', f. 2, s. xvi.

[1] Not, Dr Doyle tells me, recorded in the will of Sir Edmund Wighton, 1484 (PCC 21 Logge).

6712 (Mun. A. 6. 89). *M. Paris, Flores historiarum; etc.*

s. xiii med.–xiv^{1}

1. ff. 1–6^{v} A graded Sarum calendar, s. xiii ex., in blue and red, the two colours alternating, adapted for use at the abbey of Westminster, O.S.B., by new and altered entries and changes of grading. The process of alteration was completed only for Jan.–July. For Aug.–Dec. only the stage of erasure was reached and there are no new names or gradings.

Original entries include the Conception of B.V.M. and 'Eductio ihesu de egypto' (8 Dec., 9 Jan.); also (erased) Edith and Hugh (16 Sept., 17 Nov.). Original gradings were for double feasts, feasts of nine lessons ('ix' always erased, but still legible at 21 Sept. (Matthew) and opposite an erased name at 4 Oct.), feasts of three lessons, and commemorations.

Added entries, s. xiv, include Milburga (23 Feb.: twelve lessons) and the feast of relics (16 July) and gradings 'in capis' (with numbers), 'in albis' and for twelve and three lessons and 'commemmoratio'. The gradings differ occasionally from *Missale Westm.*, I. v–xi.

In s. xv a hand added royal obits and coronations, none later than the coronation of Henry VI, 6 Nov. 1429.

2. ff. 7–295^{v} Incipit prologus in librum qui flores hystoriarum intitulatur. Temporum summam lineamque descendentem ab exordio mundi . . . promtissime receperunt.

Matthew Paris, Flores historiarum, continued to 1326. Printed from this copy (*Ch.*) by H. R. Luard (RS 95 (1890): 3 vols.): described in I. xii–xv and by R. Vaughan, *Matthew Paris*, 1958, pp. 92–101. The text was written at one time to 1241 and by Paris himself (scribe 3) from 1241 to 1249 and was continued at intervals, first at St Albans in 1249–50 and 1265 (?) and then at Westminster. Throughout there are many later additions in the margins and sometimes in the text space.

The St Albans part, ff. 7–239, is probably by six scribes:

MS.	Edn.	Date
1. ff. 7–19^{v} felici pertina-	i. 1–73/35	
2. ff. 20 cia restituerentur–170va annotantur	i. 73/35–ii. 250/2	
3. ff. 170vb Eodemque–200va nunciet etas	ii. 250/3–361/14	1241–9
4. f. 200vb Tempore quoque–201rb/23 faleratis	ii. 361/15–363/34	1249
5. f. 201rb/24 et bigis–38 remeauit	ii. 363/34–364/15	1249–50
6. ff. 201va Comes Ricardus–239ra/33 Segraue	ii. 364/16–iii. 6/19	1251–65

The Westminster part is probably by ten scribes (7–16), the last of whom added a bifolium (ff. 259–60), probably as a substitute for cancelled leaves of quire 24:

MS.	Edn.	Date
7. ff. 239ra/33 Bellow igitur–240rb uiolenter	iii. 6/20–11/23	1265–7
8. ff. 240va Ipsos–247vb/23 Aedwardi	iii. 11/23–44/24	1267–74
9. ff. 247vb/24 Que per–248vb/26 postularunt	iii. 44/25–51/25	1274–8
10. ff. 248vb/26 cuius postulacio–250va/31 ornabatur	iii. 51/25–61/11	1278–84
11. f. 250va/31 Iste alfonsus–250vb/33 tuta	iii. 61/11–62/22	1284
12. ff. 250vb/34 Anno gracie mcclxxxv–254va/26 circumduxit	iii. 62/25–86/26	1285–93
13. ff. 254va/27 Circa festum–258rb/17 imponi	iii. 87/3–103/3	1293–7
14. f. 258rb/17 Comitibus–258vb austrie	iii. 103/4–104/33	1297–8

16. f. 259ra belloque–260vb futurorum	iii. 104/34–112/22	1298–1302
15. f. 261ra Anno gracie–294vb/26 mercedem	iii. 112/26–232/21	1303–25
17. ff. 294vb/26 Sic que–295^{v} receperunt. Changes of ink after *procedit* (232/30) and *suspensus fuit* (234/19).	iii. 232/22–30, 232/31–234/19, 234/20–235/33	1325–6

Parts of ten pages, ff. 53, 115^{v}, 123^{v}, 126^{v}, 129, 133, 135^{v}, 141, 144^{v}, 247^{v}, contain coronation pictures of Arthur, Edward the Confessor, William I, William II, Henry I, Stephen, Henry II, Richard I, John, and Edward I, reproduced by A. Hollaender, 'The pictorial work in the Flores Historiarum', *BJRL* xxviii (1944), 361–81, and plates i–vi. The last picture, 'much weaker', is in the Westminster part of the manuscript. Cf. also Vaughan (1958), pp. 224–5, and *MERT*, p. 19 and pl. 4*a* showing the picture on f. 115^{v}.

3 (added, s. xv ex.). ff. 296–7 De penitencia Regis Anglie pro marterio Archipresulis. Diuulgato igitur letali facto . . . inflammante corruissent.

Excerpts from the 'Second quadrilogus', corresponding to *Materials for the history of Thomas Becket*, iv (RS 67, 1879), 413–416/8 *fumigant* and 409–410/33. f. 297^{v} blank.

4. Flyleaf notes in English, s. xv: (*a*) f. iv Memorandum of the descent of Richard (earl of Cambridge, †1415), son of Edmund Langley, duke of York, from Henry III; (*b*) f. iv^{v} Abiuracio publica confessio domini Reginaldi Pecoke Episcopi Cicestren'. In the name of þ^{e} holy trinite . . . into þ^{e} example and terrour of all other etc.

(*b*). At Paul's Cross, 4 Dec. 1457. Printed in a modernized form in C. Babington's introduction to Pecock's Repressor (RS 19, 1860), I. xlvii–xlviii.

ff. iv + 295 + iv. ff. ii–iv, 296–8 are medieval endleaves: 298^{v} was pasted down. An older foliation used by Vaughan and others is two or three above that now in use. Medieval column numbering of ff. 1–258rb at first in ink over pencil and from f. 81^{v} ('298') in pencil, 1–1009. 250 × 190 mm. Written space *c.*200 × 130 mm. 2 cols. 38–43 lines. The first line of writing is above the top ruled line on ff. 171–201^{r}, that is to say in the part of the manuscript written by Matthew Paris: cf. N. R. Ker in *Celtica*, v (1961), 15–16. Collation: 1^{6} $2–5^{12}$ 6^{16} $7–14^{12}$ 15^{10} 16 ten (ff. 177–86) 17, 18 doubtful (ff. 187–203: the central bifolia are 190–1 and 199–200) $19–21^{12}$ (ff. 204–39) $22–23^{8}$ 24 three (ff. 256–8) 25^{2} (ff. 259–60, an insertion: see above) $26–27^{12}$ 28^{12} wants 12, perhaps blank, after f. 295.

For the scribes of art. 2, see above: (3) is Matthew Paris; (4, 5) are unskilled; (6) was perhaps a professional scribe: for (3) see R. Vaughan, 'The handwriting of Matthew Paris', *Transactions of the Cambridge Bibliographical Society*, i (1953), 376–94, with facsimile, pl. XVIII*c*, of part of f. 188 (formerly f. 191): facsimile of f. 173 (formerly f. 176) by T. D. Hardy, *Catalogue of materials relating to the history of Great Britain*, iii (RS 26, 1871), pl. XVIII.

Ten pictures (see above). Initials on ff. 7–203: (i) gold on blue and pink grounds; (ii) 2-line, red or blue, plain or with ornament of the other colour; (iii) on ff. 170^{v}–191^{v}, 202^{v}–203, 1-line, red or blue. Initials on ff. 204–238^{v}: 3-line or 2-line, red or blue with ornament of the other colour. Initials on ff. 239–247^{v}, 250^{v}–295^{v}, 2-line, red. Initials on ff. 247^{v}–250: 2-line, red or blue with ornament of the other colour. Capital letters in the ink of the text are filled with red on ff. 7–200^{v} and sometimes on ff. 201 onwards. Binding of s. xix. Secundo folio (f. 8) *Burgund'*.

Written at the Benedictine abbeys of St Albans and Westminster: see above. 'Iste liber est ecclesie beati petri Westm' ', f. 1, s. xv. 'Dnompnus (*sic*) T. Gardener Anno Domini m. 503°

... In vigilia Sancti I. Baptist' and 'R. Teddyngton', f. 298: for these people see E. H. Pearce, *The Monks of Westminster*, 1916. 'Liber Westmonasterii / siue / Flores historiarum / per Matthhæum Westmonasteriensem / Alias Florigerum / Collecti Ex dono / Nicholai Higginbotome / De Stockport Generosi et ibidem seneschalli / 1657', f. iii. *CMA* ii, no. 7148. *MERT*, no. 13.

6713 (Mun. E. 8. 21). *Missale Sarisburiense* s. xiv ex.

Fragments of a large and very handsome missal. The calendar, the ordinary and canon of mass, and all but two leaves of the sanctoral are missing, and the temporal lacks more than twenty leaves. According to the Governors' minutes, December 1848, mutilated leaves were removed before rebinding in 1845 and further mutilations took place after rebinding.

1. ff. 1–107v Temporal, beginning imperfectly in the full rubric for the first Sunday in Advent 'euangelium. facie crucifixi ad ipsum legentem conuersa. Quandocumque uero legitur epistola in pulpito'.

The secret for the second Sunday after Epiphany is Ut tibi grata.

2. ff. 107v–108v In dedicatione ecclesie, ending imperfectly.

3. ff. 109–110v Sanctoral, beginning in the secret for All Saints, 1 Nov., and ending in the secret for Edmund, king and martyr, 20 Nov.: *Sarum Missal*, pp. 342/16–347/23.

4. ff. 111–23 Common of saints beginning imperfectly 'et comodat' (*Sarum Missal*, p. 358/12).

5. ff. 123v–132v Votive masses,[1] ending imperfectly and with a gap after f. 131: (4–6) B.V.M., with heading 'Ordinacio misse cotidiane beate marie uirginis que dicitur Salue sancta parens. pulsato . . .'; (1) Ad missam de trinitate; (3) Holy Cross (with long rubric); (2) Holy Spirit; (7) Pro fratribus et sororibus; (11) Ad missam de pace; (28) Ad missam pro serenitate aeris; (27) Ad missam ad pluuiam postulandam; (43) In tempore belli; (23) Pro quacumque tribulacione; (p. 459) De angelis, ending imperfectly, f. 131v; (13) *(Pro prelatis et subditis); (15) *Pro rege; (16) *Pro rege et regina; (17) Pro semetipso sacerdote; (18) *Item . . . pro semetipso, ending imperfectly.

6. ff. 133–136v Marriage service, beginning imperfectly in the rubric 'ante ostium ecclesie coram deo sacerdote et populo'.

English forms on f. 133. The rubric on second marriages, f. 135v, is said here, as usual, to have been determined in 1321 and brought to England by master John Haystede: cf. *Manuale Sarum*, pp. 55–7.

[1] An asterisk shows that only collect, secret, and postcommunion are provided. For the numbers and page reference in brackets see below, All Souls College, Oxford, 302.

7. ff. 136^{v}–138 Ordo ad seruicium peregrinorum faciendum.

Manuale Sarum, pp. 60–3.

8. ff. 138–9 Ordo ad uisitandum infirmum. In primus induat se . . .

Manuale Sarum, pp. 99–107.

9. f. 139^{rv} Priusquam ungatur infirmum . . . ut nec ad corrupcionem (*ends imperfectly*).

Manuale Sarum, pp. 107–9/7 (Extreme unction).

10. f. 140^{rv} (*begins imperfectly*) exuta contagiis . . . intrabunt in eam. Quibus peractis. dicantur uigilie mortuorum et postea completorium de die more solito.

Cf. *Manuale Sarum*, pp. 121/5–124/35 (Commendation of souls).

11. f. 140^{v} Ubi uero in die sepulture deportatur corpus ad ecclesiam: tunc immediate post predictam orationem scilicet Suscipe domine seruum tuum tunc dicitur commendacio animarum sollempniter hoc modo. A'. Requiem eternam . . .

Manuale Sarum, pp. 143–52 (Commendation of soul and mass for the dead).

12. ff. 143^{v}–145 Collect, secret, and postcommunion of masses for the dead on special occasions.

Of the nineteen sets in *Sarum Missal*, pp. 434–42, nos. 2–4, 6, 7, 5, 10, 13 are here in that order on ff. 143^{v}–144^{v}: no. 13 ends imperfectly. f. 145 begins in the collect of the mass *Pro quibus orare tenemur* (cf. below, Oxford, Corpus Christi College 394, art. 11). Fidelium (*Sarum Missal*, no. 18) follows.

13. ff. 145–146^{v} Item Missa Generalis.

Four forms. *Sarum Missal*, pp. 442–5.

14. ff. 146^{v}–147^{v} Ad missam pro defunctis. quando corpus adest presens accedant . . . ab infernalibus claus (*ends imperfectly*).

Sarum Missal, pp. 446–8/12.

ff. ii + 147 + ii. 522 × 360 mm. Written space 395 × 230 mm. 2 cols. 36 lines. Quires normally of eight leaves, but of the twenty-four remaining quires only 1, 2, 4, 8, 9, 16 are complete (ff. 1–16, 23–30, 49–64, 96–103). Written in an elaborate hand: the crosses at each end of the horizontal stroke of *x*, of the nota for *et* and of the abbreviation for *per* are remarkable. Some quires marked 'cor' at the end. Initials: (i) on now missing leaves; (ii) 2-line, patterned blue or pink on grounds of punched gold, decorated and with short ivy-sprig and acorn prolongations; (iii) 1-line, gold on coloured grounds. The decoration of cadels with green penwork, the fillings of capital letters in the ink of the text with colour, usually green and yellow, and the frames to catchwords are all unusually elaborate: thirteen framed catchwords remain, ff. 8^{v}, 16^{v}, 22^{v}, 30^{v}, 37^{v}, 56^{v}, 70^{v}, 95^{v}, 103^{v}, 112^{v}, 119^{v}, 126^{v}, 137^{v}. Line fillers blue, red, and gold. Binding of 1845: see above.

Written in England.

6714 (Mun. A. 4. 106). *Comment. in Ovidii Metamorphoseos* s. xv² (1470?)

Ars Ovidii methamor^eos continet xv libros parciales et quilibet illorum continet plura capitula . . . (f. 6ᵛ) In noua fert animus etc. Ouidius hic wlt incipere materiam suam dicens quod . . . (f. 147) presagia viuam. Et sic finitur liber methamor[. . .] ad aliqualem expositus et translatus a quodam libro in gallico quem compilauit magister phi de vilaco.

ff. 1–6 contain a summary of the fifteen books. The commentaries on them begin on ff. 6ᵛ, 16ᵛ, 22ᵛ, 28, 36ᵛ, 44ᵛ, 52ᵛ, 62ᵛ, 70ᵛ, 78, 85ᵛ, 94ᵛ, 102, 116, 133ᵛ. The first word or two of lemmata underlined in red. Writing damp-stained and faded throughout. f. 147, torn, contains two 2-line epitaphs on Ovid, 'Hic ego qui iaceo . . .' and 'Ac tu qui transis . . .', after which the scribe wrote in blacker ink 'Anno domini M 1470 finitus est p[. . .]'.

ff. i + 147 + i. Paper. 202 × 145 mm. Written space *c.*155 × 100 mm. 34 long lines. No visible ruling. Collation impracticable. Written in a set round cursive with, usually, straight ascenders. 3-line red initials. Capital letters in the ink of the text touched with red. Bound by W. Boddington, Todd St., Manchester, in s. xix.

Written in France.

6717 (Mun. A. 6. 74). *Psalterium; Horae; etc.* s. xv med.

1. ff. 1–97 Psalms 1–150.

2. ff. 97–107 Six ferial canticles, followed by Te deum, Benedicite, Benedictus, Magnificat, Nunc dimittis, Quicumque vult.

3. ff. 107–116 Litanies.

A special set of names is provided for each weekday, Tuesday–Saturday, nearly as in *Brev. ad Usum Sarum*, ii. 255–9, but 'Terenciana' is a thirteenth virgin on Wednesday. Thomas apostle has been erased, f. 107ᵛ, instead of Thomas martyr, f. 111!

4. ff. 116–126ᵛ Hours of B.V.M. of the use of (Sarum).

Memoriae after lauds of Holy Spirit, Holy Trinity, Holy Cross, Michael, John Baptist, John Evangelist, Peter and Paul, Andrew, apostles (naming James, Bartholomew, Philip, James), martyrs (naming Vincent, George, Alphege, Blaise, Pantaleon, Christopher, Quintin, Denis, Leger, Polycarp), Nicholas, Julian hospitaller, confessors (naming Gregory, Ambrose, Jerome, Augustine, Benedict, Leonard, Giles, Hilary, Remigius, Germanus, Audoenus, Severinus, Julian), Katherine, Margaret, and Mary Magdalene (Katerina margareta uirginis (*sic*) sanctissime . . . : not in *RH*), virgins (naming Margaret, Katherine, Agatha, Agnes, Lucy, Cecilia, Juliana, Radegund, Mildred, Bridget), relics, All Saints, peace. Hours of Holy Cross worked in. Cross references to leaf numbers of art. 1 in the margins, as also in arts. 6, 10.

5. (*a*) f. 126ᵛ Salue regina . . . ; (*b*) ff. 126ᵛ–127 Virgo mater ecclesie . . . , and prayer 'Omnipotens sempiterne deus qui gloriose uirginis marie . . .'; (*c*) f. 127ᵛ Gaude uirgo mater cristi . . . ; (*d*) f. 128ʳᵛ De sancta maria. Gaude flore uirginali Honoreque *spirit*uali (*sic*) . . .

(*a–d*). *RH*, nos. 18147, 21818, 7017, 6809.

6. ff. 128v–133v Hours of Holy Spirit.

Hymn at matins Ueni creator spiritus mentes tuorum . . .

7. ff. 133v–135 Hic incipiunt mat' de sancta trinitate . . . Hympnus. Quicumque uult animam firmiter saluare . . .

Hours of Holy Trinity. *RH*, no. 16566.

8. f. 135rv In manus tuas et in misericordia tua domine deus meus creator . . . et consolacionem. Cf. *Lyell Cat.*, p. 383.

9. ff. 135v–136 Dicitur oracio sequens quam fecit sanctus bonefacius papa (*erased*) quartus et concessit omnibus uere confessis . . . Gracias tibi ago domine ihesu criste qui uoluisti pro redempcione mundi . . . Cf. *Lyell Cat.*, p. 63.

10. ff. 136–142v Hic incipiunt uigilie mortuorum. Office of the dead.

11. f. 142v Commendacio animarum. Beati immaculati . . . Tibi domine commendamus animas famulorum famularumque tuarum et animas (*ends imperfectly*). *Manuale Sarum*, pp. 143–4/1.

12. ff. 143–6 Fifteen Oes of St Bridget, beginning imperfectly in the first O, followed by 'Bona oracio. Gracias tibi ago domine ihesu criste qui passionem tuam . . .'.

13. ff. 146–148v. Oracio. Aue uirgo graciosa stella celi clarior . . . (206 lines). *RH*, no. 2215. f. 149rv left blank.

ff. ii + 149 + ii. A medieval foliation in red, incorrect after 'lxxxv', ends at 'cxv' (f. 106). 272 × 196 mm. Written space 182 × 125 mm. 21 long lines (24 on ff. 143–48). Collation: $1\text{–}3^8$ 4^8 wants 2 after f. 25 $5\text{–}17^8$ 18^8 wants 8 after f. 142 19^8 wants 1 before f. 143. The hand changes at f. 80 (quire 11^1): catchwords are to be seen after this. Initials: (i) 5-line (ff. 1, 116), 4-line (Pss. 26, 38, 52, 68, 80, 97, 109) and 3-line (Ps. 51), in colours, including green and brick red, on gold grounds decorated in colours and with prolongations (forming a continuous border on f. 1); (ii) 2-line, gold with violet ornament or blue with red ornament. Line fillers in red and blue. Binding of s. xix. Secundo folio *circumdantis*.

Written in England. 'Istud psalterium dedit Iohannes Gyste armiger ad vsum monialium monasterii Sancti Iohannis baptiste de Godestow (O.S.B.) et si quis illud alienauerit a dicto monasterio anathema sit amen', f. 148v, s. xv. Frere, no. 633.

6720 (Mun. A. 6. 59). *Terentius* 1427

1. ff. 1–3v A preliminary damp-stained quire, containing: (*a*) f. 1 A notice of Terence, 'Terentius genere extitit afer ciuis cartaginensis . . . captarent fauorem'; (*b*) f. 1 A note on why the first play is called Andria, 'Fabula prima andria . . .'; (*c*) f. 1 Six couplets on the plays, 'Andria quod roma (?) . . . captus amore sue'; (*d*) ff. 1–3v Prose introductions to each play: (Andria) Orto bello athenis . . . ;

(Eunuchus) Quo tempore (?) [. . .] hec fabula . . . uti personis; (Heauton Timorumenos) Acta est . . . emulorum respondet; (Adelphi) Acta est . . . plenius legendo uidebuntur; (Hecyra) Hechira dicta a loco . . . quem peperit philomena; (Phormio) Argumentum istius fabule . . . plenissime manifestabi[t]. Expliciunt e[. . . .] sex infrascriptarum comediarum.

2. ff. 4–83 The six plays: f. 4 'Andria'; f. 17v 'Eunucus'; f. 32 'Eutuntumerumenos'; f. 45v 'Adelphe'; f. 58 'Hechira'; f. 69v 'Phormio'. Argumenta before and 'Caliopius recensui' after each play. Andria is preceded by the epitaph on Terence 'Natus in excelsis . . . cautus erit', ed. E. Baehrens, *Poetae Latini minores*, v. 385. f. 83 ends 'Mccccxxvii die ultima maii. Explicit liber terencii Deo gracias Amen'.

The argumenta are: (Andria) 'Sororem . . . coniugem'; (Eunuchus) 'Meretrix . . . illuditur' and 'Sororem . . . ephebo'; (Heauton.) 'In miliciam . . . accepit'; (Adelphi) 'Duos cum . . . duro suo demea'; (Hecyra) 'Uxorem . . . cum filio'; (Phormio) 'Cremetis . . . agnitam'. Running numbers I–VI. Leaves at the end damaged by damp. f. 83v blank.

ff. iv + 83 + ii. 295 × 200 mm. Written space 192 × 100 mm. 34 long lines. Collation: 1^4 wants 1, perhaps blank, $2–11^8$. Initials: (i) 10-line, beginning plays, red and pink on blue and gold grounds, decorated; (ii) 2-line, blue with red ornament or red with violet ornament. English binding, s. xix, with Chetham arms as centrepiece. The direction on f. 1, 'Marble paper and Board leather on ye back' refers to an older binding. Secundo folio (f. 2) illegible; (f. 5) *Quin tu*.

Written in Italy in 1427.

6721 (Mun. A. 4. 109). *Terentius* s. xv/xvi

The six plays: f. 1 'Andria'; f. 22v 'Eunuchus'; f. 44v 'Heautontimorumenos'; f. 66v 'Phormio'; f. 89v 'Adelphis'; f. 111 'Ecyra'. Argumenta before and 'Calliopius recensui' after each play.

The arguments are: (Andria) 'Sororem . . . coniugem'; (Eunuchus) 'Meretrix . . . illuditur'; (Heauton Timorumenos) 'In militiam . . . accipit'; (Phormio) 'Cremetis . . . agnitam a patruo'; (Adelphi) 'Duos quum . . . duro demea'; (Hecyra) 'Uxorem . . . cum filio'. Leaves at the end damaged by damp. f. 129v blank.

ff. iv + 129 + iv. ff. (iv) and 130 are parchment flyleaves. 157 × 120 mm. Written space 112 × 72 mm. 29 long lines. Collation: 1^8 wants 1 $2–16^8$ 17 two (ff. 128–9). Written in set hybrida. Initials: (i) beginning argumenta and plays, in patterned blue, pink, or magenta on coloured grounds, with sprays into the margins; (ii) 2-line, blue or metallic red. Red morocco binding, s. xvii/xviii. Secundo folio *Propterea*.

Written in Germany, probably. 'Iste liber pertinet [. . .] Si quis inueniat. amore dei [. . .]edeat', f. 129, in an English hand, s. xvi.

6722 (Mun. A. 4. 92). *P. Cantor, Verbum abbreviatum* s. xiii in.

1. ff. 1–134v De breuitate (?) [. . . .] in uerbis et eorum superfluitate. Titulus primus. Verbum abbreuiatum fecit dominus super terram. Si enim uerbum de

sinu patris . . . insufficientes et inualidi sumus (*ends abruptly at the foot of the page*).

Stegmüller, no. 6447. Bloomfield, no. 6387. *PL* ccv. 23–366/1. The last words are in ch. 'cxlv' (edn., ch. 152). f. 135^{rv} blank.

2. (*a*) ff. 136^{v}–137^{v} Quelibet persona uerbi personalis regit nominatiuum casum . . . vt doceo te gramaticam. (*b*) f. 138^{r} Notes on Ps. 1 and on confession.

(*a, b*) in one hand. (*a*), notes on grammar, includes the words 'Vbi es? rome. Rothomagi. Lundoniis. Vernone . . .' and four mnemonic verses to illustrate *Quo, Qua, Ubi, Unde*, 'Romam. Rothamagum. Vernonem tendit athenas . . .'. ff. 136^{r}, 138^{v} blank.

ff. ii + 138 + ii. ff. ii, 139 are medieval leaves, flyleaf and pastedown respectively. 240 × 160 mm. Written space 170 × 100 mm. 33 long lines. The first line of writing is above the top ruled line. Collation: 1–13^{10} 14 five (ff. 131–5: 134–5 are a bifolium) 15 three (ff. 136–8: 137–8 are a bifolium). Quires 1–13 numbered at the end in red. Art. 2 is semi-current. Initials: (i) f. 1, silver on punched gold ground decorated in colours and gold; (ii) outside the written space, gold (rarely) or red with blue ornament or blue with red ornament. Binding of wooden boards, perhaps medieval, but covered with brown leather in s. xviii (?). Secundo folio *hereticum. tum*.

Written in England. 'Decimus octauus liber Tercii gradus', f. ii^{v}, s. xv.[1] 'Andrew Barton' is named in a scribble on f. 139, s. xvi in. 'Will' Drake', f. ii^{v}, s. xvii.

6723 (Mun. A. 2. 160). *New Testament (in English)* s. xv in.

1. ff. 2–11^{v} Here biginniþ a rule þat telliþ in whiche chaptris of þe newe testament ȝe may fynde þe pistils and gospels þat ben red in þe chirche at masse after þe use of salisbiry . . . and a clause of þe ending þerof also. First sunday in aduent . . .

A table giving the first and last words of lessons of 'dominicals and ferials', 'commemoracions' and the 'propre' (of saints), but not the common of saints.

2. ff. 12–291^{v} The New Testament in the later Wycliffite version, with the usual prologues.

Forshall and Madden, no. 143. Chapters are divided by letter-marks in the margins *a–g* or *a–e*, but the letters are often omitted, if they do not serve to show the beginning of a lesson: thus only *c* and *d* are written against Mt. 7 and only *a*, *b*, and *e* against Mt. 8. The first and last words of lessons are covered with a pale yellow wash and the point at which a lesson ends is marked also by a pair of strokes in the margin.

ff. iv + 290 + iv, foliated i–iii, 1–291, (292–5). ff. 1, 292–3 are medieval parchment flyleaves. 178 × 126 mm. Written space 122 × 82 mm. 2 cols. 30 lines. Collation of ff. 2–291: 1^{10} 2–26^{8} 27^{8} 6, 7 cancelled after f. 216 28–35^{8} 36^{10}. Quires 2–34 signed a–z, þ, ⁊, ɔ, 1–7. Probably all in one hand. Initials: (i) of books, handsome, in colour on gold grounds, decorated and with prolongations in gold and colours, which, sometimes, form a continuous

[1] B.L., Royal 2 D. xxvii has the mark 'xxxviii liber tercii gradus': facsimile in *New Palaeographical Society*, i, pl. 17 (10*c*).

border; (ii) of the prologue to the Gospels on f. 12, gold on coloured ground; (iii) of other prologues and of chapters, 3-line, blue with red ornament. Capital letters in the ink of the text filled with pale yellow. Binding of s. xix. Secundo folio *Sunday* (f. 3) or *biut* (f. 13).

Written in England. 'Margret Elyngbrygge wrytt thys wyth her owne honde', f. 1, s. xvi. 'Codice hoc MS^{to} Bibliothecam Chethamensem ornauit vir Reverendus Joannes Clayton A:M: 1732' f. iii.

8001 (Mun. A. 4. 94). *Aristotle, Ethica* s. xv med.

Premissio quædam ad euidentiam noue translationis. Aristotelis ethicorum libros facere latinos nuper instituti . . . (f. 5) cum antea non essent. Ad sanctissimum. ac beatissimum patrem dominum martinum papam v leonardi aretini prephatio in libros ethicorum lege feliciter. Non nouum esse constat . . . quædam præmisi. Omnis ars omnisque doctrina . . . (f. 135^{v}) et quibus legibus et moribus. Explicit feliciter.

Leonardo Bruni's translation: printed often (*GKW*, nos. 2367–9). The two prefaces printed also by Hans Baron, *Leonardo Bruni Aretino*, Leipzig 1928, pp. 75–81. Six (?) leaves missing after f. 26 contained the end of bk. 1 and beginning of bk. 2. The few marginalia there are well written. ff. 136–137^{v} blank.

ff. ii + 137 + ii. 240 × 167 mm. Written space 165 × 100 mm. 26 long lines ruled with a stylus. Double vertical bounding lines. Collation: 1–2^{10} 3^{4} 4 four (the two outer bifolia) 5–14^{10} 15^{10} wants 10, blank. Quires signed by letters at the end. Initials to books 4-line, gold on blue and brown grounds, decorated with white vine-stem interlace: usually a butterfly or bird has alighted on a corner of the ground (cf. *Humanistic Script* (Bodleian Picture Book, no. 12, 1960), pl. 8). Binding of s. xix bearing ticket of 'Wilde, Book-binder, Manchester'. Secundo folio *ut de*.

Written in Italy.

8002 (Mun. A. 4. 90). *Aeschines (in Latin)* s. xv med.

'Oratio Aeschinis contra demosthenem a Leonardo Aretino'. Quanti conatus parentur . . . (f. 32^{v}) ex dictis et omissis iuste pro re.p. decernatis. Explicit deo gratias Amen.

Printed with Cicero, De oratore, in 1485 and 1488: *GKW*, nos. 6750–1. Much damaged by damp. ff. 33–40 blank, except for the words 'Charte xxviiii sine coopertorio' on f. 39^{v}.

ff. ii + 40 + i. f. ii is a parchment flyleaf bearing offset of writing on f. 1. 237 × 160 mm. Written space 150 × 100 mm. 25 long lines. Collation: 1–4^{10}. Upright textura. The only initial is a 3-line red *Q* on f. 1. Italian binding of wooden boards covered with stamped brown leather: rebacked: central clasp.

Written in Italy.

8003 (Mun. A. 4. 102). *Iacobus de Cessolis, O.P., etc.* s. xv^2

1. ff. 1–15v (*text*) Loqui prohibeor. et tacere non possum . . . (f. 1v) Incipit exposicio eiusdem epistole. Pro quo sciendum est quod si queratur an valerius fuerit ille qui historias romanorum scripsit prosaice. siue valerius marcialis poeta dubium non est hunc valerium et Ruphinum familiares fuisse. qui quidem valerius (*text ends*, f. 15) sed ne horresten (*sic*) scripsisse videar. Vale . . . (*commentary ends*) rugose frontis et tristis offenditque correptos etc. Explicit Epistola Valerii ad Ruphinum de vxore non ducenda.

Walter Map's Dissuasio Valerii, included by him in his De nugis curialium: ed. M. R. James, 1914, pp. 143–58/6 (chapters 3, 4, and part of chapter 5 of De nugis). Eight chapters here, each followed by a commentary. The commentary is that ascribed in Cambridge, U.L., Ff. 6. 12 to John Ridewall: cf. R. Dean in *Mediaeval and Renaissance Studies*, ii (1950), 130–1, and James, op. cit., pp. xxxii–iii. Queens' College, Cambridge, 10 is another unascribed copy.

2. ff. 16–63v Multorum fratrum ordinis nostri . . . huius ludi scaccorum. Explicit prologus. Inter omnia mala signa in homine . . . optimum et perfectum. Deo igitur sit honor . . . amen. Explicit tractatus super ludo scaccorum.

Iacobus de Cessolis, De ludo scaccorum, ed. Köpke 1871 and often earlier. *SOPMA*, no. 2066.

3. ff. 64–80v Historia Daretis Frigii Entilii historiographi de uastacione Troie in greco facta et a Cornelio nepote salustii de greco in latinum sermonem translata. Incipit prologus. Cornelius nepos salustio crispo suo salutem. Cum volumina multa legerem athenis curiose . . . reuertamur etc. Incipit historia Troianorum Frigii de greco translata in latinum a Cornelio. Peleus rex fuit in poloponenso opido qui esonem fratrem habuit . . . Diomedes mesten et alios quinque hucusque historia daretis frigii perscripta est quam athenis litteris mandauit.

Dares Phrygius, Historia troianorum, with the two supplementary paragraphs: cf. *Catalogue of Romances*, i. 12–25. The present copy, in thirty-eight paragraphs, has a title like B.L., Burney 280 (*Cat.*, p. 21).

4. ff. 81–98 Superius autem excidio secundum daretem explicito Iter Enee In Italiam casusque quidam Paulus persequitur. Eneas ergo cum Anchise . . . Rome subiecta esse. Explicit tractatus tractans de itinere Enee post discidium troie.

5. ff. 98v–99v Three paragraphs headed: (*a*) Diuisio orbis inter filios Noe; (*b*) De concepcione et natiuitate Cristi; (*c*) De etatibus mundi.

6. ff. 100–15 Gesta Alexandri. Nectanabus Rex egipti peritissimus in astrologia et mathematica . . . spiritum exalauit etc. Expliciunt gesta Alexandri.

Printed from this copy by S. H. Thomson, 'An unnoticed abridgment of the Historia de preliis', *Univ. of Colorado Studies*, i (1941), 241–59. f. 115v left blank.

7. ff. 116–123v Quia consulit apostolus hebreos . . . Aluredus anno regni sui 18 mortuus est et anno domini 441 (*sic*) et anno domini 106 (*sic*) venit Willelmus conquestor etc.

An amplified version of the (legendary) history of the founding of the University of Cambridge printed by Thomas Hearne in *Thomae Sprotti Chronica* (1719), pp. 246–79. The present copy includes many references to Alfred of Beverley, Giraldus Cambrensis, Bede, Geoffrey of Monmouth, and William of Malmesbury. 'E. Br.' wrote on f. 115ᵛ, s. xvii, 'Sequitur historia Academiæ Cantabrigiensis vocata Niger Academiæ Codex. de hoc plura apud Londinensem eius defensorem, et Twinum eius aduersarium' and a later hand added a reference to Hearne's edition.

8. f. 123ᵛ In cronicis Wintonie legitur in epistola secundum bonam graciam de villa dei ad nigros monachos que incipit O quam pulcra (*altered to* preclara) etc'. et pendet super sepulcrum vel feretrum sancti Swythuni quod sanctus swythunus erat doctor theologie in vniuersitate cantabrig' plane in terminis qui swythunus erat instructor adelulfi patris aluredi qui aluredus primo fundauit vniuersitatem Oxon' vt habetur in cronicis. legitur eciam Wintonie in alia tabula quod aluredus oxoniam fundauit et eius successor Edwardus senior vniuersitatem cantabrig' restaurauit etc'.

Extracts from 'Tabulae' hanging in Winchester Cathedral.

9. ff. 124–6 Anglia modo dicta olim albion dicebatur . . . de primis habitatoribus huius terre. Explicit tractatus declarans quomodo Anglia primo vocabatur Albeon etc.

10. ff. 126ᵛ–129ᵛ In principio creauit deus celum et terram . . .

A chronology of English kings from Brutus to the coronation of Henry IV in 1399, after which six lines have been erased. f. 130ʳᵛ blank.

ff. i + 130 + i. 220 × 140 mm. Written space 135 × 94 mm. 30–8 long lines. Ruled in pencil. Frame ruling ff. 48–63. Collation: 1^8 2^8 wants 8, probably blank, after f. 15 $3–12^8$ 13^6 wants 5, 6, probably blank, after f. 99 $14–16^8$ 17^8 wants 8, blank, after f. 130. Secretary by several scribes, the last of them (arts. 7–10) skilful. 4-line blue initials with red ornament. Capital letters in the ink of the text filled with yellow in arts. 2, 7–10. Binding of s. xix. Secundo folio *scribendo tibi*.

Written in England. Belonged to Richard Farmer: his sale, at T. King's, King St., Covent Garden, London, 7 May 1798, lot 8091, to Chetham's Library, for £1. 2*s*.

8005 (Mun. A. 6. 88). *Justinus, Epitoma in Trogum Pompeium*

s. xv^2

Principio rerum: gentium: nationumque . . . (f. 213ᵛ) tot periculorum miserati (*ends imperfectly in bk. 44*).

Printed often. The last words correspond to Teubner edn., p. 300/3: the missing text was supplied in s. xviii (?) on ff. 214–215ᵛ. The preface was perhaps on the missing first leaf of quire 1. Well written contemporary scholia in red and black inks.

ff. 27, 140 and some other leaves have washed-out underwriting in a late Italian rotonda: 2 cols.

ff. i + 215 + i. 325 × 230 mm. Written space 185 × 115 mm. 25 long lines. Collation of ff. 1-213: 1^{10} wants 1 $2\text{-}21^{10}$ 22 four. Catchwords written vertically. Upright large humanistica, not very good. 4-line initials, gold paint on blue, green, or red grounds, decorated in gold paint and framed in black. Binding of s. xix. Secundo folio *nem auxit*.

Written in Italy. 'libraria di 5to in O. piazo', f. 1, at top, s. xvi. Bought for the library in the Farmer sale, 7 May 1798, lot 8075, for £1. 9*s*.

8007 (Mun. A. 2. 161). *Horae (partly in French)* s. xv^2

Arts. 8, 11-16, 18, 20, 21, 23, 25*a* are in French.

1. ff. 1-12^v A rather empty calendar in French in red and black.

Entries in red include 'La dedicace s' iehan', 'Saint claude', 'La passion s' ferruel et s' fergeul', 'Saint anthide', 'La dedicace s' estiene' (2 May; 5, 16, 17 June; 3 Oct.); also Visitation of B.V.M., 2 July.

2. ff. 13-16^v Sequentiae of the Gospels. 'Protector in te sperantium . . .' after John.

3. ff. 17-19^v Hours of the Cross, beginning imperfectly.

4. ff. 20-23^v Hours of the Holy Spirit.

5. ff. 24-53^v Hours of B.V.M. of the use of (Besançon). ff. 54-55^v blank.

6. ff. 56-68^v Penitential psalms and (f. 63) litany.

Thirty-three martyrs: (1-6) Stephane Agapite Ferreole Ferruci Germane Anthidi . . .

7. ff. 68^v-85^v Cy apres sensuiuent vigiles de mors. Three lessons only.

8. ff. 86-88^v Ie te prie dame sainte marie . . . Sonet-Sinclair, no. 846.

9. ff. 88^v-90 De nostre dame. O intemerata . . . orbis terrarum. Inclina . . . Ego peccatrix . . .

10. ff. 90-94^v Oroison deuote a nostre dame. Domina mea sancta maria perpetua uirgo uirginum . . .

11. ff. 94^v-98 Cy apres sensuiuent les xv ioyes nostre dame. Doulce dame de misericorde mere de pitie . . . Sonet, no. 458.

12. ff. 98^v-101 Cy apres sensuyuent les sept requestes . . . Doulx dieu doulx pere sainte trinite . . . Sonet, no. 504.

13. f. 101 Deuote meditation a nostre seignur. Ihesus soit en ma teste et mon entendement . . . Sonet-Sinclair, no. 991.

14. f. 101 Aultre deuote meditation. Qui du tout son cueur met en dieu . . . (4 lines).

15. ff. 101–102v Sensuit vne deuote oroison de nostre dame. Stabat mater dolorosa. Sur pieds estoit la uierge mere . . . Ten 6-line stanzas.

16. f. 103 Deuote oroison a nostre dame. O des cieulx royne couronnee . . . Sonet–Sinclair, no. 1311.

17. f. 103rv Memoria of Katherine of Siena.

18. ff. 104–12 Pater noster. Aue maria. Iesu eternelle doulceur. Ioye de tes vrays amateurs . . .

The Fifteen Oes of St Bridget.

19. ff. 112–13 Ceste oroison est de grant merite. Domine ihesu criste fili dei redemptor mundi . . .

20. ff. 113–15 Deuote oroison a nostre seigneur. Ihesu crist filz de diuine bontey aide moy . . . Sonet–Sinclair, no. 948.

21. ff. 115–118v Se aucuns ha tribulacion . . . E tres doulx sire ihesu crist que su soing de dieu le pere . . .

According to the 14-line heading, this prayer helps those who say it 'xxv iours continuellement . . . Et la composa monseigneur saint augustin'.

22. ff. 119–21 Omnibus consideratis . . . *RH*, no. 14081.

23. ff. 121–122v Les sept vers saint bernard en franscois lesqueulx sont de grant vertuz. Illumina oculos meos. Doulx dieu qui me creastes . . .

24. ff. 122v–124v Memoriae of John Baptist, John Evangelist, Peter and Paul, Stephen, Christopher, Nicholas (*ends imperfectly*).

25. f. 125rv (*a*) (*begins imperfectly*) . . . Et en ce monde preseruer. De tonnairre. et de mort subite. Amen. (*b*, *c*) Memoriae of Anne and All Saints.

(*a*). The last 13 lines of a verse prayer to a virgin saint.

26. ff. 125v–127 Ceste oroison est de grant indulgence. O domine ihesu criste adoro te in cruce ascendentem . . . uulneratum . . . mortuum et sepultum . . . descendentem . . . resurgentem . . . saluatorem uenturum . . . pastor bone . . .

The Seven Oes of St Gregory.

27. ff. 127–8 Auete omnes fideles . . .

A heading in French conveys indulgence of as many days 'que y ha de corps enseueliz ou dit cymitiere iusques a celle heure'.

28. f. 128rv Prayers at mass: (*a*) Salue saluator mundi . . . ; (*b*) O sanguis cristi qui passus amore fuisti . . . da nobis regna beata. Amen. (*c*) Ceste oroison . . . Domine ihesu criste qui hanc sacratissimam carnem . . .

(*b*). Three couplets, *RH*, no. 31018, *AH* xv. 57. (*c*). The heading conveys unspecified indulgence and pardon. ff. 129–132v are ruled, but blank.

ff. vi + 132 + iii, excluding blank parchment and paper leaves inserted to protect pictures. ff. iv–vi are old parchment flyleaves. 178 × 126 mm. Written space 104 × 72 mm. 19 long lines. Collation: $1\text{–}2^8$ 3^8 wants 1 before f. 17 $4\text{–}15^8$ 16^8 wants 6–8 after f. 124 17^8. Catchwords in *lettre bâtarde*. Four 16-line pictures, one before each of arts. 4–7. Fifteen smaller pictures, *c*.37 × 37 mm, seven in art. 5, four in art. 24 (John Baptist, Peter and Paul, Stephen, Nicholas) and one before each of arts. 11, 12, 16, 26 (vision of Gregory). Initials: (i–iii) 3-line (or more), 2-line, and 1-line, gold on coloured grounds patterned in white. Capital letters in the ink of the text filled with pale yellow. Line fillers in blue, red, and gold. The larger picture pages have continuous floral borders on grounds of gold paint and the smaller picture pages a similar border in the outer margin the height of the written space. Binding of s. xix.

Written in France for female use (arts. 9, 26) in the diocese of Besançon. A shield in the border on f. 24 bears or an eagle displayed sable and another in the border on f. 56 barry of six sable and gules, a canton (blurred). 'N° 98', f. ivv.

8008 (Mun. A. 4. 103). *Prick of Conscience (in English)* s. xiv ex.

(*begins imperfectly*) Of the las worlde . . . þat gode men in heuyn schal fele and se (*ends imperfectly*).

The first line now is line 1048 and the last line line 9082 of the edition by R. Morris, 1863. Probably four leaves are missing after f. 42: 42v ends 'Til we come vnto purgatory' (line 3929); 43 begins 'þat god cursed as clerkes can telle' (line 4204). Part of f. 39 is torn away and part of f. 1 cut out.

ff. iii + 115 + ii. 204 × 137 mm. Written space *c*.165 mm high. 32 long lines. Collation: $1\text{–}5^8$ 6^8 wants 3–6 after f. 42 $7\text{–}14^8$ 15^8 wants 8 after f. 115. Upright anglicana formata (single compartment *a*), all in one hand. Latin in red ink. Initials: (i) of each part, blue and red with ornament of both colours; (ii) 2-line or 1-line, blue with red ornament. Binding by Bramhall and Menzies in 1931.

Written in Ireland (?): cf. A. McIntosh and M. L. Samuels in *Medium Aevum*, xxxvii (1968), 4, where this manuscript is listed as one of three copies of the Prick of Conscience 'for which the evidence of Irish provenance is wholly or mainly linguistic'. 'hyt is master Hart is boke', f. 19, s. xvi. 'Charles Fotherby: given by C. Foth: Esq', f. 2, s. xvii.

8009 (Mun. A. 6. 31). *Ipomadon, etc. (in English)* s. xv²

Thirteen pieces in verse and (arts. 1, 4, 12, 13) prose, written by probably nine scribes. Described by E. Kölbing in *Englische Studien*, vii (1884), 195–201, and by G. Guddat-Figge, *Catalogue of manuscripts containing Middle English romances*, 1976, pp. 238–40. J. Hardres writing in 1732, Bryan Faussett, and J. O. Halliwell gave their opinions of the date of the manuscript on f. v, suggesting respectively the reigns of Richard II, Henry III–Edward I, and Edward IV. Arts. 7, 8, 13 are quire fillers.

1 (quire 1: hand 1). ff. 1–2^{v} The right glorious virgyn seint Dorothea . . . by all þe worlde of world*es* Amen.

2 (quire 2: hand 2 (on f. 3^{rv}) and hand 3). ff. 3–17^{v} A merye tale tell I may . . . That lastithe evire w^{t} owte end. Explicit Assumpcio Sancte Marie Amen. *IMEV*, no. 2165.

3 (quire 3: hand 4). ff. 18–29^{v} O blessed Ihesu that arte full of myght . . . And when we dye to haue eternall blise. Here endyth the lyff of Seynt Anne. *IMEV*, no. 2392.

4 (quires 4, 5: hand 5). ff. 30–47 Here begynnyth the lyf of Seynt Katerin And how she was maried to oure lord. Here begynnyth the liffe of seynt katryne that ys a ryght glorious virgyn . . . to the eternall light amen. Amen. Here endyth the lyf of Seynt Katerin And the maryage to oure lorde. f. 47^{v} blank.

5 (quires 6–8: hand 6). ff. 48–75 Cum anima aduerterem . . . When I aduertice in my Remembraunce . . . Not causeth me but symplenes of wit. Explicit liber Catonis quod scripci da michi quod merui quod N (?) P Vna p valde d tantum d me Quod non p ire ad l nisi S me.

IMEV, nos. 3955, 854. Benedict Burgh, Cato Minor and Cato Major, preceded stanza by stanza by the Latin text 'Cum . . . ferto amorem. Si deus . . . binos' (Walther, nos. 51, 17703: ed. M. Boas, 1952) in red. The English collated as M by Max Förster in *Archiv für das Studium der neueren Sprachen*, cxv (1905), 302–23; cxvi (1906), 25–34. f. 75^{v} blank.

Arts. 6–8 are on quires 9–11 in hand 7 (to f. 93^{v}) and hand 5.

6. ff. 76–119^{v} Here begynneth a good tale of Torrence of Portyngale. God that ys worthy and Bold . . . Oute of this world whan we shall wend Amen. Explicit Torent of Portyngale.

IMEV, no. 983. Printed from this copy by E. Adam, EETS, Extra series, li, 1887.

7. ff. 119^{v}–121 Of all women that euer were born . . . Wnto the blis where is my son dere.

IMEV, no. 2619. A lamentation of B.V.M. printed from this copy by M. Förster in *Anglia* xlii (1918), 167–72.

8. f. 121^{rv} Mary moder well thou be . . . To heuyn blis that I may wend Amen. A prayer of oure lady Explicith.

IMEV, no. 2119. Printed from this copy by M. Förster, ibid., 172–5.

9 (quires 12–16: hand 5). ff. 122–190^{v} Here begynnyth a good tale of Bevys of hamton A good werriour. Lystenythe lording*es* yf ye will dwell . . . That for

vs died vppon a tree Amen. Here endyth a good tale of Beuis of hamton that good verriour.

IMEV, no. 1993. A leaf is missing after f. 124.

10 (quires 17–27: hand 5). ff. 191–335 Here begynnyth a good tale of Ipomadon. Off love were lykynge of to lere . . . To brynge vs to the blysse that lestis aye Amen ffor Charyte.

IMEV, no. 2635. Printed from this copy by E. Kölbing, *Ipomadon*, 1889, pp. 1–253. A leaf is missing after f. 237. f. 335v blank.

11 (quire 28: hand 5). ff. 336–355v A boke of kervyng and Nourtur (*title on f. 336, otherwise blank: 336v blank*). A good boke of kervyng and Nortur. In nomine patris god kep me et filii for Cherite . . . þt never shall haue endynge Amen. Explicit the boke of nvture and of kervynge quod Ego.

IMEV, no. 1514/5. Differs much from ed. F. J. Furnivall, *Early English Meals and Manners: the Boke of Norture of John Russell* . . ., EETS xxxii (1868), 117–98 (line 1234). The line which names Russell is here 'Praye ye for the soule of Iohn Russell in London dwellynge'.

Arts. 12, 13 are on quire 29, art. 12 in hand 5, and art. 13 in hand 8.

12. ff. 357–366v The Lady of Comynes the best and the derrest of my spirituelle Doughters. To you I recomaunde me humbly . . . whome I beseche to send you all þat ye desire. Writen at þe sayd Saint Maximien beside Tresues the xxviith day Octobr'.

An account of the meeting of Charles the Bold, duke of Burgundy, and the emperor Frederick III at Trier in 1473. A leaf is missing after f. 358. ff. 356rv, 367r blank.

13. ff. 367v–368v 'The Namys of Wardeyns and Balyffys' (later, mayors and sheriffs) of London from 1189 to 1217. f. 369rv blank.

14 (quire 30: hand 9). ff. 370–2 Ihesu that arte Ientyll ffor' Ioye of they dam . . . ye shall heyr' the best behynd. A fytte. Here begennethe anod*er* fytte ye sothe for to sey (*nothing follows: f. 372v blank*).

IMEV, no. 1751. Printed from this copy by Wright and Halliwell, *Reliquiæ Antiquæ*, 1841–3, ii. 196–9.

ff. v + 372 + v. Paper. 262 × 190 mm. Written space *c.*190 mm high. 30–3 long lines. Frame ruling with pencil. Collation: 1 two (ff. 1, 2) 2^{16} wants 16, blank, after f. 17 $3\text{–}4^{12}$ 5^{6} 6^{8} 7 eleven (ff. 56–66) 8 nine (ff. 67–75) 9^{16} 10^{14} 11^{16} 12^{14} wants 4 after f. 124 $13\text{–}19^{14}$ 20^{14} wants 6 after f. 237 21^{12} 22^{14} 23^{12} $24\text{–}26^{14}$ 27^{10} 28^{20} 29 thirteen (ff. 356–68) 30 four (ff. 369–72). In quires 17–27 the leaves in the first half of each quire are numbered continuously from 'I' to 'LXXIII'. In nine hands, all current: see above. The main scribe (5) wrote ff. 30–47, 94–366: his hand is more secretary than anglicana. The other hands are secretary (1, 2, 4, 6, 9), current anglicana (3), more anglicana than secretary (7), and a mixture of the two scripts (8). A few red initials. Binding of s. xx. Secundo folio *with thy wychecrafte*.

Written perhaps in London (cf. art. 13), art. 12 after 1473. 'This booke I fownde ymoungest my fatherris 20 Ianuarie 1598 Pe. Manwood', p. v: Peter Manwood's father was Sir Roger Manwood, 1525–92. Later owners were perhaps J. Hardres in 1732 and Bryan Faussett, †1776: see above. J. Monro sale, 23 April 1792, lot 3399, to Richard Farmer for £29.[1] Bought for the library in the Farmer sale, 7 May 1798, lot 8062, for £14. 14*s.*[2]

8023 (Mun. A. 6. 96). *'Questiones magistri Roberti de meduana supra librum philareti de pulsibus', etc.*

s. xiii ex.–xiv med.

Arts. 1–3 (quires 1–3) are of s. xiv med.

1. ff. 1–10ᵛ [V]num in ternario . . . (f. 2ᵛ) Differencia prima. Quod necessarium non sit medico . . . ideo etc.

Thorndike and Kibre. An abbreviation of the Conciliator of Petrus de Abano (first printed in 1472; Goff, P. 431). Differentiae IV and VI are absent. 'Suanensem uel cognomine suo de albano ad 2 leucas prope paduam constructus pro hem' generale anno cristi 1331 constructus' is at the head of f. 1, s. xiv.

2. (*a*) ff. 11–16ᵛ Omnes significationes oporte(n)t precongruare . . . Hec ypo. 3 pronosticorum ca. 38 . . . exposita et ideo sensibilior [. . .]. Expliciunt questiones magistri Roberti de meduana supra librum philareti de pulsibus deo gracias scriptos (?) 1340 in nocte sancti andree in vico clob*er*nelli (?).[3] (*b*) ff. 17–19ᵛ Perhaps part of (*a*).

(*a*). On f. 14 the scribe had to avoid defects in the parchment. (*b*). The text does not appear to be continuous from leaf to leaf. On ff. 17 and 18 paragraphs begin as in (*a*) 'Consequenter queritur'. The subject is the pulse on f. 18: 'Consequenter queritur vtrum magnus pulsus sit signum caliditatis et etiam an velocitas . . .'. On ff. 17, 19 it seems to be the liver and heart: f. 19, 'Alia est opinio aristotelis et auer'. voluit enim aristoteles vt patet 13 de animalibus quod solum sit vnum membrum principale scilicet cor . . .'. The last words on f. 19ᵛ are 'Sic igitur apparet quod ista seruiuntur'.

3. ff. 20ʳᵛ, 66–74ᵛ, 32ʳᵛ (*begins imperfectly*) *Capillorum* et est quoddam dubium scilicet . . . (*ends imperfectly*).

Eleven consecutive leaves of a commentary on the *Ars medica* (beginning *Tres sunt omnes*) of Galen, covering the text on ff. 7–9ᵛ, 14–22 of the edition of the *Ars* printed in *Articella*, Venice 1493. Commentary on the text of edn. ff. 10–13ᵛ is lacking at the point where the scribe left space on f. 68ᵛ, after which a leaf may be missing. On f. 32ʳᵛ sections of the commentary begin 'Determinatis de signis sanis' and 'Docet de signis morborum aliquorum membrorum', and the last lemma on the verso is 'Ita vero et secundum ventrem'.

4 (quire 4, s. xiii ex.). (*a*) ff. 33–40 Non solum etc'. Istud commentum potest diuidi in duas partes . . . de tercia particula ibi et in sermone suo in vino. (*b*) f. 40ᵛ Notandum autem secundum astronomos incepcio anni . . . ad frigiditatem et siccitatem.

[1] The buyer's name and the price are given in the annotated copy of Halliwell's catalogue in the Local History Collection of Manchester Public Library.

[2] The marked catalogue in Glasgow University Library gives the name of the buyer as 'Leigh and Sotheby'. This firm was presumably acting for Chetham's Library.

[3] Mlle. M. T. d'Alverny suggests the Clos Bruneau in Paris: see above, Liverpool Univ. Libr., F. 4. 20.

(*a*). A commentary on the commentary of Galen on the De regimine acutorum of Hippocrates. (*b*). A space-filler on the signs of the zodiac.

5 (quires 5–9, s. xiii ex.). ff. 41–65^{v}, 21–31^{v}, 75–80^{v} '[. . .] pta [. . .] super [. . .]'. Circa introitum febrium ysaac queritur primo utrum medicina sit sciencia et uidetur quod non . . . interpolabit xlviii horis. hec sufficiunt de fe. ysaac. Expliciunt glosule super febres ysaac.

On the De febribus of Isaac Judeus.

6 (quire 10, s. xiv in.). ff. 81–87^{v} Incipit liber de simplici medicina translatus a magistro girardo cremonensi qui albigephi uocatur. liber in quo est pars prima medicinarum simplicium et ciborum secundum editionem abegnefid. [E]x antiquorum libris hunc aggregaui . . . et hoc est ubi incepi.

Thorndike and Kibre. Printed in *Tacuinum sanitatis*, Strasbourg 1531, pp. 119–39, and later.

7. f. 88 Notes, s. xiii, on medical and other properties of animals and birds, for example, 'De pauone. oua eius ad aurem colorem faciendum prosunt sicut anserina. cerebrum huius auis amatorium poculum . . .'.

A flyleaf. The verso is blank.

ff. ii + 87 + iii. For f. 88 see art. 7. 260 × 180 mm. Written space 200 × 143 mm. 2 cols. 52 lines (art. 5). Frame ruling in quires 1, 2, 4. Collation of ff. 1–20, 66–74, 32–65, 21–31, 75–87 in that order: 1^{14} + two singletons, ff. 6, 15 2 three (ff. 17–19) 3^{10} + 1 leaf after 6 *or* 3^{12} wants 5 after f. 68 (ff. 20, 66–74, 32) 4 eight (ff. 33–40) 5 eight (ff. 41–8) 6^{8} (ff. 49–56) 7^{10} (ff. 57–65, 21) 8^{10} (ff. 22–31) 9 six (ff. 75–80) 10 seven (ff. 81–7: 84–5 are a bifolium). A small neat textura for art. 5, a larger textura for art. 6, and cursiva for the rest. A red *C* on f. 41: a few spaces for coloured initials elsewhere not filled. Binding of s. xix. Secundo folio *An. 20^{a}*.

Written probably in France, art. 2*a* or its exemplar in 1340 and probably in Paris.

11362 (Mun. A. 6. 91). *Poems of Alain Chartier, etc. (in French)* s. xv med.

Described by L. E. Kastner in *Modern Language Review*, xii (1917), 45–58. Arts. 1–4, 7–10 occur in the 1617 edition of Chartier's works at pp. 402, 549, 542, 581, 502, 525, 523, 525 respectively. Arts. 4 and 7 are signed at the end 'Ieunesse'. The reader who added the title of art. 5 wrote in the margin of f. 31^{v}, opposite the point in the Quadrilogue where Chartier speaks of those who come from abroad to aid the French, 'nota hic pour larmee descoce qui vint au secours de france contre les anglois ou mois daoust mil iiii^{c} xix'.

1. ff. 1–36^{v} Sensuit le quadrilogue fait par maistre Alain charretier.

2. ff. 37–59 Le debat des deux fortunes damours.

3. ff. 60–64^{v} (Le lay de Paix).

4. ff. 65–72v Le Breuiaire des nobles.

5. ff. 73–9 'Sensuit vn lay que fist feu maistre Rogier haultpin'. En cheuauchant par vn matin naguiere . . .

Printed from this copy by Kastner, pp. 47–56.

6. ff. 79v–80 Balade. Du liz plaisant tresexcellente fleur . . .

Printed from this copy by Kastner, pp. 57–8.

7. ff. 81–97v La belle dame sans mercy. Naguere cheuauchant pensoie . . .

8. f. 98 Coppie des lettres enuoiees par les dames a Alain.

9. ff. 98v–99 Copie de la requeste baillee aux dames contre Alain.

10. ff. 99v–104 (Excusacion de M. Alain) Mes dames et mes demoiselles. f. 104v blank.

ff. ii + 104 + ii. 262 × 196 mm. Written space 170 × 105 mm. 28 long lines. Ruling in pencil. Collation: 1–13[8]. *Lettre bâtarde* by a skilled hand. Initials: (i, ii) 6-line (f. 1) and 3-line or 2-line, blue or pink patterned in white on decorated gold grounds; (iii) 2-line, gold on grounds of blue and pink patterned in white. Floral borders on pages with initials of types (i, ii), continuous on f. 1. Capital letters in the ink of the text filled with yellow in arts. 7–10. Binding of red morocco, s. xviii. Secundo folio *naissent*.

Written in France. '74', f. 1, at the top. Duc de la Vallière sale, Paris, 1783, lot 2791. William Roscoe sale, Liverpool, 19 Aug. 1816, lot 1804: bought for the library for £6. 6*s*.

11366 (Mun. A. 4. 101). *R. Bacon, Opera medica* s. xv ex.

Described by A. G. Little, *Opera hactenus inedita Rogeri Baconi*, ix (1928). Little called it a 'collected edition of Roger Bacon's medical treatises', closely related to Bodleian MSS. Bodley 438 and e Mus. 155, pp. 591–700. He prints arts. 1–9: ix. 1–83; 90–5; 96–7; 98–102; 103–19; 120–43; 144–9; 150–79; 181–6 (App. I).

1. ff. 1–32v Incipit liber quem composuit frater Rogerus Bacon' de ordine minorum de retardacione senectutis et senii . . . [D]omine mundi . . . debilitas nature. Explicit tractatus fratris Rogeri Bacon' . . .'. A leaf missing after f. 11.

2. ff. 32v–34v De vniuersali regimine senum et seniorum. [E]t summa regiminis vniuersalis . . . linicionem.

3. ff. 34v–35v De balneis senum et seniorum. [S]enes sunt balneandi . . . frigide nature.

4. ff. 35v–37v De composicione quarundam medicinarum . . . [I]ncipiamus in nomine domini excelsi . . . in corpore toto.

5. ff. 37v–45v Incipit primum capitulum antitodarii quem fecit Rogerus Bacon'. [P]ost completum medicinalis sciencie . . . uel morsibus.

6. ff. 45v–55v [I]ntendo componere sermonem . . . in eis purgetur.

7. ff. 55v–58 Incipit quidam tractatus perutilis ediccione siue comparacione fratris rogeri Bacon' ordinis fratrum minorum de graduacione medicinarum . . . [O]mnis forma inherens . . . difficilis plurimum.

8. ff. 58–60v, 63–74 De erroribus medicorum secundum fratrem rogerum Bacon' de ordine minorum. [V]ulgus medicorum . . . enim hoc probabit.

9. ff. 74–77v, 61rv Frater Rogerus Bacon in libro 6 scienciarum . . . in hoc mundo et cetera.

10. ff. 61v–62v, 78–82v Item alius tractatus eiusdem fratris rogeri Bacon . . . diffuse pertractatam. [C]orpora vero ade et eue . . . multis modis. Explicit tractatus de predicto libro Rogeri Bacon.

As Opus minus, ed. Brewer, RS xv (1859), 373/7–374/7, and Opus maius, ed. Bridges, ii. 204–13. The heading 'Item . . . pertractatam' is written, as in e Mus. 155, immediately after the last words of art. 9: Little prints it, ix. 179. f. 83rv blank.

11. On the flyleaves, s. xvii: (*a*) f. xxi A careful table listing arts. 1, 2, 5–9 and after them 'Tractatus de simplici Medicina . . . Editus, vt putatur, a fratre Rogero Bacono, et é vetusto exemplari MSS., licet mendoso, transcriptus per J. Cobbes';[1] (*b*) f. xxiv A discussion of authenticity of the Liber de simplici medicina, ending 'Vale. J. Co. 16 Januarii 1650'.

ff. xxi + 82 + xxv, foliated (i–xxi), 1–24, 26–83, (84–108): '26'–'83' is a medieval foliation in red. The first and last flyleaves are modern, the rest of s. xvii. 221 × 167 mm. Written space 165 × 105 mm. 35 long lines. Collation: 1^8 2^8 wants 4 after f. 11 $3\text{–}7^8$ 8^8 (ff. 57–60, 63–6) 9^8 (ff. 67–74) 10^8 (ff. 75–7, 61–2, 78–80) 11^4 wants 4, blank. Round set hybrida, verging on *lettre bâtarde*. Initials not filled in. Bound in limp parchment, s. xvii. Secundo folio *mulsa*.

Written in France (?). In England in s. xvii and owned by J. Cobbes (cf. *MMBL* ii. 219). Sale of Cox Macro's collection of manuscripts, Feb. 1820, lot 26, to Dawson Turner: his sale, 6 June 1859, lot 17, to Chetham's Library for 10*s.*[2] A descriptive note by Francis Palgrave dated 1840 is on a piece of paper attached to f. iiv.

11379 (Mun. A. 6. 90). *Polychronicon, etc. (in English)* s. xiv/xv

St John's College, Cambridge, 204 and B.L., Add. 24194 contain the same three translations by John Trevisa. Arts. 1, 2 were collated as Ch for the EETS edition (clxvii, 1925) by A. J. Perry.

[1] Cf. the next footnote.

[2] In the copy of the sale catalogue in the Bodleian Library the name of the buyer is given as Bell. Bell bought also lot 18, Bacon, De simplici medicina, for 3*s.*, probably Cobbes's transcript (see above art. 11*a*) which, however, does not appear to be in Chetham's Library.

1. ff. 1–5^{v} Dialogus inter militem et clericum. Ych wondre syre noble kny3t . . . vor þe holy day. Explicit dialogus inter clericum et militem.

A translation of Pseudo-Ockham, Dialogus inter militem et clericum. Perry, pp. 1–37.

2. ff. 5^{v}–18^{v} Incipit sermo domini archiepiscopi Armacani. Demeþ no3t be þe face . . . bote ry3tfol dom 3e deme.

A translation of Richard Fitzralph's tract against the mendicant orders, Defensorium curatorum, Avignon, 8 Nov. 1357. Perry, pp. 39/1–9, 47/1–93. Two leaves missing after f. 5.

3. Tables to art. 4: (*a*) ff. 19–27^{v} in Latin, beginning 'Abraham 2. 10' and ending, imperfectly, in the letter *V*; (*b*) ff. 28–34^{v} in English, beginning imperfectly in the letter *D* and ending 'Wynchelse ybrend 7. 44'.

Cf. above, Liverpool Public Library, f091 HIG, art. 1. Book and chapter numbers are given.

4. ff. 35–178^{v} (*begins imperfectly*) lost and for3ete . . . aboute þe feste of (*ends imperfectly*).

Polychronicon. In Babington's edition the first words here are at i. 17/1 and the last at viii. 325/12 in the annal for 1327. Between these points probably nearly one hundred leaves are missing. The gaps—four of them large—are after ff. 45, 69, 74, 86, 89, 100, 109, 118, 122, 123, 125, 127, 140, 164, 177, with the text in edn., i. 157/19–319/13, ii. 289/4–301/6, ii. 361/18–iii. 423/12, iv. 115/2–285/8, iv. 327/10–415/2, v. 107/16–123/6, v. 257/7–273/11, v. 409/11–vi. 11/2, vi. 71/5–255/1, vi. 269/1–297/1, vi. 325/14–357/17, vi. 387/2–415/13, vii. 111/17–255/3, viii. 75/18–103/12, viii. 283/6–311/6. Sometimes the wording differs much from edn.: for example, chapter 18 of bk. 6 begins 'Canutus þe dane was ymad kyng alone whanne Edmund was ded . . . he delede þe kyngdom of engelond a voure and assignede'.

ff. iii + 178 + iv. 347 × 265 mm. Written space *c.* 250 × 185 mm. 37 long lines. Collation: 1^{12} wants 6, 7 2^{12} 3^{12} wants 6, 7 after f. 27 4 two (ff. 33, 34) 5^{12} wants 1 (ff. 35–45) 6 six (ff. 46–51) 7^{12} 8^{12} wants 7 after f. 69 9^{12} (ff. 75–86) 10^{12} wants 4–9 after f. 89 11^{12} wants 9 after f. 100 12^{12} wants 7 after f. 109 13^{12} wants 5–8 after f. 118 14 six (ff. 123–8) 15^{12} 16^{12} wants 1 before f. 141 17^{12} 18^{12} wants 2, 3 after f. 164 19 five (ff. 174–8). *Ad hoc* pencilled signatures: within a quire the first recto has no mark or letter, the first verso and second recto have a mark followed by *a*, the second verso and third recto the same mark followed by *b*, and so forth. Written in anglicana formata, probably by the same scribe throughout: regular *v* for *f*. The leaves on which the books of art. 4 began have all been removed. The remaining initials are: f. 1, 4-line blue and red *D* with ornament of both colours; (ii) 2-line, blue with red ornament or gold with violet ornament, or (rarely) red with blue ornament. Binding of s. xix. Secundo folio *no3t iuge*.

Written in England. Listed in Halliwell's catalogue of 1842 as no. 8037.

11380 (Mun. A. 4. 91). *Medica* s. xiii/xiv

Many more or less short medical texts, mainly in one hand. Many of them end exactly at the end of a column, page, or leaf.

1 (quire 1). (*a*) ff. 1–6 Incipit liber ypo. de aere et aqua. Omnis quis (*sic*) ad medicine studium accedere curat . . . non errabit a veritate amen. Explicit liber

ypo. de aere et aqua. (*b*) ff. 6^{v}–7 Creator omnium deus a quo omne bonum . . . lapis lazuli et similia. Hic autem finem secrete practice imponamus. Explicit etc. (*c*) ff. 7^{v}–8 Quomodo debes visitare infirmum secundum precepta ypo. Non omnem infirmum vl'r[1] visites. Sed si integre . . . qui solus est medicus. amen. Expliciunt precepta ypocratis. (*d*) f. 8^{rv} Dicta ypocratis de luna in qua infirmi decidunt. Luna prima qui decubuerit . . . exibitis:' curabitur. (*e*) f. 8^{v} Incipit dictamen de saporibus. Dulcia mundificant gustus instrumentum . . . Cui uero debet aliquis adhibere fidem.

(*a–d*). Thorndike and Kibre. (*c*). Three paragraphs. Cf. Beccaria, p. 424 (Non omnem infirmum uniter . . .). (*d*). Beccaria, p. 420. (*e*). Lines 540–93 of Flos medicinae scholae Salerni, ed. Renzi, v. 15–16.

2 (quires 2–5). (*a*) ff. 9–28^{v} Incipiunt signa Ricardi. Finis medicine laudabilis existit . . . precipue cum lingue denigracione. signum est mortale. Expliciunt signa Ricardi etc. (*b*) ff. 29–34^{v} Incipit modus medendi archimethei (*sic*). Cum igitur medice ad egrum vocaberis . . . petita licencia vade in pace. Explicit modus medendi archimathei etc. (*c*) f. 35^{rv} Incipiunt exposiciones sompniorum secundum G. Aues in sompno videre. et cum aliis pugnare . . . Qui fontem videt. sibi securitatem significat. etc. Expliciunt Exposiciones sompniorum secundum Magistrum G etc. (*d*) ff. 35^{v}–36^{v} Incipiunt dicta B' (?) de lunacionibus. Luna prima. In omnibus rebus agendis . . . Interdum caute cauendum est etc. Expliciunt lunaciones secundum M. (*e*) f. 36^{v} Ver. estas. dextras autumpnus hiemsque sinistras . . . (10 lines). (*f*) f. 37 Incipit epistola G. contra morbum contagiosum. Ad euitandum morbum contagiosum siue morbos sic poterit medicus precauere . . . et quecumque talia. Explicit epistola G. contra morbum contagiosum. (*g*) f. 37 De fluxu uentris. Dicit magister Gillebertus quod nunquam . . . et super aspergatur paruum vini etc. (*h*) ff. 37^{v}–39^{v} Incipiunt amphorismi Iohannis Damaceni filii serapionis. Liberet te deus . . . translatorem inueni etc' etc'. Expliciunt amphorismi Iohannis Damacheni filii serapionis. (*i*) f. 40^{rv} Philosophia quedam. Vt ait seneca in quadam epistola ad lucilium. studeas et addiscas sciencias cum viuere sine litteris sit mors anime . . . Quod alias declarabitur etc.

(*a–e, h*). Thorndike and Kibre. (*a*). Wickersheimer, p. 696 (Ricardus Anglicus). (*c*). Cf. M. Förster in *Archiv für das Studium der neueren Sprachen*, cxxv (1910), 47. The alphabetical series reaches only to Q. (*d*). Cf. the texts printed by E. Svenberg, *De latinska lunaria*, 1936. (*e*). Walther, no. 20125. (*f*). Diseases are said to be more contagious in France and England than in Provence and Italy. (*g*). On the virtues of goat's flesh and cabbage. (*h*). Printed often.

3 (quires 6–9). (*a*) ff. 41–71 Secundum quod vult auic' in primo libro . . . in hoc capitulo nominabis. Explicit secundum quod vult auic'. (*b*) f. 71^{rv} Recipes, the first 'Unguentum quod in unctione manuum prouocat vomitum . . .'. (*c*) f. 72 Verses 'de ustione', 'de ablucione', 'de coctione', 'de contricione', 'de pressione' and on 'operaciones calidi . . . frigidi . . . humidi . . . sicci', 28 lines in all.

(*a*). Thorndike and Kibre (commentary of J. de Sancto Amando on Antidotarium Nicholai). (*c*). The first piece begins 'Ustio. locio. coctio. trictio. pressio facta' and the second 'Ustio quinque facit. dat acumen. tollit acumen'.

[1] The word here should be *uniter*.

4 (quire 10). (*a*) ff. 73–8 Incipit musandina de preparacione ciborum et potuum infirmorum. De cibis et potibus preparandis . . . delectetur. multum iuuant. Explicit musandina deo gracias. (*b*) ff. 78v–80v Incipit practica puerorum secundum Rasim et primo de assahaphati. Assahaphati accidit pueris . . . oleo antiquo vel oleo de ben.

(*a, b*). Thorndike and Kibre. (*a*). Wickersheimer, p. 652. Printed often. (*b*). Printed in 1481 (Goff, R. 175).

5 (quire 11). (*a*) ff. 81–8 Incipiunt flores dietarum. Corpus hominis ex quatuor constat . . . et valde bonum erit. (*b*) f. 88v Incipit ars medicinarum laxatiuarum . . . Idem ducit dyaprimis Hec sufficiant de quantitate laxacionis medicinarum secundum Magistrum Iohannem Stephani. (*c*) f. 88v Nota generaliter secundum magistrum Ricardum Quod omnis artherica . . . (10 lines).

(*a*). Thorndike and Kibre (Johannes de S. Paulo: Wickersheimer, p. 480). (*b*). Thorndike and Kibre. Wickersheimer, p. 793.

6 (quires 12, 13). (*a*) ff. 89–96 Incipit liber virtutum medicinarum siue liber graduum. quem composuit Plat'. Cogitanti michi de simplicium medicinarum virtutibus . . . parare vtilitatem. Explicit Cogitanti michi. qui dicitur liber virtutum. (*b*) ff. 96–104v Incipit compendium M. Salomonis de Salerno breue et vtile et valde bonum. Duplici causa me cogente socii dilectissimi . . . Medicina est sciencia apponendi . . . corpus perungatur. Explicit.

(*a*). Thorndike and Kibre (J. de S. Paulo: Wickersheimer, p. 480). (*b*). Thorndike and Kibre. Ed. Renzi, iii. 52 and v. 201.

7 (quires 14, 15). (*a*) ff. 105–108v Incipit liber de conferentibus et nocentibus . . . Conferunt cerebro fetida . . . nimis ventosum. Explicit etc. (*b*) ff. 109–10 Incipit tractatus qui dicitur quid pro quo. Quoniam ea que vtilia sunt . . . Pro aristol. ro: ruta domestica. dup' . . . Pro ianti flore: mirta. Explicit. Quid pro quo. (*c*) ff. 110v–116v Incipiunt addiciones Thesauri Pauperum Magistri Petri Yspani. De casu capillorum. Lac asine summe . . . singulariter curat. Dya. Expliciunt addiciones. (*d*) ff. 117–120v Incipit breuiarium de antid' M. Barth'. Cum dieta et medicina maxime . . . Et in hoc terminatur istud breuiarium. Explicit breuiarium magistri barth'. (*e*) f. 120v Notes on clisters and powders.

(*a*). Thorndike and Kibre. Wickersheimer, p. 172 (Pseudo-Agilon). (*b*). Thorndike and Kibre. (*d*). Thorndike and Kibre have the incipit *Cum dieta et medicina* from *Ancient Libraries*, p. 482, a short Modus medendi in a manuscript belonging to the priory of Dover.

8 (quire 16). (*a*) ff. 121–2 Incipiunt canones vrinarum secundum magistrum Bart'. Urinarum xix sunt colores scilicet albus . . . cognoscuntur. Expliciunt canones etc'. (*b*) ff. 122v–124 Incipiunt contenta vrinarum secundum M. Galterum dictum ag*ui*llon. Iste est modus iudicandi vrinas. Et quod dictum est . . . significant dissolucionem tocius corporis vniuersalem. Expliciunt contenta M' Galteri. (*c*) ff. 124–5 Syrupus contra tercianam de colera ru. per quem . . . Alia circa febres plana sunt quare etc' explicit. (*d*) f. 125v Prognostications from the age of the moon and from dreams 'secundum Danielem'. (*e*) f. 125v A recipe and a charm

against fevers. (*f*) f. 126 Fert aqua plurima. fert aqua maxima dampna bibenti . . . defectisque solet facere salutis opem (30 lines of verse). (*g*) f. 126 Quatuor humores humano corpore constat . . . (48 lines). (*h*) ff. 126^{v}–128^{v} Incipit tractatus de saporibus. Rerum cognicio duobus modis . . . (f. 127rb/25) et iuncturarum corporis separatu. De saporibus ergo est dicendum. De saporibus tractaturi. videamus quid sit sapor . . . sunt in suis qualitatibus etc'. Explicit.

(*b*). Thorndike and Kibre (Iste modus est). Wickersheimer, p. 171. (*c*). Thorndike and Kibre (Siripus). On fevers. (*f*). On food and drink. (*g*). Walther, no. 15321. Lines 1, 14–25 are Flos medicinae (cf. art. 1*e*), lines 1682, 2100–11 (signs of recovery); with lines 26–41 cf. edn. lines 2044–55 (signs of death). (*h*). For the text beginning at f. 127rb/25 cf. Thorndike and Kibre and edn. by G. F. Hartmann, *Die Literatur von Früh- und Hochsalerno* (Leipzig 1919), pp. 55–7 (Urso).

9 (quire 17). (*a*) ff. 129–32 Incipit tractatus de 4 qualitatibus. Cum questionum omnium fere soluciones . . . in grossitantem consumit. quare etc'. Explicit tractatus de 4 qualitatibus secundum Cardinalem. (*b*) ff. 132^{v}–133 Sicut scribit aueroys in primo sui colliget. omnes artes vt artes dicuntur . . . medicus in suum finem. De aliis sufficiant. (*c*) ff. 133–4 Secundum quod dicit philosophus secundo celi et mondi. modicus error in principiis . . . et ex consequenti naturali philosophie. (*d*) f. 134^{rv} Secundum quod scribitur quarto metheororum et secundo phisicorum et pluribus aliis locis Ars imitatur naturam . . . magis quam alia via etc'. Iste tres philosophie fuerunt edite a Magistro Iohanne de corpo dum legit etc'. (*e*) f. 135 Dicta G. de luna in qua incumbunt infirmi . . . (*f*) f. 135 Quisquis prima die cuiuslibet mensis ceciderit . . . (*g*) f. 135 Recipes for making wine 'pulcrum ad vendendum', etc. (*h*) f. 135^{v} De probacione sanguinis. (*i*) f. 135^{v} De signis mortis. (*j*) ff. 135^{v}–136^{v} Recipes 'Contra vicia oculorum', 'Contra gutam', and 'De syropo contra arthericam'.

(*a*). Thorndike and Kibre (Urso). (*d*). For questions of Johannes de Corpo on the Prognostica of Hippocrates see Bodleian, Laud Misc. 558, art. 2. (*e, f*). Prognostications. (*h*) Six ways of proving that blood is 'correptus'.

10 (quire 18). (*a*) ff. 137–9 Incipit tractatus de aquis. Quoniam aquarum nonnullus est vsus in medicinis . . . fac bullire in aqua. Explicit. (*b*) ff. 139–41 Aqua vite secundum thadeum. Notandum est autem quod omnes passiones . . . Et fiat vt supra. Explicit composicio aque vite secundum M. Thadeum. (*c*) ff. 141^{v}–142^{v} Incipit secundus philosophus. Secundus philosophus sic philosophisatus est omni tempore silencium seruans . . . secundi philosophi digitis. Explicit. (*d*) ff. 143–144^{v} Incipiunt secreta ypo. Peruenit ad nos quod cum ypocras . . . lepram pronosticat. Expliciunt secreta ypocratis.

(*a*). Arnaldus de Villanova, De aquis laxatiuis, ed. 1585, pp. 603–8/1. (*c*). Thorndike and Kibre (Secundus fuit). (*d*). Thorndike and Kibre. Pseudo-Hippocrates, Capsula eburnea.

11 (quires 19–21). (*a*) f. 145 Incipit practica canum secundum M. G (?). Vt canes pulcros habeas . . . assidue pascantur etc'. Explicit practica canum composita a M' [.]. (*b*) ff. 145^{v}–148 Incipit practica auium secundum M' P. Ex primis legum cunabulis . . . plumatam et sanabitur. Explicit. (*c*) ff. 148^{v}–167 Incipit philosophia supra dietas particulares et etiam questiones. Vt ait Galienus in 2°

de complexionibus . . . Queriter consequenter de castaneis et oliuis et similibus. Set quia questiones istorum que remanent habeo alibi. inde est quod ibi pono finem quam ad questiones huius libri etc'. (*d*) ff. 167v–172v Incipit philosophia quedam supra librum tegni. Sicut dicit philosophus in policiis quas ordinauit et scripsit . . . capillos generat. Et sic ad illud etc'. (*e*) f. 172v A recipe for laxative pills 'Magistri Iohannis de rupe'.

(*a*). Thorndike and Kibre (Simon de Herbrad). (*b*). Thorndike and Kibre.

12 (quires 22–3). (*a*) f. 181rv Sicut scribit aristotiles in principio metaphisice Omnes homines . . . error in principiis etc'. (*b*) ff. 181v–183v Incipit summus tractatus de ornatu mulierum. Vt ait ypo in libro quem de sciencia . . . et decenter conseruent. Explicit tractatus necessarius de supplecione Pulcritudinis mulierum. (*c*) ff. 183v–186v Incipiunt notabilia Senece. Beneficium nec dare scimus . . . nec eripi nec dari potest. etc'. Expliciunt notabilia Senece de beneficiis. (*d*) ff. 187–188v, 173–4 Incipiunt Notabilia super librum tegni G. Paruum in omni re simile est in forma magno completo . . . nisi per artem dyaletice solum. Expliciunt notabilia supra librum Tegni Galieni. (*e*) ff. 174v–175 Incipiunt Notabilia supra librum reg' acut'. Omne quo fit iuuamentum. in sanacione egritudinum . . . contrarii cum contrario. (*f*) ff. 175v–177 Brief notes on words in Justinian, Institutes. (*g*) ff. 177v–180v Notes on fevers, the first 'De allopicia'.

(*b*). Thorndike and Kibre. (*c*). Cf. the beginnings of De beneficiis, bks. 1, 6. (*d, e*). From Galen and Hippocrates. (*g*). Headings in red. 'De terciana' begins, f. 179v 'Nota dicit Magister de bona fortuna. quod de terciana non vidit aliquem mori. Set Magister suus vidit vnum mori . . .'.

13 (quire 24). (*a*) ff. 189–90 Notes 'De epilencia' and 'De ebrietate'. (*b*) ff. 190v–192 Incipit practica M. Iohannis de Parma. Quoniam quidam de melioribus amicis . . . renes. que dicte sunt supra etc'. Explicit practica M. Iohannis de Parma compilata bononie. et est valde bona. (*c*) ff. 192v–196v Incipit tractatus de interpretacionibus sompniorum. Philosophantes antiquos siue indos siue persos . . . potest conuenienter pro homine proporcionali (*ends imperfectly in pt. 2, ch. 6*).

(*b, c*). Thorndike and Kibre. (*c*). William of Aragon on dreams, is printed among the works of Arnaldus de Villanova, edn. 1585, pp. 623–37 col. 1/4: the last six chapters are missing.

14. f. 197 Dico quod est habitus . . . quamuis in hac falsa opinione viuant.

This leaf may belong to quire 13. It is torn and the verso is pasted over.

15. Medical pieces neatly written in the hand of arts. 12*g*, 13*a* fill nine or ten lines in the lower margin of ff. 158v–174v, 177v–197.

One piece ends (f. 167) 'Dicit m. de bona fortuna' and five pieces end 'Hoc (*or* Hec, *or* Vt) dicit magister de bona fortuna' (ff. 161, 174v, 178v, 180v (Vt dicit magister de bona fortuna super primum capitulum libri), 190v (after a piece 'Nota etiam quod vidi quemdam qui a corpore cuiusdam eduxit plenam scutellam de pediculis . . .'. On f. 189 is 'Ego autem m. de bona fortuna aliquando in primis tribus diebus nichil dedi nisi . . .'. Cf. above art. 12*g* and, for a commentary on the Viaticum of Constantinus by 'Bona Fortuna', Thorndike and Kibre, col. 623.

16. f. 197, below the last piece of art. 15, a memorandum about money: 'nota detuli mecum in festo (?) [. . .] de paris'. In flor' 9 lib' et d'. Item in albis [. . . . .] Item in bursa de serico in dup[. . . . . .] ii alb' et d'. Item alb' den' et alb'[. . . .].

ff. ii + 197 + ii. 242 × 175 mm. Written space *c*.176 × 126 mm. 2 cols. 39–49 lines. The first line of writing above the top ruled line. Collation: $1\text{-}18^8$ 19^{12} $20\text{-}23^8$ 24^{10} wants 9, 10 after f. 196 25 one (unless f. 197 was 24^{10}). Quires 22 and 23 are wrongly bound: see above, art. 12. Quires appear to be lost after f. 136 (17^8) and f. 144 (18^8) to judge from 'hic d*efici*t Pe(cia) [. . .]' in the margin of f. 136^v, s. xiii/xiv, and the offset writing on f. 144^v: the next page bore decoration like ff. 1, 9, 73, but was not any of these pages. *Ad hoc* quire and leaf marks in pencil here and there. Written mainly in one informal textura which varies in size: a better hand wrote arts. 12*g*, 13*a*, 15. Initials: (i) f. 1, 7-line *O* in colour on a gold and coloured ground, historiated (doctor and patient ?) and with prolongations into the margins: on the horizontal bar in the lower margin a dog chases a hare; (ii) 5-line, as (i), but decorated, not historiated: the dog and hare motif in the lower margins, ff. 9, 73 and cf. f. 144^v; (iii) gold on coloured grounds; (iv) 4-line, blue or red (or blue and red) with ornament of both colours; (v) 2-line, blue or red with ornament of the other colour: sometimes violet takes the place of blue in the ornament. Capital letters in the ink of the text filled with red. Bound by Bramhall and Menzies in 1931 for 15*s*. 6*d*. Secundo folio *que yleos*.

Written in France. For some connexion with 'Magister de bona fortuna' see above arts. 12*g*, 15; with Paris, above art. 16. A later owner recorded the birth of the son 'comitis (?) clairevallis B[. . .] de val', 17 Oct. 1593, on f. 36^v. No. 8038 in the Halliwell catalogue of Chetham manuscripts, 1842.

27857 (Mun. A. 3. 134). *Medica quaedam* s. xv^2

1. ff. 1–285^v 'Capitulum primum de Natura sperme generantis et non generantis 2^m etates humanas.' Dixit auic' 20. 3^{ii} Quod sperma ebrii decrepiti et infantis et hominis multi coitus non generat . . . est proprie epatis et non matricis egritudo.

A gynaecological work in sixty-five chapters in which Gilbertus, Gordonius, Paulus, and Consiliator (P. de Abano) are quoted. Marginalia in a late fifteenth-century English hand are numerous on ff. 1–60. Projecting tabs of parchment cut from a manuscript of English origin, s. xv, show where the chapters begin. f. 119^v blank; also 239^{rv}.

2. ff. 286–302^v Reuerendissimo in cristo patri ac domino domino diuina fauente gratia summo pontifice petrus de abano minimus medicorum cum deuocione presens scriptum . . . Quia venenosum cibus fit pars nostri corporis . . . a medicis tiriaca est appellata.

P. de Abano, De venenis. Thorndike and Kibre, cols. 1234 (Quia venenum), 1357. *GKW*, nos. 2521–3.

3. ff. 303–5 Intendo mediocriter docere medicos quam breuius potero de natura balneorum . . . et hoc ad presens de balneis nos circumstantibus sufficiant etc. Deo gratias scripsit Ia. cristi*ani* 2^m (*sic*).

Thorndike and Kibre (Gentile da Foligno).

4 (on flyleaves). (*a*) f. i Richardus Marchall de mulieribus. Ad restringenda menstrua . . . secundum kyng golsmyth. (*b*) ff. i^v–ii^v Partus Mulieris. Tempus vero

egressus de vtero materno . . . (*c*) f. 307^{v} Secundum Iohannes herdern. Medicus ad Regem henrycum v. Ad prouocand' Menstrua . . . (*d*) f. 308^{rv} Recipe 'For a woman y^{t} is bolned as she were w^{t} chylde' and two other recipes.

(*a–d*) added in England in the hand which annotated art. 1.

5 (on flyleaves). ff. iv, v, 306–307^{v} Tables of arts. 1–3, s. xvi in.

ff. v + 306 + viii, foliated i–v, 1–72, 72*, 73–313. The medieval numbering runs to 285 and then begins afresh with art. 2, 1–20. Paper. 211 × 150 mm. Written space 140 × 90 mm. 29 long lines. Verticals are ruled with pencil, horizontals with hard point. Collation: 1–28^{10} 29^{6} (ff. 280–5) 30–31^{10} (ff. 286–305). Strips of thin parchment between and in the middle of the quires. Arts. 1, 2 in current sloping humanistica, perhaps by a German or Netherlandish scribe. Art. 3 in a neat textura, with humanistic *g*. Art. 4 and annotations to art. 1 in current anglicana. Initials: (i) red with pink ornament or blue with red ornament; (ii) 3-line, as (i). Nearly contemporary English binding of wooden boards half covered with once white leather: 3 bands: 2 clasps, now mostly missing: a title 'Liber [. . . .]' on the back cover.

Written in Italy (?), but soon in England: cf. arts. 1, 4. 'R. Marchal', f. v^{v}, s. xv^{2}: cf. art. 4*a*. 'Robertus Syddallus me iure possidet 1600', f. v^{v}. A price, '8 s' ', on the pastedown, on f. v^{v}, and on f. 312^{v}, s. xvi (?). 'J. Byrom', f. v^{v} and elsewhere, is the signature of John Byrom of Kersall, Lancashire, 1692–1763. Listed on p. 244 of the Byrom catalogue printed in 1848. Given by Miss Eleanora Atherton in 1870.

27894 (Mun. A. 3. 128). *Evangelistarium* s. xv med.

Gospel lections of Sarum use, bound in a confused order.

Arts. 1, 2 are on quires 1–7.

1. ff. 1–40^{v}, 65–72^{v}, 45^{rv}, 47–52^{v}, 46 Temporal from Advent to the 25th Sunday after Trinity. Parts of the Palm Sunday Gospel, ff. 15–16, 18, 21^{v}–23 are noted.

2. f. 46^{rv} Dedication of church and octave.

Arts. 3–5 are on quires 8, 9.

3. ff. 61^{rv}, 41^{rv}, 63^{rv}, 43–44^{v}, 64^{rv}, 42^{rv}, 62^{rv}, 53–55^{v} Sanctoral.

Saints' names have been blotted out. Largely by cues. No office of Anne.

4. ff. 56–60^{v}, 73–6 Common of saints.

5. (*a*) f. 76 Vigil of Pentecost. (*b*) f. 76^{rv} Hugh of Lincoln. (*c*) f. 77^{rv} Cena domini (John 13: 1–15).

(*a*, *b*) in the main hand. (*a*) does not occur on f. 67 where there is a reference in the margin to f. 76. (*b*). As *Sarum Missal*, p. 348, footnote 3. (*c*). Added in s. xv^{2}.

ff. iii + 78 + ii. 262 × 182 mm. Written space 164 × 111 mm. 24 long lines. Collation: 1–9^{8} (ff. 1–40; 65–72; 45, 47–52, 46; 61, 41, 63, 43, 44, 64, 42, 62; 53–60) 10^{6} (ff. 73–7 and the pastedown). Initials: (i) ff. 3v (Christmas), 38 (Easter), 64 (John Baptist) and beginning arts. 2–4, 4-line or 3-line, blue or pink shaded to white on decorated gold grounds: borders continuous or (ff. 46, 64) on three sides; (ii) 3-line or 2-line, gold on coloured grounds, with sprays of green and gold into the margin: a continuous border on f. 1; (iii) 1-line, blue with red ornament or red with pale green ornament. Capital letters in the ink of the text filled with yellow. English binding, s. xvi, of wooden boards covered with brown leather: centrepiece of a blank shield and corner-pieces: two clasps missing, except the metal pieces. Secundo folio *leprosi mundantur*.

Written in England. Many scribbles, s. xvi, include names: James Madewell, f. 1; Willhelus (*sic*) Cooke, f. 2; Thomas Cooke, ff. 2, 77v; Jhon hyllysley, f. 4; Willelmus Howarde, ff. 6, 49v; Henre frelond, f. 23; Mr Hughe Nalinghurst Gente, f. 59v; Willyam Lottysham, f. 64. 'Fulke Wallwyne', f. iii, s. xvii, probably denotes ownership: cf. *MMBL* ii. 939. 'J. Byrom' inside front cover and on f. 1. Byrom catalogue, p. 239. Given as MS. 27857. Frere, no. 636.

27900 (Mun. E. 8. 23). *Aulus Gellius* s. xv^2 (*c.* 1472)

Incipiunt capita librorum auli gellii noctium atticarum. Quali proportione . . . (*table of chapters of the twenty books*) . . . (f. 16) summa de noctium ordine. (f. 17) Auli gellii noctium atticarum liber primus incipit feliciter. Quali proportione quibusque collectionibus . . . uiueret. Capitulum primum. Plutarchus in libro . . . (f. 251) inuenirique possit. Auli Gellii noctium atticarum liber uicesimus explicit.

The Greek is written—by Bartolomeo Fonzio—in red in spaces left blank. As in all 'codices deteriores' and in all editions before that of Gronovius (1651), Gellius' preface is attached to the end of bk. 20 (bk. 20, ch. 11): cf. ed. Hertz (1873–5), II. lxx–lxxv. ff. 16v, 252rv blank.

ff. i + 252 + i. 335 × 230 mm. Written space 208 × 113 mm. 34 long lines. Double vertical bounders. Collation: 1^{10} 2^6 $3\text{–}25^{10}$ 26^6. Quires signed AA, bb, A–Z, Ↄ. Written in a good humanistic hand. Initials: (i) of each book, 9-line, gold on blue and green grounds covered with convolutions of white vine stem, which on f. 17 extend into the margins; (ii) '2-line', blue, outside the written space. Binding of stamped and gilt red leather over wooden boards for Matthias Corvinus, King of Hungary, †1490 (see A. R. A. Hobson in *The Book Collector*, 1958, pp. 265–8; C. Csapodi, K. Csapodi-Gárdonyi, T. Szántó, *Biblioteca Corviniana: The Library of King Matthias Corvinus of Hungary*, 1969, pp. 55, 138, and pl. xxiv; C. Csapodi, *The Corvinian Library*, 1973, no. 293): repaired conservatively by W. H. Woods and Co. of Manchester in 1879: two clasps missing.

Written in Florence for Francesco Sassetti: see A. C. de la Mare in *Essays in honour of P. O. Kristeller*, ed. C. H. Clough, 1976, p. 186, no. 66, where the scribe is identified as Hubertus and the illuminator as Antonio di Niccolò di Lorenzo. A strip has been cut from the head of f. 1 and arms (of Sassetti) defaced in the lower border on f. 17. '5367' on the pastedown at the end. 'J. Byrom' on both pastedowns. Byrom catalogue, p. 246. Given as MS. 27857. *MERT*, no. 72.

27902 (Mun. A. 5. 14)[1] *G. de Chauliac, 'Inuentorie . . . in Cirurgicale parte of medicyne' (in English)* s. xv^2

1. Here bigynnethe the Inuentorie or the Collectorie in Cirurgicale parte of medicyne compiled and complete in þe ȝere of our lorde 1363 by Gwydonem

[1] See p. 335 n. 2.

id est Gy de Caulhiaco Cirurgien Maister in medicyne *id est* doctor of phisic in þe fulle clere studie of Montis pessulani *id est* Mountpelers wt some addiciouns of oþer doctoures necessarii to þe forsaide arte or crafte. Forsoþe after þt thay haue first done lovinges . . . For emeroidez it is best for to cese (*ends imperfectly in bk. 7, doctrine 2, chapter 7*).

Two leaves missing after f. 1, two after f. 85, and one at the end. The introduction and bks. 1 and 5 are printed by Wallner, Lund 1964, 1969. Other copies are New York, Academy of Medicine 12, Cambridge, U.L. Dd. 3. 52, Gonville and Caius College, Cambridge, 336, ff. 1–42v (bk. 1), and Glasgow, Hunterian 95, ff. 35–74v (imperfect). Another translation was edited by M. Ogden, EETS cclxv (1971): the last words here occur there, p. 638/24.

2. Inserted pieces: (*a*) 'A certeyn medicyn for restorytyf' and two other recipes in English, s. xvi, on a slip of parchment loose at f. 39; (*b*) 'For a fistula an approved medicine', s. xvi ex., on a paper sheet loose at f. 112; (*c*) a prescription, s. xvi/xvii, on a loose scrap of paper at f. 112; (*d*) notes of payments to the poor at Chedburgh (Suffolk) in 1618–20 by John Frost of Whepstead under the will of Sir Robert Drurie, on a piece of paper tied in at f. 63**.

(*d*). For Drurye see J. Gage, *Thingoe Hundred*, 1838, pp. 429, 437–8.

3. The pastedown at the beginning is a bifolium of an ordinal, s. xiv, in an English hand (anglicana formata): 2 cols. 43 lines. Text blurred.

For example, 'Feria 2a ebdomade iiiite incipiunt epistole canonicales' (cf. *Brev. ad usum Sarum*, I. dccccxxxviii).

ff. 153, foliated 1, 4–35, 35*, 36–61, 61*, 62, 62*, 62**, 63–96, 96*, 97–121, 123–7, 127*, 128–36, 136*, 137–49. Paper and—for the outside and middle leaves of each quire—parchment. *c*.375 × 260 mm. Written space *c*.315 × 208 mm. 2 cols. 49–53 lines. Frame ruling in pencil. The first line of writing above the frame line. Collation: 1^{12} wants 2, 3 (ff. 1, 4–12) $2–7^{12}$ 8^{12} wants 6, 7 after f. 85 $9–13^{12}$ 14 one (f. 249). Quires numbered a–o. Written in a current mixture of anglicana and secretary by one hand throughout. Initials: (i) of each book, in colours on gold grounds decorated in colours and with sprays into the margins; (ii) 3-line, blue with red ornament. Binding of wooden boards covered with brown leather, bearing Oldham's roll HM h. 30 and a crested roll, s. xvi^2; metal corner-pieces and centrepiece; two clasps missing; repaired in 1879 by W. H. Woods and Co. Manchester, whose ticket is at the end. Secundo folio missing: f. 1v ends 'as sheres' (cf. edn., p. 4/33).

Written in England. In Suffolk in s. xvii^1. '15s', f. 1. 'J. Byrom' on pastedown. Byrom catalogue, p. 244. Given as MS. 27857.

27907 (Mun. A. 3. 129). *Hymnale* s. xv^2

1. ff. 1–52v Temporal.

The order here, as compared with *Brev. ad usum Sarum* III. ciii–v is: nos. 1–4, 9–12, 81, 17 (?: only the doxology remains on f. 9), 18–58, Alma chorus (*Brev. ad usum Sarum*, ii. 236), 59–66. Two settings of nos. 2, 51, 65, 66. Eight leaves missing after f. 8.

2. ff. 52v–54 In dedicatione ecclesie.

Ibid. nos. 67, 68. f. 54v blank.

3. ff. 55–88v Sanctoral.

Ibid. nos. 79, 80, 82–3, 86–7, 84, 85 (two settings), Crux fidelis (*Brev. ad usum Sarum*, iii. 279), 88–90, 91 (two settings), 93–4, 110–12, 113–15, together with ten hymns not in *Brev. ad usum Sarum*:

ff. 60v–71 (after Crux fidelis) Ruine celi, Signum magnum, and O celebre conuiuium (*AH* xxiii. 150–1) for the translation of Bridget, with settings for use at Christmas, Easter, and Ascension. In all but first settings, the last verse of each hymn, Tu esto nostrum gaudium . . . , has been erased;

ff. 76–8 (after no. 91) Sacre virginis marie pietas clementie, and f. 80rv (after no. 94) Festiuis laudibus (*ends imperfectly*), both for Visitation of B.V.M.;

f. 81rv, after a gap of nine leaves, the last words of a stanza 'lis reduxit orbita' and five complete stanzas of a hymn which includes the words 'Conemur totis uiribus iungamus preces precibus ut augustini meritis celi fruamur gaudiis', followed on ff. 81v–82 by Celi ciues applaudite, also for Augustine;

ff. 84–86v (after no. 112) Hora consurgit, Celi perornant, and Dies salutis (*AH* lii. 145; xliii. 100; iv. 116) for the canonization of Bridget.

On f. 88v the heading 'In commemoracione beate birgitte' is followed by a cross-reference to her translation.

4. ff. 89–122v Common of saints.

Ibid. nos. 69–78. From two to six settings of each piece. Three leaves missing after f. 120 contained the end of no. 77 and the beginning of no. 78.

5. f. 122v Ad primam ympnus. Iam lucis orto . . . (*ends imperfectly*).

A good hand of s. xvi² completed the text on f. 122v and added elsewhere variant readings and additional stanzas of hymns and also notes on metre and authorship (Vexilla regis by Theodulf of Orleans; Aurea luce by Elpis, the wife of Boethius).

ff. 122. A former foliation 1–8, 17–88, 98–137, 141–2 takes account of the leaves now missing from arts. 1, 3, 4. 250 × 175 mm. Written space 177 × 107 mm. 8 long lines and music. Collation: $1–8^8$ 9^6 (ff. 65–70) 10 three (ff. 71–3) 11^8 wants 8 after f. 80 $12–16^8$ 17^8 wants 1–3, 6–8 (ff. 121–2). In quire 8 the first two and last two leaves are singletons. Initials: (i) 2-line, blue with red ornament; (ii) 1-line, red or blue. Contemporary binding from the 'Caxton bindery' (Oldham, stamps 233, 234 (as border), 243), rebacked and repaired by W. H. Woods and Co., Manchester: two clasps missing, but the metal pieces to which they were attached remain on the back cover. Secundo folio *sul ad custodiam*.

Written in England for the use, presumably, of the brothers of Syon. 'J. Byrom', ff. 1, 65. Byrom catalogue, p. 239. Given as MS. 27857.

27911 (Mun. A. 2. 166). *Life of Christ (in English)* s. xv¹

(*begins imperfectly*) [. . . . . .] (f. 1v) schamed sore of hem self. and token leffis of a fig tree . . . (f. 85r) . . . gaderþ togeder þe reliff. þat it be noȝt lost. þei went (f. 85v) [. . . .] (*ends imperfectly*).

ff. 1r, 85v are all but illegible. The last words on f. 85r translate John 6: 12. Of twenty-seven remaining headings the first is on f. 4, 'How Anne conseyued Marie þe moder of ihesu crist.

þoroȝ whome helþe of Adam and Eue was restored and to al hem þt were in helle wiþ hem' and the last on f. 83, 'Of þe woman take in avowtrie', beginning 'In time sone after ihesus went into þe hille of Olyuete'. A leaf missing after f. 78.

The text corresponds with Trinity College, Dublin, D. 4. 3, pp. 245–92 and is combined with Love's Mirror in Trinity College, Cambridge, B. 2. 18.[1]

ff. 85. Formerly foliated, s. xvi (?), [20]–104. 132 × 90 mm. Written space *c.* 72 × 44 mm. 17 long lines. Collation: 1^8 wants 1 2–8^8 9^8 wants 8 after f. 78 10^8 wants 8. Written in a neat short-*r* anglicana formata. Catchwords have distinctive ornament. Initials: (i) 2-line, blue with red ornament; (ii) 1-line blue. Evidently long coverless: ff. 1r, 85v are badly stained. 'Bound by W. H. Woods, Manchester, 1879'.

Written in England. Scribbles of s. xvi/xvii: 'Robert Bunting', f. 17v; 'Robert Barton: booke', f. 45v; 'John Barton', f. 79. Byrom catalogue, p. 239. Given as MS. 27857.

27929 (Mun. A. 3. 131). *Coluccio Salutati, Opera* s. xv in.–xv med.

No. 17 in the Bodleian exhibition catalogue, *Duke Humfrey and English humanism in the fifteenth century*, Oxford 1970; no. 21 in A. Sammut, *Unfredo duca di Gloucester e gli umanisti italiani*, 1980.

1. ff. 1–89v Incipit feliciter Liber Primus de Seculo et Religione editus a Colucio Pyeri de Stignano Cancellario Florentino. ad fratrem Ieronimum de Vzano ordinis Camaldunensium in Monasterio Sancte Marie de Angelis de florentia. Et primo prohemium. Memor semper fui . . . indiuisibili perseuerat Amen. Explicit felicite(r) Liber Secundus et Vltimus de Seculo et Religione compositus a (*etc., as above*).

No. 15 of the manuscripts listed by B. L. Ullman, *Colucii Salutati De seculo et religione*, 1957. Bk. 2, f. 47v. f. 90rv blank.

2. ff. 91–200 Colucii Pyeri Salutati de fato et fortuna liber incipit ad felicem Abbatem Monasterii Sancti Saluatoris de Septimo ordinis Cisterciensis et primo prohemium. Quotidianum esse uidemus et communiter . . . et operam perdidisse. Colucii Pyeri Salutati de fato et fortuna liber explicit ad Domnum felicem (*etc., as above*).

Tractatus 1 (3 chapters), f. 92v; 2 (11 chapters), f. 99v; 3 (13 chapters), f. 140; 4, f. 195v; 5, f. 197v. Three leaves missing after f. 117. Cf. B. L. Ullman, *The Humanism of Coluccio Salutati*, 1963, pp. 30–1.

3 (added in the space remaining blank in quire 22 and on two additional leaves). ff. 200v–205 Declamations of Salutati: (*a*) Colucii Pyeri Salutati Declamacio quedam. Lucretia Spurii Lucrecii filia et golatiui . . . vetat pater et coniux; (*b*) Quod Lucrecia non se interimat. Pars una. Noli te afflictare Lucretia . . . Supplicio affecit. Caue; (*c*) Pars altera Lucrecie. Nolite me pater sanctissime . . . licitam fore vitam; (*d*) Eiusdem Colucii declamacio. Sententia prima Reprobata. Questio est coram decem viris quid iure Ciuili statuendum sit de hiis qui fecerunt carmen famosum contra aliquem. vel ipsum recitauerunt. Pars una. Utile ni fallor est peccata . . . ridiculum tribuatis; (*e*) Pars altera contra delacionem. O preclarum

[1] Information from Dr A. I. Doyle.

consilium. O lex . . . aut iniusticie prenotare. Vale amen. Finiunt Notabiles Declamaciones Colucii. Deo gracias.

Cf. Ullman, *Humanism*, p. 34. (*a–c*) are printed as a letter of Aeneas Sylvius in early editions of his letters (edn. Nuremberg 1481, no. 428).

ff. i + 205. 225 × 160 mm. Written space 140 × 100 mm. 25 long lines. Pencil ruling. Collation: 1^{10} 2 cancelled $2\text{–}4^{10}$ 5^{10} wants 10 after f. 48 $6\text{–}9^{10}$ 10^{2} (ff. 89–90) $11\text{–}12^{10}$ 13^{10} wants 8–10 after f. 117 ($13^{6,7}$ were cut out and then sewn in again) $14\text{–}21^{10}$ 22^{6} + 2 leaves after 6 (ff. 204–5). Arts. 1, 2 in an Italian textura, by the same hand throughout;[1] art. 3 added in English textura. Initials of art. 1: (i) f. 1, 7-line *M* in colour on a decorated gold ground, with prolongations into the margin; (ii) f. 2, 2-line *A* on coloured ground; (iii) 3-line, blue or red, with ornament of the other colour. Initials of arts. 2, 3: (i) ff. 91, 99ᵛ, in colour on decorated gold grounds with prolongations which, on f. 91, form a continuous border; (ii) 3-line, blue with red ornament. Capital letters in the ink of the text are filled with yellow in arts. 1, 3. Line fillers in blue and red in art. 2. Medieval binding of wooden boards covered with stamped leather by a binder who worked at Salisbury, *c.*1460 (Oldham, pl. xxvii, binder I; G. D. Hobson, *English Binding before 1500*, 1929, pl. 16; N. R. Ker in *BLR* v (1955), 179–80): Oldham, stamps 402, 405 form a double frame, within which are three vertical rows of stamps, Oldham 402 in the middle and the same fleur-de-lys stamp as occurs on Bodleian, Laud Misc. 558, on either side of it: repaired and rebacked by W. H. Woods and Co., Manchester, in 1879. Secundo folio *eius deceptos*.

Arts. 1, 2 written in Italy and art. 3 in England. Art. 1 decorated in Italy (Florence) and arts. 2, 3 in England. Belonged to Humfrey, duke of Gloucester, according to erased inscriptions: (f. 205) 'Cest li[. . . .] Homfry duc de Gloucestre', followed by two erased lines the first of which ended 'Gloucestre'; (ff. 2, 91) 'Mon bien mondain Gloucestre au duc'. Belonged later to William Witham (Emden, *BRUO*, p. 2066: †1472): 'Liber magistri Willelmi Witham legum doctoris' on the pastedown; 'Witham' in large letters on f. i. 'Laurentius Stubys' (*BRUO*, p. 1809: fellow of Magdalen College, †1536), f. 205. 'Thomas Smith', f. iᵛ, s. xvi. 'J. Byrom' on pastedown and f. 147. Byrom catalogue, p. 246. Given as MS. 27857.

27938 (Mun. A. 3. 127). *Medical recipes (in English)* s. xv/xvi

1 (quire 1). (*a*) f. 1ʳᵛ An alphabetical list of herbs, 'Alleluia wodseur . . .'. (*b*) ff. 2–5 Hic incipiunt Capitula libri subsequentis de diuersis medicinis humano genere congruis incipient' in descendendo. Et primo pro dolore capitis. Set transmutatur in Anglicum vt forte medicine possunt eo leuius intelligi. For the hed ach For Fantony or Vanite . . . For a man that may not wele pisse. etc. etc. (*c*) ff. 5ᵛ–6 Recipes.

(*b*). A table of contents of art. 2 which shows that bk. 3 continued after oils with syrups, clisters, suppositories, pessaries, and 'pilotes' and that there was among the syrups a 'Medicina pro petra per Magistrum Glaston'. (*c*). Added in s. xvi in the space after (*b*). Includes a charm for healing a wound, 'Take a pese of led and make yt iiii square . . .'.

2. ff. 7–56ᵛ Omnia medicinarum et oracionum continencium in presenti libro et materiarum. Sic incipiens per capud a uertice usque ad plantam pedis diuersimodis materiis et languoribus humanis generibus cognoscendis. For the hedde ach. Take veruayne or Betony or filled Wormode . . .

[1] Or so I think. According to *Duke Humfrey* . . . (op. cit.), art. 2 is in a different hand from art. 1.

Three books, the third ending imperfectly in a section on oils, 'Also thou may make oyle of hey': cf. art. 1*b*. A mass against the falling evil is on ff. 24–5 and remedies for it are on f. 25, for example 'Takes and write the names of the iii kyng*is* of Coleyn with his awne blode and hang hem aboute his nek'. A recipe on f. 38 begins 'Take a blak Catte and prykke hym in the ballok that is to the mene man the carle Cat the Woman the quene'.

3. (*a*) ff. 57–60v Recipes and the virtues of seventeen waters. (*b*) ff. 63–68v Fifteen recipes, the first 'For to knaw qwedyr ye dropcy be hott or cold'. (*c*) ff. 68v–72 A repetition of ff. 57–60/3. (*d*) f. 72v Five recipes.

(*a*) and (*c*) are in different hands and spellings differ slightly. (*b*) ends 'Explicit Ryc' Thomas (*cancelled*) denyas spens'. ff. 61–62v blank.

ff. iii + 72 + iii. Paper. 228 × 155 mm (less on ff. 57–62). Written space *c.* 170 × 110 mm. 31–3 long lines. Faint frame ruling with a hard point. Collation: 1^6 $2\text{–}3^8$ 4^8 wants 1 before f. 23 5^6 6 five (ff. 36–40) $7\text{–}8^8$ 9 six (ff. 57–62) 10^{10} wants 9, 10. Arts. 1*a*, *b* and 2 in a clear secretary hand (see below). Art. 3 in current anglicana by two hands. Initials: (i) red with ornament in the ink of the text; (ii) 2-line, red. Contemporary parchment binding: modern endleaves. ff. 57–72 have been mended skilfully, s. xx.

Written in England, art. 1*a*, *b*, and art. 2 probably by 'Richard Wermyncham Spens' who wrote his name and designation on f. 5v in the hand of the text, and art. 3*b*, *c* by another steward, Richard Denyas (see above): Warmingham is a Cheshire place-name. '[...] asfordeby C. d. k' is scribbled on f. 61v. 'J. Byrom', ff. 1, 61. Given as MS. 27857.

27941 (Mun. A. 2. 171).[1] *Medica quaedam* s. xv²

1 (quires 1–9). ff. 1–90v Incipiunt versus medicinales editi a Magistris et doctoribus Salernitanis in Aprilia (*sic*) scripti karolo magno . . . Francorum regi scribit tota scola selerni (*sic*) . . . deus et facientem. Cui sit . . . Explicit florarium versuum medicinalium scriptum cristianissimo Regi francorum karolo magno a tota vniuersitate doctorum medicinalium preclarissimi studii salernitani tempore quo idem rex Saracenos deuicit in Runciuale quod lituit (*sic*) usque tarde et deo uolente nuper prodiit in lucem.

In five parts. Thorndike and Kibre note four manuscripts of this version of the Schola Salernitana: Bodleian Ashmole 1475 and e Mus. 228 (*Sum. Cat.* 3544) are others and cf. *CMA* ii. 98, no. 3806. The first two leaves of quire 1, ff. i, ii, were left blank.

2 (quire 10). ff. 91–98v The peynes of the tethe ben nombrede of haly abbas in sermone xxo primo (*sic*) partis libri disposicionis regalis. There ben v or six aches as ache fretyng . . . lackynge of norysschment and (*ends imperfectly: a quire missing*).

3 (quire 11). (*a*) ff. 99–100v Circa inspecciones vrine 7tem sunt necessario consideranda . . . (*b*) ff. 101–5 Conferunt capiti et cerebro fetida in graui racione et oppressione cerebri . . . (*c*) ff. 105v–106 Notes on weights. (*d*) ff. 106v–107v De proprietatibus planetarum et conpleccionibus earundem. (*e*) A list of the

[1] See p. 335 n. 2.

thirty-two 'dies periculosi' (ff. 107v–108), a 'Tabula fleobotomie' (ff. 109–110v), etc.

(*a*, *b*). Cf. Thorndike and Kibre, 223 (Circa urine inspectionem), 246 (Conferunt cerebro).

4 (quires 12–19). ff. 111–201 Felix qui poterit rerum cognoscere causas . . . Quare egritudines generantur . . . 3o propter purgacionem scabiei Amen. Completa est sentencia abstracta causarum problematum Aristot'. assistente prime cause subsidio. ex qua. in qua. et per quam omnia cui laus et gloria.

In four parts and thirty-eight particulae, according to the preface. Thorndike and Kibre; L. Thorndike in *Bulletin of the History of Medicine*, xxix (1955), 517–23, refers to copies in Cambridge, U.L., Ee. 1. 22 and Bodleian, Digby 77, 153, and 161.

5 (quires 20–6). (*a*) ff. 203–17 Aquarum quatuor sunt qualitates . . . sanguinem impurum denunciant. (*b*) ff. 217–59 Incipiunt signa distinctiua vrinarum manifestissima . . . vt citrini subcitrini Ruffi subruffi dicuntur medii etc'. (*c*) ff. 259–260v Siliqua est quinta pars denarii . . .

(*a*, *b*) on urines. (*b*). Thorndike and Kibre, from Corpus Christi College, Oxford, MS. 132, ff. 118–34. (*c*). On weights.

ff. 262, foliated i, ii, 1–260. Paper. 147 × 107 mm. Written space *c.*90 × 65 mm. 14–20 long lines. Frame ruling. Collation: $1\text{–}6^{12}$ (ff. i, ii, 1–70) $7\text{–}8^{8}$ 9^{4} (ff. 87–90) 10^{8} $11\text{–}18^{12}$ $19\text{–}21^{8}$ 22^{16} $23\text{–}25^{8}$ 26 two (ff. 259–60). Current secretary and (ff. 219–260v) a mixture of current anglicana and secretary: headings and explicits are in short-*r* anglicana formata. Initials: (i) 3-line or 4-line, red with brownish ornament; (ii) 1-line, red. Contemporary binding of wooden boards covered with brown leather bearing stamps 254 and 259 and panel REL 7 in Oldham (Crucifer binder: cf. p. 28): rebacked by W. H. Woods, Manchester, in 1879: two clasps missing. Secundo folio *Fetus testantur.*

Written in England. 'Salern' et Gyleys v s' and 'Memorandum (?) Iohn Irton in Irto(n) in Copland (*Irton, Cumbria*) et (?) pro vxore [. . .] paraletic' et cum mola matricis', f. i, s. xv ex. 'Robertus Syddallus', f. 1: cf. MS. 27857. Perhaps the Hoby manuscript in *CMA*: see above, art. 1. 'J. Byrom', ff. iiv, 1. Byrom catalogue, p. 245. Given as MS. 27857.

27971 (Mun. A. 3. 132). *Horae* s. xv²

1. ff. 1–12v Calendar in gold and black.

Entries in gold include 'Dedicacio ecclesie constan' ', 'Clari martiris', 'Laudi episcopi. Mathei apostoli', 'Reliquiarum constan' ' (12, 18 July, 21, 30 Sept.). f. 13rv blank.

2. ff. 14–59v Hours of B.V.M. of the use of (Coutances).

Hours of Cross and Holy Spirit are worked in. 'Gaude virgo concipiens . . .' (6 lines: *RH*, no. 27179; *AH* xlvi. 132, lines 1–6) in the space after lauds. The first leaf is missing and its place is taken by a leaf of another smaller book of hours—14 long lines—with a damaged Annunciation picture on the recto. f. 32v blank.

3. ff. 60–5 Sequentiae of the Gospels. f. 65v blank.

4. ff. 66–80^{v} Penitential psalms and (f. 75) 'letania maiora'.

Twenty-three confessors: . . . (8, 9) Laude Taurine.

5. ff. 81–107^{v} Office of the dead.

6. ff. 108–111^{v} Doulce dame de misericorde fontaine de pitie . . .

Fifteen Joys of B.V.M. Sonet, no. 458.

7. ff. 111^{v}–114 Obsecro te . . .

8. ff. 114–115^{v} Passio domini nostri ihesu xpristi secundum iohannem. In illo tempore apprehendit pylatus . . . testimonium eius. Deus qui manus tuas . . .

Cf. *Lyell Cat.*, pp. 65–6. Leroquais, I. xxiii–iv.

9. ff. 115^{v}–118 Oratio valde deuota de beata maria. O intemerata . . . orbis terrarum. De te enim . . . f. 118^{v} blank.

10. f. 119 Memoria 'Des cinq principales festes de la virge marie. Aue cuius conceptio . . .' (*RH*, no. 1744).

11 (added, s. xvi). ff. 119^{v}–120^{v}, 122^{rv} Prayers in Latin and French.

Includes: f. 122, Paraphrase sur le libera me domine eterna. Deliure moy seigneur de la mort eternelle . . . (11 couplets: Sonet, no. 1377); f. 122, a prayer in French 'a mon^{r} St. Sebastien'.

ff. ii + 119 + v. ff. 120–2 are flyleaves of old parchment. 192 × 142 mm. Written space 102 × 70 mm. 16 long lines. Collation: 1^{12} + an inserted blank, f. 13, after 12 2^{8} wants 1 (supplied, see above) 3–7^{8} 8^{4} (ff. 62–5) 9–14^{8} 15^{6} (ff. 114–19). Ten pictures, 12-line or 11-line, eight in art. 2, at each hour except matins (missing: see above) and compline, and at matins of Holy Cross and Holy Spirit, one before art. 4, and one before art. 5. Initials: (i) in pink or blue patterned in white, decorated or (compline in art. 2) historiated (coronation of B.V.M.); (ii, iii) 2-line and 1-line gold on coloured grounds patterned in white. Capital letters in the ink of the text filled with yellow. Line fillers in red, blue, and gold. Framed floral borders on two or three sides of picture pages: the decoration is mainly by means of sprays on reserved white grounds, but on four pages (33, 53, 66, 81) part of the ground is of gold paint which bears more elaborate decoration. Binding of s. xix: ticket of Thomas Carter, Bookbinder, 7 Bridgewater Place, Manchester.

Written in France for use in the diocese of Coutances. 'J. Byrom', f. 1. Byrom catalogue, p. 239. Given as MS. 27857.

28024 (Mun. A. 3. 130). *G. de Vino Salvo, Nova poetria; etc.*

s. xiv/xv (art. 1), xv^{1}

1 (quires 1–3). ff. 1–25^{v} Prologus G. anglici in nouam poetriam. Papa stupor mundi si dixero papa nocenti . . . Crescere non poteris. quantum de iure mereris.

Geoffrey of Vinsauf, Poetria nova, ed. E. Faral, *Les arts poétiques*, 1923, pp. 197–262. Lines 488–1028 are not here: a quire is missing after f. 8. f. 26^{rv} blank.

2 (quires 4–7). ff. 27–53 Ad rethoricam dictandi facultatem tam in prosis quam in metris species sunt colorum diuerse . . . non pudebit accedere. Explicit tractatus rethorice.

By an Englishman, who gives a long example of 'apostropha' on f. 51 'ad nostrum . . . regnum': 'O anglia regnorum decus et regina. rege tibi ricardo superstite securus . . . O anglia clipeo regis nuper edwardi defensa . . .'. Ten chapters. ff. 46–52 are out of order. ff. 53^{v}–54^{v} blank.

3 (quires 8, 9). ff. 55–69 Glorioso principi potestates aereas debellanti domino theobaldo dei gracia regi nauarrie . . . accio et vox laudis. Explicit sompniale dilucidarium pharaonis. compositum per Iohannem lemouicensem.

Ed. C. Horváth, *Iohannis Lemouicensis opera omnia*, 1932, pp. 71–126. ff. 69^{v}–70^{v} blank.

4 (quires 10–20). ff. 71–152^{v} Prologus in epitalamicum beate virginis carmen. Per orbis ambitum . . . (*text*) Aulam sacre uirginis cano triumphalem . . . Concordi corda. musica dulcis erit.

John of Garland, Epithalamium beate Marie virginis. Walther, no. 1577. This copy noticed by Paetow, *Morale scholarium*, 1927, p. 113. Single leaves are missing after ff. 72, 91, 149. f. 153^{rv} blank. After it, the stubs of at least two excised quires can be seen.

5. f. i, a binding leaf formerly pasted down, is from a manuscript in current short-*r* anglicana,[1] s. xiv. Chapter 6, 'De ypocrasi', begins 'Et nunc ad membra de[scen]damus'.

On vices. Hypocrisy is the first branch of pride. 2 cols. 36 lines.

ff. i + 153. For f. i see above. A medieval foliation was made when the leaves were in their right order and before loss of eight leaves after f. 8 and of single leaves in quires 10 and 12. 253 × 185 mm. Written space *c.* 175 mm high (arts. 1, 4), *c.* 172 × 115 mm (arts. 2, 3). Long lines, 33 (art. 1) and 38 (arts. 2–4). Ruling in ink for arts. 1, 4. Frame ruling in pencil for arts. 2, 3. Collation: 1–2^{8} 3^{10} 4–5^{8} 6^{8} (ff. 43–5, 51–2, 46–8) 7^{4} (ff. 49, 50, 53–4) 8–9^{8} 10^{8} wants 3 after f. 72 11^{8} 12^{8} wants 7 after f. 91 13–19^{8} 20^{8} wants 2 after f. 149 and 7, 8, probably blank. Quires 1–3 are signed a, c, d, quires 4–9 a–f, quires 10–20 a–l. Written in textura and (arts. 2, 3) secretary, each art. in a different hand. Initials: (i) art. 1, bks. 2, 4–10, gold on coloured grounds, with floral sprays into the margins; (ii) blue with red ornament; (iii) 2-line or 3-line, red; (iv) 1-line red (art. 1) or blue (art. 4). Capital letters in the ink of the text sometimes marked with red. Contemporary binding of wooden boards covered with white leather, repaired: five bands (VIV); two strap-and-pin fastenings missing. Secundo folio *Tota trahet*.

Written in England. No. 19 of the manuscripts of Francis Bernard listed in *CMA*: *CMA* ii, no. 3588. 'J. Byrom', ff. 1, 153^{v}. Byrom catalogue, p. 247. Given as MS. 27857.

33667 (Mun. A. 2. 163). *Horae (in Netherlandish)* s. xv ex.

Arts. 2–6 are the translations of Geert Grote, ed. N. van Wijk, *Het Getijdenboek van Geert Grote*, Leiden 1940.

[1] Normally, anglicana in which the short *r* is used is not current.

1. ff. 1–12^v Calendar in red and black.

Entries in red include the usual Utrecht saints and (17 Aug.) Ieron.

2. ff. 13–47^v Hours of B.V.M. of the use of (Utrecht), followed on f. 47, after 'sonder eynde Amen' (edn., p. 70), by a translation of Regina celi letare, with versicle and collect.

3. ff. 48–62 Hier beghint die vii psalme.

4. ff. 62^v–81 Hier beghint die wijsheits tijde.

5. ff. 81^v–101^v Hier beghint die ghetijde uan den heilighen gheest.

6. ff. 102–120^v Hier beghint die langhe cruus ghetide.

7. ff. 121–53 Hier beghint die vighelie.

After Magnificat the scribe left a page (124^v) blank, except for 'Circumdederunt me gemitus': the *M* of *Mi*, f. 125, is a type (i) initial.

8. (*a*) ff. 153–4 Dit ghebet salstu lesen alstu wilste gaen totten helighen sacramente. O almachtighe ende goedertieren god. ic alder onweerdichste sondaer . . . (*b*) f. 154 Dit salstu lesen alstu ontfangheste dat heilighe sacrament. Here ihesu criste des leuende gods soen . . . (*c*) ff. 154–5 Alstu ontfanghen heueste dat helighe sacrament ghebet. O vader van hemelrijc hoe sal ic arme . . .

9 (added in s. xvi). (*a*) ff. 155^v–157 Dit is een geestelick wijngart. Men vindt geen beter dranc dan wijn . . . (27 couplets); (*b*) f. 157^{rv} Een deuote oefeninge voer een kerstenmensche. Sint dat ick bekende . . .

ff. 158 + i. f. 159 is a parchment flyleaf. 160 × 114 mm. Written space 95 × 59 mm. 22 long lines. Collation: 1^{12} 2–19^8 20^2. Initials: (i) of arts. 2–7 and on f. 125, 10-line, red and blue, with green, blue, yellow, and red ornament; (ii) as (i), but 4–6 line, and blue instead of red and blue; (iii, iv) 2-line and 1-line, red or blue. Good penwork borders, nearly continuous on pages with initials of type (i) and short on pages with initials of type (ii). Capital letters in the ink of the text touched with red. Binding of s. xvi: wooden boards covered with brown leather bearing a heads-in-medallions roll and a crested roll: rebacked: two clasps missing.

Written in the Low Countries (Holland). 'Desen bock hoort Toe eef Ians dochter van Amsterdam', f. 157^v, s. xvi. 'S. (?) Haudelair', f. 159, s. xix. 'Ex libris F. G. H. Culemann Hannoverae' inside the cover, s. xix: his sale at Sotheby's, 8 Feb. 1870, lot 200.

MANCHESTER. PUBLIC LIBRARY[1]

BR. 310 D. 5. *J. Calderinus, Repertorium utriusque iuris* s. xv med.

(*begins imperfectly in* Appellatio) viua voce de ap. c. l. in glo . . . Zoillus similiter ut C de he. insti cum proponas. Explicit repe*r*torium Chalderini deo gracias.

A legal dictionary, A–Z: cf. Schulte, ii. 249. Printed at Basel in 1474: *GKW*, no. 5904. Leaves are missing at the beginning—for the first words now see edn. signature d^{10} recto, col. 1, last line—and there are other gaps. The extra leaf in quire 20 (f. 215) is in the main hand and supplies an omission.

ff. i + 256 + i. Strong paper and—for the outside and central sheets of each quire—parchment. 405 × 285 mm. Written space *c.*300 × 195 mm. 2 cols. *c.*74 lines. Frame ruling in pencil. Collation: 1^{12} wants 1 and 12 2^{12} wants 1 before f. 11 $3\text{–}5^{12}$ 6^{12} wants 6, 7 after f. 62 7^{12} wants 12 after f. 78 8^{12} 9^{12} wants 10 after f. 99 and 12 after f. 100 10^{12} wants 1 before f. 101 and 6, 7 after f. 104 11^{12} 12^{12} wants 12 after f. 132 13 four (ff. 133–6) 14^{12} wants 1 and 12 (ff. 137–46) 15^{12} wants 1 and 12 (ff. 147–56) 16^{12} wants 1 before f. 157 $17\text{–}19^{12}$ 20^{12} + 1 leaf after 11 (f. 215) 21^{12} $22\text{–}23^{14}$. Written in a current hand, with hybrida and some cursiva letter-forms. Metallic red initials, 5-line, 2-line, and 1-line. Capital letters in ink of text touched with red. Contemporary wooden boards covered with brown leather bearing small stamps of three designs, one, a roundel, only round the edges, a second only within the rectangular border formed by two pairs of widely separated fillets, and the third, a fleur-de-lys, only in the lozenges of the panel within the border: 'rebacked by Hodgins'. Four bosses were on the back cover only: they are now missing.

Written in Germany. 'Liber Iohannis Stammel clerici Lubicen' ', s. xv ex., on the pastedown. 'G. Sumner, Woodmansey, 1856' and his pressmark, E, 3/23, are on f. 1: his sale, Beverley, 31 Oct. 1877, lot 595 (£1. 16*s.*).

BRm. 343 Lt. 13. *Officium in agenda mortuorum, etc.* s. xv ex.

1. Antiphons, etc.: (*a*) ff. 1–10v 'In die palmarum quando fit processio'; (*b*) ff. 10v–14v 'In festo purificationis beate marie'.

2. ff. 14v–43v Ordo fratrum heremitarum secundum consuetudinem romane ecclesie. quando anima a corpore egressa est. pulsetur campana magna ter immediate. et tunc dicatur hoc Responsorium recitando Subuenite sancti dei . . . pietatis absterge. R' Amen. Noted office of burial.

3. ff. 43v–92 Incipit officium in agenda mortuorum. Noted.

4. ff. 92v–93v Six settings of 'Requiem eternam dona eis domine et lux perpetua luceat eis'.

[1] I have not included in these descriptions a very large quire book, perhaps seventeenth-century and from Spain. Leaves measure *c.*700 × 520 mm and minims are 26 mm high. Two fragments in f091. F. 9 are included. This and f091. M. 14 are both large collections of fragments.

ff. 94. 222 × 160 mm. Written space *c.*157 × 110 mm. 15 long lines. Collation: 1^8 $2–9^{10}$ 10^6. Initials: (i) in colours on gold grounds: historiated on ff. 1v (bishop) and 10v (B.V.M.); (ii) red with violet ornament or blue with red ornament. A continuous border on f. 1 includes at the foot a roundel in which the Flight into Egypt is depicted. Binding of brown leather (s. xvi/xvii ?) over wooden boards: rebacked. Secundo folio *interrogauit*.

Written in Italy for the use of Austin Friars. 'Ad usum Conuentus Sanctæ [. . . .] de [. . . .] Almæ Vrbis [. . . .] anno Domini 1669',[1] f. 92. Phillipps MS. 12291.[2] Phillipps sale 17 May 1897, lot 14, to Avondale (£1. 13*s*.). Given by Henry Watson in 1899.

BRm. 343 Lt. 15. *Antiphonale, pars aestivalis* s. xv ex.

1. ff. 1–144 Antiphons of the temporal, beginning imperfectly at Easter Eve and ending at Dominica in kalendis nouembris. 'Finis ferialis', f. 144. ff. 144v–146v are ruled for music, but otherwise blank.

2. (*a*) ff. 147–155v Facta communione sacerdotis in missa. statim incipitur in choro pro uesperis R' Alleluia . . . Ps. Laudent d. A' Uespere autem sabbati . . . Finis hy diurni. (*b*) ff. 157–60 Ad Mag' antiphona. Tradent enim uos in conciliis . . . Estote fortes . . . Deus tuorum militum . . . Finis hymni noct' '.

Day and night hymns of the common of saints and In dedicatione ecclesie. ff. 156rv, 160v blank.

ff. iii + 160 + iii. Thick paper. 196 × 153 mm. Written space 150 × 110 mm. 8 long lines and music. Collation: 1^{10} wants 1–3 $2–14^{10}$ 15^{10} wants 8, probably blank, after f. 144 16^{10} 17^4. The signatures are z, marks of abbreviation for *-que, con-, -rum, -bus,* aa–kk, 3, 5: they suggest that probably twenty-two quires are missing at the beginning—they were perhaps bound as a separate volume—two quires before f. 147 and one quire before f. 157. Art. 2 in current hybrida. Red initials. Binding of s. xix.

Written in Italy. Book-stamp of a Cremona library, f. i: 'Biblioth. S. Angeli Cremonæ'. The relevant slips from an Italian and an English bookseller's catalogue, s. xix, are inside the cover. Book-plate of the Henry Watson Musical Library.

BRm. 360 Py. 35. *Psalterium, etc.* s. xv med.

1. ff. 1–3 Litany. Bruno and Hugh were added later.

2. ff. 3v–9 Calendar of Carthusian use in red and black.

Entries in red include 'Bernhardi abbatis', Bruno (added), 'Festum reliquiarum', 'Commemoratio fratrum nostrorum', Hugh (of Lincoln) at 21 Aug., 6 Oct., 8, 9, 17 Nov. Entries in black include Hugh (of Grenoble) and 'Adelarii episcopi et martyris' (traditionally bishop of Erfurt, †755), at 1, 20 April.

3. f. 9v 'Sanctus Bernardus.' Loquitur deus in psalmo . . .

[1] Of the three illegible words, the first may begin with a *C*, the second probably ends *lo*, and the third may begin *Ca*.

[2] Cf. A. N. L. Munby, *Phillipps Studies*, iv. 180.

4. ff. 10–141v Liturgical psalter.

Projecting tabs show the main divisions of the Carthusian psalter at Pss. 20, 32, 45, 59, 73, 95, 109. Noted antiphons, etc.

5. ff. 142–154v Six ferial canticles (Audite celi divided at Ignis succensus), followed by Benedicite, Benedictus, Magnificat, Nunc dimittis, Quicumque vult.

6. ff. 154v–161 Office of the dead.

7. Additions at the end of quire 17, include, f. 163v, a table of psalms of the common of saints, with leaf references to art. 4, s. xv², and—on a paper leaf attached to f. 163—settings of Alleluia, s. xvi in.

ff. 163. ff. 10–155 have a medieval foliation '1'–'147'. 182 × 132 mm. Written space 130 × 90 mm. 19 long lines. Collation: 1^{14} wants 1 $2\text{–}5^{10}$ 6^{8} $7\text{–}8^{10}$ 9^{8} $10\text{–}13^{10}$ $14\text{–}15^{8}$ 16^{10} 17^{10} wants 8, 9 after f. 162. Clear black hands, changing at ff. 55, 154v. Flex punctuation in art. 6 only. Initials: (i) red and blue, with ornament mainly in red; (ii) 2-line or 1-line, red or blue. Cadels and capital letters in the ink of the text touched with red. Contemporary German binding of wooden boards covered with stamped pigskin: five small bosses removed from each cover: central clasp missing: offset of manuscript pastedowns.

Written in Germany for Carthusian use and perhaps at Erfurt (art. 2). 'liber cartusiæ Erfurt', f. 1, s. xvii (?). 'Fol. 161. d. 13. April . 1835. Bibl. Bülov. Beyern. G. H. Schr', f. 1: probably lot 1681 in the Bülow sale, 10 Oct. 1836.[1] 'G. Sumner, Woodmansey, 1854', f. 1: not identifiable in his sale (see above BR. 310 d. 5). The book-plate of 'W. H. C.' is inside the cover; also a slip from an English bookseller's catalogue, s. xix, and the book-label of the Henry Watson Musical Library, with date of acquisition, 4 July 1917.

G. 091 B. 1. *Legenda, etc., Sanctae Bonae* s. xiii¹

A 'libellus' of the acts and miracles of St Bona, which belonged formerly to the church at Pisa where her body lay and was presumably written for use there. Probably the manuscript used by the Bollandists.

1. (*a*) f. 1rv Incipit prologus in legendam sancte bone de ciuitate pisana. Bonus deus bonorum omnium conditor . . . gratiam impetrabit. (*b*) ff. 1v–3v A table of eighty-five numbered chapters. (*c*) ff. 4v–40 Incipit legenda sancte bone uirginis de ciuitate pisana. Et primo de natiuitate eius. Igitur sancta bona nata est in ciuitate pisana . . . uoluntarie uouit. deuote compleuit.

The legend of St Bona of Pisa, †1208, printed in *Acta Sanctorum* at May 29 'ex pervetusto MS. codice Ecclesiæ Pisanæ' (Maii VII, 145–63). ff. 4r, 40v blank.

2 (added, s. xiv²). f. 40 A note that when Bona's body was translated to the new church of St Martin a leaden tablet was found and on it the words 'Anno dominice Incarnationis mo ccviiio iiiio kl' Iunii. venerabilis Re et nomine Bona deuota huius eclesie et Ministra requiescit'. This inscription was seen by several friars

[1] For G. H. Schäffer and F. G. J. von Bülow see *MMBL* ii. 592.

minor, among them the writer 'frater Bettus Stephanii dicte capelle sancti martini de pisis qui pro tunc erat actualiter Sororum visitator. Scriptum Anno domini m° ccc° lxiiii° die xiii Aprilis'.

Printed ibid., p. 160 (reading *Corporum* instead of *Sororum*). f. 40v blank.

3. The flyleaves, ff. 41–2, contain an office of St Bona, s. xiv, 'quod fit post vesperas feria 3a pent' '.

The three lessons are each preceded by noted antiphons, etc. The third says that Bona died on 28 May. The final prayer, f. 42, is printed ibid., p. 142F (cf. C). f. 41 is rubbed and may have been pasted down once. f. 42v blank.

ff. i + 40 + iii. ff. 41–2 are medieval flyleaves: cf. art. 3. 223 × 170 mm. Written space 150 × 110 mm. 2 cols. 24 lines. The first line of writing is above the top ruled line, except on some leaves where what looks like an extra line has been ruled across the top. Collation: $1–5^8$. Well written. Initials: (i) ff. 1, 4v, red with red and blue ornament; (ii) outside the written space, red. Binding of crimson velvet, s. xix/xx. Secundo folio *a quo*.

Written in Italy (Pisa). The ex-libris of the Augustinian priory (later Franciscan convent) of St Martin, Pisa, is in good uncials of s. xiii (?) on f. 40v: LIBER SANCTI MARTINI PISANI NEGATHOL'. Quaritch, *General catalogue of books*, Suppl. for 1875–7, no. 18390. Armorial book-plate of Henry White, J.P., D.L., F.S.A.: his sale at Sotheby's, 21 Apr. 1902, lot 300. Book-plate of the Thomas Greenwood Library for Librarians.

G. 091. H. 2. *Horae* s. xv med.

1. ff. 1–6v Rather empty calendar in French, in red and black.

2. ff. 7–13v Hours of the Cross, followed by the prayer 'Domine ihesu criste qui hanc sacratissimam carnem . . .', with heading in French, conveying indulgence of 2,000 years.

3. ff. 14–17v Hours of the Holy Spirit, beginning imperfectly.

4. ff. 18–57v Hours of B.V.M. of the use of (Tournai).

5. ff. 57v–60v Obsecro te . . . Et michi famule tue . . .

6. ff. 60v–62v O intemerata . . . orbis terrarum. Inclina . . . ego miserrima peccatrix . . .

7. Devotions to B.V.M.: (*a*) ff. 62v–64v vii especiales goyes a la viergene marie sensieuent. Gaude flore uirginali . . . (*b*) f. 64v Encore a nostre dame. Aue regina celorum . . . (*c*) f. 64v Item a nostre dame. Regina celi letare . . .

(*a–c*). *RH*, nos. 6809, 2070, 17170.

8. ff. 65–8 Memoriae of Christopher, Barbara, and Sebastian, St John 1: 1–13, and a memoria of Elizabeth of Hungary.

9. ff. 69–80v Penitential psalms and (f. 77) litany.

Ten martyrs: Stephane Laurenti Vincenti Sebastiane Quintine Nichasi Piate Adriane Cristofore Valentine. Ten confessors: ... (8–10) Franscisce (*sic*) Anthoni Ludouice. Deus cui and Fidelium are the only prayers.

10. f. 81rv Les viii vers s' bernart. Illumina oculos meos ...

11. f. 81v Orisons a son bon angele. Angele qui meus es ...

ff. iv + 81 + v. 182 × 128 mm. Written space 118 × 75 mm. 18 long lines. Collation doubtful: mostly eights and sixes: all larger pictures are on singletons. Poor script and decoration. Ten 14-line pictures with continuous borders, eight in art. 4 and one before arts. 2 and 9 (Christ on the rainbow). Five smaller pictures, four to illustrate the memoriae in art. 8 and one before art. 5 (B.V.M. and Child in glory). Initials: (i) pink patterned in white on gold and blue grounds, the gold decorated and the blue patterned in white; (ii) 2-line, gold on coloured grounds patterned in white; (iii) 1-line, blue with red ornament or gold with grey-blue ornament. Line fillers of red and blue penwork in litany. Binding by Ramage, s. xx: gilt edges.

Written for female use in the diocese of Tournai. Book-plate of the Thomas Greenwood Library for Librarians.

q411. G. 2. *G. Barzizius, De orthographia; etc.* 1474

1. ff. 2–17v Orthographia Gasparini Pergamensis Oratoris Optimi foeliciter Incipit. Quoniam recta scriptura quam greca appelacione orthographiam dicimus ... rationemque scribendi daturum pollicitus fui. Orthographia Gasparini oratoris optimi finit. H.V.G.

The first part of the Orthographia of Barzizius. Printed in 1471 (*GKW* 3691) and later. The last words here are thirty lines short of the end, sign. d(iiiiv), in the edition listed by Pellechet, no. 1991.

2. ff. 18–19v On punctuation. (*a*) a summary account of the marks used, 'Restat ut de modo punctuandi breuia subnectamus . . .', is followed by extracts on punctuation from (*b*) f. 18 Catholicon, (*c*) f. 18v Isidore, (*d*) f. 18v Hugutio, (*e*) f. 19 Papias, (*f*) f. 19 'Franciscus Petracha', and by (*g*) f. 19v, a prayer 'in qua omnia puncta habentur iam supradicta', beginning 'Si decernas in solitudine te conferre'.

(*a*), after two sentences in praise of punctuation, is a briefer version of lines 3–25 of (*f*). (*b–e*) are printed by M. Hubert in *Archivum Latinitatis Medii Aevi*, xxxvii (1970), 131–2 (XIIIh, lines 1–45), 118–19 (XIIk, lines 7–34), 70–1 (VIIa, lines 55–81), 98–100 (XIa, lines 39–59, 107–9). (*f*). Lines 3–25 differ slightly from the text printed by L. Gai in *Memorie Domenicane*, n.s. iii (1972), p. 306/3–26. The showing of a parenthesis by means of brackets or of points above the line is noted as one of 'tres alii puncti quorum usus iam apud nos non est' and discussed in lines 26–35. (*g*) is as Gai, p. 306/30–8.[1]

[1] I owe the references to Hubert and Gai to Mr Jean Vezin.

3. ff. 19v–20 Liber donati de accentibus sequitur. Tonos alii accentus. alii tenores . . . addita vel detracta significatur. Finit liber donati de accentibus.

Hubert, loc. cit., p. 29 (IVa). Donatus, Ars Grammatica, ed. Keil, 1864, pp. 371–2.

4. ff. 20–1 Aelegantis Guarrini Oratoris differencialia feliciter incipiunt. Dicitur esse nepos de nepa luxuriosus . . . Assurgo dominis. insurgo durus in hostes. Aelegantis Guarrini oratoris differencialia feliciter finiunt. H.V.G.

Walther, no. 4425. Printed with Guarino's Regulae grammaticales, but the last six lines here differ from the last five in the editions. Verses were added on f. 21, s. xv ex., 'Carceribus deditum (?) studentem crebro petisti / Præsul. cur clericum zodomitam non tenuisti Stoker. inhumanum tu nosti pontifex suum (?)'.

5. f. 21v Alique abreuiaciones romanorum more que plurimum in auctenticis libris offenduntur quod quidem ut scire opere precium est. sic ignorare turpissimum. A aulus. C caius dicitur . . . Sunt alie que non in auctenticis libris. set forte scissuris lapidis inueniuntur . . . et huiusmodi multa etc. Dixi.

Another hand adds a note on conventional abbreviations in law books.

6. f. 22 (*begins imperfectly*) circumque discipline et non ex hiis que . . . equiuocacio (*ends abruptly*).

7. ff. 22v, 23v Notes on the months and indictions.

8. f. 23rv Incipiunt precepta breuiuscula memorie digna guarrini oratoris permaximi. Tametsi dicendi venustas . . . cedere soleat. Hec itaque precepta sunt de arte dicendi agregata ac ea memorie si mandaueris te et doctum et facundum efficient.

Thirty-four precepts.

9. ff. 24–36v Clarissimi uiri ac prestantissimi philosophie doctoris Augustini dachi senensis de variis loquendi figuris seu de modo dictandi ad andream ciuem senensem hysagogicus libellus incipit feliciter. Si quis id operis diligens examinator . . . a quo paternum offitium requiras: vale. Dixi.

Pseudo-Datus, Rhetorica minor. Often printed (*GKW*, 8139–58).

10. ff. 38–40 Summa preceptorum ad partem composicionis pertinentium que ad collationem et ordinem spectant. Primum preceptum quod se oracio augeat ut nobilis et egregius . . . Vltimum preceptum quod non utamur preceptum que themasis dicitur in diccionibus simplicibus . . . sunt reperta.

The right order of the leaves is 39, 38, 40.

11 (in very small current writing). Notes on Greek grammar (f. 36v), names, forms, and values of the Greek letters (f. 37v), 'Littere persarum' (f. 37v), 'Littere Galilee', and 'Littere Penteptone' (f. 40), 'Littere Egipciorum', 'Littere Tartarorum', 'Littere Caldeorum' (f. 40v).

12. The flyleaf (f. 1) has a title in the main hand on the recto, 'Orthographia Gasparini foeliciter Incipit 1474' and a note about Barzizius in a hand of s. xvi ex. on the verso.

ff. ii + 39 + i, foliated (i), 1-41. Paper. For f. 1 see art. 12. 280 × 210 mm. Written space *c.* 190 × 120 mm. 39-55 long lines. Collation of ff. 2-40: 1^{10} (ff. 2-11) 2^{12} wants 11, 12 after f. 21 3 two (ff. 22, 23) 4^{12} (ff. 24-35) 5 five (ff. 36-40: the bifolium 38-9 is now turned the wrong way round). Written in small skilful current hybrida (occasional humanistic *g*), all but art. 6 probably in one hand, but art. 11 is smaller and more current, like the marginalia in art. 1. Red initials, 5-line (f. 1) and 3-line: spaces unfilled, ff. 27-40. Capital letters in the ink of the text touched with red. Rebound in 1961 by Sangorski and Sutcliffe: the earlier binding was German, s. xix.

Written in Germany (?) by 'H. V. G.' (?: cf. arts. 1, 4). Book-plate of Georg Kloss, s. xix. Bought 25 June 1866. The price then (?) paid, '£1. 15. 0', was inside the cover of the nineteenth-century binding.

f091. F. 9 ff. 20-1, 26-31, 36-41, 48-51, 77-8. *Breviarium (fragm.)* s. xv med.

Twenty leaves of the sanctoral of a breviary, fragments of seven quires. Ten pages, formerly pasted down, are badly blurred: 20^r, 26^r, 29^v, 31^v, 37^v, 39^v, 40^r, 48^r, 51^v, 78^v.

Quire 1. ff. 20, 40 Andrew. Two consecutive leaves.
Quire 2. ff. 38, 30, 50-1, 31, 39 Nicholas (6 Dec.), octave of Andrew (7 Dec.), Conception of B.V.M. (8 Dec.: ff. 50-1, 31, 39). A leaf is missing after f. 30 and a leaf after f. 51.
Quire 3. ff. 41, 21 Lucy (13 Dec.), Thomas apostle (21 Dec.), Canute, 'cuius festum celebratur sequenti die post festum epiphanie domini. cum ix leccionibus' (f. 21^v). Two consecutive leaves.
Quire 4. ff. 77, 36-7, 78 Prisca (18 Jan.), Fabian and Sebastian (20 Jan.), Purification of B.V.M. (2 Feb.). Leaves are missing after f. 36.
Quire 5. ff. 26-7 Vincent (22 Jan.), Conversion of Paul (25 Jan.), and memoriae of Proiectus and Agnes 'post benedicamus'. Two consecutive leaves.
Quire 6. ff. 28, 48 Vitalis (28 Apr.), 'Petri noui martiris' (29 Apr.: nine lessons), Philip and James (1 May), and a memoria of Walburga 'post benedicamus', Invention of Cross (3 May), John before Latin gate (6 May). Leaves are missing after f. 28.
Quire 7. ff. 49, 29 Vitus (15 June), William (of Eskill, 16 June), Botulph (17 June), Nativity of John Baptist (24 June), a memoria of Canute 'post Benedicamus', translation of Canute (25 June: nine lessons), John and Paul (26 June). Leaves are missing after f. 49.

On ff. 50-1 imperfections in the parchment were patched with pieces of a manuscript of s. xv.

ff. 20. Written space 230 × 162 mm. 2 cols. 40 lines. The following are bifolia: 38-9, 30-1, 50-1, the first, second and fourth in quire 2; 77-8, 36-7, the first and second or the second and third in quire 4; 26-7, the fourth in quire 5.[1] f. 21 was on the last leaf of quire 3 and f. 29 the last leaf of quire 7, as catchwords show. 2-line initials, red or blue.

[1] I call the outermost bifolium the first and the innermost bifolium the fourth, presuming that the quires were of eight leaves (four bifolia).

Written in Denmark.[1] Used as pastedowns and flyleaves in bindings, presumably in a 5-volume set. Part of a collection of fragments taken from bindings (except ff. 87–98, q.v.) and put in a binding by Riviere, almost certainly for Thomas Greenwood (†1908: *DNB*).

f091. F. 9 ff. 87–98 *Exempla* s. xiii^2

A collection of stories for use by preachers, beginning imperfectly. The subject headings are: (f. 87) [. . . .] mentis siue cogitacionum; (f. 87^v) De uoto et peregrinacione; (f. 90^v) De religione; (f. 92^v) De morte iustorum; (f. 93^v) De pena purgatorii; (f. 95^v) De diabolo et eius temptacionibus; (f. 96^v) De fide chatolica; (f. 96^v) De aqua benedicta; (f. 96^v) De perseuerantia; (f. 97^v) De sacramento altaris.

Sources are 'Petrus Cluniac' ' (the De miraculis of Peter the Venerable, abbot of Cluny 1122–56: *PL* clxxxix. 851–954), Gregory's Dialogues, Vitas patrum, Bede's Historia ecclesiastica, Barlaam, and lives of SS Jerome, John Evangelist, John the almoner, James, Nicholas, and Leonard. Several stories concern Dominicans. An added note on f. 87 begins 'Nota bone frater in isto sexternulo habentur plura exempla . . .'. ff. 87, 90, 93, 97, 98^v are partly blank.

ff. 12. 142 × 100 mm. Written space 110 × 80 mm. 26–8 long lines. A quire of 12 leaves. Written in current anglicana. 2-line initials not filled in.

Written in England. ff. 55–66 of a larger manuscript, if '55' in a medieval hand on f. 87 at the foot is a leaf number. Now part of a collection of fragments: see preceding item.

f091. J. 12. *Codex Justiniani* s. xiii^2

In nomine domini nostri ihesu cristi la aptis Iustiniani liber primus incipit de summa trinitate et fide catholica. et ut nemo de ea publlice contendere audeat lāa Rubrica. Gratum (*sic*) ual' en (*sic*) āa ad populum urbis constanti Rubrica. Imperator. Cunctos populos quos . . .

Bks. 1–9 without the preliminary constitutions (ed. P. Krueger, pp. 1–4), De nouo codice faciendo, etc.: bk. 2, f. 32^v; 3, f. 53^v; 4, f. 71^v; 5, f. 100; 6, f. 136; 7, f. 176; 8, f. 203; 9, f. 226^v. The scribe missed a piece of bk. 5, which was added by another contemporary hand on f. 116. Many glosses, most of them ascribed to 'ac' and some to 'az', are written in more or less current hands in the wide margins, but there is no continuous apparatus, except the beginning of the commentary of Accursius as a rather later addition on ff. 1–2^r, 'In nomine domini de summa trinitate. De iusticia tractaturus de eius parte . . .'. A drawing of an open coffin with a man partly in it is among notes and scribbles on f. 241^v: the caption is 'Si alterum pedem haberem in sepulcro adhuc [. . .]', to which another hand added 'anno domini m^o ccc^o xxx^o'.

ff. ii + 241 + ii. 395 × 255 mm. Written space *c.* 235 × 115 mm. 2 cols. 50 lines of text and sometimes up to 130 of commentary. Collation: 1^{12} 2 ten 3 ten 4 ten $5–7^{12}$ 8 nine (ff. 79–87) $9–10^{12}$ 11^{12} + 1 leaf inserted after 12 (f. 116) $12–13^{12}$ 14^{16} + 1 leaf after 14 (f. 163) $15–19^{12}$ 20^{14} + 2 leaves after 14. Quires numbered at the beginning a–v. Initials:

[1] Dr Tue Gad tells me that the office of St William is in the Odense breviary, but that elsewhere the fragments agree with the breviary of Slesvig.

(i) outside the written space, blue with red ornament; (ii) 1-line, red. Each book, except the third and eighth, begins with a line of long narrow blue capitals, with red ornament. Bound by Riviere, s. xix/xx. Secundo folio *statum pertineat*.

Written in France (?). Book-plate of the Thomas Greenwood Library for Librarians.

MANCHESTER. JOHN RYLANDS UNIVERSITY LIBRARY

The John Rylands Library in Deansgate, Manchester, was founded by Mrs Rylands as a memorial to her husband, John Rylands, 1801–88, to form a scholarly reference library in the centre of Manchester in which the main emphasis was to be on theology. This conception was broadened after Mrs Rylands had acquired the Spencer collection in 1892. The library was opened on 1 January 1900. E. Gordon Duff's 3-volume catalogue of the printed books published in 1899 contains at the end (iii. 1983–6) a brief list of manuscripts: of the medieval manuscripts twenty-one are in Latin (Lat. 136–8, 140–52, 168, 169, 171, 366, 395), fifteen in English (Eng. 75–87, 92, 94), and one in French (Fr. 66). The manuscript holdings became vastly greater in 1901 when Mrs Rylands bought the collection of Lord Crawford for £150,000: see N. Barker, *Bibliotheca Lindesiana*, 1977, pp. 350–4, 359–60. Since 1901 they have been added to steadily by gift and purchase. A general account of the library as it was in 1920 is given by the librarian, Henry Guppy, in *BJRL* vi. 11–68, and as it was in 1941 by Moses Tyson in *BJRL* xxv. 44–66.

The medieval manuscripts of the University of Manchester are partly manuscripts which came to Owens College after the death of J. P. Lee in 1870: they are mentioned in *The Library*, v (1893), 22–3. Their number was increased by the bequest of R. C. Christie in 1901. All the medieval manuscripts are in Latin, except two, one in English and one in German, which formerly belonged to the Medical Society.

The John Rylands Library and the library of the University were merged in 1972 to form the John Rylands University Library. At the time of the merger the manuscripts and rarer printed books belonging to the University were moved to the building in Deansgate which now forms the special collections section of the new joint library.

Catalogues and Handlists. The Latin manuscripts belonging to the John Rylands Library in 1910 were catalogued, except for a few recent acquisitions, by M. R. James, *A descriptive catalogue of the Latin manuscripts in the John Rylands Library at Manchester*, 2 vols. (i, Letterpress; ii, Plates), 1921: a reprint, with additional notes and corrections by Dr Frank Taylor, was published in 1980. James's numbers run from 1–183. Latin manuscripts not catalogued by him and other manuscripts in other Western European languages are described in handlists: by R. Fawtier, 'Hand-list of additions to the collection of Latin manuscripts in the John Rylands Library, 1908–20', *BJRL* vi (1920), 186–208, covering Lat.

184–332; by M. Tyson, 'Hand-list of additions to the collection of Latin manuscripts in the John Rylands Library, 1908–1928', *BJRL* xii (1928), 581–609, covering Lat. 184–395: the descriptions of Lat. 184–332 are taken almost verbatim from the earlier list; by M. Tyson, 'Hand-list of the collection of English manuscripts in the John Rylands Library, 1928', *BJRL* xiii (1929), 152–219, covering Eng. 1–508; by M. Tyson, 'Hand-list of the collections of French and Italian manuscripts in the John Rylands Library, 1930', *BJRL* xiv (1930), 563–619, covering Fr. 1–117 and It. 1–61; by M. Tyson, 'The Spanish manuscripts in the John Rylands Library', *BJRL* xvi (1932), 188–99 (no medieval manuscripts); by M. Tyson, 'Hand-list of additions to the collection of English manuscripts in the John Rylands Library, 1928–1935', *BJRL* xix (1935), 230–54, 458–85, covering Eng. 509–865 (no medieval manuscripts); by F. Taylor, 'Supplementary Hand-list of Western Manuscripts in the John Rylands Library, 1937', covering Lat. 396–447, Eng. 866–907, Dutch 1–13, French 118–29, German 1–18; by F. Taylor, 'Hand-list of additions to the collection of English manuscripts in the John Rylands Library, 1937–51', *BJRL* xxxiv (1951), 191–240, covering Eng. 908–1157 (no medieval manuscripts); by F. Taylor and G. A. Matheson, 'Hand-list of additions to the collection of English manuscripts in the John Rylands University Library of Manchester, 1952–1970', *BJRL* lx (1977), 1–49, covering Eng. 1158–309 (no medieval manuscripts). Typescript descriptions of Lat. 448–72, acquired between 1937 and 1972, are available in the library. Descriptions of the medieval manuscripts acquired from the Congregational Library in 1976 are also available in typescript.

C. W. E. Leigh, *Catalogue of the Christie collection*, 1915, includes brief descriptions of the manuscripts on pp. 461–9.

A catalogue of MSS. Lat. 184–530 and of the Latin manuscripts in the Christie collection by Dr Taylor and myself is planned for publication. I have not therefore included these manuscripts in this volume of *MMBL*, apart from providing a hand-list of Lat. 448–530 of which there is as yet no description in print. The non-Latin manuscripts are described in the shorter form used for manuscripts at Gray's Inn, Lincoln's Inn, Society of Antiquaries, and University College, London, in vol. i and for Canterbury in vol. ii.

Manuscripts in Netherlandish

Dutch 8, 9 are foundation books from the Crawford library. Dutch 10 was acquired in 1923 and Dutch 12, 13 in 1936.

Dutch 8. *Hours* s. xv^2

1. Calendar. 2–7. Hours, etc. in the translation of Geert Groote. 8, 9. Prayers. ff. ii + 133 + ii. ff. i, 135 were formerly pasted to the covers. 183 × 130 mm. Written space 100 × 70 mm. 20 long lines. Collation: 1^8 2^2 3–5^8 6^2 (ff. 36–7) 7^8 8^8 + 1 leaf after 8 (f. 55) 9^8 10^6 11^2 (ff. 71–2) 12–14^8 15^6 (ff. 99–104) 16–18^8 19^4, together with a picture leaf in front of quires 3, 7, 9, 12, 14, 16 (ff. 11, 38, 56, 73, 90, 105). Simple, but effective pictures on the versos of these leaves:

Annunciation, Crucifixion, Christ with the doctors, Pentecost, Christ in Judgement, Christ rising from the Tomb: the direction for the artist is sometimes legible in the margin, for example (f. 38v) 'cruys'. Contemporary binding of wooden boards covered with brown leather bearing a worn panel of good design, apparently the same as Weale, no. 295: the inscription '[SIET DAT LAM GOEDES] DAT BOERT DIE SONDEN [DER VERL]' is only partly legible: a fleur-de-lys above, below, and on each side of the panel: five bands: two clasps.

Written in the Low Countries. A shield in the margin, f. 49, bears or a cross gules. Howell Wills label, marked A/III/75, inside the cover: his sale at Sotheby's, 11 July 1894, lot 415, to Lord Crawford (£7. 10*s*.). An earlier mark, s. xix, is 'No 236 du lat. 133 feuillets . . .', f. ii; also 'BAS', f. iv, top left.

1. ff. 1–10v A full calendar in red and black, written without gaps between the months. The usual Utrecht saints in red, but Jeroen does not occur at 17 Aug. 2–7. ff. 12–37, 39–55, 57–72, 74–89v, 91–103, 106–132v Hours of B.V.M., 'die lange cruus getide', Hours of Eternal Wisdom, Hours of the Holy Spirit, the seven penitential psalms and litany, and the office of the dead. The litany (ff. 97v–103) has twenty-one confessors and twenty-two virgins, Anne last. ff. 37v, 55v, 72v blank. 8. Communion prayers as quire fillers after art. 6: (*a*) ff. 103v–104v Les dit eer tu toten heiligen sacrament gaetste. O here allene der engelen glorie. Ic arme sondige mensche . . . ; (*b*) f. 104rv Leest dit nader ontfanc. O here ihesu criste lof si dijnre minliker goedertierenheit . . . 9. Prayers to B.V.M. as quire fillers after art. 7: (*a*) ff. 132v–133 Een gebet van die moeder gods ende maget maria. Weest gegruet alre heilichste maria moeder gods coninghinne des hemels. vrouwe des paradijs . . . ; (*b*) f. 133rv Een gebet van die moeder gods. Vrouwe heilige moeder gods maria om die eer ende minne . . .

Dutch 9. *Imitation of Christ, etc.* s. xv/xvi and s. xvi[1]

1. ff. 1–44v Translation into 'dietshe' of De imitatione Christi, bk. 1. 2. ff. 45–134v Life and miracles of St Barbara. 3, 4. ff. 135–158v, 159–66. Sermons.

Paper. ff. 166. 195 × 140 mm. Written space varies from 135 × 100 mm to 150 × 105 mm. 20 long lines in art. 1; then *c*.26. Collation: $1\text{–}2^{12}$ $3\text{–}4^{10}$ 5^{12} + 1 leaf after 4 (f. 49) 6 six (ff. 58–63) $7\text{–}10^{12}$ 11^{10} (ff. 112–21) 12^{12} 13 one (f. 134) $14\text{–}17^{8}$. Set hybrida (art. 1), current hybrida (art. 2) and current cursiva, set in art. 3.

Written in the Low Countries. The spine, s. xviii, bears the title 'Hofken van devot' 1492 oock een oud M. S.' and on a round label at the top '843'. The title shows that there was a now missing printed piece at the beginning and this is confirmed by the width of the spine. An edition of the *Hookijn van devotien* of 1492 is not recorded: editions of 1487 and 1496 are Goff, J. 217–18. Howell Wills label marked 'A. IV. 92' inside the cover: his sale at Sotheby's, 11 July 1894, lot 98, to Lord Crawford for 5*s*., evidently without the *Hoofkijn*.

1. Quires 1–4. This and other copies listed by C. C. de Bruin, *De middelnederlandse vertaling van* De imitatione Christi *van Thomas à Kempis*, Leiden 1954. 2. (*a*) ff. 45–94v Legend of Barbara, beginning on f. 50, after a 5-leaf 'prologhe' (Allen ghelouighen in gode . . . : see *Hand-list*), 'Binnen der tijt dat tytus ende vespasiaen regneerden' and ending 'Dar hij ons dor har bede wil verleenen die . . . Amen'. Twenty-five numbered chapters. (*b*) ff. 100–105v A 'legende' for the translation of Barbara in four chapters, 'Ghebenedijt sij die heere

god van israhel . . .'. (*c*) ff. 106–134ᵛ A prologue and thirty-four unnumbered miracles of Barbara, the last ending imperfectly. Cf. W. B. Lockwood in *BJRL* xxxvi (1953), 25–37, who prints no. (6) from f. 110ᵛ and notes other Netherlandish manuscripts containing collections of miracles. Most miracles of the present collection took place in the Low Countries, no. (15) when the English lay before Ypres. The latest date seems to be 1446. **3.** Sermons 'Van den woerden christi' (Matthew 18: 3, *except ye be converted and become as little children*) and an Advent and Lent sermon, on three quires, s. xvi^1. **4.** A sermon on Qui habitat (Ps. 90: 1–14), s. xvi^2.

Dutch 10. (R. 55690.) *Usuard; calendar* 1472

1. ff. 1–102 Martyrology of Usuard. **2.** ff. 102ᵛ–114 Calendar. ff. ii + 116 (foliated 1–93, 93*, 94–115) + ii. 200 × 135 mm. Written space 135 × 97 mm. 29 long lines. Collation: $1–13^8$ 14^{12}.

Written in 1472 for the use of the nuns of St Lucy, Amsterdam, of the third order of St Francis:[1] 'Item dit boec is ghescreuen int iaer ons heren M cccc. ende lxxii. ende hoert toe den susteren van sinte Lucien', f. 115 in contemporary textura. 'J. Kendall' stamped on the pastedown, s. xviii (?); 'Nº 3' also on the pastedown. Bought from P. J. and A. E. Dobell for £7. 11*s.* 3*d.* (£8. 8*s.*, less 10% discount) in 1923: invoice dated 24 Nov.

1. Preceded on f. 1 by an extract from the All Saints entry in the Netherlandish translation of Legenda aurea, 'Die feeste ende eerwaerdicheit der heilighen is ingheset . . . hemelsche dingen ende emighe dinghen', as in Leiden, Univ. Libr., Ltk. 273 (Lieftinck, *Maatschappij*, p. 87). Each day is marked with its Sunday letter, A–G, A–G . . . A). At the end 'God si gheloeft'.

2, not in the same hand as **1**, includes for the most part only red-letter saints, among them 'Ieroen martir' (17 Aug.) and other saints of the Utrecht calendar; also 'Onser vrouwen visitacio' (2 July) and 'Lucia ioncfrau van ciracusanen' (13 Dec.). Many added obits, mostly by one scribe who often begins his entry with a number (year of death ?), sometimes referring to benefactions, for example, (2 July) lxxi iacop claes z(oen) ewige memor*ie*, (5 Feb.) lxvi ghijsbert claes z(oen) v' ewige memorie, (31 Aug.) Aue louwen dochter v' m' x gulden ewig[e] rent[e], goesen dircz(oen) iiii wilhelmus scilt ewig[e] rent[e]: the lowest number is 'lxiii' and the highest 'xc'. Later additions, fairly numerous, run from (14)93 to 1587. f. 114ᵛ left blank.

Dutch 12. (R. 77720.) *Hours* s. xv med.

1–4. Hours in the translation of Geert Groote. ff. i + 76 + i. 168 × 117 mm. Written space 94 × 83 mm. 21 long lines. Collation: $1–2^8$ 3^4 (ff. 17–20) 4^8 5^{10} 6^8 7^{10} wants 1 before f. 47 and 9, 10, blank, after f. 53 $8–9^8$ 10^8 wants 8. Each piece begins with an historiated initial, (f. 1) Pentecost, (f. 21) Christ stands blessing, a book in his left hand, (f. 39) Christ in Judgement, (f. 54) two naked figures, man and woman, in prayer: on f. 39 the upper and lower borders supplement the initial by showing respectively trumpeting angels and the resurrection

[1] I owe the identification to Professor G. P. Gumbert, who refers me to I. H. van Eeghen, *Vrouwenkloosters en begijnhof in Amsterdam*, 1941, pp. 156–93 (and especially for G. Dircsz in 1465, pp. 160, 163, 179) and tells me that the Wilhelmus scilt was first coined by William VI of Holland in 1411.

of the dead: on f. 54 the border on the right includes a skull and a scroll inscribed 'o mensce spiegelt [. . .] sul di werden'. Old sewing on five bands.

Written in the Low Countries. One of twenty medieval manuscripts given by Mrs Ernest Hartland in May 1936. '4/4', f. i.

1 (ff. 1–19^{v}), **2** (ff. 21–38), **3** (ff. 39–53^{v}), **4** (ff. 54–76^{v}) correspond to Dutch 8, arts. 5, 4, 6, 7 respectively, q.v. Art. **1** is followed on ff. 19^{v}–20 by a memoria of B.V.M., 'Regina celi letare alleluia. Verblide di coninghinne des hemels alleluia . . .': f. 20^{v} blank. f. 38^{v} blank after art. **2**. In art. **3** the litany begins on f. 46, but lacks all names between Mary, Michael (f. 46^{v}) and Gereon, Patrokel in the list of martyrs, where thirty-one names remain (f. 47^{rv}): forty-two confessors, beginning with Martin: thirty-one virgins, beginning with Anne: names are usually latinized, for example 'aghata' not *aecht*, 'nycolaus' not *niclaes*. Art. **4** ends imperfectly in the second psalm after lesson 9: f. 76^{v} is hardly legible.

Dutch 13. (R. 77721.) *Communion prayers, etc.* s. xv med.

Fourteen pieces: **2–9** are communion prayers and devotions. ff. ii + 137 + ii. 97 × 67 mm. Written space 58 × 40 mm. 14 long lines. Collation: 1–10^{8} 11^{8} + 1 leaf after 8 (f. 89) 12–17^{8}. Hybrida.

Written in the Low Countries. No. 190 in an English bookseller's catalogue, s. xix^{2}: a fragment of the relevant notice is inside the cover and the number is also at the foot of the spine. Given as MS. Dutch 12.

1–9 are on quires 1–11 and **10–14** on quires 12–17.

1. ff. 1–27^{v} Die wijse horen de wordt hy noch wijser . . . deser elleyndiger werelt. A miscellany of sayings strung together in paragraphs most of which begin 'Item'. f. 2^{v} is on six things hateful to God 'ende dat seuende versmaet god': the seventh is a maker of discord 'tusschen bruederen of susteren'. ff. 14^{v}–23^{v} are largely quotations from authorities, Seneca, Cyprian, Ambrose, Chrysostom, and Vitas Patrum among others.

2. ff. 27^{v}–42^{v} Hier volght een ynnighe groete totten heylighen sacramente. O wonderlijc werc o godlike ghifte . . . Lof wonderlijc ghebenedijt sacrament. Fifteen 15-line stanzas written as prose: in each, the last line is 'Lof . . . sacrament'.

3. ff. 43^{v}–50 Dese sequencie ende louesanc makede Sinte thomas van aquinen een licht der heilig' kerken van den weerden heylighen sacramente ons heeren lichamen. O scouwende syon berch der heyligher kerken . . . te ghebruyken. amen.

4. ff. 50–55^{v} Dit ghebet van den heylighen sacramente sprack die selue thomas van aquinen. O verborghen wairheyt die onder dese figure . . . glorificeren. Dair du leues . . . amen. Cf. Meertens, vi. 47.

5. ff. 55^{v}–65^{v} Dit is een hoech weerdich gebet totten heyligen sacramente ende lichaem ons heeren ihesu cristi. Wonder scouwe ic ende sie . . . ghebenedijt moet wesen. amen.

6. ff. 65^{v}–74 Dit ghebet makede sinte ambrosius archibisscop van meylaen. Een doctoer van der heyliger kerken. Dat hy altoes voer sinen missen plach te sprekene. O ouerste ende ghewarighe priester . . . openliken te ghebruyken. Dair du regneeis . . . amen. Cf. Meertens, vi. 9.

7. ff. 74–83 Dit is een soete ghebet van nutscap vrucht ende orbare diese gelengen die weerdelic dat heylighe sacrament ontfangen gheestelic oft sacramentelic. Ach here god my verstricket dat. dat ic in diner tafelen sie ende smake . . . in tide ende in ewichede. Amen.

8. ff. 83–7 Dit ghebet salmen lesen eer men dat heylighe sacrament ontfaet. O ghenadighe almachtighe god. Ic arme onweerdich soendich mensche Beghere te gane . . . troest ende sekerheyt. Amen.

9. ff. 87–9 Dit sijn die groeten totten heyligen sacramente. Wes ghegruet heere ihesu criste woert des vaders sone der maget lam godes . . . des ewich leuens. Amen. Meertens, vi. 180. f. 89^{v} blank.

10. ff. 90–109^{v} Van den xii punten die den menschen hinderen dat sy gode nyet ghewinnen en connen. Hout v bedect ende onbeulect . . . ende den heyligen gheest. Amen. Cf. Lieftinck, *Maatschappij*, pp. 37, 75, 119, 192. Red headings, thirty-two in all, introduce quotations from scripture and the Fathers.

11. ff. 109^{v}–110 Van sinte barbaren der maget een deuoet ynnich ghebet. Suuerlike bistu geheeten barbara . . . Meertens, iii. 10.

12. ff. 110^{v}–117 Van der oetmoedicheyt Sinte augustijn seyt. Dat beghin ende fondament van allen doechden is oetmoedich*eyt* . . . groeter sijt voer god. Quotations from the Fathers.

13. ff. 117–134^{v} Dit sijn die graden der oetmoedich*eyt* die den religiosen toebehoren. Item in den yersten sal die mensche gheestelijc . . . is beghin van allen sonden. Sixteen heads, followed by quotations from the Fathers, introduced by 'Iheronimus', 'Barnardus', etc.

14. ff. 134^{v}–137^{v} Van ons lieuen heeren aensichte. Weest ghegruet soete minlike aenschijn mijns lieuen heeren . . . menischfondigen lydens. Amen. Cf. Meertens, ii. 70–80, vi. 34.

Manuscripts in English

Eng. 1–3, 7 are foundation books from the Crawford library and Eng. 75–87, 92 foundation books from the Ashburnham Appendix collection which Henry Yates Thompson bought in May 1897 and re-sold almost immediately to Mrs Rylands.[1] The other manuscripts were acquired in: 1905, Eng. 98; 1908, Eng. 88–90, 102–5; 1910, Eng. 63, 94, 109, 113, 404; 1913, Eng. 206–7; 1916, Eng. 288; 1919, Eng. 50, 51; in or before 1923, Eng. 91; 1926, Eng. 412–13; 1937, Eng. 895. Eng. 1310 was transferred from the University Library in 1972.

Eng. 1. *J. Lydgate, Siege of Troy* s. xv med.

ff. ii + 174 + iii. 450 × 325 mm. Written space 305 × 200 mm. 2 cols. 44 lines at first, 43 from f. 89 (11^{1}) and 45 from f. 113 (14^{1}). Collation: $1\text{–}21^{8}$ 22 six (ff. 169–74). Anglicana formata by two hands: see below. A picture in the text space before the prologue and bks. 2–5 (ff. 1, 28^{v}, 78^{v}, 112, 151^{v}: continuous borders on these pages) and more or less large pictures in 64 margins: see below. Secundo folio *To bathe*.

Arms of Carent on a red ground hatched in gold, with floral ornament and a frame, take up the whole of f. 173^{r}: the decoration is like that elsewhere, but

[1] A London binder, Zaehnsdorf, took charge of Eng. 75–87, 92 soon after they were acquired. He rebound Eng. 80 for £1. 6*s*. and put Eng. 75–8, 80–4, 92 into the 'fireproof boxes' in which they are still kept, at prices ranging from £2. 12*s*. to 16*s*. 6*d*. He also made cheap slip cases for Eng. 79, 85–7 at a cost of sixpence a case: only one of these four cases survives. Zaehnsdorf's invoice (J. R. L. invoices, ii. 1. 881) is dated March 1898 and has '31 Dec.' against the first item. Presumably 31 Dec. 1897 is the day on which Zaehnsdorf received these books. (Information from Dr Frank Taylor.)

the leaf, if original, is not likely to be in its original position. For Carent and later owners before Henry Perkins, see below. Perkins sale at Sotheby's, 3 June 1873, lot 634, to Quaritch (£1,320). In Quaritch catalogues 332 (1880), no. 47 and 343 (1882), no. 7375 (£1,720).[1] Bought by Lord Crawford in 1882: Barker, pp. 256–7, 278.

Ed. H. Bergen, EETS Extra Series xcvii, ciii, cvi, cxxvi (4 vols., 1906–35): collated as Cr. and described at iv. 29–36. *IMEV*, no. 2516/18. Bergen notes a special textual resemblance to Bodleian, Douce 230 which also contains the verses 'Pees makith plente . . .' (*IMEV*, no. 2742: printed by Bergen, iv. 26: here on f. 172^{v}). f. 174^{rv} left blank.

Script. The second hand begins at f. 113rb/27 at the words 'And of my herte' (edn., iv. 189): in this and the next 69 lines (iv. 189–257) the new scribe writes ⁒ as a mark of punctuation within the line, instead of //.

Pictures. The principal initials, other than those on the five pages listed above, occur at irregular intervals and not always at an obvious point: bk. 1, lines 1, 429, 623, 723, 1015, 1197, 1345, 1513, 2373, 2723, 3201, 3431, 3589, 3721, 3907, 4069; bk. 2, lines 203, 479, 1067, 1323, 1697, 1903, 2063, 2305, 3319, 3755, 4097, 4255, 4509, 5067, 5391, 8015; bk. 3, lines 821, 2365, 2667, 3323, 3755, 4077, 4889, 5423; bk. 4, lines 343, 545, 1223, 1701, 2029, 2401, 2525, 3107, 3271, 3363, 4281, 4637, 6023, 6731; bk. 5, lines 217, 697, 1011, 1207, 1665, 1839, 2111, 2315, 2623, 2937. The decoration in the margins of these sixty-four pages is continuous, consisting partly of a picture which takes up the lower margin and often some part of the side margins and partly of border work like that on the five pages where the borders are continuous. The pictures are listed and described by Bergen, iv. 32–6. In 'William Abell "lymnour" and 15th century English illumination', *Kunsthistorische Forschungen Otto Pächt zu Ehren'*, ed. A. Rosenauer and G. Weber, Salzburg 1972, J. J. G. Alexander noted (p. 169) that the artist is close in style to Abell. Facsimiles: of f. 28^{v}, much reduced, in *John Rylands Library, Manchester, Catalogue of a selection of mediaeval manuscripts . . .*, 1939, pl. 12; of part of f. 25^{v}, reduced in M. R. Scherer, *The legends of Troy in art and literature*, 1963, p. 244, fig. 2.

Owners. For members of the Carent family, one or other of whom is likely to have been the original owner, see Alexander, loc. cit. For owners in s. xv ex., s. xvi, 1786 and 1818, see W. G. Clark-Maxwell, 'An inventory of the contents of Markheaton Hall made by Vincent Mundy Esq. in the year 1545', *Journal of the Derbyshire Archaeological and Natural History Society*, li (1930), 117–40, who gives reasons for supposing: (*a*) that this is the copy of the 'Seege of Troy' mentioned in 1492 in the will of Sir Humphrey Talbot (†1494) and in 1503 in the will of his executor, Thomas Booth, who left it to *his* executor, Sir John Mundy (goldsmith and lord mayor of London in 1522, †1537), failing the daughter of Dr Roger Marschall, physician of London (Emden, *BRUC*, p. 392: †1477), to whom Talbot had bequeathed it; (*b*) that it is to be identified with 'a booke of parchment of the syege of Troy pres' xiii^{s} iiii^{d}' entered in the Markheaton inventory: the evidence for this is a now very difficult inscription on f. 173^{v}—not as Clark-Maxwell says a now missing inscription—which was read and, traces suggest, read correctly by H. Smedley (see below) in 1818 as an inscription of gift from John Mundy to his son Vincent, 25 May 1553; (*c*) and (*d*) that it is the copy of the Siege of Troy referred to in two letters to the owner of Markheaton Hall, one in 1786 from Samuel Pegge, who saw the manuscript in the possession of Thomas Barrett of Lee, Kent, and the other from H. Smedley who saw it in 1818 when it was in London with the bookseller, Longman.[2]

[1] I am grateful to Mr E. M. Dring for telling me the dates of these catalogues. The entries were copied in Quaritch's *General Catalogue*, 1887, nos. 47, 7375.

[2] Probably, as Seymour de Ricci saw, the gap between 1615 and 1786 can be partly filled, since this is likely to be the copy of the Siege of Troy entered as Poet. 7 in the catalogue of manuscripts of John, Baron Somers, †1716 (B.L. Harley 7191) and sold for £8. 15*s*. in the Somers–Jekyll sale, 26 Feb. 1739, lot 416, 'John Lydgate's Poem on the golden Fleece and Siege of Troy, finely written on Vellum, and illuminated, being the original Book presented by the Author to K. Henry V'.

Eng. 2. *Lydgate, Fall of Princes* s. xv med.

ff. ii + 185 + ii. 415 × 295 mm. Written space 285 × 200 mm. 2 cols. 43–51 lines: the number changes often and is 49 (seven stanzas to a column) only on the first two quires. Collation: $1\text{–}10^8$ 11^8 wants 6 after f. 85 $12\text{–}22^8$ 23^{10}. Signatures of the usual late medieval kind, but only 't 1' remains intact (f. 144: 19^1). A rather ugly and unstable anglicana formata, with a change of ink, but perhaps not of hand, at f. $151^{va}/27$, after the word 'Poncius' (viii. 372). A continuous border on f. 1 and L or I borders where bks. 2–8 begin. Secundo folio *For. lordis.*

An owner, s. xvi^2, wrote 'a note of all my Bookes' (but not including this one) on f. 185^v. Belonged to V. A. G. C. Villiers, 7th Earl of Jersey, of Osterley Park, Middlesex: his sale 6 May 1885, lot 238,[1] to Quaritch (£234); passed to Lord Crawford at 5% above this price (Barker, p. 284).

IMEV, no. 1168/19. Ed. H. Bergen, EETS, Extra series cxxi–cxxiv (1924–7). This copy collated by him as J and described at iv. 21–3, where he notes the close relationship to Pynson's edition (1494: *STC* 3175). Bk. iv, lines 98–288 are missing after f. 85. The 28 lines on f. 184, 'Greenacres a lenuoye vpon Iohn Bochas. Blake be thy bondes . . .' (*IMEV*, no. 524/2: ed. Bergen iii. 23), occur only here and in Pynson's print.

Numbers added in the margins throughout bks. 7, 8 correspond to pages of the Pynson edition, the first, 'xiiii' (f. 140), covering only four stanzas, because only these four are on sign. A 7^v in the edition. The series then runs xv, xvi, b i–xvi, c i–xvi, d i–xvi, e i–xvi, f i–xvi, g i–xvi, h i–v at intervals of 11, 12, or 13 stanzas, according to the number of stanzas on any one page of the edition, sign. A 8^r–H 3^r (103 pages), and finally h vi opposite the line 'Explicit Iohn Bochas' (f. 184) which is on sign. H 3^v in the edition. For this and other evidence that Pynson used MS. Eng. 2 see M. M. Morgan in *BJRL* xxxiii (1950), 194–6.

The book-list on f. 185^v is printed by Bergen, iv. 22. The forty-three titles, all English, include (28) The vysyon of pers plowman, (31) Raynold the Foxe, (32) The golden asse, and (40) Wytegyft*es* admonysyon (i.e. An answere to . . . An Admonicion (*STC* 25427–9), which was printed in 1572 and 1573).

Eng. 3. *Gospels* s. xv in.

The four Gospels in the later Wycliffite version. ff. xii + 200 (including a slip, f. 47: foliated 7–206) + iii. 173 × 120 mm. Written space 130 × 82 mm. 2 cols. 24 lines. Collation of ff. 7–206: $1\text{–}4^8$ 5^8 + a slip after 8 (f. 47) $6\text{–}16^8$ 17^6 (ff. 136–41) $18\text{–}24^8$ 25^{10} wants 10, blank. A fairly large textura. Secundo folio *in his natyuyte*.

According to an elaborate title-page, f. v, s. xix, the manuscript was a present to Queen Elizabeth from 'Frauncis Newport Mdlx Restored by James Dix, Bristol, Mdccclx'. Sold by Dix to Lord Crawford in 1861 for £250 through Quaritch (Barker, p. 200).

[1] According to a note in the Bodleian copy of the Jersey sale catalogue this was 'Fairfax 2343', that is to say, lot 2343 in the Bryan Fairfax sale, 26 April 1756.

The order is Luke, (71^{v}) John, (119^{v}) Matthew, (172^{v}) Mark. The usual prologue precedes each Gospel. The scribe missed all between 'Be glad wiþ' (Luke 15: 6) and 'me. for' (Luke 15: 9) and made good his error on a slip, f. 47.

ff. 1–6, s. xix, contain what purports to be a long address to the Queen by Newport. Probably Fawtier is right, in considering this to be a fabrication.[1]

Eng. 7. *'Fourme of cury'* s. xv^{2}

ff. iii + 35 + i + 50 + ii, foliated 1–91. 140 × 98 mm. Written space 92 × 50 mm. 14 long lines. Collation of ff. 4–89: 1–2^{8} 3^{8} + a slip after 7 (f. 26) 4^{8} 5^{8} + a modern leaf inserted after 2 (f. 39) 6–10^{8} 11^{8} wants 1, 2 before f. 86 and 7, 8 after f. 89 + a modern supply leaf after 6 (f. 90). Written in anglicana formata. Bound in contemporary leather stuck to pastedowns conjoint with ff. 1 and 91.

Bought by Lord Crawford in 1872 for £31 through Quaritch, as appears from a note on a loose piece of paper. A name on f. 1, s. xvi, seems to be 'Dominus Iohannes Walsh'.

One hundred and ninety-four numbered recipes, but nos. 184–6 and part of no. 187 are missing after f. 85 and no. 194 is missing at the end. No. 37, Blank dessorree, was missed at first and added by the main hand on a slip, f. 26. Preceded on ff. 4–11^{v} by a brief preface and numbered table of recipes. Closely related to the *Forme of cury* printed by Samuel Pegge in 1780 from the 'Brander Roll', now B.L., Add. 5016, except in the preface which is shorter and altered slightly.[2] ff. 39 and 90 contain modern copies from the 'Brander Roll', the latter supplying no. 194 and the former giving the text of a recipe which was added to the 'Brander Roll' in a blank space.

Eng. 50. (R. 45388.) *Prick of Conscience; Guy of Warwick* s. xiv ex.

1. pp. 1–204 Prick of Conscience. 2. pp. 205–24 Guy of Warwick, Speculum (ends imperfectly). ff. vi + 112 (paginated 1–224) + v. 250 × 150 mm. Written space 190 × 87 mm. 33 long lines. Collation: 1^{8} wants 7, 8 (pp. 1–12) 2–4^{8} 5^{8} wants 6 after p. 70 (a tiny scrap remains) and 8 after p. 72 9^{8} 10^{8} wants 2–7 after p. 90 11–18^{8} 19 two (pp. 221–4). Anglicana formata.[3] Secundo folio *In her manere*.

Belonged to 'Andrew Clerke', f. 1, s. xviii; to the Norfolk antiquary Peter Le Neve (†1729), f. 1; to Thomas Martin (†1771), f. v^{v}; to R. Farmer, master of Emmanuel College, Cambridge: his sale, 7 May 1798, lot 8061; to C. H. Harford (admitted at Emmanuel College in 1785) who wrote a note on f. v signed C. J. H. and dated 1813 in which he says that the book had been in Benjamin Uphill's

[1] Description of MS. 3 in his manuscript 'Catalogue of the English manuscripts in the John Rylands library'. Holinshed records, edn. 1808, iv. 166–7, 176, the presentation of an English Bible to Queen Elizabeth in Cheapside, 12 January 1559. It was no doubt a printed Bible.

[2] Dr Lorna J. Sass tells me that the orthography is closer to the Bühler manuscript in the Pierpont Morgan Library, New York, than to Add. 5016. The PML copy begins imperfectly at recipe 15.

[3] Professor Angus McIntosh tells me that B.L., Harley 1205 is in the same hand.

catalogue for 1800 and that he had bought it when Uphill 'lived in Bridge Street 1802'; to H. C. Harford: his sale, Sotheby's, 6 May 1907, lot 229. Quaritch catalogue 344, item 28 (£35). Bought from Quaritch in 1919 for £35: invoice dated 28 Jan.

1. Ed. R. Morris, 1863. *IMEV*, no. 1193/3. A variant version, as in Bodleian, Douce 156 (*Sum. Cat.* 21730), beginning with a 20-line prologue (running title 'Entre'), 'Her beginneþ þe soþ to say . . . God hit vs graunte say all Amen'. The text begins 'Befor þat e[ny] þ[ing] was wrouȝt' and ends 'That for oure heele on roode con hinge'. Probably thirty-four leaves are missing between these points in gaps after pp. 12, 70, 72 (probably 17 leaves), 90, and 140 (probably 8 leaves): the missing lines are between 394 and 528, 2551 and 2626, 2704 and 3957, 4594 and 5017, and 6824 and 7392. The removal of almost the whole of bk. 4, on purgatory, may have been on purpose, since the two lines on p. 11 referring to book 4 have been erased (lines 356–7): the gap in passing from the last line on p. 72 (2704) to the first line on p. 73 (3957) is not very obvious.

2. Lines 1–659 only. EETS, Extra series lxxv (see p. xxxi). *IMEV*, no. 1101/10. The text begins 'Herknes alle to my speche' and ends 'wolde þou shone'. It accompanies Prick of Conscience also in Cambridge, Univ. Libr., Dd. 11. 89, and B.L., Arundel 140 and Harley 1731.

Eng. 51. (R. 45387.) *Prick of Conscience, etc.* s. xv in.

1. ff. 5–116ᵛ Prick of Conscience. 2. ff. 117–123ᵛ, 127–134ᵛ Commentary on the seven penitential psalms. ff. viii + 119 + iii + 8 + iv, foliated i–iii, 1–138. ff. 1–4, 124–6, 135 are medieval flyleaves. 175 × 120 mm. Written space 148 mm high. 39 long lines. Collation of ff. 5–123, 127–34: 1^8 wants 1 and 3 2^8 3^8 wants 6, 7 after f. 23 $4\text{–}14^8$ 15^{10} (ff. 113–22) 16^{10} wants 10, perhaps blank (ff. 123, 127–34). Untidy anglicana formata, with lapses into current anglicana. Secundo folio *and ȝaf* (f. 5).

'Thomas Day of Brystow' is scribbled, upside down, on f. 125, s. xv ex. Belonged to John Hardy, 12 May 1708 (f. 4) and in 1710 to Maurice Johnson of Ayscough Fee Hall, near Spalding (f. 4), who (?) noted on f. i that 'My learned Friend The reverend Mʳ John Hardy' had the manuscript 'bound up by a Bookbinder at Nottingham' (in, no doubt, its present binding). The Johnson armorial bookplate of sixteen quarterings is inside the cover. Maurice Johnson sale at Sotheby's, 21 March 1898, lot 966. Quaritch catalogues 328, item 584, and 344, item 29, at £36. Bought from Quaritch in 1919 for £36: invoice dated 28 Jan.

1. *IMEV*, no. 3428/61. Ed. R. Morris, 1863. Begins at line 76 'and ȝaf hym skylle witt and mynde'. Ends 'þat for vs made heuen erþe and al þinge. Her endeþ þe pricke of conscience. Finito libro reddatur gloria cristo. Qui scripcit carmen sit benedictus amen'. A leaf is missing after f. 5ᵛ which ends 'haue no knowings' (line 153): f. 6 begins 'and amende wiþ al' (line 230). Two leaves are missing after f. 23ᵛ which ends 'soule and body' (line 1687), followed by the heading 'Of þe maner of gostly deþ': f. 24 begins 'Whan þe soule' (line 1839).

2. *IMEV*, no. 3755/7. Begins 'To goddes worschipe þat der' vs bouȝt'. Ends 'graunte oon god and persones þre. Amen amen amen. Explicit comentum super 7 ps' penitenciales in anglicis'. '1223' is written in what might be the main hand on f. 134ᵛ in a line by itself between *persones þre* and the three Amens; also on f. 135.

1, 2 are the first two of thirteen items listed on f. 2, s. xvi in.: (1) the prycke of concyence, (2) vii salmes in Inglysche, (3) the name of Ihesu, (4) for fyschyng and fowlyng, (5) a ballett of lente, (6) Ayenst ye yoke of maryage w^t^ mery ballett', (7) A blynd ballett, (8) A maryners boke, (9) A ballett of eduerd ye iiii^th^ kyng, (10) byll' of bok*es* abbrogated, (11) of the passyon of o^r^ lord Ihesu chryst, (12) A ballett of o^r^ ladyes ault^r^, (13) the bond of norfolke men.

Eng. 63. *Chaucer, Canterbury Tales (fragm.)* s. xv²

Fragment of the Miller's Tale. ff. iv + 2 + iv. 272 × 195 mm. Written space 212 mm high. 38 long lines. A bifolium, leaves 2 and 7 in a quire, if the quire was of 8 leaves. Round anglicana formata. A 19-line pen-and-ink drawing of the miller, 101 × 128 mm within the frame, fills the upper half of the text space on f. 1ᵛ. Binding by Fazakerley, Liverpool, for the Rylands Library.

A label 'e bibliotheca Spenceriana' is pasted inside the cover.

The last 29 lines of the prologue to the Miller's Tale and lines 1–19, 323–400 of the Tale itself. The picture comes after the prologue. Described and printed by G. Vine in *BJRL* xvii (1933), 333–47, with facsimile of all four pages; also by J. M. Manly and E. Rickert, *The Text of the Canterbury Tales*, 1940, i. 396–8, who show that the Rylands leaves were part of lot 157 in the George Mason sale at Leigh and Sotheby's, 25 Apr. 1799, and that eleven other leaves of the same manuscript (*IMEV* 4019/62b) belong to the Rosenbach Company, New York, 1084/2.

Eng. 75. *Pauline Epistles, etc.* s. xiv/xv

Pauline Epistles, Acts, Catholic Epistles, and Apocalypse in the later Wycliffite version, beginning 'accordinge wiþ' in the prologue to Romans (ed. Forshall and Madden, p. 303, line 6 of the third prologue) and ending 'moyses þe' (Apoc. 15: 3). 160 × 110 mm. Written space 110 × 75 mm. 26 long lines. Collation: 1^8 wants 1, 2 $2\text{–}5^8$ 6^8 wants 4–6 after f. 41 7^8 8^8 wants 5, except a scrap, after f. 63, 9^8 wants 1, except a scrap, after f. 66 10^8 11^8 wants 3–5 after f. 83 $12\text{–}14^8$ 15^8 + 1 leaf after 2 (f. 112) wants 7 after f. 116, replaced by a bifolium, 117–18, in a larger contemporary hand (25 long lines) $16\text{–}20^8$ 21^8 wants 7 after f. 165 22^8 wants 3 after f. 168 23^8 wants 8 after f. 180 24^8 25^8 wants 8. Quires signed (a)–t, w, x, y, þ, z, ȝ.

Belonged presumably to James Forster who signed neatly written verses on ff. 56ᵛ, 61, 64ᵛ (dated 1593) and wrote many calligraphic scribbles. Seen by Forshall and Madden in the possession of Rev. C. Fletcher, Southwell, Notts: his sale at Sotheby's, 22 July 1850, lot 69, to Lord Ashburnham, for £13. 5*s*. Ashburnham Appendix 23.

Forshall and Madden, no. 167. Usual prologues, two (2 Cor., 2 Tim.) missing. f. 61 is defective, ff. 83ᵛ–84 are badly stained, some initials have been cut out and there are seven gaps where leaves are missing: f. 41ᵛ ends 'I am her-' (1 Cor. 16: 19) and f. 42 begins 'of israel' (2 Cor. 3: 3); f. 63ᵛ ends 'reproue' (Eph. 5: 11) and f. 64 begins 'of ȝoure' (Eph. 6: 5); f. 66ᵛ ends 'i ȝou boþe' (Phil. 2: 13) and f. 67 begins 'israel' (Phil. 3: 5); f. 83ᵛ ends in 1 Tim. 1: 4 and f. 84 begins 'by tymes' (2 Tim. 1: 9); f. 165ᵛ ends 'honourid' (1 Peter 2: 5) and f. 166 begins 'Also' (1 Peter 3: 1); f. 168ᵛ ends 'Vertu' (2 Peter 1: 3) and f. 169 begins 'of pardicion' (2 Peter 2: 1); f. 180ᵛ ends 'stire to pa–' in the prologue to Apocalypse (edn., p. 640/8) and f. 181 begins 'golden' (Apoc. 1: 13).

Eng. 76. *New Testament* s. xv in.

1. ff. 1–9v (*begins imperfectly at Thursday before Easter*) . . . Thus endiþ þe kalender of lessons. Pistils and gospels Of al the ȝere. 2. ff. 10–185v New Testament in the later Wycliffite version, ending imperfectly 'liflode and' (1 James 2: 16). ff. iv + 185 + iii. 207 × 145 mm. Written space *c.* 150 × 100 mm. 2 cols. 35 lines. Collation: 1 five 2^4 (ff. 6–9) $3–24^8$. Catchwords centred. Secundo folio *in hir* (f. 11).

Scribbled names, s. xvi: Hedgman, f. 98; John Hedgem, f. 139; John Dowty, f. 167; Jarves, f. 185v. Ashburnham App. 24.

1. Forshall and Madden, iv. 686–98, but the text here and in Eng. 77, 78, 80, 91 differs substantially from theirs, which goes with the earlier Wycliffite version. A table for the common of saints is not provided here or in Eng. 77, 78, 80, 91: cf. edn., p. 696, footnote. The proper of saints is followed by commemorations for B.V.M., Holy Trinity, Holy Spirit, Holy Cross, angels, 'For briþren and sustryn and for saluacion of þe puple', peace, fine weather, rain, battles, 'A man for hymself', pestilence of beasts, pilgrims, weddings, sinners, and the sick. The word 'pope' has been erased; so too the name of St Thomas at 7 July.

2. Not listed by Forshall and Madden. Usual prologues. A quire is missing after f. 161v which ends with the catchword 'schal be' (Hebr. 2: 13): f. 162 begins 'me of ihesu' (Acts 8: 12).

Eng. 77. *New Testament* s. xiv/xv

1. ff. 4–12 Here bigynneþ þe calender of pistlis and gosp[els] þat ben red bi al þe ȝer in þe chirche after þe vse of Salisbery. 2. (*a*) ff. 13–15 Seynt austyn seiþ in þe secunde book of cristen doctryne . . . be more holpen. (*b*) ff. 15–16 Oure lord ihesu crist verri god and verri man seiþ in þe gospel . . . for þi lawe. amen. ihesu for þi merci. 3. ff. 16–266v New Testament in the later Wycliffite version. ff. iv + 266 + ii, foliated (i, ii), 1–270: ff. 1, 2 are medieval parchment flyleaves. 190 × 130 mm. Written space 122 × 80 mm. 2 cols. 36 lines. Collation of ff. 3–268: 1^{10} $2–33^8$. Quires, except the last, numbered 1–32 on the last verso but one. Good initials on gold grounds. Secundo folio (f. 14) *aduersariis*.

'This booke [. . .] my moder (?) iiiil vis viiid And wisse (?) and holy mon [. . .] And hit was overseyn And redd by doctor Thomas Ebbrall and Doctor Yve or þt my moder bought it', f. 267v, s. xv/xvi.[1] 'Carvyle', f. 2v, s. xv/xvi. 'Mr edgcombs booke', f. 2v, s. xvi. On f. 268v John Picard, 'pastour of pluckleye (*Kent*)' noted that he had 'bene at pluckleye thes 30 yeares I praise god and as muche synce as the thirde of Aprill 1598. The 20 daye of June nowe'. 'Mr J. T. Barrett', f. i (see below). Duke of Sussex, sale 31 July 1844, lot 432. Belonged to Lea Wilson (cf. MS. 81). Ashburnham App. 20.

1. Forshall and Madden, iv. 683–98: see above, Eng. 76. The commemorations are those in Eng. 76, but they come before the proper of saints. The word 'pope' has been blotted out; so too the name of St Thomas at 29 Dec. and 7 July. ff. 3r, 12v left blank.

[1] For Thomas Eborall, master of Whittington College, London, 1444–64, †1471, and his successor, William Ive, †1486, see Emden, *BRUO*, pp. 622, 1008.

2 printed hence by J. T. Barrett of Trinity College, Dublin. Both (*a*) and (*b*) are prefaces to the Gospels.

3. Forshall and Madden, no. 15. They note that this copy is the basis of the text in The English Hexapla edition of the New Testament printed in 1841. Usual prologues. Fairly frequent omissions by homoioteleuton have been supplied neatly in the margins. ff. 267–268^{v} left blank.

Eng. 78. *New Testament* s. xv in.

1. ff. 1–8^{v} (*begins imperfectly at Thursday before Palm Sunday*) . . . Thus eendiþ þis kalender of lessouns pistils and gospels. 2. ff. 9–173^{v} New Testament in the later Wycliffite version, ending imperfectly 'we han' (2 Cor. 7: 2). ff. iii + 173 + iii. The parchment on ff. 25–55 (quires 3–7) is thinner than elsewhere. 160 × 108 mm. Written space 128 × 80 mm and (ff. 25–55) *c.*110 × 70 mm. 2 cols. 32 lines and from f. 56 where the hand changes, 30 lines. Collation: 1 eight (probably 1^{10} wants 1 and 9) $2\text{–}5^{8}$ 6^{8} wants 8, blank, after f. 47 $7\text{–}15^{8}$ 16^{8} wants 1 before f. 120 17^{8} 18^{8} wants 1 before f. 143 $19\text{–}21^{8}$. Quires signed as usual, (a)–x. Matthew in three hands, changing at ff. 25 (4^{1}) and 26. The first quire of Mark, ff. 48–55^{v}, is in a fourth hand and the rest of the book in a fifth. Secundo folio *gat sadoc* (f. 10).

Scribbles of s. xvi include names: f. 72 'this is John dishe is Boke' (cf. f. 128^{v}); f. 96 'To all crystyan peple to whome thes present wrytyng Indentyd shall com hugh sidnam p*ar*sone of coryemalace sendeth gretyng . . .'; f. 84^{v}, as f. 96, but the name is 'george Repe of corymalot'; f. 132^{v} 'my lorde byschop of Baathe and Wells'; f. 58^{v} 'John Hurman hathe beten his wyfe on candelleve'. The second, third, and fourth of these scribbles are in one hand. Belonged to W. S. Higgs: his sale, 26 Apr. 1830, lot 719 (Wilkes, £4. 4*s*.). J. Wilkes sale, 12 Mar. 1847, lot 101. Ashburnham Appendix 21.

1. Forshall and Madden, iv. 686–98: see above Eng. 76. The commemorations precede the proper of saints as in Eng. 77. A leaf of the proper is missing: f. 7^{v} ends with Cyriac (8 Aug.) and f. 8 begins with Mark Marcellus and Apuleius (7 Oct.).

2. Forshall and Madden, no. 160. Usual prologues. Two gaps: f. 119^{v} ends 'My' (John 5: 17) and f. 120 begins 'how schulen' (John 5: 47); f. 142^{v} ends 'to parten' (Romans 1: 11) and f. 143 begins 'knowist' (Romans 2: 4).

Eng. 79. *New Testament* s. xv in.

Later Wycliffite version of NT. ff. iv + 240 + iii, foliated (i–iii), 1–241, (242–4). f. 1 is a parchment flyleaf. 165 × 115 mm. Written space 117 × 85 mm. 2 cols. 31 lines and from f. 58 35 lines. Collation of ff. 2–241: $1\text{–}16^{8}$ 17^{2} (ff. 130–1) $18\text{–}30^{8}$ 31^{6}. Binding of s. xvi. Secundo folio *gidere*.

Belonged to Lea Wilson: cf. MS. 81. Ashburnham Appendix 22.

Forshall and Madden, no. 159: they note peculiar readings by a second hand.[1] The order is Gospels, Apocalypse (ff. 114^{v}–130^{v}), Pauline Epistles, Acts, Catholic Epistles. Usual prologues. f. 131^{rv} blank before Romans which begins a new quire. ff. 239–240^{v} left blank.

[1] A corrector has mended errors of omission. I was unable to find more than this.

Eng. 80. *New Testament* 1444 (?)

1. Preliminaries to 2: (*a*) f. 1^{v} Table of movable feasts; (*b*) ff. 2–7^{v} Calendar in red and black; (*c*) f. 8 Table to find Easter, 1448–1520; (*d*) ff. 9–22^{v} . . . þus endiþ þe kalendir of lessouns pistlis and gospels of al þe ȝeer; (*e*) f. 23 The first place in augrym noumbre . . . 2. ff. 24–271^{v}, 317^{rv} New Testament in the later Wycliffite version. 3. ff. 272–316^{v} Epistle lections from the OT. ff. iii + 317 + iv. f. 318 is a parchment flyleaf. 215 × 147 mm. Written space 160 × 108 mm. 2 cols. 36–8 lines in quires 4–9 and 30–2 lines in quires 10–40. Collation: 1–2^{8} 3^{8} wants 8, blank, after f. 23 4^{8} wants 1 before f. 24 5–22^{8} 23^{8} + 1 leaf after 4 (f. 179) 24–34^{8} 35^{8} wants 1 before f. 272 36–39^{8} 40^{8} wants 8, blank. A new hand begins at f. 272 (art. 3). A handsome initial and C-shaped or I-shaped border at the beginning of most books. Secundo folio *sterre* (f. 24).

'26 Jan 1692 this Booke was shewne to Mr Wm Fox at his Examination on the behalfe of John Cullum at ye suit of Thomas Shaftoe in the Court of Excheq^{er} before me John Powell', f. 1. Belonged to Anthony Merry and by his gift in 1834 to the Reverend Wilmot Marsh of Bangor: 'obtained after his sale in 1847 by the Earl of Ashburnham' (Forshall and Madden). Ashburnham Appendix 18.

1*b*. Entries erased at 7 July and 29 December, but 'Utas of seint thomas' not erased, 5 Jan. 1*d*. Forshall and Madden, iv. 683–98: see above, MS. Eng. 76. The commemorations precede the proper of saints, as in MS. 77. 1*e*. An explanation of arabic numbers. ff. 1^{r}, 8^{v}, 23^{v} left blank.

2. Forshall and Madden, no. 157: their *r* in Laodiceans and the prologue to Romans (iv. 438, 301: see below). All before 'sterre' (Matthew 2: 2) came on the leaf missing before f. 24. 'Here endiþ þe Apocalipis Anno domini m ccc^{o} (*sic*) xliiii' (f. 271) is followed by a prologue not usually found in English, 'Romayns ben þei þ^{t} of iewes and heþen . . . to pees and acorde' (cf. Stegmüller, no. 674), which is squeezed in on f. 271^{rv} and overflows onto a half leaf now pasted to f. 317: the hand is that of ff. 1–271. Other prologues as usual. The leaf added to quire 23 contains the Epistle to the Laodiceans and its prologue.

3. The first leaf is missing with all before 're him. And þei schulen clepe hem'. The temporal ends on f. 307^{v} and is followed by a cue for the feast of relics and 'Here enden þe pistlis and lessouns of þe olde lawe for sonedaies and ferials: and begynnen commemoraciouns'. Commemorations, ff. 307^{v}–308: of Our Lady, for brothers and sisters, for clear weather, for rain, for pestilence of beasts, and 'In masse of requiem or for deede'. Sanctoral, ff. 308^{v}–312: twelve feasts, Andrew, Conception of B.V.M., Purification of B.V.M., Philip and James, 'on mydsomer euyn', 'on mydsomer dai', Mary Magdalene, vigil, day, and octave of Assumption of B.V.M., Decollation of John, Nativity of B.V.M. Common of Saints, ff. 312–316^{v}. For other copies see *MMBL* i. 7, 288. f. 317^{rv} left blank.

Eng. 81. *New Testament* s. xiv/xv

Earlier Wycliffite version of NT. ff. vii + 153 + xi. 270 × 192 mm. Written space 207 × 133 mm. 2 cols. 48 lines. Collation: 1–18^{8} 19^{8} + 1 leaf after 8 (f. 153). Quires signed in red, a–v, in the usual late medieval way. Secundo folio *nazareth*.

A gift to the abbey of Syon 'on myddellent Sunday', 1517, from 'Dame Anne Danvers widowe' of Sir William Danvers, who asks 'good m^{r} Confessor of Sion wt his brethren' for their prayers for her family alive and dead: she names them individually, together with John and Thomas, servants of William Danvers, and Margaret Langford, f. 153v. 'Fowller', f. 1. Inscription of gift by William Simonson, fellow of Merton College, Oxford (elected 1598, †1651) to Edward Reynolds (fellow of Merton 1620 and warden 1660–1, bishop of Norwich 1661–76), f. 1. Belonged to Lea Wilson. Ashburnham Appendix 19.

Forshall and Madden, no. 156. They note that this copy is the source of Lea Wilson's text in *The New Testament in English translated by John Wycliffe*, printed by Pickering in 1848.[1] The order is Gospels, Acts, Catholic Epistles, Pauline Epistles, Apocalypse: '. . . here endiþ þe apocalips. Blesside be þe holy trinite Amen'. f. 153v left blank. No prologues. The page containing 1 Cor. 13, 14 is in reduced facsimile in a Rylands exhibition catalogue, *History of the Translation of the Bible*, 1911, facing p. 10.

Eng. 82. *Old Testament (part)* s. xv^1

Later Wycliffite version of part of OT. ff. ii + 242 + iii. 257 × 175 mm. Written space 160 × 108 mm. 2 cols. 24 lines. Collation: 1^{10} $2\text{–}18^8$ 19^8 wants 4, 5 after f. 149 $20\text{–}25^8$ 26^8 wants 3–5 after f. 202 27^8 wants 1 before f. 206 28^8 29^8 wants 8 after f. 227 30^8 31^8 wants 8 after f. 242. Quires signed in the usual late medieval way, f–z, ⁊, A–E, H–O, except that the number of the leaf within the quire is written beneath the letter, instead of beside it.

'No 83' at the head of f. 1, on the left, s. xviii, shows provenance from the library founded in 1684 by Archbishop Tenison in the church of St Martin in the Fields, London: catalogue of 1786 by S. Ayscough (B.L., Add. 11257), no. 36; sale 1 July 1861, lot 12 to Lilly (£150) for Lord Ashburnham. Ashburnham Appendix 27.

Not in Forshall and Madden. A handsome and large-scale copy which contained originally the four books of Kings, the second book of Chronicles, and the five sapiential books on well over 300 leaves—the text goes straight on within quires from 4 Kings to 2 Chronicles and from 2 Chronicles to Proverbs—but contains now only 1 Kings 28: 5 'filisteis'–Ecclesiasticus 16: 2 'traueilis of hem', with probably 23 leaves missing between these points, including all between Proverbs 19: 4 'richessis' and Ecclesiastes 2: 6 'wode of' after f. 192, where two quires are missing. f. 242 is damaged.

A pair of ruled lines in each margin. The running title is between the lines at the top and the quire signature is in the box where the lines in the lower margin cross those in the outer margin on rectos. Good initials and continuous borders on the five remaining pages where new books begin (2–4 Kings, 2 Chronicles, Proverbs: ff. 5, 40v, 83v, 124, 174). Elaborately framed catchwords: 'in god is al euer was and euer schal' is in the frame on f. 18v.

Eng. 83. *Proverbs and extracts from other sapiential books* s. xiv/xv

1. ff. 5–88 Proverbs in the later Wycliffite version. 2. Extracts from (*a*: f. 88) Ecclesiastes, (*b*: f. 92v) Song of Songs, (*c*: f. 93) Wisdom, and (*d*: f. 117) Ecclesiasticus in the later Wycliffite version. 3. ff. 146–153v Quotations from the

[1] MSS. 81, 77, and 79 are nos. 1–3 of the manuscripts of the New Testament in *Bibles in the collection of Lea Wilson*, 1845, pp. 137–140.

Bible and the Fathers in twenty-nine paragraphs. ff. v + 149 + vii, foliated i, 1–160. ff. 1–4, 154–7 are parchment endleaves, 1^r and 157^v once pasted down; they come no doubt from the sixteenth-century binding (see below). 98 × 65 mm. Written space 70 × 50 mm. 16 long lines. Collation of ff. 5–153: 1^8 2^6 (ff. 13–18) 3–14^8 15^8 wants 3 after f. 116 16–19^8. Secundo folio *þou wiþ vs.*

'This booke (honorable Syr) amongest others of great pryce wrytten in parchment. were preserved from the fyer in the tyme of the late kynge E. the vi^th^ by my stepfather and after by me new covered and reserved as holy reliques the others in latyne this in the olde Saxon English tongue wch I am bolde to presente to your vewe and readynge yf you can take delyghte therin', f. 4, s. xvi, in a good bold hand. Ashburnham Appendix 27A.

1 is headed 'þese ben þe parablis of salamon'. No prologue. 2*a*. . . . and here suen a fewe textis of ecclesiastes. Weyward men . . . eiþer yuel. Extracts from chapters 1, 2, 4, 5, 7–10, and all chapter 12. 2*b*. Song of Songs 8: 6, 7. 2*c*. Here sueþ a part of sapience fro þe bigynninge til nyne chapitris ben eendid. Wisdom, chapters 1–9 and 16: 29. 2*d*. Ecclesiasticus, chapters 1–3, beginning imperfectly 'þat wisdom' (1: 9), extracts from chapters 4–8, 10–12, all chapter 13, extracts from chapters 14–16, all chapter 19, and extracts from chapters 20–3, 25, 27–9, 32, 33, 35. 3. The wraþþe of god is turned in to merci to men þat forsakiþ synne . . . deeþ of soule. Spaces for 29 headings not filled: directions for the headings in the margins have been cut into by the binder.

The present binding is red morocco, s. xviii. 'peytetoo' and 'Pulcra dies operi nox conuenit atra quieti' on f. 2.

Eng. 84. *Acts* s. xiv/xv

Acts in the later Wycliffite version, except 7: 31–10: 6 (ff. 29^v/14–44^v/4) which are in the earlier version. ff. ii + 124, foliated 1–126. 122 × 85 mm. Written space 78 × 50 mm. 17 long lines. Collation of ff. 3–126: 1–8^8 9^8 wants 1 before f. 66 and 8 after f. 71 10^8 11^8 wants 6 after f. 84 12–16^8. Changes of ink, but perhaps not of hand at ff. 72 (10^1), 104^v/7, 111 (15^1) and 122^v/1. Old boards re-covered: three bands. Secundo folio *ke. and to hem.*

'W. B.', f. 2^v. 'Tho. Miles The Gift of Mr Dyer', f. 1, s. xviii. Belonged to Lea Wilson. Ashburnham Appendix 25.

Forshall and Madden, no. 161. Three leaves missing: f. 65^v ends 'and from þens' (14: 25) and f. 66 begins 'syn vp' (15: 5); f. 71^v ends 'spiritt of dyuy-' (16: 16) and f. 72 begins 'kepe ham' (16: 23); f. 84^v ends 'to repreef: but' (19: 27) and f. 85 begins 'houris' (19: 34). Prologue, ff. 3–4. In the part of Acts taken from the earlier version there are red headings in the text at 8: 5, 8: 14, 8: 26, and 9: 1 and the word 'eende' is written in red at 8: 9 after 'cyte', at 8: 17 after 'gost', and at 9: 22 after 'crist'. The headings are: (f. 34) The thursdai pystil in witsone weke; (f. 35) þe tewsday pistil in witsone weke and in commemoracyoun of the holy gooste'; (f. 36^v) The fyrst þrusday pistyl after paske; (f. 38^v) The pistyl of þe conuersyoun of seynt poule. The lessons at these points are those of the earlier Wycliffite version: cf. Forshall and Madden, iv. 688, 697, 687, 691. 'DEO GRACIAS' at the end, f. 125. ff. 125^v–126^v left blank.

Eng. 85. *On the Lord's Prayer, etc.* s. xiv/xv

1. ff. 2–37 Here bigynneþ þe abcde. and next pater noster aue marie and crede and next þe heestis and oþer þingis shortli touchid to helþe of euery persoone þat þenkiþ to be saued. 2. ff. 37–54 þe pater noster (*this and the next three titles are running titles*). Siþ þe pater noster is þe best praier þat is . . . in blisse and ioie wt hym to wone wt outen eende. Amen. 3. ff. 54v–64 þe mirrour of synners. 4. ff. 64–72v þe chartir of heuene. 5. ff. 72v–81v þe þre arowis. Who þat wole haue in mynde þe dredful day of dome . . . upon þe rode tre. Amen. 6. f. 1rv Text on flyleaf. ff. v + 80 (foliated 2–81) + iv. ff. ii–iv, 1, 82–4 are parchment flyleaves. 142 × 95 mm. Written space 93 × 65 mm. 19 or 20 long lines. Collation of ff. 2–81: $1–4^8$ 5^4 (ff. 34–7) $6–10^8$ 11^4 (ff. 78–81). Quires 1–9 signed a–i in the usual late medieval way, except that in quires 1–5 the leaf number is written below the quire letter. Catchwords much reduced, for example (f. 9v) *fe*: f. 10 begins *feend*. The hand changes at art. 2. Secundo folio *kide crist* (f. 3).

'Iste liber constat Iohanni Ade Cum magno gaudio et honore', f. 83v, s. xv ex.[1] For other names see *Hand-list*. 'No 90' (altered to '75'), f. ivv and f. v, s. xviii: the older number is in the same hand as the number in Eng. 82. No. 75 in Ayscough's catalogue of the Tenison collection (cf. Eng. 82). Sale, 1 July 1861, lot 97, to Lilly for Lord Ashburnham (£37. 10*s*.). Ashburnham Appendix 27B.

1. Divisible into eighteen sections: (*a–e*) f. 2rv The alphabet (a–z, þ, 7, ꝫ, :, est, amen), Lord's Prayer, Hail Mary, Creed, Blessing; (*f*) ff. 2v–9 On the ten commandments, 'Alle manere men shulde holde . . . ony man doiþ', printed from this copy by A. L. Kellogg and E. W. Talbert in *BJRL* xlii (1960), 371–6. (*g*) ff. 9–13 On the deadly sins, 'Pride and Enuye . . . do to ihesu crist': Jolliffe, F. 21a; (*h–n*) ff. 13–19 Seven pieces setting out the five wits of body and of soul, the seven spiritual virtues, the seven works of corporal and of spiritual mercy, the seven gifts of the Holy Spirit and the seven sacraments; (*o*) f. 19rv A prologue, 'This litil compilation biginneþ wiþ praier . . . and not oonli bi drede', which looks back to (*b, d, f*) and forward to (*p–r*) and occurs with (*p–r*) also in Durham Cathedral A. IV. 22, pp. 98–116; (*p*) ff. 19v–24v þe twelue lettyngis of preier: Jolliffe, M. 4; (*q*) ff. 24v–25v Of beleeue in general. Also touchinge þe crede . . . and come to bliss; (*r*) ff. 25v–37 Of diuerse degrees of loue: Jolliffe, G. 3.

2. Cf. Eng. 90, art. 2. 3. Jolliffe, F. 8. 4. Part of Pore Caitif: Jolliffe, B. 5. Basically the same, but fuller than the text printed by C. Horstmann, *Yorkshire Writers*, ii. 446–8. 6. Twenty-three lines on the recto and twenty-five on the verso, all more or less faded: the first sentence begins 'Wymen schulden make ensaumple as hester þt was a qwene to aray hem' and another sentence begins 'Also seint poul repreueþ'.

Eng. 86. *John Wyclif, Tracts (Latin and English)* s. xiv/xv

A collection of works by or perhaps by Wyclif, all in Latin, except 1, 3, 4. ff. iii + 122 + iii. ff. 1–121 have a medieval foliation 1–118, 121–2. 158 × 110 mm, except the leaves of quires 7, 8, 14 and leaves 2–7 in quire 6 which are shorter than the rest (*c.*145 mm) and except ff. 119–21, where a greater width has been preserved by the binder (*c.*115 mm). Written space 135 × 82 mm, except on

[1] For this expression, current in East Anglia, see Ker, *MLGB*, p. 328.

ff. 119–21 where the width is *c.*100 mm. Frame ruling, if any. 34–44 long lines. Collation: $1\text{–}6^8$ 7^6 (ff. 49–54) 8^6 (ff. 55–60) $9\text{–}12^8$ 13^4 (ff. 93–6) $14\text{–}15^8$ 16^6 (ff. 113–18) 17^2 (ff. 119–20) 18^2 (ff. 121–2). Catchwords not only on last versos, but on all versos in the first half of a quire. Current anglicana by one hand throughout. Secundo folio *þe contrarye*.

Ashburnham Appendix 27C.

Arts. 1–5 are on quires 1–6.

1. ff. 1–21ᵛ þer ben two offisis . . . to shyne frely. Amen. Explicit tractatus de officio pastorali. 32 numbered chapters. W. W. Shirley, *Catalogue of the original works of John Wyclif*, 1865, English 61. *The English works of Wyclif hitherto unprinted*, ed. F. D. Matthew (EETS lxxiv, 1880), pp. 408–57.

2. ff. 21ᵛ–24ᵛ Ad declarandum veritatem fidei . . . acceptanda. Explicit tractatus de ordine cristiano. Five numbered chapters. J. Loserth, *Catalogue of the extant Latin works of John Wyclif* (revision of Shirley), 1925, Latin 78. *Opera Minora*, ed. J. Loserth, 1913, pp. 129–39: this copy, called D, the basis of the text.

3. ff. 25–34ᵛ God seiþ bi ieremye. þᵗ he wakide . . . bifore þou bie hem. Explicit tractatus de papa. Twelve numbered chapters. Shirley, English 62. Ed. Matthew, op. cit., pp. 460–82.

4. ff. 35–42ᵛ Two vertues ben in mannus soule . . . no ground in god. Explicit tractatus de confessione et penitencia. Thirteen numbered chapters. Shirley, English 51. Ed. Matthew, op. cit., pp. 327–45.

5. ff. 43–48ᵛ Sicud est vnus verus et summus dominus . . . ecclesia exemplante. Explicit tractatus de contrarietate duorum dominorum suarum partium et etiam regularum. Eight numbered chapters. Loserth, Latin 84. *Opera polemica* (ed. Buddensieg, 1883), ii. 698–713, from this manuscript.

6. ff. 49–54 Sepe assumptum est ut fides catholica . . . deus et homo multis regnis. Explicit purgatorium secte cristi. Loserth, Latin 98. Ibid. i. 298–316, from this manuscript.

7. f. 54ᵛ Videtur autem sanctis doctoribus quod superfluit . . . multipliciter istum mundum. Explicit dictum de gradibus cleri ecclesie militantis. *Opera minora*, pp. 142–4 (chapter 3 of De gradibus ecclesiae, Loserth, Latin 96).

Arts. 8, 9 are on quires 8, 9.

8. ff. 55–64ᵛ Quia euangelium istud est multis absconditum . . . melius intellecta. Explicit exposicio textus Matthei 24ᵗᵒ. Eight numbered chapters. Loserth, Latin 44. *Opera minora*, pp. 354–82.

9. ff. 65–68ᵛ, slip before f. 65, and f. 89ᵛ Questio. Si papa uel eius vicario . . . seruiat libertate Amen. Explicit tractatus de citacionibus friuolis et aliis versuciis anticristi. Loserth, Latin 73. *Opera polemica* ii. 546–64 (this copy called Ash.).

It looks as though the scribe originally intended this piece to follow art. 11, but after copying as much of it as would fit on f. 89ᵛ he continued his writing inadvertently, or after a change of mind, on the then still blank second half of quire 9. He then recopied the text on f. 89ᵛ on a slip to go in front of f. 65 and marked f. 89ᵛ 'va cat'.

Arts. 10–12 are on quires 10–13.

10. ff. 69–82ᵛ Cum sapiencia dei patris . . . in istis perfidis sine fine. 12 numbered chapters. Loserth, Latin 43. *Opera minora*, pp. 313–53.

11. ff. 82v–89v Cum secundum philosophos sit relatiuorum eadem disciplina . . . multiplici atque graui. Explicit tractatus de seruitute ciuili et dominio seculari. Six numbered chapters. Loserth, Latin 69. *Opera minora*, pp. 145–64, from this manuscript.

12. ff. 90–96v Cum secundum veritatis testimonium . . . homines spoliantes. Explicit tractatus de noua preuaricancia mandatorum. 13 numbered chapters. Loserth, Latin 80. *Opera polemica*, i. 107–50.

Arts. 13–15 are on quires 14–18.

13. ff. 97–116v Cum idempnitas sit mater fastidii . . . consenciant in hac parte. Explicit speculum ecclesie militantis. Chapters numbered 1–28, 33–6. Loserth, Latin 63. Ed. A. W. Pollard, 1886, pp. 1–60/14, 78/10–80/29: this copy the basis of his text. The scribe noted on f. 114v 'Hic deficiunt 4or capitula. scilicet 29. 30. 31. 32': see below, art. 15.

14. f. 117 Vnus amicus fidelis in domino quesiuit sensum misticum huius euangelii M 21o ite in castellum . . . compleatur. Extracts from two of Wyclif's sermons (ed. Loserth, pp. 200/27–201/5 (with slight differences) and 233/10–26), with a linking sentence, 'Sensum autem alium de verbis istis et aliis verbis euangelii nouit vestra discrecio fideliter dilatare'.[1] f. 117v blank.

15. ff. 118–21 These four leaves and two others now missing after f. 118 contained the missing chapters of art. 13 and a further chapter numbered 37: (*a*) f. 118rv ch. 29 and ch. 30 as far as 'a titulo elimosine' (ed. Pollard, pp. 60/15–63/20); (*b*) missing, except for a few letters remaining on the two stubs after f. 118; (*c*) ff. 119–20 Capitulum 32m. Sed adhuc arguitur. Si clerus . . . sancto spiritu per dona sua septiformia edocente. Ibid., pp. 69/19–78/9; (*d*) ff. 120–1 Capitulum 37m Sed demum recensius arguunt populares . . . per diabolum introductis. Ibid., pp. 73–8. Pollard calls (*c*) chapter 31 and (*d*) chapter 32 against the evidence of the manuscript: see his introduction, pp. xxv, xxvi. Probably ch. 31, which, like ch. 32, was not known to Pollard in other copies, was here on the second of the two missing leaves. ff. 121v–122v are blank, except for a note of s. xv on 122v, 'carencia diuersorum capitulorum dialogi que apud alios libros communiter sunt repert[a]', a reference to art. 13.

Eng. 87. *Pore Caitif* s. xiv/xv

1. ff. 1–119v Pore Caitif. 2. f. 120 (flyleaf): on recto, directions for masses, etc.; on verso, a prayer. ff. v + 119 + v. ff. 120–1 are parchment flyleaves. 145 × 105 mm. Written space 93 × 65 mm. 22 long lines. Collation: 1^8 wants 2 after f. 1 and 7 after f. 5 2^8 3^8 wants 8 after f. 21 $4–14^8$ 15^8 wants 2 after f. 110 16^8 wants 5–8 after f. 119. Quires signed b–r in the usual late medieval way, except that the leaf numbers are written below the quire letters, as in MS. Eng. 85. On f. 85v a catchword is reduced to its first syllable, *wa*: f. 86 begins *watir* (cf. Eng. 85).

'George Ratlyfe oweth Thys bocke god macke hym a good man', f. 68, s. xvi. 'THOMAS DODE est verus possessor huius libri 1555 20 agusti', ff. 76v–77. For other names see *Hand-list*. Belonged to Thomas Martin, †1771, who wrote his name, the number '155', and the remark 'Note all old English Mss are very valuable' on f. iiiv. 'No 6', f. iv. Ashburnham Appendix 27D.

[1] I owe this identification to Dr Anne Hudson. (Art. 14 has now been published by C. R. Thomson in *Medieval Studies*, xliii (1981), 531–6, with a reduced facsimile of ff. 116v–117.)

1. Jolliffe, B. This and twenty-two other manuscripts containing all fourteen parts are listed by M. T. Brody in *Traditio*, x (1954), 529–48: the first part, on the Creed, begins imperfectly (f. 1) 'do but also of dedis left vndo' (probably eight leaves missing), lacks a leaf after f. 1 and ends imperfectly at f. 5^{v}, 'Seynt symond seide. I bileeue forȝifnesse of' (one leaf missing); pt. 2, on the Commandments, begins imperfectly (f. 6) 'þerfore ech man and womman' and lacks a leaf after f. 21; pt. 3, on the Lord's Prayer, f. 52; pt. 4, f. 66^{v}; pt. 5, f. 70; pt. 6, f. 73; pt. 7, f. 74; pt. 8, f. 81^{v} (running title 'þe hors'); pt. 9, f. 90^{v}; pt. 10, f. 94^{v}; pt. 11, f. 98^{v}; pt. 12, f. 102; pt. 13, f. 103^{v}; pt. 14, f. 106^{v}: it lacks a leaf after f. 110 and all after 'þis is my filosofie. þis is my victorie'.[1]

2*a*. (*begins imperfectly*) of all the apostolus w^{t} xii candelys xii almysdedys and offyr as tohu (*sic*) dydys before . . . proued of the Court of Rome. Directions for (Wednesday), Thursday, Friday, and Saturday votive masses and for saying the eight verses of St Bernard to help deliver souls from purgatory.

2*b*. Domine ihesu criste fili dei viui qui gloriosum corpus tuum . . . per eundem cristum dominum nostrum Amen. s. xv in.

Eng. 88. (R. 14777.) *Psalms and canticles* s. xiv^{2}

1. Psalms in the later Wycliffite version, followed on ff. 67^{v}–74^{v} by 2, the six ferial canticles and Benedicite, Te deum, Magnificat, Benedictus, Nunc dimittis, and Quicumque vult. ff. vii + 74 + iii. 168 × 115 mm. Written space 128 × 80 mm. 2 cols. 32 lines. Collation: 1–8^{8} 9 two (9^{8} wants 2–7 ?) 10^{8}. The hand changes at f. 41 (6^{1}: Ps. 81). Secundo folio *hooli man*.

'Robert Hay' crossed through, f. i^{v}. Presumably in the John Hey sale at Leigh and Sotheby, 29 May–2 June 1815, but not in the sale catalogue. 'R. W.' (Roger Wilbraham) notes the sale, f. i^{v}, and was no doubt the buyer. Armorial bookplate of George Wilbraham, s. xix. Noted as a Wilbraham manuscript in HMC, *Third Report* (1872), Appendix, p. 293.[2] Bought from Bull and Auvache for £50 in 1908: invoice dated 27 Feb.

1. Here biginniþ þe sauter. Beatus uir. Blessid is þe man . . . (f. 74^{v}, after Quicumque vult) Explicit psalterium. f. 65^{v} ends 'he schal speke' (Ps. 126: 5) and f. 66 begins 'speke þi power' (Ps. 144: 11). 2. (*a*) Confitebor. I schal knowledge to þee. for þou were wroþ to me . . . (*b*) Ego dixi. I seide in þ^{e} myddil of my day . . . (*c*) Exultauit cor meum. Myn herte fulli ioiede . . . (*d*) Cantemus domino. Synge we to þe lord: for he is magnified gloriously . . . (*e*) Domine audiui. Lord I herde þin heryng . . . (*f*) Audite celi que loquar. Ȝe heuenys here what þingis I schal speke . . . (*g*) Benedicite. All werkis of þe lorde blesse ȝe to þe lord . . . ; (*h*) Te deum laudamus. Thee god we preisen thee lord we knoweleche . . . (*i*) Magnificat. My soule magnifieth þe lord . . . (*j*) Nunc dimittis. Lord now þou leuest þi seruant . . . (*k*) Quicumque vult. Who euere wole be saaf . . .

Eng. 89. (R. 16265.) *Old Testament (part)* s. xv in.

1. Parts of OT: (*a*) ff. 1–10^{v} Ezekiel, abbreviated; (*b*) ff. 11–50 Daniel; (*c*) ff. 50^{v}–76 Minor Prophets, abbreviated; (*d*) ff. 76–90^{v} 1 Maccabees, abbreviated, ending imperfectly at 9: 39 'greet appairel and'. (*a, c, d*) are in the earlier and (*b*)

[1] In Bodleian MS. Douce 288 these words are on f. 82^{v}/15, one leaf from the end of Pore Caitif.

[2] Cf. *MMBL* ii. 214.

is in the later Wycliffite version. 2. f. 50^{rv} 'Glose of Daniel'. ff. i + 90 + i. 140 × 100 mm. Written space 105 × 68 mm. 2 cols. 25 lines. Collation: 1^8 2^2 (ff. 9, 10) 3-12^8. Binding by D. Cockerell, dated 1901. Secundo folio *þe secunde*.

Book-plate of Laurence W. Hodson, Compton Hall, near Wolverhampton: his sale 3 Dec. 1906, lot 666. Bought from Quaritch in 1908 for £50: invoice dated 23 October.

1. In (*a, c, d*) the scribe writes 'et cetera' at the point at which he omits words, for example 'and y siȝe visions of god. et cetera and of þe middil of it' where *etc.* takes the place of Ezekiel 1: 2-4. (*b*). No prologue. 2. f. 50^{rv} Here endiþ þe book of daniel and bigynne þe glose of daniel. The first visioun is of a stoon . . . is figurid in þis. Lyre on þe bigynninge on þe ii^{e} c' of daniel.

Eng. 90. (R. 16586.) *Prick of Conscience, etc.* s. xiv/xv

1. ff. 2-62^{v} Prick of Conscience, interpolated. 2. ff. 63-65^{v} Sith the pater noster ys the beste preyer þat is . . . blisse and ioye with him with outen ende Amen. 3 (flyleaves). ff. 1, 66^{v} Accounts. ff. v + 64 + v, foliated (i-iv), 1-70. 343 × 245 mm. Written space 277 × 200 mm (art. 2). 2 cols. 48-52 lines. Collation of ff. 2-65: 1-7^8 8^4 (ff. 58-61) 9 four (ff. 62-5). More or less current anglicana, art. 2 in a different hand from art. 1. In art. 1 *n, m,* and *u* are usually made of straight, backward-sloping strokes.

At St Albans in s. xv/xvi, to judge from a scribble on f. 1^{v}, 'Iste sunt testes hugone Chattok Taylor of Sint Albons Wyllyham scheddebolt Bayly araunt dwelling in the same Tovne'. 'Ph: Mainwaringe pre: 3^{s}', f. 2, s. xvii: for his identity see below, Rylands Fr. 63. No doubt in the same Mainwaring sale as Fr. 63, either lot 497, 'Poetical Commentary on the Pater Noster, MS. on vellum, *very curious*' bought by (James) Crossley (1800-83: *DNB*), or lot 498, 'A curious MS. of Devotional Poetry, Eng. and Lat. on vellum', bought by Crossley for £4. Probably Crossley passed it on to Thomas Corser (1793-1876; rector of Strand, near Manchester: *DNB*): his sale at Sotheby's 28 July 1868, lot 697. Ashburnham Appendix sale at Sotheby's, 1 May 1899, lot 165 (Ellis, £39. 10*s.*). J. Scott sale at Sotheby's, 27 March 1905, lot 1961. Bought for £54 from J. and J. Leighton in 1908: invoice dated 6 July.

1. The myȝt off þe fadur almyȝti . . . þ^{t} for ous fouched saff to henge. Ed. R. Morris, 1863. For this version in eight instead of seven parts, much as in Bodleian Ashmole 60, see K. D. Bülbring in *Englische Studien*, xxiii (1897), 23-8 and H. E. Allen, *Writings of Richard Rolle*, 1927, pp. 388-93. The two points at which the largest amounts of Latin and English are interpolated into the text are: between line 192 and line 193, 440 lines of English verse interspersed with Latin prose (ff. 2^{v}-7); between line 6894 and line 6895, Latin prose (ff. 39-41, 46-8) and 563 lines of English verse interspersed with Latin tags and longer pieces of Latin (ff. 41-6). After line 9474 come 112 lines of English verse, f. 61rb/19-61vb/41, most of them taken from lines 6346-401, which do not occur in their usual place after f. 37ra/3. Part 8 begins in this section (61rb/29) 'Nou off þe viii part . . .'. At the end (f. 62^{v}) is a note in Latin, 'Hoc nomen consciencia componitur ab hoc preposicione . . . agendorum et non etc'.[1]

[1] Professor Robert Lewis helped me with this description.

2. W. W. Shirley, *Catalogue of the original works of John Wyclif*, 1865, English 64. *Select English works of John Wyclif*, ed. T. Arnold, 1869–71, iii. 98–110.

3. Two pieces cut from a roll (?) of which the dorse (ff. 1v, 66r) was left blank. f. 66v is hardly legible. f. 1r contains thirty-five entries, s. xiv, all but five of them beginning 'la paroessz de . . .': no. 34 begins 'lislle de bellislle' and no. 35 'lissle de quibeuron'. The formula continues after the place-name with 'Ransone et paie au dit stanlou' and a sum of money in francs which varies from 30 to 350. The places referred to are in the diocese of Vannes. Presumably these accounts belonged to an English receiver (Stanlow ?) during Edward III's wars in Brittany.[1]

Eng. 91. (R. 55397.) *Bible (vol. 1)* s. xv[1]

1. ff. 1–9 Heere bigynneþ a reule þt telleþ in whate chapiters of þe bible ȝe may fynde all þo pistles and þe gospels in al þe ȝer after Salisb*ery* vs markid wt letter*is* of þe a.b.c at þe begynning and endiþ wt strikys. 2. ff. 10–272 The second volume of a Bible in the later Wycliffite version, beginning at Proverbs.

ff. 272. 380 × 270 mm. Written space 272 × 180 mm. 2 cols. 52 lines. Collation: 1^8 + 1 leaf after 8 $2–19^8$ $20–21^6$ (ff. 154–65) $22–34^8$ 35^4 wants 4, blank. Catchwords sometimes abbreviated, for example (f. 229v) *he acur*: f. 230 begins *he acursid*. Continuous borders on ff. 10, 46v (Isaiah), 126v (Minor Prophets), 166 (Matthew) and C-shaped or I-shaped borders on other pages where principal books begin. Binding of wooden boards, bevelled on the inside, earlier probably than the crimson velvet which covers them. A hole in the middle of each piece of velvet reveals a blurred coloured armorial on the board. Secundo folio *þin iȝe*.

Belonged to John Symonds Breedon, Bere Court, (Pangbourne) Berkshire, in 1789. Armorial book-plate of Charles Lilburn. No record of acquisition.

1. Forshall and Madden, iv. 683–98: see above Eng. 76. Commemorations precede the sanctoral, as in MS. Eng. 77. They differ from other Rylands copies by making no mention of Salus populi as part of the commemoration of brothers and sisters.

2. Usual prologues throughout NT, but in OT only at Isaiah and Baruch. Some damage by damp, mainly in the middle. From quire 11 (ff. 82–9) onwards the outside leaves of every quire show offset from other outside leaves: for example, part of f. 238 (31^1) has offset onto f. 89v (11^8), except for the red ornament of the blue initial *T*.

Eng. 92. *Apocalypse with commentary* s. xiv/xv

ff. ii + 46 + iii. f. 47 is a parchment flyleaf. 208 × 133 mm. Written space 140 × 87 mm. 2 cols. 31 lines. Collation: $1–5^8$ 6^8 wants 7, 8 blank. Secundo folio *of holi chirche*.

'Edoardus Dering Miles et Baronettus' surrounds the arms of Dering on the cover, as on Bodleian, Lyell 1 and Lyell empt. 3 and other manuscripts: the owner was Sir Edward Dering, †1644. Sale of the Surrenden (Dering) collection at Puttick

[1] A John de Stanlow was with the army in France in 1346 (*Calendar of Patent Rolls, 1345–1348*, p. 507, and see p. 74).

and Simpson, 8 June 1858, lot 1596. 'L. 1. 8' inside the cover, s. xviii (?) is a Dering shelfmark.[1]

Collated, but not fully, as Ry, by E. Fridner, *An English fourteenth century Apocalypse version*, Lund Studies in English xxix (1961). Modernized as compared with Fridner's base text. Each section of text is underlined in red and followed by a section of commentary. There are usually three or four sections in each chapter. The commentary begins 'þe openynge of seint ioon bitokeneþ prelatis of holi chirche' and ends 'in bodi and in soule and dwelle wiþ him wiþouten ende AMEN'.

Eng. 94. *Mirror of the Life of Christ, etc.* s. xv med.

1. ff. 1–125 Pseudo-Bonaventura, Mirror of the life of Christ, in the translation of Nicholas Love: Quecumque scripta sunt . . . comforte oure wretchede life. 2. ff. 125–137v Here begynneth the boke of the crafte of dyinge. 3. ff. 137v–152 Here begynneth a tretyse of gostely bataile right deuoute. 4. (*a*) f. 152rv Here begynneth a lytil shorte tretyce that telleth howe there were vi mastirs assemblede togedir . . . The firste mastir sayde . . . (*b*) ff. 152v–153 Nota de paciencia infirmitatis ut sequitur. Si sciret homo quantum ei infirmitas utilius fuisset . . . et glorificet qui est super omnia deus benedictus in secula. Amen. (*c*) ff. 153–168v Here sweth a prologe upon the xii prophetis of tribulacioun . . . ff. i + 168 + ii: f. 169 is a parchment flyleaf. 362 × 240 mm. Written space 265 × 153 mm. 2 cols. 36 lines. Collation: $1\text{–}21^8$. Signatures of the usual late medieval kind, [a]–t, +, ꝉ. Short-*r* anglicana formata. Secundo folio *to the grave*.

William Northamton wrote his name on ff. 147, 148, s. xvi. Given by Humfrey Wanley to Coventry School before 1696: no. 16 in the list in *CMA* ii. 33–4[2] and, under the title 'Speculum vitæ Christi', the first of seven manuscripts listed under Wanley's name in the Donors' Book now Cambridge, U.L., Add. 4467. Chained in the school library: the mark of the chain can be seen in the side margins, ff. 168–9. Advertised at £50 in a catalogue of Bull and Auvache dated Christmas 1893: see below, MS. Eng. 413, f. (ix).

1. Here anonymous. Ed. L. F. Powell, 1908. A table of the 64 chapters of the seven parts on ff. 1–2 (as edn., pp. 1–5) is followed by two paragraphs in Latin, (f. 2) 'Attende lector . . . apparere' (edn., p. 6), (f. 2) 'Memorandum quod circa annum domini Millesimum quadringentesimum decimum originalis copia . . . et hereticorum siue lollardorum confutacionem', a notice to the effect that Love's translation was inspected and approved by Archbishop Arundel, which Tanner prints in his *Bibliotheca* (1748), p. 533.

2. Jolliffe, L. 4(a). 3. Jolliffe, H. 3. It follows 2 immediately not only here, but in four of the other manuscripts listed by Jolliffe. Horstmann, *Yorkshire Writers*, ii. 420–36. 4. (*a*)–(*c*) go together in this order in the six manuscripts listed by Jolliffe, J. 2(c), J. 3(b). They were printed by Horstmann, ii. 390–406.

[1] John Anstis, †1744, took notes of such Dering manuscripts as interested him when the collection belonged to Sir Chumley Dering (All Souls College Oxford, MS. 297 (vii), ff. 46–50). The shelfmarks he noted range from L. 1. 9 to L. 8. 57.

[2] The second piece in Wanley's description in *CMA* is the last chapter of art. 1.

Eng. 98. (R. 12144.) *Mirror of the Life of Christ* s. xv med.

Pseudo-Bonaventura, Mirror of the Life of Christ in the translation of Nicholas Love. ff. ii + 140 + i. 300 × 200 mm. Written space 188 × 130 mm. 2 cols. 35 lines. Collation: 1^8 wants 1, 2 $2-11^8$ 12^8 wants 5 after f. 90 $13-16^8$ 17^8 wants 2 after f. 126 18^8: 8 was pasted down. Quires signed in the usual late medieval way.

Records of the Roberts of Willesden and Horde of Ewell families, s. xvi med., are in legal hands in blank spaces of quire 18, ff. 137v–138: cf. *Hand-list*. 'Robert Knyuett oweth this booke', f. 138v, s. xvii. Armorial book-plate of Thomas William Evans inside the back cover, s. xix. Bought from Bull and Auvache for £25 in 1905: invoice dated 12 July.

Ed. L. F. Powell, 1908. The text begins imperfectly 'and euery age an euery dignite' (edn., p. 8/5) and ends (f. 136v) 'with outen endinge amen' (as edn.) after which it continues on f. 137 with two paragraphs, 'And for als moche as þat blessid and worthy feste of þe precious sacrament . . . of alle false lollardes. Thus endith the contemplacion . . . nowe and euere wt outen ende Amen', and on f. 137rv in red ink, 'Memorandum quod circa annum . . . (as in MS. 94, f. 2) Explicit speculum vite cristi conplete'. In the second of the two paragraphs on f. 137 the reader is advised to pick and choose as suits him rather than keep to the Monday–Sunday divisions of the text.

A leaf is missing after f. 90v which ends 'grace inwardly' (edn., p. 214/7): f. 91 begins 'the fairest the wisest' (216/3 up); also a leaf after f. 126v which ends 'of þe holy' (299/5): f. 127 begins 'haue mynde of' (302/13). ff. 138–140v were left blank.

Eng. 102. (R. 15384.) *Brut Chronicle* s. xv med.

Brut Chronicle, beginning imperfectly 'and our' soueraiegne' and ending with the death of King Edward III in 1377, 'god haue mercy amen': ed. F. W. D. Brie (EETS cxxxi, cxxxvi, 1906–8), pp. 7/24–332/19. 239 numbered chapters. ff. ii + 101 + ii. 320 × 235 mm. Written space 235 × 190 mm. 2 cols. 34 lines. Collation of ff. 1–43, 45–57, 60–101: 1^8 wants 1 before f. 39 and 7, 8 after f. 43 7^8 8^8 wants 6 after f. 57 $9-13^8$: for ff. 44, 58–9 see below. Secretary hand, with some influence from anglicana.

Among scribbles in law hands, s. xvi, are: f. 101v 'M Willelmus Yong petit hunc librum Testante . . .'; f. 10v 'M Lionelius (? *sic*) Wodward petit hunc librum Testante . . .'; f. 37v 'Nouerint *uniuersi per presentes me Thomam Colepeper in comitatu* Kancie Armiger teneri . . . Richardo Colepeper de Grays Inn . . . Armigero viginti minus anglice legalis monete Anno domini 1568': the words in italics are illegible on f. 37v, but are likely to be the same words as occur in the same hand on f. 39v, where the scribble stops at 'comitatu'. Arms of Sir James Ley (earl of Marlborough, †1629) on the binding. 'George Leigh Wasey' inside the cover. Item 1175 in a bookseller's catalogue, said to be 'Leighton 1908'. Bought from J. and J. Leighton for £22. 10*s*. in 1908: invoice dated 18 June.

f. 38v ends 'bi way þei met' in ch. 129 and f. 39 begins 'nne himself king of Englonde'. f. 43v ends in the title of ch. 145 'come aȝen' and f. 45 begins in ch. 149 'me other bisshopryche'. f. 57^v ends 'his pees þurght' and f. 60 begins 'M^o vii'. For the missing text see edn., pp. 132/11–135/23, 152/26–159/8 and 202/19–205/18. Part of the second gap—as far as edn., p. 158/11—and all the third gap was supplied in s. xv/xvi on three added leaves. On f. 86 after 'calenge of any man' (edn., p. 286/9, battle of Halidon Hill, 1333) is 'Deo gracias dicamus omnes Amen' in red. f. 60^v is damaged.

Eng. 103. (R. 15385.) *Brut Chronicle* s. xiv med.

Brut Chronicle to 1333, continued in another hand and ending imperfectly at 1346 'fast by Crescy' (ed. F. W. D. Brie, EETS cxxxi and cxxxvi (1906–8), p. 298/24). ff. iv + 130 + ii: ff. iii, iv are parchment flyleaves containing lists of early English kings and a list of archbishops of Canterbury from Augustine to Matthew Parker, s. xvi. Parchment of good quality, thick and soft. 275 × 183 mm. Written space 182 × 112 mm. 34 long lines. Collation: 1^8 2^8 wants 2–7 after f. 9 $3\text{–}7^8$ 8^8 wants 1, 2, 4, 5, 7, 8 (ff. 51–2) $9\text{–}17^8$ 18^8 wants 7, 8. Quires signed in the usual late medieval way a, b, d–s. The fifth leaf in each quire is marked on the recto, bottom right, with a cross made without raising the pen. Anglicana formata by two hands, the second beginning at f. 126^v/30 after 'chalaunge of eny man' (edn., p. 286/9). A nearly continuous border on f. 9. The second leaf of the text is missing, but its first words were no doubt *al this*, since f. 9^v ends 'herden' (edn., p. 3/9).

The owner, s. xix, wrote 'MSS: A' at the foot of f. 1 and noted on f. 84^v that 'my MS. B is deficient for the remainder of this reign' (so it lacked edn., pp. 199/15–247) and that one piece of text on f. 126 was 'as MS. B' and another 'as MS. C'. Bought from J. and J. Leighton in 1908 for £36: invoice dated 18 June.

(f. 9) Here may a (man) hure Engeland was first called Albyon and þoruȝ wham it hadde þe name. In the nobele lande of Syrrye . . . The preceding quire contains a table of 223 numbered chapters (ff. 1–7^v) and a blank leaf (f. 8^{rv}). Five gaps: six leaves between f. 9^v which ends 'þe ladyes herden' and f. 10 which begins 'and feete'; a quire between f. 18^v which ends 'and whanne he' and f. 19 which begins 'wheder to wende'; two leaves after f. 50^v which ends 'hertes' and f. 51 which begins 'loued þat þey bicomen sworne breþeren'; two leaves after f. 51^v which ends 'he had of ham' and f. 52 which begins 'to þe englisshmen'; two leaves after f. 52^v which ends 'and after' and f. 53 which begins 'come aȝen vnto king Edward'. The missing text is in edn., pp. 3/9–14, 33/20–50/6, 115/17–119/17, 121/23–125/30, 127/30–132/5.

'oooooo 7111' at the foot of f. iii, s. xvi (?). 'A $\overset{P}{X}$ Ω' at the head, f. 9.

Eng. 104. (R. 15386.) *Brut Chronicle* s. xv ex.

A Brut Chronicle which begins imperfectly a page before an account of Cadwallader's going to Rome and ends imperfectly at 1415 'at þe dise and an [archer]', edn. cit. (Eng. 103), p. 378/14. 248 × 190 mm. Written space 203 × 123 mm. 39 long lines. Collation: $1\text{–}2^8$ 3^8 wants 7 after f. 22 $4\text{–}8^8$ 9^8 wants 2 after f. 64 $10\text{–}16^8$ 17^8 wants 8. Mixed, but mainly secretary script: *a* in one compartment or two, the latter more commonly: strokes of *m* and *n* sometimes linked and sometimes not.

'Eles Tomlynson', f. 14, and 'Robart Tomlynsone', f. 55, are scribbles of s. xvi. Item 7450 in a bookseller's catalogue, said to be 'Leighton 1908', at £18. Bought from J. and J. Leighton in 1908 for £16. 4*s.*: invoice dated 18 June.

f. 1v/22 begins 'Howe king Offa was soueraine' (edn., p. 102/21). The preceding 21 lines, 'Thanne kyng Aleyn did sende for the Clergie of his londe . . . vic lxxix' are not in edn. and are derived, no doubt, from Geoffrey of Monmouth (ed. Griscom, 1929, p. 534): f. 1r is barely legible. f. 22v ends 'Englande' and f. 23 begins 'tharchebisshop'. f. 64v ends 'layen xi' and f. 65 begins 'and afterwarde he'. For the missing text see edn., pp. 147/21–149/26, 238/33–240/21. No chapter numbers before '203' on f. 61: the last remaining chapter is numbered '244'. 'Deo gracias' at f. 87/2 (edn., p. 286/9, battle of Halidon Hill, 1333).

Pencil drawings in the margin of f. 32, s. xvi: a man and an acorn, the man saying 'Iohn geue me sum acornes ho'.

Eng. 105. (R. 15391.) *Brut Chronicle* s. xv ex.

Brut Chronicle, ending imperfectly at 1413. ff. iii + 134 + iii, foliated (i), 1–136, (137–8). Paper and for the outside, fourth, and middle sheets of each quire, parchment, except that parchment was saved in three quires by using singletons, ff. 32, 86, 133, instead of bifolia: see the collation. ff. 1, 2 are parchment binding leaves: 1 was pasted down. 275 × 205 mm. Written space 175 × 135 mm. 28–38 long lines: the closer spacing begins at f. 68, where the number of lines rises from 31 to 34. Collation of ff. 3–136: 1^{16} wants 2 2^{14} + 1 leaf after 14 (f. 32) 3^{16} wants 15, 16, perhaps blank, after f. 46 4–5^{16} 6^{14} + 1 leaf after 7 (f. 86) 7–8^{16} 9^{14} + 1 leaf after 7 (f. 133), wants 11–14 after f. 136. Several secretary hands: changes at f. 45/18 and at f. 47 (4^1).

'Iste liber constat hugoni Wyniard', 'Iste liber partinet ad Thomam Pawlyn Surgion in Ciuitate London' and 'Iste liber pertinet ad me Nicholaum Stevinson gent' ', f. 2, s. xvi. '93' at the head of f. 2v. T. Thorpe's catalogue for 1836, item 251. 'Phillipps MS. 9486', f. 2v: sale 15 June 1908, lot 361. Bought then through Bull and Auvache for £21: invoice dated 19 June.

Here begynneth a boke in Englysshe tunge called Brute . . . the whiche conteyneth ccxxxviii chapiters withoute the prolog or protogoll. The prolog of this booke declareth . . . of hem many oon. Some tyme in the noble lond of Surry . . . (f. 136v) ihesu haue mercy amen. Of kinge Henry the vth borne at Monmouth in Wales son to king Henry the iiiith (*ends imperfectly*). Ed. F. W. D. Brie, EETS cxxxi and cxxxvi (1906–8), as far as p. 373. f. 3v ends 'evell taches and governaunces' (edn., p. 2/18): f. 4 begins 'shuld comme to much honor and worship' (edn., p. 6/3). Chapters are not numbered after 'Capitulo cxmo' (edn., ch. 108) on f. 57.

Eng. 109 (R. 21638) + Norwich Cathedral 5.[1] *'Mirrour' and other sermons in English and Latin* 1432; s. xv[1]

1–3. Three collections of sermons, 2 in Latin: 1, ff. 4–17v; 2, ff. 18–36v; 3, ff. 37–126 + Norwich. 4. ff. 1–2v Table of 1–3 added in s. xvi[1]. ff. vi + 123 + ii in Manchester, foliated (i–iii), 1–126, (127–8). ff. i + 8 + i in Norwich. Paper,

[1] Norwich Cathedral 5 is deposited in the Norfolk and Norwich Record Office: see below.

except ff. 75–8. A now damaged foliation in the hand of art. 4, 1–143, repeats two numbers, 23 or 24 and 27 or 28, and takes account of fourteen of the leaves missing from art. 3: it was made when arts. 1, 2 were in their present state, when the first leaf of art. 3 was out of place and the second leaf missing and when the gap after f. 101 already existed. 280 × 205 mm. Written space *c.* 215 × 155 mm at first, rising to 232 × 175 mm on f. 126. 40–54 lines (40 lines throughout quires 3–8). Ruling with a hard point in quires 3–7: frame ruling in ink in quires 9–12. Collation of ff. 4–126 and Norwich ff. 1–8: 1^{20} wants 1, 16–20 (16–20 probably blank: 1–9 are lettered b–k) 2 nineteen (ff. 18–36) 3^{12} wants 2 and 12 (ff. 54, 37–45) 4^{12} wants 7 and 11 (ff. 46–51; Norwich ff. 5–7; f. 52) 5^{12} wants 2, 3 after f. 53 and 7–9 after f. 57 (ff. 53, 56–60) 6^{12} wants 7–9 after f. 66 7^{12} wants 10–12 (ff. 70–4; Norwich ff. 1–4) 8 four (ff. 75–8) 9^{14} (ff. 79–92) 10^{12} wants 5–7 after f. 96 11^{16} (ff. 102–17) 12^{10} (ff. 118–22; Norwich f. 8; ff. 123–6). Current anglicana, arts. 1, 2 in different hands and art. 3 in two other hands, changing at f. 79: in art. 1 the scribe wrote a catchword on each verso and on some rectos.

'Iste liber constat A[. . . . .] de W[. . . .] 'domino Roberto Prestwold'. Si quis hunc librum a predict' [. . . .] alienauerit anatema sit. amen. Et scriptus erat Anno domini Millesimo CCCC^{mo} xxx^{mo} secundo', f. 126^{v}, may apply to art. 3 only, but art. 4 shows that the whole manuscript was together by s. xvi^{1}: M. R. James (see below) read the third and fourth letters of the erased place-name as *lb* (the third letter can be seen to be an ascender) and was almost certainly right in suggesting Welbeck, Ord. Praem., in the north of Nottinghamshire, and traces suggest that the two other erased words were *Abbathie* and *Abbathia.*[1] The list of contents (art. 4) and the foliation are in a distinctive current mixed anglicana-secretary which seems to be the same as the hand in lists of contents, foliations, etc., in manuscripts now at Gray's Inn, London (see *MMBL* i. 50–1) and at Shrewsbury School, most of which come from Cheshire, but one probably from Staffordshire and one from Derbyshire, not very distant from Welbeck, whence the manuscript had been alienated, it seems, before s. xvi^{1}. 'Iste liber pertinet bear this in mind ad me Iohannem Voudon (?) both' is scribbled on f. 78^{v}, s. xvi.[2] 'Tho. Gibbon', f. i, s. xvii. Lot 215 in the John Henley sale, 21 June 1759. No. 1157 in Thomas Thorpe's catalogue for 1836 at £1. 11*s.* 6*d.*: the relevant cutting from his catalogue—inside the cover of the fragment in Norwich—refers evidently to Rylands + Norwich, since it gives the date as 1432. The 'book-*plate*' of Charles Clark of Totham Hall, Essex, inside the cover of Rylands, consists of twenty lines of verse headed 'A pleader to the needer when a reader': the date 1859 is added in pencil at the end. Lot 1688 in a sale at Sotheby's, 28 Nov. 1861.[3] Bought from Quaritch in 1910 for £35: invoice dated 24 March.

Rylands is described by M. R. James, *Catalogue*, pp. 305–6, when it was MS. Lat. 179: he follows the foliation of s. xvi.

[1] Professor Angus MacIntosh told me that a north Nottinghamshire origin for this copy of the 'Mirrour' would suit the linguistic evidence.

[2] *courteous and kind* is the conventional ending of this form of ex-libris.

[3] Seymour de Ricci knew of the entries in these sale catalogues and asked for information about the present whereabouts of this manuscript in a letter to *The Times Literary Supplement*, 12 Febr. 1938, p. 112.

1. ff. 4-17 (1-14 in the old foliation). (*begins imperfectly*) hert when þ^{u} kepes it clene . . . (f. 4^{v}) In rogacionibus. Estote prudentes . . . Gode men and women euere cristen man is holden to here cristes worde . . . Eight sermons of the temporal, listed by James: the first was on the text 'In omni tempore benedic deum', as appears from art. 4. f. 17^{v}, left blank, contains seventeen lines in two hands of s. xv med., 'y^{o} might `and y^{o} through´ of ye fader almighte of heuen . . . is madde of noȝt'.

2. ff. 18^{v}-36^{v} (15-31 in the old foliation, wrongly). Dominica prima aduentus domini. Cum appropinquasset . . . Appropinquacio cristi versus hierusalem significat . . . in altitudine multipli- (*ends imperfectly*). Seven sermons, nos. 1-5, 20, 21 of the series of temporal sermons in Bodleian, Laud Misc. 200 ff. 1-18^{v}, 52^{v}-64^{v} (first four Sundays in Advent, Christmas Eve, Septuagesima, Sexagesima): the sixth sermon here follows the fifth immediately on f. 29^{v}.

3. ff. 54, 37-51; Norwich 5-7; 52, 53, 55-74; Norwich 1-4; 75-122; Norwich 8; 123-6 (54, 32-46, [49-51], 52, 53, 55-7, 61-9, 73-80, [81-4], 88-109, 113-38, [139], 140-3 in the old foliation: the numbers on the Norwich leaves seem to have been obscured deliberately). Assit principio sancta maria meo. M[*any more ther ben that*][1] haue will' to here rede romance and iestes . . . ne eigh of wordely man se. Amen. Explicit iste liber. The Mirrour, a translation of the Miroir of Robert de Gretham: this and five other copies noted by T. G. Duncan in *Neuphilologische Mitteilungen*, lxix (1968), 204. About twenty leaves are missing and ff. 59, 60 are damaged. The text is a series of temporal sermons from Advent to the 24th Sunday after Pentecost, preceded by a preface and followed as in Bodleian, Holkham misc. 40, etc. by a miscellaneous tail (ff. 102-126^{v}: cf. James, *Catalogue*, p. 306). The first scribe finished his work on f. 78^{v}, 'but þei lost non fisshe and þ^{t}' at the foot of the first column and left the second column blank. The second scribe began f. 79 with the same seven words, 'bot þei loste no fysshe. And y^{t}'. f. 101^{v} ends 'ne for `no´ noþer letting' and f. 102 begins a new sermon 'Missus est gabriel . . .': in the copy in Bodleian, Holkham misc. 40, these words come on f. 103^{v} at lines 8 and 28 respectively, so the leaf which is presumably missing after f. 101 may have been mostly blank.

The eight leaves in Norwich contain the sermons for Septuagesima, Sexagesima, and Quinquagesima (ff. 5-7), for Trinity and the two Sundays after Trinity (ff. 1-4) and on the Creed and Pater Noster (f. 8). The Quinquagesima, Trinity, and Pater Noster sermons are now divided between Norw. and Rylands (Norw. f. 7, Ryl. ff. 52-3; Ryl. ff. 73-4, Norw. f. 1; Norw. f. 8, Ryl. f. 123).

4. ff. 1-2^{v} A table of arts. 1-3, with leaf numbers running from 1-144. Begins 'In omni tempore Benedic deum fo 1', For the hand see above. f. 3^{rv} blank.

Charles Clark (see above) printed the sermon on 'The rich man and Lazarus' in a book called *The style of preaching four hundred years ago* . . . , printed on his private press, Great Totham, 1837. (Information from Dr A. I. Doyle: a copy, one of 100, is in the Routh Collection in Durham University Library).

Eng. 113. (R. 24403.) *Chaucer, Canterbury Tales* s. xv^{2}

1. ff. 6-194 Canterbury Tales. 2, 3. Additions on flyleaves and in blank spaces of quire 8. ff. v + 190 + ii, foliated 1-197. Paper, except f. 5, conjoint with the pastedown, and ff. 196-7, a conjoint pair, of which 197 was formerly a pastedown. 297 × 210 mm. Written space *c.*235 × 102 mm in Parson's Tale. 54-60 long lines. Collation: 1-7^{24} 8^{22}. A strip of parchment down the gutter in the middle of each quire. Current anglicana of a rather legal sort. Medieval binding

[1] Letters in italics supplied from Magdalene College, Cambridge, Pepys 2498.

of brown leather over wooden boards: six bands: five bosses on each cover, now missing: two clasps, missing. Secundo folio *musyng* (f. 4) or *vnder his* (f. 7).

'Constat Iohanni Brode Iuniori etc' ', f. 194, is in the hand of the text. Probably art. 1 is in Brode's hand and art. 2 was added by him on various occasions. Belonged probably to John Hull, 'customer of Exceter and Dartmouthe', in s. xvi, whose scribbles are on ff. 1, 194^{v}, 195^{v}, 196^{rv}. Book-plate of L. W. Hodson, Compton Hall, near Wolverhampton: not in the catalogue of his sale, 3 Dec. 1906. Bought for £180 from Quaritch in 1910: invoice dated 24 May.

1. Described by J. M. Manly and E. Rickert, *The text of the Canterbury Tales*, 1940, i. 349–55, who note that the text is closely related to Cn, the Brudenell Chaucer, and that the hand is like that of Bodleian Digby 181, ff. 1–39, which ends with the words 'Explicit Edorb quod'.

2. (*a*) f. 3^{rv} King Edward the iiiith. Wher is this Prynce that conquered his right . . . for hym to pray Explicit. *IMEV*, no. 4062. Printed from here by F. J. Furnivall in EETS xv, pp. xlvi–viii. (*b*) f. 4^{rv} Musyng alone voide of consolacion . . . and wo. Baradoun Henricus transtulit istud opus per semetipsum. *IMEV*, no. 2227. Printed from here by Furnivall in EETS xv. 289. (*c*) ff. 4^{v}–5^{v} Articuli passionis cristi. Cristus imminente passione . . . custoditus est. Sixty-three heads.

3. (*a*) f. 194^{v} Periculum animarum periuratorum secundum diuersos autores. Twelve lines, each beginning 'Cristus Qui iurat voluntarie': swearing on Book, putting hand on Book, kissing Book. (*b*) f. 195 Dates of death or cessation of English kings, Edward I–Edward V: Memorandum quod Rex E' primus post conquestum filius Regis Henrici tercii obiit die translacionis sancti Thome Martiris anno regni sui xxxv^{to} sicut continetur in Rotulo xxxv^{o} dicti Regis E primi in Surr' et Sussex' in titulo Vic' . . . Memorandum quod E v^{tus} cessauit a regimine xxvi^{to} die Iunii anno regni sui primo Et Rex Ricardus tercius incepit regnare. (*c*) f. 197 Qui cepit vxorem cepit absque quiete laborem . . . (4 lines).

Eng. 206. (R. 33820.) *Brut Chronicle* s. xv^{2}

Brut Chronicle, ending imperfectly at 1326. ff. iv + 102 + ii, foliated (i, ii), 1–104, (105–6). 262 × 195 mm. Written space *c.* 197 × 118 mm. 34–8 lines. Frame ruling. Collation of ff. 3–104: 1–5^{8} 6^{8} wants 5, 6 after f. 45 7–13^{8}. A good secretary hand, the same throughout. Secundo folio *othir into*.

Scribbled names, etc., s. xvi, include 'W. CAMPINET' in large capitals on f. 99^{v} (cf. f. 95^{v}) and 'William Campinet de Kilworty' on f. 15; also 'John Peele de Stoke' on f. 10 and 'dracon de elton in Com' lincolne' on f. 37^{v}. Armorial book-plate, s. xviii/xix, of D. P. Coke, fellow of All Souls College, Oxford (†1825). 'G. D. 1899', f. 1. Bought at the George Dunn sale, 2 Feb. 1913, lot 440 (£9), through P. M. Barnard: invoice dated 25 Feb.[1]

(f. 3) 'Here may a man heren how that Englonde was first called Albion and thurgh whom it had the name. In the noble londe of Surrey . . . (f. 104^{v}) then shuld he cloo–': catchword 'then hym in a'. Ed. F. W. D. Brie, EETS cxxxi and cxxxvi (1906–8), as far as p. 244/18. f. 45^{v} ends 'lorde' and f. 46 begins 'Englonde': for the missing text see edn., pp. 90/27–95/4.

[1] The eleven manuscripts bought at the Dunn sale are Eng. 206, 207, Fr. 64, Lat. 193, 203, 204, 206, 211, 216, 217, 218.

Divisions into chapters as in edn., but no chapter numbers. No chapter headings after f. 48, 'How Cadwalader . . .'. Spaces for initials not filled.

A legal note in the margin of f. 103, s. xvi: 'The xxith of Henry the viiith it is inacted that no bysshope archedecun Chaunselor comysary officyall or other maner of persone' with authority 'to probatte eny will' shall charge more than sixpence if the goods do not amount to more than £5 (etc.). A recipe on f. 102^{v} 'for to make tethe faste': 'Take of ye barke of thelme . . .'.

The binding leaves, ff. 1, 2, s. xiv^{2}, are from indexes to two different works (cf. *MMBL* ii. 498). On f. 1^{rv} entries are mainly theological, letters N, O, P, for example 'Nomen cristi secundum hominem in eternum et qualiter 134.3.13'. On f. 2^{rv}, letters P, R, S, there are longish entries under Princeps, Puer, Rex and shorter entries like 'Percussionum plura genera sunt 3° libro 63 per totum' and 'Portare scire onera est vtile bellantibus 3° libro 63 a'.

Eng. 207. (R. 33821.) *Brut Chronicle* s. xv^{1}–xv^{2}

Two incomplete manuscripts put together in or before 1749 to make a nearly complete Brut Chronicle to 1415: 1. ff. 1–103, s. xv^{2}; 2. ff. 104–24, s. xv^{1}. ff. iii + 123 (foliated 1–77, 80, 78–9, 81–7, 89–124) + ii. As far as '103' the foliation is of s. xvi. 2 is on paper. 272 × 200 mm. Written space: 1, 172 × 130 mm. 27–32 long lines; 2, 220 × 130 mm. 40 long lines ruled with a hard point. Collation: (1) 1^{8} wants 1, 2 $2–8^{8}$ 9^{10} (ff. 63–72) 10 eleven (ff. 73–83) 11^{10} + 1 leaf after 6 (ff. 84–95) 12 six (ff. 96–101: three outer bifolia) 13 two (ff. 102–3: first two leaves); (2) 14 three (ff. 104–6: last three leaves) $15–16^{8}$ 17 three (ff. 122–4: first three leaves). Signatures in 1 of the usual late medieval kind: the first to be seen now is b 1 on f. 7, so the now missing first quire may have been outside the series beginning with *a* (cf. *MMBL* ii, p. viii). Both 1 and 2 are current, a mixture of anglicana and secretary. Binding of red morocco, s. xviii, probably for Palmer: 'HISTORY / OF / BRITTAIN' on the spine.

1 was perhaps in Lancashire in s. xvi: scribbles of that date include (f. 19^{v}) 'By yt knowen . . . that I thomas dycconson of Eccleston', (f. 20) 'Thomas Heaton of Knowisley', (f. 47) 'Wyllyam Aston est possessor vjus lybry'. 'Bibliotheca Palmeriana' and a note dated 30 July 1749 and signed 'Palmer' on f. ii.[1] 'G. D. Nov. 1899', f. ii. Bought at the George Dunn sale, 2 Feb. 1913, lot 441, for £10. 10*s.* (cf. MS. 206): invoice dated 25 Feb.

1. Begins imperfectly 'heir vnto the' (ed. F. W. D. Brie, EETS cxxxi and cxxxvi (1906–8), p. 23/16). Ends imperfectly (f. 103^{v}) 'Tormentours. ys more chame vnto Crystenmen and schewen' (cf. edn., p. 297/4). f. 98^{v} ends 'of Sir Edward dethe hys' and f. 99 begins 'quarell' and ther Right title' (cf. edn., pp. 262, 275/30). The text often varies from that printed by Brie and tends to be shorter. The last remaining chapter is numbered 220 (edn., ch. 226). The leaves of quire 10 were at one time out of order, as the foliation shows and also signes de renvoi of s. xv ex. on ff. 77^{v}, 79^{v}, 80^{v}. 1, unlike 2, has references to the Polychronicon in the margins, s. xv.

2. Begins imperfectly 'Englond. The xx yer' (ed. Brie, p. 297/11). Ends imperfectly in the story of Agincourt 'And englisshe peple was dede yat day the duke of ȝorke and the erle of Sothfolke Sirr' Cam and sir Ric' lyȝtley. These ii knyghtes assemblet first in the batayll'

[1] For Palmer see below, Oxford, Worcester College, 213.

and wer' slayne And of all' other' off englisshemen er' nacion yer' wer' not dede not passed xxxvi bodies thonket be Ihesu. Anone ye kynge' (cf. edn., p. 379/25-9). Brie's chapters 227-39, 341-4 are here numbered '233'-'248', '250'. The history of Richard II is abbreviated by the omission of the whole of Brie's chapter 240 (11-18 Richard II) on f. 116^v and of part of his chapter 239 (here '245') on f. 116, where edn., 338/22-339/20 and 339/30-340/29 do not occur.

Eng. 288. (R. 39329.) *Littleton, Tenures and other pieces in English, French, and Latin* s. xv/xvi

1. ff. 1-23 Formulary proceedings at a court leet, in Latin and English. 2 (missing). *A generall rule to teche euery man that is willinge for to lerne to serue a lorde or maystr in anything to his Plesure*. 3. ff. 25-57^v Littleton, Tenures, in French. 4. ff. 58-155^v Legal pieces, principally (ff. 71-155^v) a Natura brevium in French. 5. ff. 156-188^v Legal notes in French. ff. 189, foliated 1-36, 36*, 37-188. Paper. 222 × 150 mm and (ff. 167-78) *c.*200 × 135 mm. Written space *c.*175 × 100 mm. *c.*30 long lines. Collation: 1^{12} wants 1 $2\text{-}4^{12}$ 5^{12} wants 12 after f. 57 6^{18} (ff. 58-75) 7^{80} (ff. 76-155) 8^{32} wants 32, blank, + two singletons, ff. 162, 179: for this quire see art. 5, below (ff. 156-88). Full-length strips of parchment between quires and two short strips, each *c.*70 mm long, in the middle of each quire as strengthening at the points where the sewing holes come. Written in a mixture of secretary and anglicana and (arts. 3, 5) current legal anglicana, sometimes of a very scribbly sort. Contemporary binding made of a triple thickness of parchment: the quire strings are brought out at four places on the spine and knotted together in pairs.

'Liber Iohannis Wolff', f. 23^v, s. xv ex. 'Iohn Willoughby', f. 188^v, s. xvi². Lot 447 in a sale, s. xx in: the relevant cutting is loose inside the cover. Eng. 287 and 288 were bought from Quaritch for £10 in 1915: invoice dated 2 July.[1]

1 (quires 1, 2). (*a*) ff. 1-14^v In primis preceptum factum balliuo per Seneschallum . . . (*b*) ff. 14^v-18^v Modus diuersarum naturarum factarum de Copiis Rotularum de terris et tenementis acceptis et habitis secundum Consuetudinem Manerii tent' ad voluntatem domini per virgam qualiter Clericus debet eas in Curia rotularum etc' . . . (f. 18^v) Nunc de leta . . . (*c*) f. 21 Modus qualiter Balliuus vel Bedellus qui seruiet Curiam debet vocare assisam panis et seruicie quando Curia cum visu totaliter finitur . . . (*d*) ff. 21-22^v Oaths of constable and others and form of granting seisin. (*e*) ff. 22^v-23 Modus faciendum (*sic*) extract' Cur'.

(*a*). Proceedings of the court presided over by Thomas B., chief steward of the archbishop of Canterbury, at Plumstead (Kent), Monday after St Augustine, 22 Edward IV. In Latin, except for 'The charge of the Courte' under 21 heads and 'the charge of the lete' under 36 heads. (*b*) and (*e*) are in Latin. ff. 23^v-24^v were left blank: 24^{rv} contains added formulary documents.

2 Recorded in the sale catalogue (s. xx in.) as item 2. At the time of the sale the manuscript had 203 leaves.

3 (quires 3-5). ff. 25-57^v Vne lyuer de Exposicion . . . Tenaunt en fee simple . . . *que* lun carne est (ends imperfectly). Printed very often from (1482): *STC* 15719-15759. bk. 2, f. 34^v; 3, f. 55^v. The last two-thirds of the text, from edn. (1482), cvii^v/9, is missing.

[1] Eng. 287 was lot 448 in the sale in which Eng. 288 was lot 447. It is a legal formulary of Lancashire interest, s. xvi, and like Eng. 288 belonged to John Willoughby.

4 (quires 6, 7). (*a*) f. 58 . . . (line 7) Ceo vous monstre T. Northall' que . . . (*b*) ff. 58v–68v Notes in French on statutes of the realm, Quia emptores (*SR* i. 106), Westminster I, Marlborough, and others. (*c*) ff. 70–155v Proc' de natura breuium . . . (table of writs De debito–De homine replegiando) . . . (f. 71) Dicitur que il y a breue de droit patent et breue de droit de clos . . . (f. 151) Expliciunt breuia originalia. Et incipiunt breuia iudicialia . . . Explicit. Very much shorter than the *Natura brevium* printed in (1494) and later (*STC* 18385–18411). Twenty judicial writs, ff. 151–155v. ff. 62r, 63v–64, 67v–68, 69rv left blank.

5 (quire 8). (*a*) ff. 156–162v Legal notes in French headed 'Ml' xiiii H viti, and beginning 'Detinu de box et charters'. 'Explicit quarto decimo h. vi' at the end. (*b*) ff. 163–188v Law cases, etc., in French in various hands: many pieces begin 'home'.

ff. 156–88 are now a single quire wrapped in a strip of a legal document, s. xv/xvi, but they appear to have been originally four quires in different hands and of rather different dates, which have been put one inside the other: (8.1) ff. 156–62, 184–8, a twelve, wants 12, blank, + 1 leaf after 6 (f. 162); (8.2) ff. 163–6, 180–3, an eight; (8.3) ff. 167–70, 175–9, an eight + 1 leaf after 8 (f. 179); (8.4) ff. 171–4, a four.

Eng. 404. (R. 24458). *Medical recipes, charms, etc.* s. xv^2

1. ff. 1–33v Medical recipes, etc. 2. ff. 34–46v Charms, recipes, notes on urine, etc. ff. i + 46 + i. 210 × 140 mm. Written space *c.*163 × 115 mm. 26–8 long lines. No ruling or coloured letters. Collation: 1 three 2^6 3^8 4^{16} 5 thirteen (ff. 34–46: 37–42 are three bifolia). The script changes at f. 26v from secretary (mainly) to anglicana: the anglicana is current, except sometimes in headings. 'Unbound' in 1929 (*Hand-list*): now in a Rylands binding by Bramhall and Menzies.

Perhaps from Kent, in view of art. 1*d*. Entered in the accessions register in September 1928 as being perhaps from the bequest of Mrs Rylands.

1 (quires 1–4). (*a*) A numbered table of (*b*), added rather later. The scribe began with 'Ihesu mercy lady helpe' at the head of f. 1. His numbers run to 'vic iiii iiii' (644); but in fact (*b*) has only about 142 heads and the numbers are wildly wrong after 'lxix'. (*b*) ff. 4–31 Recipes, the first 'For Swellyng Take watir Crasses and crommys of brede . . . ': numbered by the scribe of (*a*). (*c*) ff. 31v–33 More recipes in other hands. (*d*) f. 33v *Latin*. Non omittas propter alliquam libertatem quin distr*ahis* . . . : two copies of a letter from the sheriff of Kent to William Rothley and Richard Vane, bailiffs, bidding them summon Robert Sottesherst and twenty-three other named jurors.

2 (quire 5). (*a, b*) f. 34 *Latin*. Two charms; (*a*) Omnipotens sempiterne deus qui locutus pretro (*sic*). fac hunc famulum tuum Iohannem vt non amplius frebrum nec dolores habeant. Moneo vos frebres que estis vtem (*sic for* 7tem) sorores Prima vocatur helya . . . (*b*) Alia. In nomine patris et filii et spiritus sancti Amen. Ante portam zerusalem petrus sedebat supra petrum marmoriam + de febre mala . . . tu me famulum tuum Iohannem liberare digneris . . . (*c*) ff. 34v–35v On the *dies mali* and days not to let blood. (*d*) f. 35v A charm to avoid ill fortune, to be worn around the head, 'cum istis catarectaribus (*sic*) [. .]M.K.E.r (?) r (?) R.E.E.V'. (*e*) f. 36 Seven recipes. (*f*) f. 36v *Latin*. Charm of the holy names, 'Ihesu crist + Missias sother . . . Ista nomina protegant famulum tuum I. C. . . .': the heading is damaged. (*g*) f. 36v *Latin*. Charm naming the apostles and evangelists 'vt me defendant ab omni malo et periculo et ab omni tribulacione hic et in futuro amen'. (*h*) ff. 37–42v, 46v Recipes, mainly herbal, beginning with Mugwort. (*i*) ff. 42v–43v Wryne is seid of whaye of blode for as þe whay comes of þe milke . . . : on colours of urine, qualities of waters, four seasons of the year and four humours. (*j*) ff. 43v–44v Vryn' es departed in iiii regionys . . . (*k*) f. 44v

To knowe a manys water froe a womanys . . . (*l*) f. 44v To torne a chelde if it lye ouerthwart in the motheris belle. (*m*) f. 45 Notes on differences in urine, the first beginning 'The iiide þinge is sexus þat is to saye manhede or womanhede'. (*n*) f. 46 Two recipes for invisible ink and a third 'And you will see the son' in a Glasse . . . probatum per [. . .] etc' '. (*o*) f. 46 A charm to overcome enemies, 'Take erbe fluelly . . .'. (*p*) f. 46v Seven recipes, the first 'For evyl in þe stomake'. (*q*), added in s. xv/xvi, 'Howe to know yf a woman be wt chylld or no geyve her i clowe of garlyke to hete when she goeyth to bede ande yf she felle the sawer of yt when she doeythe awake of her fvrst slepe thene she ys wt chyllde'.

Eng. 412. (R. 61716.) *Pore Caitif, etc.* s. xv in.

Nine quires of a larger manuscript. 1. ff. 1–34v Parts 1, 2, 8 of Pore Caitif. 2. ff. 34v–39 Mirrour of sinners. 3–8. ff. 39v–72v Six theological pieces. ff. xii + 72 + vii. 202 × 130 mm. Written space 145 × 90 mm. 31–2 long lines. Frame ruling. Collation: $1\text{–}9^8$. Quires signed f–o, but not quite in the usual late medieval way, since leaves 2–4 in each quire are marked ii–iiii, without a quire letter. Anglicana formata by one hand throughout: *a* sometimes in one compartment and sometimes in two compartments. Initials not filled in.

Belonged perhaps to John Stow (†1605), whose distinctive hand is on ff. 19, 30, 34v, 59v ('of prelates') and elsewhere. Notes on f. 1 are said to be in the hand of Thomas Percy, Bishop of Dromore, †1811: sale of his books at Sotheby's, 29 Apr. 1884, lot 285 to Wake for £3. Acquired by H. T. Wake, bookseller, Fritchley, Derbyshire, in whose catalogue 86 it is listed, and bought from him by J. J. Green, 30 May 1884: the preliminary leaves have attached to them, among much else,[1] Wake's receipt and letters to Green about his manuscript from W. W. Skeat, 22 and 24 July 1884. Bought from Mrs E. Green in Jan. 1927 for £10.

1. Jolliffe, B. Begins imperfectly in pt. 1 (Creed), 'þe þridde is sorowe'. Pt. 2 (Commandments) begins on f. 6v and pt. 8 (Horse) on f. 30.

2. [F]or þt we ben in þe wey . . . wt his herte blood. Amen. Jolliffe, F. 8.

3. ff. 39v–42 De officio militis. [S]eþ no man mai come to blisse . . . to þe blisse euerlastinge Amen.

4. ff. 42–3 [I]ohannes est nomen eius. Manie men han þis name . . . makinge redi his wey.

5. ff. 43–8 [S]eint Austyn þe holi doctour techeþ . . . haue mercy on me. Amen. Jolliffe, I. 32.

6. ff. 48–49v [T]his lore þat folewt techeþ crist . . . stinkynge bifore god. and so knowen to god. Jolliffe, K. 12: this copy only.

7. ff. 50–72 [M]emorare nouissima. ecclesiastici 7. þe help and þe grace . . . þe siȝt of þi face. Amen. Also in Bodleian, Rawlinson C. 751.[2]

8. f. 72rv [T]hou shalt loue þi lord god . . . for to deceyue men wiþ (*ends imperfectly*: *catchword* whanne he). Jolliffe, G. 27.

[1] Including two letters from C. W. Le Bas, written in 1822 and 1826, which seem to have no immediate relevance.

[2] Information from Dr A. I. Doyle.

The process of correction can be seen in this manuscript. A corrector supplied longer omissions in the lower margin and shorter omissions in the side margin. These were then copied by the scribe of the text in the margins near the point where they were to be taken into the text.

Eng. 413. (R. 61717.) *Mirror of the Life of Christ* s. xv in.

A very imperfect copy of the Mirror of the Life of Christ, the translation by Nicholas Love of Pseudo-Bonaventura, Speculum Vitae Christi. ff. ix + 50 + v. 225 × 170 mm. Written space 170 × 110 mm. 31 long lines. Ruling in red ink. Collation: 1^8 wants 1, 3 2^8 wants 1-3 3^8 wants 2, 3 after f. 12 4^8 5^8 wants 1 before f. 25 6^8 7^8 wants 6 after f. 44 and 8 after f. 45 8^8 wants 5, 7, 8 (ff. 46-50). Textura.

'Joseph J. Green, 182 Up Grosvenor Road Tunbridge Wells. Bought of Henry Thomas Wake, of Fritchley, near Derby, Quaker Bookseller, circa 1891 cost about £ (*cypher*)', f. i. Letters to Green from W. W. Skeat, 21 Apr. 1891, Randel Harris, 5 June 1908, and L. F. Powell, 11 Aug. 1911 and 19 Dec. 1920, are attached to the preliminary leaves. Green's own notes on the manuscript are on ff. i^v, ii, vi–viii^v (dated 26–7 Nov. 1920) and on ff. 51–2 (dated 2 Dec. 1920). Bought from Mrs J. Green for £10 in January 1927.

Ed. L. F. Powell, 1908. The first words are in chapter 32, 'as þei diden we mowe' (edn., p. 155/11), and the last in chapter 55, 'medicine ayens swiche' (edn., p. 274/12: f. 50 is damaged). The ten leaves missing between these points are equivalent to twenty pages of the Roxburghe Club edition: f. 1^v ends 'souereynly euer' (edn., p. 157/21) and f. 2 begins 'of vertues' (159/22); f. 6^v ends 'þer with þei' (169/8) and f. 7 begins 'but wheþer' (175/4); f. 12^v ends 'in þat preciowse' (186/28) and f. 13 begins 'he cam nyh' (190/22); f. 24^v ends 'and his preci', followed by the catchword 'owse blood' (215/16) and f. 25 begins 'al his inward' (217/23); f. 44^v ends 'of þin fowleste' (256/18) and f. 45 begins 'but a litel' (258/13); f. 45^v ends 'And so' (260/11) and f. 46 begins 'restre. where þat' (262/9); f. 49^v ends 'wiþ us in ma' (270/12) and f. 50 begins 'and þe disciples' (272/12). The upper margins contain chapter numbers and running titles in red: 'Die iouis', ff. 1–24^v; 'Die ueneris', ff. 25–44^v; 'Die sabbati' f. 45^{rv}; 'Die dominica', ff. 46–48^v.

Eng. 895. (R. 78096.) *Passion and Resurrection of Christ, etc.* s. xv med.

The stories of the Passion and Resurrection of Christ based on Pseudo-Bonaventura, Passio et Resurrectio Christi, together with the Gospel of Nicodemus and Harrowing of Hell. ff. 125. ff. 111–24 have a medieval foliation iii–x, xiii–xv, xv, xx, xxi. 230 × 137 mm. Written space 140 × 65 mm and (ff. 115–7) 140 × 55 mm. 21 long lines. Collation: 1^{16} wants 1, 16 (ff. 1–14) 2–9^{12} 10^{12} wants 1, 2, 11, 12 (ff. 111–18) 11^{12} wants 5–8 after f. 122 and 12, blank, after f. 125. A secretary-influenced short-*r* anglicana formata: *a* in one compartment: one hand throughout.[1] The blank spaces on ff. 14^v, 58^v, 62^v, 69^v, 100 may have been intended for pictures. Contemporary binding of pink-stained leather over

[1] Dr Ian Doyle tells me that B.L., Egerton 2658 (see below) and Trinity College, Dublin, 71 (Rolle's English psalter) are probably in the same hand.

bevelled wooden boards: 6 bands (VVV): of 2 strap-and-pin fastenings the upper pin and lower strap remain. Secundo folio *lete hym*.

'John Senleger knight' is named in a legal scribble on f. 57. 'Robert Worthye', f. 125ᵛ. 'Iohn Hockm[. .] 1576' on the wood inside the back cover, above which is 'John Hockmon 1576 Tho: Taylor 1756'. Ex-libris of George Dunn inside the cover: his sale 2 Feb. 1913, lot 604. Bought from Messrs. Maggs for £30 in 1937: invoice dated 19 Feb.

Probably a continuous narrative as in B.L., Egerton 2658 and Stonyhurst College, 43 B. xliii, but the transition from the Resurrection section to the Nicodemus section came on a now missing leaf. Rotographs of twenty-two pages of the Stonyhurst manuscript (ff. 21-3, 29ᵛ-32, 82ᵛ-84, 88ᵛ-90, 91ᵛ-94) are kept with Eng. 895 to supply the text on its ten missing leaves: (1) a leaf before f. 1 which begins 'lete hym go thus' (Stonyh., f. 22ᵛ/11: St. begins on f. 21/1, 'Passio domini nostri Ihesu cristi sit nostra salus et proteccio. That tyme yᵗ oure lord Ihesu Cryst was xxx ȝere'); (2) a leaf between f. 14ᵛ which ends 'and comanded watyr' (St., f. 30/10) and f. 15 which begins 'þinges he sayde hem' (St., f. 32/2); (3, 4) two leaves between f. 110ᵛ which ends 'and sleeþ oure hertes', followed by the catchword 'And wiþ all' (St., f. 83/5) and f. 111 which begins 'ken hem abyde. We had no myght' (St., f. 84/21); (5, 6) two leaves between f. 118ᵛ which ends 'wende to hys dysciples' (St., f. 89/1) and f. 119 which begins 'Furthe[. . .] þey wreten and sayden' (St., f. 90/3); (7-10) four leaves between f. 122ᵛ which ends 'and þow layst dede in' (St., f. 92/16) and f. 123 which begins 'de a lytell' (St., f. 94/23). Latin pieces on ff. 18-19ᵛ, 22ᵛ, Christ's prayers to the Father, on ff. 23ᵛ-24ᵛ, St Michael's message to Christ, and on f. 90, Ecce rex noster . . . adoremus eum', are in red ink. 'Here endeþ þe processe of þe passion' and begynneþ þe Resurreccion', f. 79ᵛ.

'A wanton wyfe and a backe dore Sonne will make a ryche man poore' is in the blank space after the text, f. 125, s. xvi: see *Oxford Dictionary of English Proverbs*, s.v. *Nice wife*.

Eng. 1310. *On urines* s. xvi in.

1. ff. 1-13ᵛ Blac vryn hath evermor' a swartnesse and a dymnes . . . and make a confection therof and vse it often τελοσ.

Diagnosis by colour of urine. The colours are in the same order as in B.L., Sloane 568, ff. 201-14, black, 'bloo', white, 'glauk', milky, 'karapos', pale, 'citrine', 'rufe' and 'subruf', rubicund, 'ynopos' and green.

2. ff. 13ᵛ-21 Ther ben iiii Regions in mannys body vrin . . . Uryn blac and watry in a fat man Mortes significat.

The 'regions', 'circles', and contents of urine and its sediment (f. 19ᵛ To the ypostasis shuld long v condicions . . .). A similar Latin text is in B.L., Harley 1612, ff. 4ᵛ-9ᵛ (Regiones urine sunt quatuor . . . (f. 9ᵛ) Ypostasis debet habere v condiciones . . .).

Both in art. 1 and in art. 2 sentences usually end with the name of an authority, for example Ysaac, Avicenna, Egidius, Walterius, Gordianus.

ff. 21. Paper. Contemporary foliation in red ink. 305 × 215 mm. Written space 230 × 150 mm. c. 40 long lines. No ruling: the edge of the leaf has been folded to make a vertical bounder. Collation: $1\text{-}2^8$ 3^6 wants 6, probably blank. Secretary hand: the bracket is employed to show a parenthesis (f. 16v Also it is to be vnderstond that (as techeth the commentoure vpon gilis) that iii thing*is* . . .). Red initials, 5-line, 3-line, and 2-line. Bound in paper covers, s. xix. Secundo folio *Blac vrin*.

Written in England. 'Perfect T. W. 1879': cf. Germ. 24. The relevant slip from a sale catalogue is pasted inside the cover.

Manuscripts in French

Fr. 1–7, 66, 88 are foundation books, all but Fr. 66 being from the Crawford collection. The other manuscripts were acquired in: 1908, Fr. 99; 1909, Fr. 62; 1910, Fr. 75; 1911, Fr. 55, 57 + 71, 58; 1912, Fr. 72; 1913, Fr. 63, 64; 1916, Fr. 73; 1918, Fr. 65; 1919, Fr. 54, 56; 1923, Fr. 74; 1925, Fr. 87; 1926, Fr. 98; 1975, Fr. 142; 1976, Fr. 143.

Fr. 1 + Oxford, Bodleian, Douce 215. *Arthurian romances*

s. xiv in.

The Lancelot, Queste (f. 182) and Mort Artu (f. 212) sections of the cycle of Arthurian romances which form vols. 5, 6 of the edition by H. O. Sommer (8 vols., 1909–16). The rest of the set was in cat. 153 (1979) of H. P. Kraus, New York, item 31, at $400,000.[1] Fr. 1 is described in *BJRL* xxxi (1948), 318–44,

[1] Kraus cat. 153, item 31, is three volumes, (1) Grail, (2, 3) Merlin and Lancelot, 118, 233, and 104 leaves respectively. (2, 3) were bought by Sir Thomas Phillipps in the Robert Lang sale, 17 Nov. 1828, lot 1305, and given the number 3630. Subsequently Phillipps noticed that (1), one of his earlier acquisitions, belonged with (2, 3). He therefore changed the number previously assigned to (1), replaced it with the number 3630 (see below), and added a note on the same flyleaf: 'Bought I believe in Yarnold's Sale or of Longman and Co. It is the first vol. of the copy of this work of which I bought the two other vols. in Lang's sale. See 3630 in my catalogue, thus making the set complete'.

The relationship between the three Kraus volumes and the present Douce 215 had not escaped the notice of Francis Douce, who wrote a note on a piece of paper now attached to Douce 215 f. iii and, later, added to it on the other side of the paper: (*a*) on the recto, 'I have seen 3 other volumes or parts of the present work certainly belonging to each other originally. Vol. I the roman de Merlin bound in 2 vols.* Ending "son frere agrauain" and then a rubrick "Ci comenche le livres de li branque agrauain". This was sold at Evans in May 1815. It belonged to (*blank*). Vol. II. A single volume of the Sang graal. Sold at Paris's sale at Leigh and Sotheby May 1815 (*P. C. Parris sale, 18 May 1815, lot 1035, 'The Romance of Saint Graal'*). The present MS (*Douce 215*) is that part which has followed the rubrick above mentioned. It came from the Crevenna library (*P. A. Bolognaro-Crevenna sale, Amsterdam, 1790, lot 5138 (15 florins, 10 sols): the number is on a label inside the cover*) and originally from the D. de la Vallieres (*Duc de la Vallière sale, Paris 1783, lot 4006*) where probably all the other parts were that is of the same size and transcription'; (*b*) on the verso: '* (*in reference to the * on the recto*) Vol. 1 begins Mout furent (*cf. edn., ii. 3/1*) ends Chi entre li duc de Clarence en un chastel. Vol. 2 begins Chi endroit dist li contes que quand li duc de Clarence (*edn., iv. 89/5*) ends Chi comence li livres de le branque agrauain. These 2 Vols. are now (July 1817) in Dulau's shop for sale at £15 `? afterwards in Mr Lang's library''. The two volumes at Dulau's in 1817 duly appeared in Lang's sale, 17 Nov. 1828, lot 1305, 'Lancelot du Lac 2 vol. old red morocco 352 leaves and 77 curious miniatures' which the cataloguer, or Lang himself, took to be English from the style of the painting. Douce bid for it, but only eleven guineas. It went for £43. 1*s.* to Evans, who was bidding for Phillipps, presumably. The number of leaves given in the Lang sale catalogue seems to confirm Douce's and Fr. 1 + Douce by A. Micha in *Romania* lxxxiv (1963), 479–80, 486, and by M. A. Stones in *Scriptorium* xxii (1968), 42–5, with facsimiles of parts of ff. 73, 188, 232 and Douce, ff. 14, 32, 35. The angel in the margin of f. 82, the whole of f. 82, much reduced, and part of the margin of f. 212 are plates 3, 54, 523 in L. Randall, *Images in the margins of Gothic MSS*, 1966.

ff. ii + 129 + i in Rylands, vol. 1. ff. ii + 128 (foliated 130–257) + ii in Rylands, vol. 2. ff. ii + 46 + iii in Douce. Good parchment. 393 × 282 mm. Written space 285 × 200 mm. 2 cols. 44 lines. Pricks in both margins of ff. 82–181. Collation: 1^{8} (Douce ff. 1–8) 2^{8} wants 5 after f. 4 3^{8} 4^{8} wants 3 after f. 17 $5\text{–}6^{8}$ 7^{8} wants 8 after f. 45 $8\text{–}9^{8}$ 10^{10} 11^{8} wants 3–6 after f. 73 12^{6} (ff. 76–81) $13\text{–}24^{8}$ (vol. 2 begins at quire 19) 25^{4} (ff. 178–81) 26^{8} wants 1 before f. 182 $27\text{–}28^{8}$ (ff. 189–204) 29^{8} (Douce ff. 9–16) 30^{8} wants 6 (Douce ff. 17–23) 31^{8} wants 3–6 (Douce ff. 24–7) 32^{6} wants 3, 4 (Douce ff. 28–31) 33^{8} (Douce ff. 32–9) 34^{8} wants 2 (ff. 205–11) 35^{2} (Douce ff. 45–6) 36^{8} wants 3–6 (ff. 212–15) 37^{8} wants 4, 5 (ff. 216–21) 38^{8} 39^{8} wants 2, 3 after f. 230 and 6, 7 after f. 232 $40\text{–}42^{8}$ (ff. 234–57) 43^{8} wants 1, 7, 8 (Douce ff. 40–4). In five quires (3–7), each leaf in the first half of a quire was marked with a pair of letters: the letters are partly cut off, but enough remains to show that the series is bb, bc, bd, be (ff. 8–11), cd, ce, [cf], cg (ff. 16–18), de, df, dg, dh (ff. 23–6), ef, eg, eh, ei (ff. 31–4), fg, fh, fi, fk (ff. 39–42). Two hands: (1) quires 1–12, 26–43; (2) quires 13–25 (ff. 82–181), a fine hand of earlier type than (1). Eighty pictures: see below.

guess that these volumes at least came from the Duc de la Vallière: lot 4004 in the 1783 sale was a copy of 'Lancelot du Lac' on 352 leaves, ending 'et retorne a parler dagrauain son frere' (cf. edn., iv. 362).

The three volumes were a part of the Phillipps collection which remained unsold in 1977 and was sold then *en bloc* to H. P. Kraus. The two plates in cat. 153, p. 124, show two pictures and some lines of writing by two hands. One of the hands, that in the lower plate, taken from one of the Lang-Phillipps volumes, is the main hand of Rylands + Douce. The over-all dimensions are given as 405 × 290 mm, the number of leaves as 118 + 233 + 104, the number of lines as 44 in two columns to the page, and the bindings as English red morocco, s. xix (but see below). Arms in the lower border of f. 1 of vol. 1 are said to be of La Rochefoucauld, s. xvii. The number of leaves in vols. 2 + 3 is fifteen less than we should expect from the evidence of the Lang and La Vallière catalogues. The discrepancy is probably due to errors in the old foliation: Dr Roland Folter tells me that vol. 2 has no old foliation now (as a result of rebinding ?) and that an old foliation on every fifth leaf of vol. 3 runs to '110' on f. 100, because the foliator went wrong at f. 90 which he marked '100'. Dr Folter also tells me that the number originally assigned to vol. 1 by Phillipps was 1045 (not 1046, as printed in the catalogue). This number 'is still clearly visible on the fly-leaf of Vol. 1; later he wrote "3630" over it without erasing the previous number. At the foot of the spine we find the usual printed slip bearing the number 1045. However its last digit has been corrected in ink into 7 and then everything was crossed out in pencil.' The number 1045 or 1047 is puzzling, because these and 1046 are numbers assigned by Phillipps to three Arthurian manuscripts which he bought in an anonymous sale (Yarnold's ?), 27 May 1825, and which surfaced again in the sale of Phillipps manuscripts by Messrs Robinson on 1 July 1946:

1. 27 May 1825, lot 855, written in 1357, sold to Thorpe for £89. 5*s*. Phillipps 1045. Sale, 1 July 1946, lot 14. Now Yale University 227.

2. 27 May 1825, lot 856, sold to Thorpe for £73. 10*s*. Phillipps 1047 (241 leaves, 2 cols., 50 lines). Sale 1 July 1946, lot 10 (Scheler, £1,100).

3. 27 May 1825, lot 857, sold to Thorpe for £52. 10*s*. Phillipps 1046. Sale 1 July 1946, lot 8. Now Cologny-Genève, Fondation Martin Bodmer 147.

Dr Folter also tells me that the uniform red morocco bindings of all three volumes are not English, s. xix, as they are said to be in the Kraus catalogue, but probably French and s. xvii.

The opening words of the second leaf of vol. 1 are *tai bailliet. Et ie dis.*

Three pages with principal initials and elaborate borders, Douce f. 1, Rylands f. 82 (edn., v. 256/8), Rylands f. 212: a fourth page of this kind was the recto of the leaf now missing before f. 182 (26^1). Douce and Fr. 1 are in uniform bindings of gilt red morocco: the Crevenna sale number is inside the cover of Douce and his reference to La Vallière, 'V. 4006' on f. 49: the spines bear titles in the second compartment, 'HISTOI / DE ST / GREAL' (Douce) and 'HISTOIRE / DU ROI / ARTUS' (Fr. 1) and the two volumes of Fr. 1 are distinguished by 'TOM I' and 'TOM II' in the third compartment. Secundo folio (Douce f. 2) *si naures.*

Written in northern France. Perhaps in s. xvii in the library of the Duc de la Rochefoucauld, whose arms are said to be in the first volume of the set (see above, footnote).

Fr. 1 belonged to Charles Spencer, 3rd Earl of Sunderland, †1722, and is entered on p. 1870 of the catalogue of his library made in 1728 (Rylands MS. Eng. 62), with the pressmarks KK 2-7 and KK 2-8: 'L'Histoire du Roy Artus, et des Compagnons de la table Ronde. Avec des figures. Fol. In membran.'. Vol. 1 has the shelfmarks KK. 2. 8 and (later) 105. l. 13 on f. i^v and vol. 2 the shelfmarks KK. 2. 7 and (later) 105. l. 14 on f. i^v. The two volumes were in the Sunderland sale at Puttick and Simpson, 1 Dec. 1881, lot 670 and were bought by Quaritch (£535), who sold them to Lord Crawford. The description in the sale catalogue shows that they consisted in 1881 of: (1) ff. 212-57, 1-81 (127 leaves); (2) ff. 82-211 (130 leaves). This mis-arrangement was devised, no doubt, in order to bring an important page into first place in each volume.

Douce 215 must have been separated from Fr. 1 before the latter left France. It was in the collection of the Duc de la Vallière (sale catalogue, Paris 1783, lot 4006: see above). Douce bought it at the Crevenna sale, lot 5138 (see above).

Begins (Douce f. 1) 'Chi endroit dist li contes ke quant': edn., v. 3.[1] Ends imperfectly (Douce f. 44^v/44) 'Et quant il' (edn., vi. 386/30), but the last 14½ lines are an addition in a later hand and the original ending of Douce was an abrupt one in the middle of line 30, 'ne lui estoit' (edn., vi. 386/24). Probably twenty-seven leaves are missing between these points: (*a*) 2^5: f. 4^v ends 'sentresaluent' (edn., v. 34/5) and f. 5 begins 'ent tere virent' (v. 36/20); (*b*) 4^3: f. 17^v ends 'praiel' (f. 70/11) and f. 18 begins 'ele quide' (v. 72/26); (*c*) 7^8: f. 45^v ends 'de chestre chose' (v. 144/3) and f. 46 begins 'e du lupart' (v. 147/38); (*d*) 11^{3-6}: f. 73^v ends 'quant lanc' ' (v. 233/18) and f. 74 begins 'nature' (v. 233/37); (*e*) 26^1: f. 181^v ends 'esmerueillier. Mais a tant finist chi endroit maistre gautiers map son liure de lancelot del lac. Si commence a parler du saint graal. Chi commenche li liures du saint graal' (cf. v. 409) and f. 182 begins 'ke on fait' (vi. 6/1); (*f*) 30^6: Douce f. 21^v ends 'comenchierent' (vi. 102/35) and f. 22 begins 'soloient' (vi. 105/16); (*g*) 31^{3-6}: Douce f. 25^v ends 'eusse loisir' (vi. 116/4) and f. 26 begins 'Ha cheualiers' (vi. 126/11); (*h*) $32^{3,4}$: Douce f. 29^v ends 'bohort voloit' (vi. 136/20) and f. 30 begins 'quil le fendi' (vi. 141/3); (*i*) 34^2: f. 205^v ends 'fist de partir' (vi. 176/18) and f. 206 begins 'chele nef' (vi. 178/36); (*j*) 36^{3-6}: f. 213^v ends 'monsignur' (vi. 208/25) and f. 214 begins 'damoisiele' (vi. 218/22); (*k*) $37^{4,5}$: f. 218^v ends 'gau. auoet' (vi. 231/17) and f. 219 begins 'Maintenant' (vi. 236/28); (*l*) $39^{2,3}$: f. 230^v ends 'en auroie iou' (vi. 270/3) and f. 231 begins 'roi son oncle' (vi. 277, footnote 1, line 34); (*m*) $39^{6,7}$: f. 232^v ends 'crueil' (vi. 287/29) and f. 233 begins 'eslirent' (vi. 293/26); (*n*) 43^1: f. 257^v ends 'haute persone' (vi. 368/26) and Douce f. 40 begins 'ent molt bien' (vi. 371/28). ff. 140vb/41-167ra/27 contain the text printed by Sommer in an appendix (v. 413-74).

Stones lists the pictures, loc. cit., pp. 44-5. Sixty of them are in the text space, usually column width and 10-line in height (*c.*60 × 92 mm). Twenty, of later date, s. xiv ex., *c.*48 × 88 mm, are in the margins. Forty-nine of the original pictures are by one artist and eleven by another artist who made all the pictures in quires 26-9. The lower margins of

[1] The heading which should precede these words, 'Chi comenche li livres de le branque agravain', is on the last leaf of the Lang-Phillipps manuscript, as Douce noted (see above) and as is noted in the description of item 31 in the Kraus catalogue.

pages with pictures in the text space usually contain erased writing in, first, a smaller and then a larger hand. According to Pickford, who examined the erasures by ultra-violet light, the smaller writing gives directions to the artist and the larger writing provides copy for the scribe who put titles above the pictures in red ink. If, as sometimes, the copy for the scribe is omitted, the titles above the pictures follow the directions to the artist: so, for example, on ff. 101^{v}, 109^{v}. By ordinary light only a very little of this erased writing is legible, for example 'galaadz' in a direction on f. 185^{v} and 'foudre' in a direction on f. 39^{v}. The description of item 31 in Kraus's catalogue 153 shows that the Phillipps manuscripts referred to above in the footnote also had erased directions on picture pages. Professor Stones, who has seen these manuscripts, tells me that some of the directions are fairly clear still.

Fr. 2. *Deguileville, Pélérinages* s. xv^{1}

Guillaume de Deguileville, O.C. († after 1358): (*a*) ff. 1–101 Pelerinaige du corps humain; (*b*) ff. 101–173^{v} Pelerinaige de lame; (*c*) ff. 175–247^{v} Pelerinaige Ihesucrist; (*d*) ff. 247^{v}–249 Oroison . . . Doubz Ihesus filz de dieu le pere . . . auoir nostre estre. ff. ii + 249 + i. 323 × 250 mm. Written space 205 mm high. 2 cols. 39 lines. Collation: 1–21^{8} 22^{6} (ff. 169–74) 23–30^{8} (ff. 175–238) 31^{6} 32^{6} wants 6, blank. *Lettre bâtarde* by one hand. 176 pictures, column width (80 mm) and taking up 6–11 lines of text. Secundo folio *Maintes.*

Written in France. A gift from Marguerite Chenbellain, widow of Etienne Bourcier, to her niece Marguerite Gandrem, nun of the Franciscan convent of Auxonne, to go to the convent after her death: the inscription of s. xv^{2} on f. 249 is given in full in *Hand-list* and by Lofthouse, p. 194.

First printed in 1499 (Goff, G. 637). This copy collated as C^{2} from line 2811 of (*b*) in the Roxburghe Club edition by J. J. Stürzinger, 3 vols., 1893–7.[1] Described by M. Lofthouse in *BJRL* xix (1935), 191–215, with special reference to (*a*) which was not used by Stürzinger: she lists the pictures on pp. 196–200. ff. 174^{rv}, 249^{v} blank. (*d*). Sonet-Sinclair, no. 533. According to M. Meiss the pictures are related to those of the Master of the Berry Apocalypse (*The Limbourgs and their contemporaries*, 1974, p. 370). *MERT*, no. 27.

Quires signed in the usual late medieval way, a–z, ɔ, A–G. Catchwords in *lettre bâtarde* as far as f. 168^{v} and then in current cursiva. A continuous border on f. 1. French binding of s. xvi: two 'Heads in medallions' rolls: bosses.

Fr. 3. *Salutations to B.V.M., etc.* s. xiv/xv

Salutations to B.V.M. in verse and prose, the Psalter of St Jerome, and prayers to the Father, the Son, and B.V.M. ff. ii + 53 + ii. 237 × 165 mm. Written space *c.* 163 × 113 mm. 28 long lines. Collation: 1^{10} + 1 leaf before 1 2^{6} 3^{8} 4^{12} 5–6^{8}. A full-page picture of the Crucifixion and Arma Christi on f. 1^{v}. An 18-line grisaille picture on alternate double openings from 2^{v}–3 to 24^{v}–25 (except that the fifth picture is on 10^{r} not 10^{v}): the pictures form a normal hours-of-B.V.M. series (1–8), followed by a Passion series, Betrayal–Longinus (9–18), Descent from the Cross (19), Entombment (20), Resurrection (21), Christ and Mary

[1] For Lord Crawford's loan of this manuscript to Stürzinger in 1893 see Barker, p. 320.

Magdalene (22), Ascension (23), Pentecost (24). A grisaille picture, 60 × 110 mm (Christ blesses a man kneeling at an altar) before the Psalter of St Jerome, f. 35v.

Written in France for male use. Henry Perkins sale at Sotheby's, 3 June 1873, lot 581. William Bragge sale at Sotheby's, 7 June 1876, lot 303, to Lord Crawford.

Fully described by K. V. Sinclair, 'On a French Manuscript Collection in the John Rylands Library', *Essays presented to G. I. Lieftinck*, ii (Litterae Textuales, 2, 1972), 97–105, and facsimile of f. 10. Eight of the twenty-two pieces in the main hand, all anonymous here, occur in the same order in Brussels, B.R., 11065–73, ff. 272v–276v. Art. 1 is an Ave Maria by Baudouin de Condé. Art. 2, on the Nine Joys, is commonly attributed to Rutebeuf. A twenty-third piece, added at the end in *lettre bâtarde*, f. 53rv, is legible by ultra-violet light, '[O] tres certaine deffenderesse et dame . . . denfer qui' (*ends imperfectly*): Sonet–Sinclair, no. 1538, the last words here five lines from the foot in the edition by Leroquais, *Livres d'heures*, ii. 332.

Fr. 4. *Jean de Courcy, La Bouquechardière* s. xv ex.

Jean de Courcy's world history to the time of the Maccabees: six books, ff. 7v, 115v, 175v, 231, 303, 392. ff. i + 441. 425 × 295 mm. Written space 295 × 190 mm. 39–42 long lines. Collation: $1\text{–}24^8$ 25^8 7 cancelled after f. 198 $26\text{–}28^8$ 29^6 + 1 leaf inserted after 6 (f. 230) $30\text{–}50^8$ 51^8 8 cancelled after f. 405 52^8 wants 4, 5 after f. 408 $53\text{–}55^8$ 56^8 wants 7, 8 blank, after f. 441. Quires signed from (a) in the usual late medieval way, but most of the marks have been cut off: a new series began with the new hand,. f. 231. Cursiva by two hands changing at f. 231 (30^1, beginning of bk. 4). Ascenders in the first line on a page and descenders in the last line are prolonged and often cadelled and filled with colour: the work by the second hand is particularly expert. The first line of each book is in textura and the next dozen lines are in script akin to *lettre bâtarde*. A large decorated initial begins each book and is accompanied by a border. A similar initial, but smaller (3-line or 4-line), begins each chapter and has a short border beside it. Contemporary binding of wooden boards covered with brown leather bearing stamps of two patterns, one a bird and the other S-like: rebacked and repaired: five shell-shaped bosses remain on the back cover and four out of five on the front cover. Secundo folio *de cephalus*.

Written in France. Belonged in s. xvi to the family of Laurencin (of Lyon), whose arms and the name 'Marguerite de Laurencin' are added in the border on f. 175v. Howell Wills label, marked A/I/18, inside the cover: his sale at Sotheby's, 11 July 1894, lot 551, to Lord Crawford (£27. 10*s*.).[1]

The world history by 'iehan de courcy cheualier normant', completed in 1422 and generally known as La Bouquechardière from the home of its author: cf. *Cat. of Romances*, i. 897–9; P. Meyer, *Alexandre le Grand*, 1886, ii. 347–55; Sotheby sale catalogue, 28 Nov. 1967, lot 112. Preface, f. 2, printed by J. Monfrin (cf. below, Fr. 63), pp. 162–4. Table of chapters, ff. 2–7v. Books divided into 93, 65, 58, 65, 84, and 42 numbered chapters. Two leaves missing after f. 408 which ends 'par parolles' near the beginning of bk. 6, ch. 13: f. 409 begins

[1] Barker, p. 323. Lord Crawford's son, Lord Balcarres, bid in person at the sale, to the annoyance of Bernard Quaritch (Barker, pp. 322–4).

'le cueur leur remut' in ch. 14. The leaf added to quire 29 contains the last chapter of bk. 3 in a hand which did not write any part of the text elsewhere: it is no doubt referred to in a note at the foot of f. 229^v, 'Nota quil fault yssi apres mettre vng feueillet (*altered to* deux feueilletz) en blank'.

The foliation, top right, followed in *Hand-list* missed four numbers, 160-3 and is four ahead of that now in use from f. 160.

Fr. 5. *Pictures illustrating Genesis* s. xiii med.

Forty-eight pictures, with captions in French. ff. ii + 48 + ii, interleaved with blank paper, s. xvi. 185 × 150 mm. Binding of s. xvi, repaired in 1963: a strip of a service book inside the back cover.

Reproduced in full by R. Fawtier, 'La bible historiée toute figurēe de la John Rylands Library', *Bulletin de la société française de reproductions de manuscrits à peintures*, vii (1923), plates accompanying pp. 34-87.

Fr. 6. *Lives of saints, etc., in verse and prose* s. xiii^1

A fragment of a much larger manuscript. Six of the ten pieces are complete (arts. 2-5, 9, 10). ff. ii + 12 + xxvi. 272 × 190 mm. Written space 183 × 125 mm. 2 cols. 42 lines (40 lines, ff. 3^r-4^r; 44 lines, ff. 11-12^v). The first line of writing above the top ruled line. Collation: 1^8 (ff. 3-5, 2, 1, 6-8) 2 four (ff. 9-12: two adjacent bifolia: a gap between 10 and 11). ff. 9-12 may have preceded or followed ff. 1-8, which formed the 20th quire in the manuscript as it once was: the signature 'xx', perhaps in the main hand, is at the foot of f. 8^v. Bound for Lord Crawford in stiff parchment in the same style as Rylands Lat. 26, 42-6, all of which are fragments of books obtained in the Libri sale in 1859.[1]

Written perhaps in England. Perhaps part of lot 1119 in the Libri sale, 28 March 1859 (Quaritch, £1. 1*s*.).[1]

The ten pieces are listed in *Hand-list* and by R. Fawtier and E. C. Fawtier-Jones in *Romania* xlix (1923), 321-40, where arts. 8-10, Alexis, the poem on Antichrist written by a templar for Henri d'Arci,[2] and a versification of the Fifteen Signs before the Day of Judgement, are printed (pp. 325-31; 331-40; 340-2). Four of the eight verse pieces are written as prose.

Fr. 7. *Régime de santeé* s. xv^2

ff. i + 95. Thick parchment. 252 × 180 mm. Written space 150 × 118 mm. 24 long lines. Collation: 1-11^8 12^8 wants 7: 8 is a pastedown. Quire 9 has traces of signatures of the usual late medieval kind. Written in *lettre bâtarde*. A 12-line picture on f. 1, 77 × 72 mm, shows the presentation of a book: continuous border. Medieval binding of bevelled wooden boards: four bands: the cover, green velvet, is later. Secundo folio *plest*.

[1] Information from Dr Frank Taylor.

[2] As Professor Ruth Dean tells me. Attributed by Fawtier to Henri d'Arci himself.

Arms in the border on f. 1 are blazoned there as 'ung escu de noir a iii piegnes dargent': *Hand-list* notes that these are the arms of Tunstall. 'Gilbert North', f. 1, s. xvii.[1] 'William Bury' inside the cover, s. xix; also a Howell Wills label inscribed 'Aa/II/52'. H. Wills sale at Sotheby's, 11 July 1894, lot 1700, to Lord Crawford (£21. 10*s.*).

(f. 1) Cy commence le regime de sante fait pour entretenir lomme en bonne disposicion. Dieu qui par sa grant puissance tout le monde crea . . . (f. 94) comme dessus est declaire plus amplement. Four parts: 1 (f. 3^{v}) in twenty chapters, the first 'De lair'; 2 (f. 35^{v}) in eight chapters, the first 'Des cheveux'; 3 (f. 48^{v}) in nine chapters, the first 'Du froument'; 4 (f. 91), 'De la fizonomie des hommes', undivided. Basically the same as the *Régime du Corps de maître Aldebrandin de Sienne*, edited by L. Landouzy and R. Pépin, 1911. Cf. the Latin text in Bodleian, Can. misc. 288 beginning 'Deus qui summa potestate . . . Aer est unus de quatuor elementis' (Thorndike and Kibre, cols. 70, 410). f. 95^{rv} left blank: on f. 95 is 'madomosella pinpernella votre chemesa ce ne pa bella'.

Fr. 54. (R. 45954.) *Roll Chronicle* s. xv^{1}–xv med.

Roll chronicle of popes, emperors, kings of France, and kings of England. *c.* 5110 × 600 mm. 4 cols. Secretary and, on the dorse, textura. Drawings of Constantine (monk holding crown), Arthur, Charlemagne, and William I. Many conventional towns, mostly in roundels. A handsome cruciform church with a central tower against Henry III of England.

Written in England. Numbered on dorse, s. xix, 550/2, 2528/2 and, on a round label, 640. Phillipps MS. 24971. Phillipps sale, 24 June 1919, lot 640: bought then through Quaritch for £20. 18*s.*: invoice dated 30 June.

Mainly in four columns, each *c.* 80 mm wide, except the third which is *c.* 100 mm wide. Cols. 1, 2, 4 end nearly at the same point, after which the matter of France takes up the whole space in two columns. The headings and first words of each column are set out in *Hand-list*. Col. 1 ends at 1378 with Pope Urban VI, 'dommage et pitie pour toute cristiente. Cy ne parle plus des papes'. Col. 2 ends 'Et apres regna loys de bauiere. Et lors les Romains firent vn antipape. Cy ne parle plus des empereurs'. Col. 4 should take the English history to 1396, but it runs in fact to Henry IV and ends with the sending to France of Richard's queen (1401), 'qui depuis fu duchesse dorleans' (1406).

The part of the French history in two columns begins in the *second* column at 1286 and continues in the *first* column from 1314 to the coronation of Charles VI, 4 Nov. 1380, and the events of 14–15 Nov. following, '. . . Sy furent les Corps des Iuifs Ramenez. Et aucuns des Biens mais ce fu pou etc' '. A roundel for Charles VII has 1423 against it and below it a roundel for 'Loys daulphin de Viennoys', who was born in that year.

On the dorse, a table of years 1067–1448 is flanked by a descent of the kings of England from 'Willelmus conquestor' to Henry VI. Kings' names are in larger roundels and their children and grandchildren in smaller roundels. Events in English history are entered against some years, including 'Obsidio castri de ledes' at 1321, 'Furiositas lollardorum vi^{o} die ianuarii' at 1413, the death of John, Duke of Bedford, 'die sancte crucis septembris' at 1435,

[1] The same name is in Cambridge, Univ. Libr., Dd. 1. 20, Worcester Cathedral Q. 80, and a Mostyn manuscript (HMC 4th Report, Appendix, p. 350, no. 91) sold at Sotheby's, 13 July 1920, lot 24, and 25 July 1929, lot 357. A Persian manuscript in the Bodleian Library (*Sum. Cat.* 3246) came to John Selden 'ex dono viri nobilissimi Gilberti North, Jan. 1641'.

and (the last entry) 'Obitus henricus Cardinallis' at 1447. At 1162 is 'Nota quod hec (*sic*) anno celebratum primo fuit de festo trinitatis in ecclesia cristi' and at 1260 'Institucio festum (*sic*) corporis cristi'. The roundel for the daughter of William I, inscribed 'Gumdrada (?) nupta Willelmus (*sic*) com' Warrenie', has against it 'Hic fundauit prioratum de lewes' and the roundel for their son contains the words 'Willelmus hic fundauit prioratum de castelat' (? *sic*: Castleacre). A more or less illegible line of verse in red follows the name of each king: for example, (Stephen) 'Hic stephano strictum fit iter [. . .] iure relictum', (John) 'Cunctis annis anglis [. . .]', (Henry III) 'Scutus (?) baronensis [. . .]que lewensis'.

Fr. 55. (R. 26216.) *E. de Monstrelet, Croniques* s. xv ex.

1. E. de Monstrelet (†1453), Croniques, bk. 1, abbreviated. 2. Pastedown. ff. iv + 181 + ii, foliated (i–iii), 1–182 (183–4). ff. 10–181 have a medieval foliation in red, i–clxx, clxxiii, clxxiiii. Paper, except ff. iii, 183, which were once pastedowns. f. 1 is a binding leaf ruled like the rest of the manuscript and is probably a leaf from quire 16. 380 × 275 mm. Written space 238 × 180 mm. Ruling in red ink. 2 cols. 36 lines. Collation of ff. 2–182: 1^8 $2\text{–}15^{12}$ 16^{10} wants 3, 4 and (blanks) 8–10: usual late medieval signatures, a–p. Secundo folio *deuant le roy*.

Written in France. 'Cest liure et a hault et puissant prince mon^r Engelbert de cleues conte de neuers deu (*sic*) de Rethel et dauxerre per de France et gouerneur et lieutenant pour le Roy en Bourgoignie', f. iii^v: below the inscription 'k' and '[.]OLON';[1] also 'Pierrepont'. Phillipps MS. 3950. Acquired at the Phillipps sale on 24 Apr. 1911, lot 219 (£12); invoice from Quaritch dated 3 May.

1. Chronicle from 1400 to the death of Charles VI in 1422. Table of chapters, ff. 2–8^v, with leaf references in red: f. 9^{rv} blank. (*prologue*, f. 10) Prologue ou proheme du liure. Extrait de hystores et croniques faites et compilees par noble homme enguerran de monstrelet . . . (f. 10^v) mil iiii^e et xxii. le xxii^e iour doctobre. (*text*) Cy parle de la generacion . . . Cy dist Enguerran de monstrelet pour donner congnoissance aux lisans . . . (f. 181) mercy de son ame. Amen. The first eighteen lines on f. 10 were left blank over both columns, probably for a picture. Two leaves missing after f. 179 which ends 'et il y mist vne grosse' (edn., 1603, f. 324: ch. 265/5): f. 180 begins 'gaboit de paroles. Par ma foi' (edn., f. 326^v/4, near end of ch. 265).

2. f. 183, formerly pasted down, is a leaf from a rental (?) of the bailliwick of Lens (between Arras and Lille) concerned especially with desperate rents: the dates 1422 and 1435 occur, the name of Jacques de Humbertus as receiver, and several times a parish name, 'Vremelle'.

Fr. 56. (R. 45959.) *History of the dukes of Normandy, etc.* s. xiv^2

1. ff. 5–64^v History of the dukes of Normandy to 1217. 2. ff. 65–80^v Chronicle of the kings of France to 987. ff. v + 76 + vii, foliated (i), 1–86, (87). ff. 1–4, 81–6 are parchment endleaves: 1 and 86 were pasted down. 205 × 135 mm. Written space 135 × 88 mm. 29 long lines. Collation of ff. 5–80: $1\text{–}7^8$ 8^4 (ff. 61–4) $9\text{–}10^8$. A continuous border on f. 5.

Belonged in s. xvi to Nicholas Verdier (f. 2^v) and to François Telles or Toilles (f. 1^v). Telles was gaoler—at Evreux ?—in 1548 (f. 83^v: cf. *Hand-list*) and

[1] The first letter is a monograph, perhaps of M, E, and D.

entered the births of his children on ff. 3^{v}, 4: Jacques, 27 Oct. 1536; Loys, 27 Jan. 1537(–8); Gy, 29 Nov. 1546, at Orbec; Barbe 18 Oct. 1540. 'J. B. Hautin', f. i^{v},[1] s. xvii. Inside the cover are 'L 249' (altered to '272') and 'A la Librairie Française et Etrangère (de Galignani) Rue Vivienne, N° 18' on a printed label. 'Mr Rennie's Library', f. 1^{v}. John Rennie sale at Evans', 19 Mar. 1833, lot 848, to Phillipps. Phillipps MS. 3777: sale 27 Apr. 1903, lot 843; sale 24 June 1919, lot 840. Acquired then through Quaritch for £99 (invoice dated 30 June).

1. Par la diuision que li ancien sage firent de toutes les terres sauons que . . . par toutez les terres pour aller en iherusalem. The last words here are at f. 99 in the printed text, Paris, *c.* 1510–20, from which this differs greatly.

2. Si comme nous trouuons es anciens liures. Troyes fu anciennement la plus noble . . . lun nomme *karlers.* et lautre loys. Explicit Ci faut la lignee du Roy Karlemaigne Qui aporta les saintes reliques de la sainte cite de iherusalem.

Fr. 57. (R. 26217.) *N. de Fribois, Chronique de France* s. xv/xvi

1. Chronicle, here anonymous. 2. ff. i, 142 Pastedowns, now raised. ff. i + 141 + i. Paper, except the binding leaves. The medieval foliation of art. 1 runs to 143 and takes account of the leaves missing from quires 1 and 3. 203 × 140 mm. Written space 137 × 90 mm. 30–40 long lines. Frame ruling. Collation: 1^{16} wants 1 2^{16} 3^{16} wants 11 after f. 41 $4–8^{16}$ 9^{16} wants 16. Current cursiva: every page begins with a capital letter. Contemporary binding of green stained leather over a pad, mainly of paper, now kept separately as Fr. 71, q.v. The pad was secured in place by the pastedowns, art. 2 and by eight leather tabs, four inside each cover: three bands: two ties missing.

'J. B. Hautin', f. i^{v}, as in Fr. 56, q.v. 'L. 97', f. i^{v} (cf. Fr. 56). Phillipps MS. 6968. Phillipps sale, 25 Apr. 1911, lot 221 (£4. 10*s.*): bought then through Quaritch, whose invoice is dated 3 May.

1. This and fifteen other manuscripts of the chronicle beginning 'Cest chose prouffitable' are listed by P. S. Lewis in *Transactions of the Royal Historical Society*, 5th series xv (1965), p. 10, footnote 5. The present copy runs to 1498 (f. 136^{v}), 'Remut en france auec ses gens', after which is (ff. 137–141^{v}) a 'Recapitulation sure le deuant dit. Lon trouue en anciennes cronicques . . . ny auoient point de' (*ends imperfectly*): this covers 1328–39. f. 41^{v} ends 'fut tousiours piteable' and f. 42 begins 'De vie a trespas': one leaf is missing. The missing first leaf of quire 1 was perhaps blank.

2. (*a*) f. i, part of an inventory in French, s. xv/xvi. (*b*) f. 142, part of a notarial document in which Michel Allegrin acknowledges a debt of 500 'livres parisis' to 'Demoiselle Iehanne C[. . .]', 25 March 1503. The notary's sign at the foot bears the name 'Bourdier'.

Fr. 58. (R. 26215.) *Customs of Brittany, etc.* s. xv^{2}

1. ff. 1–209^{v} Customs of Brittany. 2. ff. 210–212^{v} Treaty of Senlis, 23 Dec. 1465. 3, 4. Pastedowns. ff. i + 215. ff. 210–15 are paper. 225 × 163 mm. Written space of 1 125 × 82 mm, with 24–5 long lines; of 2, 185 × 115 mm, with 33–6

[1] For manuscripts belonging to J. B. Hautin, †1640, in Paris and Cambridge, see L. Delisle, *Cabinet des manuscrits*, i. 365, iii. 370. The Moore Bede is the best known.

long lines. Collation: 1^{14} 2^{16} 3^{10} (ff. 31–40) $4\text{–}6^{16}$ $7\text{–}15^{8}$ 16^{10} 17^{8} wants 8 after f. 177 $18\text{–}21^{8}$ 22^{6} (ff. 210–15). Signatures of the usual late medieval kind have been cut off as a rule: a new series seems to begin at f. 97 (7^{1}). Some catchwords written vertically. Cursiva. Contemporary binding of wooden boards covered with brown leather bearing eight vertical rows of stamps: (*front*) 1, 7 dragon, 2, 8 stag, 3 dromedary, 4 crown and heart, 5 fleur-de-lys, 6 quatrefoil; (*back*) 1, 7 dog, 2, 8 rabbit, 3 bird, 4 crown and heart, 5 lamb and flag, 6 fork-tailed beast (all beast and bird stamps are sideways): five bands. Secundo folio *commencement*.

Written in France (Brittany). J. Chauniry wrote an ex-libris on f. i^{v} dated 20 April 1558 (see *Hand-list*) and a note on f. 14^{v} that Claud de Guyime was ill 'chez nous' on the same day; also a note at the foot of f. 1 dated 20 May 1555 that 'Franzois chauncler' and others compeared at our court of Rennes 'Ce iour auiourduy . . . dauent nous Iehan Chauniry et Claud de Guyines notaries et Tabellions Iurez et Recuz'. For other names see *Hand-list*. 'Achetee a Rennes 18^{e} juillet 1741, consequament Elle mapartient. Desabaye (?) Hariot (?)', f. i^{v}. Phillipps MS. 21859. Bought through Quaritch at the Phillipps sale, 24 April 1911, lot 131, for £22: invoice dated 3 May.

1. (*Prologue*) Aucunes foiz est aduenu que aucunes terres . . . de ceulx dont nous diuisons. (*Table of numbered chapters*, ff. 3–14^{v}). (*Text*, f. 15) Qui vouldroit entendre a viure honestement . . . (f. 209^{v}) ne vinrent pas en bon estat (*ends imperfectly in chapter 332*). For the last words here see edn. Planiol (cf. below, Fr. 74), p. 309/19, chapter 334. The table of chapters does not go beyond the title of chapter 331. f. i^{rv} has the nine chapter-heads printed in edn., p. 72, in a hand of s. xv/xvi.

2. Pierre pean seigneur du grant bois . . . mil iiii^{c} soixante quinze. Ed. P. H. Morice, *Mémoires pour servir de preuves à l'Histoire de Bretagne*, iii (1746), 293–4. ff. 213–215^{v} were left blank.

3. Pastedown in front. Antiphons, etc. of B.V.M., perhaps a waste leaf of a book of hours, s. xv: written space 115 × 90 mm. 17 long lines.

4. Pastedown at the back. The end of a document in French in which occur the name 'Thomas le vaireur' (line 1) and place 'in parochia de montegermondo' (line 6) and date 1443 (line 21).

Fr. 62. (R. 18106.) *Grandes Chroniques de France* s. xv med.

A copy of the Grandes Chroniques ending at 1380. ff. ii + 502 (counting 8 supply leaves) + ii, foliated (i–iii), 1–111, 113–24, 124–501, (502–3). A contemporary foliation in red goes badly wrong and ends at CCCCIIII^{xx}. A correct modern foliation at intervals of ten leaves begins at 50. 410 × 285 mm. Written space 280 × 195 mm. 2 cols. 49 lines. Ruling in red ink. Collation of ff. iii, 2–7, 13–499: 63 quires, all eights, except 48^{6} (ff. 376–81), but 1^{2}, 2^{1-5} and $63^{7,8}$ were missing in s. xvii and were supplied then for Abbé Antoine de Sève on added leaves of parchment (ff. 1, 8–12, 500–1). Cursiva. Twenty-four pictures, column width and about 15 lines in height: see below. Part borders on picture pages. Binding for de Sève, whose arms are on the cover and on f. 1. Secundo folio *le iiie*.

Belonged to de Sève (see above) and to J. B. Denis Guyon, whose name, 'Guyon de Sardiere' is at the head of f. 1: his sale, Paris 1759, lot 1626. According to Delisle, *Cabinet des manuscrits*, i. 550, the Guyon manuscripts were bought *en bloc* by the Duc de la Vallière, but Fr. 62 is not identifiable in his sale catalogue (1783). In Sotheby sales on three occasions: John Broadley sale, 12 July 1832, lot 179; sale of the 6th Duke of Buccleuch, 25 Mar. 1889, lot 292 (the arms of Scott, dukes of Buccleuch, have been added on the covers); H. White sale, 21 Apr. 1902, lot 494. Given by Mrs Rylands in June 1909.

Printed in 1476 and later (*GKW* 6676-7); last by P. Paris, 1836-8 (6 vols.). Begins imperfectly (f. 2) in the heading of ch. 4 'le iii^{e} Comment ils conquistent' (ed. Paris, i. 9). Five leaves and probably a picture are missing between f. 7^{v} which ends 'a la pucelle et lui porta' (edn., i. 39/21) and f. 13 which begins 'le xvi^{e} de la mort saint benoist' in the table of chapters of bk. 2. From f. 416 the text is in the edition of the chronicle for 1350-1380 by R. Delachenal (1910-20, 2 vols.). It ends imperfectly at 1380 'sur vne schaufault' (edn., ii. 373/1 up; Paris edn., vi. 463/1 up). A numbered table of chapters before each reign. f. iii^{rv} left blank.

A picture has been cut out of f. 13 (Childebert), but after this the series of pictures is complete: f. 64 Dagobert; f. 78^{v} Clovis; f. 85 Pippin III; ff. 88^{v}, 101^{v}, 108^{v}, 119^{v}, 128, in front of each of the five books covering the reign of Charlemagne; f. 135 Louis I; f. 158 Charles the Bald; f. 187 Robert II; f. 191 Henry I; f. 206^{v} Louis VI; f. 227^{v} Louis VII; f. 239^{v} Philip II; f. 281^{v} Louis IX; f. 317^{v} Philip III; f. 335 Philip IV (King Edward I of England does homage); f. 360^{v} Louis X; f. 362 Philip V; f. 367 Charles IV; f. 377^{v} Philip VI; f. 416 John II; f. 459 Charles V.

Fr. 63. (R. 33634.) *Valerius Maximus (in Latin) with Latin and French commentaries* s. xv in.

Books 1-5 of the Facta et dicta memorabilia, with the Latin commentary of Dionysius de Burgo Sancti Sepulchri, O.E.S.A., †1342, and the French expanded translation of Dionysius by S. de Hesdin. ff. iv + 431 + iii. A medieval foliation stops at xxix. 407 × 290 mm. Written space *c.*280 × 203 mm. 2 cols. 43 lines by scribe 1, 42 lines, usually, by scribe 2.[1] Collation: 1^{12} (1^{1} was pasted down) $2\text{-}3^{12}$ 4 seven (ff. 37-43: probably 4^{12} wants 7-11 after f. 42) $5\text{-}36^{12}$ 37 four (ff. 428-31: f. 431^{v} was pasted down). Signatures of the usual late medieval kind, (a)-z, aa-ff, began presumably on quire 9, but cannot be seen there: no traces on quires 1-8. Cursiva by two hands, the second beginning at f. 95 (9^{4}). Initials in colour on gold grounds and part borders of ivy leaf on the five main pages. Bound in 1851 and repaired in 1892 (f. iv^{v}). Secundo folio (f. 3) *Qui quod.*

'Ph. Mainwaringe', f. 1, s. xvii, is presumably Philip Mainwaring of Over Peover, †1647: see G. Ormerod, *History of Cheshire* (1882 edn.), i. 483. Bought for the Portico Library, Manchester, by James Crossley at the Mainwaring of Peover Hall, Cheshire, sale, 28 Aug. 1837, lot 291, for £8. 5*s.*:[2] see W. E. A. Axon,

[1] Scribe 2 wrote 40 lines on ff. 95-100^{v}, but was forced to change to 43 lines when he came to ff. 101-103^{v}, since these leaves had already been ruled at the same time as ff. 92-4. He settled for 42 lines on f. 104.

[2] Mr H. Horton kindly told me of this catalogue which is not in the British Museum's *List of Catalogues* (1915). The copy in the Manchester Central Library, SC 1837, no. 2, was

Handbook of the Public Libraries of Manchester and Salford, 1877, p. 10. Bought from the Portico Library, 10 Apr. 1913, for £52.

Printed in 1476 and later: Goff, V. 44-5. This and other manuscripts listed by J. Monfrin in *The late Middle Ages and the Dawn of Humanism outside Italy*, ed. G. Verbeke and J. IJsewijn, Louvain 1972, p. 140: an earlier list by D. M. Schullian in *Studies in honor of B. L. Ullman*, 1960, pp. 81-95, is here amplified. Each section consists of the Latin text ('Textus'), the Latin commentary ('Expositio'), and the French 'translation' ('Translateur') interspersed with passages headed 'Acteur'. Bk. 1, ff. 8-108^{v}, dated 1375 at the end; bk. 2, ff. 108^{v}-209^{v}, dated 2 May 1377 at the end; bk. 3, ff. 210-285^{v}; bk. 4, ff. 286-357; bk. 5, ff. 357^{v}-431^{v}, ending 'a mourir. Et yci fine le dernier Chapitre du quint liure. Cy fine le quint liure de Valerius maximus'. Preliminary matter before bk. 1: f. 1^{rv}, a table of bks. 1-9 and the chapters of each book in Latin; ff. 1^{v}-2^{v}, an alphabetical 'Tabula expositoria libri Valerii Maximi' in Latin, 'Abstinencia-Vlcio'; f. 2^{v}, the prohemium of Valerius Maximus, 'Urbis Rome . . .'; ff. 2^{v}-5, the introductory letter of Dionysius and his commentary on the prohemium; ff. 5-8, the introduction by S. de Hesdin, 'La briefte et fragilite . . .', and his translation of the prohemium: cf. *Hand-list.* Perhaps five leaves are missing between f. 41^{v}, which ends 'At cecilia etc'. Ad intelligenciam huius' in the commentary on 1. 5. 4 and f. 42 which begins 'ou iettement de voix' in the translation of 1. 5. 8.

Up to the point where the hand changes, that is to say before f. 95, there are many unerased directions for the rubricator in the margins and also a few unerased or only half-erased directions for the corrector, for example on f. 41^{v}: these are written in ink with a very fine pen.

Fifteenth-century marginalia in a French hand include, as Tyson saw, one on f. 56, which refers to the part played by France in aiding Henry IV to gain the English crown: the writer saw a contrast with the story of King Demeratus of Lacedemonia who, in exile with Xerxes, king of Persia, gave his country warning of Xerxes' plans to invade Greece, as Hesdin noted from Justinus (ii. 10) in his long commentary on Valerius 1. 6, Externa 1.

Fr. 64. (R. 33819.) *English chronicle* s. xiv in.

An English chronicle, ending with the council of Lyons in 1274. ff. ii + 53 + iii. 235 × 162 mm. Written space *c.*170 × 120 mm. 29-32 long lines. Collation: $1\text{-}4^{12}$ 5^{6} wants 6, blank. Current anglicana. Contemporary binding of bevelled wooden boards covered with pink leather: five bands: two strap-and-pin fastenings missing. Secundo folio *de genz*.

Written in England. 'Fairfax', f. 1, is the signature of Thomas, Lord Fairfax, †1671: to it is added 'nunc e libris Rad: Thoresby Leodiensis'. Listed in Thoresby's *Ducatus Leodiensis*, 1715, p. 529, no. 100: the number and page reference are at the head of the front cover, outside, s. xviii. Not identifiable in the miserable sale catalogue of Thoresby's library, 27 Feb. 1764. Sale of Sir F. A. T. C. Constable (Tixall library) at Sotheby's, 6 Nov. 1899, lot 142. 'G. D. Nov. 1899', f. ii. Bought at the George Dunn sale, 2 Feb. 1913, lot 439, through P. M. Barnard for £18: invoice dated 25 Feb.

Crossley's and is marked with prices and names of buyers and at the end a Who's who of buyers. The twelve medieval manuscripts went to the London trade (Thorpe 2, Rodd 1), a Manchester clergyman (Rev. G. Dugard, St Andrew's Church, Ancoats, 2), a Warrington bookseller (Haddock 2), a local Cheshire landowner (P. S. Brooke, Mere Hall, near Knutsford, 1) and Crossley himself (4). One of Dugard's is now B.L., Egerton 2204. For one of Crossley's see above, Eng. 90.

Nus deuoms sauer al comencement ke le isle de bretaigne . . . (f. 51) qe fust conferme de la curt de roume. ff. 51^{v}–53^{v} are blank and, except 51^{v}, without ruling. On f. 21/13–21 the scribe copied what he had already copied in its right place on ff. 19^{v}/32–20/7: the lines are marked 'va cat'. The text was printed by J. Glover from Trinity College, Cambridge, R. 14. 7, RS xlii (1865), pp. 32–300, with readings from a Vatican manuscript. The period before 900 is dealt with very briefly: here on ff. 1^{v}–4. Vising, no. 298 (2).

Fr. 65. (R. 45318.) *Guillaume de Tignonville, Dits moraux* s. xvi in.

(*a–d*) Les dits moraux des philosophes (of Guillaume de Tignonville), with supplements. ff. ii + 129 (including two supply leaves) + ii. The contemporary foliation in red begins with i on the first leaf of quire 2 and ends with vi^{xx} vi. Thick parchment. 275 × 198 mm. Written space 190 × 133 mm. 2 cols. 30 lines. Ruling in red ink. Collation: 1 three (ff. iii–v: ff. iii, iv are a bifolium) 2^8 wants 4, 5: supplied on ff. 4, 5 in s. xvii (?) 3–8^8 9^6 10^8 11^6 12–13^8 14–18^6 19^4. Written in hybrida.

No. 157 in the collection of Paul Barrois, bought by Lord Ashburnham in 1849: his sale 10 June 1901, lot 165, to Maggs (£7. 10*s*.). The Barrois number is on a round green label at the foot of the spine and the Ashburnham sale number in blue pencil on f. i^{v}. Item in catalogue xxii (New Series) of Davis and Orioli (1918) at £45: the relevant cutting is attached to f. i. Bought from Davis and Orioli in 1918 for £40. 10*s*. (the price reflects a discount of 10%): invoice dated 16 Dec.

(*a*) ff. (iii–v) Tables of chapters of (*b–d*), with leaf numbers. For the headings of the three tables, see *Hand-list*. f. v^{v} blank.

(*b*) ff. 1–89^{v} Sedechias fut phylozophe le premier par qui de la volunte . . . soy fier en celluy dont on a este autresfoiz deceu. Cy finist le liure des ditz des philosophes. Printed *c.* 1477 and later (*GKW* 8319–20). This and many other manuscripts listed by C. F. Bühler in the edition of the English *Dictes* (EETS ccxi), pp. xiii–xv. Two leaves are missing and have been supplied in s. xvii (?): f. 3^{v} ends 'Fiez vous en dieu qui scet' and f. 6 begins 'en temps de pourete'.

(*c*) ff. 89^{v}–121^{v} Sensuiuent aucuns dits de philozophie de aristote et autres philozophes. Aristote qui fut le souuerain philozophe trouua alexandre qui plouroit . . . sauue vostre honneur.

(*d*) ff. 121^{v}–126^{v} Sensuiuent plusieurs notables enseignemens que fist Seneque en son liure de meurs. Senecque dit ou liure de meurs. Nourriture . . . ne fait elle acconuoiter. Explicit.

Fr. 66. (R. 4598.) *Roman de la Rose* s. xiv med.

1. ff. 2–4 Treatise on love. 2. ff. 7–163^{v} G. Lorris and J. Chopinel de Meun, Le roman de la rose. ff. ii + 163 + ii. 280 × 195 mm. Written space 208 mm high. 2 cols. 34–5 lines. Collation: 1^6 2–3^{10} 4–20^8 21 one. Quire 4 numbered III on f. 34^{v}. Changes of hand at ff. 27 (see below), 147 (19^1). Changes of ink, but perhaps not of hand, at ff. 51, 140ra/13. Three small framed pictures, f. 22 before

line 2077, f. 87 before line 10495, and f. 87v before line 10565, measure respectively 30 × 55 mm, 43 × 55 mm and 33 × 60 mm within the frames. *M* of *Maintes*, f. 7, historiated: the border ornament includes dog, hare, and grotesque in the lower margin. Bound for the John Rylands Library by Fazakerley, Liverpool. Secundo folio (f. 8) *Enclos*.

Written probably in north-eastern France. Belonged to the convent of Minims at Mons in s. xvii: 'De Conventu Patrum Minimorum Montensium', f. 2 at top. Their pressmark, P. 1. 1, f. 2 at foot. A foundation gift by Mrs Rylands.

Described by C. E. Pickford in *BJRL* xxxiv (1952), 333–44, 349–65.
1. On voit souuent aucunes gens de diuerses manieres . . . non gratos de inuentis sed veniam de omiscis. Printed by Pickford, pp. 354–65, from this manuscript. He follows Langlois in suggesting that Richard de Fournival is the author.
2. Chi commenche li romans de la Rose. Maintes gens dient . . . Delitables a damoiseles (*ends imperfectly at edn. Langlois, 1914–25, v. 21008*). Many contemporary marginalia in red ink.

Lines 2833–7 are in this copy (f. 31v): beside them another hand wrote in the margin the six lines, 'Vne femme et i vilain homme . . . qui a droit conte', noticed by E. Langlois, *Les manuscrits du Roman de la Rose*, 1910, pp. 241, 260.

Lines 2152–2742 (or most of them) were copied twice, by one scribe on ff. 22va/34–26vb/35 (589 lines) and by another on ff. 27ra/1–31ra/12 (555 lines).[1] A corrector crossed out the lines written by the second scribe, put a signe-de-renvoi from f. 26vb/35 to f. 31ra/13, and wrote in red on f. 27 'chil quatre foeillet sont écrit deuant'. The differences in wording and spelling and number of lines show that the texts on ff. 22v–26v and 27–31 come from different exemplars.

The preliminary quire, ff. 1–6, contains: f. 1v (1 is blank), a 43-line introduction to art. 2, 'Le primier capitle enseigne . . . et le veut amender', printed from this manuscript by R. Fawtier in *Romania*, lviii (1932), 270–3; ff. 2–4, art. 1; ff. 4v–6v, a table of chapters of art. 2, 'Comment li faisieres proeue . . . Au fait et enseignement comment le rose fu ceu'i'llie', numbered in red to CXXXIII, but most of the numbers have been erased. This quire is in the same hand as ff. 7–26v.

Fr. 71. (R. 52731.) *Accounts of Royal Artillery* s. xv^2

Twenty-eight pieces of paper and parchment cut to form the pad of the binding of Fr. 57, q.v., consist of accounts, etc., of the French royal artillery. ff. 1–12 are complete or nearly complete leaves of a paper book. ff. 13–23 are parts of leaves of a paper book in larger format than 1–12. ff. 24–8 are parts of single-sheet documents of small size on parchment, blank on the dorses.

Described and partly printed by R. Fawtier in *Essays in Medieval History presented to T. F. Tout*, ed. A. G. Little and F. M. Powicke, 1925, pp. 367–77.

Fr. 72. (R. 29093.) *Nova statuta Angliae* s. xiv ex. (1390 ?)

1, 2. Statutes of 1–50 Edward III and 1–14 Richard II. ff. ii + 251 + ii. 157 × 115 mm. Written space 110 × 78 mm. 26–8 long lines. Frame ruling, the first line of writing above the frame line. Collation: 1^8 2^8 + 1 leaf after 8 (f. 17) 3^8

[1] The first scribe left out lines 2322 and 2450 by mistake. The second scribe left out lines 2181–2 (as in Langlois' *L*), 2223–4, 2267–94, and 2349–52 (as in *L*).

wants 1 before f. 18 4^8 5 eight (ff. 33–40) $6–27^8$ $28–29^{10}$ 30^8 31^8 wants 7, blank, after f. 250. Current anglicana: two-compartment and one-compartment *a* indifferently: the hand changes at f. 243 (30^7). A king's head in the initial *R* on f. 169. Secundo folio (f. 18) *e le commune.*

Written in England. 'Tho. Taylor. The Gift of Wm Lane of Coffleet, May 1789 . . . found among Lumber at Bradley in a Room that had been the Chapel. Messrs Polwhele, Andrew and Swete were with me in a Ride from Denbury', f. i. Armorial book-plate of 'Thos Taylor Arm: de Denbury in Com. Devon:'. Item 266 in P. M. Barnard's catalogue 51 (1912) at £10. 10*s.*: the relevant slip is attached inside the cover. Bought from P. M. Barnard for £10. 10*s.* in 1912: invoice dated 8 Feb.

1. Consists of: (ff. 1–16^v) a table of statutes ending imperfectly at 37 Edward III; (f. 17) notes from cases in Easter term, 42 Edward III—the verso blank; (ff. 18–168^v) statutes of Edward III, beginning imperfectly in statute 1 of anno 1. Differences from *SR* i. 252–398 include:
Anno 1. A third statute, 'Come nadgairs en temps le Roi E fitz le Roi henr' . . . , not in *SR* (ff. 23–24^v).
Anno 2. The statute ends with a paragraph not in *SR*, p. 201, on the repeal of oyers and terminers, 'Acorde est . . . a ce parlement de Northampton . . .', in which the abbeys of Bury and Abingdon are excepted (f. 28^v).
Anno 7. Statute of the staple, 'Edward . . . as maire et baillifs de loundres . . .', not in *SR* (ff. 37–38^v).
Anno 9. Statute 1 only.
Anno 10. A fourth statute, not in *SR*, 'A soun chier et foiale William de Clynton . . .' (ff. 46^v–48) and a fifth, 'Statutum de retinencia malefactorum editum dicto anno x^mo. Rex vic' Lincoln' salutem. Quandam concordatam . . .' (f. 48^rv).
Anno 12. A statute made at York, not in *SR*, 'Pur ceo que plusures gentz . . .' and writ on it addressed to the justices of the Bench.
Anno 14. Statutes 1, 2, 4 only.
Anno 15. Statute 2 is followed by 'Incipiunt prerogatiua regni Anglie ne subiciatur regno francie . . . Sachez que come ascuns gents . . .' (ff. 66^v–67^v), and not by statute 3 (see below, anno 18).
Anno 17. No statute.
Anno 18. Statutes 3, 2, 1 in that order, and between 3 and 2, statute 3 of anno 15.
Anno 23. The statute in *SR* is followed by statutes 2 and 3 of anno 25.
Anno 25. Five statutes corresponding to statutes 5, 4, 7, 6 of anno 25 and statute 1 of anno 27 in *SR*. Statute 1 does not occur; for 2, 3, see above, anno 23.
Anno 26. 'Edward par la grace . . . au Maire et viscountz de loundres. Purceo que plusours foith . . .', not in *SR* (ff. 102–104^v).
Anno 27. Between statute 2 and the ordinance of fees in *SR* come: 'Quedam ordinacio. Et puis apres estoit ordeigne . . .', appointing a staple at Kingston upon Hull (f. 117^v), 'Sequitur declaracio quorundam articulorum Stapule eodem anno. Come contenu soit en les ordeignaunces de lestaple . . .' (ff. 117^v–119^v); 'Quoddam aliud statutum de Stapula editum eodem anno. Fait a remembrer que ia soit . . .' (ff. 119^v–120).
Anno 31. Statutes 1, 3, 2 in that order. Statute 4 does not occur.
Anno 43. Statute 2 is the statute of anno 45 in *SR* (i. 393).

2. ff. 169–245 Statutes of 1–14 Richard II. As *SR* ii. 1–77, except for the absence of the statute of anno 10 (ii. 39–43). The writ in anno 12 is addressed to the sheriff of York. The hand changes at f. 243 (anno 14), where the space for the initial *P* has not been filled. ff. 245^v–251^v blank.

Fr. 73. (R. 41487.) *Customs of Normandy* s. xv^2

'Coustumier du pays et duchè de Normendie' (title of s. xvii). ff. ii + 246 + i, foliated 1-249. 112 × 85 mm. Written space 78 × 55 mm. 23 long lines. Ruling in red ink. Collation of ff. 3-248: 1-17^8 18^6 (ff. 139-44) 19-31^8. Cursiva by two or perhaps more hands, unstable after the hand changes at f. 27 (4^1).

'Perrette le brel 1639', f. 144. 'May 11-84 0.2.9', f. 1, is perhaps in the hand of Peter Le Neve (†1729: *DNB*), whose ex-libris, 'Liber Petri Le Neve Norroy', is on the same page. Bought at the Le Neve sale, 19 March 1731, by N. Hardinge (Nicholas Hardinge, †1758: *DNB*), whose note to this effect is on f. 1. Bought from Davis and Orioli in 1916 for £5. 13*s*. 8*d*. (invoice dated 30 December): the relevant strip from their sale catalogue (New series xvii (1916), item 8 at £6. 6*s*.) is attached to f. 1.

(*Begins imperfectly*, f. 3) [. . .]ler les droiz des tenebres de [. . .] si que par le trauail de mon corps soient esclairer . . . Le droit. Droit est diuise en deux parties . . . (f. 240^v) ne sont par vrayes. (f. 241) excepte le hebergement . . . (f. 248^v) perdra sa querelle. Explici[. . . .] istius libri. ff. 3-240^v. Basically the French text printed in 1483 and later (Goff, C. 955-6) a translation of the Latin Summa de legibus in 124 chapters printed by E. J. Tardif, *Le plus ancien coutumier de Normandie*, ii (1896), 3/16-339/21 *deneget esse vera*. The beginning of the preface is missing and the end of ch. 123, De lege apparenti, and all ch. 124. Part 1 is in five distinctions: 2, f. 31; 3, f. 50; 4, f. 98^v; 5, f. 111. Part 2 begins at f. 123. Chapters are not numbered, except for a late *ad hoc* numbering from 1 to 194. The text includes over fifty notes of proceedings at the Easter exchequers at Rouen, Falaise (twice), and Caen (once) at various dates in s. xiii and s. xiv, and especially in the 1390s: the latest date is 1398 (f. 45^v). It includes also some documents, an ordinance of 1212 at Nogent le Robert (f. 93), and royal and episcopal letters (ff. 82^v-85, St Louis, 1269; f. 195, William archbishop of Rouen to King Philip).

ff. 241-248^v. Begins imperfectly. Short paragraphs, except the last which begins on f. 246^v 'Les gens du Roy a Rouen ne veull' souffrir que les gens de leglese pour cause de leur meffait entrent en maisons qui soient en fieu lay sans appeller le bras secullier'.

Fr. 74. (R. 55795.) *Customs of Brittany* s. xv med.

1. ff. 1-136^v Customs of Brittany. 2. f. 136^v Assize of Count Geoffrey. ff. ii + 136 + ii. ff. 13-136 have a medieval foliation i-vi^{xx} iiii. f. ii is a parchment flyleaf. 247 × 173 mm. Written space 178 × 115 mm. 32-5 long lines. Frame ruling. Collation: 1-17^8. Cursiva: ascenders in the top line are prolonged and elaborated, with use of chain interlace for diagonals but not verticals. Secundo folio *des autres*.

Written in France (Brittany). No. 299 of the manuscripts bought by Lord Ashburnham from Paul Barrois in 1849: Ashburnham-Barrois sale, 10 June 1901, lot 82, to Ellis for £9. 15*s*. Davis and Orioli, cat. xxxvi (New Series), item 4 (£18). Bought from Davis and Orioli for £18 in 1923: invoice dated 26 March.

1. Printed in 1480 and later, last as *La très ancienne coutume de Bretagne*, ed. M. Planiol, Rennes 1896, pp. 51-312/20. (f. 1) Aucune foiz est auenu en plusieurs terres . . . (f. 2) plus plenierement trouuer. Cy fine le prologue de ce present liure Et commencent les chapitres

ou le Repertoire diceulx . . . (*table numbered incorrectly to* xvii^{XX}xviii) . . . (f. 13) Qui veult viure honnestement . . . (f. 136^{v}) et venir a son Royaume des cieulx Amen Explicit liber iste Consuetudinum Britannie. Chapters are numbered from i to xvi^{XX}iii`i'. The last chapter is 'Pourquoy Iustice fut faite et establie', as edn., p. 308: in the table this is number 'xvii^{XX} ix' and is followed by the nine chapter-headings printed in edn., p. 72, numbered here 'xvii^{XX}' to 'xvii^{XX}xviii'.

2. As often, the 'coutume' is followed here immediately by the assize of Count Geoffrey at Rennes in 1185, 'Notum sit omnibus . . .', but all that remains of it are the fourteen lines on f. 136^{v} which ends 'perpetuum denarios', ed. Planiol, op. cit., p. 322/6.

Fr. 75. (R. 21238.) *Britton* s. xiii/xiv

Britton. ff. 138, foliated 1–93, 93*, 94–137. 245 × 167 mm. Written space 190 × 117 mm. 38 long lines. Collation: 1^{12} wants 1 2^{12} 3^{12} 11 or 12 cancelled (ff. 24–34)[1] $4–10^{12}$ 11^{12} wants 8 after f. 124 12^{12} wants 10, 11 (stubs remain, unnumbered), 12. Quires 1–4 numbered at the end a–d. Set current anglicana: split-topped ascenders. 2-line initials, blue or red with ornament of the other colour. Loose in quires and without covers: six bands once. Secundo folio (f. 1) *mentz* (?) *des Iurours*.

Written in England. Bought from P. M. Barnard in 1910 for £5. 5. 5: invoice dated 26 Jan.

Ed. E. Wingate, 1640; F. M. Nicholas, 1865 (2 vols.); Vising, no. 333. Begins imperfectly '[. . .] des Iurours ne des pleintes' (edn., 1865, i. 6/15). A leaf missing between f. 124 which ends 'vnges douweyr illoekes' (edn., ii. 265/10) and f. 125 which begins 'tie de aucun' (edn., ii. 270/11). f. 136^{v} ends 'si com de Contes et de Barons e de touz' (edn., ii. 347/5). Quires 1–6 (ff. 1–70) are damaged, but the decay extends into the text space only in quires 1–4 (ff. 1–46) and not too seriously there.

Fr. 87. (R. 59238.) *Theological tracts* s. xiv/xv–xv med.

Five pieces: **1**, **3**, s. xiv/xv; **2**, **4**, **5**, s. xv med. ff. i + 121 + i. *c.* 168 × 130 mm. Written space *c.* 135 × 95 mm. Long lines: 26 (ff. 1–24, 42–76), 23 (f. 25), 22 (ff. 77–121) and 20 (ff. 26–41). Collation: 1^{12} 2^{12} + 1 leaf after 12 (f. 25) 3^{12} 4 four (ff. 38–41, two bifolia) 5^{6} + 1 leaf before 1 (f. 42) 6^{8} $7–8^{10}$ $11–13^{8}$ 14^{6} wants 6, blank. Textura in quires 1, 2, 5–8. Cursiva in quires 3, 4, 9–14.

'Cest present liure est a moy Claude Chaulmont', f. 76^{v}, s. xvi. 'Ad vsum frater (*sic*) Claudius Gaiche', f. 121, s. xvi. 'Ex libris Richard Hancock' book-plate, s. xix/xx, and 'Sermons etc £7/7' inside the cover. Bought at this price (less 10% discount) from P. J. and A. E. Dobell in 1925: invoice dated 9 Jan.

Probably art. **1** is an early addition to art. **3** and modelled on it. Arts. **2**, **4**, **5** may have been added as they were written.

1. (*a*) ff. 1–23^{v} Cy commance la vangille de la toussains laquelle Euua(n)gile Est contenu et faite de lautin En francois. Beati pauperes spiritu . . . Nous veons senciblement que ou lieu

[1] Only ff. 26–33 in quire 3 are still conjoint. The other leaves in this quire and in quires 1, 2, 4 are now singletons, as a result of damage.

qui est communs a toute gens . . . A commentary on Matthew 5: 3–8, the Gospel for All Saints. (*b*) ff. 23v–25v Cy apres sensuit Lenseignement. Que S. ysidores aprent a humaine creature pour sauuer lame. Sainte escripture nous aprent. Et saint ysidorez. Coment nous pouons . . . Exp(l)icit. Deo gracias.

2. ff. 26–41v Cy commence un sermon translate de latin en francoys appelle le miroir des pecheurs . . . Mes tres chiers freres. Nous sommes en ce monde . . . A translation of Pseudo-Augustine, Speculum peccatoris, *PL* xl. 983–92.

3. ff. 42–76 Cest cy le commencement de la vertu de la vraie foy. Les gens qui ne croient mie come les bougres et autres . . . de bonne oeures faire. pour venir a la glore de paradis. On faith, hope, and charity, on the kinds of divine love, on the seven things for which God loves us, on ten signs to love God, and on contemplation. For the sub-headings see *Hand-list*.

4. ff. 77–120v . . . Saint augustin dit monseigneur mon dieu tu es grant . . . ame dieu sains en terre. Explicit les dis des tres excellans docteurs et mirouer de lumiere. A piece called 'le mirouer de vraie lumiere' in thirty-seven chapters, most of which begin 'Saint augustin dit'. ff. 77–81 contain a table of the chapters and two prologues, 'Sainte escripture nous enseigne . . .' and 'Sachent ceulx qui lirent . . .'. The text ends with a reference to the opinion of 'vn maistre . . . appelle Guill*aumes* bouquin'.

5. ff. 120v–121v Qui en paradis veult aler Ainssi puet on la voie trouuer . . . Qui lame en paradis conuoie. 39 lines. Sonet–Sinclair, no. 1748.

Fr. 88. *Armorial roll* s. xv[1]

Five membranes. *c.* 3000 × 240 mm. Secretary, with occasional long *r*: the ink and probably the hand change after the description of shield 127. 1-line initials not filled in.

Written in England (Yorkshire?). Belonged to S. Grimaldi, †1863. Formerly Crawford English 19.

Described by A. Wagner, *A catalogue of English Mediaeval Rolls of Arms* (Aspilogia i, 1950), p. 62 (cf. pp. 144, 163): 'Early 15th century copy of a compilation of *c.* 1350'. Printed by S. Grimaldi in J. G. Nichols, *Collectanea Topographica et Genealogica*, 1835, ii. 320–8. 167 shields, four in a row at first (nos. 1–32: row 1 rather damaged) and then five in a row, each row followed by names and blazonings, for example (no. 167) '[R]obert Wyclyff port dargent oue vne cheueron et trois croiceletz de goules'. As Wagner notes, the hand of nos. 1–127 is probably the same as that of a paper book of arms with Yorkshire connections, B.L., Add. 40851 (Wagner, p. 73, with reduced facsimile of one page, pl. 6). From no. 128 the script is larger and more regular[1] and the names in these last eight rows are mostly of persons living in the north-west of Yorkshire, beginning with Adam Stavelay of Dent.

No. 157 in the heraldic exhibition at Burlington House, London, in 1894.

Fr. 98. (R. 61214.) *Commentary on Westminster II, etc.* s. xv med.

1. ff. 3–39v Commentary on chapters 3–7 of the second statute of Westminster (*SR* i. 74–7). 2. f. 43 Chapter 6 of the statute of 6 Richard II (*SR* ii. 27): on rape. 3. f. 2rv Flyleaf verses in English. ff. ii + 41 + i, foliated 1–44. Paper,

[1] Spelling is also more regular from no. 128 onwards, for example *port* and *fees* always as against *port* or, less often, *porte*, and *fees*, *feesse*, or *fesse* before no. 128. The scribe of Add. 40851 also writes *porte* instead of *port* now and then.

except f. 2. 213 × 148 mm. Written space 130 × 95 mm. 22–4 long lines. Ruling on three sides (not at the bottom) of the written space with hard point and (ff. 37–9) pencil. Collation impracticable. Current anglicana. No coloured letters.

Written in England. '83' on a label on the cover and '807' on f. 2. Bought from J. E. Cornish for 21*s.* in 1926: invoice dated 18 June.

1. In casu quando vir implacitatur . . . Sur cest estatut fuist reherce *que* si vn home . . . ff. 40–43v are blank, except the page containing art. 2, and ff. 41–2 are still joined along the top edge. 3. Verses 'We (*sic*) wyll be war' in purchesyng concederyng þe poynt*is* þt ben suyng . . . in non morgage' in a hand of s. xv/xvi: 'Ihesus maria' at the head of the recto. Cf. *IMEV*, no. 4148 (Who so wylle . . .).

Fr. 99. (R. 14335.) *Chronicle roll* s. xv²

A chronicle of popes, emperors, kings of France, and kings of England, in roll form, like Leeds University, Brotherton Collection 100, q.v. *c.*17,230 × 686 mm. *Lettre bâtarde*. Sixty-six pictures.

Bought from Mrs Coppock, Newquay, for £10 in January 1908.

In two or four columns, beginning, after the heading printed in *Hand-list*,[1] 'In principio creauit deus celum et terram etc'. Cest a dire que au commencement'. The basic 2-column arrangement, each column *c.*245 mm wide, ruled in red ink, changes to four columns for a period after the destruction of Troy and becomes set in four columns—the first wider than the rest—at: (col. 1) Roboam le filz salemon . . . ; (col. 2) Iheroboam apres la mort salemon . . . ; (col. 3) Apres siluain tint le regne . . . ; (col. 4) Briut le filz siluain . . . Col. 1 takes the line of popes to 1378, crowning of Urban VI, '. . . a tres grant sollennite etc'. Explicit. Cy ne parleray plus des papes pour la diuision qui a puis este en saincte eglise que dieu vueille amender amen. etc' ': the column is then blank. Col. 2 takes the line of emperors to the coronation of Louis of Bavaria 'mil trois cens trente (*sic*) huit . . . Et lors les rommains firent a romme vng antipape. Explicit. Cy ne parle plus des empereurs de romme etc' ': the column is sometimes used after this point for roundels containing names belonging to col. 3. Col. 3 runs to 1461, death of Charles VII of France 'le xxie iour de Iuillet entre vne heure et midi. Et gist son corps a saint denis en france. etc.' '. Col. 4 ends with the coronation of Henry IV of England in 1399, '. . . Et fut henry de lenc`e´astre couronne roy dangleterre le quel a fait mourir des plus nobles du royaume dangleterre. Sicomme les croniques le dient plus a plain. etc'. Cy fine des Roys dangleterre. etc' ': the column is then blank. The first 350 mm of the text are damaged on the left side and there is some damage on the right side a little further down. A framed floral border bounds the text on the left at first, but only the last 200 mm of it remain.

The pictures are in roundels usually about 78 mm in diameter, with toothed edges. Most of them illustrate headings written above them in red or black. The following list is in 'Fitzwilliam order' (see above, Leeds, Brotherton 100) with the Fr. 99 number in brackets after the italicized Fitzwilliam number, and the number of the column in which the roundel comes in last place in each entry. The main differences between Fitzwilliam and Fr. 99 seem to be at nos. *10, 12, 38, 41–3*, and Fr. 99 has pictures after nos. (28), (37), (65), which do not occur in Fitzwilliam.

[1] The heading has 'de Wandes' in error for *Londres*, like the copy noticed in *Notices et extraits*, v (1798), 154.

1 (1) (lost).
2 (2) Creation of herbs and trees, almost all missing.
3 (3) Creation of waters and fishes.
4 (4) Creation of beasts and birds.
5 (5) Creation of angels.
6 (6) 'Comment dieu trebucha les mauuais anges'.
7 (7) Creation of Adam and Eve. (1)
8 (9) God instructs Adam and Eve beside the tree. (2)
9 (8) Adam and Eve and the serpent. (2)
10 Conviction. (no picture)
11 (10) God drives Adam and Eve, both naked, out of Paradise. (2)
12 Angel clothes Adam. Eve already dressed (11) Adam plants 'le Raincel' of the apple tree. (1)
13 (12) Adam digs—with great energy. (Centred)
14 (13) The Ark. (Centred)
15 (14) Tower of Babel. (2)
16 (15) Abraham and Isaac. (1)
17 (16) 'Iosue premier preux'. (2)
18 (22) 'Dauid ii^{e} preux'. (1)
19 (17) Troy destroyed. (2)
20–3 (18–21) Four roundels of loaded ships in a horizontal row: headings 'Comment eneas (priamus, turtus, helenus) se mist en mer . . .'
24 (23) 'Comment briut conquit lisle dalbion et occist les gens'. (4)
25 (27) 'Samarie'. (2)
26 (25) 'Sedechias'. (1)
27 (26) 'Comment nabugodonosor fut mis en iii^{e} pieces'. (1–2)
28 (24) Founding of 'Sincambre'. (3–4)
(28) Battle scene, headed 'Comment briut occist les gens'. (4)
29 (29) Founding of Rome. (Centred)
30 (31) 'Balthasar qui fut occis'. (1–2)
31 (30) 'Comment Romus et ses gens rauirent les dames'. (3)
32 (32) Founding of 'lutesse'. (3–4)
33 (33) 'Lexillement de la royne Vasti'. (2)
34 (34) Poisoning of Alexander 'le iour quil fut couronne empereur de tout le monde. iiii^{e} preux. etc' '. (2)
35 (35) 'Macabeus v^{e} preux'. (1–2)
36 (36) Birth of Christ. (1)
37 (37) Crucifixion under the heading 'Ihesus nazarenus rex iudeorum'. (1)
(38) Fifteen signs before Judgement. (3) *38* Resurrection (41) Christ seated, wearing a simple tiara, the orb in his left hand, blessing with his right, under the heading 'Comment ihesus sist en humanite en cest monde come premier pape'. (1)
39 (40) Murder of Julius Caesar. (2)
40 (39) 'Comment neufue troye fut nommee Londres en angleterre'. (4)
41 Battle of Sicambrians and Romans (42) Tournament: no heading. (3)
42 Constantine and Bishops (43) 'Bucie (*sic*) premier Roy crestien de la grant bretaigne'. (4)
43 Le duc Priant (44) 'Comment les francois occirent les Rommains en bataille'. (3)
44 (45) 'Comment conain fut fait le premier roy de la petite bretaigne'. (4)
45 (46) Crowning of Pharamond, first king of France. (3)
46 (47) Baptism of Clovis. (3)
47 (48) 'Comment anglist occis xxx mille bretons en trahison'. (4)
48 (49) Founding of St Denis. (3)
49 (50) Arthur kills 'mordet' in battle. (4)
50 (51) A ruined town to illustrate 'comment la grant bretaigne fut du tout destruite par les aufricois qui la donnerent aux sanxoinis et la nommerent du tout angleterre'. (4)
51 (52) Crowning of Pepin. (3)
52 (54) St Gregory. (1)
53 (53) Duke William kills Harold in battle. (4)

54 (56) 'Comment hue capet fut fait a force roy de france'. (3)
55 (57) Godfrey 'de billon' riding to the crusade. (4)
56 (55) Crowning of Charlemagne as emperor. Between (1) and (2)
57 (58) Crowning of 'le duc godesfroy de billon' as king of Jerusalem. (4)
58 (60) 'Saint Louys qui fut roy de france': he is seated alone. (Centred)
59 (59) 'Berengier premier de ce nom empereur de romme'. (2)
60 (61) Edward I. (4)
61 (62) Philip de Valois. (Centred)
62 (63) 'Comment le Roy iehan fut prins et mene en angleterre'. (Centred)
63 (64) Charles V.
64 (65) Charles VI.
(66) Charles VII: 97 mm in diameter and damaged.

Fr. 142. (R. 136830.) *Denis Piramus, La vie S. Edmund le Rei*
s. xiii/xiv

ff. vi + 68 + ii. 175 × 115 mm. Written space *c.* 130 mm high. 32 long lines. Collation: $1\text{-}2^{12}$ 3^{16} 4^{12} 5^{16}: quires 3–5 are numbered at the end 4–6. Forty-two rough but lively pen drawings, coloured in green and red, in the margins. Limp parchment cover, s. xvii (?).

Written in England. Belonged to James Cobbes (cf. *MMBL* ii. 219 and *BJRL* lviii. 2) in 1642: see below. Bought in March 1975 from Mrs J. C. Campbell of Wick, Caithness, for £4,000.

Described by W. Rothwell in *BJRL* lx (1978), 135–80. The first quire is missing and the first words now are 'Edmund le fiz mun cusin', line 685 of the edition by Kjellman, 1935. Ends imperfectly at a point 926 lines beyond the end of the only manuscript known to Kjellman. f. vi is made up as a title-page: 'La uie et Les miracles / De Saint Edmund Roy / et Martir Anglois. escrit / en vers / deest principium et finis / Adiectus est ad calcem Tractatus de Cauteriis / Item alius de ventositati/bus Incerti Authoris / (*these four lines cancelled*) omnia Tineis et Blattis erepta / per Iacobum Cobbes Armigerum / 1642.' The two medical pieces are now missing.

Fr. 143 (Cong. Coll. 10). (R. 136854.) *Horae (in French and Latin)*
s. xv in.

Arts. 1a, 2–5, 10–32, 38 are in French.

1 (added, s. xvi in.). (*a*) ff. 1–4v Oryson de la magdelainne. O Magdelainne par celle grant liesse . . . de dieu la Chambrette. (*b*) f. 4v O salutaris hostia que celi pandis hostium bella premunt hostilia da robur fer auxilium. (*c*) f. 4v O vere digna hostia per quem tracta sunt tartara redempta plebs captiuata reddita uite premia. Amen.

(*a*). Fifteen 12-line stanzas signed at the end 'Payot'. (*b*). *RH*, no. 13680.

2. ff. 5–16v Calendar—not very full—in French, in gold, blue, red, and black.

Includes in black 'Translacion s' martin de boillant' and 'Miracles nostre dame' (4 July, 20 Oct.). The only added saint is Dominique, 5 August.

3. f. 17rv John 1: 1–14 in French.

4. ff. 17v–18v Ci commencent plusurs antenez de nostre dame: (*a*) Regina celi Royne du ciel esioy toy. alleluya vault autretant come loenge soit . . . ; (*b*) Salue regina misericordie. Ie te salue royne mere de misericorde . . . ; (*c*) Ante thronum trinitatis. Debonnaire mere de pitie soies pour nous . . . ; (*d*) Aue regina celorum. Aue domina. Ie te salue royne des cielx Ie te salus . . . ; (*e*) Aue regina celorum mater regis. Ie te salus royne des cielx. mere le roy . . . ; (*f*) Alma redemptoris. Sainte mere de nostre racheteur . . .

(*a*). Cf. Sonet, no. 1797. (*b, d*). Sonet, nos. 883, 890.

5. f. 19rv Au cuer dois auoir grant douleur Quant icy uois mort ton seigneur . . . (40 lines of verse). f. 20r blank.

6 (added, s. xv). f. 20v Confiteor deo . . . quia ego miser peccator . . .

7. ff. 21–47v Hours of B.V.M.

Antiphon and capitulum at prime, Quando natus and Hec est uirgo; at none, Ecce maria and Felix namque.

8. ff. 48–54v Penitential psalms.

9. ff. 54v–55 John 1: 1–14 (cf. art. 3). f. 55v blank.

10. ff. 56–82 Ce sont les heures nostre dame en rommant.

The capitulum at none does not go with art. 7, but is Paradi por.

11. f. 82 Antene . . . Ie te salue royne des cielx . . . As art. 4*d*.

12. ff. 82v–87v . . . Hymne. Patris sapiencia. Pere de sapience uerite diuine . . .

Hours of the Cross in French.

13. ff. 88–97 Pour moy et pour mes amis et pour toutes nos gent . . . et sa grace lor dont (4 lines). Dieu en ton iugement ne margue . . .

Penitential psalms in French verse. Längfors, p. 92.

14. ff. 97–100v Litany in French.

Twenty-five virgins: (4) Susanna . . . (12) Katherine of Siena. Anne is absent.

15. ff. 101–120v Office of the dead in French.

The ninth lesson at matins is 'En icel iour dit saint iehan uint a moi . . . ce que sauf les fera'.

16. ff. 120v–121v Contre les sept pichies mortel. Douce uierge marie en cui humanitei . . . : Sonet-Sinclair, no. 490.

17. ff. 121v–124v Cy apres sensuit les xv ioye nostre dame. Douce dame de misericorde mere de pitie . . . : Sonet, no. 458.

18. ff. 124v–127v Quiquonques veut estre bien consilliez . . . Doux Dieu doux pere . . . Biau sire dieu ie vous requier . . .

The Seven Requests: Sonet–Sinclair, nos. 1760, 504.

19. ff. 127v–131v Orison de saint pierre de lucenbourc. Dieu le pere qui creas le monde . . . (150 lines).

Sonet, no. 405. Thirty-five stanzas, thirty of 4 lines and five (nos. 9, 18, 33–5) of 6 lines.

20. ff. 131v–134 Royne qui fustes mise et asise . . .

Sonet–Sinclair, no. 1804. Twelve 8-line stanzas. The heading conveys 800 years of pardon 'pour sez pichiez venielz et pour son temps perdus'.

21. ff. 134v–136 Vrai dieu si com tu desis vii parolles quant mort preis . . .

Sonet–Sinclair, no. 2366. Eighty lines of verse.

22. ff. 136v–157 Apres la sainte passion Ihesu crist a lascencion . . .

A verse life of St Margaret. Längfors, p. 19. Spaces for fourteen pictures remain blank.

23. ff. 157v–158v E tres douce sainte gertrux Ancelle et amie de ihesus . . . (37 lines of verse).

24. ff. 158v–160v O mere et fille anne et marie Secoures . . .

A prayer to St Anne in twenty 4-line stanzas.

25. ff. 161–163v A ceste ymage Ie fais hommage Tant nette et clere . . .

Seventeen 6-line stanzas to B.V.M., rhyming aabccb.

26. ff. 163v–164 Per vng aiournant trouuay en vng prey Pastorel seant . . .

Twenty-seven lines of verse marked 'vacat' by the main hand and lined through lightly.

27. ff. 164v–166 A vous chante uirge marie Vng chant piteux et plein de pleur . . . (65 lines of verse).

28. ff. 166–7 Qui vuet en paradis aler . . . (34 lines of verse).

Sonet–Sinclair, no. 1748.

29. f. 167rv Eight sentences, each beginning 'Helas', the first 'Helas ie ne cuidoye mie si tost morir'.

30. ff. 167^{v}–173^{v} Glorieuse uierge marie En cui per la uertu diuine . . .

Sonet-Sinclair, no. 695. Forty 6-line stanzas.

31. ff. 174–5 Ottroye nous sire tous puissans . . . et espris. Saint cristofe martir tres doulz Prie le roy . . . (31 lines of verse).

Sonet-Sinclair, no. 1816, with prose heading. f. 175^{v} blank.

32. f. 176^{rv} (*a*) Quant on vuet receuoir le corpz nostre*signeur*. Mon tres doulz creatour vrais et tous puissans . . . : Sonet-Sinclair, no. 1220. (*b*) f. 176^{v} Apres la recepcion. Mon tres doulz creatour doucement . . .

33. ff. 176^{v}–177 On doit dire ceste orison sus les mors qui sensuit cy apres. Auete omnes cristi fideles . . .

34. f. 177 Cy apres sensuit lez vii vers seint bernard. Illumina oculos meos . . .

Nine verses: Illumina; In manus; Locutus sum; Et numerum; Disrupisti; Periit; Clamaui; Fac mecum; Domine exaudi. The prayer 'Omnipotens sempiterne deus qui ezechie . . .' follows.

35. f. 178 On doit dire ceste orison entre la leuacion nostre signeur. Domine ihesu criste qui hanc sacratissimam carnem . . .

36. ff. 178–179^{v} Memoriae of Barbara, Salue barbara uirgo prudentissima neupmatis almi . . . (4 lines) and Katherine.

37. f. 179^{v} Cy commence lez salmes que saint hilaire li euesque trait hors du psaultier . . . Heading only.

38 (added, s. xv). (*a*) f. 180 Sainte char precieuse ie vous aoure . . . (*b*) ff. 180–1 Crois en toy voy mon pere dieu pendre . . . (*c*) f. 181^{rv} Vierge pucelle nette et pure Vierge de tres plaisant figure . . .

(*a*). Sonet-Sinclair, no. 1855. (*b*). Cf. Sonet, no. 301. Twenty-three couplets, each beginning Crois (or Croix), and a final triplet. (*c*). Five 6-line stanzas, rhyming aabaab.

39 (added by another hand, s. xv). (*a*) ff. 182–183^{v} O intemerata . . . orbis terrarum. Inclina . . . ego peccatrix . . . (*b*) ff. 183^{v}–184 Te inuocamus te adoramus . . . f. 184^{v} blank.

40. f. 185 and both pastedowns are paper leaves containing coloured woodcuts of saints, s. xvi, each 50 × 37 mm, six to a page: on the pastedown at the end, John Baptist, John Evangelist, Peter, Stephen, Christopher, Laurence; on the pastedown at the beginning, Ecce homo, Julian, Claude, Paul, Andrew, James; on f. 185^{v}, Roche, Sebastian, Nicholas, Francis, Jerome, Anthony.

Printed titles in French. f. 185^{v} is blank and so no doubt were the hidden sides of the pastedowns.

ff. 184 + i. For f. 185 see above, art. 40. 212 × 147 mm. Written space 130–40 × 90 mm. 20 long lines. Ruling in red ink. Collation: 1^4 $2\text{–}6^8$ 7^4 wants 4, blank (ff. 45–7) $8\text{–}23^8$ 24^4 (ff. 176–9) 25^6 wants 6, blank (ff. 180–4). Catchwords in *lettre bâtarde*. Spaces for 10-line pictures were not filled: except on ff. 145v–174 a line of pricks runs along the head and usually the foot of the picture space. Initials: (i) 4-line or 5-line, blue or red patterned in white on gold grounds decorated in colour and with bar prolongations in gold and red or gold and blue; (ii–iv) 3-line, 2-line, and 1-line, gold on coloured grounds patterned in white. Borders of ivy leaf, etc., on each recto of art. 2, on pages where pictures were to come and on pages with initials of type (i): the style is heavier in arts. 7, 8 than elsewhere. Line fillers in gold, blue, and red. Capital letters in the ink of the text filled with yellow. Binding of s. xvi.

Written in France. The owner was a woman when art. 39*a* was added. 'Henrico-Mariæ Dupré de Geneste, 1764', in red on f. 1. Given to the Lancashire Independent College by Joseph Thompson, Pin Mill, Ancotes, 22 Nov. 1866. Bought in April 1976.

Manuscripts in German.

Germ. 1 is a foundation book from the Crawford library. Germ. 11 was acquired in 1926 and Germ. 13 in 1936. Germ. 24 was transferred from the University Library in Oxford Road to Deansgate in 1972.

Germ. 1. *'Vera sciencia alhimie in figuris'* s. xv/xvi

ff. ii + 14 + vi. 217 × 180 mm. Written space of f. 2 160 × 110 mm in 29 long lines; of f. 7 155 × 120 mm in 34 long lines. A single quire of good parchment. Hybrida: except on ff. 2r, 7rv the writing is small and current, often in red. Nearly contemporary wooden boards covered with brown leather bearing a pattern of rolls: 3 bands: 5 bosses on each cover: central clasp.

Written in Germany. 'Hunc mihi libellum uere aureum donationis titulo dedit C.S. natione ut dixit Germanus die primo mensis 9mbris 1677(?)', f. 14v. A probably rather later name is on f. 1, 'Petrus Bortieler Honscheynischer . . .', below a couplet 'Mercurium quaeris . . .': higher on the page is 'alcamistica res est longa spes dulcis depauperacio et lepus quem nemo capere potest' in the same hand. In the collection of Lord Crawford in 1896 (see below).

Described by R. Priebsch, *Deutsche Handschriften in England*, i (1896), 190–2, no. 180, when part of the Crawford collection at Haigh Hall, Wigan. The only texts of any length are the verses written as prose on f. 2, 'Dis gewalt peynigt mich nackendes weib . . . ', and on f. 7rv, 'Platonis tochter ruft unde schreit also . . . Aber diser Elixir ist die warheit etc.': all the first piece and the first two and last sixteen verses of the second piece are printed by Priebsch. For the rest, the manuscript consists of seventeen picture pages, with captions and short pieces of text distributed in blank spaces. The first two pictures appear to show the bird-filled tree of sun and moon (ff. 2v, 3) and the last is an apparatus for distilling, enlivened by cocks on taps, without any accompanying text (f. 13v). The 'forma speculi trinita(ti)s' on f. 8v shows Christ with wounded feet and hands and a crowned head emerging at mid point between the heads of a double-headed black eagle. The facing page 9, 'figura speculi Sancte trinitatis' has another smaller eagle-Christ crucified on a green shield supported by B.V.M., below figures of God the Father, B.V.M. crowned, and God the Son, marked respectively 'Sapiencia', 'Corpus', and 'Anima': a symbol of an evangelist in each corner. ff. 1rv, 11v–13r, 14rv were left blank. The title, 'Vera sciencia . . .' was supplied on f. 1, s. xvi.

Germ. 11. (R. 61197.) *Büchlein von der Liebe Gottes, etc.* s. xv^2

1. ff. 1–146v Büchlein von der Liebe Gottes. **2.** ff. 148–71 H. Suso, O.P., sermon on Lectulus noster floridus. **3–11.** ff. 171–218v Short pieces. **12.** ff. 219–55 On the sacrament of communion. **13.** ff. 255–7 Von ainer saligen pegeinen. **14.** f. 262, formerly a pastedown. ff. 262 + i, foliated 1–46, 46a, 47–262. Paper, except f. 262. 150 × 100 mm. Written space *c.*100 × 65 mm. 16–18 long lines. Frame ruling. Collation: 1^{10} $2\text{–}22^{12}$: parchment strips in quire centres. Cursiva, changing to hybrida by another hand on f. 226, the first leaf of quire 20. Contemporary binding of wooden boards covered with red-stained leather: 3 bands: 5 bosses on each cover: 2 clasps missing.

Written in southern Germany, probably for the use of nuns. Bought from J. E. Cornish in 1926 for £1: invoice dated 18 June.

Described, except art. 14, by F. P. Pickering in *BJRL* xxii (1938), 466–92, as follows: 1, based on N. von Dinkelsbühl (†1433), De dilectione Dei et proximi, with introductory letter of a Carthusian, on pp. 466–71; 2, Suso, printed by K. Bihlmeyer, *Heinrich Suese. Deutsche Schriften* (1907) pp. 495–508, on pp. 471–4; 3, ff. 171–2, on pp. 474–5; 4, ff. 172–91, a sermon of J. Tauler for the sixth Sunday after Pentecost, no. 39 in the edition by F. Vetter (*Deutsche Texte des Mittelalters* xi, 1910), on pp. 475–6; 5, ff. 191v–199v, and 6, ff. 199v–203, on pp. 476–80; 7, ff. 203–204v, verses beginning 'O mensch wildu geistlich sein', on pp. 481–2; 8, ff. 204v–208v, printed by Pickering, pp. 482–4; 9, ff. 205–211v, a prose translation of Salve mater salvatoris, on pp. 484–5; **10**, ff. 211v–216v, a 'Stucklein . . . aus dem taller', on pp. 485–7; **11**, ff. 217–218v, on pp. 487–8; **12**, on pp. 488–92; **13**, on pp. 476, 480. ff. 147rv, 257v–261v blank.

14. A now raised pastedown which is taken round the last quire and comes up as a stub between f. 249 and f. 250 seems to be part of a leaf of a 2-column manuscript. It contains 56 lines of verse, 28 on each side, in a German textura, s. xiii, beginning on the 'recto' 'Fac ut ameris. ama quos fructus amoris amicos. Predicat. est brauio dignus amoris amor' and ending on the 'verso' 'Non credas fame titulis. [t]e consule. crede'. Lines 21–3 on the 'recto' are 'Quinque precor famulos rege quos natura ministros Vsibus humanis officiosa dedit. Visus. odoratus. auditus. tactus. amicus'. Lines 9, 10 on the 'verso' are 'Tactus adulatur falsus dum uendit amanti Plana superficies que scabiosa latent'. Another piece of the same manuscript was the pastedown at the beginning: offset shows and the stub remains between f. 10 and f. 11.

Germ. 13, ff. 75–90, 93–102. (R. 77737.) *Penitential psalms, etc.* s. xv/xvi

'Syben psalmen' and their antiphons and (ff. 93v–102) litany. Cut down to 83 × 65 mm: part of the border ornament is lost. Written space 63 × 45 mm. 15 long lines. Collation: $1\text{–}3^8$ 4 two (ff. 101–2).

Written in southern Germany: the names in the litany suggest Augsburg. Bound in s. xvi with a collection of prayers mainly in one hand of s. xvi med.: see *Handlist*, where an earlier date is assigned to this part of the manuscript. Book-plate of W. A. Copinger. Given as MS. Dutch 13.

Litany: twelve confessors, (1, 2) Gregory, Ulrich, (6, 7) Othmar, Gall, (10) 'gilg', (12) Erasmus; ten virgins, (1, 2) Mary Magdalene, 'otilg' (Ottilia), (7) Affra, (10) Anne. At the end are the litany prayers Deus cui proprium, Exaudi, Ineffabilem, Deus qui culpa, and Actiones nostras translated into German and a prayer 'fur vater vnd muter. Got der du [vns] gebotten hast vater und muter in eren zu halten . . .'.

Germ. 24. *On diseases, etc.* s. XV ex.

Das ist das erst puch. [D]ie weysen die hie vor waren vnd die nu sind . . .

Four books: the first on the elements, humours, etc., in fourteen chapters; the second, f. 8^v, on foods and drinks in 79 chapters; the third, f. 25^v, 'von den dingen die da wol smekchunt' in eighteen chapters; the fourth, f. 29^v, on diseases, ending abruptly in ch. 6 'von den haubtwe' (f. 35^v/5). A table of chapters precedes each book. A leaf missing after f. 27 and the excised nine lines at the head of f. 28 contained chapters 16 and 17 of bk. 3, '[v]on wacher' and '[v]on minne', according to the table. The table of bk. 4 lists 92 chapters.

ff. i + 35 + i. Paper. 215 × 150 mm. Written space 140 × 90 mm. 28 long lines. Frame ruling. Collation: 1-2^{12} 3^{12} wants 4 after f. 27. Current hybrida. 3-line and 2-line initials not filled in.

Written in southern Germany or Austria. A note on f. i is signed 'T(homas) Windsor 1876': cf. MS. Eng. 1310.

Manuscripts in Icelandic

Ice. 1. *Rimbegla, etc.* s. XV

1-4, 6, 7. Computistical and other pieces. **5.** A calendar in Latin. Described by Eiríkr Magnússon, 'Codex Lindesianus', *Arkiv för Nordisk Filologi*, xiii (1896), 1-14, by O. Skulerud, *Catalogue of Norse Manuscripts in Edinburgh, Dublin and Manchester*, 1918, pp. 59-60, and by B. S. Benedikz in *BJRL* lx (1978), 292-6. Presumed by P. E. K. Kålund to have been AM 462 12° of the Árni Magnússon collection in the University of Copenhagen (Alfrædi Íslenzk, *Islansk Encyclopædisk Litteratur*, iii (1918), xiv-xvi). This manuscript was missing before Kålund catalogued the collection (2 vols., 1894-6). There, ii. 500, he reproduces the description in Jón Ólafsson's catalogue of 1731-2, which shows that AM 462 began with a computistical piece (Rimbegla: cf. 1) and ended with 'the year of the book's composition reckoned from various points' (cf. 7) and had in between these items papal decrees and an exposition of mass (cf. 2), a treatise 'on the bodily shape of man and of his limbs and how to recognize his character from his bodily shape' (cf. 4) and a 'calendar grid' (Rimstockur) and 'computational tables' (cf. 5, 6).[1] ff. iii + 94 + iii. ff. ii, iii, 95-6 are medieval parchment endleaves. 78 × 57 mm. Written space 45 × 35 mm. 15 long lines. Collation: 1-6^8 7^8 wants 8 after f. 55 8-11^8 (ff. 56-87) 12^8 wants 2 after f. 88 *or* 12^6 + 1 leaf after 5 (f. 93). Quires 2-10 were signed later b-k on first rectos. Written in

[1] I owe the references to Ólafsson and Björnsson and English translation of Ólafsson's titles to Dr Benedikz, who tells me that he would not expect to find any manuscript which had belonged to Árni Magnússon without his annotations.

a script equivalent to anglicana formata, arts. 1–3 and art. 4 (except ff. 64–6) by one hand.[1]

'sra Finnur Jons*son*', f. 1v, s. xvii: cf. Benedikz, p. 295. Very probably once AM 462 12° at Copenhagen University: see above. If so, it is likely to have been lost before 1780 when Stefán Björnsson edited Rimbegla without mention of AM 462. F. G. H. Culemann sale at Sotheby's, 7 February 1870, lot 575, to F. S. Ellis. Bought from Ellis by Lord Crawford in or soon after 1872.

1. ff. 1–38 Gud baud moysi . . . A computistical piece, Rimbegla, printed from a longer version in Copenhagen, GKS 1812 4° by L. Larsson in *Samfund til Udgivelse af Gammel Nordisk Literatur*, ix (1883), 8/7 sqq. Magnússon, pp. 3–8.

2. ff. 38v–47/6 Alexander enn fyrsti papa baud . . . fyrer aunduerdu. Notes on forms of service, Gloria in excelsis Deo and others, and on church services from Advent to Easter, some of which is paralleled in Honorius, Gemma animae (*PL* clxxii. 646–7, 652). Magnússon, pp. 8, 9.

3. ff. 47/7–48 Ef þu uillt idraȝt synda þinna . . . og lofa suo skapara sinn. Virtues of certain psalms. Printed by Benedikz, p. 293.

4. ff. 48v–66 Almattigur guds son . . . skal rada eppter. A treatise on the mystical significance of the parts of the human body, consisting of an introduction and three sections with headings in red. Magnússon, pp. 9–10 and 11–14, and p. 2, where he notes that the gap after p. 55 is filled by Copenhagen, AM 435 12°, f. 7.

5. ff. 66v–78 A calendar in Latin, two pages to a month. Entries include: 7 Feb. Dorothy (in red); 6 Mar. Thomas Aquinas (in red); 7 May John of Beverley; 15 May 'Halluardi m' '; 2 June '[. . .] episcopi m' ' (in red); 17 June Botulf; 21 June 'Leofredis abbatis con' ' (of La Croix-S.Leufroy); 22 June Alban; 23 June Etheldreda; 2 July Visitation of B.V.M.; 20 July 'Translacio thorlaci episcopi'; 26 July Anne (in red); 29 July Olaf, king and martyr; 3 Aug. Olaf king and martyr; 5 Aug. Transfiguration; 9 Aug. 'Passio sancte margarete de nordnes' (in red); 4 Sept. Translation of Cuthbert; 13 Sept. 'Festum sanctarum reliquiarum'; 8 Nov. Willehad; 20 Nov. Edmund king and martyr; 23 Dec. 'Sancti thorlaci episcopi et confessoris'. Magnússon, pp. 10–11.

6. (*a*) ff. 78v–79 Table of a great cycle of 532 years, 1140–1671. Magnússon, p. 11. (*b*) f. 79v Rule for finding the number of days between Christmas and Ash Wednesday. Magnússon, p. 11: he notes that there is an erased table on f. 80. ff. 80v–87v blank.

7 (quire 12). Erased or (ff. 90v–94v) blank, except f. 89v, where there are notes in one hand of the age of the world (6,138 years) and of the number of years from the flood (4,148), the incarnation (1,473), and the death of archbishop Thomas (of Canterbury) (280), and of the ages of Adam and Eve. These notes were continued on f. 90 where five lines have been erased. Magnússon, pp. 2–3.[2]

Ice. 5. (R. 45386.) *Horae (?)* s. xv in. (?)

Underwriting on probably all the leaves of twenty-five quires and on two endleaves, 185 leaves in all, of a handsome mid-sixteenth-century copy of the lawbook Jónsbók, for which good parchment was procured by blotting out the text

[1] I do not see a change of hand at f. 47/7, where the writing becomes rather larger.

[2] Icelandic 1 was sent to King's College, Cambridge, for cataloguing by M. R. James early in 1901 and James may have had these erasures in mind when he wrote asking if he might be allowed to 'revive erased inscriptions' (Barker, p. 347).

of a Latin book of hours (?) and reusing the leaves which measure now 170 × 115 mm. The underwriting is in a fairly large hand and seems to have been in 19 (+ ?) long lines. Consecutive text can be read on p. 351 (the recto of the second leaf of quire 25), which begins in the genealogy of Christ 'genuit iudam et fratres eius' and ends 'genuit osiam' (Matthew 1: 2–8) and on p. 350 which begins 'Osias autem genuit' and ends, probably, 'mathan' (Mt. 1: 9–15). Since p. 351 was originally a verso, the genealogy must have begun on p. 352 a little below the point where a 2-line blue *O* (?) with red ornament can be seen. Line 1 on this same page began with a 2-line blue *B* with red ornament. A few words can be read by ultra-violet light on other pages, for example on 354/2 'nolebat nec', 354/5 'Amen dico uobis', 354/11 'in te confido non' and there are obvious traces of writing on many pages, for example 175, 180, 283, 289, 302, 356–7.

For the earlier history of this Jónsbók see B. S. Benedikz in *BJRL* lx (1978), 298–9.

Manuscripts in Irish

Irish 35. *Medical treatises (in Gaelic)*[1] s. xv/xvi

1. ff. 1–57v Aron barba iarus pes vituli. id est tri hanma in geagair . . .

A dictionary of materia medica based on Latin herbal dictionaries such as Thorndike and Kibre list, cols. 5, 6. It occurs, more or less as here, in a number of other copies: see especially the very full description of N.L.S., Adv. 72. 1. 3, art. 1, by J. Mackechnie, *Catalogue of Gaelic Manuscripts in selected libraries in Great Britain and Ireland*, 1973, i. 129–34. It ends here with Zinciber, after which there is no colophon: some manuscripts note here that the translation from Latin is by Tadhg Ó Cuinn in 1415. Leaves are missing at four points: after f. 14 which ends in Auellana (A 46): f. 15 begins in (Barba filicana: B 2); after f. 15 which ends in Bilonia molena (B 9): f. 16 begins in (Burneta: B 14); after f. 25 which ends in Diuretica (D 6): f. 26 begins in (Endiuia (?): E 4); after f. 37 which ends with Isopus: f. 38 begins with Nasturcium. On ff. 1–36 the entries under each letter of the alphabet are numbered A 1–(50), B (1)–16, C 1–34, D 1–( ), E (1)–12, F 1–18, G 1–8, H 1–4, I 1: cf. below, art. 9*b*. Whitley Stokes notes the beginning of each chapter on ff. 1v–12, 17–24v, 47v–57 in *Academy*, no. 1254 (16 May 1896), 406–7. Latin headings added often in the margins, s. xv/xvi, for example, f. 53v, 'contra frigiditatem stomoci et pectoris et lapides': many of them have been cut off partly. On f. 31v the scribe saw that there was too much show-through on part of his parchment and avoided writing on it.

The main hand added pieces on f. 57v after Zinciber: on wine (line 1), Aurea alaxandrea (line 5), Antimeron (line 12), hawk (line 18), and eagle (line 30). Another hand added charms in a blank space after F 14 (f. 34, lines 29–34): one begins 'Procul recedant somnia' and the other, against worms, cites Colum cille; both are also in N.L.S., Adv. 72. 1. 2, f. 130v. The same hand and brown ink occur also in additions on ff. 47v, 58v.

Arts. 2, 3 are on four bifolia (58–65), followed by two singletons.

2. ff. 58–60, 61–66v Medical recipes and charms and pieces on simples (f. 58), poisons (f. 61, 'Capitulum aureum id est caibidil . . .) and quotidian fever (f. 62).

For f. 59rv see Stokes, loc. cit., p. 407. f. 60v was left blank: see art. 3.

[1] I could not have made this description without the help of Mr Ronald Black.

3 (added in s. xvi and later). (*a*) f. 60v below two erased lines, a 2-line note of the nine symptoms of diseases, arranged as three triads. (*b*) f. 60v Descent of Archibald MacDonald of Islay, †1568, from Tuathal Techtmar, a pre-historical high king of Tara. (*c*) f. 60v A definition of the difference between raw and undigested material, signed Fergus. (*d*) f. 67, lines 1–4 Verses. (*e*) f. 67, lines 5–8 A charm (?), beginning 'Sgris a De an mac fallain'. (*f*) f. 67, lines 9–11 A list of persons cured by the writer in Largie and Oa, Islay. (*g*) f. 67, lines 12, 13 An alphabet. (*h*) f. 67, lines 14–17 Verses, 'Gabh sin romhad ga coir . . .' ending 'In nomine patris et filii et Sp*ir*atai Sanctai amen . . .'. (*i*) f. 67v Notes on royal traits, indulgences and the soul after death. (*j*) f. 67v Notes in two hands, including a charm. (*k*) Scribble 'Amen digo uobis . . .'. (*l*) Five lines on orthography by Donald, son of Kenneth.

4 (two bifolia) ff. 68–71v Medicina est que corporis uel tuetur uel restaurat . . .

The Latin sentences beginning the first four paragraphs are taken from the opening words of chapters 1–4 of bk. 4 of Isidore, Etymologiae, *PL* lxxxii. f. 69 is numbered at the top '87', f. 70 '90', and f. 71 '108': this suggests that ff. 68–71 are the first and nineteenth bifolia of a quire of twenty bifolia.

5 (four bifolia). ff. 72–79v De dolore capitis id est doteineas . . . lat foss (*ends imperfectly*).

Leaves, presumably a bifolium, are missing after f. 75. The headings before the gap are (f. 74v) Capitulum secundum de rubore oculorum and (f. 75v) Capitulum tercium; after the gap, (f. 76) Capitulum secundum de tonitrua et sibera, (f. 76) Tercium capitulum de dolore aureum, (f. 76v) Capitulum quartum de uermibus, (f. 76v) Capitulum quintum de apostematibus auereum, (f. 77) Capitulum sextum de ulceribus et sanie et aqua in auribus, (f. 77) Capitulum septimum de sanguine exeunte ab aurebus, (f. 77v) Tractatus tercius libri terci, (f. 78v) Quartus tractatus terci (*sic*) libri. The headings show that this is part of bk. 3 of a work in at least three books. Cf. Stokes, loc. cit., p. 407.

6 (a quire of seven bifolia followed by a quire of six bifolia, followed by three singletons and two bifolia). (*a*) ff. 80–112 Apostemata et tumor idem sunt secundum anticos ut dixit galienus . . . (*b*) f. 112v Thirty-two lines of cures mainly for ailments of the eye ending with a charm in Latin, '. . . sana oculos meos saluator et deus medice diuine . . . hoc septies canitur . . . posuisti dies meos'.

(*a*). See Thorndike and Kibre, col. 114, where a 'Latin and Irish' text in Trinity College, Dublin, E. 3. 3 (1432) is referred to. Paralysis is discussed after tumours (f. 94), then dropsy (f. 97), smallpox (f. 108: Varioli sunt parua apostemata id est iseadh . . .), and dropsy again (f. 111v).

7 (a quire of 8 wanting the last leaf). Miscellaneous medical pieces: (*a*) f. 113rv, digestion of the humours; (*b*) ff. 113v–114, head wounds; (*c*) ff. 114–116v, cure of wounds, 'Labrum anois . . .'; (*d*) ff. 117–18 Pastinaca id est athair l*iath* . . . ; (*e*) ff. 118–119v, cure of felon, etc., with ingredients for ointments; (*f*) f. 119v, a list of ingredients, ending imperfectly.

(*d*) is printed from this copy by Whitley Stokes in *Archiv für celtische Lexikographie*, i (1900), 333–7.

8. (*a*) f. 120 A list of electuaries. (*b*) f. 120 A charm added in brown ink. (*c*) ff. 120v–123v Notes on simples and syrups.

9. (*a*) f. 124 On the primary and secondary qualities of matter. (*b*) f. 124v An index to art. 1, ending imperfectly.

(*b*). Only A, B, C remain under 50, 16, and 34 numbered heads respectively: C is numbered wrongly 1–10, 12–35.

ff. ii + 124 + ii. 197 × 140 mm. Written space *c.* 190 × 110 mm. 33–7 long lines in arts. 1, 2. 2 cols. of 28–37 lines in arts. 4–8. Pencil ruling, except in art. 4, where the ruling is with a blunt hard point. Collation: of art. 1, 1^{14} 2 one (f. 15) 3^{22} wants 11, 12 after f. 25: 3 and 20 (ff. 18, 33) are singletons 4 four (ff. 36–9) 5^{8} (assuming that ff. 40 and 47 were once conjoint) 6^{10} (ff. 48–57: ff. 48–52 have slits in the inner margin to guide ruling); of arts. 2–7, see above under each art. Insular minuscule, except for Latin marginalia and for the Latin part of art. 6*b*, mainly by four hands: (1) arts. 1, 2, 9, a hand which occurs also in N.L.S., Adv. 72. 1. 2, ff. 1–3v (hand 1) and 72. 1. 4 (hand 5); (2) art. 4; (3) arts. 5, 7, 8; (4) art. 6*a*. The Latin part of art. 6*b* is in a modified textura and the Latin marginalia in art. 1 in anglicana (long *r*: single compartment *a*). Mr Black comments on four of the hands in art. 3: 3*b* and 3*f* 'apparently in the hand of an Ollamh Ìleach, head of the Beaton medical family of Islay'; 3c in the hand of 'Fearghus Ó Fearghail, whom I believe to be an early member of the MacRyrie bardic family of Skye'; some verses on f. 67 'may be by Revd. James Currie, minister of Kildalton and Oa, Islay, 1698–1712'; the writer of 3*l* is 'probably the MacConacher physician who flourished in Argyll *c.* 1560'. Facsimiles of twelve pages in N.L.S., MS. 14901 show the hands: ff. 1, 57v, 66v, hand 1; f. 68, hand 2; ff. 79v, 119v, 120, hand 3; ff. 80, 105, hand 4; ff. 60v, 67rv, the later hands. More or less elaborate 3-line and 2-line penwork initials, some zoomorphic, for example, f. 34v dragon, f. 35 dog, f. 57v bird. Binding of s. xix labelled on the spine 'ANCIENT MANUSCRIPT': the binder then or earlier cut into the last line of text on many leaves.

Written in Ireland or the Western Highlands of Scotland. In Islay in s. xvi and perhaps still *c.* 1700. 'Edmond Mc Kaey' is on f. 67v below two hardly legible lines, s. xvii (?). Described by Ewen MacLachlan in 1828 in Royal Highland and Agricultural Society, MS. A. i. 19 (50) as 'Mr Thomson's Gaelic Manuscript' (Thomas Thomson, 1768–1852: *DNB*). Belonged to John Archibald Campbell, W.S. (1788–1866): his name inside both covers. 'No 32 (*altered to* 33)', top left inside the front cover, is probably a Campbell number. B. Quaritch, catalogue 196 (May 1863), no. 3733, at £25: bought then by Lord Crawford.

Manuscripts in Italian

It. 1–4, 43 are foundation books from the Crawford library. It. 49 was acquired in 1907, It. 51 in 1911, and It. 53 in 1923.

It. 1. *Petrarch, Rime; Dante, Canzoni* s. xiv²

1. ff. 2v–148 Petrarch, Rime. 2. ff. 149–74 Dante, Canzoni. ff. ii + 175 + ii, together with unnumbered modern paper leaves inserted after ff. 2, 104, 148. Parchment of good quality. 240 × 165 mm. Written space 142 mm high. 29 long lines. Collation: 1^{2} $2–13^{8}$ 14^{6} (ff. 99–104) $15–19^{8}$ 20^{4} (ff. 145–8) $21–23^{8}$ 24^{4} wants 4, blank. Catchwords centred. Historiated *U, I, C* (ff. 3, 105, 149). Elaborate continuous borders on these three rectos include a lady in each outer border and the arms of Strozzi in the lower borders on ff. 3, 105.

Written in Florence (presumably), by a scribe Paul, working for Lorenzo di Carlo Strozzi (†1383), according to the colophon in the main hand on f. 174: Gratissimi spetiosique huius voluminis adepto fine. laus sit et gloria deo. qui Laurentio karoli di strozis qui ipsum fieri fecit. Pauloque scriptori eiusdem. felicem tribuat uitam per tempora longiora. Amen. Belonged in or before 1854 to T. O. Weigel of Leipzig (cf. *Hand-list*: his initials are on the binding) and later to Libri: Libri sale 28 March 1859, lot 784 to Quaritch for Lord Crawford (£250: Barker, pp. 175–6).

1. Fully described by N. Mann in *Italia medioevale e umanistica*, xviii (1975), 343–4.

2. No. 179 in D. de Robertis, 'Censimento dei mss. di Rime di Dante', *Studi danteschi*, xxxvii (1960). Fifteen canzoni: in the edition by M. Barbi (1921), nos. CIII, LXXIX, LXXXI, LXXXII, XC, XCI, omitting lines 81–96, CI, CII, C, LXVII, LXXXIII (lines 77–95 follow lines 58–76), L, CIV, CVI, lines 1–147, CXVI.

ff. 1–2ᵛ are blank, except for fourteen lines in red on f. 2ᵛ, Prima uedi . . . esser lettore': in line 8 a dozen letters have been altered or erased and written over so that what was 'a[. . . . .]' is now 'atiro Strozi'. ff. 174ᵛ–175ᵛ are blank.

It. 2. *Dante, Divina Commedia; etc.* s. xv^2

1. Inferno (ff. 2–36), Purgatorio (ff. 38–73ᵛ), and Paradiso (ff. 75–100ᵛ). 2. Poems on ff. 1ʳᵛ, 36ᵛ–37ᵛ, 74ᵛ, 111–113ᵛ. ff. v + 113 + iv. Paper. ff. i, 118 are parchment flyleaves conjoint with the pastedowns. 280 × 210 mm. Written space 212 mm high. 2 cols. 32–6 lines. Frame ruling: the scribe usually fitted in one or two more lines in the second column than in the first. Collation: $1\text{–}6^{10}$ 7^8 $8\text{–}11^{10}$ 12^6 wants 6 (ff. 109–13). Narrow strips of parchment between and in the middle of quires. Catchwords centred. Italian binding, s. xvi: brown leather over wooden boards bevelled on the inside: small metal bosses and centrepiece: two clasps from back to front.

Book-plate of Tolomei Gucci, s. xviii. '41' on a label at the foot of the spine. S. Kirkup sale at Sotheby's, 6 Dec. 1871, lot 1176.

See K. Speight in *BJRL* xliv (1961), 176–7.

2. Pieces in terza rima, except (*e*).

(*a–c*) Fifty, sixty-four, and twenty stanzas in front of Inferno, Purgatorio, and Paradiso respectively: f. 1ʳᵛ Uoi che siete del uerace lume . . . per uirtu diuino. Nel mezo del camin di nostra uita; ff. 36ᵛ–37ᵛ Pero che sia piu frutto et piu diletto . . . suo simperende. Fortificando la cristiana fede (Carboni, no. 2951: Bosone da Gubbio); f. 74ᵛ (74ʳ is blank) Ora soni a mo . . . pero che piu dimori. Presso alla scala per la qual si monta.

(*d*) ff. 111–112ᵛ Fifty-one, nineteen, ten, and four stanzas on respectively the Creed, the Ten Commandments and seven deadly sins, the Lord's Prayer, and Salve Regina: '[I] scrissi gia damor piu volte rime . . . con digiuno; [D]ieci da dio abbiamo i commandamenti . . . ; [O] padre nostro che nel cielo stai . . . ; [S]alue Regina vergine maria . . . (Carboni, nos. 1688–9, 3386; Dante).

(*e*) f. 113ʳᵛ Nineteen 8-line stanzas, 'Fattor del cielo . . . piu tosto riposare (*ending imperfectly* ?).

It. 3. *Guido da Pisa, Ord. Carm., Istorie antiche* 1472 (?)

ff. i + 96. Paper. Contemporary foliation. 292 × 217 mm. Written space 202 × 127 mm. 40–4 long lines. Frame ruling. Collation: 1–8[12]. Catchwords centred. Strips of parchment wrap quires and lie in quire centres as strengthening. Cursiva. Contemporary binding of thin wooden boards, quarter-covered with leather stained pink: rebacked: three bands: two strap-and-pin fastenings, front to back, missing.

The scribe headed a summary of the four parts on f. 94v, 'Questo sono le concordanze dal quante ystorie antiche conposte e compilate per frate Guidoni da pisa . . . Escritte per me Gherardo di Giouanni Vanucci da Pisa habitante al presente in Vinegia a di vii dottobre mccccxi', but the hand looks later and the memorandum in a rough hand at the foot of f. iv '1472 e di 29 di luglio libro fato' may give the date of completion, or possibly the date of binding. 'Questo libro e di filippo degli alberti di firenze', f. i, s. xv/xvi. 'Questo libro E di 'lorenzo' strozi', f. iv, s. xv ex.: 'lorenzo' is over erasure of another name.

Preface, ff. 1–2, 'Tuti li homini segondo che scriue Aristotile . . . ', and four parts, the first beginning (f. 4) 'De nomi de Ytalia e del suo sito e delle suoe conditioni. Italia secondo che dice e scriue ouidio': pt. 2, f. 30; 3, f. 41; 4, f. 57. Printed as *Fiori di Italia*, Bologna 1824; pt. 4 also by A. Marenduzzo, *I fatti d'Enea*, Biblioteca di classici italiani annotati, i, 1906. Chapters are not numbered in the text, except at first, where the numbers were added later, but are numbered 54, 32, 36, and 53 in the table of chapters preceding each book. ff. 3v, 29v, 95–96v were left blank.

It.4. *J. Climacus, Scala Paradisi* s. xv in.

1. ff. 1–141v St John Climacus, Scala Paradisi, translated from Latin. 2. ff. 141v–145 Life of John Climacus by Daniel, monk 'de raithu'. 3. ff. 145–6 Letter of John, abbot 'di raithu' and reply of John Climacus. ff. i + 146 + i. 272 × 195 mm. Written space 168 × 130 mm. 35 long lines. Collation: 1–14[10] 15[10] wants 7–10, perhaps blank. Quires numbered in the usual late medieval way. Catchwords centred on quires 1–4; then to right of centre. Some fading of writing on flesh sides. Historiated initials—the author writing—ff. 1, 134v; others gay with gold and colours. A striking picture of a town full of people and the thirty steps to Paradise which fills three margins of f. 2 is in the style of Cristoforo Cortese of Venice, for whom cf. I. Toesca in *Scriptorium*, i (1946–7), 73–4 and *Paragone* iii (1952), Arte 29, pp. 51–3 and pl. 21 (reduced[1] facsimile of f. 2). Binding of wooden boards covered with cuir-bouilli, s. xvi (?): the floral pattern has 'ihs' as a centrepiece within a double circle 110 mm in diameter and 'ave maria gratia plena' round it in the space between the circles: five bands: twenty-three out of twenty-four brass knobs remain on the edges of the boards: four brass bosses on each cover: rebacked.

Written in the Veneto (?). '370' in pencil inside the cover.

[1] Information from Dr J. J. G. Alexander.

1. Printed often: Goff, J. 308-11. 1-3. Edn., Bologna 1875, pp. 19-515; 3-14; 14-19. 1 begins like edn. with a prologue referring to John Climacus, a table of the thirty steps, and 'un altro prologo' in which the translator refers to the difficulty of rendering Latin in the vulgar tongue. The manuscript differs from edn. 1875 and edn. 1478 by having the word 'Glosa' in red in front of some short passages which in edn. 1875 are sometimes printed in footnotes, for example on p. 25, but more often appear in the text without any indication of what they are, as, for example *andando sempre a un modo* (p. 32/3 up), where It. 4 has 'Glosa. andando sempre a uno modo'. The glosses are referred to in the second prologue. At the end of the thirtieth step It. 4 has 'Salite sorelle' (f. 134) instead of the *Salite frati* of edn. 1875. The 'Sermone . . . al pastore' follows on f. 134^{v}, as in edn. 1875, p. 491. 'Orate pro scriptore', f. 146. f. 146^{v} blank.

It. 43. *Description of Venice (in Italian verse)* 1464

(f. 3) Qui comenzia el sommo de la chondicione. e stato. E prencipio. della cita di uenecia. e del suo teritorio conposto [. . .]. ff. i + 28. Paper. 315 × 225 mm. Written space 240 mm high. 2 cols. 50-6 lines. Frame ruling. Collation: 1^{2} $2\text{-}3^{10}$ 4^{6} (6 pasted down). Written in current hybrida: for the scribe see below.

Written in Venice, presumably. Howell Wills sale at Sotheby's, 11 July 1894, lot 1878, to Lord Crawford, for 11*s.* (?): the Wills label, marked ab/I/154, is inside the cover, top left.

(f. 2) Table of sixteen chapters. (f. 2^{v}) Prose preface, 'Auendo io per longo tenpo . . . chonposto `per sier andrea uituri . . . nicholo abitador dela contrada de sancta agniexe sumareto de le cose partichulat in ditto libro scrito. Et conposto neli anni del nostro signior mis*er* yhesu cristo 1442 adi xx de mazio in la zita (?) de ueniexia´'. (ff. 3-25) Qui comenzia . . . conposto [. . .]. Di tuta italia lombardia e toscana . . . regniano in paze senza altra ranchura amen. (f. 25) Io `andrea vituri´ fu fatore di questi uersi. e di questo tentato . . . (*21 lines of verse*) . . . Scrito per mi andrea uituri 1464 copiaui et fini ad' 17 f[. .]. ff. 1^{rv}, 25^{v}-28^{v} blank.

The addition to the preface on f. 2^{v} is partly over erasure and about six words have been erased from the heading on f. 3 and two words where the author gave his name on f. 25. The scribe Vituri has substituted his own name on ff. 2^{v}, 25.

The crossed-arrows watermark has the proportions of Briquet, no. 6272 (Treviso 1464), but is not quite the same.

It. 49. (R. 21097.) *Dante, Divina Commedia; etc. (in Italian and Latin)* 1416, 1426, s. xv^{1}

1. ff. 1-174 Dante, Divina Commedia. 2-7. ff. 174^{v}-260 Theological and other texts in Latin and Italian. ff. i + 260 + i. Paper, except the flyleaves. 282 × 220 mm. Written space of art. 1 *c.*178 mm high; of arts. 2-7 varying from *c.*180 to *c.*228 mm in height and from *c.*140 to *c.*150 mm in width. Long lines, 41-5 in art. 1 and 33-51 in arts. 2-7. Frame ruling with hard point and (from f. 78) pencil: the first line of writing is above the top frame line. Collation: $1\text{-}4^{16}$ 5^{18} $6\text{-}9^{16}$ 10^{12} 11^{10} 12^{10} wants 9, 10, probably blank after f. 176 13^{8} wants 1, perhaps blank, 14^{16} 15^{18} wants 18, probably blank, after f. 226 16^{10} $17\text{-}18^{12}$. Rotonda and (art. 4, from f. 206^{v}) current hybrida. All written by the scribe

Landi (see below), except ff. 115–139/4 up, 206v–226v, and 249–60. In the prose pieces Landi places a hyphen both at the beginning and at the end of a line. Catchwords centred. Spaces for initials not filled. Medieval Italian binding of wooden boards covered with stamped brown leather: rebacked: two clasps from front to back missing: five bosses on each cover.

Written in Italy, mostly by a scribe who finished art. 1 on 28 June 1416 and art. 6*a* on 23 December 1426 at Volterra, and gives his name in both his colophons: 'Scripta fuit per me bartolomeum landi de landis de prato notarium', f. 174; 'Bartholomeus olim landi de landis de prato notarius', f. 245v. '340' or 'z 40' at the foot of f. 1, s. xviii. The late-nineteenth-century Dante scholar G. L. Passerini signed a note on f. iv. Given by Mrs Rylands, 14 Dec. 1907.

Described by A. Cassio in *The Antiquary*, n.s. vi (1910), 209–13, by K. Speight in *BJRL* xliv (1961), 177–8, and by N. Mann in *Italia medioevale e umanistica*, xviii (1975), 344–5.

1. The scribe began Purgatorio and Paradiso on new leaves (54, 113: 53v, 112v are blank). Many scholia added in the wide margins in Latin and a few in Italian.

2, 3 are space fillers in quire 12. 2, f. 174v Nescio qua tenui sacrum meo carmine dantem . . . laudibus Euo: 26 lines of verse, Walther, no. 11737.

3. ff. 174v–176v Augustinus. Epistolam fili Petre tue caritatis accepi . . . actio percipitur: two extracts from Pseudo-Augustine, De fide ad Petrum (*PL* xl. 753–755/20 up, 767/19–768/40).

4 (quires 13–15). ff. 177–226v Summum bonum deus est . . . letificando includit. Isidore, Sententiae. *PL* lxxxiii. 537–738. Bk. 2, f. 189; 3, f. 203. f. 202v blank.

5 (quire 16). (*a*) ff. 227–30 Prouerbiorum. Ne delecteris semitis impiorum . . . Sapiens in populo hereditabit honorem. Sayings from Proverbs and Ecclesiastes set out one to a line. (*b*) ff. 230–3 Incipit viridarium Consolationis. Quoniam vt Petrus apostolus ait . . . mentem subiugat. Part 1 of the Viridarium of Jacobus de Benevento, O.P. This copy listed in *SOPMA*, no. 2052: cf. Bloomfield, no. 5058. (*c*) ff. 233v–235 Parliamento facto tra Scipione ducha de Romani e Anibale ducha de Cartaginesi. Volendo parliamentare in sieme Scipione e Anibale . . . Segiera per fatale dispositione . . . ai potuta patire. (*d*) f. 235rv Oratione di Quinto fabio massimo. Mandata a lutio emilio paulo electo nuouo consulo in sieme com Marco terenzo varrone contro a Anibale. Si tu auessi lutio emilio . . . e sproueduta e ciecha. (*e*) ff. 235v–236 Canzone di dante aleghieri e parla di firenze. Patria degna di triumphal fama . . . sempre augusto. Carboni, no. 2860 (Fazio de gli Uberti). (*f*) f. 236 Oratio sancti Augustini . . . Domine deus meus sis michi custos peccatori omnibus diebus . . . f. 236v blank.

6 (quire 17). (*a*) ff. 237–245v Cicero, De senectute, translated into Italian. (*b–f*) fill the space on the last four leaves of the quire: (*b*) ff. 245v–246v Ps. Bernard, Epistola ad Raimundum (*PL* clxxxii. 647–51: Ep. 456) translated into Italian; (*c*) ff. 246v–247 Canzone di fazio degluberti. A donna grande possente . . . e Tabernaculo (Carboni, no. 47); (*d*) f. 247 Canzone di Mughione da lucha. Spente la cortesia . . . con ragion difesa; (*e*) f. 247rv Pistola di Senecha a Nerone scritta per Cornelio tacito . . . Questo e lanno quarto decimo Cesare chio fui aggiunto . . . Riposta di Nerone . . . Che io possa rispondere subitamento . . . , and (f. 248v) notes on these two letters (for the Latin see Tacitus, *Annales*, xiv. 52. 2–56); (*f*) f. 248v Canzone di Messer Francesco Petrarca. Io uo pensando . . . mappiglo (Carboni, no. 1786; Mann, loc. cit.). f. 248r was left blank.

7 (quire 18). ff. 249–60 Quoniam pluries rogasti me ut aliquem tractatum scriberem de gratia . . . Circha primum capitulum tria uidenda sunt . . . non autem mali. Explicit 6a

distintio. The preface explains that the six questions on grace in the Prima secundae of St Thomas Aquinas (questions 109-14) are here simplified so that those who are not accustomed to read the questions and articles of the said doctor can more easily understand them: the arrangement is by distinctions, each subdivided into chapters.

Narrow strips of a manuscript on parchment written in a small and faded hand, s. xiii (?), separate quires and lie down the centre of quires of art. 1.

It. 51. (R. 26222.) *Fioretti of St Francis, etc.* s. xv med.

1. pp. 1-117 Fioretti of St Francis. 2. pp. 119-238 Legend of St Clare. ff. i + 69 (paginated 1-138) + i. 288 × 198 mm. Written space 215 × 140 mm. Long lines and (art. 2) 2 cols.: 32-4 lines. Frame ruling. Collation: 1^{12} wants 1, perhaps blank, $2\text{-}5^{12}$ 6^{10}. Current hybrida in a remarkably back-sloping, widely spaced hand: the scribe kept a level line, in spite of the absence of ruling. Spaces for initials not filled.

Written in Italy. Belonged to the Franciscan nuns of Fabriano (between Perugia and Ancona): 'Iste liber est pauperarum sororum de fabriano', p. 1, s. xv. A slip bearing a handwritten bookseller's description of this manuscript is inserted before p. 1: 'No XIX Sancto Francesco, Li Fioretti . . .'. Phillipps MS. 12302, bought by Sir Thomas from Payne and Foss in 1848—'Payne 1848' is on p. 1—and bound for him in 1849: 'Bretherton ligavit 1849' inside the cover. Bought through Quaritch at the sale of Phillipps manuscripts, 24 April 1911, lot 412, for £16: invoice dated 3 May.

1. In 65 numbered[1] chapters, listed on pp. 115-17. For the main divisions of the text, ch. 1-52 'a different version of the usual text', ch. 53-62 (on the Stigmata), ch. 63 (fr. Marinus), ch. 64-5 (Michael Bernardi) see *Hand-list*. Printed in 1476 and later: Goff, F. 284-90. After ch. 65 the scribe wrote on p. 114 'Forniti e li fiorícti del nostro patre Mesere santo Franceschо. Prego qualunqua persona glie legera et dissy alcuno fructo o consolatione auera se dignie dire vna aue maria per la salute de lo scriptore et questo voglio sia lo mio salario. DEO GRATIAS AMEN. p. 118 is blank.

2. Questa e la legenda della deuota vergene sposa de yhesu cristo santa chiara. Capitolo primo. La mirabele donna santa chiara de vertu chiarissima . . . de vita eterna amen Finita e la legenda della vergene gloriosa sposa de yhesu cristo madonna sancta chiara. DEO GRATIAS AMEN. Eleven chapters.

It. 53. (R. 56063.) *Antoninus Florentinus, etc. (partly in Latin)* s. xv med.

1. ff. 1-73v Antoninus Florentinus, O.P., Confessionale. 2 (in Latin). (*a*) ff. 74-8 Six ferial canticles. (*b*) ff. 78-97v Hymns of temporal, sanctoral, and common of saints. (*c*) f. 97v Memoriae of B.V.M. ff. iii + 97 + iii. ff. ii, iii, 96-7 are old parchment endleaves. ff. 2-73 have a contemporary foliation in red 1-72. 245 × 155 mm. Written space 162 × 95 mm. 29 long lines. Ruling with hard point. Double vertical bounders. Collation: 1^{10} + 1 leaf before 1 $2\text{-}7^{10}$ 8^{2} (ff. 72-3) $9\text{-}10^{10}$ 11^{4}. Written in a good set current humanistica. 5-line historiated

[1] The numbers 4 and 7—but not 5—have their present shapes.

gold *O* on f. 2 shows Antoninus: the ground is blue with patches of red and green and patterning of white vine stem.

Written in Italy. A blackened shield at the foot of f. 2. '46' on a label and the book-plate of Vernon, s. xix, inside the cover. Vernon shelfmark and title on f. ii: 'Cabinet 1 c. 47 e (47 e *cancelled*). Antonino. Cat. N° 161'. Sale of Lord Vernon at Sotheby's, 10 June 1918, lot 17. Item 1 in a catalogue of P. J. and A. E. Dobell at £18. 18*s*. Bought from Dobell in 1923, together with MS. Lat. 342, for £21, less a discount of £2. 2*s*.: invoice dated 6 June.

1. Printed often (*GKW* 2152–76). This and many other manuscripts of the Confessionale in Italian, beginning with a text from Boethius, 'Omnis mortalium cura . . .', listed in *SOPMA* i, no. 257. The text begins on f. 2 and is preceded on f. 1rv by a table of chapters with leaf references, but not chapter numbers. 'YH̄S' at the head of f. 2.

2*b*. Ninety-six hymns: (1–28) for the week, Sunday–Saturday; (29–59) Advent–Corpus Christi, including hymns for Chair of Peter and Ave maris stella, Quem terra pontus, and O gloriosa domina for feasts of B.V.M.; (60–79) sanctoral: Anthony of Padua (En gratulemur, Laus regi, Ihesu lux uera, Chori nostri: *RH*, nos. 5408, 10530, 9561, 2791), John Baptist (3), Peter and Paul (3), Chains of Peter, Michael (2), Francis (Proles de celo, In celesti collegio, Plaude turba, Decus morum: *RH*, nos. 15573, 8544, 15058, 4310), Mary Magdalene (Nardi maria), All Saints (2); (80–92) common of saints; (93–4) dedication of church; (95–6) Martin (Rex criste martine, Martine pas (*sic for* par) apostolis).

2*c*. 'Ave regina celorum' at vespers and 'Virgo maria non est tibi similis . . . tui yhesus. FINIS' at matins.

Latin manuscripts

For Lat. 1–447 see above, pp. 393–4.

Lat. 448. (R. 78951.) *Postilla studencium Pragensis super dominicalia ewangelia* s. xv med.

Schneyer, p. 101 (Conrad Waldhausen, O.S.A.). Reduced facsimile of f. 1 as frontispiece of *Prague Essays*, ed. R. W. Seton-Watson, 1949.

ff. 158. Paper and parchment. Written in cursiva of German type. Nearly contemporary binding: title label on front cover. Bought from Gilhofer and Ranschburg, Vienna: invoice dated 15 Dec. 1937.

Lat. 452. (R. 91698.) *Horae B.V.M.* s. xv med.

The capitula at prime, Ego quasi vitis, and at none Que est que progreditur are not preceded by antiphons. Pictures on ff. 15–18 only: they accompany memoriae of Cross, John Baptist, Blaise, and Katherine and appear to be from another book of hours of slightly earlier date.

ff. 172. Written in France. In a Sotheby sale 15 June 1926, lot 291 (£16). Given in 1942.

Lat. 453. (R. 52199.) *Horae B.V.M.* s. xv^2

Use of (Angers). ff. 102. Written in France. Bequeathed by D. Lloyd Roberts in 1921.

Lat. 454. (R. 82918.) *R. de Sancto Victore, In Ionam; Albertinus Causidicus, De doctrina dicendi et tacendi* s. xiii med.

ff. 152. Written in France. 'Iste liber est. Pauperum magistrorum de sorbona. ex leg' M. petri de lemouicis quondam socii domus huius In quo continetur summa albertini 'Item exposicio Ricardi de sancto victore super ionam prophetam que prius fuerat cum abdia et Erat tercius inter Rich'' Pretii xx s' 66us inter morales'. For the donor, †1304, see L. Delisle, *Le Cabinet des Manuscrits de la Bibliothèque Nationale*, ii. 167–9 and for this book in the Sorbonne catalogue of 1338, ibid. iii. 46: cf. 75, 104. Bought from E. P. Goldschmidt: invoice dated 13 May 1939.

Lat. 458. (R. 79243.) *Speculum mortis maius, etc.* 1458, 1459, 1464

Seven pieces, 1 and 4 De cognoscendo Deum ascribed in a later hand to Bernhardus de Waging, prior of Tegernsee (†1472), 2 De fine religiose perfectionis and 3 De natura et gratia gloria et beatitudine ascribed to Johannes Castellensis, 5 Laudatorium docte ignorancie, and 6, 7, pieces for and against 5, ascribed to Bernhardus de Waging and Vincentius de Aggsbach.

ff. 236. Paper. Written in hybrida, partly at least at Melk, O.S.B., diocese of Passau, 2 'copiatus in mellico, 3 'In castello compilatus mellici copiatus'. 'Scriptum per cristoferum lieb de ysni Anno domini m^{o} 1458 inchoante', f. 130^{v} after 1. Melk pressmark 'H (in red) 115' on a label on the front cover of the contemporary binding. F 44 in the Melk catalogue of 1483 (T. Gottlieb, *Mittelalterliche Bibliothekskataloge Österreichs*, 1915, p. 240), when there was a 'modus scribendi artificialis notularum' at the beginning[1] and three further pieces at the end. Round stamp 'Bibliothek des Stiftes Melk', f. 236^{v}. Bought from the abbey by E. P. Goldschmidt, probably in the 1930s. Bought from Goldschmidt, together with Lat. 459; invoice dated 14 March 1938. Fully described by Goldschmidt, cat. 47 (1938), item VII.

Lat. 459. (R. 79244.) *Nicholaus de Cusa, De visione Dei; etc.* s. xv^{2}

ff. 105. Paper. Written in hybrida. Melk pressmark 'I (in red) 53' on a label on the front cover of the contemporary binding. Bought from E. P. Goldschmidt at the same time as Lat. 458, q.v. Fully described by Goldschmidt, ibid., no. VI.

Lat. 466. (R. 95248.) *Horae B.V.M.* s. xv in.

Use of (Rome). ff. 144. Written space 35 × 27 mm. Written probably in the southern Low Countries: Donatianus is in red in the calendar. Belonged in s. xvi to 'Ursula Abbtissin Olspergensis' (near Aarau, Switzerland), f. 1, s. xvi. Given by J. D. Hughes: registered in April 1950.

Lat. 467. (R. 95219.) *Bernardus, etc.* s. xv^{1}

St Bernard, Apologia ad Willelmum, (f. 25) De diligendo Deo, (f. 47) Liber de quatuor instinctibus, (f. 76) Richard of St Victor on Ps. 28 (Stegmüller, no. 7326) and (f. 100) an abbreviation of Ludolphus de Saxonia, Vita Christi. ff. 190. Paper and parchment. Written in German cursiva. Belonged in s. xv to the canons regular of St Augustine at Gaesdonck, Westphalia. Sotheby sale, 24 Nov. 1947, lot 68. Bought from Myers and Co.: invoice dated 23 March 1950.

[1] Now Cambridge, Mass., Harvard College, Typ III H.

Lat. 469. (R. 96458.) *Horae B. V.M.* s. xv in.

Use of (Tournai). Hugh and Aicadre are added to the calendar at 30 Sept. and a 'Memoire de saint hue et de saint akaire, Magnifici patres pietatis . . .' (not in *RH*) is on f. ii^v. ff. 189. Panel binding (Annunciation), s. xvi^1. Given by Sir J. J. Conybeare, 13 May 1951.

Lat. 470. (R. 96499.) *Missale 'secundum usum sancte romane ecclesie'* s. xiv/xv

ff. 160. Written in Italy. Given as Lat. 469.

Lat. 471. (R. 96500.) *Cassiodorus, Variae,* (ff. 128–160^v) *De amicitia* s. xiv^1

ff. 160. Written in Italy. Belonged to the Dominican friars of Casali in 1582 (f. 63). Given as MS. Lat. 469.

Lat. 472. (R. 96501.) *Psalterium cum glossa Petri Lombardi* s. xiii^1

ff. 213. Written in Italy. 'Istud Psalterium Glosatum est concessum ad vsum fratri Benedicto ordinis Minorum de Ari*mino*', f. 213^v, s. xiv/xv. Armorial book-plate of Lee. 'J. Lee. Doctors Commons. 28 March 1828', '3/13/6' and 'N° 5315 of Messrs Howell and Stewarts Catalogue' inside the cover. Given as MS. Lat. 469.

Lat. 474. (Cong. Coll. 1). (R. 136854.) *Biblia* s. xiii med.

ff. 420. Line numbering by fives between the columns, ff. 161^v–379. Written in England. At Christ Church, Canterbury, O.S.B., in s. xiv ex., to judge from 'Per Iohannem Wodnysbergh' on f. 297, and in s. xv ex.: cf. Ker, *MLGB*, pp. 37, 241 (Langdon). Three fragments of the mortuary roll of William Molashe, prior of Christ Church, † 19 Feb. 1437–8, have been taken over from the old binding and form ff. iii, iv, 421–3. Bought from the Congregational College, Manchester, in 1976.

Lat. 475. (Cong. Coll. 2). (R. 136854.) *Correctiones Bibliae* (Correctorium D, etc.); *Lucidarium Legendarum* s. xiii/xiv

Correctorium D (Stegmüller, no. 856) is followed on f. 107 by a piece beginning 'Quoniam quedam mencionem faciunt' (cf. Berger, *Quam notitiam*, p. 37) and on f. 121 by 'Correctiones Bibliae' beginning 'Fons ascendebat de terra. heb. habet nubes ascendebat de terra'. The Lucidarium (ff. 162–192^v) is Franciscan and begins 'Utilitatem operis'.

ff. 192. Written in Italy. Belonged in s. xiii/xiv to the Franciscan convent 'de S[. . .]s' (Siena ?), 'quem procurauit frater matheus de buofere . . .'. Bought as Lat. 474.

Lat. 476 (Cong. Coll. 3). (R. 136854.) *Gregorius, Moralia in Job, lib. 17–24* s. xv^2

ff. 136. Contemporary stamped binding. Written at Bethleem, near Louvain, O.S.A., in part by fr. Peter Maes: cf. E. Persoons in *Monasticon Windesheimense*, i (1976), 24, for this and other manuscripts written by Maes. Bought as Lat. 474.

Lat. 477 (Cong. Coll. 4). (R. 136854.) *Cassiodorus, In Psalmos 1–50* s. xv ex.

'In nomine domini et Oswaldi' at the head of f. 1. ff. 193. Paper. German cursiva. Belonged to J. Gurlitt, whom a later hand identifies as the friend and patron of Neander (J. G. Gurlitt, 1754–1827). Bought as Lat. 474.

Lat. 478 (Cong. Coll. 5). (R. 136854.) *Sermones* s. xiii med.

Sermons of Petrus de Remis on the common of saints (Schneyer, *Rep.* iv. 752–61). ff. 12 (81–92 of a larger book). Written probably in the Low Countries. 'Io de louanis presbiterum 1 f' ', f. 12ᵛ. Bought as Lat. 474.

Lat. 479 (Cong. Coll. 6). (R. 136854.) *Pontificale* 1405

ff. 44. The main hand wrote at the end 'Domino francisco Athenarum archipresuli De saraūllo Cenet' diocesis scripsit 1405 Veneciis'. Bought as Lat. 474.

Lat. 480 (Cong. Coll. 7). (R. 136854.) *Breviarium* s. xv in.

ff. 357. Perhaps from the church of Le Château d'Oléron, diocese of Saintes. Its dedication in black and the dedication of the cathedral of Saintes in red, with octave, are in the calendar at 28 July and 26 Aug. Bought as Lat. 474.

Lat. 481 (Cong. Coll. 8). (R. 136854.) *Psalterium, etc.* s. xv in.

Psalms, canticles, and litany are followed by hymns (ff. 27ᵛ–36ᵛ), antiphons, etc. (ff. 36ᵛ–45), and collects for the year. ff. 63. Written in Germany for a Praemonstratensian house under the patronage of St Potentinus, presumably Steinfeld. Bought as Lat. 474.

Lat. 482 (Cong. Coll. 9). (R. 136854.) *Horae B.V.M.* s. xv^2

Use of Rome. A rather bare calendar includes Bavo and Donatian in red (1, 14 Oct.) and Visitation of B.V.M. (2 July). ff. 219. Cursiva approaching *lettre bâtarde*. Seventeen pictures. Written in the southern Low Countries. Bought as Lat. 474.

Lat. 483 (Cong. Coll. 11). (R. 136854.) *Officium mortuorum* s. xiv/xv

(Sarum) use. ff. 69. Written in England. Belonged to Thomas Hylbrond in s. xvi. Bought as Lat. 474.

Lat. 484. (R. 147436.) *Officium mortuorum, cum notis* s. xv med.

ff. 27. Written in Germany. Belonged in s. xvii and s. xviii to the hospital of the Holy Spirit at Horb (Horb am Neckar, 60 km south-west of Stuttgart, founded in 1352). Memoranda of anniversaries observed there in 1615 and 1766–8 include those of Dieterich Guterman, 'Erster Stifter des Spitals', and of Ita, countess of Toggenburg, 'ain stifter des Spitals'. Bought from Professor G. L. Brook in 1980.

Lat. 485. (R. 147437.) *Collectarium ad usum ordinis Carthusiensis* s. xiv[1]

ff. 115. Written in Spain (?). Flex punctuation. Belonged to the charterhouse of Paular, diocese of Segovia, as appears from the obit of John king of Castile (†1390), 'fundator istius domus beate marie de Paulari'. Bought at the same time as Lat. 484.

Lat. 486. (R. 147438.) *Vita, miracula et officium Sanctae Clarae de Cruce* s. xv[2]

Life and miracles (*BHL*, no. 1818) and (ff. 53–8) office of Clare, abbess of Montefalco in the diocese of Spoleto, †1308, canonized in 1881. Twenty-four disordered paper leaves of a larger book: a foliation in red shows the original order, 1, 23–6, 16, 49, 37, 44, 20, 2, 15, 38–43, 53–8. Begins 'Cum sancte recordationis domina Clara'. Written in Italy. Book-plate of Lord Guilford. Phillipps MS. 7514. Sale 9 May 1913, lot 641. Bought at the same time as Lat. 484.

Manuscript in Welsh

Welsh 1. *Gutun Owain, Pedigrees (in Welsh)* 1497 (?)

'An incomplete volume of Welsh pedigrees, largely of Gwynedd, Powys, and the March, written in the paper, as distinct from the parchment, hand of Gutun Owain (fl. *c.*1460–*c.*1498), poet, scribe, and genealogist, of Dudleston in the lordship of Oswestry, together with some seventeenth-century additions. Much of the contents of the volume corresponds to Peniarth MS. 129.'[1] ff. vi + 67 + vii. Paper. 200 × 140 mm (f. 50). Written space *c.*170 × 100 mm. *c.*29 long lines. Frame ruling with hard point. All leaves now probably singletons and all more or less damaged. The script is a current mixture of anglicana and secretary. No ornament. Binding of s. xix.

'oed krist eleni Mcccclxxxxvii o vlynyddoedd (*the age of Christ this year Mccccixxxxvii*)' is in the margin of f. 10 in the main hand: the text here is concerned with pedigrees of 'this age', 'lest the generation of the next age should be ignorant'. 'Peter Davies of Eglwyseagle his book 1730', f. 44v, and the same in Latin, f. 51.[2] 'J. Price Trin. Coll. Oxon.', f. 66. 'Sam. Meyrick 1811', f. 66. S. R. Meyrick sale at Sotheby's, 20 July 1871, lot 1390, together with Welsh 2. Quaritch catalogue 279 (1871), item 417 (£12. 12*s.*). Acquired from Quaritch by Lord Crawford.

(*begins imperfectly*) a Chaswallon llawir i kefnderw . . . For manuscripts by Gutun Owain other than this one see Thomas Roberts in *Bulletin of the Board of Celtic Studies*, xv (1953), 99–109 (in Welsh) and P. C. Bartrum in *Transactions of the Honourable Society of Cymmrodorion* for 1968, pp. 71–2; for this manuscript Bartrum, ibid. for 1976, pp. 111–12.

[1] So the description of the negative photostat of Welsh 1, MS. 11114B, acquired by the National Library of Wales in 1959 (*Handlist of Manuscripts*, iii. 310). I owe my knowledge of the photostat and much help to Mr Daniel Huws.

[2] More probably Eglwyseggl near Wrexham than Eglwyseggl near Llangollen.

NLW, Peniarth 129, of which there is a full description by J. Gwenogvryn Evans in HMC, *Report of Manuscripts in the Welsh language*, is considered to be a copy of Welsh 1, s. xvi.

The order in which the leaves were bound in s. xvi, 1–26, 28, 30, 29, 32–3, 35, 34, 36–7, 27, 38, 41–2, 39, 40, 43–65, 31, 66–7, can be established from the numbers on the page-for-page copy made by Meyrick, now MS. Welsh 2,[1] and from the foliation of s. xvi which can still be seen on many leaves, top right. Illegible numbers in square brackets are derived from Welsh 2. The numbers on ff. 28, 39, 40 are legible in the photostat in NLW.[2]

ff. 1–8 liiii–lxi. Strips of six torn-out leaves are visible after f. 8: there is writing on four of them.
ff. 9–22 lxiiii–lxxvii. Strips of two torn-out leaves show after f. 14.
ff. 23–4, small fragments. [lxxviii], [lxxix]
ff. 25–6 lxxx, lxxxi
f. 27 [cv]
f. 28 lxxx[ii]
f. 29 lxxxiiii
f. 30 lxxxiii
f. 31 [cxxxviii]
ff. 32–3 lxxxv, lxxxvi
f. 34 cii
f. 35 ci
ff. 36–7 ciii, ciiii
f. 38 cvi
ff. 39, 40 [cx], [cxi]
ff. 41–2 cviii, cix
ff. 43–7 cxii–cxvi
ff. 48–54 cxviii–cxxiv
f. 55, a small fragment. [cxxv]
f. 56 cxxvi
ff. 57–8 cx[xviii], c[xxix]
ff. 59–61 cxxx–cxxxii
ff. 62–5 cxxxiiii–cxxxvii
f. 66 cxxxix
f. 67, a small fragment. [cxlii].[3]

The genealogical pieces in Gutun Owain's hand on ff. 56^{v}, 59^{v}, 62–66^{v} were probably copied in Peniarth 129, but are not there now: f. 56^{v}, 'bits of pedigrees'; ff. 59^{v}, 63^{v}–66^{v}, 'Denbighshire pedigrees'; ff. 62–3, 'a tract, headed "Deheubarth" (i. e. S. Wales), on the descendants of the Lord Rhys (Rhys ap Gruffydd, 1132–97: a rather different version of this tract is printed by P. C. Bartrum in *NLWJ* xiv (1965), 97–104)'.

Other pieces not in Peniarth 129 are additions to Welsh 1: ff. 55–6, 'pedigrees added in the hand of Edward ap Roger of Ruabon (ob. 1587), best known for his great collection of

[1] At least 18 of Meyrick's numbers, for example lxxviii, lxxix, must be supposititious. Gaps in the foliation of Welsh 1 and the appearance of stubs led him to assign numbers: see also the next two footnotes.

[2] Welsh 2 and the photostat are of special value, because Welsh 1 is now in a worse state than when they were made: for example, the photostat shows 'Mam' and 'oedd' beginning the last two lines on f. 32, where we now have '[.]am' and '[. . .]d'. Welsh 2 records a few letters on [lxii], [lxiii], [cxlv], and [cxlix], leaves which do not now exist in Welsh 1 or the photostat, and the photostat shows a now non-existent fragmentary leaf conjoint with f. 66 and not, it seems, recorded by Meyrick.

[3] The foliation of Welsh 2 runs liiii–lxxxvi, ci–cxvi, cxviii–cxlix. Ten of these leaves, cvii, cxxvii, cxxxiii, cxl, cxli, cxliii, cxliv, cxlvi–cxlviii, have no text written on them, but only a series of dashes.

pedigrees in Peniarth 128'; f. 56^v, 'part of an elegy in *cywedd* metre (lines 4–6) and an *englyn* (lines 7–8)': 'I think the hand is that of Gutun Owain. But they look like later additions'; f. 60^v, 'pedigrees in the hand of Thomas ap Llewelyn ap Ithel, who signed his name on f. 59^v: for identification of his hand see Bartrum, loc. cit. (1976), pp. 111–12'; f. 66, 'a note about paying for two windows in Ruabon church'. 'The main 17th-century annotator (e.g. ff. 4^v, 8, 8^v) is John Salusbury of Erbistock, Denbighshire (ob. 1677), a good genealogist about whom nothing has been written'.

'The correction in the second line of the recto' of f. 38, 'which I take to be Gutun Owain's, is an interesting one: the title of David ap Ievan is changed from lord abbot of Llanegwestl (Valle Crucis) to lord bishop. He became bishop of St Asaph in 1500.' Peniarth 129, p. 97, follows the correction.[1]

MANSFIELD. QUEEN ELIZABETH'S SCHOOL FOR BOYS

Psalterium, etc.[2] s. xiii in.

1. ff. 1–117^v Psalter, beginning imperfectly at Ps. 9: 4, Quoniam fecisti.

Many leaves removed, some evidently in s. xix or earlier for the sake of their initials: nineteenth-century notes in English on ff. 12, 15, 27, 39, 50 draw attention to the loss of the leaves on which Pss. 21, 26, 38, 52, 68 began. Other leaves (ff. 73–81, 87–9) have been cut away except for a wide stub on which some writing remains and many (ff. 13, 14, 53, 55, 56, 70–2, 82–6, 90–6) have been slit without damage to the text. The fact that f. 14^v is almost entirely blank after Ps. 25 suggests that principal psalms began on a new leaf.

Signes-de-renvoi are by *a* in red in the text space answering to *b* in red in the margin: see, for example, f. 58^v.

2. ff. 117^v–131 Six ferial canticles, followed by Te deum, Benedicite, Benedictus, Magnificat, Nunc dimittis, Quicumque vult.

3. ff. 131–133^v Litany.

Twenty-three confessors: martine machute lupe siluester hilari marcialis nicholae gregori ambrosi augustine ieronime bricci remigi germane gregori maurici albine benedicte maure georgi egidi maxenti leonardi. Fourteen virgins: maria egiptiaca felicitas perpetua agatha agnes cecilia genouefa radegundis lucia scolastica columba margareta katerina petronilla. Maurice and George are listed both as confessors (!) and martyrs. The prayers at the end are Deus cui omne cor patet (instead of Deus cui proprium est), Fidelium, Actiones nostras, Deus qui nos patrem et matrem (*ending imperfectly* 'claritatis gau').

ff. 133 (but see above) + i. Thick parchment. 245 × 180 mm. Written space 153 × 97 mm. 21 long lines. Collation (uncertain in seven quires): 1 three 2^8 3^8 wants 1, 3, 6 (ff. 12–16) 4^8 5^8 wants 4 after f. 27 6^8 wants 8 after f. 38 7 six (ff. 39–44) 8^8 wants 6 after f. 49 (ff. 45–51) 9 four (ff. 51–5) 10^8 wants 6–8 after f. 60 11^8 wants 1, 2 before f. 61 12^6 (ff. 67–72) 13 five (ff. 73–7) 14 eight (ff. 78–85) 15 six (ff. 86–91) 16^8 17 three (ff. 100–2) 18–20^8 21^8 wants 8 (ff. 127–33). Initials: (i) on now missing leaves; (ii) 4-line, gold on red and

[1] Quotations in these three paragraphs are from letters to me from Mr Daniel Huws.
[2] Mr Michael Brook told me of this manuscript.

blue grounds patterned in white, with heavy projections running the full height of the written space or further: the patterns inside initials are often fairly elaborate and sometimes become zoomorphic drawing (eagle, ff. 4, 45^{v}, 91; dragon, f. 11); (iii) '1-line' outside the written space, as (ii), but only the ground inside an initial is patterned. English binding, s. xviii.

Written in France. Corrections and additional punctuation seem to be in English hands, s. xv.

MARLBOROUGH. VICAR'S LIBRARY[1]

E. 32. *Sermons, etc. (mostly in English)* s. xvi^{1}

Five leaves in front and thirty-four leaves at the back of a copy of the homilies of Gregory on Ezekiel, sine anno et loco (Paris, U. Gering or C. Wolff: Hain 7943 = *7945; Pellechet, *Catalogue général des incunables des bibliothèques publiques de France*, no. 5373), contain mainly holograph sermons—to judge from the cancellations and additions between the lines—and some 80 pages of the Gregory contain extracts from patristic and other authorities.

1. ff. 5–8 (*begins imperfectly*) nowe ys made saluatyon and strenthe . . .

Writing can be seen on four stubs in front of f. 5. The sermon ends on f. 7^{v} where a longer cancelled ending included the words 'holy holy and Ive' which are taken up in an addition on ff. 7^{v}–8 'holy holy and Ive. hoo whatt man art þ^{u} to remember such word*es* . . . bounde vnto the', followed at the foot of f. 8 by a signe-de-renvoi to a now missing continuation.

2. ff. 8^{v}, 10^{rv} Notes from sermons in Latin, except one note on f. 10^{v}.

In green ink. Beginnings are: 'Dionysius. Alii secundum suam voluntatem . . .'; 'In dominica 3 post pascha sermone 4 Hoc inter Iustos discat ac impios . . .'; 'Item in eadem sermone. Sed iniusti qui sunt filii seculi huius . . .'.

3. ff. 11–47 Seven sermons: (*a*) ff. 11–16^{v} `12 post trinitatem' Marke vii$^{c}$. adducunt ei surdum et mutum . . . They browght vnto hym one that was dyffe and dome . . . (*b*) ff. 16$^{v}$–21$^{v}$ `14 post trinitatem' Agaynst ypoccrisye and soo howe to obey god . . . (*c*) ff. 22–5 16 post trinitatis festum Ephes iii^{c} patiens yn aduersyty. Huius rei gratia flecto genua mea . . . For þ^{is} cause do I bowe my knes . . . (*d*) ff. 25–31^{v} Howe man ys browght to grace and soo to trewe penans by the mercy and Iustyce of god . . . (*e*) ff. 31^{v}–35^{v} 23 post trinitatem S. m^{t} 22 c. S. marke 12 c. S. Luc' 20 c. cuius est hec imago When Iesus hade sayde þ^{t} he was kynge of þ^{e} Iuyse: then þ^{e} pharyses . . . (*f*) ff. 36–41^{v} Quotquot autem receperunt eum dedit eis potestatem filios dei fieri . . . As many as haue receuyde hym: to them he hathe geuyn . . . (*g*) ff. 44–7 Quare non in vulua mortuus sum . . . O that I hade not dyed in þ^{e} wombe . . . (*ends imperfectly: f. 47, partly torn away, is blank on the verso*).

[1] Housed in Marlborough College.

(*c*). The words 'to be but titivilitium þ^{t} is nothinge' in the text on f. 23 were enlarged upon in a note at the foot of the page: 'titiuilitium þ^{t} is no more þ^{an} the blossom of a thistle þ^{t} fleith w^{t} þ^{e} wind and is nothinge weighty'. (*d*). Writing can be seen on the stub after f. 26, but the text seems to run on from f. 26^{v} to f. 28. The space left blank on f. 35^{v} after (*e*) includes among other notes 'the 9 orders of angels I haue writen in St Austen 5 boke' and 'I haue also writin Beniamin and Erod in paper'. (*f*) includes on f. 41 a lively translation of the tale of the three sons, each of whom claims to be his father's heir and is told to shoot his corpse: cf. F. C. Tubach, *Index exemplorum*, 1969, no. 1272.

4. The lower margins of all pages of the Gregory from c1 to h8 and of a few pages outside these limits are filled with writing in the hand of arts. 1–3, all of it in English, except on g2^{v}–3^{v} and g6^{v}–h8. It consists mostly of extracts from patristic and other authors whose names are given in headings in green ink.

'S. thomas wyth the golden chayne' (c2: Aquinas, Catena aurea) and 'Guil' parisiensis in De opere quadrage(simali) sermone 87' (g3^{v}: the lenten sermons of William of Auvergne) seem to be the latest works excerpted. The Fathers include 'Leo papa in sermone de ieiunio' (g1) and Theophylact (e8^{v}).

ff. 39, foliated in modern pencil to allow for missing leaves: 5–8, 10 in front; 11–26, 28–41, 44–7 at the back. 200 × 130 mm. Written space *c.*170 × 115 mm. *c.*32 long lines. No ruling. Collation: 1^{8} wants 1–4 + 1 leaf after 8 (ff. 5–8, 10) 2–3^{8} 4^{8} 1 cancelled (ff. 28–34) 5^{8} wants 8 (ff. 35–41) 6 four (ff. 44–7). All by one hand, a current secretary in which the anglicana forms of *a, e, w* are used throughout. No coloured initials, but the beginning of a new sermon is preceded by a handsome horizontal band of green in which is a narrow bar of black with a smaller and larger helix wound on it.

Bound with a printed book in Oxford about or perhaps a little before 1570 (Ker's centre-piece vii and ornament 28: Ker, *Pastedowns*, no. 1595 and cf. pp. 216, 222): the scribe of ff. 5–47 wrote on the pastedown in front 'nother masse nother holy trinity in þe holl' byble'.[1] Part of the library given to the Mayor and Corporation of Marlborough by William White in 1678 for the use of successive vicars of St Mary's, Marlborough: see *Parochial Libraries of the Church of England*, ed. N. R. Ker, 1959, p. 89.

MINEHEAD. PARISH CHURCH OF ST MICHAEL

Missale — s. xiv/xv

1. ff. 1–6^{v} Calendar in red and black.

Sarum use. Anne and All Souls in red (26 July, 2 Nov.). Swithun in black, 2 July, and (translation of Swithun) 15 July. Richard (of Chichester) in black, 3 April and (translation of Richard) 16 June. No additions: David, Chad, Visitation of B.V.M., Transfiguration, Frideswide, Winefred do not occur. Only Epiphany is graded (principale duplex). 'pape' and the name of St Thomas at 5 Jan. and 29 Dec. are lightly erased, but the 'Translacio sancti Thome episcopi et martiris' in red at 7 July is untouched.

2. ff. 7–8^{v} Omnibus dominicis per annum post capitulum . . .

Salt and water service.

[1] In *Pastedowns* I presumed (wrongly ?) that the pastedowns had been taken over from an earlier binding.

3. ff. 8v–10 Omnibus dominicis aduentus domini ad processionem a' Missus est . . . Quilibet autem . . . (f. 9) set statim post antiph' Missus est. Sacerdos conuersus ad populum in lingua materna dicat Oremus pro ecclesia romana pro papa pro archiepiscopo et specialiter pro episcopo nostro N. et decano uel rectore istius ecclesie. Scilicet in ecclesiis parochialibus (*these four words in red*) et pro terra sancta et pro pace ecclesie et terre et rege et regina et eorum liberis . . . Oracio. Deus qui caritatis dona . . . Oremus. Absolue quesumus domine animas famulorum tuorum . . . et habitu consuetis.

Cf. *Missale Sarum* (Burntisland edn.), cols. 37**–42** (taken from printed Sarum processionals).

4. ff. 10–184v Dominica prima in aduentu domini peracta processione . . . (f. 11) Ad te leuaui . . .

Temporal from Advent to Easter Eve. The secret at the 2nd Sunday after the octave of Epiphany is Ut tibi domine grata. On ff. 50v–51 the office of St Thomas of Canterbury is lightly cancelled.

5. (*a*) f. 184v Oracio sancti Augustini dicenda a sacerdote in missa (*ends imperfectly at the eighth word of the heading*). (*b*) ff. 185–6 Gloria in excelsis deo . . . Credo . . . (*c*) ff. 186–193v Noted prefaces, ending imperfectly in the rubric after the common preface at the words 'Sequatur Sanctus. Item in aliis'. (*d*) ff. 194–203v Canon of mass beginning imperfectly in the prayer *Hanc igitur oblacionem* at the words '(at)que ab eterna dampnacione'. (*e*) ff. 203–205v Iste preces sequentes fiunt quotidie ad missam in ecclesia sar' cum prostracione . . . Ps. Dum uenerunt . . . et cetera more solito.

(*d*). f. 195v on which is the prayer for the dead 'Memento eciam domine . . .' has at the foot 'Orate pro animabus Iohannis Nuborgh. Iohannis Fitziames Alicie vxoris sue. et Magistri Ricardi Fitziames `olim Londoniensis Episcopi´ in the bishop's hand (cf. Bullivant (below), figs. 2 and 6). (*e*). *Missale ad usum Sarum* (Burntisland edn.), cols. 631–4: cf. *Sarum Missal*, p. 209.

6. ff. 206–292v (*begins imperfectly in the versicle* Confitemini—*one leaf missing*) bonus quoniam in seculum misericordia eius . . .

Temporal from Easter Sunday to the 25th Sunday after Trinity.

7. ff. 292v–296v Dedication of church, octave of dedication, and 'In reconsiliacione ecclesie'.

On f. 295 the sequence Quam dilecta (*PL* cxcvi. 1464–8) is squeezed in by a later hand over erasure of a shorter version: here there are twenty-four verses, the initials not filled in colour, against eighteen in the Burntisland edition.

8. ff. 297–394v Sanctoral, Andrew–Linus.

One-leaf gaps after ff. 335 and 387: the offices for John Baptist and All Saints began on the missing leaves. An office for Richard of Chichester at 16 June, but not at 3 April. An office for Swithun at 15 July and a memoria at 2 July. Feast of relics in July, f. 344. Two added notes in the margins: f. 379v 'Sancti thome herfordie episcopi et confessoris (*2 Oct.*) omnia de communi preter or'. Require in fine libri'; f. 380v 'Translacio sancti hugonis episcopi et confessoris (*6 Oct.*) omnia sicut in alio festo preter or'. Require in fine libri': cf. art. 22. The office of Thomas of Canterbury at 7 July (f. 343v) is lightly cancelled.

9. ff. 394v–416 Common of saints.

10. ff. 416–441v Votive masses:[1] (4–6) B.V.M., with long heading 'Sabbato celebratur . . . requieuit et cetera. Ordinacio misse . . .', as in Burntisland edn., cols. 759*, 760*; (1) Holy Trinity; (2) Holy Spirit; (3) Holy Cross; (p. 459) angels; (7) Pro fratribus et sororibus; (11) Pro pace; (15) Pro rege; (16) *Item alie oraciones; (23) Ad inuocandam graciam sancti spiritus; (17) Pro semetipso sacerdote; (18) *Item pro semetipso alia or' non sarum; (34) Ad poscendum donum sancti spiritus; (25) Pro peccatoribus; (31) Pro penitentibus; (33) Pro inspiracione diuine sapiencie; (37) Pro tribulacione cordis; (26) Pro quacumque tribulacione; (39) Pro infirmo; (19) Pro salute amici; (20) *Pro amico; (p. 410, footnote) *Pro infirmo proximo morti; (28) Pro serenitate aeris; (27) Ad pluuiam postulandam; (43) Tempore belli; (35) Pro eo qui in uinculis tenetur; (29) Contra mortalitatem hominum; (42) Pro peste animalium; (30) *Pro iter agentibus; (10) *Pro uniuersali ecclesia; (9) *Pro papa; (12) *Pro episcopo; (14) *Item alie oraciones pro episcopo; (13) *De prelatis et subditis; (21) *Contra temptaciones carnis; (22) *Contra malas cogitaciones; (24) *Pro peticione lacrimarum; (32) *Contra aereas potestates; (36) *Contra inuasores ecclesie; (38) *Pro nauigantibus; (40) *Pro benefactoribus uel salute uiuorum; (41) *Contra aduersantes; (p. 406, footnote) *Contra paganos; *Missa de incarnacione domini nostri ihesu cristi; *Ad memoriam de sanctis katerina margareta et maria magdalena; (8) *Commemoracio generalis de omnibus sanctis.

Agrees exactly in contents and order with All Souls College, Oxford, 302, q.v., and Keble College 58 (Catalogue as Parkes, p. 266).

11. ff. 442–447v Ordo ad facienda sponsalia.

English on ff. 442v, 443. In the rubric on second marriages this copy has 'Morardum doctorem' (*Manuale Sarum*, p. 57/4) and does not mention Haysted or the constitution of John XXII, the words *et translata . . . Haysted* and *et causa discussionis . . . dispensare* (*M.S.*, pp. 57/5–6, 57/6–58/3) being omitted.

12. ff. 447v–450v Ordo ad seruicium peregrinorum faciendum.

Manuale Sarum, pp. 60–3.

13. ff. 450v–453v The same eleven benedictions, sword–eyes, as in *Manuale Sarum*, pp. 63–70.

The last heading is 'Benedictio oculorum magister Willelmus de montibus matricis ecclesie lincolniensis benediccionem oculorum infirmorum quando necessitas inducit et deuocio postulancium et potest fieri in hunc modum'.

[1] For the numbers see below, Oxford, All Souls College, 302. An asterisk shows that only collect, secret, and postcommunion are provided.

14. ff. 453v–456v Ordo ad uisitandum infirmum.

Ends imperfectly 'exoptata remissio'. *Manuale Sarum*, pp. 97–110/10.

15. ff. 457–8 (*begins imperfectly*) (appa)ricionem tuam . . . angustiis amen.

Extreme unction. *Manuale Sarum*, pp. 117/2–118/22.

16. ff. 458–61 Sequatur commendacio animarum . . . R'. Subuenite . . . requiescant. Amen. Statim exeat sacerdos . . . incipiatur missa pro defunctis.

Manuale Sarum, pp. 118–124/33, 125/4–10, 124/34–125/3.

17. ff. 461–6 Sciendum est eciam quod cotidie per aduentum . . . uel aliquod trigintale ad (*sic: no mark of punctuation*) missam pro defunctis officium. Requiem eternam . . .

Mass of the dead, with heading as in Burntisland edition, cols. 859*, 860*. As in *Manuale Sarum*, pp. 145, 150–1, 152, the collects, secrets, and postcommunions Ante diem sepulture, In anniuersario, and In die tricennali are each in a group.

18. ff. 466–470v Special forms of collect, secret, and postcommunion of the mass of the dead for use on seventeen occasions: (*a*) Pro episcopo; (*b*) Pro abbate; (*c*) Pro sacerdote; (*d*) Pro patre et matre; (*e*) Pro parentibus et benefactoribus; (*f*) Pro fratribus et sororibus defunctis; (*g*) Pro amico defuncto; (*h*) Pro defuncto morte preuento; (*i*) Pro masculis familiaribus; (*j*) Pro femina defuncta; (*k*) Pro feminis familiaribus; (*l*) Pro trigintalibus euoluendis; (*m*) Pro benefactoribus nostris; (*n*) Pro quiescentibus in cimiterio; (*o*) Ordo trigintalis quod quidam apostolicus . . . proximiores prime oracioni; (*p*) Pro quibus orare tenetur; (*q*) Oracio generalis pro omnibus defunctis.

(*a–n, q*) are *Sarum Missal*, pp. 434–42, nos. (2–4), (6), (7), (10), (15), (13), (14), (16), (17), (12), (8), (18), (19). (*o*). Ten feasts specified in the heading, the second, Epiphany, under the name Apparicio. No mention of Gregory. The collect begins 'Deus summa spes'. Cf. below, Oxford, Corpus Christi College, 394, art. 13. (*p*) is as Burntisland edn., col. 878*.

19. ff. 470v–472 Item missa generalis . . .

The four sets in *Sarum Missal*, pp. 442–4.

20. ff. 472v–477 Post missam pro defunctis quando corpus adest presens accedant duo clerici . . .

Office of burial. Cf. *Manuale Sarum*, pp. 159–62.

21. ff. 477–8 Istud euangelium compositum fuit per dominum iohannem papam uicesimum secundum apud auionem (*sic*) tercio die . . . In illo tempore Apprehendit pilatus . . . testimonium eius. Dominus uobiscum . . . Domine iesu xpiste qui manus tuas . . .

Cf. *Lyell Cat.*, p. 66, for this catena and its heading.

22 (*added early in another hand*) f. 478 Collects for Thomas of Hereford and Hugh of Lincoln (cf. art. 8): (*a*) Deus qui ecclesiam tuam . . . (*b*) Deus qui beatum hugonem confessorem atque pontificem . . .

f. 478v left blank: see below.

ff. ii + 478 + ii. 210 × 140 mm. Written space 137 × 85 mm. 2 cols. 32 lines and (ff. 185–203v, where the hand is larger) 24 lines. Collation: 1^6 $2\text{–}23^8$ 24 eight (ff. 183–90) 25^6 wants 4 after f. 193 26^8 27^8 wants 3 after f. 205 $28\text{–}42^8$ 43^8 wants 6 after f. 335 $44\text{–}49^8$ 50^8 wants 3 after f. 387 $51\text{–}58^8$ 59^8 wants 1, 2 before f. 457 $60\text{–}61^8$. The hand changes at f. 89 (12^4) and at f. 386 (50^1): the scribe who completed quire 12 and wrote quires 13–49 placed his catchwords unusually high up the margin.

Initials: (i) 5-line, blue or pink, patterned in white, on gold grounds, historiated: ff. 7 (priest and acolyte), 11 (Ad te leuaui: vision of Gregory ?), 45v (Christmas), 54v (Epiphany), 231v (Ascension), 238 (Pentecost), 248v (Trinity), 251 (Corpus Christi), 293 (dedication), 297 (Andrew), 311v (Purification of B.V.M.), 359 (Assumption of B.V.M.), 369v (Nativity of B.V.M.), 377v (Michael), 394v (beginning art. 9): the Te igitur page and three other main pages, Easter, John Baptist, All Saints, are missing; (ii, iii) 2-line and 1-line, blue with red ornament or gold with violet ornament. Capital letters in the ink of the text filled with pale yellow. Borders in gold and colours either all round or on three sides of pages with initials of type (i). On ff. 7–88v blank spaces at line ends are not filled, but from f. 89 where the new scribe begins, larger spaces were filled with blue line fillers by the illuminator and smaller spaces with diagonal strokes (//) by the scribe (for example, f. 92/2). Reduced facsimiles of two pages with borders, ff. 7v, 231v, and of f. 196v, in C. Bullivant's pamphlet, *The Missal of Richard Fitzjames* (Minehead, no date). Binding of s. xx[1] by Gray of Cambridge (cf. Bullivant, p. 14). Secundo folio (f. 8) *cens priuatim*.

Written in England. Belonged to Richard Fitzjames, warden of Merton College, Oxford, 1483–1507, vicar of Minehead 1485–97, bishop of Rochester 1497–1506, bishop of London 1506–22, † 15 Jan. 1522: his request for prayers for his soul and the souls of his grandfather and parents is on f. 195v (see above, art. 4, and Bullivant, p. 9 and fig. 2). 'Missale Reuerendi Patris Richardi Fitziames nuper London' episcopi anno 1506 vsque ad annum 1521 quo obiit et sucessit ei Cutbertus Tonstall in episcopatu', f. 478v (Bullivant, fig. 9). Belonged to George Payne of Sulby, Northants, in s. xviii[2], to Lord Ashburnham (App. xlv: his sale, 1 May 1899, lot 92), to J. M. Falkner (his sale, 12 Dec. 1932, lot 297) and to R. L. Harmsworth (his sale, 29 Nov. 1949, lot 13). Bought then for Minehead Church in memory of Mrs Nellie May Bullivant (Bullivant, p. 13).

MIRFIELD. COMMUNITY OF THE RESURRECTION

1. *Beda, Historia ecclesiastica gentis Anglorum*[1] s. xiv med.

1. . . . (3v/12) Britannia oceani insula . . . (f. 74) intercessionis inueniam. Explicit liber quintus (historie) ecclesiastice gentis anglorum.

Ed. B. Colgrave and R. A. B. Mynors, 1969: this copy not listed. Bk. 2, f. 8v; 3, f. 31; 4, f. 52v; 5, f. 61 (begins imperfectly). A table of chapters before each book. Probably twenty-one leaves are missing, four after f. 3, sixteen (two quires) after f. 60, and one after f. 73, with the text in edn., pp. 16/3–46/11, 384/5–486/22, 562/1 up–568/26. Some leaves are

[1] Deposited in York Minster Library, MS. Add. 299.

damaged and f. 1, containing Bede's preface, is no more than a strip on which are some letters in each of the last twenty-eight lines, recto and verso, the first complete word being 'bonis' and the last 'ad' (edn., pp. 2/11, 6/20): the next leaf, f. 3, begins 'arriane' in ch. 8 of the table of bk. 1 (edn., p. 8). Quire 3 and the last leaf of quire 1 are misbound: see the collation below.

A c-text occurs in that the prayer 'Preterea . . . inueniam' (edn., p. 6/22–9) comes at the end of the whole work, not at the end of the preface, but iv.14 is here, though not a separate chapter from iv.13 (ff. 59v/15–60/42: the word at edn., p. 378/9 is *gracia*). The other readings which distinguish a c-text, set out by Mynors, p. xli, cannot be checked here, as they came on now missing leaves.

Marginalia, s. xv/xvi, suggest perhaps a special interest in St Chad: see, for example, ff. 52v–53v. f. 74v, left blank, contains some difficult memoranda, s. xvi in., including a mention of the cloister and the words 'pro lignis in parlatorio'.

2. f. 75 is part of an antiphonal in an English hand, s. xiv, used in binding. The text is from the office of St Anthony of Padua, 13 June.

8+ long lines and music. The text runs from a little before '[pre]sentabat' in the response Sanctus hic de titulo of the third nocturn to 'cordis organo laudet' in the antiphon at lauds Sono tube timpano (*Haymo*, p. 124).

ff. i + 74 + ii. f. 75 is a medieval binding leaf: see above. 250 × 170 mm. Written space 195 × 130 mm. 42 long lines. Collation: 1^8 wants 3–6 (ff. 1, 3, 4, 2) 2–9^8 (ff. 13–20, 5–12, 21–68) 10^6 wants 6 after f. 73 + 1 leaf after 6. Anglicana formata. The ink is brown, rather than black, as often in English manuscripts of this date. Initials: (i) cut out of ff. 3v, 8v, 31; (ii) 3-line or 4-line, blue with red ornament; (iii) 1-line, blue or red. Binding of s. xix. Secundo folio *arriane*.

Written in England. Belonged perhaps to a monastic house in the diocese of Lichfield: see above.

2. *Miracula B.V.M., Sermones; Exempla*[1] s. xiii²

1 (quires 1, 2). (*a*) ff. 1–21v De fide. Fides est religionis sanctissime fundamentum . . . (*b*) ff. 21v–22 Additions to (*a*) in contemporary hands. (*c*) f. 22v De diuisione articulorum due sunt opiniones. Quidam dicunt quod xiiii quidam quod xii . . . quedam sunt de humanitate quedam. etc.

(*a*). Notes on virtues, etc., each with a heading underlined in red. Authorities are noted in the margins, the Fathers, Seneca, 'Tulius' (often), the gloss ('glo'), Ricardus (f. 15), 'peregrinus sacerdos docet' (f. 16v), Fulgentius (f. 18v), Pelagius (f. 20v), 'Aureolus philosophus' (f. 21v). (*c*). On the articles of the creed. The scribe went only as far as he could in the space he had.

2 (quires 3–5). ff. 23–54v Brief sermons or heads of sermons for the temporal from Ash Wednesday to the first Sunday after Easter.

The three Ash Wednesday sermons are on the texts Nolo mortem peccatoris, Memor esto . . . and Conuertimini ad me . . . and begin respectively 'Hoc uerbum isto tempore in ecclesia

[1] Deposited in York Minster Library, MS. Add. 300.

frequentatum peccatores', 'Sicut ait seneca', and 'Reges terreni uolentes'. Sermons mostly begin at the head of a column. Authorities are noted in the margins.

3 (quire 6). ff. 55–58v De theophilo. qui renunciauit auxilium domine. Erat theophilus cuiusdam ciuitatis ciliciorum . . . et statim disparuit.

Twenty unnumbered miracles of B.V.M., each with a heading in red. The second is 'De quodam clerico debriato et necato liberato per dominam quia sepe dicebat aue' and the third 'De monacho deuoto domine cui in morte apparuit'. The seventeenth, 'De clerico dissoluto qui horas deuote dicebat quod domina de purgatorio traxit', begins 'Prior quidam monasterii sancti saluatoris de papia'. The twentieth is followed by fourteen lines about abbot Elsinus (here called 'Helphinus') and the origin of the feast of the Conception: cf. R. W. Southern in *Mediaeval and Renaissance Studies* iv (1958), 194.

4 (quire 7). (*a*) ff. 59–68 Incipiunt miracula Beate virginis. Inmense pietatis et uenerandi nominis marie genitricis dei miracula recitaturus . . . infundat. Hildefonsus archiepiscopus dulce uolumen . . . presentibus commitans. (*b*) f. 68 Crisostomus de maria. Que est ista que progreditur sicut aurora . . . (*c*) f. 68v Item bernardus (?) in sermone tempus loquendi etc' sileat inquit . . .

(*a*). Preface and miracles in 114 paragraphs, the last beginning 'Petronilla petri apostoli filia'. Apparently the same collection as in Amiens, Lescalopier 7, ff. 61v–66v, which ends imperfectly. (*b, c*) are space-fillers, s. xv.

5 (quire 8). (*a*) ff. 69–74v Incipiunt auctoritates sanctorum de beata virgine. Bernardus In sermone de annunciatione. Marie priuilegium non datur alteri . . . (*b*) ff. 75–76v Sermo de angelis. Numquid nosti ordinem celi . . . Verba ista sicut nostis scripta sunt in iob . . .

(*a*). A collection of patristic extracts, to which the scribe of art. 4*b,c* added a piece from Augustine 'in sermone de assumpcione' on a blank page, f. 71v. (*b*) fills the space at the end of the quire.

6 (quires 9–11). ff. 77–97v 'Unius martiris' Beatus uir qui inuentus est sine macula eccl. 33 . . .

Sermons and heads of sermons in several hands, at first on the common of saints. ff. 90v–94v are in many short paragraphs, each beginning with a text from the Bible. The scribes tend to begin a new sermon at the head of a column, ending the previous sermon abruptly with 'etc'. ff. 94v–97v were added rather later.

7 (quire 12). (*a*) ff. 98–99v 'Cesarius' (*over erasure of a longer title*). Venire ad eremum summa perfectio est . . . uota non susscipi. (*b*) f. 100rv Solinus. Mulier solum animal menstruale est ut ait democrihtus . . . (*c*) f. 101rv Incipit Seneca de paupertate. Honesta inquid epicurus res est paupertas leta . . . insolenciam. (*d*) ff. 101v–103v Incipit Seneca de iiiior uirtutibus. Quatuor uirtutum species . . . puniat ignauiam.

(*b*). Twenty-six short paragraphs on human marvels and strange customs. (*c*). Ed. Haase, iii. 458–61. (*d*). *Clavis*, no. 1080 (Martin of Braga). Ed. C. W. Barlow, 1950. Bloomfield, no. 4457.

8 (quire 13). (*a*) f. 104 (*begins imperfectly*) modis naturales efficiantur . . . De referendariis rubrica. Seruus pro mortuo reputatur . . . et exibitione reorum. (*b*) ff. 105–6 A table of art. 9*a*, 1 De penitentia. Et de memoria mortis . . . 39. De largitate contra auaros. (*c*) f. 106 A table of art. 9*c*. 1. De condicione inferni . . . 11. De hiis que prosunt illis qui sunt in purgatorio. (*d*), added in blank spaces after *a* and *c*, ff. 104^{rv}, 106^{rv} Three sermons 'de consecracione'.

(*a*). A little more than a column from the end of a text in short paragraphs. (*b*) lists and numbers the exempla on each page of art. 9*a*.

9 (quires 14, 15). (*a*) ff. 107–22, 123–125^{v} Fuit quidam nobilis et magnarum opum et maximus impietatis . . . sed quid me dare. (*b*) f. 122^{rv} Tractatus de anthycristo. Ad habendam notitiam eorum que de anticristo . . . ut superius patet et hec sufficiant. (*c*) ff. 126–130^{v} Incipit tractatus de inferno. De inferno agendum est. Et primo ostendemus quod infernus ait. Secundo de hiis . . . et restituendum indulsit.

(*a*). Two hundred and fifty exempla on pages numbered in red at the foot 1–15, 16 and 17, 18–39. Petrus Alphonsus and Petrus Damianus are quoted. On each page the exempla are usually numbered from 1: thus, for example on f. 107^{r} 1–9 and on f. 107^{v} 1–7. On f. 114^{v} where there are two red numbers, 16 and 17, the sixth exemplum begins against 17. f. 112^{v} ('12') was left blank and there are other blank spaces, in two of which the scribe put as much as he had room for of a piece on antichrist, (*b*). (*c*) is on pages numbered from 39 (*sic*) to 48.

10 (quire 16). (*a*) ff. 131–4 Ad detestacionem luxurie. Cum quidam sanctus homo fuisset a sarracenis . . . lapides clamabunt. (*b*) ff. 134^{rv}, 136^{rv} Mundus dicitur quasi vndique motus . . . ignis gehenna enim terra dicitur. (*c*) ff. 135–6 Reolus (?) theofasti composuit de nupciis in quo querit. an uir sapiens ducat uxorem . . . simul sequerentur.

(*a*). Stories against vices, etc., in short paragraphs. (*b*), added in blank spaces, s. xiv, begins as Imago mundi (*PL* clxxxii. 119).

11 (flyleaves). Heads for sermons on the Annunciation of B.V.M. and Christmas Eve (f. 137, s. xiii) and other notes (ff. ii^{rv}, iii^{v}).

ff. iii + 136 + iii. ff. ii, iii, 137–8 are medieval flyleaves: cf. art. 11. 163 × 120 mm. Written space 120 × 80 mm. 2 cols. 44–54 lines. Two vertical bounders on left and one bounder on right of ff. 29–58^{v}, 77–83 and three verticals between columns on these leaves and on ff. 1–20^{v}. Collation: 1^{14} 2^{8} 3^{6} 4^{12} 5^{14} 6^{4} 7^{10} 8^{8} 9^{8} wants 1 before f. 77 10^{6} 11^{8} 12^{6} 13^{4} wants 1 before f. 104 14–15^{12} 16^{6}. Small hands. Initials only on ff. 84–85^{v}: 1-line, red. Binding of s. xix. Secundo folio *Caritas*.

Written in Italy. Five inscriptions, all except (*e*) erased, but (*a*) and (*c*) are partly legible by ultra-violet light and show Dominican ownership in s. xv: (*a*) f. iii Iste liber est fratris philippi [. . .] de ancona ordinis predicatorum; (*b*) f. 1, illegible; (*c*) f. 138, as (*a*); (*d*) f. 138^{v} Iste liber est fratris [. . .]; (*e*) f. 138^{v}, over part of (*d*), Iste liber est ad usum fratris nicol' tholssith (?) de s*anct*ibenito altoris (?).

3. *Graduale* s. xiii ex.

1. ff. 7–215v (*begins imperfectly*) V'. Ostende nobis domine . . . Offer' Ad te domine leuaui . . .

Temporal from Advent. A leaf missing after f. 25v which ends 'Off'. Deus enim firmauit orbem terre' (Christmas): f. 26 begins in the gradual Viderunt omnes at 'salutare dei nostri' (Christmas). Two leaves missing after f. 75v which ends 'misereatur no-' in the versicle Ita oculi nostri (3rd Sunday in Lent: f. 78 begins 'bellans tribulauit me Offerenda. Exaudi deus . . .' (Monday in 3rd week of Lent).[1] Crux fidelis . . . (*RH*, no. 4019) on ff. 131v–134v. Litany, ff. 136v–143: eleven martyrs: (10, 11) thoma petre; twelve confessors: siluester ylari martine augustine ambrosi gregori nicholae Dominice (the *D* stroked in red and a rubric before the name, 'Uox exaltetur et bis dicatur') francisce ieronime benedicte antoni. Thomas and Vincent are added to the confessors; also, erased, Bernard and two others, illegible. Martha, Margaret, and Herena are added to the virgins. No office of Corpus Christi.

'[I]nfixus sum in limo . . .' is an early addition to the office for Ash Wednesday in the lower margins, ff. 42v–43. Many late alterations, s. xvi, xvii. On f. 48v the Latin rubric that the masses on the Friday and Saturday before the first Sunday of Lent are the same is rendered in the margin (s. xvii ?): 'Toda a Missa do sabado [. . .] a da Sexta feria' f. 48 Audiuit'.

2. ff. 215v–218v In die consecrationis et in anniuersario dedicationis ecclesie et per oct'.

3. f. 218v In vigilia sancti andree apostoli.

Heading only. At the foot of the page the catchword of the introit 'Dominus secus'.

ff. 210 + i, foliated 7–75, 78–218, (219). On the first seven leaves (ff. 7–13) the only visible foliation is in modern blue pencil (W. H. Frere's ?). On the next fifteen leaves there are two foliations, 14–28 in blue pencil and 13–24, 26–8 in a hand of s. xvi. From 29 onwards the only foliation is of s. xvi: it predates the loss of leaves after ff. '24' (now 25) and 75. 415 × 300 mm. Written space 310 × 200 mm. 7 long lines and music. Writing is between a pair of ruled lines: two pricks to guide ruling are in the inner margin opposite each line. Collation: 1 four (ff. 7–10) 2^8 3^8 wants 8 after f. 25 4^8 5^8 5 cancelled after f. 37 $6–9^8$ 10^8 wants 4, 5 after f. 75 $11–14^8$ 15^{10} 16^4 (ff. 123–6) $17–24^8$ 25^{10} (ff. 191–200) $26–27^8$ 28^2 (ff. 217–8). *Ad hoc* pencil signatures in quires 7, 15, 17 only: in quires 7 and 17 the first *five* leaves are marked (a–e) and in quire 15 the first *six* (a–f). Catchwords centred. Initials: (i) ff. 21 (Christmas), 27 (Sunday after Christmas), 28v (Epiphany), 100v (Passion Sunday), 143v (Easter), 166 (Ascension), 171 (Pentecost), red or blue, with ornament which is usually of both colours; (ii, iii) blue or red with ornament of the other colour. Binding of wooden boards covered with brown leather bearing a broad crested roll: two clasps, one of them missing, fasten from front to back: five bosses on each cover: twelve small studs on the lower edges, six on each board (one stud now missing).

Written for Dominican use, perhaps in Spain, where it seems to have been at one time. Book-plate of John Waterhouse of Halifax. Bequeathed by his widow in 1916, as appears from a letter from C. E. McDougall-Rawson, dated 16 Oct. 1916: this letter, kept with MS. 3, begins 'Dear Father Longridge, Mrs. Waterhouse had always destined this book for your College at Mirfield and I am therefore sending it on to you . . .'

[1] In this manuscript the words Offerenda and Communicanda are written often in full.

4. *Processionale*[1] s. xiv/xv

1. ff. 3–49v Temporal, Advent–Trinity. Here and in arts. 2–4 there is a complete absence of rubric, save to indicate versicles thirty-three times and psalms twice.

f. 3 (*begins imperfectly* Ecce) dies ueniunt . . . (1st Sunday in Advent).
f. 3v Ecce radix iesse . . . (3rd Sunday in Advent: *PS*, p. 10).
f. 3v Nascetur nobis paruulus . . . (4th Sunday in Advent: *MPE*, p. 137).
f. 4 O uirgo uirginum . . . (Advent).
f. 4v *Sanctificamini filii israel dicit dominus in die enim crastina descendet dominus . . . aufert a nobis. cum gloria patri (vigil of Christmas: *CAO*, no. 7593).
f. 5v Descendit de celis . . . (Christmas: *PS*, p. 12).
f. 6 Te laudant alme rex tellus pontus celi . . . (Christmas: *PS*, p. 13).
f. 6v In principio erat uerbum . . . (Christmas).
f. 7 Hodie cristus . . . (Christmas: *PS*, p. 13).
f. 7v Lapides torrentes . . . V'. Lapidauerunt stephanum . . . (Stephen).
f. 8 *Aue senior stephane aue paradoxe qui inter agmina plebis iudaice . . . (Stephen).
f. 8v Intuens in celum beatus stephanus . . . (Stephen).
f. 9 Apparuit caro suo iohanni . . . V'. Cumque complesset . . . (John).
f. 9v In medio ecclesie . . . induit eum alleluya alleluya. Amen (John).
f. 10 *In medio ecclesie . . . intellectus. V'. Iocunditatem et exultacionem . . . (John: *CAO*, no. 6913).
f. 10v In circuitu tuo . . . V'. Lux perpetua . . . (John: *PS*, p. 163, Common of martyrs).
f. 12 (*begins imperfectly in* Hi empti sunt *at*) primicie deo . . . (John: *PS*, p. 17).
f. 12 *Igitur thomas subiit exilium . . . V'. Misertus enim est deus . . . (Thomas of Canterbury).
f. 12v *O caput preciosum ecclesie anglorum . . . (Thomas of Canterbury).
f. 13 Confirmatum est cor uirginis . . . V'. Domus pudici pectoris . . . (Circumcision).
f. 13v Tria sunt munera preciosa que (no more). (Epiphany: *PS*, p. 23).
f. 15 (*begins imperfectly in* Hodie in iordane *at*) est filius meus . . . V'. Celi aperti sunt . . . (Epiphany).
f. 15 Hodie celesti sponso . . . (Epiphany).
f. 15v Abscondi tamquam aurum . . . V'. Quoniam iniquitatem . . . (Sundays after Epiphany: *PS*, p. 24).
f. 16v *Criste pater misericordiarum qui tempus acceptabile . . . (*CAO*, no. 1784).
f. 17v Alma redemptoris mater . . . (B.V.M.: *PS*, p. 130).
f. 18v Ubi est abell . . . (Septuagesima Sunday: *PS*, p. 24).
f. 19 Speciosa facta est . . . (B.V.M.: *PS*, p. 131).
f. 19v Benedicens ergo deus noe . . . (Sexagesima Sunday: *PS*, p. 25).
f. 19v *Aue uirgo specialis stella maris certa nautis per quam uiget rerum ordo . . . (B.V.M.).
f. 20 Ecce nunc tempus acceptabile . . . (1st Sunday in Lent).
f. 20v Ductus est ihesus in desertum . . . V'. Et cum ieiunasset . . . (1st Sunday in Lent: *PS*, p. 31).
f. 21v *Uere dominus est in loco isto . . . (2nd Sunday in Lent: *CAO*, no. 7842).
f. 21v Igitur ioseph ductus est . . . (3rd Sunday in Lent).
f. 22 *Adduxi uos per desertum . . . (4th Sunday in Lent: *CAO*, no. 6030).
f. 22v In die quando uenerit . . . (3rd Sunday in Lent: *PS*, p. 41).
f. 23v Circumdederunt me . . . (Passion Sunday: *PS*, p. 42).
f. 24 Adiutor et susceptor . . . (Passion Sunday).
f. 24v Ante sex dies solempnitatis pasche . . . (Palm Sunday: *PS*, p. 49).
f. 25 Prima autem azimorum . . . (Palm Sunday: *PS*, p. 48).
f. 26 Dominus ihesus ante sex dies pasche . . . (Palm Sunday: *PS*, p. 52).

[1] The pieces in arts. 1–3 which do not occur as antiphons or responses in the printed Sarum and York processionals (*PS*, *MPE*), or in *Brev. ad usum Sarum*, are marked with an asterisk. Some of them are in *CAO*, as noted. I have supplied occasions, following printed sources, if possible.

f. 26^{v} Occurrunt turbe . . . (Palm Sunday: *PS*, p. 51).
f. 27 Salue quem ihesum testatur . . . (Palm Sunday: *PS*, p. 50).
f. 27 Salue lux mundi rex regum . . . (Palm Sunday: *PS*, p. 51).
f. 27^{v} Salue nostra salus pax uera . . . (Palm Sunday: *PS*, p. 51).
f. 27^{v} *Aue rex noster fili dauid redemptor . . . (Palm Sunday: *PS*, p. 53).
f. 28 *Ceperunt omnes turbe descendencium gaudentes laudare . . . (Palm Sunday: *CAO*, no. 1840).
f. 28^{v} Cum audisset turba . . . (Palm Sunday: *MPE*, p. 149).
f. 29 Gloria laus et honor . . . (Palm Sunday: *PS*, p. 52).
f. 30 Ingrediente domino . . . (Palm Sunday: *PS*, p. 53).
f. 30 Cogitauerunt autem . . . (Palm Sunday: *PS*, p. 52).
f. 31 Mandatum nouum . . . (Cena domini: *PS*, p. 64).
f. 31 *In hoc cognoscent omnes . . . (Cena domini: *CAO*, no. 3239).
f. 31^{v} Diligamus nos inuicem . . . (Cena domini: *PS*, p. 65).
f. 31^{v} *Ubi est caritas et dileccio . . . (Cena domini: *CAO*, no. 5259).
f. 32 Maria ergo unxit . . . (Cena domini: *PS*, p. 65).
f. 32^{v} Postquam surrexit . . . (Cena domini: *PS*, p. 65).
f. 33 *Surgit ihesus a cena et ponit . . .
f. 33 *Misit denique aquam in peluim et cepit lauare . . .
f. 33^{v} *Postquam ergo lauit . . .
f. 33^{v} Vos uocatis me magister . . . (Cena domini: *PS*, p. 65).
f. 34 Domum istam protege domine . . . (Dedication of Church).
f. 34^{v} *Dominus ihesus postquam cenauit . . . in lege domini. Ps. Beati qui scrutantur . . . (Cena domini: *CAO*, no. 2413).
f. 35 Inuentor rutili . . . (Holy Saturday: *PS*, p. 79/1–4).
f. 35^{v} Salue festa dies . . . qua deus infernum . . . (Easter: *PS*, p. 93).
f. 35^{v} Sedit angelus . . . V'. Crucifixum in carne . . . (Easter: *PS*, p. 94).
f. 36^{v} Cristus resurgens ex mortuis . . . (Easter: *PS*, p. 92).
f. 37 Respondens autem angelus dixit mulieribus . . . (Easter).
f. 37 Rex noster in cruce debellans . . . (Easter: *MPE*, p. 180).
f. 38 Surgens ihesus mane . . . (Sundays after Easter).
f. 38 Ego sum alpha . . . V'. Ego sum uestra redempcio . . . (Sundays after Easter: *PS*, p. 103).
f. 39 Saluator mundi salua nos omnes sancta dei genitrix . . . (for Rogationtide in the Holyrood Ordinal: *PS*, p. 136).
f. 40 Salue festa dies . . . qua deus . . . tenet (Ascension: *PS*, p. 122).
f. 40 Non relinquam uos . . . V'. Pacem meam . . . (Friday after Ascension).
f. 40^{v} O rex glorie . . . (Friday after Ascension).
f. 40^{v} Viri galilei . . . V'. Cumque intuerentur . . . (Ascension: *PS*, p. 123).
f. 41^{v} Salue festa dies . . . qua noua de celo . . . humo (Pentecost: *PS*, p. 124).
f. 41^{v} Repleti sunt omnes . . . (Pentecost: *MPE*, p. 187).
f. 42 Ueni sancte spiritus . . . (vigil of Pentecost).
f. 42^{v} Omnis pulcritudo domini . . . V'. Nisi ego abiero . . . (*Brev. ad usum Sar.* has Omnis as a response at Ascension and Si ego non abiero as a response on Friday after Ascension).
f. 43 Aduenit ignis diuinus . . . V'. Inuenit eos . . . (Tuesday after Pentecost: Aduenit is a versicle, *PS*, p. 125).
f. 43^{v} Summe trinitatis . . . V'. Prestet nobis graciam . . . (Trinity: *PS*, p. 125).
f. 44^{v} Honor uirtus . . . V'. Trinitati lux . . . (Trinity: *PS*, p. 126).
f. 45 Te deum patrem ingenitum . . . (Trinity).
f. 45^{v} Benedictus dominus deus israel . . . (Trinity: *MPE*, p. 190).
f. 45^{v} *Salue fes (*ends imperfectly in the second word*). Cf. *RH*, no. 17934 for Trinity.
f. 48 *(*begins imperfectly*) punctum aculeo alleluia. Spiritum.
f. 48 Crux fidelis inter omnes . . . iacula (Saturdays after Trinity: *PS*, p. 130).
f. 48^{v} Gracias tibi deus . . . (Trinity).
f. 48^{v} Crux splendidior cunctis astris . . . (Saturdays after Trinity: *PS*, p. 129).
f. 49^{v} *Benediccio et claritas et sapiencia . . . (Trinity: *CAO*, no. 1710).

2. ff. 49v–81v Sanctoral, Andrew–Katherine.

f. 49v Ambulans ihesus . . . secuti sunt eum. Magnificat (Andrew).
f. 50 O pastor eterne o clemens . . . (Nicholas: *MPE*, p. 206).
f. 50v Biduo uiuens pendebat in cruce . . . (Andrew).
f. 50v Solem iusticie regem paritura . . . V'. Ipsa suo nato nos reddat florida cristo. Stella (Conception of B.V.M.: for response see *PS*, pp. 137, 155).
f. 51 *Generosa uirgo beata barbara . . . (Barbara).
f. 51 *Aue pater wlstane pastor egregie dirige nos in uiam iusticie refoue in loco celestis pascue ut cum sponso cubantis in meridie introduci mereamur in ortum glorie. Amen (Wulfstan).
f. 52 Beata agnes in medio flaminarum . . . (Agnes).
f. 52v Sacram huius diei solempnitatem . . . (Vincent).
f. 53 Stans beata agnes in medio flamine . . . (Agnes).
f. 53v Lumen ad reuelacionem . . . israel. Ps Nunc dimittis . . . pace. Lumen ad reuel' (Purification of B.V.M.: *PS*, p. 143).
f. 54 Aue gracia plena dei genitrix uirgo . . . (Purification: *PS*, p. 143).
f. 54v Adorna thalamum tuum . . . (Purification: *PS*, p. 143).
f. 55 Responsum accepit symeon . . . (Purification: *PS*, p. 143).
f. 55v Hodie beata uirgo puerum ihesum . . . (Purification: *PS*, p. 143).
f. 56 Cum inducerent puerum ihesum . . . (Purification: *MPE*, p. 195).
f. 56v Stirps iesse uirgam . . . spiritus almus. V' Uirgo dei genitrix . . . (Conception of B.V.M.).
f. 57 Xpisti uirgo dilectissima uirtutum operatrix . . . iugiter. V' Quoniam peccatorum mole . . . (Annunciation of B.V.M.: *PS*, pp. 144–5).
f. 58 *Uiribus acceptis oculis resurgit . . . crucifixo alleluya. V' Amor ipsa domo qui uite tempore toto Discurrit.
f. 58v Per tuam crucem salua nos criste saluator . . . reparasti. V' Miser(er)e nostri iesu . . . (*PS*, p. 156, Exaltation of Cross).
f. 59 *Ibant gaudentes a conspectu consilii . . . (Philip and James: *CAO*, no. 6873).
f. 59v Gabriel angelus apparuit . . . (John Baptist).
f. 60 Innuebant patri eius . . . V' Apertum est os . . . (John Baptist).
f. 60v Inter natos mulierum non surrexit . . . V' Fuit homo missus . . . (John Baptist: *PS*, p. 148).
f. 60v Petre amas me tu scis domine . . . V' Symon iohannes diligis me plus hiis tu scis domine quia amo te. Pasce . . . (Peter and Paul: *MPE*, p. 197).
f. 61 Isti sunt due oliue candelabra . . . (John and Paul: *Brev. ad usum Sarum*, iii. 353).
f. 61v *Uenerantes et dignam memoriam beate margarete . . . (Margaret).
f. 62 *Eterni regis inmensam collaudemus pietatem qui marie magdalene . . . (Mary Magdalene).
f. 62v *Sub iugulo mortis stat apostolus ut leo fortis fitque deo carra quasi uictima martir in ara, V' Cumque scriba mas (?) celi subit ense iosyas (James).
f. 63 Ciues apostolorum et domestici dei aduenerunt . . . populum domini. V' Audite preces supplicum . . . hodie. Portantes (James: *PS*, p. 162, Common of apostle).
f. 63v *Inclita stirps iesse uirgam produxit amenam . . . odore. V' Est hec uirga dei mater flos . . . (Anne).
f. 64 *Solem iusticie matrem qui peperit anna . . . ortum. V' Cernere diuinum lumen gaudete fidelis. Hodie (Anne).
f. 64v *[A]d felicis anne festum omnes fluant populi cuius proles effugauit . . . (*RH*, no. 34894: Anne).
f. 65v [C]andida uirginitas . . . (Assumption of B.V.M.: *PS*, p. 155).
f. 66 Felix namque es sacra uirgo maria . . . (Assumption: *PS*, p. 154).
f. 66v *[C]ongaudentes uirtutes angelice matris cristi occurerunt hodie . . . V' Vocem enim eius suauissimum . . . (Assumption).
f. 67 *Ecce adest dies preclarus in quo sancta dei genitrix . . . (Assumption: *CAO*, no. 6572).
f. 67v *Salue festa dies . . . qua mater domini . . . (Assumption).

f. 68 Ascendit cristus super celos et preparauit . . . (Assumption: *MPE*, p. 198).
f. 68v *Sanctus bartholomeus apostolus . . . (Bartholomew).
f. 69 *[U]lnerauerat caritas cristi cor eius . . . uastatores. V' Ascendenti a conualle ploracionis . . . (Augustine: in Bodleian, Rawlinson C. 939, f. 206v, and Lyell 9, f. 75v).
f. 69v *Agmina sacra angelorum letamini pro conciui uestro augustino . . . (Augustine: *CAO*, no. 6033).
f. 70v *Adest dies celebris quo solutus nexu carnis sanctus presul Augustinus . . . (*RH*, no. 22479: Augustine).
f. 71 [I]ohannes baptista arguebat herodem . . . (Decollation of John Baptist: *Brev. ad usum Sarum*, iii. 747).
f. 71 Misit herodes rex manus ac tenuit iohannem et uinxit eum in carcerem quia dicebat ei non licet habere uxorem fratris tui. Magnific (Decollation: cf. *Brev. ad usum Sarum*, iii. 748–9).
f. 72 Beata progenies unde cristus natus est . . . genuit. V' Regali ex progenie maria exora . . . (Nativity of B.V.M.).
f. 72 Solem iusticie regem paritura . . . (Nativity: *PS*, p. 155).
f. 72v Natiuitas tua dei genitrix virgo . . . (Nativity: *PS*, p. 156).
f. 73 Dum sacrum misterium cerneret iohannes . . . (Michael).
f. 73v Celorum candor splenduit nouum sidus emicuit sacer franciscus claruit . . . (*RH*, no. 3589: Francis).
f. 74 Salue festa dies . . . Qua sponso sponsa . . . (Dedication of church: *PS*, p. 134).
f. 74v Quam dilecta tabernacula tua . . . atria domini alleluya. V' Beati qui habitant in illa domo tua (Dedication).
f. 75 O quam metuendus est locus iste . . . (Dedication).
f. 75 Audi domine ympnum et oracionem . . . (1st Sunday after Trinity).
f. 75v *Beata uere mater ecclesia quam sit honor . . . (All Saints: *CAO*, no. 6170).
f. 76v Laudem dicite deo nostro omnes sancti . . . (All Saints: *MPE*, p. 199).
f. 77 Beati estis sancti dei omnes . . . (All Saints).
f. 77v *Sacra letantes solempnia suscipiamus que beatis- (*ends imperfectly*).
f. 80 (*begins imperfectly*) *regis nostri et hominibus offera ei . . . aromata. V' Que in mundo distillauit uere uite balsamum et in celo collocauit uirgo sibi thalamum. Offera. Gloria . . . Offera. (Presentation of B.V.M.)
f. 80v *Eterno regi templum speciale futura virgo maria . . . (Presentation).
f. 81 *Offer nos beata uirgo xpisto regi domino quo oblata es in templo huius festi terminum fac odorem ut nostrorum acceptat libaminum . . . (Presentation).
f. 81v Inclita sancte uirginis katerine solempnia . . . (Katherine: *MPE*, p. 153).

3. ff. 82–83v Common of saints.

f. 82 Miles xpis(ti) gloriose N sanctissime tuo pio interuentu . . . V' Ut celestis regni sedem . . . (Confessor: *PS*, p. 163).
f. 82v Ciues apostolorum et domestici dei . . . (response and versicle for apostles, as on f. 63: *PS*, p. 162).
f. 83 Regnum mundi et omnem ornatum seculi contempsi propter amorem . . . (Virgin: *PS*, p. 164).

4. f. 83v Concede nobis domine quesumus ueniam delictorum . . . V' Adiuuent nos eorum merita . . . (Relics and All Saints: *PS*, pp. 150, 159).

5. ff. 84v–85 Dormiuit habraham cum patribus et plauxerunt . . . ysaac. V' Qui orauit dominum et dedit illi . . .

For Quinquagesima Sunday in Hereford Breviary (*HBS* xxvi), p. 249.

6 (added, s. xv[1]). ff. 85v–86v Exultat infans gaudiis . . . marie Propter archam domini . . . zacharia (*sic*). Regalis stirpis virginem . . .

Visitation of B.V.M.: responses and versicles in *Brev. ad usum Sarum*, iii. 398, 404.

ff. ii + 78 + ii. The modern foliation (i, ii), 3–10, 12, 13, 15–45, 48–77, 80–6 (87–8) is designed to take account of missing leaves in quires 1, 2, 6, 9. 190 × 120 mm. Written space 118 × 77 mm. 7 long lines and music. Collation: 1^8 wants 1, 2 (ff. 3–8) 2^8 wants 3, 6 (ff. 9, 10, 12, 13, 15, 16) $3–5^8$ 6^8 wants 6, 7 (ff. 41–5, 48) 7^8 8^{10} (ff. 57–64, 73–4) + a quire of 6 and a quire of 2 inserted after 8 (ff. 67–70, 71–2) 9^8 wants 4, 5 (ff. 75–7, 80–2) 10^2 (ff. 83–4) 11 two (ff. 85–6). Usual late medieval signatures beginning with (a), b on quires 2, 3: presumably the first quire was either not marked or was marked +: cf. *MMBL* II. viii. Catchwords centred. Red initials. Binding of s. xix.

Written in England, probably in the diocese of Worcester and for use in an Augustinian house which had an office for the Presentation of B.V.M. by *c.* 1400: cf. ff. 51, 69, 70, 80–1. Scribbles of s. xvi include 'F. Dorington' (f. 25), 'John Doryngtone' (f. 28), 'William Yates did write this sentense. William Yates is but a foole' (f. 29v). A number '50' at the head of f. 1, s. xviii (?), and a label marked '2 J (?). 31' at the foot.

5. *Officium mortuorum, etc.* s. xvi in.

1. ff. 1–3v Incipit officium mortuorum. Adiutorium nostrum in nomine domini . . . Homo natus de muliere . . . Suscipiat te sanctus michael . . . Subueniant angeli dei . . . Suscipiat te sanctus petrus apostolus . . . Adiuuet te sanctus paulus . . . Intercedat pro te sanctus iohannes electus dei . . . Oret pro te beatissimus pater noster antoninus qui per singnum crucis cecos inluminauit. Orent pro te omnes sancti et electi appostoli dei . . . Intercedat pro te Sanctus franciscus . . . Intercedant pro te omnes sancti dei . . . Oremus. Inclina domine . . . Deus qui nos patrem et matrem . . . Oratio. Deus uenie largitor . . . Fidelium deus . . . O mater dei memento mei.

A short office of the dead, consisting of one lesson, eight sentences asking for the aid of saints, and four prayers.

2. (*a*) f. 4rv Benedictio agni. Oratio. Yhs. Deus uniuerse carnis qui noe . . . (*b*) ff. 4v–5 Domine sancte pater omnipotens eterne deus benedicere digneris hunc panem . . . (*c*) f. 5 Benedic domine creaturam istam panis . . . (*d*) f. 5rv Benedic domine creaturam istam N ut sit remedium . . . ff. 6–10v blank: 6–9r are ruled.

ff. 10. 200 × 140 mm. Written space 145 × 90 mm. 16 long lines. One quire of ten leaves. 2-line red initials with red ornament. Capital letters in the ink of the text washed with pale yellow and stroked with red. Binding of red morocco, with handsome tooling, s. xvi: an egg-shaped centre has an inscription round it in which 'FRANCISCVS V[. . .]' is legible.

Written in Spain (?). The relevant strip from an English sale catalogue of s. xix is pasted inside the cover. Apparently a gift to Mirfield from Amy S. Robinson, The Old Manor, Ham, Shepton Mallet, whose letter of 3 Feb. 1937 which accompanied 'a nice scrap', presumably this manuscript, is kept with it.

6. *Horae; Preces* s. xv/xvi

1. ff. 1–12^{v} Calendar in red and black.

Entries in red include translation of Nicholas, Anthony of Padua, Visitation of B.V.M. (no octave), Festum niuis, Januarius, Francis, 'Sancti saluatoris', 'Dedicatio apostolorum Petri et Pauli' (9 May, 13 June, 2 July, 5 Aug., 20 Sept., 4 Oct., 9, 16 Nov.).

2. ff. 13–86 Hours of B.V.M. of the use of (Rome).

Advent office, f. 77^{v}. f. 13 is a later supply, s. xvi ?: cf. arts. 9, 10, 12. f. 86^{v} blank.

3. f. 87 (*begins imperfectly*) uirginis intercessione . . .

Mass of B.V.M. beginning in the secret.

4. ff. 87^{v}–92 Deuotissima oratio de domina nostra sancta maria. Oratio. Obsecro te . . .

Masculine forms. Followed by the antiphon 'O uirgo uirginum O uirgo regia sola spes hominum . . .' (*RH*, no. 13920), versicle, response, and prayer 'Deus qui uirginalem aulam . . .'.

5. ff. 92–6 Confexio generalis et oratio. Creator celi et terre deus rex regum dominus dominantium qui ex nihilo me fecisti . . . Masculine forms.

6. ff. 86–97^{v} Seven verses of St Bernard (no heading) and prayer 'Omnipotens sempiterne deus qui ezechie regi . . .'.

7. ff. 97^{v}–98 Oratio quando eleuatur corpus et sanguinem (*sic*) christi. Domine iesu christe fili dei uiui qui hanc sacratissimam carnem . . .

8. ff. 98–99^{v} Beatus gregorius papa ix^{a} missarum sollempnia quodam die celebranti . . . de indulgentia concessit. O domine iesu christe . . .

The Five Oes of St Gregory. The heading conveys an indulgence of 14,000 years.

9. ff. 100–107^{v} Hours of the Cross.

The text on f. 100^{rv} is a later supply, but the leaf itself is conjoint with f. 101. Presumably quire 11 was originally a four, 3, 4 blank: 1 and 4 were removed and the text on 1 was recopied on 3, which was then turned round so that it came before 2.

10. ff. 108–31 Penitential psalms and (f. 120) litany.

f. 108 is a later supply. Four monks and hermits, Benedict, Francis, Dominic, and Anthony. Nine virgins, not Anne: . . . (8, 9) clara elizabeth. The text continues after 'Sed libera nos a malo' as in Oxford, Lady Margaret Hall, Borough 1, q.v.

11. ff. 131–5 Athanasian creed. f. 135^{v} blank.

12. ff. 136–183^{v} Office of the dead.

f. 136 is a later supply. ff. 184–185^{v} blank.

13. ff. 186–197^{v} Passio domini nostri iesu christi. Secundum Ioannem. In illo tempore. Egressus est iesus . . . quia iusta erat monumentum posuerunt iesum.

John 18: 1–19: 42. A 2-line gold initial *P* at *Post hec* (19: 38).

14. ff. 197^{v}–200 Quicumque hanc orationem sequentem omni die dixerit uel secum portauerit. remissionem omnium peccatorum optinebit. et si uis iter facere dicas illam ea die et nullum (*sic*) et nullus scit uirtutem istius orationis nisi solus deus. oratio. Deus omnipotens pater et filius et spiritus sanctus da mihi famulo tuo k. uictoriam contra inimicos . . . et eterna protectio. amen.

See *Lyell Cat.*, p. 373.

15. ff. 200–2 Oratio ualde deuota ad dominum nostrum iesum christum. Iuste iudex iesu christe. rex regum et domine . . . *RH*, no. 9910.

16. ff. 202–3 Domine deus meus qui es uerus omnipotens. dies incipit ab eterminum (*sic*) a mane usque ad sero et a sero usque a(d) mane multa pericula occurrunt ex quo ignoro an moriar uel uiuam cum deo. ut uerus christianus firmiter credo omnes articulos sancte fidei contenti in credo minori . . . animam meam peccatricem Qui uiuis . . . Amen.

17 (added early). f. 203^{rv} Si queris miracula mors herror calamitas . . .

Memoria of Anthony of Padua, *RH*, no. 18886, followed by Ora pro nobis beate antoni . . . Oremus. Ecclesiam tuam deus beati antonii confessoris . . .

ff. ii + 203 + i. 102 × 90 mm. Written space 73 × 53 mm. 15 long lines. Collation: 1^{12} 2^{10} wants 1, supplied (f. 13) 3–8^{10} 9 seven (ff. 83–9) 10^{10} 11^{2} (see above, art. 9) 12^{6} (ff. 102–7) 13^{10} wants 1, supplied (f. 108) 14^{10} 15^{8} (ff. 128–35) 16^{10} wants 1, supplied (f. 136) 17–21^{10} 22^{8}. Initials: (i) missing: see above, art. 1; (ii) at the hours in arts. 2, 9 and beginning art. 13, 5-line or more, blue or red patterned in white on gold grounds decorated in gold and colours and with a floral border in the inner margin: handsome; (iii) 2-line, gold on grounds of red and blue patterned in white; (iv) 1-line, blue with red ornament or gold with violet ornament. Binding half old and half new, the front board perhaps contemporary, thin wood covered with leather bearing a centrepiece and angle-pieces within a border, all gilt, the back cover new; patterned gilt edges: old pastedowns and one old flyleaf, f. i.

Written in Italy. Januarius (art. 1) suggests Naples. A seal (portcullis) on f. i^{v}.

MOUNT ST BERNARD CISTERCIAN ABBEY

1. *Antiphonale Cisterciense, pars hiemalis* s. xiii^{1}

1. ff. 1^{v}–146 (paginated 1–290). Sabbato ante primam dominicam aduentus domini ad Vesperas super psalmos antiphona. Custodit dominus et cetera. Ps. Confiteantur . . . (p. 2) Aspiciens a longe . . .

Temporal to Holy Saturday, followed on p. 288 by the hymn for Palm Sunday, Magnum salutis gaudium. In s. xiii med. thirteen leaves, six bifolia preceded by a singleton (ff. 66–78:

pp. 130–55), were added to quire 7 after the fifth leaf to supply the ferial antiphons, responses, and versicles for Monday to Friday: Priuatis diebus. Secunda feria. Inuit'. Uenite . . . iherusalem. Euouae. This insertion follows the office for Saturday in Septuagesima, p. 129. The stub of an inserted leaf projects after p. 19 and bears traces of writing, but no text is missing at this point. Many alterations were made in s. xviii, some on added slips, for example, after p. 163. f. 1^{r} is a blank unnumbered page.

2. ff. 146–53, 157–221^{v} (paginated 290, 1–15, 22–151). In natali sancti andree. Ad vesperas. R'. (p. 1) Uenite post me . . .

Sanctoral for thirteen feasts, Andrew, Nicholas (cues only), Stephen (p. 22), John Evangelist, Innocents, Agnes, Vincent (cues only), Conversion of Paul, Purification (p. 78), Agatha, Chair of Peter, Benedict, Annunciation (p. 137).

In s. xviii the office for the Conception of B.V.M. was added on three leaves, pp. 16–21.

3. ff. 221^{v}–260^{v} (paginated 151–229) Common of saints.

4. ff. 261–262^{v} (paginated 230–3) Monastic canticles for Christmas (Populus qui ambulat, Letare, Urbs fortitudinis) and for the common of virgins (Audite me diuini fructus, Gaudens gaudebo, Non uocaberis).

Mearns, *Canticles*, pp. 87, 92.

ff. 262 (including insertions), paginated (one unnumbered page) 1–290, 1–233. 425 × 300 mm. Written space 325 × 205 mm. Nine long lines and music or 27 long lines. Collation: 1–24^{10} 25^{10} wants 7–10, probably blank, together with thirteen leaves inserted in quire 7, three leaves inserted after quire 14 and one now missing leaf inserted after quire 1 (see above). Flex punctuation is used only in art. 4. Initials (no gold): (i) a 15-line *A* of *Aspiciens* (art. 1, p. 2), *c.*180 mm high and *c.*140 mm wide at the base, formed of two dragons, one red and white in stripes, the other green on a blue and red ground decorated with foliage among which is a man, a lion (?), a bird, and a stag, and centred below them a human head with foliage coming from the mouth: a monkey sits atop the dragons nursing a human child in swaddling clothes: narrow green border; (ii) 9-line (art. 2, p. 22, Stephen) and 6-line (art. 2, pp. 81, 140, Purification and Annunciation), blue and red on a brown ground, decorated mainly with curled leaf ornament; (iii) 6-line, blue and red with ornament of both colours; (iv) 3-line, blue or red with ornament of the other colour; (v) 1-line, blue or red. Medieval binding of thick wooden boards bevelled on the inside, covered with brown leather, plain except for repetitions of a seven-petalled flower on the front cover: seven bands: five bosses on each cover formerly, but all now missing, were each attached to the wood by four pins: two strap-and-pin fastenings from back cover to front cover and a presumably later central clasp are also missing. Secundo folio (p. 4) *tur. Et* or (p. 2) *Aspiciens.*

Written probably in northern France, for Cistercian use. In use still in s. xviii.

2. *Vita Sancti Bernardi; etc.* s. xii/xiii

This copy described by J. Morson, O.C.R., in *Collectanea Ord. Cist. Ref.*, xvi (1954), 30–4, 214–21, and in *BJRL* xxxvii (1955), 485–8. Facsimile of f. 1, reduced, in *Bernard de Clairvaux* (Comm. d'Hist. O.C.), 1953; of part of f. 1, slightly reduced in *BJRL*, loc. cit. Arts. 1–3 are in this order also in York Minster, XVI. L. 18, written in 1481.

1. ff. 1–110 Incipit prephacio dompni Guillelmi uenerabilis abbatis sancti theoderici in uita sancti bernardi clareuallis abbatis. Scripturus uitam serui tui . . . et tu super omnia deus benedictus in secula amen. Explicit.

The life in five books partly by and partly edited by Geoffrey of Auxerre, with the preface of William of St Thierry. *PL* clxxxv. 225–366. Recension B: cf. J. Morson, 'The life of St Bernard', *Collectanea Ord. Cist. Ref.*, xix (1957), 58. Single leaves are missing after ff. 32, 34. Bk. 2 ('2'), f. 32ᵛ; 3, f. 59ᵛ; 4 ('2'), f. 76; 5 ('3'), f. 98. Books are in unnumbered sections, except the third which is written continuously.

2. ff. 110–116ᵛ Sermo de eodem in anniuersario die depositionis ipsius. Quam dulcis hodie dilectissimi . . . unus est \`super omnia′ deus benedictus in secula amen. Explicit.

PL clxxxv. 573–88: attributed to Geoffrey of Auxerre. Only a corner of f. 115* remains. On f. 112ᵛ line 28 runs 'non uidetis:′ spiritualiter tamen (*sic*) eum qui circa uos': here the scribe left out everything between *spiritualiter* and *Iam eum qui circa vos* in the edition (cols. 576/5 up–582/23).

3. ff. 116ᵛ–123ᵛ Item de eodem. Sermo nouus ex ueteri a sancto hylario arelatensi ępiscopo de beato honorato editus. et detractis uersibus aliquantis ad beati nostri memoriam cum offerre ipse uideretur assumptus. Agnoscite dilectissimi diem publicis fidelium memoriis . . . aliquatenus obtinere mereamur amen.

PL L. 1249–72, adapted, for example by writing 'pater' for *antistes . . . honoratus* in the second sentence.

4. ff. 123ᵛ–125ᵛ In memoria ęterna iustus domini constitutus . . . a uite corruptionibus alienus.

PL clxxxv. 366–8, as a supplement to bk. 5 of art. 1.

5. ff. 125ᵛ–163ᵛ Incipit prephacio dompni bernardi clareuallis abbatis in uita malachie dunensis ępiscopi et apostolice (*sic*) in hybernia legati. Semper quidem opere precium . . . tenuimus presentiam eius. et (*ends imperfectly*).

PL clxxxii. 1073–1114/16 up. Lacks two leaves after f. 126, one leaf after f. 149 and all but a fragment of f. 160*.

6. The pastedown in front is a bifolium of the Tobias of Matthew of Vendôme, s. xiii.

Thirty-three lines, chapter 1, lines 110–42 in *PL* ccv. 937–8, on one of the exposed pages: the other page is blank.

The pastedown at the end has writing on it of s. xvi (?) which I cannot read.

ff. i + 165 + i, foliated i, 1–115, 115*, 116–60, 160*, 161–(4). ff. i, 164 are modern flyleaves. ff. 115*, 160* are small fragments. 265 × 170 mm. Written space 220 × 125 mm. 29 long lines. Collation: $1–3^8$ 4^6 5^8 wants 3 after f. 32 and 6 after f. 34 $6–16^8$ 17^8 wants 4, 5 after f. 126 $18–19^8$ 20^8 wants 5 after f. 149 21^8 22 four (ff. 160*, 161–3). A heavy ugly hand, the same throughout. Punctuation includes the flex. The 16-line picture of St Bernard on f. 1, 93 × 30 mm not counting the frame, is described by Morson in *Collectanea*, pp. 30–2 and in *BJRL*, pp. 485–6. Initials: (i) f. 126, 3–6 line, red or blue patterned in white, with ornament of the other colour; (ii) 2-line, red with green ornament. Medieval binding of thick wooden boards covered with pink-stained leather: rebacked and repaired: two bands: a strap-and-pin fastening from front to back: two bosses at the head and one centred at the foot of the back cover: the same originally on the front cover, but the bosses have been removed. Secundo folio *Bernardus*.

Written probably in the Low Countries. Ashburnham Appendix 232: sale at Sotheby's, 1 May 1899, lot 159. Book-plate of James P. R. Lyell, †1949. 'N° 15' and '£120' on f. i. Bought from Messrs Quaritch in 1951.

NEWCASTLE UPON TYNE. CATHEDRAL

For the parochial library at the church of St Nicholas (which became a cathedral in 1882) see *Parochial Libraries of the Church of England*, ed. N. R. Ker, pp. 91, 110. The collection given by Robert Thomlinson in 1735 and 1745 was transferred to the Public Library in 1885 and the four medieval manuscripts which bear TH numbers were included in the transfer apparently, although there is no evidence that any of them were Thomlinson books and one (TH. 1678) was given to the church in 1660: for these manuscripts see below, Newcastle, Public Library.

Biblia s. xiii med.

A Bible in the usual order and so far as one can now tell, probably a 'normal' Bible.[1] 'Explicit biblia' at the end. The whole of 2 Chronicles, 1 Ezra, Judith, and Catholic Epistles are missing in gaps after pp. 204, 214, and 514, and there are smaller gaps (one or two leaves) after pp. 4, 124, 264, 286, 308, 330, 358, 360, 386, 396, 400, 402, 404, 406, 422, 430, 446, 456, 484, 488, 492, 494, 496, 518.

Thirteen remaining leaves have been damaged by having initials cut out of them, f. 1 and the leaves on which Exodus, Leviticus, 3 Kings, 3 Ezra, Esther, Pss. 1, 68, 97, 109, Ecclesiastes, Wisdom, and Amos begin. Eight prologues remain, all of the common set, Stegmüller, nos. 284, 285, 311, 328, 482, 538, 620, 624. Psalms (pp. 233–64) are numbered in a late medieval hand.

ff. i + 260 + i, paginated on rectos (i, ii), 1–(360), 363–(84), 361–(2), 385–(520), (521–2). 320 × 215 mm. Written space 235 × 135 mm. 2 cols. 58 lines. Collation impracticable, but pp. 1–342 consisted probably of sixteen quires of 12, the missing leaves being 1^{3} after p. 4, $6^{4,5}$ after p. 124, 9^{10-12} after p. 204, seven leaves of quire 10, 11^{1} before p. 215, 12^{8} after p. 250, 13^{4} after p. 264, $14^{4,5}$ after p. 286, $15^{5,6}$ after p. 308, 16^{6} after p. 330. Clear and not too small writing. Initials: (i) of books—the twelve survivors begin Numbers, Deuteronomy, Joshua, Ruth, 2 Kings, 4 Kings (King Ahaziah of Israel falls from his window), 1 Chronicles, Pss. 26, 38, 52, Haggai, John—9-line, patterned blue or red on coloured grounds, historiated; (ii) of prologues—for the eight survivors see above—6-line, as (i), but

[1] See above, Liverpool Cathedral 13.

decorated, not historiated; (iii) of chapters and psalms, other than principal psalms, 2-line, red or blue, with ornament of the other colour; (iv) of verses of psalms, 1-line, red or blue. A little (tarnished) silver is used in the decoration of initials of types (i, ii). Binding of wooden boards, s. xix, with modern chain attached. Secundo folio *et oculi mei.*

Written in France (?). The ex-libris of the Augustinian priory of Hexham, 'Liber sancte Andree de Hexham', is at the foot of f. 1, s. xv in. and, below it, a difficult 9-line note signed by Richard Morton at 'S[. . .]houses', Northumberland, in which the date August 1660 occurs.

NEWCASTLE UPON TYNE. PUBLIC LIBRARY

TH. 1678. *Psalms and Canticles in Latin, with Rolle's translation and commentary in English; etc.* s. xiv²

1. ff. 1–102 Psalms, six OT canticles and Magnificat with Rolle's verse-by-verse translation and his commentary in the original uninterpolated version. Begins imperfectly at Ps. 39: 1, 'michi'. Probably thirteen leaves are missing between this point and the end of Magnificat.

Edited from other manuscripts by H. R. Bramley, *The Psalter . . . by Richard Rolle of Hampole*, 1884. No. 15 of the copies listed by Allen, *Writings*, p. 172. ff. 49a, b lie loose after f. 49: see below. Some leaves have been damaged by damp and exposure.

Begins at edn., p. 146/6. f. 1ᵛ ends 'and þai presse' (Ps. 39: 16, edn. 149/7) and f. 2 begins 'sall noght to keste' (Ps. 40: 9, edn. 152/12). f. 7ᵛ ends 'heritage is' (Ps. 46: 4, edn. 170/23) and f. 8 begins 'telles in toures' (Ps. 47: 11, edn. 173/21). f. 8ᵛ ends 'of þe mane' (Ps. 48: 10, edn. 176/23) and f. 9 begins near edn. 179/21 (Ps. 49: 4). f. 78ᵛ ends 'vsed in thy' (Ps. 118: 27, edn. 414/20) and f. 79 begins 'Iusticia tua' (Ps. 118: 142, edn. 431/last line). f. 85ᵛ ends 'of þe myddis of' (Ps. 135: 11, edn. 457/14) and f. 86 begins 'þe and þou' (Ps. 138: 12, edn. 465/4). f. 95ᵛ ends near edn. 499/20 (canticle Exultavit) and f. 96 begins at edn. 505/31 (canticle Cantemus domino).

2. ff. 102–4 Benedictus dominus . . . plebis sue. Blessed be lord god of israel for he hath viseted and mad þe byeng of his folk. þe holy man zacharie . . . and stedfast of pees in þe wilke we sal rest wᵗouten endynge amen.

A commentary on the canticle Benedictus. Also in Lambeth Palace, 472, art. 6. This copy collated by B. Wallner, *A commentary on the 'Benedictus'*, Lunds Universitets Årskrift, N.F. Avd. 1, Bd. 53, Nr. 1 (1957), with facsimile of part of f. 102.

An extract from *Notes and Queries* (see below) and two leaves containing a modern copy of Rolle's prologue in Bodleian, Laud Misc. 286, f. 1, are attached to f. ii.

ff. ii + 106 + i, foliated (i, ii), 1–49, 49a, 49b, 50–(105), together with fifteen leaves of modern blank paper in place of leaves now lost. 280 × 200 mm. Written space *c.* 215 × 138 mm. 2 cols. 48 lines. Collation: probably 1^{12} wants 1, 3, 10, 12 $2\text{–}7^{12}$ 8^{12} wants 1–5 before f. 79 9^{12} wants 1, 2 before f. 86 10^{12} wants 1–3 before f. 96. Text and commentary are distinguished by the size of the script: the larger is anglicana formata (short *r*) as far as f. 49* and after this mainly textura; the smaller is anglicana. Initials: (i) of psalms, 3-line, blue with red ornament; of psalm-verses, 1-line, blue or red. Line fillers of several patterns in red. Binding of s. xix ex. by Andrews, Newcastle.

Written in England. Found 'in the library of St Nicholas's Church, Newcastle-on-Tyne, in several portions, tumbling about in a drawer among old magazines and Newcastle dirt'. The finder, Rev. J. T. Fowler, described his discovery and his method of cleaning the leaves in *Notes and Queries*, Fifth Series, i (17 Jan. 1874), 41–2. He applied sulphide of ammonium to a now illegible inscription on f. 104^{v} and copied it on f. (105) as 'October the 20th. 1660. The gift of Doctor Thomas Burwell Chancellor of this Diocese'. Presumed to have been transferred to the Public Library in 1885 with the Thomlinson collection to which it now belongs. ff. 49a and 49b, the central bifolium of quire 5, were given by Mr H. H. Peach of Crowbank, Old Knighton, Leicester, in 1934: see his letter to *The Times*, 21 Dec. 1934, p. 13.

TH. 5045 [A]. *Peregrinus de Oppeln, O.P., Sermones de tempore* s. xv in.

(*begins imperfectly*) sed deo. Audiens ananias cecidit . . . visionem tamen (*ends imperfectly*).

All or part of nos. 4–24, 45, 46, 48–50, 52–4 of the series of sixty-four sermons of the temporal, 1st Sunday in Advent to 25th Sunday after Pentecost, by Peregrinus de Oppeln, O.P., †1322 (?), as found in Bodleian MSS. Laud Misc. 400 and Hamilton 36.[1] The remains here run, with gaps, from the 4th Sunday in Advent to Thursday in Holy Week and from the 6th to the 15th Sundays after Pentecost. A quire or more is missing after f. 17, and three leaves have gone after ff. 19 and 21 and single leaves after ff. 5, 7, 8, 16. ff. 1 and 5 are bound back to front. The sermons are numbered.

In s. xix each leaf was mounted separately on a large sheet of paper and forty-three other sheets of paper of the same size were supplied. Twenty-four of them were used for a copy of ff. 1–12 into English and an English translation of the text on these leaves.

ff. iv + 23 + iii and interleaves (see above). 210 × 155 mm. Written space *c.*160 × 100 mm. *c.*40 long lines. Collation: 1^{12} wants 1–3, 9, 12 (ff. 1–7) 2^{12} wants 2, 11 (ff. 8–17) 3^{12} wants 3–5, 8–10 (ff. 18–23). In the first half of each quire the leaves are numbered 1–6. Neatly written in a mainly secretary hand but with anglicana forms of *d, g*, and sometimes *r*. 2-line initials, blue with red ornament. Bound in 1978.

Written in England. Probably once part of TH. 5405 [A], q.v. Kept as part of the Thomlinson collection transferred from the Cathedral in 1885.

TH. 5403 [A]. *Johannes Calderinus, Repertorium utriusque iuris* s. xv med.

Probably less than half the dictionary of Calderinus (printed in 1474: *GKW* 5904), lacking all A–E, all but two leaves of F, all G, H, nearly all Q, all Y, Z, and some leaves elsewhere.

The letter F begins on f. 1, 'Fabricare fabrica tam (?) dicitur de fabricis quam de hospitalibus'. The letter X begins on f. 136^{v} 'Xenon xenodochium locus venerabilis est'. Leaves are frayed at the edges, but the writing is only badly damaged on ff. 1, 2.

[1] The sermons of Peregrinus, De tempore, are set out in Schneyer, *Repertorium*, iv. 548–56. The sixty-four sermons in the two Bodleian manuscripts are nos. 1, 3, 5, 7, 8, 13, 14, 16, 17, 20–7, 29–32, 34, 35, 41, 45, 46, 48, 52, 53, 55, 57, 59, 60, 64, 67, 68, 71, 72, 74, 77, 81–104 in Schneyer's list. The manuscripts differ from the early printed editions, Goff, P. 263–9.

ff. 136. Paper. *c.*400 × 275 mm. Written space *c.*300 × 190 mm. 2 cols. *c.*75 lines. Frame ruling. No collation possible, except on the evidence of the remaining quire numbers: these numbers are XII–XVIII, XXI–XXIII on ff. 7^{v}, 14^{v}, 26^{v}, 37^{v}, 47^{v}, 59^{v}, 76^{v}, 96^{v}, 107^{v}, 115^{v} respectively. A few sheets are still conjoint, for example all but the outside sheet in the 10-leaf quire numbered XVI and the central sheet in the quire after that numbered XXIII (ff. 121–2, where a strengthening strip of parchment lies down the gutter). Written in cursiva. Initials: (i) red and black with red ornament; (ii) 2-line or more, red.

Written in north-west Germany or the Low Countries or perhaps by a scribe from this area in England: a side note on f. 62 is in an English hand, s. xv. A scribble on f. 76, s. xvii: 'm^{r} Pearsonne and Josias basnott persuaded me to my wronge'. Kept as part of the Thomlinson collection transferred from the Cathedral in 1885.

TH. 5405 [A]. *Sermones abbreviati* s. xv in.

Divisions of themes of sermons on the Sunday gospels through the year, beginning in the sermon before that for the 2nd Sunday after Epiphany.

The sermons are numbered (81)–188 and the medieval foliation shows that thirty-seven leaves are missing at the beginning. The last three sermons are for the 25th Sunday after Pentecost, the dedication of a church, and angels. No. 86 begins 'Ascendente ihesu in nauiculam. Nota quod per nauiculam illam crux cristi intelligitur'; no. 179 (23 after Pentecost) 'Magister scimus quia verax es etc. Nota quod hoc nomen magister bene conuenit cristo'; no. 187, 'Fac tibi archam . . . Per archam istam', and no. 188 'Lauda ysa vi. Seraphim stabat super illud'. ff. 1, 2 are badly stained. f. '110'^{v} is blank, except for the catchword 'abiciamus' which suggests that sermons on the epistles followed: cf. Schneyer, pp. 2–10.

ff. x + 67 + lvii. The medieval foliation, partly erased, is (38–47), (49)–60, 62–71, 73–89, 92, 94–110. 215 × 152 mm. Written space *c.*140 × 95 mm. 2 cols. 31–6 lines. Collation: 1^{12} wants 1 and 12 2^{12} 3^{12} wants 1 and 12 4^{12} 5^{12} wants 6, 7, 9 6^{14}. The hand is like that of TH. 5045 [A], but not the same: in addition to the non-secretary forms of *d*, *g*, and *r* which occur here as well as there, *a* is sometimes in two compartments and *e* is often 'reversed'. 2-line initials, blue with red ornament, similar to those in TH. 5045 [A], but the ornament does not extend so far up and down the margins. Bound in 1979.

Written in England. Probably once part of the same manuscript as TH. 5045 [A]. Kept as part of the Thomlinson collection transferred from the Cathedral in 1885.

091. 01173 *Hugo de Novo Castro, O.F.M., De victoria Christi; etc.* 1475, s. xv^{2}

1. ff. 1–67^{v} Pro excitandis cordibus nostris ad deuotam meditacionem passionis dominice multum videtur congruere verbum illud ysaie (*canc.*) 83 ps. Respice in faciem cristi tui. Et videtur nobis ad propositum duobus modis scilicet ad introducendum et prosequendum dominice passionis historiam . . . quippe generaliter dicuntur que lino texuntur. Hec Aug' etc.

A reference to 'Henricus de Hassia in sermone de festo lancee et clauorum' is in the text on f. 58^{v}. ff. 68–72^{v} blank.

2. ff. 73–76v De hora mortis cristi. Cum cristus dominus sit mortuus circa horam terciam post meridiem. Cur et vnde venit in falsam estimacionem multorum et omnium quasi quod sit mortuus in meridie. Respondeo quod . . .

Apparently by a Dominican who quotes among others, Aquinas, Albertus Magnus, Holcot, Thomas Waleys, Lactantius, Michael de Bononia, Leonardus de Utino, Johannes de Essendia, Johannes Scorpe, and refers, f. 76, to the argument in favour of hora sexta being meridies which Master 'Iacobus de Zosato in vniuersitate coloniensi' put forward in a work 'qui habetur in libraria conuentus nostri in gottingen'.

3. ff. 77–127v Incipit tractatus de victoria cristi contra Anticristum Magistri Hugonis de nouo castro Sacre Theologie et Decretorum doctoris parisien'. Sequitur ergo prologus huius libri quem ponit in principio. Non sum propheta n(e)c filius prophete. Amos vii. Humilis ille Amos considerans . . . scire futura dei. Explicit tractatus de victoria cristi contra Anticristum Editus (per) Reuerendum Magistrum Hugonem de Nouo Castro Sacre Theologie ac decretorum doctorem parisien' Anno domini MCCCClxxv.

Two books of 35 and 36 chapters. No doubt copied, together with art. 4, from the edition printed at Nuremberg in 1471 (Goff, H. 502). For the author, *fl.* 1320, see *DNB*.

4. ff. 127v–130 Incipit coniectura Reuerendissimi In cristo patris ac domini domini Nicolai de Cusa Cardinalis tituli sancti petri ad vincula et episcopi parisiensis Necnon doctoris eximii atque illuminatissimi de vltimis diebus mundi. Uniuersus hic mundus . . . sit omnis sapiencia qui est in secula benedictus. Explicit coniectura domini Nicolai de Cusa cardinalis de vltimis diebus.

Follows art. 3 in the Nuremberg edition. In copying the incipit the scribe stumbled over the south German form of Brixen, *prixiensis*.

ff. i + 130 + i. Paper. 214 × 145 mm. Written space 155 × 95 mm. 34–6 long lines. Frame ruling. Collation: $1\text{–}6^{12}$ 7 four (ff. 73–6) $8\text{–}11^{12}$ 12^{6}. Art. 1 in good cursiva. Art. 2 in unusual, very current hybrida. Arts. 3, 4 by one hand in current hybrida. Initials: (i) f. 1, 6-line, red with blue ornament; (ii) 4-line (f. 77) and 2-line, red or blue. Capital letters in the ink of the text touched with red. Binding of s. xix in. Secundo folio *respice quem.*

Written in Germany, perhaps in the Cologne region. Phillipps MS. 749, one of many manuscripts acquired from Leander van Ess in 1823. Phillipps sale, 6 June 1910, lot 448. Bought from Bernard Halliday, Leicester, 16 May 1911.

NEWCASTLE UPON TYNE. UNIVERSITY LIBRARY

1. *'Passionarium'* s. xiii[1]

Arts. 1 and 2 are two series of abbreviated saints' lives (etc.), each beginning at 1 September. The first series is for a full year, the second virtually for four months. Described by B. C. Raw, *Lives of the Saints* (University Library, Newcastle upon Tyne, Publications, no. 2, 1961), who prints the tables of chapters (ff. 1, 120v–121: edn., pp. 1–4, 28–30): reduced facsimile of f. 130v.

1. ff. 1–120v One hundred and twenty-one pieces, preceded by a table numbered i–cx (see below). (1–18: *September*) Giles, Bertin, Adrian 'cum sociis', Gorgonius and Dorotheus, Protus and Jacinth, Maurilius, 'Quomodo signum sancte crucis constantino imperatori innotuit et reuelatio sancte crucis a perside. et exaltatio eius' (title from the table), Cyprian, Eufemia, Lambert, Matthew, Maurice, Tecla, Firminus, Justina and Cyprian, Cosmas and Damian, Michael, Jerome. (19–29: *October*) Remigius, Leodegarius, Faith, 'Argumentum quod dionysius areopagita parisius passus est', Calixt, Luke, Justus, 11,000 Virgins, Crispin and Crispinian, Simon and Jude, Quintin. (30–44: *November*) All Souls, Eustace, Leonard, Quatuor coronati', Theodore, Mennas, Martin, Brice, Machutus, Cecilia, Clement, Katherine, Maximus of Riez, Chrisanth and Darias, Andrew. (45–53: *December*) Eligius, Nicholas, translation of Nicholas, Lucy, Barbara, Thomas the apostle, Anastasia, 'Dormitio sancti Iohannis apostoli et euangeliste', Silvester. (54–9: *January*) Basil, Genovefa, Paul first hermit, Sebastian, Agnes, Vincent. (60, 61: *February*) Agatha, Vedast. (62–8: *March*) Macra, Gregory, Gertrude, Benedict, translation of Benedict, Theodosia, Ambrose. (69–74: *April*) Mary of Egypt, Euphrosina, Macarius, 'Mirabile quoddam de quodam feneratore', beginning 'Traditur a catholicis quod quidam fenerator accesserit ad episcopum tharentinum cupiens insigniri sancta cruce', George, Mark. (75–81: *May*) Philip, James, Invention of Cross, Alexander Eventius and Theodolus, Nereus and Achilleus, Servatius, Petronilla. (82–91: *June*) Marcellinus and Peter, Medard, Primus and Felicianus, Vitalis, Gervase and Protase, invention of Gervase and Protase, John and Paul, 'Conflictus apostolorum contra Simonem magum', Peter, Paul. (92–106: *July*) Processus and Martinianus, Arnulf of Tours, Margaret, Julia, Mary Magdalene, translation of Mary Magdalene, Apollinaris, Christina, James, Christopher, Cucuphat, Seven Sleepers, Pantaleon, Abdon and Sennes, Germanus. (107–21: *August*) 'Qualiter sollempnitas sancti Petri ad vincula sit instituta', Maccabees, Stephen, invention of Stephen, Sixtus, Laurence, Hippolytus, 'Visio Elisabeth de assumptione beate Marie virginis', Agapitus, Arnulf of Soissons, Timothy and Apollinaris, Symphorian, Bartholomew, invention of relics of John Baptist, invention of head of John Baptist.

According to the table, no. xxxvii should be a life of Anianus, but no life is provided and the (added) numbering in the text passes from xxxvi to xxxviii. A reader noted in the margin of f. 31, 'xxxvii sancti aniani deficit'. Elsewhere also table and text go together in their numbering: nine lives, nos. (34) Theodore, (62) Macra, (64) Gertrude, (67) Theodosia, (70) Euphrosina, (71) Macarius, (72) De quodam feneratore, (80) Servatius, and (85) Vitalis are unnumbered later additions to the table and are supernumerary in the text; the lives of Martin and Brice (36, 37) are counted as one number in both table and text, and so also are the lives of Philip and James (75, 76). Evidently the numbers in the text are derived from the table.

2. ff. 121–153v Seventy-four pieces, preceded by a table numbered i–lxxi. All are short, except no. 71. (1–18: *September*) Lupus, Antoninus, Remaclus, Victorinus, Regina, Evurtius, Humbert, Audomarus, Syrus and Eventius, Maximus, Cornelius, Aychadrus, Lucy and Geminianus, Fausta and Evilasius, Alexander bishop and martyr, Florianus and Florentius, Florentius, Emmeram. (19–39: *October*) Bavo, Piaton, 'Duorum Ewaldorum', Sanctinus, Benedicta, Richarius, Gillenus, Gereon, Bruno archbishop of Cologne, Therachius Probus and Andronicus, Vanantius of Tours, Donatian, Basolus, Mummolinus, Gallus, Amatus,

Ethbinus, Severinus, Salvius, Pharo, Foillanus. (40–57: *November*) Benignus, Cesarius, Maturinus, Vigor, Hubert, 'Passio innumerabilium martyrum' (3 Nov.), Adelaida, Columba, Winnoc, Willibrord, Theodore, Cunibert, Livinus, Maxellenis, Mumbolus, Columbanus, Trudo, Peter of Alexandria. (58–69: *December*) Nicetius, Sabinus, Eucharius, Valerius and Maternus, Leochadia, Eulalia, Fuscianus, Victoricus and Gentianus, Waleric, Judoc, Autbertus, Nichasius, Folquinus, Victoria. (70, 71: *January*) Martina, Julian. (72, 73: *March*) Macra, Gertrude. (74: *April*) Theodosia.

According to the table, no. xxii should be a life of Caprasius, but no life is provided and the (added) numbering in the text passes from xxi to xxiii. No. 56 is an unnumbered addition to the table and supernumerary in the text. Nos. 16, 17, nos. 37, 38, and nos. 45–7 are counted under one number in both table and text. Nos. 72–4 are repetitions of art. 1, nos. 62, 64, 67, where they are supernumerary.

3. ff. 153v–158 Thirty-four stories listed in a table on f. 153v. The first begins 'Quidam monachus dum frixuras in refectorio deferret' and the last 'Refert Petrus Damianus quod helyas propheta'.

Raw, op. cit., prints the table (pp. 45–6) and identifies nos. 4–19, 21–6, 29–34 in the works of Peter Damian (pp. 47–50: cf. xiii–xv) and nos. 20, 27 with items in *Cat. of Romances*, iii. 664 (no. 237) and 694 (no. 16).

ff. iii + 158 + ii. ff. ii, iii, 159 are medieval endleaves: iir, 159v were pasted down. 290 × 190 mm. Written space 200 × 113 mm. 2 cols. 47 or 48 lines. Pricks in both margins to guide ruling. The first line of writing above the top ruled line. Collation: $1\text{–}19^8\ 20^6$. 2-line initials red or blue with ornament of the other colour. Binding of s. xix: red velvet cover. Secundo folio *gis gottorum*.

Written probably in north-east France: for connections with the diocese of Thérouanne and manuscripts of Brussels (7460–1) and St Omer (716) see Raw, op. cit., pp. xv–xviii. Ex-libris and pressmark of the Benedictine abbey of St Mary, York, on f. iiiv: 'Liber Mon' beate Marie Ebor' ', s. xiv, and 'In N. xv' within a frame. 'Passionarium G. de Lacy', f. 159, s. xiv. Armorial book-plate of William Constable Maxwell, of Everingham Park, York, s. xix. Listed among the manuscripts at Everingham Park in HMC, *First Report* (1874), App. p. 45. Given to Armstrong College by J. H. Burn, 19 July 1932.

2. *Missale ad usum Sarum* s. xv in.

1. ff. 1–6v Calendar in blue, red, and black.

Anne in red, 26 July. 'pape' and feasts of St Thomas of Canterbury erased.

2. ff. 7–9 Holy water service.

3. ff. 9–123 Temporal from Advent to Easter Eve.

The secret for the 2nd Sunday after the octave of Epiphany is Ut tibi domine grata. On ff. 28v–45 the red numbers recording in the margins the chapter numbers of lessons are set out on neat scrolls; so too the catchwords on ff. 30v, 38v. Exultet noted. In quire 15 the middle sheet is misplaced before the third sheet: the correct order is ff. 114, 113, 116, 115.

4. (*a*) ff. 123–31 Ad missam dicendum executor officii cum suis ministris . . . Ueni creator spiritus . . . (*b*) ff. 131–134v Noted prefaces, ending imperfectly in the general preface. (*c*) ff. 135–8 Canon of mass, beginning imperfectly 'to cancellatis manibus' (*Sarum Missal*, p. 223/16). (*d*) f. 138rv Cum uero sacerdos exuerit casulam . . . (*e*) ff. 138v–141 Rubric for special occasions, 'Predictus modus et ordo . . .' and psalms and three noted prayers in prostration. (*f*) f. 141rv Settings of Benedicamus and Ite missa est.

(*a*). Ordinary of mass. Between the prayer Aufer a nobis (f. 124) and Credo in unum deum (f. 129v) there are: ff. 124–125v, nine kyries, Deus creator, Kyrie rex genitor, Kyrie fons bonitatis, Kyrie omnipotens, Kyrie rex splendens, Lux et origo, Cunctipotens, Conditor, Orbis factor (*Sarum Missal*, pp. 1–4, nos. 1, 6, 7, 2, 4, 5, 3, 9, 8); ff. 125v–127r, settings of and directions for singing Gloria in excelsis; ff. 127–129v, directions, including noted specimens of the epistle for the Annunciation (f. 127rv: Isaiah 7: 10, 11, 13) and of Gospels (ff. 128v–129v: Cum appropinquasset . . . ; Osanna filio dauid . . .) and the notation to be used for the endings of 'barbare dicciones', Michael, Gabriel, Raphael, Ierusalem, Israel, Syon, and 'greca' (*sic*), Adam, Abraham, Ihesus, Moyses, Cephas, Mammona, Dauid, Iuda, and when two or three monosyllables come together: the first of four examples is Hoc est corpus meum. Much of this is not in the ordinals printed by Frere (W. H. Frere, *Use of Sarum*, i. 61–75, 265–8), but occurs in missals of s. xiv ex. and s. xv in.: in Oxford it is in Bodleian, Barlow 1, All Souls College. 302, q.v., Corpus Christi College, 394, q.v., and Keble College, 58.

5. ff. 142–95 Temporal from Easter.

Corpus Christi, f. 167.

6. ff. 195v–198v Offices in dedication of church and within the octave and at consecration and reconciliation.

In the postcommunion Deus qui ecclesiam tuam the last 8½ lines 'et ecclesia tua . . . mereatur' (*Sarum Missal*, p. 204/2–6) have been lightly erased: cf. below, Corpus Christi College, Oxford, 394, art. 6.

7. ff. 199–264 Sanctoral, Andrew–Linus.

The leaf on which the office of the Assumption of B.V.M. began is missing. f. 264v blank.

8. ff. 265–281v Common of saints.

9. ff. 281v–301 Ordinacio misse quotidiane beate uirginis que dicitur Salue. Pulsato . . .

Exactly the same series of 48 votive masses as in Corpus Christi College 394, art. 10, and in the same order and with the same variation between a full office and three prayers, except that a full office is not provided here at Pro quacumque tribulacione. 'papa' erased in the heading 'Pro papa'.

10. ff. 301–8 Sciendum est quod quotidie per aduentum . . .

The mass for the dead is followed on f. 304v by twenty sets of collect, secret, and postcommunion for special occasions. The first eighteen and the twentieth are in *Sarum Missal* in the order (1, 9, 11, 2, 10, 7, 3, 4, 12, 6, 8, 14, 5, 15–17, 13, 18, 19). No. 19 is Pro quibus orare tenemur, as in Corpus Christi College, 394, art. 11, no. 18.

11. ff. 308–9 Oracio generalis. Four sets of collect, secret, and postcommunion, as *Sarum Missal*, pp. 442–5.

12. f. 309rv Ordo trigintalis quod quidam apostolicus pro liberacione . . . prime oracioni. Oracio. Deus summa spes . . .

As Corpus Christi College, 394, art. 13, except that (by error ?) the ten feasts on which three masses are said are reduced in the heading to eight: Ascension and Pentecost are not mentioned.

13 (added in s. xvi med. on f. 310). Collect, secret, and postcommunion for Queen Mary in childbirth.

The prayers are: (collect) Omnipotens sempiterne deus qui beatissimam virginem . . . ; Secreta. Suscipe quesumus domine preces et hostias humilitatis nostre . . . ; Postcommunio. Adesto supplicationibus nostris . . .

ff. iii + 309 + ii. ff. iii, 310–11 are medieval flyleaves. 260 × 170 mm. Written space *c.* 160 × 98 mm. 2 cols. 37–8 lines. Ruling in violet ink. Collation: 1^6 $2–17^8$ (for the dislocation in quire 15 see above) 18^8 wants 1, 2 before f. 135 19^8 wants 2 after f. 141 $20–30^8$ 31^8 wants 5 after f. 239 $32–39^8$ 40 three (ff. 307–9). Initials: (i) in blue and pink shaded to white on decorated gold grounds: continuous or I or C borders in gold and colours; (ii) 2-line, gold on grounds of red and blue patterned in white: sprays of colours and gold into the margins; (iii) 2-line, blue with red ornament: the style of the ornament becomes better at f. 212 (28^1); (iv) 1-line, blue with red ornament or gold with violet ornament. Line fillers in gold and blue. Binding of s. xix. Secundo folio (f. 8) *ubicumque*.

Written in England. Given to Armstrong College by J. H. Burn, 25 January 1933.

3. *P. Lombardus, Sententiae* s. xiii med.

Bk. 2 of the Sentences of Peter Lombard, followed by bk. 4 in a very different style of writing.

1. ff. 1–50v Bk. 2, ending imperfectly in Distinction 43.

A leaf is missing after f. 44. Distinction numbers not entered after the first two. ff. 45–50 are misbound (see collation, below) and cropped, so that part of the last line on ff. 45–8 and all of it on ff. 49, 50 has been cut off. f. 51 is an inserted blank.

2. ff. 52–83v Bk. 4, ending imperfectly in Distinction 41.

No distinction numbers: perhaps cut off.

3 (binding leaves in front, s. xv). ff. i–ivv Antiphons and hymns of the common of saints.

Two bifolia, f. i pasted down. Written space 185 × 130 mm. 12 long lines. Interlinear spaces for music not filled. Written in an unsteady mixture of anglicana, secretary, and textura. f. iv begins in an antiphon for the common of martyrs, 'sunt sequenti et quia pro' (*Brev. ad usum Sarum*, ii. 396) and f. ivv ends in an antiphon of the common of confessors, 'sempiternum in quo' (ibid., ii. 440).

4 (binding leaves at the back, s. xi/xii). (*a*) ff. 87–88^{v} (in the order 88^{vr}, 87^{vr}) Office of burial. (*b*) ff. 85–86^{v} (in the order 86^{vr}, 85^{vr}) Votive masses for the dead.

(*a*) and (*b*) are two adjacent bifolia formerly laid flat sideways as pastedown and flyleaf: the pasted sides were 85^{r} and 88^{v}. Written space 188 × 80 mm. 40 long lines. Small hand (Norman ?). Red headings and initials.

(*a*) begins (f. 88^{v}) 'Non intres in iudicium cum seruo tuo domine. quoniam nullus apud te iustificabitur' (cf. *Pontifical of Magdalen College* (HBS xxxix), p. 195) and ends (f. 87^{r}) 'A'. Clementissime domine qui pro nostra miseria ab impiorum manibus . . . super peccatore. Laudate . . . P. Domine miser'. Pater noster. Et ne nos. Requiem eternam. Requiescat. A porta inferi'. 'Benedictio sepulchri' is a heading on f. 88^{r}: the blessing which follows is that in *Missale Westm.*, col. 1291. (*b*) begins on f. 86^{v} in (1) a mass *Pro sacerdote* 'dotis N quam de huius seculi \`eduxisti′ laborioso certamine' and ends on f. 85^{r}, probably in (12) a mass *Pro quiescentibus in cimiterio*, as *Sarum Missal*, p. 441, but f. 85^{r} is hardly legible. The legible headings (in capitals) are (3) Missa pro episcopis vel sacerdotibus, (4) Missa plurimorum, (5) Missa pro anniuersario, (6) Pro uno defuncto, (7) Missa unius defuncti, (8) Pro pluribus defunctis, (9) Missa pro famulabus dei, (10) Pro omnibus fidelibus. (1–3, 5–8, 10–12) are collect, secret, and postcommunion only. (4) and (9) contain lessons also. The three pieces in (2) and (8) go with *Missal of Robert of Jumièges* (HBS xi), pp. 304–5 (*Pro sacerdote defuncto*) and 306–7 (*Item alia unius defuncti*); those of (10) with *Missale Westm.*, col. 1177 (Pro omnibus fidelibus defunctis); those of (11) with *Sarum Missal*, p. 440 (Pro uno defuncto).

ff. iii + 50 + i + 32 + iii. For the binding leaves foliated i–iv, 85–8 see above, arts. 3, 4: 84 is a blank flyleaf. 228 × *c.*180 mm.

Art. 1. Written space 190 × *c.*140 mm. 34–9 long lines. Pricks in both margins. Collation: 1^{8} 2^{10} 3^{8} 4^{10} 5^{8} 6^{8} wants 1 and 8 (ff. 47, 45–6, 49, 50, 48). 2-line red or blue initials.

Art. 2. Written space 210 × 118 mm. 2 cols. 50 lines. Pricks in both margins. Collation: 7–10^{8}. 2-line initials, red or blue with ornament of the other colour.

Late medieval binding of thick bevelled boards covered with white leather: five bands: central strap and pin missing: chain mark at foot of front cover.

Written in England (?). A damaged armorial book-plate inside the back cover, s. xvii, is of Robert Spearman of Oldacres, co. Durham. The King's College, Newcastle, book-plate inside the front cover is marked 'Robert White collection'.

4. *Petrarch, Trionfi (in Italian)* s. xv med.

F. Petrarce amoris Triumphus primus incipit. Nel tempo che rinuoua i miei sospiri . . . Or che fia dunque a riuederla in celo. Finis.

This copy fully described by N. Mann, 'Petrarch manuscripts in the British Isles' (*Italia medioevale e umanistica*, xviii, 1975), pp. 347–8.

ff. iv + 47 + iii. 215 × 140 mm. Written space 120 × 75 mm. 24 long lines. Collation: 1–4^{10} 5^{10} wants 8–10 blank. Well written in humanistica. 6-line (f. 1) and 4-line gold initials on grounds coloured blue, pink, and green, and decorated with white vine ornament. A border on three sides of f. 1. Red morocco binding, s. xix in.

Written in Italy (Florence ?). Arms in the lower border of f. 1, gules a pig rampant proper girt with a band argent, and above them two quails (?). They seem to be of the Acquanegra family of Mantua: cf. Rietstap, pl. 8.[1] Arms of George Spencer-Churchill, Marquess of Blandford, in gilt on each cover. Bought in 1925 from the J. A. D. Shipley bequest.

5. *Gualterus de Brugis, O.F.M., Quaestiones de correctione fraterna; etc.* s. xiii ex.

1. ff. 3–19^{v} (*begins imperfectly*) sum quam ille qui agit contra conscienciam . . . uoluntatem ad peccandum. Explicit.

Begins in no. 17 of the 34 numbered questions of Gualterus de Brugis: ed. E. Longpré (*Les philosophes Belges*, x, Louvain 1928), pp. 145/2–238.[2]

2. Questions concerning B.V.M.: (*a*) f. 19^{v} Utrum assumpcio et resurreccio domine nostre debuerit preuenire generalem corporum et sanctorum resurreccio(nem); (*b*) f. 21^{v} Utrum debuerit esse mora aliqua inter glorificacionem anime et glorificacionem corporis gloriosissime virginis marie. f. 23^{v} was left blank.

3. ff. 24–89 Questio est utrum a mente paterna procedat verbum in diuinis vere et proprie et vtrum nomen verbi bene translatum sit ad diuina. Ad primum respondeo quod sit. hoc tenet sana fides . . .

Twenty-three numbered questions, listed on f. 89^{v}. Nos. 5, 8, 9, 19, 21–3 begin with the words 'Utrum anima cristi'. No. 23 is 'Utrum anima cristi omnia ea que cognoscit habitu in uerbo cognoscit actu. an plura possit actu cognoscere. Respondeo in beatis 3 est apprehensio apprehensio essencie uerbi . . .'.

ff. ii + 87 + ii, foliated 1–91. 288 × 205 mm. Written space 216 × 138 mm. 2 cols. 53 lines. Collation of ff. 3–89: 1^{12} 2^{8} + 1 after 8 (f. 23) 3–7^{12} 8^{6}. Several hands, one of them, ff. 24–6 (first three leaves of quire 3) an incipient anglicana book-hand; the others, not English-looking, include a more or less current textura (ff. 39–89). Book-plate of David Richardson, The Gables, Newcastle.

6. *Vincentius Ferrer, O.P., Sermones aestivales* s. xv^{2}

1. ff. 2–328^{v} In die sancto pasche sermo etc. Surrexit non est hic M^{t} 16. Vt in presenti sermone resurreccionis domini nostri . . .

Sermons of the temporal from Easter to the twenty-fifth Sunday after Trinity. Printed in 1572 and earlier. The author died in 1419. The series here includes also, ff. 169^{v}–172, a sermon for the octave of St Dominic 'patris nostri' on Non veni soluere legem (Mt. 5: 17) from the Sermones de sanctis (edn. Antwerp 1573, p. 304) and, ff. 206^{v}–209, a 'Sermo speculatiuus de quatuor virtutibus cardinalibus. Virtus de illo exibat . . . et sanabat omnes. Deo gracias'.

2. ff. 329–330^{v} Sequitur de predestinacione vnus sermo b. vincentii. Quos presciuit et predestinauit . . . ut per bona opera etc. usque ihesu cristi 2^{m} petr 1° patet sermo. ff. 331–333^{v} blank.

[1] As James Wardrop told me in a letter of 30 May 1957.
[2] I owe the identification of art. 1 to Dr H. V. Shooner.

ff. i + 332 + i, foliated 2–335. Paper. 315 × 215 mm. Written space 230 × 135 mm. 2 cols. 40–7 lines. Frame ruling. Collation of ff. 2–333: 1^{12} wants 1, perhaps blank, $2–27^{12}$ 28^{12} wants 10–12, blank. Current hybrida. 2-line red initials. Binding of s. xix. but the original (?) pigskin covers, each with metal centrepiece and corner-pieces, have been pasted over the new covers: repetitions of a rectangular floral stamp form a border enclosing a panel divided into compartments by diagonal double fillets. The stamps in the panel are (1) a swan in a roundel and (2) a running deer in a square frame. A lozenge stamp of a double-headed eagle is outside the border. A label was stuck to the front cover. Secundo folio *bat et.*

Written in Germany. Book-plate of David Richardson, The Gables, Newcastle.

7. *Officia liturgica* s. xvi in.

1. Musical parts of offices: (*a*) ff. 1–7 Mass of the Nativity of B.V.M.; (*b*) ff. 7–13 Missa In festo Assumptionis beate Marie Virginis; (*c*) ff. 13–21 De beata virgine marie tam in mis. votiuis quam festis. Kyrieleyson . . . Gloria . . . Sanctus . . . Agnus dei . . . Da nobis pacem; (*d*) ff. 21–47v Officium defunctorum; (*e*) ff. 48–79v Missa defunctorum.

2. ff. 71–9 Sacerdos et ceteri in gradu suo ordinate. in circuitu feretri stent. Et incipiat absolute in alta voce hanc orationem. Non intres . . .

Office of burial. ff. 79v–81v blank.

3. ff. 87v–88 Christe fili dei uiui miserere nobis . . . propter nomen tuum. Noted. ff. 86rv, 87r, 88v blank.

4 (added, s. xvi). (*a*) ff. 82–85v Incipit Oratio Hieremie Prophetę. Recordare Domine . . . in Ciuit. Iuda. Ieru. Ieru conuertere ad dominum deum tuum. (*b*) f. i Ad cognoscendum Tonos. Pri: re la . . . Oct: ut fa. Iste modus Incipiendi Psalmos de quolibet sit tono. Primus cum sexto Fa sol la. semper habeto . . . (4 lines of mnemonic verse).

(*a*). Lamentations 1: 5–11 + seven words. Noted.

ff. iv + 89. Strong parchment. Contemporary flyleaves. 185 × 130 mm. Written space 120 × 80 mm. 4 long lines and music. Collation: $1–10^{8}$ 11^{4} + 1 leaf after 3 (f. 84) 12^{4}. Art. 4*a* in a humanistic hand. Red initials. Contemporary binding with arabesque patterning in gilt on the covers, which are inscribed (front) ESTO MEMOR MORTIS and (back) GEORGIVS CAPITANEVS LACTANTIVS: a centrepiece and small metal corner-pieces on each cover: repaired and furnished with two clasps by Roger Powell, Froxfield, in 1962.

Written in Italy. For an owner, s. xvi, see above. Armorial book-plates of: (i) Henry Thomas Ellacombe (probably no. 628 in his sale, Sotheby's, 13 May 1886); (ii) H. C. Embleton. Given by J. H. Burn in 1933.

8. *Breviarium (Diurnale)* s. xv^{2}

1. ff. 1–20 Graded calendar written without breaks between the months.

Notes of variations on special occasions follow many entries in the same script; for example, after 'Lebuini confessoris ix lc' ' (25 June, f. 10) 'In octaua trinitatis uel sacramenti tantum memoria habet ad vtrasque vesperas ad mat' et ad missam. Et missa de eo legitur'. The Visitation of B.V.M., 'Augustini episcopi et confessoris patris nostri', and 'Dyonisii et sociorum eius' are in red and graded 'Solempne festum' (2 July, 28 Aug., 8 Oct.) and have 'Solempnes octauas'. Usual Utrecht saints in red. 'Frederici episcopi' (of Utrecht) in black, 18 July.

2. ff. 20–21v Hic notandum est quod xxiii sunt officia dominicalia inter octauas penth' et aduentum domini . . . scilicet lebuini post martini'.

3 (quires 4, 5). ff. 22–34v De aduentu domini nostri ihesu cristi. Ordinarius capituli de syon. Aduentus domini nostri ihesu cristi proxima dominica . . . per cristum dominum nostrum Amen.

Provisions for services. The last heading is 'De cursu beate marie'.

4. ff. 35–109v Antifone et psalmi feriales. Cap. Sobrie et iuste et pie . . .

Temporal from Advent to Good Friday.

5. ff. 110–29 Sanctoral from Andrew to Annunciation of B.V.M.

6. ff. 129v–130v Canticum ambrosii et augustini. Te deum . . .

7. ff. 131–208v Dominicis diebus ad laudes. Dominus regnauit decorem . . .

Liturgical psalter at lauds, (f. 159v) prime, (169) terce, (172) sext, (175) none, (178) vespers, (202v) compline.

8. ff. 208v–214 Litany

Denis twenty-third of twenty-six martyrs. Twenty-five confessors: (1) augustine . . . (11–15) seruati willibrorde patriti theobalde malachi. Seventeen virgins: . . . (10, 11) walburgis gheertrudis . . . (16, 17) anna elysabeth. f. 214v blank.

9. ff. 215–40 Sixty-six hymns for the course of the year, including two for Augustine (ff. 232v–234) and two for Denis (ff. 235–6).

Advent: (vespers) Conditor, (compline) Ueni redemptor, (lauds) Uox clara.
Christmas: (V) A solis ortus, (C) Enixa est.
Christmas–Epiphany: (prime) Agnoscat, (terce) Maria ventre, (sext) Presepe poni, (none) Adam vetus.
Epiphany: (V, C 'et noct') Hostis herodes, (L) Lauachra puri gurgitis.
Purification of B.V.M.: (V, C) Quod chorus, (L) O gloriosa.
Annunciation and commemoration of B.V.M.: (V) Aue maris stella, (C) Fit porta.
Ash Wednesday: (L, V) Clarum decus.
1st Sunday in Lent–Passion Sunday: (V) Ex more docti, (C) Criste qui lux es, (L) Audi benigne.
Passion Sunday: (V) Vexilla regis, (C) O crux aue, (L) Lustra sex.
Palm Sunday: (C) Magno salutis.
Octave of Easter–Ascension: (V) Ad cenam agni, (C) O uere digna hostia, (L) Sermone blando.
Invention and Exaltation of Cross: (V) Salue crux sancta, (L) Signum crucis.
Ascension: (V) Festum nunc, (C) Ihesu nostra redempcio, (L) Tu criste nostrum.
Pentecost: (V, C) Veni creator, (L) Beata nobis.

Trinity: (V, L) Adesto sancta, (C) O trinitas laudabilis.
Corpus Christi: (V, C) Pange lingua, (L) Verbum supernum.
Octave of Trinity–O sapientia (16 Dec.), on Saturdays and Sundays: (V) O lux beata.
John Baptist: (V 'et noct') Ut queant, (L) Antra deserti, (C) O nimis felix.
Peter and Paul: (V) Aurea luce, (L) Iam bone pastor, (C) Oliue bine.
Visitation of B.V.M.: cue to Annunciation of B.V.M.
Mary Magdalene: (V, L) Uotiua cunctis.
Anne: (V, L) Salue sancta parens.
Laurence: (V, L) En martiris.
Assumption of B.V.M. 'ad omnes horas diei': O quam glorifica.
Augustine: (V, L) Magne pater, (C) Celi ciues.
Nativity and Presentation of B.V.M.: (V, C) Maria mater domini.
Michael: (V, L) Criste sanctorum, (C) Tibi criste.
Denis: (V) Iubilent[1] filii sumpta victoria, (C) Diem sanctum recolentes o fideles populi (neither hymn in *RH*).
All Saints: (V, C, L) Ihesu saluator seculi.
Elizabeth: (V, L) Nouum sydus emicuit.
Dedication of church: (V) Urbs beata, (L) Angulare fundamentum, (C 'et ad minores horas') Hoc in templo summe deus.
Apostles: (V, L) Exultet celum. Martyr: (V, L) Martyr dei. Martyrs: (V) Rex gloriose, (L) Sanctorum meritis. Confessor: (V, L) Iste confessor. Virgin: (V, L) Ihesu corona. f. 240v blank.

10. ff. 241–291v Temporal from Easter Eve to the twenty-third Sunday after the octave of Pentecost.

A leaf missing after f. 265: beginning of Corpus Christi.

11. ff. 291v–293 Incipit commune sanctorum tempore paschali de vno martire ad vesperas.

12. ff. 293–353v Sanctoral beginning with Ambrose and ending with Radbodus (archbishop of Utrecht) and Saturninus on 29 Nov.

Includes an office 'In festo sancti dyonisii patroni nostri', f. 338v, and cues for the Presentation of B.V.M., f. 350v. A note in the margin, f. 293v, 'In translacione sancti dyonisii Coll' vt ante in primo folio'. A leaf missing after f. 319: beginning of Assumption of B.V.M.

13. ff. 353v–356v Dedication of church.

14. ff. 357–373v Common of saints.

15. (*a*) ff. 373v–376v In commemoratione beate marie. (*b*) ff. 376v–377 De sancto augustino ad vesperas . . . (*c*) f. 378 In secundis vesperis de sancta elizabeth. Exultet vox ecclesie. nam caput superbie . . . (not in *RH*).

(*a, b*) are space-fillers in the main hand. (*c*) is a later addition supplementing art. 12, f. 350v. ff. 377v, 378v are blank.

ff. 378. 155 × 110 mm. Written space 95 × 65 mm. 20 long lines. Collation: $1–2^8$ 3^6 wants 6, blank, after f. 21 4^6 (ff. 22–7) 5^7 wants 8, blank, after f. 34 $6–27^8$ 28^4 (ff. 211–4) $29–31^8$ 32^2 (ff. 239–40) $33–35^8$ 36^8 wants 2 after f. 265 $37–42^8$ 43^8 wants 1 before f. 320

[1] The illuminator put *S* instead of *I*.

44–46⁸ 47⁸ wants 7, 8, blank, after f. 356 48–49⁸ 50⁸ wants 7, 8, blank. Initials: (i) of arts. 4, 10, 7-line and 6-line, gold on coloured ground or blue on gold ground; (ii) gold on decorated pink grounds; (iii) 4-line (art. 12), 3-line, or 2-line, blue with red ornament and red and blue projections into the left margins; (iv) 2-line or 1-line, blue or red. Borders: continuous on ff. 35, 241; in upper and lower margins of pages with initials of type (ii): on f. 50 and f. 292 birds hold scrolls inscribed, respectively, 'disce mori' and 'deus videt'. Binding of wooden boards covered with brown calf, s. xvi: border roll, panel ornament, and cornerpieces: five bands: central clasp missing.

Written for the use of an Augustinian convent in the diocese of Utrecht under the patronage of St Denis.[1] Book-plate of Bannerman of Elsick (Kincardineshire), s. xix. Bought in April 1963 from Arthur Rogers for £100, through the Friends of King's College.

9. *Horae* s. xiv²

1. ff. 1–12ᵛ Full calendar in French in red and black.

Geneviève and Denis are among feasts in red.

2. ff. 13–46ᵛ Hours of B.V.M. of the use of (Paris).

All beginnings lost except prime (f. 31ᵛ) and terce (f. 37ᵛ).

3. ff. 47–52ᵛ Hours of the Holy Cross, incomplete at both ends.

4. ff. 53–6 Hours of the Holy Spirit, imperfect at the end. f. 56ᵛ blank.

5. ff. 57–75 Penitential psalms, imperfect at the beginning, and litany.

Genovefa last of virgins.

6. ff. 76–103ᵛ Office of the dead, incomplete at both ends.

7. f. 104ᵛ The Fifteen Joys of B.V.M. in French (Sonet–Sinclair, no. 458), imperfect at both ends.

8. ff. 105–106ᵛ Doux dieu doux pere sainte trinite . . .

The Seven Requests in French. Sonet, no. 504.

9. ff. 106ᵛ–112 Sequentiae of the Gospels.

10. ff. 112–115ᵛ Obsecro te . . . Et michi famule tue .N. . . .

11 (added in 1522). ff. 116–17 Glorieuse vierge pucelle Fille de dieu mere et ancelle . . . mon corps et mon ame [soit] mis ant Reaume de paradis affin que de mon [. . .] le doux salut ie te [. . . .] que lange [. . .]

Sonet–Sinclair, no. 638. Continues two—damaged—lines further than the text in Leroquais, ii. 312.

[1] Dr Pieter Gumbert tells me that this 'can only be St Dionysius, also called "ter Lelie" or Nieuwe Nonnen, in Amsterdam'.

ff. i + 117 + i. 170 × 120 mm. Written space 95–100 × 70 mm. 15 long lines. Probable collation: 1^{12} 2^{8} wants 1, 2 (ff. 13–18) 3^{8} wants 2 after f. 19 $4\text{–}5^{8}$ 6 two (ff. 42, 43, a bifolium) 7^{8} wants 4 after f. 46 8^{6} wants 3 after f. 52 + 1 leaf after 6 (f. 56) 9^{8} wants 1 before f. 57 10^{8} 11^{8} wants 5 after f. 75 $12\text{–}14^{8}$ 15 four (ff. 103–6) 16^{8} 17 three (ff. 115–17). Initials: (i) in colours on gold grounds, decorated in colours and with sprays of colour and gold into the margins; (ii, iii) 2-line and 1-line, gold on coloured grounds. Line fillers of red, blue, and gold. Capital letters in the ink of the text touched with red. Rebound in 1976: the former binding was of s. xviii, with emblems of the Passion as centrepiece. The centrepiece has been retained.

Written in France, art. 10 for use by a woman. Two inscriptions on f. 117^{v} are in the hand of art. 11: (*a*) Memoire du Iour que Ie ecript sette oresson sevenant eceple et fut le Ioir de Paques qui etouet le xxme Iour dauril lan mil v^{c} xxii par moy anthoine patoillet; (*b*) Ie sartifye auoir ecript sette or[. . . .] sy deuant e a prennt a [. . .] mon syne fait le mardi xvi^{e} Iour setampbre mil v^{c} lvi anthoine patoillat. Given to the Literary and Philosophical Institute of Newcastle by Thomas Davidson, according to the supplement of 1803 to the library catalogue printed in 1800. Acquired in 1975.

Pybus Cv. 5. *J. Arderne, etc.* s. xiv^{1}–xiv ex.

1 (quire 1). (*a*) f. ii^{v} A diagram of the winds. (*b*) ff. iii–iv Sciendum quod ista subsequencia [. . . . . .] in Nundinis de Lenton' Et in N' [. . . . . .] botulphi Anno domini M^{o} ccc^{mo} [. . . . . .] De Galbano libra [. . .] De lapide calaminar' [. . . .] Sciendum quod venditores vtr' *scilicet* ves*tr*i [. . . . . .] pondus quod portant pro v s'. (*c*) ff. iv^{v}–vi. A table of chapters of art. 2.

(*a*). In manuscripts of Arderne this diagram is usually on the first page between the paragraph ending *suspendatur* and that beginning *Macerare*. In Glasgow, Hunterian 339 it is on the lower part of f. 1^{r}. (*b*). A list of materia medica obtainable at the Lenton (Notts) and St Botolph (Lincs) fairs in a year near the end of s. xiv. Eighty-seven items, including two added at the foot of f. iii. The price per pound is usually given. The leaves are damaged on the right so that most prices of items 1–27 (f. iii^{r}), 58–87 (f. iv^{r}) are more or less illegible and parts of the two sentences beginning *Sciendum* are illegible. On the other hand, the list of items itself is not seriously damaged on f. iii^{v}, since it is written down the middle of the page. (*c*). An addition, s. xv in. The titles of the chapters are usually taken from the first words of paragraphs in art. 2. They are numbered from 1 to 185 and corresponding numbers have been inserted in the margins of art. 2, 1–87 (2*a*), 88–170 (2*b*), 171–82 (2*c*), 183–4 (2*d*), 185 (2*e*).

2. (*a*) ff. 1–59 Ad cancrum in virga virili . . . uulnera maxima sanat.[1] (*b*) ff. 59–124^{v} Practica Magistri Iohannis de Newerk Arderne Cyrurgici. Ego Iohannes predictus a prima pestelencia . . . et cessabunt menstrua etc. (*c*) ff. 125–133^{v} De mixtura conficienda . . . (*d*) ff. 133^{v}–135 Incipit bonum regimen vite et cura contra pestilenciam. In primis omnem auferas timorem grauedinem . . . et bibere aquam frigidam cum aceto mixtam. (*e*) ff. 135–140^{v} Alegans (*sic*) est nature cognicio que per exteriores formas . . . hanc autem in nomine cristi in hoc opere nostro. primo desposcimus. Humana corporis fabrica ab elementis disponente deo . . . Irascentem ex leui causa (*ends imperfectly: the catchword is* guttur planum).

[1] This seems to be a broken sentence. It occurs thus in all manuscripts I have seen. In Glasgow, Hunterian 339, there is a possible reason for the break in that the words 'uulnera maxima sanat' are at the end of the last line on the verso of the last leaf of a quire.

(*a, b*). The general treatise on medicine and the surgery of John Arderne, † in or soon after 1378: cf. D. Power in EETS cxxxix (1910), ix–xxxv; Thorndike and Kibre; Talbot and Hammond, p. 111. One leaf of (*a*) is missing. (*b*) ends like Bodleian, Barlow 34 and Glasgow, Hunterian 339. It is followed by a 10-line recipe 'ad menstrua prouocanda' ending 'oleo violac' '. (*c*). Recipes, mainly herbal, set out in paragraphs, four of them in French, and a 'Coniuracio pro rauclo vel pro dolore uel pro plaga et dicas In nomine dei . . .' (f. 127). A French piece on f. 128, 'Pernez burnet . . .', has against it in the margin 'Sauue secundum magistrum Willelmum de Anstan (*or* Austan)' and another French piece, f. 129ᵛ, gives instructions for 'le grand boyuer (*or* boynet) de antioche'. (*d*). Thorndike and Kibre (Dilectissime frater). Singer and Anderson, 1950, no. 16 (this copy not listed). Corresponds to lines 5–94 of the text printed by K. Sudhoff in *AGM* v (1912), 75–7. (*e*) Thorndike and Kibre (Elegans). They refer to V. Rose, *Anecdota*, i. 175, and three English manuscripts. One leaf is missing.

3. ff. 141–6 are three bifolia of an older, legal (?) manuscript, probably preserved here for the sake of the recipes and charms added to it. (*a*) f. 141 Ex quo autem placitum est coram Iusticiariis de banco quare debent visores ponere languido diem apud turrim Lond'. cum non sedeant ibi Iusticiarii. In hoc breui mittet (*sic*) quatuor legales milites. sic dicitur. si sit langor . . . (*b*) ff. 141ᵛ–146ᵛ Recipes and charms in Latin, French, and English.

(*a*). s. xiv[1]. Twenty-nine lines showing how the writ Mitte quatuor legales milites could be applied in vacation. The writ is printed by de Haas and Hall, p. 320, no. 45 of the Register of Judicial Writs 'J' (s. xiii med.). (*b*). s. xiv med. Probably all in one hand, but written at different times.[1] f. 146ᵛ is hardly legible. The other pages contain about fifty-six pieces, 34 in Latin, 15 in French, and 7 in English. About fourteen of the Latin pieces are charms: four for staunching blood (ff. 141ᵛ, 145), three of them beginning 'Longius (*sic*) miles'; four against fevers (ff. 141ᵛ, 142, 145ᵛ), the first beginning 'Coniuro vos febres calidas siue frigidas que septem sorores estis', and the second, 'breue propter febres', asking for the intercession of six confessors, 'Augustinus Nicholaus Germanus Albinus Sewaldus et sanctus Sigismundus'; one for snake bite (f. 141ᵛ); one for nose bleed (f. 142); two for toothache (f. 143); two to find stolen goods (ff. 143ᵛ, 144ᵛ). Two of the French pieces are prayers for recovery (f. 146), 'Dow (?) sir' dieux ieo vous pri . . . donez a N gareyson . . .', 'Dame seynt Marie Mere et sauueour pur les v ioies . . .'. (*a*) is in formal and (*b*) in informal current anglicana.

ff. i + 150 + i, foliated (one unnumbered leaf), i–vi, 1–10, 12–135, 137–46, (147). The foliation is partly of s. xviii (?), before leaves were lost after ff. 10, 135. 195 × 140 mm. Written space 130 × 80 mm. 29–31 long lines. Frame ruling. Collation of ff. i–vi, 1–140: 1^6 2^4 + 1 leaf after 1 (f. 2) and 1 leaf after 2 (f. 4) 3^6 wants 5 (ff. 7–10, 12), 4–18^8 19^8 wants 4 after f. 135. Arts. 1, 2 in neat current anglicana. 2-line blue initials with red ornament. Bound by Zaehnsdorf, London, s. xx in.: wooden boards covered with half pigskin. Secundo folio *distilletur*.

Written in England. The names 'W. Harrysson' and '[Mis]ter Rowlestone' are on f. iᵛ, s. xvii; 'Rowlstone' also on f. ii. Scribbles of s. xviii include 'Richard Pearson his Book' (f. 28ᵛ), Sarah Ridall (ff. 6, 6ᵛ, 28ᵛ), Christopher Wainman (f. 83ᵛ), Mster Rutter (f. 28ᵛ): the names suggest that the manuscript was in the north of England before it was acquired by Professor F. C. Pybus: his gift in 1965.

[1] The spelling 'Iehu' with stroke through the *h* as an abbreviation of *Ihesu* is a curiosity. In English *þ* is distinguished from *y* only by the absence of a dot over the letter. The spelling 'þo' for *the* is regular.

NORWICH. CASTLE MUSEUM

99.20. *Glossaria* s. xiii ex.

Arts. 1, 3–5 occur in Balliol College, Oxford, 155, s. xiv.

1. ff. 1–90v Incipit pars prima glosarum a Beato Eusebio Ieronimo. Sophronio Hebrayce. Grece. Latine composita et exposita. A litera in omnibus gentibus Ideo prima . . . Zmirna vrbs vel ciuitas libie. Zmirne mirram.

Substantially, it seems, as Balliol College, 155, art. 4; cf. G. Goetz, *Corpus glossariorum latinorum*, i. 186, and Stegmüller, nos. 7586, 11595. A disturbance here in the letter A: quire 1 runs to 'Affecta', followed by the catchword 'Affectat' (f. 12v: Balliol, f. 43ra/28); quire 2 begins with 'Acerbus' (f. 13: Balliol, f. 41ra/23) and continues with Ac-, Ad-, and Af- words to 'Affabilis' (f. 18v) before 'Affectat' is reached. Many nearly contemporary additions in the upper and lower margins, among them 'catubulum punefolde' (f. 35v).

2. f. 91rv Deriuatio fit principaliter tribus modis . . . nobisque sunt occulta.

3. ff. 92–115v Incipit prologus sancti Ieronimi presbiteri in librum glosarum. Eusebius: qui a beato pamphilo . . . me credo. Philo vir disertissimus . . . cristianus impleret. Expliciunt prefaciones. Incipit liber Glosarum sancti ieronimi. Aaron mons fortitudinis . . . Zozomin. hee cogitaciones.

The prefaces are those to the Liber de situ et nominibus locorum hebraicorum and the Liber hebraicorum nominum. After them these two works (*PL* xxiii. 859–928 (903–82) and 771–858 (815–904)) appear to be combined in a single alphabet. Cf. Balliol 155, art. 1.

4. f. 115v Vox est aer ad linguam ictus: auditu sensibilis . . . Voces mutorum animalium. Aquila dicimus clangere . . . Ranas. Ranire uel coaxare.

Fifty-three birds and beasts and the verb for the noise each makes. In Balliol 155 this comes on f. 172rv as part of the glossary, above, art. 1, s.v. *Voces*.

5. ff. 116–43 Incipit prefacio pauli doctoris eximii ad regem karolum. (in) Glosarium ex libris sexti festi pompei . . . dictis. Diuine largitatis munere . . . ad pociora excitabit. Abacti. Magistratus dicebantur . . . palatina erquilina. collina.

The glossary of Festus (ed. W. M. Lindsay, Teubner series) abbreviated by Paulus Diaconus and here rearranged in a more strictly alphabetical order. Balliol 155, art. 5. f. 143v blank.

6. ff. 144–155v Abominor. aris uerbum deponens Inde abominatus . . .

A and most of B of a glossary arranged in two series under each letter: under A, first from 'Abominor' to 'Apostolus' (ff. 144–9) and then from 'Abauus' to 'Azora (*sic*) .dii ita vocati. extra celi zonam exsistentes. Marcianus. Dii quos azonos uocant' (ff. 149v–153v); under B, first from 'Babiger' to 'Buxus' (ff. 153v–155) and then from 'Baburra' to the word after 'Baro' where it ends imperfectly: catchword 'Barritus quarte declina'. In the first series there are fewer words but fuller entries, with references to classical authors, Augustine, Rabanus, and at *Ager* 'Auianus in exposicione super matheum'. Some glosses in French, for example 'aluta id est pellis sutorii que gallice dicitur corneis'.

7. The binding strip at each end is from a bifolium of a theological manuscript in an English hand, s. xv in.

ff. i + 155 + i. 320 × 220 mm. Written space 220 × 148 mm. 3 cols. 44 lines. Collation: $1-7^{12}$ 8^{8} wants 7, perhaps blank, after f. 90 $9-12^{12}$ 13 four (ff. 140-3) 14^{12}. Quire numbers on first rectos, top right, 'ix' (f. 92), 'xiiii' (f. 144) and traces elsewhere. Several hands. Well-drawn initials: (i) blue and red with ornament in red and blue-green; (ii) 2-line, blue with red ornament or red with blue-green ornament: omitted in art. 6. Brown calf binding, s. xvii in. Secundo folio *est:hoc*.

Written in England. 'H. xlvii', altered to 'H. xlv', at the head of f. 1 on the left is the pressmark of Norwich Cathedral Priory. 'Liber fratris Ade de Aldeby `monachi'' to the right of it is probably earlier. Alienated in s. xvi and at Cambridge University Library by 1600. The Cambridge number 151 is at the foot of f. 1 and on the fore-edge, and the Cambridge mark, # F. z. 9 inside the cover, top left: cf. N. R. Ker in *Transactions of the Cambridge Bibliographical Society*, i (1949), 14. MS. 67 in the collection of Lord Mostyn: cf. HMC, *4th Report*, 1874, App., p. 349. Mostyn sale at Sotheby's, 13 July 1920, lot 47. Bought for the Museum for £41. 10*s*.

149.938/1. *Horae* s. xv in.

1. ff. 1-7 Sequentiae of the Gospels.

2. ff. 7-8v Omnibus dicentibus . . . Domine ihesu criste qui hanc sacratissimam carnem . . .

The heading conveys an indulgence of 2,000 years granted by Pope Boniface 'ad supplicacionem philippi condam regis francie'.

3. ff. 9-14v Papa innocencius concessit . . . sicut uidisti et audistis. Obsecro te . . .

Masculine forms. The heading conveys an indulgence of 100 days granted by Pope Innocent.

4. ff. 14v-17v O beata et intemerata . . . orbis terrarum. Inclina . . .

5. ff. 17v-22v Oracio. Domine exaudi oracionem meam quia iam cognosco . . .

6. ff. 22v-25v Memoriae of Michael, guardian angel, and Cosmas and Damian.

7. ff. 26-28v Domine ihesu criste qui septem uerba . . . benedictum in secula seculorum amen.

The prayer of the Seven Words often ascribed to Bede.

8. ff. 29-103 Hours of B.V.M. of the use of (Rome).

9 (added as a space-filler in quire 14). ff. 103v-104 Memoria of Joseph, f. 104v blank.

10. ff. 105-128v Penitential psalms and (f. 117v) litany.

Nine pontiffs and doctors: (2) amantii. Six monks and hermits: paule anthoni benedicte seuere geraldi dominice.

11. ff. 129–72 Hours of the Cross.

The hymns are In passione domini (etc.): *RH*, no. 8722, etc.; *AH* L. 568–70 (Bonaventura ?).

12 (added as space fillers in quire 23). (*a*) ff. 172–174ᵛ De sancto michaele oracio. [D]eus propicius esto michi peccatori . . . (*b*) ff. 174ᵛ–176 Gaude uirgo mater cristi . . . Cum pudoris lilio . . .

(*a*). Memoria of Michael. (*b*). *RH*, no. 7017. f. 176ᵛ blank.

13. ff. 177–204ᵛ Hours of the Holy Spirit.

14 (added as a space-filler in quire 27). ff. 204ᵛ–107 [I]hesu crist filz de dieu le pere tu qui es dieu des angelz . . .

Sonet-Sinclair, no. 945. The heading in French says that this prayer was found beneath the sepulchre of Our Lady 'en la ual de iosaphat' and that it is good against mortality, epidemics, fire, water, and battle. f. 207ᵛ blank.

15. ff. 208–60 Office of the dead.

16 (added). ff. 260ᵛ–261ᵛ Oracio ad deum patrem. Domine ihesu criste qui mundum proprio sanguine redemisti . . .

17. ff. 262–265ᵛ Legitur quod cum beatus thomas martir ecclesie cantuarien' archiepiscopus septem gaudia . . . Gaude flore uirginali que honore speciali . . .

The Seven Joys of B.V.M. *RH*, no. 6810. Cf. *Lyell Cat.*, p. 381.

18. ff. 265ᵛ–267 Commemoracio sancti michaelis archangeli. Cristiane uir fidelis. Qui regnare . . .

RH, no. 24515. f. 267ᵛ blank.

ff. iii + 269 + iii, foliated i–iii, 1–107, 107*, 108, 108*, 109–267. 110 × 80 mm. Written space 64 × 48 mm. 13 long lines. Collation: $1–3^8$ 4^4 (ff. 25–8) $5–13^8$ 14^4 (ff. 101–4) $15–16^8$ 17^{10} (ff. 119–28) $18–26^8$ 27^8 wants 8, probably blank, after f. 207 $28–34^8$ 35^6. Catchwords written vertically. Six 11-line pictures, two in art. 8 (Annunciation at matins, Coronation at vespers) and one before each of arts. 10 (God the Father seated, blessing, orb in left hand), 11, 13, 15. Borders on three sides of picture pages. Initials: (i) in colour on gold grounds, decorated in colours; (ii–iv) 3-line, 2-line, and 1-line, gold on coloured grounds patterned in white. Line fillers in red and blue. Capital letters in the ink of the text filled with yellow. Continental binding, s. xvi, rebacked.

Written in France. Blurred arms in the border on f. 105. Armorial book-plate of John Buxton Esq. Given by Mrs Maud Buxton in 1938.

158.926/4a–f, g(1–5, 7)

The twelve medieval manuscripts referenced 158.926/4 were lent by the executors of Col. R. W. Patteson in 1926 and given by his sister, Mrs J. Perowne, in

1961. They are manuscripts of English origin and most if not all of them have been together for more than 200 years. They bear no indications of their history in the eighteenth century, however, and the only indications for the nineteenth century are the name of W. F. Patteson in 4b, 4f, and 4g(3). The Reverend William Frederick Patteson was born in 1801, a younger son of the John Patteson who had inherited the manuscripts of Cox Macro (1683–1767) through his wife, Elizabeth Staniforth.[1] The present collection is mostly, if not entirely, a Macro residue, which was presumably reserved by John Patteson for his son when he sold the rest of the manuscripts.[2] W. F. Patteson died unmarried in 1881. His elder brother, John Staniforth Patteson, was the great grandfather of R. W. Patteson and Mrs Perowne.

Seven of the twelve manuscripts are identifiable in the catalogue of Macro's manuscripts, London, B.L., Add. 25473, ff. 1–8, made in 1766: 4b is 12° 15; 4c, 4° 64; 4g(1), 4° 11; 4g(2), 4° 30; 4g(5), 4° 52; 4e and 4g(4), 12° 11 and 24.

The spines of the bindings bear or bore paper labels on which is a number, s. xviii (?). The still legible numbers are '9' on 4g(2), '10' on 4g(1), '11' on 4g(7), '12' on 4b, '13' on 4g(4), '14' on 4g(5), '15' (?) on 4c, '16' on 4g(3), and '17' (altered from another number) on 4e.

158.926/4a. *Psalterium, etc.* s. xv/xvi

1. ff. 1–12^{v} Full calendar in red and black.

Gradings for main feasts. Entries include the Visitation of B.V.M. and Name of Jesus in red and the Transfiguration, Osmund, and (30 Dec.) translation of James in black. The word 'pape' and entries of Thomas of Canterbury at 7 July and 29 Dec. not cancelled.

2. ff. 13–152 Liturgical psalter.

Cues only for the gradual psalms (119–33) and Pss. 148–50.

3. ff. 152–162^{v} Six ferial canticles, followed by cues for Te deum, Benedicite, Benedictus, Magnificat, and Nunc dimittis and by Quicumque vult in full.

ff. v + 163. The modern foliation in fives misses a leaf between 55 and 60. Flyleaves of medieval parchment. 120 × 90 mm. Written space 75 × 50 mm. 20 long lines. Ruling in red ink. Collation: 1^{12} 2–19^{8} 20^{8} wants 8, perhaps blank. Good textura. Initials: (i) of the usual eight psalms, 7-line, blue on grounds of gold paint, historiated; (ii, iii) 2-line and 1-line, gold paint on red grounds. Framed floral borders, the grounds of gold paint, on pages with

[1] See *DNB*, Macro. The descent from Macro was through his daughter Mary (†1775) to her husband William Staniforth and from him to his daughter and heiress, Elizabeth, who married John Patteson in 1781. I am grateful to Mr Frank Sayer for details about the Patteson family.

[2] The introduction to the catalogue of the 1820 sale at Christie's says of Macro, 'His valuable library, with these Manuscripts, descended by marriage to the present Possessor, John Patteson, Esq. of Norwich', which seems incompatible with what is said in *DNB*, that in 1819 Patteson 'sold the manuscripts for a trifling sum . . . to Richard Beatniffe', bookseller of Norwich, 'who resold them at a very large profit' at Christie's in 1820.

initials of type (i) and on each recto of art. 1, where the sign of the zodiac is at the head of the page and the occupation of the month at its foot. Lasko and Morgan, no. 89: reduced facsimile of f. 126 shows initials of types (i) and (iii) and a border. Binding of red velvet over pasteboard. Secundo folio (f. 14) *cum tremore*.

Written in the Low Countries (?) for English use. A memorandum of s. xvi on f. i^{v}: 'Nicholas vexe *ser*unt to the duches of Suffolk hathe by her comaundment in his kepyng [t]he decre or composission of the Sevyn Townes hey[. . .] w^{t} in the Countie of Lyncoln'. Given by Mrs J. Perowne in 1961.

158.926/4b. *P. Riga, Aurora* s. xiii med.

1. ff. 1-236 (*a*) Fraterne caritatis . . . comodius fiat. (*b*) De laude [libri] Stringere pauca libet . . . vana fugat (60 lines). (*c*) Omnis scriptura diuinitus inspirata . . . (f. 2^{v}) quod humilitas superbiam. (*d*) Frequens sodalium m(e)orum peticio . . . (f. 3) patenter illuxit. (*e*) Incipit aurora. Primo facta die . . . docuere fidem. Expliciunt recapitulationes. Hic liber est scriptus qui scripsit sit benedictus amen.

P. Riga, Aurora. Ed. P. E. Beichner, 1965. Stegmüller, nos. 6823-5. A copy of the recension by Giles of Paris. (*a–d*). Preliminaries: Beichner, pp. 4-10, nos. IV, V, II lines 1-70, III. (*e*). The order is Genesis-4 Kings, Tobit, Esther, Judith, Daniel, Maccabees, Song of Songs, Job, Gospels, Acts, Recapitulationes. The later medieval titles on f. i^{v} are 'Biblia versific' ' and 'Hic liber Aurora dicitur'.

2. f. 236 Mnemonic verses: (*a*) De ieiunio iiiior temporum. Dant crux. lutia . . . ; (*b*) Quomodo et quando debent fieri xii lecciones in anno bisextili. Bisextum sexte . . . ; (*c*) Versus patronomicorum. Nomine de proprio patronomica . . . formatur et acrisione.

(*a*). 2 lines. Walther, *Sprichwörter*, no. 4943a. (*b*). 2 lines. Walther, *Initia*, no. 2203. (*c*). 13 lines. Walther, *Initia*, no. 11941.

3. ff. 236^{v}-238 Viri venerabiles uiri literati Hostes iniustitie . . . Sic sit salus omnibus nunc et in fine. amen.

Twenty-nine 4-line stanzas. Walther, *Initia*, no. 20580. ff. 238^{v}-239^{v} blank.

ff. i + 239 + i. Late medieval foliation to f. 26. Medieval flyleaves. 137 × 95 mm. Written space 105 × 48 mm. 37 long lines. Collation: $1\text{-}23^{10}$ 24^{10} wants 9, probably blank. Initials: (i) f. 1, gold on blue and pink ground, patterned in white; (ii) beginning books, 4-line or 5-line, red and blue with ornament of both colours or one colour; (iii) 2-line, red or blue, with a pair of vertical strokes of the other colour. Capital letters in the ink of the text lined with red. Binding of wooden boards covered with plain dark calf, s. xvi: armorial centrepiece, presumably of Sir William Cecil (1520-98) before he was created Baron Burghley in 1571, quarterly 1 and 4 Cecil, 2 Caerleon, 3 Walcot, but without the chevron ermine seen in Burghley's sexpartite armorial (A. R. Wagner, *Historic heraldry of Britain, pl. 15*):[1] two clasps, the upper one remaining. Secundo folio *ad arguendum*.

[1] The same arms, but with the chevron ermine, are, as Miss Pamela Black told me, on the back cover of B.L., Add. 36705, acquired by Cecil in or about 1569, but the armorial, imposed on an oval centrepiece, may be later. Cecil, Caerleon and Walcot are 1, 3 and 5 of the sexpartite armorial. Wagner notes that 1, 2 (Winstone) and 3 of this armorial were granted to William Scicill of Allt yr ynis at the visitation of Herefordshire in 1569: he was probably Burghley's cousin. The Walcot arms are those of Burghley's maternal grandmother.

Written in England. Number 129 of the Latin manuscripts in the Burghley sale, 21 Nov. 1687; bought by Sir Richard Gipps whose name 'Rich: Gipps' is on f. i^{v}. Belonged to Cox Macro: see above, p. 510. 'This book belongs to Rev. W. F. Patteson St. Helen's Norwich' on pastedown, s. xix: he was vicar, 1824–81. '12' on label on spine. Given by Mrs J. Perowne in 1961.

158.926/4c. *Psalterium, etc.* s. xv med. (except art. 13)

1. (*a*) f. 3^{rv} Lecciones de commemoracione sancti thome. Dormiente cum patribus suis . . . theobaldo . . . (*b*) ff. 3^{v}–4^{v} Hymns for Mary Magdalene. (*c*) f. 4^{v} Twelve blessings in octaves of B.V.M.

(*a*). Three lessons. (*b*). The three hymns of Philip de Grève, Collaudemus magdalene . . . , Estimauit ortholanum . . . , O maria noli flere . . . , *RH*, nos. 3655, 580, 13208; *AH* L. 532–4.

2. ff. 5–10^{v} Graded Sarum calendar.

Entries in red include the dedication of Norwich cathedral, 24 Sept., and Thomas of Hereford, 2 Oct.; in black, Felix, 8 March. The word 'pape' and feasts of St Thomas have not been cancelled. 'Obitus M. Howgonis damplet' and 'Obitus patris mei iohannis howton' added at 15 Apr. and 20 Sept.: Damlett was master of Pembroke Hall, Cambridge, 1447–50 and rector of St Peter's, Cornhill, London, 1447 until death, will proved 20 Apr. 1476 (Emden, *BRUC*, p. 176).

3. ff. 11–93^{v} Liturgical psalter.

4. ff. 93^{v}–100^{v} Six ferial canticles, Te deum, Benedicite, Benedictus, Magnificat, Nunc dimittis.

5. ff. 100^{v}–105 Litanies for each day of the week, Monday–Saturday, written continuously.

As *Brev. ad usum Sarum*, ii. 250–1, 255–60, except that the Wednesday martyrs include 'Austroberte Wlstane' instead of *Germane Ausberte Wilfranne*.

6. ff. 105–116^{v} Hoc modo dicuntur exequie mortuorum.

As *Manuale Sarum*, pp. 132–142/10, 123/29–124/33. Noted.

7. ff. 116^{v}–118 Memoriae of Holy Cross (as *PS*, pp. 129–30) and of B.V.M.

8. ff. 118–19 Benedictions of salt and water.

9. f. 119^{rv} In illo tempore quo beatus gregorius in roma fuit presul una die dum cantabat missam quando uoluit consecrare corpus cristi. sibi dominus ihesus cristus in tali effigie qua hic depingitur apparuit . . . Et hoc scriptum est in capella sancte marie de ierusalem in templo et est registratum in Roma.

Includes an indulgence of 20,006 years, thirty-six days, granted by Gregory and other popes. Cf. *Lyell Cat.*, p. 66. No picture here, but the side margin has been cut off.

10. ff. 119v–120 Illumina oculos meos . . . et consolatus es me.

The verses of St Bernard, here eight. Cf. Leroquais, I. xxx and *Lyell Cat.*, p. 62.

11. ff. 120–6 Lecciones de sancta (maria): Advent, Easter, Christmas, and 'per estatem'.

12. Collects: (*a*) ff. 126–7 David, Chad, Thomas of Hereford, Francis, Winifred, John of Beverley (2), Dominic, Felix; (*b*) ff. 127v–129 Sundays after Trinity from Deus in te sperancium to Excita quesumus domine. f. 129v blank.

The nine collects in (*a*) are: (1) Omnipotens sempiterne deus qui beato dauid confessori tuo atque pontifici nondum nato . . . ; (2) Deus qui sanctorum tuorum meritis . . . ; (3) Deus qui ecclesiam tuam beati pontificis tui thome . . . ; (4) Deus qui ecclesiam tuam . . . ; (5) Deus qui beatam Wenefredam . . . ; (6) Deus qui hunc diem sanctissimi Iohannis confessoris tui . . . ; (7) Alia. Deus qui presentem diem beati iohannis . . . ; (8) Deus qui ecclesiam tuam sancti dominici confessoris . . . ; (9) Deus cuius gracia beatus felix pontifex . . .

13. ff. 1, 2, 130 are single inserted leaves: (*a*) f. 1v, s. xv (?), a picture of Christ rising from the tomb: the recto is blank; (*b*) f. 2, s. xiii med., Gaude virgo graciosa uerbum uerbo concepisti. Gaude. Gaude tellus fructuosa . . . iunge tuo filio. Deus qui beatam uirginem mariam in conceptu et partu . . . (*c*) f. 2, s. xiii med., Encuntre tonerre die cest. Ecce dominice crucis uiuificans . . . Quant il escleire seignez uus e diez A signis celi ne timueritis . . . (*d*) f. 2v, s. xiii Christ, seated, blessing, in a framed mandorla, an evangelist's sign filling the space in each corner of the frame. (*e*) f. 130, s. xiv/xv, emblems of the passion and, in red, 'Quicumque hec arma domini nostri ihesu `cristi´ deuote inspexerit . . . tria milia annorum penitencialium et tria milia annorum venialium'.

(*b*). Memoria of the Conception of B.V.M.: *RH*, no. 7006; *AH* xxix. 31. (*c*). A charm against thunder and lightning. (*e*). Indulgenced by St Peter and his successors, and Pope John XXII. A blank lozenge-shaped space in the middle of the page is surrounded by the words 'Vera mensura vulneris domini nostri ihesu cristi latere suo non dubitetur'. f. 130v blank.

ff. i + 2 + 127 + 1 + i. For ff. 1, 2, 30 see art. 13. 190 × 135 mm. Written space *c.* 135 × 84 mm. 27 long lines. Collation of ff. 3–129: 1–16⁸. Quires signed +, a–p. Two inserted pictures: see art. 13*a*, *d*. Initials: (i) in colours on gold grounds decorated in colours, including green and brick-red: prolongations form a continuous border on f. 11; (ii) 2-line, blue with red ornament; (iii) 1-line, red or blue. Cadels in art. 6. Medieval binding of wooden boards covered with pink leather: five bands, VIV: two strap-and-pin fastenings missing. Secundo folio (f. 4) *mundatorem.*

Written in England, for use in the diocese of Norwich. 'Thys boke longgyth to [. . . . . .]', f. 129v, s. xv. 'Ex bibliotheca Dni Ham: Lestrange', f. iv, s. xvii: for Hamon L'Estrange, 1605–60, see *DNB*. '15' (?) on a label on the spine, s. xix in. (?). Belonged to Cox Macro: see above, p. 510. Given by Mrs J. Perowne in 1961.

158.926/4d. *Statuta Angliae* s. xiv¹–xiv med.

1 (quire 1). ff. 1–12 A table of chapters of arts. 2–7, 10, 15, 26. f. 12v blank.

2. ff. 13–19 Magna carta. Edwardus dei gracia . . .

The confirmation of 1300, dated at the end 28 March anno 28. *SR* i, Charters, p. 38.

3. ff. 19–23 Incipit carta Foreste. Edwardus dei gracia . . .

Dated as art. 1. *SR* i, Charters, p. 42.

4. ff. 23–6 Prouisiones de Merton. *SR* i. 1.

5. ff. 26v–35 Marleberge. *SR* i. 19.

6. ff. 35v–53 Westmonasterium Primum. In French. *SR* i. 26.

7. ff. 53–57v Incipit Statutum Gloucestrie. Pur les grantz meschiefs . . . henri sisme.

SR i. 47–50, chapters 1–15, preceded as often by a short introduction in place of the longer text printed in *SR*.

8. ff. 57v–58 Iste articulus in quadam billa scriptus consutus est statuto consignato in Banco. Come contenu soit en nostre estatut . . .

SR i. 216. Heading as in Cambridge, U.L., Mm. 5. 19, where this piece follows art. 7.

9. ff. 58–9 Articulus statuti Gloucestr' per dominum E. quondam Regem anglie Patrem Regis nunc anno regni sui nono et consilium suum correctus pro ciuibus London' de forinsecis vocatis ad Warantum in Hustengo London'. Purveu est ensement que si homme . . . pledent la garantie. Memorandum quod iste articulus in forma predicta consignatus fuit sub magno sigillo domini E. Regis filii R.E. anno regni sui nono et missus Iustic' de Banco in modum litere patentis cum quodam breui clauso sub dat' Regis apud Westm' ii die Marcii anno predicto quod ipsi omnia et singula in articulo predicto contenta facerent et exequerentur non obstante quod articulus ille in omnibus cum dicto statuto Gloucestr' non concordat.

SR i. 52, but without the Memorandum. The corrected form of chapter 12 of the statute of Gloucester: cf. *MMBL* i. 33 (Liber Horn, art. 77).

10. ff. 59–94v Incipit statutum Westm' secundi. *SR* i. 71.

11. ff. 94v–97 Incipit statutum. Quia fines. *SR* i. 128.

12. ff. 97–98v Statutum de Religiosis. *SR* i. 51.

13. ff. 98v–99 Incipit statutum West' tercii. *SR* i. 106.

14. ff. 99–100v Statutum de mercatoribus. In French. Ends imperfectly. *SR* i. 98.

15. ff. 101–106v Articuli super cartas. In French. Begins imperfectly. *SR* i. 136.

16. ff. 106^{v}–109 De coniunctim feoffatis. *SR* i. 45.

17. ff. 109–111^{v} Incipit addicio de Foresta. *SR* i. 147.

18. ff. 112–114^{v} Incipit statutum de apport' Religiosorum. *SR* i. 150.

19. ff. 114^{v}–116 Incipit stat' Lincoln' de Escaetoribus. *SR* i. 142.

20. ff. 116–17 Statutum Lincoln' de vicecom'. In French. *SR* i. 174.

21. f. 117^{rv} Incipit modus faciendi homagium et fidelitatem. In French. *SR* i. 227.

22. ff. 117^{v}–118 Incipit statutum de conspiratoribus. In French. *SR* i. 145.

23. ff. 118–122^{v} Articuli cleri. *SR* i. 175.

24. ff. 122^{v}–125^{v} Incipit statutum Ebor' anno regni R.E. secundi xii^{o}. In French. *SR* i. 177.

25. ff. 125^{v}–126^{v} Incipit Commissio ordinacionum. In French. Dated 16 Mar. 3 Edward II. Rymer, *Foedera*, iii. 204.

26. ff. 126^{v}–144^{v} Incipiunt ordinaciones. In French. *SR* i. 157. Running title 'Noue ordinaciones'.

27. ff. 145–212^{v} Statutes of 1, 2, 4, 5, 9, 10, 11, 14 Edward III, 17 Edward II, and 18 Edward III, ending imperfectly.

So far as it goes, exactly the same collection as in 4g.1, below, except that the statute of Northampton is here preceded by a writ to the sheriff of Northampton, 22 May anno 3. A new hand, s. xiv med., begins at anno 9, f. 171^{v}.

ff. viii + 212 + iv. Medieval endleaves. 142 × 92 mm. Written space 92 × 55 mm. 27 long lines. Collation: 1^{12} 2–26^{8}. The quire signatures (in ink) on quires 2–20, +, b–m, o–x, show that a quire is missing after f. 100. Written in anglicana formata by an able scribe as far as f. 171^{v}, where the hand changes for the worse. Initials: (i) f. 13, 9-line blue *E* on pink ground, framed in gold and historiated (a seated king): floriated border bars of gold and colours, a musician and a bird standing on the uprights; (ii) 6-line or less, in colours on gold and coloured grounds, decorated and with prolongations into the margins, the uprights ending sometimes in human or animal heads. Contemporary(?) binding of wooden boards covered with white leather: four bands: two strap-and-pin fastenings now missing. Secundo folio (f. 14) *non capiat*.

Written in England. 'Iste liber pertinet ad me Willielmus (*sic*) sunman', f. 215, s. xvi ex. 'September 1664 bought of Mr Nowell in little Breton', f. ii^{v}. Given by Mrs J. Perowne in 1961.

158.926/4e. *Processionale* s. xv in.

1 (quire 1). ff. 1–8 Dominica prima aduentus domini post primas uesperas regulares non ad crucem sed ad sanctam mariam fit processio . . . Ecce uirgo concipiet . . . : followed by Christmas, Stephen, John Evangelist, Thomas (of Canterbury: Ihesu bone per thome merita . . .), Circumcision and Sundays after Epiphany 'ad crucem'.

2 (quires 2–9). ff. 9–73v Dominica prima aduentus domini. Processio in die ad s' mariam. R'. Missus est gabriel . . .

Temporal, Advent to Pentecost.

3 (quire 10). ff. 74–81v Six antiphons and two prayers: (*a*) Asperges me domine ysopo . . . ; (*b*) Salue regina . . . ; (*c*) Speciosa facta es . . . ; (*d*) Alma redemptoris mater . . . ; (*e*) Beata es uirgo maria . . . ; (*f*) Cum uenerimus ante conspectum . . . ; (*g*) Omnipotens deus supplices te rogamus ac petimus ut intercessio archangelorum . . . ; (*h*) Oremus dilectissimi nobis deum patrem omnipotentem ut cunctis mundum purget erroribus . . .

(*a–d, f*). *PS*, pp. 4, 190, 131, 130, 31.

4. ff. 82–126 Twenty-seven feasts of the sanctoral: f. 82 Purification of B.V.M. (2 Feb.); f. 86v Benedict (21 Mar.); f. 88 Dedicatio ecclesie; f. 92 Annunciation of B.V.M. (25 Mar.); f. 93 Invention of Cross (3 May); f. 93 De sancto pancrasio. Martir gloriose pancrati . . . (12 May); f. 96 Etheldreda (23 June); f. 97 Nativity of John Baptist (24 June); f. 99 Peter and Paul (29 June); f. 102 translation of Thomas of Canterbury (7 July); f. 103 translation of Benedict (11 July); f. 103v Margaret (20 July); f. 104v Mary Magdalene (22 July); f. 105v Anne (26 July); f. 106v Invention of Stephen (3 Aug.); f. 108 Transfiguration (6 Aug.); f. 109v Assumption of B.V.M. (15 Aug.); f. 111 Decollation of John Baptist (29 Aug.); f. 112v Nativity of B.V.M. (8 Sept.); f. 115 In festiuitate sancti Philippi episcopi et martiris Gloria et honore coronasti eum domine . . . Post matutinas. Proc'. R'. Posuisti domine . . . ; f. 116 'In exultacione (*sic*) sancte crucis' (14 Sept.); f. 117 Michael (29 Sept.); f. 118 In excepcione sancti pancrasii. Incipiat armarius respon'. Ihesu fili dei cuius precepto . . . (20 Oct.); f. 119 All Saints (1 Nov.); f. 120 Quintin (31 Oct.); f. 121 Edmund king and martyr (20 Nov.); f. 122 Katherine (25 Nov.); f. 124 Nicholas (6 Dec.).

Perhaps Philip between 8 and 14 Sept. is Philip of Alexandria, bishop and martyr, 13 Sept.

5. ff. 126–133v Processions on the 3rd Sunday in Advent (Suscipe uerbum . . .) and at Epiphany (Tria sunt munera . . .) and, from f. 129, on Wednesdays and Fridays in Advent and Lent.

f. 129 Incipiat armarius Respon'. Tua est potencia tuum regnum . . .

6 (added). ff. 133v–134 Stella celi extirpauit . . .

RH no. 19438. ff. 134v–135v are blank, except for scribbles.

7. ff. iv–vi^{v} Procession for rain, 'Domine rex deus abraham dona nobis pluuiam super faciem terre . . . ne auertas faciem tuam a singultu nostro'.

ff. vii + 135. ff. i–vii are medieval endleaves: see art. 7. 123 × 85 mm. Written space 85 × 60 mm. 7 and (ff. 1–6, 82–134) 6 long lines and music. Collation: 1–3^{8} 4^{10} 5^{8} 6, 7 cancelled after f. 39 6–8^{8} 9^{10} 9 cancelled after f. 72 10^{8} 11^{8} + 1 leaf after 5 (f. 87) 12–15^{8} 16^{4} + 1 leaf after 3 (f. 126) 17^{8}, 8 formerly pasted down. Quires 1–17 signed b–s. Initials: (i) 3-line, blue, plain or with red ornament; (ii) 1-line, red or blue. Cadels are not coloured. Contemporary binding of wooden boards covered with pink leather: three bands: central clasp missing. Secundo folio *nomini* (f. v) or *re. iacob* (f. 2).

Written in England. Art. 4 suggests that the provenance is a Benedictine house in East Anglia (?) where there was a special devotion to St Pancras and a little known St Philip and a festival of dedication between 21 and 25 March.[1] Belonged to Cox Macro: see above, p. 510. Given by Mrs J. Perowne in 1961.

158.926/4f. *Horae, etc. (partly in French)*

s. xiv^{1} and (arts. 9–17) xiv med.

1 (added, s. xiv). ff. 1^{v}–2 Memoriae of (*a*) B.V.M., (*b, c*) Kentigern, Leonard, and (*d*) Olave in three hands. f. 1^{r} is blank and pasted over with paper.

2. ff. 2^{v}–8 Calendar in gold, blue, green, and red (these colours varied for effect), and black.

Translation of Edmund and 'Dedicacio ecclesie Norwyci' (29 April, 24 Sept.) in red. The word 'pape' and feasts of St Thomas of Canterbury have not been cancelled. 'Obitus Domine Katerine bakun Anno m^{o} cccc^{o} lxxvii^{o}' added at 31 March.

3. f. 8^{v} Table of a cycle of 532 years. 'anno domini m^{o} ccc^{mo} xxxix' in the margin may show the date of writing.

4. ff. 9–26^{v} Ici comencent les matines a ihesu crucifie les queles si home chescun iour die e pense de sa passiun ke il suffri a chescun ure: il ne murra ia de male mort . . . Oreysun. Domine ihesu criste qui hora matutina pro nobis . . .

Hours of the Cross. Memoriae of B.V.M. and St John follow lauds and other hours. Headings in French.

5. ff. 27–75^{v} Hours of B.V.M. of the use of (Sarum).

Memoriae after lauds of Holy Spirit, Holy Trinity, Holy Cross, Michael, John Baptist, Peter, Andrew, John Evangelist, apostles and evangelists, Stephen, Laurence, Thomas of Canterbury, Edmund king and martyr (Aue rex gentis anglorum miles regis angelorum . . . : *RH*, no. 23809), martyrs, Denis (in another hand over erasure), Edmund 'de punteni' (O edmunde singularis signum ferens gracie . . .), Nicholas, confessors, Mary Magdalene, Margaret, All Saints, 'de la pes'; also of the Annunciation, 'e deyt estre dite apres checune oure'. f. 30 should follow f. 31. Single leaves beginning lauds and vespers are missing after ff. 34, 65.

6. ff. 76–95 Penitential psalms and (f. 86^{v}) litany.

[1] The Cluniac priory of Lewes was dedicated to Pancras and had an East Anglian dependency at Castle Acre, Norfolk.

Nineteen martyrs: (6) Edmunde . . . (14) Olaue. Twenty-three confessors: (3) Taurine. Twenty-one virgins: (6) Editha . . . (19–21) Etheldreda Osytha Milburga. One confessor, Francis, added after (20) Antoni. Three virgins added, Clare, Juliana, and Alburga.

7. ff. 95–105^{v} Ici comencent les quinze psalmes. Ad dominum cum tribularer . . . Pss. 119–33.

8. ff. 105^{v}–142^{v} Ici comence placebo.

Office of the dead.

9. ff. 142^{v}–145 Aue dei genitrix et inmaculata. Virgo celi gaudium toti mundi nata . . .

RH, no. 1761; *AH* xxx. 274–5. Thirteen 4-line stanzas. After each stanza, 'Aue maria. Cent iours de pardoun' and at the end 'La summe de iours de pardoun. Mil tres. Cens. e Cesze Cardinals de la Curt de Rome checon par sei. xl iours de pardoun'.

10. ff. 145–149^{v} Ci comence le meindre sauter nostre dame en fraunceys e en latin e contient sulement cynkaunte aues . . . La prime ioye de la concepcion nostre dame. En le honuraunce duz sire ihesu de cele seintisme aue Dont uostre mere en terre . . . (f. 149) Gaude uirgo mater cristi . . .

The Five Joys of B.V.M. in French verse (Sinclair, no. 2834), with prayers in Latin, followed by the Five Joys in Latin, *RH*, no. 7017.

11. ff. 150–2 Duce dame seynte anne ancele ihesu crist . . .

Five Joys of St Anne in French prose. Cf. Sinclair, no. 2771.

12. f. 152^{rv} Memoria of Thomas of Lancaster.

Antiphon, 'Generose miles cristi tu thoma lancastrie . . . (8 lines)'. Versicle, 'Martyr de celis . . . '. Prayer, 'Deus qui beato thome comiti lancastrie pro iuramento prestito ac pace regni anglie martirii palmam contulisti . . .'

13. ff. 152^{v}–153^{v} Ihesu le fiz marie ky uerais deux uerais hom . . . eiez merci de mei pecheresse . . .

14. ff. 153^{v}–154 En le honurance de deu et de ma dame seynte marie la treglorius e uirgine mere et pucele . . . delieueras ausi moy N. ta sergaunte . . .

15. ff. 154–5 Oreison de seinte Katerine. Seinte pucele Katerine uous pri pur icele honur ke deu vous dona . . .

16. ff. 155^{v}–157 Li apostolie ioh' xxii ad graunte a tuz ceuz que dirrunt ces matines en memorie de la passiun ihesu i an e xl iors de pardun. Domine labia mea . . . Patris sapiencia . . .

17. f. 157 Li apostolie Clement . . . Deprecor te sancta maria mater dei pietate plenissima . . .

The heading conveys an indulgence of 260 days from Pope Clement to all saying this prayer. f. 157^{v}, pasted down, is presumably blank.

ff. iii + 157 + iii. 205 × 145 mm. Written space 155 × 93 mm. 15 long lines, between double ruled lines. Collation: 1^{8} 2^{14} 3^{4} (ff. 23–6) 4^{12} wants 9 after f. 34: 4, now a singleton, is misplaced after 5 $5–6^{12}$ 7^{12} wants 5 after f. 65 $8–11^{8}$ 12^{14} $13–14^{10}$ 15 three (ff. 155–7). Arts. 4–8 are in a 'sine pedibus' textura. In art. 1 the occupations of the months are in roundels on gold grounds. Initials in arts. 4–8: (i) six, once eight, in art. 5 and one before each of arts. 4, 6–8, in colours on gold grounds, historiated: art. 5, B.V.M. and Child, Presentation, Resurrection, Harrowing of Hell, Ascension, Death of B.V.M.; art. 4, bishop at altar; art. 6, Coronation of B.V.M.; art. 7, Christ showing his wounds; art. 8, the dead rising: prolongations into which human figures, animals, and grotesques are introduced, make a continuous border on ff. 27, 76 and fill three margins on other pages; (ii) 2-line, in colours on gold and coloured grounds, decorated or containing heads, etc., with prolongations into the margins: on f. 35^{v} the *I* of *Iubilate* is an elegant goat-headed monster in green socks; (iii) 1-line, blue with red ornament or gold with grey-blue ornament. The type-i initial on f. 27 and decoration on f. 95 are reproduced by Selma Jónsdóttir, *Illumination in a manuscript of Stjórn*, Reykjavik 1971, pls. 8, 50, and Lasko and Morgan, no. 25 shows a type-i and a type-ii initial in a much reduced facsimile of f. 76. Initials in arts. 9–13, 2-line, blue with red ornament; in art. 14, 2-line, red; in art. 15, 2-line, blue with red ornament or red with green ornament and 1-line, red or blue. Line fillers in red and blue. Capital letters in the ink of the text lined with red. Binding of s. xviii, lettered 'Missale romanum'. Secundo folio (f. 10) *bra tergens* or (f. 2) *Iste cognouit*.

Written in England for use in the diocese of Norwich: arts. 13, 14 are for use by a woman. The style of decoration is East Anglian. Bacon (art. 1) is a well known Suffolk name. Armorial book-plate of William Frederick Patteson. Given by Mrs J. Perowne in 1961.

158.926/4g.1. *Nova Statuta Angliae* s. xv med., xv^{2}

1. ff. 1–29^{v} An index to art. 2, beginning imperfectly in the letter F, 'Forcible entre. Vide forcible entre'.

The last six headings are Vtlages, Wast, Wexchaundelers, Wrek en meere, Worstede, Wynchester and the last words 'Anno septimi Ricardi capitulo quinto etc'. 23 Henry VI under the heading Viscountz seems to be the latest date. ff. 30–32^{v} blank.

2. ff. 33–371 Statutes of Edward III, (f. 132) Richard II, (f. 194) Henry IV, (f. 230^{v}) Henry V, and (f. 257^{v}) Henry VI, ending 'Expliciunt statuta Regis henrici sexti'. In French and—a few statutes—Latin. 'Ex*aminat*ur' is at the end of quire 17 (f. 137^{v}) and there are traces of the same word at the end of some other quires.

Edward III. As compared with *SR* i. 251–398: statute 3 of anno 10, statutes 1, 2 of anno 15 and statute 3 of anno 25 are omitted; statutes 2 of anno 10 begins on f. 49 'Come en lestatut' (*SR* 276/16) and the passage 'Ceux sont les choses accordez . . . pointz' (276/1–15) is added on a slip, f. 48; the statute of Ireland of 17 Edward II (*SR* i. 193), 'Sachez qe a lamendement . . .', is entered as a statute of anno 17; the ordinance of justices of anno 20 ends at 'preignent' (305/13); ff. 81–3 contain a statute of the staple of 16 Sept., anno 26, 'Pur ceo qe plusours foitz . . .' (6 chapters); statutes are in a different order at anno 9 (2, 1), anno 14 (1, 3, 4, 2), anno 25 (2, 7, 6, 1, 4, 5 and after 6 the oaths of justices and clerks printed in *SR* under 20 Edward III), anno 31 (1, 3, 2 and the fourth statute in edn. (p. 357), here in first place under anno 36).

Richard II. As compared with *SR* ii. 1–110, the statutes of anno 10 and anno 21 are omitted and the statute of anno 17 includes chapters 1–10 only.

Henry IV. As *SR* ii. 111–74.

Henry V. As *SR* ii. 175–212, except that the statute of anno 8 is preceded by an 18-line Latin piece which refers to it, '. . . Teste Duce Humphredo 10 Ian. anno 8'.

Henry VI. As *SR* ii. 213–379, except that the statute of anno 1 contains chapters 1–5 only. In the statute of anno 8 there are additions to chapters 12 and 13 in the margins by another hand: they are not printed in *SR*. Anno 23 is the last to be written in the main hand: a new hand begins on f. 345.

ff. ii + 371 (foliated 1–47, 49–255, 255*, 256–371), together with an inserted slip (f. 48). 255 × 180 mm. Written space *c*.150 × 100 mm. 33 or 34 long lines usually. Collation: $1\text{–}5^8$ 6^8 (ff. 41–7, 49, and added slip, f. 48) $7\text{–}40^8$ 41^6 (ff. 321–6) $42\text{–}43^8$ 44^6 6 cancelled after f. 347 $45\text{–}47^8$: quires signed in the usual late medieval way b–z, â–ẑ, 7, ɔ. ff. 1–344 are in current anglicana of a rather legal sort (but the two-compartment *a* is not much used) and ff. 345–71 in secretary. Initials: (i) blue and red, with ornament of both colours; (ii) blue and red with red ornament; (iii) 3-line, blue with red ornament; (iv) 3-line, blue. Contemporary binding of wooden boards covered with leather, now a dirty pink: four bands: two strap-and-pin fastenings missing.

Written in England. 'Constat Iohanni Fyncham', f. 371, s. xv ex.: the name is common in Norfolk. 'Leonard filloll one This Boke Iohannes fillol witnes', f. 371, s. xvi. Belonged to Cox Macro: see above, p. 510. '10' on a label on the spine. Given by Mrs J. Perowne in 1961.

158.926/4g.2. *Paupertas* s. xiv²

Hic incipit prologus pauperis in librum qui vocatur paupertas. Optatus michi dies aduenerat in quo visitante me diuina clemencia exoneratus sum ab ecclesiastici regiminis grauissima cura . . . in manus tuas commendo spiritum meum. Deo gracias.

For six other copies of these 'flores spiritualium doctorum' in twenty-two 'diuisiones', see Bloomfield, no. 0599. f. 125ᵛ, left blank, has quotations from Augustine, 'Philosophus', etc. A reader in s. xvi made notes in the margins and collected them on four paper leaves, ff. iv–vii. A seventeenth-century reference to the copy in Lincoln College, Oxford, now MS. Lat. 18, is on f. iii.

ff. vii + 125 + i. f. iii is a late medieval parchment flyleaf. For ff. iv–vii see above. The foliation is late medieval. 195 × 140 mm. Written space 152 × 105 mm. 32 long lines. Collation: $1\text{–}10^{12}$ 11^6 wants 6, probably blank. Written in anglicana formata. Initials: f. 1, 7-line, red and blue, with red and violet ornament; (ii) 2-line, blue with red ornament, or red with violet ornament. Calf binding, s. xvii. Secundo folio *debeant. et*.

Written in England. 'Libellus qui dicitur paupertas. De Adquisitione fratris Henrici de Tylmanstone (cf. Emden, *Donors*, p. 18: floruit s. xiv²) de librario Sancti Augustini Cantuarie (*erased*) Distinctione 9ª Gradu 6º', f. iii, s. xiv ex. It is the first of two copies of the 'Liber qui dicitur paupertas' recorded in the medieval catalogue of St Augustine's, Canterbury (*Ancient Libraries*, p. 286, no. 844): the second copy, no. 845, s. xv ex., is now Lambeth Palace 498. Belonged to Cox Macro: see above, p. 510. Given by Mrs J. Perowne in 1961.

158.926/4g.3. *Theological treatises (in English)* s. xv med.

Manuscripts of arts. 1–3 are listed in the chapter, 'Wyclif and his followers', by J. Burke Severs, *Manual of the writings in Middle English*, 1970, nos. 52, 14, 58. Additions to these lists by A. Hudson in *Notes and Queries*, ccxviii (1973), 451–2, include the present manuscript.

1. ff. 1–64 Prestis dekenes. eiþer curatis shulden not be lordes . . . and þe blys of heuene wiþ outen ende. amen par charite amen.

2. ff. 64v–75 þe pater noster. Siþ þe pater noster is þe beest praier . . . wiþ hym to reste wiþouten ende.

T. Arnold, *Select English works of John Wyclif*, iii. 98–110.

3. ff. 75–78v Aue maria. Heyle be þou marie ful of grace . . . þe archaungel gabriel sent of god . . . in parfite charite amen.

F. D. Matthew, *The English works of Wyclif hitherto unprinted* (EETS, lxxiv, 1880), pp. 204–8.

4. ff. 78v–82v Credo. Alle maner of men and wymmen shulden stydfastliche bilieu . . . þus it endiþ wiþouten more Amen.

5. ff. 82v–105 þe prologe of þe ten comaundementis. Euery man and womman shuld bisily descre and coueite . . . and þus here in þis wise it endiþ wiþouten more Amen.

6. ff. 105v–106v It is wryten in þe book of daniel þe þridde capitle how þt nabulgodonosor . . . he confounde hem not.

7. ff. 106v–108v Lo frendis if it is ȝoure wille for to lerne good wordis . . . here endiþ þe prolog of þese wordes. It is written in þe book of exodi þe foure and þretti capitle. god seiþ if þat ȝe wolen here my voice . . . do to hym þe same.

A series of texts from scripture.

8. ff. 108v–117 Frendes I praie ȝou all þt heren þese wordes radde if ȝe wol not amende hem . . . and in her soules aȝens oure lord good merciable god.

On meekness and mercy.

9. ff. 117–19 Here bigynneþ a prologe of þe mercy of god. Euery man and womman shuld bisily axe for to lerne . . . to bileue and telle better amen.

10. f. 119rv þe moste þing þt holdiþ a man in goddis loue . . . or putte truth from him and turne to synne. Eight lines.

11. ff. 119v–120v Of antecrist. To speke generally antecrist is a man lyuynge synfully aȝens crist . . . þus seiþ thomas alquyn in his book þt he made of þe truþe of dyuynyte þe seuenþ book þe eiȝte capitle.

ff. i + 120 + i. 168 × 118 mm. Written space 115 × 90 mm. 26 long lines. Collation: 1–15[8]. Written in poor hybrida, by one hand throughout: the scribe does not use a capital letter to begin a sentence, nor a hyphen at a line-end when a word is broken, and he uses few abbreviations. 2-line blue initials. Contemporary binding of wooden boards covered with pink leather: four bands: a central strap-and-pin fastening missing. Secundo folio *þis pastorals*.

Written in England. 'Ro: Cotton Connintonensis', f. 1: a stray therefore from the great collection of Sir Robert Cotton (1571–1631), now in the British Library. 'W. F. Patteson 1818' inside the cover. Given by Mrs J. Perowne in 1961.

158.926/4g.4. *Processionale* s. xv med.

A processional of Bury St Edmunds, O.S.B.

1. ff. 1–82v Dominicis diebus per aduentum. Missus est angelus gabriel . . .

Temporal. In the litany on Quinquagesima Sunday the martyrs are Stephen, Edmund, Laurence, and Vincent and the confessors Benedict, Botulph, and Jurmin (f. 21v). At Easter forms are provided for use 'ad pontem sancti botulphi' (f. 59v), 'apud teyfen' (f. 65v), and 'ad portam de Rysby' (f. 63v).

2. ff. 82v–125 Sanctoral from Edward king and confessor (5 Jan.) to Nicholas (6 Dec.).

f. 82v (Edward, king and confessor) Agnus in altari . . . Aue sancte rex edwarde . . .
f. 83v (Vincent) Criste miles preciose . . .
f. 84 (Conversion of Paul) Sancte paule apostole predicator ueritatis . . . R'. Magnus sanctus . . .
f. 85 (translation of Edmund, king and martyr) Salue festa dies toto uenerabilis euo Qua sacer . . . Cant'. Hanc tua sancta diem reddit translacio claram . . . Cant'. Rex martir uirgo sublimis . . .[1]
f. 86v (Botulph) R'. Sint lumbi uestri precincti . . .
f. 87v (Etheldreda) Gaude et exulta angelorum ecclesia . . .
f. 88v (John Baptist) Gabriel angelus apparuit . . . In capella Responsorium. Inter natos mulierum . . .
f. 89v (Peter and Paul) Cornelius centurio . . . In cripta a'.
f. 90 (translation of Benedict) Alme pater qui precius|tu . . .
f. 91 (Mary Magdalene) Relinquens maria . . .
f. 91v (James) Salue festa dies toto uenerabilis euo Qua decorat . . .
f. 92v (Transfiguration) Coram tribus discipulis . . .
f. 93v (Laurence) Laurea laurenti . . .
f. 94 (Hippolytus) Yppolite si credis . . .
f. 95 (vigil of Assumption) O decus uirginitatis . . .
f. 95v (Assumption) Salue festa dies toto uenerabilis euo qua celos subiit . . . Ante magnam crucem. Rex noster in cruce . . . V' a sex monachis cantatur. O mira cristi regis potencia . . . Ascendit cristus . . . Ibo michi in montem . . . Quam pulcra es . . .
f. 99 (Bartholomew) Gloriose bartholomee . . .
f. 100 (Decollation of John Baptist) Puelle saltanti . . .
f. 100v (Nativity of B.V.M.) Stirps iesse . . . In cript' cantetur hoc R'. Solem iusticie . . . Prosa. Hodie prodit uirga iesse . . .
f. 102 (Exaltation of Cross) Nos autem gloriari . . . R'. Crux fidelis . . .

[1] The procession went 'non circa claustrum set directe in capella sancti Stephani', as against *circa claustrum et . . . in capella S. Stephani* in the Bury ritual (M. R. James, *On the abbey of S. Edmund at Bury*, 1895, pp. 185–6).

f. 105v (Matthew) Cue to common of apostle.
f. 106 (Michael) Te sanctum dominum in excelsis laudant . . .
f. 106v (Sunday within octave) R'. Archangeli michaelis . . .
f. 107 (Denis) Preciosus domini dionisius . . .
f. 108v (relics) Concede nobis domine quesumus . . .
f. 109v (All Saints) Laudem dicite deo nostro . . .
f. 109v (Martin) Martinus abrahe . . .
f. 111v (vigil of Edmund) Felix edmundus suorum . . .
f. 112 (Edmund) Salue festa dies toto uenerabilis euo martiris edmundi laude colenda pia . . . Chorus cant' O decus angelorum celi preclare senator . . . Per totum annum R'. Sancte indolis puer edmundus . . .
f. 120 (Andrew) Mox ut uocem domini . . .
f. 121 (Sabas) Beatus uir sabas qui suffert . . . Prosa. Mirandis modis preparatam Gemmis auroque decoratam . . . (f. 122v) Aue spes et flos anglorum tu choeres angelorum edmunde . . .
f. 123 (Nicholas) Ex eius tumba marmorea sacrum resudat oleum . . . Sospitati dedit egros olei perfusio . . .
f. 124v R' de s. maria cantand' feria iii rogationum. Felix namque es sacra uirgo maria . . .

3 (added). ff. 125v–126 Mater domini mei venit ad me facie rutilans vultu coruscans pulcrior luna . . . (*ends abruptly*). Noted.

ff. i + 126. 155 × 125 mm. Written space 105 × 76 mm. 7 long lines and music. Collation: 1^8 2^8 6 cancelled after f. 13 3–10^8 11^6 + 1 leaf after 6 (f. 86) 12–16^8. Initials: (i) 3-line, blue; (ii) 1-line, red or blue. Cadels have green pen-work ornament and red linings. Contemporary binding of wooden boards covered with pink leather: three bands: central strap and pin missing. Secundo folio *perueniet*.

Written for use at the abbey of Bury St Edmunds, as James Cobbes noted on f. iv, s. xvii.[1] Belonged to Cox Macro: see above, p. 510. '13' on a label on the spine. Given by Mrs J. Perowne in 1961.

158.926/4g.5. *Theological treatises (in English)* s. xv[1]

1. ff. 1–30 A pistle of sent Ierom sent to a mayde demetriade: þat hadde vowed chastite to oure lord ihesu criste. The firste besynesse and þe firste studie . . . he þat for us deide on þe roode tre. Qui cum patre . . . Amen.

Jolliffe, H. 5, O. 11. A translation of part of Pseudo-Jerome (Pelagius: cf. *Clavis*, no. 737), Epistola ad Demetriadem (*PL* xxxiii. 1105–20). f. 30v blank.

2. ff. 31–58v Crist þat deyde on the tre for þe sauacion of mankende. Graunte vs grace for to skape the sleye fleyt of þe fende. That we be noch for synne lost at oure deth with outyn ende. Amen. These thingis þat I haue purposid þrow godis grace to don in þis lityl tretys . . . ȝeue me grace. De superbia. Pride is not ellis but a badde desyre . . . and take oure soule after oure deth to his blisful place Amen. Explicit tractus de septem peccatis mortalibus et de eorum speciebus.

[1] James Cobbes owned the Bury psalter now at Bury St Edmunds School (*MMBL* ii. 219), Manchester, Chetham's Library 11366 (q.v.), and John Rylands University Library Fr. 143 (q.v.), and a 'Popish Missal or Breviary with a Calendar 3 inches long and 2 broad', no. 28 of the duodecimos in the Macro catalogue of 1766 (cf. above, p. 510).

Jolliffe, F. 2(a). This copy collated by J. P. M. van Zutphen, *A litil tretys on the seven deadly sins by Richard Lavynham O. Carm.*, 1956. For Lavynham see Emden, *BRUO*, p. 1110.

3. ff. 58v–88 Pater noster qui es in celis. Oure fader þat art in heuene . . . but delyuere us fro euery wikked. Amen. So mote it ben. þis is cleped oure lordis prayeris for oure lord ihesu crist made it . . . (f. 61v) and þouh wullene and lynene ben nedful. Pater noster qui es in celis. Oure fadir þat art in heuene. God is oure fadir . . . he þat for us alle deyȝed on þe rode tre. Amen.

Jolliffe, M. 9. Next to art. 2 also in B.L., Harley 1197.

4. f. 88rv Legitur in cronicis Romanorum quod tempore Antonini Imperatoris in ciuitate romana accidebat pestilencia . . .

The answers of four philosophers, Ȝifte is domysman . . . and treue may no man fynde (16 lines). *IMEV*, no. 906. f. 89rv left blank.

ff. iii + 89. The pastedown inside the front cover and ff. i–iii are medieval parchment leaves. 190 × 130 mm. Written space 142 × 90 mm. 27 long lines. Collation: $1\text{–}3^8$ 4^4 5^2 (ff. 29, 30) $6\text{–}12^8$ 13^4 (4 is pasted down). Quires, except the fifth, signed +, a–l. A fairly large textura. Initials: (i) 4-line, gold on pink grounds patterned in white, with sprays into the margins; (ii) 2-line, blue with red ornament. Capital letters in the ink of the text lined with red. Binding of wooden boards (s. xv ?) covered with leather, s. xvi, bearing Oldham's roll FP. g. 5, and as centrepiece the Burghley gilt armorial as on 926.4b, q.v.: four bands. Secundo folio *is suffred*.

Written in England. Belonged to William Cecil, Lord Burghley (1520–98). The Burghley armorial book-plate, s. xvii, with motto 'Cor vnum via vna' inside the cover. An erasure, f. i. No. 52 of the manuscripts in English in the Burghley sale, 21 Nov. 1687. Belonged to Cox Macro: see above, p. 510. '14' on a label on the spine. Given by Mrs J. Perowne in 1961.

158.926/4g.7. *Prophetae minores glosati* s. xii ex.

Minor Prophets in a central column, glossed between the lines and with a column of gloss on each side. Text and apparatus are on one grid. The two prologues at the beginning, Non idem ordo and Temporibus ozee (Stegmüller, nos. 500, 507), are in the same size of script as the text, as in Eton College 23 (*MMBL* ii. 649). Other prologues are in the size of script used for the gloss.

Two leaves missing after p. 264 which ends in Zechariah 14: 18 'ascenderit et non uenerit'; p. 269 begins in Malachi 1: 7 'pecta est. Si offeratis'. p. 280 blank.

The prologues written in with the gloss are hard to distinguish from it. Stegmüller, nos. 511, 510, and 509 are on p. 71 (Joel); 515, 512, and 513 on p. 95 (Amos); 519 on p. 142 (Obadiah); 524 and 521 on p. 150 (Jonah); 526 and 525 on p. 163 (Micah); 528 on p. 184 (Nahum); 531 on p. 194 (Habakkuk); 534 on p. 207 (Zephaniah); 538 on p. 219 (Haggai); 539, 540 on p. 227 (Zechariah); also passages not listed as prologues by Stegmüller, but which occur as prologues in some English Bibles, (p. 142) 'Abdias quanto breuior . . . mutans quibusdam uerbis' (Obadiah), (p. 150) 'Ionas qui columba interpretatur . . . ascendat in celum (Jonah), (p. 163) 'Sermo dei qui semper . . . a parentibus imposita sunt' (Micah), (p. 219) 'Cum cyrus rex persarum . . . prohibentibus' (Haggai): cf. his index.

Running chapter numbers. Hosea is in 33 chapters, Joel in 12, Amos in 23, Obadiah in 4, Jonah in 7, Micah in 10, Nahum in 5, Habakkuk in 6, Zephaniah in 5, Haggai in 4, Zechariah in 19+, Malachi in 7.

ff. ii + 138, paginated i–iv, 1–264, 269–80. 298 × 210 mm. Written space *c.*200 mm high and from 165 to 130 mm wide. 20 or less lines of text, spaced differently from page to page. 37–41 lines of gloss. Pricks in both margins of some quires. The first line of gloss above the top ruled line in quires 1–4, 12–18. Collation: $1–16^8$ 17^8 wants 4, 5 after p. 264 18^4. Initials: (i) of books, red and blue with ornament of both colours; (ii) of some prologues, 2-line, blue or red with ornament of the other colour; (iii) 1-line, blue or red. Medieval binding of wooden boards covered with white leather: two widely separated bands: central strap and pin missing: slits in the leather near the top of the back cover may have held a title label. Secundo folio *simulacrorum*.

Written in England. 'Iste liber est [. . . .] et in hoc uolumine continentur xii prophete glosati', p. iv, s. xiii in. Over the erasure is 'Iohannis Duffeyld', s. xv.[1] '1570 Liber Roberti Staunton. De Staunton Armiger', p. iv. '11' on a label on the spine, s. xix^1. Given by Mrs J. Perowne in 1961.

181.27. *Horae* s. xv ex.

1. ff. $1–12^v$ Calendar in red and black.

Entries in red include Rumold and Lambert (1 July, 17 Sept.). The text is written on the last six leaves of quire 1 and the first six of quire 2: $1^{1,2}$ and $2^{7,8}$ remain blank.

2. ff. 16–20 Incipiunt hore sancte crucis.

3. f. 21^{rv} Imnus. Veni creator spiritus . . .

4. ff. 22–3 Dese bedinge es gescreuen in de kerke van sinte Ian te latranen te Rome ende diese dagelijcx leest . . . Die verdient lxxx^m iair aflaets . . . amen. Domine ihesu criste Rogo te et amoneo in honore illius gaudii . . . (f. 23) papa eugenius. Sancte et indiuidue trinitati ihesu xpristi crucifixi . . . amen. f. 23^v blank.

5. ff. $24–67^v$ Hours of B.V.M. of the use of (Tournai).

6. ff. 70–87 Penitential psalms and (f. 80^v) litany.

Nineteen martyrs: (2) Rumolde repeated. Twenty-nine confessors: (1) Lamberte . . . (7) Gommare . . . (14) Gommare. f. 87^v blank.

7. ff. 89–112 Incipiunt vigilie mortuorum.

Office of the dead. Three lessons. f. 112^v blank.

ff. 114 + i, foliated (one unnumbered leaf), i, 1–113. 172 × 120 mm. Written space 90 × 60 mm. 16 long lines. Ruled in violet ink. Collation: 1^8 (pastedown, i, 1–6) $2–9^8$ 10^6 + 1

[1] One of this name owned Lincoln College, Oxford, Lat. 26: Emden, *BRUO*, p. 600.

leaf after 6 (f. 79) 11–14⁸, together with three singleton picture pages, blank on the rectos (ff. 15, 69, 88). Written in a good set hybrida. Three full-page pictures, ff. 15ᵛ, 69ᵛ, 88ᵛ (raising of Lazarus): only the stub of a leaf cut out before art. 5 remains. Initials: (i) in colour on gold grounds, historiated (ff. 33ᵛ, 50ᵛ, 56ᵛ, 89) or decorated; (ii, iii) 2-line and 1-line, red or blue: framed floral borders on pages with pictures or initials of type (i), continuous on ff. 16, 24, 70, and in the lower margin of other pages. Binding of wooden boards, covered with green velvet, perhaps contemporary: four bands.

Written for use in the southern Low Countries, perhaps at Mechlen where Rumold was patron. Given in September 1827; 'T. Bignold Esq. donor' inside the cover.

228.961. *Horae* s. xv med.

1. ff. 1–11ᵛ Sarum calendar in red and black, lacking January.

'pape' erased. The name of St Thomas of Canterbury in red at 29 Dec. was erased and later replaced, but his name at 7 July has not been touched.

2. ff. 12–42 Hic incipiunt matutine de beata maria uirgine.

Hours of B.V.M. of the use of (Sarum). Memoriae of Holy Spirit, Holy Trinity, Holy Cross, Michael, John Baptist, Peter and Paul, John Evangelist, Andrew, Stephen, Laurence, Nicholas, Thomas of Canterbury (erased and then replaced), Mary Magdalene, Katherine, Margaret, relics, All Saints, and peace follow lauds. Hours of the Cross worked in.

3 (added) f. 42ʳᵛ Gaude virgo mater cristi . . . *RH*, no. 7017.

4. ff. 43–9 Hic incipiunt septem psalmi penitenciales.

5. ff. 49–50ᵛ Hic incipiunt quindecim psalmi. Cues only of the first twelve psalms.

6. ff. 50ᵛ–56ᵛ Litany.

Twenty-five virgins: (1) Anna . . . (14) Pandonia. The prayers after Deus cui proprium are the six in *Brev. ad usum Sarum*, ii. 254–5.

7. ff. 58–60ᵛ Hic incipiunt vigilie mortuorum. Ends imperfectly.

ff. ii + 60 + ii. 141 × 98 mm. Written space 95 × 52 mm. 22 long lines. Collation: 1¹² wants 1 2–7⁸ together with a picture page, the recto blank, inserted after 7⁵ (f. 57). The picture, f. 57ᵛ, is full page, but badly rubbed. Initials: (i) ff. 12, 43, 58, in colour on gold grounds, decorated and with prolongations which form continuous borders; (ii) 6-line, gold on coloured grounds, patterned in white and with prolongations; (iii) 2-line, gold on coloured grounds; (iv) 1-line, gold with grey-blue ornament or blue with red ornament. Capital letters in the ink of the text touched with red. Line fillers in art. 6 only: red, blue, and gold. Binding of s. xix. Secundo folio (f. 13) *nouerunt*.

Written in England. The church at Eltisley, Cambridgeshire, is dedicated to Pandonia (*VCH, Cambridgeshire*, ii. 197; vi. 56–7). Cf. *MMBL* i. 382. Given by Mr M. D. B. Hickie of Bracondale (Norwich), before 1830.

NORWICH. CATHEDRAL[1]

1. *Chronicon Angliae, etc.* 1270–2, s. xiii^2

1. ff. 1–43^v (quires 1–6). A chronicle written at Norwich in or soon after 1270 and continued at short intervals to 1292. Described on pp. xxi–xxv of H. R. Luard's edition (RS, 1859), with facsimile of f. 1. The title 'Cronica Cotton' on f. 1 is probably of s. xv/xvi. In the later and inferior manuscript, B.L., Cotton Nero C. v, the chronicle is ascribed to Bartholomew Cotton, monk of Norwich (Magister Celarii, 1282, 1284), but his part in its compilation is doubtful and he may have had nothing to do with the present manuscript, most of which, ff. 1–32^v and 45–53 (arts. 1*a*, 3), is in the hand of the Norwich monk Ralph de Fretenham, as appears by comparison with the script of the account roll headed 'Recept' Camere Prioris Norwic' per manus Radulfi de Fretenham Anno W. de Kirkeby Prioris secundo (1273–4)'.

(*a*). ff. 1–32^v Ab origine mundi usque ad annos gracie tantummodo . . . exceptis tribus. As edn., pp. 47–146/26 (1272). In one hand, with a change of ink at f. 32/15, 'Lodowicus rex francorum' (edn., p. 144/9: in 1270), and changes on f. 32^v which looks as if it may have been written on six occasions, with pauses after 'recedens', 'arripuit', 'potiretur', 'Allemannie' and 'extremum' (edn., p. 145/20, 25; p. 146/8, 16, 17). After f. 32 three leaves have been cut out: traces of writing can be seen on the edges of the stubs, enough to show that there was more text on these leaves than is printed in edn., pp. 146/26–150/20: at most half a page was left blank on the verso of the third leaf.

(*b*). ff. 33–35^v Anno gracie M^o cc^o lxxiii . . . propria interfecit. Ma–. As edn., pp. 150/21–161/22 (1273–81). Perhaps all in one hand as far as f. 34/22, 'profecta' (*sic*), in 1279, where the Oxford manuscript ends (edn., p. 159/17), but with pauses, probably, after 'confirmatus' and 'incarcerati' (f. 33^v/15, 29: edn., pp. 156 end, 157/28). The amount missing cannot be estimated, since f. 35 is the last leaf of a quire; the text in edn., pp. 161/22–166/9 is not here.

(*c*). ff. 36^v–41^v Annals for 1285–91. As edn., pp. 166/10–182/32 and 427–8 (Appendix B), where a passage on f. 40^v/1–13 marked 'va cat' is printed. Changes of hand after 'pecunialiter', f. 36^v/15, after 'incarcerauit', f. 36^v/16, and after 'scociam', f. 40^v/30 (edn., pp. 167/2 *pecuniariter*, 167/3, 180/23). ff. 36^v/16–40^v/30 may all have been written at one time. The recto of f. 36 was left blank.

(*d*). ff. 42–3 The matter printed from this manuscript in edn., pp. 428–33 (Appendix D: 1291–2), except the first fifteen words, 'vbi Rex cepit inpungnare homines de scocia qui illico terram Scocie in Manu regis subiugarunt', which Luard omitted because he had already printed them on p. 180/23–5. A large blue *B* in the margin of f. 42 shows that the text on these two leaves—which are the last two leaves of quire 6, not interpolated leaves, as Luard says—is to be taken after 'scociam' on f. 40^v/30, where there is a corresponding red *A* in the margin. The hand is the same as that which wrote ff. 40^v/31–41^v. f. 43^v is blank.

2. f. 44^{rv} The letter from Pope Gregory X to the bishops of London and Ely, 1273, printed in edn., pp. 421–7 (Appendix A).

3. (*a*) ff. 45–8 Carta Regis Iohannis de communis libertatibus Anglie. I. dei gracie Rex Anglie . . . Dat' per manum nostram in prato quod uocatur runingemedwe

[1] MSS. 1–5 are on permanent deposit in the Norfolk Record Office, DCL/1–5.

inter Stanes et Windesoures xv° die Iunii anni regni nostri decimo (*sic*). (*b*) ff. 48–49ᵛ Incipit carta Henrici Regis de Foresta. H. dei gracia rex Anglie . . . (*c*) ff. 49ᵛ–50 Sentencia formidabilis super transgressores cartarum subscriptarum. Anno gracie M° cc° liii° Idus maii . . . apponenda. Et ut memoria huius sentencie memoriter perpetuetur et in cordibus omnium indelibilius imprimatur. pupplicari dicta sentencia `statuitur´ per totam angliam in ecclesiis parochialibus. accensis candelis et pulsatis sollempniter campanis dominicis ac festiuis diebus de precepto omnium episcoporum. Set in episcopatibus lincoln' et london' ubicumque populi conueniebant. sicuti in comitatibus. hundredis. et curiis laicorum. Vicini sacerdotes accedentes cum crucibus et campanulis manialibus dictam sentenciam horribiliter fulminandam (*altered to* fulminarunt). Protegat diuina clemencia omnes ecclesie (*sic*) regnique (*sic*) fideles: a tanta excommunicacionis voragine terribiliter metuenda. (*d*) f. 50 References to art. 1 for the assize of bread (1202) and the new laws of King Henry at Winchester (1236). (*e*) f. 50ᵛ Capitula ad uisum francpleg'. De pace domini Si bene custodiatur . . . De coterellis qui pascunt in communi quo waranto exigunt communam pasturam: 31 heads. (*f*) f. 51 Expositio anglorum nominum in cartis secundum consuetudinem scacarii . . . (*g*) f. 51ᵛ De Regibus Anglie . . . : coronation and death dates of English kings from William I, ending at Henry III with 'et anno regni sui', to which another hand or the same hand later—it resembles the hand of the passage beginning 'Lodowicus' on f. 32—added 'lvi diem clausit extremum. Anno gracie M.cc.lxx iiii Dominus Edwardus coronatus est vna cum Regina et anno regni sui'. (*h*) f. 52 Archbishops of Canterbury to Kilwardby (1273–8) whose name is an addition in the hand which added to (*g*). (*i*) f. 52ᵛ Bishops of Norwich to William de Middleton (1278), whose name has been added in another hand, together with the date of death and number of years of his predecessor, Ralph de Skerning. (*j*) f. 53 Priors of Norwich to William de Brunham (deposed in 1273), after whom comes 'Willelmus de Kyrkebi' as an addition in the same hand, 'Henricus de Lakenham' and 'Robertus de Langele' as additions in a hand like that of art. 2, and later priors: the list ends with Robert Catton and William Castleton.

(*a*). *SR* i, Charters, p. 9. (*b*). *SR* i, Charters, p. 26. (*c*). *SR* i. 6, but continuing further. (*f*). Printed hence by Luard, op. cit., pp. 439–40 (Appendix G). (*g*). In B.L., Add. 30079, which belonged to Fretenham a notice of the death of Henry III is added in a large textura and the same words, 'diem clausit extremum', are used. f. 53ᵛ was left blank.

4 (added on flyleaves). (*a*) f. 54ᵛ A contemporary account of the arrest of Thomas Wolsey, 5 Nov. 1530, and the great wind at the time. (*b*) f. 55ᵛ 'Ormisby' and below it 'Simplice sub wltu liuor latet absque tumultu Tempore quo valeat nititur vt noceat', s. xiv.

ff. v + 53 + v. ff. iii–v, 54–6 are medieval parchment binding leaves. 285 × 180 mm. Written space 213 × 122 mm. 35 or 36 long lines and (ff. 37–43) 37 or 38 long lines. Collation: 1^4 2^4 + 2 leaves after 4 (ff. 9, 10) $3\text{–}4^8$ 5^{12} wants 7–9 after f. 32 6^8 7 ten (ff. 44–53: ff. 46–51 are three bifolia). The first line of writing below the top ruled line. Fretenham's hand is a modified textura. The first sixteen lines of art. 1*c* are in anglicana formata, which is used also for ff. 40ᵛ/31–41/21: the scribe changed to current anglicana for f. 41/21–41ᵛ and used it also for art. 1*d*. Art. 2 is in current anglicana. Initials: (i) f. 1, blue with red ornament; (ii) 1-line, red or blue. Binding of s. xviii. Secundo folio *Anno gracie*.

Written at Norwich, mainly by Ralph de Fretenham (see above). The pressmark 'C. xi' and inscription 'Radulphi de fretinham Monachi', f. 1, are reproduced in Luard's edition: cf. B.L. Add. 30079, 'C. xii Radulphi de fretinham Monachi'. 'C. xix' (f. 55v). 'Liber Ecclesiæ Cathedralis Norwici ex dono Arthuri Branthwayt Armigeri ejusdem Ecclesiæ Seneschalli Anno 1709', f. iii.

2. *J. Boccaccio, De genealogiis deorum; etc.* s. xv^2

1. Preliminaries to art. 2: (*a*) ff. 1-6v 'Figure' illustrating bks. 1-7, 9-12; (*b*) ff. 7-17 An alphabetical table of names in art. 2, Abasten-Zetus, preceded by an introduction, Memo^{it} thesaurus deliciarum . . . , ego dominicus de arecio presens opus pro mea multorumque vtilitate confeci': the A-E part is fuller than the rest and in a different hand; (*c*) Name-lists, (1) Atropos-Ypologus, (2) Affrodite-Venus. ff. 4v, 21-22v left blank.

2. ff. 23-152v Genealogie deorum gentilium ad Hugonem inclitum ierusalem et ciprorum regem Secundum magistrum Iohannem boccachium de clertaldo. liber primus incipit. Prohemium incipit. Si satis ex relatis domini permensis egregii militis tui . . . (*text*, f. 26) Summa cum maiestate tenebrarum arbore . . . set nomine tuo da gloriam amen. Genealogie deorum gentilium . . . liber quintus-decimus et vltimus explicit feliciter deo laus.

Printed in 1472 (*GKW* 4475) and later.

3 (quires 15-18). Moralized tales, etc.: (*a*) ff. 154-62 Incipiunt ymaginaciones Fulgencii. Refert fulgencius de ornatu orbis. quod cum Romani . . . de quibus tormentis nos preseruet deus amen; (*b*) ff. 162-163v Incipiunt enigmata aristotelis moralizata. Quod non debemus diuicias nimis appetere. Valerius libro 3o ponit enigmata aristotelis. Primum est stateram . . . disperdet te etc. a quo nos conseruet etc. Expliciunt enigmata aristotelis; (*c*) ff. 163v-170v Narraciones antiquorum. Legitur in cronicis quod erat in ciuitate troie quedam ymago minerue . . . ecclesiasticus vocatur; (*d*) ff. 170v-173v Tres habet leo naturas. prima cum ambulat . . . tollens peccata mundi; (*e*) ff. 173v-185 Theodosius de vita Alexandri. Rex cecilie alexandrum ad conuiuium inuitauit . . . a tali pigricia nos conseruet altissimus amen; (*f*) ff. 185v-188v De iiii^{or} virtutibus cardinalibus. Iusticia est preclarissima virtutum . . . sunt conseruantia castitatem; (*g*) ff. 188-9 Incipiunt mithologie Fulgencii. Intencio venerabilis Fulgencii in sua mithologia que est sub tegmine fabularum . . . odoramenta succendere; (*h*) ff. 190-1 Prohemium in moralizationem poematum ex libris ouidii metamorphosios intitulati exce`r´ptarum per (*blank*). [A] veritate quidem auditum auertent. ad fabulas autem conuertentur ad timotheum. Dicit apostolus paulus . . . ymaginem siue figuram. Saturnus supponebatur et pingebatur . . . libido et (*ends abruptly*).

(*a, b, e-g*). The same or similar pieces are in many of the manuscripts listed by H. Liebeschütz, *Fulgentius metaforalis*, 1926, pp. 47-53, 115. (*b*). Seven enigmas. (*c*). Divided into sections by paragraph signs and thirty-five coloured letters, blue or red. The sections on f. 164v begin 'Narrat solinus de pellicano', 'Refert cassiodorus quod fuerunt duo reges', 'Legitur de quodam pisce monstruo marino', 'Narrat ouidius magnus de bello troiano'. The running title is 'Narraciones venerabilium antiquorum moralizate'. (*d*). Running title 'De naturis animalium'. (*e*). R. Holcot, Moralitates. Printed in 1505 and later. Most of the fifty-four pieces set out in *Catalogue of Romances*, iii. 106–13, occur here, but not always in the same order. No. 15 there is here on f. 181^v and has against it 'Ne desperetis. Ye that haf in synne mysthougth Trast in god and dispeyr' ye nowgth. Exemplo. Of myn exampul take good heed And reward in hevyn xal be your med'. (*g*). The beginning of John Ridevall's preface to his commentary on the Mythologiae of Fulgentius, ed. Liebeschütz, op. cit., pp. 65–66/22. (*h*). The preface and thirty-one lines of ch. 1 of Pierre Bersuire's moralization of Ovid, bk. 15 of his Reductorium morale in the earlier recension, as Bodleian MS. Bodley 571, ff. 1–2va/17.[1] f. 191^v blank.

ff. ii + 191 + i, foliated (i, ii), 1–86, 86*, 87–154, 156–91, (192). ff. 154–88 paginated 1–67 in a medieval hand. Paper, except f. ii, a medieval flyleaf. 297 × 220 mm. Written space *c.*195 × 140 mm. 44–53 long lines. Frame ruling in pencil. Collation: 1 six 2^{12} 3^4 (ff. 19–22) 4–16^{12} 17^8 18 five (ff. 187–91). Quires 4–17 signed A–O. A good secretary hand in two sizes, the smaller beginning at f. 83. Initials: (i) f. 23, blue and red, with ornament of both colours forming a continuous border; (ii–iv) 4-line, 3-line, and 2-line, blue with red ornament. Contemporary binding of wooden boards, rebacked: a little of the old white leather cover remains on the front board. Secundo folio (f. 24) *si inter mortales*.

Written in England. 'Liber ecclesie cath' norwiensis (*sic*) per dompnum Robertum de Iernemuth'. monachum dicti loci' and, in another hand, the pressmark 'F. lxxv', f. 22^v. 'D. R. Catton alias bennys canonicus et subdecanus istius ecclesie' precedes a table of contents in the same hand, f. ii^v. 'N° 36' (altered to 25), f. 1, s. xviii. St Martin in the Fields, London (Tenison) sale, 1 July 1861, lot 13. Acquired in 1883 for £12. 12*s*.

3. *Psalterium* s. xv^1

1. ff. 1–6^v Sarum calendar in red and black, graded.

Translation of Edmund and Thomas of Hereford (29 April, 2 Oct.) are marked 'sinod'. Winefred (3 Nov.) is marked 'prouinc'. An erased entry at 24 Sept. probably recorded the dedication of the cathedral of Norwich. 'pape' erased and the December feast of Thomas of Canterbury, but his name was not touched at 5 Jan. and 7 July. Botolph and Osmund added, 17 June, 16 July.

2. ff. 7–112. Psalms 1–150. Four leaves missing.

3. ff. 112–121^v Six ferial canticles, Benedicite, Benedictus, Te Deum, Nunc dimittis, Magnificat, and Quicumque vult.

A leaf missing after f. 121. The end of Quicumque vult was upplied on ff. 122, 123 in s. xvi (?).

4 (added). Local notices in the lower margins of the August–September opening and the November page of art. 1: The yere of ow^r lord god m^{lmo} v^c lii ye xxvii day of August ye Erle of Warwyke put downe Robard Kett of wyndam [. . . . . .] (*a line cut off*) qwhyce ye citey of Norwych haue kepte for y^t day a sole*m*ny messe and ryngynge geuynge laude and prayse to allmyghty god for geuy*n*ge ye vyctory; Ad festum sancti leonardi (*6 Nov.*) Magnum flumen In hac ciuitate Norwycen' Anno domini my^{lmo} quingentesimo decimo nono.

[1] I owe this identification to Mr C. Mainzer.

ff. vi + 121 + ii (ff. 122–3: see above) + v. 179 × 130 mm. Written space 120 × 75 mm. 22 long lines. Collation: 1^6 2–5^8 6^8 wants 5 after f. 42 7–8^8 9^8 wants 5 after f. 65 10^8 wants 8 after f. 75 11^8 12^8 wants 1 before f. 84 13–15^8 16^8 wants 8 after f. 121. Quires 2–15 signed (a)–o. Initials: (i) of Pss. 1, 26, 38, 68, 109 (Pss. 52, 80, 97 missing), 6-line or 7-line, in colours on gold and coloured grounds decorated in colours, including brick-red and green, and with prolongations into the margins: a continuous border, f. 7; (ii) 2-line, gold on coloured grounds, with short sprays into the margins; (iii) 1-line, blue with red ornament or gold with violet ornament. Lasko and Morgan, no. 48: reduced facsimile of f. 23 shows initials of types (i) and (iii). Line fillers in blue and red. Binding of s. xviii. Secundo folio (f. 8) *meus es*.

Written in England. In use in Norwich in s. xvi. Lot 35 in a Sotheby sale, 23 May 1889. Bought in 1912: see *Norfolk Archaeology*, xix. 82.

4. *Liber sextus cum tribus glosis* s. xiv[1]

1. ff. 1–67 (*begins imperfectly*) nito prebendam illi debere eam sibi dimiserit . . . versus finem. Nam si dominus dederit et domina melansa mea vxor non interrumperit maiores et summe vtiles eis in posterum labores meos offeram Iam licet nouiter inchoatos. iste versiculus vtiliter remansisset in calamo Iohannes Andree.

The commentary on the Sextus liber decretalium and Regulae iuris by Johannes Andreae, beginning near the end of the commentary on III. iv. 13. The printed editions do not have the seven words after 'dederit'. f. 67v is blank.

2. ff. 68–273v The Sext, with prologue addressed to the university of Oxford (bonon' *interlined*), together with the commentary of Johannes Monachus which follows the text, chapter by chapter.

The commentary begins 'Secundum philosophum scire est rem per causam cognoscere'. A table of the Regulae iuris is in a blank space on f. 273v.

3. ff. 274–301 Premissis casibus singularibus . . . in nouem C. ult'. Explicit apparatus domini digni super ti. de regulis iuris. Nec vi.

The commentary of Dinus de Mugello on the Regulae iuris printed in 1472 and later (*GKW*, nos. 2854–67), ending originally in sect. 87. The rest was supplied in s. xiv ex. on f. 301. f. 302rv is blank.

4. ff. 303–465v Venerabilibus et discretis uiris . . . cum percussio. in fine.

The commentary of Guido de Baysio on the Sext.

Arts. 5, 6 are additions on three of four leaves left blank at the end of quire 40.

5 (added, s. xiv[1]). ff. 466–8 Incipit summa aurea Iohannis Andree vocat' Rosa obriza siue speculum matrimoniale. In nomine inuocato ad honorem ipsius . . . quid dicunt vide per te etc. Explicit summula domini Iohannis Andree etc'.

Printed *c.* 1473–5 and later (*GKW*, nos. 1751–6: Summa de sponsalibus et matrimoniis).

6. f. 468v (*a*, *b*) Extracts headed 'Constitutiones de Merton' and 'Lameth'. (*c*) Norwyc constitucio de fructibus percipiendis. Walterus dei gracia etc'. Dominus

Walterus de Sowthfeld episcopus Norwyc' in synodo sancti Michaelis Norwic' presidens de consensu capituli dioc' . . . diffinimus . . . vt . . . omnes rectores et vicarii . . .', followed by a testamentary clause.

(*a*). s. xiv med. On tithes, 'Quoniam propter diuersas consuetudines in petendas decimas . . .'. (*b*). s. xiv/xv. (*c*). s. xiv/xv. A constitution of Walter Suffield, bishop of Norwich, 1255, printed by D. Wilkins, *Concilia*, 1737, i. 708.

ff. iii + 470 + i, foliated (i–iii), 1–371, 371*, 372–469, (470). 357 × 210 mm. Written space *c.*275 × 150 mm. 2 cols. 33 lines of text (art. 2), 65 lines of commentary (arts. 1–4) and 71 lines of commentary (art. 4). Collation: $1\text{–}5^{12}$ 6^{8} wants 8, blank, after f. 67, $7\text{–}25^{12}$ 26 seven (ff. 296–302: five singletons followed by an inserted bifolium) $27\text{–}40^{12}$. Contemporary (?) signatures in pencil, repeated and revised in ink: a new series begins at f. 315 (quire 28) and runs to f. 440 (quire 38), a–i, c, d in pencil and a–l in ink. The ink signatures are like those commonly found in late medieval manuscripts and the pencil signatures seem to be an early and not quite regular example of the same system. Arts. 2–4 in textura (two sizes in art. 2). Art. 1 in anglicana, usually current: single compartment *a*: the hand changes at f. $46^{ra}/16$ and at f. $56^{rb}/16$. Initials: (i) red and blue, with ornament of both colours; (ii) 2-line, blue with red and blue or (art. 1) red ornament; (iii) red. Capital letters in the ink of the text are filled with pale yellow. Binding of s. xviii ex.: the mark of a chain attached to a former binding shows on ff. 468–9.

Written in England. Formerly in a chained library: see above. 'I J. xi/Law 56' inside the cover. 'Phillipps MS. 3623', f. 1, at foot. Lot 133 in the sale of Phillipps manuscripts at Sotheby's, 10 June 1896, lot 133, to Leighton (£4). Sale at Puttick's, 29 June 1916, lot 527. '£15. 15' inside the cover.

5. *Sermons in English* 1432

A fragment of a paper manuscript containing sermons in English. The eight leaves and the binding were removed, some time between 1836 and 1859, from what is now Manchester, John Rylands University Library, Eng. 109, q.v.

Sequentiae, etc. s. xv/xvi

A printed quarto Roman missal (Weale–Bohatta, no. 882: Venice, E. Ratdolt, *c.*1483) was added to in England, *c.*1500. Arts. 2–6 are on twenty leaves at the end.

1. On the title-page, recto and (*c–f*) verso, several hands wrote: (*a–c*) collects for Mellitus, Presentation of B.V.M., Alexis (17 July: Deus sancte humilitatis et deuote pauper(tatis) amator cui beatus alexus . . .); (*d*) collect, secret, and postcommunion for Dunstan; (*e, f*) collects for translation of Monica (Omnipotens sempiterne deus qui hunc diem translacionis gloriosissime matris monice . . .) and Peter Martyr.

2. pp. 1, 2, 33–4 (*a*) p. 1 Sequence, Solemne canticum, for Thomas of Canterbury. (*b*) p. 2 Collect for Ivo. (*c*) pp. 2, 33 Collect, tract (O patriarcha inclite . . .) and secret for Joseph. (*d, e*) pp. 33–4 Collects for David and Chad.

(*a*) and the tract in (*c*) are referred to in *Brev. ad usum Sarum* III. xcvii–viii, as being 'in Mr Sherbrooke's MS.'.

3. pp. 4–16, 27–30 Sequences: (*a*) p. 4, for John Baptist, Sancti baptiste cristi preconis; (*b, c*) pp. 4, 5, for Visitation of B.V.M., Celebremus in hac die and Veni mater gracie; (*d*) pp. 5, 6, for Anne, Testamento veteri; (*e*) p. 6, for Assumption of B.V.M., A rea virga; (*f*) p. 10, for Christmas, Letabundus exultet; (*g*) pp. 10–11, for Epiphany, Epiphaniam domino; (*h*) p. 11, for Purification of B.V.M., Hac clara die; (*i*) pp. 11–12, for Annunciation of B.V.M., Aue mundi spes maria; (*j*) p. 12, for Ascension, Rex omnipotens die hodierna; (*k*) pp. 12–13, for Trinity, Benedicta sit beata trinitas; (*l, m*) pp. 13–15, for the Five Wounds, Plangat syon saluatorem and Cenam cum discipulis; (*n*) p. 16, for Nicholas of Tolentino, Tibi criste redemptori; (*o–u*) for feasts of B.V.M., p. 27 (Conception) Dies leta celebretur, p. 28 ('tempore paschali') Virgini marie laudes, p. 28 Dulcis aue penitentis (*RH*, no. 4903), pp. 28–9 Uerbum bonum et suaue, p. 29 Aue marie gracia plena. Dominus tecum virgo serena, pp. 29–30 (Advent) Missus gabriel de celis, p. 30 Gaude uirgo mater cristi.

All but (*q*) and (*u*) are in C. Wordsworth's list of 'Sequences of the English Church', *Brev. ad usum Sarum* III. xcii–xcix. His only reference for (*l, n, o*) is the present manuscript. p. 3 is blank.

4. pp. 5*–8* Sequences: (*a*) p. 5*, for Advent, Salus eterna indeficiens; (*b–f*) pp. 6*–8*, for the common of evangelists, martyrs, martyr, confessor, and virgin martyr, respectively: (*b*) Plausu chorus; (*c*) Mentis pie propulsu (*RH*, no. 11502); (*d*) Adest dies leticie e qua de valle miserie (not in *RH*); (*e*) Ecce venit lux optata; (*f*) Letare syon filia; (*g*) p. 8*, for dedication of church, O quam locus metuendus O quam locus venerandus est iste per seculum . . . (7 stanzas not in *RH*).

(*a, b, e–g*) are in Wordsworth's list, op. cit. His only reference for (*e–g*) is the present manuscript. 'Ihc' is written inside the *O* beginning (*g*).

5. pp. 16–26 Collects, secrets, and postcommunions on seventeen occasions from 18 Feb. to 6 Nov., (*a*) Edward confessor, (*b*) Patrick, (*c*) Edward king and martyr, (*d*) Cuthbert, (*e*) Richard (of Chichester), (*f*) Ambrose, (*g*) Alphege, (*h*) Augustine of England, (*i*) Alban, (*j*) Etheldreda, (*k*) translation of Thomas of Canterbury, (*l*) relics (Sarum), (*m*) Margaret, (*n*) Giles, (*o*) 11,000 virgins, (*p*) Crispin and Crispinian, (*q*) Leonard, and—in other hands—(*r–t*) collects, secrets, and postcommunions for Barbara, Erkenwald, and Aldhelm, and (*u–y*) collects for Paul first hermit, Frideswide, John (of Beverley), Wilfred (Deus cuius gracia beatus Wilfridus . . .) and William archbishop (of York: Deus qui nos beati Willelmi confessoris . . .).

6. pp. 9–10 Oratio pro trientali. Deus qui es nostra redempcio (*altered to* Deus summa spes nostre redempcionis) . . .

Trental collect, secret, and postcommunion. They occur again, 'Deus summa spes nostre redempcionis . . .', on pp. 31–2. For the two closely similar forms see *Sarum Missal*, p. 460 and Burntisland edition, col. 883*. *Both* forms are also in Corpus Christi College, Oxford, 394, arts. 4*d*, 13, q.v.

7. Additions to the printed calendar (which lacks Sept.–Dec.) include seventeen English saints, among them Milburga and William archbishop of York (23 Feb.,

8 June), graded respectively 'Maius duplex' and 'Semi duplex', an octave for Monica ('Semi duplex') and 'Maius duplex' against the feast of Monica itself (4 May). The entry of St Thomas of Canterbury at 7 July has been erased.

The twenty added leaves are paginated 1–4, 5*, 6*, 5, 6, 9–26, 7, 8, 27–32, 7*, 8*, 33–6. Paper. About 27 long lines to the page. Current anglicana more or less influenced by secretary and (pp. 9, 10 and the collect for Alexis only) textura.

The printed calendar is for the use of Austin friars and entries added in an English hand suggest a special devotion to St Monica. Art. 2*e* is followed on p. 35 by a request for prayers 'pro statu Iohannis Haynes de haddam', for the souls of John Hardiman (whose name is cancelled), William Some (?) and Cecily his wife, and 'pro anima Iohannis Drory pro statu Willelmi'. Used for *Brev. ad usum Sarum* iii (1886) when in the possession of the Sherbrooke family (of Oxton Hall, Notts): cf. the references there on pp. xcii–xcix. Sherbrooke sale at Sotheby's, 27 June 1912, lot 442 (Barnard, £4). Item 56A at £7. 10*s*. in Barnard's catalogue 64 (n.d.: the Bodleian Library copy is stamped 30.11.1912). The modern (Sherbrooke) number '44' is on a piece of paper pasted to f. ii^{v}.

Fragments in the bindings of Dean and Chapter records

1. Domesday Book of Norwich,[1] pp. 559–60. A leaf of the Decretum of Gratian. s. xii ex.

The leaf, now back to front, begins near the beginning of Causa 7 'talis culpa deiecerit' and ends in 7.1.11 'uirum suum ut alteri'. Enough remains of the conjoint leaf to show that it contained Causa 6, q. 4. The apparatus was added in s. xiii in. 'Ego M dico quod non potest hodie collegium excommunicari per dec' ' is written against the end of C. 7. 1. 9. Written space 293 × 165 mm. 2 cols. 47 lines. Well written. 2-line initials, blue or red, with ornament of the other colour.

Written in England. A flyleaf in the late medieval binding of Domesday.

2. Domesday Book of Norwich, f. v. and pp. 563–4. Two leaves of the Decretum of Gratian. s. xiv.

One leaf (pp. 563–4) from Causa 15 and one (f. v) from Causa 16 with surrounding apparatus. Written space 337 × 200 mm. 2 cols. 78 lines (text). 2-line red initials.

Written in England. Formerly pastedowns in the same binding as no. 1.

3. DCN 10 R 236 A.[2] A leaf of a commentary on the Liber Sextus of the Decretals. s. xiii/xiv.

On 1.6.5,6. The commentary on 1.5.5 Avaricie begins 'Electus ante confirmacionem administrare non debet' and ends with a reference 'secundum Gwill*elmum* *Sup*ra e dudum ii'. Written space 270 × 165 mm. 2 cols. 68+ lines. Current anglicana. Spaces for 3-line initials not filled.

Written in England. A flyleaf at the end of a rebound medieval register: perhaps taken over from a medieval binding.

[1] For the Domesday Book see H. C. Beeching and M. R. James in *Norfolk Archaeology*, xix (1917), 83–4.

[2] On deposit in the Norfolk Record Office.

NORWICH. DIOCESAN RECORD OFFICE[1]

Fragments in bindings

Much of what is said in *MMBL* ii. 312–14 about the use of fragments of manuscripts at Canterbury as pastedowns, flyleaves, and wrappers, applies also to Norwich. The Canterbury fragments have been much disturbed, however. The Norwich fragments, except a very few, are still *in situ*: as pastedowns inside parchment covers (nos. 11, 12, 23, 24, 59, 61, 79, 97); as flyleaves inside parchment covers (nos. 2, 4–8, 10, 15, 16, 19, 35–8, 60, 90, 92–6); as pastedowns inside leather covers (nos. 14a, 18, 20, 22, 25, 27, 29, 32, 34, 39, 62, 63, 70 (1 + 2), 71 + 14, 73, 76, 77, 80, 82–6, 88, 91, 98); as flyleaves inside leather covers (nos. 1, 9, 14b, 21, 26, 28, 30, 31, 33, 70 (3, 4), 72, 74, 75, 78, 81, 87, 89); as wrappers (nos. 3, 13, 17, 40–58, 64–9).

Fragments were used as wrappers mainly on deposition books of the 1560s and on seventeenth-century records of the Archdeaconry of Norwich. They were used as pastedowns and flyleaves mainly in the twenty years from 1550 to 1570. Their being *in situ* allows us to see how the binder used them: that pastedowns often have the thongs taken through them, are often taken round the spine as a single piece of parchment, and are sometimes in double thickness (nos. 14a, 18, 29, 76); that flyleaves are sometimes tied to the central strap (nos. 4, 7, 35, 72) or to the pastedown (no. 81). The covers within which we find these pastedowns and flyleaves are either plain parchment or calf. A few of the calf-bound volumes may not be local work—one seems to be an import from the Low Countries (no. 1), but the great majority are the work of a Norwich binder whose rolls, Oldham's DI. e. 3 (signed L. W.) and FP. g. 13, were first distinguished by J. B. Oldham.[2] FP. g. 13 is by itself on the bindings of twenty volumes, blank books used for records of the 1550s and 1560s (nos. 20, 22, 25, 27, 28, 29, 34, 62, 70, 71, 73, 76, 80, 81, 84, 85, 86, 88, 91, 98). FP. g. 13 and DI. e. 3 are together on the binding of one volume used for records beginning in 1570 (no. 77).[3]

Sixteen of the twenty-one FP. g. 13 bindings (nos. 20, 22, 27, 28, 29, 34, 62, 70, 71, 73, 76, 81, 84, 86, 88, 98) are stamped with the initials W.M. Evidence as to the person for whom they stand comes from no. 73 (1559), where we find 'Willelmus Mingay' inside the cover, together with a paraph flanked by W and M, and from no. 76 (1563), where the first leaf has a rather shaky 'W.M.' on it above which is a notice recording the death on Thursday, 3 August 1564 of

[1] The Norwich Diocesan Record Office is part of the Norfolk Record Office.

[2] J. B. Oldham, *Shrewsbury School Library Bindings*, 1941, p. xxvii.

[3] The roll FP. g. 13 is used on the bindings of two manuscripts described in *MMBL* (i. 268 and below, p. 558), on five books printed in the 1560s which belonged to John Parkhurst, bishop of Norwich 1560–75, and are now at Guildford Grammar School, nos. 243–4, 287–8, 290 (G. Woodward and R. A. Christophers, *The Chained Library of the Royal Grammar School*, Guildford, 1972, M 8, 10 and W 5, 7, 9), on a copy of the *Commonplaces* of Musculus in English, London 1563 (*STC* 18308), belonging to the church of St Mary Coslany, Norwich, and on two City of Norwich books (see the next note but one).

William Mingay, citizen and alderman of Norwich and principal registrar of the diocese 'Cuius anime propicietur deus. Amen'. When Mingay became registrar is uncertain. His appointment dates from 1544, but was to take effect only when Thomas and John Godsalve were dead.[1] Thomas Godsalve the elder died in 1544, probably near the end of the year: his will proved on 8 Jan. 1544/5 includes bequests to his sons John and Thomas and to 'William Mingay my servant'. John Godsalve died in 1557. That Mingay had by this time been effectively registrar for some five years seems likely from the presence of his initials on seven volumes containing wills and records of diocesan business for the years 1552–6 (nos. 20, 27, 34, 62, 70, 81, 84).

William Mingay had a son John, whose appointment as registrar in 1557 was to take effect after the deaths of his father and of Thomas Godsalve. John was registrar in 1570 to judge from two bindings bearing the initials I.M. (nos. 32 and 77). The only other initials are R.H. on a will register for 1563–6 (no. 39).[2]

1–24. Fragments other than service books

1. ACT/5/bk. 5, 1533–8. A bifolium of Jan van Boendale, Die Brabantse Yeesten, in Netherlandish. s. xiv med.

Lines 1845–2047 of bk. 3 and lines 305 (?)–482 of bk. 4 in the edition of J. F. Willems, Brussels 1839.[3] Two leaves, the central bifolium of the quire, are missing in the gap. Written space *c.* 175 mm high. 2 cols. *c.* 52 lines.

Written in the Low Countries. A flyleaf at the back inside a cover of brown leather bearing stamps of six patterns, one of them a square dragon stamp. The pastedowns are of paper, damaged printer's waste from an almanack for the year 1531[4] to which is attached a small piece of a paper manuscript in good Netherlandish cursiva, s. xv.

[1] The dates of appointment of registrars were given to me by Miss Jean Kennedy.

[2] Miss Jane Alvey tells me that the covers of the Administration Act Book of the Norfolk Archdeaconry for 1541–1601/2 are also stamped 'R.H.' and I owe to her references to the 'Liber ruber Civitatis' among the Norwich City records (case 17, shelf b), begun in 1561–2, when William Mingay was mayor, and bearing rolls FP. g. 13 and DI. e. 3 on the covers, and the 'Mayor's book of the Poor', 1571–9 (case 20, shelf e), bearing rolls FP. g. 13 and IN (5) on the covers.

[3] I owe the identification and line references to Dr P. F. J. Obbema.

[4] Roman type. Month headings in red capitals, for example MARTIVS 1531 and NOVEMBER 1531. Sundays in red. Calendar entries are in Latin. The name of a saint is not entered on a Sunday, nor on the three days before Easter, nor on the six days after it (6–8, 10–15 April). Elsewhere a saint is entered on each day, but often not the expected saint. Thus in the runs from 27 Feb. to 24 Mar. and from 4 to 22 April we find: 27 Feb., Maximi episcopi et confessoris; 28, Pigmenii presbiteri et martyris; 1 Mar., Brigidæ virginis 1 februa.; 2, Dorotheæ virginis; 3, Susannæ virginis; 4, Alexandri episcopi et martyris; 6, Simplicii martyris; 7, Perpetuæ et felicitatis virginum et martyrum; 8, Romani abbatis et confessoris; 9, Sanctorum xl martyrum; 10, Nestoris episcopi et martyris; 11, Juliani confesso.; 13, Gregorii papæ et confessoris duplex (in red); 14, Celidonii martyris; 15, Longini martyris; 16, Firmini abbatis et confessoris; 17, Patricii episcopi et confessoris; 18, Ancelmi episcopi et confe.; 20, Joachim confessoris; 21, Benedicti abbatis et confessoris; 22, Lucii papæ et martyris; 23, Maximi et asterii martyrum; 24, Eufrasiæ virginis; 4 Apr., Balbinæ virginis; 5, Vincentii confessoris; 17 Aniceti papæ et martyris; 18, Desiderii martyris; 19, Thomæ de Aquino; 20, Magni martyris; 21, Joseph confessoris; 22 Sotheris et Gaii paparum.

2. ACT/5/bk. 6, 1544–50. Two leaves of theological questions. s. xiv in.

A section begins 'Sequitur quesita circa prelatos ecclesiasticos quo ad spiritualem dispensacionem' and a paragraph begins 'An autem gracia iustificans fuerit eis collata a deo in creacione cum suis naturalibus de hoc nichil iudico nisi quod sic fuisse factum potest sed an fuerit factum quia a voluntate mera dependet scio quod nulli naturali illam deprehendi potest certitudinaliter'. Written space 265+ × 155 mm. 2 cols. 54+ lines.

Written in England. Flyleaves at beginning and end.

3. ACT/6/bk. 7a, 1550–3. A bifolium of a commentary on bk. 1 of the Sentences of Peter Lombard. s. xiii ex.

On distinction 27. A section begins 'Postquam magister determinauit de proprietatibus personalibus hic specialiter determinat de eis in comparatione ad ypostases'. Written space 220 × 155 mm. 2 cols. 55 lines. 3-line initials, blue or red, with ornament of the other colour.

Written in England. In use as a wrapper.

4. ANF Wills, Manclerke 1542–8. Eight bifolia of a commentary on Proverbs. s. xiii[1].

Includes beginnings of chapters 2, 3, and 19 (Melior est pauper etc. Inmediate supra pretulit mansuetudinem et amicabilitatem sermone rigido. hic similiter . . .). Written space 272 × 122 mm. 2 cols. 43 and 47–8 lines. The first line of writing above the top ruled line.

Written in England. Four bifolia at each end as flyleaves. ff. 1–3 are tied to the central strap, so that only 3[v] is visible.

5, 6. ANF Wills, Hynde 1546–9 and Craneforth 1550–6. Three leaves of a life of Remigius (1 Oct.). s. xiii[1].

The text agrees as a rule with the life abridged from Hincmar in Bodleian MS. Bodley 732 (*Sum. Cat.* 2711), ff. 239–48, which begins 'Post uindictam scelerum' (*BHL*, no. 7155). Written space 263 × 157 mm. 2 cols. 35 lines. The first line of writing above the top ruled line.

Written in England. The running number '15' at the head of each page suggests that this was the fifteenth item in a volume of saints' lives. Flyleaves, one at each end of Hynde and one at the beginning of Craneforth.

7. ANF Wills, Bulloke 1553–5. Two bifolia of a formulary of ecclesiastical law. s. xiii/xiv.

Apparently the two innermost bifolia of a quire containing a series of forms, each with a heading in red and, except on three pages, a number. The numbers run from (28) to 48. '32' is 'Forma litterarum pro fabricato pontium. I miser etc'. Quoniam ut ait etc' uel eterni patris etc'. Cum igitur. loco superfluo quod taliter nuncupatur vbi in yemali tempore . . .'. An unnumbered heading is 'Qualiter Episcopus compellet Rectorem et clericos quod administrent in scolis sociis suis fructus porcionis sue'. There are several references to the city and diocese 'Anag' ' (Anagni). Written space 180 × 130 mm. 34 long lines. Anglicana formata.

Written in England. A flyleaf at each end, each tied at one point to the central strap.

8. ANF Wills, Stoorye 1555–6. Two bifolia of Legenda Sanctorum. s. xiv in.

Two adjacent leaves contain part of a life of Edward the Confessor, including the beginning of the Visio Brihtwoldi derived from William of Malmesbury, Gesta pontificum. Two adjacent leaves contain parts of two consecutive pieces in the Legenda Sanctorum of Jacobus de Voragine, the Vita Pelagii, end, from edn. Graesse, p. 838, and De dedicatione ecclesiae (the first fifteen words only, ending 'templum', edn., p. 845/4). Probably this was a copy of Legenda Sanctorum with additions of English interest. Written space 135 mm wide. 2 cols. 35+ lines.

Written in England. A flyleaf at each end: for the binding see no. 34.

9. ANW/19/1, Registrum indictionum from 1532. A bifolium of J. de Voragine, Legenda Sanctorum. s. xiii ex.

Lives of Gervase and Protase and of Peter (19, 29 June: ed. Graesse, pp. 354, 369). Written space 185 × 140 mm. 2 cols. 35 lines. Current anglicana.

Written in England. A flyleaf in a binding of pasteboard covered with brown leather bearing two indistinct rolls.

10. ANW/21/1, Registrum diversorum from 1574. Two bifolia of P. Lombardus, Sententiae. s. xii ex.

Bk. 2, distinctions 15, 29, 30. A handsome copy on thick soft parchment. Written space 220 × 135 mm. 2 cols. 41 lines. Pricks in inner margin to guide ruling. 2-line initials, red, blue, or green.

Written in England. Flyleaves.

11, 12. ANW Wills, Barnham 1553–6 and Bootton 1557–8. Two bifolia of sermons. s. xiii^1.

A sermon begins '[Mi]licia[1] est uita hominis super [terram] (Job 7: 1). [Dicit] dominus per ieremiam prophetam. Ce[rua in] agro peperit . . .'. Written space 165+ × 117 mm. 2 cols. 37+ lines.

Written in England (?). Pastedowns at the end of both registers. The pastedowns which formerly lined the front covers are missing: offset shows.

13. DEP/15/bk. 16, 1574–6. A bifolium of Augustine, Confessiones. s. xiii ex.

From bk. 1 (*PL* xxxiii. 664). Written space 232 × 153 mm. 2 cols. 42 lines.

Written in England. Used as a wrapper.

14. NCC, Administration Act Book 1557–9 (as no. 71). Part of a leaf of a theological text. s. xv^2.

On the seventh house of the soul: quotations on gluttony from 'Giraldus Cambrensis de mirabilibus hibernie libro 2 c. 11' and from (pseudo-)Bede, De imagine mundi. Written space 275+ mm high. 2 cols. 51+ lines. Written in a modified textura.

The leaf ekes out no. 71, which was too short.

[1] The initial *M* has been cut out.

14a. NCC, Administration Act Book 1563–70 (as no. 76). Bifolium of a Bible (?). s. xv (?).

Beginning of 4 Kings 5, but not much can be read. Written space 270 (+?) mm high. 2 cols. 35 (+?) lines. Not a small hand.

The inner of two thicknesses of parchment taken round the spine of an FP. g. 13 binding: see no. 76.

14b. NCC, Administrative Act Book 1563–70 (as no. 76). Two leaves of canon law with surrounding apparatus. s. xiv in.

One of the leaves has 39 lines of apparatus below the text, which is in 2 cols.

A flyleaf in front and at the back a leaf pasted to 14a.

15. NCC Wills, Underwood 1536–7. Two leaves of sermons (?). s. xiii[1].

A section (sermon ?) begins 'Nabuchodonosor obsedit ierusalem . . . Audite quod dicit apostolus. Quicumque uiolauerit templum' (1 Cor. 3: 21). Written space 235 × 165 mm. 2 cols. 40 lines. The first line of writing is above the top ruled line.

Written in England. Flyleaves at beginning and end.

16. NCC Wills, Thyrkyll 1540–3. Two leaves of the Sentences of P. Lombardus. s. xii/xiii.

From bk. 3, dist. 34 and 35. 293 × 215 mm. Written space 215 × 145 mm. 2 cols. 48 lines.

Written in England. Flyleaves at beginning and end.

17. NCC Wills, Craforde 1532–47. A bifolium of Jerome, Epistolae. s. xiii[2].

Parts of letters '44', '45' (headed 'Ieronimus ad Euagrium de Melchisedech'), '(50)' and '51' (headed 'Ieronimus ad Dardanum de terra promissionis'). The remains on the first leaf are *PL* xxii. 660/18–664 and 675–677/12 (parts of letters 69 and 73). The remains on the second leaf are *PL* xxx. 123D–125D and *PL* xxii. 1099–1103/12 (parts of Ep. suppos. viii (see *Clavis*, no. 633: a translation of Origen, hom. 5 on Jeremiah) and letter 129). Letter numbers and column numbers applying to each letter are in the hand of the scribe at the head of each page: (f. 1^r) co. 6 Epistola 44 co. 7; (f. 1^v) co. 8 Iero. co. 9 Epistola 45 co. 1; (f. 2^r) co. 3 Epistola 51 co. 1; (f. 2^v) co. 2 Iero. co. 3. 360 × 230 mm. Written space 265 × 150 mm. 2 cols. 63 lines.

Written in England. Formerly in use as a wrapper: now detached and kept in the same box as Register Craforde.

18. NCC Wills, Punting 1532–45. Two bifolia of scholastic theology (commentary on St Luke ?). s. xv in.

Chapters numbered 15–24. 18 begins 'Ad secundum argumentum principale ⁊ cuius vis stat in isto Quod cristus dixit discipulis suis vicesimo secundo capitulo. Reges gentium' (Luke 22: 25). Written space 188 × 145 mm. 2 cols. 39 lines. Hybrida: punctuation includes the flex. 3-line initials not filled in.

Written in France (?). Taken round the spine in a double thickness. The two leaves at the back are pasted together.

19. NCC Wills, Wymer 1547–9. Two leaves of a commentary on Liber sextus decretalium. s. xiv[1].

On V.7.2–V.9.1: for example (on V.7.10) 'Si papa in aliquo. et de hoc nota per innoc' et host' . . .'. Written space 270+ × 183+ mm. 2 cols. 68+ lines.

Written in England. A flyleaf at each end.

20. NCC Wills, Lyncolne 1552–3. A bifolium of a commentary on bk. 2 of the Sentences of Peter Lombard. s. xiii med.

On distinctions 24 and 34. A paragraph of dist. 34 begins 'Secundo queritur utrum malum sine malicia'. Written space 207 × 140 mm. 2 cols. 50 lines.

Written in England. Taken round the spine as pastedowns in an FP. g. 13 binding.

21. NCC Wills, Jagges 1556–7 (as no. 85). A leaf of a commentary on canon law. s. xiv med.

Written space 245 × 165 mm. 2 cols., 53 lines.

Written in England. A flyleaf at the back: for the binding see no. 85.

22. NCC Wills, Jerves 1557–8. A bifolium of a Bible. s. xiii[1].

One leaf begins in 2 Maccabees 4 and the other in Matthew 13. Written space 252 × 162 mm. 2 cols. 52 lines. The first line of writing is above the top ruled line.

Written in England. 'Magister G[uardia(?)]nus frater Robertus Cooke' is at the foot of the leaf of Maccabees, s. xv ex. Taken round the spine as pastedowns of an FP. g. 13 binding: cf. no. 87.

23. NCC Wills, Folklin 1566–7. Two leaves of biblical history. s. xiii[1].

End of bk. 2, '. . . fluctuacione turbetur', and beginning of bk. 3, 'Liber tercius de misteriis rerum gestarum a moyse usque ad iosue continens capitula xxii. Nota est ystoria de natiuitate moysis . . .'. Written space 225 × 133 mm. 2 cols. 55 lines.

Written in England. A pastedown at each end.

24. NCC Wills, Brygge 1570–2. A leaf of a Bible. s. xiii med.

End of Exodus and beginning of Leviticus. Written space 205 × 115 mm. 2 cols. 58 lines. The first line of writing below the top ruled line. Double vertical bounders and three vertical lines between the columns. 6-line red and blue *U* of *UOCAUIT*, with ornament of both colours: red and blue capitals for *OCAUIT*.

Written in England. A pastedown at the back. Offset of another leaf of the Bible shows inside the front cover.

25–98. Fragments of service books, all of them English

25. ACT/6/bk. 7b, 1550–3. A bifolium of a gradual. s. xv in.

Sanctoral (Michael; Martin, Edmund king and martyr): cf. *Sarum Missal*, pp. 328, 349. Written space 280 (?+) × 185 mm. 2 cols. 13+ lines. Cf. no. 80.

Taken round the spine as pastedowns of an FP. g. 13 binding.

26. ACT/6/bk. 7b (as no. 25). Two leaves of a noted missal. s. xii^2.

One leaf of the sanctoral (Martin, Menna, Brice) and one of the common of an apostle: cf. *Sarum Missal*, pp. 345, 356. Written space 240 × 150 mm. 2 cols. 29 lines. 2-line initials, blue or red with ornament of the other colour, or green with red ornament.

Flyleaves in the same binding as no. 25.

27. ACT/7/bk. 8, 1553–5. A bifolium of a missal. s. xv med.

Sanctoral (Alban–John Baptist and Benedict–Arnulf): cf. *Sarum Missal*, pp. 279–80, 290–2. Written space 243 × 165 mm. 2 cols. 42 lines. See also no. 34.

Taken round the spine as pastedowns of an FP. g. 13 binding.

28. ACT/8/bk. 9, 1560–2. Two bifolia of a liturgical psalter. s. xv in.

Psalms 6 and 23. Written space 183 × 115 mm. 20 long lines. Ornamental line fillers.

Flyleaves, a bifolium at each end, in an FP. g. 13 binding: the pastedowns are blank parchment.

29. ACT/9/bk. 10, 1562–4. Two bifolia of an antiphonal. s. xv in.

One bifolium is from the sanctoral (Vincent) and one from the common of a confessor: cf. *Brev. ad usum Sarum*, iii. 104; ii. 420. Written space 220 mm wide. 2 cols. 16+ lines and music.

The bifolia form a double thickness of parchment taken round the spine as pastedowns of an FP. g. 13 binding.

30. ACT/9/bk. 10 (as no. 29). A leaf of a missal. s. xiv/xv.

Temporal (Thursday and Friday in the 4th week of Lent): cf. *Sarum Missal*, p. 83. Written space 253+ × 145+ mm. 2 cols. 36+ lines.

A flyleaf inside the front cover: see no. 29.

31. ACT/9/bk. 10 (as no. 29). A leaf of a noted breviary. s. xiv in.

Sanctoral (2–11 Nov., All Souls–Martin: prayers only for Eustace cum sociis, Leonard, Quatuor coronati, Theodore): cf. *Brev. ad usum Sarum*, iii. 948–1009. Written space 255 × 163 mm. 2 cols. 42 lines. 2-line initials, blue or red with ornament of the other colour.

A flyleaf inside the back cover: see no. 29.

32. ACT/11/bk. 12, 1570–2. A leaf of an antiphonal. s. xiv ex.

Temporal (Wednesday after Pentecost): cf. *Brev. ad usum Sarum*, I. mxix–mxx. Written space *c.*320 × 220 mm. 2 cols. 17 (?) lines and music. See also no. 77.

Taken round the spine as pastedowns inside a binding of brown calf bearing a crested roll (not recorded by Oldham) and a small centrepiece flanked by I and M: see above, p. 536.

33. ACT/11/bk. 12 (as no. 32). A leaf of a large noted breviary. s. xiv/xv.

Sanctoral (Denis): cf. *Brev. ad usum Sarum*, iii. 894–7. Written space 245 mm wide. 2 cols. 48 (?) long lines. See also no. 78.

Cut in two and used as flyleaves, one piece at each end of the same binding as no. 32.

34. ANF Wills, Stoorye (as no. 8). Bifolium of the same missal as no. 27.

Sanctoral (6 Dec.–17 Jan., Nicholas–Sulpicius): cf. *Sarum Missal*, pp. 234–9. The middle bifolium of a quire.

Taken round the spine as pastedowns of an FP. g. 13 binding.

35. ANF Wills, Beales 1556–8. Two bifolia of a customary of Norwich Cathedral Priory. s. xii/xiii.

The bifolium in front is tied to the central strap and one side of each leaf is mostly invisible: the exposed pages contain directions for services, (1) within the octave of Trinity and (2) for the 25th and 26th of June, corresponding more or less to *Customary of Norwich* (HBS lxxxii, 1948), pp. 126/11 up–127, 138, and 'Die tercia' (27 June) can be seen on the tied-down verso of (2). The bifolium at the back is concerned with bloodletting, the 'capitulum puerorum', and other matters not treated of in the printed text: musical notes for settings of Benedicamus domino have not been filled in. Written space 147 × 98 mm. 2 cols. 34 lines.

Flyleaves, a bifolium set sideways at each end.

36. ANF Wills, Wolston 1556–8. A leaf of an antiphonal. s. xv.

Dedication of church: cf. *Brev. ad usum Sarum*, I. mccclxii. Written space 235 mm wide. 15+ long lines and music. Cadels have faces.

Cut in two and used as flyleaves, one piece at each end.

37. ANF Wills, Lyncolne 1557–9. A leaf of the same antiphonal as no. 36.

Office of the dead: cf. *Brev. ad usum Sarum*, ii. 278–9.

Cut in two and used as flyleaves, one at each end.

38. ANF Wills, Postyll 1560–2. A leaf of a breviary, s. xiv/xv.

Lessons within octave of dedication of church: cf. *Brev. ad usum Sarum*, I. mcccclxviii–mcccclxx. Written space 290 × 206 mm. 2 cols. 43 lines.

A flyleaf at the beginning. Traces remain of another leaf at the back.

39. ANF Wills, Waterladde 1563–6. Two bifolia of a missal. s. xiv med.

Sanctoral (23 June; 28–9 June; 2, 4 July, vigil of John Baptist, memoria of Etheldreda, John Baptist; vigil and day of Peter and Paul; Processus and Martinianus, translation of Martin): cf. *Sarum Missal*, pp. 280; 283–4, 286–7. Written space 200+ × 130 mm. 2 cols. 44+ lines. Four leaves from one quire, including the middle bifolium.

Set sideways as pastedowns inside a brown leather cover bearing Oldham's roll MW. d. 13, another narrower roll, and a centrepiece flanked by R and H: see above, p. 000.

40. ANW/1/7, 1573. A bifolium of a noted missal. s. xiii².

Temporal (Sabbato 4 temporum Adventus and vigil of Christmas): cf. *Sarum Missal*, pp. 23 (the secret is Sacrificiis presentibus not Super has hostias) and 25–6. Written space 250 × 160 mm. 2 cols. 27 lines (9 lines and music).

Wrapper.

41. ANW/1/18, 1605. A bifolium of a handsome missal. s. xiii ex.

Sanctoral (29 Nov.; 24 Feb.–18 Mar., vigil of Andrew; Matthias, Perpetua, and Felicitas, Gregory, Edward king and martyr); cf. *Sarum Missal*, pp. 232, 255–7. Written space 250 × 160 mm. 2 cols. 36 lines. For other leaves see nos. 49, 56 (?).

Wrapper.

42. ANW/1/23, 1614. A leaf of an antiphonal. s. xv in.

Temporal (1st Sunday in Lent): cf. *Brev. ad usum Sarum*, I. dlxxxi–iv. Written space 345 × 225 mm. 17 long lines and music.

Set sideways as wrapper.

43. ANW/1/24, 1615. A leaf of a noted breviary. s. xiv/xv.

Sanctoral (Vincent): cf. *Brev. ad usum Sarum*, iii. 101–3. Written space 290 × 210 mm. 2 cols. 42 lines. The last leaf of a quire: catchword. For other leaves see nos. 48, 50 (?), 52 (?), 53–5.

Set sideways as wrapper.

44. ANW/1/28, 1631. A leaf of a handsome noted missal. s. xiii ex.

Temporal (Sabbato 4 temporum Adventus): cf. *Sarum Missal*, pp. 22–3. Written space 325 × 210 mm. 2 cols. 36 lines (12 lines and music). Initials with vertical prolongations in red and blue, from which leaves and animal heads project into the margin.

Set sideways as wrapper.

45. ANW/1/29, 1634. Part of a leaf of a large and handsome antiphonal. s. xv in.

Temporal (1st–3rd Sundays after Easter): cf. *Brev. ad usum Sarum*, I. dccclxiv–vii, dcccxciii–iv, dccccix–xi. Written space 210+ × 270 mm. 2 cols. The ten last lines on the page.

Set sideways as wrapper.

46. ANW/1/31, 1664. A leaf of an antiphonal. s. xiv/xv.

Common of time, Wednesday–Thursday: cf. *Brev. ad usum Sarum*, ii. 127, 204, 128, 148. Written space *c.* 290 × 212 mm. 2 cols. 14 lines and music.

Set sideways as wrapper.

47. ANW/2/5, 1569–70. Part of a leaf of a gradual. s. xv.

Common of a martyr: cf. *Sarum Missal*, pp. 360–2. Written space 220 mm wide. 2 cols. The 7 last lines on a page.

Set sideways as wrapper, but the upper half of the leaf, which should form the back cover, has been removed.

48. ANW/62, 1617–18. A leaf of the same noted breviary as no. 43.

Temporal (Tuesday and Wednesday in Holy Week): cf. *Brev. ad usum Sarum*, I. dcclxviii–lxx.

Set sideways as wrapper.

49. ANW/3/12, 1606. A bifolium of the same missal as no. 41.

Temporal (Sabbato 4 temporum Septembris): cf. *Sarum Missal*, pp. 198–200. The middle bifolium of a quire.

Wrapper.

50. ANW/3/18, 1613–14. A leaf of a noted breviary, s. xiv/xv, probably from the same manuscript as no. 43.

Common of martyrs: cf. *Brev. ad usum Sarum*, ii. 382–3. Written space *c.*295 × 215 mm. 2 cols. 42 lines.

Set sideways as wrapper.

51. ANW/3/20, 1614–15. A leaf of an antiphonal. s. xv.

Temporal (within octave of Epiphany): cf. *Brev. ad usum Sarum,* I. cccxxxi–xl. Written space 230 mm wide. 2 cols. 17 lines and music. See also nos. 57, 58.

Set sideways as wrapper.

52. ANW/3/21, 1617–18. A leaf from the same noted breviary as no. 50.

Common of martyrs: cf. *Brev. ad usum Sarum*, ii. 399–401.

Set sideways as wrapper.

53. ANW/3/22, 1618–23. A leaf from the same noted breviary as no. 43.

Common of time (Monday: end of Splendor paternae gloriae and memoriae of B.V.M. and All Saints): cf. *Brev. ad usum Sarum*, ii. 88–94.

Set sideways as wrapper.

54. ANW/3/23, 1619–22. A leaf from the same noted breviary as no. 43.

Temporal (4th Sunday in Lent): cf. *Brev. ad usum Sarum,* I. dcxci–ii.

Set sideways as wrapper.

55. ANW/3/25, 1622. A leaf from the same noted breviary as no. 43.

Temporal (5th Sunday after octave of Epiphany to Septuagesima Sunday): cf. *Brev. ad usum Sarum,* I. cccclxix–lxxiii. The first of the lessons 'per ebdomadam' is 'Factum est sacramentum . . . ', followed by 'Alie lecciones. Obsecro itaque . . .'.

Set sideways as wrapper.

56. ANW/3/35, 1640. Bifolium of a missal. s. xiii med.

Temporal (vigil of Epiphany and Sunday after the octave): cf. *Sarum Missal*, pp. 27, 39–41. Written space 255 × 155 mm. 2 cols. 36 lines. Perhaps from the same book as no. 41, but the hand looks rather earlier.

Wrapper.

57. ANW/6/7, 1609–23. A leaf of the same book as no. 51.

Temporal (Epiphany): cf. *Brev. ad usum Sarum,* I. cccxxviii–ix. Written space 342 × 225 mm. 2 cols. 17 lines and music.

Set sideways as wrapper.

58. ANW/17/1, 1612. A leaf of the same book as nos. 51, 57.

Temporal (2nd Sunday after Easter): cf. *Brev. ad usum Sarum,* I. dcccxciii–vi.

Set sideways as wrapper.

59. ANW Wills, Aleyn 1545–51. A leaf of an antiphonal. s. xv.

Common of apostle and common of martyr: cf. *Brev. ad usum Sarum*, ii. 370–1. Written space 217 mm wide. 14+ lines and music.

Cut in two: half a leaf set sideways at each end as pastedown: the half leaf at the end is covered with paper.

60. ANW Wills, Ayer 1561–4. Half a leaf of a gradual. s. xv.

Temporal (Ascension Day): cf. *Sarum Missal*, pp. 155–6. Written space 215 mm wide. 2 cols.

Flyleaf at the beginning.

61. DEP/5/bk. 5A, 1550–1. A leaf of a noted breviary. s. xiv^{2}.

Sanctoral (decollation of John Baptist): cf. *Brev. ad usum Sarum*, iii. 751–4, but the ninth lesson begins here 'Factumque est adulterium pupplicum'. Written space 233 × 165 mm. 2 cols. 40+ lines.

Pastedown at the back, now raised.

62. DEP/7/bk. 6A, 1556–8. A bifolium of a breviary or lectionary. s. xiv/xv.

Sanctoral: Chad (2 March) and translation of Edmund, king and martyr (29 Apr.). This and the two leaves, no. 85 below, make four consecutive leaves of what may have been a supplement to a Sarum breviary containing synodal feasts for the diocese of Norwich. The remains are: on the first leaf of no. 62, lessons 1–6 for Chad (1 ends 'tam episcopatu'; 2 begins '[...] merciorum simul et'; 3 begins 'Qui cum in illa prouincia'; 4 begins 'Qui increscente'; 5 begins 'At . . .'; 6 begins 'Instituta quoque'); on the two leaves of no. 85, lessons 8, 9 for Chad (8 ends 'miracula sanitatum operari'; 9 begins 'Denique nuper freneticus') and lessons 1–7 for Felix (1 begins 'Felix episcopus'; 3 ends 'sordida gestanti'; 4 begins 'Animaduertit honorius'; 5 begins 'Mira res gentem anglorum'; 6 begins 'In ecclesia namque'); on the second leaf of no. 62, lessons 5 and 6 for Edmund (5 ends 'uirtutes locuntur'; 6 begins 'Ostenso tanto miraculo'). Written space *c.*235 × 140 mm. 2 cols. 33 lines.

Taken round the spine as pastedowns of an FP. g. 13 binding.

63. DEP/7/bk. 6A (as no. 62). A leaf of a noted missal. s. xiv/xv.

Temporal (Tuesday and Wednesday in the 1st week of Lent): cf. *Sarum Missal*, pp. 60–1. Written space 295+ × 180 mm. 2 cols. 45 (?+) lines.

A pastedown for the flap of the same binding as no. 62.

64. DEP/8/bk. 7D, 1560. A leaf of an antiphonal. s. xv.

Temporal (Trinity): cf. *Brev. ad usum Sarum,* I. mxlviii–mliii. Written space 335 × 225 mm. 2 cols. 15 lines and music. Cf. no. 69.

Set sideways as wrapper.

65. DEP/8/bk. 7E, 1561. A leaf of an antiphonal. s. xv.

Temporal (Advent Sunday): cf. *Brev. ad usum Sarum,* I. xxix–xxxii. Written space *c.*315 × 225 mm. 2 cols. 18 lines and music.

Set sideways as wrapper.

66. DEP/9/bk. 8, 1562. Two leaves of a noted breviary. s. xv.

Temporal (Easter; 2nd and 3rd Sundays after Easter): cf. *Brev. ad. usum Sarum,* I. dcccix–xi; dcccxcvi–dccccix. Written space 225 mm wide. 2 cols. Cf. no. 68.

Set sideways in double thickness as wrapper, but the upper half of the Easter leaf has been removed, no doubt for the sake of an initial: the lower half has a border at the foot and between the columns.

67. DEP/10/bk. 11A, 1565–7. Two leaves of an antiphonal. s. xv.

Temporal (Christmas; John Evangelist): cf. *Brev. ad usum Sarum,* I. cxciii–iv; ccxv–xvi. Written space 225 mm wide. 2 cols.

Set sideways in double thickness as wrapper.

68. DEP/11/bk. 12, 1567–8. A leaf of a noted breviary, probably from the same manuscript as no. 66.

Temporal (1st Sunday after Easter): cf. *Brev. ad usum Sarum,* I. dccclxiv–v. Written space 225 mm wide. 2 cols.

Set sideways as wrapper.

69. DEP/12/bk. 13B, 1569–70. Two leaves of an antiphonal. s. xv.

Sanctoral (Michael): cf. *Brev. ad usum Sarum*, iii. 865–9. Written space *c.*320 × 220 mm. 2 cols. 15 lines and music. Perhaps from the same book as no. 64, but the hand is not the same.

Wrapper (folded in).

70. NCC Administration Act Book 1555–7. Three and a half leaves, two of them a bifolium, of a gradual. s. xiv².

Sanctoral (1, vigil of Laurence; 2–4 vigil and day of Assumption of B.V.M.): cf. *Sarum Missal*, pp. 303, 307–9. The fragments of sequences include the words 'Uirgo preelecta ut sol pulcra' (3ᵛ: not in *S.M.*). Written space 275 (+?) × 205 mm. 14 (+?) long lines and music. (2) is the upper half of a main leaf which had no doubt an initial of some size on the missing lower half: the *B* of *Beata viscera* is a zoomorphic cadel. See also no. 83.

In an FP. g. 13 binding, (1) as a pastedown sideways, (2) as a pastedown for the flap and (3, 4) as flyleaves: (1) and (3, 4) are taken round the spine.

71. NCC Administration Act Book 1557–9. A leaf of an antiphonal. s. xv in.

Common of time (prime): cf. *Brev. ad usum Sarum*, ii. 54. Written space 300 (+?) × 215 mm. 2 cols. 36+ lines.

Set sideways as a pastedown in an FP. g. 13 binding. It is taken round the spine, and—being too short—is eked out with no. 14.

72. NCC Administration Act Book 1557-9 (as no. 71). Two leaves of an ordinal. s. xiv med.

Dedication of church and vigil of Andrew. Written space 215 × 135 mm. 2 cols. 42 lines. Written in anglicana formata.

Flyleaves in the same binding as no. 71. The leaf in front is tied to the piece of leather on to which the strap fastens.

73. NCC Administration Act Book 1559-63. A bifolium of a noted breviary. s. xiv^2.

Sanctoral (2-11 Nov., All Souls-Martin): cf. *Brev. ad usum Sarum*, iii. 986-1011. Recto of (1) only partly visible. Written space 255+ × 235 mm. 2 cols. 45 (+?) lines.

Taken round the spine as pastedowns of an FP. g. 13 binding. The leaf in front, (1), is backed by a leather cover bearing a roll like Oldham's HE. a. 1 and both it and the leaf at the back are separated from the FP. g. 13 cover by a piece of plain leather which is also taken round the spine.

74. NCC Administration Act Book 1559-63 (as no. 73). Bifolium of a gradual. s. xiii.

Temporal (12th and 13th Sundays after Trinity): cf. *Sarum Missal*, pp. 184-5. Written space 175+ × 115 mm. 10 long lines and music.

Set sideways as a flyleaf in front, in the same binding as no. 73.

75. NCC Administration Act Book 1559-63 (as no. 73). A leaf of a gradual. s. xv in.

Common of martyr: cf. *Sarum Missal*, pp. 358, 360. Written space 233+ × *c*.177 mm. 2 cols. 12 (+?) lines.

A flyleaf at the back, in the same binding as no. 73.

76. NCC Administration Act Book 1563-70. Bifolium of an antiphonal. s. xiv/xv.

Sanctoral (relics and (22 July) Mary Magdalene): cf. *Brev. ad usum Sarum*. iii, 459, 516. Mostly obscured by no. 14a. Written space 270 (+?) mm high.

Taken round the spine as pastedowns of an FP. g. 13 binding. Cf. no. 14a.

77. NCC Administration Act Book 1570-8. A leaf of the same antiphonal as no. 32.

Temporal (1st Sunday after 28 July): cf. *Brev. ad usum Sarum*, I. mcclvii-viii.

Taken round the spine as pastedowns of a binding bearing rolls FP. g. 13 and DI. e. 3 and the same small centrepiece as on no. 32: as there the centrepiece is flanked by I and M.

78. NCC Administration Act Book 1570-8 (as no. 77). A leaf of the same noted breviary as no. 33.

Sanctoral (Matthew): cf. *Brev. ad usum Sarum*, iii. 849-51.

Cut in two and used as flyleaves, one at each end of the same binding as no. 77.

79. NCC Wills, Briggs 1514–27. A leaf of a noted breviary. s. xv in.

Common of time (compline): cf. *Brev. ad usum Sarum*, ii. 224–6. Written space 275+ × 185 mm. 2 cols. 42+ lines.

A pastedown at the back inside a parchment cover, probably of s. xvi²: another now missing leaf was at the beginning.

80. NCC Wills, Wilkins 1553–4. A bifolium probably from the same gradual as no. 25.

Sanctoral (Andrew, Nicholas (sequence) and Conception of B.V.M. (cue only); Tractus. Sicut ceruus desiderat . . .): cf. *Sarum Missal*, pp. 233, 432. Written space 244+ × 192 mm. 2 cols. 12 (+?) lines and music.

Taken round the spine as pastedowns of an FP. g. 13 binding.

81. NCC Wills, Walpoole 1554–5. A bifolium of a noted breviary. s. xiv ex.

Common of time (prime, terce): cf. *Brev. ad usum Sarum*, ii. 49–50, 58. Written space 293(+?) × 215 mm. 2 cols. 41 (+?) lines.

Taken round the spine as flyleaves of an FP. g. 13 binding: the leaf in front is tied to no. 82.

82. NCC Wills, Walpoole (as no. 81). A leaf of a gradual. s. xiv².

Temporal (Christmas): cf. *Sarum Missal*, pp. 28–9. Written space 273+ mm high. 14 long lines and music.

A pastedown in front: the inner side is tied to no. 81.

83. NCC Wills, Walpoole (as no. 81). A leaf of the same gradual as no. 70.

Sanctoral (Assumption of B.V.M. (sequence A rea virga)): cf. *Sarum Missal*, pp. 309, 479.

Set sideways as a pastedown at the back.

84. NCC Wills, Beales 1555–6. A leaf of a missal. s. xiv¹.

Temporal (feria 5 post Cineres): cf. *Sarum Missal*, p. 53. Written space 275+ × *c.* 200 mm. 2 cols. 37+ lines. 2-line blue initials.

Originally a bifolium taken round the spine as pastedowns of an FP. g. 13 binding, but the leaf at the back has been removed: offset shows.

85. NCC Wills, Jagges 1556–7. A bifolium of the same breviary as no. 62.

Lessons for Chad and Felix: see no. 62.

Taken round the spine as pastedowns of an FP. g. 13 binding.

86. NCC Wills, Hustinges 1557. A bifolium of a graded calendar. s. xiv².

The outside sheet of a Sarum calendar, Feb. and Nov. exposed. 'Oswaldi episcopi et confessoris' added, 28 Feb. 'pape' erased, 23 Nov.

Taken round the spine as pastedowns of an FP. g. 13 binding.

87. NCC Wills, Jerves (as no. 22). Two bifolia of a breviary, s. xiii med.

Sanctoral (Blasius, Agatha): cf. *Brev. ad usum Sarum*, iii. 147–56. Written space 187 × 125 mm. 24 long lines. The two middle bifolia of a quire. Large hand. 2-line initials, blue or red, with ornament of the other colour.

Set sideways as flyleaves at each end: for the pastedowns see no. 22.

88. NCC Wills, Veysye 1558. A bifolium of a missal. s. xiv ex.

Temporal (Easter Eve and ordinary of mass): cf. *Sarum Missal*, pp. 119, 216. Written space 285+ × 180 mm. 37+ lines. 2-line initials, blue with red ornament and 1-line, blue or red.

Taken round the spine as pastedowns of an FP. g. 13 binding: supplemented by (88a) a strip of another missal, s. xv^1, containing part of the office for Saturday after Pentecost (cf. *Sarum Missal*, p. 167): written space 263 mm high: 2 cols. (?) 42 lines.

89. NCC Wills, Veysye (as no. 88). Two leaves of a lectionary. s. xv^2.

Sanctoral (lessons 1–4 for Cuthbert, (1) Dum quadam die adolescens . . . , (2) Occurrunt consolaturi . . . , (3) Quadam die dum famuli . . . , (4) Cum predictus adolescens nocte quadam . . . ; lessons 8, 9 for John Baptist, as *Brev. ad usum Sarum*, iii. 346). Written space 250 × 160 mm. 2 cols. 27 lines, ruled in violet ink. Capital letters in the ink of the text filled with pale yellow.

Flyleaves.

90. NCC Wills, Woodcocke 1558–9. A leaf of a gradual. s. xiv^2.

Temporal (vigil and day of Ascension): cf. *Sarum Missal*, pp. 152–5. The recto ends with the first two words of the officium Omnes gentes, which continues on the verso 'plaudite mani/bus iubilate deo' against which is a marginal note 'war' wel her' '. Written space 233 × 157+ mm. 12 long lines and music. See also nos. 92–5.

Formerly a flyleaf inside a parchment binding, now, after rebinding, kept separately in the same box as the register.

91. NCC Wills, Colman 1559. Three leaves of an antiphonal. s. xv med.

Sanctoral (6–7 Aug., Transfiguration and Name of Jesus): cf. *Brev. ad usum Sarum*, iii. 612; 618–9, 450; 631. 450 × 297 mm. Written space 340 × 225 mm. 2 cols. 18 lines and music.

Taken round the spine as overlapping pastedowns in an FP. g. 13 binding.

92. NCC Wills, Goldingham 1559–60. The last six lines of a leaf of the same gradual as no. 90.

Temporal (Passion Sunday): cf. *Sarum Missal*, p. 85.

Formerly a flyleaf inside a parchment binding, now, after rebinding, kept separately in the same box as the register.

93. NCC Wills, Bircham 1560–1. A leaf of the same gradual as no. 90.

Temporal (Annunciation of B.V.M.): cf. *Sarum Missal*, p. 259). The sequence *Ave mundi spes maria* is complete.

Flyleaf at the back.

94. NCC Wills, Cowles 1561–2. Two leaves of the same gradual as no. 90.

Sanctoral (Marcellinus and Peter, translation of archbishop Edmund (2, 9 June); John Baptist, John and Paul (24, 26 June)): cf. *Sarum Missal*, pp. 272, 477, 283.

Flyleaves at each end.

95. NCC Wills, Knightes 1563. Two leaves of the same gradual as no. 90.

Sanctoral (Invention of Cross, Nereus and Achilleus, Pancras (3, 12 May); memorial of Etheldreda, John Baptist (23, 24 June)): cf. *Sarum Missal*, pp. 265–7, 281. Blue and red *D* of *De ventre*, the officium for John Baptist, with ornament of both colours and cross hatching inside *D*.

Flyleaves at each end.

96. NCC Wills, Martin 1564–5. The last seven lines of a leaf of an antiphonal. s. xv med.

Temporal (Christmas): cf. *Brev. ad usum Sarum,* I. clxxiv–vii. Written space 220 mm wide. 2 cols. Border ornament.

A flyleaf in front. The flyleaf at the back has been removed: offset shows.

97. NCC Wills, Bun 1567. Two leaves of a noted missal. s. xiv med.

Temporal and sanctoral (12th Sunday after Trinity; (16, 18, 19 Oct. Michael in Monte Tumba, Luke and Justus, Frideswide): cf. *Sarum Missal*, pp. 184–5, 336. Written space 260 × 155 mm. 2 cols. 38 lines.

Pastedowns at each end.

98. SUN 3 (Register of miscellanies, 1550–1618). A leaf of a handsome breviary, s. xii ex.

Sanctoral (25–8 July: James, end of last lesson, from 'Estote uos ergo humiles et sic ad dignitatem . . .', and noted cues to the common of an apostle, 'R' Ciues apostolorum . . . ; Eodem die sanctorum cristophori et cucufati Memoria. Deus per quem fides igne . . . ; collect for Seven Sleepers, 'Deus qui gloriosos . . .', and three lessons, Regnauit, Malcus, Contigit; collect for Pantaleon, 'Uotiuos nos . . .', and three lessons, In diebus, Cui sanctus, Inperator; collect for Sampson, 'Omnipotens sempiterne deus . . .', first lesson, Sanctus samson, and part of second lesson, Hoc etiam): cf. *Brev. ad usum Sarum*, iii. 539, 555–8. Written space 267 × 170 mm. 2 cols. 46 lines. 2-line initials, blue, brown, green, or red.

A flyleaf at the back inside an FP. g. 13 binding.

NORWICH. NORFOLK RECORD OFFICE

Rye 38. *Book of arms, notes on French grammar (in English and French), etc.* s. xv med.

Described by N. Davis and G. S. Ivy, 'MS. Walter Rye 38 and its French Grammar', *Medium Aevum*, xxxi (1962), 110–24.

1 (quires 1-3). pp. 1-71, 74-5 Coats of arms, mainly of Norfolk families, with a description in English below each coat and the name of its bearer.

Listed in A. Wagner, *A catalogue of English Mediaeval Rolls of Arms*, Aspilogia i (1950), 200; ii. 274. The coats are listed by O. Barron in *The Ancestor*, x (1904), 87-97. Reduced facsimile of pp. 20-1 in *Norwich Public Libraries* (see below, Norwich Public Library), p. 39. pp. 72-3, 76-80 blank. For pp. 81-2 see below.

2 (quire 5). (*a*) pp. 115-17 ye pedigru of anus paston dowter of sir E barrei knyth. (*b*) pp. 118-21 Twenty-four entries, all obits, except no. 11, 'Combustio magne grangie aput markynford anno gracie m^o^ ccc lxxxviii. (*c*) p. 126 A descent from Thomas Hengham.

(*a-c*) printed by E. Farrer in *Norfolk Antiquarian Miscellany*, iii (1887), 424-38. (*a*) 11 lines on p. 116 and all 8 lines on p. 117 crossed out. The first, if not the second, of the two leaves cut out after p. 116 had writing on it. (*b*), nos. 1-5, 9, 10, 12, 24 are Barrey obits and nos. 13-16 Paston obits: cf. Davis and Ivy, p. 114. pp. 83-114 (quire 4), 123-5 blank, except for scribbles.

3 (quire 6). pp. 127-32 Memorand(um) y^t^ ho hath affeccion to lerne y^is^ langage must first considr*e* viii thingg*is* . . .

Notes on French grammar printed by Davis and Ivy, pp. 117-22, with slightly reduced facsimiles of pp. 127, 130 (ff. 65, 65^v^). pp. 133-42 blank.

ff. i + 40 + i + 30, paginated i, ii, 1-142. Paper. pp. i, ii, 81-2 are a parchment bifolium wrapping quires 1-3. 147 × 105 mm. Written space *c.*130 × 90 mm. 19 long lines. Collation of pp. 1-80, 83-142: 1^{16} 2^{8} $3\text{-}4^{16}$ 5^{8} wants 2, 3 after p. 116. Current secretary-influenced anglicana by several hands. No coloured initials. Parchment wrapper.

According to Davis, loc. cit., pp. 114-16, art. 3 is in the hand of William Paston II, 1436-96, and art. 2 is partly by him and partly by a scribe whose hand occurs often in Paston letters. Davis dates Paston's hand as probably a bit before 1454 and notes that the latest obit in art. 2 is of 1448, although misdated by the scribe 1468. The name 'olyuer Ingham' is on p. 82, s. xv/xvi. Belonged to Francis Blomefield, †1752 (his hand on f. i), and then in quick succession to Thomas Martin (†1771: his signature, faint but distinctive, inside the cover), John Ives (†1776: his name on f. i: his sale, 3 March 1777, lot 384), Edward Thomas (his sale, 1 July 1787, lot 540), and Samuel Tyssen (his sale, 7 Dec. 1801, lot 2719). Towneley of Towneley Hall sale at Sotheby's, 27 June 1883, lot 5. Belonged to Walter Rye in 1897 and bequeathed by him in 1929 (cf. *Bulletin of the Institute of Historical Research*, viii (1930-1), 59).

NORWICH. PUBLIC LIBRARY

G. A. Stephen, *Three Centuries of a City Library*, Norwich 1917: see pp. 27-8, 45-50, 52-6 for the manuscripts, the Donation Book, and the catalogues. P. Hepworth and M. Alexander, *Norwich Public Libraries*, Norfolk and Norwich Record Office, Norwich 1965. The Donation Book was begun in 1659, but takes account of earlier gifts back to the beginning in 1608. The catalogue by Benjamin Mackerell printed in 1732 lists TC 27/1, 2, 3(?), 4, 5, and TC 28/2, q.v., and two now missing manuscripts: p. 29, Glanville de proprietat. a MSS. Fol. K. 58; p. 48 Statutes of King Edward 3d a MSS 8° F. 141. Both have '*Kir*' against them, showing that they were the gift of John Kirkpatrick, †1728.

TC 27/1 (S. A. 1. 1.) *Berengaudus, In Apocalypsin; Qui bene presunt* s. xiii med.–xiii/xiv.

Two manuscripts bound together by the time art. 4 was added.

1 (s. xiii/xiv). ff. 6–77v Incipit expositio prime uisionis . . . Apocalipsis ihesu cristi . . . Apocalipsis reuelatio interpretatur. Quod reuelationis donum . . . ut uite eterne participes esse mereamur. qui . . . amen.

PL xvii. 765–970. This copy described by M. R. James, *The Apocalypse in Art*, 1931, pp. 19–20, 23–5, where the pictures are listed: 'very rude'.[1]

2 (space fillers at the end of quire 7: current anglicana, s. xiv in.). ff. 78–9 Notes 'De anticristo et ortu eius', on Adam and the reasons for his fall, and 'De vii miraculis natiuitatis cristi'. f. 79v blank.

3 (s. xiii med.). ff. 80–107 Incipit summa magistri Ricardi edita de vita prelatorum et de eorum doctrina aliis predicanda. Qui bene presunt . . . consummatus. valete in domino.

For the probable author of this popular text, R. de Wetherset, see Emden, *BRUC*, p. 632, and frontispiece, and *MMBL* i. 43.

4 (added, s. xiv). ff. 2–5. A table of arts. 1, 3. f. 5v blank.

5 (binding leaf). f. 1rv A numbered table, s. xiii med., of the last 134 chapters of a work on sacraments in 178 chapters.

Chapter 55 is 'Quare aqua misceatur' and chapter 178 'De virginibus'.

ff. iii + 106 + ii, foliated (i, ii), 1–107, (108–9). For f. 1 see above, art. 5. The other flyleaves are modern paper. 260 × 190 mm. Collation of ff. 2–107: 1^{4} 2^{12} 3^{10} 4^{10} + 1 leaf after 10 (f. 39) $5\text{–}6^{12}$ 7^{14} $8\text{–}10^{8}$ 11^{4}, together with inserted picture-pages, ff. 35, 54, 74. Medieval binding of bare wooden boards: five bands. Secundo folio *dotes dei*.

Arts. 1, 2. Written space 180 × 140 mm. 2 cols. 34–5 lines. Art. 1 in two hands, the second beginning at f. 28. For the pictures see James, op. cit., and *Norwich Public Libraries*, p. 38 (reduced facsimile of f. 6: St John writing). Initials: (i) f. 6, 5-line blue and red *A*, with ornament of both colours; (ii) 2-line, blue with red ornament, or, less often, red with blue ornament. Capital letters in the ink of the text marked with red.

Art. 3. Medieval foliation 1–28. Written space 200 × 135 mm. Pricks in both margins to guide ruling in first quire only. The first line of writing above the top ruled line. 1-line initials, red or green, with ornament of the other colour. Capital letters in the ink of the text marked with red.

[1] According to James there is a large gap after f. 27: this seems wrong.

Written in England. An erasure at the head of f. 2. Recorded in the Donation Book as the gift of Thomas Atkins, merchant of Norwich, in 1618. 4° V. 65 in 1732. A Norwich number '287' is on labels on the front cover, s. xviii ?.

TC 27/2 (S. A. 1. 2). *Biblia* s. xiii^2

A Bible with three large gaps: (quires 1–13) pp. 1–300 Genesis–2 Chronicles 13: 17; (quires 14–17) pp. 301–90 Five Sapiential Books, Matthew, Mark 1–3: 31; (quires 18, 19) pp. 391–426 Pauline Epistles, beginning in the prologue to Philippians, and Apocalypse.

The books were probably in the same order as in B.L., Royal 1 B. viii and some other manuscripts of English origin in which Matthew follows Ecclesiasticus and Apocalypse follows Pauline Epistles. Proverbs begins a new quire, p. 301. The scribe started to copy Wisdom for a second time when he had finished Ecclesiasticus (p. 365), but he saw his mistake on turning the page and began p. 366 with the prologue to Matthew. The Epistle to the Laodiceans follows 2 Thessalonians without heading (pp. 396–7).

The remaining prologues are nineteen of the common set of 64 (see above, Liverpool Cathedral 13), Stegmüller, nos. 284, 285, 311, 323, 328 (to 2 Chronicles); 457, 462, 468, 590, 589, 607; 736, 747, 752, 765 (. . . ab urbe), 772, 780, 783, 793, and one prologue not of the common set, Stegm., no. 834.

Books are written continuously and do not have running titles or chapter numbers, and the only indication of a new chapter is a small space in the text containing two diagonal strokes. There are some signs of use, nevertheless.

ff. iv + 213 + ii, paginated (i–viii), 1–148, 148*, 148**, 149–391, 391*, 391**, 392–422, (423–6). 233 × 180 mm. Written space 180 × 105 mm. 2 cols. 52 or 53 lines. Collation: $1\text{–}3^{12}$ 4^{12} wants 11, 12 after p. 92 $5\text{–}6^{12}$ 7^{10} $8\text{–}11^{12}$ 12 twelve (pp. 253–76) $13\text{–}14^{12}$ 15^{10} 16^{12} 17^{12} wants 2 after p. 370 18^{12} 19^{4}. A small clear hand. Initials: (i) of books and some prologues, blue and red: ornament (of both colours) on pp. 1, 7 only; (ii) of prologues, 2-line, blue. Capital letters in the ink of the text are touched with red. Binding of s. xx. Secundo folio *sunt breuiter*.

Written in England. 'Bassingbonus Throckmorton generosus D.D. Bibliothecæ publicæ Nordouicanæ', f. iii^v: the Donation Book records his gift under the year 1614. 4° W. 129 in 1732.

TC 27/3 (S. A. 3. 1). *Medica* s. xiii med.

Arts. 1–5 are in B.L., Royal 12 B. xii, arts. 15, 6, 4, 17, 16. For arts. 1–4 see H. H. Beusing, *Leben und Werke des Richardus Anglicus*, Leipzig dissertation, 1922.

1 (quires 1–4). ff. 1–18^v (*begins imperfectly and hardly legibly: a chapter begins on f. 1^v*) Aurium passiones ueteres post annum . . . liberati sunt a fistula.

The Micrologus of Richardus Anglicus. Thorndike and Kibre, s.v. Acutarum. Beusing, pp. 19–22. Many leaves missing. A corner of the leaf before f. 1 remains.

Arts. 2–5 are on quires 5, 6.

2. ff. 19–24v Incipit anothomia Ricardi. Galieno testante in tegni. Quicumque . . . omnium membrorum habent commune. Explicit anathomia. Sic nichil ob malum de membris preterit hec ars / Set hec cuncta satis breuiter liquideque notata.

K. Sudhoff, 'Der Micrologus Text der Anatomia Richards des Engländers', *AGM* xix (1927), 209–34. Thorndike and Kibre. Beusing lists thirty-eight manuscripts, pp. 12–17.

3. ff. 24v–29v Qui cupit urinas mea per compendia scire / Hec legat assidue. nec oportet longius ire. Incipiunt regule urinarum secundum M. Richardum. Circa urinas quinque attenduntur . . . cognicionem hic ergo sit regularum finis congruus.

Thorndike and Kibre. Beusing, p. 25.

4. ff. 30–33v Incipiunt repressiue. Laxatiua solent . . . et fortius addita frugine.

Thorndike and Kibre. Beusing, pp. 25–6.

5. ff. 33v–34v Faciei decor et uenustas . . . poteris euellere.

On cosmetics. Thorndike and Kibre. Printed in the *Opera* of Arnald of Villanova (ed. 1504, f. 298v: cf. Glorieux, no. 211*ep*). A corner of f. 34 missing.

Arts. 6–9 are on quires 7, 8.

6. ff. 35–6 (*begins imperfectly*) cum carnem sallitam . . . uentrem si fluat constipaberis. Explicit de cibis.

Only two complete chapters remain: the second begins 'Diximus qualiter fastidium in conualescentibus auferendum'.

7. ff. 36–43v Incipit compendium Salerni. (*prologue*) Duplici causa me cogente . . . (*text*) Medicine est scientia . . . precedentium informentur.

Renzi, v. 201–32. Thorndike and Kibre. A table of 83 heads follows the prologue. A leaf is missing after f. 37 which ends in a recipe for 'syrus acetosus' at the words 'bulliant lento igne': f. 38 begins—in a new hand—'pio debet fieri per antipasim' in the chapter before those beginning 'De adustionibus' and 'De sternutatoriis'.

8. ff. 44–5 Oportet te o Alexander. Cum a sompno . . . et unguentis ungui congruis temporibus.

Pseudo-Aristotle, Letter to Alexander. Thorndike and Kibre.

9. f. 45rv Pleuresis est uera cum spirandi grauitate . . . Vnctus acetosus subtiles sunt et acutus (*ends imperfectly*).

The first 86 lines of the cento from Regimen Salernitanum printed by K. Sudhoff in *AGM* x (1916), 91–9 (202 lines).

Arts. 10–13 are on quire 9.

10. ff. 46–48ᵛ De oleo rosata. Inter cetera que spectant ad usum practice: non modicum tenet locum usus oleorum . . . et potest dari similiter loco zᵉ uiol'. On oils and syrups.

11 (added in blank space). (*a*) Recipes. (*b*) Verses, including 'Collige triticeis . . .' and 'His signis moriens . . . (18 and 9 lines: Walther, nos. 3027, 8211: Renzi, v. 44, 62).

12. ff. 49–51ᵛ Incipit modus tractandi in clisteribus pessariis et suppositoriis. Inter cetera laxatiua medicaminum genera: non indigniorem tenet locum usus clisteriorum . . . et ideo ista de pessariis sufficiant. A leaf missing after f. 50.

13. f. 52ʳᵛ Mania est infectio anterioris cellule capitis . . . expulsis ad exteriora.

Definitions of diseases, noted by Thorndike and Kibre in B.L., Harley 5228, f. 58ᵛ.

Arts. 14, 15 are on quires 10, 11.

14. ff. 53–7 De fleobothomiis noticia liber. Presentis negocii propositum est breuiter tractare in quibus egritudinibus . . . quasi creta reperitur.

Begins like the flebotomy sometimes ascribed to Richardus Anglicus (Thorndike and Kibre, col. 1086).

15. ff. 57ᵛ–62ᵛ Presentis negocii propositum est breuiter tractare de speciebus que . . . Alfita farina ordei . . . set spinis caret (*ends imperfectly in* Lupulus).

Thorndike and Kibre. The preface is in B.L., Royal 12 B. iii, f. 93. The rest is printed in a rearranged form, Renzi, iii. 271–322.

ff. 62. 190 × 130 mm. Written space 135 × 80 mm. 2 cols. 40–7 lines. The first line of writing above the top ruled line. Collation: 1 two (ff. 1, 2) 2^8 wants 1 before f. 3 3 three (ff. 10–12) 4^6 (ff. 13–18) $5–6^8$ 7^8 wants 4 after f. 37 8^4 (ff. 42–5) 9^8 wants 6 after f. 50 10^8 11 two (ff. 61–2): gaps after quires 6 and 8. Written in several small hands. Initials 2-line, red or blue with ornament of the other colour. No binding: kept in a case.

Written in France (?). 'Nup' (?) Jackson his Booke 1653', f. 15. 'Ezekell Danvers his booke', f. 36ᵛ, s. xvii. 'Thomas Marmion his booke 1656', f. 41ᵛ. 'Radulfas Doyly his booke 1656', f. 55ᵛ. Perhaps the miscellany, 4° L. 1, in the 1732 catalogue, recorded as the gift of John Kirkpatrick in 1728.

TC 27/4 (S. A. 1. 3). *Manuale cum notis* s. xv in.

1. ff. 1–3 Omnibus dominicis diebus per annum . . . in hoc habitaculo. per . . . Amen.

Blessings of salt and water. *Manuale Sarum*, pp. 1–4.

2. ff. 3–11v Ordo ad catechuminum faciendum. In primis inquirat sacerdos ab obstetrice . . .

Manuale Sarum, pp. 25–38/12. Litany, f. 6rv Twelve confessors, not as edn.: (6–12) Martine Nicholae Edmunde Swithine Cuthberte Benedicte Egidi; twelve virgins (not Anne), not as edn.: (7–12) Iuliana Agnes Agatha Cecilia Lucia Etheldreda.

3. ff. 11v–17v Ordo ad facienda sponsalia statuantur ante ostium ecclesie . . . dimittat eos in pace.

Manuale Sarum, pp. 44–59. English passages on f. 12rv. In place of the last part of the rubric on second marriages (edn., pp. 57/4 *Morandum*–58/17 *sacramenti*) we have here 'Morardum doctorem. Et sciendum est quod ista questio discussa erat et determinata in sacro pallacio domini pape. Anno domini mo iiimo xxio. Hic queri potest . . . sacramenti (edn., p. 58/4–17). Iohannes seruus seruorum . . . Concertationi . . . dispensare (edn., pp. 57/11–58/3). Et notandum quod capellanus benedicens secundas nupcias aliquando debuit adire curiam romanam pro absolucione habenda per primum capitulum extra de secundis nupciis. Set modo potest absolui a suo diocesano per extrauagantem I*ohannis* (?) pape que talis est' (*no more*).

4. ff. 17v–20 Ordo ad seruicium peregrinorum faciendum. In primis dicantur . . . et ita recedat in nomine domini.

Manuale Sarum, pp. 60–3.

5. ff. 20–3 The eleven blessings in *Manuale Sarum*, pp. 63–70.

The last heading is 'Benedictio oculorum Magister Willelmus de montibus ecclesie lincolniensis cancellarius benediccione oculorum infirmorum necessitas inducit. ut deuocio postulancium et potest fieri hunc modum cum Dominus uobiscum et Oremus'.

6. (*a*) ff. 23–4 Ordo ad uisitandum infirmum. In primis induat . . . cum deo patre. (*b*) ff. 24–8 Priusquam ungatur . . .

Manuale Sarum, pp. 97–100, 106–7 (cf. p. 100, footnote 11); 107–12. Feminine forms interlined.

7. (*a*) ff. 28–30 Cum uero anima in exitu . . . angustiis amen. (*b*) ff. 30–3 Sequatur commendacio animarum . . . intrabunt in ea(m). (*c*) ff. 33–50v Quo peracto incipiantur uigilie mortuorum ut postea sequatur. Dicantur uigilie mortuorum quotidie per aduentum . . . (*d*) ff. 50v–54v Commendacio dicitur a choro . . . Requiescant in pace amen.

Manuale Sarum, pp. 114–18; 118–125/10; 125–42; 142–4. The names in the litany in (*a*), ff. 28v–29v, are nearly as in edn., but in a different order and without Æthelwold among confessors.

8. ff. 54v–60v Post missam accedant duo clerici . . .

Burial service. *Manuale Sarum*, pp. 152–62.

9. f. 60v Forma ad absoluendum quemcumque per bullam concessam de plena remissione peccatorum . . . Deinde dicitur ista oracio. Pretende domine . . .

Cf. *Manuale Sarum*, pp. 105–6.

10. ff. 60v–61v In nocte natiuitatis domini . . . Liber generacionis . . . qui uocatur cristus . . . Laudes deo dicam . . . In qua cristi lucida uaticinatur (*ends imperfectly*).

Manuale Sarum, p. 5. Noted.

11. ff. 63–9 Alphabets and abbreviations of this manuscript, with extensions, in the hand of John Kirkpatrick, s. xviii in., on six paper leaves. The script is imitated.

12. ff. i, 70, flyleaves and the pastedowns, front and back, make two leaves of a missal, each laid sideways and folded across the middle.

Written space *c.*245 × 170 mm. 2 cols. 31 lines. English hand, s. xv in. The leaf at the back contains part of the office for Thomas of Canterbury (the name not interfered with) and the leaf in front part of the office for the second Sunday after the octave of Epiphany: *Sarum Missal*, pp. 32–4, 41–2.

ff. i + 62 + viii. For ff. i, 63–70 see above. 250 × 180 mm. Written space 185 × 140 mm. 2 cols. 27 lines. Collation: $1\text{–}4^8$ 5^8 wants 3 after f. 34 $6\text{–}7^8$ 8^8 wants 8 after f. 62. Initials: (i) f. 1, in colour on gold ground, decorated and with prolongations forming a continuous border; (ii) 3-line, gold on coloured grounds; (iii) 2-line, blue with red ornament; (iv) 1-line, red or blue. Cadels in art. 7*b*–*d*. Capital letters in the ink of the text filled with yellow. Contemporary binding of white leather over wooden boards: two straps now missing, but the pins remain on the back cover. Secundo folio *cionibus*.

Written in England. 'John Kirkpatrick Sept 12: 1704', f. i. Kirkpatrick gave his library to the city of Norwich in 1728. 'K. 147' inside cover. 'Mass Book MSS 4to K 147' in the 1732 catalogue.

TC 27/5. *Bible (in English)*[1] s. xv in.

1. ff. 1–208 A Bible in the later Wycliffite version, ending imperfectly in Proverbs 7: 10, 'maad redi wiþ'.

Listed as no. 144 and collated as W by Forshall and Madden. St. Jerome's general prefaces and all prologues to books are omitted. Only the upper half of f. 208 remains. A reduced facsimile of the verso on which Leviticus begins is no. 45 in Lasko and Morgan and pl. 11 in T. Kelly, *Early Public Libraries*; see also *Norwich Public Libraries*, p. 38, for this verso and the page facing it, much reduced.

2. f. 209 A binding-leaf taken from a large antiphonal of s. xv, one side pasted over, the other containing part of the sanctoral for 29 and 30 June (cf. *Brev. ad usum Sarum*, iii. 378).

Written space 373 × 240 mm. 2 cols. 18 lines and music.

ff. ii + 208 + i. f. ii and f. 209 (see above) are medieval endleaves backed by modern paper. 440 × 300 mm. Written space 335 × 210 mm. 2 cols. 59 lines. Collation: $1\text{–}26^8$. Written by one hand throughout. Initials: (i) of most books, in colour on gold grounds decorated in colours and with long prolongations into the margins forming continuous borders on ff. 1,

[1] On deposit in the St Peter Hungate Museum, Norwich.

207 (Proverbs): for a facsimile, see above; (ii) of some books, for example Ruth, and the main subdivisions of the psalter, gold on coloured grounds, with less decoration than with initials of type (i); (iii) 3-line, blue with red ornament; (iv) of psalm-verses, 1-line, blue or red. Rebound in s. xix, but the old leather covers were preserved and pasted over the new covers: they bear Oldham's rolls FP. g. 13 and IN. 5, which were used by a Norwich binder in s. xvi med.: see above, p. 535. The initials 'C H' are stamped lightly within the frame near the foot of the front cover, as on the front cover of Sion College MS. Arc L. 40. 2/L. 5, by the same binder (roll FP. g. 13: see *MMBL*, i. 268). Secundo folio *doon so*.

Written in England. 'liber Iacobi Boolene manens in Blickling', f. ii^v, s. xvi: Sir James Boleyn of Blickling Hall, Norfolk, died in 1561. Recorded in the Donation Book as the gift of Richard Ireland, rector of Beeston, Norfolk, in 1692. Fol. G. 15 in 1732.

TC 28/1 (S. A. 3. 2). *Astronomica* s. xv², xv/xvi

Until s. xix, as a foliation and quire signatures show, ff. 50–69 were at the end. This arrangement, which brings arts. 5 and 6 together, is followed here.

1 (quire 1). (*a*) f. 1 Tabula longitudinis et latitudinis stellarum fixarum. (*b*) ff. 1^v–2 Ars operandi per probas in speciebus algorismi est valde vtilis in equationibus planetarum . . . in omnibus poligoniis. Explicit ars probarum algorismi. (*c*) ff. 2^v–12 Septem sunt planete scilicet Saturnus . . . Et dicuntur sidera errantia.

(*a*). Forty-eight stars are named, Sceder . . . Pliades. (*b*). Thorndike and Kibre, who refer to Cambridge, U.L., Ee. 3. 61, f. 30. (*c*). Cf. Thorndike and Kibre. Dates from 1452 to judge from a passage on f. 4^v, 'Anno domini 1452 litera dominicali a sabbato ante festum apostolorum Simonis et Iude fuerunt planete in talibus signis et gradibus ad nonam'.

2 (quire 2). (*a*) ff. 13–16^v Aries domus martis est signum mobile calide et sicce nature . . . in omnem rem. Explicit complexio signorum cum suis influenciis. (*b*) ff. 17–18 Saturnus est frigidus et siccus . . . nasus fimus. Explicit complexio planetarum.

(*a, b*). Cf. Thorndike and Kibre. (*a*). Cf. Bodleian, Wood D. 8 (*Sum. Cat.* 8538), f. 4. f. 18^v blank.

3 (quire 3). ff. 19–30^v Prohemium in composicionem et vtilitatem quadrantis magistri *pre*faci (*sic*) Iudei marsiliensis sapientis astronomi in monte pessulano. Quoniam sciencia astronomie . . . (*text*) Describemus circulum a.b.c.d . . . doctrinam aliam. Explicit maximus prefacius non feyacius.

Thorndike and Kibre. Sixteen chapters.

4 (quire 4). (*a*) ff. 31–4 Tractatus de anulo. In latitudine fixe partis anuli sunt 4^or circuli . . . australis est archus. (*b*) ff. 34^v–35^v Ad noticiam huius Kalendarii est notandum quod in prima linea kalendarii descendenti secundum longitudinem . . . a dextero ad sinistrum procedes cum linea (*ends imperfectly*).

(*b*). Directions for the use of a calendar (which followed ?): cf. *MMBL* ii. 555. A leaf, or perhaps a quire, missing after f. 35. Three paragraphs remain and part of a fourth. Para. 1 begins 'Iste ciclus incipit anno domini 151° (*sic*) et finetur anno domini 1519'. Para. 2 begins 'Hec tabula prima docet pro 84 annis ab anno domini 1500'.

5 (quire 5). (*a*) ff. 36–9 In unum collecta que ad 'idem' pertinent diutius conseruantur . . . et atthasir ex consequenti. Expliciunt canones super tabulam completam domorum secundum Magistrum Iohannem Walter'. (*b*) ff. 39v–40 Notes beginning 'Quilibet planeta habet 3a signa'. (*c*) ff. 40v–47 Volentibus pronosticare futuros effectus . . . non oportet. Expliciunt canones tabularum extractarum a tabulis alfonsi per venerabilem Magistrum Willelmum Reed Cicestrensem episcopum et sacre theologie doctorem. (*d*) ff. 47v–49v Quia secundum ptolomeum in suo centilogio . . . hic et ibi. Explicit canon pro minutionibus purgationibus et medicinis recipiendis.

(*a, c, d*). Thorndike and Kibre; also Emden, *BRUO*, under John Walter, William Rede, and Nicholas of Lynn respectively. (*a*) is the canon for art. 6*a* and (*c*) the canon for art. 6*f*.

6 (quires 8, 9) ff. 71–100v Tables: (*a*) ff. 71–6 Tabula completa domorum secundum Magistrum Iohannem; (*b*) f. 77 Tabula augmenti longissime diei super diem equinoctii in omni terra habitabili; (*c*) f. 77v Tabula declinacionis solis cum diuersitate ascensionis signorum in omni terra habitabili; (*d*) f. 78 Tabula ad inueniendum dignitates planetarum in signis; (*e*) f. 78v A table headed 'Altitudo solis pro quadrante' for years 1385–1469; (*f*) ff. 79–100v Tabula mediorum motuum omnium planetarum secundum magistrum Willelmum Reed in annis collectis . . .

(*a*). Cf. art. 5*a*. (*f*). Tables of William Rede (cf. Emden, *BRUO*, p. 1560, and art. 5*c*), ending imperfectly. The table on ff. 79v–80v is for 1320–1600. Ends now with a 'Tabula stationum mercurii ad equationem centri eiusdem' (f. 100v): cf., for example, Bodleian, Wood D. 8 (*Sum. Cat.* 8538), ff. 67v–81.

7 (quires 10, 11). (*a*) ff. 101–16 (*f. 101 is a small fragment and continuous text begins on f. 102*) leuis per naturam naturalem ascendit sursum . . . patitur aut tota mundi machina dissoluitur etc. Explicit tractatus de spera. (*b*) Diagrams of earth and moon (f. 116v), the arctic and antarctic poles (f. 116v), and the spheres, fourteen concentric circles, the centre marked 'Centrum' (f. 117).

(*a*). J. de Sacro Bosco, De sphera. The first words here come in Bodleian, Digby 228 f. 62/43 in a passage which does not occur in Thorndike's edition (1949): it is shortly before edn., p. 84/1. ff. 117v–119v blank.

8 (quire 6). ff. 50–59v A repetition of art. 3, reading 'profacii' and 'in montepessulano editi' in the title and ending in the heading of chapter 16: two leaves missing after f. 59.

9 (quire 7). ff. 60–9 (*begins imperfectly*) terre ad zodiacum per centrum planete . . . in suis differentibus ideo luna non retrogradatur. Explicit theorica planetarum secundum Brytt'.

Thorndike and Kibre. Emden, *BRUO*, p. 270. The first words here are in Bodleian, Digby 58 f. 79/1. ff. 69v–70v were left blank: 69v has now some notes in English. s. xvii.

10. The parchment strips used as strengthening to the central openings of quires 5 and 8 (after ff. 42 and 78) are from a noted service book, s. xiii.

ff. 119. Paper, with parchment strips as strengthening between the quires (art. 10). 150 × 105 mm. Written space *c.* 105 × 70 mm. 29–34 long lines. Frame ruling, quires 6, 7 with a hard point. Collation: 1^{12} 2^{6} 3^{12} 4^{6} wants 6 after f. 35 5^{14} 6^{12} wants 11, 12 after f. 59 7^{12} wants 11, blank, after f. 69 8^{16} 9^{14} 10^{12} wants 1, 2, and nearly all 3 (ff. 101–10) 11^{10} wants 9, blank, after f. 118. Written in several neat secretary hands: straight ascenders in art. 8. Red initials, 3-line or 2-line. Capital letters in the ink of the text touched with red. Contemporary binding formed of a double thickness of leather lined inside with linen: the quires are stitched to the leather only near the head and foot. Secundo folio *Si proba*.

Written in England.

TC 28/2 (S. A. 1. 4). *Registrum brevium* s. xv med.

(*begins imperfectly*) quando quadraginta solidi capiuntur de Scuto set modo valent . . . ac animabus omnium benefactorum (*ends imperfectly*).

The first and last words correspond to f. 2/9 and f. 253ᵛ/31 of the edition printed in 1687. The writs are arranged nearly as in St John's College, Oxford, 256 (q.v., below), but are not in numbered chapters. The point at which a new chapter begins in St John's is usually marked here by a 3-line or larger initial: f. 7ᵛ (chapter 2); 12ᵛ (3: 1-line initial); 16ᵛ (4); 18ᵛ (5); 21ᵛ (6); 25 (7); 37 (8); 48 (9); 50ᵛ (10: 1-line initial); 54 (11); 60ᵛ (12); 66 (13); 76 (14); 101 (15); 103ᵛ (16); 106ᵛ (17); 108 (18: 5-line initial); 119ᵛ (19); 124 (20); 125 (22); 128 (21); 130ᵛ (23); 132 (24: 5-line initial); 150ᵛ (25: 5-line initial); 154 (26: 7-line initial); 168 (26: 7-line initial). The text is very defective after f. 175 where a quire or more is missing at a point corresponding to edn., f. 161. For ff. 76–83 see collation, below: they contain parts of St John's, chapters 34, 37, 38.

'Henricus' instead of *Rex* begins writs on ff. 132 and 154. The last item of (chapter 25) is dated 29 Nov., anno 8 'Teste Willelmo cheyne apud Westmonasterium' (f. 154). The writs of protection in St John's, chapter 4, do not occur here. Running titles occasionally, especially 'De statuto' on ff. 135–50. The third and fourth sheets of quire 17 are wrongly bound: the right order of this quire is 128–9, 131, 130, 133, 132, 134–5. f. 59 lacks its upper half.

ff. iii + 183 + iii. ff. 1–175 are foliated '10–183' and ff. 176–83 '120', '127', '129–34' in a hand of s. xvii (?). 290 × 212 mm. Written space 185 × 120 mm. 36–7 long lines. Collation: 1^{8} wants 1 $2–22^{8}$ 23^{8} wants 2–7 after f. 176 24^{8} wants 1 and 8 (ff. 177–83). Written in an untidy secretary hand. 7-line, 5-line, 4-line, 3-line, 2-line, and 1-line initials (see above), blue with red ornament or red with violet ornament. Binding of s. xviii. Secundo folio (f. 1) *quando quadraginta*.

Written in England. 'Mary frere', f. 69, s. xvii (?). Identifiable by the mark 'K. 60' inside the cover with 'Miscellany MSS. Fol. K. 60' in the printed catalogue of 1732. According to the catalogue it was given by John Kirkpatrick in 1728.

TC 28/4 (S. D. 4. 3). *P. Lombardus, Sententiae* s. xiv in.

A handsome copy of the Sentences of Peter Lombard: bk. 1, f. 5; 2, f. 41; 3, f. 76; 4, f. 103. Distinction numbers in red in the margins are part of the original design. f. 40ᵛ ends in dist. 38 of bk. 1: a quire is missing here with the rest of the book and the table of chapters of bk. 2. Unnumbered tables of chapters of bks. 1, 3, 4 on ff. 3–4ᵛ, 75–6, 101ᵛ–103, as in edn. 1971 (Spicilegium Bonaventurianum, iv), pp. 5–18, 31–53.

The wide margins are mainly blank, but there are many ink notes in contemporary current anglicana on ff. 103-13 (bk. 4, dist. 1-14) and extracts from 'Hilarius in libro de synodis' in fanciful shapes on ff. 33^{v}-34; other notes are mainly in pencil. Couplets on f. 111, 'Rex sedet in cena . . . ille cibus' (Walther, *Sprichwörter*, no. 26863) and 'Pixide seruato poteris copulare dolorem / Innatum. set non illatus conuenit illi' and on f. 112 'Hostias diuinorum in partes cuncta beatos / plene. sicca notat viuos. seruata sepultos'. 'loke', f. 106. 'x^{a} p^{a} [. . .]' on f. 81 (bk. 3, dist. 8) is perhaps a pecia mark.

ff. ii + 132 + ii. 400 × 260 mm. Written space 255 × 160 mm. 2 cols. 56 lines. The ruling includes a double line right across the upper and lower margins and a single line down each side margin. Collation: 1^{4} $2\text{-}4^{12}$ 5^{10} $6\text{-}11^{12}$ 12^{10}. Initials: (i) excised, but some of the fairly elaborate ornament remains on ff. 5, 76, 103; (ii, iii) of distinctions 3-line, and of chapters 2-line, blue or red, with pale ornament often touched with green; (iv) 1-line, blue or red. Capital letters in the ink of the text touched with yellow. The second and third lines of bk. 1 and the second line of bks. 3 and 4 are between rows of coloured patterning. Binding of s. xx. Secundo folio (f. 6) *frueris*.

Written probably in France, but soon transferred to England: see above. 'John Ladd owe this booke', f. 4^{v}, s. xvi ex.

S. A. 3. 7, ff. 150-67. *De noviciis* s. xv med.

(*begins imperfectly at chapter 5*) Quid in primis insinuandum sit nouicio. Recedente ab eis prelato quamuis de hiis que subsequentur . . . ad capitulum pertinentibus diligentissme instruatur.

Thirty-six (?) chapters, 5-16 numbered. The rule 'sancti patris nostri Augustini' is quoted on f. 156.

ff. 18, foliated in a hand of s. xix. 198 × 136 mm. Written space 150 × 105 mm. 29-32 long lines. Collation: 1^{8} 2^{4} 3^{2} 4^{4}. Written in current anglicana. 2-line red initials. The binding, s. xvii, rebacked, covers four pieces: (1) J. F. Picus Mirandola, *De morte Christi* (etc.), Bologna 1497 (Goff, P. 644); (2) Guillermus Parisiensis, *Super septem sacramentis*, Paris 1492 (Hain 8313); (3) MS. De noviciis; (4) *Enchiridion de institutis graecorum*, Cambridge 1619 (*STC* 636).

Written in England.

NORWICH. ST PETER MANCROFT CHURCH

A catalogue, s. xvii, printed in *Norfolk Antiquarian Miscellany* ii (1883), 359-63, appears to record both manuscripts.

Biblia s. xiii^{2}

1. ff. 1-435^{v} A Bible in the usual order (see Liverpool Cathedral 13) and with the usual contents, apart from the absence of the Prayer of Manasses, 3 Ezra, and Psalms.

Isaiah begins a new quire (f. 220). The prologues are 43 of the common set of 64 (see Liverpool Cathedral 13) and 23 others shown here by *: Stegmüller, nos. 284, 285, 311, 323, 330, 332, 335, 341 + 343, 344, 357, 482, 487, 491, 492, 494, 500, 507, 510, 512, 519 + 517, 516*, 524, 522*, 526, 525*, 528, 527*, 531, 529*, 534, 532*, 539 (as prologue to Haggai), 535*, 540*, 545*, 544*, 551, 590, 607, 620, 624, 677, 651* (. . . appositas), 683*, 688*, 701*, 706*, 721*, 730*, 736, 748, 752, end of 753* (*Scribit hanc epistolam* . . .), 766* (. . . monet esse uitandos hymeneus et alexander quos tradidi satane: ut discant non blasphemare: the last ten words marked 'vacat'), 772 + 770*, 780, 783, 793 (. . . composuit. Et quia apud hebreorum eclesias quasi destructor legis . . . excluderet lectionis), 640, 631*, 809, 807*, 806*. Luke 1: 1-4 is not treated as a prologue.

Notes of s. xiii ex. and later in English hands. f. 436^{rv} blank.

2. ff. 437-441^v Aaz apprehendens uel apprehensio . . . [Z]oe astrahens uel attractio.

Apparently a short form of the common Interpretationes nominum hebraicorum. Here there are, for example, only 28 entries under L, instead of over 100.

3. f. iv A calligraphic title-page bearing nine lines of verse, 'All-conq'ring *Labour*! thou such mighty *Things* . . . While Ragged *Sloth* with bosom'd *Hands Will* Starve, and Dye with *Shame*', followed by 'Norwich: Compos'd, Written and Illustrated by Samuel Greenvill, the Tenth Day of January, Anno 1720'.

ff. iv + 440 + iii, foliated (i-iv), 1-125, 125*, 126-75, 178-207, 209-38, 238*, 239-441, (442-4). A late medieval foliation from 1 to 435. For f. iv, see above, art. 3. 165 × 110 mm. Written space 118 × 75 mm at first, but from f. 220 the width is *c.*68 mm. 2 cols. (3 cols., ff. 436-40). 48 lines. Collation: 1^{14} $2\text{-}10^{16}$ 11^{14} + 1 leaf after 11 (f. 169) $12\text{-}13^{16}$ 14^{12} (ff. 207-19) 15^{12} 16^{14} $17\text{-}28^{16}$ 29 five (ff. 437-41). Initials: (i) of books, red and blue with ornament of both colours; (ii) of prologues and where a new letter begins in art. 2, blue with red ornament and (art. 2 only) red with blue ornament; (iii) of chapters, 1-line, blue with red ornament; (iv) in art. 2, 1-line, blue or red. Binding of s. xix. Secundo folio *`sacris' litteris*.

Written in England. 'anno domini 1340' at the end of the text, f. 435^v, may be in the hand of the foliator (s. xv ex. ?). 'Wyll*ia*m Wylles' is scribbled in pencil, f. 380^v. 'S. Greenvill 1720' (f. 435^v: cf. f. iv) cannot imply ownership, if this is the 'Biblia Hieronymi manuscripta' given by 'Mr. Rosse', entered in the catalogue (p. 361).

Epistolae Pauli, cum glossa Petri Lombardi s. xii/xiii

(*preface*) Principia rerum requirenda . . . salutacionem dicens. Hanc epistolam scribit apostolus romanis. (*text*) Paulus seruus . . . (*commentary*) Hucusque enim pendet littera . . . (f. 202) et alia dei munera sit cum omnibus uobis. Amen.

Stegmüller, nos. 6654-68. *PL* cxci. 1297-696; cxcii. 10-520. Four leaves of Colossians and two leaves of Hebrews are missing. 'emendatum est' is written at the end of many quires and sometimes on leaves within quires in the bottom left corner of versos. Ten lines of verse, 'Pauli doctoris quem rexit uirtus amoris . . . Legitur obscura sapienter litteratur' (Walther, nos. 13848 + 6124) follow the text. They are printed by M. R. James in his *Catalogue of manuscripts at Trinity College, Cambridge*, i. 523, from MS. 387 where they are laid out in the same way as they are here. f. 202^v blank.

ff. ii + 202 + ii. 370 × 265 mm. Written space 250 × 185 mm. Text in central column of 25 lines. Gloss in broader columns of 50 lines on each side of the text. The first line of gloss is written above and the first line of text is written below the top ruled line. Pricks in both margins to guide ruling. A change in the pattern of ruled lines at f. 72. Collation: $1\text{-}18^8$ 19^8 wants 3-6 after f. 146 $20\text{-}22^8$ 23^8 wants 4, 5 after f. 175 $24\text{-}26^8$. Quires 1-7 numbered at the end. Quires 9 onwards have catchwords instead of numbers and on the first four leaves of each quire *ad hoc* pencil signatures in the lower margins arranged so that the mark on a verso side is the same as the mark on the recto side facing it, for example, f. 74^v is marked + and so is f. 75^r. Two hands changing at f. 71va/16: the second hand is excellent. The nota sign standing for *et* is not crossed. Initials: (i) of each epistle, in colour on gold and coloured grounds framed in green and decorated or (ff. 2, 105^v, 122, 143, 171^v, Romans, Galatians, Ephesians, I Thessalonians, Hebrews) historiated in good style (Kauffmann, no. 101 and plates 288-90); (ii) of prologues and the gloss to each epistle, as (i), but smaller; (iii) 1-line, red, blue or green. Binding of s. xix. Secundo folio *Paulus*; tertio folio *qui etiam alio*.

Written in England. 'Epistole Pauli Roberti de Nouell' ', f. 1, above col. 1, s. xiv in. The form of the inscription suggests a gift to a Benedictine house[1] and later inscriptions make it likely that this house was the abbey of Peterborough, O.S.B.: (1) at the end, 'Liber fratris Rogerus (*sic*) Birde monachi', s. xvi in.: cf. Ker, *MLGB*, p. 293; (2) in the margin of f. 172, 'Galfrid Parrysche vicar of Lyllford', s. xvi: he was instituted to Lilford, Northants, in 1544 and is described as aged 63 and 'quondam monachus' in 1576 (*Northamptonshire and Rutland Clergy*, ed. H. I. Longden, x (1941), 171) and has been identified with Geoffrey Paris, one of the Peterborough monks extruded in 1539 (W. T. Mellows, *The last days of Peterborough monastery* (Northants Record Soc., xii, 1947), p. xcvi). No doubt the 'Annotationes in Epistolas Pauli manuscriptæ' entered in the catalogue, p. 362, as the gift of William Gargrave and his wife, Alice.

NORWICH. UNIVERSITY OF EAST ANGLIA

PA 6280. *Cicero, Philippica* s. xv^2

M. Tul. Ciceronis in M. Antonium Orationes Quæ Demostenis in Regem Philippum Macedonem exemplo Philippicę nuncupantur: Prima. Antequam de Re P. Pa. Co. dicam ea quę dicenda . . . (f. 183^v) faciendumque Vrbem.

The fourteen Philippica: 2, f. 13^v; 3, f. 58^v; 4, f. 73; 5, f. 78; 6, f. 96^v; 7, f. 102; 8, f. 109^v; 9, f. 119^v; 10, f. 125; 11, f. 134; 12, f. 146^v; 13, f. 156^v; 14, f. 173. For the last words see Loeb edn., p. 644/13. Fairly numerous contemporary scholia and interlinear glosses, probably by the scribes, except on ff. 1-4/10, 9-13, 16^v-24^v. In each book, except 1, 5, the scholia begin with an Argumentum actionis. In the argumentum of bk. 11 the scribe could not read his copy and left blank spaces: Argumentum A [*blank*] Numanta cede . . . Dolabella [*blank*] fatum M. Tullii de [*blank*] octut^i (?) quod Senatum . . . Dolabelle [*blank*] in hac oratione [*blank*] exordium Incipit . . . Aperat. He wrote ':iē: cr̄' at the head of f. 1. f. 184^{rv} blank.

ff. vii + 184 + ix. Paper. 207 × 140 mm. Written space 130-45 × 70-82 mm. 18-23 long lines. Ruling is with a hard point in quires 1-3, 20-2; with pencil in quires 4, 5; perhaps absent on quires 6-19, where the bounding line is made by folding the paper: in quires 6-14 three vertical fold lines can usually be seen, one of them within the written space.

[1] Dr C. de Hamel suggests (Oxford D.Phil. thesis) that the donor was the Robert de Novelle who witnessed Peterborough charters in the time of Abbot Benedict (1177-94): cf. *Northants Record Soc.* xx (1960), 247.

Collation: $1-3^{8}$ 4^{12} $5-15^{8}$ 6^{10} $17-21^{8}$ 22^{10}. Vertical catchwords in quires 1-5, horizontal inside a frame in quires 16-21. Current humanistica, changing at f. 25 (4^{1}) and perhaps elsewhere: less and less use is made of round backed *d* from bk. 5 onwards. 2-line, 3-line, or 4-line spaces for initials not filled. Contemporary binding of wooden boards half covered with leather: three bands: two clasps, now missing, fastened from front to back. 'M. T. PHILLIPICÆ' on the fore-edge. Secundo folio *uerbis*.

Written in Italy. Acquired by Sir Thomas Phillipps from T. Thorpe in 1824. Phillipps 2338. Book-plate of A. N. L. Munby. Given by him in 1963.

OAKHAM CHURCH

Biblia s. xiii[1]

A Bible in the order Genesis–2 Chronicles, prayer of Manasses, Ezra, Nehemiah, Tobit, Judith, Esther, 1, 2 Maccabees, Isaiah, Jeremiah, Lamentations, Baruch (in the order 6, 1-5), Ezekiel, Daniel, Minor Prophets, Job, Psalms, five Sapiential Books, Gospels, Acts, Catholic Epistles, Pauline Epistles, ending imperfectly at Hebrews 9: 4 'optulit imma' (f. 421v). 3 Kings 25: 25–4 Kings 22: 17 is missing after f. 110 and ten leaves elsewhere before f. 422. Isaiah begins a new quire (f. 206). Psalms, ff. 301-13, is on a quire by itself, originally of sixteen leaves. Job is preceded by a blank space, f. 292. No breaks between chapters, which are indicated only by red and blue numbers in the margins and a 1-line initial in the text. f. 1 is slightly damaged.

In Psalms only as much of each verse is written as fits in one line. Larger initials distinguish Pss. 51 and 101, as well as the eight liturgical divisions.

The prologues are 32 of the common set of 64 (see above, Liverpool Cathedral 13) and two others shown here by *: Stegmüller, nos. 284, 285, 311, 323, 328, 330, 332, 335, 341 + 343, 551, 491, 492, 494, 500, 457, 590, 624, 640, 809, 670* + 676*, 700, 707, 715, 728, 736, 748, 752, 765 (de Laodicia), 772, 780, 783, 793.

f. 422 contains a list of the books in the order in which they occur here, ending with Hebrews and Apocalypse, and other notes, s. xiii. Marginalia, s. xiii, are mainly in Minor Prophets and NT. Book numbers of Gregory's Moralia are entered in the margins of Job.

Kept with the Bible are: a description of it by M. R. James and a letter from him dated 25 Nov. 1925 ('. . . I have spent the morning over your Bible . . .'); a printed note about it by James (*Guardian*, 24 Dec. 1925, p. 1115); a record of marriages, christenings, and burials of members of the Pilkington family, compiled from Oakham registers in s. xix: it includes a Thomas Pilkington born 1577, died 1615.

ff. 422. 212 × 156 mm. Written space 150 × *c.*80 mm. 44 long lines (2 cols. only for Psalms, ff. 301-13). The first line of writing above the top ruled line. Collation: 1 three 2^{12} wants 2 after f. 4 $3-10^{12}$ 11 five (ff. 111-15) $12-15^{12}$ 16^{12} wants 6, 7 after f. 168 $17-24^{12}$ 25^{12} wants 12 after f. 276 $26-27^{12}$ 28^{16} wants 9, 12, 16 (ff. 301-13) $29-31^{12}$ 32^{12} wants 9, 10 after f. 357 $33-35^{12}$ 36^{12} wants 10 after f. 404 37^{12} 38 four (ff. 419-22). Probably all by one hand. Initials: (i) of books and some prologues, 4-line or 5-line, red and blue ornamented in red, blue, and green; (ii) of some prologues and main psalms, 4-line red or blue with ornament of the other colour or (psalms) without ornament; (iii) of psalms, other than main psalms, 2-line, blue with red ornament or red without ornament; (iv) of chapters and psalm verses, 1-line, red or blue. Binding of s. xvii[1] with gilt centrepiece and on the spine six stamps in gilt depicting a pair of snails: two strips of parchment as strengthening are from a writ of King's Bench, 19 James I. Secundo folio *uehiculo*.

Written in England. A cancelled inscription at the top of f. 1 has '1599' beside it. 'EX DONO THOME PILKINGTON' stamped in gold on the front cover: cf. above. The names 'John Beamount' and 'Jhon Scaresmore' occur in scribbles on f. 184ᵛ, s. xvi.

OSCOTT COLLEGE

Nos. 516, 518, 519, 583-6 are listed in *A catalogue of pictures, woodcarvings, MSS. . . . in St Mary's College, Oscott*, compiled by Rev. William Greaney, sine anno, and nos. 714 and 820 are listed in an *Appendix* printed in 1899. Nos. 516, 518, 519 and the 'Oscott Psalter' (Greaney, no. 515), now B.L., Add. 50000, are listed in HMC, *First Report*, 1874, pp. 89, 90. The psalter was sold to C. W. Dyson Perrins in 1908 and is fully described as no. 11 (pp. 40-6) in Sir George Warner's catalogue of the Perrins manuscripts published in 1920.

516 + 599.[1] *Missale* s. xv med.

A Sarum missal noticed by W. Perry in *The Oscotian*, 3rd series ii (1911), 118-27.

1. ff. v-x^{v} Calendar in red and black.

Entries in red include 'Translatio sancti edmundi regis et martyris . . . non sar' ' and 'Dedicacio ecclesie Norwicensis ix lc' non sar' ' (29 Apr., 24 Sept.), both in the main hand. Feast of Sarum relics on Sunday after St Thomas of Canterbury in July. The word 'pape' and feasts of St Thomas of Canterbury erased, but the December feast has been restored on a piece of stuck-on parchment. The list of holy days decreed by archbishop Islip, 'Decretum domini symonis . . . In primis ordinamus . . . peculiariter indicuntur' (cf. Lyndwood, *Provinciale Angliae*, bk. 2, tit. De feriis), is in the main hand at the foot of f. v.

2. ff. 1-80 Temporal from Advent to Easter Eve.

The secret for the second Sunday after the octave of Epiphany is Ut tibi grata. Noted exultet and preface, ff. 73^{v}-75^{v} and 78-79^{v}. Litany, f. 77^{rv}. On f. 14^{v} the office of Thomas of Canterbury has been erased and then restored, partly on stuck-on pieces of parchment.

3. ff. 80-92 Ad missam dicendam executor officii . . .

Ordinary, as in Newcastle, Univ. libr. 2, noted prefaces and canon of mass. Te igitur, f. 89. Before it a leaf is missing with the end of the common preface and probably a picture of the crucifixion. In its place is a blank leaf of parchment, to the verso of which a parchment leaf of a printed Sarum missal, s. xvi in. (sign. l. iii), has been pasted: the leaf, now raised, is headed 'Prefationes', begins 'In omnibus festis' and has the prefaces for B.V.M., for apostles and evangelists, and for Chair of Peter (as *Sarum Missal*, pp. 215, 214) on the recto and a full-page woodcut of the Crucifixion on the verso.

[1] Greaney's *Catalogue* assigns the number 599 to the printed leaf in art. 3.

4. (*a*) f. 92^rv Qua finita erigat se sacerdos . . . sub una determinacione. (*b*) ff. 92^v–94 Predictus modus et ordo . . . sine prostracione. Ps. Deus uenerunt . . . proteccione defendi. Per eundem cristum. (*c*) f. 94^rv Benedicamus and Ite missa est, both noted.

(*a*). *Sarum Missal*, p. 230 (Graciarum actio post missam). (*b*). ibid., pp. 209–10, but preceded here by a long rubric on the order of services.

5. ff. 95^v–132^v Temporal from Easter to the 25th Sunday after Trinity.

A leaf missing after f. 130 contained part of the offices in *Sarum Missal*, pp. 198–9.

6. ff. 132^v–134 In dedicacione ecclesie, and at the octave.

7. ff. 134–175^v Sanctoral from Andrew to Katherine, followed by feast of relics.

Cues for the offices of John of Beverley and Winefred added in the margins, ff. 146, 172^v. Office of translation of Thomas of Canterbury cancelled on f. 153. After it, a note in the text refers to the date of the feast of relics: Notandum est quod proxima dominica post festum translacionis \`sancti thome martiris′ (*restored over erasure*) celebretur festum reliquiarum quod nuper celebratum fuerat in oct' nat' beate marie. quere omnia in fine sanctorum ante commune. On f. 174 the collect for Martin on the octave of his feast, 'Concede quesumus omnipotens deus. ut beati martini . . .', is over erasure.

8. ff. 175^v–189^v Common of saints.

9. Votive masses: (*a*) ff. 189^v–197 Ordinacio misse cotidiane beate marie uirginis que dicitur Salue. Pulsato ad missam . . . ; (*b*) f. 197^rv Ordo que sanctus gregorius [papa] pro liberacione . . . proximiores prime oracionis. scilicet sub uno Oremus. et sub uno Per dominum. Or'. Deus summa spes . . . ; (*c*) ff. 197–200 Pro papa . . .

Offices of B.V.M. (4–6),[1] Trinity (1), angels (p. 459), Holy Spirit (2), Holy Cross (3), Pro fratribus et sororibus (7), Pro pace (11), Pro serenitate aeris (28), Ad pluuiam postulandam (27), In tempore belli (43), Pro iter agentibus (30), Pro quacumque tribulacione (26). (*b*). Collect, secret, and postcommunion. Cf. below, Oxford, Corpus Christi College 394, art. 13. (*c*). Collect, secret, and postcommunion: Pro papa (9: *all rewritten over erasure*), Pro pontifice (12), De sancto saluatore (as Burntisland edn. of Sarum missal (1861–3), col. 825*), De sanctis Katerina, Margareta et maria magdalena (as ibid., col. 823*), Pro penitentibus (25), De omnibus sanctis per totum annum (8), Pro uniuersali ecclesia (10), Pro pace (11), Pro prelatis (13), Pro rege (15), Pro rege et regina (16), Pro semetipso sacerdote (17), Item pro semetipso sacerdote (18), Pro salute amici (19), Contra temptacionem carnis (21), Contra malas cogitaciones (22), Ad inuocandam graciam sancti spiritus (23), Ad petendum lacrimas (24), Pro eo qui in uinculis tenetur (35), Pro nauigantibus (38), Pro infirmo (39).

10. ff. 200–1 Missa de trinitate in sponsalibus . . .

Marriage service, including the constitution on second marriages, 'Concertationi antique . . . dispensare' (*Manuale Sarum*, pp. 57–8), but the only rubric before the constitution is 'Notandum . . . nupciis' (edn., pp. 51/19–55/2), followed by 'Ideo super hoc statuitur constitucio noua iohannis pape xxii que sic incipit'.

[1] For these numbers and the page reference, see below, All Souls College, Oxford, 302, art. 9.

11. ff. 201–5 Missa pro defunctis.

Manuale Sarum, pp. 144–145/23, 147/21–152, 145/24. Followed on f. 203v by fifteen sets of collects, secrets, and postcommunions for a bishop and for other persons, as *Sarum Missal*, pp. 434–42, nos. (2–8, 10, 14–19), but the postcommunion in no. (14) is not Hec nos communio, but Propiciare quesumus domine supplicacionibus nostris et animas . . .

12. ff. 205–6 Oratio generalis.

Four forms, as *Sarum Missal*, pp. 442–5.

13. f. 206rv Omnibus uere confessis et contritis d*omp*n*u*s Iohannes xiius (?) concessit audientibus sequens euangelium ccc annos uenie et dicentibus totidem. Passio domini nostri ihesu cristi secundum Iohannem. In illo tempore Apprehendit pilatus . . . testimonium eius . . . Oremus. Deus qui manus tuas et pedes tuos . . .

John 19: 1–34, etc. (see *Lyell Cat.*, pp. 65–6). In the heading the name and number of the pope have been erased.

14. ff. 206v–208v Legitur quod ubi maius uertitur periculum ibi caucius et studiosius . . . uel alibi remanere.

On accidents at mass.

15. ff. 208v–209v Sequencie de sancta maria ad placitum.

Seven sequences: (*a*) Aue mundi domina uirgo mater maria; (*b*) Saluatoris mater pia; (*c*) Salue maris stella uerbi dei cella mater et puella uena uenie . . . extreme suspiria; (*d*) Aue maris stella uerbi dei cella singulare; (*e*) Gaude salutata uirgo fecundata; (*f*) Stabat iuxta cristi crucem uidens pati ueram lucem; (*g*) Salue celorum regina salue dulcis. (*a, b, d–g*) are *RH*, nos. 1969, 17821, 23616, 27126, 19412, 17858. (*c*) has six stanzas.

16. ff. 209v–210v Offices of David, Chad, Felix, translation of Edmund king and martyr, Dominic, Thomas of Hereford, Francis, Winefred.

17 (added, s. xv/xvi). (*a*) ff. 210v–211 Missa pro pestilencia. Recordare domine . . . (*b*) ff. 211v–212v Officium. In nomine ihesu . . . Oracio. Deus qui gloriosissimam . . . (*c*) ff. 212v–213v Missa de passione . . . Officium. Humiliauit . . . (*d*) f. 213v Passio domini nostri ihesu cristi Secundum Iohannem. (*e*) f. 213v Secret and postcommunion of mass of the anniversary, no. (9) of the masses for the dead in *Sarum Missal*, p. 438: singular forms. (*f*) f. iirv Commemoracio sancti Thome. (*g*) f. iiv Mass of the Visitation of B.V.M., 'Officium. Gaudeamus omnes . . .' (*h*) f. iii Mass of St Roche. (*i*) ff. iii–iv Missa compassionis et lamentacionis beate Marie virginis. (*j*) f. iv Prayer, 'Domine ihesu criste qui pro mundi redempcione crucis lignum ascendisti . . .'.

(*a*). *Sarum Missal*, Burntisland edn., p. 886*. (*b, g, i*). See Pfaff, *New Liturgical Feasts*, pp. 62–8, 54–6, 97–103. The respective sequences are Dulcis ihesus nazarenus, Celebremus in hac die, and Meste parentis cristi marie (*RH*, nos. 4909, 2729, 11671). (*c*). The sequence is Cenam cum discipulis (*RH*, no. 3616). (*d*) repeats art. 13, but without the heading *Omnibus . . .* (*f*). The heading, collect, and sequence, Gaude thoma de cuius (*RH*, no. 37580) have been crossed out. (*h*). The sequence is In honorem saluatoris sancti Rochi confessoris (*RH*, no. 8631).

ff. v + 218 + ii, foliated (two unnumbered leaves of modern paper), ii–x, 1–190, 192–213, (two unnumbered leaves of modern paper). ff. ii–iv are medieval flyleaves: see art. 17*f–j*. Stout parchment. 395 × 272 mm. Written space 282 × 176 mm. 2 cols. 39 lines. Collation of ff. v–x, 1–213: 1^{6} $2\text{–}11^{8}$ 12^{8} wants 8 after f. 87 + 1 leaf inserted after 7 (f. 88: see above) $13\text{–}17^{8}$ 18^{8} wants 3 after f. 130 $19\text{–}26^{8}$ 27^{10} 28 three (ff. 211–13). An ugly back-sloping textura: the writing is no bigger in the canon (art. 3) than elsewhere. Initials: (i) beginning arts. 2, 5, 8, at Christmas and Epiphany in art. 2, at *Per, Uere,* and *Te* in art. 3 (ff. 87^{v}, 89), at Ascension, Pentecost, Trinity, and Corpus Christi in art. 5, at Purification, Assumption, and Nativity of B.V.M. in art. 7, in colours on gold grounds, decorated and with border prolongations in colours and gold: a continuous border on f. 89; (ii) beginning arts. 3, 9*a*, 9*b*, 11, at John Baptist, Peter and Paul in art. 7 and for the *S* of *Salue* at the first mass of art. 9*a*, gold on coloured grounds, with border prolongations; (iii, iv) 3-line and 2-line, blue with red ornament; (v) 1-line, blue or red. Capital letters in the ink of the text filled with a more conspicuous yellow than is usual. Medieval boards (?), re-covered and re-backed: two strap-and-pin fastenings now missing. Secundo folio (f. 2) *Alleluia*.

Written in England for use in the diocese of Norwich (cf. arts. 1, 16). 'Bib: Harvin: Cler: Sec:', f. ii: transferred to Oscott from the library of the Midlands Secular Clergy at Harvington, Worcestershire, *c.*1838. '1824' on a paper label on the back cover.

518. *Alexander de Villa Dei, Doctrinale* s. xv med.

1. ff. 1–44 Scribere clericulis paro doctrinale nouellis . . . credo deitatis.

A. de Villa Dei, Doctrinale, ed. D. Reichling, 1893. Many contemporary scholia in the wide margins in a neat hybrida; also glosses between the lines. The scholia include an introduction (f. 1), 'Causa principalis huius libri talis est. Quod magister Alexander de villa dei. de cuius uita quidam scripsit quod tres fuerunt inter se socii precordialissimi scilicet Magister Alexander. alius vocabatur yuo qui duo erant de villa dei alius uero vocabatur ydelphus et hic erat anglicus et morabatur parisius . . .' (cf. P. Leyser, *Historia Poetarum et Poematum medii aevi*, 1721, p. 768). Line 42, 'Femineis abus sociabitur ut dominabis' has against it 'Laurentius Valla dicit non debere dici dominabus nec animabus. Vnde cicero . . . sed ego de vsu loquendi disputo non de abusu . . .'.

2 (added on endleaves). (*a*) f. 45 Discit homo ut lucretur et est simonia . . . (5 lines). (*b*) f. 45 Hoc tibi mando prius librorum theca meorum Nullius ignaui vel rudis esto comes . . . Te colo sed pridem proximus ipse michi (28 lines). (*c*) f. 46 A notice in Italian, headed 'yhesus', of an agreement between Jeronimo da Cremona in Monza and Antonio da Meda 'in Vedano' (near Varese) in 1529. (*d*) on the pastedown, now missing, record of a debt the parties to which were 'anbroxio da homa in lisono' (Lissone, near Monza, ?) and 'ludouicho da sirono'.[1]

(*a, b*) in one current hand, s. xv ex.

ff. ii + 44 + ii. ff. 45, 46 are medieval, a paper and a parchment flyleaf: see above, art. 2. Medieval foliation. 280 × 200 mm. Written space 175 × 90 mm. 30 long lines. Collation: $1\text{–}4^{8}$ 5^{12}. Initials: (i) f. 1, brown *S* on coloured ground, historiated (a teacher in red cap):

[1] My description was made before the binding was repaired and the removal of a leaf containing art. 2*d*, a blank medieval paper flyleaf at the beginning, and a label of s. xviii (?) on the spine inscribed 'Cod. CXVI': 'Cod. CXVI' is stamped on the new spine.

border ornament; (ii) red. Binding of wooden boards covered with brown leather, s. xv, re-backed: strap-and-pin fastenings at side (2), head, and foot, now missing: five bosses on each cover, now missing. Secundo folio *Par est*.

Written in Italy. In the neighbourhood of Monza in 1529 (art. 2). 'Cod: CXVI' in an eighteenth-century (?) library (see footnote).

519. *Palladius, etc.* s. xv med.

1. ff. 1–2v Incipit de Cura Equorum et bouum. Aliorumque animalium secundum Palladium. Plerumque Iumenta morbos concipiunt ex lassitudine . . .

Two non-adjacent leaves of extracts from Palladius on veterinary surgery, corresponding on f. 1rv to sections 22–4 and 12 and on f. 2rv to sections 64 (3, 4), 65, 28 (1–3, 6–8) and 4–6 (6) of the edition by J. Svenning, 1926, together with a section in last place on f. 1v, which does not occur in the edition: Ad Crepacias. Ad Crepacias que frequenter accidunt in iuncturis expellantur seu abradantur (*ends imperfectly*). Thorndike and Kibre note the incipit *Plerumque* from Vatican, Barberini 12, f. 88. The leaves may not be in their original position.

2. ff. 3–71v Palladii Rutili Emiliani Viri Illustris Senatoris De Agricultura ex diuersis Autoribus Liber Incipit. . . . Pars est prima prudentie . . . habet pedes 29. Explicit liber palladii. de agricultura.

Ed. J. C. Schmitt (Teubner series, 1898), pp. 1–260. Thirteen parts, each preceded by a numbered table of chapters (42, 29, 55, 31, 8, 17, 12, 9, 12, 17, 21, 25, 6). In headings Rubrica is used at first, but Capitulum from March onwards. A leaf is missing after f. 17. The scribe missed a passage and supplied it in hybrida on an added leaf, f. 23. f. 49 should follow f. 50.

3. ff. 71v–83v De Curis et reparatione vinorum ac vasorum a domino burgundione ciue pisano translatus liber incipit. Non est facile dignoscere quando oportet uindemiare uineas . . . libram unam litargiri. Explicit liber reparationis uinorum similiter et vasorum.

Thorndike and Kibre. Galen, De vindemiis, in the translation of Burgundio of Pisa. A leaf is missing after f. 81.

4. ff. 84–119v Incipit liber de disciplina et curis equorum. Cum inter cetera animalia a summo rerum opifice euidenter creata . . . neruosis adiacent uel ueriosis.

Thorndike and Kibre, col. 310: cf. cols. 311, 1282. Jordanus Rufus of Calabria. Ed. Molin, Hippiatria, 1818. Sixty-three numbered chapters. Ch. 6 is divided into sixty-three parts, listed on ff. 90v–91. Leaves missing after ff. 95, 111, 118 contained chapters 42–6, 60, 61, and parts of chapters 10, 11, 41, 47, and 62. Also in Lincoln College, Oxford, 131, q.v. below.

5. f. 119v De Signis qualitatis equorum. Equus habens garretta ampla . . . aut mollis existit.

Thorndike and Kibre. Eight paragraphs.

ff. 119 + i. Paper. 293 × 218 mm. Written space 190 × 100 mm. 34 long lines. Collation: 1 two (ff. 1, 2) 2^{16} wants 4 after f. 5 3^{16} wants 1 before f. 18 + 1 leaf inserted after 6 (f. 23) 4^{16} (ff. 34–48, 50) 5^{16} (ff. 49, 51–65) 6^{16} 7^{16} wants 1 before f. 82 and 16 after f. 95 8^{16} 9 eight (ff. 112–19: leaves missing before f. 112 and after f. 118). Written by one hand throughout: humanistic forms are introduced into a mainly rotonda script towards the end, *d* at f. 97 and *g* at f. 100 and the ampersand instead of *et* or the nota for *et* at f. 98v. 4-line and 2-line red initials. Capital letters in the ink of the text stroked with red. Binding of brown leather over thin pasteboard, perhaps original: the stamps on each cover are a leaf and a very small shell.

Written in Italy. 'S. Andreocci et amicorum (?)', f. 1, at foot, s. xviii (?). 'Luigi degli Andreocci Patrizio Castellano Figlio del Auuocato Giuseppe Maria Andreocci ed Auuocata parimente de Rei Vel 5. Off*icio* come fu Tian Francesco Andreocci mio Nonno', f. 90v. 'E. 3. 25' is on a label on the front cover, s. xix.

583. *Horae* s. xv ex.

1. ff. ii–xiiiv Full calendar in French in gold, red, and blue, the two colours alternating. 'Genevieve' and 'Marcel' in gold.

2. ff. 1–5 Sequentiae of the Gospels, beginning imperfectly. The prayer 'Protector in te sperancium . . .' after John.

3. ff. 5v–8 Obsecro te. Masculine forms, as also in art. 4.

4. ff. 8v–10v O intemerata . . . orbis terrarum. Inclina mater . . .

5. ff. 11–62v Hours of B.V.M. of the use of (Paris).

Vespers and the beginning of sext missing.

6. ff. 63–77v Penitential psalms and (f. 73v) litany.

Twelve martyrs: Victor 2nd and Denis 'cum sociis' 5th. Fourteen virgins: Genovefa 1st and Clotildis 11th.

7. ff. 78–80 Hours of the Cross, beginning imperfectly.

8. ff. 80v–83 Hours of the Holy Spirit.

9. ff. 83v–120 Office of the dead.

10. ff. 120v–125 Doulce dame de misericorde mere de pititie (*sic*) . . .

The Fifteen Joys of B.V.M.: Sonet, no. 458.

11. f. 125 Saincte uraye croix aoree . . . : Sonet, no. 1876.

12. ff. 125v–128v Doulx dieux doux pere saincte trinite . . .

The Seven Requests: Sonet, no. 504.

13. ff. 128^{v}–132^{v} Memoriae of Michael, John Baptist, James, Christopher, Sebastian (O quam mira refulsit . . . : *RH*, no. 30905), Nicholas, Katherine, and Barbara.

14. Prayers and salutations at mass: (*a*) f. 132^{v} Ad eleuacionem corporis cristi dic Aue salus mundi uerbum patris . . . ; (*b*) ff. 132^{v}–133 Ad eleuacionem sanguinis dic Aue uere sanguis domini nostri ihesu cristi . . . ; (*c*) f. 133^{rv} Deinde dic oracionem istam. Salue sancta caro dei per quam salui fiunt rei . . . ; (*d*) f. 133^{v} Anima cristi sanctifica me . . . ; (*e*) f. 134^{rv} Oracio. Domine ihesu criste qui sacratissimam carnem . . . ; (*f*) ff. 134^{v}–135 Domine ihesu criste rogo te ut amore illius gaudii . . . ; (*g*) f. 135^{rv} Salutacio deuota ad dominum. Aue ihesu criste uerbum patris filius uirginis agnus . . . ; (*h*) ff. 135^{v}–136 Deinde ad corpus et sanguinem. In presencia corporis et sanguinis tui domine . . . ; (*i*) f. 136 Oracio. Aue uerum corpus natum . . . ; (*j*) f. 136^{rv} Ecce agnus dei qui tollis peccata mundi . . .

(*c, g, i*). *RH*, nos. 18175, 1844, 2175.

15. ff. 136^{v}–140 Canticum. Quicunque vult saluus esse . . .

16. ff. 140–1 Hymnus. Criste qui lux es et dies . . .

17. ff. 141–142^{v} Oracio ad dominum. O bone ihesu o dulcissime ihesu . . .

18. ff. 142^{v}–143^{v} Pro defunctis antiphona. Auete omnes anime fideles . . . (*prayer*) Domine ihesu criste salus et liberacio . . .

19. Prayers in Latin and French: (*a*) ff. 143^{v}–144 Oracio. Fiat michi queso domine deus firma fides in corde . . . ; (*b*) ff. 144–5 Oroison deuote quant on recoit son createur. qui se commence O sanctissima anima. O tressaincte tresdoulce tresneite (*sic*) plaine de toute uertu . . . ; (*c*) f. 145^{rv} Salue sancta caro dei . . . (as art. 14*c*); (*d*) ff. 145^{v}–146^{v} Autre oroison quant on a receu le corps nostre seigneur ihesu crist et se commence. Gracias ago. Mon dieu mon createur de tes gres misericordes . . . ; (*e*) ff. 146^{v}–147 O dulcissime domine ihesu criste respicere digneris super me miseram peccatricem . . . (*f*) ff. 147–9 Alia oracio. Dieu soyes moy propices et me pardonnes mes peches . . .

(*f*). Sonet-Sinclair, no. 420.

20. ff. 149–50 Hymnus. Vexilla regis prodeunt . . .

21. Salutations to B.V.M.: (*a*) ff. 150–1 Aue cuius concepcio solenni plena gaudio . . . (*prayer*) Deus qui nos . . . ; (*b*) f. 151 Inuiolata integra et casta es maria . . . ; (*c*) f. 151^{v} Salue regina . . . ; (*d*) ff. 151^{v}–152 Aue regina celorum aue domina angelorum . . .

(*a–d*). *RH*, nos. 1744, 9094, 18147, 2070.

22. ff. 152–3 De saint claude. O desolatorum consolator . . . Oremus. Oracio. Deus qui beato claudio . . .

Memoria of Claud.

23. ff. 153–154v Les vii vers saint be(r)nard.

The seven paragraphs beginning Illumina, In manus tuas, Locutus sum, Et numerum, Dirupisti, Periit, Fac mecum (Leroquais, I. xxx) are preceded here by three more verses of psalms, 4: 7 (Dignatum (*sic*) est), 24: 7 (Delicta) and 24: 4 (Uias tuas). The usual prayer, 'Omnipotens sempiterne deus qui ezechie regi . . .', follows.

24. ff. 154v–155v Hympnus. Veni creator spiritus mentes . . . Qui paraclitus . . . Oremus. Deus qui corda fidelium . . .

ff. iii + 168 + v, foliated (2 unnumbered leaves), i–xiii, 1–17, 17*, 18–160. ff. i, 156–8 are contemporary or nearly contemporary flyleaves. 163 × 115 mm. Written space 97 × 60 mm. 18 long lines. Collation of ff. ii–xiii, 1–155: $1\text{–}2^6$ 3^8 wants 1 before f. 1 4^4 (ff. 8–11) $5\text{–}8^8$ 9^8 wants 4 after f. 45 10^8 11^8 wants 1, 2 before f. 58 and 8, probably blank, after f. 62 12^8 13^8 wants 8 after f. 77 $14\text{–}22^8$ 23^6. Eleven 14-line pictures, six in art. 5 (sext and vespers missing) and one before each of arts. 6, 8, 9 (Job and his friends), 10, 12. Thirteen 7-line pictures, *c.*38 × 38 mm, eight in art. 13, three in art. 2 (Matthew writes his Gospel in Greek (?) on a scroll) and one beginning each of arts. 3, 4. A picture of Claud in the side margin of f. 152. Initials: (i) 3-line, in colour on grounds of gold paint and red, decorated; (ii, iii) 2-line and 1-line, gold on coloured grounds. Capital letters in the ink of the text washed with pale yellow. Line fillers in blue, red, and gold. Continuous framed floral borders on pages with pictures and a framed border in the outer margin of all other rectos, the height of the written space: borders are compartmented and partly on grounds of gold paint. Binding of s. xviii, rebacked.

Written in France, perhaps for the use of a woman: cf. art. 19*e*, as against arts. 3, 4. 'Claude Poirier' and 'Ex libris Bleniel (?)', f. i, s. xvii.

584. *Horae* s. xv ex.

1. ff. i–xii Calendar in French in red and black.

Entries include Remy, Savinian, Loup in red (13, 23 Jan., 28 July) and Frobert, Savine, Mastie, in black (8, 29 Jan., 7 May); also Fale (16 May) for whom compare Falle at 16 May in the Troyes calendar in Cambridge, Fitzwilliam Museum, 115. The Visitation of B.V.M. does not occur (2 July).

2. ff. 1–5v Sequentiae of the Gospels.

3. ff. 6–7v Hours of the Cross, beginning imperfectly.

4. ff. 8–10v Hours of the Holy Spirit.

5. ff. 11–48 Hours of B.V.M. of the use of (Langres), beginning imperfectly. f. 48v blank.

6. ff. 49–64v Penitential psalms and (f. 60v) litany.

Twelve martyrs: (4) brici, (6) verole, (10–12) claudi frodoberte benigne. Twenty-two virgins: (10) syria, (13–18) maura anna radegondis sauina helena mastidia.

7. ff. 65–101v Office of the dead, beginning imperfectly.

The ninth lesson is Vir fortissimus (2 Macc. 12: 43–6).

8. ff. 102–5 Obsecro te . . .

Masculine forms, as also in art. 9.

9. ff. 105–7 O intemerata . . . orbis terrarum. Inclina . . .

10. Salutations to B.V.M.: (*a*) f. 107 Salue regina . . . ; (*b*) f. 107v Inuiolata integra . . . ; (*c*) f. 107v Regina celi letare . . . ; (*d*) f. 108 Aue regina celorum. Aue domina angelorum. Radix . . .

(*a–d*). *RH*, nos. 18147, 9094, 17170, 2070. f. 108v blank.

ff. ii + 120 + ii, foliated (two unnumbered leaves), i–xii, 1–110. ff. 1–108v have an earlier pagination 1–216. 175 × 115 mm. Written space 115 × 70 mm. 17 long lines. Ruling in red ink. Collation of ff. i–xii, 1–108: $1–2^6$ 3^8 4^8 wants 3 after f. 10 5^8 6^8 wants 6 after f. 27 7^8 8^8 wants 3 after f. 39 9^4 (ff. 45–8) $10–11^8$ 12^8 wants 1 before f. 65 $13–15^8$ 16^8 wants 8, probably blank. Vertical catchwords. 13-line pictures begin arts. 2, 4, 6. Initials: (i) blue on gold grounds, decorated in colours; (ii, iii) 2-line and 1-line, gold on coloured grounds. Capital letters in the ink of the text filled with yellow. Line fillers in red and blue, the colours separated by blobs of gold. Continuous framed floral borders on picture pages. Borders on three sides of pages with initials of type (i): the grounds are sometimes compartmented and partly of gold paint. French binding, s. xix.

Written in France: calendar and litany point to Troyes, rather than Langres (art. 5). 'Rev. Théodore Fauvel' and, in another hand, 'Presented to the Library of Oscott College, Jany 11th 1851' on the first of the two unnumbered leaves at the beginning.

585. *Horae* s. xv¹

1. ff. i–viv Sarum calendar in gold, blue, red, and black.

The word 'pape' and the entries for Thomas the Martyr have not been erased. Osmund added over erasure at 4 Dec. 'Nat' Thome Elyot Anno viii h. viii' added at 26 March.

2. ff. 1–16v Hours of B.V.M. of the use of (Sarum).

Defective and out of order: ff. 3–5, 1 matins; ff. 2, 6–13 lauds, followed by memoriae of Holy Spirit, Holy Trinity, Holy Cross, Michael, John Baptist, Peter and Paul, Andrew, Stephen, Laurence, Thomas of Canterbury (Tu per thome sanguinem . . .), Nicholas, Mary Magdalene, Katherine, Margaret, All Saints and peace; f. 14 prime; f. 15 sext; f. 16 none.

3. f. 17rv Salue regina, beginning imperfectly, and Gaude flore virginali (*RH*, no. 6809: cf. *Lyell Cat.*, p. 381), ending imperfectly.

4. ff. 19–20v A fragment of the litany, as *Brev. ad usum Sarum*, ii. 253/11–255/14.

5. ff. 18rv, 21–36v Office of the dead, imperfect at beginning and end.

Begins in Ps. 137 and ends in Ps. 29: *Manuale Sarum*, pp. 133–41.

6. ff. 37–44v Commendatory psalms (Pss. 118, 138), imperfect at the beginning.

7. ff. 45–8 Special psalms for use at matins of B.V.M., (*a*) on Tuesdays and Fridays, Pss. 44, 45, 86, and (*b*) on Wednesdays and Saturdays, Pss. 95–7.

Ps. 44 begins imperfectly at verse 13.

8. ff. 48–55v Special forms of art. 2 for use at Advent and other seasons.

9. ff. 55v–57v Memoriae of Holy Spirit, 'de festo loci et aliis ad placitum. Item memoria de reliquiis', of All Saints (5 forms) and 'De pace'.

10. ff. 57v–59v Oracio de sancta maria et Iohanne. O intemerata . . . orbis terrarum. Inclina . . .

11. f. 59v Alia oracio de eisdem. Sancta maria dei genitrix semperque virgo . . . ut spiritum fornicacionis a me procul elongetis et ardorem libidinis in me prorsus orando extinguatis . . .

12. ff. 60–64v The Fifteen Oes of St Bridget, beginning and ending imperfectly.

13. f. 65rv (*begins imperfectly*) guinem preciosum quem pro nobis . . .

The prayer of the Holy Name: cf. *Lyell Cat.*, p. 386.

14. ff. 66–70 The fifteen gradual psalms, beginning imperfectly. Cues only of Pss. 22–4, 26.

15. f. 70v Prayers: (*a*) Oracio miraculosa ad beatam mariam. Aue et gaude maria mater dei . . . ; (*b*) Oracio in leuacione hostie. Salue lux mundi uerbum patris . . . verus homo. Aue uerum corpus natum . . .

16. ff. 70v–72 Qui dicit oracionem sequentem coram passione cristi habet xlvi milia et xii annos et xl dies indulgencie. Adoro te domine Ihesu criste in cruce pendentem . . .

Seven invocations followed by the prayer 'Benignissime domine respice super me miserum peccatorem oculis misericordie tue . . .', as Hoskins, p. 112. Cf. *Lyell Cat.*, p. 367, for an older form. A large red cross at the head of f. 70v.

17 (added early). f. 72rv Prayers: (*a*) Domine ihesu criste qui voluisti pro redempcione mundi . . . ; (*b*) Oracio deuota data sancte Birgitte per reuelacionem dei. Domine ihesu criste ego cognosco me grauiter peccasse . . .

ff. iii + 178 + v, foliated (three unnumbered leaves), i–vi, 1–77. ff. 73–4 are leaves of medieval parchment, blank except for frame ruling in red. 135 × 95 mm. Written space 82 × 42 mm. 20 long lines. Ruling in red ink. Collation of ff. i–vi, 1–72: 1^6 2^8 wants 1 and 6 (ff. 3–5, 1, 2, 6) 3^8 wants 8 after f. 13 4 two (ff. 14, 15, a bifolium) 5 two (ff. 16, 17, an outside bifolium) 6 two (ff. 19, 20, a central bifolium) 7 one (f. 18, the last leaf of the quire) 8–9^8 10^8 wants 1 and 8 (ff. 37–42) 11^8 wants 3 after f. 44 12^6 (ff. 50–5) 13^4 (ff. 56–9) 14^8 wants 1, 2 before f. 61 and 7 after f. 64 15^8 wants 1 before f. 66. Initials: (i) on now missing pages; (ii) 2-line, gold on coloured grounds: sprays into the margins; (iii) 1-line, gold with grey-green ornament or blue with red ornament. Capital letters in the ink of the text washed with yellow. Bound in green morocco, gilt, s. xviii. Secundo folio (f. 3) *nam regentem*.

Written in England, perhaps for or by Richard Elyot, since 'Orate pro Ricardo Elyot' in the main hand fills up blank space in the bottom line on f. 5^{v}: cf. art. 1. 'C. J.' on verso of first unnumbered leaf. Said in *Catalogue* to have been 'Given by Charles Jefferies, Esq.'.

586. *Prayers, etc. (mainly in Netherlandish)* s. xvi in.

Arts. 1, 3–5, 7–16 and the litany in art. 6 are in Netherlandish.

1. ff. iv–xv^{v} Calendar in red and black.

Entries in red include Omaer, Baue, and Nichasis (8 Sept., 1 Oct., 14 Dec.) and 'typre Tuyndach', 8 Aug.

2. ff. 1–3^{v} (*begins imperfectly*) sus christus sine macula cum gaudio ad vitam eternam. Amen. Non nobis domine non nobis. Sed nomine tuo . . . hereditatem meam michi.

3. ff. 4–11^{v} Pater noster in vlaems . . .

Versions of Pater noster, Ave Maria, Maria mater, Credo in deum, Credo in spiritum, Magnificat, Nunc dimittis, Ave salus, 'De corte benedicite', 'Die corte gratie', Agimus tibi, Fidelium, a form of confession ('Item des auonts als ghy slapen gaet zo zult ghy met berau van uwen zonden dese biechte deuotelic spreken zegghende. Ic gheue my besculdich die heere god . . . Ende ic belide . . .'), Salve regina (*ends imperfectly*).

4. ff. 12–14^{v} Van den helighen gheest. de hymnie . . . Coemt scepper gheest . . .

Hymn, antiphon, and collect.

5. ff. 14^{v}–16^{v} Als ghy in der kercke comt. Ueest ghegruet onse coninc . . . ; also on taking holy water.

6. ff. 17–36^{v} Penitential psalms, beginning imperfectly, and (f. 30) litany. 'ioriis' is last of thirteen martyrs.

7. Prayers: (*a*) ff. 36^{v}–37^{v} Leest dese bedinghe voer alle ghelouighe zielen als ghy up een kerchof gaet . . . Ueest ghegroet alle ghelouighe zielen wiens lichamen hier ende elder in der eerden rusten . . . : conveys indulgence of 'Iohannes de vierde'; (*b*) ff. 37^{v}–39 Een schoon beuelinghe tot onsen heer*n*. Die benedictie gods des vaders . . . ; (*c*) f. 39^{rv} Een schoon beuelinghe tot onser lieuer vrauwe. O mijn vrawe heylighe maria ic beuele my . . . ; (*d*) ff. 39^{v}–40^{v} Oratie tot den vader . . . O heere heilighe vader almachtich euwighe god die uwer ghelike . . . ; (*e*) ff. 40^{v}–41^{v} Oratie tot god den zone . . . O onser heere iesu christe leuende gods zone . . . ; (*f*) ff. 41^{v}–42^{v} Oratie tot heilighen gheest . . . O heere god heilighe gheest die daer zijt euen ghelijc . . . ; (*g*) ff. 42^{v}–44 Hier naer volcht een deuote bedinghe van die heilighe drieuuldicheit . . . Antif'. Wy aenroupen di. Wy aenbeden di . . . ; (*h*) ff. 44–5 Tot die euwighe wijsheit. O wijsheit die mit den mont

des alder uppersten ghecommen zijt . . . ; (*i*) ff. 45-6 Een scoone godlike benedictie tot welcke die paues Innocentius de vierde heift ghegheuen ccc iaer aflaets. Ii (*sic for* Mi) ghebenedie die keyserlike moghentheit . . .

8 (quire 11). (*a*) f. 46rv Die dese nauolghende woerden daghelike lessen zy en sullen ghene haestighe noch onuersienige doot steruen. Ihesus van nazarenen coninc der ioden . . . (*b*) ff. 46v-51v Dit es sinte Ambrosius oracie ende van yeghelike articulen der passien ons heeren gheeft Anastasius de eerste alle diese lesen vijf hondert daghen aflaet. O eere ihesu christe des leuende gods zone schepper. ende makere . . .

(*b*). Meertens, vi. 72.

Arts. 9-13 are on quires 12-15.

9. ff. 51v-55 Dit es die oracie van den eerwaerdighen priester Beda . . . O heere Iesu christe die de zeuen woerden . . .

Bede's prayer of the seven words: Meertens, ii. 111.

10. ff. 55-57v, 63rv Die dese oratie met deuocie leest . . . Iek bidde v alderminlicste heere Iesu christe deur de ouergroote liefde . . .

The heading conveys indulgence of as many days as Christ had wounds from 'paeus Gregorius de verde uut beede van een coninghinne van inghelant'.

11. ff. 64-66v Een schoen bedinghe van den soeten naem Iesus ende es seer deuoet on lessen alle kersten menschen. O Goede Ihesu O alder soetste ihesu. O iesu marien sone . . .

Meertens, i. 109.

12. ff. 67-75v Hier beghint onser lieuer vrauwen gulden rosencranskin. Aue maria gracia plena . . . Dien ghy heilighe ioncvrauwe maria van herten . . .

13. ff. 76-81v Ic bidde v helighe maria moeder gods . . .

A translation of Obsecro te, with heading conveying indulgence of 100 days from Pope Innocent. Meertens, vi. 83.

14 (quires 16, 17). ff. 58rv, 60-61v, 59rv, 62rv, 82-83v Fragments of the fifteen 'bloetstortinghe', beginning imperfectly in the ninth at 'die ic met minen handen habbe ghedaen'. The beginnings of the tenth, twelfth, and fifteenth bloodlettings remain, 'Iek dancke dij ghebenedijde here Ihesu criste dat ghij vtstorte dijn heilighe dierbaer (15, preciose) bloet'.

Meertens, vi. 3.

15. Prayers: (*a*) f. 84rv Dese oracie heeft ghemaect papa Sixtus ende gheeft den ghenen diese deuotlijc lezen voor onse lieue vrauwe in die sonne xi duust iaer af.

Ueest ghegroet alder heylichste maria moeder gods. coninghinne des hemels poorte des paradijs . . . ; (*b*) ff. 84^{v}–88 The Seven Joys of B.V.M. 'die sint thomaes van cantelberghe ghemaect heeft. Verblijt v heilighe maria moeder ende maghet: want die grote glorie . . .'; (*c*) f. 88^{v} So wie dit nauolghende ghebet leest: die verdient C.M. iaer aflaets ende xc karenen . . . (*ends imperfectly in the heading*); (*d*) f. 89 (*begins imperfectly*) dat ick steruen zal . . . ; (*e*) ff. 89–90^{v} The prayer vouchsafed to St Bernard by an angel, 'Veest ghegruet alderheilichste dienstmaghet der heiligher drieuuldicheit maria . . . (*ends imperfectly*)'. (*f*) ff. 91–93^{v} A translation of O intemerata, beginning and ending imperfectly; (*g*) ff. 94–96^{v} Oes of St Gregory, beginning imperfectly: nine oes (?). (*h*) ff. 96^{v}–98 Een deuote bedinghe van sint' michiel. Sinte michiel archangel ons heeren Ihesu christi die den volcke gods . . . ; (*i*) ff. 98–99^{v} Een deuote bedinghe tot uwen goeden inghe*l*. Iek bidde v heilighe inghel gods wien ic van gode . . .

(*b*). Meertens, vi. 37 sub 18. Single leaves are missing after ff. 88, 91, and 93.

16. Communion prayers, (*a, b, e*) before, (*f*) during, and (*c, d*) after mass: (*a*) ff. 99–100^{v} O heere ihesu christe heeden begheere ic te ontfanghen . . . ; (*b*) ff. 100^{v}–101* O heere ihesu christe der inghelen glorie. Ic aerm zondich mensch scame . . . ; (*c*) ff. 101*^{v}–102^{v} O heere ihesu christe lof si der ontsprekeliker ende minliker . . . ; (*d*) f. 102^{v} O vriendelike heere Iesu christe nv bidde ic v om de minlicke weerdicheit . . . ; (*e*) ff. 103–5 O ontfermhertige lieue heere ic begheere nv dese messe te horen . . . ; (*f*) ff. 105–107^{v} Veest ghegruet licht der werelt woort des vaders . . .

(*a, c*). Lieftinck, p. 123.

17. ff. 107^{v}–109^{v} Dese naeruolghende oratie leerde een inghel eender ioncvrouwe segghende dat si lx duysent iaer aflaets . . . So veel aflaets alst dropelen waters op eenen dach reenen mochte. O alderminlijcste ende begheerlicste soete maria. O schoon rosa . . .

18. ff. 110–123^{v} Prayers to John Baptist, apostles, Anthony, Nicholas, Roche, Agnes, Barbara, Katherine, Mary Magdalene, Anne, Apollonia.

ff. v + 135 + ii, foliated (two unnumbered leaves), i–xv, 1–76, 78–101, 101*, 102–25. ff. ii, iii are a parchment bifolium. 130 × 92 mm. Written space 82 × 50 mm. 15 long lines. Collation of ff. iv–xv, 1–125: 1–2^{6} 3^{8} wants 1, 2 before f. 1 and 8 after f. 5 4^{6} 5^{6} wants 1 before f. 12 6^{6} wants 1 before f. 17 7–15^{6} (ff. 22–57, 63–81) 16^{6} wants 5 (ff. 58, 60–1, 59, 62) 17 two (ff. 82–3, a bifolium) 18^{6} wants 1 before f. 84 19^{8} wants 1 before f. 89, 4 after f. 90, and 8 after f. 93 20–22^{6} 23^{6} wants 4 after f. 113 24^{8}. 11-line pictures illustrate the tenth, twelfth, and fifteenth 'bloetstortinghe' in art. 4: nailing of hands and feet and piercing with lance (ff. 58^{v}, 61^{v}, 82^{v}). Ten smaller pictures of saints, 43 × 33 mm, in art. 18. The margins of ff. 12, 67, 76, 84 are decorated so as to suggest that the written space on these pages covers part of a picture: the Visitation and Annunciation in two compartments on f. 76. Initials: (i–iii), 4-line, 2-line, and 1-line, gold paint and dark red on coloured grounds. Capital letters in the ink of the text touched with red. Binding probably of s. xvii.

Written in the southern Low Countries. Decorated under strong Italian influence. Faint memoranda on f. ii, all in one hand, include a note of ownership by 'Ioncfrauue M[. . .] van gheghenen' and, lower down, the date 1588. 'From Laur^{e} Adamson to The Revd Peter Mc Grath / Douglas / Isle of Man / May 1838', f. i^{v}: his gift to Oscott College.

714. *Psalterium, etc.* s. xv in.

1. ff. i–vi^{v} Sarum calendar in red and black, the red in a different hand from the black.

Red is used for 'Translatio sancti edwardi regis' (13 Oct.), but not for other English saints apart from Thomas of Canterbury, whose name is blotted at 7 July and 29 Dec., but not at 5 Jan. The word 'pape' not damaged. Spellings are 'dinistani', 'zwichini', 'edite' (Dunstan, Swithun, Edith). 'Edwardi regis' added, 5 Jan.

2. ff. 1–7^{v} Memoriae of John Baptist, Thomas of Canterbury, Christopher, George, Adrian, Anthony, Anne, Katherine, Barbara, Margaret.

The rhymed antiphons are Gaude iohannes baptista, Gaude lux londoniarum, Sancte cristophore martyr ihesu cristi, Georgi martyr inclite, Gaude felix anne, (Gaude virgo katherina, *beginning imperfectly*) reginam. cernens: a leaf missing before f. 6, Gaude barbara regina, Gaude virgo margareta (*RH*, nos. 26988, 26999, 18445, 7242, 6773, 6991, 6714, 7011). The missing leaf probably contained a memoria of Mary Magdalene: cf. *MMBL* i. 47.

3. ff. 9–141^{v} Psalms 1–150. Two leaves missing.

4. ff. 141^{v}–154^{v} Six ferial canticles followed by Benedicite, Benedictus, Magnificat, Te deum, Nunc dimittis, Quicunque vult.

5. ff. 155–61 Litany.

Thirty-two martyrs: (22–5) Thoma Edwarde Oswalde Al(b)ane. Sixteen confessors: (16) Birine. The prayers after Deus cui are the six in *Brev. ad usum Sarum*, ii. 254–5.

ff. ii + 169 + ii, foliated (two unnumbered leaves), i–vi, 1–165. 200 × 135 mm. Written space 108 × 70 mm. 21 long lines. Collation of ff. i–vi, 1–163: 1^{6} 2^{8} wants 6 after f. 5 $3\text{–}8^{8}$ 9^{8} wants 6 after f. 53 $10\text{–}15^{8}$ 16^{8} wants 6 before f. 112 $17\text{–}21^{8}$ 22^{10}: 10 (f. 163) was pasted down; together with single leaves inserted after 3^{7}, 11^{1}, 12^{8} and 16^{5} (ff. 8, 65, 81, 111). Pictures: (*a*) in art. 1, a pair at the head of each month show occupations of the months and signs of the zodiac; (*b*) full-page in two compartments before Pss. 1, 68, 80, and 109 (ff. 8^{v}, 65^{v}, 81^{v}, 111^{v}: the rectos blank) and no doubt at one time also before Pss. 26, 38, 52, and 97: each upper compartment shows a scene from the life of David and each lower compartment a scene from Christ's passion. Initials: (i) beginning each memoria in art. 2, 8-line in colours on gold grounds, historiated; (ii) 8-line in colours on gold grounds decorated in colours; (iii) 3-line, gold on coloured grounds; (iv) 1-line, blue with red ornament or red with slate-blue ornament. Blue and gold line fillers in art. 5. Continuous framed borders in art. 3 on picture pages and pages with initials of type (ii). English binding of s. xvi in., rebacked in s. xx: the brown leather bears a worn flower and acorn roll and half-stamps: two clasps missing. Secundo folio (f. 2) *speciali*.

Written in the Low Countries for English use: the calendar suggests a special interest in Edward the Confessor. Scribbles on ff. 162^{v}, 163 are in English law hands, s. xvi. The name 'Havers' on the outside of the front cover. Given by Monsignor J. H. Souter.[1]

[1] When I first saw this manuscript, in the 1950s, it had a flyleaf, now lost, on which was 'Havers' and 'J. H. Souter Oct. 20 1886'.

820. *R. de Pennaforti, Summa de penitentia; etc.* s. xiii^2

Arts. 1–4 are on quires 1–6.

1. ff. 1–40^v Incipit summa de penitencia. Quoniam ut ait ieronimus . . . Venite Benedicti percipite regnum Amen.

R. de Pennaforti, Summa de penitentia, in three books. The preface is followed by a table of chapters of bk. 1. Probably seventeen leaves are missing in two gaps, the first of twelve leaves after f. 13 where the text passes from bk. 1, tit. 13, Bloomfield no. 5054, to bk. 2, tit. 7, and the second of six leaves after f. 14 where the text passes from bk. 2, tit. 7, to bk. 3, tit. 15. The chapters are not numbered.

2. ff. 40^v–46 Quoniam frequenter in foro penitentiali . . . Incipit summa de matrimonio. Quoniam matrimonium sponsalia . . . et corrigat et emendet.

The Summa de matrimonio which commonly follows the Summa de penitentia. Probably four leaves are missing after f. 45 where the text passes from tit. 10 to tit. 25. The chapters are not numbered. A table of them follows the preface.

3. ff. 46–47^v Beatus diues qui inuentus est sine macula . . . in vita sua. ecclesiastici xxxi. Competunt ista uerba commendationi beati Nicholai . . . uoluntatem habendi plura.

A title in the margin of f. 46, 'Rigilium (?) de beato Nicholao . . .' has been partly cut off.

4. ff. 47^v–49^v `De beato thoma'. Misi tibi uirum prudentem et scientissimum etc. Sicut dicit Iere. in tabernaculo domini . . . hodie pro domo israel. Et cetera.

A sermon for Thomas the apostle. The scribe left small blank spaces where he could not read his exemplar.

5. ff. 50–88^v Rubrica. dominica 1^a in aduentu domini sermo de epistola. Hora est iam nos de sompno surgere. Ro. iiii. est triplex sompnus ignorancie . . .

Sermons on the Epistles and Gospels of the temporal of Petrus de Remis, O.P., †1249, listed by Schneyer, *Rep.*, iv. 725–31, nos. 1–47, 49–77 (*ends imperfectly*), 86 (*begins imperfectly*), 87–90, 92, 91, 93, 94 (*ends imperfectly*), 101 (*begins imperfectly*), 102–3. Probably four leaves are missing after f. 81 where the text passes from sermon 77 to sermon 86 and three leaves after f. 86 where it passes from sermon 94 to sermon 101. An addition in a current hand in the margin of f. 70, s. xiii^2, refers to Schneyer, no. 103a: 'Cantate domino canticum nouum. alleluia etc'. Introitus est misse et predicauit frater P. de Remis. et notandum . . .'.

6. ff. 88^v–107^v Qui sunt isti qui ut nubes uolant et quasi columbe ad fe. etc. Profectus apostolorum uolatui nubium . . .

Substantially the collection of sermons for the common of saints of Petrus de Remis, Schneyer, *Rep.*, iv. 752–61, nos. 461–506, but with differences, particularly the presence here of two sermons on 'In omnem terram exiuit sonus eorum' (Ps. 18: 4) in place of no. 471 on ff. 91^v–93 and of a final sermon (f. 107^v) 'Ubera tua botris id est sicut botrus plenus musto ita ubera tua . . . nec in occasione auaricie sic scitis. q. nec in uentre'.

ff. vi + 110 + ii, foliated (two unnumbered leaves), i–iv, 1–58, 58*, 58**, 59–70, 70*, 71–107, (108–9). Rather poor parchment for arts. 1, 2: tears on ff. 35, 42, were mended before the scribe came to them; he had to avoid a large hole on f. 46. 306 × 213 mm. Written space *c.*230 × 135 mm. 2 cols. 60 lines. First line of writing above top ruled line. Collation probably: 1^{12} 2 one (f. 13, the first leaf of a quire), 3^{12} wants 1, 2 before f. 14 and 4–9 after f. 14 $4–5^{12}$ 6^{12} wants 5–8 after f. 45 7^{12} 8^{8} 9^{12} 10^{12} wants 4–7 after f. 81 11^{12} wants 1–3 before f. 87 12^{12}. Quires numbered at the beginning in pencil I–XII and sometimes at the end also: II is on f. 13 and IIII on f. 18. Several small hands. Initials: (i) red and blue with ornament of both colours; (ii) 2-line, red or blue. Medieval binding of wooden boards covered with pink leather: two strap-and-pin-fastenings, now missing, ran from the back to the front: rebacked. Secundo folio *i. q. vii.*

Written probably in France and presumably for Dominican use. In Germany in s. xviii, when J. J. Rasch wrote a long note about Summa Reymundi on ff. ii–iv^{v} and dated it Hamburg 1753. Small printed book-plate of W. P. Turnbull inside the cover, s. xix. 'Ex libris Mauritii Philippi Clifford', f. i: bequeathed by him in 1881.

1042. *Horae* s. xv med.

1. ff. i–xi^{v} Rather empty calendar in French in gold, blue, and red, lacking January.

Loys, Denis, Romain in gold (25 Aug., 9, 23 Oct.), Mellon in blue (22 Oct.), and Ouen in red (5 May).

2. ff. 1–6^{v} Sequentiae of the Gospels. Protector in te sperancium after John.

3. ff. 7–10^{v} Obsecro te . . . Masculine forms.

4. ff. 10^{v}–14 De beata maria. O intemerata . . . orbis terrarum. De te enim . . . Masculine forms.

5. ff. 15–59 Hours of B.V.M. of the use of (Rouen).

Headings in French. Memoriae after lauds of Holy Spirit, John Baptist, and Laurence. f. 59^{v} blank, except for the heading of art. 6. Two leaves missing.

6. ff. 60–77^{v} Les sept pseaumes. Litany, f. 73.

Fifteen martyrs: (15) Eutropi. Nine confessors (9) Francise (*sic*). Eleven virgins. Fidelium is the only prayer after Deus cui proprium.

7. ff. 78–80 Hours of the Cross, the first leaf missing.

8. ff. 80^{v}–83^{v} Hours of the Holy Spirit.

9. ff. 84–115^{v} Office of the dead, ending imperfectly.

The heading 'Uigilles de mors' should have been written on f. 83^{v}, but is by mistake on f. 80.

ff. 126, foliated i–xi, 1–115. 186 × 126 mm. Written space 100 × 63 mm. 15 long lines. Collation of ff. i–xi, 1–115: 1^{12} wants 1 2^{6} $3–4^{8}$ 5^{8} wants 8 after f. 28 $6–7^{8}$ 8^{8} wants 2 after f. 45 9–11⁸ 12² (ff. 76–7) 13⁸ wants 1 before f. 79 and 8, probably blank, after f. 83 14–17⁸. Ten 12-line pictures, seven in art. 5 (sext missing) and one before each of arts. 6, 8, 9. Initials: (i) 3-line, blue patterned in white on gold grounds decorated in colours; (ii, iii) 2-line and 1-line, gold on coloured grounds. Capital letters in the ink of the text filled with yellow. Line fillers in red and blue patterned in white and separated by pieces of gold. Framed floral borders compartmented and partly on grounds of gold paint, on three sides of pages with initials of type (i). English binding, s. xviii ex., labelled 'Missal'.

Written in France for use in the diocese of Rouen (but there are no Rouen saints in the litany). A mostly illegible inscription of ownership in French, f. i, s. xvii. Belonged to John Ives, †1776: 'Bibliotheca Invesia', f. i. Probably lot 382 in his sale, 3 March 1777, 'Horæ on vellum and illustration'. 'E libris Car' [. . .]pe A. M. E Coll. Reg. Oxon. 1798', f. i.

1043. *J. Wallensis, O.F.M., Communiloquium, etc.* s. xiv med.

1. ff. iii^{rv}, 1–191 (*begins imperfectly*, f. 1) ad seruos et e conuerso . . . (f. 5) Cum doctor siue predicator euangelicus sapientibus et insipientibus debitor sit . . . gracia illuminante studeat aduenire. Explicit summa collacionum fratris Io. Gallensis Ordinis fratrum minorum.

Bloomfield, no. 1086. The running title is CO/LEC. The text is preceded by a table of the distinctions of the seven parts, the second leaf missing and the first, f. iii, missing except for a corner: the first words on f. 1 are from the title of pt. 2, dist. 1.

2. ff. 191^{v}–245 Nunquit nosti ordinem celi et racionem eius pones in terra 38 Iob sicut angelica ierarchia . . . manus leuet. Et in hoc finis istius collacionis. Explicit dietarium fratris et magistri Iohannis Wallensis. De ordine fratrum minorum.

The three parts of the Ordinarium vitae religiosae, Dietarium, Locarium (f. 224^{v}) and Itinerarium (f. 229^{v}). Little, *Grey Friars*, pp. 144–5, lists seven manuscripts and three printed editions. Below the end of the text on f. 245 an English hand, s. xv, wrote 'Dieta salutis edita fuit a fratre guill(el)mo lanicia equitanico de ordine fratrum minorum'. ff. 245^{v}–247^{v} are blank, or were so at first: ill-written memoranda on f. 245^{v} include the personal names 'Iohannes Lee', 'domini Willelmi vyrsy' and 'Robertus Vyrsy', the place-names 'lymerston' (three times) and 'arreton' (Limerston and Arreton, Isle of Wight), the name Malpas, and the date 1 August 1453.

ff. ii + 250 + ii, foliated i–iii, 1–21, 21*, 22–110, 110*, 111–247, (248–9). A medieval foliation 1–244 on ff. 5–247 predates the loss of 9¹². 180 × 142 mm. Written space 125 × 90 mm. 2 cols. 32–3 lines. Collation: 1¹² wants 2 (ff. iii (a corner only, 1–10) 2–8¹² 9¹² wants 12 after f. 104 10–21¹². Initials: (i) ff. 191^{v}, 224^{v}, 229^{v}, 5-line, pink or blue patterned in white on gold grounds decorated in colour and with prolongations into the margins ending in ivy leaves: the remains suggest that f. iii had similar decoration; (ii) 3-line, red or blue with ornament in both colours running the full height of the margin. Binding of s. xx².[1]

Written probably in France. Marginalia of s. xiv/xv are in a French hand, but rather later marginalia are in English hands. Probably in the Isle of Wight in 1453: see above.

[1] There were no covers when I saw this manuscript in 1949, except for a small fragment of the wood of the back board adhering to the end of one of the bands.

OXFORD. BODLEIAN LIBRARY

Catalogues

All western manuscripts acquired before 1916 and the Lyell collection acquired in 1949 are described more or less fully in printed catalogues which, for the older collections, generally take the place of the lists in *CMA*, ii. 46–374. The best account of the history of Bodleian cataloguing of western manuscripts up to 1953 is in R. W. Hunt's 'Historical Introduction' in *Sum. Cat.*, i (1953), ix–lxxiv: see especially pp. l–lvii (pp. xxv–xxxv for *CMA*), for the volumes published in large quarto and (Douce) folio sizes between 1840 and 1900, and pp. lviii–lxv for the *Summary Catalogue* of manuscripts not described in the quarto catalogues. See also Craster (below), chapters vi and xi.

Coxe's Douce catalogue in folio was published in 1840. After this the quartos, excluding Greek, are: Ashmole, 1845 and (index) 1866; Canonici Lat., 1854; Laud, 1858 and (MSS. Misc. 750–9 and index) 1885: reprinted with new introduction and fifty pages of notes and hand-written textual corrections and minor additions to the text in 1973; Tanner, 1860: reprinted, with hand-written corrections and additions, in 1966; Rawlinson A and B, 1862; Canonici Ital., 1864; Rawlinson C and indexes of A, B, and C, 1878; Digby, 1883: revision in progress; Rawlinson D (3 vols.), 1893–1900.

Six volumes of *Sum. Cat.*, numbered ii part i, ii part ii, iii–vi, were published between 1895 and 1937 and introductory and index volumes (i and vii) in 1953. Vol. iv includes a new catalogue to replace the 1840 folio catalogue of the Douce collection. *Sum. Cat.*, although it does not include descriptions of manuscripts catalogued in the quarto series, does list these manuscripts in a continuous serial numeration of all western manuscripts in the library. From 1 to 8716 the numbers are those of *CMA*. From 8717 to 37299 they were assigned in order to show as nearly as possible the order of accession from 1698 to 1915. The *Sum. Cat.* number was an important part of the reference to any manuscript described in *Sum. Cat.* until the conspectus of shelf-marks was published in 1953 (*Sum. Cat.* i. 1–46) and it is still a useful aid to finding descriptions in *Sum. Cat.*

CMA may be fuller than *Sum. Cat.* (cf. the two descriptions of the letters of Senatus in Bodley 633 under no. 1966) and treats miscellanies like Bodley 57, 487, 677, 807 (2004, 2067, 2594, 2689) in more detail: for miscellanies a reference to *CMA* is usually given in *Sum. Cat.* The fact that the descriptions of nos. 1840–3133 (Classis VI) in *CMA* are largely Langbaine's work gives them special value. (Reprinted 1980 with corrections in vols. i and vii.)

Sum. Cat. ends with accessions of 1915. *Lyell Cat.* (1971) is the only printed catalogue of a later accession. Descriptions of the great majority of the other western medieval manuscripts acquired between 1915 (Bywater) and the present day[1] are available to readers in the library in a typescript volume 'Western medieval MSS'. More or less brief printed accounts of many of these manuscripts are to be found in six places: (1) *BLR*; (2) O. Pächt and J. J. G. Alexander, *Illuminated manuscripts in the Bodleian Library, Oxford* (3 vols., 1966–73);

[1] The post-*Sum. Cat.* typescript includes descriptions of some manuscripts which belonged to the University of Oxford before 1915 but were not part of the Bodleian Library until later. Latin manuscripts in this category are Finch e. 25 and g. 1, transferred from the Taylor Institution in 1918, and Kennicott 13–16, Radcliffe Trust d. 2, 5, e. 4, 30, f. 1, deposited by the Radcliffe Trustees in 1872 (cf. Craster (below) pp. 283, 128), and Radcliffe Trust d. 60, permanently transferred in 1982.

(3) S. de Ricci, *Handlist of manuscripts at Holkham Hall* (Bibliographical Society, Supplement 7), 1932; (4) Watson, *Oxford*; (5) Annual Reports of the Curators; (6) Annual Reports of the Friends of the Bodleian.

(1). *BLR*, i (1939–41), 14, 37, 53, 71, 115–16, 173–4, 177–8, 222, 238–9, 255–6; ii (1941–9), 6–9, 15, 53, 66, 72, 146–8, 169–70, 226–8, 260; iii (1950–1), 223, 281–2; iv (1952–3), 173–4, 227–8, 341–2; v (1954–6), 52–3, 109, 166–7, 275, 332–3; vi (1957–61), 388–9, 443, 571–2, 625, 662–3; vii (1962–7), 53, 106–7, 165, 219–20, 230, 274 (notice of Lat. th. e. 32 bought in 1953); viii (1967–72), 51; ix (1973–8), 134, 188, 291–2, 357–60; x (1978–82), 128–9, 188–9, 254–6, 327–38. In all, over 100 medieval post-*Sum. Cat.* manuscripts have been noticed in *BLR*.

(2). See the indexes to Pächt and Alexander under the headings Buchanan, Bywater, Donation, Douce d. 19, Dutch, Finch, French, Holkham, Italian, Kennicott, Latin bibles, Latin classics, Latin history, Latin liturgies, Latin miscellaneous, Latin theology, Radcliffe Trust. In all, over 160 of the entries refer to medieval post-*Sum. Cat.* manuscripts, including all fragments containing illumination. An amalgamated concordance of press-marks by B. C. Barker-Benfield was published in 1974.

(3). Of de Ricci's list nos. 8, 32, 40, 50, 66, 71, 83, 117, 153–6, 159, 161, 166, 174, 191, 193, 206, 211, 222, 223, 245, 308, 333, 340, 380, 410, 420, 460–2, 468–9, 497, 531, 574, 658, 661–3, 672–3, 675, 705, 707, 718, 754 are medieval manuscripts now in the Holkham misc. series in the Bodleian Library. See also *BLR* x (1978–82), 327–38.

(4.) Fifty-eight manuscripts: see the headings Broxbourne, Buchanan, Bywater, Germ., Holkham, Ital., Lat. bibl., Lat. class., Lat. hist., Lat. liturg., Lat. misc., Lat. th.

Histories, etc.

W. D. Macray, *Annals of the Bodleian Library, Oxford, A.D. 1598–A.D. 1867*, 1868. 2nd edition, revised and brought down to 1881, 1890. Sir Edmund Craster, *History of the Bodleian Library 1845–1945*, 1952.

Binding fragments

The system now in use for referencing and binding up fragments detached from bindings dates from the 1890s: see especially the notice at *Sum. Cat.* 30479. Fragments of special interest are usually bound on their own; others are collected together in guard-books. Fragments belonging to named collections usually keep the name; others are classified by language, subject, and size according to the system devised by E. W. B. Nicholson in 1887 for miscellaneous accessions (cf. Hunt in *Sum. Cat.*, I. xlv). Before 1890 there were a few important collections of medieval binding fragments already referenced and bound, Rawlinson D. 893-4, 913 (given shelf-marks *c.*1862–*c.*1875: Hunt, p. 67) and MS. Douce 381 (21956),[1] and a first trial of separating out was made in 1885 by the creation of Add. C. 277 (30281). Since 1890 the following have come into existence: Barlow 55, Douce c. 4 (30452), Douce d. 3, 4 (21980–1), Douce f. 1 (21999), Eng. hist. e. 49 (30481), Eng. misc. c. 674, Eng. poet. c. 3 (30516), Eng. th. e. 1 (30521), Fr. c. 4 (30528), Germ. d. 1 (30530), Lat. bib. b. 1 (30550), Lat. class. c. 2 (30551), Lat. hist. b. 1, Lat. liturg. a. 6 (30556), 8, 9, 12, Lat. liturg. b. 3 (30588), 7, 16, 17, Lat. liturg. d. 16, Lat. liturg. e. 16, Lat. misc. a. 3, Lat. misc. b. 3 (30562), 12, 13, 22, 23,

[1] Not all the pieces in these four volumes are binding fragments. Some are bits of books and many in MS. Douce 381 are cut-outs.

Lat. misc. c. 10 (30565), 17 (30567: now 102 pieces), 18*, 21 (36216), 91, 92, Lat. misc. d. 13–15 (30572–4), 30 (30584), Lat. misc. e. 122, Lat. th. a. 1, Lat. th. c. 10, 37, Lat. th. d. 10 (33199), Mus. d. 143 (30645), Rawl. Q. b. 4 (16032), Savile 106 (33671), Selden supra 102 (3490b), 102*, Tanner 471 (30692), Top. Lond. c. 4 (30733), Top. Lond. e. 6 (30736). In addition to what has been in some sense 'found in the library' a few collections of fragments and single pieces have been given or bought: Lat. bib. d. 1 (P) (31089) by gift in 1891; fragments bought with the Crawford charters in 1891: see the notice of Eng. hist. a. 2 (31346); Eng. poet. c. 4 and Eng. th. f. 10 (31791 and 31801) by purchase in 1895; Eng. poet. e. 94 by purchase in 1961; the Lanhydrock fragments, Lat. misc. b. 17, by purchase in 1963; the Dring fragments, Lat. misc. b. 19, by gift in 1964; Lat. liturg. b. 19 by purchase in 1982.

The three large Rawlinson collections of fragments were described in detail by Macray. Cataloguing on this scale was not attempted in *Sum. Cat.*, except as an afterthought in the 'Corrections, etc.' section of *Sum. Cat.* vi, where Craster added to what Madan had written about Crawford fragments. Some pieces have been itemized elsewhere, however: fragments dating from before 1200 by Craster in *BQR* xxii (1920); fragments removed from Oxford bindings by Ker, *Pastedowns* (see the index of guard-books, p. 270 (Dring, Lanhydrock) and p. 278);[1] illuminated fragments by Pächt and Alexander, but these are mainly cut-outs.

OXFORD. COLLEGE AND OTHER LIBRARIES

Catalogues. All college libraries except Christ Church, Pembroke, and post-1852 foundations: H. O. Coxe, *Catalogus Codicum MSS. qui in collegiis aulisque Oxoniensibus hodie adservantur*, 2 vols., 1852. Earlier brief lists are in T. James, *Ecloga Oxonio-Cantabrigiensis*, 1600, and in *CMA*, ii. 1–88. Coxe was able to follow existing numerations in listing the manuscripts of University College (*CMA*, MSS. 1–178), Balliol College (Gerard Langbaine[2] in Bodleian MS. Wood donat. 4, MSS. 1–230), Merton College (*CMA*, MSS. 1–323), Oriel College (*CMA*, MSS. 1–72), New College (*CMA*, MSS. 1–323: for 1–308 *CMA* follows the catalogue of 1624, now Bodleian MS. Langbaine 7, pp. 330–75, which Langbaine copied out and checked in 1655), Magdalen College (*CMA*, MSS. Lat. 1–223), and Corpus Christi College (*CMA*, MSS. 1–278).

Balliol College. R. A. B. Mynors, *Catalogue of the Manuscripts of Balliol College, Oxford*, 1963.

Christ Church. G. W. Kitchin, *Catalogus Codicum Manuscriptorum qui in Bibliotheca Ædis Christi apud Oxonienses adservantur*, 1867.

Corpus Christi College. A brief supplement to Coxe by Charles Plummer covering MSS. 394–438 was privately printed in 1886.

Keble College. M. B. Parkes, *The Medieval Manuscripts of Keble College, Oxford*, 1979.

[1] On p. 278, 'Douce c. 1' is an error for 'Douce c. 4 (30452)'.

[2] For the excellent work done by Gerard Langbaine (1609–58) in cataloguing college (and Bodleian) manuscripts, see R. W. Hunt in *Sum. Cat.* I. xviii–xxv.

Histories, etc. All libraries. Paul Morgan, *Oxford Libraries outside the Bodleian*, 2nd edn. 1980.
All Souls College (C. 96 + K. 7).[1] Sir Edmund Craster, *The History of All Souls College Library*, 1971. N. R. Ker, *Records of All Souls College Library, 1437–1600* (Oxford Bibliographical Society, new series xvi), 1971.
Allestree Library (K. 3). Morgan, p. 28. W. G. Hiscock, *A Christ Church Miscellany*, 1946, pp. 14, 15. The library is housed in Christ Church and administered from Christ Church Library.
Balliol College (C. 317. M. 320). Mynors, op. cit., pp. xi–liii. Coxe was unable to find MSS. 90 and 142, which are still missing.
Blackfriars (K. 2).
*Brasenose College (C. 19 + K. 2).
Campion Hall (K. 4).
Christ Church (Kit. 38 + K. 2).
*Corpus Christi College (C. 204 + K. 7). J. R. Liddell, 'The Library of Corpus Christi College, Oxford in the Sixteenth Century', *The Library*, 4th series xviii (1938), 385–416, based on his Oxford B.Litt. thesis, 'The Library of Corpus Christi College, 1517–1617' (1933).
Exeter College (C. 70 + K. 3).
*Hertford College, formerly Magdalen Hall (C. 3 + K. 2). The three medieval manuscripts catalogued by Coxe are MSS. 3–5.
*Jesus College (C. 89 + K. 1). C. J. Fordyce and T. M. Knox, *The Library of Jesus College, Oxford* (Oxford Bibliographical Society, v (1937), 49–115). MS. 14 was not found when the manuscripts were deposited in the Bodleian Library in 1886 and has not been found since.
Keble College (P. 66). Parkes, op. cit., pp. vii–xv.
*Lady Margaret Hall (K. 6).
*Lincoln College (C. 116 + K. 8). R. Weiss, 'The earliest Catalogues of the Library of Lincoln College', *Bodleian Quarterly Record*, viii (1937), 343–59.
*Magdalen College (C. 222 + K. 16). Coxe included MSS. Lat. 36, 210, 213, but could only say of them what is said in *CMA*, since they had been temporarily mislaid. 36 and 213 are noted in the supplement to Coxe by W. D. Macray, *A Register of the Members of St Mary Magdalen College, Oxford*, new series, ii (1897), 212–8. All three manuscripts are described below.
Mansfield College (K. 1).
Merton College (C. 325 + K. 5). F. M. Powicke, *The Medieval Books of Merton College*, 1931. H. W. Garrod and J. R. L. Highfield, 'An indenture . . . 22 October 1374', *BLR* x (1978), 9–18 (William Rede's gift of 100 manuscripts). Coxe included MS. 33, a companion volume to MS. 34, but was unable to describe it, since it had been temporarily mislaid. Two manuscripts he describes, 318 and 325, are now in other libraries, Wye College, Kent, and Worcester College, Oxford, q.v.

[1] The numbers in brackets show how many western medieval manuscripts (excluding Greek) are described by C(oxe: approximately), by Kit(chen), M(ynors), and P(arkes), and in this volume (K). Only the principal descriptions of libraries are noted. For others see Morgan, pp. x, xi, and under each library. An asterisk shows that the manuscripts, with a few exceptions, are (1982) deposited in the Bodleian Library.

*New College (C. 253 + K. 2). R. W. Hunt, 'The Medieval Library', chapter xi of *New College, Oxford, 1379–1979* (eds. J. Buxton and P. Williams, 1979, pp. 317–45). A fuller account of the library by Dr Hunt is being revised for the Oxford Bibliographical Society. Coxe recorded five manuscripts (MSS. 85, 99, 103, 200, 295) he was unable to find: they seem to have been missing already by 1688 and are not included in the total of 253. MS. 248, listed by Coxe as missing, may be B.L., MS. Royal 16 c. xix.
*Oriel College (C. 79). *The Dean's Register of Oriel, 1446–1661*, eds. G. C. Richards and H. E. Salter, 1926, pp. 386–97.
Pembroke College (K. 17). Titles first (?) listed by Haenel, col. 896. HMC, *6th Report*, 1877, Appendix, pp. 550–1 (MSS. 2, 3, 6, 5, 4, 21, 13, 12, 10 in that order). Full descriptions of MSS. 8, 10–13, 15, 21 by Dr A. Anderson, 'Some Medical MSS. in the Library of Pembroke College, Oxford', are in typescript in the library and in the Bodleian Library (Ref. 758).
Queen's College (C. 52 + K. 2). J. McGrath, *The Queen's College* (1921), i. 76–80, 126–9, 161–2, 359–60.
Regent's Park College (K. 1).
*St Edmund Hall (K. 2).
St Hilda's College (K. 1).
St John's College (C. 170 + K. 5).
Somerville College (K. 2).
Taylor Institution (K. 5).
*Trinity College (C. 83 + K. 2).
*University College (C. 120 + K. 2). R. W. Hunt, 'The manuscript collection of University College', *BLR*, iii (1950), 14–34.
Wadham College (C. 11 + K. 5).
Worcester College (C. 1 + K. 3).

Binding fragments. Most college libraries have collections of binding fragments, which have a special interest because they are likely to contain pieces of manuscripts which existed as whole books in Oxford in the Middle Ages. Such of these fragments as are known to come from the bindings of books bound in Oxford are listed by Ker, *Pastedowns*: see there, pp. x–xii and the Index of Guardbooks, pp. 271–8. One guardbook, Queen's College MS. 389, existed early enough to be included by Coxe. Seven manuscripts of which considerable fragments remain are listed below: All Souls Coll., 332, Magdalen Coll., 262–4, Merton Coll., E. 3. 1, E. 3. 30, Queen's Coll., 35. c. 1–15 + 35. d. 1–12 (still in use as pastedowns).

OXFORD. ALL SOULS COLLEGE

302. *Missale* s. xv[1]

A Sarum missal from which all but one of the principal leaves have been stolen. All main articles, except 6, 8, 12, are headless.

1. ff. 1–5^{v} Graded calendar in red and black.

March–April missing. Feasts of St Thomas and the word 'pape' erased and restored, s. xvi. An addition at 22 Oct., 'Obitus M' Willelmi Kele tercii custodis huius collegii (*1445–59*) anno domini m.cccc^{mo} lix^{no}'.

2. f. 5* (*begins imperfectly*) teriori parte post suos ministros procedat.

Holy water service. Only the top corner of the leaf remains. The first words are in *PS*, p. 6/2 and such other words as can be read here occur there on p. 6.

3. ff. 5*^{v}, 6–78^{v} Temporal, Advent–Easter Eve.

With the fragmentary text on f. 5*^{v} cf. *Sarum Missal*, p. 14/7, sqq. The office of St Thomas of Canterbury was probably on the two leaves missing after f. 14. The secret for the second Sunday after the octave of Epiphany is Ut tibi domine grata.

4. (*a*) f. 78^{rv} [S]umme sacerdos . . . (*ends imperfectly*). (*b*) ff. 79–84 Ordinary of mass. (*c*) ff. 84–85^{v} Prefaces of mass, the end missing. (*d*) ff. 86–8 Canon of mass. (*e*) f. 88^{rv} Cum vero sacerdos exuerit . . . (*f*) ff. 88^{v}–89^{v} Rubric for special occasions, 'Predictus modus et ordo . . .', followed by psalms and prayers in prostration, ending imperfectly in the prayer 'Deus qui admirabili prouidencia . . .'. (*g*) f. 90^{rv} Rubric on accidents at mass, imperfect at both ends.

(*a*). Cf. below, Corpus Christi College 394, art. 4a. (*b*). As in Newcastle, Univ. Libr. 2, q.v. (*d*). 'Habeatur in memoria Henricus Chichele Cantuariensis Archiepiscopus 'fundator [. . .]'' is added below the text on f. 86, s. xv. (*e*). Gratiarum actio post missam. (*f*). Cf. Corpus Christi Coll. 394, art. 4*f*.

5. ff. 91–124 Temporal from Easter.

Corpus Christi on f. 106.

6. ff. 124–125^{v} Offices in dedication of church, octave of dedication, and reconciliation of church.

7. ff. 126–152^{v} Sanctoral, Andrew–Cecilia, imperfect at both ends.

Anne, f. 139^{v}, the initial cut out. 'De sanctis Dauid et Cedda quere missam in fine libri', f. 129^{v}.

8. ff. 153–63 Common of saints.

9. ff. 163–175^{v} Votive masses: (4–6) B.V.M., with long heading 'Sabbato celebratur . . . requieuit. Ordinacio . . .'; (1) Holy Trinity; (2) Holy Spirit; (3) Holy Cross; (p. 459) angels; (7) Pro fratribus et sororibus; (11) Pro pace; (15) Pro rege; (16) *Pro rege et regina;[1] (23) Ad inuocandam graciam sancti spiritus; (17) Pro semetipso; (18) *Item alia pro semetipso oracio non sarum; (34) Ad poscendum donum sancti spiritus; (25) Pro peccatoribus; (31) Pro penitentibus; (33) Pro inspiracione diuine sapiencie; (37) Pro tribulacione cordis; (26) *Pro quacumque

[1] An asterisk shows that only collect, secret, and postcommunion are provided.

tribulacione; (39) Pro infirmo; (19) Pro salute amici; (20) *Pro amico; (p. 410, footnote) *Pro infirmo proximo morti; (28) Pro serenitate aeris; (27) Ad pluuiam postulandam; (43) In tempore belli; (35) Pro eo qui in uinculis tenetur; (29) Contra mortalitatem hominum; (42) Pro peste animalium; (30) *Pro iter agentibus; (10) *Pro uniuersali ecclesia; (9) *Pro `papa' (the word restored over erasure); (12, 14) *Pro episcopo (two forms); (13) *Pro prelatis et subditis; (21) *Contra temptaciones carnis; (22) *Contra malas cogitaciones; (24) *Pro peticione lacrimarum; (32) *Contra potestates aereas; (36) *Contra inuasores ecclesie; (38) *Pro nauigantibus; (40) *Pro benefactoribus uel salute uiuorum; (41) *Contra aduersantes; (p. 406, footnote) *Contra paganos; *De incarnacione domini nostri ihesu cristi; *Ad memoriam de sanctis katerina margareta et maria magdalena; (8) *Commemoracio generalis de omnibus sanctis.

The masses commonly found in missals of this date and in the common order: cf. Parkes, p. 266. Except two, they are in *Sarum Missal*. References are to pages there or, by number, to the series of forty-three votive masses printed (but not actually numbered) on pp. 384–412.[1] The mass of the Incarnation and the mass asking for the intercession of Sts Katherine, Margaret, and Mary Magdalene occur in early printed Sarum missals (Burntisland edn., cols. 825*, 823*).

10. ff. 175^v–177^v Ordo ad faciendum sponsalia . . . ad bigamiam (*ends imperfectly*).

English on f. 176. The last words are in *Manuale Sarum*, p. 55/2: the catchword 'transiens' follows.

ff. i + 178 + i, foliated before present binding 1–5, 5*, 6–177. 390 × 275 mm. Written space 275 × 190 mm. 2 cols. 36 lines. Collation: twenty-three quires, all once eights, except 1^6, but lacking twenty-eight leaves, 1^2, 2^1, $3^{4,5}$, 4^2, 11^2, 11^8, 12^8, $13^{1,2}$, 13^7, 14^1, 15^4, 15^7, $16^{3,4}$, 19^1, 19^{4-6}, 20^8, 21^1, 21^3, 22^1, 22^5, 22^8, 23^4, 23^7: the gaps are after ff. 1, 5, 14 (2 leaves), 18, 73, 78, 85 (3 leaves), 89, 90, 100, 102, 105 (2 leaves), 125, 127 (3 leaves), 136 (2 leaves), 137, 142, 145, 147, 150, 152. Initials: (i) all gone, except the *T* on f. 124, shaded pink on gold ground, decorated in colours and with prolongations on three sides; (ii) all gone, except on ff. 86^v, 130^v (Annunciation of B.V.M.), 175^v (art. 12), gold on red and blue grounds patterned in white; (iii) f. 153 (art. 8), 3-line, red and blue, with red and violet ornament; (iv) 2-line, blue with red ornament; (v) 1-line, blue with red ornament or red with violet ornament. Capital letters in the ink of the text filled with pale yellow. Bound in 1841: see below. Secundo folio (f. 5*) *teriori parte*.

Written in England. At All Souls College in s. xv (see art. 1). Identifiable with the sixth of nine missals listed in a chapel inventory of s. xv, Vellum Inventory, f. 18, 2 fo *teriori*. 'Hic liber emptus a garbrando for x^s and if it do lacke anie parte he dothe promisse to make it complete', f. 1, s. xvi/xvii. The reference is presumably to Richard Garbrand, bookseller at Oxford 1573–1602, but the book may be one of those which Richard's father, Garbrand Herks, bought from the college in 1549–50, as Sir Edmund Craster suggested in *BLR* iii. 120: cf. Ker, *Records*, p. 167. 'Found unbound in the Chapel at Tusmore Co: Ox: and given

[1] The page numbers of this series are: (1) pp. 384–5; (2) pp. 385–6; (3) pp. 386–7; (4–6) pp. 387–91; (7) pp. 392–3; (8) p. 394; (9) pp. 394–5; (10) p. 395; (11) pp. 395–6; (12) p. 396; (13) p. 396; (14) p. 397; (15) p. 397; (16) p. 398; (17) p. 398; (18) p. 399; (19) pp. 399, 400; (20) p. 400; (21) p. 400; (22) p. 401; (23) p. 401; (24) p. 402; (25) p. 402; (26) p. 403; (27) pp. 403–4; (28) p. 404; (29) pp. 404–5; (30) p. 405; (31) pp. 405–6; (32) p. 406; (33) p. 407; (34) p. 407; (35) pp. 407–8; (36) p. 408; (37) pp. 408–9; (38) p. 409; (39) pp. 409–10; (40) pp. 410–11; (41) p. 411; (42) p. 411; (43) pp. 411–12.

to H.D. by Miss Ramsay Aug. 1841. Bound for H.D. by Wiseman, Cambridge Dec. 1841. Binding and repairing £2.10.—and new vellum £2. 6. 9', on a label inside the cover. Bought from the executors of Sir Henry Dryden in 1899. Frere, no. 536.

315. *Justinianus, Institutiones* s. xiii^2

(*begins imperfectly*) ius nostrum aut ex quo utimur scripto . . . (f. 59) deo propicio aduentura est. Expliciunt instituciones.

Begins in bk. 1, tit. 2. 3. Wide margins, mainly blank. Marginalia include some verses, for example, f. 9^v, 'Occupat accipit plantat serit edificatque . . .' (4 lines), f. 16^v, 'Testari nequeunt Impubes religiosus . . .' (5 lines), f. 20 'Si vis scire leges noctu dieque leges'. f. 59^v, left blank, was filled later with legal notes.

ff. 59. 323 × 220 mm. Written space 167 × 110 mm. 2 cols. 41 lines. Collation: 1^{10} wants 1 $2\text{-}4^{10}$ 5^8 6^{12}. Initials: (i) red and pale violet with ornament of both colours; (ii) outside the written space, red or blue with ornament of the other colour. Medieval binding of wooden boards covered with white leather: four bands: two strap-and-pin-fastenings from the front to the back cover now missing. Secundo folio *ius nostrum* (f. 1).

Written in southern France (?). Three erasures, f. 59: (1) Iste liber est [. . . .]; (2) Iste liber est Iacobi [. . . . .] qui costitit ei xxxx^{ta} s' prouinc. cor' (?)'; (3) [. . . .] qui decostitit ei xxxx^{ta} s' p(ro)uinc. Cor' (?). Later in Germany, to judge from '59 B11.' inside the cover, s. xix. 'E Libris Henrici Goudy Jur. Civ. Prof. Reg. in Univ. Oxon.'. Goudy noted on a separate sheet 'Seems to have belonged to the Monastery of Buxheim', but the reason for this supposition is not now apparent. 'Presented by Professor Goudy July 1919'.

316. *Digestum Novum* s. xiii med.

1. (*begins imperfectly*, f. 8) firma edifitia . . . (f. 207) causa abesse non potest. Explicit.

The beginning was already at XXXIX. 2. 43/7 in s. xv ex. when the missing text was supplied on ff. 1*, 2-7^v, together with apparatus on ff. 1^v-3, where it stops abruptly. On ff. 8-207^v the apparatus (in another hand) is continuous round all four sides of the text and often in more than 100 lines to the page. Fairly numerous interlinear glosses.

2. f. 208, a binding leaf, is from a commentary on bk. 4 of the Decretals of Gregory ix (tit. xix. 4-8) in an Italian hand, s. xiv.

2 cols. 54 lines.

ff. iii + 208 + iv, foliated (i-iii), 1, 1*, 2-207 (208-11). An older foliation begins with 3 on f. 10. 390 × 240 mm. Written space *c.* 240 × 120 mm. 2 cols. 52 lines. Collation: 1^8 (supply leaves, s. xvi) $2\text{-}17^8$ 18^{10} (ff. 136-45) $19\text{-}24^8$ 25^6 (ff. 194-9) 26^8. Quires numbered at the end and catchwords. Initials: (i) of books and (ii) of tituli, not filled in; (iii) of authors, red or blue outside the written space; (iv) of chapters, 1-line, red or blue. Beside the blank spaces for the initials of books the first letters of each book are written in tall narrow blue and red capitals. Binding by Zaehnsdorf, s. xx^1.

Written in Italy. 'Johannes conrardi', f. 194^v, s. xv. 'Est domini Iohannis de Amila (?) emit Cremone', f. 200, s. xv. 'E libris Monasterii Wiblingensis (O.S.B., diocese of Konstanz)', f. 1*, s. xvi. 'H. Goudy', f. i. Bequeathed by him in 1921: cf. MS. 315.

322. *Alexander de Alexandria, Expositio librorum Aristotelis de Anima* 1477

Bonorum honorabilium. Liber iste cuius exposicionem intendimus . . . (f. 297) bene esse determinatas. Explicit sentenciosa atque studio digna exposicio venerabilis Alexandri super 3^m^ librum de anima Scripta a I. Alexandro Anno necessarie regencie sue Anno 1477mo tunc temporis socio Collegii animarum omnium fidelium defunctorum in Oxon'.

Glorieux, no. 340*b*. The commentary on bk. 2 ends (f. 192^v^) 'Explicit elucidantissima exposicio egregii Alexandri super 2^m^ librum de anima Scripta a M^o^ I. Alexandro (*etc., as above, but reading* 'existente' *instead of* 'temporis')'. Very closely related to the edition printed at Oxford in 1481 (*GKW* 869); the likeness extends to the placing of the red paragraph signs and the wording of the explicits of bks. 2 and 3. John Alexander began copying bk. 1 at ch. 2, abandoned it on f. 19^v^ after writing the words 'antiqui opiniones' (edn. b7^vb^/3), and began bk. 2 on f. 21.[1] f. 20 is blank on the recto and contains on the verso the prologue addressed to Philip de Melduno, 'Interrogasti . . . esse subiectum', and the first thirteen words of ch. 1, 'Ubi non . . . trinitate'. Three leaves are missing after f. 167 with the text in edn. t5^vb^/12-v1^vb^/20. The scribe copied the last two leaves of quire 8 in the wrong order: the words 'istud folium esset sequens subsequens folium' at the head of f. 79 points out his mistake. f. 297^v^ was left blank.

ff. iii + 297. f. ii is modern paper. 202–212 × 140 mm. Written space *c.* 130 × 80 mm. 30–3 long lines. Frame ruling. Collation: $1\text{–}2^8$ 3^6 wants 5, 6, probably blank, after f. 20 $4\text{–}8^{12}$ 9^{12} 11 cancelled after f. 91 $10\text{–}11^{12}$ 12^8 13^{10} $14\text{–}15^{12}$ 16^{12} wants 11, 12 after f. 167 17^{12} wants 1 before f. 168 18^{10} 19^4 (ff. 189–92) $20\text{–}28^{10}$ 29^8 30^8 wants 8, blank. Quires signed in the usual late medieval way, a–c, a–(q), A–L (quires 1–3, 4–19, 20–30). Secretary hand by a named scribe. Blue initials with red ornaments, 3-line and 2-line. Capital letters in the ink of the text marked with red. Contemporary Oxford binding of brown leather bearing stamps of three patterns, staff-and-scroll border stamp, rabbit, fleur-de-lis, rebacked (the old leather preserved): four bands: two clasps missing: D. M. Rogers discusses the binding and reproduces the staff and scroll and rabbit stamps in *The Book Collector*, xxiv (1975), 69. Watson, *Oxford*, pl. 749 illus. f. 10. Secundo folio *anime proficit*.

Written in 1477 by J. Alexander (Alysaunder), fellow of All Souls College (1471) and vicar of St Laurence, Evesham, 1502–13): see above, Emden, *BRUO*, p. 22, and N. R. Ker in *BLR* ii (1947), 186–7. 'I will that Master parson schall chewis wich boke he will haue and gyff the Good prest the todyr and I pray you be good to yo^ur^ Clerke at Evesham per me Iohannem Norris (?)', f. 297^v^, s. xvi. 'Liber collegii Animarum Ox' Ex domo (*sic*) Magistri Iohannis Alysaunder in artibus M' ', f. 2^v^, s. xvi in. In Wales in s. xvi/xvii, as appears from scribbles, 'Jane Lloyd Jones' (f. 287^v^: cf. f. i) and in the same hand 'Plas Madoc' (ff. 55, 297^v^). Sale of Sir F. S. Powell, Bt., Horton Old Hall, Bradford, 16 Dec. 1929, lot 667. Bought from Messrs. Maggs in 1929.

331. *Aphorismi Hippocratis cum expositione Magistri Cardinalis* s. xv med.

Vita breuis ars longa. tempus autem acutum . . . Corpora humana continua resolucione . . . (f. 83) ponendo ipsos vapores (*ends abruptly in bk. 4, aph. 43*).

Thorndike and Kibre. Wickersheimer, p. 94. Text followed by commentary, aphorism by aphorism. Particula 2, f. 20; 3, f. 44; 4, f. 63. The aphorisms are numbered in part. 1 and 2

[1] The signatures and the size of quire 3 (see below) suggest that the copying of bk. 1 was an afterthought.

(1–25, 1–54), but only occasionally in part. 3 and not in part. 4. Some marginalia. ff. 83v–84v blank. 'Cardinalis super librum am*forismo*rum' inside the back cover and '2o folio Oribasius' outside it. For this copy see *Manuscripts at Oxford*, p. 47.

ff. 84. Parchment (outside and in the middle of quires) and paper. 210 × 150 mm. Written space *c.*150 × 95 mm. 36 long lines in the smaller size of script. Ruled with frame lines (only ?). Collation: $1–6^{10}$ 7, 8^{12}. Secretary hand in two sizes, the larger not current as a rule. A space for an initial at the beginning of each particula not filled. Capital letters in the ink of the text marked with red. Contemporary limp parchment wrapper: the quires are stitched to the spine near head and foot only. Secundo folio *Oribasius dicit.*

Written in England. Belonged to a member of Beam Hall, Oxford: 'Iste liber constat Iohanni [. . .] de Aula Trabina' inside the front cover; also 'liber Magistri Willelmi Goldwyn' (fellow of All Souls College 1455, †1482: Emden, *BRUO*, p. 787). 'Liber Collegii animarum omnium defunctorum in Oxon' ex dono Magistri Willelmi Goldewyn', f. 2. Listed in college inventories, s. xv ex. and s. xvi in. (Ker, *Records*, pp. 132, 187, no. 538): in s. xvi in. it was one of the 'concurrentes' circulating among the fellows of All Souls. Bought for £40 in January 1948 from Mr James Fairhurst, Cranford, Kitts Moss Lane, Bramhall, Cheshire.

332. *Liber novem iudicum, etc.* s. xii ex.[1]

Binding leaves found in sixteen Oxford bindings, s. xvii in., at Magdalen College and Queen's College, Oxford, and given to All Souls College in 1948: see *BLR*, iii. 6, and Ker, *Pastedowns*, p. 115. ff. i–iv contain notes by Sir Edmund Craster and (iv) N. R. Ker. ff. v, vi are letters from Ker to Craster, 16 June and 23 Oct. 1948.

1. ff. 1, 2, 11–36 `Liber de naturis et iudiciis planetarum et stellarum secundum 9 iudices videlicet Aris. Albu*ma*zar. Alkynd'. Aomar. Abanalhan. Doroch'. Ierg'. Meshalla et Zael.' Celestis circuli forma sperica. idem cum terra . . .

Thorndike and Kibre. Carmody 1956, pp. 103–12. *Liber novem iudicum*, ed. Paris 1506 (without part 1). The text is complete on ff. 1, 2, 11, 12, 19–22, 28–34. It follows on from leaf to leaf on ff. 14–22, except for a gap of one leaf after f. 16; so too on ff. 23–6, 27–9, and 30–2. Craster identified all of it in MS. Digby 149 and in the edition, except a chapter 'De furto', ff. 21v–22/15: see his notes, ff. ii, iii. Medieval leaf numbers are on ff. 1, 2, 11, 12, 21, 22, 29, and 34: they are '1', '8', '53', '57', '125', '12[6]', '172', and '194 (?)'. Red running titles were added in s. xiv (?) on ff. 27–34, '9a domus' and '10a domus'. An omission on f. 35 is supplied in a good contemporary hand.

2. (*a*) f. 3 (*begins imperfectly*) quadam debilitate implicant. Luna in xia . . . predicere finem. (*b*) ff. 3–5v Descriptio quinquaginta preceptorum in omnibus negociis et questionibus notanda occurrunt. Zahel. Hactenus de circuli particionibus stellisque . . . grauari insinuat. (*c*) ff. 5v–6v De ac(ci)dentali stellarum proprietate alkindius. His igitur taliter exsecutis' inter cetera . . . (*d*) ff. 6v–7v De gaudio stellarum. Amplius. planetarum et gaudium' prout xii domorum . . . cum peruersis e contrario promittit. (*e*) ff. 7v–10v De significatione vii stellarum in oriente habita. Saturnus in oriente' pro lege aut agris reddit sollicitum . . . sed potius omnia quasi (*ends imperfectly*).

[1] This manuscript is earlier than the time of the emperor Frederick II (1220–50) to whom the Liber novem iudicum is supposed to have been sent by the sultan of Babylon.

Eight consecutive leaves. (*a*). Only the last sixteen lines remain. (*b, c, e*). Thorndike and Kibre refer to Carmody 1956, pp. 43–4; 82–3, 106; 72, and note that all three pieces are in Erfurt, Amplonian Q. 372. (*b–d*) are in Bodleian, Digby 47, ff. 100–3, and on f. 99v there there is a marginal reference to (*e*) 'in alio libro iudiciorum quem fecit Iergis'.

Possibly art. 2 is really part of art. 1, but there is no evidence that it was nor of where it came, if it was.

ff. viii (two unnumbered, i–vi) + 36 + ii. Medieval foliation of art. 1 (see above). Written space 235 × 175 mm. 2 cols. 29 lines. The fragments are parts of bifolia, complete half sheets (ff. 1, 2, 11, 12, 14–17, 20–2, 27–34), and strips (ff. 13, 35, 36). ff. 3–10 are probably a complete quire of eight leaves and ff. 14–22 are a quire of ten leaves, complete except for leaf 4 after f. 16. Perhaps all in one hand. The scribe uses the tailed *e* occasionally. Initials: (i) f. 1, blue with red and blue ornament; (ii) 2-line, red or blue. Bound in 1948. Secundo folio (*mutacionem ab alia natura*): the leaf is missing, but f. 1v ends 'conuersiuam' and the words following 'conuersiuam' in Digby 149, f. 205va/2–3 are 'mutacionem ab alia natura'.

Written in England. The copy of the Liber novem iudicum, 'secundo folio mutacionem ab al[. . .]', belonged to All Souls College by 1443 and was probably one of the manuscripts taken from the library desks *c.*1540 to make room for printed books: cf. Ker, *Records*, pp. 8, 130, 182 (no. 128), 220. For the later history, see above.

dd. 2. 9. *Fallentiae regularum iuris* s. xv ex.

1. ff. 1–10v Table, Appellans–Verus contumax.

2. ff. 11–152v Nota quod si heres non confecit inuentarium . . . Primo fallit quia in foro conscientie . . . L. quam ius C ad turpilia imur (?).

Apparently a version of the De regulis incipientibus or Fallentiae regularum iuris of which editions were printed under the name of Bartholomaeus Socinus in 1515 and later.[1] The order of the printed editions is not that found here. The first piece here, numbered '1', occurs at f. lxxvi in edn. 1515. The last piece here, numbered '489', 'Fragmenti fidem . . . Primo fallit nisi facta excutio . . .', seems different from the *Frangenti fidem* section in edn. 1515, f. lxviii. ff. 28–30v, 153–155v blank.

ff. 165. Paper. 418 × 285 mm. Written space 270 × 160 mm. 2 cols. 50–60 lines. Frame ruling in pencil. Collation: $1\text{–}13^{10}$ 14^{8} 15^{10} 16^{10} 17 seven (ff. 159–65). Quires numbered A 1, A 2, A 3, B–P. Ten scribes. Five of them wrote more than one quire: (1) quires A 1, D, P, leaves 2v–10v of quire N and leaves 5–8v of quire O; (2) quires A2, A3; (4) quires C, M and leaves 1–2r of quire N; (5) quires E, K; (7) quires G, I. Four of them wrote one quire each: (3) quire B; (6) quire F; (8) quire H; (9) quire L. One scribe (10) wrote leaves 1–4v of quire O. Scribes 1–3, 6, 7 write current humanistica, scribes 4, 5, 9 cursiva, and scribes 8, 10 current hybrida. Initials not filled in. Bound after law tracts of Angelus de Gambilionibus and Albertus de Gandino printed in the last decade of s. xv: cf. D. Rhodes in *The Library*, 5th series xxvii (1972), 46–50, and Ker, *Records*, no. 1432. The binding is nearly contemporary, English (London ?), with Oldham's roll AN. b. 2 and pineapple ornament A. 1.

Written in Italy. At All Souls by the middle of s. xvi, apparently by the gift of John Weston: cf. Ker, op. cit., and in *BLR*, iii. 105.

[1] I owe this suggestion to Dr P. Weimar of the Max-Planck-Institut, Frankfurt (Main).

OXFORD. ALLESTREE LIBRARY (AT CHRIST CHURCH)

F. 1. 1. *Bernardus, Sermones; etc.* s. xiii[1]

Arts. 1–3 are nearly the same collection of sermons as Balliol College 150, s. xiii in., from the Cistercian abbey of Buildwas. Cf. *SBO* iv. 146 and *Receuil*, ii. 242–3, 246, 294–5. Collated as *O* and Bd^2 in *SBO*.

1. ff. 1–117v Incipit liber beati Bernardi abbatis. Sermo in aduentu dominica prima. Hodie fratres celebramus aduentus initium . . . esse sentimus. Explicit prima pars sermonum beati Bernardi abbatis primi clareualis.

Seventy numbered sermons, all in Balliol 150 art. 1: 1–3, Balliol 1–3; 4–19, Balliol 5–20; 20–4, Balliol 23–7; 25–7, Balliol 29–31; 28–65, Balliol 34–71; 66–70, Balliol 74–7, 77a. For Balliol, no. 4, etc., cf. art. 4.

With three exceptions, the sermons are printed in *PL* clxxxiii: cf. *SBO* iv, v. 1–7, Adv. 1–3, 7, 4–6; 8–13, Vig. Nat. 5, 3, 1, 6, 4, 2; 14–18, Nat. 1, 4, 3, 2, 5; 19, Innoc.; 20–2, Circ. 3, 1, 2; 23–5, Epi. 3, 1, 2; 26, Oct. Epi.; 27, 28, 1 post Epi. 1, 2; 29, 30, Conv. Pauli 1 (1–4), 1 (5–8); 32–4, Purif. 3, 1, 2; 35, 36, Sept. 1, 2; 37–42, Quad. 1, 2, 7, 3–5; 43–6, Qui hab. 1–4; 47, Qui hab. 5, 6; 48, 49, Qui hab. 7; 50–6, Qui hab. 8–14; 57, 58, Qui hab. 16, 17; 61, Ben. 1; 62, 63, Annunc. 2, 3; 64, De div. 46; 65, Annunc. 1; 66–8, Palm. 2, 1, 3; 69, Fer. iv Hebd. Sanct.; 70, Cena dom. One leaf is missing: Adv. 2 ends and Adv. 3 begins imperfectly.

The three sermons not in *PL* are:
31. ff. 49–51v (*Conversion of Paul*) Item eiusdem in eadem sollempnitate de lectione euangelica. Dixit simon petrus ad ihesum. Ecce nos reliquimus omnia . . . Verba lectionis huius fratres. ea esse arbitror . . . benedictus in secula amen. Cf. *MMBL* ii, Eton College 39, f. 135v.

59. f. 96rv De languido iacente iuxta piscinam. Ecce iacet iuxta piscinam aque . . . Quid est aqua piscine . . . humanitate prospiciunt.

60. ff. 96v–97 De transfiguratione domini. Quis ascendet in montem domini? Sumus hic in valle lacrimarum:' in loco horroris . . . mittit timorem.

2. ff. 117v–166v Hic secuntur quidam sermones generales. Sermo beati Bernardi exhortatorius ad conuersionem. Eternam celestis patrie . . .

Thirty-one sermons, numbered, except the last, 71–100, in continuation of art. 1. All are provided for in the table of contents in Balliol 150, but only the first thirty were actually copied there, ff. 81v–108. With one exception the sermons are printed in *PL* clxxxiii (cf. *SBO* iv, v). 1, 2: De div. 111, 8; 4–11: De div. 40, 41, 17, 31, 6, 23, 24, 13; 12: Dom. 5 post Pent. 2; 13–15: De div. 22, 27, 25; 16: Quad. 6; 17–30: De div. 26, 15, 5, 4, 19, 42, 29, 93, 14, 45, 83, 7, 12, 28; Parabola 1 (*PL*, cols. 757–61; *SBO* vi. (2), 261–7).

The sermon not in *PL* is:
3. ff. 121–124v Item eiusdem sermo ad nouiter conuersos:' de contentione uoluntatis et rationis. Uideo uos dilectissimi multa cum auiditate . . . gratiam in oculis eius amen.

3. ff. 167–270 Sermo beati Bernardi abbatis in die sancto pasche. de septem signaculis que soluit agnus. Vicit leo de tribu iuda. Vicit plane malitiam . . .

Unnumbered sermons from Easter to St Andrew, followed by sermons for the dedication of a church and one for Humbertus, fifty-seven in all (out of fifty-nine ?). All but no. 45 are in

Balliol 150, art. 3: 1–9 Balliol 1, 2, 4, 8, 10, 11, 15, 14, 13; 10–13 Balliol 17–20; 14–25 Balliol 22–33; 26–8 Balliol 35–7; 29, 30 Balliol 39, 40; 31–44 Balliol 42–55; 46–57 Balliol 56–8, 58 bis, 59–66. With one exception (40) the texts are in *PL* clxxxiii (for the series cf. *SBO* iv. 130): 1–3: Pasc. 1–3; 4, 5: Oct. Pasc. 1, 2; 6: Rog.; 7–10: Asc. 2–5; 11–13: Pent. 1–3; 14: Joh. Bapt.; 15: Vig. Pet. et Pau.; 16–18: Pet. et Pau. 1, 2 (*ends imperfectly*), 3 (*begins imperfectly*); 19: 4 post Pent. 1; 20, 21: 6 post Pent. 1, 3; 22–5: De div. 36–9 (*ends imperfectly*); 26–8: Assumpt. 2 (*begins imperfectly*), 3, 4 (*ends imperfectly*); 29: Dom. in oct. Ass. (*begins imperfectly*); 30: Nat. B.V.M.; 31: De div. 35; 32, 33: Mich. 1, 2; 34–8: Omn. SS. 1–5; 39: Mal. 40; 40: Epistola de eodem (*Malachi*) Ep. 374 (*PL* clxxxii. 579); 41–5: Dom. 1 Nov. 1–5; 46: Mart.; 47: Clem.; 48: Vig. And. 1; 49, 50: And. 1, 2; 51–6: Ded. 1–6; 57: Humb. Gaps after ff. 193, 210, 214: probably Assumpt. 1 was in the second (Balliol, no. 34) and Assumpt. 5 in the third (Balliol, no. 38). f. 270ᵛ blank. The foot of f. 270 has been cut off: the verso is blank.

4. ff. 271–91 Hos subsequentes sermones in quodam exemplari inter sermones superiores mixtim repperi. quorum nullus in pluribus exemplaribus que inspexi reperitur. excepto primo qui de triplici inferno inscribitur. qui tamen sicut ceteri sequentes á stilo beati Bernardi discordat. qua de causa separaui eos ab inuicem.

Sermons numbered on versos i–xvi by a later hand. Nos. 1–7 are listed in the table of contents of Balliol 150 and nos. 1, 4–7 were copied there as part of art. 1.

1. f. 271 Sermo in aduentu domini de triplici inferno. In celebratione aduentus domini. sanctorum patrum desideria . . . hesterna que preteriit.

2. f. 274 Sermo in natali sanctorum Innocentium. In illo tempore. Angelus domini apparuit . . . Proles de uirgine matre:' veritas est . . . per contemplationem dei . . . amen.

3. f. 276 Item sermo in natali innocentium. Tolle puerum . . . Mater mentis puritas . . . abimatu et infra.

4. f. 276ᵛ Sermo in apparitione domini. Festiuitas hodierna theophania uocatur. Theophania diuina apparitio . . . ignis inferni. quod ipse . . . amen.

5. f. 278 Sermo de sex ydriis purificationis. Erant ibi posite . . . Has sex ydrias . . . proueharis in filium.

6. f. 279ᵛ Sermo in annuntiatione dominica. Omnia per sapientiam dei facta sunt. Ad ipsam sapientiam . . . magnificat anima mea dominum.

7. f. 281 Sermon de passione domini. Circuire domine possum celum . . . incautum precipitat.

8. f. 281ᵛ Sermo de triplici descensu et ascensu. Nemo ascendit in celum . . . Dominus et saluator noster ihesus cristus uolens nos docere . . . ceteris instruendis.

9. f. 282ᵛ Item sermo de triplici ascensu et descensu. Ascensiones disposui in corde meo. Homo in peccatum corruens . . . in corde meo disposui.

10. f. 283ᵛ Sermo in decollatione sancti Iohannis baptiste. Inter natos mulierum . . . Magnum preconium iohannis karissimi . . . percipiendam:' quam nobis . . . amen.

11. f. 285 In natali beatorum apostolorum Petri et Pauli. Isti sunt due oliue. etc. De beatorum petri et pauli apostolorum triumphali gloria . . . et mortis amaritudine.

12. f. 285ᵛ Sermo de triplici mortificatione. In presenti loquitur spiritus sanctus ad eos . . . Laudat in eis rigorem mortificationis . . . possidetur premium:' quod nobis . . . amen.

13. f. 286ᵛ Sermo de uerbis psalmi. Audiam quid loquatur in me dominus. Dauid regum summus et prophetarum eximius . . . sicuti est ihesus cristus dominus noster:' qui . . . amen.

14. f. 287ᵛ Sermo de sex alis cherubin. Quis dabit michi pennas . . . Ecce alius petrus qui periclitatur in mari . . . potare dignetur qui . . . amen.

15. f. 288v Sermo exortatorius ad monachos. Exi de terra tua et de cognatione tua . . . Quia fratres scientibus enim legem dei loquimur . . . in melle diuinitatis.

16. f. 290 De triplici fuga. scilicet quid. quomodo. et quando fugere debeamus. Qui habitatis in terra austri . . . Quare fratres scriptura sacra tantopere fugam nobis persuadet . . . filii ad exultationem.

The heading is printed by J. Leclercq in *Mediaeval Studies*, xxii (1960), 216, 218–26. Cf. *SBO* iv. 146. 1. *SBO* vi. 9–20. 5. De div. 55, 56. 7. Drogo, Meditatio in Passionem et Resurrectionem Domini. Cf. *Recueil*, i. 105. 8. De div. 60. 9, 13, 14. In B.L., Royal 7 F. x, ff. 164v, 166v, 165v.

Arts. 5–7 are numbered xvii–xix in continuation of art. 4: 5 and 6 were together in R. 20 at Syon Abbey (*Catalogue of the library of Syon monastery*, ed. M. Bateson, 1898, p. 173).

5. ff. 291–294v Stephanus. Sermo in die pasche de tribus mulieribus. Maria magdalene et maria iacobi . . . Proxima ebdomada sicut grauis suppliciis . . . participes nos faciat ihesus cristus dominus noster: qui . . . amen.

6. ff. 294v–299v Incipit tractatus domini eylredi abbatis Rieuallensis de decem honoribus Sancti Iohannis baptiste. Hodie dilectissimi dies illuxit insignis . . . demonstrat. dominum ihesum cristum: qui . . . amen.

In B.L., Royal 3 B. x, f. 116v and 8 E. xiii, f. 215v.

7. ff. 299v–300 Sermo in assumptione beate marie uirginis. In illo tempore: Intrauit ihesus . . . Omelia lectionis eiusdem beati Anselmi archiepiscopi. Quid ad gloriosam uirginem . . . filium eius: qui est benedictus in secula amen.

PL clviii. 644–9 (Anselm, Homelia 9). A leaf missing after f. 299. ff. 300v–301v blank.

ff. 301. 395 × 283 mm. Written space 290 × 193 mm. 2 cols. 40 lines. The first line of writing above the top ruled line. Throughout, twelve ruled lines, 1, 2, 4, 5, 18, 19, 21, 22, 36, 37, 39, 40, are continued across the margins. Collation: 1^8 wants 4 $2\text{–}20^8$ 21^8 wants 8, probably blank, after f. 166 $22\text{–}24^8$ 25^8 wants 4, 5 after f. 193 26^{10} 27^{10} wants 5, 6 after f. 210 $28\text{–}37^8$ 38^8 wants 6 after f. 299: a quire is missing after f. 214 (27^8). Quires 1–20 numbered at the end, s. xv ex. Initials: (i) ff. 1, 117v, 167, red and blue with ornament of both colours; (ii) 3-line, red or blue with ornament of the other colour; (iii) 1-line, red or blue. Binding of wooden boards covered with brown leather, s. xv: five bands: two clasps missing. Secundo folio *homines uniuersos*.

Written in England. Scribbled names, 'Jhon Clarkson' and 'Jhon Perius' on the pastedown at the beginning, s. xvi, and 'Timothy Barney', f. 301, s. xvii. A label inside the cover: 'In usum / Reg. Prof. Theol. Oxon. / Dono Dedit / Ricardus Allestree S.T.P.R. / Jan. 18. 1680'.

L. 4. 1. *Clement of Lanthony (in English)* s. xiv/xv

1. Preliminaries to art. 2: (*a*) ff. 1–7v Here bigynneþ a kalender of þe gospels þt ben rad in chirche. Firste sonday in aduent ix part vio capo a Whanne þei hadden neiȝed . . . ; (*b*) ff. 9–10v Seynt austyn seiþ in þe seconde boke of cristen doctrine . . . bi þat we heringe as drinking ben more holpyn. (*c*) f. 11 Clement a prest of

þe chirche of lantony gadride . . . of þe bible. (*d*) ff. 11v–16 Here begynneþ þe chapiters of þe first part . . .

(*a*). Divided into temporal, 'reule of þe sanctorum' and 'þe commemoraciouns'. No common of saints. References to art. 2 are by part and chapter numbers and letter marks. f. 8rv blank. (*b*). Forshall and Madden, i. 44–9. (*d*). Tables of chapters of the twelve parts. ff. 8rv, 16v blank.

2. ff. 17–126 Here bigynneþ þe first part. capitulum 1 in 1o capitulo of ioon. In þe bigynnynge *eiþer first of alle þingis* was goddis sone . . . shulden be wrytyn. Here endiþ oon of foure þat is book of alle þe four gospelers gadrid shortli into o storye bi Clement of lantony.

Cf. Wells, *Manual*, p. 407. Running titles in red, red chapter numbers, and red letters in the margins subdividing chapters permit ready use of art. 1*a*. Only letters useful in the table are entered: thus there are none against 5: 16 and only *a, c, e* against 6: 1. One leaf missing. f. 126v blank. Richard James, Sir Robert Cotton's librarian, †1638, wrote a note about Clement on f. iii.

ff. iii + 126 + ii. f. iii is a medieval flyleaf. 180 × 130 mm. Written space 125 × 80 mm and (ff. 9–16) 150 × 95 mm. 28 long lines and (ff. 9–16) 32–4 long lines. Collation: 1^6 + 2 leaves after 6 $2\text{–}4^8$ 5^8 wants 1 before f. 33 $6\text{–}15^8$ 16^8 wants 8, blank. Initials: (i) blue and red, with red and violet ornament; (ii) 3-line, blue with red ornament. Capital letters in the ink of the text marked with red. Secundo folio *Tewisday* (f. 2), *first is* (f. 10), *ben fourteen* (f. 18).

Written in England. Allestree label as in F. 1. 1.

M. 1. 10. *Augustinus* s. xii med.

Four works of St Augustine. Not listed by Römer. The table of contents, f. iiiv, s. xv, is headed 'Augustinus'. Neat corrections by the main hand, for example on f. 123, where two extra lines, omitted in error, have been fitted in.

1. ff. 1–70 Incipit Proemium Sancti Augustini De Libro Retractationum. In Libro De Doctrina Cristiana. Libros de doctrina cristiana . . . de phi'l'osophia scripsit. Hoc opus sic incipit. Incipit Prologus Eiusdem De Doctrina Cristiana. Sunt precepta quedam . . . (f. 3) oççurrit exordium. Aurelii Augustini Egregii Doctoris Liber Primus Incipit De Doctrina Cristiana. Due sunt res . . . disserui. adiuuante domino . . . amen. Explicit Liber Sancti Augustini De Doctrina Cristiana.

PL xxxiv. 19–121. Preceded by the relevant passage from the Retractationes.

2. ff. 70v–103. Incipit Liber Sancti Augustini De Uera Religione. Cum omnis uite bone . . . beate uiuimus: unum deum ex quo omnia . . . amen. Explicit Liber Sancti Augustini De Uera Religione.

PL xxxiv. 121–72. Written without break.

3. ff. 103^{v}–115 Incipit Liber Sancti Augustini Episcopi De Cura Pro mortuis Agenda Ad Paulinum Episcopum. Diu sanctitate tue coepiscope uenerande . . . responsio defuisset. Explicit Liber Ad Paulinum.

PL xl. 591–610.

4. ff. 115^{v}–126 Aurelii Augustini De Decem Cordis Sermo Incipit. Dominus et deus noster misericors et miserator . . . ibi inueniamus amen. Explicit Sermo Sancti Augustini De Decem Cordis.

PL xxxviii. 75–91 (Sermo 9).

ff. iii + 126 + iii. f. iii is a medieval flyleaf. 256 × 178 mm. Written space *c.* 190 × 123 mm. 28 long lines. Ruling with pencil. Collation: $1–15^{8}$ 16^{8} wants 7, 8: 6 (f. 126) is a fragment. Quires numbered at the end. A good round hand. Initials: (i) green, blue, or red, patterned in white, with ornament in two or three of these colours; (ii, iii) in art. 1 only, 2-line and 1-line, green, blue, or red, usually without ornament. Capital letters in the ink of the text filled with pale yellow. Binding of s. xviii. Secundo folio *et sine*.

Written in England. Belonged to 'Reginaldus Metcalfus' who notes on f. iii^{v} and at the end that he read the whole book between 16 April and 7 July 1598. An Allestree label as in F. 1. 1 is at each end.

OXFORD. BLACKFRIARS

1. *Graduale* s. xiii^{2}

1. ff. 1–2 Ad introtus (*sic*). De primo Tono . . .

Eight settings of Gloria patri et filio.

2. f. 2^{rv} Ad aspersionem aque benedicte extra tempus paschale. A'. Asperges me . . . Tempore paschali. A'. Vidi aquam . . .

Forms for use at Easter and at other times.

3. ff. 3–135^{v} Temporal from Advent to the 23rd Sunday after Trinity.

Litany, ff. 86–89^{v}: f. 86^{v} ends in apostles 'Sancte mathia' and f. 87 begins in virgins 'Sancta felicitas'. Kyrie eleyson and Sanctus, ff. 89^{v}–90^{v}. The Easter office begins on f. 90^{v}. The office for the first Sunday after Trinity, 'Domine in tua misericordia . . .', is marked in a post-medieval hand, 'hoc officium Non dicitur' (f. 115^{v}). No Corpus Christi: see art. 5.

4. ff. 135^{v}–136^{v} In die consecrationis et in aniuersario (*sic*) dedicationis ecclesie et per oct*auas*.

5 (added early on quire 13). ff. 137–40 In festo corporis cristi ad introtum misse . . .

f. 140^{v} was left blank. The original text has been erased on f. 137, but from 'Cibauit' to 'hominum (*sic*) in te' was rewritten, s. xv/xvi.

6. ff. 141–171v In uigilia Sancti andree apostoli . . .

Sanctoral, Andrew–Katherine. Peter Martyr, f. 152v. 'In festo corone domini', f. 154. Cue for translation of Dominic, f. 155. Dominic, f. 161rv, but only the alleluia verse, Pie pater dominice, is proper. 'In commemorationem (*sic*) omnium defunctorum', f. 168v. The only pre-1500 additions seem to be Martial and Procopius (ff. 155v, 160, s. xv). For later additions see art. 12.

7. ff. 171v–172v, 177–201. Common of saints.

Two leaves missing after f. 172 were supplied later: see art. 12.

8. ff. 201–203v In commemoratione beate uirginis.

9. ff. 203v–205v, 216–223v Kyrie eleyson, Gloria in excelsis deo, Sanctus, Agnus dei, Benedicamus domino, Ite missa est, all in various settings, Aue regina celorum (*RH*, no. 2072: f. 205v), Credo in unum deum (ff. 217–18), and Requiescant in pace (f. 223v).

10. ff. 223v–241v Fourteen sequences: (1) In natale domini et duobus diebus sequentibus et in epyphania et in purificatione. Letabundus exultet . . . ; (2) Victime paschali . . . (Easter); (3) Omnes gentes plaudite . . . (Ascension); (4) Sancti spiritus assit nobis gratia . . . (Pentecost); (5) Ueni sancte spiritus et emitte . . . (the two days after Pentecost); (6) Profitentes unitatem . . . (Trinity); (7) Rex salomon fecit templum . . . (consecration and anniversary of dedication of church); (8) Aue maria gratia plena . . . (Annunciation of B.V.M.); (9) Adest dies celebris quo lumen . . . (Peter Martyr); (10) In utroque festo beati Dominici. In celesti ierarchia . . . ; (11) Salue mater saluatoris uas . . . (Assumption of B.V.M.); (12) De profundis tenebrarum . . . (Augustine); (13) Natiuitas marie uirginis . . . (Nativity of B.V.M.); (14) Superne matris gaudia representat . . . (All Saints).

(1–14). *RH*, nos. 10012, 21505, 14047, 18557, 21242, 15555, 17511, 1879, 343, 8547, 18051, 4245, 11881, 19822.

11. ff. 241v–247v A now imperfect collection of sequences for use in commemorations of B.V.M. (cf. art. 13*a*): Verbum bonum et suaue . . . ; Letabundus . . . (cue only); Uirgini Marie laudes . . . ; Hodierne lux diei . . . ; Aue mundi spes maria . . . ; Iubilemus in hac die quam regine . . . complet deus (*ends imperfectly in stanza 9, f. 245v*): *Tibi cordis in altari . . . , beginning imperfectly on f. 246 in stanza 2* inepta . . . ; Stella maris o Maria . . . spei mater (*ends imperfectly in stanza 3, f. 246v*); *Saluatoris mater pia . . . , beginning imperfectly on f. 247v in stanza 2* benigna operum suffragio . . . Reis ergo fac regina apud regem (*ends imperfectly in stanza 9*).

RH, nos. 21343, 10012, 21656, 7945, 1974, 9813, 20459, 19456, 17821. *AH* liv, nos. 218, 5, 21, 219, 217, 284, 279, 283, 280. One leaf is missing after f. 245 and, to judge from the old foliation, six leaves are missing after f. 246: f. 247r is pasted over.

12. Additions of s. xvi, xvii: (*a*) f. 140v Alleluia. Magnificat anima mea Dominum et exultauit spiritus meus in deo salutari meo; (*b*) cues in several hands for more than a dozen saints in the margins of ff. 154–167v to supplement art. 6:

(March) Thomas Aquinas; (April) Vincent (Ferrer); (May) Antoninus (of Florence), Servatius; (June) Antony (of Padua); (Aug.) Transfiguration, Ludowicus confessor; (Oct.) Leodegar, Edward (king and confessor), Calixt, Hilarion: some other names are indistinct or have been cut off by the binder; (*c*) ff. 173–6, the supply to art. 7; (*d*) f. 206 Agnus: de Angeles. Agnus dei. Qui tolis peccata mundi miserere nobis; (*e*) ff. 207–209^{v} Missa Ss. Rosarii. Salve radix sancta salve mundi gloria o Maria . . . ; (*f*) ff. 210–15, two settings of the Nicene creed, the first beginning imperfectly 'homines et propter nostram', the second marked for 'Duo' and 'Chorus'; (*g*) f. 215^{rv} Sanctus; (*h*) on a paper leaf pasted to f. 247^{r}: Quassi stella Matutina in medio nebulę . . . ; (*i*) on a paper leaf loose at the end: Himno a Completas para qualquiera Fiesta Solemne. Te lucis ante terminum . . .

13. The edges of fourteen leaves have been strengthened with pieces cut from two manuscripts: (*a*) ff. 189, 216^{rv}, 217; (*b*) ff. 145–6, 177, 182, 187–8, 194, 201, 203–5, 216^{v}.

(*a*). Fragments of the sequence Ave virgo gloriosa[1] (*RH*, no. 2205) written in the main hand and taken no doubt from one of the missing leaves of art. 11. The remains include the beginnings of stanzas 7, 11, 12, 14 of the sequence printed in *AH* liv. 417–8 (no. 277). (*b*). Fragments of a handsome noted hymnal of Dominican use, s. xiii^{2}. Beginnings of hymns are: f. 188 [M]agne d[ies letitie] and Adest t[riumphus] (*RH*, nos. 10942, 435: vespers and matins of Peter Martyr); f. 194^{v} Hostis h[erodes] and A patre [unigenitus] (*RH*, nos. 8073, 14: Epiphany); f. 204^{v} Xpiste redemptor omnium ex patre (*RH*, no. 2960: Christmas).

ff. 247, including later insertions. A medieval foliation, top left of versos, now mostly cut off, runs to ccxxxiii on f. 246^{v}: it was repeated and revised after the new leaves had been inserted into quires 16 and 19 and runs to ccli on f. 246^{v} and cclviii on f. 247^{v}. Still later a pagination was entered on rectos, top right, by someone who was not interested in arts. 10, 11, since the last number, 463, is on f. 228. 358 × 255 mm. Written space 272 × 165 mm. 10 long lines and music. Collation (late insertions in italics): $1\text{–}7^{12}$ 8^{12} wants 3 after f. 86 $9\text{–}11^{12}$ 12^{4} + 1 leaf after 4 (f. 136) 13^{4} (ff. 137–40) $14\text{–}15^{12}$ 16^{12} wants 9, 10 after f. 172: *two bifolia of thick parchment, ff. 173–6, inserted as supply leaves* $17\text{–}18^{12}$ 19^{12} (ff. 203–5, 216–24) + *quires of 4 and 6 leaves of thick parchment, ff. 206–9, 210–15, inserted after leaf 3* 20^{12} 21^{12} wants 10, 12 (ff. 237–46) 22 one (f. 247: apparently leaf 6 of the quire). Initials: (i) ff. 3, 90^{v} (Easter), 114^{v} (Trinity), red and blue, with ornament of both colours, some of it saw-pattern; (ii) 1-line, blue or red, with ornament of the other colour. Running title **GRA/DV** in red and blue letters. Binding of wooden boards covered with brown leather, s. xvi: narrow rolls enclose a central corner-pieced panel: a missing central clasp fastened from front to back: ff. 1 and 247 have been pasted down and the front board shows offset from another noted service book: repairs by the Clarendon Press Bindery in 1925.

Written for Dominican use probably in Spain. Writing in a cursive Spanish (?) hand, s. xv (?), f. 136^{v}: see also art. 12. Bought in northern Spain by Charles Stewart Smith, HM consul in Bilbao 1894–1900. Given by his daughter, Jean Smith.

2. *Petrus Lombardus, Sententiae* s. xv med.

1. A very imperfect copy of the Sentences, beginning 'usque a deo (*sic*) paratum' in dist. 16 of bk. 1 and ending 'confusione prolacionis' in dist. 24 of bk. 4: *PL* cxcii. 563/30–902/2.

[1] I owe the identification to Father Osmund Lewry, O.P.

'It (?) xxi sixterni vii *foliorum*' inside the back cover, s. xv, may be a memorandum of the number of leaves: if so 141 are missing. Bk. 2, f. 27; 3, f. 60v; 4, f. 87v. The note 'Hilarius . . . perpessio' (Quaracchi edn., 1916, p. 620) is inset, occupying twenty-eight lines half a column wide in the first column on f. 69. ff. 25–26v, 59–60v, 86–87v contain numbered tables of chapters of bks. 2–4 agreeing with those in the 1916 edition. Links: from bk. 2 to bk. 3 on f. 60v, 'Huius voluminis continencia sub compendio constringitur. Hic enim racionis ordo . . . accedat'; from bk. 3 to bk. 4 on f. 87v, 'Hiis tractatis que ad doctrinam . . . accedamus'. Distinction numbers in red in the margins. Many notes in the main hand in side and lower margins: those on the sides are confined between vertical bounders.

2. The pastedowns and strips lying down the centres of quires are from a twelfth-century copy of Priscian, Institutiones Grammaticae.

A bifolium was used at each end, but that on the back is now mostly lost or remains only as offset on the board. The exposed pages on the front board are from bk. 8 (ed. Hertz, 1855, pp. 402/15–404/22, 428/13–430/9). The bifolium at the end was a sheet of the same quire: it begins at edn., p. 412/12 *doctum* and probably ended at about p. 420/20. The Greek is well written. Written space 163 × 90 mm. 33 long lines.

ff. 118. Paper and (ff. 22–3, 94, 115–16) parchment. Parchment was used for the middle sheet of quire 3 and probably for the outside sheet of all quires, but only three half-sheets remain. 318 × 215 mm. Written space 227 × 135 mm. 2 cols. 48–51 lines. Frame ruling. Collation: 1 five 2^{12} 3^{12} wants 1, 11, 12 (ff. 18–26) 4^{12} wants 1, 12 (ff. 27–36) 5^{12} wants 1, 12 (ff. 37–46) 6^{12} wants 1, 12 (ff. 47–56) 7 five (ff. 57–61) 8^{12} wants 1, 9–12 (ff. 62–8) 9^{12} wants 1, 12 (ff. 69–78) 10^{12} wants 1, 9–12 (ff. 79–85) 11^{12} wants 1–3, 12 (ff. 86–93) 12^{12} wants 12 (ff. 94–104) 13^{12} wants 1 (ff. 105–15) 14 three (ff. 116–18). Set cursiva by one hand (see below): ascenders often not looped; *n* and *u* not well distinguished; black ink. Red initials: (i) beginning books and tables of chapters, 6-line or 5-line; (ii) of chapters, 2-line; (iii) in tables of chapters, 1-line. Medieval binding of wooden boards covered with pigskin bearing a pattern of fillets on each cover: and projecting at head and foot of the spine: bevelled edges: three bands: seven of ten bosses and two of four metal corner-pieces remain: of two strap-and-pin fastenings running from the front cover to the back cover the only remains are the pins, part of one strap and the round pieces of metal placed on the inside of the boards at the points where the straps were tied in: a chain of three links is attached to the upper edge of the back cover: a title label on the upper part of the front cover is illegible.[1]

Written in Germany by the same hand as Bodleian, Lat. th. c. 34, St Thomas on the 2nd book of Sentences, which belonged to Johann von Helb, parish priest of Ebern, near Bamberg, 1427–59 (or later) and was no doubt given by him to the library he founded at Ebern in 1463.[2] The present manuscript does not bear Helb's name, but is likely to be, like Lat. th. c. 34, one of the books which he 'hat thuen Schreiben': cf. S. Krämer, 'Neue Nachrichten über die ehemalige Pfarrbibliothek von Ebern', *Mainfränkisches Jahrbuch für Geschichte und Kunst*, xxviii (1976), 36–47; also the catalogue description of Leiden, d'Ablaing 10 (P. C. Boeren, *Catalogue des manuscrits des collections d'Ablaing et Meijers*, 1970, p. 35). 'Poss. Ebern. XIV' inside the cover, s. xviii/xix (cf. above Leeds, Univ. Libr., Brotherton Collection 101). Listed as no. XIV when at Ebern in 1833–4 by J. W. Rost, whose brief description is printed by E. G. Krenig, 'Nachrichten zur ehemaligen Pfarrbibliothek in Ebern', *Mainfränkisches Jahrbuch*, xii (1960), 299. Sold with 55 other volumes in 1878. 'XXXI 1678' and the price cypher 'MRSJ' inside the cover are marks of Ludwig Rosenthal of Munich: his catalogue 31, *c.*1884, no. 1678, at 130 marks (cf. Krämer, pp. 38, 40, 46).[3]

[1] The binding of Bodleian, Lat. th. c. 34 (see below) has all the features listed here, but its fillets are closer together, its bosses smaller, and its round pieces of metal on the inside of the back board larger.

[2] Cf. *Manuscripts at Oxford*, p. 135.

[3] The price suggests that the manuscript was more complete then than it is now.

'972' on a round label inside the back cover, top right. Labels on the spine are illegible, but one of them, s. xix, is like a fragmentary label on Lat. th. c. 34.

OXFORD. BRASENOSE COLLEGE

24. *Averroes, Colliget; etc.* s. xiv[1]

1. ff. 2–82^v Incipit colligeth in medicina editus in arabico a mahamet auentost qui a latinis dicitur aueroys. Quanto uentillata fuit super me ... existit tunc illud (*ends imperfectly*).

Thorndike and Kibre. Printed often: *GKW* 3103. The last words here are in edn. 1552, f. 72ra/56 (bk. 7, sect. 10). The end of bk. 4 and beginning of bk. 5 are in a gap (12 leaves ?) after f. 47 which ends at edn., f. 39ra/35: f. 48 begins at edn., f. 46vb/67.

2. ff. 83–95^v Post tractatum de creatore et anima mundi et demonibus ... illius actiones non sint.

PL clxxii. 48/35–98/4 (William of Conches, Philosophia mundi, i. 20–iv. 31). Particula 2, f. 85^v: 3, f. 89^v; 4, f. 92. Each is preceded by an unnumbered table of chapters. Within parts the writing is continuous. Recipes were added in s. xv in the space left blank on f. 95^v.

ff. 97, foliated 1–35, 35*, 36–40, 40*, 41–95. 242 × 170 mm. Written space 200 × 128 mm. 2 cols. 49–51 lines. Collation: $1\text{–}7^{12}$ 8^{12} + 1 leaf after 10 (f. 93). Art. 1 in anglicana, usually formata, but sometimes current. Art. 2 in textura. Initials of art. 1: (i) ff. 1, 68^v (bk. 6), red and blue with red and violet ornament; (ii, iii) 2-line, red with violet ornament or blue with red ornament, those of type (ii) patterned in white. Initials of art. 2 not filled in. Bound in front of a printed book, J. de Tornamira, *Clarificatorium super nono Almansoris cum textu ipsius Rasis*, Lyon 1490. The binding is Cambridge work by the 'Unicorn Binder' (Walter Hatley) and is no. ix in Oldham's list in *EBSB*, p. 17: stamps 50 and 74 form a border containing lozenges in which are stamps 58 and 69 and stamp 63 is on the edges outside the border. The pastedowns are two leaves, one numbered '79', of a manuscript of grammatical questions, s. xiii[2] in current anglicana. The recto of '79' begins 'Disputacio Magistri Guidonis questio prima. An uerbum substancialiter secundum operacionem intelligitur. Quod non quia ...' On the verso are two questions 'An verbum ...', 'in aula', the first complete.

Written in England. A chain-mark at the head of the front cover.

91. *Genealogia regum anglorum* s. xv[1]

Considerans cronicarum prolixitatem ... phaleratus dicior hec ille.

A genealogical chronicle in roll form to show the descent of Henry VI from Adam. It seems to be a blend of the roll chronicle attributed to Roger Albon, beginning like it with the short preface 'Considerans ... vsque ad henricum sextum originaliter finem perduxi' (cf. *Lyell Cat.*, p. 84, and below, Magdalen College, lat. 248), and the roll chronicle noticed in *MMBL* ii. 229: as there the last piece of consecutive text is on the newly quiet character of the Welsh in the time of Henry V. 'Henricus Quintus' is the last name in a roundel: below it a large pencilled 'H' surmounted by a crown is just visible. Regnal years are given as a rule from Hengist to Richard II. Roundels in the left margin contain the names of archbishops of

Canterbury from Augustine to 'Henricus Chicheley' (1414–43). The paragraph 'Adam in agro damasceno . . .' is on a level with 'Considerans . . .'. The four paragraphs below 'Considerans . . .' do not occur in the Magdalen manuscript: (1) 'Dicit autem Iosephus . . .', on the great age of the patriarchs; (2–4) on Adam, 'Adam vero cognouit . . .', 'Cognouit quoque adam . . .', and 'Legitur adam habuisse xxx filios . . .'.

A roll of eight membranes measuring *c.*6040 × 285 mm. Written in a secretary hand (long-tailed *r* common). The roundel for Adam and Eve at the beginning, 60 mm in diameter, is blank, and so are smaller roundels for Noah, Christ, and Brutus. The only filled roundel is for Lucius, a pencil sketch of the head and shoulders of a king. Above the Adam and Eve roundel is a faint drawing of B.V.M., Child, and a kneeling man with scroll inscribed 'Plasmator mundi Baten miserere Iohanni'. Initials: (i) 9-line blue *C* of *Considerans* with red ornament; (ii) beginning ten paragraphs near the head of the roll, 2-line, blue with red ornament; (iii) 1-line, blue or red. The main line of descent is a broad red line: thinner red, green, or brown lines are used for side branches and the archbishops.

Written in England, probably for John Baten: for one of this name at the right date see Emden, *BRUO*, p. 132. 'George Powlet Plita (?)' is written in red ink in a legal hand, s. xvi, on the dorse of membrane 7.

OXFORD. CAMPION HALL

1. *Prayers at mass and St John 1: 1–14 (in German: fragm.)* s. xvi[1]

(*a*) f. 1rv (*begins imperfectly*) gnad vnd andacht verlihen hast. das ich dein fronleichnam und plut deins suns vnsers herren iesu christi . . . gesetzt werden. Amen. (*b*) ff. 1v–2v Das gebet sprich zu der lesten collect vor dez segen. O herr hailiger vatter der du den leib den du deinem sun . . . vnd des hailigen gaistes. Amen. (*c*) ff. 2v–3v Dar nach soltu den segen mit andacht von dem priester entpfahen. vnd begern den segern des vaters. vnd sprich. Kaiserliche kron aller seligen. iesu christe. gib mir taglichen den väterlichen segen. das durch . . . zu welt on ende. A. (*d*) ff. 3v–4 Empfach den segen des priesters kniend mit genaigtem haubt. Vnd sprich mit andacht. O barmhertziger ewiger got mein herr vnd mein schöpffer. Mein sel . . . vnd geopffert werd. Amen. (*e*) ff. 4v–5 Ewangelium Iohannis. Nach dem segen sprich das hoch ewangeli. vnd wann du komst. Et verbum caro factum est. Vnd das wort ist flaisch worden etc . . . vor tod sinden. etc. (*f*) ff. 6–8 Der an+fang des hai+ligen ewan+gelii sancti Iohannis. Gloria tibi domine. In dem anfang war das wort . . . Vol gnaden vnd warhait. Got sey gedancket dises hailigen euangelii. der dar durch vns wölle vergeben vnser sind. vnd vns behietten vor allem ybel. Amen.

(*e*) is in red. For ff. 5v, 8v see below.

ff. 8. 147 × 113 mm. Written space 92 × 64 mm. 15 long lines. One quire of 8 leaves. Written in formal hybrida (footed *m, n*). Full-page framed pictures on ff. 5v (St John (?) sitting in a wood sees a vision of B.V.M. and Child in glory) and 8v (Christ instructs his disciples in a church: the catchword in red *Pater* on f. 8v shows that the Lord's Prayer was the next item). Initials: (i) f. 6, 8-line blue *I* with red ornament on a green ground patterned in gold paint; (ii) 3-line, gold or black on patterned grounds of blue, red, or green. No binding.

From Southern Germany (Nuremberg ?).[1] According to the Donation Book, 'Illuminated portion of German manuscript, found on a German soldier in the war of 1914–18 . . . Presented by B. Bisgood, Esq.'.

2. *Horae* s. xv/xvi

1. ff. 1–3v Sequentiae of Gospels. 'Protector in te sperancium . . .' follows John.

2. ff. 3v–5v Oracio deuotissima ad beatam mariam. Obsecro . . . Masculine forms.

3. ff. 5v–6v Le benoist doulx ihesucrist vne foys entres les autres apparut . . .

The Five Oes of St Gregory here beginning Domine, not O domine. The heading conveys an indulgence of 14,000 years.

4. ff. 6v–7v Oracio deuotissimam (*sic*) ad beatam mariam. O intemerata . . . orbis terrarum. Inclina . . . Masculine forms.

5. ff. 8–32v Hours of B.V.M. of the use of (Rome), ending imperfectly in vespers. A memoria of All Saints after each hour.

6. ff. 33–42 Penitential psalms and (f. 38v) litany.

Nine pontiffs, confessors, and doctors: . . . (8,9) ludouice iuliane. Four monks and hermits: benedicte francisce antoni dominice. Eight virgins: . . . (7, 8) clara elizabeth. The prayers after Deus cui are Exaudi, Ineffabilem, Deus a quo, Ure igne, Actiones nostras, Fidelium. f. 42v blank.

7. ff. 43–55v Office of the dead, ending imperfectly.

ff. 55. 192 × 125 mm. Written space 120 × 67 mm. 28 long lines. Collation: $1–6^8$ 7^8 wants 8. Catchwords written vertically. *Lettre bâtarde*. Twelve 19–22-line pictures, seven in art. 5 (two shepherds and a woman at terce: slaughter of Innocents at vespers: compline missing) and one before each of arts. 1, 2 (angels crown B.V.M.), 3, 6 (David and Bathsheba), 7 (three dead and three living). Four smaller pictures, three in art. 1 and one before art. 4. Initials: (i) 4-line, blue patterned in or shaded to white on grounds of gold paint and red, the gold decorated with flowers; (ii) 2-line, gold paint on red grounds; (iii) 1-line, either as (ii) or on blue grounds. Line fillers blue or red patterned in gold paint. Compartmented borders, continuous on pages with larger pictures and on three sides of smaller pictures; floral, except that the parts of the borders flanking the larger pictures are made up of architectural patterns in penwork on gold paint which include small pictures: at art. 1, John in the cauldron; at art. 2, angels; at art. 5: (i) angels and saints; (ii) Joseph; (iii) shepherd and saints; (iv) shepherd; (v) kings riding; (vi) flight into Egypt; at art. 6, destroying angel; at art. 7, a man holding a stick (?), arm raised. Only the front cover of the binding remains, pasteboard covered with brown leather bearing an acorn panel which is much worn at the foot, but is probably identical with Oldham's panel AC 3, s. xvi. Secundo folio *misericordiam*.

Written in France. The binding appears to be English.

[1] Information from Mrs Elżbieta Temple.

3. *Horae* s. xv med.

A normal abroad-for-the-English-market type of Sarum hours, like Dulwich College 25 and Edinburgh University 303 (*MMBL* i. 46, ii. 592).

1. ff. 1–5^v Calendar in red and black, lacking January and February.

The Visitation of B.V.M. is included. Names of English saints are misspelt: Dinistani, Zwichini, Kenelini. The word 'pape' and entries of St Thomas of Canterbury not damaged.

2. ff. 6–10^v Oracio deuota ad ihesum xpristum. O domine ihesu xpriste eterna dulcedo . . .

The Fifteen Oes of St Bridget.

3. ff. 11^{rv} Memoria de sancta trinitate. Domine deus omnipotens . . . da michi famulo tuo N. victoriam . . . Oratio. Libera me domine . . . (*ends imperfectly*).

4. ff. 12–20 Memoriae of nine saints, John Baptist–Barbara, one to a leaf, as in Dulwich College 25 and in the same order, except that Christopher precedes Thomas of Canterbury, and with the same antiphons. The tenth saint there, Margaret, is missing here.

5. ff. 21–46^v Incipiunt hore beate marie virginis secundum usum sarum.

Single leaves missing where lauds, vespers, and compline begin. The memoriae after lauds are the same and in the same order as in Dulwich College 25. Hours of the Cross are worked in.

6. (*a*) ff. 46^v–47^v Ad salutandum virginem mariam. Salue regina . . . (*b*) ff. 47^v–51 Has videas laudes . . .

(*a*, *b*) as Dulwich 25, art. 6.

7. ff. 51–52^v Oratio de sancta maria. O intemerata . . . orbis terrarum inclina . . . Masculine forms.

8. ff. 52^v–54 Alia oratio ad virginem mariam. Obsecro te . . . Masculine forms.

9. ff. 54^v–56^v Quicumque hec septem gaudia . . . Uirgo templum trinitatis . . .

The Seven Joys of B.V.M.: *RH*, no. 21899. The heading conveys an indulgence of 100 days 'a domino papa clemente qui hec predicta (*sic*) gaudia proprio stilo composuit'.

10. ff. 57–59^v Ad ymaginem domini nostri ihesu xpristi. Omnibus consideratis . . . (f. 59^v) Oratio. Omnipotens sempiterne deus qui vnigenitum . . .

11. ff. 59^v–61^v Incipit oratio uenerabilis bede presbiteri de qua fertur quod . . . preparatam. Oratio septem uerborum domini nostri ihesu cristi. Domine ihesu criste . . . Oratio. Precor te piissime . . .

12. ff. 61v–63 Saluationes (*sic*) ad sacrosanctum sacramentum altaris.

Six prayers, (*a–f*), as Dulwich College 25, art. 14. The heading of (*f*) begins here 'Cuilibet dicenti' and ascribes the indulgence to Pope Boniface VI. f. 63v blank.

13. ff. 64–75v Penitential psalms and (f. 70v) litany.

Twelve confessors: ... (11, 12) suuichine vrine. Thirteen virgins: (1) anna ... (11–13) editha affra elizabeth. The prayers after Deus cui are Omnipotens sempiterne deus qui facis, Deus qui caritatis, Ineffabilem, Fidelium, Pietate.

14. ff. 76–92v Office of the dead.

15. ff. 93–101v Incipiunt commendationes animarum. Ends imperfectly.

16. ff. 102–105v Incipit psalterium de passione domini. Deus deus meus ...

17. ff. 106–114v Beatus uero iheronimus in hoc modo disposuit ... regnum eternum. Amen. Oratio. Suscipere digneris ... (f. 107) Incipit psalterium beati iheronimi. Uerba mea auribus ... (f. 114v) Oratio. Omnipotens sempiterne deus clemenciam tuam ...

ff. i + 114 + i. An old foliation 1–141 (s. xvi ?) took account of 26 or 27 missing leaves. 222 × 157 mm. Written space 125 × 83 mm. 22 long lines. Collation: 1^6 wants 1 2^8 + 1 now missing leaf after f. 11 3^4 (ff. 14–17) 4^4 wants 4 after f. 20 5^8 wants 6 after f. 25 $6–7^8$ 8^8 wants 1 before f. 44 and 3 after f. 44 9^8 10^6 (ff. 58–63) $11–16^8$ 17^4 wants 4, blank, after f. 114, together once with some 25 singleton picture pages, all of which have been removed.[1] Four 16-line pictures in art. 5, Annunciation at matins, manger at prime, kings at sext, Presentation at none: (the picture at terce has been cut out of f. 28 and the pictures at lauds, vespers, and compline removed, no doubt). Initials: (i) 7-line, red or blue patterned in white on grounds of gold or colour, historiated: eight in art. 5, the same eight as are provided with small pictures in Edinburgh, U.L. 303 (*MMBL* ii. 594); ten in art. 10 (in Edinburgh 303 there are nine small pictures and an historiated initial); one beginning art. 6 (B.V.M. in glory); one beginning art. 7 (Pietà); one beginning art. 9 (B.V.M. on the steps of the Temple); (ii) 5-line or 6-line, blue or red patterned in white on grounds of the other colour and gold, the gold decorated; (iii) 3-line, gold on grounds of red and blue patterned in white, with short sprays into the margin; (iv) 1-line, blue with red ornament or gold with violet ornament. Framed floral borders, continuous on picture pages and on recto sides which once faced now missing picture pages, and on three sides of pages with historiated initials: some outer borders have been cut off (ff. 11–15, 19, 22). Line fillers in blue and red, with gold blobs between the colours. Capital letters in the ink of the text filled with pale yellow. Binding of s. xvi[1], rebacked: wooden boards covered with brown leather: four repetitions of a panel, *c.*80 × 55 mm, on each cover divided vertically by a ragged-staff strip and horizontally by a fleur-de-lis strip: the 'flemish animals' on the front cover are surrounded by an inscription 'Ora pro nobis sancta / dei genitrix ut / digni efficiamur promis/sione xpristi' (cf. Weale, no. 314): the back panel has small beasts in a floral scroll and a narrow ragged-staff strip: five bands: central clasp missing.

Written in the Low Countries for England. 'Alex*ande*r Murray', f. 6v, s. xvii (?). 'Frank Brangwyn' (†1956): his gift to Campion Hall.

[1] The old foliation and comparison with Edinburgh, U.L. 303 suggest that there were nine or ten pictures in art. 4, a passion series in art. 5, and one picture before each of arts. 2, 3, 13–17.

4. *Apollinaris Offredus, Cremonensis; P. Mantuanus* 1442 (?), s. xv med.

Art . 2 is a complete copy and arts. 1 and 3 are incomplete copies of works of Offredus.

1. ff. 1–14^{v} Omnis doctrina et omnis disciplina . . . Pro introductione expositionis huius libri posteriorum sub breuitate videnda sunt quedam. videlicet primo. que fuerit causa . . . plures adducuntur raciones stat vnam (*ends abruptly*).

Commentary on the Posterior Analytics of Aristotle. Printed in 1493 and later (Goff. O. 56–7). The last words are in edn. Cremona 1581, p. 49C. Lohr, p. 367. Marginalia include (f. 2) 'Hoc est contra Marsilium in 3^{a} questione' and (f. 8) 'Contra paulum venetum'. ff. 15–20^{v} blank.

2. ff. 21–84 'Apollenaris Cremonensis in Librum Posteriorum Ar' Questiones'. Primo queritur vtrum demo(n)stratio . . . inuicem repugnant. Et sic est finis vltime huius questionis posteriorum ad laudem dei patris et filii et spiritus sancti et sanctarum Marie Magdalene Katerine et Polonie (at)que totius curie celestis triumphantis Amen finitum fuit die vi^{o} mensis Ianuarii m^{o} (c)ccc^{o} xlii Deo gratias Amen. Hoc opus scriptum fuit per me et cetera Spectabili et subtili artium et medicine doctori domino magistro [. . .]to[. . .]arsa[. . . .] quem deus altissimus conseruet prosperitate longeua sospitate continua letitia et honore per longissima tempora et semper sit in g[. . . . .].

Printed with art. 1. As edn. 1581, pp. 173–343. Lohr, p. 368. The first six of the forty-seven questions are dated at the end: (1) Et sic sit finis questionis ad laudem dei omnipotentis ac beate mathyie apostolli die 28 februarii 1435; (2) Et sic est . . . 20° aprilis 1435. Ad laudem dei omnipotentis et sacratissime resurreccionis yhesu filii dei que occurrit die 17 eiusdem Aprilis amen; (3) Et sic est . . . ad laudem . . . ac beatorum dyonisii Episcopi et urbani pape die 25 maii 1435; (4) Et sic est . . . die 21 Iullii 1434. Ad laudem . . . et beate braxedis virginis amen; (5) Et sic est . . . die 2° Iullii 1435. Ad laudem . . . ac beate simeonis monaci amen; (6) Et sic est . . . 3^{a} augusti 1435. Ad laudem . . . et beati Gaudentii episcopi.

In the colophon on f. 84 all from *Hoc opus* is crossed out and part of it is erased.

3. ff. 84^{v}–90 'Appolinaris Cremonensis. Suppositionum tractatus Incipit fœliciter'. Queritur primo vtrum diffinitio suppositionis sit bona qua communiter dicitur quod suppositio est acceptio termini . . . principaliter dependit. Dubitacio (*ends abruptly*).

Five questions. A note in the margin, f. 86^{v}, 'Hoc erat in margine libri appollinaris iuxta locum significatum. + A. uide quod per idem ita uidetur dicendum de termino demonstratiuo uocali de quo dubitabas in margine . . .'. The nine lines on f. 90 are in another hand. f. 90^{v} blank.

4. ff. 91–2 [D]icemus naturaliter loquentes primo quod sola forma secundum se . . . quam aliquis illorum acquiret et habebit (*ends abruptly*).

Petrus Mantuanus, De instanti,[1] but less than a seventh of the text is here: the last words are in edn. 1492, sign. H 4ra/12. Thorndike and Kibre. Goff, P. 499, 500. ff. 92^{v}–96^{v} blank: 96^{v} is pasted down.

[1] I owe the identification to Professor Charles Lohr.

ff. ii + 96. Paper. Late medieval foliation. 403 × 285 mm. Written space *c.*275 × 175 mm. 2 cols. 59–61 lines. The horizontal ruling does not project into the margins and is only to be seen within the written space where there is no writing. Collation: $1\text{–}6^{10}$ 7^{10} 10 cancelled 8^{10} 9^{10} 10 cancelled 10^{10} wants 9, 10, blank: 8 pasted down. A strip of parchment as strengthening in the middle of each quire. Arts. 1, 2 are in fere-textura; cursiva forms of *a, f, g, s*. Arts. 3, 4, rather later than the rest, are in current sloping humanistica. Initials: (i) f. 1, 16-line red *O* patterned in white on blue ground patterned in white and historiated: a Cistercian monk stands at a desk on which is an open copy of the Posterior Analytics: a border of leaf scrolls and roundels with the word 'yhesus' in them; (ii) f. 21, 16-line blue *P* in red patterned in white and blue and decorated in colours; (iii) 3-line, red, but the spaces are not filled after f. 56^{v}. Parchment binding, s. xvii (?): 'Appoll / Cremo / in Libr / Poster' on the spine. Watson, *Oxford*, pl. 414 illus. f. 21. Secundo folio *sed sillogismus*.

Written in Italy, art. 2 in 1442, if the date is not taken over from the exemplar.[1] A note in art. 3 suggests that the scribe may have been following the author's autograph. A shield at the foot of f. 1 is empty, except for the letters P.A. and splodges of dark red on a ground of lighter red. Belonged to the Cistercian abbey of Chiaravalle, near Milan: 'Est monasterii carevallis mediolani ad usum n. [for *enim* ?] fratris (?) Bernardi san.', s. xvi in., interlined above the date in the colophon, f. 84. 'N° 102' in an Italian collection, s. xix: the number is on the outside of the front cover and inside it on a piece of paper. 'G. 94' and '290' inside the cover are rather earlier. Item 1382 in an English auction sale (s. xx in. ?).

OXFORD. CHRIST CHURCH

(*See also Allestree Library, above*)

507. *Ovidius, Heroides* s. xiv med.

1. ff. 2–49^{v} Hanc tua penelope . . . Quos uereor paucos non uelit esse michi. D.G.A.

S. G. Owen notes readings of this copy in *Classical Quarterly*, xxxi (1917), 1–15. It is not laid out for marginal scholia or interlinear glosses.

2. ff. 1, 50 (perhaps once the cover of art. 1). Two parts of a document dated in 1363 and endorsed (f. 1^{r}) 'Inuestitura (?) dominarum Mon' noui facta m' thomasinum et gaspereolum fratres de Ruyno' and (f. 50^{r}) 'pro decano M^{o} [. . .] mccclxiii'.

The first thirty-one lines, 'In nomine domini . . .', are on f. 1^{v} and the last sixteen before the subscriptions are on f. 50^{v}. Faded, but probably all legible by ultra-violet light. Ends of lines cut off. A notarial document relating to four pieces of land in Milan (?)—'Mediolani' occurs in lines 9, 16, 23 and M*ediolan*o in an endorsement (see above). The date is in line 1 on f. 1^{v} and the names of the abbess and eight professed nuns 'monasterii suprascripti' follow in lines 2–5. On f. 50^{v} 'dicti Thomasinus et gaspereolus' is in line 2, 'sito in port*a* Vercellina' in line 13, 'Presentibus domino presbitero' in line 14, and 'ecclesie dicti monasterii noui habitan' in parochia dicti mon' noui' in line 15. The subscriptions (50^{v}) are: (1) Ego Egidiolus natus domini Pasini de serono Ciuit' mediolani port*a* Vercell / parroch' sancti protasii in campo public' imperiali auct[. . .]; (2) Ego vpoforus Nat' condam domini Alcherii de guaschis de iuliano (?) ciuitatis mediolani porta [. . .] parroch' [. . .] Egidioli notarii scripsi.

[1] Dr A. de la Mare pointed out to me that what can be read of the name after *magistro* on f. 84 is over erasure of an earlier name.

ff. iii + 48 + iii, foliated i, ii, 1–52. ff. ii (paper), iii, 50, 51 (paper) are medieval endleaves. The paper leaves are damaged and now pasted to modern paper, so that only ii^v and 51^r are visible. 252 × 175 mm. Written space 190 mm high. 36 long lines. Collation of ff. 2–49: 1–6^8. Initials: (i) f. 2, 10-line pink *H*, patterned in white on a gold and green ground, historiated with a three-quarter length figure in red robe and turban, holding a flower: prolongations in blue and red in two margins; (ii) 2-line, red. Binding of red morocco by Zaehnsdorf, s. xix ex. Secundo folio *Scirem*.

Written in northern Italy. The style of decoration is Milanese:[1] cf. art. 1. A shield at the foot of f. 2 is blank. The blank parchment endleaf, f. 50^r, and the two paper leaves were scribbled on by schoolboys, s. xv: (f. 50) Iste liber est mei francisci de remoridis qui pergit a (*sic*) scolas domini [. . . .] taodori de lucino; (f. 50) Iste liber est mei Francisci de remoridis qui pergit at scolas domini magistri taodori de lucino qui est bonus doctor in sua gramatica;[2] (f. 51) Iste ouidius est mei francisci iohannis et donati filiorum antonini de [na]ylate qui pergunt ad scolas domini magistri georgii de erba qui est bonus doctor in sua gramatica et in alliis scienciis; (f. ii^v) Iste liber ouidius est nostrorum videlicet petri Ant[. . .] filiorum domini Iohanis de Nailate pergentium ad scolas [. . .] Bertrami de Lucino qui est bonus doctor in sua gram[atica]; (f. ii^v) Iste ouidius est mei petri de nailate qui pergo ad scolas domini magistri baltrami de lucino qui est bonus doctor in sua gramatica et etiam in aliis sienciis; (f. ii^v) Ego petrus de nailate sum bonus puer quando dormio; (f. ii^v) Ego simon de n[. . .] de superiori [. . . .] xvi mensis februarii mcccclvi; (f. ii^v) Fac nos morales fieri baptista Iohannes . . . (9 lines). Bequeathed by S. G. Owen, Student, in 1948.

508. *Ovidius, Tristia* s. xv med.

Publii Ouidii Nasonis poetę clarissimi Liber primus de tristibus incipit. Parue nec inuideo . . . (f. 86^v) Comprobat acta suo Finis publii ouidii nasonis de tristibus.

Some interlinear glosses and marginal scholia. Eight quotations in the margins of ff. 29^v, 30 against 2. 447–60 are each headed 'Tibullus'. ff. 87–9^v blank.

ff. ii + 89 + ii. Paper. 237 × 160 mm. Written space 150 mm high. 21 long lines. Collation: 1–8^{10} 9^{10} wants 10, blank. Current humanistica. 2-line red initials. Russia binding of s. xviii: gilt corner-pieces and fillets. Secundo folio *Carmina*.

Written in Italy. 'Celotti', f. i^v, and above it '159': his sale, 14 Mar. 1825, lot 217, to Sir Thomas Phillipps. 'Phillipps 960 \`and 2767'', f. ii. Phillipps sale at Sotheby's, 18 June 1898, lot. 887 to Leighton (£1. 1*s*.). Lot 14 in Dobell's catalogue 48 (Oct. 1925) at £10. 10*s*.: the relevant page is fastened to f. i and S. G. Owen noted on it 'Ovid Tristia MS. Bought Oct. 1925 from Dobell'. Bequeathed as 507.

OXFORD. CORPUS CHRISTI COLLEGE

261, ff. 70–115. *Collectanea Clementis Cantuariensis* s. xv^2

Forty-six out of sixty-four leaves of a commonplace book of Clement Canterbury, monk of St Augustine's, Canterbury, *fl.* 1470 (Emden, *BRUO*, p. 350).

[1] Information from Dr A. de la Mare.

[2] A schoolboy scribble by Andrew de cochis in a grammar book sold at Christie's, 17 Nov. 1976, lot. 367, refers to Theodore de Lucino in similar terms; 'qui est bonus doctor in sua gramaticha et sic de aliis sientii[s]'. One Theodore Lucinus Comensis wrote an 'ad discipulos moralium dictorum isagogicus libellus': see *British Museum Catalogue of Printed Books*, s.v. Lucinus, for an edition printed *c.* 1500. Lucino is 4 km south-west of Como.

The date is given as 'sec. xvi ineuntis' in Coxe's catalogue. The true date and the identity of the owner were discovered by Dr B. C. Barker-Benfield: see *Manuscripts at Oxford*, p. 92 and his fuller description, 'Clement Canterbury's Commonplace-book', *The Pelican*, 1978-9, pp. 10-13. The English verses on ff. 89^{v}, 101^{v} are noted in *IMEV*, nos. 2364, 2347, and those on f. 101^{v} are printed from this copy by D. C. Baker in *Medium Aevum*, xxxviii (1969), 293-4.

ff. 46. Paper. Medieval foliation (see below). 157 × 110 mm. Written space *c.*120 × 85 mm. No ruling. Collation: 1^{16} wants 1-3 (ff. 70-81, 97, foliated 4-16) 2^{16} wants 16 (ff. 82-96, foliated 17-31) 3^{16} wants 2, 3, 6-11, 15, 16 (ff. 98-103, foliated 33, [36], [37], 44-6) 4^{16} wants 3, 5, 8, 9 (ff. 104-15, foliated 49, 50, 52, 54, 55, 58, [59-63], 64: the numbers 36, 37, 59-63 have been cut off by a binder. Mixed, but mainly secretary, hand. ff. 74^{v}-75 reproduced in *Manuscripts at Oxford*, fig. 56.

Written in England, at Canterbury, or Oxford where Clement Canterbury was in 1468-9 and 1473. Bound with other pieces in s. xvi^{2}, as the eighth of twelve volumes of collectanea formed by Brian Twyne, 1580-1644, partly out of material collected by his grandfather, John Twyne of Canterbury, †1581.

394. *Missale ad usum Sarisburiense* 1398

1. ff. 1-6^{v} Calendar in blue, red, and black.

Gradings for main feasts. Anne in red. July and December feasts of Thomas of Canterbury erased: also 'pape'. Erased additions read by Sir Edmund Craster with the aid of ultraviolet light are: (15 June) obit of Thomas W[. . . .], 1459; (18 July) 'Dedicacio ecclesie de Lappeworth'; (Nov.) 'Memorandum quod Margareta Assheby uxor Thome Assheby donatoris istius libri obiit die Mercurii prox' ante festum sancti Andree apostoli anno domini millesimo cccc^{o} xviii'.

2. f. 7^{rv} Omnibus dominicis diebus per annum post primam et capitulum . . . Ps. Miserere mei domine secundum magnam mise (*ends imperfectly*).

Holy Water service, ending now at *Sarum Missal*, p. 11/26.

3. ff. 8-90^{v} Temporal from Advent.

The first leaf and a leaf after f. 68 (Wednesday in Holy Week) are missing. 'Ut tibi domine grata . . .' is the secret for the second Sunday after the octave of Epiphany. The word 'Thoma' is lightly crossed out on ff. 21-3; also his office, f. 21^{rv}. 'Legatur' at quire ends, for example, f. 76^{v}.

4. (*a*) ff. 90-2 Oracio sancti Augustini dicenda a sacerdote in missa dum canitur officium . . . Summe sacerdos . . . (*b*) ff. 92-98^{v} Ordinary of mass. (*c*) ff. 98^{v}-102^{v} Noted prefaces of mass. (*d*) f. 102 Ordo trigintalium quod quidam apostolicus . . . cum oracionibus subscriptis. Oracio. Deus qui es nostra redempcio . . . (*e*) ff. 103-7 Canon of mass. (*f*) f. 107^{rv} Cum uero sacerdos exuerit . . . (*g*) ff. 107^{v}-110 Rubric for special occasions, 'Predictus modus et ordo . . .', and psalms and prayers in prostration. (*h*) f. 110^{rv} Settings of Benedicamus domino and Ite missa est. (*i*) f. 110^{v} Domine ihesu criste fili dei uiui qui ex uoluntate patris . . .

(*a*). Pseudo-Augustine. A. Wilmart, *Auteurs spirituels*, pp. 114–24. (*b*). As Newcastle, Univ. Libr. 2, art. 4*a*, q.v. (*d*). Collect, secret, and postcommunion as in *Sarum Missal*, p. 460: cf. art. 13. The heading does not list the ten feasts on which masses are to be said in the usual order, but from the Annunciation of B.V.M. to the Purification of B.V.M. (*e*) looks well thumbed. 'Orate pro animabus Thome Assheby donatoris istius libri ecclesie de Lappeworth et Margar' uxoris eius ac liberorum suorum' has been erased, but not very thoroughly, from the foot of the Te igitur page (f. 103). (*f*). Gratiarum actio post missam. (*g*). The psalms (77, 66, 20) are followed by prayers 'Deus qui admirabili prouidencia . . .' (*Sarum Missal*, p. 209), 'Rege quesumus uiam pacis . . .' (for bishop) and 'Da quesumus . . .' (for king).

5. ff. 111–54 Temporal from Easter.

No Corpus Christi. Single leaves missing after ff. 124, 131.

6. ff. 154–6 Offices at the dedication and within the octave, and for consecration and reconciliation of church.

On f. 155 the end of the postcommunion 'Deus qui ecclesiam tuam' from 'ut ecclesia tua' (*Sarum Missal*, p. 204) is marked 'vacat' and crossed through.

7. f. 156^{rv} Passio domini nostri ihesu cristi secundum iohannem. In illo tempore Apprehendit pilatus . . . testimonium eius . . . Oratio. Deus qui manus tuas . . .

Cf. below, Pembroke College, Oxford, 1, art. 17.

8. ff. 157–209^{v} Sanctoral, Andrew–Katherine.

Anne, f. 185^{v}.

9. ff. 210–222^{v} Common of Saints.

10. ff. 222^{v}–237^{v} Votive masses:[1] (4–6) B.V.M., with heading 'Ordinacio misse quotidiane beate uirginis que dicitur Salue. Pulsato . . .', (1) Holy Trinity; (2) Holy Spirit; (3) Holy Cross; (p. 459) angels; (7) Pro fratribus et sororibus; (11) De pace; (28) Pro serenitate aeris; (27) Ad pluuiam postulandam; (43) In tempore belli; (26) Pro quacumque tribulacione; (15) Pro rege; (16) *Pro rege et regina; (23) Ad inuocandam graciam sancti spiritus; (17) Pro semetipso; (18) *Item pro semetipso . . . non sarum; (34) Ad poscendum donum spiritus sancti; (25) Pro peccatoribus; (31) Pro penitentibus; (33) Pro inspiracione diuine sapiencie; (37) Pro tribulacione cordis; (39) Pro infirmo; (19) Pro salute amici; (20) *Pro amico; (p. 410, footnote) *Pro infirmo; (35) Pro eo qui in uinculis tenetur; (29) Contra mortalitatem hominum; (42) Pro peste animalium; (30) *Pro iter agentibus; (10) *Pro uniuersali ecclesie; (9) *Pro papa (all lightly crossed out); (12, 14) *Pro episcopo (two forms); (13) *Pro prelatis et subditis; (21) *Contra temptaciones carnis; (22) *Contra malas cogitaciones; (24) *Pro peticione lacrimarum; (32) *Contra aereas potestates; (36) *Contra inuasores ecclesie; (38) *Pro nauigantibus; (40) *Pro benefactoribus uel salute uiuorum; (41) *Contra aduersantes; (p. 406, footnote) *Contra paganos; *De incarnacione domini nostri ihesu cristi; *Ad memoriam de sancta katerina margareta et maria magdalena; (8) *Commemoracio generalis de omnibus sanctis.

[1] For the numbers and asterisks and the usual order, slightly different from this, see above, All Souls College 302, art. 9.

11. ff. 237^{v}–243 Sciendum est quod . . . Pro defunctis officium. Requiem eternam . . .

The mass is followed by twenty sets of collect, secret, and postcommunion for special occasions, the first In die sepulture and the last Pro omnibus fidelibus defunctis, all as in Bodleian, Barlow 1, ff. 422^{v}–427. The first seventeen and the last two are in *Sarum Missal*, pp. 434–42 in the order (1, 9, 11, 2, 10, 7, 3, 4, 12, 6, 8, 14, 5, 15–18, 13, 19). No. 18 Pro quibus orare tenemur has collect Concede quesumus, secret Hec munera and postcommunion Deus qui inestimabili.

12. ff. 243–4 Oracio generalis. Four sets of collect, secret, and postcommunion, as *Sarum Missal*, pp. 442–5.

According to notes in the margin the first set is for use on Monday, the second on Tuesday, the third on Wednesday and Friday, and the fourth on Thursday and Saturday. In the collect Pietate the words *dompnum papam* are crossed out.

13. f. 244^{v} Ordo trigintalis quod quidam apostolicus . . . proximiores prime oracioni. Oracio. Deus summa spes . . .

Collect, secret, and postcommunion. The collect begins as Burntisland edn., col. 883*, not as art. 4*d* and *Sarum Missal*: cf. R. W. Pfaff, 'The English devotion of St Gregory's Trental', *Speculum* xlix (1974), 75–90. The heading differs from art. 4*d*, especially at the end, and in listing the feasts in their usual order from Christmas to Nativity of B.V.M. Epiphany is called 'de apparicione', as in Newcastle Univ., 2, art. 12; Oscott 516, art. 9*b*, and the Minehead Missal, art. 18*o*, q.v.: cf. Pfaff, p. 86.

14. ff. 245–50 Office of baptism, beginning imperfectly 'pulsanti ut eternam'. Litany, f. 246^{v}. Noted prefaces, ff. 246^{v}–248^{v}.

Cf. *Manual Sarum*, pp. 27/36–38/12.

15. ff. 250–253^{v} Ordo ad facienda sponsalia . . . in pace.

Manuale Sarum, pp. 49–50. English on f. 250^{rv}.

16. ff. 253^{v}–255 Ordo ad seruitium peregrinorum faciendum.

Manuale Sarum, pp. 60–3.

17. ff. 255–7 Eleven blessings, as in *Manuale Sarum*, pp. 63–70/6.

The last blessing is of the eyes, introduced by 'Benediccio occulorum. Magister Willelmus de montibus matricis ecclesie lincolniensis cancellarius benediccionem oculorum infirmorum (quando) necessitas inducit et deuocio postulancium. et potest fieri in hunc modum'. ff. 257–258^{v} blank.

ff. ii + 258 + ii. 425 × 275 mm. Written space *c*.275 × 172 mm. 2 cols. 39 lines and (ff. 103–7, canon of mass, where the script is larger) 36 lines. Collation: thirty-five quires, all once eights, except 1^{6}, 14 two (ff. 101–2), 28^{4} (ff. 205–8), 35 three (ff. 256–8). Single leaves, 2^{1}, 9^{8}, 17^{7}, 18^{7}, 33^{5}, are missing after ff. 7, 68, 124, 131, 244. A full-page crucifixion picture, with red silk cover, f. 102^{v}: reduced facsimiles by M. Rickert, *Painting in Britain* (2nd edn., 1965), pl. 68 and cf. p. 174, and by G. M. Spriggs in *Journal of the Warburg and Courtauld Institutes*, xxxviii (1974), pl. 29e. Initials: (i) 6-line, patterned blue or pink on grounds of gold and the other colour, the gold decorated: full borders, ff. 7, 103, 157, 210: part borders, f. 154 and to mark principal feasts in arts. 3, 5, 8; (ii) beginning arts. 15, 16, 4-line, gold on grounds of pink and blue patterned in white; (iii) 2-line, blue with red ornament; (iv) 1-line, blue with red ornament and (in sequences) red with violet ornament. Blue and red line fillers in the litany. Capital letters in the ink of the text filled with pale yellow. Offset border ornament from a missing leaf shows on f. 8. Binding of brown calf, s. xvii ex., with a gilt roll and gilt corner-pieces as ornament. Watson, *Oxford*, pl. 239 illus. f. 83v. Secund folio (*ricordiam*): the leaf is missing after f. 7.

Written in England in 1398: 'Memorandum quod xiii kl' Ianuarii videlicet in uigilia sancti thome apostoli anno domini m°. ccc. nonogesimo octauo, istud missale erat plenarie et integre perscriptum [. . .]',[1] f. 257. A gift to the church of Lapworth, Warwickshire, before 1418: 'Orate pro anima Thome Assheby donatoris istius libri ecclesie paroch' de Lappeworth' et pro statibus et animabus Margarete uxoris eius ac liberorum suorum', f. 257v: see also arts. 1, 4*e*. 'Lapworthe', f. 1, s. xvi. 'Liber Col. Corp. Christi Oxon', ex dono Mri Henrici Parei in Art. Mag. et ejusdem Coll. Socii Aprilis 9° 1618': Parry gave MSS. 52, 159 on the same day.

410. *Pseudo-Bonaventura, Meditationes vitae Christi, cum picturis* s. xiv med.

Incipit prologus in meditationes uite domini nostri Ihesu cristi. Innter (*sic*) alia uirtutum et laudum preconia . . . (f. 174) benedictus et laudabilis in secula seculorum amen. Exercitatio desiderii ad patrem per mortis appotitum. Habes igitur expeditis . . . (f. 176v) Ergo iterato utriusque decorem substantie designauit. Hec B'. deo gracias amen. amen. Amen.

Printed often (*GKW* 4739–59). Stegmüller, no. 4311, 1 (J. de Caulibus, O.P.). Glorieux, no. 305*dr*. This copy listed as O12 by C. Fischer in *AFH* xxv (1932), 27. See also M. J. Stallings, *Meditationes de passione Christi olim Sancto Bonauentura attributae*, 1965, pp. 3–14.

ff. iv + 178 + iv. 248 × 158 mm. Written space 152 × 108 mm. 28 long lines. Collation: $1\text{–}11^{12}$ 12^{12} wants 8 after f. 138 $13\text{–}14^{12}$ 15^{12} wants 12, blank. One hundred and fifty-four pictures, one hundred and forty-two by one hand and twelve by another (O. Pächt in *Medium Aevum*, xxxii (1963), 235–6). A common size is *c.*100 × 85 mm. Initials: (i) f. 1, 5-line, red on blue and pink ground, decorated and with prolongations on two sides in colours picked out with gold; also St Francis, St Clare (?), and a defaced shield in the lower margin, each in a separate compartment on a gold ground; (ii) 2-line, blue with red ornament or red with violet ornament. Capital letters in the ink of the text lined with red. Binding of s. xix: gilt edges. Secundo folio *quia ibidem*.

Written in Italy. Given by Robert Trotman Coates, formerly fellow (matriculated in 1781: donor of MS. 387 also).

431. *South English Legendary, etc. (in English)* s. xiv med.

1. ff. 1–43v [A]mong oþer gospels hit ys noȝt to byleue . . . and al his fleis to rend[e].

Described by Görlach (op. cit., p. 69), p. 105 as X. ff. 2–43 contain all or part of nos. 1–26 in the South English Legendary, ed. C. d'Evelyn and A. J. Mill, EETS ccxxxv (1956), pp. 1–122/24. Lines 7–86 of Sebastian and lines 22–187 of Oswald were on missing leaves, one

[1] Two lines erased after *perscriptum*. The first two erased words are probably 'per manus'. In 1931 Sir Edmund Craster read 'anno domini cccc° quarto' (the date of gift ?) at the end.

after f. 7 and two after f. 26. No. 1 of the edition, Banna sanctorum, is preceded here by two linked pieces: (f. 1) Among oþer gospels . . . þat bygynneþ þus (26 lines); (ff. 1–2) In þe bygynnygg' of þe fader . . . Both pieces occur in Magdalene College, Cambridge, Pepys 2344, the second also in Bodley 779, f. 23^{v} (cf. *IMEV*, no. 276). Sixty-three of the lines in Bodley 779 remain here after damage to ff. 1, 2 and the loss of a leaf after f. 1: lines 1–4, 15–42, 44–7, 137–8, 144–66, 169, 170.

All leaves are more or less damaged and the text is complete only on ff. 3, 6, 9, 12, 15, 16, 19, 24, 25, 28, 34, 39. The last line on f. 43^{v} is followed by the catchword 'þulke sunne'.

2. (*a*) f. iii A list of fourteen names. (*b*) f. iv^{v} a list of twenty-six personal names, with the name of a field (?) against each of them. (*c*) f. 44 Directions for saying prayers (fifteen paternosters ?), '. . . and as offt asse he seyþ þis orisonys he schal haffe xl d[. . . .] pardon . . .'.

The relation of these leaves to art. 1 is uncertain. (*a, b*). s. xv ex., hard to read. The beginning of each line of (*b*) has gone. Names include Bowlond in (*a*) and Wylyngham in (*b*). (*c*) is 37 lines, hard to read, in a current hand, s. xv. It includes words spoken by Christ, '. . . and byfor hese deth [y] schal come wyth my dere moder and take and lede hese sowle [to] euerlastyng ioye and wan y haffe het (?) þedir brow3te y schal 3effe hym a draw3te of þe challys of my godhede' (lines 17–20). f. 44^{v} blank.

ff. iv + 44 + ii. 230 × *c.*130 mm (f. 3). Written space *c.*175 mm high. 40–1 long lines. Probable collation of ff. 1–43: 1^{12} wants 1, blank (?), 3, 10 (ff. 1–9: catchword, f. 9^{v}) 2^{12} 3^{12} wants 5, 6 after f. 26 4^{12} (catchword, f. 43^{v}). All leaves now mounted separately. Written in a mixture of textura and anglicana formata. Space for initial *A*, f. 1, not filled. Binding of s. xix.

Written in England. Found by W. H. Turner in the binding of a manuscript, according to Plummer.

457, ff. 1–40, 42–7 + pastedowns of Exeter College 9k.1590.4. *Pseudo-Augustinus, Sermones ad fratres in eremo; etc.* s. xv in.

Twenty-three bifolia removed from bindings of books at Corpus Christi College and four bifolia *in situ* in a binding at Exeter College. The text is complete on ff. 1, 3, 8, 10, 11, 14, 16, 20–1, 24, 28, 31, 34, 42, 44.

1. ff. 3, 4, 6–9, 1, 2, 10–12, 5 Twelve leaves of Sermones ad fratres in eremo (*PL* xl. 1235–358). The remaining sermons are nos. (23)–30 and (31)—or a higher number—in a numbered series. Nos. 23–9 are respectively nos. 21, 18, 23–5, 28, 38 in *PL*. 'Sermo xxx. De penitensia (*sic*). Admoneo fratres in conspectu dei timori vestro . . .' begins on f. 11^{v}. The text is continuous from f. 3 which begins 'edificarem' (edn., 1272/42) to f. 11^{v} which ends 'Omnes autem': f. 12 begins 'mente' (edn., 1272/6) in a sermon, no. 22 in *PL*, which ends on f. 5/5 'in osculo pacis et sancto': art. 2 follows immediately.

The series here is not the collection of 25 or 26 sermons found in six English manuscripts (Römer i. 353–4, nos. 11, 19, 28, 33–5). Nos. 29, 30 here are next to one another also as nos. 34, 35 in Peterhouse, Cambridge, MS. 180.[1]

[1] Information from Mr Arthur Owen.

2. f. 5rv Verses: (*a*) Vir videas . . . (6 lines); (*b*) Si tu priueris. Non nomen habere videris. Nomine priuatus sic et officio spoliatus; (*c*) Cui satis quod habet . . . (4); (*d*) Dic domo mortalis. dic de putredine . . . (4); (*e*) Est quasi muscipule . . . (2); (*f*) Quid valet ars quid opes . . . (2); (*g*) Accidiam pelle ne sompno deditus esto . . . (4); (*h*) Luctum depone pro rerum prodicione . . . (4); (*i*) Si cupias pacem linguam . . . (2); (*j*–) Thirty three lines on f. 5v, all imperfect at the beginning: the last line ends 've tibi lingua loquax'.

(*a, c, d*). Walther, *Initia*, nos. 20431, 3504, 4358. (*e, f, h, i*). Walther, *Sprichwörter*, nos. 7831a, 25204, 14014 (2 lines), 28381. (*j*–). Braces show the couplets and quadruplets.

3. ff. 13–16 Regula sancti Augustini. Ante omnia fratres karissimi . . . in temptacionem non inducatur Amen. Expliciunt regule beati Augustini.

Clavis, no. 1839b. *PL* xxxii. 1377–84. Complete, except for some damage to ff. 13 and 15.

4. ff. 16v–22v + 8 leaves in Exeter College, Glosa super Regulam sancti Augustini episcopi. Ante omnia . . . Hec igitur sunt que ut obseruetis . . .

The greater part of the commentary on the Rule attributed to Hugh of St Victor (*PL* clxxvi. 881–924): cf. Römer, i. 160–3, for copies in British libraries accompanying the Rule. ff. 16v–20v contain the text as far as 'Cum ergo' in ch. 10 (edn., 889/10). ff. 21, 22 are a central bifolium containing from 'vacui' in chapter (16) to 'exterius ges' in chapter (21): edn., 893/12 up–896/5 up. The exposed sides of the lower bifolium pasted inside the front cover of the book at Exeter College are also from this quire: edn., 890/2–16 up, 900/24–901/13. The other Exeter leaves are six out of eight from the next quire. Their exposed sides contain: (lower bifolium at the back) edn., 904/15–end and 911/1–43; (upper bifolium at the back) 905/14 up–906/32 and 909/23–910/21; (upper bifolium at the front) 907/18–908/12 up: two pages of continuous text, so this was the central bifolium.

The text is divided into shorter chapters than in *PL*: 1–9, 17–20 and parts of 10, 16, and 21 remain at Corpus Christi College, and exposed sides at Exeter College have the beginnings of 33, 34, 36–40. The titles of the chapters are longer than in *PL*: thus, for example, ch. 33 (edn., ch. 8, *De custodia rerum communium*) is headed 'Vt vestes in vno habeantur et vniusquisque accipiet sine murmure quod sibi datur'.

5. ff. 23–34v 'Decem precepta' Quoniam ut ait augustinus diuinarum scripturarum [multiplici] habundancia latissimaque doctrine . . .

Bloomfield, no. 5044. Possibly all one quire: ff. 23 and 26 are an outside bifolium, as appears from the catchword on 26v.

6. (*a*) f. 35 Incipit epistola beati Augustini [. . .] ostendit quod propter scelera cleri fugera[t ab eis.] Quoniam propter sceler[a . . .] (*b*) f. 35 [. . .] epistola per clerum yponens[is ecclesie]. Sanctissimo domino et vere om[ni laude dignissimo aug]ustino anastasius . . . (*c*) f. 35v Incipit pro[. . .] episcopi yponensis ad regularies (?) c*anonic*os [. . .] datorum dei. In omnibus o[peribus vestris sacerdotes dei dilec]tissimi memores estote . . . vel seraphin (*ends imperfectly*).

(*a, b*). These two letters of the collection of fifty-five 'Epistolae spuriae' (Römer, i. 332–4) occur together without the others also in Bodleian MS. Bodley 240 (*Sum. Cat.* 2469), p. 835. (*c*). *PL* xl. 1242–1243/22, no. 5 of the Sermones ad fratres in eremo: cf. art. 1. f. 35 is conjoint with f. 36 (art. 7).

7. ff. 36^{rv}, 47^{rv} Two leaves of the common De conflictu vitiorum et virtutum often ascribed to Augustine (Bloomfield, no. 0455; Römer, i. 49–51; *PL* xl. 1091–103). The remaining text corresponds to edn. 1097/11–1098/20 (f. 36^{rv}) and 1099/16 up–1100/34 (f. 47^{rv}). f. 47 is conjoint with f. 46 (art. 8).

8. ff. 37–8, 39–40, 42–3, 44–5 are four bifolia and f. 46 is half a bifolium (cf. art. 7) containing as yet unidentified text.

ff. 54: see above. Written space 150 × 95 mm. 34 long lines. Collation: ff. 3, 4, 6–9, 1, 2 in that order are a complete quire of 8 leaves and ff. 10–12, 5 the two outer bifolia of the next quire; ff. 13–20 are a complete quire of 8 leaves; for the rest see above, arts. 4–8. 2-line blue initials with red ornament.

Used as pastedowns by an Oxford binder, Dominique Pinart, *c.*1590: see Ker, *Pastedowns*, nos. 1296, 1305, 1322. The leaves at Exeter College are inside the covers of C. Adrichomius, *Theatrum Terrae Sanctae et Biblicarum Historiarum*, Cologne 1590, folio. Pinart used them and the other leaves in pairs of bifolia, placing one pair above the other inside each cover.[1]

479. *Letters of Phalaris (in Italian)* s. xv^2

Pistola i^a. Phalari ad Alcibo suo nimico. Polycreto messinese . . . arebeno: Val'. finiunt. Expliciunt Epistole Phalaris foeliciter.

Letters of Phalaris in the translation of Bartolomeo Fonzio, as in the edition of 1471 (Goff, P. 566). 142 numbered letters. Letters 31 and 32 were copied in the wrong order and numbered wrongly. 'A' against 'xxxii' and 'B' against 'xxxi' show that 'xxxii' should be taken before 'xxxi'.

ff. 56, foliated in s. xvi 5–60. 207 × 137 mm. Written space *c.*150 × 75 mm. 30 long lines. Collation: 1^{10} wants 1–4 $2\text{–}6^{10}$. Upright humanistica. Blue initials, 3-line (f. 1) and 2-line. Contemporary binding of wooden boards, the spine and about 50 mm of each board covered with leather: three bands: central clasp missing: offset on the back board of 16 lines of a twelfth-century copy of a Gospel book (Mark 6).

Almost certainly Florentine.[2] '532' (s. xviii ?) inside the cover and on a label at the head of the spine, where it is partly covered by a smaller label with '11' printed on it. Armorial book-plate of Henry, Baron Coleraine (†1749) inside the cover: his gift to Corpus Christi College.

546. *Virgilius, Bucolica et Georgica, cum commentis Servii* 1470

1. ff. 1–16^v Titire tu patule recumbans sub tegmine fagi . . . ite capelle.

Bucolics. Line 76 cut off with the margin of f. 2. Interlinear glosses on ff. 1–2 only. f. 17^{rv} blank.

[1] Twenty-four bifolia can be accounted for in this way, but not twenty-seven. Presumably three of the bifolia in Corpus 457 which do not bear numbers identifying them with Ker, no. 1296, or Ker, no. 1305, come in fact from another binding. In *Pastedowns*, p. 122, a strip on f. 35 of Corpus Christi College 496 is wrongly identified as coming from this manuscript.

[2] Information from Dr A. de la Mare.

2. ff. 18–59 Quid faciat letas segetes quo sidere terram . . . sub tegmine fagi.

Georgics. Bk. 2, f. 27v; 3, f. 38; 4, f. 48v. Each book is preceded by one of the four quatrains printed by Baehrens, *Poetae Latini Minores*, iv. 445–6 (Pseudo-Ovid): (1) Quid faciat . . . federe reddi; (2) Hactenus . . . ex ordine letus (3 lines only: line 3 omitted); (3) Te quoque . . . et agni (lines 3, 4 in reverse order); (4) Protinus . . . dona. They are commonly found in manuscripts and early editions and in editions of s. xvi are attributed to Herennius Modestinus: cf. the *Catalogue of printed books in the British Museum*, s. v. Modestinus. Many marginalia and interlinear glosses as far as f. 31. f. 59v blank.

3. ff. 61–84v Bucolica ut ferunt inde dicta sunt a custodia boum. id est (*blank space for Greek*) precipua . . . esse principem in scribendis bucolicis.

Commentary of Servius on Bucolics, ed. G. Thilo, 1887, pp. 1–127/19.

4. ff. 85–122v Virgilius in operibus . . . executus est titulum.

Commentary of Servius on Georgics, ed. G. Thilo, pp. 128–360/14.

ff. i + 121 (foliated 1–59, 61–122) + i. Paper: watermark changes at quire 5. 300 × 217 mm. Written space 183 mm high in arts. 1, 2; *c.*185 × 125 mm in arts. 3, 4. 27 long lines and a 28th line ruled but not written on in arts. 1, 2. *c.*47 long lines inside frame ruling, arts. 3, 4. Collation: $1–4^{12}$ 5^{12} wants 12, blank, after f. 59 $6–10^{12}$ 11 two (ff. 121–2). Quires 1–10 signed a–e, a–e. Catchwords written vertically. Current hybrida and (arts. 3, 4) cursiva by one hand. Initials: (i) ff. 1, 18, 27v, 38, 48v, 61, 85, red and blue with ornament in a different shade of red; (ii) 2-line, red. The capital letter in the ink of the text beginning each line of arts. 1, 2 is set off in a specially ruled compartment and dabbed with pale yellow. Capital letters in the ink of the text in arts. 3, 4 stroked with red. Binding of s. xix. Watson, *Oxford*, pl. 697 illus. f. 97v. Secundo folio *Nec mala.*

Written at Louvain, arts. 3, 4 probably in eighteen days: 'Scriptum louanii anno domini 1470 mensis nouembris die xviia', f. 59; 'Scriptum Louanii anno domini Millesimo cccco lxxo finitum in profesto nicholai mensis decembris die quinta', f. 122v. Bought by F. S. Ellis at a sale in which he believed many of the books to have belonged to 'Mr Octave Delepierre, the Belgium consul': writing inside the cover was, he thought, in the hand of 'old Verteist for some fifty years or more a bookseller in Brussels and who died about 15 or 20 years since' (so in a letter from Ellis, 9 May 1883, now attached to f. i). A price-mark, £1. 4, inside the cover. Bequeathed by Professor John Conington in 1869 'in usum Prof. ling. et litt. Latin.'. Deposited by the Corpus Professor of Latin in 1957.

OXFORD. EXETER COLLEGE

186. *Suetonius* s. xiv med.

For this copy of Suetonius see especially: R. W. Hunt in *Times Literary Supplement* 3056 (23 Sept. 1960), 619; G. Billanovich in *Italia medioevale e umanistica*, iii (1960), 28–58; N. Mann, ibid. xviii (1975), 494; *Manuscripts at Oxford*, pp. 140–3.

(f. 2) Versus Sydonii (*cancelled by underline*) `Ausonii' in libros Suetonii. Cesareos proceres . . . obitumque peregit (5 lines). Gaii suetonii tranquilli de uita xii cesarum. Liber primus diuus Iulius Cesar incipit feliciter. Iulius cesar annum agens sextum decimum . . . insequentium principum. Gaii suetonii Tranquilli De uita duodecim cesarum liber duodecimus domicianus Imperator feliciter explicit. Explicit liber Gaii suetonii tranquilli de uita cesarum feliciter. Versus Sydonii (*cancelled by underline*) 'Ausonii' de xii Cesaribus. Primus regalem . . . nec morte Vitellius ut uir (*ends imperfectly*).

The heading 'Gaii . . .' is on f. 2/25, separated from 'Cesareos . . . peregit' by a blank space of 21 lines probably intended for a picture. The verses before and after the text are in *Ausonii opuscula*, 1886, pp. 183–4. Each book is in paragraphs, with headings in red. Two leaves missing after f. 39 with all between *assurgere* (6. 1) and *genere* (21. 5) in the life of Claudian. Two leaves missing after f. 60 with all between *ac triumphum*[1] (2. 1) and *sima suspitione* (15. 1) in the life of Domitian. Marginalia in the main hand include translations of the Greek, for which spaces were left blank in the text: the spaces were filled later by another hand. The text was much annotated by Petrarch. The lower margin of f. 61 cut off.

ff. i + 60 + i, foliated 1–62. 340 × 240 mm. Written space *c.*223 × 148 mm. 2 cols. 44 lines. Collation of ff. 2–61: $1\text{–}4^8$ 5^8 wants 7, 8 after f. 39 $6\text{–}7^8$ 8^8 wants 6, 7 after f. 60. Catchwords centred. Well written in fairly small rotonda. Initials: (i) f. 2, 15-line, not filled in; (ii) beginning each Life after the first, 7-line, not filled in; (iii) 2-line, blue with red ornament or red with violet ornament. Capital letters in the ink of the text touched with red. Binding of gilt brown morocco over thin wooden boards, s. xvi, no. 2660 in T. De Marinis, *La legatura artistica in Italia nei secoli xv e xvi*, iii (1960): blind roundels (plaquettes) in centres, judgement of Paris (front: De Marinis, pl. after p. 16) and satyr and woman (back), as on Grolier's *Suidas* of 1499 at Trinity College, Cambridge (H. M. Nixon, *Bookbindings from the library of Jean Grolier*, 1965, pl. IV): four bands: patterned fore-edge (Grolier's arms ?): two ties missing: spine labelled down the length 'SUETONIUS MS. MEMBR: DEPICTIS INITIALIBUS'. Secundo folio *sum penitentia*.

Written in Italy: for the date and scribe see Billanovich, p. 30, who notes the likeness to a *Historia augusta* copied for Petrarch in 1356, probably at Verona, by Johannes de Campagnola (Paris, B.N., lat. 5816: facsimile of two pages by E. Pellegrin, *La bibliothèque des Visconti et des Sforza, Supplément* (1969), pls. 26, 84). Annoted by Petrarch, some of whose notes in this manuscript are reproduced by Billanovich, pls. 5, 6, by A. C. de la Mare, *The Handwriting of Italian Humanists*, i (1973), pl. III*f, h*, and in *Manuscripts at Oxford*, fig. 104. Belonged to Francesco il Vecchio da Carrara, to the Visconti library (no. 363 in 1426; no. 570 in 1459: E. Pellegrin, *La bibliothèque* . . . (1955), pp. 163, 315 and *Supplément*, p. 57), to Jean Grolier (†1565), and to 'H. Drury, Harrow' (f. i). A number '12' at the head of the pastedown. Drury sale by Evans, 19 Feb. 1827, lot 4263, to Thomas Thorpe. Thorpe catalogue for (1827), item 233 (£12. 12*s.*). Given by C. W. Boase (1825–95), fellow, in or after 1868.

187. *Petrarch, Rime and Trionfi (in Italian)* s. xv^2

1. ff. 1–140^v Petrarch, Rime.

2. f. 141 Note about Laura.

3. ff. 143–180^v Petrarch, Trionfi.

All fully described by N. Mann in *Italia medioevale e umanistica*, xviii (1975), 505–7.

[1] triumph*aliter* seems to be the reading of the manuscript.

ff. i + 180 + i. Ink ruling. Other details are given by Mann.

Ferrarese, and almost certainly by the same scribe as six other Petrarch manuscripts (Mann, p. 587, footnote 1). A number '176' at the foot of the spine and '300' on a paper label at the head. Item 1108 at £4. 4*s*. in Thomas Thorpe's catalogue of manuscripts for 1829, p. 104: the number and price-mark are inside the cover. Given by C. W. Boase, as MS. 186.

188. *Terentius* s. xv[2]

1. The six plays: f. 3 'Andria'; f. 19 'Eunucus'; f. 38 'Hentitumerumenon'; f. 54 'Adelphi'; f. 70v 'Hechirea'; f. 84 'Phormio', ending (f. 101) 'Vos ualete et plaudite caliopius recensui. Terentii affri phormio. Explicit `Liber Deo gratias Finis Amen'; also the usual argumenta of C. Sulpicius Apollinaris and the notices 'Acta ludis . . .' (except at Andria and Hecyra) and 'Caliopius recensui'.

2. Argumenta, etc., to Terence: (*a*) f. 1rv Tetrentius (*sic*) comicus quidem genere extitit affer . . . delitigat ore; (*b*) f. 1v Nomina autem fabularum siue librorum huius comici sunt ista. Andria. Eunucus. Heantontimerromenon. Adelphe. Hechira. Phormio. sed nunc de andria uideamus; (*c*) ff. 1v–2v Andria prima fabula ideo uocatur . . . qui uersiculum primi prologi in exemplum ponit; (*d*) f. 2v In prologis autem nihil aliud . . . persona laboret; (*e*) f. 2v Primus actus huius comedie est simulatio . . . filomena carino; (*f*) f. 3 Prohemium Prime comedie terentii afri. Natus in excelsis . . . cautus erit; (*g*) ff. 18v–19 Acta ludis magalensibus. ita est iungendum acta est recitata . . . ut eunucus comedia; (*h*) f. 20 Meretrix adolescentem cuius mutuo amore . . . illuditur; (*i*) f. 37rv Aliud argumentum eunuchi. Argumentum statim dicte comedie . . . uti hisdem personis; (*j*) f. 37v Acta est id est recitata est ludus . . . respondent; (*k*) ff. 69v–70 Argumentum in adelfis. Postquam poeta more suo in prologo . . . pleniter legendo uidebuntur; (*l*) f. 70rv Hechyrea incipit argumentum. Eschira dicta a loco non longe ab athenis . . . computabant; (*m*) f. 70v Aliud argumentum. Hechira est nomen huic fabule . . . peperit philomenam; (*n*) ff. 83v–84 Argumentum in phormionem. Argumentum istius fabule istud est . . . manifestabit.

(*a–f*) precede Andria: (*f*) is the epitaph of Terence, Walther, no. 11627. (*g–i*) on Eunuchus, (*g*) before it, (*i*) after it, and (*h*) after Terence's prologue 'Si quicquam . . . uelit'. (*h*) is in Prete's edn., Heidelberg 1954, p. 178. (*j, l–n*) precede Heautontimorumenos, Hecyra, and Phormio and (*k*) follows Adelphi.

ff. i + 101 + i. 245 × 160 mm. Written space 162 × 90 mm. 32 long lines. Double vertical bounders, the first letter of each line lying between them. Ruling partly with a hard point and partly with ink. Collation: $1\text{–}9^{10}$ 10^{12} wants 12, blank. Humanistica of Ferrarese type.[1] Initials: (i) f. 3, 4-line gold *N* of *Natus* (art. 2*f*) on blue ground powdered with white dots, with gold, red, blue, and green decoration extending into two margins: cf. Bodleian, Douce 247 (Pächt and Alexander, ii, no. 531, and pl. 51);[1] (ii, iii) 3-line and 2-line, blue or red. Contemporary Italian binding of stamped calf over thin wooden boards: 5 bands: rebacked. Secundo folio *filiam*.

Written in north-eastern Italy (Ferrara ?). A damaged shield at the foot of f. 3.

[1] Information from Dr A. de la Mare.

OXFORD. HERTFORD COLLEGE

1. *Biblia* s. xiii med.

1. ff. 1–18v, 407–523v, 19–406v, 524rv A Bible in the usual order of books and with the common set of 64 prologues, as in Liverpool Cathedral 13, q.v.

Three leaves missing, one after f. 209 with Jeremiah 7: 12–9: 18 and two after f. 371 with Ephesians 1: 8–Philemon 2: 7. The text of Genesis 21: 33–41: 42 is hardly legible on ff. 12rb/9–18v, 407–410ra/28: the ink seems not to have taken. Six quires containing Genesis 34: 25–2 Kings 15:2 are misbound after Apocalypse.

Proverbs begins on a new page (f. 150), but not a new quire. Psalms are numbered in red.

The heading of the first prologue to Maccabees (Stegmüller, no. 547), 'Incipit `epistola Rabani que non debet prologus sed epistola pronunciari'', is over erasure from the second word and has a note against it in the margin in red, 'Nota quod Rabanus non transtulit librum machabeorum set commentauit'.

2. ff. 525–549v Aaz apprehendens . . .

The common dictionary of Hebrew names ending imperfectly in the letter T.

3. Two leaves at the end, apparently flyleaves, contain: (*a*) f. 550rv, theological notes, s. xiii; (*b*) f. 551, in current anglicana, s. xiv med., a now much-damaged record of money payments in French, ending 'le dit M ad mys son seal. Escript [. . .] lan de regne le Roi Edd tierce [. . .]'.

ff. i + 550 + iii, foliated (i), 1–85, 85*, 86–551, (552). For ff. 550–1 see above, art. 3. 168 × 120 mm. Written space 122 × 75 mm. 2 cols. 49 lines. Collation: 1^{18} 2 seventeen (ff. 407–23) 3^{22} (ff. 424–45) 4^{18} (ff. 446–63) $5\text{–}7^{20}$ (ff. 464–523) 8^{20} (ff. 19–38) 9^{22} 10^{20} $11\text{–}15^{22}$ 16^{22} wants 21 after f. 209 $17\text{–}23^{22}$ 24^{22} wants 8, 9 after f. 371 25^{22} (ff. 385–406): ff. 524–49 doubtful. Initials: (i, ii) red and blue with ornament of both colours; (iii) 2-line, blue or red with ornament of the other colour; (iv) 1-line, blue or red. Binding of s. xix. Secundo folio *ostenditur quoniam*.

Probably French, but in England by s. xiv. *CMA* 2.

2. *Secreta secretorum* s. xiv ex.

Hic est nobilissimus liber compositus per summum Aristotilem . . . Qui liber dicitur et nominatur secretum secretorum . . . in quatuor libros. Post hec autem prologus inuenitur in principio primi libri . . . (*table of chapters of four books*) . . . (f. 3v) Domino suo excellentissimo . . . Guidono nato de Valencia ciuitatis Inpolis (*sic for* Tripolis) glorioso pontifici. Phylippus suorum clericorum minimus . . . (f. 4v) peruenire. Deus omnipotens custodiat . . . (f. 5v) omnes alie nationes. Prologus translatus de lingua arabica in chaldeam. et de caldea in Latinam. Iohannes qui transtulit librum . . . (f. 6) sub hac forma. Prologus aristotelis ad regem Alexandrum. O fili gloriosissime . . . (f. 7) salutare. Liber primus . . . Capitulum de sustentacionibus regum. Oportet itaque quemlibet regem . . . (f. 66) sua spiritualitas.

The translation by Philip of Tripoli. Printed often: *GKW* 2481–4, 2486–7. Thorndike and Kibre, cols. 465 (Domino suo), 410 (Deus omnipotens), 970 (O fili). Singer and Anderson, no. 29. Bk. 2, f. 33; 3, f. 36v; 4, f. 56v. f. 66v left blank. An English hand of s. xvii added two further chapters on f. 66rv and annotations elsewhere. Only two chapters of bk. 4 are listed in the table on f. 3.

Facsimiles of f. 1 by D. Dercsényi, *The Hungarian Illuminated Chronicle* (Corvina Press 1969), fig. 10 and (reduced) by E. Jakubovich, *Der Oxforder Codex König Ludwigs des Grossen*, 1931, pl. opp. p. 8.

ff. i + 66. Medieval foliation. 242 × 170 mm. Written space 160 × 120 mm. 2 cols. 27 lines. Collation: 1^8 wants 1 $2\text{-}3^8$ 4^{10} $5\text{-}6^8$ 7^{10} 8^{10} wants 8–10, perhaps blank. Initials: (i) f. 1, 6-line, pale violet *H* on gold and blue ground: within the *H* a ¾-length portrait of a king; (ii) 3-line or 4-line, red; (iii) 2-line, red or blue: the letter *I* is wholly outside the written space. Binding of s. xix. Secundo folio *De cautela*.

Written for Louis the Great, King of Hungary 1362–82, and of Poland 1372–82, by the same scribe as the Hungarian illuminated chronicle, Budapest, National Szechenyi Library, Clmae 404 (formerly in Vienna, Pal. lat. 405), and decorated by the same artist: cf. Dercsényi, op. cit., p. 44. In the lower margin of f. 1 a shield bearing the arms of Hungary and Anjou is flanked by shields with the arms of Hungary and Poland. 'Liber Aule Magd. Oxon 1658' and 'Ex dono Edmundi Hall Art: Mag: et Coll: Pembr: Socii', f. 1. *CMA* 3.

OXFORD. JESUS COLLEGE

146. *Johannes de Rupella, O.F.M., Sermones de sanctis; etc.*

s. xiii²

1. (*a*) ff. 1–7v, 10–11v, 14–76v In festo omnium sanctorum. Mirabilis deus in sanctis suis etc. Multa dicimus et uerbis deficimus . . . (*b*) ff. 8, 9, 12, 13 A nearly contemporary index of (*a*) on two pieces of parchment inserted between the seventh and eighth leaves of the first quire. It gives sermon numbers.

(*a*). Sermons for feasts of the sanctoral and (a few) temporal written on the scale of a small Bible. They are numbered 1–66 and as far as no. 60 (James) are mainly in the order of the church year, beginning at All Saints. With twelve exceptions they are sermons of J. de Rupella listed by Schneyer, *Rep.*, iii. 705–16: nos. 167–9, 171, 170, 179, 178, 180, (*9*),[1] 181–2, 97a, 98–100, 102–3, 105, (*19, 20*), 106, 127, 107, (*24*), 110, (*26*), 109, 108, 111, 113, 114 (first lines only and not included in the numbering), (*31*), 116, (*33*, now missing in the gap after f. 39), 119, 121, 120, 24, 22–3, 122, 62, 52, 63, 57, (*45*), 55, 64, 60, (*49*), 123, 125, 128, 126, (*54*), 127 (first lines only and not included in the numbering),[2] 139, 138, 140–2, (*60, 61*), 132, 134–5, 137 (*66*).

The sermons not listed by Schneyer are:
9. f. 10v In sancti Clementis. Qui conuertit mare . . . Triplicem legimus leticiam . . .

19. f. 22 Item de eodem (*Stephen*). Quicumque hanc regulam . . . Hic designatur meritum . . .

20. f. 23 Item de eodem. *Labidabant* (*sic*) stephanum . . . Hec sunt uerba hodierne epistole . . .

[1] Numbers in italics and within brackets are of the series here which do not occur in Schneyer's list.

[2] These lines are repeated again, sine numero, after Schneyer, no. 141.

24. f. 28 (*Circumcision*) Uocauit abraam nomen . . . Hic figuratur misterium . . .

26. f. 29^{v} (*Circumcision*) Iosue circumcidit . . . Hoc verbum legitur . . .

31. f. 37 (*Paul*) Saule saule etc. Act' 9. Predicacio uerbi domini . . .

45. f. 50^{v} (*Good Friday*) Non poterat ultra cohibere . . . Conuenienter intelligitur cristus . . .

49. f. 58^{v} (*Easter*) Pasca nostrum immolatus . . . In duobus insinuat apostolus . . .

54. f. 63^{v} In festo sancte crucis. Vidit in sompnis . . . O quam beata esset . . .

60. f. 69 De spiritu sancto. O quam bonus et suauis . . . Cum uenerit paraclitus . . .

61. f. 72^{v} In sanctorum Francisci et Dominici. Dabo duobus testibus . . . Due testes sunt duo confessores . . .

66. f. 76 Item de eodem (*John Baptist*) Erat Io. lucerna ardens . . . In hiis uerbis commendatur . . .

2. ff. 77–81^{v}, left blank at the end of quire 5, and a blank space on f. 76^{v} contain additions in several hands, s. xiii, including: (*a*) f. 77 Hec nomina cristi quicumque super se habuerit . . . Primum nomen domini. hon. hel. heley . . . adiutor michi sis in omnibus actibus meis. Amen. Amen. Amen; (*b*) f. 77 Nec te lateat satanas. Inminere tibi penas. Inminere tibi tormentas . . . ; (*c*) f. 77 In nomine dei amen. Incipiunt nomina cristi. Trinitas. sancta. agios . . . ; (*d*) ff. 77^{v}–78 Notes for sermons; (*e*) ff. 79–80 Pater noster. Hec oracio precellit in tribus . . . ; (*f*) ff. 80^{v}–81^{v} In hoc sermone premittuntur vii virtutes que et beatitudines dicuntur . . .

(*b*). Against an unclean spirit 'ut recedas a me'. (*d*). For Ash Wednesday and the next two days and within the octave of St Antony. (*f*) sets out the seven petitions, the seven deadly sins, and the seven gifts of the Holy Spirit.

3 (quire 6). ff. 86–92 Theological distinctions, one or more subjects in each column: thus, for example, f. 83rb begins 'Quedam dicuntur de deo. Causatiue. ut iustus pius misericors. conuersiue sicut dicitur deliciari'.

Each page is lettered top left, the series running C–Y on ff. 82–91^{v}, where the running title is '3' and A, B on f. 92^{rv} where it is '4'. Presumably a quire is missing before quire 6. A new column usually begins with a new subject. ff. 90 (T), 90^{v} (V), 91 (X), 91^{v} (Y), though lettered, do not contain distinctions, but miscellaneous notes in several hands, including (f. 90^{rv}) 'Quid sit nichil fieri. Confitear ergo confitear domine pater rex celi et terre miseriam meam . . . (f. 91^{v}) Transfige dulcissime ihesu medullas anime mee . . .'; (f. 91^{v}) medical recipes: Pilule. R' vnciam laudani . . . ; Colirium. R' fel leporis . . . ; Pill' portuen' contra reuma et ad oculos . . .

Arts. 4–6 (ff. 93–126) are described here in the order shown by two medieval foliations, 1–16 and 189–206 on ff. 110–26 and 17–28, and 207–23 on ff. 93–104. Art. 6, on the same quire as ff. 93–104, has no old foliation.

4. ff. 110–115^{v} Sermons for various occasions, some specified, beginning imperfectly 'habebant possessionem (?) hereditatis eterne'.

A sermon for the 3rd Sunday in Lent begins on f. 110 'Estote immitatores dei . . . Propositum uerbum su(m)ptum est . . . The sermon on f. 113^{v} continues on an inserted slip of parchment. The part of the slip projecting after f. 113 was not included in the medieval foliation beginning with '1', but is '193' in the other foliation and '114' now.

5. ff. 116–126v, 93–104v Abbreviated sermons from Advent to the 24th Sunday after Pentecost, the 'Collectio fratrum minorum' set out by Schneyer, *Rep.* vii. 2–10, from Munich, Clm. 7932.

Dominica prima de aduentu. Dominus iudex noster . . . Nos. 1–83, 86–8, 90–133 of the 'Collectio'. No. 88 ends imperfectly (f. 98v).

The part of the slip projecting after f. 118 (cf. art. 4) has quotations from Gregory, Chrysostom and other Fathers. Part of f. 93 has been torn off.

6. Early additions on leaves of quire 9 left blank at first: (*a*) f. 105rv sermons; (*b*) ff. 106–109v formulary letters.

(*b*). (1) f. 106 Excellent' et magnifico domino. Illustri Regi Aragonum O. miseracione diuina sancti angeli diaconus Car. (*Richardus de Annibaldis* ?) salutem et optatum in prosperis incrementum. Illa uera serenitas uirtutum . . . (2) f. 106 Prouido viro archipresbitero O. etc. salutem . . . Sic uos decreuit uulgaris opinio . . . (3) f. 106rv Prouidis et disscretis uiris. uniuerso Pat' capitulo dilectis amicis *suis* O. etc' salutem . . . Nuper relacionis uestre comperimus quod Parmens' mater Communis . . . (4) ff. 106v–107 Disscretis et Religiosis Viris uenerabilibus fratribus P. Guardiano Magistris et ceteris obseruantiam minorum profexis in conuentu Pars' morantibus . . . O. etc' in uero salutari salutem. Sic nobis est uestra pure gracie uinculis alligata . . . (5) f. 107rv Ang' nos specialis affeccio quam circa uos gerimus ac firma spes . . . (6) f. 107v Prouidis et disscretis viris preposito et uniuerso capitulo florentin' dilectis amicis suis O. etc' salutem in amore salutis. Quod tam pronta fiducia scribimus . . . (7) f. 107v Religiose ac nobili Mulieri B. filie Marchionis Osten' (?) O. diuina miseracione Paduan' electus . . . Quam mens nostra sit plena iocunditatis . . . (8) f. 108 Raynaldus miseratione diuina Ostien' et Vellet' Episcopus (*cardinal bishop of Ostia and Velletri 1231–54*). Nobilibus uiris P nepoti suo. Ponti et Consilio Tudert' (*Todi, Umbria*) salutem . . . Obsequia cristo accepta . . . (9) f. 108v Nobilibus et prudentibus uiris A. Roman' Consuli Potanti Tudert' dilecto nepoti suo. et Consilio ciuit' eiusdem B. Iudic' Roman' Consul salutem . . . Beneficii et honoris acceptorum a communitate Tudert' memores existentes . . . (10) f. 108v In cristo Patri uiro uenerabili et honesto domino fratri P. Assinat' episcopo reuerendo frater P custos et conuentus fratrum Minorum Viterbii commorantium . . . Paternitatem uestram credimus non latere . . . (11) ff. 108v–109 Sanctissimo patri patrum eorum reuerendissimo domino uniuersalis Ecclesie summo pontifici Domino Innoc' A. Pont' uiterbii Consilium et commune terre predicte . . . ossculum ante pedes. Quam grati filii . . . (12) f. 109rv Patri patrum et uniuersalis ecclesie summo pontifici Reuerendo domino suo A. dei et sui gracia Viterbien' et Tuscan' episcopus . . . Cunctis impendere pro futura . . . (13) f. 109v Vniuersis presentes litteras inspecturis A. salutis copiam et prosperitatis augmentum. Exultet vniuersalis mater ecclesia noui luminis illustrata fulgoribus que licet multorum lampadibus . . .

(8) refers to the abbess and nuns 'monasterii pauperum inclusarum de Fulgineo (*Foligno, Umbria*) ordinis sancti Damiani' (Peter Damian). It is followed by formulary sentences in three and four lines, Probabili presumpcione . . . , Plene fiducie . . . (12). Perhaps Alferius, bishop of Viterbo and Toscanella in 1254. (13) mentions Genoa and Apulia.

ff. ii + 121 (excluding three slips: see arts. 1, 4) + ii. Medieval foliations of art. 1, one in red roman figures on versos and one in black arabic figures on rectos, take account of leaves now missing after f. 39, but not of the slips. For medieval foliations of arts. 4, 5 see above. 155 × 110 mm. Written space 117 × 77 mm. 2 cols. 55 lines. Collation, excluding the slips: 1^{16} (ff. 1–7, 10, 11, 14–20) 2^{16} 3^{16} wants 4, 5 after f. 39 4^{18} 5^{10} + three singletons, ff. 70, 72, 73, 6^{16} wants 10–13, 15, all perhaps blank (ff. 82–92) 7^{12} (ff. 110–13, 115–22) 8 four (ff. 123–6) 9^{14} + a bifolium after 4 and a leaf after 7 (ff. 97, 98, 102). Written in very small hands. 2-line and 1-line red initials. Binding of s. xix. Secundo folio *per ordinem*.

Written for Franciscan use in Italy. An inscription of s. xiii at the foot of f. 1, erased except the last four words, is partly legible by ultra-violet light: Isti sunt sermones Iohannis de Au[. . .]lla quos accomodauit frater [. . .] Stefano de alat' (?) quando iuit parisius 'cum tali signo M.' Bought by W. M. Lindsay in Italy and given by him in 1897.

OXFORD. LADY MARGARET HALL

Borough 1. *Horae; Preces* s. xv med.

1. ff. 1–12^{v} Calendar in red and black.

Entries in red include the translation of Augustine, Monica, 'Conuersio sancti Augustini episcopi', 'Sancte marie ad niues', 'Festum transfigurationis', Augustine, Nicholas of Tollentino (28 Feb., 4, 5 May, 5, 6, 28 Aug., 10 Sept.); in black, Bernardinus, Cerbonus, translation of Augustine (20 May, 10, 11 Oct.). No Visitation of B.V.M., 2 July.

2 (added, s. xv ex.). ff. 13–14^{v} (*a*) Confiteor, (*b*) Pater noster, (*c*) Credo in unum deum.

3. ff. 15–81 Incipit officium beate uirginis marie secundum ordinem romane curie.

Salve regina and prayers follow compline and are followed, without interval, by the Advent office (f. 73). Hours of Holy Spirit after prime and later hours (not as art. 5) have been cancelled lightly. ff. 49, 50 are supply leaves, s. xvi ?. ff. 81^{v}–83^{v} blank.

4. ff. 84–92^{v} Incipit officium sancte crucis . . . Hymnus. Patris sapientia . . .

5. ff. 92^{v}–96 Incipit officium sancti spiritus . . . Hymnus. Nobis sancti spiritus . . . f. 96^{v} blank.

6. ff. 97–120 Incipiunt septem psalmi penitentiales. Litany, f. 108.

Monks and hermits are Benedict, Anthony, Dominic, Francis, and Bernardine. Psalm 69 and a series of versicles, Salvos nos fac–Domine exaudi, come between Sed libera nos a malo and Deus cui proprium, as often in Roman hours written in Italy. Deus cui proprium is followed by Exaudi, Ineffabilem, Deus qui culpa, Omnipotens sempiterne deus miserere famulo tuo N nostro, Deus a quo sancta desideria, Ure igne, Fidelium, Actiones nostras, Omnipotens sempiterne deus qui uiuorum, Confiteor (marked 'extra': cf. art. 11), Pater noster, Credo (as art. 2). ff. 120^{v}–121^{v} blank.

7. ff. 122–72 Incipit offitium pro defunctis.

8. ff. 172–183^{v} Passio domini nostri yesu cristi secundum Iohannem. Egressus est . . . posuerunt yhesum.

John 18, 19. A break at 19: 38, Post hec autem.

9. ff. 184–5 Suscipere digneris confessionem meam sancta trinitas . . . quam ego peccator . . .

Marked 'extra', like art. 11*b, e, h, i, k*.

10. ff. 185–198v Pater dulcissime propter infinitam tuam caritatem . . . sine fine et laudare. A meditation on the Lord's Prayer.

11. Prayers, mainly in adversity: (*a*) ff. 198v–199 Oratio deuotissima. Domine deus omnipotens pater et filius et spiritus sanctus: da michi famulo tuo I (?) uictoriam . . . ; (*b*) ff. 199–200 Oratio deuotissima. Deus habraam deus ysaac . . . liberare digneris me famulum tuum I (?) . . . ; (*c*) ff. 200–2 Oratio sancti augustini episcopi (*lined through, except* Oratio). Deus propi(c)ius esto michi peccatori . . . ; (*d*) ff. 202–4 Questi sono euersi di sancto bernardo abbate. Illumina . . . (*the entry crossed out*); (*e*) ff. 203–5 Oratio deuotissima pro quacumque tribulatione. Iuste iudex ihesu criste rex regum . . . ; (*f*) ff. 205–7 Oratio ad omnem aduersitatem. Domine Ihesu criste fili dei uiui redemptor mundi defende me . . . ; (*g*) ff. 207–209v Oratio ad omnem aduersitatem deuotissima. Domine yhesu criste filii (*sic*) dei uiui qui septem uerba . . . ; (*h*) ff. 209v–211 Oratio deuotissima. Liberator animarum et mundi redemptor . . . Supplico ego peccator . . . ; (*i*) f. 211rv Deprecor te domine rex celestis deus omnipotens dignare die isto . . . ; (*j*) f. 211v Omnipotens sempiterne deus ut non me perire . . . ; (*k*) ff. 211v–213 Concessit papa Bonifatius cuilibet dicenti istam orationem viginti continuatis diebus ore confessio (*sic*) corde contrito omnium peccatorum remissionem. oratio (*these 18 words crossed out*). Deus qui uoluisti pro redemptione generis humani . . . ; (*l*) f. 213 Gratias ago tibi omnipotens deus qui me dignatus es in hac die custodire . . . ; (*m*) ff. 213v–214 Salua me domine rex eterne glorie . . . ; (*n*) f. 214rv Clementissime deus qui omnium cognitor es occultorum . . .

(*c*). For the ascription to Augustine in manuscripts in British libraries see Römer, i. 374, *MMBL* i. 411, ii. 206 and above, p. 176. (*b, e, h, i, k*) are marked 'extra' in the margin.

12. ff. 214v–217 Plange fidelis anima . . .

RH, no. 14954. Fourteen stanzas (*AH* xxxi. 64, stanzas 1, 5, 7, 12, 10, 15, 23–4, 30–5, with many differences) and prayer 'Deus qui diligentibus te bona . . .'.

13. ff. 217–19 Stabat uirgo dolorosa . . . *RH*, no. 19416.

14. ff. 219–20 Aue uirgo uirginum. Que portasti filium . . . (38 lines). *RH*, no. 24023.

15. ff. 220v–221v Obsecro te o beatissima uirgo maria mater summi benignitatis . . .

16. ff. 221v–222 Beatissime ac sanctissime Iohannes baptista martir et percursor (*sic*) cristi . . .

17. f. 222rv Commemoratio sancte apollonie uirginis et martiris. A'. Christi uirgo egregia pro nobis apollonia . . . : crossed out. *RH*, no. 21744 (Virgo christi).

18. ff. 223–226^{v} Quicunque uult saluus esse . . .

19. f. 227 Memoria of Maur: crossed out.

20. f. 227^{v} [I]nclina domine aurem tuam ad me . . . : crossed out (cf. art. 24*b*). ff. 228–229^{v} blank.

21. f. 230 In nomine patris et filii et spiritus sancti. Amen. Confiteor deo omnipotenti beate marie uirgini beato francisco et omnibus sanctis . . .

Differs somewhat from the form in arts. 2*a* and 6.

22. ff. 230–237^{v} Incipit missa beate marie uirginis. Salue sancta parens . . . : crossed out, except the creed.

23. ff. 237^{v}–241^{v} Sequentiae of three Gospels, John, Matthew, Luke.

24 (added). (*a*) ff. 242^{v}–246^{v} Peccata cordis . . . Oris . . . Operis . . . Omissionis . . . (*b*) ff. 246^{v}–247 Inclina aurem . . . : as art. 20. (*c*) f. 247^{v} Record in Italian of the birth and baptism of Giulio Cesare Giosep Caracciolo, Naples, 20 Sept. 1574: parents, Hettorre and Hieronima Caracciolo; Mario Carafa, archbishop of Naples (1565–76), among godparents.

(*a*) in hand of art. 2. The words 'Finis. Venetiis mccccxc' after (*b*) seem to be a later addition. ff. 242, 247^{v}–248^{v} blank.

ff. ii + 248 + ii. *c.*193 × 132 mm. Written space *c.*120 × 82 mm. 16 long lines. (10 lines in 75 mm). Collation: 1^{12} 2 two (ff. 13, 14) $3–5^{10}$ 6^{10} wants 5, 6 (supplied, ff. 49, 50) $7–8^{10}$ 9^{10} wants 10, blank, after f. 83 10^{10} 11^{4} wants 4, blank, after f. 96 $12–13^{10}$ 14^{8} wants 6–8, blank, after f. 121 $15–19^{10}$ 20^{8} $21–23^{10}$ 24^{12} 25^{8} (ff. 222–9) 26^{10} 27 nine (ff. 240–8). The hand changes at art. 7, from which point the ink tends to be fainter than before on flesh sides. An Annunciation picture, 40 × 80 mm, on f. 15: below it a man kneels in prayer in the initial *D* of *Domine*. Initials: (i) 8-line (from art. 7) or 6-line, red, green, or blue on gold grounds, historiated or decorated: historiations at each hour of art. 3 (none, flight into Egypt; vespers, Christ in the Temple; compline, B.V.M., Child, and Joseph; terce missing) and before arts. 4 (Christ rises from the Tomb), 6, 7 (symbols of death); (ii) 2-line, gold on coloured grounds; (iii) 1-line, blue with red ornament or gold with violet ornament: the latter replaced by red with grey-green ornament in arts. 2, 24*a*. Floral borders continuous on ff. 15, 84, 97, and 122 and on three sides of other pages with historiated initials: in the lower margins of ff. 15, 122 is a rayed IHS in gold paint. Binding of s. xix/xx.

Written in Italy. Dr Pächt considered the main initials to be Umbrian and in art. 3 north Italian. Belonged in s. xvi^{2} to the Caracciolo family (art. 24*c*). Bookplate of E. F. Bosanquet: his sale at Sotheby's, 24 Jan. 1944, lot 179. Armorial book-plate of Borough and book-label of C. M. Borough. Given by Cynthia M. Borough in 1973.

Borough 3. *Breviarium, pars aestivalis* s. xiv med.

In uigilia dominice resurrectionis ad vesperos super psalmos A'. Alleluia alleluia. vt et respicientes Ps. Confiteantur. Cum aliis capitulum Si consurrexistis . . .

Offices from Easter to (f. 122^{v}) the 25th Sunday after the octave of Pentecost: f. 13^{v}, octave of Easter; f. 21, 1st Sunday after octave of Easter; f. 24^{v}, 2nd Sunday; f. 27^{v}, 3rd

Sunday; f. 31v, 4th Sunday; f. 34v, Ascension Day; f. 44, Pentecost; f. 54, octave of Pentecost; f. 59, Corpus Christi; f. 71v, 1st Sunday after octave of Pentecost.

With ff. 1–59 cf. *Monastic Ordinale of St Vedast's Abbey, Arras* (Henry Bradshaw Soc. lxxvi, lxxvii, 1957), pp. 161–80. The responses at matins at Easter, Ascension, and Pentecost are those provided ibid., pp. 91–2. Twelve lessons. Ferial lessons 'per ebdomadam' are grouped on ff. 16v, 24, 27, 30v, 34. ff. 18v–19v contain ten 'Collecte ad horas dicende' (cf. edn., p. 165), beginning with 'Deus qui credentes in te': the seventh, 'Deus qui pro salute mundi . . .' is crossed through. Four more collects were added on an inserted slip, f. 20. Faded responses and versicles on ff. 73v–74 were rewritten in s. xvii (?).

ff. 122 and a slip (see below), foliated 1–123. Medieval foliation i–cxxii on ff. 1–19, 21–123. 157 × 112 mm. Written space 120 × 70 mm. 23–4 long lines. Collation: $1–11^8$ 12^8 + 1 leaf after 5 (f. 95) $13–14^8$ 15^{10} wants 10, probably blank: a slip (f. 20) is inserted after 3^3. Initials: (i) f. 1, 4-line *S* of *Si*, blue and red with ornament of both colours; (ii) 2-line, red or blue with ornament of the other colour; (iii) 1-line, red or blue. Binding of stiff parchment, s. xvii (?). Secundo folio *mur uinculis*.

Written in northern France. Belonged to the priory of Haspres (Nord: a cell of the Benedictine abbey of St Vaast, Arras): 'Bibli. præ*positatus*[1] hasprensis', f. 1, s. xvii. Armorial bookplate of Aldis and 'Sir Chs Aldis 1825' inside the cover; also 'From the library of archdeacon Burney Surbiton' (Charles Parry Burney, archdeacon of Kingston-upon-Thames and vicar of Surbiton, †1864 or 1865;[2] also '17585', '59 C 22', and '£12–12'. Given as MS. Borough 1.

Borough 4. *Miscellanea theologica* s. xv²

1. ff. 1–2 Contemplatio beati bernardi de diuersis auctoritatibus. O qua uehementi amplexu amplexatus es me o bone yhesu . . . de te ex quo omnia in quo omnia per quem omnia. amen.

The scribe wrote six lines of art. 3 after art. 1 and then changed his mind: see below, f. 2v blank.

2. ff. 3–5 Epistola Dionisii ad Timoteum. Saluto te diuinum discipulum . . . gloria laus et cultus cum patre . . . AMEN.

Passion of Peter and Paul. Ed. J. B. Pitra, *Analecta sacra spicilegio Solesmensi*, iv (1883), 261–71.

3. ff. 5v–7v Ex meditatione beati Anselmi. Homo qui ex anima rationali . . . et princeps pacis.

PL clxxxiv. 1109–14. The scribe wrote the title of art. 4 on f. 5v and then cancelled it when he decided to copy art. 3 here instead of after art. 1.

4. ff. 7v–11v Incipit excertum (*sic*) Isidori qui dicitur Sinonima de homine plangente et ratione quietante. Anima mea in angustiis . . . Quidquid agis pro futura age mercede.

Excerpts from Synonyma, *PL* lxxxiii. 826–68.

[1] Cf. Ducange, *Glossarium mediae et infimae Latinitatis*, edn. 1883–7, vi. 463, col. 1, s.v. *Praepositatus.*

[2] Cf. *Proceedings of Society of Antiquaries of London*, 2nd series, iii. 108.

5. ff. 11v–19 Quoniam in medio aliquorum (*sic for* laqueorum) positi sumus . . . non cessant ut deum meum dilligam et in eum perseuerem usque in finem uite mee. AMEN.

Pseudo-Augustine, Manuale, chapters 1–24: *PL* xl. 951–62.

6. ff. 19–23v Incipit liber qui uocatur scala beati augustini episcopi. Cum die quadam . . . pacem in id ipsum AMEN.

Pseudo-Augustine, Scala paradisi. *PL* xl. 997–1004. Bloomfield, no. 1082 (Guigo II, Ord. Carth.).

7. ff. 23v–28v Maria stabat ad monumentum foris plorans. Omelia Origenis. Audiuimus mariam ad monumentum foris stantem . . . et hec dixit michi. Cui est honor et gloria in secula seculorum amen.

Pseudo-Origen. *Opera*, ed. Merlin, 1519, iii. 129–131v.

8. f. 28v Two short pieces (7 lines), the first said to be from Augustine and the second from Cassian.

9. ff. 28v–33v Qualiter beatus bernardus dixit et quam dulciter tractauit de sacrificio altaris. Panem angelorum manducauit homo. Non latet (*sic*) nos (*sic*) reuerendi sacerdotes . . . gratie sue auxilium ministrando amen.

No. 47 of the sermons in B.L., Royal 7 F. x, f. 123v, s. xii ex. (Non lateat uos . . .).

10. f. 33v B*ernardus*. De officio siue de oris. Consequitur homo sex utilitates . . . poterit peruenire (9 lines).

11. f. 34rv Epistola beati b*ernardi*. ex persona elie monaci ad parentes suos. Sola causa qua licet non obedire . . . in eius amore uiuamus per . . . amen.

PL clxxxii. 254–5; *SBO* vii. 283–5 (Ep. CXI).

12. ff. 34v–36 De honestate uite. B*ernardus*. Petis a me mi frater karissime quod numquam et nusquam a suo prouisore . . . et corona mea in domino Amen.

PL clxxxiv. 1167–70 (Pseudo-Bernard). Bloomfield, no. 3897.

13. ff. 36v–37v De miseria huius uite. B*ernardus*. O misera uita que tantos in prosperis decipis . . . super quo altari dicit apostolus obtulit semetipsum imaculatum deo uiuenti. AMEN.

ff. 38–40v blank: 39 nearly all cut off.

ff. iii + 40 + v. ff. 41–2 are leaves 26 and 33 of a printed astrological work, s. xvi in.: 26 is headed I. GAVRICVS. 144 × 108 mm. Written space 100 × 77 mm. 27–31 long lines. Faint hard-point ruling: see f. 38. Collation: $1–4^{10}$. Humanistic hand. 2-line red initials with a little ornament. Parchment binding, s. xx. Secundo folio *non abundat*.

Written in Italy. Probably part of a larger book. Given as MS. Borough 1.

Borough 5. *Commendatio animarum, etc.* s. xv in.–xv^2

Probably the last six quires of a book of hours.

1. ff. 1–14^v Bonitatem fecisti . . . absterge. Per . . . Amen.

Commendation of souls, beginning imperfectly at Ps. 118: 65. *Manuale Sarum*, pp. 143–144/3. f. 15^{rv} blank.

2. ff. 16–27^v Hic incipit psalmus de passione domini. Deus deus meus . . .

Psalms of the Passion, ending imperfectly 'Gloriosa pas-' in the prayer after Ps. 30 (*Horae Ebor.*, p. 116/1). The versicle is Adoremus te criste and response Quia per sanctam crucem.

3. f. 28^{rv} (*begins imperfectly in stanza 5 of* Gaude flore virginali) pater seculorum . . .

Seven Joys of B.V.M. *RH*, no. 6810; *AH* xxxi. 198.

4. ff. 28^v–30^v Oracio bona et deuota de sancta maria et de sancto iohanne euuangeliste. O intemerata . . . orbis terrarum. inclina . . . Masculine forms.

5. f. 31^{rv} (*begins imperfectly in the last stanza of* Gaude cui Symeon) dolor visus tui cordis . . . Oremus. Domine ihesu dulcis fili uirginis qui pro nobis . . .

Five Joys of B.V.M. *Horae Ebor.*, p. 179.

6. ff. 31^v–33 O bone ihesu o piissime ihesu o dulcissime ihesu . . .

ibid., pp. 179–80.

7. f. 33^{rv} Concede michi domine spacium uite et gratiam beneuiuendi . . .

8. ff. 33^v–34 Benedictio dei patris omnipotentis cum angelis suis . . .

9. f. 34^v Adoro (te) domine ihesu criste crucem ascendentem spinea coronam portantem . . . f. 35^{rv} blank.

10 (*added later in another hand*). ff. 36–38^v Domine Ihesu criste adoro te in cruce pendentem . . .

The Five Oes of St Gregory (. . . pendentem . . . vulneratum . . . in sepulcro positum . . . pastor bone . . . deprecor te . . .), versicle 'O pietas cristi que pape visa fuisti . . .' (4 lines), prayer 'Domine ihesu criste misericordissime qui pietatis tue vulnera beato Gregorio pape . . . ' and notice in red ink '[S]eynt Gregory pope the holy doctoʳ wᵗ other diuerse holy popes . . . ', conveying 29,000 years of pardon confirmed by Popes Nicholas (V, 1447–55) and Calixt (III, 1455–8), the latter of whom added 20,024 years and 23 days. ff. 39–41^v left blank.

ff. ii + 41 + ii. 128 × 85 mm. Written space *c.*78 × 50 mm. 16 long lines (14 in art. 1). Collation: 1^8 wants 1–3 2^{10} 3^8 wants 1 before f. 16 4^8 wants 6 after f. 27 5^6 wants 2 after

f. 30 6^6 + 1 leaf after 5 (f. 40). Initials: (i) 2-line, gold on grounds of red and blue patterned in white; (ii) 1-line, blue with red ornament or gold with violet ornament. Capital letters in the ink of the text filled with pale yellow. Binding of s. xvii/xviii, rebacked.

Written in England. 'Thomas Maydwell' twice on f. 39^v, s. xvi. 'A Missal' at the head of f. 1 and the monogram of Narcissus Luttrell (1657-1732) and '1693' at the foot. Armorial book-plate of C. M. Borough inside the cover. Given as MS. Borough 1.

Borough 12. *Antoninus Florentinus, O.P., Confessionale* s. xv med.

Defecerunt scrutantes scrutinio ait psalmus. Scrutantes aliorum peccata sunt confessores . . . de quibusdam statibus hominum.

The first part of the Confessionale, corresponding to Bodleian MS. Canon Misc. 77, ff. 1-27. Printed often: *GKW*, nos. 2080-102. *SOPMA* i, no. 256A.

ff. i + 20 + i. A contemporary foliation of ff. 9-14 is '18'-'23'. 202 × 143 mm. Written space *c.*130 × 90 mm. 26 long lines and on f. 1^{rv} 27. Collation: $1\text{-}2^{10}$. Catchwords written vertically. Upright humanistica, each line of writing well above the line ruled for it. A 5-line space for an initial on f. 1 and 2-line spaces elsewhere not filled. Modern cardboard binding.

Written in Italy. Part of a larger book. Given as MS. Borough 1.

Borough 19. *Homiliarium (fragm.)* s. xii med.

Leaves 122-9 of a homiliary.

1. ff. 1-3 (*begins imperfectly*) filio quem genuit. ab omni fuerit legis subiectione liberrima . . . lucę reficit. Iesus cristus dominus noster. qui uiuit et regnat . . . Amen.

For Purification of B.V.M.

2. ff. 3-6^v Dominica in septuag. secundum matheum. In illo tempore dixit iesus discipulis suis parabolam hanc. Simile est regnum celorum homini patrifamilias. qui exiit primo mane . . . Omelia gregorii. In explanatione sua multa ad loquendam . . . dicamus omnes. deus meus misericordia mea.

Gregory, In Evangelia, bk. 1, hom. 19: *PL* lxxvi. 1154-9.

3. ff. 6^v-8^v Dominica in sexagesima euangelium Secundum Matheum. In illo tempore Dixit iesus . . . Ecce exiit qui seminat . . . Omelia beati gregorii. Lectio sancti euangelii quam modo . . . consortes esse ualeatis.

Bk. 1, hom. 15: *PL* lxxvi. 1131-4.

4. f. 8^v Dominica in quinquagesima. omelia sancti augustini. Audiuimus sanctum euangelium. et loquentem in euangelio dominum cristum . . . Qui legit quidem (*ends imperfectly in seventh line*).

On John 22: 1. *Nova patrum bibliotheca* (ed. A. Mai), i. 314, sermo 134, lines 1-4 (from Vat. Lat. 1276, s. xv).

ff. i + 8 (foliated in a medieval hand cxxii–cxxviii) + i. 320 × 235 mm. Written space 240 × 165 mm. 2 cols. 30 lines. A quire of eight leaves. Brown ink. Red initials outside the written space. Parchment binding, s. xx.

Written in northern Italy.[1] Given as MS. Borough 1.

OXFORD. LINCOLN COLLEGE

Lat. 129, 131, 141 are part of a collection, Lat. 122–7, 129–42, 143 (?), 144 (?), which belonged to and were much used by John Smith, 1563–(?). Smith's notes of his birth and the places where he lived from 1581 to 1607 are in the margin of f. 84v of Lat. 122, a page on which he had written some twenty years earlier notes about his then employer John Herd, born 1512, rector of Waddington, Lincolnshire, 1564, †1588 (see *DNB* and below, MS. 131): 'Memorandum quod ego natus fui anno domini 1563 ineunte Septembri . . . Anno domini 1581 destinatus eram scriba Wadingt' `a natali Christi´. Anno 1583 inservire cepi D H circa 18 Martii . . . Anno 90 Nov. quasi decimo tertio Cantabrigiam concessi. Anno 95 `secundum Romanos´ Cantabrigia discedens Buriam S. Edmundi veni circa 21 diem mensis Martii. In octobri sequenti Coringeriam veni anno 95. Inde in anno 97 redii Wad. Vnde profectus sum Bucknellam in Oct. 97. Inde Banburiam 98. Inde Buriam . . . 98. Inde Vptoniam 1600 . . . Inde Wendlingburgum 1602 in Oct.[2] Inde Shef. in Augusto 1604. Inde W. Mar. 26 1606. Inde Gainsburg ineunte Mar. 1607 sec. Rom.'. These notes and the majority of notes in Smith's manuscripts are in humanistic script. This script was acquired evidently after the time he was with Herd, when his hand is a rather flowery secretary. The secretary hand is used for the inscription in MS. 122, f. 31, 'Iohannes Smithus librum sibi vendicat istum In quo Herdi claræ describuntur medicinæ' and, interlined as an alternative to the last four words, 'descripsit claras Herdi medicinas'. How the collection comes to be at Lincoln College is not known, but Waddington was a college living from 1755. It reveals Smith's interests in words—and horses. For a description of the parchment wrapper of Lat. 124 see A. Wathey, *Music & Letters*, lxiv (1983), forthcoming.

Lat. 129. *Miscellanea grammatica; etc. (partly in English)*

1427–8; s. xv[1]

Described by N. Orme, 'A Grammatical Miscellany of 1427–65 from Bristol and Wiltshire', *Traditio*, xxxviii (1982), forthcoming.[3] See also E. Wilson in *Notes and Queries*, ccxxiv (1979), 504–8, and D. Thomson, *A descriptive catalogue of Middle English Grammatical Texts*, New York 1979, pp. 7 (on art. 1*g*), 109 (on art. 2*d*), 129 (on art 1*f*), and 147. The contents were of much interest to John Smith (see above) who indexed them (art. 6*b*) and wrote notes throughout at intervals. On f. 2 he noted 'Prisca solent sperni gaudent novitate moderni Sub pede prisca jacent et nova cuncta placent', one of the large collection of verses forming art. 5*g* (f. 106v).

[1] Dated and localized by A. Petrucci, 11 Dec. 1975.
[2] For Wellingborough matter see below, Lat. 131.
[3] I am grateful to Dr Orme and to Mr Wilson for improvements to this description.

1 (quire 1). (*a*) f. 1 Dum manducatis cristo grates refer . . . (*b*) f. 1^{v} Names of relationship. (*c*) ff. 2–5 (*begins imperfectly*) q(uare) quia a diccione composita diriuatur . . . dolorem mentis significat. Explicit. (*d*) f. 5^{v} Omne pronomen . . . : a diagram to show the different kinds of pronoun. (*e*) f. 6^{v} Five articles of faith and seven sacraments. (*f*) ff. 7–18 Deus est noster saluator. deus regitur . . . addito quale. Expliciunt tractatus de regiminibus scriptus bristolie super nouam portam. per manus Thome Schort octauo die mensis maii Anno domini M^{o}.CCCC^{o}.XX° VII°. In cuius rei testimonium etc' etc'. (*g*) ff. 18^{v}–24 (formerly pp. 34–45) Omnia nomina terminancia in A . . . dat genus omne scola. Explicit tractatus compendiosus nec non perutilis de generibus nominum secundum vsum oxonie quem edidit Magister Iohannes Laylond. Scriptus Bristollie per manus Thome Schort xx^{o} die mensis may 2^{m} computacionem ecclesie anglicane. Anno M CCCC^{mo} XXVIII° Et anno regni regis henrici sexti post conquestum anglie sexto. Quod Schort. (*h*) f. 24^{v} Differencia inter donum et feoffamentum hec est . . .

(*a*), on good behaviour at table, and (*b*) are on a torn leaf. (*c*). Grammar in question and answer form: only the top inner corner of f. 2 remains. (*d, e*) added on blank pages after (*c*): f. 6^{r} remains blank. (*f*). Includes many verses. See Thomson, op. cit., p. 129. (*g*). For Leland, †1428, see Emden, *BRUO*, p. 1129 and Thomson, op. cit., pp. 6–12, where this and three other manuscripts of De cognitione generum are listed. (*h*). Definitions of Donum, Feoffamentum, Manerium, Messuagium, Tenementum, Curtilagium, Burgagium, Placea, Toftum, Cottagium added on a blank page after (*g*). Watson, *Oxford*, pl. 332, illus. f. 22.

2 (quire 2). (*a*) f. 25 Offic' Sar' discretis viris decano decanatus albi monasterii ac vicarii perpetui de B . . . (*b*) ff. 25^{v}–30^{v} Hic intendit autor docere de quolibet diccione nominali . . . victricia tela tulere. Expliciunt genera secundum doctrinale et precianum. quod W. beuyce (*or* benyce). Nunc finem fixi penitet me si male scripci. quod Schort. (*c*) ff. 31–3 Sciendum est quod quelibet figura in primo loco posita significat se ipsam tantum . . . (*d*) ff. 33^{v}–36 Quot modis fit ethroclisis dicendum est quod secundum autorem Ca*tholi*con . . . et liber postea vades. Expliciunt ethroclita secundum vsum lond' (?).[1] (*e*) ff. 36^{v}–42^{v} Auete reuerende pater. Carissime in cristo saluteris (*sic*). Domine si placeat fruebamini sanitate votiua ex quo recessi a presencia vestra . . . Domine qualiter placet vobis de ista seruisia. bene domine vester gracia. Nunc finem feci Secundum copiam quod Schort. (*f*) ff. 42^{v}–43^{v} Benedictus qui venit in nomine domini. Iohannis xii^{o}. Prehonorabiles magistri et viri scienciarum eximii . . . (*ends imperfectly*).

(*a*). Demands the citation of I. P. Salisbury, 13 Dec. 1435. At the foot of the page a note that I.P. is to be cited in the town of Wareham. (*b*). Mainly verses. Each section begins 'Autor dicit'. (*c*). On numbers up to 'Mille milia millesies'. (*d*). On irregular nouns. Thomson, op. cit., p. 109, notes this text or variants of it in this and twelve other manuscripts. (*e*). Sentences in question and answer form, as practice in Latin conversation. On f. 37 a scholar is asked about his hall (at Oxford): he says that it is opposite the church of St Mary and holds twenty-two scholars and that they did not have enough to eat in the past year, 'domino nostro rege recedente a Wodestoke'. Smith calls (*e*) 'Colloquia barbara obscurorum virorum'. (*f*). The subject of this address is 'spoliacio' which the author reaches on f. 43^{v}/8.

3 (quire 3). (*a*) ff. 44–5 Ywandryng ful wery and walkyng þe wayes. In somer whan þ^{e} schene sonne saylyd on hyȝe . . . þy swete helpe at nede. Amen.

[1] The first letter looks more like *k*.

(*b*) ff. 46–8 Per S tantum scribere vult lex sapientum 'of wysemen' Seco secas pro scindere 'to kut' securis 'an axe' sementum 'a morter or sement' . . . transponuntur per vicium scriptoris. (*c*) ff. 49–51 Hic incipiunt verba deponencia per modum alfabeti. Hic deponentum verborum dic documentum . . . perfectus 'p*ar*fyte' habetur. Explicit tractatus. (*d*) ff. 51–55v Primitus ambigina vadeas polisillaba lector . . . herrones vagus erro. (*e*) ff. 56–8 Thirty-four recipes in English, the first 'for to brynge brosed blod aȝene in to his kynde'. (*f*) ff. 60–1 Axioms, for example 'Bonum est omnia scire non tamen omnibus vti', an example of ambiguity (Amphibologia), explanations of biblical sentences, etc. (*g*) f. 62 Memorandum quod Robertus qui fuit primus dux Normannorum . . . : descent of St Osmund from Robert, duke of Normandy. (*h*) f. 62 Pastor pius ad gregis gaudium . . . : a memoria of Osmund, the antiphon in six lines of verse; (*i*) ff. 62v–64v Willelmus conquestor. This myȝty Duke of Normandye . . . here in his ryȝt.

(*a*). *IMEV*, no. 1378. 5. Fifteen 4-line stanzas, abab, printed by Wilson, loc. cit., pp. 506–8. (*b*). Mainly verse. Lists of words spelt with *s* alone and with *s* followed by *c* and rules for the use of *t* and *c* before *ia, io*. Many interlined English glosses on f. 46rv. (*c*). Seventy-seven widely-spaced lines of verse, most of them with interlined glosses in English. (*d*). 130 widely-spaced lines of verse, the interlined glosses in Latin and English. (*e*). Added in s. xv. (*f*). Some interlined English glosses. (*i*). *IMEV, Supplement*, no. 3632/14. Fifteen 7-line stanzas by Lydgate on the kings of England from William I to Henry VI. ff. 45v, 48v, 58v–59v, 61v blank.

4 (quire 4). (*a*) f. 65 Si tu sis pulcher magnus fortisque quid inde . . . tunc nichil inde (4 lines). (*b*) f. 65v Yff þi russet hode oppose my rede hode My rede hode schal answere thy russet hoode: also the same in Latin. (*c*) ff. 66–79 Que est differencia inter hic vesperus i.o hec vespera e . . . (*d*) ff. 71v–72 15 signa ante diem Iudicii. Ieronimus autem in annalibus ebreorum . . . et resurgent omnes. (*e*) ff. 79v–87v Chyppnam. Quot modis incipitur rectus ordo construendi. Dico quod quinque modis Primo modo . . . Iste est liber vester id est vestrum et non tui. (*f*) ff. 88–90 Chere theoron quem gignos crucis . . . misticat apotoy. (*g*) ff. 90v–91 Cuius facultatis est vos. Facultatis grammatice. Quid est grammatica . . .

(*a, b*). f. 65 has been cut out, except for the top four lines on each side. (*c*). Notes on grammar, including many verses and a few English glosses. (*d*) interrupts (*c*). (*e*). Many verses, the first 'Construe sic casum . . .'. A fresh subject at f. 85v, 'Que sunt illa nomina tercie declinacionis que faciunt accusatiuum singularem in Im tantum . . .'. (*f*). The Exoticon attributed to Alexander of Hales: Walther, *Initia*, no. 2676. Twenty couplets, with interlinear Latin glosses and an explanation, 'Sentencia istorum est . . . '. Smith added 'Festum Clementis caput . . . Symphorianus' and other verses on f. 90. (*g*). Questions on grammar. f. 91v blank.

5 (quire 5). (*a*) ff. 92–9 Schort hors sone ywhyped. lytell mete sone yflypyd. Curtus equus . . . (*b*) ff. 100–3 Chyppnam. Dum tua bursa sonat populus te laude coronat . . . (*c*, added) f. 103v Examples of 'fraus' and 'laus' and verses, including 'Clauditur in tumulo sanctus Sophista Iohannes . . . (4 lines). hec Willelmus Malmesbur' in cronicorum libro de regibus anglie. (*d*) ff. 104–5 Hostilis pater est nisi virgam sentiat heres. Si parcas pueris hiis inimicus eris . . . (*e*) f. 105 Sixteen noises of men and beasts, 'Homo loquitur Infans vagit . . . '. (*f*) ff. 105v–106 Tot video gentes . . . vilificabunt (36 lines). (*g*) ff. 106–19 Nascitur in carne veruca veru datur igni . . . (*h*) ff. 119v–120 A Sarum cisiojanus,

'Cisio ia ed epi lucianus et hil fe mau mar sulp . . .'. (*i*) f. 120ᵛ Nine names. (*j*) f. 120ᵛ Letter from Thomas, abbot of Keynsham, and his convent to Thomas (Polton), bishop of Worcester, 15 Jan. 1429/30.

(*a*). Over 100 sentences, among them many proverbs and sayings, in Latin and English versions. Facsimile of f. 97 (formerly p. 197) by N. Orme, *English Schools in the Middle Ages*, 1973, pl. 3. Headings are 'Wotton' (f. 97, 97ᵛ), 'Chyppnam' (f. 98). Printed by Orme, 'A Grammatical Miscellany' (loc. cit.). f. 99 is partly cut off: the verso is blank. (*j*). Title for ordination of Thomas S. (Schort ?).

(*b*). Differentiae verborum. Headings after the first are 'D (?) Oxon' (f. 101), and 'Wotton' (f. 102). Some entries on f. 100 are marked as in art. 5*g*. Verse pieces not on grammar are:

f. 100 Dum tua bursa . . . (2 lines: Walther, *Sprichwörter*, no. 6761)
Preterit ira cito . . . (1: no. 22257a)[1]
f. 100ᵛ Ista scias care vitas hominum breuiare . . . Hinc o ricarde non potes amodo tarde (3)
Inter omne quod est mensuram ponere prodest . . . (2)
f. 101 Hoc fuit est et erit . . . (3: no. 11012)
Vespere laudetur . . . (2: cf. no. 33226)
Triste cor ira frequens . . . (2: no. 31577)
f. 101ᵛ Cor sapit et pulmo . . . (2: no. 3428)
f. 102ᵛ The nythynggale synggyth that al the whode ryngyth. And the popyniay. But heo be my bote deyn I mote or eny day (cf. *IMEV*, no. 3439. 5 and *Anglia*, lxxxii. 12); also a Latin version, Lustrans in vastis siluis psalit philomena . . . (6)
Qui scit florescit vilescit qui bona nescit . . . (2)
Laus est doctorum profectus discipulorum (1)
Quelibet hora breuis . . . (1: no. 23129)
Dilige sudorem . . . (1: no. 5752)
f. 103 Ouidius exemplum. Cesaribus virtus contingit ante diem (Ars Amatoria, 1. 184).
Disce puer . . . pertingere metas (2: cf. no. 5874)
He þat may noȝt go before lete hym goo behynd: also a Latin version, Qui non precessor valet esse sit ipse secutor (1: no. 24412)
Qui seruit nequam . . . (1: no. 24722c).
Sumere sepe merum gula ventris amor mulierum . . . (2)
Vis peregrinari disces mendacio fari . . . (2)
Sunt ibi sermones vbi plures sunt mulieres . . . (2)

(*c*). Walther, *Initia*, no. 2866.

(*d*). Differentiae verborum, etc. Verse pieces not on grammar are, after the first:

f. 104 Potus post . . . (1: no. 22115a)
Natum virga . . . (2: no. 15922)
Gutta cauat . . . (2: no. 10508a)
Vt volo si seruis . . . (2: cf. no. 29152)
Parce michi parce quia non parcunt michi perce (1)
In pariete meo pingitur ecce leo
Carmina secessum . . . (2: no. 2380, Ovid, Tristia, 1. 1. 41-2)
f. 104ᵛ Si pir . . . (1: no. 28821)
Pauo pedem . . . (2: no. 21018)
Primo puer . . . (1: no. 22391a)
Viuet in eternum qui dat michi tale falernum (1: cf. no. 33932, line 1)
Si vis potare . . . (2: no. 29408)
Dum gramen . . . (2: no. 6546)
Omne bonum . . . (1: no. 9806)
f. 105 Affligit tortor . . . (1: no. 715)
Si dare multa . . . (1: no. 28397)
Intempestiui funduntur tempore caui (1)
Si tibi copia . . . (2: no. 29238)

[1] All references by number alone in art. 5*b*, *d*, *g*, are to Walther, *Sprichwörter*.

(*f*). Walther, *Initia*, no. 19326.

(*g*). 636 lines, nearly all verses, usually either grammatical or proverbial (etc.). Grammatical pieces are sometimes marked in the margin as 'd(ifferencia)', 'dubium', 'e(quiuoca)', 'regula', 't' (these are prose), and proverbial (etc.) pieces sometimes as 'prouerbium' or by the word 'nota'. A few pieces are attributed to their authors. Verse pieces not on grammar take up about 300 lines:

f. 106 Si quis sentiret . . . (2: no. 29074)
f. 106v Cuius semper . . . (1: no. 3978)
Iuxta mantile pendent lauacrum geminile (1)
Ingenium nisi sit . . . (2: no. 12376)
Diligit amfractus . . . (1: cf. no. 5762b)
Cordi non carte . . . (2: no. 3460)
Ad studium . . . (2: no. 477)
Qui michi dat modicum . . . (2: cf. no. 24289)
Prisca solent sperni . . . (2: cf. no. 22446)
Non emitur care . . . (2: cf. no. 17547)
Si michi marinus . . . (2: no. 28652a)
f. 107 Erroris mater . . . (1: no. 7179)
Est communis homo pariter cum nemine latro (1)
Non vox sed votum . . . (2: no. 18723)
Nec michi nec tibi . . . (2: no. 16313a)
Nil valet ille labor . . . (10: Walther, *Initia*, no. 11800)
Protinus est curtus . . . (1: cf. no. 22732)
f. 107v Haurit aquas cribris . . . (1: cf. no. 10675)
Pocula ter ferre . . . (1: cf. no. 21829a)
Ex magna cena . . . (5: 1–3 are nos 8281 + 29387)
Si quis amat ranam . . . (1: no. 28967)
In fundo condi bone consors pocula condi (1)
Qui vult cantare nolit multum vigilare (1)
Si vox sit rauca . . . (1: no. 29439)
f. 108 Fraxinus et quercus . . . (21: Walther, *Initia*, no. 6902: some interlined English glosses)
Hunc homines decorant . . . (2: no. 11294)
f. 108v Si vis vim plene mortis depellere pene . . . (2)
Plus cristo distat . . . (1: no. 21681a)
f. 109 Sospitati dedit egros . . . (8, on St Nicholas: *RH*, no. 19244)
Hic iacet in tumba (2: no. 10853)
Yn a buschel of wenyd ys not \`a' anful of wytt; also a Latin version: In modio rendi . . . (1: no. 11861)
f. 109v Martinus clamidem . . . (2: no. 14453)
Nullum peccatum pro paruo . . . (2: cf. no. 19040)
Hostis nil ledit . . . (2: no. 11230c)
Cum tu tempteris et demonis arte graueris . . . (2)
Iohannes de Garlandia. Addiscas dum tempus habes . . . (2: no. 539)
f. 110 In patria propria . . . (2: cf. nos. 11918–9)
Dura libens tolerat . . . (1: no. 6803)
Sero seram ponis . . . (1: no. 28116)
Cum rapitur fraude . . . (1: no. 4376)
Cum melior iocus est . . . (1: no. 4245)
Sero rubens celum . . . (2: no. 28113b)
f. 110v Si nisi non esset . . . (2: no. 28724)
Quatuor ista timor . . . (2: no. 23692)
Cum manibus mando sine manibus omnia tango (1)
Omne quod est rarum . . . (1: no. 19863a)
f. 111 In propriis rebus . . . (2: no. 11955a)
Stacio prolixa nec non oblacio parua . . . (2)

Pax et fama fides . . . (2, and reference to Decretals, bk. 1 Significasti, and bk. 2 De iureiurando: no. 21038)
f. 111v Unde superbimus . . . (2: no. 32162)
Unde superbis . . . (2: no. 32163)
Quid non ebrietas . . . (2: no. 25113)
Spes iubet . . . (1: no. 30197)
Me pegit (*sic*) intrare . . . (2: no. 14550)
Heu heu quam surda miseros auertitur aure . . . (2)
Tunc bonus est ignis . . . (1: no. 31786)
Potus `post´ potum . . . (3: cf. 22115a)
f. 112 Spernere mundum . . . (2: no. 30154)
Inter scanna duo . . . (1: no. 12624)
Queritur ignotum queritur qui perdit amicum (1)
A iuramento linguam proibere memento . . . (2)
f. 112v In studio nostro puer hoc quocu(m)que moratur . . . (2)
Clara dies pauli . . . (4: no. 2788)
f. 113 Dat deus omne bonum . . . (1: no. 4976)
Dum grex minatur . . . (1: no. 6546)
Sum ciphus ex murra noli me tangere sturra (1)
Si non vis calui (*altered to* falli *by Smith*) . . . (1: no. 28760)
Caluicium non est vicium (1: no. 2256. 1)
Seu bene siue male qui fert loculum imitare (1)
Cum moritur diues . . . (2: cf. no. 4256: line 2 here is 'Pauperis ad funus non currit clericus vnus')
f. 113v Sunt pueri parui . . . (2: no. 30799)
Post litis tela . . . (1: no. 22015)
Si bene regna regis . . . (1: no. 28228)
Semper ad extremum . . . (1: 27889, line 1)
Scribere disce puer ne te derideat alter (1)
Mane petas montes post prandia flumina fontes (1: cf. 14403)
f. 114 Thre thyngys me comyth a day . . . (6: cf. *IMEV*, no. 3712); also a Latin version 'Sunt tria (que) vere . . . (4: no. 30847)
Clerice tepticas (*sic*) . . . (2: no. 2826)
Panifices panes faciunt . . . (1: no. 20606)
f. 114v Do quod `non´ habeo . . . (2: no. 6169)
Qui potes et bene stas et sursum cornua gestas . . . (2)
Lucanus. Tigris et eufrates vno se fonte resoluunt (1)
Aurora. Frugifer eufrates notat `hoc´ quod plurima profert (1)
Pastor oues . . . (1: no. 20818)
Dum grex minatur . . . (see above, f. 113)
O sine p . . . (2: no. 19583)
Si tua debita sint bene reddita cuique petenti . . . (2)
Sunt derisores . . . (2: nos. 30711 + 5417)
Ut tradunt sancti . . . et exul erit. Petrus in aurora (2)
f. 115 Sepe dat vna dies . . . (2: nos. 27100 + 25784)
Perdita sola dies . . . (2: no. 21317)
Dampna fleo . . . (2: no. 4893)
Tempus transactum numquam reuocatur `ad´ actum (1)
Nate nepos frater puero dixit sua mater
Verum dicebat si quis scit soluere soluat } enigma (2)
Natus casta nitens . . . (4: *Initia*, no. 11621)
f. 115v Ignorat sedem . . . (1: no. 11413)
Commoda qui sentis . . . (1: no. 2979)
Non sis seruus opum . . . (1: no. 18477, line 1)
Vsus prestabit omnem normam superabit (1)
Dat tria temptare . . . (2: no. 5018)
De sancta sinodo . . . (1: no. 5148)

Dum iuuenile decus . . . (2: no. 6559)
Diligo te non . . . (1: no. 5786)
Roma semel quantum dat bis meneuia tantum (1)
f. 116 Mensibus in quibus R . . . (3: nos. 14736b + 1841)
Garcio siquit amat ignes quos astula flammat (1)
Amphora ceruisiæ semper sunt res fugitiue (1)
f. 116v Atria seruantem postico falle clientem. Oracius (Ep. 1. 5. 31)
Dulcius est melle . . . (2: no. 6402)
Culcitra plumalis . . . (2: no. 3989b)
Sume cibum modice . . . (1: 30642, line 1)
Bytwene þe ebbe and þe flode god may send myche good; also the same in Latin, 'Inter ledonem magnum . . .' (2)
Dum furor in cursu . . . (2: no. 6541)
Whan me proferyth þe pygge opyn þe powȝ (? *sic*); also the same in Latin, 'Cum porcum tibi do . . . (2: no. 4326)
Venit ab occeano submergens cuncta vorago teodoli (1: *Ecloga*, line 69)
Salue Waltere nam clet tua t*er*cina (?) vere (1)
f. 117 In cratera meo . . . (4: Walther, *Initia*, no. 8870)
Qui vult audire missam . . . (2: no. 24940, lines 1, 2)
Laudemus virgam flectenti que cito credit . . . (2)
Qui binos lepores . . . (2: no. 23863: linked with the next four by braces)
Ad duo qui tendis . . . (1: no. 351)
Omnia vis scire nec ad vnum sufficis ire (1)
Omnia scruteris nec in ullo certus haberis (1)
Pluribus intentus . . . (1: no. 21629)
Ob leue colloquium . . . (2: no. 19604)
Quid magis est . . . (2: no. 25069)
Qui multis duliam . . . (2: no. 24305)
Primitus est orta lis de caupone loquentem . . . (2)
Este precor memores . . . (1: no. 8020)
f. 117v Lepra febris scabies . . . (2)
Tu peruerteris . . . (2: line 1 as no. 31698)
Non tendit peritum . . . (1: no. 18574)
Per nolo et nescio soluitur omnis questio (1)
Sacra lauaturus mane petebat aquas (1)
A tauro torida . . . (4: Walther, *Initia*, no. 91, lines 1–4)
Romanus tecla bartinus cum petronilla / Hec cum noctorno dant sua festa coli (2)
f. 118 Salue plus decies . . . (10: Walter, *Initia*, no. 17138)
f. 118v Paupere ditato . . . Crudescunt . . . (2: cf. no. 20954)
Cum breuis esca . . . (2: no. 6433, *Dum*)
Tangere qui gaudes . . . (2: no. 31040, lines 1, 2). Marked 'Nota bene'.
f. 119 Bis binas plena . . . (2: no. 2029a)
Femina corpus opes . . . (2: no. 9007). Marked 'Nota'.

(*h*). As C. Wordsworth, *Ancient kalendar of the University of Oxford* (OHS xlv, 1904), pp. 166–8.

(*i*). The names are 'Galfridus Strut Smyth Scherman Lauerans Deueros Russell Cosham Sowdear'.

(*j*). Asks that Thomas S. should be promoted 'ad omnes sacros ordines quod nondum assecutus est . . . ad titulum domus nostre'. S. stands presumably for Schort who wrote this piece.

6. The flyleaf, f. 121, has on the recto (*a*) a drawing of a chalice with letters round the rim and 'Hic est calix noui testamenti', s. xv, and (*b*) in the remaining space, recto and verso, a careful index of arts. 1–5 in the hand of John Smith who continued it on space remaining blank on f. 120v.

A scrap of paper in Smith's handwriting, formerly loose, is now attached to f. 122 and marked 122a.

ff. ii + 120 + iii. Paper and—for the outside and middle sheets of each quire—parchment. f. 121 is a parchment flyleaf. ff. i, ii, 122-3 are modern flyleaves. A faulty pagination of s. xvi runs to 243 on f. 120. 220 × 150 mm. Written space *c.*165 × 100 mm. 23-8 long lines. Collation: 1^{24} wants 2 + 1 leaf after 14 (f. 14): 1 and 3 (ff. 1, 2) are corners only 2^{20} wants 20 after f. 43 3^{22} wants 1 before f. 44 4^{26} 1 (f. 65) cut off, except the top 45 mm 5^{30} (ff. 91-120). Mostly in mixed secretary and anglicana by Thomas Schort (see below and for a facsimile, above, art. 5*a*), who wrote a purer secretary in art. 2*e, f* than elsewhere, but arts 1*h*, 2*a, f*, 3*a–h, i*, 5*h* appear to be in other hands, the two verse pieces 3*a* and 3*i* in current anglicana by one hand. 2-line red initials in art. 1*a–g*. Capital letters in the ink of the text touched with red. Contemporary parchment cover, repaired: three bands.[1]

Written in England, mainly by Thomas Schort[2] and partly at least in 1427 and 1428 at Bristol (art. 1*f, g*: cf. art. 2*b, e*). Interest in Bristol and its neighbourhood is suggested also by sentences in art. 5*a* (f. 97, I have dewllyd at bristow y^s^ þre ȝere and as myche more as fro myȝelmasse hedyr to; f. 97, y kan ryde to bathe in a day and als for beȝond for nede), by art. 5*j*, and by the name 'Chyppnam' (arts. 4*e*, 5*a*). 'Johannes Smith ex dono M^ri^ Chr̄of. Bulweri Aug. 20: 1612', f. 1.

Lat. 131, ff. 9-32. *Herbal (in English)* s. xv med.

Auans gariofilate harefote sanamunda. Take auans and ȝeue to drynke w^t^ vynne and it wyl make a man to speke y^t^ hath lost speche . . . y^t^ somme men callyn clyuer' or hayryff yt (*ends imperfectly*).

A collection of recipes arranged alphabetically under the names of herbs, ending in 'Madyr'. John Smith made an index to it on f. 1^rv^ which shows that sixteen leaves are missing at the end and that they contained recipes under some eighty headings, 'Mercury' to 'Woodrooffe'.

ff. 24. A pagination (Smith's ?) 1-(48). Paper. 215 × 145 mm. Written space 168 × 103 mm. 34-6 long lines. Frame ruling. Collation: $1\text{-}3^{8}$. Current anglicana: *a* sometimes in one compartment and sometimes in two. 2-line blue initials with red ornament.

Written in England. 'Wodysend Thomas' is on a scroll on f. 16^v^, as though it were a catchword. Belonged to John Smith (cf. MS. 129) who put it with ff. 45-69^v^, q.v., and other later pieces.

Lat. 131, ff. 45-69, 75. *Jordanus Ruffus de Calabria, Cyrurgia equorum* s. xv in.

Incipit cyurgia (*sic*) equorum composita a domino Iordano Ruphi Milite Marescallo quondam domini Frederici Imperatoris etc. De generacione . . . (*table of 46*

[1] Many years ago I recorded that 'The pad of this book consists of damaged fragments of English-Latin grammar, rather like the text itself, s. xv'. These were separated and called MS. Lat. 130 and subsequently mislaid. They have now been found, but not in time to be included in this volume of *MMBL*.

[2] Schort's career has been traced by Orme. He was ordained deacon in June 1430 (cf. art. 5*h*), was a chantry priest in Salisbury Cathedral in 1436 (cf. art. 3*g, h*), and was rector of Bremilham, Wilts from 1445 to 1465.

unnumbered chapters). Prologus ad subsequentia. Cum inter cetera animalia vsui hominis deputata . . . (f. 45v) et remediis. De generacione et natiuitate pullorum. Equs debet gigni . . . ad spissitudinem etc'. Explicit liber de cyurgia equorum.

As Merton College, Oxford, MS. 230, ff. 1–11, Thorndike and Kibre, col. 311: cf. cols. 310, 1282. Printed by Hieronymus Molin, *Hippiatria*, 1818, but this version differs much from the edition and is generally shorter.[1] The last correspondence seems to be in the section De mutacione vngularum (f. 66rv: edn., p. 107). The nine sections after this, De sanguine superhabundante . . . De fluxa pilorum, are listed in the table at the beginning and are in Merton 230, unlike the last eight, ending with 'De interferitura'.

The top corner of each leaf has been eaten away, with some loss of text on ff. 51–69. Added recipes on f. 69v. f. 75rv left blank. This leaf and nine added leaves of paper (ff. 70–4, 76–9) contain notes by John Smith, mainly on the subject of horses. The title on the cover 'Chirurgia equorum Iordani Rufi militis' is probably in Smith's hand.

ff. 26, formerly paginated 1–50. 215 × 145 mm. Written space 167 × 115 mm. 32–6 long lines. Frame ruling. Collation: $1\text{–}2^{12}$ 3^{2} (ff. 69, 75). Anglicana, more or less current. 2-line blue initials with red ornament. Binding presumably for Smith, who put Jordanus here after ff. 9–32, q.v., and (ff. 33–44) collectanea on horses, s. xvi ex., inside a cover which consists of a leaf of a well-written English Bible, s. xii² (2 Maccabees 9: 26 Oro itaque– 10: 38 benedicebant dominum: written space *c.* 270 × 180 mm: 2 cols. 36 lines). The binding is strengthened by eight flyleaves, ff. 1–8, of which 1 and 8 are a bifolium of parchment and 2–7 are leaves of paper waste, including articles of agreement dated 1589, calculations of Easter, etc., for 1589, and two letters from Christopher Lauson (?) to 'his good cuntryman' John, master of the free school at Wellingborough, Northants, one dated in 1603 and the other in October (?) 1604.[2]

Written in England. 'Memorandum that I did gyve this bok de Chirurgia equorum to Ihon Smyth my man', f. 75, s. xvi, is presumably in the hand of John Herd: see above, p. 630. Acquired as MS. 129.

Lat. 141, ff. 1–6, 9–20, 23–6. *Verses (in English); Latin–English vocabulary* s. xv²

1 (quire 1). Pieces of verse: (*a*) f. 1, cut out, except a strip on which are the first letters of a few lines on the recto and the ends of a few lines on the verso, for example 'brak hys brayn', 'fell on Saule'; (*b*) began on this leaf, no doubt, but all that remains of it are (f. 2) 'Pro nobis deus exora That we may in heweyne bryȝt Inter sanctorum agmina; (*c*) f. 2 Syng we now yis holy feste Vox in rama audita . . . (10 lines); (*d*) f. 2v Agnus dei hodie natus de pura virgine Is lombe for hys fadyr is thome He is com tyll a pure virgynys wombe . . . (12 lines); (*e*) f. 3 To

[1] The preface here is 'Cum inter cetera animalia vsui hominis deputata (equs) sit nobilius de ipsius cura et regimine et infirmitatibus tractare intendimus ideo ordine secundum quod a peritis in hac arte dicimus de omnibus raciones verissimas demonstrando. Primo ergo dicemus de generacione et natiuitate equorum (f. 45v). Secundo de laqueacione et dominacione (ff. 45v–46). Tercio de custodia et doctrina (ff. 46–8). Quarto de cognicione pulcritudinis et corporis membrorum (ff. 48–49v). Quinto de infirmitatibus (ff. 49v–69v). Sexto de medicinis et remediis (*included with 5*). The preface in the edition is considerably longer than this.

[2] According to A. F. Leach in *VCH Northants*, ii. 265–6, Robert Law was schoolmaster in 1603 and was followed by Edmund James in 1604. Smith seems to have been in Wellingborough for some years from October 1602: see above, p. 630.

blysse god bryng vs all and sume Criste redemptor omnium In bedleem in y^t^ fayr cyte . . . (14 lines); (*f*) ff. 3^v^–4 A blyssyd full songe y^is^ is to vs Miserere mei deus . . . (17 lines); (*g*) f. 4^rv^ Salue mater delicie Almyty god in trinite Thow seyndyst y^i^ sone frome heuen cyte . . . (18 lines); (*h*) ff. 4^v^–5 Ihesu fili virginis miserere nobis Ihesu of a maydyn woldyst be borne To sawe mankynd y^t^ was forlorne . . . (10 lines); (*i*) f. 5^rv^ Man lat be y^i^ cruelnese . . . (18 lines); (*j*) ff. 5^v^–6 Pyrdow pyrdow pyrdowy. wows sẹ bone trenket sowterly. Lystyne lordys verament How the sowt*er* hath mad' hys testament w^t^ py(rdowy) . . . ; (*k*) f. 6^rv^ All' fresche all' fresche fresch' is my song Sa̤lomon to wytnes I schall say ȝow no wrong. Sal[o-mon] to [wyt]ne[s.] Salomon ye wise . . .

(*c*) is for Innocents and (*d, e, g, h*) for Christmas. For other copies of (*e*) and (*h*) see *IMEV*, nos. 1471, 1738 and R. L. Greene, *The Early English Carols*, 1977, nos. 21, 91. In (*f*) lines 2, 7, 12, 17 are Miserere mei deus and in (*g*) lines 1, 6, 10, 14, 18 are Salue mater delicie. The ink changes at (*j*). (*j*), the souter's testament, and (*k*), on the dangers of taking a wife, are printed hence by E. Wilson in *Notes and Queries*, ccxxv (1980), 22, 25.

2. ff. 11^v^–20^v^, 23–24^v^, 26^rv^ (for the right order see below) Hoc principium ii a Begynnyng . . . (f. 24) Hec amphora re a Tankerd.

A Latin-English vocabulary, at first (ff. 11^v^–13^v^) like T. Wright and R. P. Wülcker, *Anglo-Saxon and Old English Vocabularies*, 1884, i. 673–677/35; then more like the vocabulary on pp. 745–814, but much abbreviated and inferior. Headings are: f. 15^v^ Nomina vestimentorum; f. 14 Nomina diuersorum hominum; f. 16^v^ Nomina mulierum; f. 26^v^ Nomina arborum (et) frugum; f. 17 Nomina terrarum et planetarum et aliarum rerum; f. 18^v^ Nomina domorum et ecclesiarum; f. 19^v^ Nomina auium domesticorum; f. 20^v^ Nomina piscium aquarum retencium; f. 23 Nomina vermium; f. 23 Nomina muscarum; f. 23^v^ Nomina diuersorum lapidum; f. 23^v^ Nomina pertinencia coquine; f. 24 Nomina pertinencia botulare. The text is continuous from f. 13 to f. 15, from f. 15 to f. 14, and from f. 26 to f. 17. A leaf may be missing between f. 18 which ends on the verso 'Hec Capella le a Chapell' and f. 19 which begins 'Hec Cippa pe a plante': the entries on f. 19^rv^ before the heading are miscellaneous. Nine early additions on f. 24^r^, seven on f. 24^v^ and seven on f. 11^r^, which was left blank at first. Probably three leaves were left blank at the beginning of quire 2 and four leaves at the end of quire 3. Some of these leaves were filled later (art. 3).

3. (*a*) f. 9^rv^ Notes on grammar, English translations of Latin words and on 9^v^ the sentence 'Dum pulcra et amena dies formica laborat non pereat cum nix venerit alta fame'. (*b*) f. 25^rv^ (*begins imperfectly*) mittor . . . ciuitati uel ad ciuitatem . . . (*ends imperfectly*). (*c*) f. 10^v^ Ac^t^ of the thyngs and matter contayned in this little booke are as follow viz. First the parts and membres of a mans body . . .'.

(*a, b*). s. xv/xvi. (*b*). Schoolboy notes on grammar, for example 'Magister est doctior suis discipulis uel quam sui discipuli', 'Ego sum altior socio meo vno pollice'. (*c*). s. xvi. Notes the first sections of art. 2.

ff. 22. The modern foliation runs to 26 because the strips of manuscript, s. xvi/xvii, used as strengthening between quire 1 and quire 2 and in the middle of quire 3 are included in it (ff. 7, 8, 21–2). ff. 11^v^–20^v^, 23^r^–26^r^ were paginated in s. xvi/xvii, 1–4, 6–27. 153 × 103 mm. Written space 85–95 mm high. A bounding line on the left is the only ruling and that only in art. 2. Collation: 1^8 wants 1, 2 (ff. 1–6) 2^8 wants 2, blank (ff. 9–13, 15, 14) 3 nine (ff. 16, 26, 17–20, 23–5: 16 and 25, 19–24, and 20 and 23 are bifolia, so, unless a leaf is missing after f. 18, the quire is a twelve wanting 9–11 after f. 24). Arts. 1, 2 in current anglicana by one hand. No decoration. Binding of limp parchment, s. xvi/xvii.

Written in England. Part of a mainly lexicographical collection put together and bound in s. xvi/xvii, no doubt for John Smith, whose hand occurs throughout. The other contents include two Latin-English vocabularies, s. xvi (ff. 31-94, 163-85), a Greek-English vocabulary, s. xvi (ff. 194-211), and a printed *Nova et expedita via comparandae linguae Latinae*, Cambridge *c.*1590 (*STC* 24695a. 5: ff. 266-73).[1] Given as MS. 129.

Lat. 149. *Horae* s. xv²

1. ff. 1-12ᵛ A rather empty calendar in red and black.

Entries in red include Amandi episcopi, Visitatio marie, Remigi et bauonis (6 Feb., 2 July, 1 Oct.); in black, Milburge virginis, Brandani episcopi (23 Feb., 17 May).

2. ff. 14-21 Incipit offitium sancte crucis . . . Ymnus. Patris sapientia . . . f. 21ᵛ blank.

3. ff. 23-8 Incipit offitium sancti spiritus . . . Nobis sancti spiritus . . . f. 28ᵛ blank.

4. f. 30ʳᵛ Incipit offitium Misse beate marie. Introibo . . . Ends imperfectly.

5. ff. 32-120ᵛ Offitium beate marie uirginis. Use of (Rome).

The Advent office begins on f. 112.

6. ff. 122-44 Septem psalmi penitentiales. Litany, f. 131ᵛ.

The monks and hermits are Benedict, Bernard, Francis, Leonard, and Dominic. ff. 144ᵛ-145 blank.

7. ff. 146-95 Office of the dead. f. 195ᵛ blank.

ff. i + 195 + v. ff. i, 195-7 are parchment endleaves, the first and last pasted to paper leaves. 95 × 70 mm. Written space 53 × 33 mm. 16 long lines. Collation doubtful, mainly eights (1-2⁶: leaves missing after f. 30), together with fourteen singleton leaves with blank rectos and pictures on the versos, ff. 13, 22, 29, 31, 52, 67, 74, 81, 87, 93, 103, 111, 121, 145. Fourteen full-page pictures, nine in art. 5 (a passion series and on f. 111ᵛ, Coronation of B.V.M.), and one before each of arts. 2 (Christ rises from the tomb: instruments of the Passion), 3, 4 (B.V.M., Child and kneeling angel), 6 (Christ in judgement on the rainbow), 7. Eight 10-line or 11-line pictures in art. 5 (Innocents at vespers, Flight into Egypt at compline). Initials: (i) 8-line or less, blue patterned in white on grounds of red and gold, the red patterned in white and the gold decorated; (ii) 2-line, gold on grounds of red and blue patterned in white; (iii) 1-line, blue with red ornament or gold with blue ornament. Gold framed floral borders all round picture pages and pages facing pictures. A bird or two, including owls and peacocks, on each of these pages. Line fillers in litany only: blue and gold. Binding of s. xix. Secundo folio (f. 15) *Domine*.

Written in the southern Low Countries. The pictures are of the school of W. Vrelant of Bruges. Given by Eric Sexton, F.S.A., in 1975.

[1] Smith was at Cambridge in the 1590s: see above, p. 630.

Lat. 150. *Canon missae, etc.* s. xiii^2

Described by E. G. Millar, *The Library of A. Chester Beatty*, ii (1930), 63–5.

1. (*a*) ff. 1–2 Oratio ad manus abluendas dum sacerdos preparat se ad missam celebrandam. Largire sensibus nostri . . . (*b*) ff. 2–4 Prefaces (no music). (*c*) ff. 5ᵛ–11 Canon of mass. (*d*) f. 11 Sacerdos recedens ab altari dicat hanc a' cum sequentibus. Trium puerorum . . .

(*d*). Psalms and prayers, Deus qui tribus, Da nobis quesumus, Tribue quesumus.

2. ff. 11–26ᵛ Twelve feasts of the temporal from Christmas to Trinity and (f. 20) eleven feasts of the sanctoral from John Baptist to Andrew, together with (f. 23ᵛ) the 'officium commune de S. Maria' after the office of the Nativity of B.V.M.

3. ff. 26ᵛ–27ᵛ In dedicatione ecclesie.

4. (*a, b*) ff. 27ᵛ–29 Collect, secret, and postcommunion of (*a*) eleven masses for the dead and (*b*) a mass 'tam pro uiuis quam defunctis'. (*c*) ff. 29–30ᵛ Full office 'pro pluribus sacerdotibus defunctis'.

(*a*). (1) pro layco defuncto et pro pluribus. (2) pro femina defuncta. (3) pro pluribus defunctis. (4) pro anniuersariis. (5) (pro uno defuncto). (6) pro patribus et matribus. (7) pro quiescentibus in cymiterio. (8) pro cunctis fidelibus defunctis. (9) pro congregatione. (10) pro sacerdote defuncto. (11) pro episcopo uel pro sacerdote. (2, 3, 5–8) are as *SMRL* ii. 329–30, no. 63 (h, n, g, m, k, o, i); (1, 4, 9–11) differ more or less from edn. (*b*). ibid., p. 324, no. 37. (*c*). The collect is Concede quesumus omnipotens deus animabus, the secret Munera tibi domine dicata, and the postcommunion *Quesumus*[1] omnipotens deus ut anime.

5. ff. 30–32ᵛ Votive masses: (*a*) Oratio pro pace; (*b*) De omnibus sanctis oratio; (*c, d*) Oratio propria pro sacerdote (two forms); (*e*) Oratio cotidie ad missam in quadragesima; (*f*) Oratio pro familiaribus; (*g*) Pro pace habenda; (*h*) Oratio contra temptationes carnis; (*i*) Oratio pro infirmo; (*j*) Oratio pro iter agentibus; (*k*) Oratio pro peccatis.

(*a–c, e–h*). As *SMRL* ii. 321–4, nos. 10 (Pro persecutoribus ecclesie), 8, 18, 38, 33, 11, 24.

6. f. 32ᵛ Oratio in missa de nupciis. Exaudi nos omnipotens et misericors deus . . .

Collect, secret, and postcommunion. ff. 33–35ᵛ left blank.

7 (added). (*a*) f. 32ᵛ Mass of St Nicholas. (*b*) ff. 33–4 Mass (pro se ipso sacerdote), signed 'S. A. Lensz'.

(*a*). s. xv ex. (*b*). s. xvi ex.

ff. ii + 35. Late medieval foliation of ff. 1–35 ix–xliii. 188 × 130 mm. Written space *c.* 140 × 90 mm. 2 cols. 36 lines (18 lines, ff. 3ᵛ–10ᵛ). Collation: 1^{18} wants 1–5 2^{24} wants 20, 24,

[1] MS. *Deus*, through the rubricator's error.

blanks. Quire 1 is signed at the foot of the last verso (13^v) in red, XIIII. Two full-page pictures: f. 4^v Crucifixion; f. 5 Christ in Majesty. The double opening, 4^v–5, is reproduced by Millar, pl. 121, and, reduced, in the Sotheby sale catalogue. Initials: (i) ff. 3^v, *P* of *Per omnia* and (smaller) *U* of *Uere*, 5^v *T*, 11^v *V*, blue or blue and pink, patterned in white, on grounds of blue and red, historiated; (ii, iii) 3-line and 2-line, red and blue with ornament of both colours in saw pattern; (iv) 1-line, red or blue. Parchment binding, s. xvi (?).

Written in France. Apparently once part of a much larger book (see above) in which the last (?) forty-three leaves had an independent foliation. For an owner, s. xvi ex., see above, art. 7*b*. Inscriptions of ownership by the Premonstratensian abbey of Dommartin (Pas de Calais) in s. xviii and by G. J. Oblin, last abbot of Dommartin (1787–91: †1824), on f. 1; also a letter-mark, 'Q', in the right margin. Phillipps MS. 4448, acquired *c.*1830. Bought privately from the Phillipps collection by A. Chester Beatty in 1925: Chester Beatty MS. 58. Sale at Sotheby's, 24 June 1969, lot 52, to Messrs. Maggs. Given as MS. 149.

Lat. 151. *Brut Chronicle (in English)* s. xv^2

Here may a man here how Englond was first called Albion and thurgh whom it had the name. In the noble lond of Sirrie . . . (f. 3) Capitulo primo. In the noble Citee of grete Troye . . . was sette in reste and in governaunce.

Ends at 1419. As compared with Brie's edition (EETS cxxxi, cxxxvi, 1906–8) this manuscript contains chapters 1–222 and with some gaps 226–45: the omitted passages are chapters 227, 229, 232, 234–5 and parts of chapters 226, 228, 231, and 233 (edn., pp. 295/29–300/7, 301/20–306/29, 308/19–309/25, 310/34–313/4, 313/9–319/34, 321/13–326/18. On the other hand ff. 49^v–51^v contain two chapters on Cadwallader numbered 102 and 103, 'After þ^e dethe of Cadwalyn . . . yere of grace vi^c lxxix', which do not occur in the edition after p. 103/8. Chapters 1–152 (edn., 1–150) are numbered. After this point the hand changes and only a few chapters are numbered: the numbers are not usually in agreement with the edition. At f. 175^v/34 (edn., p. 388/13, 14) the reading is 'my mayster nevell'.

ff. i + 176 + i, foliated i, 1–25, 27–178. 237 × 180 mm. Written space 175 × 110 mm. 33–5 long lines. Collation: 1–22^8. Quires signed [a]–y in the usual late medieval way: the first scribe signed his leaves lower down than the second scribe and all his marks have been cut off, except 'h 4' on f. 69 (where one would expect 'i 4'): the first complete quire by the second scribe is signed 'l' (f. 82). Two secretary hands, changing at f. 78/10 'And whan' (edn., p. 161/18): the first hand often uses long *r*. Initials: (i) f. 1, 8-line *I*, red on gold ground decorated and with marginal prolongations in colours into three margins; (ii) blue, with red and a little gold ornament, 3-line to where the hand changes and then 4-line. Binding of s. xvii, rebacked. Secundo folio *hem of their*.

Written in England. 'Presens opusculum sibi vendicat magister Robertus turrell et vxoris eius', f. 177^v, s. xvi. Scribbles of s. xvi include: 'Rychard smyth wrytte thys', f. 153^v; 'Crystyan parker gorgyse parker mathwe chalys', f. 154; 'Necollas tomsewn (?) Tomas freman the [. . .] and Ihon freman of ascheton strethe' (*Street Ashton, Warwickshire* ?), f. 175^v; 'Thomas freman of laendoas (?)', f. 176^v; 'Thys boke ys master [. .]erey[. . .] boke and Roberd Chale[s] dede wryght yt', f. 177^v. Armorial book-plate of (Rev.) George Norris, s. xix^1: his gift to Norwich Castle Museum in 1830. Sold at Sotheby's, 11 Dec. 1961, lot 159. Given as MS. 149.

Lat. 152. *Horae* s. xv^1

1. ff. 1–86 Hours of B.V.M. of the use of (Paris). ff. 58^v, 86^v–87^v blank.

2. ff. 88–109^v Penitential psalms and (f. 104) litany.

Seven martyrs: . . . (6, 7) dyonisi quintine. Ten confessors: . . . (5–10) maglorii ludouice claudi maure fiacri anthoni. Eleven virgins: (not including Anne): . . . (5) columba . . . (10, 11) genouefa oportuna.

3. ff. 110–114v Hours of Holy Cross. '. . . (f. 110v) Ymnus. Patris sapiencia . . .'.

4. ff. 115–19 Hours of Holy Spirit. '. . . (f. 115v) Hymnus. Nobis sancti spiritus . . .'.

5. ff. 119v–177v Office of the dead.

6. ff. 177v–184v Les xv ioies nostre dame. Doulce dame de misericorde mere de pitie . . . Sonet, no. 458.

7. ff. 184v–188 Doulz dieu doulz pere sainte trinite . . . Sonet, no. 504.

8. f. 188rv Sainte uraye croix aouree . . . Sonet, no. 1876.

9 (added, s. xvi). f. 188v Orayson pour pryer pour les ames de purgatoyre. Mon tressouuerain seygneur mon benoist et pytoux redempteur . . . (*ends imperfectly*).

ff. i + 188 + i. 140 × 100 mm. Written space 70 × 48 mm. 13 long lines. Ruling in red ink. Collation: $1–6^8$ 7 seven (ff. 49–55) 8^6 9 seven (ff. 62–8) 10^8 11^{10} wants 10, blank, after f. 87 $12–24^8$ 25^8 wants 6–8, blank, after f. 188. Twelve 10-line pictures, eight in art. 1 and one before each of arts. 2–4, 5 (devil and angel, one on each side of the bed of a dying man: Death throws his dart). Initials: (i) 3-line, blue patterned in white on decorated gold grounds; (ii; iii) 2-line and 1-line, gold on blue and red grounds patterned in white. Floral borders framed in red ink are continuous on picture pages and on three sides of ff. 177v, 184v. Mirror image borders the height of the written space in the outer margin of all other written pages: flowers and gold ivy leaves. Line fillers blue or red patterned in white, with gold blobs between the colours. Capital letters in the ink of the text filled with pale yellow. Gilt morocco binding, s. xviii: 'Horæ canonicæ' on the spine. Secundo folio *Uenite*.

Written in France. G–4/9 inside the cover. Armorial book-plate of Eric Sexton, F.S.A. Given as MS. 149.

Lat. 153. *Virgilius, Bucolica et Georgica* s. xv med.

1. ff. 1–15 Titire tu patule recubans sub tegmine fagi . . . hesperus: ite capelle.

Red headings to all but the first of the ten eclogues, for example (8) 'Sequitur octaua egloga que apellatur contentio Damonis et alphesibei qui damon conqueritur de amasia sua nisa'. No scholia or glosses. A 4-line space for a heading on f. 1 left blank.

2. ff. 15–50v Quid faciat laetas segetes quo sidere terram . . . ceagrius (*sic*) hebrus.

Ends imperfectly at 4. 524: catchword 'uolueret'. Scholia and interlinear glosses on ff. 15–19 only. Verses in front of bks. 2–4, as in Corpus Christi College 546, art. 2, q.v.: [H]actenus aruorum . . . ex ordine foetus; [Te]que pales . . . carmine uates; [P]rotinus . . . dona. Spaces for headings not filled.

ff. i + 50 + i. 260 × 165 mm. Written space 160 mm high. 30 long lines. The first line of writing above the top ruled line. Collation: $1-5^{10}$. Vertical catchwords. Humanistica by one hand. Spaces for 4-line or 3-line initials on ff. 1, 15, 23^{v}, 32^{v}, 42 and for 2-line initials elsewhere not filled. Binding of perhaps contemporary wooden boards covered with white leather: three bands: two clasps fastening from front to back missing, but the metal pieces for them on the covers remain.

Written in Italy, probably the north-east.[1] In Spain in s. xviii: 'En toledo' and, lower, 'Eugenio Domingo' inside the cover. Given by Professor Martin Robinson in 1978.

OXFORD. MAGDALEN COLLEGE

Lat. 36. *Chronicon Angliae* s. xiii^{2}

1. ff. 3–197^{v} [R]omanorum nonagesimus iii^{us} Henricus regnauit . . . litteris domini pape acceptis: repatriauit.

An English chronicle from 1002–1226 edited by W. Stubbs as *Memoriale Walteri de Couentria* (RS 58 (1872): 2 vols.): this copy described in I. xl–xli and collated as M. Fairly numerous marginalia draw attention to points in the text and suggest a special interest in miracles and the history of Scotland.

2. ff. 1–2 De letania maiori et minori. [L]etanie in anno bis fiunt. scilicet in festo sancti Marchi . . . quod tangere non audent.

A bifolium, s. xv, which acted as flyleaves of another manuscript until s. xvii in. The table of contents of this other manuscript is on f. 2^{v} in a hand of s. xiv in.: 'In isto libro continentur / Cro[nica] Martini / Speculum peccatoris / Vita sancti Mat[hie] apostoli / Sancte Marie [Magd]alene / Vita sancti dyon' Archiepiscopi / Vita barlaam / Vita basilii episcopi / [. . .] de sanctis andrea apostolo / firseo / arsenio / agatono / Commemoracio omnium fidelium / Euangelium Nichodemi'. A hand of s. xvii in., which wrote tables and titles also in MSS. 53, 180 and other manuscripts given to Magdalen College by Samuel Foxe, repeated the old table, but with the addition of two items after the life of Mathias 'et Vita Iudæ Iscariotæ Vita Sancti Macharii' and an extension of the last title but one to read 'De Commemoratione omnium fidelium. Vbi agitur de Purgatorio. de purgandis de suffragiis de loco pænarum etc.': evidently the manuscript to which the table refers was still in existence at this time. 'Ex dono fratris Ricardi de Knesall' is in a hand of s. xiv in. above the old table.

ff. iv + 193 + i, foliated 1–197 (198). 248 × 177 mm. Written space 182 × 125 mm. 2 cols. 44 lines. Collation of ff. 3–197: $1-2^{8}$ $3-7^{12}$ 8^{8} (ff. 79–86) $9-15^{12}$ 16^{8} 17^{8} wants 8, blank, after f. 197. Written in current anglicana by more than one hand. Spaces for initials remain blank. Binding of smooth calf, s. xvii^{1}.[2] Secundo folio *instructus* (f. 4).

Written in England. Used by John Bale whose hand occurs, for example, on ff. 3, 40, 175^{v}. Belonged probably to John Foxe (†1587: *DNB*) who may have written 'simonia cleri' on f. 101 (edn., i. 397/3) and 'ha ha ha' on f. 150^{v} (edn., ii. 108: death of William of Poitiers). Given by his son, Samuel (fellow 1579–90, †1630: *DNB*): cf. T. James, *A manuduction*,

[1] Information from Dr A. de la Mare.

[2] Smooth calf bindings like this are also on MSS. 43, 53, 69, 70, 84, 170, 172, 180, 181, 199, 200, all, it seems, gifts of Samuel Foxe, but not on other manuscripts at Magdalen College.

1625, p. 139, and the list of Foxe's manuscripts in B.L., MS. Lansdowne 819, ff. 95–6^{v}, where this manuscript is no. 19, 'Wigorniensis Monachi historia', a title taken from Bale's on f. 3. Probably reached Magdalen College in 1614 when Foxe's servant was given 20*s.* 'adferenti Manuscript:'.

Lat. 210. *Cassiodorus, etc.* s. xiv med. (art. 4)–xiv/xv

1. ff. 1–73 In hoc op(er)e continentur historie ecclesiastice ex socrate. Sozomeno et theodorico. in vno collecte et insuper de greco in latinum translate libri xii^{cim}. Prefacio cassiodori senatoris serui dei. Utiliter nimis . . . imperatoris theodosii. Explicit liber qui dicitur tripartita historia.

PL lxix. 879–1214. No. 120 of 135 copies listed by W. Jacob in *Texte und Untersuchungen zur Geschichte der altchristlichen Literatur*, lix (1954): the latest of his mainly English group VId (cf. pp. 144–8, where this copy is referred to as M).

2. ff. 73^{v}–74^{v} Potestatem remittendi peccata . . . discutienda sunt.

3. ff. 75–138^{v} Historia eusebii de greco in latinum translata que ecclesiastica appellatur historia. Incipit prologus historiarum. Peritorum dicunt esse . . . premia meritorum. Expliciunt vndecim libri historiarum.

Ed. T. Mommsen (see below, Worcester College, Oxford, 285, art. 1). Chapters 15–18 and part of ch. 19 of bk. 11, left out on f. 136, were added on f. 138^{v} by another hand.

4. ff. 139–86 Incipiunt sermones beatissimi patris sanctissimi abbatis clareuallis domni Bernardi. de temporibus et festis. Sermo de aduentu domini et vi circumstanciis eius. Incipit. Hodie fratres celebramus . . . esse deuota. Expliciunt sermones Bernardi de tempore et festis per Annum. deo gracias. Amen.

Eighty-one sermons, most of them more or less abbreviated. They consist of: (ff. 139–65) forty-seven sermons of the temporal from Adv. 1 to Pent. 3; (ff. 165–6) Hoc mare magnum . . . (De diversis, 35: *SBO* v. 288) and Benedictus qui venit (*SBO* iv. 270); (ff. 166–184^{v}) twenty-eight sermons of the sanctoral (Conversion of Paul–Andrew); (ff. 184^{v}–186) Ded. 1, 3, 4, 5. f. 186^{v} blank.

ff. 186. ff. 139–86 (art. 4) are foliated in a medieval hand 348–70, 372–96. 370 × 255 mm. Written space of arts. 1–3 270 × 185 mm: 2 cols.: *c.*60 lines: frame ruling. Written space of art. 4 *c.*252 × 150 mm: 2 cols.: 60 lines. Collation: 1–11^{12} 12^{8} wants 7, 8, perhaps blank, after f. 138 13–16^{12}. Quires 3–5 are signed f, g, h: the leaf numbers precede the quire letters. Short-*r* anglicana formata, art. 4 under French influence. Initials of arts. 1–3: (i) f. i, 4-line and 3-line, red with green ornament; (ii) 2-line, red. Initials of art. 4: (i) f. 139, 3-line *H*, blue with red ornament; (ii) 2-line, blue or red with ornament of the other colour. Oxford binding by Robert Way of rough calf over pasteboards: peacock with garter below earl's coronet as centrepiece and Ker, *Pastedowns*, ornament 65, as corner-pieces (see there, p. 218). Secundo folio *nequaquam*.

Written in England and (art. 4) probably in Italy. Art. 4, part of a much larger book, may not have been placed with arts. 1–3 until s. xvii in., when Robert Way bound this and many other Magdalen College manuscripts.

Lat. 213. *John Gower, Confessio Amantis (in English)* s. xv²

Torpor ebes sensus . . . Of hem that writen vs tofore . . . requiesce futurus. Gower. J.

IMEV, no. 2662/C3. A copy of the 'third recension' noticed by C. G. Macaulay, *Works of John Gower*, 1901, II. clxiii, and referred to as Magd. Macaulay notes the likeness to the 'third recension' manuscript used by Caxton for his edition. A. I. Doyle and M. B. Parkes note the relationship with B.L., Harley 7184 in *Essays presented to N. R. Ker*, 1978, p. 201. Book 1, p. 14; 2, p. 54; 3, p. 95; 4, p. 127; 5, p. 169; 6, p. 255; 7, p. 282; 8, p. 341. Nine missing leaves contained bk. 2, lines 400–586, on a leaf after p. 58 and bk. 5, lines 701–2163, on a quire after p. 176. Scribbles of s. xvi in many margins. On the flyleaf, p. 380, eight lines of verse, s. xvi, 'Off deathe and lyffe which be in stryfe to treate now I intende . . .'. On p. iv^v at the top 'Blabys blamyth blechynden', s. xvi.

ff. ii + 180 + i, paginated before loss of leaves (i–iv), 1–58, 61–176, 193–377, (380–2). 475 × 330 mm. Written space 345 × 215 mm. 2 cols. 48 lines. Collation: $1–3^8$ 4^8 wants 6 after p. 58 $5–23^8$ 24^6. A large non-current secretary by one hand throughout. Initials: (i) of prologue and books, pink and blue shaded to white on decorated gold grounds: projections from part borders: (ii, iii) 3-line and 1-line, blue with red ornament or gold with blue ornament. A skilled calligrapher was employed to decorate the *E* of *Explicit* at the end of bks. 1–4 and the catchwords of quires 1–11. Calf binding, s. xvi, over (medieval ?) wooden boards: the leather bears a crested roll and Oldham's roll FP. g. 13. Secundo folio *The membres*.

Written in England. Probably in Norfolk in s. xvi med.: roll FP. g. 13 is not known to have been used outside Norwich. 'John Gibon 1581' is scribbled on p. 127. 'This is Marchadyne Hunnies his booke and he that steles this booke shall hange . . . ', p. i, looks like schoolboy work: Hunnies was 16 when admitted to Magdalen College in 1601. 'Liber collegii Beatæ Mariæ Magdalenæ ex dono Marchadini Hunnis in artibus Magistri (*M.A., 9 Nov. 1609*) Anno a partu virginis 1610[1] Feb. 28', p. ii.

Lat. 248. *Chronicon regum angliae* s. xv²

Considerans Cronicorum (*these two words in red*) prolixitatem necnon et difficultatem . . . vsque ad henricum sextum (*these two words in red*) originaliter finem perduxi. Adam in agro damasceno . . . qui natus erat in festo translacionis Sancti Edwardi regis et confessoris Anno domini Millesimo CCCC^{mo} Quinquagesimo Tercio. After this, a crown and roundel are part of the original design: on the crown is 'Corona aurea super capud eius' and in the roundel 'Edwardus iiii^{us} Rex'.

A genealogical descent from Adam to Edward IV is accompanied by text running as far as Cadwallader ('Iste kadwalladrus . . . monochus est effectus') and from 788 to 1453, the birth of Prince Edward. The chronicle is attributed to Roger Albon by Bale, *Scriptores*, II, xii, no. 71: cf. *Lyell Cat.*, pp. 84–5 and *MMBL* i. 332. Differs from Bodley Rolls 7 (*Sum. Cat.* 2965) only in having crowns above the roundels containing the names of kings from Brutus to Careticus (ninety kings) and from 'Edulphus' (Aethelwulf, AD 839) to the end, in concluding the list of popes in the left edge with Pius II (1458–64) instead of with Calixtus (III: 1455–8) and in having the Edward IV roundel at the end.

[1] Not 1620 (Macaulay).

A roll of thirteen membranes each about 800 mm long and 310 mm wide. Written in anglicana formata. The roundels are alternately green and red. The roundel against Adam is 80 mm across internally—larger than the rest—and has no name in it: it was perhaps intended for a picture. The *C* of *Considerans* and *A* of *Adam* are red and green, with red and violet (?) ornament. Kept in a box.

Lat. 251. *Seneca, Epistolae* s. xv^2

1. (*a*) ff. 1–7 Rubrice epistolarum Lucii Amei (*altered to* Anei) Senece ad Lucilum in libros. (*b*) ff. 8–172^v Incipiunt epistole Lucii amei Senece ad Lucillum. Liber primus. De colligenda et sistenda fuga temporis . . . Ita fac mi Lucili . . . infelicissimos esse felices. Liber epistolarum Annei Senece ad Lucilum explicit.

(*a*). Headings of fifteen books and titles and incipits of 124 letters in the hand which writes (*b*) from f. 92. f. 7^v blank. (*b*). Headings are not filled in beyond f. 81 (bk. 10, letter 72). Books 1–14 contain 11, 8, 9, 7, 9, 6, 7, 8, 4, 3, 4, 3, 3, 3 letters respectively. Book 15 contains 39 letters (86–124). Letter 89 begins on a new quire (12^1: f. 120) and the written space becomes larger.

2. (*a*) f. 173 Lucius Anneus Seneca cordubensis . . . interfectus est. Explicit dictum beati Ieronimi. (*b*) ff. 173–175^v Incipiunt epistole Imperatoris magistri ad Paulum et Pauli apostoli ad Senecam. Seneca pauli salutem. Credo tibi Paule . . . istic properantem. Vale Seneca carissime nobis. (*c*) f. 175^v Epitaphium Seneca. Cura labor . . . ossa tibi. Deo gratias.

(*a–c*) are the extract from Jerome, the correspondence of Paul and Seneca, and the epitaph of Seneca commonly found together and in this order (cf. *MMBL* ii. 702, 757). (*a*). *PL* xxxiii. 629. (*b*). Letters 1–10, 12, 11, 13, 14 in edn. Haase (Teubner series), iii. 476–81. (*c*). *Anthologia Latina*, ed. Riese, no. 667.

ff. ii + 175 + ii. Paper. 283 × 180 mm. Written space *c.*172 × 118 mm and on ff. 120–55 *c.*210 × 150 mm. 32–47 long lines. Collation: 1 seven $2\text{–}10^{12}$ 11^4 (ff. 116–19) $12\text{–}15^{12}$ 16^8. Written by two (?) hands in hybrida, more or less current from f. 92, where the second hand begins. Red initials on ff. 8–11 only: spaces remain blank elsewhere. Binding of s. xix by Lewis, according to the bookseller's catalogue (see below). Secundo folio *non succurrit* (f. 9).

Written in Germany (?). Item 1155 in Thomas Thorpe's catalogue for 1836. Phillipps 9476. Phillipps sale, 21 March 1895, lot 1017, to H. S. Nichols (£5. 15*s.*). Item 494 in a catalogue the relevant slip from which is fastened inside the cover. Given by A. W. Varley, demy, in 1900.

Lat. 252. *Horae* s. xv med.

1. ff. 2–13^v A rather empty calendar in red and black.

'Donaciani episcopi' in red, 15 Oct. 'Danieli martiris' and 'Venandi episcopi' in black, 8 July, 12 Oct.

2. ff. 14–17^v Incipiunt hore de sancta cruce . . . Patris sapiencia . . .

3. ff. 19–22^v Incipiunt hore de sancto spiritu . . . Nobis sancti spiritus . . .

4. ff. 23–30 Incipit missa beate marie. Introibo ad altare . . .

5. ff. 30v–36v Sequentiae of the Gospels.

6. ff. 38–98 Incipiunt hore beate marie uirginis. secundum consuetudinem romane ecclesie. Cf. art. 10. f. 93v blank.

7. ff. 98v–99v Oratio deuota ad uirginem. Salue regina . . . Oracio. Omnipotens sempiterne deus qui gloriose uirginis marie . . .

8. ff. 101–119v Incipiunt septempsalmi . . . (114v) Incipiunt letanie.

Twenty martyrs: (18–20) lupe amande donate. Seven confessors: (4–7) anthoni augustine dominice egidi. Eight virgins: (3) clara.

9. ff. 121–139v Incipiunt uigilie mortuorum.

Ends with 'Partem beate resurrectionis . . .'.

10 (in another hand). ff. 140–172 Istud offitium supra scriptum facimus die dominica . . .

Special forms of art. 6: (*a*) f. 140 Psalms on Tuesday and Fridays; (*b*) f. 146 Psalms on Wednesdays and Saturdays; (*c*) f. 151 Office in Advent, etc. ff. 172v–173v blank.

ff. ii + 172 + iii, foliated i, 1–176. ff. ii, 174–5 are post-medieval parchment. The parchment of art. 10 is softer than the rest. 83 × 62 mm. Written space 43 × 30 mm. 14 long lines. Collation: $1\text{–}2^6$ $3\text{–}8^8$ 9^8 + 1 leaf after 8 (f. 75) $10\text{–}11^8$ 12^4 (ff. 96–9) $13\text{–}16^8$ 17^6 (ff. 133–9) $18\text{–}20^8$ 21^{12} wants 11, 12, blank; together with eleven picture-page singletons. Eleven full-page pictures on versos, the rectos blank: eight are a passion series illustrating art. 6 (ff. 37, 50, 65, 71, 76, 81, 86, 94; three precede arts. 3, 8 (Christ in judgement: angels blow the last trump on long gold horns), 9. Initials in arts. 2–9: (i) blue or red patterned in white on gold and red (or blue) decorated grounds: continuous borders; (ii) 2-line, gold on red and blue grounds patterned in white; (iii) 1-line, blue with red ornament or gold with violet ornament. Initials in art. 10: (i) 2-line, red or blue with ornament of the other colour; (ii) 1-line, red or blue. Capital letters in the ink of the text touched with pale yellow. Gilt red morocco binding, s. xvii/xviii.

Written in the Low Countries, but the script and decoration of art. 10 are Italian. '466' inside the cover. College ex-libris, followed by 'ex dono viri desiderati Ioannis Rigaud S.T.B. olim socii' (†1888).

Lat. 253, ff. 1–33, + 257, ff. i, ii, 39, 40. *Comment. in Decretales, etc.* s. xiv ex.

1. ff. 1–27v (*begins imperfectly*) minime continetur ad maiores res . . .

Brief notes on the Decretals of Gregory IX, in order of books, beginning at I. iii. 15 and ending at V. xl. 3. 'Exteriores. Si Aliquis super vna causa . . .' on I. iii. 16 is the first complete piece. Most of bk. 2 and all bk. 3 were in a large gap after f. 14. ff. 28, 29 are very small pieces: 28 begins with V. xl. 4.

2. ff. 31, 32, 30, 33 (in that order). De siluis decimandis. Quamquam ex soluentibus . . .

Constitutions of Archbishop John de Stratford, †1348. Chapters 5–17 of the Concilium Londiniense printed by Wilkins, *Concilia* (edn. 1737), ii. 704–9, interrupted after ch. xiii by a chapter 'De vasis et ornamentis. Ad doctrinam presencium . . . reparari' and a 'Constitucio Willelmi de abiuracione concubinarum. Abiuraciones fornicarias . . . scripturam'.

3. The leaves in MS. 257 formed the cover of MS. 253, two bifolia of stiff parchment, blank except for a list of tituli of art. 1 written in the hand of art. 1 on ff. ii^v, 39, and a title 'De constitucionibus' and above it 'Magistri Iohannis Wayngflete decani de Chychestr' ' on f. 40^v, formerly the outside of the back cover.

ff. ii + 33 + ii. Paper (except art. 3). 302 × 220 mm. Written space 250 × *c.*190 mm. *c.*54 long lines. No ruling. Collation impracticable. Written in a large current anglicana. No coloured initials. Bound up in s. xix with six leaves of notes on logic, s. xiii/xiv, evidently taken from a binding (ff. 34–9). For the old binding see art. 3.

Written in England. Belonged (?) to John Waynflete (dean of Chichester 1455, † by Nov. 1479: Emden, *BRUO*), brother of William Waynflete, founder of Magdalen College.

Lat. 254. *Biblia (fragm.)* s. xiii[1]

1. One quire of a Bible, containing from 'et factum est grande' (Daniel 8: 9) to 'eius effusa est' (Nahum 1: 6).

The prologues are Stegmüller, nos. 500, 507, 510 (. . . continetur), 512, 516, 522, 525, and 527, the last six being all from Jerome's letter to Paulinus (*PL* xxii. 546). Table of chapters between the prologue and text of each book: (Hosea) De uxore fornicata . . . mouetur ad dominum (7 heads); (Joel) De fame et bellis . . . letari (5); (Amos) De temporibus . . . premiorum (10); (Obadiah) Arguuntur illi . . . referuntur (1); (Jonah) De iona . . . subsecuta (2); (Micah) Propter idolatriam . . . mansuris (7); (Nahum) [. . .] . . . predicitur (1): cf. de Bruyne, *Sommaires*, pp. 224–32.

2. ff. 7^v–9 A formulary letter scribbled in the margins, s. xiii ex., is from R. de Ros, chancellor of London and commissary of J., bishop of London (John Chishull, bishop 1274–80). It refers to the tithes from a mill and mentions the prior of St Cross, Isle of Wight, the prior of Astley, diocese of Worcester, and the dean and sub-dean 'Leym' h. dioc' '.

St Cross and Astley were alien piories. 'Leym' ' is the cell of Reading, O.S.B., at Leominster, diocese of Hereford.

ff. 10. 220 × 158 mm. Written space 152 × 107 mm. 2 cols. 52 lines. The first line of writing above the top ruled line. A single quire. Flex punctuation. 4-line, 2-line, and 1-line spaces for initials not filled.

Written in England. Perhaps in view of art. 2 and the absence of decoration, a discarded quire used in the binding of a manuscript not long after it was written. 'Ric' Smith, f. 1, s. xv ex.

Lat. 255. *Huguitio (fragm.)* s. xiv in.

Four leaves of *P* from the alphabetical Magnae derivationes of Huguitio.

The right order of the leaves is 4, 2, 3, 1.

ff. 4. 330 × 245 mm. Written space 250 × 168 mm. 2 cols. 50 lines. Two adjacent bifolia, not from the middle of a quire. 2-line blue initials, with red and blue ornament (saw pattern). Binding of s. xix.

Written in England. The leaves do not show signs of having been used in binding.

Lat. 256. *J. Lathbury, O.F.M., Distinctiones theologicae (fragm.)* s. xv med.

[A]bstinendum est a deliciis quod patet . . . et dices populo huic audite (*ends imperfectly: catchword* audientes).

Stegmüller, no. 4758. The first quire only, ending in a paragraph beginning Audire. Corresponds to Exeter College, Oxford, MS. 26, ff. 1–20va/32. For three other manuscripts see Emden, *BRUO*, p. 1105: another is Leyden, Univ. Libr., D'Ablaing 30.

ff. iii + 12 + xix. 332 × 255 mm. Written space 220 × 165 mm. 2 cols. 48–51 lines. Frame ruling, col. 2 wider than col. 1. A quire of twelve leaves signed in the usual late medieval way. Current secretary: long *r* common. Spaces for a 5-line initial on f. 1 and for 3-line initials elsewhere not filled. Binding of s. xix. Secundo folio *pontificis*.

Written in England. A price mark 'ii s' at the head of f. 1, s. xv.

Lat. 257, ff. 1–38. *Quaestiones disputatae in philosophia* s. xiv ex.–xv in.

1. (*a*) ff. 1–8 (*begins imperfectly*) ad formas contrarias et incomparabiles (?) . . . et tanta de hac questione. (*b*) ff. 8–17 Utrum in ordine naturalium sunt tantum 4or genera causarum. Ad argumenta igitur in opposicionem laborancia respondendum est per ordinem (*ends abruptly in paragraph beginning* 'Ad 15m argumentum quod est primum principale dicitur').

(*a*). Twelve arguments, the first four and part of the fifth now missing. ff. 17v–22v blank.

2. ff. 23–24v (*begins imperfectly*) [. . . .] Primo notandum est quod licet ab auctoribus multis . . .

A paragraph on f. 23 begins 'Primo articulo. In isto articulo teneo 3am opinionem quamuis non parue difficultatis est videre quomodo anima . . .'.

3. ff. 25–38v Vtrum anima intelectiua est quodomodo anima quod non arguitur . . . (line 34) Primus ergo articulus est utrum anima intelectiua est forma substancialis hominis in quo dimissis opinionibus alexandri et aliorum qui negant . . .

Four articles: 2, f. 28; 3, f. 30v; 4, f. 34. A summing up, f. 38v.

ff. 38. Paper. 297 × 220 mm. Written space 240 × 190 mm. *c.*50 and (ff. 23, 24) 80 long lines. No ruling. Collation: 1^{22} 2^{16}. Mixed, but mainly secretary hands. Art. 2, current anglicana, looks older than arts. 1, 3. No coloured initials. Binding, s. xix.

Written in England (Oxford ?).

Lat. 258. *Justinianus, Institutiones (fragm.)* s. xii/xiii

Twenty-nine leaves of the Institutes. f. 29 is from 1. xii–xiv. ff. 1–24 contain consecutive text from 1. xxiv–3. vi. ff. 25–8 are from 3. ix–xiv, xix–xxv. Apparatus, not continuous, in the margins.

Bk. 2, f. 2; 3, f. 20. 3. vi is interrupted by a table of consanguinity which occupies the whole of f. 24v. The manuscript is discussed and nearly all its apparatus printed by P. Legendre, 'Commentaires pré-accursiens', *Tijdschrift voor Rechtsgeschiedenis*, xxxiii (1965), 358–425. Dolezalek, ii.

ff. 29. 252 × 180 mm. Written space *c.*160 × 108 mm. 2 cols. 34–6 lines. Collation: 1 one (f. 29) $2\text{-}4^{8}$ (ff. 1–24) 5^{8} wants 1, 4, 5, 8 (ff. 25–8). Quires 2–4 are numbered at the end II–IIII. 4-line and 2-line initials, red or blue with ornament of the other colour; also at 3. vi. 10, *S* of *Soli*, 1-line, red. Bound in s. xix.

Written in England.

Lat. 259, ff. 1–6. *Replicationes scholasticae* s. xv med.

Six paper leaves, damaged at the top, but not seriously. Described by Macray as 'notes of an argument before a university or some ecclesiastical court in a cause 'inter me patremque honorandum sacri Predicatorum ordinis', in defence of the doctrine of the Immaculate Conception. . . . The writer clearly was a Carmelite' (*Register*, ii. 215–16). The leaves are probably consecutive, the three inner bifolia of a quire of twelve leaves, but a gap between f. 1 and f. 2 is possible.

(*a*) f. 1. *The last twenty-one lines of a piece. In lines 11–14 the writer condemns an opinion of doctor Franciscus (de Mayronis) in* distinccio 42 q. 4 . . . ideo velem quod meus pater et frater dictis facta compensans suum doctorem in isto procesu luculenter declararet *and in lines 18, 19 he refers to Scotus* sicuti me edocuit per libelum quem michi in presencia carmeli principisse . . . donauit.

(*b*) ff. 1–3 Ihesus. Equum iudicium sit inter nos Leu' 24. et pro nostre huius replicacionis radicali fundamento . . . (f. 1/38) Cum ergo pater meus honorandus sacri ordinis predicatorum sancti dominici ordinatim sentenciarius principisse carmeli dei genitrici. virginum virgini intacte peccatorum consollatrici omnia peccata pellenti fedus et maculam originalis peccati imposuisset suo in introitu . . . (f. 2) [. . .] Porticula celica lux sine macula . . . (f. 2v) *the writer mentions the university of Salamanca and (line 26) approves the assertion of Pope Eugenius IV that the Virgin was not conceived in original sin* per eiusdem bulam habitam apud locum ord(in)is fratrum beatissimi francisci. in ista vniuersitate que est vna de 5 principalibus vt patet in clementinis de magistris (*bk. 5, tit. 1*) que quidem bulla perlecta erat coram tota vniuersitate diuersas per vices.

(*c*) ff. 3–4^{v} Ihesus. Iudica deus et discerne causam meam Ps' 42 et pro nostre huius replicacionis radicali fundamento. Agonis scolastici milites strenuissimi magistri recolendi patres predeuoti et domini. Ne forte . . . Sic ergo ex hiis tribus articulis in primo contexte nostri 3^{tii} test' patet quod virgo benedicta in peccato non sit concepta quapropter . . . humiliter deuoteque posco et exoro Iudica deus et discerne causam meam. *The authorities noted by Macray, among them* Guido quondam nostri ordinis professor *are cited on f. 3^{v}/31–35.*

(*d*) ff. 4^{v}–6 Solaris perspicue in telure claritatis hodierne radiosa lumina aurora . . . sua in pura innocens. *The theme of this section is the innocence of the Virgin.*

(*e*) f. 6^{rv} Ihesus. Veritas et iusticia obuiauerunt sibi Ps' 84 et pro nostre . . . fundamento. Agonis scolastici . . . et domini . . . (f. 6/21–2) per illud argumentum ego probabam quod necessario quicumque teneretur affirmare hic in anglia partem meam . . . (f. 6/29–32) Cum uero 2° illud dixisses quod cauerem ne forte ista bulla sublatim esset adquisita in 2° paterno concilio bassiliensi a felice antipapa importuno quem deus a suis cogitacionibus auertat ac prope (*sic*) tranquilitatem ecclesie in viam salutis conuertat certe frater bulla incipit eugenius episcopus seruorum etc'. vide frater an tunicula hec eugenii silicet (?) sanctissimi vel felicis importuni . . .

For the mid-fifteenth-century interest in this much-debated question see H. Ameri, *Doctrina theologorum de Immaculata B. V. Mariae Conceptione tempore Concilii Basileensis*, Rome 1954.

ff. 6. Paper. 300 × 220 mm. Written space *c.*245 × 180 mm. *c.*47 long lines. Leaves now mounted separately, formerly 4–9 of a quire of 12, if the numbers 4 on f. 1^{r}, 5 on f. 2^{r}, and 6 on f. 3^{rv} are leaf numbers of a quire. Current hybrida. No ornament. Bound in s. xx in. in front of ff. 7–18, q.v.

Written soon after 1439 and in England, as appears from (*e*) above rather than from the script.

Lat. 259, ff. 7–18. *Extracta a Ludolpho de Saxonia, De vita Christi* s. xv^{2}

A quire or part of a quire of a notebook containing large extracts from chapters 50 onwards of the second part of the Vita Christi arranged under subjects alphabetically by first letter, closely written, but with spaces to allow for additions: ff. 8^{v}, 10^{v}–12^{r}, 14^{r}, 17^{v}, 18^{rv} are blank. This quire contains words beginning with the letter P. Probably the compiler usually began a new word on a new page, but the tops of the pages are now damaged and the only complete entries are short ones begun in the middle of a page, Proditores (f. 15^{v}), Palma (f. 16, added), Pretorium (f. 16). The headless entries are on Predestinacio (f. 7^{rv}), Pascha (f. 8), Passio (ff. 9–10), Pylatus (ff. 12^{v}, 13, 16^{v}), Princeps (?: f. 13^{v}), Petrus (f. 14^{v}), Peccator (?: f. 17). The extracts are taken in order of chapters and all references to chapters above about 65 appear to be additions: for example, the last for Pilate, 'Pylatus post mortem cristi . . . deportatus est in exilium lugdunum vnde et oriundus 3m 66o'. The compiler seems to have intended to go further: for example, the collection for Peter ends 'scribe ex extracto 3m 79o e'.[1]

ff. 12. Paper. *c.*300 × 220 mm. Long lines: 10 or 11 lines in 50 mm. ff. 12, 13 are still conjoint: ff. 7–18 are probably, therefore, either a quire of 12 or the six inner bifolia of a larger quire. Current hybrida: long *r* common. No ornament.

Written in England. Bound with ff. 1–6 in s. xx in.

Lat. 260. *Evangelium Nicodemi* s. xv²

[F]actum est in anno nono decimo . . . (f. 13v) que facta sunt de ihesu in pretorio meo.

Gospel of Nicodemus, beginning and ending as Magdalen College 53, pp. 169–89. As there, the letter of Pilate which concludes the piece (cf. Stegmüller, no. 183, 1) is addressed to Claudius, not to Tiberius. Some blank spaces, presumably because the scribe could not read his exemplar. f. 14rv blank.

ff. 14. 230 × 132 mm. Written space 160 × 125 mm. 32 long lines. Collation: 1^6 2^8. Anglicana formata (short *r*). Spaces for 4-line initials not filled, ff. 1, 5v. Binding of s. xix.

Written in England. Formerly bound after W. Durandus, *Rationale divinorum officiorum* (Lyon) 1494 (*GKW*, no. 9139), a gift from John Rawstone, chaplain, in 1807: the printed book is now Arch. C. I. 1. 4.

Lat. 261. *Justinianus, Codex cum apparatu* s. xiv med.

In nomine domini nostri ihesu cristi domini iust. sacratissimi principis perpetuis augustis codicis repetite preelectionis. Incipit constitucio prima de nouo codice faciendo. Rubrica (*blank space of eleven lines*). Imperator iust. augustus ad senat'. [E]a que necessario . . . testem habeant. Explicit liber Codicis [. . .].

Bk. 2, f. 39; 3, f. 57v; 4, f. 78; 5, ff. 93–127, 'Explicit prima pars textus codicis' in main hand; 6, f. 127v; 7, f. 165; 8, f. 187; 9, f. 210. A continuous apparatus begins with the last leaf of bk. 1, f. 38. Bk. 1 may not have been with the rest at first since there is no sign on ff. 1–38v of a small annotating hand of s. xiv (English) which occurs often thereafter: see also below. 'Explicit Appitatus (*sic*) tercii libri per Nich', f. 77v. f. 186rv, left blank before bk. 8, has a list of tituli of bks. 1–8: the writing on the recto has been erased. An alphabetical table, '[A]postatis . . .' to 'Vt intra cetera tempora . . . Expliciunt Rubrece codicis secundum alphabetum. `Cuius secundum folium incipit macione´', was added in current anglicana, s. xiv ex., on f. iiiv.

ff. iii + 229 + iv. For f. iii see above. ff. 228–9 are parchment endleaves, 229 backed with modern paper. 408 × 252, but ff. 1–38 were rather shorter and have been eked out with a 15 mm strip of parchment pasted across the foot. Written space *c.*245 × 135 mm. 2 cols. *c.*50 lines of text (48, ff. 1–38) and up to 106 lines of apparatus. Collation: $1\text{–}2^{10}$ 3^8 4 five (ff. 29–33) 5 five (ff. 34–8) 6^{12} wants 1 before f. 39 7^{12} wants 1 before f. 50 + 1 leaf

[1] All references to the Vita Christi begin '3m', not as one might expect '2a'.

after 11 (f. 60) 8^{12} 9^{12} wants 9–12 after f. 81 10^{10} + 1 leaf after 10 (f. 92) 11^{14} 12^{12} 13^{8} (ff. 119–26) 14^{8} wants 4 after f. 129 15–16^{8} 17^{12} 18^{8} 19^{10} 20^{8} wants 7 after f. 185 21^{12} 22^{12} wants 5 after f. 202 23^{12} 24^{6}. Changes of hand at ff. 38, 162 (18^{1}), 210 (23^{1}) and elsewhere. In the first halves of quires the leaves are numbered in red roman figures. A blank space for a picture or large initial is in front of each book, except 7, and except 2 which has lost its first leaf. Initials: (i) 3-line or 2-line, blue with red ornament; (ii, iii) 2-line and 1-line, blue or red. The type (iii) initials beginning sub-sections of *tituli* are outside the written space, except on ff. 1–38^{v}, 162–186^{v} (quires 1–5, 18–20). The remains of the old white leather covers are pasted over a rebinding of s. xix. Secundo folio *macione electi*.

Written in England. 'Caucio d. Willelmi Clerk exposita ciste de Nele[1] anno domini M^{o} cccc^{o} xlix^{o} xi die Marcii et habet 2° supplementa scilicet petrum de aquina et vnum conflat' et iacet pro xvi s' ', f. 227^{v}. 'Iste liber constat Edwardo Hancok ex emtione eiusdem de magistro (?) Garet Stacioner' hiis testibus Yordans et aliis', f. 229^{v}, s. xv med.[2] 'prec' xvi s' viii d' ', f. 228^{v}.

Lat. 262. *Aristoteles, De caelo, Meteora; Avicenna, De congelatis* s. xiii med.

Twenty-four bifolia. Described in *Aristoteles Latinus*, no. 1918. Half the text was formerly pasted down and is hard to read. Many contemporary marginalia in a very small hand.

1. ff. 1–28 (*begins imperfectly*) centis de eo quod est factum . . . nostram in eo. Explicit liber celi et mundi.

The 'Vetus translatio'. Bk. 2, f. 6; 3, f. 15. Here and in art. 2 a running title in black capitals is written on the page on which a new book begins. The first words are in Corpus Christi College, Oxford, 111, f. 156vb/22.

2. (*a*) ff. 28^{v}–46 Postquam precessit rememoracio nostra . . . (*b*) ff. 46–48^{v} [Terra pura] . . . res quedam extranee. amen. Explicit liber metheororum.

(*a*). The 'Vetus translatio'. Bk. 2, f. 33; 3, f. 41. Some side notes, for example on ff. 40, 41, 44^{v}, are ascribed to 'Alwredus' (Alfred of Shareshull). (*b*) begins near the top of f. 46 at a point where the text is hard to read. Evidently it followed (*a*) without a break, as it does in Corpus Christi 111 and 114. Thorndike and Kibre. Ed. E. J. Holmyard and D. C. Mandeville, *Avicenna de congelatione et conglutinatione lapidum*, Paris 1927, pp. 45–55. They assign the translation to Alfred of Shareshull: cf. J. C. Russell, *Writers of thirteenth-century England*, 1936, pp. 18–20.

ff. 48. Written space 142 × 87 mm. 26–8 long lines. Collation: 1–2^{10} 3 six 4^{10} wants 1 before f. 27 and 10 after f. 34 5^{10} 6^{4} (ff. 45–8). Initials: (i) f. 28^{v}, 5-line, red and blue with ornament of both colours; (ii) f. 6, red and black with red ornament and (ff. 15, 33) blue with red ornament; (iii) 2-line, blue with red ornament or red with ornament in blue or in the ink of the text. Binding of s. xix.

[1] There were Nele chests at both Oxford and Cambridge.

[2] The persons named here may be Edward Hancock, fellow of King's College, Cambridge, 1447–57, Roger Jordan, fellow of King's 1454–9 (cf. Emden, *BRUC*, pp. 284, 333), and the Cambridge stationer Gerard Wake: Wake was stationer in the middle of the century (cf. G. J. Gray, *The Earlier Cambridge Stationers and Bookbinders*, 1904, pp. 10–11).

Written in England. Used in bifolia by an Oxford binder, probably Thomas Middleton, to line the boards of the 12-volume set of Aquinas, *Opera*, Venice 1593: cf. Ker, *Pastedowns*, no. 904 and p. 211.

Lat. 263. *Henricus de Gandavo, Quodlibeta (fragm.)*[1] s. xiv in.

Querebantur in nostra generali disputacione . . .

Quodlibet I and parts of Quodlibets II, III: described by R. Macken, *Bibliotheca manuscripta Henrici de Gandavo*, i (1979), 444-6 (no. 123). Quodl. I ends at f. 20 'in v eth'. Explicit disputacio ista de quolibet questionum numero 42' and is followed by a table of the questions, 'Questio i vtrum sit ponere in deo bonitatem aliquam personalem . . .'. f. 24^{v} ends in II. 8 (edn. 1613, f. 56ra/25). ff. 25-8 are from III. 3, 4, 11-14 and ff. 29, 30 from III. 15.

ff. 30. Written space 262 × 170 mm. 2 cols. 60 lines. Collation: 1-2^{12} 3^{12} wants 1-4, 9-12 4^{12} wants 1-5, 8-12. Initials: (i) ff. 1, 20^{v}, red and blue, with ornament of both colours (saw pattern); (ii) 2-line, red or blue with ornament of the other colour. Bound in 1950. Secundo folio *ere autem*.

Written in France, but came early to England. Used in bifolia by an Oxford binder, Dominique Pinart, after 1590, to line the boards of *Biblia sacra latina* (b. 13. 1-6: 6 vols., Lyons 1590) and two other volumes: cf. Ker, *Pastedowns*, nos. 1036, 1167, 1924, and pp. 211, 218. ff. 25-8 were given in 1950 by the President and Fellows of St John's College and ff. 29, 30 in the same year by the Curators of the Bodleian Library.

Lat. 264 + pastedowns of Arch. C.II.3.16. *Comment. in Librum Pauperum Vacarii (fragm.)* s. xii/xiii

Fragments of a commentary on excerpts from the Digest and Code in the order in which they occur in the Liber Pauperum of Vacarius. Forty-one chapters of Vacarius, bk. 4, are covered here: 16-18 (ff. 1-2^{v}), 29-55 (ff. 3-18^{v}), 56-8 (f. 19^{rv}), 61-3 (ff. 20-21^{v}), 70-4 (f. 22): cf. edn. by F. de Zulueta, Selden Society xliv (1927), pp. 124-73. Each chapter begins with a summarizing introduction, for example (ch. 18), 'Obseruantur quidam specialia circa instrumenta ideo specialiter de eis agit . . .'.

Many contemporary scholia in the margins of ff. 4-20. Headings not filled in in quire 1 nor after the change of hand in quire 4: on f. 22 they were supplied early and differ verbally from the headings of Vacarius, for example 'De distractione pingnoris et remissione' at ch. 73.

ff. i + 22 + i. Written space *c.*230 × 150 mm (ff. 1, 2, 257 × 167 mm). 2 cols. 59-64 lines. Pricks in both margins to guide ruling. Collation: 1 two (ff. 1, 2, the central bifolium) 2^{8} (the outside bifolium, ff. 3, 10, is in Arch. II. 3. 16) 3^{8} 4^{8} wants 1, 3, 6, 8 (ff. 19-22).[2]

[1] Nos. 1214, 1516, 1824 in Ker, *Pastedowns*, are probably also from this 60-line copy. They contain fragments of Quodlibets XIII, VII, and VIII respectively. One of the pages of Quodlibet XIII.5 has the mark 'pecia ii^{a}' opposite 'secundum aug' xiii de trinitate' (edn., f. 297rb). Pecia 2 of q. 13 begins at this point in Paris, Arsenal 454: cf. R. Macken in *Miscellanea codicologica F. Masai dicata*, 1979, ii. 307.

[2] My old notes record also a small piece of 4^{6}, now missing: it contained fragments of chapters 64, 67, 69.

Three hands, changing at ff. 3, $21^{va}/26$. 2-line initials, blue or red with ornament of the other colour: on ff. 3–18 they are outside the written space. Binding of s. xix^1.

Written in England. Used in bifolia by an Oxford binder, probably Nicholas Bokebynder, s. xv ex.,[1] as pastedowns and (ff. 6, 7, 12, 13, 16, 17, 19, 22) as flyleaves in a 3-volume Latin Aristotle (*GKW* 2439, etc.: now Arch. B. III. 4. 1–3) and as pastedowns in a copy of the college statutes, s. xv ex., now Arch. C. II. 3. 16 (rebound, s. xvii in.): cf. Ker, *Pastedowns*, nos. 16, 905.[2]

Lat. 405. *Horae* s. xv^2

1. ff. $1–12^v$ Calendar in French in red and black.

Entries in red include 'Saint Lubin', 'Saint Cheron', and 'Saint Arnoul' (all saints of Chartres, 14 March, 28 May, 18 July) and 'La dedicacion nostre dame' (Chartres Cathedral, 17 Oct.); in black 'Saint Aignan' (of Chartres, 10 June, 7 Dec.).

2. ff. 13–17 Sequentiae of the Gospels, beginning imperfectly. 'Protector in te sperantium . . .' follows John.

3. ff. 17–18 Passio domini nostri ihesu cristi secundum Iohannem. Gloria tibi domine. In illo tempore Apprehendit pylatus ihesum . . . testimonium eius.

The catena from John and Matthew, nearly as *Horae Ebor.*, p. 123. Cf. *Lyell Cat.*, p. 65.

4. ff. 18–21 De beata virgine oracio. Obsecro te . . . Et michi famule tue . . . f. 21^v blank.

5. ff. 23–79 Hours of B.V.M. of the use of (Chartres). Hours of Holy Cross and Holy Spirit worked in.

The beginning of matins of the Cross was on a leaf missing after f. 47. f. 80^{rv} blank.

6. ff. $81–96^v$ Penitential psalms and (f. 91^v) litany.

Twenty-five confessors: (1–7) siluester hylari aniane gaciane cypriane iuliane leobine.

7. ff. $97–110^v$ Office of the dead.

8. Prayers: (*a*) f. 111^{rv} Oratio ad xpistum. O bone ihesu per tuam misericordiam esto michi ihesus. Et quid est ihesus . . . ; (*b*) ff. $111^v–113$ In nocte quando ibis cubitum. Ihesus nazarenus rex iudeorum . . . ; (*c*) f. 113^{rv} Quando surges a lecto. Adiutorium nostrum . . . Oratio. Gratias ago tibi . . .

9. ff. $113^v–132^v$, 134–7 Memoriae: (1) Holy Cross; (2) B.V.M. (Aue cuius concepcio solemni plena gaudio . . .); (3) Michael; (4–11) John Baptist, Peter, Paul, Andrew, John Evangelist, James, Bartholomew, James the less; (12–16) Stephen, Laurence, *Christopher*, *Sebastian*, Saturninus; (17–24) Martin, Nicholas, Hilary,

[1] See G. Pollard in *The Library*, 5th series xxv (1970), 209.

[2] The Helmingham manuscript referred to in *Pastedowns*, p. 2, footnote, was in a Sotheby sale, 8 July 1970, lot 62 (to Traylen, £380).

Gregory, Claud, Anianus (Aue stella matutina vero soli co*n*nicina stellato palacio . . .), Francis, Antony; (25–30) Anne, Mary Magdalene (Gaude pia magdalena spes salutis . . .), Genovefa, *Katherine*, *Barbara*, Margaret.

(2). *RH*, no. 1744. (20). Followed by 'Domine ihesu criste adoro te . . .' in five paragraphs. (28). For use by a woman. 'Aue virginum gemma Katherine sponsa . . .' (*RH*, no. 23938) is followed by 'O uirgo pro me ora cristum beatissimum ut me ancillam suam . . .'. f. 129^{r} blank.

10. ff. 137^{rv}, 139–140^{v}, 138^{rv}, 141 De omnibus sanctis oratio. Deus pater qui creasti . . .

RH, no. 4477 (Peter of Luxembourg), adapted for use by a woman. 141 lines, stanzas 1–10, 13–24, 29, 32–6, 38, 44, 46–50 of the text printed in *AH* xv. 167–70. Stanza 47 has five lines, instead of four: the extra line is the third, 'consolator miserorum'.

11. ff. 141–2 De defunctis commemoratio. Auete omnes anime fideles . . .

12. ff. 142^{v}–144 Salue sancta facies nostri redemptoris . . .

A memoria of Holy Face, *RH*, no. 18189.

13. ff. 144–146^{v}, 133^{rv}, 147 Six hymns: (*a*) Veni creator spiritus mentes tuorum visita . . . ; (*b*) Veni redemptor gentium ostende partum . . . ; (*c*) Vexilla regis prodeunt . . . ; (*d*) Ut queant lapsis . . . ; (*e*) Katherine collaudemus . . . ; (*f*) Criste qui lux es . . .

RH, nos. 21204, 21234, 21481, 21039, 2693, 2934.

14. f. 147^{rv} De beata maria. Inuiolata integra et casta es maria . . . *RH*, no. 9093.

15. ff. 147^{v}–148^{v} Versus sancti bernardi. Illumina . . .

Seven verses, Illumina, In manus, Locutus sum, Dirupisti, Periit, Clamaui, Hac mecum, and prayer 'Omnipotens sempiterne deus qui ezechie regi . . .'.

ff. ii + 148 + ii. 132 × 93 mm. Written space 75 × 50 mm. 17 long lines. Collation: 1–2^{6} 3^{8} wants 1 before f. 13 4–6^{8} 7^{8} wants 5 after f. 47 8–17^{8} (ff. 51–130) 18^{8} (ff. 131–2, 134–7, 139, 140) 19^{8} (ff. 138, 141–6, 133) 20 two (ff. 147–8). Written in *lettre bâtarde*. Nine 14-line pictures with continuous framed borders, five in art. 9 (as shown by italics) and one before each of arts. 5–7, 12. At art. 7 three dead men with spears confront three horsemen. Initials: (i, ii) 3-line and 2-line, grisaille on grounds of gold paint and red; (iii) 1-line, gold paint on blue or red grounds. Line fillers of red or blue patterned in gold paint. Framed and compartmented borders on three sides of pages with initials of type (i). Binding of s. xix. Secundo folio (f. 13) *mundus*.

Written in France for the use of a woman (arts. 4, 9, (28), 10) in the diocese of Chartres. Given by Patrick Thompson, fellow 1942–9, in 1949.

OXFORD. MANSFIELD COLLEGE

1. *Missale* s. xv[1]

Slightly more than one third of a missal. Eighty leaves are missing at the beginning and at least fifteen leaves at the end.

1. ff. 81–7, 91^{v}–105 (*begins imperfectly*) leluia. V'. Veni sancte spiritus . . . est in mundum. Si alia dominica aderit fiat ut supra in dominica precedenti. Expliciunt offitia dominicalia.

Temporal, beginning in the office for Pentecost and interrupted after Corpus Christi by art. 2. The church year recommences with 'Dominica prima post oct' pentecost' ', f. 91^{v}. Noted preface for Trinity, f. 86^{rv}. Corpus Christi, ff. 86^{v}–87. The last words, apart from rubric, are in the lesson from John 6: 5, Cum subleuasset . . . , for the 25th Sunday after the octave of Pentecost. Spellings with *cum–* are as common as or commoner than those with *con–* in the words *cumpleta, cumplendum, cummemoratio*. The lower margins of ff. 93–6, 104 have been cut off.

2. ff. 87–91^{v} Incipiunt prephationes.

Noted prefaces (feasts of B.V.M., apostles, Lent), Per omnia (noted), the common preface (noted), Sanctus, Gloria (noted: two settings), Communicantes and (ff. 89^{v}–91^{v}) canon of mass. f. 89 is damaged where a 19-line crucifixion picture, *c.*90 × 65 mm, has been cut from the second column on the verso in front of *Te igitur*.

3. ff. 105–133^{v} Incipiunt festiualia. In natiuitate Sancti stephani.

Sanctoral, beginning at 26 December and ending imperfectly in the lesson from Matthew 18: 1, Accesserunt . . .', for the 'Dedicatio ecclesie sancti michaelis' (29 Sept.). A full office for Thomas of Canterbury (ff. 106^{v}–107), but cues only for Bernard 'Sicut in sancto antonio' (f. 126): no saints of later date. Exaltation of Cross, f. 129, has a noted preface, f. 129. Offices for Wednesday, Friday, and Saturday 'quatuor temporum' (as *Missale romanum*, i. 282–90) come between Eufemia and the vigil of Matthew, ff. 129^{v}–132^{v}.

Two additions in red in the margins, s. xv: f. 121^{v} 'Officium visitacionis beate uirginis marie quod celebratur secunda die mensis Iulii solemniter. fit sicut ˋfol. cxxviiˊ natiuitate eiusdem uirginis preter euangelium quod est Exurgens maria abiit. quere fol. iii. De martiribus (*i.e. Processus and Martinianus*) uero fit tantum commemoracio'; f. 123^{v} 'Officium misse beate anne quere in fine libri. fol. cxlviii'.

ff. 53. The medieval foliation lxxxi–cxxxiii (followed here) is bottom left of versos. 283 × 198 mm. Written space 200 × 147 mm. 2 cols. 39 lines (10 lines in 50 mm). Collation: 1^{8} 2^{10} 3^{6} (ff. 99–104) $4–6^{8}$ 7^{8} wants 6–8. Some fading of the script on flesh sides. Flex punctuation. A picture missing: see art. 2. Initials: (i) for Trinity and Corpus Christi in art. 1, *T* of *Te igitur* in art. 2 and twelve feasts of art. 3, Stephen, John Evangelist, Purification and Annunciation of B.V.M., nativity of John Baptist, Peter and Paul, James, vigil and day of Assumption of B.V.M., Bartholomew, Nativity of B.V.M., Matthew, pink patterned in white on blue grounds (outside) and green grounds (inside), the green decorated with flowers and leaves: short acanthus leaf prolongations into the margins; (ii, iii) 3-line and 2-line, red with violet ornament or blue with red ornament. Capital letters in the ink of the text filled with pale yellow. Binding of rough calf bearing a pattern of fillets (s. xviii) over old boards: four bands.

Written in Italy. Given by J. L. Cherry in 1909.

OXFORD. MERTON COLLEGE

256B (E. 1. 6). *N. Trevet et T. Wallensis, Expositiones super Augustinum de Civitate Dei* s. xiv[1]

Described by F. M. Powicke, *Medieval books of Merton College*, 1931, p. 137, no. 362; and by B. Smalley, *English Friars and Antiquity*, 1960, p. 88.

1. ff. 3–74v Incipit exposicio hystoriarum extranearum dictorumque poet\ic/orum que tanguntur ab augustino in libris de ciuitate dei facta per fratrem Nicholaum treueth ordinis fratrum predicatorum. Gloriosa dicta sunt de te ciuitas dei. Ps. lxxxvi. Cum romani . . . reddere clariora. Explicit prologus. Incipit tractatus. Capitulum primum. Ad intellectum eorum . . . ad eternam beatitudinem. Ad quam . . . Amen.

Twenty-two books, the last twelve printed often: cf. art. 2.

2. ff. 75–208v Exposicio fratris thome Waleys doctoris sacre theologie ordinis predic' super libros Augustini de ciuitate dei facta Anno domini M° CCC.XXXII°. Fluminis impetus . . . qui ab eis uocantur (*ends abruptly*).

Printed in 1473 and later, together with bks. 11–22 of art. 1: cf. B. Smalley in *AFP* xxiv. 86. The last words here are soon after the beginning of bk. 8, ch. 1. The scribe left blank spaces here and there, for example on f. 194, and on f. 75 he left half the recto blank, omitting much of the prologue: the gap is between the sentence beginning 'Fluuius tamen' and the sentence beginning 'Quia igitur ut supra tactum est'. For a passage on ff. 103v–104 which contains more than the printed text, see Smalley, *English Friars*, p. 93. ff. 209–210v were left blank and without ruling.

ff. v + 208 + ii, foliated (i–iii), 1–210, (211–12). ff. 1, 2 are medieval flyleaves. 220 × 150 mm. Written space 155–178 × 102–110 mm. 2 cols. 36–43 lines. Collation of ff. 3–210: $1\text{–}6^{12}$ $7\text{–}8^{8}$ $9\text{–}18^{12}$. Textura by two scribes: the second, ff. 75–89r, used quires of 8 instead of 12 leaves and ruled a larger written space, with more lines to the page. Initials: (i, ii) 5-line and 2-line, blue or red, with ornament of the other colour. Capital letters in the ink of the text marked with red. Binding of s. xviii, rebacked. Secundo folio *culum continue.*

Written in England. John Grandisson (†1369: *DNB*) wrote a note of the contents on f. 2v in his distinctive large hand. After it is 'Iste liber quondam Iohannis Episcopi Exon'; assignatur alicui pauperi scolari Oxon' in theologia studenti; in eius memoriam cuius erat. et eo promoto vel decedente aliis sic studentibus relinquatur; in aula de Merton' ad usum huiusmodi extunc perpetuo remansurus'; at the foot of the same page 'Tradatur I. Gardener. socio dicte aule (*fellow, c.1382*) illuc deferendus'. Identifiable by the secundo folio with the 'Triuet super Augustinum de Ciuitate Dei' which John Hanham (fellow, 1427) received from the Warden of Merton probably in 1433 (Powicke, p. 73) and probably with the 22nd book in the 'electio' of Richard Frendship, fellow, in 1519 (Powicke, pp. 73, 252). S. R. Meyrick sale, 20 July 1871, lot 1404. Quaritch, cat. 279 (1871), item 410 (£3. 16*s*.). No. 582 in a catalogue of Sotheran and Co., Piccadilly, London, at £6. 10*s*.: bought for Merton College in 1878.

297B. *Vetera et nova Statuta Angliae* s. xv^1–xv med.

A large collection of statutes, etc., noticed briefly by F. M. Powicke, *Medieval Books of Merton College*, 1931, p. 245. Damage by damp at the head of leaves has only affected the text seriously in quire 2.

1. ff. 1–2^v A table of arts. 5, 6, one hundred and eight 'Vetera Statuta' and eighty-six statutes from 1 Edward III to 3 Henry VI.

The last item of art. 6 is not listed. Henry V is called 'illustrissimus' and Henry VI 'serenissimus' in headings.

2. ff. 3–8^v Sarum calendar in red and black. Added gradings.

Erkenwald in red, 30 April. 'Diluuium incipit', 12 Apr. John of Beverley, John of Bridlington, and 'Dedicacio noui templi London ix lc' added in red at 7, 11, and 31 May in the same hand as the gradings, which are for 9 and 3 lessons, and in the August and September octaves of B.V.M., (17–19 Aug., 9, 11 Sept.) 'memoria tantum'. No entries of Visitation and Transfiguration (2 July, 6 Aug.). Entries of Thomas of Canterbury and the word 'pape' have not been touched.

3. ff. 9–18 Sachez qen court Baron si poet . . . que aueerer nous deuons etc'. Explicit Curia Baronis.

Cf. Powicke, p. 245, footnote, and *MMBL* ii. 838. Fifteen lines in English, f. 13, are about payment of debts.

4. Tables of contents and lists of chapters: (*a*) ff. 18^v–34, of art. 5; (*b*) ff. 35–62, of art. 6.

(*a*) ends 'Expliciunt abbreuiamenta veterum statutorum videlicet Henrici tercii Edwardi primi et Edwardi secundi'. It is the same piece as occurs in Lincoln's Inn, Hale 74, ff. 9 sqq., and in Bodleian, Douce 362, ff. 13–27^v and takes account of the twenty pieces which are in these manuscripts, but not in art. 5, q.v.

5. One hundred and eight 'vetera statuta' numbered in roman figures and marked (except 49, 71, 76, 80, 83–5, 90–3, 96–104) by the scribe at the end either 'Examinatur' or (1, 2, 6, 52, 55, 56, 59–61, 66, 69, 75, 81–2, 87, 108) 'Examinatur per rotulum'. 5–10, 12–16 are dated in the headings. Explanatory side notes in French against 1, 2, 4–9.

All the pieces here occur in exactly the same order in Hale 74, ff. 56–204^v, and in Douce 362, ff. 64–213. There, however, the numbers run to 128 to take account of twenty pieces which do not occur in art. 5: three on the New Ordinances (*SR* i. 257; *Foedera*, ii. 105; *SR* i. 189); five on Gaveston and the Despensers (*SR* i. 169, 170, 181, 185, 187 footnote); the statute of the Jewry (*SR* i. 221); the statute of Kenilworth (*SR* i. 12); the ten law treatises listed in *MMBL* i. 128. These twenty pieces are nos. 81, 82, 88, 93, 94, 102–4, 111, 124, 114–23 in the Hale-Douce collection, which was put together in the time of Edward III, presumably, since Henry III is called 'Henricus ultimus' in the explicits of Hale and Douce.

1. f. 69 Magna carta.[1] Henricus dei gracia . . . Westminster 12 Feb. 1225. *SR* i, Charters, p. 22.
2. f. 71 Carta de libertatibus Foreste. *SR* i, Charters, p. 26.

[1] I omit the first word of titles, *Incipit* or *Incipiunt*, and the second word if it is *Statutum* or (6, 7, 9 only) *Statuta*, except at 70. Neither *Incipit* nor a following noun occurs in the titles of 106, 107.

3.	f. 72	Sentencia lata super Cartas.	*SR*, i. 6
4.	f. 72^{v}	Prouisiones de Merton.	i. 1
5.	f. 74	De Marlbergh.	i. 19
6.	f. 77	Westmonasterii primi. In French.	i. 26
7.	f. 83^{v}	Gloucestr'. In French. Followed by a reference to no. 28 in Latin.	i. 45
8.	f. 85^{v}	Explanaciones Gloucestr'.	i. 50
9.	f. 86	Westm' secunda.	i. 71
10.	f. 102	De emptoribus terrarum.	i. 106
11.	f. 102^{v}	De religiosis.	i. 51
12.	f. 103	De mercatoribus.	i. 98
13.	f. 104	De finibus.	i. 128/55
14.	f. 105	Articuli super cartas.	i. 136
15.	f. 108	De bigamis.	i. 42
16.	f. 108^{v}	De coniunctim feoffatis.	i. 145
17.	f. 109^{v}	De vocatis ad warantum.	i. 108
18.	f. 109^{v}	De quo waranto. Quia breuia . . .	i. 107
19.	f. 110	Modus calumpniandi essonia.	i. 217
20.	f. 110^{v}	Dies communes in banco.	i. 208
21.	f. 110^{v}	Dies communes in banco in placito dotis.	i. 208
22.	f. 111	Wynton. In French.	i. 96
23.	f. 112^{v}	De recognicionibus in finibus.	i. 215
24.	f. 112^{v}	Exonie de inquisicione facienda super coronatores. In French.	i. 210
25.	f. 113^{v}	Articuli super precedens statutum Exonie. In French.	i. 211
26.	f. 114^{v}	Modus faciendi homagium et fidelitatem. In French.	i. 227
27.	f. 115	Articuli cleri.	i. 171
28.	f. 116^{v}	Articulus statuti Gloucestr' correctus pro Ciuibus London in forinsecis vocatis ad warantum in Hustengo London'. In French and (the final 'Memorandum . . .') Latin.	i. 52
29.	f. 117	Apud Ebor. In French.	i. 177
30.	f. 118	Visus franciplegii. In French.	i. 246
31.	f. 118^{v}	Lincolnie de Vicecomitibus. In French.	i. 174
32.	f. 119	Iuramentum Vicecomitis. In French. The final clause, 'E que vous demanderez nulle allowance . . .', is not printed in *SR*.	i. 247
33.	f. 119^{v}	Assisa panis et seruisie.	i. 199
34.	f. 120	De Pistoribus et Brasiatoribus et aliis Vitellar'. et de Venis et Bussellis et de forstallariis.	i. 202
35.	f. 120^{v}	Iudicium pillorie.	i. 201
36.	f. 121	De appellatis.	i. 141
37.	f. 121^{v}	De wardis et releuiis.	i. 228
38.	f. 122	De Scaccario.	i. 197
39.	f. 123	Districciones Scaccarii.	1. 197*b*
40.	f. 123^{v}	Extenta Manerii.	i. 242
41.	f. 124	De apportis Religiosorum.	i. 150
42.	f. 125	Prerogatiua Regis.	i. 226
43.	f. 126^{v}	Quod vocatur Ragman de Iusticiariis assignatis. In French.	i. 44
44.	f. 127	De Gauelet.	i. 222
45.	f. 127	De Militibus faciendis.	i. 229
46.	f. 127^{v}	De cambii parte. Berwick, 20 Edw. (I). In French.	i. 216
47.	f. 128	De frangentibus prisonam.	i. 113
48.	f. 128	De tenentibus per legem Anglie.	i. 220
49.	f. 128	De Regia prohibicione. Sub qua forma . . .	i. 101/24
50.	f. 128^{v}	Circumspecte Agatis. Rex talibus . . . sub qua forma etc' vt supra prox'. Dat' Parasceue E. secundi tercio decimo. In *EHR* xliii (1928), 14, Graves listed eight manuscripts in which this piece is dated—the regnal year is 14 (not 13) Edward II.	i. 101/1-23
51.	f. 129	De recognicionibus et Iuratis siue de ponendis in assisis.	i. 103
52.	f. 129	Lincoln de Escaetoribus.	i. 142

53.	f. 129v	Diffinicio de conspiratoribus. In French and (the final clause) Latin.	i. 145
54.	f. 130	De conspiratoribus.	i. 216, para. 2
55.	f. 130	Diffinicio de excepcione. Notandum quod quatuor modis dicitur excepcio . . .	
56.	f. 130v	Composicio Monete et Mensurarum 'Anno xx^{o} Regis E primi statuto primo'. Per discrecionem tocius regni . . . (7 lines).	i. 219
57.	f. 130v	De foresta Nouum siue addicio de foresta.	i. 147
58.	f. 131v	Consuetudines et Assise de Foresta.	i. 243
59.	f. 132v	De anno et die bisextili.	i. 7
60.	f. 133	De quo waranto Novum. Del brief . . .	i. 107
61.	f. 133	Composicio de Ponderibus. Nunc dicendum est de ponderibus plumbi et aliarum rerum. Notandum est quod le chare de plumbo . . .	Cf. i. 205
62.	f. 133v	Armorum. In French.	i. 230
63.	f. 134	Exposicio vocabulorum. Sok hoc est secta . . . pro aueragio domini Regis.	
64.	f. 134v	De accione vasti facti tempore alieno.	i. 109
65.	f. 135	De defensione Iuris de superuenientibus ante Iudicium.	i. 110
66.	f. 135v	Hibernie de coheredibus de Homagio participando.	i. 5
67.	f. 136	De proteccionibus reuocandis. In French.	i. 217
68.	f. 136	De malefactoribus in chaceis parcis et Warennis.	i. 111
69.	f. 136v	Westm' quarti de vic' et aliis de viridi cera. In French.	i. 180
70.	f. 137	Statutum siue tractatus de antiquo dominico. Cf. *MMBL* i. 142.	
71.	f. 137v	De quo waranto magnum. Alia duo precedencia. Anno domini millesimo duocentesimo septuagesimo octauo . . . , followed by four forms of writ.	Cf. i. 45/1-21
72.	f. 138v	De quo waranto quartum. Dominus rex tercio die Nouembris . . . secundum naturam constitucionis etc'.	Cf. i. 107
73.	f. 138v	Confirmacio cartarum de libertatibus angl' et foreste anno (xx)v^{to} E primi. In French.	Cf. i. 114
74.	f. 139v	Sentencia lata super confirmacionem Cartarum. In French.	i. 126
75.	f. 139v	De tallagio non concedendo.	i. 125
76.	f. 140	De visu terre et Esson' de seruicio domini Regis.	i. 218
77.	f. 140	De magna assisa iniungend' sine duello. In French.	i. 218
78.	f. 140v	De Moneta paruum. Edwardus . . . Quia mercatores . . . 21 June 20 Edward (I).	Cf. i. 220, 219, n.
79.	f. 141	De moneta magnum. In French.	i. 219
80.	f. 141v	Articuli de moneta. In French.	i. 219*a*
81.	f. 141v	De mercatoribus apud Acton' Burnellum editum. 12 Dec. 20 Edward (I). In French.	i. 98
82.	f. 142v	Capitula Itineris. que tangunt Coronam. De veteribus placitis . . . et eorum subditis. *SR* i. 233-234*a*/1 and footnote 1/1-3.	
83.	f. 143v	Capitula de Paruis Balliuis et eorum Subditis in Itinere. De hiis qui colligere . . . suffocantur. *SR* i. 234*a*, footnote 1/3-5, and 234*a*/1-21 and footnote 12.	
84.	f. 144	Alia Capitula Itineris. Quot et que maneria . . . parliamentum. *SR* i. 235-237*a*.	
85.	f. 145	Adhuc capitula coram iustic' itinerantibus. De vic' et aliis balliuis quibuscumque . . . conquesti fuerint. *SR* i. 235*a*/15-237/16.	
86.	f. 146	Panis et seruisie. Quando quarterium frumenti venditur pro tribus solidis vel quadraginta denariis . . . et castigari noluerit. Differs from 33 above and *SR* i. 199.	
87.	f. 146	De defensione portandi arma. In French.	i. 170
88.	f. 146v	De terr' Templar' Anno regni regis E secundo xvii^{mo}.	i. 194
89.	f. 147v	Ordinacio pro statu terre Hibernie Anno regni regis E. secundo xvii^{mo}. In French.	i. 193

90. f. 148^{v}	Composicio vlnarum et particarum.	i. 206, n.
91. f. 148^{v}	Modus leuandi fines in Curia domini Regis. In French.	i. 214
92. f. 148^{v}	De inquisicionibus pro domino Rege capiendis.	i. 143
93. f. 149	De Iusticiariis assignatis. Cum dominus Rex vltimis statutis . . . nisi de speciali gracia domini Regis. Number of assize judges for each county.	
94. f. 149^{v}	Litera patens super Prisis bonorum Cleri.	i. 175
95. f. 150	De regia prohibicione et consultacione.	i. 108
96. f. 150^{v}	De forma mittendi Extractas ad Scaccarium. In French.	i. 190
97. f. 151^{v}	De terris et tenementis amortizandis. In French.	i. 131
98. f. 152	Distincio de socagio. Socage poet estre . . .	
99. f. 152	Officium coronatoris.	i. 40
100. f. 153	Tractatus de Warantia Carte. De simplicibus cartis . . . pro defectu donatoris.	
101. f. 153	Constituciones Kancie. In French.	i. 223
102. f. 154^{v}	Articuli et sacramenta Ministrorum Regis in Itinere Iustic'.	i. 232
103. f. 154^{v}	Modus admensurandi terram.	i. 206–207/1
104. f. 155	Statuta Wallie.	i. 55
105. f. 162^{v}	Assisa seruisie. Quando quarterium . . . sex denariis etc'.	Cf. i. 200
106. f. 162^{v}	De breui de inquisicionibus concedend' de terr' ad manum mortuum ponend'.	i. 111, 1
107. f. 162^{v}	De terris et tenementis non amortizandis.	i. 111, 2
108. f. 163^{rv}	Tractatus de ponderibus et mensuris. Per ordinacionem . . . ex occies xx^{ta}. Expliciunt vetera statuta. videlicet Henrici tercii. Edwardi primi. et Edwardi secundi. Post conquestum Regni Anglie. f. 164^{rv} blank.	i. 204

6. Statutes from 1 Edward III to 4 Henry VI in French and Latin, numbered in Roman figures in a continuous series 1–87: (*a*) ff. 165–227^{v}, Edward III; (*b*) ff. 228–275^{v}, Richard II; (*c*) ff. 276–305^{v}, Henry IV; (*d*) ff. 307–329^{v}, Henry V; (*e*) ff. 331–340^{v} Henry VI.

(*a*). Forty statutes as numbered here, but forty-two as set out in *SR* i. 251–398. Six statutes in *SR* (XIV. 1, XV. 1–3, XXXI. 4, XXXV do not occur here.

i *SR* i. 251 (I. 1)
ii *SR* i. 255 (I. 2)
iii *SR* i. 257 (II)
iv *SR* i. 261 (IV)
v *SR* i. 265 (V)
vi *SR* i. 269 (IX. 1)
vii, addressed to William de 'Chitton', constable of Dover. *SR* i. 273 (IX. 2)
viii *SR* i. 275 (X. 1)
ix *SR* i. 278 (X. 3)
x, ending at 'de partie'. *SR* i. 276–277/27 (X. 2)
xi *SR* i. 280 (XI)
xii *SR* i. 281 (XIV. 1)
xiii *SR* i. 293 (XIV. 3, 4)
xiv *SR* i. 300 (XVIII. 2)
xv *SR* i. 302 (XVIII. 3)
xvi *SR* i. 299 (XVIII. 1)
xvii, ending abruptly 'ministres preignent'. *SR* i. 303–305/13 (XX)
xviii *SR* i. 307 (XXIII)
xix *SR* i. 311 (XXV. 2, 3ii–iv)
xx *SR* i. 314 (XXV, 3i)
xxi *SR* i. 319 (XXV. 5)
xxii *SR* i. 310 (XXV. 1)

xxiii *SR* i. 316, 324 (XXV. 4, 6)
xxiv *SR* i. 332, 344 (XXVII. 2 and 'Ordenance')
xxv *SR* i. 329 (XXVII. 1)
xxvi *SR* i. 345 (XXVIII)
xxvii *SR* i. 349 (XXXI. 1)
xxviii *SR* i. 353 (XXXI. 2)
xxix *SR* i. 355 (XXXI. 3)
xxx *SR* i. 364 (XXXIV)
xxxi *SR* i. 371 (XXXVI)
xxxii *SR* i. 378 (XXXVII)
xxxiii Stat' de libertatibus ville Cales' anno xxxvii edit'. *Foedera*, edn., 1816–30, iii. 690
xxxiv *SR* i. 383 (XXXVIII. 1)
xxxv *SR* i. 385 (XXXVIII. 2)
xxxvi *SR* i. 388 (XLII)
xxxvii *SR* i. 390 (XLIII)
xxxviii *SR* i. 393 (XLV)
xxxix *SR* i. 395 (XLVII)
xl *SR* i. 396 (L)

(*b*). Nos. xli–lxii. *SR* ii. 1–110, less two statutes, X and XIII. 3 (pages 39, 74).

(*c*). Nos. lxiii–lxxi. *SR* ii. 111–69.

(*d*). Nos. lxxii–lxxxiii. *SR* ii. 170–212.

(*e*). Nos. lxxxiv–lxxxvii. *SR* ii. 213–32 (1–4 Henry VI).

7 (added). ff. 340^v–391 Statutes of 6, 8–11, 14, 15, 18, 20, 23 Henry VI, without numbers.

SR ii. 232, 238–258/29 (end of chapter 26), 263, 272, 278, 289, 295, 301, 315, 326; that is to say all statutes, except the second of anno 10. In anno 15 (p. 295), chapter 4 is here an addition at the end (f. 371), with a *signe de renvoi* to f. 369^v, where 'Vide statutum quartum in fine ad hoc signum' is written in the margin. ff. 391^v–395^v blank.

ff. iii + 395 + i. ff. i–iii, 396 are medieval flyleaves; i–iii ruled like the rest. 295 × 200 mm. Written space 200 × 132 mm. 41–2 long lines. Collation: 1^8 $2–3^{12}$ 4^{16} 5^{12} 6^8 (ff. 61–8) $7–8^{12}$ 9^6 (ff. 97–102) $11–13^{12}$ 14^{14} (ff. 151–64) $15–26^{12}$ 27^{12} + 1 leaf after 8 (f. 318) $28–31^{12}$ $32–35^8$ 36^4; together with two blank leaves, 306 and 330, inserted after 26^9 and 29^7. Textura in art. 1 and for the rest secretary by two hands, changing at f. 103 (11^1), and for art. 7 a mixed legal hand of good quality. Initials: (i) f. 331, pink and blue elaborately patterned historiated *A* in a gold frame: Henry VI is shown as a boy, seated and holding two crowns: scroll inscribed 'Uiuere pacifice michi sit et utrique corone': a handsome continuous border; (ii) beginning arts. 5, 6*a–d*, gold on grounds of gold and pink, patterned and bearing within the initial an eagle (f. 69), a leopard (f. 165, Edward III), a hart (f. 228, Richard II), a dog (f. 276, Henry IV), and a horned dog-like spotted animal (f. 307, Henry V): each beast is gorged with a coronet, stands on grass, and bears an inscribed scroll, (f. 69) 'Laus legislate volat undique cum probitate', (f. 165) 'Uiuat vis legis quia ius est gloria regis', (f. 228) 'Sauns departier', (f. 276) 'Ma soueraine', (f. 307) 'Un sanz pluis': continuous border; (iii) f. 9, gold *S* on pink and blue ground; (iv) 6-line, blue with red ornament. Binding of rough calf with a triple fillet round the edges, Oxford work, s. xvii in. Secundo folio xix *Statutum* (f. 2) or *Large meis* (f. 10).

Written in England. The second of the two chief scribes finished art. 6 after 18 Feb. 1426 and presumably before 6 Nov. 1429, when Henry VI was crowned. Arts. 1–6 were a gift to Christ Church, Canterbury, in 1435: 'Liber ecclesie Cristi Cantuar' de statutis et legibus Anglie quem librum Iohannes Pyrye de Cantuar' iurista legauit eidem ecclesie anno domini millesimo ccccxxxv^{to}. cuius anime propicietur deus', f. 9^{v} (cf. ff. 110^{v}, 214^{v}, 299^{v}).[1] Art. 7 is likely to have been added at Canterbury in or soon after 1445: it begins on the fifth leaf of quire 30. 'Liber Collegii Mertonensis ex dono Magistri Iacobi Leeche quondam socii eiusdem' (†1589).

E. 3. 1, etc. *R. Rolle (fragm.)* s. xiv ex.

Binding fragments of a fairly early and handsome copy of works of Richard Rolle, †1349, consisting of two complete quires and parts of four other quires.

1. ff. 1–26^{v} + Emmanuel Coll., Cambridge, 318. 3. 14 (2 leaves) . . . (f. 26) que in anima est. Iste liber docet . . . (f. 26^{v}) profundos sensus scripture.

Commentary on the Psalms. Stegmüller, no. 7298. Allen, *Writings*, pp. 165–9. Printed in 1536. The text is complete from f. 7, 'Hoc opus eorum' (Ps. 108: 20: edn., f. lxv/27), except on ff. 14, 31, which are slightly defective, but it is hard to read in places, owing to staining. On ff. 1–6 the beginnings of nine psalms occur: 49 (f. 1^{v}); 54 (f. 2); 94 (f. 3); 95 (f. 3^{v}); 99 (f. 4); 100, 101 (f. 4^{v}); 105 (f. 5); 107 (f. 6^{v}). Emman. has the beginnings of Pss. 82 and 87 on the exposed sides.

2. ff. 26^{v}–31^{v} Confitebor tibi domine id est laudabo te nunc quoniam . . . ex populo suo. Explicit compendiosa exposicio super psalterium per Richardum Heremitam de Hampole. August^{n} de laude psalmorum.

On the canticles of the psalter. Stegmüller, no. 7302. Allen, *Writings*, pp. 62–88. Printed in 1536, after art. 1 (ff. lxxxiii^{v}–lxxxviii^{v}).

3. (*a*) f. 32 Canticum psalmorum animas decorat . . . peccatum agere. (*b*) f. 32 Ter quinquagenas cantat dauid ordine psalmos. Versus bis mille sex centum sex canit ille.

(*a*). Stegmüller, no. 369. Römer, i. 196 (Pseudo-Augustine). The title seems to have been transposed to the end of art. 2. f. 32^{v} blank.

4 (four leaves *in situ* in Merton Coll. 58. c. 8). (*a*) (*begins imperfectly*) istarum semitarum . . . et graciarum accio in secula seculorum. amen. (*b*) Notandum est ut homo possit amplius proficere . . . diffinire dicunt. (*c*) Expulsus . . . ita et opus tuum nam unde saluas (*ends imperfectly*).

Continuous text: three leaves of (*a*) and one leaf of (*b, c*). (*a*). The end of Rolle's Emendatio vitae. Allen, *Writings*, pp. 230–45. The first words are in edn. 1536, f. cxxxix/28. (*b*). Ten things a man should try to possess in himself. (*c*). Rolle's Oleum effusum, Stegmüller, no. 3707 (IV). Allen, *Writings*, p. 63. The fragment here corresponds to Bodley 861, f. 85rb/52–85va/49.

ff. 38 (thirty-two leaves in Merton E. 3. 1, four leaves *in situ* in Merton 58. c. 8 and two leaves *in situ* in Emmanuel College, Cambridge, 318. 3. 14). Written space *c.*225 × 140 mm. 2 cols. 51 lines. Collation of E. 3. 1: 1 two (ff. 1, 2, bifolium), 2 four (ff. 3–6, two bifolia),

[1] The donor may be the John Pyrye, who, Dr William Urry told me, was a junior 'juratus' on the Canterbury City Council in 1400–1 and bailiff in 1401–2. A John Pyrye became a monk of Christ Church, Canterbury, in 1435 and died *c.*1449.

3^{12} (ff. 7–18) 4^{14} (ff. 19–32). Quires 3, 4 signed g, h. The leaves in 58. c. 8 are two adjacent bifolia from the centre of a quire. The leaves in Emman. are a bifolium. Written in an unusual textura: the ascender of *l* slopes back and is deeply split and *b* and *h* (but not *l*) are provided with angular heads made separately from the ascenders. Initials: (i) f. 7 (Ps. 109) and beginning art. 4*c*, red and blue with ornament of both colours and violet; (ii) 4-line, blue with red ornament; (iii) 1-line, blue or red.

Written in England. Used in binding F. de Ripa, Lyons 1542 (54. b. 12: leaves removed to E. 3. 1), Bertachinus, Bas. 1573 (5 vols., 58. c. 4–8: leaves from 58. c. 4–7 removed to E. 3. 1) and the fifth of seven volumes of M. Flacius, *et al., Historia ecclesiastica*, Bas. 1560–74 (Emman.). These books were bound by the Cambridge binder who worked for John Betts of Trinity Hall, Cambridge, †1599 (cf. Ker, *Pastedowns*, p. viii, and Oldham, *EBSB*, p. 49) and marked Emmanuel Coll., Cambridge, 312. 1. 5 and 318. 3. 10–16 with the initials 'C. E.' and the date 1592.

E. 3. 30, etc. *Hugo de S. Victore, De sacramentis (fragm.)*

s. xii med.

Binding fragments of about half a fine copy. The original first leaf, New College 363, f. 4, is followed immediately by the two bifolia *in situ* in Lambeth Palace **H 1936 and by New Coll., f. 5.

(*New Coll., f. 4*) Incipit prologus / [libri] magistri / hugonis sancti / uictoris de sa/cramentis. ab / initio usque / ad finem in / unam seriem / [. . .] / ad [. . .].[1] Librum de sacramentis cristiane fidei . . . formam exhiberet. Explicit prologus. Primus liber a principio . . . (*Lamb., front pastedown*) Quod tria sunt genera sacramentorum in lege. Expliciunt capitula. Cum igitur de prima eruditione . . . (*Lamb., back pastedown*) promitto. Unum esse principium a quo facta sunt omnia de nichilo. In principio creauit . . . (*Merton Coll., Stack, 111. b. 5, back pastedown*) si deum nemo (ends in II. xviii. 16: *PL* clxxvi. 613/26).

The consecutive runs after the first are: Merton Coll. E. 3. 30, ff. 1, 2 (containing I. iii. 26–30); ff. 3–6; ff. 7–11; ff. 12–14; ff. 15–18; ff. 19–26; ff. 27–31; ff. 32–4, 36, 35, 37, 38; ff. 39, 40; (**bk. 2**) f. 41; ff. 42–4; ff. 45–51; All Souls Coll., 401 (Building accounts), back pastedown (bifolium); Merton Coll., E. 3. 30, ff. 94, 95; All Souls Coll., 401, front pastedown (bifolium); Merton Coll., E. 3. 30 ff. 52, 53; ff. 54–77, 96, 78–83, 97, 84, 85 (34 consecutive leaves); ff. 86–8; ff. 89, 90; f. 91; f. 92; f. 93; Merton Coll., Stack 111. b. 5, front pastedown; Stack 111. b. 5, back pastedown.

ff. 109. 330 (+ ?) × 245 (+ ?) on E. 3. 30, f. 96, 97, now the largest leaves. Written space 263 × 168 mm. 2 cols. 40 lines. Collation: the quire-number IX is at the foot of f. 97, so probably E. 3. 30, ff. 54–77, 96, 78–83, 97 are four complete eights (quires six to nine) of the part of the manuscript which began with bk. 2. A handsome round hand. Initials: (i) New Coll. 363, no. 4, 13-line blue and brown *L* on decorated gold and red ground: after it the letters *IBRV̄* in gold are included on the red ground and beside it the heading is in colours, red for every other line and blue alternating with green for lines 2, 4, etc.; Lambeth, gold and blue *I* and after it the letters *N PRINCIPIO* red, green, or blue; Merton E. 3. 30, f. 41, *M* of *Magnę* sketched, but not coloured. (ii) beginning parts, red, green, or blue, with ornament in all three colours; (iii) beginning chapters, as (ii), but smaller and the ornament often in two colours only; (iv) 2-line, red, green, or blue, with ornament in one of the other colours; (v) 1-line, red, green, or blue. ff. 1–93 were bound in s. xix and ff. 94–7 are loose

[1] There were about thirty letters in five lines after *seriem*.

insertions. The other leaves are in a guard book (New Coll.) or are *in situ* in bindings. Secundo folio (*in semetipsis*): the leaf exists (Lambeth Palace), but is defective at the top.

Written in England (the West ?). 'Iste liber pertenet ad me iohannem (?) [. . .]ttan[. . .] fratris [. . .]' at the foot of the first leaf, s. xvi. Used by an Oxford binder for binding more than 30 volumes in the last years of s. xvi: cf. Ker, *Pastedowns*, pp. xii, 88. Used in bifolia for larger books—one leaf is usually complete, or nearly so, and the other a fragment only —and in singletons for smaller books.

E. 3. 31. *Psalterium (fragm.)* s. xiii²

Psalms 26: 6 (cantabo et . . .)–68: 5 (mei iniuste . . .), with gaps.

ff. 31. Written space 230 × 125 mm. 21 long lines. ff. 12–23 are a quire of 12 leaves, complete except for one leaf, f. 18, which is only a small fragment. ff. 24–31 are a quire of 10 leaves, lacking 1 and 10. Initials: (i) removed: cut out of ff. 19, 31 (Pss. 52, 68); on missing leaves (Pss. 38, 51); (ii, iii) 2-line and 1-line, blue or red with ornament of the other colour. Red and blue line fillers of many different patterns.

Written in England. Used in Oxford as pastedowns, probably in 1590–1: see Ker, *Pastedowns*, no. 1104 and p. 211.

OXFORD. NEW COLLEGE

358. *Psalterium, etc.* s. xiii med.

1. (*a*) f. ii^v Table of a great cycle of 532 years, 1140–1671. (*b*) f. iii Rota to show the 'Terminus lxx^e', etc., in each year of a decennovenal cycle. (*c*) ff. iv–ix^v Calendar in gold, blue, green, and red, the colours alternating: often two and even three colours are used in one word.

(*c*). The base manuscript for the St Albans calendar in F. Wormald, *English Benedictine Kalendars after A.D. 1100*, i (HBS lxxvii, 1939), 34–5. Edmund Rich, canonized in 1246, is in the main hand at 16 Nov. Obits of Humfrey, Duke of Gloucester, 24 Feb., and of the father, mother, and uncle of Abbot John VI (Whethamstede), 5 March, added. The first and second battles 'apud Sanctum Albanum', 1455 and 1461, are noted at 22 May and 18 Feb. The word 'pape' and feasts of Thomas of Canterbury erased lightly. ff. ii^r, iii^v blank.

2. ff. xi^v, 1–122^v Psalms 1–150.

No headings. No signs of the Benedictine psalm-divisions, apart from an added 'Gloria' (s. xiv ?) before Ps. 68: 17, Exaudi me, and Ps. 77: 36 Et dilexerunt. The foliator, s. xvi in., numbered the psalms 1–171, counting Ps. 118 as 118–139. ff. x–xi^r blank.

3. ff. 122^v–134 Six ferial canticles, Benedicite, Te deum, Benedictus, Magnificat, Nunc dimittis, and Quicumque uult.

Numbered 172–83 in continuation of art. 2.

4. ff. 134–8 Litany, partly scratched out.

Thirty-nine martyrs: (1, 2) Albane II Amphibale cum sociis II . . . (20) Oswine. Thirty-seven confessors: (30) Benedicte II; Edmund (Rich) and Hugh added, s. xiv (?).

5. ff. 138–140^v Subuenite sancti dei . . .

Commendation of souls. Cf. J. B. L. Tolhurst, *Monastic breviary of Hyde Abbey*, vi (HBS lxxx, 1942), 77–81.

6. ff. 140^v–145 In agenda mortuorum.

Office of the dead. The responses are Tolhurst's set C, as in the St Albans manuscripts he used (*Mon. brev.*, p. 110).

7 (added, s. xiii ex.). f. 145^v Salue regina . . . V'. Virgo mater ecclesie . . . V'. Virgo clemens . . . V'. Funde preces . . . felle potato. o dulcis maria salue. V'. Aue maria . . . Omnipotens sempiterne deus qui gloriose uirginis et matris marie . . .

Tolhurst, op. cit., pp. 131–2.

8 (added, s. xvi in.). ff. 146^{rv}, 148 A table of the psalms.

ff. i + 157 + iii, foliated (i–xi), 1–104, 104*, 105–149. ff. 1–130 are foliated in a hand of s. xvi in. 257 × 182 mm. Written space 160 × 100 mm. 21 long lines. Pricks in both margins to guide ruling. The first line of writing above the top ruled line. Collation: 1^8 (ff. ii–ix) 2^2 (ff. x, xi, a bifolium of superior parchment) 3–16^{10} 17^{10} wants 8–10. Initials: (i) f. xi^v, an elaborate nearly full-page *B* of *Beatus*, cut by the binder at head and foot; (ii) at the usual liturgical divisions and at Pss. 51, 101, 6-line or 7-line, pink or blue patterned in white on grounds of gold and the other colours and framed in gold; (iii) for *EATUS UIR* on f. xi^v and for the rest of the words beginning with initials of type (ii), gold on blue or red grounds patterned in white; (iv) beginning other psalms, 2-line, gold or blue, with red and blue ornament running the height of the page; (v) for verses of psalms, 1-line, gold with blue ornament or blue with red ornament. A sloping streamer of gold, red, and blue along the lower margin of each page springs usually either from the type (v) initial in the last line on the page, or, if there is none, from the last line filler. Line fillers in red and blue or gold and blue. Binding of s. xviii: gilt spine. Secundo folio *qui non abiit*.

Written for the abbey of St Albans, O.S.B.: see above. 'Ex dono ricardæ (?) [. . . .] 1589 december 10 `vidua quondam vxor iacobi Harcote Londinensis´', f. 148. 'Will and Walke aright Will: Walker', ff. ii, x, s. xvii. 'W. Busby', f. i. The words 'legauerunt Robert Wetherell Ann Wetherell' are added to the college ex-libris inside the cover, s. xviii.

Mun. 9182. *2 Henry V, Stat. 1, cap. 7* s. xv in.

A contemporary copy of the chapter on Lollards in 2 Henry V, statute 1: vii Item per ceo q*ue* grandes rumours . . . et autres officers du Roy desius declarez etc. Item etc. (*SR* ii. 181–4).

A roll of one membrane. 645 × 205 mm. Written space 560 × 170 mm. 83 lines in current anglicana on one side, the other left blank. Formerly in use as a cover for a bundle of documents, as appears from a note of contents on the dorse, 'In this little bundle are writing*es* of dyvers thing*es* videlicet of Indentures expired . . .', s. xvi.

OXFORD. PEMBROKE COLLEGE

1. *Missale* s. xv[1]

1. ff. 1–6v Calendar in red and black, graded.

'Translacio sancti Ricardi' in red, 16 June. Additions: 'Dunstani' pencilled in the margin at 19 May; 'Translacio Sancti Osmundi mag' duplex', 16 July; 'Hic predicabit frater carmelitanus Oxon' ', 1 Aug. Feasts of Thomas of Canterbury erased at 7 July, 29 Dec., and 5 Jan. The word 'pape' erased.

2. ff. 7–8 Omnibus dominicis per annum post primam . . .

Holy water service, noted.

3. ff. 8–116v Temporal from Advent to Easter Eve.

Begins with texts corresponding to *PS*, pp. 6–8. Long rubrics, ff. 9–17v. The secret for the second Sunday after the octave of Epiphany is Ut tibi domine grata. The office of Thomas of Canterbury scrubbed out, f. 33rv. An erasure in the margin, f. 15v. Two leaves missing, one before f. 9 (Advent) and one after f. 30 (Christmas).

4. (*a*) ff. 117–18 Summe sacerdos . . . (*b*) ff. 118–20 Ordinary of mass. (*c*) ff. 120–122v Prefaces of mass. (*d*) ff. 123–125v Canon of mass. (*e*) ff. 125v–126 Cum uero sacerdos . . . (*f*) ff. 126–7 Notandum est quod a Domine ne in ira . . . (*g*) f. 127rv Settings of Benedicamus domino and Ite missa est. (*h*) ff. 127v–129v De diuersis casibus et periculis in missa contingentibus presbyter . . . corpus et in glosa.

(*a*). Cf. above Corpus Christi College 394, art. 4*a*. (*b*) consists only of nine kyries (as in Newcastle, Univ. Libr., 2, q.v.), Gloria in various settings and Credo in unum deum. (*c*) ends imperfectly and (*d*) begins imperfectly: three leaves missing. (*e*). Gratiarum actio post missam. (*f*). No rubric for special occasions, but psalms and prayers in prostration as in 394, art. 4*g*.

5. ff. 129v–171v Temporal from Easter.

Five leaves missing. f. 149 is a fragment and most of the office for Corpus Christi was in the gap after it.

6. ff. 172–173v Offices at the dedication of a church, the first leaf missing, and at the anniversary of the dedication, collect, secret, and postcommunion 'In consecratione ecclesie' and office 'In reconciliacione ecclesie'.

7. ff. 174–224v Sanctoral from Andrew.

Includes Anne. Four leaves missing, including the first and last.

8. ff. 225–41 Common of saints.

Alternative forms for a confessor have been added on ff. 234–235v.

9. ff. 241–56 Votive masses: (4–6) De sancta maria, (1) De trinitate, (2) De sancto spiritu, (3) De sancta cruce, (p. 459) De angelis, (7) Pro fratribus et

sororibus, (11) Pro pace, (15) Pro rege, (16) *Pro rege et regina,[1] (23) Ad inuocandam gratiam spiritus sancti, (17) Pro semetipso sacerdote, (34) Ad poscendum donum spiritus sancti, (25) Pro peccatis, (31) Pro penitentibus, (33) Pro inspiracione diuine sapiencie, (37) Pro tribulacione cordis, (26) Pro quacumque tribulacione, (39) Pro infirmo, (19) Pro salute amici, (20) *Pro amico, (p. 410, footnote) *Pro infirmo proximo morti, (28) Pro serenitate aeris, (27) Ad pluuiam postulandam, (43) In tempore belli, (35) Pro eo qui in uinculis detinetur, (29) Contra mortalitatem hominum, (42) Pro peste animalium, (10) *Pro uniuersali ecclesia, (9) *Pro papa (*the word lightly erased*), (12) *Pro episcopo, (21) *Contra temptaciones carnis, (22) *Contra malas cogitaciones, (24) *Pro peticione lacrimarum, (32) *Contra aereas potestates, (36) *Contra inuasores ecclesie, (38) *Pro nauigantibus, (40) *Pro benefactoribus uel salute uiuorum, (41) *Contra aduersantes, (p. 406, footnote) *Contra paganos, *De incarnacione domini nostri ihesu cristi, *Ad memoriam de sanctis Katerina margareta et maria magdalena, (8) *Commemoracio generalis de omnibus sanctis.

For the order and the numbers and page references see above, All Souls College 302, art. 9.

10. ff. 256–60 Ordo ad facienda sponsalia . . . eos in pace.

Manuale Sarum, pp. 44–59. English on ff. 256v, 257. Has the rubric on second marriages.

11. ff. 260–261v Ordo ad seruicium peregrinorum faciendum.

Manuale Sarum, pp. 60–3.

12. ff. 261v–263v Eleven forms of blessing, as in Corpus Christi College 394, art. 17, q.v., and *Manuale Sarum*, pp. 63–70/7.

The heading of the blessing of eyes is 'Benediccio oculorum magister Willelmus de montibus ecclesie lincolniensis cancellarius cum benediccionem oculorum necessitas inducit et deuocio postulancium potest fieri hunc|modum.'

13. ff. 263v–268v Ad missam pro defunctis officium.

The mass is followed by (1) grouped secrets and postcommunions for three occasions, burial, anniversary, and trental, and by (2) collects, secrets, and postcommunions for special persons. The former are the secrets and postcommunions of nos. (1, 9, 11) and the latter are nos. (2–4, 6, 7, 5, 10, 15, 13, 14, 16, 17, 12, 8, 18) of the eighteen sets provided in *Sarum Missal*, pp. 434–41.

14. ff. 268v–269 Ordo trigintalis quod quidam apostolicus . . . proximiores prime orationem (*sic*). Oracio. Deus summa spes . . .

As Corpus Christi College, Oxford, 394, art. 13, q.v.

15. f. 269 Missa generalis pro omnibus defunctis.

Sarum Missal, p. 442.

16. ff. 269–70 Missa generalis.

Four forms. *Sarum Missal*, pp. 442–5.

[1] An asterisk shows that only collect, secret, and postcommunion are provided.

17. ff. 270^v–273^v Post missam pro defunctis quando corpus est presens . . .

Sarum Missal, pp. 446–50.

18. f. 273^v Istud euangelium compositum fuit per do*mp*n*u*m iohannem papam (*lightly erased*) xxii apud auinionem tercio die ante decessum suum . . . In illo tempore Apprehendit pilatus. ihesum . . . uerum est testimonium eius. Dominus uobiscum. Oremus. Domine ihesu criste qui manus tuas . . .

Cf. *Lyell Cat.*, p. 86. The heading conveys an indulgence of 300 days.

19 (added on the flyleaves, s. xv/xvi). ff. 274–5 Office of Visitation of B.V.M. f. 275^v blank.

The main divisions of the text are shown by projections from the edges of the leaves made either by sewing a piece of parchment to the edge or by cutting the edge and bringing the cut piece back through a slit.

ff. ii + 273 + ii. Heavy parchment. 432 × 300 mm. Written space 275 × 178 mm. 2 cols. 36 lines and (ff. 123–125^r where the writing is slightly larger) 33 lines. Collation: thirty-seven quires, all once eights, except 1^6, 17^6 (ff. 123–8) 24^4 (ff. 171–3), but lacking fifteen leaves, 2^3, 5^2, $16^{7,8}$, 17^1, 18^3, $20^{1,3}$, $21^{2,3}$, 24^2, 25^1, 26^1, 27^7, 31^7: the gaps are after ff. 8, 30, 122 (3 leaves), 129, 142, 144, 149 (2 leaves), 171, 173, 179, 193, 224. Quire 36 (ff. 258–64) has a cancelled leaf after 7 and quire 37 an extra leaf after 2 (f. 267). Initials: (i) shaded red or (f. 7 only) blue and red on decorated gold grounds: prolongations form continuous borders on ff. 7, 37 (Epiphany), 205^v (Assumption of B.V.M.), 211 (Nativity of B.V.M.), 220^v (All Saints) and short borders on ff. 215 (Michael) and 263^v; (ii) 3-line and 2-line, gold on grounds of red and blue patterned in white; (iii) 2-line, blue with red ornament; (iv) 1-line, blue with red or red with violet ornament. Capital letters in the ink of the text filled with pale yellow. Contemporary binding of wooden boards covered with white skin: eight bands: two clasps missing. Secundo folio (f. 8) *circumquaque*.

Written in England. For a connection with Oxford see art. 1.

2. *J. Mirfeld, Breviarium Bartholomei; etc.* s. xiv/xv

1. (*a*) f. 1 `secundum fratrem I Somur′ Istud kalendarium subsequens fuit factum ad meridiem vniuersitatis Oxon'. Anno domini millesimo $ccc^{mo}$ octogesim`o′ `septimo′ (*over erasure*) Premittens . . . figure Eclipsium depinguntur. (*b*) f. 1 Hic incipit Canon kalendarii subsequentis Magistri Walteri Elueden `sicut habetur in Rosa Magistri de Cadesden′. Istud kalendarium fuit factum anno domini 1327 et durat . . . in meridie diei precedentis. (*c*) f. 1 Ad sciendum horas diei et noctis rubrica. Cum volueris scire . . . (*d*) Ad habendum coniuncciones ueras. Coniuncciones autem inuenies . . . (*e*) f. 1 Declaraciones abbatis sancti Albani supra kalendarium Regine. Si fiat questio de Natiuitate . . . ac multas diuicias. (*f*) f. 1^{rv} Dignitates planetarum. Sunt autem in signis quedam fortitudines . . . in istis inferioribus. (*g*) f. 2 Proprietates planetarum et tabula eorum. Septem sunt planete scilicet Saturnus . . . (*h*) f. 2^{rv} Exposicio signorum Rubrica. Multum prodest scire in quo signo est luna . . . notabilibus. (*i*) f. 2^v Et notandum quod quando luna impediatur . . . (*j*) f. 2^v De tabula planetarum Rubrica. cuius

figura protrahitur ex altera parte folii. In hanc tabulam planetarum intrandum est . . . perambulare. (*k*) f. 3 Eclipsis solis. (*l*) f. 3 Hic notantur quibus partibus humani corporis planete assimulantur. Saturnus frigidus et siccus . . . : followed by a table of planets and zodiacal signs 'pro menbris humanis sicut patet'.

(*a*), the canon to art. 2, is printed from this copy by J. L. G. Mowat, *Sinonoma Bartholomei*, 1882, p. 5. For John Somur, O.F.M., see Emden, *BRUO*, p. 1727, where seven manuscripts of his calendar are listed, but not this one. (*b–d*). Cf. B.L., Egerton 831, f. 7/6–34 and for Elveden, Emden, *BRUC*, p. 210. (*e–h*), Thorndike and Kibre, are also in Bodleian, Ashmole 191, ff. 7^{rv}, 9–10. (*j*), Thorndike and Kibre, is in explanation of (*g*). (*k*). A table to show 28 eclipses in the four decennovenal cycles 1387–1462. Against 1436 is 'Vix vel non videtur'. (*l*). Thorndike and Kibre. f. 3^{v} blank.

2. ff. 4–9^{v} Calendar.

Ruled for 37 columns, 14 columns to the left of the calendar and 20 columns to the right of it. Basically Somur's calendar (cf. Bodleian, Digby 5, ff. 73^{v}–86) with a set of festivals for Abingdon, O.S.B., substituted for Somur's Franciscan set. The entries are the same as in the Abingdon calendar, s. xiii ex., printed by F. Wormald, *English Benedictine Kalendars after A.D. 1100* (HBS lxxvii, 1939), 15–30, apart from the absence of some octaves and the presence of Anne, 26 July. January is printed by Mowat, op. cit.

3. f. 10^{rv} Table of lunar eclipses in four decennovenal cycles, 1387–1462.

4. ff. 11–342 Incipit liber qui intitulatur Breuiarium Bartholomei compositus per venerabilem virum Iohannem Mirfeld commorant' in Monasterio sancti Bartholomei London' a quo liber iste denominatur. In principio huius compilacionis . . . benedictus sullimis (*sic*) et gloriosus viuens et regnans in secula seculorum Amen.

Fifteen parts, each divided into distinctions, and each distinction into chapters. Described, and five sections (the proemium, I. vi. 19, IV. i. 13, XIII. iv. 12, and XIII. viii. 9), printed by P. H.-S. Hartley and H. R. Aldridge, *Johannes de Mirfeld*, 1936, p. 167. The names of authorities not mentioned in the text are occasionally entered in the margin by the main hand: 'secundum M.A. de sutwille', f. 114; 'secundum M. Rog' Fucard', f. 177; 'Arnaldus de villa noua', f. 131; 'Magister W. de conrado', f. 177^{v}; 'In cyrurgia salern' ', f. 217^{v}; 'Experimenta fratris Nicholai de Polonia', f. 269: cf. Mowat, op. cit., p. 2. Mirfeld's opinion about the value of charms—of which there are many—is expressed on f. 149^{v} (Hartley and Aldridge, p. 44), as a reader noted on the front pastedown: 'Nota quod compilator huius libri non adhibuit spem neque fidem in carminibus et empiricis licet talia sint in multis locis sui libri recitata. vt patet parte 6 d' 3 c' xi in fine. ait enim ibi. Quidam fiduciam habent in talibus empiricis forte illis valebunt sed non multum sapiunt in iecore meo. parcat michi deus. Reuera nec aliquo modo in iecore meo quod palmer. `Et hoc idem `dicit´ Ric' Lofthous´ (*probably R. L., fellow of New College 1416–45: Emden,* BRUO)[1] quia non procedunt ex racione set pro maxima parte ex sola fide´'. A prayer to staunch blood has against it 'Nota istud theologum expertum', f. 21, s. xv.

Part 7 and part 13, dist. 5, begin on new quires, ff. 155 (14^{1}) and 299 (26^{1}). ff. 153^{v}–154^{v} were left blank at the end of quire 13 and ff. 297^{v}–298^{v} at the end of quire 25 where the rubricator wrote an explicit (f. 297^{v}), 'Explicit distinccio 4 huius 13 partis. Et in proximo quaterno videlicet in 2° folio ab isto. quod habet tale numerum 145 `in superiori angulo´ incipit distinccio quinta partis eiusdem': the space is filled by an 'Unguentum exon'´ secundum doctrinam primi componentis' in the main hand on ff. 297^{v}–298 and four recipes, the

[1] The name here lends support to Dr Emden's suggestion that Lofthouse is the same person as the physician, master Richard Loftes (or Lostes) who was paid 26*s.* 8*d.* by the treasurer of the abbey of Abingdon in 1440–1 (as an annual retainer ?).

first for a sleeping draught, 'Dormitorium Magistri Iohannis Wyke' (J. W., fellow of Merton College 1357, † by June 1387: Emden, *BRUO*, p. 2109; Talbot and Hammond), on f. 298, s. xv in. The rubricator also put in a cross-reference on f. 335v, 'Item de tractatu fleobotomarii quere post 6m folium cum sua figura', but no such treatise or diagram is now to be found. f. 342v blank.

5. ff. 343–348v Incipiunt sinonoma Bartholomei. Aaron iarus pes vituli . . . Zodoarium radix est id est cetewale. Expliciunt sinonoma bartholomei.

Alphita (Renzi, iii. 272–322), but with many English equivalents. Printed from this copy by Mowat, op. cit., pp. 9–44. The English words are collected by Mowat on pp. 45–6.

6. ff. 348v–349v Incipit hic. Quid pro quo. Quoniam ea que sunt vtilia . . . Pro asara potest poni zinziber . . . Pro zuccra potest poni aqua mellis. Et prodest pauperibus. Pro benedicta vide infra 253 d. Explicit quid pro quo.

Cf. Thorndike and Kibre.

7. f. 349v Incipit de ponderibus et mensuris. Oportet modo pondera medicaminum mensurasque eorundem cognoscere . . .

Printed (mostly) from this copy by Hartley and Aldridge, op. cit., pp. 92–4.

8. ff. 349v–350 Virtutes Roris Marini. Recipe flores eius . . .

Cf. Thorndike and Kibre, cols. 1365–6. ff. 350v–352v blank.

9. ff. 353–9 Incipit tabula libri Iohannis Mirfeld'. quem ipse composuit et breuiarium Bartholomei nominauit. eo quod ipsum compilauit in monasterio sancti Bartholomei London'. eundemque diuisit in partes quindecim . . .

A table of the parts and the distinctions of each part of art. 4. f. 359v blank.

ff. i + 359. A faulty medieval foliation begins at f. 11 and runs 1–151, 1–188: the second series begins at f. 155. 375 × 240 mm. Written space 270 × 180 mm. 2 cols. 55 lines. Collation: 1^{12} wants 11, 12, perhaps blank, $2–28^{12}$ 29^{8} (ff. 335–42) 30^{12} wants 9 and 11, blank (ff. 343–52) 31^{21} wants 8–12, perhaps blank. From f. 59 (6^{1}) the quires are numbered e–m, a–[q]: in the first series, quires 6–13, the leaf number within the quire is written below the letter in roman; in the second series it is written above the letter in arabic. Anglicana formata by several hands: one change is at f. 155. Initials: (i) f. 11, historiated *I* (John Baptist) on gold ground: decoration in gold and colours forms a continuous border; (ii, iii) of parts and distinctions of parts, gold on grounds of blue and red patterned in white; (iv) 4-line or less, blue with red ornament. Initials of type (ii) are accompanied by part borders and on f. 155 by a nearly continuous border. Red and blue line fillers in arts. 5–7. Capital letters in the ink of the text filled with pale yellow. Medieval binding of wooden boards covered with white leather and a chemise over all: seven bands: two strap-and-pin fastenings: five bosses on each cover. Secundo folio (f. 2) *Set quia*; (f. 12) *at de*.

Written in England and perhaps at or for the Benedictine abbey of Abingdon: the abbey arms are in the lower border of f. 11 and the Abingdon entries in art. 2 are not additions. 'Iohannes Batcumbe', 'Richardus Lofthovs' (cf. art. 4), 'Wille Baker', 'Dauid Iohnys' on the pastedown at the end, s. xv; also 'Richardus Bartlet in medicinis doctor', s. xvi. Bartlett's gift to All Souls College, Oxford, according to an erased inscription at the foot of f. 12, 'Liber collegii animarum omnium fidelium defunctorum in Oxon' ex dono venerabilis viri

Ricardi Bartlett in medicinis doctoris et quondam huius collegii socii' (fellow 1495, †1557: Emden, *BRUO*, p. 121). The gift was probably in 1550 or 1551 and the book appears in the inventory of 1576: N. R. Ker, *Records of All Souls College Library 1437–1600*, 1971, no. 1277, pp. 64, 117, 126, 148. Used by Brian Twyne, who wrote a note on f. 42; cf. Hartley and Aldridge, op. cit., p. 21.

3. *Beda, Historia ecclesiastica* s. xii/xiii

(*begins imperfectly*) lino euangelizante conuersam esse . . . pie intercessionis inueniam. Explicit liber ecclesiastice hystorie gentis anglorum.

Noticed in the edition by R. A. B. Mynors and B. Colgrave (1969), p. lii. A C-type manuscript of the Gloucester sub-group, with (as usual) the last paragraph of the preface, 'Preterea . . . inueniam', at the end of the text. Begins at edn., p. 194/3 (2. xvii). Bk. 3, f. 4v; 4, f. 30v; 5, f. 56. Two missing leaves contained 4. xii and parts of 4. xi and 4. xiii (edn., 364/5 up, *si non obstina*–374/2 *gens suscepit*). The 'recapitulatio' at the end of bk. 5 runs to 734. A table of chapters before each book.

ff. ii + 85 + iii, foliated (i, ii), 1–20, 20a, 21–52, 52a, 53–8, 58a, 59–83, (84, 85). f. 83, a medieval endleaf, was pasted down. 362 × 266 mm. Written space 229 × 170 mm. 2 cols. 33 lines. Pricks in both margins. The first line of writing above the top ruled line. 1–3, 16–18, 31–3 of the ruled lines are continued over the margins. Collation: 1^8 wants 1 2–5^8 6^8 wants 1, 2 before f. 39 7–11^8. Quires 1–10 numbered at the end VI–XV: catchwords also. Initials: (i) of books, blue or red, patterned in the other colour and white, on decorated brown grounds; (ii) of chapters, 3-line, green with red ornament, or red with blue, or blue with red; (iii) in tables of chapters and the 'recapitulatio', 1-line, alternately red, green, red, blue. Contemporary binding of wooden boards covered with white leather, rebacked: four bands; central strap and pin missing. In repairs the back cover was put at the front and the front cover at the back.

Written in England. Scribbles s. xvi include 'Anthonye Cole of Cadwych', f. 46v, 'James Parsal (*or* Pursal)', f. 52a, 'Anthonye Cole', ff. 47, 67v.

4. *P. Lombardus, Sententiae* s. xiii ex.

1. ff. 1–230v Cupientes aliquid de penuria . . . (1v) premisimus. Incipiunt capitula primi libri sentenciarum. Omnis doctrina . . . (f. 3) Expliciunt capitula . . . Incipit ius liber. Ueteris ac noue legis . . . uia duce peruenit. Explicit liber senten-ciarum iiii.

PL cxcii. 521–962. Bk. 2, f. 69; 3, f. 124; 4, f. 169. The usual table of unnumbered chapters in front of each book. Chapter headings in current anglicana in the lower margins to guide the rubricator, at first in ink, but from f. 10v in pencil. Distinction numbers in arabic figures in the margins in pencil are perhaps nearly contemporary: they are repeated in red and blue ink. Some contemporary ink and pencil marginalia. f. 168v blank.

2. f. 231v A wheel of vices with (*a*) forty-two lines of verse as the spokes, (*b*) seven lines as the rim, and (*c*) three lines in the hub.

(*a*) begins on pride, 'Ipocrisis. Quod uidear grata michi dat uirtus simulata': Walther, no. 16326. (*b*) begins on pride, 'Cetera que supero memet transcendere curo': Walther, no. 2666. (*c*) begins 'Circumdor uiciis capitalibus ac speciebus . . .'. f. 231v left blank.

3. ff. 232–7 Versus primi libri senten(ci)arum. Incipit eternus et fit factura creator . . . Ex hoc gaudentes nichil ipsis compacientes. Expliciunt versus quarti libri.

Twelve preliminary lines (Walther, no. 9188) followed by lines which vary in number from one to nine and apply to each distinction of each book of the Sentences of Peter Lombard. A letter marks each group of verses, the series running A–Z, Al–Z (mainly Hebrew letters), Abs, B for the forty-eight distinctions of bk. 1 and similarly for bks. 2–4. The first line for bk. 1, d. 1 is A. Res et signa sunt doctrine . . . : Walther, no. 16620; Stegmüller, *Sent.*, nos. 18, 19. f. 237^{v} blank.

ff. 238. 335 × 230 mm. Written space 235 × 150 mm. 2 cols. 40 lines. Collation: $1\text{–}18^{12}$ 19^{14} 20^{8} wants 7, blank, 8 pasted down, + 1 leaf before 1 (f. 231). Pencil signatures on the first six leaves of each quire, *ad hoc* at first, but from f. 73 on a system whereby the letters a–f which distinguish the leaves (a–g in quire 19) have above them, before them, below them, or after them, a stroke or, from f. 121, a number on a regular pattern: a horizontal or vertical stroke is used for quires 7–10, the figure 3 for quires 11–14, the figure 4 for quires 15–18 and the figure 5 for quire 19. Thus, for example, ff. 121, 133, 145 and 157 are marked $\frac{3}{a}$ 3a $\frac{a}{3}$ a3 respectively. Initials: (i) of books, 3-line or 4-line, red and blue with ornament of both colours; (ii) of chapters (distinctions are not marked by a special initial) 2-line, red or blue, with ornament of the other colour; (iii) in tables of chapters, 1-line, red or blue. Contemporary binding of wooden boards covered with red leather, repaired and rebacked, but keeping the old leather on the spine: five bands: no clasps. Secundo folio *non ueni*.

Written in England.

5. *T. Wallensis In Bibliam; Interpretationes nominum hebraicorum* s. xiii in.–xiv/xv

1. (*a*) ff. $1\text{–}105^{v}$ Ecce populus filiorum israel multus et forcior nobis est. philosophus libro de animalibus capitulo 5 . . . (*b*) ff. $105^{v}\text{–}9^{v}$ Aduentus cristi et eius effectus exo. 19 . . . referre cessant iosue 6. Explicit tabula sentencialis super lecturam Magistri thome Wallensis. (*c*) ff. $109^{v}\text{–}112^{v}$ Incipit alia tabula vocalis super eandem. Adamas exo. 4 . . . Yrundo deut^{o} 25. Explicit tabula vocabulorum etc.

(*a*). Thomas Wallensis, O.P., Commentary on ten books of the Bible, Exodus, f. 18 Leviticus, f. 23 Numbers, f. 31 Deuteronomy, f. 44^{v} Joshua, f. 52^{v} Judges, f. 61 Ruth, f. 63 Ecclesiastes, f. 75 Song of Songs, f. 85 Isaiah. Stegmüller, nos. 8237, 8238, 8239. 1, 8240. 1, 8241. 1, 8242. 1, 8243. 1, 8249. 1, 8250. 1, 8251. Beginnings and ends are as Bodleian, Laud Misc. 345, ff. $98\text{–}185^{v}$, except the end of Song of Songs, here 'sub ficu uidi te', the commentary from *Capite* (2: 15) onwards being absent, and the beginning of Isaiah which lacks the prologue *Nosque* and begins 'Lauamini'. (*b, c*). Stegmüller, nos. 8260. 2, 8260. 3. As Laud Misc. 345, ff. $185^{v}\text{–}91^{v}$. f. 113^{rv} blank.

2. ff. 114–92 Hec sunt interpretationes hebraicorum nominum. Incipientium per A litteram. Aaz apprehendens . . . vel consiliatores eorum. 'Hic liber istud opus. Iordano cedit honori Pro mercede quies. sit succedente labori'.

The Interpretations of Hebrew names usually found at the end of thirteenth-century Bibles. Coloured initials break each letter into alphabetical groups, for example Saa, Sab, Sac, Sad + Sae, Saph, Sag + Sah + Sai. f. 192^{v} blank.

ff. ii + 194 + i. 268 × 185 mm. Written space of art. 1, 185 × 135 mm, of art. 2, 185 × 120 mm. 2 cols. *c*.31 lines (art. 1) and 35 lines (art. 2). Frame ruling in art. 1, but the scribe has put short horizontal pencil strokes in the margins here and there on many pages to act as a guide. Collation: $1-9^{12}$ 10^{6} wants 5 blank after f. 113 $11-19^{8}$ 20^{8} wants 8 blank. The first six leaves of quires 1-9 are each marked i-vi. Quires 11-19 are numbered at the end in red i^{us}–ix^{us}. Art. 1 in current anglicana. Initials of art. 1 (omitted on ff. 106-112^{v}): (i) f. 1, blue and red, with red, blue, and violet ornament forming a nearly continuous surround; (ii) 2-line, blue with red ornament. Initials of art. 2: (i) blue and red with ornament of both colours, or blue or red with ornament of the other colour; (ii) 2-line, blue or red with ornament of the other colour; (iii) 1-line, blue or red. Binding of modern boards covered with old white leather: five bands: probably a single central clasp was replaced by a pair of clasps, but all are missing. Secundo folio (f. 2) *de fluuio vertetur*; (f. 115) *meus superfluus.*

Written in England. Art. 2 was given to Christ Church, Canterbury by Jordanus de Rofa (monk before 1239):[1] 'Interpretationes hebraicorum Nominum Secundum Remigium. Iordani de Rofa', f. 114 at the top and beside it the mark 'Jor'. It is entered among the *Libri Jordani* in Eastry's catalogue (*Ancient Libraries*, no. 1305), and was probably bound up after art. 1 in s. xv. Art. 1 is listed in the library catalogue of 1508 when it was on desk 7 (*Ancient Libraries*, p. 157, no. 146, 'Opera Wallensis 2 fo de fluuio uertetur').

6. *Philippus Cancellarius, Sermones in Psalterium* s. xiii^{1}

Exurge psalterium, etcetera . . . (*table of 305 numbered chapters*) . . . (f. 9^{v}) De custodia quinque sensuum. (f. 10: *begins imperfectly near the end of sermon 1*) spiritus etcetera. Iocundum est ergo . . . (f. 240^{v}) diei. Preterea ypocrite similes sunt (*ends imperfectly in a chapter numbered 250*).

Stegmüller, no. 6952. Glorieux, no. 119*b*. The first words remaining here occur in Bodleian MS. Bodley 745, p. 504, col. 1/31. Fairly numerous notes, s. xv^{2}, in English hybrida. f. 240 is defective at the foot and blurred.

ff. i + 240 + i. 263 × 190 mm. Written space 195 × 125 mm. 2 cols. 34 lines and (from f. 198) 39 or 40 lines. Ruling on ff. 1-197^{v} is between a pair of ruled lines. The first line of writing above the top ruled line from f. 198. Collation: $1-21^{12}$, with twelve leaves missing, $1^{10,11}$, 6^{12} after f. 69, 8^{12} after f. 92, 10^{3} after f. 106, $12^{6,7}$ after f. 192, 16^{4} after f. 176, $19^{5,12}$ after ff. 212, 218, 20^{1} before f. 219, 21^{12} after f. 240. Quires numbered at the end and catchwords. The hand changes for the better at f. 193vb and the new scribe changed the pattern of ruling and number of lines as soon as he began a new quire (f. 198). Initials 2-line, red or green with ornament of the other colour. Parchment binding, s. xx. Secundo folio *De tribus* (f. 2).

Written in England. 'Guliel. Gardiner in Artibus magister (Hart Hall, M.A. 1582, unless another of this name) et vicarius de Lynton 1582', f. 10 at the top: cf. f. 2.[2]

[1] See W. G. Searle, *Christ Church Canterbury* (Cambridge Antiq. Soc., octavo publications xxxiv, 1902), p. 172 for references to Jordanus by Gervase of Canterbury; also Wilfred Wallace, *Life of St Edmund of Canterbury*, 1893, p. 502. Art. 2 is in his own writing, to judge from the couplet on f. 192.

[2] He owned MS. 18, q.v., Glasgow, Hunterian 223 in 1596, Lincoln Cathedral 204 in 1573, New York, Columbia U.L., Plimpton 270 in 1582, and Oxford, Bodleian, e Mus. 130 (*Sum. Cat.* 3514) in 1586.

7. *Biblia* s. xiii[1]

1. ff. 15–308v Bible in the order Genesis–Nehemiah, Judith, Esther, Tobit, 1, 2 Maccabees, Psalms, Isaiah, Jeremiah, Baruch, Lamentations, Ezekiel, Daniel, Minor Prophets, Job, five sapiential books,[1] Gospels, Acts, Catholic Epistles, Pauline Epistles (Colossians follows 2 Thessalonians), Apocalypse. Fourteen lines, 'Deus. Filius. Vox. Timor . . . capitis. dentium. signa. Res. Sen. Tau' precede Lamentations, f. 195v. A heading, 'Sequitur canticum eiusdem prophete de incarnacione et passione domini nostri ihesu cristi', precedes Habakkuk 3, which is given an initial of type (i). 'Expliciunt oracula xii prophetarum. qui secundum ieronimum pro uno computantur libro' follows Minor Prophets, f. 226.

Books are written continuously, the beginning of a new chapter being shown only by a paragraph mark in the text, against which is a number in black in the margin: thus, for example, Amos has 42 paragraph marks numbered in the margins 1–42. Red numbers in the margins show the chapter divisions now in use.

Prologues are 47 of the common series of 64 (see above, Liverpool Cathedral 13) and 23 others (shown by *): 284, 285, 323, 328, 330, 335, 341 + 343, 332, 482, 487, 492, 494; (*Minor Prophets, general prologue*) 500; (*Hosea*) 507; (*Joel*) 511 + 510 + Iohel qui interpretatur filius dei . . . et micheas* + 509*; (*Amos*) 515 + 512 (. . . audiendi uerbum dei); (*Obadiah*) 519 + 517 + 516*; (*Jonah*) 524 + 522*; (*Micah*) 526 + 525*; (*Nahum*) 528 + 527*; (*Habakkuk*) 531 + 529*; (*Zephaniah*) 534, Iosiam regem . . . tunc temporis tribuendam*, 532*; (*Haggai*) 539 + 535* (headed 'Incipit prologus in aggeo et zach' '); (*Zechariah*) Secundo anno darii filii hitaspis . . . regis imperium* + 540*; (*Malachi*) 543, Ultimus xii prophetarum . . . uenit in ierusalem* + 545* + 544*; 344 + 349* + 350*, 596* (. . . hereticis quam ecclesiasticis esse emendas), 595*, 590, 607, 620, 624, 640, 809, 670*, 674* (Quoniam sunt ex iudeis gentibus qui crediderant . . .), 676*, 685, 699, 707, 715, 728, 747, 752, 736, 765 (. . . discipline), 772, 783, 793, 834*.

Numbers, Psalms, Isaiah, and Job begin on new quires, ff. 48, 157, 171, 227. The scribe had difficulty in packing Psalms into fourteen leaves, ff. 157–70v. ff. 47v, 156v blank.

A reader, s. xiii, accustomed to a more normal type of Bible, noted that 3 Ezra, the Prayer of Manasses, and the prologue to Ecclesiastes are not here. Pauline Epistles were annotated in s. xv.

2. ff. 309–320v Hic sunt interpretationes nominum hebreorum per a literam. Aaz apprehendens . . . consiliatores eorum.

The usual dictionary of Hebrew names. Not written to match art. 1.

3 (added). (*a*) f. 2v A list of the books of the Bible in the order of art. 1. (*b*) ff. 3–6v A table of lessons of temporal, dedication of church, sanctoral, and common of saints and at votive masses and masses 'pro mortuis' and 'in nupciis'. (*c*) ff. 7–13v A table of contents of chapters of the Bible. (*d*) f. 14rv Titles of sermons (?) for example—the last two 'Sermo domini super tirum', 'De ruina babilone'.

(*a*). Anglicana, sometimes current, s. xiv. (*b–d*). Secretary, s. xv. (*b*). The votives are 'In commemoracione sancte trinitatis', followed by Holy Spirit, Holy Cross, B.V.M. at special seasons, angels, Pro pace, Pro rege, Pro salute amici, Pro benefactoribus, Ad poscendum

[1] Ecclesiasticus begins 'Stultorum' instead of *Multorum*!

donum sapiencie, Ad poscendum donum caritatis, Pro penitentibus, Pro infirmo, and In tempore belli. (*c*). The four gospels are under one heading 'De contentis in iiii^{or} euangeliis'. ff. 1^{rv}, 2^{r} blank.

ff. iii + 320 + i. ff. ii, iii are medieval parchment leaves. (Art. 1) 242 × 165 mm: written space 195 × 112 mm: 2 cols. 59–61 lines. (Art. 2) 205 × 145 mm: written space 180 × 132 mm: 3 cols. 82 lines. Collation: 1^{12} + 2 leaves after 12 (ff. 1–14) $2\text{-}3^{12}$ 4^{10} wants 10, blank, after f. 45 5^{12} 6^{14} $7\text{-}10^{12}$ 11^{10} + 1 leaf after 4 (f. 126) $12\text{-}13^{12}$ 14^{8} (ff. 157–64) 15^{6} (ff. 165–70) $16\text{-}19^{12}$ 20^{8} (ff. 219–26) $21\text{-}26^{12}$ 27^{10} (ff. 299–308) 28^{12}. Quires 2–26 numbered at the end I–XXV; also catchwords. Initials in art. 1: (i) of books and many prologues and principal psalms, red and blue with ornament of both colours; (ii) of psalms and some prologues, red or blue with ornament of the other colour; (iii) of verses of psalms, 1-line, red. Initials in art. 2: (i) f. 309, blue *A* with red ornament; (ii, iii) 3-line or 2-line and 1-line, red or blue. Limp parchment binding, s. xx (?). Secundo folio *Euangelium* (f. 4), *Omnisque legis* (f. 16).

Written in England. 'Liber Collegii Pembrokiæ in Universitate Oxon'. Ex dono Georgii Townsend Armigeri A.D. 1682'.

8. *Alexander Trallianus, Therapeutica* s. xii/xiii

Incipit primus liber Alexandri yatros Sophiste De Allopicia et ophyasi. Contingit hec duplex . . . (f. 119) incohantem marasmon. Explicit liber Alex'. (f. 119^{rv}) Incipiunt capitula primi libri. De allopicia et offiasi . . . (f. 121^{v}) De marasmode perfectius existente.

Thorndike and Kibre. Printed in 1504. Bk. 2, f. 43; 3, f. 108. One leaf missing. The wide margins contain many notes in a very small good hand on specially ruled lines and between ruled verticals. Corrections were first written further out in the margins and then carefully rewritten in the main hand in the space between the ruled verticals or, if short, inserted between the lines of text: see f. 81 for both methods. 'Sancti spiritus assit nobis gracia' at the head of f. 1.

ff. i + 121 + i. Parchment of high quality. 240 × 180 mm. Written space *c.*145 × 90 mm. 34 long lines: 1–3, 17–19, 32–4 are prolonged into the margins. Collation: $1\text{-}13^{8}$ 14^{8} wants 6 after f. 109. Initials: (i) f. 1, cut out; (ii) ff. 43, 108, gold on blue and red decorated grounds; (iii) 2-line, blue or red with ornament of the other colour; (iv) 1-line spaces not filled on ff. 119^{v}–121^{v}. Limp parchment binding, s. xvii. Secundo folio *Si ergo ex siccitate.*

Written in France (?). A conspicuous red '104' at the head of f. 1.

9. *Summa Reymundi, etc.* s. xiii ex.

1. ff. 1–182 Quoniam ut ait Ieronimus . . . (f. 1^{v}) corrigas et emendes. De symonia . . . (*table*) . . . De symonia. Quoniam inter crimina . . . percipite regnum meum amen.

Reymundus de Peniaforti, †1275, Summa de poenitentia, in three books. Printed very often. Bloomfield, no. 5054. 'Secunda particula', f. 53; 'Tercia particula', f. 96. Each is preceded by a table (6, 8, and 34 heads).

2. ff. 182^{v}–208 Incipit prohemium de tractatu de matrimonio. Quoniam frequenter in foro penitenciali . . . pertinentes. De sponsalibus . . . (*table of 15*

heads) . . . De sponsalibus. Quoniam matrimonium . . . animo set benigno corrigat et emendet. Explicit summa de matrimonio.

Printed with art. 1. Bloomfield, no. 4943. The running title calls it bk. 4. f. 208^{v} left blank.

3. Additions on flyleaves and in blank spaces include: (*a*) f. ii^{rv} Notes in faint pencil, s. xiv, including a list of personal names; (*b*) f. 209 A list of words, s. xiv, widely spaced for interlined interpretations in English; (*c*) f. 208 A recipe, 'Accipe triticum . . .', s. xv; (*d*) f. 208 A list of payments 'pro Blidegrove xxii s' . . . pro Chesturshethe (?) domino Toneworthe iii s' x d' per annum', s. xv/xvi; (*e*) f. 208^{v} Memorandum y^{t} I pay yerly fo(r) my tuyth hay to þ^{e} parson whather I mowe lytell or myche xx^{ti} d', s. xvi; (*f*) f. 208^{v} Memorandum quod Willelmus Sheldon habet (?) de bonis et catallis patris mei quatuor Iuga bovium . . . , s. xvi in., in a law hand; (*g*) f. 209 Item predict' Iohanna bedyll asportauit [. . .] a domo mea apud clark in Wythworth anno regni regis h viii octauo per mandat Willelmi Sheldon.

(*b*). 7½ lines in anglicana formata. 'Hoc sulcus ci co hec lira re prima longa hec lyra re prima breuis . . .': the interlined words up to this point are 'waterforugh', 'a backe', 'harpestreng'. (*f, g*) in one hand.

ff. ii + 208 + ii. ff. ii, 209 are medieval flyleaves. Faint medieval pencil foliation. 235 × 168 mm. Written space 157 × 105 mm. 2 cols. 30 or 31 lines. Collation: 1-20^{10} 21^{8}. Initials: (i) f. 1, red and blue with ornament of both colours; (ii) 2-line, blue or red, with ornament of the other colour; (iii) in lists of chapters, 1-line, blue or red. Contemporary boards, re-covered s. xx (?): 3 bands: the parchment which shows in the holes in the front cover where the bands are brought through has writing on it. Central strap-and-pin fastening missing. Secundo folio *consuluit.*

Written in England. 'Sheldon', f. 206^{v}. 'Iste liber pertinet ad Rychardum Sheldon', f. 208^{v}, s. xvi. 'Sheldon Richard de Blakegreve', f. 209^{v}. The place is perhaps Blackgrave in King's Norton, Birmingham: cf. f. 209 ('. . . de la Blackgreve') and art. 3*f, g*. 'Liber francisci Harewell de Birlingham (*Worcestershire*) Armig.', f. 208, s. xvi/xvii: he also owned Worcester Cathedral MS. Q. 36.

10, ff. 1-107. *Medica* s. xii med.-xiii in.

Seven originally separate pieces.

1 (quires 1-4: s. xiii in.). ff. 1-22^{v} Verba albubecri filii Zacarie a rasi. Ventilata fuit in presentia . . .

Bk. 1 of Rasis, Liber divisionum, ending imperfectly, f. 21^{v}, at the seventeenth word, 'melancoliam', of ch. 126, 'De verrucis' (edn., Lyon 1510, f. liii, cap. 124), followed by a leaf of bk. 2 (ed. ff. lxxxii^{v}-lxxxiv^{v}), with the running title 'III'. Thorndike and Kibre.

The title at the head of f. 1, 'Liber diuisionum translatus a magistro Giraudo Cremonensi in Toleto et antidotarium rasis et quidam alii tractatus de simplici medicina' shows what the contents originally were: only quires 1-3 and a fragment of quire 4 now remain.

2 (quire 5: s. xiii in.). (*a*) ff. 23-25^{v} Dicitur urina quoniam fit renibus una . . . tangere dignus. Expliciunt urine egidii. (*b*) ff. 25^{v}-26 Urina alba et subtilis in

acuta febre: malum . . . (*c*) f. 26 Recipes in Latin and French. (*d*) ff. 26v–29v Incipiunt anathomie. Galienus in tegni testatur . . . uel feminas generant. Expliciunt anathomie. (*e*) ff. 29v–30 Incipit regimen sanitatis. Alexander. Cum sit homo corrup(tibilis) et ei accidit . . . medicis non indignisset. Explicit regimen sanitatis. (*f*) f. 30rv Cura fistule. In principio digeratur . . . (*g*) f. 30v Verses: (1) Gaudet epar . . . (2 lines); (2) Incaustum uino . . . (2 lines); (3) Quatuor hii menses . . . (4 lines).

(*a*). Thorndike and Kibre (Aegidius of Corbeil, De urinis, in verse). Glossed in the margins and between the lines. (*b*). Table of prognostications from urine. (*c*) added in current anglicana, s. xiii/xiv, in blank space. (*d*). See MS. 15, art. 5. (*e*). Thorndike and Kibre. The letter to Alexander which begins pseudo-Aristotle, Secreta secretorum. (*f*). Fourteen paragraphs of remedies for various ills: set out in Dr Anderson's description. (*g*1). Walther, no. 10190*b*. (*g*3). Renzi, v. 1870–2.

3 (quire 6: s. xiii[1]). (*a*) ff. 31–4 Questiones phisicales. [S]epe michi dubiam traxit sententia mentem . . . Fetidus est sudor et copia tanta pilorum. (*b*) ff. 34v–35 [R]es aloe lignum preciosa sit hoc tibi signum . . . pix greca nigrescit. (*c*) Verses: (1) De proprietatibus complexionum. Largus amans hilaris . . . nigrique coloris; (2) De ponderibus. Collige triticeis . . . ; (3) Dat scrupulum: nummus . . . ; (4) Constat sex solidis . . . ; (*d*) ff. 35v–36v Recipes in twelve paragraphs, the first in French, 'Pur la destresce del piz . . .'.

(*a*). 257 lines of verse. Printed by B. Lawn, *The Salernitan questions*, 1963, pp. 160–6, 170–6, from B.L., Sloane 1610, ff. 43v–5. Five neatly written side notes. (*b*). 140 verses on aromatic simples. Walther, no. 16604. Lines 133–7, 'Albam . . . probanti', are marked 'vacat'. (*c*1–3). 8, 6, and 2 lines, Walther nos. 10131, 3027, 4071. Printed in *Traditio*, xi, 179–80. Lines 1695–703, 1589–91, 1604–5 of the Flos scholae Salerni (ed. Renzi, v. 1–104). (*c*4), 7 lines, was added in the lower margin. (*d*). The paragraphs are set out in Dr Anderson's description.

4 (quires 7–9: s. xii med.). (*a*) f. 37 In nomine domini incipit epistola messahalah in rebus eclipsis lune . . . Dixit messehalah. quia dominus altissimus . . . aptatio quoque (*ends abruptly*). (*b*) ff. 37–51 Sexta particula practice de faucibus. Si (i)n faucibus calidum nascitur apostema . . . Tempera cum fuco scariol' aut solatri aut lupuli. (*c*) ff. 51–56v Incipit liber chirurgie. Quia infirmitates potione et dieta curare ducuimus (? *sic*) . . . proficiunt aposita. Explicit liber chirurgiarum. (*d*) ff. 56v–57v Incipit liber flebothomię. Flebothomia est uenę incisio Et sanguinis effusio . . . flebothomatur uirtutem abere fortem (*ends imperfectly*).

(*a*). The scribe began copying Messahala on eclipses (Thorndike and Kibre), but changed his mind and ceased in the first chapter. (*b*). Cures of diseases, beginning with the throat and ending with the liver. f. 37 is headed, s. xiii, 'Summa magistri Perrotin' and 'Alani' is at the foot of the page. (*d*). Thorndike and Kibre. A slip of parchment after f. 57 seems to have been cut from the flyleaf of some book. It has on one side a title, 'Lgica (*sic*) quatern' de barbarismo `et summas Galteri hic habet [. . .]'', and on the other side seven lines on the virtues of bleeding for those over 40, written in an English hand, s. xiii[2].

5 (quires 10–13: s. xiii[1]). (*a*) ff. 58–80v [C]irca instans negocium . . . hic leto fine concludimus. (*b*) ff. 80v–84* [D]e bato [D]e butiro [D]e bullo. [B]atus herba stiptica . . . [D]e xilocaracta quando est in materia delet uerrucas fricata

decoccio eius lotam [. . . .]ntium uentrem et constringit. (*c*) ff. 58–63v, lower margins, Contra a[. . . . .]tatem uocis infundatur furfur . . .

(*a*). Thorndike and Kibre. Aloes–Zucara. Cf. MS. 12, art. 1, and MS. 15, art. 8. (*b*). An alphabetical herbal like (*a*), letters B–X. It probably ended at the foot of col. 1 on f. 84*: col. 2 has been cut off. The verso is blank. (*c*). Recipes, six lines to a page, added in s. xiii. Both (*a*) and (*c*) contain some interlinear glosses in French, but not after f. 62.

6 (s. xiv). f. 85. (*a*) recto, a quarter circle with degrees, 1–90, marked on it round the rim, and the names of the months, six signs of the zodiac, and 'umbre verse' and 'umbre recte' within it. (*b*) verso, a diagram of the brain showing sense centres. McKinney, no. 125. 1.

7 (s. xiii in.). ff. 86–107 [L]iber iste quem in presenti legendum assumsimus . . . Si ex flegmate cum vino decoc' polip contra.

Thorndike and Kibre. Platearius on Antidotarium Nicholai, ending in Yeralogia. Printed in 1495 (Goff, M. 516) and later. f. 107v is blank and was probably once pasted down.

ff. 108, foliated 1–84, 84*, 85–107, bound before a sermon for the Annunciation of B.V.M. in German, s. xvi ex. (ff. 108–23). 220 × 160 mm, except that in art. 1 20 mm of the outer margin has often been folded in to preserve side notes. Limp parchment binding, s. xvii, as on MS. 8. Secundo folio *assicuracio* (? *sic*) *acceptionis*.

ff. 1–22. Written space 180 × 120 mm. 2 cols. 48 lines. The first line of writing above the top ruled line. Collation: 1^8 $2\text{–}3^6$ 4 two (ff. 21–2, the outside bifolium). Initials: (i) f. 1, red and brown, with red ornament; (ii) 2-line, red, plain or with red ornament.

ff. 23–30. Written space 167 × 120 mm. 2 cols. 52 lines. The first line of writing above the top ruled line. Collation: 5^8. 3-line initials to (*a, c, d*), the first two blue with red ornament and the third red with blue ornament.

ff. 31–6. Written space of (*a*): 155 × 50 mm in 40–2 long lines; of (*b–d*) 155 × 110 mm in 2 cols. of 41–2 lines. Collation: 6^6. Initials omitted or (*d*) in the ink of the text.

ff. 37–57. 195 × 108 mm at first, increasing later to 205 × 140 mm. 2 cols. 41–3 lines. Ruling with a hard point. Collation: $7\text{–}8^8$ 9^8 wants 6–8 after f. 57. 2-line initials, blue or red at first, but from f. 54 in the ink of the text and lined with red.

ff. 58–84, 84*. Written space 170 × 115 mm at first, increasing later to 185 × 125 mm. 2 cols. 51–6 lines. The second quire is pricked in both margins. The first line of writing below the top ruled line in the first quire and above it in the three other quires. Collation: 10^6 11^8 12^4 + 2 leaves after 2 (ff. 74, 75) 13^8 (ff. 78–84, 84*). The four quires are numbered at the beginning 1–4 and the number of leaves in each quire is entered above the quire number. Spaces for initials not filled.

f. 85. A single leaf.

ff. 86–107. Written space 175 × 115 mm. 2 cols. 37–9 lines. The first line of writing above the top ruled line. Collation: 15^{12} 16^{10}. Spaces for initials not filled.

Arts. 1–5, 7 are probably French. Art. 6 is English. The manuscript, or parts of it, was in England before 1300: cf. 2*c*, 4*d*.

11, ff. 1–68. *Recepta medica, etc.* s. xiv/xv

1. ff. 1–27v (*begins perhaps imperfectly*) Electuarium laxatiuum quod fecit magister Si pro domino gri pro tempore hyemali set multum est amarum propter agaric' et aloes et coliquint' Recipe . . . cum succo mente et aque ro.

A tidily written collection of recipes.

2. ff. 27v–34 Nota de flobocomia (*sic*). Presentis operis est breuiter pertractare in quibus egritudinibus . . . audaces et cito cessantes. Explicit liber de fleubocomia.

Cf. Thorndike and Kibre (Presentis negotii. . .).

3. ff. 34–44 Vnguentum quod dicitur gracia dei . . . zuccarri quod sufficit etc.

A further collection of recipes, like art. 1. ff. 44v–48v blank.

4. ff. 49–66v Dixit G. quod ignis qui descendit super altare conbuxit libros regis Michi autem conbuxit . . . set si plus acquisiuimus alias. in fine huius tractatus scribemus.

Thorndike and Kibre. Pseudo-Galen. *Hippocratis et Galeni Opera*, 1679, x. 561–70. Also in Balliol College 285, ff. 198–207, and in Merton College 228, ff. 51–57v.

5. ff. 67–68v, left blank, contain added recipes 'de libello M. Thadei', 'De aquis spiritualium', etc. Cf. Bodleian MS. Bodley 585, f. 107v (Thaddeus of Bologna).

ff. 68, bound before two paper quires (ff. 69–87) containing notes in an English hand, mainly on diseases of the eye, and recipes, s. xvi/xvii: the names 'maystres blakwell', 'magistro polen de suthfolke', 'magistro bulle', 'magistro kyrton', 'my lady marquese of exceter', 'Willelmo Martyn', 'Skynner de Soper Lane' and 'magistro turke aldermanno in parochia sanctis magnetis' are in the headings of recipes on ff. 82–7. Paper and—for the outside and middle leaves of quires 1–5—parchment. 220 × 150 mm. Written space 142 × 88 mm. 27–9 long lines in arts. 1–3. Frame ruling. Collation: $1\text{–}5^{12}$ 6^{12} wants 9–12, blank. Art. 1 in short-*r* anglicana formata. Art. 4 in a current mixture of anglicana and secretary. Initials of art. 4: (i) red 4-line *D*, f. 49; (ii) 2-line, not filled in. No spaces for initials in arts. 1–3. Binding of limp parchment, as on MS. 8. Secundo folio *quater uel quinquies.*

Written in England.

12. *Medica* s. xii/xiii–xiii/xiv

Two manuscripts bound together: arts. 1, 2, s. xii/xiii; arts. 3, 4, s. xiii/xiv.

1 (quires 1–9). ff. 1–66v [C]irca instans. negocium in simplicibus medicinis . . . leto fine illud concludimus. Hactenus archanum salerni diximus urbis/Littera iam lasso pollice sistat opus. Explicit circa instans. alleluia alleluia.

See MS. 10, art. 5*a*. 'assit principio sancta maria meo' at the head of f. 1. The blank space on f. 66v contains a table of the herbs of art. 2, with leaf references, in an English hand, s. xiv². Many marginalia, for example on f. 1v 'asparagus genus herbe gallice brusk anglice kneholm', are also in this hand, which appears to be that of Simon Bredon, fellow of Merton College, Oxford, †1372, to judge from the similarity of the index on f. 66v to Merton College 231, f. 152, Merton College 250, f. 154rv, and Balliol College 89, ff. 2–3v, 393v–397v, but the present manuscript is not identifiable with any book listed in Bredon's will (Powicke, *Medieval Books of Merton College*, 1931, pp. 82–6). As in other Bredon indexes the references are to the double opening, not to recto and verso.

2 (quires 10–17). (*a*) ff. 67–123v Incipit practica magistri Rogeri de baronia. [S]icut ab antiquis habemus auctoribus . . . ad cura predictas. et hec de sinthomatibus dicta: ad presens sufficiant. (*b*) ff. 123v–130v Cum medicinalis artis

due sint partes integrales . . . ácc' succ' uermicularis scar' (*ends imperfectly in chapter* De oleis).

(*a, b*) are also in MS. 15, arts. 2, 3, q.v. In the edition printed in 1499 the last words of (*b*) are at f. 169vb/21. Many margins cut off.

3 (quires 18–21). ff. 131–167v Incipiunt diete particulares. Compleuimus in primo libro uniuersales significationes . . . et lapidem in renibus creat. Expliciunt particulares diete.

Isaac Judeus. Thorndike and Kibre.

4 (quires 22–7). ff. 168–213v Capitula . . . (*table of chapters*) . . . Incipiunt diete uniuersales. Quod coegit antiquos disputare . . . delectabiliora sunt. et utiliora. Explicit liber dietarum.

Isaac Judeus. Thorndike and Kibre (Quod in primis coegit).

ff. i + 213 + i. 200 × 150 mm. Limp parchment binding, s. xvii, as on MS. 8. Secundo folio *est fetidum*.

(Arts. 1, 2). Medieval foliation on versos of art. 1 1–66 and on rectos of art. 2 1–(64). Written space 145 × 110 mm (art. 1) and 150 × 98 mm (art. 2). 2 cols. 36 lines. Collation: $1–8^8$ 9 two (ff. 65–6) $10–17^8$. A few red initials, ff. 74v–77: elsewhere spaces are left blank. Written in England. Belonged to Simon Bredon: see above.

(Arts. 3, 4). Written space *c.*150 × 98 mm. 2 cols. 35–7 lines. Collation: 18^8 + 1 leaf after 7 (f. 138) 19^{10} 20^8 21^{10} (ff. 158–67) $22–26^8$ 27^6: 2 and 9 are half sheets in quire 19. Initials: (i) red with blue and red ornament; (ii, iii) 2-line and 1-line, red or blue with ornament of the other colour.

Written in France (?).

13. *Medica* s. xiii in.–xiii med.

Four parts (1, s. xiii^1; 2, s. xiii med.; 3, s. xiii^1; 4, s. xiii in.) assembled before 1500 and perhaps in s. xiii: cf. 1*d, e*, 2*c*.

1 (quires 1, 2). ff. 1–15. (*a*) f. 1 [Aurea alexandrina datur] eunti dormitum cum [uino] calido in modum castanee . . . (*b*) ff. 2–13 A[. . .] diuus Aaron id est d[. . .] . . . Zuccocaria R. in metridato flos agni casti. (*c*) f. 13 Dragea quod interpretatur mixtura specierum . . . (*d*) ff. 13–15 Recipes, etc., added at different times in blank spaces, including: f. 13v, s. xv, a reference to art. 4*b*(4), 'vno folio ante librum parui Micrologi'; f. 14v, s. xiii/xiv, a piece on 'ydropsis' in current anglicana; f. 15, s. xiii, a recipe for 'yliaca domine Luc' de Chauncy' and other recipes, and directions for making an astronomical instrument, 'Accipe rotulas ex au^do^ secundum numerum et magnitudinem quam uis . . .'. (*e*) f. 15rv A table of the 160 chapters of art. 2*a*.

(*a, b*). Herb lists. (*a*) ends with Yera constantini: cf. art. 3*c*. In (*b*) Aurea alexandrina is in seventh place. (*c*). Recipes. f. 1v blank.

2 (quires 3–10). ff. 16–75 (*a*) ff. 16–74v Incipit liber magistri Rogerini (*sic*). Sicud ab antiquis habemus auctoribus . . . cum aqua calida in mane. Explicit Rogerina dei gracia. (*b*) ff. 74v–75v Recipes, s. xiii ex., in current anglicana. (*c*) f. 75v A table of the 126 chapters of art. 3*a*.

(*a*). The Rogerina maior (ff. 16–66) and minor (ff. 66v–75v) are here run together as one work in 160 chapters: cf. MS. 15, arts. 2, 3.

3 (quires 11–17). ff. 76–137. (*a*) ff. 76–117 Incipit liber practice bartholomei. Practica diuiditur in duo . . . fuerit audacter utere. Explicit practica magistri Bartholomei. (*b*) ff. 117–25 Incipit liber de uirtute simplicis medicine. Cogitanti michi sepe de simplicium medicinarum virtutibus . . . et clare cutis reddunt homines. (*c*) f. 125rv Aurea alexandrina datur eunti dormitum . . . Yera constantini purum est lax. Ex receptione purgat principaliter co. nigram. Explicit. (*d*) ff. 126–137v [A]lphita farina ordei . . . Zimia est apostema factum ex fleumate ut in Ioh'. Explicit.

(*a*). Renzi, iv. 321–406, and a final paragraph on Podagra. (*b*). Thorndike and Kibre. J. de S. Paulo. Lacks the final paragraph in MS. 21, art. 2. (*c*). A list of purgatives: cf. art. 1*a*. (*d*). Thorndike and Kibre. The editions by J. L. G. Mowat, 1887, and by Renzi, ii. 272–322 are rearranged in a more strictly alphabetical order.

4 (quires 18–27). (*a*) ff. 138–176v Assiduis peticionibus meis karissime compendiose . . . dirigente deo omnipotente. (*b*) ff. 176v–177v Recipes and charms in the space at the end of quire 23, including: (1) f. 176v + arla + farla + tarla + arlaus + farlaus + tarlaus + on + on + on + Iohannes Lucas. Marchus. Matheus; (2) f. 176v Medicorum illiteratorum. simplicium. adolescentium. negligentium. luxui subiacentium: plurimi homicide . . . ; (3) f. 176v A recipe 'contra fistulam'; (4) f. 177 Pillule Regis Rogeri cicl' (*Roger of Sicily, †1154*) quibus utebatur fere singulis diebus . . .', and other recipes; (5) f. 177, at foot, + In nomine + patris + et filii + et spiritus sancti + amen + hugor + sudor + + neor + exi foras; (6) f. 177v, upper margin, + Sleral: gustus: guttanla: + droso + drosudro +. (*c*) ff. 178–200v Hic incipit paruus Micrologus de causis signis et curis earum de quibus agitur passionum. Cum uetustati sicut moderne nouitati exosa fuisset olim studiorum negociorumue prolixitas . . . minora. Acutarum alia est terciana de colera rubra . . . melius tinguntur quam alii. (*d*) ff. 201–211v De signis egritudinum. De signis et causis et curis egritudinum sub compendio tractaturi. quoniam teste G in actionibus corporum . . . De quibus aliqua utilia breuiter dicamus. (f. 202) Tractatus urinarum. De urina ergo uideamus quid sit. et quot modis consideratur . . . (f. 205) et maxime in pleuretico et peripl*eti*co. De tracta(tu) sanorum egrorum. et neutrorum: consequenter de pulsu. Hiis sufficienter et compendiose determinatis ad curarum accedamus tractatum. quare . . . et ita fiat donec curetur.

(*a*). Thorndike and Kibre. Johannes de S. Paulo, Breviarium. (*c*). The Micrologus of Ricardus Anglicus, with a preface in which the author says that he wrote at the request 'cuiusdam domini scilicet decani beluacensis': this preface is also in Edinburgh Univ. Libr. 174, f. 82, and in Paris, B.N., lat. 6957, f. 37 (whence printed by K. Sudhoff in *Janus*, xxviii (1924), 401–3) where the dean's name is given as Ancelinus (Talbot and Hammond, p. 271, suggest Lancelinus, archdeacon of Beauvais 1178–90). A table of the two parts, 64 and 16 chapters, is added on f. 177v. Part 2, chapters 14–16, are the De decoratione printed among the works of Arnold of Villanova (edn. 1504, ff. 298v–299) and listed by Thorndike and Kibre *s.v.* Faciei decor: (14) De ornatu faciei. Faciei decor et uenustas . . . ; (15) De decoratione dentium. Dentium non minus . . . ; (16) De decoratione capillorum. Capillos multiplicant . . .

ff. i + 211 + ii. ff. 2–15, 117–37 and 201–11 are foliated 1–14, 1–21, and 1–11 by a writer who noted on f. 211 'pro prima parte contenta 14 pro secunda parte 21 pro 3a part 11'. 210 × 145 mm. Limp parchment binding, s. xvii, as on MS. 8. Secundo folio (f. 17) *aurea.*

ff. 1–15. Written space *c.*175 × 120 mm. 2 cols. 64 lines. The first line of writing below the top ruled line. Collation: 1^8 2^8 wants 7, perhaps blank. No initials.

ff. 16–75. Written space 135 × 105 mm. 2 cols. 35 lines. Pricks in both margins to guide ruling. The first line of writing below the top ruled line. Collation: $3–6^8$ 7^{12} $8–10^8$. Initials: (i) f. 16, 5-line, blue with red ornament; (ii) 2-line, red.

ff. 76–137. Written space 155 × 85 mm. 2 cols. 37 lines and (ff. 117–37) 37 long lines. The first line of writing above the top ruled line. Collation: $11–14^8$ 15^{10} (ff. 116–25) 16^8 17^8 wants 5–8 after f. 137. Initials: (i) f. 76, red and green; (ii) outside written space, red, green, or (ff. 116, 117 only) blue: no green after f. 115v.

ff. 138–211. Written space *c.*155 × 100 mm. 2 cols. 38 lines. Pricks in both margins of quires 25–7. The first line of writing above the top ruled line. Collation: $18–20^8$ 21^4 (ff. 162–5) $22–23^6$ $24–26^8$ 27^8 + 2 leaves after 8. Quires numbered 1–10, usually at the end. Hands change at f. 178 and near the foot of f. 193va. Initials: (i) f. 138, blue (dragon motif) on decorated red ground; (ii) red and blue with ornament of both colours; (iii) 2-line, red or blue with ornament of the other colour; (iv) 1-line, red or blue.

Written in England. 'continet (?) [. . .] 14 quater' [. . .] anno 1445to' and 'Liber Iohannis Somyngley de Louth in Comit' Lincoln', f. 211v. 'E. S.', ff. 15, 211v: cf. MS. 15.

15, ff. 1–230. *Medica* s. xii²–xiii med.

Three parts (arts. 1–10, s. xiii med.; art. 11, s. xiii¹; art. 12, s. xii²) bound together probably before 1500.

1 (quires 1, 2). ff. 1–21 Ego Nicholaus rogatus . . . (*ends imperfectly in* Zinziber).

Antidotarium Nicholai, printed in 1471 and later (Goff, N. 160–3). f. 21 is badly damaged. f. 22 contains recipes in the main hand on the recto, including one for 'Trocissci iiiior magistrorum', and is blank on the verso.

Arts. 2, 3 are on quires 3–7.

2. ff. 23–62 'Rogerina'. Sicut ab antiquis habemus auctoribus . . . recurras ad superiora. Et hec dicta de sinthomatibus sufficiant.

Thorndike and Kibre. Rogerius de Baron, Practica. Printed with Guy de Chauliac in 1499 and later (Goff, G. 558).

3. ff. 62–68v Cum artis medicinalis due partes . . . vel pannus illesus (*ends abruptly*).

Thorndike and Kibre. Rogerius de Baron, Rogerina minor, ending in the section 'De aqua ardente', Follows art. 2 in the editions. The last words here are in edn. 1499, f. 169va/21. f. 69rv was left blank.

4 (quires 8, 9). ff. 70–90 Cum omnis sciencia ex fine et utilitate . . . in uasis cupreis. quemadmodum axungie. in testis. Explicit.

Thorndike and Kibre. Gerardus, De modo medendi. An 'Emplastrum laxatiuum' follows. ff. 90^{v}–91^{v} were left blank.

Arts. 5–7 are on quire 10.

5. ff. 92–96^{v} Galienus testatur in tegni quod quicumque interiorum membrorum . . . tantum masculos uel tantum feminas generant.

Thorndike and Kibre (Galieno testante). H. H. Beusing, *Richardus Anglicus*, 1922, pp. 12–17 (Anathomia Ricardi, ed. K. Sudhoff in *AGM* xix (1927), 209–39). The scribe began art. 5 and art. 8 with 'Sancti spiritus assit nobis gracia'.

6. ff. 97–103 Alfita farina . . . Zirbus omentum ut in o`ribosio . . . Zuccarium . . . agni casti′.

Cf. MS. 13, art. 3*d*.

7. f. 103 Sixteen sets of verses: (*a*) Aurea quando datur capud a langore . . . apta dolori (29 lines); (*b*) Gaudet epar . . . (2); (*c*) Si medicina datur . . . (3); (*d*) Succor macelli . . . (2); (*e*) Pruna ser' lactis . . . (2); (*f*) Sambucus autem . . . (2); (*g*) Camed`e′os . . . (1); (*h*) Mirabolanorum species . . . (5); (*i*) Vtraque spica . . . (4); (*j*) Thus mastix . . . (4); (*k*) Hec lapidem frangunt . . . (4); (*l*) Publica solemnem . . . (4); (*m*) Lingua manus uenter . . . (3); (*n*) Saluia catoreum . . . (4); (*o*) Sunt hec diuretica . . . (4); (*p*) Restam sume bouis . . . (2).

(*a*). Thorndike and Kibre. Walther, no. 1807. Renzi, v. 35. (*b*, *i*). Thorndike and Kibre. f. 103^{v} blank.

8 (quires 11–13). ff. 104–143^{v} Circa instans negotium . . . in cibis et potibus eorum. Explicit.

Thorndike and Kibre. On simples, Aloes–Zucara. Printed in 1497 (Goff, S. 466) and later: Renzi, ii. 18. Differs a good deal from MS. 10, art. 5*a* and lacks the last fourteen words there.

9 (quires 14–16). ff. 144–176^{v} Amicum induit . . . Et bene desiccati:/ reseruentur. Explicit.

Thorndike and Kibre. Platearius. Printed in 1497, together with art. 8, and later. f. 167 ends in Diarria and f. 168 begins in Yctericia: one leaf missing.

10. Blank spaces after arts. 1, 3–5, 8 were used by a reader, s. xv, who fitted in recipes on ff. 22^{rv}, 68^{v}–69, 90–1, 96^{v}, 143^{v}.

11 (quires 12–19). (*a*) ff. 177–205^{v} Liber iste quem in presenciarum legendum assumpsimus . . . yera constantini et tantumdem seruatur. (*b*) ff. 205^{v}–206^{v} Twenty-seven short paragraphs, the first beginning 'De repressuris omnium acuminum dicendum est et primo scamonee. que apud modernos' and the last ending 'puluerem predictorum confities'.

(*a*). Thorndike and Kibre. Platearius. Cf. MS. 10, art. 7.

12 (quires 21-3). ff. 207-230v Quoniam disputacionem simplicium medicine . . . hec solebant mensis apponere. 'Finit'.

Thorndike and Kibre. De gradibus simplicium. Begins with Rosa, Viola, and Absinthium and ends with Rafanum.

ff. 230, bound in front of 116 separately foliated paper leaves containing mainly medical recipes (on ff. 77v-82 also a 'Composicio horalogii horizontalis') in a current English hand, s. xvi[1]: the name 'hasard' (? William Hasard of Magdalen College, Oxford: Emden, *BRUO*, p. 883) is attached to a 'puluis contra lapidem' on f. 38v. 220 × 140 mm. Limp parchment binding, s. xvii, as on MS. 8. Secundo folio *lapidem.*

ff. 1-176. Written space *c.*130 × 100 mm. 2 cols. (art. 6, 3 or 4 cols.). 31-4 lines. The first line of writing above the top ruled line. Collation: 1^{12} $2\text{-}6^{10}$ 7^{8} wants 8, blank, after f. 69 8^{10} $9\text{-}10^{12}$ 11^{14} (ff. 104-17) 12^{12} $13\text{-}14^{14}$ 15^{10} 16^{10} wants 1 before f. 168. In quires 8, 9, 11-14 the leaves in the first half of each quire bear pencilled numbers i-iiii, xvi-xx, i-vi, vii-xi, iiii-ix respectively. In each quire, the numbers run consecutively, except the first, which is the same number on both the verso of the first leaf and the recto of the second leaf: $8^{1,2}$ are marked I (ff. 70v, 71) $9^{1,2}$ XVI, $11^{1,2}$ (I), $12^{1,2}$ VII, $13^{1,2}$ IIII, $14^{1,2}$ X. Initials: (i) red and blue with ornament of both colours; (ii) 2-line or 1-line, blue with red ornament or red with blue or blue-green ornament: ornament omitted ff. 71-167.

ff. 177-206. Written space *c.*165 × 100 mm. 42 long lines. The first line of writing above the top ruled line. Collation: $17\text{-}19^{8}$ 20^{8} wants 7, 8 after f. 206. Quires 17-19 numbered at the end (I)-III. Red initials, plain or with ornament in red or (f. 177 only) blue.

ff. 207-30. Written space *c.*160 × 95, and rather more from f. 219v where the hand changes. 27-33 long lines. Collation: $21\text{-}23^{8}$. 3 and 6 are half-sheets in quire 21 and 1, 2, 7, 8 half-sheets in quire 22. Initials: f. 207, 2-line, red and black with red ornament; (ii) 2-line or 1-line, red.

Written in England. 'Ricardus Som*ur*uill' ', f. 96v, s. xv. 'E. S.' at the foot of f. 1 as in MS. 13, and a number '8' at the head of f. 1.

18. *Apocalypsis, cum glossa* s. xii ex.

1. (*a*) Continuous text, ff. 2-56, in a column of varying width. Chapters are noted only by a much later hand, but some 270 sections are shown by red or blue letters. The gloss on either side of the text is not continuous or extensive and is sometimes in framed shapes, for example on ff. 39, 43. (*b-h*) ff. 1-2 Preliminaries in seven paragraphs: (*b*) Incipit prefacio Ieronimi presbiteri in ueram apochalipsim. Iohannes apostolus et euangelista . . . doctrina seruetur; (*c*) Apocalipsis inter reliquos noui testamenti . . . Visio ysaie; (*d*) Alpha: principium . . . (3 lines); (*e*) Causa que beatum iohannem scribere monebat (*sic*). quia interim dum ipse exul . . . de remuneracione; (*f*) Nomen etiam autoris . . . intellexit; (*g*) Deus pater preuidens . . . configurauit; (*h*) Asia minor est . . . (f. 2) scripsit euangelium.

(*b, c, g*). Stegmüller, nos. 835, 828, 832. (*e*) occurs in the Christ Church, Canterbury, Bible, now Paris, Mazarine, 5.[1]

[1] Information from Miss M. Dulong.

2. f. 56rv Iaspis uiridis: uirorem fidei inmarcescentem significat . . . uirtutum multiplicitas. Finit de xii lapidibus.

Thorndike and Kibre.

3 (added on flyleaves). ff. 57v, 60v–61v Notes on the Apocalypse, s. xiii, including seventeen lines of verse on the seven visions: Visio septena septem sunt ecclesiarum . . .

The amount of alteration suggests that these may be original verses.

ff. ii + 56 + v. The five flyleaves and the pastedown at the end are three bifolia. 198 × 150 mm. Written space 128 mm high and from 35 to 80 mm wide. 13 long lines. Ruling for interlinear glosses and marginal scholia. Collation: $1-7^8$. Initials: (i) on f. 2, cut out; (ii) 2-line (f. 1rv) and 1-line, red or blue. Modern boards, but the covers and sewing may be original. Secundo folio *misit*.

Written in England. Erasures, f. ii. 'Guliel. Gardiner in Artibus magister et vicarius de Linton 1583', f. 1: cf. MS. 6.

20. *Horae de S. Matthia, etc.* s. xv in.

Fully described by J. J. G. Alexander, 'A Book of Hours made for King Wenceslaus IV of Bohemia', *Studies in late medieval and renaissance Painting in honor of Millard Meiss*, ed. I. Lavin and John Plummer, 1978, pp. 28–31, with facsimiles of f. 40v and of parts of ff. 13, 35, 39, 44, 46, and 47v.

1. (*a*) ff. 1–3v Confiteor tibi domine deus quia peccaui in celum et in terram . . . omnium peccatorum meorum. Amen. (*b*) ff. 3v–8 Sequitur alia confessio. Confiteor tibi domino meo omnipotenti et vbique presenti . . . resistere valeo omnipotens deus. Qui viuis . . . (*c*) ff. 8–10v Domine ihesu criste qui mundum proprio sangwine redemisti exaudi me peccatorem . . . ff. 11–12v blank.

2. ff. 13–28v Cursus de sancto mathia apostolo ad matutinas. Deus in adiutorium meum . . . Ps. Beatus quem elegisti . . .

In each hour the intercession of Matthias is asked for on behalf of the royal suppliant: thus, at matins, f. 14v, '. . . michi W. seruo tuo obtinere digneris. vt qui me inter electe plebis sue numero recensuit. et eiusdem ceptrigerum regimen commendauit. dignum vite sue sectatorem efficiat. Amen'; at terce, f. 18v, '. . . michi vero in die tui gloriosi natalis in orbem terrarum exorto. te in patronum speciali dono concessit';[1] at sext, f. 20v, '. . . me W. seruum tuum . . . absolue. vt qui in sublime solium regia dignitate conscendi . . .

3. ff. 29–49 Hore canonice congeste ad laudem dei et omnium sanctorum eius et primo pro matutine hore principio. de sancta trinitate quia scriptum est. In matutinis domine meditabor in te. quia fuisti adiutor meus. et incipit hoc modo.

The headings after the first are: Pro matutine hore medio. De gloriosa virgine maria. quia . . . ; Pro matutine hore terminio de nouem choris angelorum ipsi enim . . . ; Pro prima de

[1] Wenceslaus was born on the day of St Matthias, 26 Feb. 1361.

sanctis patriarchis et prophetis. nam . . . ; Pro hora tercia de sanctis apostolis. quia . . . ; Pro hora sexta de sanctis martiribus. ipsi namque . . . ; Pro hora nona de sanctis confessoribus. nam . . . ; Pro hora vespertina de sanctis virginibus. nam . . . ; Pro hora completorii de sanctis viduis. ipse enim . . . ; Pro completorii progressu de sanctis coniugatis. nam . . . ; Pro completorii complemento de omnibus sanctis et electis dei. nam . . .

4. ff. 49–56v *Hec est* nimirum *dies* votiua celebritate colenda *quam* profecto . . . *fecit . . . dominus . . .*

For Christmas. The italicized words are in blue and by themselves make up a prayer of 47 words.

5. ff. 56v–86v Incipiunt vii psalmi penitenciales.

Followed by a litany, f. 78. Nine martyrs: Stephane Laurenci Vincenti Vite Wenceslae Adalberte Sigismunde Georgi Mauricii cum sociis tuis. Twelve confessors: Siluester Leonarde Martine Nicolae Procopi Egidii Gregori Ieronime Augustine Ambrosi Francisce Galle. Ten virgins: Maria Magdalena Lucia Cecilia Katherina Margaretha Dorothea Barbara Elyzabeth Ludmilla Ursula cum sodalibus. Ends abruptly 'Per eum qui ven. est in iu–'. ff. 87–92v blank.

ff. iii + 92 + i. 162 × 120 mm. Written space 97 × 70 mm. 11 long lines. Collation: 1^4 $2–12^8$. Initials: (i) 4-line, blue or green with leaf patterning in shades of the same colour on grounds of gold and patterned colours, historiated: eleven in art. 3 and one beginning each of arts. 2, 4, 5, listed by Alexander, loc. cit.; they include Matthias (ff. 13, 37), Wenceslaus (f. 39), Adalbert of Prague (f. 40v), and Ludmilla (f. 44); (ii–iv) 3-line, 2-line, and 1-line, gold with blue ornament (art. 1 only) or blue with red ornament. Floral decoration in three margins of pages with initials of type (i). Blue headings. Capital letters in the ink of the text filled with pale yellow. Binding of s. xvi in.: wooden boards covered with brown leather, each cover bearing a panel 150 × 98 mm over all containing two repetitions of a 'triple' panel of the general type of Oldham's TRIP. 7 and between them a horizontal strip 25 mm wide containing wyvern, saint (Margaret ?), and griffin, each in a compartment. The borders round the 'flemish animals' are inscribed: 'Adiutorium nostrum / in nomine / domini qui fecit celum / et terram'; 'Sit nomen domini / benedictum / ex hoc nunc et usque / in seculum'. Secundo folio *Peccaui*.

Written for the use of King Wenceslaus of Bohemia, †1419, and decorated at Prague, probably in the last decade of the king's life by the leading masters of an important workshop. Probably in the Low Countries in s. xvi in. 'Franciscus muijlwijch' at the head of f. 1, s. xvi.

21. *Medica* s. xiii ex.–xv med.

Two parts (arts. 1–20, s. xiii ex.; arts. 21–3, s. xv med.) put together in s. xv or later. Arts. 1–4 are on quires 1–5.

1. ff. 1–17v Reuerentissimo domino salernitane ecclesie archipresuli A Constan. africanus montis cassinensis monachus . . . consequi ualeam . . . (*table of 26 chapters*) . . . Oportet intelligere. quia prima accio nature . . . omnia indigestibilia. Explicit liber stomachi constantini.

Thorndike and Kibre (Oportet nos). Ends with no. 38 of the 39 chapters in edn. Bas. 1536, pp. 215–70.

2. ff. 18–36v Cogitanti michi de simplicium medicinarum virtutibus . . . non modicam prestare vtilitatem. Explicit liber de Simplici Medicina Editus a Magistro Iohanne de Sancto Paulo deo gracias Ammen (*sic*).

Thorndike and Kibre. Cf. MS. 13, f. 117.

3. ff. 37–48 Galieno attestante in tegni quicumque . . . nutrimentum omnium menbrorum habent. sic nil omissum.

Thorndike and Kibre. Differs much from MS. 15, art. 5.

4. f. 48rv Natura pingues homines facit atque iocantes . . . dinoscitur affore fuluus (28 lines of verse).

On the humours. Cf. Renzi, v. 48, lines 1690 sqq.

5 (quire 6). ff. 49–60v Regule vrinarum secundum magistrum Ricardum Anglicum et primo de hiis que attenduntur in vrina principaliter vnde versus Qui cupit . . . longius ire. Quinque circa vrinam . . . credo cognicionem. Explicit vrinarum tractatus pars medicine secundum magistrum Ricardum Anglicum.

Thorndike and Kibre (Qui cupit; Quinque: cf. Circa urinas).

Arts. 6–10 are on quires 7–10.

6. ff. 61–75 Scribitur in libro viatici constantini quod quicumque uult continuam custodire sanitatem . . . et baccarum lauri et hec sufficiant. Explicit summa de sanitate conseruanda a Magistro Iohanne de Coleto Edita Deo gracias ammen.

John of Toledo. Thorndike and Kibre (Ut dicit Constantinus, and (from this copy) Scribitur). The last two chapters here, on poisons and their cure, are not in the text in Bodleian, Rawlinson D. 238, ff. 49–58, which differs a good deal throughout. The scribe wrote 'Assit principio sancta maria meo' at the head of f. 61. A leaf missing after f. 72.

7. ff. 75–8 Sperma hominis descinditur (*sic*) ex omni humore . . . masculi creantur. Explicit composicio hominis et cetera.

Thorndike and Kibre (Galen, De spermate).

8. ff. 78–9 Vilis est materia de qua forma detur . . . finit nec doletur. Twelve 4-line stanzas.

9. ff. 79v–95v Incipit summula de preparacione ciborum et potuum infirmorum secundum Muszandinum. De cibis et potibus preparandis . . . et humores. In (*ends imperfectly, but only the last few lines are missing*).

Thorndike and Kibre. Petrus Musandinus. Renzi, v. 254–268/9.

10. (*a*) ff. 96–7 A collection of emplastra, beginning imperfectly. (*b*) f. 97 Recipes added in s. xiv. f. 97v blank.

Arts. 11, 12 are on quires 11-17.

11. ff. 98^{v}-174 Incipiunt signa prognostica secundum magistrum Ricardum Anglicum. Finis medicine est laudabilis ita dumtaxat . . . cum denigracione lingue mortale est signum. Expliciunt signa Magistri R. anglici et cetera.

Thorndike and Kibre. f. 98^{r} blank.

12. ff. 174^{v}-175^{v} Decidit allopitiis lux flauea turget . . . dant cretica signa. 55 lines of verse.

Arts. 13-16 are on quires 18, 19.

13. ff. 176-89 Cum auctor vniuersitatis deus in prima mundi origine . . . domestica et similibus. Explicit trotula senior deo gracias.

Thorndike and Kibre. The explicit is followed by 5½ lines, 'Item si mulier parum de folio lauri . . .'.

14. ff. 189^{v}-192 Cum igitur o medice ad egrum uocaberis . . . et tempus anni sit calidum. Explicit etc.

This entertaining piece corresponds to the beginning of Practica Archimathei, but lacks the preface there (Thorndike and Kibre, col. 329). As Bodleian, Digby 79, ff. 119^{v}/11-121/25. Renzi, ii. 74-80 is more or less the same at first.

15. ff. 192-5 De urinarum scienciis tractaturi sumus. primo videamus quid sit vrina secundo que et quot . . . admixtionem. et hec de urinis dicta sufficiant. deo gracias etc.

Cf. Thorndike and Kibre, col. 394.

16. (*a*) f. 195 Medicina est quedam sciencia medicinalis et celestis que suum opificem facit quasi miraculis coruscantem honestum amabilem . . . et si que secreciora fuerint illi tam sanctorum sanctissimo reuelantur. (*b*) f. 195^{v} Table of the twenty colours of urine. (*c*) ff. 196-8 Table of herbs, 'Electuaria calida. Dragagantum . . . (*d*) ff. 198^{v}-199^{v} Recipes in several hands, s. xiii-xiv and s. xiv, the first 'Collirium optimum ad oculos secundum magistrum H. de H.'.

(*a*-*d*) fill the space left blank at the end of quire 19. (*a*). Thorndike and Kibre, who refer to this manuscript only. Seven lines on the advantages of being a doctor. (*c*). Thorndike and Kibre (Electuaria . . . Diamargariton . . .).

Arts. 17, 18 are on quires 20-2.

17. ff. 200-21 Incipit dosys medicinarum secundum magistrum Walterum. Medicinarum quedam sunt simplicia . . . vsque ad z i. hec de dosy medicinarum sufficiant. Explicit etc.

Thorndike and Kibre. Walter Agilon.

18. ff. 221–225v Et (*sic*) testatur philosophus nos sumus quodam modo fons omnium . . . multum iuuat. et hec de alteracione et preparacione ciborum et potuum vobis data sufficiant. explicit etc.

Cf. Thorndike and Kibre, col. 1499. A regimen sanitatis.

Arts. 19, 20 are on quire 23.

19. ff. 226–7 Incipit ars medecinarum laxati(u)arum. Hec est ars medicinarum laxatiuarum tam simplicium . . . ter ducit. Idem facit dyaprunis. hec sufficiant de quantitate laxacionis medicinarum secundum magistrum Iohannem Stephani de(o) gracias.

Thorndike and Kibre. Ed. K. Sudhoff in *AGM* xi. 212–13.

20. ff. 227–241v Corpus hominis ex quatuor constat humoribus . . . ordei farina et bis uel ter coletur. Explicit flores dietarum.

Thorndike and Kibre. The last sentence here is the last sentence but one in Bodleian, Ashmole 1470, f. 314.

Arts. 21–3 (s. xv) are on quires 24–6.

21. ff. 242–255v Euax rex arabum legitur . . . Pars negat et multis p(ro)hibetur in partibus orbis.

PL clxxi. 1737–70. The poem of Marbodus.

22. Miscellaneous recipes, etc., tending towards magic: (*a*) f. 256 A recipe 'for the gret pockys'; (*b*) f. 256 Syr and it plese yu yis ys . . . ; (*c*) ff. 256v–258 Twenty-five paragraphs: (1) Si quis absciderit li(n)gua(m) anseris et posuerit super pectus viri aut mulieris dormientis . . . ; (2) for killing mice; (5) Si vis scire de viro aut muliere quis earum sit sterilis . . . ; (25) Vt capilli fiant crocei . . . ; (*d*) ff. 258–60 Herba que dicitur alitropia id est solsequium . . . (*e*) ff. 260–1 Est animal quod dicitur bubo . . . ; (*f*) ff. 261–2 Cum ego Iohannes paruulus essem in alexandria ciuitate . . . vlterius augmentari etc.; (*g*) 262–5 Accipe de argento viuo . . . ; (*h*) ff. 265–6 Iste sunt virtutes aque preciose et efficacie . . . ; (*i*) ff. 266–8 Actus mirabilis aquarum quas composuit petrus hispaneus cum naturali industria . . . Recipe rutam feniculi . . . ; (*j*) ff. 268v–270v De aqua ardente et non ledente sic fit . . .

(*b*). Hard to read. (*d*). Magical properties of sunflower and twelve other herbs. (*e*). Magical properties of owl, hoopoe, crow, and kite. (*f*). Thorndike and Kibre (Johannes Paulinus). Twelve experiments 'de corio serpentis'. (*g*). Twenty-three paragraphs of recipes for making wine, candles, gold and silver heavier; 'Ad faciendum literam que non legetur nisi carta calefacta ad ignem', 'Ad delendum literam sine rasura', etc., most of them more or less magical. (*i*). Cf. Thorndike and Kibre, col. 1328, but *Recipe limaturam* . . . is here the third of eight recipes. (*j*). Ten paragraphs. Miscellaneous recipes like (*g*).

23. ff. 271–278v To make colour of gold or siluer . . .

Forty-five paragraphs in English, (1-30) mainly recipes for colours, (31) To lay gold on a emage, (32) To make wyȝt led, (33, 34) To 'goo knkkskblf' (cf. *MMBL* i. 207), (38) a good oynement for cold feet and cold handis, (45) To mak heere growe . . . and it xal grow probatum est.

ff. ii + 278 + ii. Parchment and (ff. 242-78) paper. 155 × 110 mm. Binding of limp parchment, s. xvii, like MS. 8. Secundo folio *enim composita*.

ff. 1-241. Written space *c.*110 × 80 mm and (art. 1) 128 × 78 mm. 20-4 long lines (3 cols. in art. 15*c*) and (art. 1) 2 cols. 42 lines. Ruling sometimes poor, for example on f. 87. Collation: $1\text{-}2^{12}$ $3\text{-}5^{8}$ 6^{12} 7^{16} wants 13 (ff. 61-75) 8^{8} 9^{12} 10^{12} wants 3-6 after f. 97 (ff. 84-95) $11\text{-}12^{12}$ 13^{8} 14^{10} $15\text{-}16^{8}$ 17^{14} 18^{16} 19^{8} (ff. 192-9) 20^{10} $21\text{-}22^{8}$ 23^{16} (ff. 226-41). A quire or more missing after quire 9. Quires 3-9, 11-23 have quire and leaf signatures at the foot of rectos on the left, usually in pencil: they consist of a letter on each leaf in the first half of the quire, a-d, a-e, a-f, or a-h, according to the size of the quire, followed by a quire number, 16, 17, 11, 9-11 on quires 3-9 and 2-8, 12, 13, 12, 14, 15, 13 on quires 11-23.[1] Current anglicana by one hand for arts. 2-16*c*, 17-20. Textura for art. 1. Initials of art. 1: (i) f. 1, 4-line *R*, blue and red with ornament of both colours; (ii) 2-line, blue or red with ornament of the other colour. Initials of arts. 2-20, 2-line, blue with red ornament.

ff. 242-78. Written space 113 × 75 mm. 20-3 long lines. Frame ruling. Collation: 24^{10} 25^{14} wants 11-14 after f. 262 26^{16}. Current anglicana. Spaces for initials not filled.

Written in England.

OXFORD. QUEEN'S COLLEGE

405. *Horae* s. xv med.

1. ff. 1-12v Full calendar in French in gold, blue, and red, the two colours alternating. 'Ursin' in gold, 9 Nov., also the Visitation of B.V.M., 2 July.

2. ff. 13-17v Sequentiae of the Gospels.

3. ff. 18-79v Hours of B.V.M. of the use of (Bourges). Headings in French.

4. ff. 79v-82v La messe de nostre dame. Salue sancta parens . . . Ps. Post partum . . .

5. ff. 82v-86v Oroison deuoute de nostre dame. Obsecro te . . . Et michi famule tue . . .

6. ff. 86v-90 Oracio deuota. O intemerata . . . orbis terrarum inclina . . . Esto michi peccatori . . .

7. ff. 90-95v Aultre oroison deuoste de nostre dame. Les quinze Ioyes. Doulce dame de misericorde . . . Sonet, no. 458.

[1] An early example of the method of marking quires which became common in s. xiv ex.: cf. *MMBL* i. x.

8. ff. 95v–98v Sensuiuent les sept requestes a nostreseigneur. Quiconques veult . . . Doulx dieu doulx pere . . . Sonet, no. 504.

9. ff. 99–117v Penitential psalms and (f. 112) litany.

Fourteen confessors: (1–6) Ursine Guillerme Sulpici Ambrosi Nicholae Austregisille.

10. ff. 118–21 Hours of Holy Cross.

11. ff. 121v–124v Hours of Holy Spirit.

12. ff. 124v–164 Pro deffunctis ad vesperas . . . Office of the dead.

13. f. 164v Quicuonques dira ceste oroison il aura viii mille ans de pardon. Domine ihesu criste saluator et redemptor tocius mundi rogo te et ammoneo pro honore illius gaudii . . .

14. ff. 165–6 Memoriae of Sebastian and Katherine.

15. f. 166rv Anthems of B.V.M.: Salue regina . . . ; Aue regina celorum. aue domina angelorum salue radix sancta . . . ; Regina celi letare . . .

RH, nos. 18150, 2070, 17170.

ff. i + 166 + i. Thick parchment. 182 × 145 mm. Written space 102 × 70 mm. 15 long lines. Collation: $1\text{–}2^6$ 3^6 wants 6, blank 4^8 5^6 + 1 leaf after 1 (f. 27) $6\text{–}8^8$ 9^{10} $10\text{–}12^8$ $13\text{–}14^4$ (ff. 91–8) $15\text{–}22^8$ 23^4. Twelve 11- or 12-line pictures, eight in art. 3 and one before each of arts. 9–12. Initials: (i) blue or red, patterned in white, on gold grounds, decorated or (f. 83) historiated (B.V.M. and Child); (ii) ff. 87, 90v, 4-line, blue or red patterned in white on grounds of red or blue patterned in white and decorated with gold; (iii–v) 3-line, 2-line, and 1-line, gold on grounds of red and blue patterned in white. Blue and red line fillers with gold pieces between the colours. Capital letters in the ink of the text filled with pale yellow. Conventional lightly-framed borders on picture pages. A spray falls from the initials beginning arts. 4–7. Limp parchment binding, s. xvii: gilt ornaments in centre, at the corners, and on the spine: kept in a box.

Written in France. 'Hoc Psalterium Manuscriptum ex Seculo decimo tertio emi pro ducentis florenis 7tem die Martii 1697. Hans Heinrich von Herwart bairische (?) Kanzler' inside the end cover. His torn armorial book-plate dated 1674 inside the front cover: cf. F. Warnecke, *Die deutschen Bücherzeichen*, 1890, no. 826, and for the quartered arms of Hörwarth von Hohenburg (near Lenggries, Upper Bavaria), Rietstap, pl. 227. The armorial book-plate of William Jackson, Archdeacon of Carlisle (and later Provost of Queen's College, †1878) is attached to f. i. Given by his daughter, Georgiana (Mrs J. R. Macgrath, †1899).

35.c.1–15 + 35. d.1–12. *Johannes et Lucas glosati* s. xiii¹

108 leaves *in situ* as pastedowns, two, a bifolium, laid sideways at either end of each of the twenty-seven volumes of *Tractatus Juris Universi*, Venice 1584, given in 1597. John is complete (quires 1–7). Luke, which presumably followed it, as in Jesus College, Oxford, 98, and in a copy given to New College, Oxford, by

William of Wykeham (Oxford Hist. Soc., *Collectanea*, Third series (1896), p. 227),[1] ends in ch. 13 (quires 8–14).

Text flanked by gloss and with shorter notes in spaces between the text. The recto of the first leaf is by ill luck pasted down (vol. 9, front pastedown): the verso ends in the prologue (Stegmüller, no. 624) 'tamen post omnes scripsit euan' and in the gloss to the prologue 'contra eos addit'. A good many contemporary notes in the wide margins, some perhaps belonging to a commentary which begins on John 1: 1 (vol. 9, front pastedown) 'In principio erat uerbum. In principio huius euangelii ponuntur iiii^{or} clausule siue distinctiones et est prima'. A few later notes, among them an extract from Holcot, 'Cristus figurabatur per serpentem . . . ' at John 3: 14 (vol. 4, front pastedown, s. xiv). The prologue to Luke is Stegmüller, no. 620. Luke 1: 1–4 is treated as part of the Gospel, not as a prologue.

ff. 108. Written space 235 × 160 mm. 23 lines of text and 46 lines of gloss. The first line of writing above the top ruled line. Text and gloss ruled on one grid. Pricks in both margins to guide ruling. Probable collation: $1\text{–}13^8$ 14^8 wants 1, 2, 7, 8. Initials: (i) *Q* of *Quoniam* (Luke 1: 1) not filled in; (ii) 1-line, red or blue with ornament of the other colour. Running titles in red and blue capitals. Secundo folio in textu (*gelium*); in glosa (*hoc id est uerbum*).[2]

Written in England. Used by an Oxford bookbinder, almost certainly Thomas Middleton, s. xvi/xvii: cf. Ker, *Pastedowns*, no. 939 and p. 212.

OXFORD. REGENT'S PARK COLLEGE

Angus d. 54. *Horae* s. xv med.

1. ff. 4–15^v Calendar in French in red and black.

No entries at 2 and 26 July (Visitation of B.V.M., Anne). Spellings are 'bietremien', 'franchois', 'mikiel', 'lucq', 'thumas'.

Arts. 2–4 are on quires 4–6.

2. ff. 16–22 Sequentiae of the Gospels.

3. ff. 22^v–29^v Sensieult le messe nostre damme. Introibo ad altare . . . Confiteor deo . . . Misereatur uestri . . . Introitus. Salue sancta parens . . .

In *Confiteor* the forms are feminine, 'ego infelix peccatrix' and 'oretis pro me peccatrice'.

4. (*a*) ff. 30–4 Orison de nostre dame. Obsecro te . . . (*b*) ff. 34–36^v Aultre orison. O intemerata . . . orbis terrarum. Inclina . . . (*c*) f. 37^{rv} Orison de nostre dame. A'. Salue regina . . . Oratio. Concede nos famulos tuos . . .

(*a*). Masculine forms, with feminine interlined. (*b*). Feminine forms.

[1] In Wykeham's copy the second leaf began in the gloss with the words *alii concederent* (cf. *Biblia sacra cum glossa ordinaria*, Lyon 1589, v. 1015), which in the Queen's copy begin the last line of the gloss on f. 1^v (vol. 9, front pastedown). The two manuscripts appear to have had almost exactly the same amount of matter on their first leaves.

[2] The secundo folio references are on the pasted-down, and therefore invisible, leaf forming part of the bifolium at the end of vol. 9.

5 (quires 7–14). ff. 38–94^v Heures de nostre dame: use of (Rome).

A 'memore de tous sains' at each hour from lauds. No special section for the office in Advent (etc.). Three leaves missing.

Arts. 6, 7 are on quires 15, 16.

6. ff. 95–102 Hours of the Cross.

7. (*a*) ff. 102^v–107^v Heures du saint esperit. (*b*) f. 108^{rv} Ueni creator spiritus mentes tuorum uisita . . .

Arts. 8–10 are on quires 17–22.

8. ff. 109–126^v 'Les vii psalmes' and (f. 121^v) litany.

Eight pontiffs and confessors: (8) ludouice. Six monks and hermits: francisce benedicte anthonii dominice ludouice bernardine. Eight virgins: (6, 7) clara elyzabeth. No prayers after Deus cui proprium.

9. ff. 127–155^v Office of the dead.

10. ff. 156–160^v Memoriae of Sebastian, Christopher, Anthony hermit, Nicholas, Trinity, Barbara, Katherine, Margaret.

11 (added, s. xv^2, on a preliminary quire). (*a*) f. 1 O salutaris hostia que celi pendis (*sic*) ostium bella premunt hostilia da robur fer auxilium: repeated three times. (*b*) f. 1 Uni trinoque domino sit sempiterna gloria . . . in patria Amen (*c*) f. 1 Agnus dei . . . (*d*) f. 1 Miserere mei deus secundum magnam misericordiam tuam . . . : repeated three times. (*e*) f. 1 In manus tuas . . . domine deus ueritatis. (*f*) ff. 1^v–3 In passione domini quia (*sic*) datur . . . Oremus. Oracio. Deus qui sperantibus uite misereri poscius eligis quam . . . (*g*) f. 3^{rv} De nostra domina. Inuiolata integra et casta es maria . . . permansisti.

(*a*). *RH*, no. 13680. (*f*). A memoria of the Passion, *RH*, no. 8722. (*g*). *RH*, no. 9094. f. ii^{rv} blank.

ff. i + 161 + i, foliated i, ii, 1–161. 218 × 150 mm. Written space 102 × 62 mm. 15 long lines ruled in red ink. Collation of ff. ii, 1–160: 1^4 (ff. ii, 1–3) 2–3^6 4–5^8 6^6 (ff. 32–7) 7–9^8 10^8 wants 8 after f. 68 11^8 wants 4, 5 after f. 71 12–13^8 14^4 (ff. 91–4) 15^8 16^6 (ff. 103–8) 17–21^8 22^{12} (ff. 149–60). Twelve of fourteen 11-line pictures remain, six in art. 5 (terce and sext pictures missing: at prime a turbaned figure in red kneels behind B.V.M.) and one before each of arts. 2, 3 (B.V.M. and Child enthroned, backed by a red wall inscribed 'Ihesus maria'), 6–9. Initials: (i) 4-line, red or blue, patterned in white, on decorated gold grounds; (ii, iii) 2-line and 1-line, gold on grounds of red and blue patterned in white. Line fillers red and blue, patterned in white, with a central blob of gold. Capital letters in the ink of the text filled with pale yellow. Continuous floral borders on picture pages, broad (30 mm) at the foot and on the outer side: a bird at mid point in the outer border. Mirror-image borders the height of the written space in the outer margin of all other pages: a red and blue acanthus scroll is the central motif.

Binding of brown leather over wooden boards, rebacked: a cock and tree stamp (1) on the front cover and a dragon stamp (2) on the back cover form borders containing stamps of three patterns in five vertical rows, (3) (4) (5) (4) (3) on the front cover and (3) (6) (5) (6) (3) on the back cover, (5), a swan (?), being the narrowest: five bands: two strap-and-pin fastenings, front to back, now missing.

Written in north-eastern France for the use of a woman. Given by the executors of Mr Horsepool in 1885.

OXFORD. ST EDMUND HALL

1. *Processionale* s. xiv/xv

1. ff. 1–101 Omnibus dominicis diebus per annum de [quocumque fit seruicium] preterquam a pascha usque ad festum trinitatis et dicitur in dominica passionis et ramis palmarum. cum Gloria patri et Sicut. Ant' Asperges me . . . (f. 1v) Omnibus dominicis per aduentum ad processionem A' Missus est . . .

Temporal. Corpus Christi, ff. 87v–92.

2. ff. 101–3 In dedicacione ecclesie.

3. (*a*) ff. 103–4 Fiunt autem quedam processiones ueneracionis causa . . . (*b*) ff. 104–20 Fiunt autem quedam processiones causa necessitatis.

Cf. *PS* (reprint of edition of 1508), pp. 164–7, 169–70.

4. ff. 120–46 Sanctoral, Andrew–Katherine.

The occasions provided for are the same as in *PS*, except for the presence here of cues for James, Invention of Stephen, and Bartholomew, and the absence here of John and Paul, Visitation of B.V.M., Transfiguration, Name of Jesus, and Brice.

5. ff. 146–149bv Common of saints.

6. ff. 149bv–150v Processio ad recipiendum corpus R' Libera me do. Item Introitu ecclesie A' In paradysum . . .

Cf. edn., pp. 167–8.

7. (*a*) ff. 151–153v Dominus uobiscum . . . Liber generacionis ihesu xpisti . . . uocatur xpistus. (*b*) ff. 153v–156 Dominus uobiscum . . . Factum est autem cum baptizaretur . . . regressus est in iordane. (*c*) ff. 156–157v Exultet iam angelica turba . . . perficiat. Per . . . (*d*) ff. 157v–162 Vere quia dignum . . . in hiis paschalibus gaudiis conseruare digneris Qui . . . Amen. f. 162v blank.

Noted. (*a*). Mt. 1: 1–6. (*b*). Lk. 3: 21–4: 1. (*c, d*). Blessing of wax taper and preface on Easter Eve. *Sarum Missal*, pp. 118–19.

ff. iii + 164 + ii, foliated i–iii, 1–3, 4a, 4b, 5–148, 149a, 149b, 150–64. 185 × 130 mm. Written space 142 × 90 mm. 8 long lines and music. Collation: $1–20^8$ 21^4. Traces of signatures remain, for example M 3 (f. 90). Initials: 3-line (f. 1) and 2-line, blue with red ornament. Cadels and capital letters in the ink of the text stroked with red. Binding of s. xix in. Secundo folio *ponsatam*.

Written in England. From the Throckmorton library at Weston Underwood, Bucks: 'Bibl. Weston' at the foot of f. 1, s. xvii. 'Ex libris Domini Throckmorton' is in a modern hand on a flyleaf. Given by A. B. Emden in 1925.

2. *De sacramentis* s. xv^2

(*begins imperfectly*) deuotionem et subiectionem . . . (f. 135^v) C de pac. conuer. 1. hac lege. Explicit tractatus de matrimonio.

A treatise on sacraments, beginning in baptism, shortly before the heading 'Quid est baptismus'; followed by: f. 5 De confirmatione; f. 5^v De penitentia; f. 12 De contritione; f. 15 De confessione; f. 74 De satisfactione; f. 90 De remissionibus siue indulgentiis; f. 106 De eucharistie sacramento; f. 113 De extrema unctione; f. 113^v Tractato in superioribus de sacramentis necessitatis nunc subsequenter tractandum est de sacramentis uoluntatis . . . ; f. 122 De sponsalibus; f. 123^v De matrimoniis. Johannes Calderinus is referred to. A side note on f. 112 is 'hodie est declarandum per extrauagantem Eugenii iiii^{ti} quod laici possunt sumere corpus cristi per octo dies ante pascha resurrectionis et octo post et sic inteliguntur satisfecisse ecclesie'. A 'Rep*er*torium operis precedentis' is on ff. 136–8 and a table of 'Festiuitates colende. Omnis dominica dies . . . Antonii et similium' on f. 139. ff. 138^v–139^v blank.

ff. ii + 138 + ii, foliated i, ii, 2–141. Paper. 340 × 240 mm. Written space 200 × 138 mm. 2 cols. 42–6 lines. Frame ruling in pencil. The first line of writing is above the top ruled line. Collation: 1^{10} wants 1 $2\text{–}13^{10}$ 14 nine. A strip of manuscript of s. xii (?) lies down the centre of each quire as strengthening: it is best seen between f. 5 and f. 6. 3-line initials, blue with red ornament or red with pale violet ornament. Binding of s. xx. Secundo folio *deuotionem*.

Written in Italy. Item 843 in a catalogue of T. Thorp, Guildown Road, Guildford: the relevant strip is pasted inside the cover. Armorial book-plate of W. M. Wright, Wold Newton (Lincs). His gift in 1934: cf. *St Edmund Hall Magazine*, 1934, p. 31.

OXFORD. ST HILDA'S COLLEGE[1]

1. *Horae (in Netherlandish)* s. xv ex.

Arts. 2, 3, 9, 11, 12 are the translations by Geert Grote printed by N. van Wijk, *Het Getijdenboek van Geert Grote*, 1940.

1. ff. 1–12^v Full calendar in red and black.

Utrecht saints in red, including 'Sinte Iourijs', 10 Aug.

[1] MS. 2, a small book of devotions (ff. 67, parchment, written space 85 × 50 mm, 11 long lines within a gold frame) in a humanistic hand is much too late for *MMBL*, but deserves mention for the inscription on f. 53: 'Claude Ruffin Chanoine de S. Anian en Leglise Nostre Dame de Paris, estant Aagé de quatre vingt et quatre an, à escrit et enluminé ce liure de deuotion. 1637'. 'Anagrame. Claude Ruffin. Icy nul fraude', f. 67^v.

2. ff. 13–40 Hier begint die vrouwe getide. Domine. Here du selte op doen . . . Inuitat'. In der eerlijcheit . . . Gode seggen wij danck.

Ends at edn., p. 70/10. f. 40^{v} blank.

3. ff. 41–57^{v} Hier begint die wijsheit getide. Mijn ziel heuet dij begeert . . . rusten in vreden Amen. Edn., pp. 92–112.

4. f. 58^{rv} Sixtus die vierde paus (†1471) heeft dit vierde ende dit vijfte gebet gemaect ende daer mede heuet hij die aflaten ghedubbeleert alsoe dat wise leest verdient xlvi^{m} iaer aflaets ende xl dagen. Ende die niet lesen en can. macht verdienen mit xv pater noster ende xv Aue marien. O here ihesu criste . . .

The Five Oes of St Gregory increased to seven: (4) nederclimmende . . . ; (5) opuerisende . . . : cf. Meertens, ii. 86–7 and 87, footnote 20.

5. (*a*) f. 59^{rv} Alsmen ten heiligen sacramente gaen wil soe suldi dit gebet lesen. Wes ghegruet alre heilichste lichaem . . . (*b*) ff. 59^{v}–60 Alsmen ten heiligen sacramente geweest heeft. O here ihesu criste die all tijt . . . (*c*) f. 60^{rv} Dit salmen lesen alsmen onsen here heffen sel. O here ihesu criste ewige god die dit heilighe vleisch . . .

(*a*). Cf. Meertens, iii. 63–4. (*b, c*). Meertens, iii. 88, 8.

6. ff. 60^{v}–61 Dit gebet suldi lesen daer mede verdien di veertich daghe oflaets. Ghegroet sijstu warachtich god . . . Oratio. O lieue here ihesu crist warachtich god ende mensche . . .

7. ff. 61–61* Hier begint een gebet van sinte Anna der heiligen vrouwen. Uerblijt v heilige anna salige vrouwe . . . Memoria of Anne.

8. f. 61* Dit sijn die tien gheboden gods. Mint god wt al dijns herten gront . . . (16 lines of verse). f. 61*^{v} blank.

9. ff. 62–83 Hier begint die langhe cruus getide. Here du selte op doen . . . Inuitat'. Dien behouder . . . wordes beweent (*ends abruptly*).

Cf. edn., pp. 113–138/4. The invitatory differs. f. 83^{v} blank.

10. ff. 84–101 Hier begint die heilige geest getide. Here du selte . . . Inuitat'. Die geest des heren . . . Venite. Coemt laet ons vrolic wesen . . . Ps. Salich is . . . Die erste les. Als veruolt waren . . . seggen wij danc.

Only sometimes as edn., pp. 71–86. f. 101^{v} blank.

11. ff. 102–13 Hier begint die seuen salm Dauid. Here in dijnre verbulgentheit . . . Litany, f. 108^{v}.

Psalms as edn., pp. 139–45. Names in litany differ from edn.: Iorijs 24th of twenty-eight martyrs; Bavo last of eighteen confessors. Fifteen virgins, (1) Maria magdalena . . . (15) Elizabeth. f. 113^{v} blank.

12. ff. 114–41 Hier begint die lange vigilie mit ix les. Mi hebben onbeuangen ... int leuen ouer te gaen. Bi onsen here ihesum cristum Amen.

Edn., pp. 165/5–195/18. f. 141^v blank.

ff. ii + 142 (foliated 1–61, 61*, 62–141) + ii. 190 × 130 mm. Written space 110 × 75 mm. 22 long lines. Collation: 1–5^6 6^6 + 1 leaf before 1 (f. 31) 7^6 + 1 leaf after 6 (f. 44) 8–10^6 (ff. 45–61, 61*) 11^8 12–13^6 14^2 (ff. 82–3) 15–17^6 18^8 19^4 (ff. 110–13) 20–23^6 24^6 wants 5, 6, blank. Initials: (i) beginning arts. 2, 3, 9–12, 11-line, blue patterned in white, historiated, framed in gold; (ii) beginning lauds and other hours in arts. 2, 3, 9, 10, twenty-eight in all, as (i), but 6-line; (iii) ff. 58, 59, 108^v, 5-line and 3-line, gold with red ornament; (iv) 2-line and (f. 61) 3-line, red or blue, with ornament of the other colour; (v) 1-line and (f. 61*) 2-line, red or blue. The historiations in arts. 3, 9 are mainly passion scenes; in art. 10, Christ rising from the tomb, B.V.M. and St John at f. 84, Pentecost at f. 87, Christ and the Magdalene at f. 93, and a naked Christ-Child (?) playing a psaltery at f. 96. Borders: (i) framed in red ink, on three sides of pages with initials of type (i); (ii) above and below the written space on pages with initials of type (ii): the grounds are flecked with dots. A lady kneels in the lower border, f. 13. On twenty-six pages the motif in the lower border is a shield, usually gold, bearing an emblem or design—on f. 62 emblems of the passion, and supported by a human figure, angel, animal, or monster. An angel is usually playing an instrument in the outer border (ff. 55^v, 62, lute players and women; f. 84, man and woman at a well). Line fillers blue and gold in the litany and elsewhere red. Capital letters in the ink of the text lined with red. Binding of gilt speckled calf, s. xviii.

Written in the Low Countries for use in Holland (art. 1). '9/2073' and '£13/10/', f. i^v. Given by Miss Helen Smith in November 1944.

OXFORD. ST JOHN'S COLLEGE

256. *Registrum brevium* s. xv med.

A register of writs described by W. S. Holdsworth, *History of English Law*, ii (1909), 525–7; 1923 edn., ii. 615–17.

1. ff. 3–7^v An index to art. 3, Attachiamentum–(De) Vicis et Vinellis mundandis, with leaf references. Not in the main hand. ff. 2^{rv}, 8^{rv} blank.

2. ff. 9–14 (K)alendarium.

Table of contents of the forty-six chapters. Printed by Holdsworth, op. cit., ii. 527–46 (617–36), where references are given in round brackets to the leaf numbers of art. 3, according to the old foliation 1–222 (see below), and in square brackets to the leaf numbers of the 1687 edition of *Registrum Omnium Brevium*. f. 14^v blank.

3. ff. 15–229^v A register of writs beginning with a writ of right of 5 Oct., 15 Henry (VI).

Forty-six chapters, numbered at the head of each verso on the left and of each recto on the right. Headings in the left margin of versos and the right margin of rectos are in a shorter form than in art. 2. f. 230^{rv} blank.

4. f. 231 Three writs in the main hand: (*a*) De frumento traducendo; (*b*) De peregrinis traducendis; (*c*) Aliter inde.

(*b*) is a licence to a shipowner to take 100 pilgrims to St James of Compostella and back. ff. 231v–237v blank: 237v has probably been pasted down.

ff. ii + 236 + i, foliated (i), 1–238. f. 1 is a medieval parchment endleaf. ff. 15–236 are also foliated at the foot of rectos on the right, 1–28, 28–222, s. xv. 255 × 170 mm. Written space 170 × 113 mm. 41 long lines. Collation 1^6 2^6 + 1 leaf after 6 3–19^8 20^8 wants 5, perhaps blank, after f. 154 21–30^8. Current anglicana of a set legal kind. Initials: (i) f. 15, 8-line *H*, pink patterned in white on a decorated gold ground: a continuous border has been cut by the binder: (ii) of chapters, 3-line, blue with red ornament. Binding of s. xvii, re-backed. Secundo folio (f. 16) *infra regnum.*

Written in England.

257. *Nova Statuta Angliae (in French and English); etc.* s. xv/xvi

Arts. 1–5 are closely related to Bodleian, Hatton 10 (*Sum. Cat.* 4135), ff. 7–42, 274–379.

1 (quires 1–8). ff. 1–63 Index, Accusacions–Wurstede, of statutes of Edward III, Richard II, Henry IV, Henry V, and Henry VI.

The first words are 'Null' soit attache' and the last 'anno xxo h. viti cao x'. Cf. *MMBL* i. 18, 190. Runs to 20 Henry VI (s.v. Staple, Wurstede). Three leaves (2, 3, 11) are out of order: see below, collation. f. 63v blank.

2 (quires 9–11). ff. 64–85 Statutes of 25, 27, 29, 32, 33, 39 Henry VI, as in *SR* ii. 344–79.

f. 85v is blank, except for the title of art. 3.

3. ff. 86–142v Statutes of Edward IV, as in *SR* ii. 380–476.

Anno 2 in edn. is here called anno 3, as in Hatton 10. f. 143r blank.

4. ff. 143v–154 Statutes of Richard III, as in *SR* ii. 477–98. ff. 154v–155v blank.

5 (quires 21–9). ff. 156–221 Statutes of 1–11 Henry VII, anno 1 in French, as *SR* ii. 499–506, anno 3 in French, as *SR* ii. 509–23, and anno 4–11 in English, as *SR* ii. 524–52.

f. 168v blank: a change of aspect and possibly of script at f. 169 where a new quire begins and the language changes to English. In anno 4 the readings agree with those noted in edn. 'Ex lib. Scacc. Westm. XI' (E 164/11: *MMBL* i. 190). Anno 7 is in eleven chapters, as in Hatton 10: 1–3, edn. 1–3; 4, edn. 10; 5, edn. 4; 6, 7, edn. 5; 8, edn. 24; 9, edn. 9; 10, edn. 7; 11, edn. 6. Anno 11, ff. 192–221, is preceded by a table of 28 chapters and a 9-line notice, 'The kynge oure soueraigne lorde . . . in maner and fourme folowynge', as in Hatton 10: headings differ from those in edn. ff. 221v–224v are blank.

6. ff. 225–50, three quires, are coeval with the rest, to judge from the ruling, but were not used for further statutes, but, if at all, for miscellaneous additions:

(*a*) f. 238^{v} Letters under the privy seal concerning a grant to John Michell Esq. of the sole right of making writs of supersedeas in the Court of Common Pleas, 25 Nov. 1616; (*b*) f. 243^{rv} 'Herafter do insue good Ordinances and Rules . . . for the good rule and ordre' of the Court of Common Pleas, as enrolled in Trinity Term 1457 'Ro ccccIxxxxiiii'; (*c*) ff. 244–6 Fees payable to officials of the Court of Common Pleas; (*d*) f. 249^{v} 'Memorandum that there ys owyng to Thomas Grene of Audenham (*or* Andenham) 'for the Caryage of the Kynges Recordes' from Seynt Albons to Westminster after the terme of saynt Michell anno xxxv^{to} H. viii there holden and fynysshid vi^{s} viii^{d}'; (*e*) f. 250^{v} 'Paid vnto Master Hall . . .'.

(*b, c*) in one large set legal anglicana, s. xvi/xvii, are the pieces printed by Margaret Hastings, *The Court of Common Pleas in Fifteenth Century England*, 1947, pp. 249–51, 251–5, from a manuscript of s. xvii in. in the Public Record Office, which includes a heading and colophon to (*b*) not found here. (*c*) specifies forty-seven fees under eight headings. (*e*). Payments for a window in the 'Tresor hows' and for repairs at 'The comon place' (at Westminster), s. xvii in.

7. f. 251, formerly pasted down, has on the recto a memorandum 'Pascha xxvi^{to} H viii Ro Clxxxii' and below it a list of seven volumes of statutes in a hand of s. xvi ex.: (1) Henry III–1 Henry VIII; (2) Henry VIII; (3) Edward VI and 1, 2 Mary; (4) 1, 8, 13, 14, 18, 27, 29, 31 Elizabeth; (5) Rastell's abridgment of the Statutes; (6, 7) 'Item ii statute bookes of the old statutes in frenche wch are written'.

ff. xix + 250 + xx. f. 251 is a parchment flyleaf, formerly pasted down. 270 × 180 mm. Written space 165–75 × 115 mm: the shorter height begins at f. 169 (23^{1}). 34 and (ff. 207–21) 35 long lines. Collation of quires 1, 2 (ff. 1, 4–9, 11, 10, 12–17 in that order) doubtful; then $3–4^{8}$ 5^{8} (ff. 34–5, 2, 3, 36–9) $6–10^{8}$ 11^{6} $12–19^{8}$ 20^{6} (ff. 150–5) 21^{8} 22^{8} wants 6–8, blank, after f. 168 $23–29^{8}$ 30^{6} (ff. 225–30) 31^{8} 32^{12} (ff. 239–50). Written in a set non-current legal anglicana by the same scribe as Hatton 10.[1] Initials: (i) the first letter of the king's name, *E* (f. 86), *R* (f. 143^{v}), *H* (f. 156), 12-line, patterned in pink and blue on gold grounds, historiated: the king seated, crowned, with clergy on his right and laity on his left: continuous framed floral borders, the borders at the foot containing the royal arms;[2] (ii) 5-line and (art. 5) 4-line, gold on pink and blue patterned grounds, with sprays into the margin: the style changes for the worse at f. 116. Binding of s. xviii. Secundo folio *Anno secundo* (f. 3) or *plusours* (f. 65).

Written in England. Belonged in 1535 to an official who had care of the king's records at Westminster, to judge from art. 6*d*, and in s. xvi and s. xvii in. to an official of the Court of Common Pleas (art. 6*a–c, e*). The binding bears the gilt armorial of Franklin (of Gonalston, Notts). 'Sr John Francklin. Dorothea Franklin', f. 1, at the head.

265. *Breviarium Praemonstratense* s. xv ex.

1. f. 1 Benedictiones. In dominicis et in omnibus festis nouem leccionum. Benedictione perpetua . . . gracia. ut supra.

Fifteen blessings.

[1] I owe this identification to Mr J. J. Griffiths.

[2] Cf. the plate of Hatton 10, f. 290 ('King Edward IV and his court') in *Manuscripts at Oxford*, fig. 74.

2. f. 1^{v} Regula specialis ad inueniendum diem pasche. Quando sydus currit per i . . .

Nineteen variations.

3. ff. 2–7^{v} Calendar in red and black, graded.

Very like the calendar in the Parc breviary, N.L.W. 495.[1] The gradings are Quadruplex (Christmas), Triplex (Augustine, 28 Aug.), Duplex, and for nine lessons. Duplex feasts in red include Servatius (13 May), translation of Augustine (11 Oct.: octave in black), and, as an addition, Presentation of B.V.M., 21 Nov. The Visitation of B.V.M. in red, 2 July, but not graded and without octave. 'Anne electe' duplex in black, 26 July. Thomas of Canterbury, 'celebre festum ix lc', in black, 29 Dec. 'Norberti episcopi fundatoris nostri ordinis' and Christina added in black, 6 June, 24 July: Christina is added in N.L.W. 495 also. No entry of the Transfiguration, 6 Aug.

4. ff. 8–42^{v} In dominicis (et) ferialibus Inuit'. Venite exultemus domino. Beatus vir . . . Psalms 1–108.

'Secunda quinquagena' before Ps. 51. f. 43^{rv} left blank: on the verso the Epiphany hymn Hostis herodes was added.

5. f. 44^{rv} Ps. 94, hymns Nocte surgentes and Consors paterni, Credo in deum patrem, Pater noster, Aue maria, and hymn Verbum supernum.

6. ff. 45–286^{v} Dominica prima aduentus domini. Inuitatorium. Ecce uenit . . .

Temporal from Advent to the 25th Sunday after the octave of Pentecost. The OT lessons for Sundays and weekdays after Pentecost are on ff. 198^{v}–267^{v} and lessons for Corpus Christi on ff. 269^{v}–271. f. 271^{v} is blank and homilies on the Gospels for the twenty-five Sundays after the octave of Pentecost begin on a new quire, f. 272.

7. ff. 286^{v}–290^{v} In dedicacione ecclesie.

8. ff. 291–400^{v} In festo sancte Katherine gloriose virginis . . .

Sanctoral, Katherine–Clement. Feasts provided with lessons within the octave include the deposition and translation of Augustine (ff. 366, 382^{v}), Lambert (f. 375), and 11,000 Virgins (f. 385). The common of saints between Easter and Pentecost is on ff. 320^{v}–321^{v}, between the Annunciation (25 March) and Ambrose (4 Apr.).

9. ff. 400^{v}–406^{v} Incipit commune sanctorum.

10. ff. 406^{v}–415^{v} Nine lessons 'In die Sancti Gregorii' (12 March) and for Nativity of B.V.M., Jerome, Peter, Gertrude (f. 413), and John Baptist.

ff. i + 415 + i. Paper. ff. 296–411 have a medieval foliation i–cxi. 198 × 140 mm. Written space 145 × 95 mm. Frame ruling. 2 cols. 31–9 lines. Collation: 1^{6} + 1 leaf after 6 2–35^{12}. Written in set hybrida: ascenders and *t* are split at the top. Initials: (i) f. 8, blue *B*, patterned in white on a ground of gold paint patterned in red and with ornament in red and violet forming a border on three sides; (ii) red patterned in white: in art. 4 this type of initial distinguishes Pss. 51 and 101 as well as the main liturgical divisions; (iii, iv) 2-line

[1] Mr Daniel Huws kindly sent me details of this calendar.

and 1-line, red. Binding of brown leather, s. xviii, with the lilies of the abbey of Parc (not erased) on each cover and the gilt title '**BREVIARIVM / ORDINIS / PREMONSTRATE**' in the second of six compartments on the gilt spine: the armorial stamp is of the smaller size noted by E. van Balberghe in *Archives et Bibliothèques de Belgique*, Numéro special 11 (1974), 528 and pl. 4.

Written for Premonstratensian use in the southern Low Countries. Belonged in s. xviii to the abbey of Parc, near Louvain, as appears from the binding and the pressmark 'J theca xi' inside the cover: cf. van Balberghe, loc. cit., p. 531 and pl. 8. Given by George Hart Morley, commoner, in 1831 (f. 1). Morley may have got it in the sale of John Peckham in Oxford, 5-9 May 1831, in which there were Parc manuscripts.[1]

266. *J. Lydgate, Siege of Thebes* s. xv ex.

[H]ere Begynnyth the prolog off the Story of Thebes. [W]han bright Phebus . . . (f. 61v) I make an ende Amen. [H]ere now Endeth as ye may se The Destruccion of Thebes þe Cite.

Ed. A. Erdmann, EETS Extra Series cviii. *IMEV*, no. 3928/28. For this copy, its owners, Roger Thorney (†1515) and William Myddelton, who married Thorney's widow, and its use by Wynkyn de Worde as the exemplar for his edition (1497 ?: *STC* 17031, Duff no. 268) see G. Bone in *Transactions of the Bibliographical Society*, 2nd series xii (1931), 284-306, with facsimile of f. 42. ff. 62-67v blank.

ff. 67. Paper: dog and quatrefoil watermark, Briquet, no. 3624. 265 × 190 mm. Written space 190 mm high. 39 long lines, ruled with red ink. Collation: $1-8^8$ 9^4 wants 1 (ff. 65-7). Secretary hand, the same throughout. A 4-line space for the *W* on f. 1 and 2-line spaces for other initials not filled.

Written in England. Bound up after Caxton's editions of Troilus and Cressida (*c.*1482), Canterbury Tales (*c.*1484) and Quattuor sermones of John Mirk (1483). 'Roger Thorney mercer of London' is on a flyleaf at the end: probably Thorney owned the whole book. 'W.M.', f. 1 at the foot, as on a. ii of the Troilus. 'Constat Wyllelmi Myddelton', f. 61v, as on the last leaf of Mirk. Given by Sir William Paddy, s. xvii in. and rebound in Oxford probably in the first or second decade of s. xvii (Ker, *Pastedowns*, no. 1509).

293. *Psalterium, etc.* s. xv med.

1. ff. 2-7v Calendar in blue, red, and black.

Conception of B.V.M. in blue, Anne and Erkenwald (30 Apr.) in red. Visitation of B.V.M. and Transfiguration not entered. 'pape' and feasts of St Thomas of Canterbury erased.

2. ff. 8-137v Psalms 1-150.

A leaf missing after f. 44 with the end of Ps. 37 and the beginning of Ps. 38. Quire 9 is misbound: see below.

3. ff. 137v-147v Six ferial canticles, followed by Te deum, Benedicite, Benedictus, Magnificat, Quicunque vult.

[1] This suggestion and the reference to N.L.W. 495 are in a note about the manuscript (and kept with it) in the hand of Dr Eric Millar of the Department of Manuscripts, British Museum.

4. ff. 147^v–153^v Sarum litanies, one for each day of the week.

Six prayers after Deus cui proprium, as in *Brev. ad usum Sarum*, ii. 254–5.

ff. iii + 152 + ii, foliated (i, ii), 1–154, (155). ff. 1, 154 are parchment flyleaves. 245 × 162 mm, except the pages with borders, which have been folded in and when unfolded measure *c.*260 × 180 mm. Written space 160 × 105 mm. 22 long lines. Collation of ff. 2–153: 1^6 2–5^8 6^8 wants 6 after f. 44 7–8^8 9 six (ff. 63, 65, 64, 67, 66, 68) 10^8 11 seven (ff. 77–83) 12–13^8 14 seven (ff. 100–6) 15 seven (ff. 107–13) 16–20^8. Four pictures, 80 × 105 mm, including the frame: Pss. 1 (anointing of David), 26 (David, crowned, kills a lion), 51 (David and man with two swords), 52 (David with Goliath's head on the point of his sword: queen and two women at castle gate). Initials: (i) 8-line, in colours shaded to white, on gold grounds historiated (Pss. 68, 80, 97, 109), or decorated; (ii) 2-line, gold on red and blue grounds patterned in white: sprays into the margins; (iii) 1-line, gold with blue-green ornament or blue with red ornament. Antiphons begin with a cadelled letter. Line fillers in gold and blue. Continuous borders on pages with pictures and initials of type (i) have been partly spared by the binder: see above. Binding of s. xix. Secundo folio (f. 9) *subsannabit.*

Written in England. 'Liber Gulielmi smalwoodi socii collegii diui Iohannis Ba`p´tiste Oxoniæ 1557', f. 1. Smalwood wrote his name also on ff. 8, 32^v (1553), 57, and 68. On f. 109 someone scribbled 'the honer of thys [book] y[s and] hathe bene and shall be ye popes owne derlyng'. On f. 151 'Fuit homo missus a papa cuius nomen est W. Smallwod. a doble p[. . . .] 1551. [. . . .] P.M. 1551' all crossed out and partly scribbled over. An armorial book-plate (Heathcote), s. xix, inside the cover, and below it, in print, 'Godfrey Heathcote'. Bought in 1953.

OXFORD. SOMERVILLE COLLEGE

1. *Horae* s. xv ex.

1. ff. 1–12^v Calendar in red and black.

Entries in red include 'Hylarii episcopi pict' ', 'Translatio s. Nicholay', 'Lodouici regis francie' (13 Jan., 9 May, 25 Aug.). 'Serenedi episcopi and 'g' ' in black, 21 July. No entries at 2, 26 July (Visitation of B.V.M., Anne).

2 (quires 2–8). ff. 13–65^v Hours of B.V.M. of the use of (Angers).

The first leaf missing. Hours of Cross and Holy Spirit worked in.

3 (quires 9, 10). ff. 66–78 Penitential psalms and (f. 73) litany, both beginning imperfectly.

A leaf is missing before f. 66 and a quire after f. 72. Twelve confessors: martine nicholae iuliane hylari germane gregori ieronime egidi francisce guillelme ludouice yno. Fifteen virgins: (8) radegundis; not Anne or Barbara. The only prayers at the end are Fidelium deus and Inclina domine aurem tuam. f. 78^v left blank.

ff. ii + 78 + ii. 87 × 68 mm. Written space 50 × 35 mm. 13 long lines. Collation: 1^{12} 2^8 wants 1 before f. 13 3^8 7, 8 cancelled after f. 25 4–8^8 9^8 wants 1 before f. 66 10^8 wants 7, 8, perhaps blank, after f. 78. Written in *lettre bâtarde*. Initials: (i, ii) 3-line and 2-line, grisaille on grounds of gold paint; (ii) ff. 16, 18, 19^v, 2-line, gold on grounds of blue and red patterned in white; (iv) 1-line, gold paint on ground of blue or dark red. Capital letters in the ink of the text filled with pale yellow. Line fillers in the litany blue or red, the red patterned in gold paint. Binding of gilt red morocco, s. xx. Secundo folio (f. 13) *et in psalmis.*

Written in France, for use in the diocese of Angers. 'Ce present livre appartient a moi Breton si[. .] de sa mere', f. 78^v. Given anonymously by an old Somervillian in 1961.

2. *Horae* s. xv med.

Hours of the use of Rome of a type commonly produced in the southern Low Countries in which hours of the Cross and of the Holy Spirit are in first place after the calendar: cf. for example, Cambridge, Fitzwilliam Museum, 80–4 and Oxford, Bodleian, Canon. liturg. 17, 91, 183, 238, 255, Douce 256 and Rawlinson liturg. e. 10.

1. ff. 1–12 Calendar in red and black.

Entries in red include Basil, Translacio Thome, Remigius and Bavo, Donatian (13 June, 3 (*sic*) July, 1, 14 Oct.); in black 'Visitacio marie' and 'Anne matris marie' (2, 26 July).

2. ff. 14–21^v Incipiunt hore sancte crucis . . . Ymnus. Patris sapiencia . . .

3. ff. 23–28^v Incipiunt hore de sancto spiritu . . . Ymnus. Nobis sancti spiritus . . .

4. ff. 30–36^v Incipit missa beate marie uirginis. Introibo ad altare . . .

Masculine forms in *Confiteor.*

5. ff. 37–43 Sequentiae of Gospels. f. 43^v blank.

6. ff. 45–131^v Incipiunt hore beate marie uirginis secundum usum Romanum.

Psalms for particular week days are included in matins. Advent office begins on f. 122.

7. ff. 133–56 Incipiunt septem psalmi penitenciales: litany, f. 146.

Monks and hermits are Benedict, Paul, Nicholas, Anthony, Bernard, Francis, Dominic, Alexius. Nine virgins: (9) Monica: not Anne or Mary of Egypt. From Sed libera nos to Omnipotens sempiterne deus qui uiuorum the pieces are the same as in Lady Margaret Hall, Borough 1, art. 6, q.v. f. 156^v blank.

8. ff. 158–163^v, 179–194^v, 171–178^v, 169–70, 195–197^v Incipiunt uigilie mortuorum. ant' Placebo. Dilexi quoniam . . .

Office of dead. The quires are out of order. Leaves missing after f. 170 contained the end of the third nocturn of matins and the beginning of lauds.

ff. ii + 197 + ii. 112 × 77 mm. Written space 60 × 37 mm. 17 long lines. Collation: 1–2^6 3–5^8 6^4 (ff. 40–3) 7–14^8 15^6 wants 6 blank (ff. 116–20) 16–18^8 19^8 + 1 leaf after 8

(f. 157) 20^6 (ff. 158–63: ff. 160–1 are single leaves) $21–23^8$ (ff. 179–94, 171–8) 24^6 + 1 leaf after 3 (ff. 164–70) 25 three (ff. 195–7: 195 and 197 are conjoint), together with fourteen single leaves with pictures on the versos and blank rectos (ff. 13, 22, 29, 44, 66, 80, 86, 92, 98, 104, 114, 121, 132, 157). Fourteen pictures, in which brown rocks picked out in gold are an outdoor feature: nine are in art. 6 and one is before each of arts. 2, 3, 4 (B.V.M. and Child and kneeling angels), 7, 8. In art. 6 the slaughter of Innocents comes at vespers, the flight into Egypt at compline, and the coronation of B.V.M. before the Advent office, as often in this type of hours: at prime (Nativity) there is no ox or ass, but a standing angel, at vespers no sword, and in the coronation picture no crown, but only angels hovering above the seated Christ and B.V.M. Initials: (i) on rectos of double openings with pictures, 5-line, blue patterned in white on gold grounds decorated in colours; (ii) 2-line, gold on grounds of pink and blue patterned in white; (iii) 1-line, blue with red ornament or gold with blue-grey ornament. Continuous floral borders framed in red on the fourteen picture pages and the fourteen pages facing them. Blue or gold line fillers in the litany. Capital letters in the ink of the text filled with pale yellow. Binding of s. xix: silver cornerpieces and clasps. Secundo folio (f. 15) *et animarum*.

Written in the southern Low Countries. 'D paula Cagnola', ff. 1, 69, 116, s. xvi. Given as MS. 1.

OXFORD. TAYLOR INSTITUTION

8° E. 1. *Statuta Angliae* s. xiv[1]

A pocket copy, rather smaller than Glasgow, U.L., Gen. 336 (*MMBL* ii. 910).

1. (*a*) ff. 2–8 Tables of chapters of arts. 2–7. (*b*) ff. 8–13v Incipiunt Notabilia super Statuta. Dampna in triplo . . . Dampna in Duplo . . . Grauia Dampna . . . Prisona vnius anni . . . Prisona duorum annorum . . . Prisona trium annorum . . . Prisona xla dierum . . . Prisona dimidii anni . . . Prisona incerta et voluntaria . . . Prescripcio temporis . . . Secta regis . . . In quibus casibus procedendum est ad iudicium post magnam Districcionem . . . In quibus casibus procedendum est ad inquisicionem post magnam Districcionem . . . Expliciunt quedam notabilia super Statuta.

(*b*). References are to the statutes of Merton, Westminster 1, 2, Gloucester, etc.

Arts. 2–7 are abbreviations. Especially in arts. 2, 3 sentences often begin with *Statuitur* or *Preterea*.

2. ff. 14–21v Magna carta. Edwardus dei gracia . . . Inspeximus . . . Explicit magna carta abbreu'. Cf. *SR*, Charters, p. 33.

3. ff. 21v–25 Incipit statutum de Merton. Prouisiones de Merton' de hiis que agunt ad iuuamen placitorum et iudiciorum sub breuibus comprehendi possunt quia per primum capitulum. Statuitur quod vidua . . .

4. ff. 25–31 Dicendum est de statut' de Marleberge. Ordinatur quod omnes in Curia regis . . . Dictum est de Marleberge abreuiat'.

5. ff. 31–46 Dicendum est de stat' Westm' primi. Precipit Rex quod pax ecclesie . . . Dictum est de Westm' primo abreu'.

6. ff. 46–51 Dicendum est de Statut' Gloucestr'. Statuitur in primo capitulo quod si disseisitor . . . Dictum est de stat' Glouc'.

7. ff. 51–71 Dicendum est de stat' Westm' secundi. Statuitur quod in donis condicionalibus . . . Dictum est de West' secundo abbreuiat'.

8. ff. 71–72v Incipit statutum Westm' tertii. Quia emptores . . . *SR* i. 106.

9. ff. 72v–73v Incipit sententia lata super cartas. En le non . . . Nous Roberd Erceuesqe . . . *SR* i. 126 (1297).

10. ff. 73v–106 Incipiunt noue ordinaciones. In French. *SR* i. 157.

11. ff. 106–8 Incipit visus franci plegii. Nous (*sic*) nous dirrez . . . a sauoir la uerite. Differs much from *SR* i. 246.

12. ff. 108–109v Incipit Extenta Manerii. Ade primes de chescun Maner . . . Cf. *SR* i. 242 (Latin).

13. ff. 109v–111 Incipit modus faciendi homagium et fid' Manerii.

In French. *SR* i. 227, but with an extra first paragraph, 'Ceo oyez vous bailiff . . . qe ieo R de ceo iour en auant au Roi Edward . . . a son chief plegge'.

14. ff. 111–113v Incipit assisa panis et Ceruisie. Quando quarterium frumenti . . . *SR* i. 199.

15. ff. 113v–114v Incipit Statutum de prohibicione. Edwardus . . . Iustic' suis itinerantibus in Com' Cantebrig' salutem. Scire facit . . . forma. Primus articulus. Circumspecte agatur . . . licet porrigatur. etc.

SR i. 101/1–24. Three copies of the form of the statute found here were known to Graves (*EHR* xliii. 14).

16. ff. 114v–115v Incipit sub qua forma laici impetrant. Sub qua forma . . . prohibicione non obstante etc. *SR* i. 101/24–102.

17. f. 116 Incipit Composicio Mensur' et Monete. Per discrecionem . . . partem quarterii. Cf. *SR* i. 204.

18. ff. 116–19 Incipit statutum de bigamis. In presencia venerabilium patrum W. Roff' et Roberti Bath' et Well' Episcoporum. Walteri Scamell Decani Sarum. Magistri Thome Bek. Archid' Dors' domini Francisci filaccursi domini Legum Magistri de Scardeburg Archid' Eastriding'. Magistri de Seiton' Magistri Ricardi de Stanes. Magistri G de haspal R. de Hengham Walteri de helion et aliorum optimatum . . . *SR* i. 42.

19. ff. 119–20 Incipiunt dies communes in Banco. *SR* i. 208.

20. ff. 120–1 Incipiunt dies communes dotis. *SR* i. 208.

21. ff. 121–122^{v} Incipit statutum de Antiquo dominico. Licet . . . de Recto clausum.

Edn. in RS, *Yearbooks 20–21 Edward I*, pp. xviii–xix/29.

22. ff. 122^{v}–124 Incipit Stat' de Gauelette in Lond'. *SR* i. 222.

23. ff. 124–5 Incipit Stat' de Conspiratoribus. Dominus Rex mandauit . . .

SR i. 216/15. The writ dated at Westminster, 3 Nov. anno xxii.

24. f. 125^{rv} Incipit Stat' de Chaunpart'. In French. *SR* i. 216/1–14.

25. ff. 125^{v}–126 Explicit (*sic*) Stat' de anno et die bisextili. *SR* i. 7.

26. ff. 126^{v}–128 Incipit statutum de Religiosis. *SR* i. 51.

27. ff. 128–35 Incipit stat' de scaccario. In French. *SR* i. 197.

28. ff. 135–7 Incipiunt districciones scaccarii. In French. *SR* i. 197*b*/5–46.

29. ff. 137–9 Incipit statutum de Iustic' assign' . . . Explicit Stat' de Ragemen. In French. *SR* i. 44.

30. ff. 139–43 Incipit Statutum Exon'. In French. *SR* i. 210.

31. ff. 143–148^{v} Incipiunt articuli Exon'. In French. *SR* i. 211.

32. ff. 148^{v}–153^{v} Incipit Statut' Wynton'. In French. *SR* i. 96.

33. ff. 153^{v}–159^{v} Incipit Statutum de Mercatoribus. In French. *SR* i. 53.

34. ff. 159^{v}–162 Incipit Statutum de Moneta. In French. *SR* i. 219. f. 160 is damaged at one corner.

35. ff. 162–163^{v} Incipiunt articuli de Moneta. In French. *SR* i. 219*a*.

36. ff. 163^{v}–165^{v} Incipit Statutum de Militibus. *SR* i. 229.

37. ff. 165^{v}–167^{v} Incipit Statutum de ponend' in assis'. Quia dominus Rex . . . Writ follows, dated xiii Dec. anno xxi. *SR* i. 113.

38. ff. 167^{v}–171^{v} Incipit Statutum de finibus. Quia fines in Curia . . . *SR* i. 128.

39. ff. 171^{v}–174 Incipit Statutum de vocatis ad Warrantum. *SR* i. 108.

40. ff. 173–5 Incipit Statutum de vasto. *SR* i. 109.

41. ff. 175–176v Incipit Statutum de Wardis et Releu'. In French. *SR* i. 228.

42. ff. 176v–181 Incipit Statutum de quo warranto primo. Anno gracie Mo cco lxxviiio . . . Latin text equivalent to the French in *SR* i. 45/1–21, followed by four forms of writ.

43. ff. 181–182v Incipit statutum de quo warranto secundo. Per ceo qe les brefs . . . en celes parties. Cf. *SR* i. 107 (in Latin).

44. ff. 182v–184 Incipit de terris perquis' de gracia Regis. Fait asauoir qe le Roi ordona a Westm' le premier iour de aueril Lan de son Regne xxme qe ceux qe voudrount purchaser nouele emparkementz . . . et la terce en la Garderobe.

45. f. 184 Incipiunt proteccciones domini Reg'. In French. *SR* i. 217.

46. ff. 185–95 Incipiunt noui articuli facti tempore Regis Edwardi. *SR* i. 235 (Capitula Itineris).

47. ff. 195–196v Incipit tractatus de antiquo Dominico corone.

As art. 21, but continuing a little further with 'tamen vxor sokemanni . . . consuet' manerii' (cf. edn. cit., p. xix/32–4).

48. ff. 196v–198 Incipit modus calumpniandi esson'. *SR* i. 217.

49. ff. 198–209 Incipit dictum de Kinlinworth. *SR* i. 12.

50. ff. 209–13 Incipit Statutum de coniunctim feoffatis. [E]dwardus die gracia . . . *SR* i. 145.

Seven pages (ff. 213v–216v) were left blank. The first two contain notes on Magna Carta in English, s. xvii/xviii, perhaps Mickleton's. An erasure, f. 216.

ff. iii + 215, foliated (i, ii), 1–216. ff. i, ii, 1 are post-medieval parchment flyleaves. 80 × 63 mm. Written space 63 × 40 mm. 21 long lines. Collation: $1\text{–}10^{12}$ 11^{12} + 2 leaves before 1 (ff. 121–2) $12\text{–}17^{12}$ 18^{12} wants 11, blank: 12 pasted down. Written in anglicana. Initials: (i) f. 14, 12-line gold *E* with blue ornament; (ii) 7-line or less, blue with red ornament or (a few times only) red with green-blue ornament. Parchment binding, s. xvii ex. (?). Secundo folio (f. 15) *secundum antiquam*.

Written in England. 'Ja. Mickleton Furnivalls Inn Ano 1705', f. i. 'George L. Wasey Bridgnorth', f. i, s. xix. The names show that this is a Mickleton manuscript which, like the Glasney cartulary (Davis, *MC*, no. 750)[1] did not form part of the Wasey gift to Durham in 1817: cf. *MMBL* ii. 517. Acquired in 1878.

[1] I owe the reference to Dr Ian Doyle.

8° It. 1. *Cecco d'Ascoli, Acerbo (in Italian)* s. xiv med.

Incipit liber acerbe etatis compositus per magistrum cechum de esc`h´ulo. Oltra non segue . . . Et questa `vita´ e luce di noi. Explicit liber acerbe etatis cechi de esculo. Facto fine pia laudetur virgo maria. Qui dedit expleri angelo det premia celi.

Printed in 1476 and later: *GKW* 6445–55; ed. F. Stabili, 1927. For this copy see J. P. Rice, 'Notes on the Oxford manuscripts of Cecco d'Ascoli's "L'Acerbo" ', *Italica*, xii (1935), 137–8. The poem is in ten books and each book in chapters, with headings in red which are often over erasure, for example on f. 70^{v}. Lines 2551–72 and 4359–668 are not in this copy. f. 98^{v} blank.

A scribe of s. xiv/xv began a Latin commentary, 'oltra non seque. Hic dicit quod ultra primum celum . . .' on f. 1, but abandoned it on the same page. It corresponds to pp. 223–4 of the partial edition of the commentary by H. Pflaum, *Archivum Romanicum*, xxiii (1939), who refers to this manuscript as Da and notes (p. 215) its relation to Flor., Bibl. Naz., Magl. VII. 701.

ff. ii + 98 + ii. Thick paper. 298 × 225 mm. Written space 195 mm high. 25–8 long lines, widely spaced. Frame ruling (double vertical bounders), the first line of writing above the frame line. Collation: 1–8^{12} 9 two. Strips of blank parchment in quire centres as strengthening. Written in the Italian equivalent of anglicana formata ('cancelleresca'). Initials: (i) f. 1, 6-line, blue and red *O* with ornament in red and violet; (ii) 2-line, blue with red ornament or red with violet ornament. Binding of s. xviii stamped on the spine in gold '**CECCHI / DE ESCULO / LIBER ACERBÆ / ÆTATIS / M.S.**' and inscribed 'd'Ascoli / L'Acerba. Poema / sec. xiv'.

Written in northern Italy. Item 3895 in the catalogue of the library of M. Pinelli (†1785), printed at Venice in 1787 (vol. 5, p. 98): the number is on f. i^{v}, top right. Pinelli sale, London 26 March 1789, lot 4895. '7^{s} M: Wodhull F. 25th 1790', f. ii. J. E. Severne sale of the Wodhull collection at Sotheby's, 11 Jan. 1886, lot 633, to Quaritch, for the Taylor Institution (£15).

8° It. 2. *Leonardus Bruni, Historiae florentini populi* s. xv med.

(f. 2) Historiarum florentini populi liber primus incipit feliciter. Leonardi opus. Diuturna mihi cogitatio fuit . . . (f. 3) clariora reddantur. Florentiam urbem Romani condidere . . . (f. 141) libertatem consecuti sunt.

Bks. 1–6 only: 2, f. 21^{v}; 3, f. 44; 4, f. 61; 5, f. 88; 6, f. 117. Ed. E. Santini and C. di Pierro, *Rerum Italicarum Scriptores*, XIX. 3 (1914–26), 3–166: of twenty-five manuscripts listed there, four, nos. 2, 11, 18, 19, contain bks. 1–6 only, and one, no. 10, containing bks. 1–6 and the first few lines of bk. 7, has the same heading as is found here. Main events are picked out in the margins, more at first than later. f. 141^{v} blank. 'Hirundinem in contubernio ne habeto', 'Fide deo soli mundo sine fine caduco' (cf. Walther, *Sprichwörter*, no. 9438) and 'Tu decies fęlix fęlix O Patria: si non / Gentibus externis subdita colla dabis' on the flyleaf, f. 1, s. xvi.

ff. i + 140, foliated 1–141. 302 × 215 mm. Written space 192 × 125 mm. 31 long lines. Ruling with a hard point: double vertical bounders. Collation of ff. 2–141: 1–14^{10}. Catchwords centred. The hand is basically humanistic, but *a* is single compartment and *f, s* are often descenders: the *-bus* sign (bɔ) and final round *s* are distinctive. Initials: (i) f. 2, 9-line gold *D* on blue ground decorated with white vine stem and gold dots in threes; (ii) f. 3 and beginning books 2–6, as (i), but 4-line or 5-line and pale yellow, instead of gold. Contemporary binding of wooden boards covered with brown leather: repeated stamps within fillets form a broader outer and a narrower inner border enclosing a panel containing three repetitions of a knotwork ornament: repaired and edges speckled: two clasps fasten from front to back. Secundo folio *noticia.*

Written in Italy. '+ yhesus maria Est Ioannis flisci de Caneuali d. x° fori', 'Dico quod non est Ioannis. sed est x° fari et eius fratris ac amicorum'', f. 1, s. xvi. 'RD Naples 26 June 1733' inside the back cover. 'R.S.D. (?)' and, in pencil, 'Libri (?) 6/18/–', '655', and 'Bought for £1-10-0' inside the front cover. Book-plate of the Taylor Institution marked 1877, the date of acquisition.

8° It. 3. *Francesco da Buti, Commentary on the Paradiso of Dante (in Italian)* s. xv in.

Impaurito dellaltezza della materia . . . intentione. La gloria di colui . . . Impero che nella prima chantica . . . immense et debite. A quali sia sempre honore . . . Amen.

Printed by C. Giannini, *Commento sopra la Divina Comedia*, iii (1862), 1–871. For this copy see E. Moore, *Contributions to the textual criticism of the* Divina Commedia, 1889, pp. 549–50. The date in the author's colophon is the day of St Barnabas, 11 June 1395.

ff. ii + 251 + ii. Paper. 290 × 147 mm. Written space 203 × 147 mm. Commentary in 50–4 lines. Frame ruling, the first line of writing above the frame line. Collation: $1\text{–}20^{12}$ 21^{12} wants 12, blank. Traces of quire signatures of the usual late medieval kind, (a)–y. Written in two sizes of current hybrida, the larger for Dante's text (10 lines in *c.*55 mm) and the smaller for the commentary (10 lines in 37 mm): in the smaller script *h* is looped when it follows *c*. Initials: (i) f. 1, patterned blue *I* and pink *L* decorated in colours in gold grounds, the *L* historiated: Christ blessing holds an open book inscribed on one page $\overline{A}$ and on the other $\bar{\omega}$; (ii) beginning each 'chanto' and 'lettione' of a canto, 12-line or less, blue or red. Binding of red morocco for Pope Pius VI: see below. Secundo folio *La gloria.*

Written in Italy. An armorial book-stamp at the foot of f. 1 bears a partly legible name round its edge, '. . .]do Saluiata', s. xviii (?). The binding bears the arms of Gian'Angelo Braschi after he became pope (Pope Pius VI, 1775–99): cf. D. L. Galbreath, *Papal heraldry*, 1930, p. 103 and fig. 190, which differs slightly from the stamp on these covers; also *Legature papali de Eugenio IV a Paolo VI*, Exhibition catalogue, Biblioteca apostolica vaticana, 1977, no. 262 and pl. cxci. 'Purchased for £30 from Italy (Dura, Naples) through Lisieux (?) and Nutt's Apr. 1877', f. ii^v. Book-plate as in MS. It. 2.

8° It. 4. *F. Petrarch, Trionfi; etc. (in Italian)* s. xv med.

1 (quires 1–5). ff. 1–41 Petrarch, Trionfi, fully described by N. Mann in *Italia medioevale e umanistica*, xviii (1975), 486–7. ff. 41^v–42^v blank.

2 (quires 6, 7). ff. 43–54^v Auendo in questi giorni . . . di suo ruote FINIS FINIS.

A life of Dante, ed. A. Solerti, *Le vite di Dante*, 1904, pp. 97–104. ff. 55–56^v blank.

3 (quire 8). ff. 57–62 Francescho Petrarcha huomo di grande ingegno . . . dare si puo. FINIS [. . . .].

L. Bruni's life of Petrarch, ed. Solerti, op. cit., pp. 288–93. ff. 62^v–64^v blank. A leaf and the text in edn., pp. 290/13–291/10, are missing after f. 58.

ff. iv + 64 + iv. f. iv is a parchment flyleaf. 215 × 130 mm. Written space 142 × 68 mm. 27 long lines. Pencil ruling: double vertical bounders. Collation: 1–4^{10} 5^2 (ff. 41–2) 6^{10} 7^4 (ff. 53–6) 8^{10} wants 3 after f. 58 and 8, blank, after f. 62. Humanistica, current from f. 43 where the hand changes. Initials: (i) f. 1, 5-line *N* in gold on a ground of blue, pink, and green, decorated with white scrollery and black dots; (ii) 2-line, blue. Binding of s. xix. Secundo folio *Le sue.*

Written in Italy. For Italian owners, s. xvi, see Mann, loc. cit. No. 438 in a French bookseller's catalogue, s. xix, at 60 francs. Book-plate as in 8° It. 2.

OXFORD. TRINITY COLLEGE

93. *Summary of the Bible (in English)* s. xiv/xv

In þis first chapiter is made mencion . . . in persecucions wirkes pacience (*ends imperfectly*).

A summary of the Bible, book by book, in the common order, and chapter by chapter. Described by N. R. Ker, 'A Middle-English summary of the Bible', *Medium Aevum*, xxix (1960), 115–18, and by D. Fowler in *Manuscripta* xii (1968), 67. 2 Maccabees is missing in the gap after f. 150. The last words on f. 200^v are very near the beginning of Catholic Epistles. For other damage see Ker, p. 115. Notes by James Ingram on ff. iii^v, iv show that he thought John Trevisa was the author.

ff. v + 200 + v. 208 × 140 mm. Written space 165 × 122 mm. 39–41 long lines. Collation: 1^8 wants 2 2^8 3^8 wants 7, 8 after f. 21 4–19^8 20 one (f. 151) 21^8 wants 3 after f. 153 22–25^8 26^8 wants 1 after f. 189 27 four (ff. 197–200). Quire and leaf signatures of the usual late-medieval kind, mostly cut off: g iii on f. 48 is the first to be seen and p iiii on f. 113 the last. Written by one hand in current anglicana. 2-line and 1-line initials, blue or red. Binding of s. xix in. (1808 ?): 'Trevisa's Comm / on the Bible / M.S.S. Ant.' on the spine.

Written in England. Much scribbled on in s. xvi, mainly by Thomas Shawe. Other writings are: 'John Bewleye', f. 58; 'This is William Daunce book Record of Thomas Shawe and of many more of his fellowes I beare wytnes to the same William Daunce is my name', f. 60^v, on specially ruled lines (cf. f. 34^v); 'John Nott is a knave by mee William Daunce 1576', f. 87^v; 'Thomas pim is m[y] name', f. 103. 'Iacobo Ingram / Coll: S: Trin: Apud Oxon: Soc: / Hoc opus MS: / D.D. / Iacobus Dallaway M.B. / eiusd: coll: olim scholaris / quod ibidem / perpetuo adseruandum / voluerunt ambo / qui clepserit / aut alio quocumque modo / fraudem faxit / deae fidei sacer esto / MDCCCVIII', f. v^v, in handsome red capitals. Presumably bequeathed by Ingram, who was president of Trinity College from 1824 until his death in 1850.

94. *Missale* s. xv med.

1. ff. 1–6^{v} Calendar in red and black, graded.

Misbound in the order 1, 2, 5, 6, 3, 4. Includes ten feasts not in *Sarum Missal*, pp. xxi–xxxii, but all commonly found in later Sarum missals, David, Chad, Richard, 'Sancti Erkynwaldi', translation of Edmund, translation of Richard, Anne, Cuthburga, translation of Edward, Hugh (1, 2 March; 3, 30 April; 9, 16 June; 26 July; 31 Aug.; 13 Oct.; 17 Nov.). Three entries there do not occur here, Germanus, Francis, octave of Andrew (28 May, 4 Oct., 7 Dec.). Feast of relics on first Sunday after 7 July. 2 Feb., 15 Aug., and some other important feast days are blank; perhaps the intention was to use blue ink or gold.[1]

2. ff. 7–9 Omnibus dominicis diebus . . .

Holy water service.

3. ff. 9–121^{v} Temporal from Advent to Holy Saturday.

Four (?) leaves missing after f. 22 which ends in the farcing of the lesson from Isaiah on the vigil of Christmas at the words *Datus est nobis* (*AH* xlix. 170/5: the last eleven letters are part of the catchword): f. 23 begins *uit in nobis* (*Sarum Missal*, p. 29). The next two leaves are in the wrong order. On ff. 24^{v}, 26 the office of St Thomas of Canterbury has been crossed out. The secret at the 2nd Sunday after the octave of Epiphany is Placare, not Ut tibi grata.

4. ff. 121^{v}–134^{v} Ad missam dicendam executor . . .

Ordinary and noted prefaces of mass, ending imperfectly at *Celi celorum* (*SM*, p. 220/5).

5. ff. 135^{v}–186 Temporal, beginning imperfectly at Tuesday after Easter in the lesson from Acts 13 (*SM*, p. 139).

Pentecost and later offices (*SM*, pp. 159–67) missing in a gap after f. 151. Corpus Christi, f. 155.

6. ff. 186–9 Offices for the dedication, consecration, and reconciliation of a church.

7. ff. 189–248^{v} Sanctoral from Andrew to Linus.

No office of the Visitation of B.V.M. at 2 July. A rubric at f. 232^{v}, 'Nota quod festum natiuitatis beate marie non habet vigiliam secundum usum sarum in multis uoluminibus inuenimus scriptum est quod haberet vigilia per omnia sicut in vigilia assumpcionis'. Cues 'de communi' for a memoria of John of Beverley at 25 Oct., f. 242.

8. ff. 248^{v}–263^{v} Common of saints.

9. ff. 263^{v}–280^{v} Votive masses: (i–iii) B.V.M., beginning with rubric 'ordinatio misse quotidiane beate marie uirginis que dicitur Salue. Pulsato . . . (4–6);[2]

[1] 2 July is not blank, but has the normal pre-Visitation entry of Processus and Martinianus.

[2] For the meaning of the arabic numbers and page references in brackets and the asterisks, see above, All Souls College 302, art. 9.

(iv) Holy Trinity (1); (v) Holy Spirit (2); (vi) Holy Cross (3); (vii) angels (p. 459); (viii) Pro fratribus et sororibus (7); (ix) De pace (11); (x) Pro serenitatem (*sic*) aeris (28); (xi) Ad pluuiam postulandam (27); (xii) In tempore belli (43); (xiii) Pro quacumque tribulacione (26); (xiv) Pro rege (15); (xv) *Pro rege et regina (16); (xvi) Ad inuocandum graciam spiritus sancti (23); (xvii) Pro semetipso (17); (xviii) *Pro semetipso (18); (xix) Ad poscendum donum spiritus sancti (34); (xx) Pro peccatoribus (25); (xxi) Pro penitentibus (31); (xxii) Pro inspiracione diuine sapiencie (33); (xxiii) Pro tribulacione cordis (37); (xxiv) Pro infirmo (39); (xxv) Pro salute amici (19); (xxvi) *Pro amico (20); (xxvii) *Pro infirmo proximo morti (p. 410, note); (xxviii) Pro eo qui in uinculis tenetur (35); (xxix) Contra mortalitatem hominum (29); (xxx) Pro peste animalium (42); (xxxi) *Pro iter agentibus (30); (xxxii) *Pro uniuersali ecclesia (10); (xxxiii) *[Pro papa], the collect cancelled (9); (xxxiv) *Pro episcopo (12); (xxxv) *Pro episcopo (14); (xxxvi) *Pro prelatis et subditis (13); (xxxvii) *Contra temptacionem carnis (21); (xxxviii) *Contra malas cogitaciones (22); (xxxix) *Pro peticione lacrimarum (24); (xl) *Contra aereas potestates (32); (xli) *Pro nauigantibus (38); (xlii) *Pro benefactoribus uel salute amicorum (40); (xliii) *Contra aduersantes (41); (xliv) *Contra paganos (p. 406, note); (xlv) *De incarnacione domini nostri ihesu cristi (Burntisland edn., col. 825*); (xlvi) *Ad memoriam de sanctis Katherina Margareta et Maria Magdalena (ibid., col. 823*); (xlvii) *Commemoratio generalis de omnibus sanctis (8).

In (xv), f. 272, for king and queen, nine words of the collect, *triumphum . . . semper*, have been replaced, s. xvi, by 'ut incedant coram te semper corde perfecto et per unigenitum tuum', and in the secret *hostias* has been changed to 'vota'.

10. ff. 280v–286 Pro defunctis.

The nineteen sets of collects, secrets, and postcommunions in *Sarum Missal*, pp. 431–2, are here in the order 1, 9, 11, 2, 10, 7, 3, 4, 12, 6, 8, 14, 5, 15, 16, 17, 13, 18, 19, and there is a set in the last place but one, Pro quibus orare tenemur, as in Burntisland edn., col. 878*.

11. ff. 286–287v Oracio generalis.

Four forms, as *Sarum Missal*, pp. 442–5.

12. f. 287v Ordo trigintalis quod quidam apostolicus . . . proximiores prime oracioni. Oracio. Deus summa spes . . .

Collect, secret, and postcommunion as in Burntisland edn., col. 883*. The heading as in Corpus Christi College, Oxford, 394, f. 244v, q.v.

13 (additions, s. xv). (*a*) f. 288v Lessons for Wednesday in the week following the first Sunday after the octave of Epiphany. (*b*) ff. 289–90 (*begins imperfectly*) secrets and postcommunions of nine of the votive masses in art. 9.

(*b*). Presumably the collects of these masses were in the gap between f. 288 and f. 289. The gap (two leaves ?) may also have contained the seven prayers said daily from Monday after the first Sunday in Lent until Holy Thursday to which reference is made in a side-note on f. 50, 'Nota quere oraciones istas insimul in fine libri'.

14 (additions, s. xvi). (*a*) f. 290 Domine deus omnipotens qui nos per spiritum tuum . . . (*b*) f. 290 Suscipe piissime Iesu in sinu patriarche tui Abrahe animam famule tue Margarete eamque sanctis et electis omnibus adiunge. Sed ne noceat culpam carnis ad penam prosit ille tue miseracio pietatis ad ueniam per christum dominum nostrum Amen. (*c*) f. 290 Omnipotens sempiterne deus cui numquam sine spe misericordie supplicatur: propiciare anime famule tue Margarete vt que de hac vita in tui nominis confessione decessit sanctorum tuorum numero facias aggregari per christum dominum nostrum Amen. Tho: pope. (*d*) f. 290^{v} Deus patrum nostrorum et domine misericordie . . . Custodi nobis quesumus HENRICVM quem elegisti regem populo tuo . . .

(*b, c*). Margaret, wife of Sir Thomas Pope, died 16 Feb. 1539.

15. The flyleaf, f. 291, contains: (*a*) cues for Oraciones ad missam pro defunctis, the same as occur in art. 10 (*Sarum Missal*, nos. 9, 11, 2, 10, 19); (*b*) cues for the office of St Osmund, s. xv ex.

(*b*) is referred to in the margin, f. 191. The feast, 3 Dec., was instituted in 1480. f. 291^{v} was pasted down.

ff. iii + 290 + iv. f. 29, a medieval flyleaf, was pasted down. 268 × 162 mm. Written space 182 × 100 mm. 2 cols. 39 lines. Collation: 1^{6} (ff. 1, 2, 5, 6, 3, 4) $2\text{-}3^{8}$ 4 four (ff. 23, 25, 24, 26) $5\text{-}10^{8}$ 11^{8} 1 cancelled before f. 75: its stub remains, with an X (to show cancellation ?) on the verso $12\text{-}17^{8}$ 18^{8} wants 6-8 after f. 134 $19\text{-}20^{8}$ 21^{8} wants 2-7 after f. 151 $22\text{-}30^{8}$ 31 four (ff. 225-8) $32\text{-}38^{8}$ 39^{4} 40 two (ff. 89, 90, bifolium). Initials: (i) 4-line or 5-line, blue or pink or (f. 28) both colours, shaded to white, on gold grounds decorated in gold and colours, including green (a pineapple motif sometimes), with prolongations into two or three of the margins; (ii) 2-line, blue with red ornament; (iii) 1-line, red or blue. Binding of diced russia, gilt, s. xviii. Secundo folio (f. 8) *nanter*.

Written in England. Belonged to Sir Thomas Pope, founder of Trinity College, †1559: see art. 14.[1] f. 1 was scribbled on in s. xvii, 'There was a man had 9 woodes and euery wood . . .': cf. ff. 290^{v}, 291. 'John Darell Scotney (Kent) N° 48' and 'Wm Braban his Book the gift of John Darell Esq. 26 August 1774' on f. 1, at foot. In Quaritch's Catalogue 369 (1886), no. 35671 (£36). Belonged to Lord Amherst in 1906: cf. S. de Ricci, *Handlist*, MS. 12. R. Leicester Harmsworth sale, 16 Oct. 1945, lot 2030, to Trinity College (£180).

Danson 1. *W. Peraldus, Summa de virtutibus.*[2] s. xiv^{2}

Incipiunt capitula prime partis in summa uirtutum. Presens opus habet v partes principales . . . (f. 1^{v}) Expliciunt capitula. Incipit prologus uirtutum. Cum circa

[1] Mr Michael Maclagan kindly told me of the printed Sarum missal, Paris 1527, now at the Groot Seminarie, Mechlen, in which Pope wrote—on a leaf of the canon—'Orate pro animabus Thome Pope Militis et Margarete et Elizabeth vxoris eius nec non Willelmi patris et Margarete Matris ipsius Thome Pope ac Alicie filie eorundem Thome et Margarete. Tho: Pope'. Probably MS. 75 and MS. 94 are the two books referred to in the list of Pope's gifts to Trinity College in College Register A, f. 6: 'Item a Faire masse booke of parchment lyned w^{t} gold and covered w^{t} black velvett. Item a massebooke of parchement covered w^{t} leather'.

[2] Neil Ker learned of the existence of this manuscript from Dr A. de la Mare only a few days before his death. He never saw it but hoped that at least a short description might appear in this catalogue even although proofs had already begun to reach him. This description attempts to follow his method, and I am grateful to Dr de la Mare for help with it. A. G. W.

utilia studere debeamus . . . (f. 218^{v}) celestem hereditatem. Benedictus dominus. Amen. fiat fiat fiat. Explicit summa uirtutum. Incipiunt capitula in summa uirtutum . . . (f. 220^{v}) de patientia persecutionum.

For manuscripts and printed editions see A. Dondaine, 'Guillaume Peyraut', *AFP* xviii (1948), 193-7, *SOPMA* ii. 133-42 no. 1622, Bloomfield, no. 1628. For printed editions see also Goff, P. 84-90. Capitula to book 1 on ff. 218^{v}-219 repeat the capitula on f. 1^{v} but the capitula to books 2-5 appear for the first time, perhaps by an oversight of the scribe. The scribe seems to have underestimated the space required and rather than continuing for a few lines on a new leaf wrote the last five lines on f. 220^{v} in a smaller, more documentary, hand.

ff. (i) + 220 + (i). 323 × 215 mm. Written space 198 × 130 mm. 2 cols. 44 lines. Collation: 1^{12} + 1 leaf after 12 $2\text{-}18^{12}$ 19^{2} + 1 leaf after 1. With the exception of the first, all quires are arranged with flesh sides outwards. Almost all quires have signatures in the bottom centre of the first six leaves in small roman numerals, probably contemporary with the writing. Decoration: f. 1^{v} a border of blue, blue-grey, red, and green flowers in the left-hand margin links initials *P* (9-line) and *C* (7-line) which are on heavily gilded backgrounds. Heavily gilded balls between leaves. Spaces left for other initials. Binding of s. xix. Secundo folio *patum est conuiuio*.

Written in north (?) Italy. The illuminated initial *P* contains a coat of arms: argent a fesse azure. On f. 1 is the ex-libris of the monastery of S. Giustina at Padua: Iste liber est monachorum congregationis de observantia sancte Justine deputatus monasterio sancte Justine paduane. Quem librum condam Bone memorie dominus Antonius Zeno `de mediolano' decretorum doctor ac Vicarius domini episcopi pad' testamento suo legauit eidem monachis. obijt 1445 mense octobris repositus est in eodem monasterio. Oretur pro anima eius. This is preceded by ·A 13· and followed by '278'. f. 218^{v}, Iste liber est monachorum congregationis sancte Justine ad usum monasterii eiusdem sancte Justine de padua. This is followed by '278' and ·A 13·. No. 278 (with A13 at end of entry) in inventory of S. Giustina printed by G. Mazzatinti, *Inventario dei manoscritti italiani delle biblioteche di Francia vol. ii. Appendice all'inventario dei manoscritti italiani* . . . , 1887, pp. 579-661. f. 218^{v}, erased, Iste summa de virtutibus empta a domino Iacobo de [. . .] est mei gasperini de barziziis de pergamo, i.e. Gasparino Barzizza, †1431. Some notes appear to be in his hand. f. 1, erased, Liber domini [. . .] de perusio decretorum doctoris quem emi (?) a fratre (?) Abeldati (?). Inside the cover a large pencil number 291 (s. xix ?) and bookseller's marks a/e/j and i/e/. No. 188 in a sale catalogue, the relevant entry from which is pasted to f. 1—no doubt the sale at which the book was acquired by John Raymond Danson, whose book-plate is inside the cover and who bequeathed it to Trinity College in 1976.

OXFORD. UNIVERSITY COLLEGE

190 + 113, ff. 166-9. *P. Comestor, Historia Scholastica; etc.* s. xiii in.-xiii med. (art. 2)

1. ff. 1-115^{v} Incipit epistola magistri petri ad archiepiscopum synonensem. Reuerendo patri . . . benedictus deus amen. Prologus siue prefacio in scolasticis histor*iis*. Imperatorie maiestatis . . . in cathacumbis. Explicit liber.

PL cxcviii. 1053-722. Very many marginalia, mostly of s. xiii, including some verses, for example: f. 93 In matutino dampnatur tempore cristus . . . (7 lines): Walther, no. 8988

(Hildebert); f. 98 Consummant pene mortem cristi duodene . . . (5); f. 115^{v} Prima caput membris in cristo uult sociare . . . (8).

2. ff. 115^{v}–135^{v}, MS. 113 ff. 168, 166–7, 169. Miscellaneous theological pieces added in s. xiii on the part of quire 12 which remained blank after art. 1 and on three more short quires. They are: (*a*) f. 115^{v} 'vii regule tychonii' from Augustine, De doctrina christiana, bk. 4; (*b*) ff. 116–135^{v}, MS. 113 ff. 168^{rv}, 166^{r} Notes on biblical history, often with reference back to the column numbers of art. 1: the longest piece is at the end, ff. 133^{v}–135^{v}, 168^{rv}, 166, 'De inicio et fine lxx^{a} annorum captiuitate . . . super desolatum', with reference back to '301 f' (= f. 73vb); (*c*) interrupting (*b*) on ff. 119^{v}–123^{v} Theological questions, mainly 'De personis: on f. 121 col. 2, on hypostasis, a section begins 'Opponit autem magister W' and on f. 121^{v} one begins 'Sicut igitur dicit W'; (*d*) MS. 113 ff. 167–9 Extracts from 3, 4 Kings and 2 Chronicles in Hebrew, preceded by a brief Latin introduction referring back to art. 1, f. 53va: De duabus columpnis in portico templi salomonis Supra 220 e agitur . . . Vt autem melius pateat earum factura; ecce ipsum ebraicum uerbo ad uerbum interpretandum et recte intelligendum pono. quatinus et ebraicum et latinum scientibus innotescat. quia ipsa uerba pondus habent et succincte multa insinuant.

Slips were added to (*b*), ff. 117 + 122 and ff. 129 (blank) + 134. In MS. 133 f. 166^{v} (numbered '543', '544') and f. 169^{v} were left blank.

3. f. 136 A plan of the 'atrium tabernaculi'. f. 136^{v} blank.

Arts. 4–6 were once in front of arts. 1, 2, as appears from the chain mark on f. 137.

4. ff. 137–43 Incipit liber Sancti Ieronimi de locis qui in scripturis inueniuntur sacris per alfabetum editus. Eusebius qui a beato pamphilo martire . . . lege paralipomenon. Explicit.

PL xxiii. 859–928.

5. (*a*) f. 143 Fausto presbitero insulano Eucherius episcopus. Ierosolimitane vrbis situm . . . a solis occasu etc. (*b*) f. 143 Balanus id est quercus luctus . . .

(*a*). An extract from Pseudo-Eucherius, De situ orbis. *CSEL* xxxix (1898), 125–131/4. (*b*). Interpretations of eleven Hebrew names beginning with B, Balanus–Betharan.

6. ff. 143^{v}–144^{v} An index to art. 1, Anima–Ymber, with leaf and letter references.

7. (*a*). f. 145 x precepta. Non tibi sint plures dii; sed verus deus vnus . . . (*b*) f. 145 x plage egipti. Sanguis. rana. culex . . .

Ten lines on the ten commandments and two on the ten plagues of Egypt added on the flyleaf, s. xiii/xiv. (*b*) is Walther, *Sprichwörter*, no. 27492c.

ff. iii + 145 (including two double slips: see above) + ii in MS. 190 and ff. 4 in MS. 113. MS. 190 foliated (i–iii), 1–92, 92b, 93–145, (146). f. 145 is a medieval flyleaf. Arts. 1, 2 have medieval column numbering, 1–549, 560 (*sic*): the slips, ff. 122 and 134, are given the same numbers, 492 and 531, as the columns to which they are additions. 330 × 220 mm. Written space 210 × 125 mm and (arts. 3, 4) 260 × 170 mm. 2 cols. of 57–9 lines in arts. 1, 2, lettered a–g between the columns at intervals of nine or ten lines. 2 cols. of 63 lines in arts. 4, 5. The first line of writing is above the top ruled line in arts. 1, 2. Collation, excluding f. 136 and the slips added to quires 12 and 14: $1–10^{10}$ 11^{14} (ff. 110–13) 12^{8} (ff. 114–16, 118–21, 123) 13^{4} (ff. 124–7) 14^{6} (ff. 128, 130–3, 135) 15^{4} (MS. 113 ff. 168, 166–7, 169) 16^{8} (ff. 137–44).

Art. 1 is in one hand, except for the last two leaves. Another scribe wrote arts. 5, 6. Art. 2 was added by several scribes in modified textura and incipient anglicana formata, s. xiii med. Initials in art. 1 (art. 2 has none): (i) f. i, 6-line, red and blue with ornament of the other colour. Initials in arts. 4, 5, 2-line and 1-line, blue or red. Binding of s. xix. Secundo folio (f. 138) *in tribu iuda* or (f. 2) *rant ea*.

Written in England. Belonged to the Dominicans of Beverley in s. xv, if not in s. xiii: 'Fratrum predicatorum' at the head of f. 1 and 'fratris Roberti de Eston' at the foot, both probably in the same hand, s. xiii; 'Conuentus Beuerlaci', f. 137, s. xv. 'C. Hyldyard', MS. 113, f. 169, s. xvi, may have been written before or after the last four leaves of art. 2 were transferred to MS. 113: the same name is on MS. 113, f. 1. Both manuscripts were the gift of Obadiah Walker, master 1676–9: see Hunt, loc. cit. (p. 586), p. 27.[1]

191. *Gregorius, Homeliae in Evangelia; etc.* s. xii med.

1. ff. 6–127v Reuerentissimo et sanctissimo fratri secundino episcopo: gregorius . . . fiant. Explicit prologus. Incipit liber primus omeliarum beati Gregorii. In illo tempore . . . Dominus ac redemptor noster . . . mentibus loquatur: cui est . . . amen. Explicit liber quadraginta omeliarum beati Gregorii pape. quas . . . idem papa uenerabilis edidit.

PL lxxvi. 1075–312. Bk. 2, f. 50. Four leaves are missing after f. 6v which ends 'Et tunc' in homily 1 (edn. 1079A): f. 7 begins 'est. Quibus notis uerbis' in homily 3 (edn. 1086C). The middle sheet of quire 5 (ff. 34–41) is misplaced as the outside sheet: the correct order is 35–7, 34, 41, 38–40.

Part of the text is marked in pencil by a perhaps contemporary hand for a series of twelve lessons, for example 'lc' xii' on f. 36, and notes of s. xiv on ff. 12v, 31v, 40v, 54v, 103, 112v show where the reader in refectory is to begin, for example in the middle of homily 6, f. 12v, 'Hic incipiatur ad mensam'. Nota marks, s. xii, usually within a circle, include 'D.M.' ('dignum memoria' in full, ff. 115, 121v), 'A.L.' ('audi lector' in full, f. 121v) and 'R.L.' ('retine lector' in full, f. 109v).

2. ff. 128–40 Incipit expositio beatissimi Ieronimi presbiteri super Marcum ewangelistam. Incipit prologus. Curis fratrum occupatus . . . furtum laudabile faciens. Appropinquante passione: appropinquat temptatio . . . Incipit liber.

[1] Hunt notes Walker's connection with the Hildyard family. In or about 1635 Sir Christopher Hildyard of Winestead, East Yorkshire, owned the chronicle of the abbey of Meaux, near Beverley, now Manchester, John Rylands University Library, MS. Lat. 219, and in 1553 or 1563 an earlier Sir Christopher owned the cartulary of Meaux, now B.L., Lansdowne 424 (Davis, *MC*, no. 653).

Et factum est . . . Marcus euangelista sicut ceruus . . . concordans enarrat. Explicit expositio beatissimi ieronimi presbiteri super marcum euangelistam.

Pseudo-Jerome. From *Factum est* as *PL* xxx. 594/19-644.

3 (in another hand). ff. 140v-142 Descriptio cuiusdam sapientis breuiter de codicibus excepta ad reginam Gerbertam Heinrici saxorum (*sic*) nobilissimi Regis filiam. de anticristo in omnibus malefico. atque omni inprobitate digno. In primo proferendum est nobis: quare dicitur anticristus. Ideo scilicet quia . . . iudicandum esse ante predixit. Finiunt gesta anticristi.

Adso of Montier-en-Der. Ed. E. Sackur, *Sybillinische Texte und Forschungen*, 1898, pp. 105/19-113/16: cf. p. 104, footnote a, for the heading and p. 105, footnote a, for this beginning. f. 142v blank.

4. Pieces added on flyleaves, s. xii: (*a*) ff. 1v-2v Sanctus Augustinus. Presentia mala . . . (*b*) ff. 2v-3 Ieronimus de passione reciproca uel subalterna inter duas personas rationem scilicet ammonentem: et hominem deflentem. Homo. Anima mea in angustiis est . . . Ploratu enim: (*ends abruptly*). (*c*) f. 3v Extracts from Bede, Historia ecclesiastica, bk. 4. 11, on 'Scebbi', king of the East Saxons, who became a monk, and from bk. 5. 19 on 'Conredh', king of Mercia, and Offa, son of the king of the East Saxons, who went to Rome and became monks, and from Historia Francorum on the 'celsitudo monastici ordinis'; (*d*) f. 3v Isidorus. Non sunt promouendi . . . istosque diligamus.

(*a*). Three short paragraphs and a longer paragraph, 'Locutus est ad nos sermo dei et depromptus est . . . Accipite disciplinam . . . thesaurum in celo'. (*b*). An abbreviation of most of the first part of Isidore, Liber synonymorum, *PL* lxxxiii. 827-840/21. (*d*). Extracts from Isidore, Gregory, and Jerome on the qualities needed in a good bishop.

5. f. 5rv Incipiunt capitula libri primi omeliarum uenerabilis Bede presbiteri . . .

A leaf which appears to have been taken from the beginning of a copy of Bede's homilies on the Gospels, s. xii². It contains a list of fifty homilies in two books of twenty-five each, in the order of Boulogne MS. 75: cf. M. L. W. Laistner and H. H. King, *A Hand-List of Bede manuscripts*, 1943, pp. 114-18, and G. Morin in *RB* ix (1892), 316. Written space 223 × 135 mm. 2 cols. 35 lines.

6. The pastedowns are two leaves of a noted breviary, s. xiv.

The exposed side at the end contains part of the office for St Andrew and the exposed side at the beginning part of the office for St Lucy, as *Brev. ad usum Sarum*, iii. 8-10 and 51. On the front pastedown the spaces for the musical notation have not been filled. Written space 273 × 190 mm. 2 cols. 51 lines.

ff. v + 138, foliated 1-41, 41b, 42-142. ff. 128-39 are numbered in pencil 1-12, s. xiv (?). 310 × 210 mm. Written space 215 × 132 mm. 32 and from f. 65 33 long lines. Pricks in both margins to guide ruling. Collation of ff. 6-142: 1^8 wants 2-5 2-17^8 18^4 (ff. 137-40) 19^2 (ff. 141-2). Signatures in ink of the usual late medieval kind, a. 1-g. 4, were added later, probably at the time of rebinding, on quires 2-8, and the four leaves of quire 1 were marked at the same time +1, +6, +7, +8. The hand changes at f. 65 (9^1). Flex punctuation: most of the marks in art. 1 appear to be additions to the original punctuation. Initials: (i) f. 6rv,

6-line green *R* with red ornament and blue and red *D*; (ii) usually 3-line, green or red, and usually with some ornament and patterning. Late medieval binding of wooden boards, now bare of leather, repaired and rebacked in 1883: five bands: two clasps missing. Secundo folio [*uidebunt*].

Written in England. The punctuation suggests ownership by a Cistercian house in s. xii. Its inscription of ownership, '[Liber] sancte M[arie] d[e . . . .] anathema sit', is on f. 4^v^, s. xii ex.

OXFORD. WADHAM COLLEGE

A. 5. 28. *Psalterium, etc.* s. xiv med.

1. ff. 1–6^v^ Calendar in red and black, graded.

The calendar of Norwich cathedral priory printed in *Customary of Norwich* (HBS lxxii, 1948) has all the feasts here except 'Resurreccio domini', in red, 27 March. Thirteen entries there do not occur here: octave of Thomas of Canterbury, Benedict, Eusebius, Audoenus, Hermes, Sabina, Eufemia, Lambert, octave of translation of relics, Remigius, octave of Michael, Eustace, Menna (4 Jan., 21 March, 14, 24, 28, 29 Aug., 16, 17, 23 Sept., 1, 6 Oct., 2, 11 Nov.). Taurinus, 11 Aug., is here graded 'xii lc' and Osyth, 7 Oct., 'in albis'. There are no obits of bishops of Norwich apart from Herbert (not in calendar of the customary) in red on 23 July. The translation of relics, 16 Sept., and the dedication of Norwich, 24 Sept., both in red, have been erased, but the entry at 1 Oct., 'Oct' dedic' in cap' ', also in red, has not been erased. 'Sancti alphegi episcopi' added, 19 May.

2. ff. 7–163^v^ Psalms 1–150.

Probably twenty-nine leaves are missing. The gaps are after ff. 31 (2 leaves), 35 (4), 65 (6), 66 (4), 68 (5), 85 (1), 89 (2), 100 (4), 140 (1). Leaves are out of order in quires 12 and 14: see below, collation. Pss. 9, 17, 36, 77, 88, 103–6, 138, 143, 144 are divided, as no doubt were 67 and 68 which came in the gap after f. 68.

3. ff. 164–78 Six ferial canticles—Audite celi divided at Ignis succensus—followed by Te deum, Benedicite, Benedictus, Magnificat (*ends imperfectly*), Quicumque vult (*begins imperfectly*).

Three leaves are missing after f. 177.

4. ff. 178–197^v^ Penitential psalms and (f. 187) litany.

Twenty-three martyrs: . . . (17–23) albane osuualde eadmunde aelfege thoma blasi uuilelme. Twenty-six confessors: . . . (2, 3) marcialis taurine . . . (13–26) audoene dunstane cuthberte felix iuliane bonite edmunde benedicte maure leonarde paule antoni egidi noethe. Twenty-two virgins: . . . (13) austroberta . . . (16) honorina . . . (20–2) etheldreda mildreda osida. Deus cui is preceded by Pss. 69, 70 and followed by Mentem famuli tui episcopi nostri, Omnipotens sempiterne deus qui facis, Pretende, Ure igne, Actiones, Ecclesie tue, A domo tua, Deus a quo, Deus qui inter apostolicos sacerdotes, Animabus, Deus qui es sanctorum (*ends imperfectly*).

5. ff. i–ii^v^ Notes by William Baynton to show the descent of William Latton (see below) and his own descent from John Wadham, the father of the founder of Wadham College.

ff. ii + 195 (foliated 1–8, 10–132, 134–97) + ii. 162 × 95 mm. Written space 110 × 58 mm. 18 long lines. Probable collation: 1^4 + 2 leaves after 4 $2\text{-}4^8$ 5^8 wants 1, 2 before f. 32 and 7, 8 after f. 35 6^8 wants 1, 2 before f. 36 $7\text{-}9^8$ 10^8 wants 1–6, 8 (f. 66) 11^8 wants 1–3, 6–8 (ff. 67–8) 12^8 wants 1, 2 (ff. 69–72, 73, 74) 13^8 14^8 wants 3 (ff. 84–7, 83, 88, 89) 15^8 wants 1, 2 before f. 90 16^8 wants 6–8 after f. 100 17^8 wants 1 before f. 101 $18\text{-}21^8$ 22^8 wants 1 before f. 141 $23\text{-}25^8$ 26^8 wants 7, 8 after f. 177 27^8 wants 1 before f. 178 28^8 29 five (ff. 193–7). Initials: (i) of principal psalms, including Pss. 51, 101, 4–6 line, red and blue patterned in white on grounds of both colours and gold, the gold decorated in colours: prolongations into the margins in gold and colours; (ii) 2-line, gold on grounds of red and blue patterned in white; (iii) 1-line, blue with red ornament. Binding of s. xvii ex., labelled 'MISSAL ROMAN': the arms of the family of Latton and motto 'Mors potior macula' on both covers. Secundo folio (f. 8) *tutus sum.*

Written in England for the use of the Benedictine cathedral priory of Norwich, whose pressmark 'A. x' is at the head of f. 7 in the middle. 'Wm L.', f. 1 (William Latton, fellow of Wadham College, librarian 1682). 'Wm Baynton of Chadlington and Grays Inn, Esqr F.A.S. . . . present owner of this Mss.', f. ii^v^, s. xix. 'E libris A. J. V. Radford', f. i. Given by Arthur Rau in 1927.

A. 7. 8. *Missale* 1521

1. ff. 2–7^v^ Calendar in red and black, not graded.

'Huberti episcopi' in red, 3 Nov.

2. ff. 8–9^v^ Benedictio salis et aque.

3. (*a*) ff. 10–20^v^ Masses of Holy Spirit, Holy Cross, B.V.M., angels. (*b*) ff. 20^v^–24^v^ Collect, secret, and postcommunion of twelve masses: Pro pace; Pro peccatis; Pro tribulatione; Pro familiaribus; Pro iter agentibus; Pro serenitate; Pro pluuia; Pro infirmo; Pro papa; Pro prelatis; Pro rege; Pro uiuis et defunctis generalis.

(*b*). *SMRL* ii. 321–7, nos. 11, 25, 10, 33, 13, 35, 34, 62, 12, 21, 43, 38, except the postcommunions Sumpta domine celestis (13), Plebs tua domine (35), and Tuere nos (34).

4. (*a*) ff. 24^v^–25 Pro mortuis. Introitus. Requiem eternam . . . (*b*) ff. 25^v^–28^v^ Ten sets of collects, secrets, and postcommunions for the dead: Pro pontifice; Pro sacerdote; Pro episcopis et sacerdotibus; Pro famulo; Pro femina; Pro defunctis nobis insciis. In anniuersario; Pro fratribus et sororibus; Pro patre et matre; Generalis; (*c*) f. 28^v^ Collect, secret, and postcommunion 'Pro uiuis et defunctis. Omnipotens sempiterne deus qui viuorum . . .'. (*d*) ff. 28^v^–29^v^ Lessons for the dead: Ecce mysterium . . . ; Omne quod dat . . . ; Nolumus vos ignorare . . . ; Dixit martha . . .

(*b*). (1, 2, 4–10) are *SMRL* ii. 329–30 (e–h, n, l, i, m, o), except that the postcommunions are sometimes different. (3) is Concede, Munera, Quesumus ut anime. (*c*). ibid., p. 324, no. 37.

5. ff. 30–69^v^ Offices for eleven occasions: Christmas Eve; Christmas Day; John Evangelist; Circumcision; Epiphany; Purification of B.V.M.; Ash Wednesday; Annunciation of B.V.M.; Palm Sunday; Cena Domini; Easter Saturday.

(2–6, 8–10) are preceded by a picture. A rubric in 'De cena domini', f. 62, refers to the abbot, 'Deinde abbas accepto calice . . .'.

6. ff. 70–88v Ordinary, (f. 72) noted prefaces, and (f. 81) Canon of mass.

7. ff. 89–131 Offices for seventeen occasions: Easter; dedication of church; Ascension; vigil of Pentecost; Pentecost; Corpus Christi; Trinity; John Baptist; Visitation of B.V.M.; Assumption of B.V.M.; Nativity of B.V.M.; Augustine; 'In festo recollectionis omnium festiuitatum beate marie virginis'; All Saints; All Souls; Conception of B.V.M.; Presentation of B.V.M.

(1–3, 5–17) are preceded by a picture.

8. ff. 131–135v Sequuntur sequencie in missis votiuis de domina dicende.

The heading on f. 132v, 'Infrascripte sequencie dicuntur vicissim de domina in sabbatis' is followed by Aue preclara maris stella, Aue plena singulari gracia, Imperatrix gloriosa potens, Hodierna lux diei celebris, Marie preconio seruiat cum gaudio, and Tibi cordis in altari (*RH*, nos. 2045, 2036, 8487, 7945, 11162, 20459).

9. ff. 135v–137v Office of St Katherine.

The sequence is 'Hac in die mentes pie . . .', *RH*, no. 7516.

ff. ii + 136 + i, foliated (i), 1–137, (138). f. 1 is a parchment leaf which was formerly pasted down. ff. 8–69, 89–137 have a contemporary foliation i–cxi. 428 × 310 mm. Written space *c.*290 × 185 mm. 2 cols. 24 lines and (ff. 71v–88v) 18 lines of text or 9 of music. Ruling with violet ink. Collation of ff. 2–137: $1\text{–}3^8$ 4^4 (ff. 26–9) $5\text{–}9^8$ 10^{10} (ff. 70–9) 11^8 + 1 leaf before 1 (f. 80) $12\text{–}16^8$ 17^8 + 1 leaf after 8 (f. 137). Punctuation includes the flex.

A full-page crucifixion picture, f. 80v: six haloed figures, one a bishop (Augustine) holding a pierced heart in his left hand, stand beside the Cross: a monastery (Parc) in the background. Twenty-five 7-line pictures, eight in art. 5, sixteen in art. 7, and one before art. 9. Initials: (i) in bronze and gold paint, f. 81 historiated (Christ rises from the tomb: instruments of the Passion) and f. 30 decorated (strawberry); (ii) 4-line, as (i), on coloured grounds and with a little floral ornament; (iii) 2-line, as (i, ii), but on grounds of gold paint, without ornament; (iv) 1-line, red or blue. Floral borders are continuous on main pages (for example, Assumption of B.V.M.) and run down the space between the columns; on secondary pages they fill three margins. Butterflies, snails, caterpillars, and a few birds and flies occur among the flowers. In the side border on f. 81 St Ambrose holds a scourge and in a compartment below him a tonsured surpliced figure, kneeling at an altar, holds a pastoral staff: no doubt he represents Ambrose, abbot of Parc. Capital letters in the ink of the text stroked with red.

Binding of s. xviii/xix, rebacked, bearing the lilies of the abbey of Parc and 'Bibliothecæ Parchensis' in gilt on each cover. The armorial stamp is of the larger size described by E. van Balberghe (see above, St John's College, Oxford, 265), p. 528 and pl. 5: as commonly on bindings of Parc service-books, the arms have not been erased. Secundo folio (f. 9) *cedant*.

Written by a named scribe to the order of Ambrose van Engelen, abbot of Parc, in 1521: 'Istud missale scribi fecit reuerendus pater dominus Ambrosius de angelis (*these three words in red*) Abbas modernus huius monasterii Parchensis Ordinis Premonstraten' prope louanium

Per Franciscum weert.[1] Anno uirginei partus M° CCCC° XXI°. Finit feliciter', f. 1v, in the hand of the text, as three lines lower down the same page, 'Presbyter in mensa domini quid agas bene pensa. Aut tibi vita datur aut mors eterna paratur. Missam dicturus viuas quasi cras moriturus' (cf. Walther, *Sprichwörter*, no. 22340: 2 lines). Arms of van Engelen of Louvain (cf. Rietstap) in the lower margin of ff. 33v, 81, 89, 91, 102, 104v, 114, 124. Parc pressmarks 'I theca xii' inside the cover and 'I/XII i' on f. 1v: cf. van Balberghe, pp. 531–2. Book-plate of Henry Boucher, commoner: his gift in 1852. In Burlington Fine Arts Club Exhibition, 1908 (*Catalogue*, p. 85, no. 172). *Flemish Art 1300–1700*, 1954, p. 165, no. 618. Watson, *Oxford*, pl. 813 illus. f. 31v.

A. 10. 18. *Cicero, etc.* s. xv²

1. ff. 1–30v Liber de senectute. O tyte si quid ego . . . probare possitis `vos scipio et leli´. MARCI TULLII CICERONIS DE SENECTUTE LIBER EXPLICIT.

Some currently written scholia in the margins and glosses here and there and between the lines. f. 31rv blank.

2. ff. 32–63v Liber de amicitia. Quintus mutius augur sce`u´ola memoriter et iocunde solebat . . . de amicicia que dicerem. Deo gratias. Hoc opere expleto cape mox altrum. capucine Antoni et referens magnalia scribe libenter. MARCI TULLII CICERONIS DE AMICITIA LIBER EXPLICIT.

Annotated like art. 1. The first scholium begins 'Intentio auctoris est velle de amicitia tractare': the scribe uses a *de* ligature which looks like a *q* with the vertical stroke rising above the line.

3. ff. 64–71 De somnio scipionis. Cum in africam venissem . . . solutus sum a somno. Marci tullii ciceronis particula voluminis de Re publica pertractans somnium Scipionis explicit. reliquam partem dicti uoluminis non inueni.

Annotation almost ceases at f. 66. f. 71v blank.

4. ff. 72–7 Epistola ad laudem cuiusdam nobilissimi romani. Cum rebus bellicis semper ceteris . . . (f. 72v) De presidentia certant. (f. 73) Alexander loquitur. Me o libice preponi decet . . . hic spernendus est. et hic est finis. Finis.

Johannes Aurispa, De capitaneis antiquis, based on Lucian's Dialogues of the dead, no. 12: cf. R. Förster in *Jahrbücher für classische Philologie*, cxiii (1876), 221–3. f. 77v blank.

5. ff. 78–9 Querela vrbis Rome erga ciues. Si canas comas lacerare non desino . . . de meritis extinguetur. Explicit.

Rome laments her decayed state.

[1] For Weert cf. E. van Balberghe in *Archives et Bibliothèques de Belgique*, xliii (1972), p. 119, footnote 40. He wrote a psalter now in Brussels, BR 11556, for van Engelen in 1527; also Bodleian, Douce 200, which contains the same offices as A. 7. 8 arts. 5, 7, 9, but is confined to epistles, tracts, grails, versicles, sequences, and some collects. In both Douce and A. 7. 8 the scribe varies between the 'old' spellings 'ihesus' and 'cristus' and the 'new' spellings 'iesus' and 'christus', but the latter are commoner in Douce, which has for example, 'iesus' three times in the Palm Sunday lesson from Philippians 2: 1–11, where Wadham has, each time, 'ihesus'.

6. f. 79^{v} Dice il prouerbio che vn fa male ad cento . . . le sue parole.

14 lines of verse on a lost book. 'Verissimum est' at the side in red.

7 (added, s. xv ex.). f. 80 De qualitate yhesu cristi. Temporibus Octauiani Cesaris. Cum ex vniuersis . . . sic. Apparuit temporibus nostris . . . inter filios hominum. Repertum in annalibus Rom'.

The letter of Lentulus (Stegmüller, no. 158. 1), preceded by a 6-line introduction. ff. 80^{v}–91^{v} left blank.

ff. i + 91 + i. Paper. 213 × 145 mm. Written space *c.* 125 × 65 mm. 20 long lines. Ruling in mauve ink. The first line of writing is above the top ruled line. Collation: 1^{16} 2^{14} + 1 leaf after 14 (f. 31) $3–5^{16}$ 6^{14} wants 13, 14, blank after f. 91. A strip of parchment as strengthening in the centre of each quire. Textura with a few borrowings from cursiva, for example round and long forms of *s*. 2-line red initials. Capital letters in the ink of the text touched with red. Parchment binding, s. xvii (?).

Written in Italy. 'Valerii cyllenii victoris et amicorum emptus romȩ a quodam florentino nummo vno (?) argenteo 4 caroleno', f. 80^{v}, s. xv ex. Belonged later to the Jesuits of Agen: 'Colleg. Agenen. Socie. Jesu Catal. Inscrip.', f. 1. The number '1560' above the title on f. 1, s. xviii. L. Celotti sale at Sotheby's, 14 March 1825, lot 101 (?), to Sir Thomas Phillipps. Phillipps 1014 (and 2762). Phillipps sale at Sotheby's, 10 June 1896, lot 288, to Webster for £1. 3*s*. Given by Rev. E. W. Bowell in May 1905.

A. 10. 19. *Horatius* s. xv^{2}

1. ff. 1–39^{v} Qui fit mecoenas ut nemo . . . peior serpentibus aphris. Amen. Te deum laudamus. Amen.

Sermones. Bk. 2, f. 20. No annotation after f. 13^{v}.

2. ff. 40–6 Humano capiti cerulcem (*sic*) pictore quinam (*sic*) . . . dormitat homerus (*ends abruptly*).

Ars poetica, lines 1–359. f. 46^{v} blank.

ff. ii + 46 + ii. Paper. 208 × 153 mm. Written space *c.* 150 mm. high. 28 long lines. The only ruling is of the double vertical bounders with a blunt hard point. Collation: 1^{10} $2–3^{12}$ 4^{14} wants 13, 14, blank. A strip of parchment as strengthening in the centre of each quire. Widely spaced current humanistica. Initals: (i) blue with red ornament (f. 1) or red with black ornament; (ii) 2-line, red. Parchment binding, s. xix in. Secundo folio *Forte*.

Written in Italy. L. Celotti sale at Sotheby's, 14 March 1825, lot 171, to Sir Thomas Phillipps. 'Phillipps 943', f. 1 and at the foot of the spine. Phillipps sale at Sotheby's, 21 Mar. 1895, lot 423, to Nichols (£6. 15*s*.). Given as A. 10. 18.

A. 10. 20. *Statius, Thebais* s. xv ex.

[F]raternas acies alternaque Iura prophanis . . . aggere rursus (*ends abruptly*).

Bks. 1–9 and bk. 10, lines 1–880. The scribe had difficulty with his exemplar in bk. 8, where lines 22, 542, 646 were left blank and lines 100, 204, 308, 516, 620, 724 were not completed.

ff. i + 169 + i. Paper of good quality, except for the last quire. 185 × 132 mm. Written space 142 mm high. 24 long lines. Ruling with a blunt hard point, the direct impression always on the verso. Collation: $1-2^{10}$ 3^{12} $4-19^{8}$ 20^{10} wants 10, blank. Well written in upright humanistica. Spaces for initials remain blank. Red morocco binding, s. xix^{1}, labelled on the spine 'STATII / THEBAIDOS / M.S. / SEC. XV'. Secundo folio *Turbidus*.

Written in Italy. A motto 'Post Nubila Serenum' at foot of f. 1, s. xvii. '1227' inside the cover. T. Thorpe's catalogue for 1836, item 1227, to Sir Thomas Phillipps: Phillipps 9250. Phillipps sale 21 March 1895, lot 1058, to Nichols (£1). Given as A. 10. 18.

OXFORD. WORCESTER COLLEGE

213 + 213* *Meditationes, etc.* s. xiii^{2}

1 (quire 1). (*a*) pp. 1–4 (*begins imperfectly*) m/mi/mii Memoria defunctorum in cristo ab oddilone abbate instituitur in crastino omnium sanctorum . . . (*b*) p. 5 Sancta maria fuit in etate xvi annorum: quando peperit cristum . . . ab hoc seculo. (*c*) pp. 7–9 Memorandum quod nouem sunt festa . . . (*d*) pp. 10–22 Anno domini M°.c° xcix° Obiit Rex Ricardus 'ante pascham' telo confossus . . . (*e*) p. 2 In hoc volumine continentur . . . (*f*) p. 2 ihesus nazarenus + rex iudeorum miserere nostri + amen. Incipit (epistola) domini nostri ihesu cristi ad abgarum regem missa quam ipse dominus . . . et saluus eris. Domini est terra. Si quis hanc epistolam . . . sother. messias. sabaoth. (*g*) p. 3 Anno quo supra Venerabilis pater Radyng' impetrauit ab abbate glouernie quod posset edificare in stowelstret pro scolaribus suis oxon'. (*h*) p. 2 Note of the decision to have a building for Reading monks at Gloucester College, Oxford, taken at a chapter general at Reading in 1277.

(*a*). Annals, 1000–64 (pp. 1, 2) and 1276–81 (pp. 3, 4). Only eight entries on p. 1 (1000–31) and probably only three (1040, 1042, 1048) on p. 2, but these three erased in favour of (*e*) and (*f*). (*b*). B.V.M. 63 years old at death (16 + 33 + 14). (*c*). Note of seventy-five feasts at which the convent has special food or drink and of the obit days on which the sub-prior, chamberlain, cellarer, or granetarius provides a refection: 'Summa omnium vinorum per annum c et x'. (*d*). Annals 1199–1264, including local Reading abbey entries, for example at 1261. (*e*). The earlier part of (*a*) was out of use by s. xiii^{2}, when (*e*), which lists the contents under sixteen heads, was fitted in partly over erasure of (*a*). The first nine entries in the table are 'Liber beati Ieronimi de membris domini (art. 1) In cuius principio sunt quedam parue cron' (art. 1*d*). 'Item visio sancti pauli. Item Lunar'. Item de xv signis. Item sompniale sancti danielis. Item quedam notabilia. Item quedam experimenta ypocratis. Item penitentialis' (art. 3). Presumably, since nothing can be missing between art. 2 and art. 3, items 3–8 here are short pieces which once followed art. 1*d* on a now missing quire. (*f*). s. xiii ex. An abbreviation of the letter of Christ (cf. *MMBL* ii. 306) and note of its virtues. (*g*), s. xiv/xv, and (*h*), s. xv in., in anglicana, printed from this manuscript in *Snappe's Formulary* (Oxford Historical Society, lxxx, 1924), p. 386a. p. 6 blank.

Arts. 2–5 are on quires 2, 3.

2. (*a*) pp. 61–2, 23–32 Ieronimus de membris domini. Omnipotens deus pater et filius et spiritus sanctus Vnus atque trinus . . . se manifestum demonstrare. Explicit. (*b*) p. 32 Augustinus in libro de Trinitate. de fide trinitatis et vnitatis

inuiolabiliter seruanda. Omnes quos legere potui qui ante me scripserunt de trinitate . . . operentur.

(*a*). Pseudo-Jerome. *PL* xlii. 1199-1206/8. (*b*). From bk. 1, *PL* xlii. 824.

3. (*a*) pp. 32-42 Ex penitentia affricana. In primis dicat sacerdos ad penitentem . . . ne homicidii reus sit. (*b*) pp. 42-4 Distinctione xc in prima parte Litigiosus quoque prohibetur . . . (*c*) pp. 44-6 Qualis debet esse episcopus. Et de mortalibus et venialibus peccatis. Oportet episcopum esse irreprehensibilem . . . (*d*) pp. 46-7 Item Gregorius . . .

(*a*). Eighty-six unnumbered paragraphs, each with a heading. No. (38), 'De homicidio', is 'ex penitentiali Theodori Cantuariensis archiepiscopi'. (*b*). Extracts from Gratian, Decretum, the first from D. 90. 1. (*d*). Patristic excerpts on purgation of sin.

4. pp. 48-55 De antixpisto. Excellentissime ac regali dignitate pollenti ac deo dilecte. omnibusque sanctis amabili. monachorum nutrici. et sanctarum virginum regine G. frater A . . . Ex quo domina mater misericordie . . . (p. 48/29) Ergo de anticristo scire volentes . . . que fueritis imperature. Explicit.

Adso, De antichristo. *PL* ci. 1291-3.

5. (*a*) pp. 55-7 Hic incipit quomodo sanctum dominicum diem seruare debemus. Incipit epistola de cristo filio dei et de sancto Dominico die. Quia nescitis . . . custodire debeatis in secula seculorum. Amen. Explicit qualiter sanctus Dominicus dies debet custodiri. (*b*) pp. 58-9 In nocte Natalis domini ad primam missam Aue maria . . . (*c*) p. 59 Li apostoile innocent fist cest confermement . . . Benedicatur hora qua deus natus est . . . (*d*) p. 59 Seinte marie pure pucele mere ihesu crist . . . en teu manere (8 lines). (*e*) p. 59 Anna sancta ihesu cristi matris mater protulisti . . . (*f*) p. 60 Anna salue gloriosa. Ex qua mundo . . . (*g*) p. 60 De sancto edmundo. O edmunde singularis signa ferens gratie . . .

(*a*). The letter of Christ about Sunday: cf. *Lyell Cat.*, p. 31. (*b*). Prayers at mass on Christmas Eve, ending with an 'Oratio sancti oddonis abbatis in nocte Natalis domini. O domina et mater misericordie tu nocte ista . . . (*c*). *Lyell Cat.*, p. 371. (*d*) is not in Sonet-Sinclair. (*e-g*). Memoriae, not in *RH*.

Arts. 6, 7 are on quires 4-9.

6. pp. 63-149 Incipiunt meditaciones siue orationes beati Anselmi. Domini ihesu criste redemptio mea . . .

The thirty-three pieces are taken here in three divisions:

(*a*). Nos. i-iii, v, vi, viii, xii-xxi. Prayers 2, 18, 19, 5, 7, 6, 8-16 and Meditation 1 of the collection of prayers and meditations in *SAO* iii. 3-91.

(*b*) Nos. ix-xi, xxii, xxiii. Five prayers which may be derived from the twelfth-century Reading manuscript, Bodleian MS. Laud Misc. 79, where they occur on ff. 107-109^{v} in the order xxii, xxiii, ix-xi.

ix. p. 90 Oratio de sancta cruce. Aue crux gloriosissima omnium lignorum preciosissima et splendidissima . . . (as *PL* clviii. 937-9, but continuing further with nine lines after *coniunge*).

x. p. 91 Alia oratio de sancta cruce. Ueniam peto domine coram te . . .
xi. p. 91* Alia oratio de cruce. Obsecro te domine ihesu criste fili dei uiui. per sanctam crucem tuam: ut dimittas . . .
xxii. p. 137 Oratio de sancta trinitate. Domine deus omnipotens qui es trinus et unus qui es semper in omnibus . . . (L. Gjerløw, *Adoratio Crucis*, p. 142; A. Wilmart, *Auteurs spirituels*, pp. 573–7).
xxiii. p. 139 Oratio [. . .]. Domine deus omnipotens qui fecisti celum . . .

(*c*) The remainder.
iv. p. 70 Oratio. Ego ipse tanquam homo malus . . .
vii. p. 82 Oratio ad sanctam mariam. O beatissima et sanctissima uirgo semper Maria . . .
xxiv. p. 140 Oratio de sancto spiritu. Omnipotens deus qui in nomine unigeniti tui . . .
xxv. p. 141 Oratio de sancta trinitate. Sancta trinitas et indiuisa unitas . . .
xxvi. p. 141 Oratio de sancta cruce. Sancta et ueneranda crux. in qua nos gloriari . . .
xxvii. p. 141 Alia oratio de sancta cruce. Domine ihesu criste pro benedicta cruce tua intra nos sis . . .
xxviii. p. 142 Ubi sunt misericordie tue? Quid differs . . .
xxix. p. 144 De sancta Maria et sancto Iohanne. Mulier inquit ecce filius tuus . . .
xxx. p. 146 Oratio de Sancta Maria. O uirgo uirginum dei genitrix Maria . . .
xxxi. p. 147 Oratio. Suscipere digneris domine deus omnipotens laudes . . .
xxxii. p. 148 Alia oratio. vel salutacio beate Marie. Aue maria gracia plena a deo préélecta . . .
xxxiii. p. 149 De sancto Iohanne euuangelista. Sancte iohannes euuangelista et dilecte dei apostoli. qui uirgo electus . . . Cf. *Lyell Cat.*, p. 397.

7. (*a*) pp. 150–96 Incipit epistola de commendatione meditacionis. Meditaciones que me consolantur . . . in hiis esto. Incipit prologus Meditacionis. Due sunt uite que in sacra scriptura . . . (p. 154) que in margine notantur. Incipit libellus meditacionum cuius prima pars continet de misterio trinitatis et vnitatis. hec est prima meditacio. Fac me delectari in dulcedine tua . . . (*b*) pp. 196–8 Oratio luctuosa. Confiteor tibi domine deus quia peccaui nimis cogitando . . . (*c*) pp. 198–9 Terret me domine quod tam diuites quam pauperes . . . non ut dampnes. Qui cum patre . . . Amen. (*d*) pp. 199–200 Gratias ago tibi domine ihesu criste qui me in nocte preterita . . . esse in regno tuo. Qui cum . . . Amen. (*e*) p. 201 Signa sompniorum de superfluitate humorum. Qui sepe sompniat uidere pluuias . . . obturacionem significat.

(*a*). Five parts, the third, 'de opere redempcionis nostre, containing nine meditations (pp. 158–89): at the end, five lines beginning 'Qui in predictorum contemplacione'. (*c*). Bloomfield, no. 6000. (*e*). Thirteen lines. p. 202 blank.

Arts. 8–19 are on quires 10–15.

8. (*a*) pp. 203–19 Hic incipiunt hore sancte trinitatis. Domine labia mea . . . (*b*) pp. 220–54 Prayers to Father, Son and Holy Spirit, jointly and severally, and (v, viii) forms of absolution and confession.

(*a*). The hymn is Pater fili paraclite . . . (40 stanzas: *RH*, no. 14660; *AH* xlvi. 17–19). (*b*). Twenty-two pieces: (i) p. 220 Oratio de sancta trinitate. Domine deus rex regum qui sedes . . . (cf. *Lyell Cat.*, p. 377); (ii) p. 221 De trinitate. Oratio. Sancta trinitas unus deus . . . miserere michi peccatori; (iii) pp. 221–4 Hec est oratio quam beatus Augustinus angelo dictante scripsit . . . possidebit. Domine deus pater omnipotens qui es trinus et unus qui es semper . . . (ends as Bodleian, Lyell 30: *Lyell Cat.*, pp. 336–7; (iv) pp. 225–32 Oracio ad deuocionem excitandam. Domine ihesu xpiste fili dei uiui principium et finis intencionis mee . . . humani generis amen; (v) pp. 232–4 Uice beati petri apostolorum principis cui dominus commisit claues . . . absoluo te frater N ab omni uinculo delictorum . . . ; (vi) pp. 234–42 Oratio ad deum patrem. Domine ihesu criste fili dei uiui qui in hunc mundum propter nos peccatores . . . in syon pertingere merear amen; (vii) pp. 242–4 Miserere mei deus secundum gratie tue infusionem . . . ; (viii) pp. 244–6 Confiteor tibi domine rex pater celi et terre . . . omnium peccatorum meorum Amen; (ix) pp. 246–7 Oratio ad dominum quando sudor in agone de ipso currit. Domine ihesu criste fili dei uiui in honore et memoria trium sanctissimarum orationum . . . (cf. *Lyell Cat.*, p. 378); (x) p. 247 Oratio ad dominum. Omnipotens et misericors deus te deprecor ut non me famulum tuum . . . merear. amen; (xi) p. 247 O domine ihesu criste pro benedicta cruce tua intra nos sis:' ut nos reficias . . . ; (xii) pp. 247–8 Oratio ad deum patrem. Rex uirtutum cuius nutum . . . (10 stanzas: not in *RH*); (xiii) pp. 248–9 Summe summi tu patris unice . . . dimittat debita (24 stanzas: *RH*, no. 19710; *PL* clxxxiv. 1323–6); (xiv) pp. 249–50 Oratio ad deum patrem. Omnipotens et misericors deus pater et bone domine miserere michi peccatori . . . ; (xv) pp. 250–1 Oratio ad deum et dei filium. Lux uera mundi domine ihesu criste doce me . . . ; (xvi) p. 251 Li apostoile innocent. fist cest confermement . . . la dira. Aue ihesu criste uerbum patris . . . (5 aves: for the heading cf. art. 5*c*); (xvii) p. 251 Oratio. Deus qui nobis signatis lumen (*sic*) uultus tui memoriale . . . (*Lyell Cat.*, p. 375); (xviii) p. 252 Oratio. Omnipotens sempiterne deus qui humano generi ad inuitandum humilitatis exemplum . . . ; (xix) p. 252 Oratio ad spiritum sanctum. Ueni sancte spiritus in me a quo omne bonum . . . ; (xx) pp. 252–3 Oratio. Assumus assumus. sancte spiritus . . . ; (xxi) pp. 253–4 Oratio. Ueni ueni clementissime consolator paraclite sancte . . . ; (xxii) p. 254 Ueni sancte spiritus et iunge nos tibi . . .

9. (*a*) pp. 254–71 Incipit psalterium in laude sancte crucis. Aue salutiferum sancte crucis lignum . . . (p. 271) Oratio. Respiciat ad me rector eternus . . . (*b*) pp. 272–81 Prayers, mainly of the cross and (v) a form of commendation.

(*a*) *RH*, no. 35721; *AH* xxxv. 12–25, from B.L., Royal 2 A. ix, art. 7.

(*b*) Sixteen pieces: (i) p. 272 De sancta cruce. Oratio. Sancta et ueneranda crux in qua nos gloriari . . . ; (ii) pp. 272–3 Stabat iuxta cristi crucem . . . (*RH*, no. 19412); (iii) p. 273 Oratio ad sanctam crucem. Ueniam peto . . . (as art. 5(x)); (iv) p. 273 Oratio de cruce. Deus cuius filius per tropheum . . . ; (v) pp. 273–4 Oratio. Deus qui fecisti celum. et terram. et mare . . . tibi commendo corpus et animam meam . . . ; (vi) p. 274 Oratio. In nomine sancte et indiuidue trinitatis in eius amore crucis . . . Otha precor te . . . ; (vii) p. 274 Oratio de sancta cruce. Ihesu cristi domini nostri corpore saginati . . . ; (viii) p. 274 Oratio. Deus qui illuminas noctem . . . ; (ix) pp. 274–6 De sancta cruce. Oratio. Seinte croix ie uus aur. E uus salu e nuit e iur . . . (Sonet-Sinclair, no. 1856); (x) pp. 276–7 Oratio ad dominum ihesum cristum. Iesu pere rei celestre. ki pur nus deignastes nestre . . . (part of (ix) in other copies); (xi) p. 277 Oratio de sancta cruce. Sancta et ueneranda . . . (as (i) above); (xii) pp. 277–9 Si uus uolez auer uerei pardun . . . deuant la croiz:' ces oreisuns. O pie crucifixe redemptor omnium populorum . . . (six paragraphs, each ending with Pater noster); (xiii) pp. 279–80 Domine ihesu criste qui uoluisti pro redempcione mundi . . . ; (xiv) p. 280 Oratio. Domine ihesu criste qui per crucem et passionem tuam redemisti . . . ; (xv) pp. 280–1 Oratio. Obsecro te domine ihesu criste fili dei uiui per sanctam crucem tuam . . . ; (xvi) p. 281 Oratio. Omnipotens et misericors deus:' te deprecor ut non me famulum tuum . . .

10. (*a*) pp. 281–96 Incipit psalterium beate uirginis marie. Mente concipio laudes conscribere . . . pagina. Aue uirgo uirginum parens absque pari . . . (p. 295) Aue celi gloria . . . prorsus aue graui. (*b*) pp. 296–319 Prayers, nearly all of them to B.V.M.

(*a*). *RH*, no. 29602. 11 + 140 + 10 stanzas. *AH* xxxv. 170, 153–66, 168–9: the last ten stanzas here are the fourth, sixth, ninth, first, second, third, and tenth on p. 168 and the first on p. 169 in that order.

(*b*). Twenty pieces: (i) pp. 296-7 Oratio. Maria mater gratie mater misericordie. per illam tue humilitatis . . . ; (ii) pp. 297-9 Oratio de sancta maria et de S' Iohanne. O intemerata atque in eternum benedicta . . . orbis terrarum. Inclina . . . ; (iii) pp. 299-302 Oratio de sancta maria. Singularis meriti . . . (Maurilius of Rouen: cf. A. Wilmart, *Auteurs spirituels*, p. 480: *PL* clviii. 946-8, Oratio 49); (iv) p. 302 Aue ihesu criste uerbum patris . . . (as art. 8, xvi); (v) p. 302 Gaude uirgo mater cristi que per aurem . . . (*RH*, no. 7017); (vi) pp. 302-3 Per benedictum fructum uentris tui . . .

(vii-xii) 104 stanzas, most of them to be found in the Mariale of Bernard of Morlaix, as printed in *AH* 50. 424-82: (vii) pp. 303-4 Oratio. Omni die dic marie . . . (Rhythmus II, stanzas 1, 2, 17-19; III, stanzas 1-14); (viii) pp. 304-5 Oratio de sancta maria. Reparatrix et solatrix . . . (Rhythmus III, stanzas 25-34); (ix) pp. 305-6 Salutaris stella maris . . . (Rhythmus IV, stanzas 1-13); (x) pp. 306-7 Oratio. Maris stella interpella . . . (Rhythmus IV, stanzas 14-23, 25, 24; VIII, stanza 4, . . . ; XI, stanzas 47-8; X, stanzas 34-5); (xi) pp. 307-8 Oratio. Stella maris que preclaris . . . (Rhythmus IX, stanzas 15-27); (xii) pp. 308-9 Oratio de sancta maria. O maria mater pia. plena dei gracia . . . (. . . ; Rhythmus XII, stanzas 13-18, . . . , 19-21, . . .). In (x), six stanzas follow Rhythmus VIII, stanza 4, beginning Nos conforta, Meis caris, Illis mecum, Tuam prolem, Te laudamus, Da perfectum. In (xii), the stanzas which do not occur in Rhythmus XII are (1-8) O maria, Pia prece, Qui te, Illa inquam, De mortalis, In hac vita, Pro meorum, Virgo lenis a terrenis, (15) Mater dei per quam, (19-23) Stella maris singularis spes, Vite forma, Quantas tendat, Quibus modis, Quam impie.

(xiii) pp. 309-10 Oratio. Aue rosa speciosa. aue florens lilium . . . (10 stanzas not in *RH*); (xiv) pp. 310-11 Oratio de sancta maria. O maria dei. miserere precor mei . . . (11 stanzas: *RH*, no. 13199; *AH* xlvi. 172-3, from Laud Misc. 79, f. 149v); (xv) p. 311 Oratio. Sancta et perpetua uirgo maria mater domini et aduocatrix mea . . . ; (xvi) pp. 311-12 Oratio. In mentibus nostris domine uere fidei sacramenta . . . ; (xvii) pp. 312-18 Oreisun de nostre dame en romanz. Aue seinte marie mere al creatur . . . La ioie de sun regne auer a nostre desir. Amen (Sonet-Sinclair, no. 145: 58 stanzas: a stanza, 'Dame pur la ioie de tun tres cher fiz . . .', is added in the margin of p. 318 in current anglicana, s. xiii[2]); (xviii) p. 318 Oratio. O regina angelorum mitis hera . . . (*RH*, no. 39590: *AH* xlvi. 175); (xix) p. 318 Oratio. Deus qui beatam uirginem mariam in conceptu . . . ; (xx) pp. 318-19 Oratio. Omnipotens sempiterne deus qui beate et gloriose uirginis et matris marie corpus et animam . . .

11. pp. 319-26 Prayers to angels, apostles, martyrs, confessors, and virgins, sixteen pieces in all.

(*a*) p. 319 Oratio de sancto michaele. Sancte michael arcangele domini . . . (A. Wilmart, *Auteurs spirituels*, pp. 212-13 in second column). (*b*) p. 319 Oratio ad omnes angelos. Precor uos sancti angeli et arcangeli . . . (cf. *Lyell Cat.*, p. 393). (*c*) pp. 319-20 Oratio de sancto petro apostolo. Sancte petre apostole electe dei. tu confessus es . . . (L. Gjerløw, *Adoratio crucis*, p. 137). (*d*) p. 320 Oratio de sancto Paulo apostolo. Omnipotens et misericors deus cuius misericordia reuiuiscunt miseri . . . (*e*) p. 320 De Iohanne et Iacobo. Ad uos reus fugio nati zebedei . . . (8 lines, not in *RH*). (*f*) p. 321 Oratio de Sancto Iacobo. Ad te suspiro Iacobe . . . (8 lines). (*g*) p. 321 Oratio. O columpna fidei catholice . . . O rector et protector presentis monasterii . . . (*h*) pp. 321-2 Alme pater iacobe nostra consolatio . . . (28 lines not in *RH*, to James, 'Presentis familie pater et protectio', and John). (*i*) p. 322 De sancto Iohanne ewangelista. oratio. Confratrem condiscipulum uotis inuocamus . . . (six 4-line stanzas, not in *RH*). (*j*) pp. 322-3 De omnibus sanctis oratio apostoli. Sanctissimi apostoli dilecti dei quos dominus elegit . . . (*k*) pp. 323-4 Oratio ad sanctum Stephanum. sanctum Laurentium. sanctum Vincentium. sanctum Thomam. O sancte sanctorum. conciuis et coheres glorie . . . (*l*) p. 324 Oratio ad omnes martires. Supplico uos electi dei martires . . . (*m*) p. 324 Ad sanctum Benedictum. Clarissime pater et dux monachorum . . . (*n*) pp. 324-5 Ad omnes confessores oratio. Queso uos sacratissimi confessores cristi intercedite pro me . . . (*o*) p. 325 Oracio ad omnes uirgines. O gloriose uirgines dei. et margarite precipue. Agnes. Agatha. Cecilia. Lucia. Katerina. Margareta. Obsecro uos . . . (*p*) pp. 325-6

Oratio ad omnes sanctos. Succurrite michi queso omnes sancti dei ad quorum ego peccator . . . (*Lyell Cat.*, p. 399; in Laud Misc. 79, f. 148v).

12. pp. 326–8 Benedictiones de patre. Alma dei patris ueniat benedictio nobis . . .

Benedictions of Father, Son, Holy Spirit, evangelists, at the feast of All Saints, on Sundays and week days, twelve in all.

13. pp. 328–9 Hic incipiunt lecciones in estate priuatis diebus. Feria 2a. Lectio ia. Consurge in nocte . . .

One lesson for each week-day. The set is Tolhurst's A, B, C, E, F, D, used at Battle, Winchcombe, and St Mary's, York: *HBS* lxxx. 194–5.

14. pp. 329–32 Incipiunt lecciones de domina nostra. In nocte dominica. Leccio prima. Ecce tu pulcra . . .

Three lessons for each day of the week.

15. pp. 333–7 Iste collecte dicende sunt ad vesperas . . .

Twenty-four collects at vespers and twenty-four at matins: Trinity; Holy Cross; Michael; John Baptist; Peter and Paul; Peter; Paul; John and James; John; B.V.M. (Beate marie matris apostolorum iohannis et iacobi . . .); Andrew; apostles; Stephen; Thomas of Canterbury; martyrs; Martin; Nicholas; Benedict; 'Oddo', Maiolus, Odilo, and Hugh, jointly; confessors; Mary Magdalene; Katherine; virgins; relics.

16. pp. 338–9 In aduentu collecta Deus qui de beate . . .

Notes of collects, commemorations, and antiphons at special seasons and on special occasions, including the Transfiguration.

17. pp. 339–40 Hec sunt festiuitates in quibus potest ebdomadarius reg' cantare de ipsis sine restauratione. Natalis domini . . . In omnibus aliis festiuitatibus per annum cuiuscumque dignitatis sit. Si ebdomadarius de eis celebrauerit restaurabit missam regi quam cito poterit. In omni duplici festo . . . In hiis et in altioribus omnibus festis per annum potest ebdomadarius cimiterii cantare sine restauratione. Set in aliis festis ut in uigilia natalis domini . . . postea restaurabit. Pro annuali. Nouem sunt dies in quibus potest ebdomadarius annualis cantare de festo sine restauracione. scilicet Natalis domini . . . Dies sancti Iacobi. Hos nouem dies restaurabit armarius post finem anni. Sunt alie nouem dies . . . In quibus festiuitatibus dicitur Credo . . .

18. pp. 340–4 Incipit seruitium de beata uirgine maria per totum annum . . . Ad primas vesperas super ps'. Antiphona. Anima mea liquefacta . . . angelus a deo (*ends imperfectly in lesson 10*, Missus est inquit angelus).

Office at first vespers. The special form for use in Advent begins on p. 344.

19. Two binding leaves of polyphonic music, s. xiii2, are now kept separately as MS. 213*: (*a*) f. 1r Aue uirga decoris incliti officina almi paracliti . . . uirtus altissimi (9 lines); (*b*) ff. 1v–2 Aue tuos benedic uirgo singularis . . . mater salutaris

(4 lines); (*c*) f. 2^{rv} Aue maria salus hominum cella regia qua lux luminum . . . luctus term[. . .] (8 lines); (*d*) f. 2^{v} A aue (*sic*) regina celorum aue decus angelorum aue gaudium sanctorum aue so (*no more*).

Described in *Répertoire international des sources musicales*, 1966, vol. B IV (1), pp. 594–5. Written space 185 × 120 mm. 12 lines of music and 3 or 4 lines of text on each page. Initials: (i) blue with red ornament, outside the written space; (ii) 1-line, blue. Notes by Anselm Hughes on this 'Conductus cum cauda', dated 17 Jan. 1949, are kept with it.

ff. ii + 175 + v, paginated (i–iv), 1–91, 91*, 92, 92*, 92**, 93–8, 98*, 98**, 99–344, (345–54), together with two binding leaves, foliated 1, 2, now kept separately. 212 × 145 mm. Written space *c.*155 × 100 mm. 32 long lines. The first line of writing below the top ruled line. Collation: 1 eleven (pp. 1–22: 7–14 are two bifolia) 2^{12} (pp. 61–2, 23–44) 3^{8} (pp. 45–60) $4–15^{12}$ (pp. 63–344). Arts. 2–19 in one expert hand. Art. 1*b–d* in one hand. Initials of arts. 2–19: (i) p. 203, 6-line *D* in blue and red, with ornament of both colours; (ii) p. 63, 4-line *D*, with red and blue saw-pattern ornament in two margins; (iii) 2-line (4-line, p. 130), blue with red ornament or red with blue-green ornament; (iv, v) 2-line and 1-line, blue or red. No initials in art. 1. Capital letters in the ink of the text stroked with red. Gilt morocco binding, s. xviii. Secundo folio *respectu* (p. 23).

Given to the abbey of Reading, O.S.B., by Alan, prior: 'Hunc librum dedit Alanus prior deo et beate marie de Rading' quem qui celauerit uel alienauerit uel fraudem de eo fecerit Anathema sit', p. 2, at the top, s. xiii^{2}, in the hand of the table of contents, art. 1*e*: art. 11*g*, *h* suggests that the book was written for use at Reading where St James was in special honour. 'P' in red, top of p. 2. 'Bibliotheca Palmeriana (*erased*) Londini 1747', p. iii: passed like other 'Bibliotheca Palmeriana' manuscripts[1] into the possession of Ralph, second Earl Verney (1752–91), whose bookplate is inside the cover. 'Londini ab Elmsleyo emptum Bibliothecæ Francisci Basset Baronet[ti] D.D.D. R.E. Raspe d. 14 Mart. 1787', p. 1. Book-plate of Francis 'Basset' Lord de Dunstanville (1796–1835: son of Sir Francis Basset), p. i. 'G(eorge) D(unn) Feb. 1907', p. iii. Not, it seems, in the catalogues of the Dunn sales, 2 February 1913 and later.

233 (LRA 6). *T. Netter, etc.* s. xv med.

Books 3 and 4 of the Doctrinale of Thomas Netter of Walden against the Wycliffites and Hussites, followed by Woodford against Wyclif, and pieces by John Deveros (cf. Emden, *BRUC*, p. 186). Formerly at Merton College (MS. 318) and described among the Merton manuscripts in Coxe's catalogue and by F. M. Powicke, *Medieval Books of Merton College*, 1931, p. 231: see also *Manuscripts at Oxford*, p. 86. The present volume is the second of two volumes of Netter given to Gloucester College by John Whethamstede, abbot of St Albans, in s. xv med., as appears from a handsomely written table of contents followed by four lines of verse, 'Fratribus Oxonie datur . . .', on f. 1^{v}. The first volume became the property of John, Lord Lumley, †1609, and is now B.L., Royal 8 G. x.[2]

[1] Lord Verney appears to have sold manuscripts in his lifetime: cf. H.M.C., *8th Report*, Appendix p. 234, a reference I owe to Dr David Rogers. He probably acquired them from his father, Ralph, first Earl Verney (1684–1752), of Little Chelsea, Middlesex, grandson of Ralph Palmer of Little Chelsea: cf. *The Complete Peerage*, ed. V. Gibbs and H. A. Doubleday, v (1926), 295–6. 'Bibliotheca Palmeriana' books tend to be important and in handsome eighteenth-century bindings.

[2] Royal 8 G. x has a similar table and the same four lines of verse on f. 1^{v} and also at the end a notice that Whethamstede assigned it 'ad usum monachorum studencium in collegio Gloucestrie Oxonie'.

ff. ii + 157, foliated i, 1–83, 83*, 84–157. f. i was formerly pasted down. 387 × 275 mm. Written space 255 × 170 mm. 2 cols. 49 lines. Collation of ff. 2–157: 1–10⁸ 11 three (ff. 82, 83, 83*) 12–19⁸ 20¹⁰. Quires 3–11 are signed A–I in the usual late medieval way. The hand is probably the same throughout,[1] but there is a change of ink at f. 84—it becomes lighter—and a change in the pattern of ruling at the same point: on ff. 84–157 the ruled lines above the 25th and 26th lines of writing are prolonged into the margins. Initials: (i) ff. 2, 35 (Doctrinale, bk. 4), 84, 118ᵛ, 131ᵛ, 6-line or more, blue and red with ornament of both colours or of red only: gold ornament on f. 84; (ii) of chapters, 4-line, blue with red ornament; (iii) on ff. 85–114ᵛ, as (ii), but 2-line; (iv) 1-line, blue. Continuous red and blue borders on ff. 2, 84, with a roundel at each corner (1, 4 Agnus Dei, 2, 3 Eagle);[2] part borders on the three other main leaves. Contemporary binding of wooden boards, now bare, rebacked: nine bands run to three points on each board (⩚⩚⩚): two clasps missing: four nail-marks of an unusually long (120 mm) horizontal chain staple on the back cover at the foot.[3] Watson, *Oxford*, pl. 295 illus. fol. 4ᵛ. Secundo folio *propter quesitum*.

Written in England, no doubt to the order of John Whethamstede: see above. A gift to Merton College from Robert Scherles, formerly fellow (fellow 1512–24, sub-warden 1524–5, vicar of St Peter in the East, Oxford, 1524–58: Emden, *BRUO 2*, p. 510), 'pro cuius fœlice statu orate', received by the college at his death in 1558. Given to Worcester College, as representative of the medieval Gloucester College, in 1938.

285. *Eusebius, Historia ecclesiastica; etc.* s. xiv¹

Described by R. W. Hunt in *BLR*, vii (1962–7), 23–7: pl. IV*a* shows part of f. 238ᵛ. MS. Bodl. 712 (*Sum. Cat.* 2619) is another manuscript written by this scribe for Robert Wivill. Arts. 6, 7, 3, 4, 5 occur in that order in Bodleian MS. Laud Misc. 247, ff. 45–139, 171–223, s. xi.

1. ff. 1–112ᵛ (*begins imperfectly*) celeste dei uerbum . . . premia meritorum. Explicit ecclesiastica hystoria scripta apud nouam Sarum.

Eusebius, Historia ecclesiastica, in the translation of Rufinus and with his continuation, as edited by T. Mommsen, *Die Griechischen Christlichen Schriftsteller*, ix (2 vols., 1903–8), 45/23–1040. Eleven books, each preceded by a table of contents. 'defectus exemplar(is)' in the margin of f. 31ᵛ is probably a corrector's note: the scribe added a sentence in the margin at this point. A leaf missing after f. 90.

2. (*a*) ff. 114–124ᵛ (*begins imperfectly*) regium habebant . . . gaudia agitabantur. (*b*) ff. 124ᵛ–146ᵛ Falso queritur de natura sua . . . in illo site. Qui cupis ignotum iugurthe noscere letum. Tarpeia rupe pulsus ad yma ruit. Explicit liber salustii. de bello Catiline. et de bello Iugurtino.

(*a, b*). Sallust, Catilina (beginning at ch. 5, 6) and Jugurtha written as one. A corrector noted 'Explicit Catilenarium Salustii. Incipit Salustius de bello Iugurstino' in the lower

[1] Royal 8 G. x, ff. 21ᵛᵇ–203ᵛ, is in the same unattractive hand; so too New College, Oxford, 49, ff. 14–40ᵛ, 57ᵛ–159. Dr David Howlett first drew my attention to the evidence from script, decoration, and chaining that New College 49 was at Gloucester College in the Middle Ages: cf. *Manuscripts at Oxford*, pp. 85, 87, and *BLR*, x (1978–82), 225–8 and pls. xiv, xv*a* (f. 84).

[2] Similar borders occur in other manuscripts made for Whethamstede, Eton College 103 (*MMBL* ii. 716), Royal 8 G. x, f. 2, New College, 49, f. 1, Bodleian Library, Auct. F. inf. 1. 1, f. 169 (*Manuscripts at Oxford*, fig. 57).

[3] The long chain staple is still *in situ* on the back cover of New College 49. Its length may have been a Gloucester College speciality.

margin, f. 124v. The verses at the end of (*b*) follow Sallust also in Pembroke College, Cambridge, 114, s. xii, from Bury St Edmunds.

3. ff. 147–59 Incipiunt Capitula gestorum alexandri regis . . . (f. 148) apud egypcios. Incipiunt gesta prima alexandri magni regis macedonum. Capitulum primum. Egipti sapientes. sati genere diuino . . . extinctus occubuit. Finit.

Gesta Alexandri in the epitome of Julius Valerius. Ed. J. Zacher, 1867. 42 chapters. This copy of arts. 3, 4 not included by D. J. A. Ross in his list of manuscripts in *Scriptorium*, x (1956), 129–32. 'Primus alexander pillea natus in urbe . . . dormitauerat annis' (4 lines of verse: Walther, no. 14648) follows the text on f. 159. This copy noticed by B. Hill, '*Epitaphia Alexandri* in English medieval manuscripts', *Leeds Studies in English*, viii (1975), 98–104.

4. ff. 159–166v Incipit epistola alexandri regis ad magistrum suum aristotilem de situ indie et itineribus eius et variis generibus bestiarum ac serpencium. Semper memor tui . . . optime. Aristotiles indicium. Val'.

Cf. art. 4. Thorndike and Kibre. Ed. M. Feldbusch in *Beiträge zur klassischen Philologie*, lxxviii (1976), 12a–120a.

5. ff. 167–180v Incipiunt gesta appollonii regis tyrorum. Capitulum primum. In ciuitate antiochia . . . amodo libere sitis (*ends imperfectly in ch. 34*).

The end now—two leaves are missing after f. 180—is in ch. 46 of the editions by Riese, 1893, and Raith, 1956. The text differs much from the editions and is usually fuller. Thasia's speech, ed. Riese, pp. 97–9, is here in 44 lines of verse, 'Cum releuet mestas mentes diuina potestas . . . iura negando patris', which form the first half of ch. 31.

6. ff. 183–238v Incipiunt capitula libri primi historie gentis langobardorum . . . (*numbered table of six books*) . . . (f. 186v) [Septentrionali]s [plaga quant]o magis . . . pacem custodiens. Explicit liber sextus historie gentis langobardorum. scriptus Reuerendo domino patri. domino Roberto Wiuill'. dei gracia Sar' Episcopo.

Paul the Deacon. *Clavis*, no. 1179. Ed. G. Waitz, MGH, Scriptores rerum Germanicarum in usum scholarum, xlviii (1878), 52–242. The initial *S* has been cut out of f. 186.

7. ff. 239–47 Incipit prologus de uita karoli imperatoris. [U]itam et conuersacionem . . . adimplere curauit. Explicit vita karoli imperatoris.

Einhard. Fifty-seven numbered chapters. Ed. G. Waitz, MGH, Scriptores rerum Germanicarum in usum scholarum, xxv (1911), 1–41. The initial *U* on f. 239 has been cut out. f. 247v left blank.

8. ff. 248–52 De situ ierosolimitane regionis . . . (*table of 17 chapters*) . . . Incipit libellus de situ ierosolimitane regionis. Situs ierusalem . . . temperare satagas. Explicit libellus (*etc.*).

Beda, De locis sanctis. Ed. Geyer, CSEL xxxix (1898), 301–24. Manuscripts, but not this one, listed by M. L. W. Laistner and H. H. King, *A Hand-List of Bede manuscripts*, 1943, pp. 83–6.

9. ff. 252–254v Incipit descripcio locorum que vidit Bernardus sapiens quando iuit Ierusalem uel rediit et de ipsa ierusalem et de locis circa eam. Capitulum primum. Anno dcccclxx incarnacionis cristi . . . non possunt diebus (*ends abruptly*).

Itineraria Hierosolymitana, ed. T. Tobler and A. Molinier (Publ. de la société de l'orient latin, sér. géog.), i (1879), 309–319/12. The lost Rheims manuscript ends at the same point.

10. ff. 254v–266v Incipit hystoria a Magistro fulcero composita de Ierusalem a cristianis obtenta. Capitulum primum. Anno ab incarnacione domini millesimo nonagesimo quinto . . . petierunt a raimundo comite qui proper turrim (*ends imperfectly at I. 30. 3*).

Ed. H. Hagenmeyer, 1913, pp. 119–309.

ff. 251, foliated 1–266 in s. xviii: this foliation takes account of the leaves missing from quires 12, 16, 25, and reaches 266 by leaving out the numbers 190–9 and 222. 345 × 220 mm. Written space 255 × 155 mm. 2 cols. 44 lines. Collation: 1 three (the last 3 leaves of a quire) $2–11^8$ 12^8 wants 8 after f. 90 $13–14^8$ 15^6 wants 6, blank (?), after f. 112 16^8 wants 1 before f. 114 $17–19^8$ 20 two (probably 20^4 wants 3, 4, blank, after f. 146) $21–22^8$ 23^6 wants 5, 6, blank, after f. 166 24^8 25^8 wants 7, 8 after f. 180 $26–30^8$ 31^8 wants 6, blank, after f. 238 $32–34^8$ 35 two (the first two leaves of a quire). Quires 2, 3 are marked 'corr' ' at the foot of the first rectos in the middle. Textura, but the scribe uses fancy anglicana formata for the explicits on ff. 113v, 146v, 238v (see plate), 252, and for the incipit on f. 254v. Initials: (i) of arts. and books of arts. 1, 6, 7-line, blue or red, patterned in white on grounds of red or blue patterned in white, and gold, the gold decorated or historiated: the three remaining historiated initials are on ff. 148 (a seated king: 'rex in cathedra' in pencil in the margin), 167 (king's head and grotesque), 248 (Jerusalem): prolongations into the margins in colours and a little gold include oak leaves and buds and on f. 148 a trumpeting figure atop a vertical bar; (ii) blue or red on grounds of the other colour and gold, decorated: prolongations include oak leaves, but not buds; (iii) 3-line, gold on grounds of blue and red, patterned in white; (iv) 2-line, blue with red ornament; (v) 1-line, blue or red. Capital letters in the ink of the text filled with pale yellow. Medieval sewing on seven bands: no covers: a decorative pattern on the fore-edges: kept in a box.

Written at Salisbury (art. 1) by a scribe working for Robert Wivill, bishop of Salisbury (1330–75: art. 6). Belonged in s. xvii med. to 'Ed. Shaa' who signed his name on f. i with the date '[. . .] Septembris 1636' and on f. 247v with the date 'Aug. 17 1657' and wrote a table of contents on f. 247v and many marginalia: it is he, no doubt, who 'improved' the punctuation throughout and added cedillas to *e* for *ae*.